Social Psychology

Second Edition

ARUN KUMAR SINGH

Formerly, University Professor and Head
Postgraduate Department of Psychology
Patna University, Patna

PHI Learning Private Limited

Delhi-110092
2020

₹ 695.00

SOCIAL PSYCHOLOGY, Second Edition
Arun Kumar Singh

© 2020 by PHI Learning Private Limited, Delhi. All rights reserved. No part of this book may be reproduced in any form, by mimeograph or any other means, without permission in writing from the publisher.

ISBN-978-93-89347-25-8 (Print Book)
ISBN-978-93-89347-26-5 (e-Book)

The export rights of this book are vested solely with the publisher.

Second Printing (Second Edition) ... ... **November, 2019**

Published by Asoke K. Ghosh, PHI Learning Private Limited, Rimjhim House, 111, Patparganj Industrial Estate, Delhi-110092 and Printed by Rajkamal Electric Press, Plot No. 2, Phase IV, HSIDC, Kundli-131028, Sonepat, Haryana.

To
My Wife
Kumud Rani

Contents

Preface xiii

1. INTRODUCING SOCIAL PSYCHOLOGY 1–24

Learning Objectives 1
Key Terms 1
Definition and Nature of Social Psychology 2
Social Psychology: A Historical Perspective 4
Overview of Social Psychology in Indian Perspective 11
Social Psychology as a Science 17
Fundamental Axioms of Social Psychology 18
Relation of Social Psychology with Other Sciences 19
SUMMARY AND REVIEW 23
REVIEW QUESTIONS 24

2. RESEARCH METHODS IN SOCIAL PSYCHOLOGY 25–67

Learning Objectives 25
Key Terms 25
Objectives of Social Psychological Research 26
Basic Concepts of Research 27
Basic Research Methods 29
Validity of Experiment 49
Social Psychology of Experiment 51
Role of Theory in Social Psychological Research 55
Types of Research in Social Psychology 57
SUMMARY AND REVIEW 64
REVIEW QUESTIONS 67

3. THEORETICAL FOUNDATIONS OF MODERN SOCIAL PSYCHOLOGY 68–86

Learning Objectives 68
Key Terms 68
Role Theories 70
Motivational Theories 72
Learning Theories 74
Cognitive Theories 78
Symbolic Interaction Theories 80
Socio-cultural Theories 82
Evolutionary Theories 83
SUMMARY AND REVIEW 85
REVIEW QUESTIONS 86

4. SELF AND IDENTITY 87–113

Learning Objectives 87
Key Terms 87
Meaning and Nature of Self 88
Development (or Sources) of Social Self 90
Self and Culture 93
Effects of Self Upon Thoughts, Behaviour and Emotions: Process of Self-Regulation 96
Identity: The Self We Interact 98
Self-esteem 102
Self-serving Bias 109
Self as an Object of Prejudice 110
SUMMARY AND REVIEW 112
REVIEW QUESTIONS 113

5. SOCIAL COGNITION, SOCIAL PERCEPTION AND ATTRIBUTION 114–174

Learning Objectives 114
Key Terms 114
Meaning and Nature of Social Cognition 115
Components of Social Cognition: Schema and Prototype 117
Impact of Schema Upon Social Cognition: Schematic Processing 119
Self-fulfilling Nature of Schema 121
Cognitive Heuristics: Mental Shortcuts for Reducing our Efforts in Social Cognition 122
Potential Sources of Errors in Social Cognition 125
Cognition and Affect: A Reciprocal Relationship 130
Field of Interpersonal Perception: Social Perception and Person Perception 132
Role of Non-verbal Cues in Person Perception: Forming Impression of Others 134

Recognising Deceptions in Non-verbal Cues *139*
Impression Formation *140*
Integrating Information about Others *142*
Impression Management *151*
Self-Perception *154*
Attribution: Understanding the Causes of Others' Behaviour *155*
Theories of Attribution *156*
Bias and Error in Attribution *164*
Applications of Attribution Theory *169*
Cultural Basis of Attribution *171*
SUMMARY AND REVIEW *172*
REVIEW QUESTIONS *174*

6. SOCIALISATION 175—201

Learning Objectives *175*
Key Terms *175*
Meaning and Nature of Socialisation *176*
Theoretical Perspectives of Socialisation *177*
Process of Socialisation *185*
Agents of Socialisation *187*
Outcomes of Socialisation *193*
Concept of Adult Socialisation *198*
SUMMARY AND REVIEW *200*
REVIEW QUESTIONS *201*

7. SOCIAL ATTITUDES AND PERSUASION 202–264

Learning Objectives *202*
Key Terms *202*
Brief Historical Review *203*
Defining Attitude and Its Components *203*
Functions of Attitude *206*
Attitude and Behaviour *207*
How do Attitudes Guide Behaviour? *211*
Formation and Maintenance of Attitudes *214*
Attitude Change and Persuasion *216*
Theories of Attitude Organisation and Change *229*
When do Attitude Change and Persuasion Become Difficult? *249*
Dimensions of Attitude *251*
Measurement of Attitude *252*
SUMMARY AND REVIEW *262*
REVIEW QUESTIONS *264*

8. STEREOTYPING, PREJUDICE AND DISCRIMINATION   265–303

Learning Objectives   265
Key Terms   265
Nature and Contents of Stereotypes   266
Why do People Form and Use Stereotypes?   270
Activation of Stereotypes   272
Impact of Stereotypes on Judgements and Actions   273
Changing Stereotypes and Barriers to Stereotype Change   275
Gender Stereotypes   277
Shifting Standards: Does No Difference in Evaluations Or
    Ratings Mean Absence of Stereotypic Thinking?   280
Stereotypes Associated with Single and Married Persons   281
Concept of Prejudice and Discrimination   282
Forms of Prejudice and Discrimination   284
Origin, Development and Maintenance of Prejudice and Discrimination   286
Reduction of Prejudice and Discrimination   295
Measurement of Prejudice   300
SUMMARY AND REVIEW   300
REVIEW QUESTIONS   302

9. BEHAVIOURS IN GROUP   304–342

Learning Objectives   304
Key Terms   304
Meaning and Nature of Social Group   305
Group: Some Basic Features and Aspects   306
Why do People Join a Group?: Benefits and Costs of Joining   310
Types of Groups   311
Group Development   314
Effects of Presence of Others: Social Facilitation and Social Inhibition   315
Social Loafing   318
Effects of Being in Crowd: Deindividuation   320
Group Decision-Making   322
Group Polarisation: Risky Shift Beyond Risk-Caution Dimension   323
Groupthink: Does Group Hinder or Assist Group Decision?   325
Biased Use of Information in Groups   328
Failure to Share Unique Information from Some Members   329
Ways of Improving Group Decisions   329
Guidelines for Effective Decision-making   330
Group Interaction: Cooperation versus Competition   330
Communication Network in Group   338
SUMMARY AND REVIEW   340
REVIEW QUESTIONS   342

10. SOCIAL NORMS AND CONFORMITY BEHAVIOUR 343–358

Learning Objectives 343
Key Terms 343
Concept of Social Norms 344
Formation of Social Norms 345
Meaning of Conformity Behaviour 348
Why do We Conform? 349
Factors Influencing Conformity 352
How Can We Resist Social Pressure to Conform? 354
SUMMARY AND REVIEW 357
REVIEW QUESTIONS 358

11. LEADERSHIP AND SOCIAL POWER 359–400

Learning Objectives 359
Key Terms 359
Defining Leadership 360
Emergence of Leadership 361
Functions of Leaders 362
Transformational and Transactional Leaders: Differential Impact 364
Personal Characteristics of Leaders 366
Basic Dimensions of Leader Behaviour 369
Types of Leaders 370
How is a Leader Perceived by the Followers? 373
Theories of Leadership 375
Meaning and Bases of Social Power 393
Determinants of Social Power 397
SUMMARY AND REVIEW 399
REVIEW QUESTIONS 400

12. INTERPERSONAL ATTRACTION AND RELATIONSHIP 401–426

Learning Objectives 401
Key Terms 401
Meaning and Nature of Interpersonal Attraction 402
Theories of Interpersonal Attraction 402
Determinants of Interpersonal Attraction 409
Romantic Relationship 419
SUMMARY AND REVIEW 424
REVIEW QUESTIONS 425

13. SOCIAL INFLUENCE   427–436

Learning Objectives   427
Key Terms   427

Meaning and Nature of Compliance   428
Underlying Principles of Compliance   428
Techniques of Compliance   429
Obedience to Authority   432
Factors Behind Obedience   433
Resisting the Effects of Destructive Obedience   435
SUMMARY AND REVIEW   435
REVIEW QUESTIONS   436

14. AGGRESSION AND SOCIAL VIOLENCE   437–465

Learning Objectives   437
Key Terms   437

Defining Aggression   437
Causes of Aggressive Behaviour   438
Theories of Aggressive Behaviour   450
Prevention and Control of Aggression   457
Media Violence   461
SUMMARY AND REVIEW   464
REVIEW QUESTIONS   465

15. PROSOCIAL BEHAVIOUR: ALTRUISTIC AND HELPING BEHAVIOUR   466–487

Learning Objectives   466
Key Terms   466

Defining Prosocial Behaviour and Alturism   467
Five Steps of Bystander Intervention: A Decision Tree Analysis   467
Determinants of Prosocial Behaviour   471
Basic Motivation Behind Prosocial Acts: Theories   482
How Can Helping Behaviour Be Increased?   484
SUMMARY AND REVIEW   486
REVIEW QUESTIONS   487

16. LANGUAGE AND COMMUNICATION   488–533

Learning Objectives   488
Key Terms   488

Language: Properties and Structure   489
Functions of Language   493
Critical Period Hypothesis   494

Linguistic Hierarchy *496*
Theories of Language Development *497*
Language and Thought *504*
Diversity in Language Acquisition among Indian Children *506*
Language Acquisition and Theory of Mind *507*
Bilingualism/Multilingualism in Indian Society *508*
Reading Acquisition among Indian Children *510*
Gender Differences in Verbal Communication *512*
Barriers to Verbal Communication *513*
Nature and Purpose of Communication *514*
Models of Communication *515*
Communication Network *519*
Non-verbal Communication *521*
Combining Verbal and Non-verbal Communication *524*
Gender Differences in Non-verbal Communication *526*
Communication and Social Structure *527*
SUMMARY AND REVIEW *531*
REVIEW QUESTIONS *532*

17. APPLICATIONS OF SOCIAL PSYCHOLOGY   534–583

Learning Objectives *534*
Key Terms *534*
Social Psychology: Education *535*
    School as a Social System *536*
    Classroom as a Group *537*
    Teacher Variable *538*
    Classroom Climate *539*
    Social Factors, Social Motivation and Academic Achievement *540*
    Improving the Outcome of Education *541*
Social Psychology: Personal Health *544*
    Health Behaviour and Health Attitude *545*
    Stress, Health and Illness *547*
    Causes of Stress *548*
    How Does Stress Affect Health and Well-Being? *551*
    How to Cope with Stress? *552*
    Personal Factors, Health and Illness *554*
    Promoting Healthy Lifestyles *557*
Social Psychology: Legal System *558*
    Aspects of Police Interrogation *558*
    Eyewitness Identification and Testimony *559*
    Methods of Assessing Eyewitness Accuracy *563*
    How to Increase the Accuracy of Eyewitnesses? *563*
    Criminal Defendants *564*

Social Psychology: Entrepreneurship   *566*
Social Psychology: Sports   *569*
Summary and Review   *582*
Review Questions   *583*

OBJECTIVE-TYPE QUESTIONS   *585–621*
GLOSSARY   *623–635*
REFERENCES   *637–723*
INDEX   *725–737*

PREFACE

The second edition of Social Psychology has more or less similar goals as the first edition. This edition, like the previous one, provides an introduction to social psychology through scientific consideration of concepts, models, theories and important researches. The basic aim of the book is to provide a simple, clear and understandable introduction in the discipline of social psychology. The major thrust has been given to the scientific area of enquiry, using various techniques of empirical research, including laboratory experiments. Added emphasis has been made to illustrate the area with Indian researches also.

The present book has been organised into 17 chapters for providing a systematic presentation of the materials. Chapter 1 introduces the elementary concepts of social psychology that are widely needed by those who are beginners for clarifying the basic concepts of the field. Chapter 2 emphasises the basic research methods and the requirements of conducting good researches in the field. Major types of researches in social psychology are also included in this chapter. In addition, this chapter provides the fundamental base on how to conduct research in the field of social psychology. Chapter 3 provides a fundamental and theoretical foundation of social psychology. It clarifies the major theories of social psychology that are the bases of conducting good researches. Chapters 4–6 throw light upon the development of social self, social cognition and socialisation, which are considered important for understanding the social behaviour in scientific way. Chapters 7–8 focus on social attitudes, stereotypes and prejudices. These chapters provide a wider coverage of the concerned area so that all important theories relating to attitude change, measurement techniques of attitudes, origin, development and maintenance of prejudice may be widely illustrated and also exemplified by the Indian researches. Chapters 9–10 relate to the various types of behaviour in groups and social norms.

Chapter 11 is related to the leadership and social power. This chapter lucidly explains all important aspects of leadership behaviour and their bases of power. A special attraction is the comparison of Indian leadership behaviour with the behaviours of foreign leaders. Chapter 12 is related to the most sensitive social behaviour of human being, that is, interpersonal attraction and relationship. A cogent explanation has been provided by throwing light upon different theories of interpersonal attraction. Chapter 13 deals with the various forms of social influence to which we are subjected to most of the time. Knowledge of various techniques of compliance provides a base for understanding day-to-day interactions in scientific way. Chapters 14–15 deal with two important types of social behaviour—aggression and prosocial behaviour. To provide the latest look to the materials included, text related to the current researches in the field is incorporated into these chapters. Chapter 16 discusses language and communication emphasising various theories of language development and role of critical period. The language development, in a way, affects the communication both verbal and non-verbal, and this has been nicely explained for understanding the relationship between the two. Chapter 17 discusses the wider applications of social psychology in different fields, making it a science for everyone to understand and accept. This edition expands and clarifies a number of concepts in an easy-to-understand language.

The present edition, like previous one, is extensively illustrated with examples, figures and tables so that the reader may not have any difficulty in understanding anything anywhere. The style, language and presentation are kept so lucid and simple that nowhere there should be any problem. The organisation of the chapters is highly sequential. Every chapter begins with the learning objectives, which aim at providing an idea about the contents and major concepts covered in the chapter. Towards the end of the book, there is a complete glossary, which will act as a quick guide for promoting knowledge regarding the basic concepts covered by the whole book. Reference section and index at the end of the book would also facilitate in going into more details and easily locating the desired concepts within no time.

The text has benefitted greatly from thoughtful comments and reviews of many researchers, teachers and students. My thanks go to all of them. These persons are too numerous to list here, but their inputs are gratefully acknowledged. My special thanks go to Dr. Alpana SenGupta, Retired Professor of Psychology, for taking keen interest in the text and illuminating the text with some good suggestions. I also appreciate the useful feedback I have received from the students who have gone through the first edition. On the suggestion of most of the students and teachers, the number of objective questions has been considerably enhanced in each chapter. These questions would act as an extra incentive for all those who are preparing for various civil service examinations. I am also thankful to all those authors whose research works/books have been directly or indirectly used in preparing the manuscript of this book. I also wish to thank the publisher, PHI Learning, especially the editorial and production teams for their efforts in bringing this publication in short period of time in such a presentable and useful form. My most heartfelt thanks go to my wife, who kept me out of responsibility, which I should have normally taken, but could not. In fact, I could not have done it without her, thanks a million!

I sincerely hope that teachers and students will consider this book and its material a refreshing change from those already available. I appeal to all my colleagues and students, who will use this text, to tell me whether and to what extent, I have succeeded. So, kindly send me your reactions, comments and suggestions. I shall listen to them very carefully and shall try to include constructively in planning the next edition.

Arun Kumar Singh

1. Introducing Social Psychology

Learning Objectives

- Definition and Nature of Social Psychology
- Social Psychology: A Historical Perspective
- Overview of Social Psychology in Indian Perspective
- Social Psychology as a Science
- Fundamental Axioms of Social Psychology
- Relation of Social Psychology with Other Sciences

Key Terms

Accuracy
Cognitive processes
Construction of reality
Experimental social psychology
Objectivity

Open-mindedness
Pervasiveness of social influence
Psychological social psychology
Scientific study

Skepticism
Social interaction
Social processes
Sociological social psychology

Social psychology is today more useful than ever before. Whether the person wants to understand himself or the social world around him, social psychology tends to offer valuable insights. In fact, social psychology studies our impressions on other people, our sense of personal identity, our belief about the various events, the pressure we feel to conform to social groups as well as our search for love and affectionate social relationship. In a nutshell, it can be said that social psychology examines how an individual's thoughts, feelings and actions are affected by interaction with others. Whatever definition one chooses, it is clear that social psychology covers a lot of fields and there are many diverse areas that fit well within the discipline. For example, some social psychologists focus on social interaction between two or more individuals, some focus on social influence on the individual and still others on various types of group processes.

In the present chapter, we shall concentrate upon a more formal definition of social psychology. Subsequently, social psychology will be examined in its historical perspectives. Finally, its status as a scientific discipline and relationship with the other disciplines of social sciences would also be examined.

DEFINITION AND NATURE OF SOCIAL PSYCHOLOGY

The most distinctive aspect of the human life is its social character. People tend to prefer doing things in concert. For example, they want to work together and share the understanding of their various acts. Not only that, they tend to reach to the others in terms of their meanings. In fact, everything we think, feel and do is obviously related in some way to the social side of the life. This is called *social interaction*. Social psychology tends to study the behaviours of the individuals in social context. Therefore, it is the scientific study of the experience and behaviour of individuals in relation to other individuals, groups and cultures.

Social psychology can be defined as the discipline that studies how a person's thoughts, feelings and actions affect and are affected by real, implied or imagined presence of others (Feldman, 1985, Allport, 1985, Ciccarelli and Meyer, 2006). It is a systematic study of the nature and causes of human social behaviour. In other words, social psychology is the scientific discipline, which seeks to understand the nature and causes of behaviour and experience of the individuals in social situations. Putting in a simplified way, *social psychology* is defined as the scientific study of the impact of social and cognitive processes on the ways the persons influence and relate to the others in social situations.

Analysing this definition, we get the following major points:

1. Social psychology is a scientific discipline or study. Social psychology is scientific in nature because it adopts some core values, which are essential for considering the field as scientific. Those core values are accuracy, objectivity, skepticism and open-mindedness (Baron, Byrne and Branscombe, 2008). *Accuracy* refers to collection of carefully made observations in a careful, accurate and error-free manner. *Objectivity* indicates evaluation of the obtained information in a bias-free manner. *Skepticism* indicates accepting any finding accurate only to the extent they have been verified time and again. *Open-mindedness* indicates a commitment to change one's view if the existing evidences do not support the held view.

    Social psychology is considered scientific in orientation because this branch of psychology is deeply committed to use these values for understanding the nature of social behaviour and social thought. In fact, social psychologists like other scientists, tend to gather knowledge systematically by means of scientific methods, which honour the said four core values. These methods help in generating knowledge that is less subject to biases and distortions, which generally characterise common sense knowledge (Fletcher and Haig, 1990).

2. The main concern of social psychology is social behaviour, or broadly, social processes, which are defined as the ways in which the individual's thoughts, feelings and actions are influenced by the other individuals around us, the groups to which the individual belongs, the pressure the persons experiences from others, personal relationships, teaching of parents and culture, etc. (Smith and Mackie, 2007). This entire process includes four types of themes— impact of one individual upon other individual, impact of individual members upon the group to which they belong, impact that a group has on its members and the impact that one group has on another group. Much of our social behaviour revolves around two goals–survival and reproduction.

One individual affects the other individual in many ways. Communication from other may have significant impact upon changing one's belief and attitude. There are many examples in our day today life, where we find that the persuasion by others brings changes in one's belief or attitude towards persons, groups or other objects. One person may develop a strong attitude (such as liking, disliking, loving, hating, etc.) towards other person based on who the other is and what he does and communicates. Social psychologists try to study such issues to discover why persons develop positive attitudes towards some and negative attitude towards others.

Social psychology also studies the impact of individuals on the group to which they belong. There are many examples where we find that the individuals influence the group itself. For instance, the individuals may contribute to group productivity, group decision-making and effective leadership. By way of his effects, a member may enhance group productivity and contribute to some important decision-making process. Likewise, some members, by performing functions like planning, organising, and controlling, may provide effective leadership, thereby leading to successful group performance.

Groups also have an impact upon their individual members. Groups tend to influence and regulate the behaviour of their members by establishing norms. As a consequence, there occurs conformity by which group members adjust their behaviour, and experience to bring them in line with norms of the group. For example, schools and colleges have norms, which clearly stipulate how their students should dress, what should they do and what should they not do. Groups have also a still more long-term influence on its members through what the social psychologists have termed as *socialisation*. It shapes the knowledge, values and various skills of group members. The outcome of such socialisation is the development of appropriate language skills, religious beliefs and proper self-development.

Groups also affect the other groups. Social psychologists also study the impact of one group on the activities of the other group. Relations between two groups may be friendly and hostile. Friendly relationship may lead to cooperation and hostile relationship may lead to intergroup conflict. Thus, these relationships affect the structure and activities of each group. Social psychologists have taken keen interest in studying intergroup conflict, with its accompanying tension, hostility and violence.

3. Social psychology also studies the effect of experience, or broadly, cognitive processes on the ways the incidents influence and relate to others. *Cognitive processes* are defined as the ways in which memories, perceptions, self-esteem, thoughts, emotions and motives tend to guide the understanding of the world and one's action. Cognitive processes tend to have impact upon every aspect of our lives because the contents of our thoughts and feelings we have about other people and their activities are, to a greater extent, based upon what we believe the environment or the world is like.

Although social processes and cognitive processes have been explained separately, these two processes, in reality, are inextricably intertwined. This is because social processes affect the person even when others are not physically present. In fact, we are social creatures even when we are alone. Social processes that affect us when others are present also depend, to a larger extent, on the way we interpret them and their actions. Thus, whether we are alone or in group of others, both social processes and cognitive processes operate together to affect our thinking, feeling and action.

4. Social psychology not only addresses the nature of social behaviour but also the causes of such behaviour. In other words, social psychologists try to discover the antecedents and preconditions that cause various types of social behaviour (Fisher, 1982). Causal relations are considered as important building blocks for the development of a theory, which in turn, is regarded as the single most important and crucial factor for the prediction and control of social behaviour. Social psychologists have identified five such factors that are directly or indirectly responsible for shaping social behaviour and social thoughts of persons such as attitude, belief, feeling and the inferences regarding other persons. These five factors are social cognition (Shah, 2003), environmental factors like hot, cool and comfortable weather (Anderson, Bushman and Groom, 1997), cultural factors (Baron, Byrne and Branscombe, 2006), biological and genetic factors (Schmitt, 2004, Buss and Shackelford, 1997) and the actions and characteristics of other persons (Hassin and Trope, 2000). In fact, the findings of Hassin and Trope have very clearly indicated that one cannot ignore others' appearance even when one consciously tries to do so.

Thus, we see that social psychology studies social behaviour and social thoughts of the persons, as they are influenced by real, imagined or implied presence of the others, and also tries to understand them by locating the antecedents of social behaviour as causative factors. (Allport, 1985)

SOCIAL PSYCHOLOGY: A HISTORICAL PERSPECTIVE

Social psychology is considered as a subdiscipline of both psychology and sociology. As we know, *psychology* is defined as the scientific study of individual behaviour, whereas *sociology* is defined as the scientific study of social systems such as families, societies, organisations, etc. as well as of complex processes such as social change and the process of socialisation. *Social psychology*, being a subdiscipline of both psychology and sociology, is defined as the scientific study of nature and causes of social behaviour occurring in the various social environment. Thus, it can be said that social psychology is broadly concerned with human interaction and human relationship in the social world.

If one tries to look at the history of a discipline, the first question that hits the mind is who was the founder of the discipline? Applying the same question to social psychology and making an honest attempt to answer the question, it can be said that it is very difficult to call any one individual as the founder of social psychology. A look at the historical antecedents reveal that from the time of Plato, various socio-psychological questions, especially pertaining to the relationship between the individual and political state, have been raised. Plato in his famous book *The Republic* had argued that states originate because man as the individual is not self-sufficient. He further placed the idea that in order to satisfy his own essential goal, a man needs the cooperative efforts of others. He suggested that man is committed to be a social organism because of pragmatic and voluntary entry into cooperative organisation. Plato also recognised that when individuals come together as a crowd, they are transformed into an irrational mob. This served as an impetus for Gustav Le Bon, who, in 1908, wrote about group mind and how the individual behaviour is changed into crowd behaviour. Like Plato, Aristotle conceived man to be clearly committed to social participation, but at the same time, he is bound by his inherent nature to be gregarious with others. Likewise, in the writings of Hobbes, Locke, Rousseau and many others, there are a lot of provocative thinking about relation between individual and society, but their approach, on the whole, was not scientific.

Gordon Allport (1968) made a very illuminating review of the history of social psychology and credited the French Philosopher, Auguste Comte (1798–1857), with initiating sociology and proposing an emergence of a science that obviously parallels modern psychology with social psychology. Comte clearly suggested that the behaviour of a person can be entirely studied scientifically with reference to its social and biological influences. After many decades of this assertion, sociologists and psychologists joined hands to create empirical study of individual behaviour in society. As a consequence, the first textbook entitled *Social Psychology* was written by a sociologist, E.A. Ross in 1908. Ross had obtained Ph.D. in History, Politics and Economics and had combined these disciplines together with Psychology and Sociology to write the first textbook of social psychology. In this book, the major emphasis was on the fact that how do suggestion and initiation account for the transfer of ideas, habits and attitudes among members of social groups. In fact, he took up this theme which soon became the central concern of social psychology, that people are predominantly influenced by the others whether they are physically present or not. In the same year, William McDougall, a psychologist, published second textbook of social psychology entitled *Introduction to Social Psychology*. He also explored the role of initiation and suggestion in explaining the similarity of behaviours of members of a given social group. McDougall further claimed that human social behaviour was produced by social instincts, which were defined as innate tendencies common to all people. He claimed that social interactions are caused by social instincts and each social instinct tends to induce a related emotion. McDougall (1908) emphasised the role of instincts, sentiments and socialisation in human behaviour. At that time, McDougall's view dominated the emerging field of social psychology.

Since the beginning of social psychology as a discipline with the help of these two books, it has flourished in subsequent decades. In 1968, as per the estimate of Allport (1968, p. 68), there were about 100 textbooks on social psychology. The rapid growth of social psychology has continued, and according to one estimate, today there are approximately 200 textbooks and more than half a dozen journals devoted to the field.

Apart from the appearance of these textbooks on social psychology, both sociologists and psychologists have developed the field unexpectedly. This has led to the separation and independence to the extent that it would be more accurate to speak of two schools of social psychology—*psychological social psychology* and *sociological social psychology*. Psychological social psychology deals with the person within the social context. Here, emphasis is given upon the individual—his attitudes, feeling, motives, learning and perception—as these are shaped by the society and its various groups. This approach broadly emphasises upon what has been called *within the skin processes*, that is, the internal events that shape social behaviour. It is clearly reflected in Krech, Crutchfield and Ballachey's approach (1962, p. 4), which defines social psychology as the science of behaviour of the individual in society. Secord and Backman's view (1964), according to which social psychology is the study of individuals in social contexts, is another example of the psychological social psychology. The sociological school of social psychology emphasises upon the group as a unit of study and is concerned with the individual and the social context. This approach mainly emphasises upon what happens *between skins* or *between people* and it covers some essential broad phenomena such as crowd behaviour, social norms, social power, problems of group dynamics, rumour transmission and communication process. The sociological social psychologists were critical of psychological social psychology for studying person's responses or responses of individuals, not as a part of collective. Newcomb's emphasis (1950) on the interacting group as the proper subject matter of social psychology is one of the best example of sociological approach. This approach is also reflected in the title of Newcomb's text namely, *Social Psychology: The Study of Human Interaction* (1965).

The description of these two approaches, that is, psychological approach and sociological approach should never be taken to imply that social psychology is divided into two camps with no point of contact. In fact, this implies that there are several social psychologies and not one uniformly agreed upon the subject matter. Reality is that the differences between the two approaches shape the very nature of the discipline. Sherif (1963) had rightly pointed out that despite these two approaches, social psychologists have much in common because they overall basically concerned with the following trends:

1. Social psychologists lay emphasis upon studying social behaviour within an interacting framework, rather than exclusively concentrating either on internal approach (motives, feelings, attitudes, etc.) or on external approach (groups, culture, etc.).
2. Social psychologists assert positive efforts through cross-cultural and intergroup comparisons for achieving a perspective in drawing conclusions.
3. Social psychologists emphasize upon increased utilisation of scientific methods and techniques.

From the beginning, social psychology has tried to study the human social behaviour by emphasising upon the correct methods. The first laboratory experiment in social psychology is attributed to Norman Triplett, an American researcher, who conducted it in 1897. This experiment investigated *social facilitation*, a process whereby an individual's performance on a familiar task improves in the presence of other performing the same task. In fact, he tested the hypothesis that individuals tend to perform at higher levels when they are competing with others than when they are acting alone. He had found that children winding up reels of strings to which flags were attached worked faster when they were with others as compared to when they were acting alone. This group effect on individual behaviour was also reported by Walther Moede, a German psychologist, who found that hand grip strength and pain endurance were greater when subjects were in group than when they were alone. These interesting early finding were, however, contradicted by Max Ringelmann, a French agriculture engineer, who had reached a conclusion even in an earlier study conducted in 1880. He found, using tasks such as pulling a rope or pushing a cart, that an individual puts in less effort when working with the others in group than when working alone. This phenomenon today is called *social loafing*. However, it was Allport's report of experiments measuring the influence of group on individual behaviour that attracted the attention of others and led to what we call today as *experimental social psychology*.

Following Krech, Crutchfield and Ballachey (1962), it can be said that one of the early milestones in social psychology was Starbuck's attempt (1901) to take this young discipline into the field to study the psychology of religion. Another early event contributing to the emergence of social psychology was publication of an influential book entitled *Human Nature and the Social Order* by C.H. Cooley in 1902. The book presents the idea that the self and society are intimately related and are the same thing, although viewed at different levels of attraction.

Besides these early events, which had a profound impact upon emergence of social psychology as a scientific discipline, some other subsequent developments have taken place, which expanded the field and made social psychology a full-fledged member of social science family. Those developments can be described by dividing the period into following important spans:

1. Developments in between 1908–1945 A.D.
2. Developments in between 1945–1970 A.D.
3. Social psychology after 1970 A.D.

The major developments which contributed to the growth and expansion of the field of social psychology during these span of years are briefly presented below:

1. Developments in between 1908–1945 A.D.

As described above, in 1908, two textbooks of social psychology were published—one by the sociologist, E.A. Ross and another by a psychologist, William McDougall. Although both books are titled *Social Psychology*, they differ greatly in their content. Ross emphasised upon the idea that thoughts and memories are based on the principles of imitation and suggestion. McDougall stressed the importance of instincts and innate drives in determining behaviour. Although McDougall's approach was appreciated at first, within a couple of decades, it had been largely discarded by social psychologists of that time. F.H. Allport published *Social Psychology* in 1924 and this marked the beginning of what might be called *modern era in social psychology*. Allport praised the individual approach to social behaviour proposed by McDoughall, but he refused to accept the instinctual theories of McDougall. The publication of Allport's book also marked a turning point in social psychology because it was the first social treatise, which was based on the results of experimentation, rather than on observations and speculations. Thus, it initiated a scientific trend that became a major approach in social psychology today.

Since 1920s, the most noticeable trend has been the growing importance of experimental approach to the field of social psychology. Another related trend has been the development of psychology of personality, which has been an area shared by both social psychologists and clinical psychologists. This growing interest in both social psychology and personality inspired Morton Prince in 1922 to publish the first major social psychology journal entitled *Journal of Abnormal and Social Psychology*, whose name was changed later on to become *Journal of Personality and Social Psychology*. This journal served as a major vehicle for publication of researches done by American psychologists in these overlapping fields. Carl Murchison and John Dewey in 1929 started another journal named *Journal of Social Psychology* which served as an additional source for this field. Since then, many other journals have been devoted to meet the needs of various aspects of social psychology. *Human Relation*, *Journal of Experimental Social Psychology* and *Journal of Conflict Resolution* are three best examples.

During 1920s and 1930s, the researches in the fields of social attitudes—self and stereotypes were considered very prominent. Thurstone and Chave (1929) and Likert (1932) developed scaling methods for measuring attitudes. Katz and Braly (1933) published the prominent studies relating to social stereotypes of college students. In 1934, G.H. Mead published the seminal work on the self. J.L. Moreno developed sociometry in 1934. *Sociometry* is a system of measuring patterns of social interaction based on individual's choices. This method allowed researchers to assess personal attractions within the members of the group. In the same year, that is, in 1934, R.T. LaPiere tried to investigate inconsistencies between attitude (racial prejudice) and related behaviours (discrimination) in the field situation. In 1936, Muzafer Sherif demonstrated, by creating social norms in controlled setting, that even complex, but realistic situation can be meaningfully studied experimentally in laboratory. In the same year, that is, in 1936, George Gallup developed methods for conducting public polls and surveys. In the same year, a small group of psychologists founded, what was called the Society for the Psychological Study of Social Issues (SPSSI), now a division of American Psychological Association. This organisation was mainly committed to the scientific use of social science to promote human welfare. During the period under review, there has also been an increase in the amount of cross-fertilisation between social psychology and industrial psychology. The best example of this cross-fertilisation is the classic study of production and morale at the Hawthrone plant of Western Electric Company in the late 1920s and early 1930s. This study was essentially a field study of social behaviour and much of the work done by industrial psychology can be called *applied social psychology*. Likewise, educational psychology has also moved from its earlier preoccupation with measurement and principles of learning to the concept of the classroom and school as social situations, which has been broadly called *social psychology of education*. In 1937, J.L. Moreno founded a journal entitled *Sociometry*, which published researches done on the structure and process in groups and networks. Later on, this journal was renamed as *Social Psychology Quarterly*. In 1939, Kurt Lewin, R. Lippitt and R. White, using Lewin's field theory, studied reactions of the members of the group to various style of leadership such as autocratic style, democratic style and laissez-faire style. In this way, they initiated the era of studying group dynamics experimentally by observing the effect of different leadership styles on the productivity and morale of boys' play groups. Thus, we see that by 1930s, the scientific ideals of objectivity, precision and accuracy dominated the field of social psychology (Allport, 1968).

It is commonly said that the person who has the most impact on the development of social psychology is Adolf Hitler (Cartwright, 1979). This statement apparently appears to be ironical, but it contains the element of truth. In fact, both the events that precipitated the Second World War and the war itself had a profound impact on the development of social psychology. As Nazi domination spread across Europe and persecution of Jews continued in 1930s and 1940s, a number of psychologists left their homelands to live in North America and Great Britain. One result of this was that the major growth in social psychology was conducted in North America and Great Britain for the next few decades. For example, Sherif's famous summer camp study (1936) in which teenage boys had participated, demonstrated that how conflicts develop between groups. Likewise, Adorno, Frankel–Brunswik, Levinson and Sanford (1950) developed an idea of authoritarian personality in an attempt to understand and explain prejudice and blind and strict obedience to authority. Stanley Milgram's popular experiment investigating obedience to authority was very much instrumental in understanding why too many Germans had blindly obeyed orders, which resulted in mass murder of Jews by Nazis or Holocaust during 1939–45.

2. Developments in between 1945–1970 A.D.

The developments in the starting of the decade 1940 were more prominent for the growth of social psychology. In 1941, William Foote Whyte used the technique of participant observation for studying and describing the social functioning of teenage street gangs. In 1943, Theodore Newcomb investigated the impact of social pressures on attitudes held by students at Bennington College. In 1946, R.F. Bales developed a categorical framework for systematically observing communication and role differentiation in various task groups. All these developments led to systematic explanation of the field in scientific way. However, during 1940s, there occurred a profound impact of Kurt Lewin, whose creativity and dedication had very clearly marked him as the founder of applied social psychology. He had a strong faith that the integration of theory, research and practice was the essential and very useful ingredient of social psychology. As a consequence of his dedications and integration of theory with research, he developed many original concepts such as action research, field theory and sensitivity training. In fact, it was Lewin's effort, which led to the formation of three well-known organisations in America—Commission on Community Interrelations, Research

Centre for Group Dynamics and National Training Laboratories (*NTL*). Researches conducted at these three organisations proved a boon for the further development of social psychology as a scientific discipline. Alarming situations heated by Second World War also drew social psychologists into the search for solutions to immediate practical problems. The government of United States put before social psychologists the task of convincing civilians to change their eating habits such as to eat less steak and more kidneys and lever, to drink more milk as well as to feed their babies with orange juice (Lewin, 1947). Kurt Lewin, one of the scientists who had fled Hitler, held the view that all behaviours depend on the person's life space, which was defined by him as a subjective map of the person's current goals and his social environment. He is often called as the father of modern social psychology and is one of the first researchers to study group dynamics and organisational development. Social psychologists were also requested to help the military personnel in keeping their morale up as well as in improving the performance of aircraft and task crews (Stouffer et al., 1949). They were also engaged in the task of teaching troops to resist enemy propaganda and even to teach them lesson regularly (Hovland, Janis and Kelley, 1953). Another significant and contributing development took place in 1946 when Solomon Asch demonstrated that cognitive set has an impact on what impression people form about others. In 1951, he further expanded the field by demonstrating the fact that under some conditions, individuals in group would tend to conform to the position of majority when their beliefs are questioned. During the Second World War, some other psychologists also appreciated the demand for applied theory and research for scientific development of social psychology. As a consequence, they established and developed several prominent research areas like mass communication, attitude measurement and change, morale and leadership, propaganda, group structure, intergroup prejudice, stereotyping, interpersonal relations, etc. In 1950, R.F. Bales, on the basis of his extensive research, developed a categorical framework for systematically observing communication and role differentiation in task groups. In the same year, that is, in 1950, G. Homans published a famous book *The Human Group*, which was a seminal treatise on group structure and process. In 1950s, the field of social psychology continued to expand and develop in different new directions. In 1953, Carl Hovland and his colleagues at Yale University completed the numerous studies on the effect of persuasive communication on social attitudes. In 1954, Gordon Allport published a famous and the most influential book *The Nature of Prejudice* in which he presented a very important analysis of intergroup prejudice and stereotyping. In 1957, Leon Festinger proposed *theories of social comparison and cognitive dissonance*, which proved to be very pertinent theories having high heuristic importance in the field of social psychology. The theory of cognitive dissonance reflected an approach to attitude change based on the idea that people strive for consistency between attitude and behaviour. In fact, the emergence of theory of cognitive dissonance marked a shift of attention from the study of social interaction of groups to the study of those processes, which were lying within the individual. Also, at that time, studies within a laboratory setup were being considered more standard than studies being conducted in a field work. This stand also continued during 1970s, thus establishing experimental social psychology as the mainstream of the discipline. As a result of emphasis upon studying individual processes rather than group process, social psychologists studied many individual processes, which were considered potentially relevant for behaviours of real life. Aggression, prosocial behaviour and altruism, obedience to authority interpersonal attraction and conformity to group norms were some of the examples of such individual behaviour. In 1958, Fritz Heider published a treatise entitled *The Psychology of Interpersonal Relations*, which laid the foundation for attribution theory and research. In 1959, John Thiabut and Harold Kelley published a book entitled *The Social Psychology of Groups* in which a general theory of social exchange and interpersonal relations was formulated. John Thibaut is well known for interdependence theory from 'The Social Psychology of Groups':

3. Developments after 1970 AD

After 1970, social psychology continued to expand and strengthen its base as an experimental social psychology. Social psychologists expanded the fields of attribution theory and interpersonal relations. In 1975, E.O. Wilson published a treatise entitled *Sociobiology: The New Synthesis* that produced a new craze for theorising about the role of evolution in social and psychological behaviour. Towards the beginning of 1980s, social psychologists started paying attention to the field researches. They started showing an interest in what was called *cross-cultural research* so that they could study and compare the same behaviour in different cultures. Triandis (1977) presented a general framework for linking cultural influences to social behaviour, which in turn, attracted many studies that increased the external validity or generalisability of social psychology. Since 1980, a renewed interest in the study of social self had arisen among social psychologists, who started giving more emphasis on the cognitive aspects of social behaviour. This field grew so rapidly that many new social psychology journals were started to get published. Thus, keeping an overall view over developments taking place in prosperous 1950s and 1960s, it can be said that social psychology grew and flourished well. During this period, Europe was recovering and rebuilding from the destruction of the war. Therefore, social psychologists in several countries developed theoretical and various research approaches to wide varieties of areas, particularly those concerned with group membership, influence within groups and competitive relationships between groups (Doise, 1978; Moscovici, 1980; Tajfel, 1978). By 1970s, social psychologists, on both side of Atlantic, had developed a set of reliable findings, which was definitely a sign of scientific maturity.

Also during 1960s, there was a strong move towards an integrated theoretical understanding of social and cognitive processes and towards further applications of social psychological theory to important applied problems. Although cognitive themes and theories became a natural framework for integration of both within and outside social psychology, this cognitive revolution was not a new revolution for social psychology because its formation had been laid decades earlier in Allport's, Sherif's and Lewin's research work in 1930s and Stouffer's and Hovland's studies in 1940s. Basic concepts such as attitude, beliefs, values, norms already being used in social psychology, began to be applied in the new areas of study by social psychologists. Personal relationship, aggression, prosocial behaviour, stereotyping and discrimination covered such new areas. During 1970s and 1980s, these applications were greatly facilitated by those experimental methods and research techniques that were found very relevant to the field of memory and perception by cognitive psychologists. Thus, we find that theoretical concerns and selected experimental methods and research techniques have converged, as the researchers in different areas of social psychology focus their attention on the study of cognitive processes.

Apart from paying their attention to cognitive processes, social psychologists have also shown concern for the social processes, which directly or indirectly create an impact upon everything the people do. Social psychologists consider that human behaviour is influenced by perception, attitude, beliefs and their interpretation, and simultaneously, also hold that these factors, in turn, are fundamentally shaped by person's relationship to other, his thought about the reaction and group membership that help him to define who he is (Markus, Kitayama and Heiman, 1996). This scientific understanding of the way social and cognitive processes work together for moulding all social behaviour got further impetus from the increasing integration of North American social psychology with European social psychology.

Thus, we see that social psychology, which formally started in 1908 with the publication of two textbooks, has today expanded its horizon. Nowadays, researchers from all domains of social psychology are working together for studying the effects of social and cognitive processes to provide scientific explanation of people's experience and behaviour.

OVERVIEW OF SOCIAL PSYCHOLOGY IN INDIAN PERSPECTIVE

Although we know about the practical aspects of social behaviour since our ancient times, the schematic social psychology in India started in 1920s mostly as borrowed and transported discipline from the west. Traditionally, social psychology has remained largely concerned with intraindividual processes and social cognition. However, the emergence of Second World War produced a strong demand for social psychology to attend the various practical social problems. Accordingly, social psychologists started paying their attention to such problems and targeted their researchers to find out solutions to these social problems. Majority of Indian's belief is guided by the philosophy of *Advaita Vedanta*. We know that this philosophy does not make distinction between human and society or between self and non-self. Western traditions emphasise upon the dichotomy between the self and the others. Unlike western tradition of understanding the social behaviour, the Indian view emphasises upon the interrelations of human existence, keeping in view that the important model is human society and not individual distinct from others. In fact, for Indians, the individual and the society remain in a state of symbiotic relationship, where one cannot separate each other (Sinha, 1981). Moreover, the idea of *Vasudhaiba Kutumbakam* gives strong emphasis upon the interrelatedness of the whole community. In fact, such emphasis starts from oneself and extends to the entire world.

As we know, psychology was first introduced as a subject at Master stage in India at Calcutta University in 1916. The second university department of Psychology was started in Mysore in 1924 and third at Patna in 1946. With the initiatives of the then vice-chancellor of Calcutta University (Sir Ashutosh Mukherjee), Sir Brojendra Nath Seal, who was professor of Mental and Moral philosophy, was given responsibility of drafting the first syllabus for experimental psychology in 1905. The department of experimental psychology was established in 1916. Prof. Narendra Nath Sengupta, who had doctorate degree in philosophy from Harvard University, chaired this department till 1929. He had an opportunity of studying under Hugo Munsternberg, who was a student of Wilhelm Wundt and he had received training with Robert Yerks and E.B. Holt. He had also visited the laboratory of psychology at Cornell University. When Prof. Sengupta moved to Lucknow University, he got a chance to work with an eminent sociologist, Radhakamal Mukherjee and along with him, he published the first book in the field of social psychology entitled *Introduction to Social Psychology* in 1928 from London. This fine precedence of scholars from psychology and sociology working together was, however, not followed in later works in social psychology in India. In fact, the distance between the two disciplines widened further.

Prof. Sengupta challenged the concept of group mind and was against reduction of mind to brain. Sengupta and Singh (1926) conducted one of the earliest investigations regarding social facilitation. Although this study was modeled on experiments first carried by Allport and his colleagues, it definitely laid the foundation for experimental social psychology in India. Other important studies were conducted by Prasad (1935, 1950) and Sinha (1952) on rumour. In fact, Prasad had collected and analyzed more than 35 thousand rumours, relating to the earthquake in Bihar in 1934, using the technique of serial production of Bartlett (1932). Prasad (1935), Sinha (1952) later published it in form of research article entitled *The Psychology Rumour: A Study Relating to the Great Indian Earthquake of 1935*. Subsequently, Sinha (1952) also studied rumours and related behaviour of people in various catastrophic situations. These three early studies became the base for formulation of theory of cognitive dissonance by Festinger (1957). Later Bose (1939) also opined that the themes of social psychology, although much theoretical in nature, provided a better scope for comparative analysis of social behaviour along cultural lines. Further, reviewing the work of his time, Bose (1939) lamented that it was mostly replication of Western researches. Barring few experimental studies, most of studies in social psychology of his time were nothing but simply logical analysis of the various social phenomena. Mukherjee (1940) had studied ability differentials in work in isolation and group. In fact, social psychology before independence, was comparatively less popular than other branches like Clinical psychology and General psychology (Ganguli, 1971).

After India's independence rapid unplanned expansion of this discipline occurred. Despite this, some departments were recognized for their significant contributions in specific areas such as Utkal University for the study of social disadvantage and deprivation, Allahabad University for social change and development and A.N. Sinha Institute of Social Studies, Patna for the study of social motives, social values and leadership.

During post-independent era, there also occurred shifts in the nature of discipline as well as in research themes and methodology. In post-independence days, the Government of India was also very much keen to go with western economic development because it considered the adoption of western technology as panacea for quick socio-economic development of the country. As a consequence, import of western science and technology started. Many academic exchange programmes such as Commonwealth, Fulbright etc., were started and a large number of Indian scholars went abroad for higher studies and many western scholars came to India. At that time, Gardner Murphy under UNESCO plan came to India and many Indian psychologists worked with him for understanding social-psychological consequences of communalism and social violence that occurred between Hindu and Muslim at the time of partition of India and Pakistan in 1947. These researches were summarized in Murphy's book entitled *In the Minds of Men*.

In the 60s and 70s, many social psychologists returned after their training in experimental social psychology in western universities and started working in India according to their training. In a few cases such attempt resulted in excellent programmatic research. For example, the *National Seminar on Perspectives in Experimental Social Psychology in India* at Allahabad in 1979 proved a good platform for presentation and discussion of experimental social psychology researches, which was later on published by Pandey (1981) in the book form. In later years, social psychologists continued working in areas of prejudice, stereotypes, knowledge, attitude and practice (KAP). KAP studies became very popular and about more than 240 such studies were conducted in late sixties (Sinha, 1986). Large scale surveys were conducted using various attitude measures. Adinarayan (1953, 1957, 1998) conducted studies of racial and communal attitudes and caste attitudes and this was intelligently followed by Rath and Sircar (1960) and Anant (1970) and many others. Sinha (1969) took up the lead in applied research by conducting studies of villages. Prabhu (1954) also worked a lot on Indian social psychology. However, most of the researches in early post-independent India replicated the western models (Nandy, 1974, Mitra, 1972).

The establishment of the Indian Council of Social Science Research (ICSSR) was another important milestone for the acceleration of the development of discipline of social psychology. The survey of psychological researches over the years by ICSSR have critically reviewed Indian researches. The first ICSSR survey covered the period of research from the beginning in 1920s to 1969 (Mitra, 1972). This first survey included only one chapter on social psychology (Rath, 1972). However, Ganguli (1971) found that in the period 1920–1967, social psychology ranked first with 16% of all publications. The second ICSSR Survey covered the researches conducted from 1971 to 1976 (Pareek, 1980, 1981) and devoted eight chapters to various aspects of social behaviour. The contents of these chapters reflected adequate emphasis upon applied social psychology covering areas like communication and influence processes, political processes, psychology of work, environmental issues, poverty, inequality, dynamics of social change, etc. The third ICSSR survey covered the period from 1977 to 1982 (Pandey, 1988) and one of its three volumes was exclusively devoted to *Basic and Applied Social Psychology*. It contained various, important review chapters on attitude and social cognitions, intergroup relationship and social tensions, social influence processes, social psychology of education, dynamics of rural development, etc. In fact, this third survey recorded significant progress in basic and applied social psychological researches. The fourth ICSSR Survey, *Psychology in India Revisited*: *Developments in the discipline* covered the period from 1983 to 1992 (Pandey, 2000, 2001, 2004) and was published in three volumes. Volume 3 deals with the domains of applied social and organizational psychology with chapters like attitudes, social cognition, justice, social values, poverty and deprivation, environment and behaviour, motivation and leadership and human performance. These various chapters covered definitely indicated the dominance of applied orientation in social psychology. The fifth ICSSR Survey covered the period from 1993 to 2003 (Misra, 2009) and has been published in four volumes. Of these four volumes, Volume 2 entitled *Social and Organisation Processes* comprises six chapters on different aspects of social behaviour as well as organisational behaviour. The chapters related to social behaviour are: social-psychological processes: understanding the social world, social-psychological perspectives on self and identity as well as psychology and societal development.

Another important source that has contributed to development and enhancement of the status of social psychology in India is the ICSSR-sponsored *Indian Psychological Abstracts and Reviews*, a six monthly journal edited by Prof. B.N. Puhan. The journal also published a review article in each issue. It has been found that from 1994 to 2003, there were 19 published review articles, out of which 12 were related to different areas of social behaviour like leadership and power, social cognition, values, ethical behaviour, environmental pollutions, etc. In its 17th volume (No.1+2) released in 2011 and edited by Prof. K.D. Broota, there were 40 review articles out of a total of 132 only from the area of social psychology including applied social psychology in Indian Psychological Abstracts and Reviews. All these contributed to the popularity of social psychology. Due to such growing popularity, many Indian psychologists who were trained in experimental areas later moved to the social psychology. A very good example is Prof. D. Sinha (Allahabad University) who had been trained under the guidance of Bartlett but later switched to conducting researches on social phenomena like rumours, villages in transition, etc. (Sinha, 1952, 1969).

In the historical development of social psychology in India, the 70s and 80s also witnessed the beginnings of Doctoral Programmes with course work. Such programmes first started at Indian

Institute of Technology at Kanpur and later to the Department of Psychology, Allahabad. Still later, such programmes also spread to other institutions in limited way in form M.Phil programmes (such as Delhi and Meerut). The major purpose of such programmes was to train the new generation of social psychologists and help them understand social reality in indigenous context. In such programmes greater emphasis on applied social psychology under indigenous context was clearly visible. The *National Seminar* on *Applied Social Psychology in India* held in 1987 in Bhopal further emphasised the important role of social psychology in solving social problems related to change and development. The book entitled *Applied Social Psychology in India* (Misra, 1990) was directly the outcome of this seminar.

Like in western countries, social psychology in India has been influenced by both *Zeitgeist* (that is, spirit of time) as well as by the *Ortgeist* (that is, way the sprit of time expresses itself in different places) during its post independence period. In this period, the national concern is that of a better socio-economic reconstruction and overall development. Indian Social psychologists by virtues of their researches in different fields through various enthusiastic programmes have contributed a lot in attaining the national goals. In this direction, there are large number of studies covering varied areas of social behaviour. It is not possible to attend to all those areas here but a lucid attempt has been made to cover four such important areas as under:

1. Attitude, prejudice and intergroup relations: Since Adinarayan's (1941, 1957, 1964) researches in racial, communal and caste attitudes and colour prejudice as well as Murphy's (1953) book *In the Minds of Men*, many researches have been conducted by Indian social psychologists who did attitude surveys regarding all possible kinds of social, cultural, political, economic, national and international issues (Rath, 1972). They assessed various social stereotypes and prejudice using popular attitude measurement techniques like those of Likert, Thurstone and Bogardus. There have also been studies in the area of national stereotypes and international relations. Sinha and Upadhyaya (1960) studied the attitudes of Indians toward Chinese and found significant changes in attitude from positive to negative in post Indo-Chinese war period.

Indian caste system is not only unique but also plays a significant role in determining social relationship. Social psychologists have shown interest in caste-based identities, inter-caste relationship, self-perceptions and caste-related tensions. For example, Sidana, Singh and Shrivastava (1976) reported that positive attitudes towards one's own caste and negative attitudes towards other castes develop quite early among children. Paranjpe (1970) studied caste prejudice and reported that social contacts between different castes were extremely limited. Dalits had a negative self-image whereas Brahmins had the most positive self-image. Prasad (1976) studied caste awareness in Bihari Children and reported that there was higher caste awareness among low caste children as compared to high caste children. Singh (1988 a) focused upon the developmental aspects of caste and religious prejudice and identity. Related areas covered in social psychological research are intergroup attitudes and relative deprivation (Tripathi and Shrivastava, 1981) as well as sex stereotypes (Williams et al., 1982). Still another area of special significance and relevance is terrorism and secessionism. In this area a welcome work has been done by Angomcha (1999) who has enthusiastically examined the role of relative deprivation and social identity in violent actions and secessionism.

2. Social motives, social values and development: A very important area that persisted in popularity was achievement motivation. For assessing achievement motivation of school and college students, several measures were constructed. In early 60s, several Indian psychologists, were attracted towards need-achievement theory of McClelland. Many of them were convinced by the argument of McClelland that a very important cause of India's underdevelopment was low achievement of Indians. In Kakinola, Andhra Pradesh, Small Scale Industrial Training Institute was set up where many Indian psychologists collaborated with him (McClelland) providing entrepreneurial training in light of McClelland's theory. Some social psychologists also questioned the appropriateness of need for achievement theory in the scarce resource society of India (Sinha, 1968; Sinha & Pandey, 1970). These researchers showed that in two high n-Ach groups, one who was selfish tended to hoard resources more than the altruistic type. This posed a serious question mark on the relevance of McClelland's theory in Indian context. In 1980s, research in this area took a new turn. Agrawal and Misra (1986) argued for understanding of the meaning of achievement in Indian culture and they examined achievement and means of college students in their own notion about achievement goals. Besides, several research projects were also undertaken to explore the need for achievement in improving entrepreneurial activities (Sinha, 1969; Hundal, 1971; Hundal and Singh, 1975; Muthayya et al., 1979).

Social values and their link with development have also been the major concern with various social psychology research programmes. The study conducted by Sinha and Kao (1988) is one good example of such attempt where the relationship of Hindu religion with personality, attitudinal and behavioral patterns and their association with economic development has been studied. Sinha and Sinha (1974) have identified a set of middle-class values that are hostile to the development. Sinha (1988) has argued that values that are functional to the national development and values that are dysfunctional to the national development should be clearly identified. Researches conducted in individualism and collectivism have shown collectivism as dominant Indian orientation and have also examined its relationship to the development process (Verma, 1992). Punckar (1989) accepted that some of values common to industrially successful Western and Japanese systems are necessary for the development of India's industrialization.

3. Social influence processes: Social influence processes are considered basic to social behaviour and begin when two or more persons come into contact and start interacting. A range of social behaviours related to helping and altruism, interpersonal attraction, impression management, manipulative social behaviour (ingratiation and Machiavellianism), leadership, social power and control mechanisms have been investigated by Indian social psychologists.

So far as the research on helping behaviour is concerned, it started in the 1960s in the west but later also attracted Indian social psychologists Krishnan (1981) conducted several researches on prosocial behaviour. Pandey et al. (1987) have examined the developmental and social psychological determinants of prosocial behaviour and have demonstrated the impact of birth order, age and gender on children's helping behaviour. First-born children were found to show more helping behaviour than last born or the only child in the family. Likewise, older children were found to donate more than the younger children. Pandey and Griffitt (1974, 1977) have extended the idea that dependency can be used as an instrument to seek help from others. However, Pandey (1988) has remarked that research in helping behaviour is still to get ground in India.

Interpersonal attraction and interpersonal relationship have been another important areas where social psychologists have done commendable work. In this field, several social psychologists did programmatic research (Singh, 1988b; Singh, Gupta and Dalal, 1979). In these researches, some mathematical models were used to explain structure judgments and decision within the framework of Anderson's information integration theory.

Researches on manipulative social behaviours were next important milestones in the development of social psychology. Ingratiation and Machiavellianism were extensively preferred manipulative social behaviours that have been researched (Pandey, 1981; Tripathi, 1981). Ingratiation is one of the popular behavioural tactics, which is used by a person to manipulate another person. Pandey reported that in Indian society in which there are limited resources and higher uncertainties, people take recourse to ingratiation tactics, frequently for manipulating the behaviours of others. Machiavellianism which is disposition or a personality type involving manipulation of others, aims at controlling and influencing others. Tripathi (1981) has conducted a series of studies on ingratiating tactics of the Machiavellianism. The goal of both types of manipulation is to control and influence others (Pandey & Rastogi, 1979).

Researches in the area of leadership date back to the mid-1950s. In earlier studies, the social psychologists using western frameworks, reported relationship between employee-centred supervision and job satisfaction and morale. Later work on leadership also proposed new models as a part of programmatic research. Sinha (1980, 1994) proposed the NT (Nurturant Task) model of leadership, which clearly shows that in India the effective leadership style is personalized and is centred on deference for the leader by the followers and the nurturance and affection shown by leader for their followers.

Researches in the area of social power and control mechanism are also important contributors to the development of social psychology. The research works done by Kakar (1971, 1974) are major source. His work on authority and power in the Indian context has indicated that any leadership style can be better understood with reference to the psychohistorical framework of the subordinates. His analysis further reveals that the image of superior is either nurturant or assertive, with a strong preference for the nurturnat. He suggested that the work behaviour of subordinates in response to the style of superior is dependent upon personality dynamics, the stage of life and the ideals of the group from which subordinate derive his sense of identity. Sinha (1982) has further suggested that such relationships are jointly determined by the high power need of the Indian executives and the hierarchical structure. Sinha (1977) had already proposed that due to intense power striving among Indian adults, one may experience loss of team spirit as well as widespread mistrust and suspicion. He has reported three major realities, that is, poverty, crowding and social hierarchy as major sources of power striving in Indian society.

4. Poverty, deprivation, social disadvantage and social justice: Poverty, deprivation, social disadvantage and social inequalities are the harsh realities of Indian society. The most important and first exhaustive study of poverty was started by Dandekar and Rath (1971). They had reported that 40% of rural and 50% of urban populations were below poverty line. In the first ICSSR survey there was no serious talk about poverty (Mitra 1972) but in the second ICSSR Survey, poverty and welfare politics became major issues (Pareek, 1981). The then government of India also included it as one of political agendas with popular slogan of *Garbi Hatao* (remove poverty). As a consequence, many projects on poverty and deprivation were funded by ICSSR. In third ICSSR Survey, poverty and deprivation again remained important thrust area of research (Tripathi, 1988). Many researches showed deleterious and negative consequences of poverty and deprivation on cognitive abilities and achievement motivation. Here worth mentioning research is that of Tripathi and Misra (1975) relating to the prolonged deprivation because it led to the significant changes in the measurement of deprivation in real-life situations. In fact, they have identified 15 aspects of a person's natural environment in which lack of experience results in prolonged deprivation. Social disadvantage is closely linked with deprivation. Most socially disadvantaged groups such as tribal and dalits are poor and deprived. (Dube & Sachdev, 1983; Husain, 1983) A special number of journal *Social Change* has devoted to *Social Disadvantage and Education in India* (Social Change, 1980).

Problems of poverty, deprivation and social disadvantage bring issue of providing justice for the members of these groups. Researches in this area started in 1960s and they have focused on distributive justice. A very commendable research programme on distributive justice in reward allocation in Indian context was done by Krishnan (2000). He has demonstrated that people exhibit individual and cultural variations in considering what is fair to them. Two important cross-cultural studies comparing American and Indian participants revealed that Indians tend to prefer allocating more on the basis of rule of need in comparison to US American participants. In several studies conducted by Pandey and Singh (1997) it was found that the importance of need or merit itself was dependent upon the context in which the allocation was done.

Thus we find that the development of social psychology in India has seen more ups than downs. Therefore, a contextually rooted and sensitive social psychology has to be responsive to various social behaviours and problems. Various researches done by Sinha (1984, 1993) as well as by Pandey and Naidu (1992) and many others have revealed a clear deviation from western traditions by focusing more on modifying theories, models, etc. to suit Indian socio-cultural setting and thus providing a consolidated ground for conceptual indigenisation.

SOCIAL PSYCHOLOGY AS A SCIENCE

We have seen that social psychology is broadly the scientific study of nature and causes of human social behaviour. Social psychologists not only formulate theories but also engage in putting empirical generalisations on the basis of their researches. Naturally, then one relevant question arises here — is social psychology a science? Can we consider social psychology a scientific discipline in the way we consider Chemistry, Biology and Physics as scientific ones?

Any scientific field rests upon several assumptions, of which three are important:

1. The first assumption is that scientists assume that there exists a real and external world independent of ourselves. This world is subject to investigation by the scientists.
2. Second assumption is that relations in the world are organised in terms of cause and effect. In other words, there are discoverable causes for all events in the scientists' domain of interest.
3. Third assumption is that knowledge concerning the external world is objective and there does not lie any element of subjectivity. The results obtained by one scientist can easily be verified by the others. This is called *objectivity*.

These three assumptions are basic to all branches of science. In addition to these assumptions, any field that claim to be a science should have certain critical characteristics or hallmarks like following:

1. Every science rests on the accurate observation of facts. If the field or discipline does not permit a careful, precise and error-free observation of facts, it cannot be considered as science. This is called *accuracy*.
2. Every science has an explicit and formal methodology. Scientists follow this explicit methodology in making observations. As a consequence, one scientist's finding can be repeatedly verified by the others. This is called *skepticism*.

3. Every science is primarily involved in accumulation of facts and generalisations. Sometimes, a fact many undergo reinterpretation of its meaning, but its essential characteristics remain intact. If the existing evidence suggests that the currently held views are inaccurate, then it should be reinterpreted for change. This is called *open-mindedness*.
4. Every science includes a body of explicit theory or theories, which serves to give systematic and organised facts and empirical observations. Sometimes, these theories may also serve to guide new empirical investigation.
5. Every science after obtaining a reasonable level of development, provides at least some degree of prediction and control over selected aspects of the environment.

Let us now hold social psychology up against these five hallmarks:

Social psychology very clearly meets the *first hallmark*, that is, reliance on empirical observation. Today, social psychology encompasses several thousands of empirical studies. Social psychology also meets the *second hallmark* because it uses an explicit and formal methodology for conducting empirical observation. The most common methods used by social psychologists are experimental method, survey method, field studies, etc. *Third hallmark*, that is, accumulation of observed facts is also met satisfactorily by social psychology. Social psychologists continue to accumulate facts regarding the conditions under which certain social behaviour occurs or also the conditions under which a particular social behaviour is least likely to occur. Social psychology also meets the *fourth hallmark*, that is, reliance on theory. Social psychology has two types of framework—*theoretical perspectives* and *middle-range theories*. Theoretical perspectives provide general explanations for a wide array of social behaviours in a variety of situations. Middle-range theories make predictions about specific types of social behaviour under restricted conditions. Therefore, middle-range theories are narrow, focused frameworks that identify the conditions, which produce a specific social behaviour.

However, with respect to the *fifth hallmark*, there arises some problem in considering social psychology as a science. The fifth hallmark very clearly states that after attaining a reasonable level of development, every science provides some degree of prediction and control over the phenomena investigated. The stand of social psychology with respect to this hallmark is not clear because it has so far provided only a modest degree of predictability and control over social behaviour. Although social psychology well explains the social behaviour, it does less well in predicting future events or providing a strict basis for control of behaviour. However, some social psychologists are hopeful that the capacity to predict and control social behaviour will improve to some degree. Part of the problem relating to this fifth hallmark stems from the nature of theories of social psychology. Most of the theories cover only limited range of phenomena or apply only under very restrictive and artificial conditions. These theories often fail to make accurate predictions when attempts are made to apply them to some new settings.

Thus, we see that social psychology meets many characteristics of a science and is close to a more mature physical science. However, it has not yet achieved the same degree of accuracy in making prediction and control as a mature physical science has achieved.

FUNDAMENTAL AXIOMS OF SOCIAL PSYCHOLOGY

There are two fundamental axioms or principles of social psychology, which integrates not only cognitive and social processes but also basic theory and applied research (Smith and Mackie, 2007). Those principles are as follows:

1. People construct their own reality: Every now and then people are forced to think about the world of reality twice. When we come to know that there can be different views about the same social event, we construct our own reality. Think for the time being that you are sitting in a group of five friends, who are watching a cricket match on television. You may discover that your interpretation of the players' behaviour being shown on television is different from others. This happened because you have made your own construction of reality. Social psychologists view that this construction of reality is partly shaped by our cognitive processes (that is, the ways in which our mind works) and partly shaped by social processes (that is, influence from others either actually present or imagined). Cognitive processes operate when we pay attention to the different information, draw some inferences from them, and finally, try to weave them into a meaningful whole. In this sense, an individual's view of the world of reality is definitely in the eye of the beholder like beauty lies in the eye of the beholder.

As said earlier, the construction of reality is also partly shaped by the social processes. They enable us to influence and be influenced by the others' view as we move towards agreement about the nature of reality. We construct a reality about a social event in light of views expressed by the others.

2. Social influence is pervasive: The pervasiveness of social influence is another important axiom of social psychology. It means that other people, whether they are physically present or not, influence our thoughts, feelings and behaviours. We commonly find that a person's thoughts about others' reaction and his identification with any social group tend to mould his perception, feelings, motives and even him too. Sometimes, a person's behaviour and feelings are changed only when he thinks about a particular person or event. For example, one feels very much disturbed by only remembering about an event in which he was trapped by some robbers in a compartment of a train. Sometimes, a person may experience social influence as social pressure when one encounters an aggressive neighbour who forces him to accept his viewpoints. But social influence is said to be most profound when it is least evident, that is, when the person does not have realisation about it, and it really influences one's beliefs and fundamental assumptions. For example, when an aggressive and rebellious teenager becomes a parent and tries to impose a curfew on his own teenagers. This all happens in such a natural way that we attribute it not to social influence but to the simple reality of the world. Thus, we see that social influence has powerful impact upon moulding our thinking, feelings and actions (that is, in moulding the reality we construct)—whether we are with others or alone with our thoughts.

These are two fundamental axioms of social psychology, which help us in understanding the diversity and richness of human social behaviour.

RELATION OF SOCIAL PSYCHOLOGY WITH OTHER SCIENCES

Social psychology bears a close relationship with many different fields such as general psychology, sociology, psychology of personality, anthropology, etc. Here, we shall review this relationship.

1. Social psychology and general psychology: General psychology studies the behaviour of the individual. Although this behaviour may be social, it need not be. Behaviour includes both the activation of sense organ as well as all mental activities. In fact, it arises as reaction to the stimuli, which form a part of the environment. General psychology addresses such topics as human learning, perception, memory, intelligence, motivation, emotion and personality. Being branches of psychology, both general psychology and social psychology has some points of similarities and dissimilarities. The major points of similarities are as under:

(i) Both general psychology and social psychology study behaviour of the individual. This behaviour includes both his internal experiences and external activities.

(ii) Both general psychology and social psychology use the research methods, experiments, psychological tests, etc. The methods used by both are scientific, which means that both proceed through the orderly method of observing, collecting data, classifying it and then making such generalisations, which can be varied and which may form the basis of the prediction.

Despite these similarities, the two branches of psychology do differ:

(i) General psychology studies the behaviour of the individual. It is the scientific study of individual's reactions to stimuli of any kind and his activities in a large variety of situations and has accumulated a systematic knowledge concerning the processes of perception, memory, thinking, learning, intelligence, personality, etc. Social psychology is also interested in individual behaviour, but it focuses its attention on the person's interactions and reactions in social situation. In other words, social psychology also studies individual behaviour, but only in so for as it is around, stimulated and influenced by other individuals, singly or in groups. A parent scolding a child and a teacher teaching his pupil are the examples of individual behaviour being stimulated by the other individual. The other individuals may not be present, but still they affect our thoughts, feelings and behaviour (Alport, 1985). Here, mental pictures of the individuals with whom we have been associated in the past affect our behaviour.

(ii) General psychology and social psychology differ in scope. The former has a wider scope, whereas the latter has a limited scope. This is because of the fact that general psychology studies the behaviour and experience of the individual in general, whereas social psychology limits only to the study of behaviour of the individual in society (Krech, Crutchfield and Ballachey, 1962). In other words, the major concern of social psychology is limited only to the behavioural processes, causal factors and result of interaction among persons and groups (Lindgren, 1985).

(iii) The unit of study of general psychology is the individual, whereas the unit of study of social psychology is the interaction among persons and groups.

Despite these dissimilarities, it can be said that the distinction between general psychology and social psychology is relative. In reality, there is no behaviour of the individual, which is not coexistent with the social environment.

2. Social psychology and sociology: Social psychology and sociology too have much in common and are interdependent. In fact, sociology and psychology are social psychology's parent's disciplines (Myers, 2005, p. 12). Sociology studies society and social psychology studies the individual in society, and since the individual and society cannot exist and subsist without each other, the two sciences are said to be interdependent. Both social psychologists and sociologists tend to share an interest in studying how people behave in groups (Myers, 2005).

Despite this, the two disciplines differ from each other as under:

  (i) The subject matter of sociology and social psychology differs. Sociology is the scientific study of human society. It studies social institutions such as family, religion, politics, stratification within society such as class structure, gender roles, race, caste, etc. and the structure of social units such as groups, networks, formed organisations, bureaucracies, etc. Social psychology is the scientific study of nature and causes of human social behaviour. Human social behaviour includes many things such as the activities of individuals in the presence of others, the process of interaction between two or more persons and the relationships between the individuals and the groups to which they belong. Social psychologists address not only the nature of social behaviour but also seek to discover the preconditions that may have caused the social behaviours.

 (ii) Although social psychologists and sociologists use some of the same research methods, they have a clear-cut distinction in their approach. Social psychologists rely heavily on laboratory experiment methodology, where they tend to manipulate factor such as the presence or absence of the other people in order to examine its impact upon the performance level. The primary concern of social psychology is how an individual's behaviour and social thoughts are affected by social stimuli (often other persons). Social psychologists tend to give emphasis upon the topics like self, person's perception, attribution, attitude change, social learning, modelling, altruism, aggression and interpersonal attraction. Sociologists, on the other hand, rely mainly on a sample survey and observational methods for collecting data. They are mainly interested in the relationship between the individuals and the groups to which they belong. They tend to study topics like socialisation, conformity and deviation, social interaction, leadership, cooperation and competition, social interaction, self-presentation, socio-economic status, where manipulation of factor is difficult or unethical.

Despite these differences, the fields of social psychology and sociology can be best viewed as complimentary, rather than conflicting. In fact, social psychology is such a field where both sociologists as well as psychologists can contribute with their differing approaches.

3. Social psychology and personality psychology: Social psychology and personality psychology are closely related in the sense that both tend to focus on the individual. That is the reason why American Psychological Association has included both branches in the same journal, such as Journal of Personality and Social Psychology, Personality and Social Psychology Bulletin. However, the two fields can be distinguished as under:

  (i) Social psychology mainly emphasises upon the study of the individuals, as they influence or be influenced by the others in the society. Therefore, social psychology bears a social character, whereas personality psychology gives emphasis upon internal functioning and differences between the individuals. For example, it is the main concern of personality psychology that why one individual shows aggressive behaviour or altruistic behaviour towards the other, whereas the main concerns of the social psychologists are how individuals, in general, view and affect one another, what situations lead a person to behave aggressively towards the other or forces him to behave in altruistic way, etc. Thus, as compared to personality psychology, social psychology focuses less on the differences and more on how individuals, in general, view and influence each other.

(ii) Social psychology has shorter history as compared to the history of personality psychology. The scientific study of personality started with Sigmund Freud, who formulated his famous *Psychoanalytic Theory of Personality*. If we trace the history of social psychology, we will find that a scientific study and theorisation started in 1924 when Floyd Allport published a social psychology text, which for the first time, laid emphasis upon the use of the experimental method in social psychology and set forth a research agenda for the next decade to be recognised as the beginning of modern social psychology.

Despite these differences, these two fields have proved boon for the development of each other.

4. Social psychology and anthropology: Social psychology is close to anthropology, which studies the patterns of culture in various parts of the world, particularly among primitive, preliterate and pre-urban people. It uses concepts like culture, custom, folkways and moves to explain the differences between the various cultural groups. Anthropology has branches of which cultural anthropology is very close to social psychology. We know, there are three important segments of socio-cultural behaviour—individual, society and culture. The individual is assigned to psychology, society to sociology and culture to cultural anthropology. A close look reveals that the integration among the individual, society and culture is so close and the interaction among them is continuous, and any researcher who wants to study any one of them by ignoring the other two, very soon comes to a meaningless conclusion. This description shows that social psychology is the meeting point for both sociology and anthropology.

Cultural anthropology basically studies the civilisation of the primitive man because here, we find the beginning of social organisation and social control through rituals, taboos and superstitions. Since much of human life and activities are interlinked with the use of these taboos, superstitions and rituals, anthropologists seek to reconstruct the social pattern and custom of primitive people from the remains found in the ruins of primitive culture.

The interlink of social psychology with cultural anthropology becomes more distinct and obvious when their areas of contact are mentioned. Social psychologists feel indebted to anthropologists because the factual data collected by anthropologists are of immense help in solving many problems of social psychology. In fact, it is the impact of the cultural anthropology that has made social psychology much conscious of the cultural determinants of personality and human behaviour. Social psychologists feel that the real universal content of human behaviour cannot be properly studied without considering the large amount of data obtained from real situations that are made available. In turn, social psychologists help the anthropologists in solving some problems of anthropology like those of superstitions, beliefs, taboos, etc. Not only that, methods of investigation developed by social psychologists are largely being used by anthropology in studying culture and making a comparative study of different cultures.

Despite these points of interlinking, social psychology and anthropology do differ on the following points:

(i) Cultural anthropology studies culture and cultural behaviour of the person, whereas social psychology studies the interaction among the individual, society and culture, rather than any of these three alone.

(ii) Social psychology aims at discovering some relevant laws concerning the individual social behaviour so that social behaviour both at present and in future can be meaningfully

explained. Anthropology, particularly cultural anthropology, tries to look into the past of the cultures and make little suggestions for the future.
(iii) Cultural anthropology generally uses naturalistic observation and participant observation as the main techniques of its investigation, whereas social psychology uses several methods such as experimentation, case history, field experiments, sample survey, projective techniques besides naturalistic observation and participant observation.
(iv) The approach of cultural anthropology is largely academic and it makes little contribution in solving the problems of society. On the other hand, approach of social psychology is practical besides being academic. In other words, social psychologists today have demonstrated keen interest in issues that are considered important outside the laboratory such as crime and aggression, ethnic conflict, AIDS epidemic, declining productivity and global interdependence (Rodin, 1985). Thus, the approach of social psychology is both practical and academic.

So, social psychology and anthropology, though interlinked, also display some points of differences.

SUMMARY AND REVIEW

- *Social psychology* is defined as scientific discipline that investigates the impact of social and cognitive processes on the ways other persons, real, imagined or implied influence many others in different social situations. It provides a scientific explanation of the nature and causes of social behaviour. The main concern of social psychology is the study of social behaviour, including cognitive processes. This includes four types of themes— impact of one individual upon other individual, impact of individual members upon the group to which they belong, impact that a group has on its members and the impact that one group has on another group.
- Social psychology emerged as an independent area of study in 1908, with publication of first two textbooks in the field— one textbook was published by E.A. Ross, a sociologist, and another textbook was published by William McDougall, a psychologist. Prior to this, Norman Triplett, an American researcher, had published the first research study in 1898 in the field of social facilitation and Max Ringlemann, a French agricultural engineer, had published another research study in the field of social loafing. Both Triplett and Ringlemann conducted studies, showing the impact of group effects on the performance. In 1924, the position of social psychology as an experimental disciple was further strengthened by the publication of another textbook by Floyd Allport.

  This book was one of the first systematic treatments in the field of social psychology, which emphasises the use of experimental method in social psychology. During 1930s and 1940s, many European social psychologists fled to North America, where they had a major magic influence upon the growing field of social psychology. Throughout this period, the important questions inspired by the rise of Nazism and the Second World War shaped the researches done in this field. During 1950s, emphasis was given upon the integrated theoretical understanding of social and cognitive processes and also towards the applications of social psychological theory to important applied problems. The period of 1960s saw a larger number of laboratory studies of cognitive dissonance and much emphasis was given upon the areas like altruism, aggression and interpersonal attraction. In 1970s, the growth of attribution theory and expanding interest in interpersonal relations was seen. The period of 1980s witnessed a renewed concern with social self and much emphasis was laid on the cognitive aspects of social behaviour. Since 1990, the social psychologists are continuing their scientific efforts to investigate social cognition, emotions and self, decision-making, prejudice and discrimination,

- language and communication, group performance, etc. Recently, they have also started taking interest in solving practical problems such as ethnic conflict, AIDS, epidemic, crime and aggression, and global interdependence.
- An overview of the development of social psychology in India reveals that it has moved from the study of the intraindividual processes and social cognition to the study of various practical problems of national development and social importance through indigenous means. Thus, the spirit of social psychologists shows inclination towards applied problems, rather than to mere theoretical problems.
- As social psychology is a scientific discipline, it meets the important hallmarks of science. Moreover, all core values, which are essential for considering the field as scientific one, are present in social psychology. These core values are accuracy, objectivity, skepticism and open-mindedness.
- There are two fundamental axioms or principles of social psychology— people construct their own reality and social influence is pervasive.
- Social psychology is frequently compared with general psychology, sociology, personality psychology and anthropology. There are some points of similarities and distinctions with each of the four fields.

REVIEW QUESTIONS

1. Define social psychology. Also discuss its nature.
2. Present a historical background of the development of social psychology.
3. Is social psychology a science? Give arguments with concrete examples.
4. 'Social psychology is the meeting point for both psychology and sociology.' Explain it.
5. Make a comparative study of social psychology with anthropology, general psychology and personality psychology.
6. Outline the major fundamental axioms of social psychology.

2. Research Methods in Social Psychology

Learning Objectives

- Objectives of Social Psychological Research
- Basic Concept of Research
- Basic Research Methods
- Validity of Experiments
- Social Psychology of Experiments
- Ethical Issues and Values in Social Psychological Research
- Role of Theory in Social Psychological Research
- Types of Research in Social Psychology

Key Terms

Action research	Emic approach	Mundane realism
Bio-social effect	Etic approach	Negative correlation
Cause and effect relationship	Evaluation research	Participant effect
Confidentiality	Experimenter's expectancy	Participant observation
Confounding variable	External validity	Positive correlation
Correlational research	Extraneous variable	Psychological effect
Cross-lagged panel correlation	Hypothesis	Random assignment
Debriefing	Independent variable	Rosenthal effect
Deception	Informed content	Situational effect
Dependent variable	Interaction Process Analysis	Survey method
Descriptive research	Internal validity	Systematic observation
Ecological validity	Internet research	
Effect size	Meta-analysis	

Social psychology is an empirical science, which means that its theories and conclusions about social behaviour are tested through the use of systematic data collection and observation. Like other scientists, social psychologists also believe that scientific research methods produce answers to the research questions in a more unbiased and trustworthy manner as compared to when we arrive at some conclusion through our common sense. However, scientists are not perfectly objective in their approach. Being a human being, they are also vulnerable to preconceptions, prejudices and other biases. Because scientists know that such biases can distort their reasoning and findings, they use various research methods to counter such biases and errors. With the help of these research methods, social psychologists try to arrive at the basic goal of reaching general conclusion about human social behaviour that may be as trustworthy as possible.

OBJECTIVES OF SOCIAL PSYCHOLOGICAL RESEARCH

Social psychological researches are conducted for several reasons. The major objectives of such researches include one or more of the following:

1. Describing reality in accurate and precise terms: Some of the researches in social psychology simply aim at describing some features of social process in accurate and precise term. In fact, description is considered as very important when a researcher investigates such phenomenon about which little or nothing is known. Not only that, even when a social psychologist investigates a known phenomenon, he wishes to find out the frequency with which a particular social behaviour occurs in a specified group or population. For example, during the time of pre-election period, the researchers usually conduct public opinion polls to know about how people, in general, feel about political party, its candidate and about the various issues. Here, goal lies in describing the feelings and sentiments of public with accuracy and precision.

2. Identifying correlation between variables: Another objective of social psychological research is to find out the correlation between two or more behaviours or variables. For example, a social psychologist might conduct a study to find out whether the presence of many people in the situation is associated with altruism or whether growing older is associated with the changes in sexual desire or whether caste prejudice is associated with discrimination. Through such correlational studies, social psychologists try to establish a possible reflection about causal relation, although two variables may be correlated without one causing the other and this happens when both variables are caused by a third variable. Thus, correlational evidences are alone not a sufficient evidence for causation.

3. Testing existing theories and also developing new ones: Another objective of social psychological research is to test the validity of the existing theories. If the research supports the prediction derived from the theories, the existing theories are held to be valid one. Sometimes, social psychologists juxtapose several theories that make different predictions and on the basis of the research, they are able to reject one theory in favour of another. In fact, social psychologists seek to develop theories to explain social behaviour in a scientific way. A scientific theory basically reflects a statement about the causal relationship among abstract constructs. Such statement holds for specified types of people, times and situation.

4. Discovering causes of some behaviour or event: Social psychologists also aim at discovering the cause of some behaviours by conducting experimental researches in laboratory or in field. They develop some hypotheses, which basically reflect difference of changes in other behaviour. For example, a social psychologist might hypothesise that the individuals working in the group would tend to exhibit better performance than the persons working alone. After formulating the hypothesis, he would collect the data from the participants or subjects and then test the hypothesis. For supporting the hypothesis, it is essential that the differences or changes in one variable must produce changes in the other variable. If this really happens, as it becomes clear from the analysis of the results of data collection, it is finally concluded that one has caused the other.

5. Helping in solving social problems: Social psychological research also aims at providing help in solving everyday social problems. For example, application of the knowledge of social psychology may help the individuals in learning to control their own aggressive impulses or develop a more satisfactory and intimate personal relations. Recently, social psychologists are frequently using social psychological principles for understanding prejudice against people, who are suffering from AIDS, cancer, etc., and also in helping sexually active people to engage in safer sex practices (Taylor, Peplau and Sears, 2006).

Thus, we see that social psychological research has some obvious aims.

BASIC CONCEPTS OF RESEARCH

Before discussing the various research methods and the details of the research process, it is essential to throw some light upon a few scientific and research concepts. Knowledge of these concepts is considered fundamental for doing research. A few such concepts are being discussed here:

1. Variables and hypotheses: Most of the research projects begin with some propositions called *hypothesis*, which links two or more than two variables. Hypothesis may be suggested by observation of a given social behaviour or it may be derived from a theory. One of the popular hypotheses in social psychology is the *diffusion of responsibility hypothesis*, which states that greater the number of people present in any crisis situation, the less likely is the probability of single individual offering individual assistance. Here, two variables linked by the hypothesis are the number of people present in the crisis situation and the rendering individual assistance. The dependent variable is rendering individual assistance and the independent variable is the number of people present in the crisis situation. In social psychological research, frequently, there are more than one independent variables because social behaviour often tends to be complex one.

2. Operational definitions: In social psychological researches operational definitions of the variable are preferred. An *operational definition* is a statement of operations necessary to produce and measure any concept. In simple language, it can be said that operational definition defines a concept in terms of how it is measured. Although social psychologists as well as psychologists, in general, experience difficulty in operationally defining their variables or concepts because of their abstract nature, their efforts are definitely praiseworthy which fulfil the criteria of being the operational one. For example, in one test of diffusion of responsibility hypothesis by Latane and Rodin (1969), the individual assistance (dependent variable) was defined as the participants going from one room to the next room offering assistance to a young woman, who had pretended to have fallen from a chair upon which she was standing. The independent variable was operationally defined as the number of individuals present when the accident occurred.

3. Reliability and validity: *Reliability* refers to the consistency or stability over time of measurements. Reliable operational definitions will yield the same results for different investigators if the other things are kept equal. The reliability of operational definitions can be easily assessed by having two or more observers, who independently record the same set of social behaviour. Generally, if the observers agree on about 80% to 85% of the recorded observations, they are accepted as being reliable ones.

Validity, here, refers to whether the operational definitions have actually measured what they are supposed to measure. In simple words, it ensures whether the operational definition is a real indicator of the theoretical variable. There are several techniques of assessing the validity of the operational definitions, but they suffer from some limitations. They tend to be either extremely difficult to apply or are inconclusive in demonstrating validity. The best technique is to use an alternative source of information, but unfortunately, multiple indicators are not available for most of the variables. Even when multiple indicators are available, it cannot be said with certainty that which of the different indicators is the most valid or the closest to the reality.

4. Causal relationship and non-causal relationship: In social psychological researches, two types of relationship are frequently studied by social psychologists—*causal relationship* and *non-causal relationship*. In causal relationship, it is possible to state that an independent variable causes or produces the dependent variable. The major problem in identifying causal relationship is the elimination of alternative explanation of the behaviour being studied. The failure to eliminate the alternative explanation of behaviour has been vividly shown in the Hawthorne studies conducted in 1927–1932, with the purpose of determining the factors that affect productivity in factory work environment (Roethlisberger and Dickson, 1939). In such experiments, the effect of the various work conditions such as light intensity, frequency and length of rest periods, and the type of supervision (all independent variables) upon the work performance (dependent variable) was examined. All participants were female employees and for two years, the lighting, rest periods, and supervision were kept varied. Results revealed that each change caused production to increase. However, eventually, it became apparent that it was not the change in light, rest periods or supervision, but the attention of the researchers that caused increase in the production.

Social psychologists also study non-causal relationship, also called *correlational* or *associational relationship*. For example, social psychologists may want to study the associational relationship between self-esteem and achievement of the children. After conducting the study and making the interpretation of the data, they may conclude that both variables are correlated. But at the same time, such results do not ensure that self-esteem causes higher achievement. Both are related to each other because both may be linked to the underlying and unmeasured intelligence and family social status.

5. Sampling: The primary objective of the social psychological research, like any other research in social science, is to make generalisation to all humans or at least to some significant segments of the human beings. It is not ordinarily possible for the researcher to test any proposed hypothesis or principle on every individual of the population to which he or she belongs. Therefore, the researcher has to remain satisfied with some selected individuals from the population. These selected individuals are called *samples* and the procedure is called *sampling*. The most frequently used sampling procedure in experimental social psychology is *simple random sampling*, where every individual in the population has an equal chance to be selected and included in the sample. This sampling technique although appears to be easy to execute, but this is not really the case. The whole list of the members of population is not generally available, and the researcher also tends to face difficulty in locating the selected subjects and in convincing them to participate in research. Due to these difficulties, many selected individuals are not finally included in samples and this influences the *generalisability* of the results to a greater extent.

6. Tests of significance: Social psychological researchers present their findings in terms of *significant differences* or *significant relationship*. Here, significant never means important, rather it means that the particular relationship does not occur by chance, and therefore, it occurs due to some reality. For example, suppose the researcher is interested in determining whether the observing altruistic behaviour done by others increases the probability of helping behaviour on the part of the observer. The researcher may take two groups of persons—one group having the opportunity to observe altruistic behaviour done by others and the other group may spend equal time for listening music (control group with no opportunity to observe altruistic behaviour). Subsequently, he may measure the frequency of altruistic behaviours shown by the two groups, say for 40 minutes. A test of significance of difference computed for these two groups would tell the researcher whether the observed difference in showing altruistic behaviour is real, that is, due to the opportunity of observing altruistic behaviour on the part of others.

A test of significance is usually stated as the number of times out of one hundred that the observed difference would occur by chance. Generally, two levels—0.05 and 0.01 are selected as levels of significance. The 0.05 level means that the relationship would happen by chance five times out of one hundred. Normally, 0.05 level of significance is accepted as the cut-off point in social sciences and is accepted as being an evidence for a real relationship. The 0.01 level is considered as stronger and still more effective for being accepted as an evidence for a real relationship.

These are the primary concepts, which must clearly be understood by all those who are going to do some kinds of research in any area of social psychology.

BASIC RESEARCH METHODS

Social psychology employs several methods for scientific investigation. These mainly include laboratory experiment, field experiment, natural experiment, correlational studies, field studies and naturalistic observation, survey method, archival research, case studies, meta-analysis and Internet research. A detailed discussion of these methods is as under:

1. Laboratory experiment

Social psychologists conduct experiments in laboratory. Such experiments are called *laboratory experiments*. Laboratory experiment method offers the highest degree of control over the variables. However, it never intends to replicate real-life situations. The major aim of such laboratory experiment is to establish the effect of manipulating one variable or a number of variables upon behaviour. For any study to be a true experiment, it must meet the following two *hallmarks*:

  (i) The investigator must manipulate one or more of the independent variables, which have been hypothesised to have a casual impact upon the dependent variable. An independent variable is one, which is manipulated by the experimenter and the dependent variable is one about which prediction is to be made on the basis of the experiment. Whereas the researcher simply manipulates the independent variables in any experiment, he simply measures the dependent variable.
  (ii) The investigator must randomly assign the subjects or participants to various levels of each of the independent variable. This is called *random assignment*, which denotes the placement of participants in experimental treatments on the basis of chance or with the help of using

table of random numbers. Random assignment is considered essential because it mitigates the impact of *extraneous variables*, which are defined as the variables that may affect dependent variable, but the investigator is not interested in examining their impact, and therefore, he keeps them controlled. By using random assignment, the investigator creates groups of participants or subjects that become equivalent in all respects, except their exposure to different levels of independent variables.

According to Higbee et al. (1982), social psychologists have used experimental method in about three-fourth of their research studies, and in two out of three studies, the setting has been that of a research laboratory (Adair et al., 1985). Let us illustrate the experimental method by considering the following example:

Suppose the investigator wants to examine the impact of viewing television programme upon aggressive behaviour of the children. Experiments could be done in many ways to examine this, but let us consider a group of 30 children aged 10–12 years that may be selected to act as participants. These children are having experience of viewing various types of television programmes for about an hour per day. Subsequently, they may be administered a short questionnaire to assess and match their level of aggressiveness. After that, they may be randomly assigned to two groups by using table of random numbers. One group may view the aggressive television programme in which different children are shown to exhibit aggression towards each other over the various issues. Another group may view the non-aggressive television programme in which children are shown to solve the problems by non-violent means such as by showing cooperativeness and sympathy. Then, both groups of children separately may be provided with some opportunities in which they are allowed to aggress. If the group viewing aggressive television programme actually does more aggressive act than the other group that viewed non-aggressive television programme, the researcher would have a clear reason to conclude that aggression is enhanced by viewing violent and aggressive television programme. In this particular experiment, sex and intelligence level of children might affect the level of aggression. Since the researcher is not interested in studying the impact of these two variables, they need to be controlled. These two variables, in this particular experiment, constitute the example of extraneous variables. All subjects or participants must, therefore, be either male or female for controlling sex variable and must be of more or less same IQ level for controlling the intelligence variable. In social psychology, results of many experiments, in general, have revealed higher levels of aggression among those participants who have viewed the violent and aggressive television programmes (Bandura, Ross and Ross, 1963; Singer and Singer, 1981; Bushman and Huesmann, 2001).

In this particular experiment, independent variable is television programme and dependent variable is aggressive act. Sex and level of intelligence are shown as extraneous variables.

Laboratory experiments have some strengths and weaknesses. Major *strengths* of laboratory experiments are:

(i) Laboratory experiments allow cause and effect relationship to be established firmly. An experimenter can, with confidence, tell that this variable is caused by a particular other variable.
(ii) Laboratory experiments have a higher degree of internal validity because they control or offset all factors or variables other than independent variable that may have an impact upon dependent variable.

(iii) Laboratory experiments have higher degree of *experimental realism*, which refers to the impact the experimental situation creates among the participants, that is, the extent to which the participants feel involved in the situation. This, in turn, increases the credibility of the laboratory experiment.
(iv) Since the results of laboratory experiments are generally analysed with the help of statistical tools, they are considered more objective and dependable.
(v) Laboratory experiments are easier means to test the causal hypotheses drawn from the various theories of social psychology like social exchange theory and cognitive theory. For example, several experiments have been conducted to locate the causes of racial and ethnic prejudice.

Despite these strengths, laboratory experiments have some obvious *weaknesses* as under:

(i) Laboratory experiments lack *external validity*, which refers to generalisability of the obtained results from one specific experiment to the other experiments, people, etc. or to the real-life situations. The latter part of external validity, that is, generalisability to real-life situation is also called *ecological validity*. Lack of external validity is because of two reasons. Firstly, in laboratory experiments, generally very few participants take part. These limited participants may not adequately represent the whole population, which they are seemingly thought to represent. Secondly, laboratory situation provides an artificial situation, where sometimes the participants do not behave in a natural way. For participants, such situations have low apparent realism. In other words, laboratory experiments have low *mundane realism*, which refers to the extent to which the experimental settings appear similar to natural and everyday situations.
(ii) Laboratory experiments cannot be used in some situations because of some practical or ethical considerations. In some situations, it is impossible to manipulate the independent variable and doing so would violate ethical principles of the society. For example, if the researcher wants to study the impact of pornography on unprotected sex of adolescents, by conducting a laboratory experiment, he would have to expose some adolescents to some explicit and intense pornography and some to comparatively vague and little degree pornography and then compare their unprotected sex. Theoretically, this is possible but practically, this would violate ethical consideration.
(iii) Although laboratory experiments possess a higher degree of internal validity, there occurs many threats to such internal validity too. Such threats lower the credibility of the laboratory experiments. Such important threats are *demand characteristics*, *experimenter effect* and *participant (subject) effect*. The details of these three sources of biases or error would be discussed later on in this chapter.
(iv) Laboratory experiments can study only limited number of independent variables at a time. Since human behaviour in real life is influenced by a large number of variables, it is just possible that relationship demonstrated in laboratory experiment may not be the same relationship as found in the real world. In fact, with this observation, the problem of external validity is further compounded.

Despite some drawbacks, laboratory experiments in social psychology are the most important and preferred research methods because these drawbacks can, to a greater extent, be overcome through the use of a well-designed laboratory experiment.

Simulation and games in laboratory experimentation: For the sake of injecting more social reality into the contrived laboratory situation, social psychologists frequently use methods of simulation and gaming. *Simulation* refers to intentional invitation of the essential processes and outcomes of a real social situation. Simulation is followed in order to provide a better understanding of the mechanisms of the real social situation (Abelson, 1968). Thus, simulation basically acts like an operating model of social system that generally continues for some time. Here, the researcher attempts to represent more of social reality without sacrificing the fundamentals of experimental control (Crano and Brewer, 1973). Simulations generally have been used to represent some real-life situations such as a police communication centre, a mock prism, a ward in psychiatric hospital, etc.

One very popular kind of simulation, especially when time, resources or the subject population is very limited, is the use of simulated presence of other people by means of tape recording or films in close-circuit television. Participants in such situation do react to simulation as if other people were actually present.

Simulation involves several inherent advantages. Simulation permits the study of a large number of variables in a more complex interaction than does an ordinary laboratory experiment permit. Also, in simulation, participants show a strong willingness to the experimenter in providing a help to develop the reality of social situation through their role-playing behaviour. Another inherent advantage is that simulation is frequently used as a theory-testing device in those situations, where the relationship among variables should be studied in realistic manner. Despite these, it is said that simulation does not provide as much isolation and control over the variables as a laboratory experiment provides.

In *gaming*, the participant is given a well-specified role in a situation, which is designed and controlled by the experimenter. Participants behave according to their role, which requires them to make choices for maximising task success. However, as compared to simulation, in gaming, the range of scores is more restricted. A good example of gaming is *mixed-motive game*, which studies the mixture of cooperation and competitive behaviour in conflict resolution and negotiation. Using mixed-motive game, the researchers have studied the impact of some independent variables such as amount of communication and personality characteristics upon the amount of competitive and cooperative behaviour shown by players. Mixed-motive game has also been frequently used to study conflict.

A comparative study of simulation and gaming reveals that simulation of social systems in laboratory is more complex than gaming. This is because in simulation, a large number and variety of roles are involved, and also, here, the role players exhibit a greater degree of flexibility as compared to gaming. However, in simulation, the researcher has little control over the situation due to varieties of role and flexibility in the range of behaviours of the participants.

2. Field experiment

Field experiments are another methods of experimentation in social psychology. They are defined as studies, where the researcher or the experimenter manipulates variables in the field and not in the laboratory. *Field* refers to natural, non-laboratory settings such as school, bus stand, railway platform, street, hospital, office, etc. Usually, these field settings are known to the participants or subjects. Field experiment requires the same planning and preparation as required in the laboratory experiment, that is, manipulation of the independent variable, measures of dependent variables and making a decision about the variables to be controlled. In a field experiment, the investigator tries to influence how people behave, testing various types of prediction derived from a theory. For example, a field experiment may be conducted to examine whether or not the people are more willing to take a risk when they see a model taking a risk than when it does not. Field experiment often involves a *before-and-after design*, but sometimes, it may use control group as well. A very good example of field experiment has been provided by Lupfer, Kay and Burnette (1969). They have examined the influence of picketing on the purchase of toy guns and have found that picketing, in fact, depresses the sale of toy guns.

Field experiments also have strengths and weaknesses. Its important *strengths* are as under:

(i) As compared to laboratory experiments, field experiments have higher degree of external validity. This is because of the fact that field experiments are conducted in natural and uncontrived settings that usually have greater mundane realism. (Aronson et al., 1985)

(ii) Participants in the field experiments may not be conscious of their status as experimental subjects—a fact that tend to reduce participants' reactivity. In other words, in field experiments, participants do not know that they are working in any experimental study, and therefore, they will not react in ways that may invalidate the results. All this happens because the method is non-reactive. This may enhance the internal validity of the field experiment that is supposed to be generally low here.

However, field experiments have some *weaknesses* as under:

(i) Field experiments have poor degree of internal validity because of the two reasons. Firstly, in natural settings of field experiment, the experimenter usually faces difficulty in manipulating independent variables, and secondly, in such a situation, the experimenter has a little control over the various extraneous variables.

(ii) Field experiments generally raise some difficult ethical issues like invasion of privacy, deception and lack of informed consent. All these issues put the experimenter in a difficult situation, which makes the objectives manipulation of independent variables a herculean task.

(iii) In field experiments, it is generally very difficult to assign subjects to different conditions randomly, to be certain that all subjects are experiencing the same thing as well as to get a precise measure of dependent variable. Observation has also revealed that here, it is also difficult to design pure manipulation of dependent variable (Taylor, Peplau and Sears, 2006).

Despite some weaknesses, social psychologists conduct field experiments for studying the cause and effect relationship between those variables, which can be studied in natural settings in a better way.

3. Natural experiment

Natural experiment is one where manipulation of independent variables occurs only by accidental natural occurrence, rather than by some kind of intervention by the experimenter. Here, the researcher capitalises on some natural occurrences such as earthquakes, famine, flood, tidal waves, Tsunami, etc. by studying their impact upon some appropriate dependent variable measures. The natural occurrence of the event may produce a change in conditions, which serve the purpose of manipulated independent variables (McDavid and Harari, 1999). Unlike laboratory experiment, in natural experiment, the investigator need not do much planning and exercise control and he has to simply react to the natural occurrence.

A good classic examples of natural experiment has been provided by Lieberman (1956), who examined the effects of role position on the attitudes of role occupants. He conducted a study in an industrial organisation to measure the attitudes of employees towards the management and the union. In the beginning part of the study, two categories of employees underwent role changes—one category consisted of employees, who were promoted to the rank of supervisors and another category consisted of employees, who were elected as union stewards. Results revealed that the workers, who were promoted as supervisors, exhibited more favourable attitude towards the management, and the workers, who were elected as stewards, exhibited more favourable attitude towards the union. Later on, a period of economic recession occurred in the organisation and the experimenter took advantage of such occurrence by assessing further change in the attitude. The supervisors, who were demoted to their previous rank, reverted to the attitudes they previously held and those supervisors, who remained in the role of supervisor, maintained their favourable attitude towards the management. Results with respect to union stewards were less clear-cut. Thus, on the whole, results supported the hypothesis that a person's role has an obvious impact on attitudes relevant to carrying out the role.

Natural experiments have some strengths and weaknesses. Important *strengths* are as follows:

(i) Natural experiments do not much tax the mind of the experimenter because it involves less planning and control on his part (Fisher, 1982).
(ii) In natural experiments, the investigator or the researcher is able to encompass a greater degree of reality than what is possible in laboratory or field experiments. Only requirement of this is that the researcher must be able to capitalise on natural situations that occur.
(iii) Since manipulation of independent variables occur in this kind of experiment in some natural way, it is possible to make some interpretation of causal relationship.

However, natural experiments have some *weaknesses* too, which are as under:

(i) The biggest weakness of the natural experiments is their rarity. Often it is very difficult, if not impossible at all, to anticipate appropriate kinds of natural critical events for experimental study of the issue before they have really occurred.
(ii) In natural experiments, it is very difficult for the experimenter or researcher to establish a proper control over the effects of changes other than due to critical events.
(iii) In natural experiments, the generalisability or the external validity is low probably because here, subjects or participants are not selected in a representative fashion, rather they are either self-selected or just happen to be available.

Social psychologists use all these three kinds of experimentations for studying social behaviour. Of these, laboratory experiments act as the crown jewel followed by field experiments. Natural experiments are used very infrequently due to their nature.

4. Correlational methods

Social psychologists frequently use correlational methods for studying the social behaviour. *Correlational methods* can be defined as the methods of research in which the researcher systematically observes two or more variables to determine whether or not the changes in one variable is accompanied by the changes in the other variable. Correlational methods as a research technique have the following two basic aims:

(i) To know about whether two or more variables are related
(ii) To know about the type of relationship existing between the variables under study.

Correlational methods enable the researcher to make prediction. Suppose a correlation exists between self-esteem and academic achievement of the children. Then, a prediction can be made that high self-esteem may accompany higher academic achievement. The accuracy of prediction depends on the amount of correlation between the variables under study. Correlations can range from 0 to +1.00 or –1.00. *Positive correlation* indicates similar trends of relationship, that is, if one variable increases, then the other variable also increases or if one decreases, other also decreases. *Negative correlation* indicates dissimilar trend of relationship, that is, if one variable increases, the other variable decreases. Thus, positive correlation, in the above example, means that as the level of self-esteem arises, the level of academic achievement also rises. Negative correlation means that as the level of self-esteem decreases, academic achievement increases or vice versa. The absolute size of the correlation coefficient indicates the strength of relationship between the two variables, whereas sign indicates the direction of relationship.

Suppose a social psychologist wants to study correlation between good mood and helpfulness and finds that persons in good mood tend to be related to helpful behaviour because the correlation coefficient between these two variables is 0.86. Of course, this is done by measuring mood of the participants by a questionnaire. They may also be asked to report how many times they do favours to the others by providing adequate help. Subsequently, the two measures are correlated.

In social psychology, there are many studies available to show that correlational techniques have been used for making prediction. As for example, a few studies are being cited here. A classic study involving correlational method in social psychology is that of Adorno et al. (1950), who examined the relationship between authoritarian personality and ethnic prejudice and political-economic conservations and found that these variables were positively correlated, which meant that the persons with authoritarian personalities tend to display greater ethnic prejudice and political-economic conservatism. Likewise, Carroll, Smith and Benett (1994) correlated socio-economic status and longevity of life and reported a positive correlation between these two variables.

Correlational methods have some strengths and weaknesses. Major *strengths* are as under:

(i) Correlational methods can easily be used by social psychologists in natural settings, where the researcher can examine factors like race, gender and social status that cannot be manipulated in the laboratory.
(ii) A large amount of information can be obtained by correlational method within a short spell.

Despite these strengths, correlational methods have some obvious weaknesses:

(i) The major drawback of correlational method is that it does not guarantee causation, that is, no cause and effect prediction can be done on the basis of correlational method. The fact that the two variables are correlated, even highly correlated, does not guarantee that there is causal relationship between them, that is, changes in one causes changes in the other. Reality may be that the obtained correlation between the two variables may be due to chance or random factors or due to the fact that changes in both variables are related to the third variable. For example, self-esteem and academic achievement of children may be related because both are linked to the underlying intelligence and social status of the family. Likewise, the common observation that weight gain and increase in income may be related to each other due to a third variable, that is, age. As people grow older, they tend to gain weight and also earn more income. Thus, both variables are actually related to age.

However, with the application of advanced correlational techniques, one can suggest cause-effect relations. One such popular technique is *cross-lagged panel correlation* (Campbell, 1973; Kenny, 1975). In this correlational technique, two variables are measured at more than one time and the cross-lagged correlations between the variables are computed. In other words, variables A and B are measured at two points in time 1 and 2. This yields four different sets of measures—A_1, A_2, B_1 and B_2. Scores on variable A at time 1 (A_1) are correlated with the scores on variable B at time 2 (B_2) and scores on variable B at time 1 (B_1) are correlated with the scores on variable A at time 2 (A_2). The two correlations between the two variables at two different times (A_1 with B_2 and A_2 with B_1) are called *cross-lagged correlations—cross* because they are across the two variables and *lagged* because there is lag between two times. On the basis of size of correlation, it is possible to tell which variable causes the other. If the correlation between A_1 and B_2 is greater than that of between B_1 and A_2, one can easily conclude that changes in A cause changes in B rather than vice versa. This is because A scores measured first permit the prediction of later B scores better than the prediction of later A scores by B scores measured first (that is, A_2 by B_1). Kahle and Berman (1979) used this cross-lagged panel correlation to answer the question of whether attitudes cause behaviour or vice versa and concluded that the attitude was more likely to cause behaviour, which obviously implied that the knowledge of attitude helps us in predicting people's behaviour and also that any successful attempt to change attitudes indeed produces a changed behaviour.

(ii) Correlations indicate that two variables are related, but they do not indicate the direction of these effects (Baron, Byrne and Branscombe, 2006). For example, from a high correlation (0.75) between mood and helpfulness, one can simply conclude that these two variables are related, but it is difficult to tell that whether good mood causes increased helpfulness or helping others puts us in good mood.

Despite some limitations, social psychologists frequently use correlational methods in making prediction about social behaviour.

5. Field studies and Naturalistic observation

Social psychologists frequently use field studies for studying the various types of social behaviour. *Field study* is a systematic observation about behaviours, as they occur naturally in everyday situation. *Systematic observation* is defined as a method in which the behaviour is systematically observed and recorded. Since the behaviour is here observed and recorded in natural settings, it is also called *naturalistic observation.*

In field studies, data are collected by one or more researchers, who observe the activities of the people and record the information about those activities. Field study differs from field experiment in the sense that the former is a non-experimental research method, where a researcher generally does not intervene in the situation, whereas the latter is an experimental method, which includes experimental manipulation of independent variable, appropriate control group and allowing cause-effect relationship to be shaped.

Following Bickman (1976), all types of observation are characterised by the following three dimensions:

(i) **Degree of concealment:** The researcher has to decide as to what extent his identity as observer will be concealed from the participants or subjects in research. Sometimes, the observer's identity is completely concealed from the participants, whereas at other times, observer's identity is known to the participants and also, he takes part in the interaction with the other participants.

(ii) **Extent of observer intervention:** An observer may play an active role and affect the social situation of the observation to a greater extent. Such observation is called *participant observation*. Or the observer may play a positive role and does nothing to affect the interaction through his behaviour.

(iii) **Degree of structure in the process of observation:** In observation, the degree of structure may vary. Some observations are comparatively unstructured and such observations are based upon impressions of the observer about the participant's activities. On the other hand, some observations are highly structured, where the observer is required to simply check off some predetermined categories of behaviours as they are observed. Bales' *interaction process analysis* is a good example of structural observation.

Field studies differ in how the observers collect and record the information. In some field studies, the observer watches very carefully the behaviour of the participants or events of the situation and then makes a note of important things from his memory. One advantage of such recording is that such observation is less likely to arouse suspicion or antagonism among the participants. In some other field studies, the observers may record the activities of the participant at the same time when they observe their behaviour. In still other forms of field studies, researchers make audio or video recordings of interaction, and subsequently, analyse the tape (Whalen and Zimmerman, 1987). Tape recordings may prove to be a superior alternative, but it can also inadvertently influence the behaviour of the participants if they find that their behaviours are being taped.

Participant observation is one of the very popular form of field studies in social psychological research. It is a method of research in which the observer describes a social situation in which he is actively involved. Here, the members of the research team acting as observer not only make systematic observations of others' behaviour but also interact with them and play an active role in the ongoing events. The fact of being an active participant enables the investigator to study and observe the behaviour in a way which otherwise would be inaccessible. Participant observation is relatively unstructured because here, the observer has some flexibility in deciding what to observe and how to observe and record. Usually, the observer records important elements such as participants, social setting, purpose of interaction, frequency and duration of specific behaviours, etc. In some instances of participant observation, the observer needs to use an assumed identity lest their true identity as investigators may disrupt the normal process of interaction.

Field studies sometimes use *unobtrusive measures*, which are defined as the measurement techniques that do not intrude on the behaviour under study and also cause a reaction from people (Webb et al., 1981). Usually, such unobtrusive measures depend on the physical evidence left behind by the individuals after they have exited from the situation. One important example of observation using such unobtrusive measure is the analysis of inventory records and bar bills to measure the alcohol consumption patterns at various bars and nightclubs (Lex, 1986).

Researches done by social psychologists have vividly shown that field studies have been used to investigate many forms of social behaviour in their natural settings. For example, researchers have observed and recorded data about social interaction between teachers and students in the classroom (Galton, 1987), between judges and attorneys in courtroom (Maynard, 1983) and between working-class boys and girls in school (Thorne, 1993). In some other field studies, focus has been given upon socialisation. For example, Lois (1999) made observation of a volunteer search and rescue group for about 3½ years and studied the process by which individuals became willingly ready to risk their lives in dangerous situation for saving others.

As said earlier, observation may also be structured. The most structured observational method involves behavioural checklists or categorising system. With the help of this method, the observer records the frequency of occurrence of a given behaviour during social interaction. One popular example of categorising systems is *interaction process analysis*, which was developed by Bales (1950) for observation and coding of behaviour in small groups. Bales' category system consists of 12 categories—three from social emotional area: positive reactions; three from task area: attempted answers; three from task area: questions; and three from social-emotional area: negative reaction. Bales had successfully used this technique for observing behavioural interactions and development process in different types of small groups. Later on, Flanders (1970) adapted the technique of interaction process analysis to observe and record the classroom behaviour of teacher and students. Flander's method of interaction analysis focuses mainly on the teacher's verbal behaviour that directly or indirectly attempts to influence the behaviour of students in the classroom. This technique consists of 10 categories—teacher talk: response has three sub-categories like accepts feeling, praises or encourages and accepts or uses ideas of pupils; teacher talk: initiation has four categories: ask questions, lecturing, giving directions and criticising or justifying authority; one category each for pupil talk response, pupil talk initiation and silence. Flander's technique has been modified and expanded for different categories.

Field studies also have strengths and weaknesses. Its important *strengths* are as under:

(i) Field studies or naturalistic observation allows the researchers to study the social behaviour in natural or real-world settings. This provides so much relevant information about the behaviour, which would be otherwise difficult to obtain.
(ii) Field studies are relatively unintrusive. Therefore, they can be used to investigate sensitive or private behaviour such as sexual activities or drug use. Such behaviours are difficult to be observed through intrusive methods like surveys or experiments.

The major *weaknesses* are as under:

(i) Field studies are very much sensitive to the recording methods being frequently used. Observations recorded after the events of fact are usually less reliable and valid than those recorded on the spot or those based on video or audio taping.
(ii) The validity of field studies may be destroyed if the observers operate covertly during observation and the participants suddenly discover that they are being observed by someone.
(iii) The external validity of the field studies generally remains at stake because research of this type frequently focuses on only one group or on a sample of interactions selected for convenience.

(iv) In some cases, field studies, including participants' observations, are objected on ethical grounds because generally in such researches, the researchers do not get informed consent from the persons being observed prior to the collection of data. Permission for using the data is obtained after the behaviour has been observed or tape-recorded. This creates ethical problems.

Despite these limitations, field studies are used by social psychologists for studying different types of social behaviour, particularly those social behaviours about which it is ordinarily difficult to obtain information otherwise.

6. Survey method

The survey method has a long and varied historical background. In fact, its use for social research started with social reform movements and social service professions documenting conditions of urban poverty. In the beginning, surveys were simply an overview of an area based on questionnaires and other data. Scientific sampling and statistics, which are today considered as the backbone of survey method, were absent at that time. In fact, the following four factors reshaped the earlier social survey into modern quantitative survey research:

(i) Researchers applied statistically-based sampling techniques and precise measurement to the survey.
(ii) Researchers started developing scales and indices to collect systematic quantitative data on attitudes, opinions and subjective aspects of social life.
(iii) Several researchers adapted survey method to many applied areas. For example, journalists started using survey methods in measuring public opinion and impact of radio and television. Government officials started using surveys for improving various types of social programmes.
(iv) Empirical social researches turned their attention to focus on local social problems using a mixture of methods, including scientific methods modelled after natural sciences.

Modern survey method is comparatively more objective, scientific and statistically-based technique. Today, *survey method* is defined as a systematic observation, where the researchers sample a large number of respondents, who answer the same questions, measure many variables and test multiple hypotheses. Thus, in survey method, the researcher collects information by asking members of the same population a set of questions, recording their responses and analysing them with appropriate statistical techniques. This method is considered very useful for identifying the average or typical response to a question as well as the distribution of responses within a defined population.

Purpose of survey method: Obviously, survey method is used by social scientists, including social psychologists and sociologists, for various purposes. Some important purposes are as follows:

(i) Researchers often use survey methods to obtain self-reports from persons to know about their important attributes such as their attitudes, behaviour and experiences. This type of information enables the researcher to find out the distribution of attributes in the population and also helps in determining whether a relationship exists between the variables under consideration.
(ii) Survey method is also used for knowing the political views to elections. In fact, one form of survey called *public opinion poll*, is often conducted during election period. Such surveys

measure the frequency, strength of favourable or unfavourable attitudes towards public issues, political figures, etc. and are considered very important in moulding public opinion.

(iii) Survey methods are used for obtaining data about various types of social problems like national health care, family planning, affirmative action programmes, etc. For instance, government agencies and individual researches have conducted many surveys on frequency and contraceptive used by teenagers (Levine, 2000).

(iv) Sometimes, survey method is used with the basic objective of making theoretical contributions to social psychology. For example, social psychologists have conducted many survey studies in the various fields such as prejudice and discrimination, socialisation, psychological well-being, attitude-behaviour relationship, etc. and have made significant contributions.

Types of survey method: Survey method, depending on the mode of data collection, may be basically of four types, which are discussed as under:

(i) *Personal interview:* Also known as interview survey or survey interview, it is a survey in which the interviewer asks questions from the respondent who answers them. Answers are recorded by the interviews. Survey interview is a specialised kind of interview, whose primary goal is to obtain accurate information from the respondents. Thus, survey interview can be defined as a short-term, secondary social interaction between the interviewer and the respondent, with the explicit purpose of obtaining specific and accurate information from the respondent. Here, the information is generally obtained in structured format in which the interviewer asks prearranged questions to which the respondent answers. Thus, the survey interview differs in many ways from an ordinary interview. The major features of survey interview may be outlined as under:

(a) In survey interview, the interviewer asks and the respondent answers most of time.
(b) Only the respondent reveals his beliefs, feelings and opinions.
(c) Interviewer tries to obtain direct answers to the specific question asked.
(d) All through the interview, the interviewer remains non-judgemental and does not try to bring any change in respondent's beliefs and opinions.
(e) Interviewer is interested in seeking genuine answers and not the ritual responses.
(f) Interviewer always try to control the topic, direction and pace. He keeps the respondent on task and irrelevant diversions are avoided.
(g) Interviewer does not correct the respondent's factual errors.
(h) Respondent is not allowed to evade questions and he is expected to be truthful and thoughtful in his approach.
(i) All through the interviewer maintains a consistently warm but serious and objective tone.

There are three necessary conditions for any interview survey to be successful (Singh, 2011). First is *accessibility*, that is, information required should be such that the respondent is able to convey it to the interviewer. Second is *cognition*, which means understanding on the part of the respondent of what is required of him and what type of information is required. Third is *motivation*, that is, the respondent must be motivated to give accurate answers because a highly distorted answer is not better than no answer at all.

(ii) *Questionnaire survey:* In question survey, questions are printed on a paper and the respondents read and answer them at their own pace. No interviewer is present in the survey. Researchers can give questionnaires directly to the respondents (called *self-administered questionnaires*) or mail them to the respondents (called *mail questionnaire*). When the researcher sends the questionnaire to the respondents by mail with a request to return the questionnaire after giving answers only by mail on the given address, it is called *mail questionnaire survey*. The major disadvantage of questionnaire, particularly mail questionnaire, lies in the response rate that is the percentage of respondents who really provide answer by completing the questionnaire. It has been shown that mail questionnaire rarely attain more than 50% response rate. This is a very serious disadvantage. Apart from this, mail questionnaires are not returned by most of the respondents. This creates serious problems for the survey researchers. A meta-analysis conducted by Yammarino et al. (1991) is worth mentioning here. They selected 115 articles on mail survey responses taken from 25 journals, which had been published in between 1940 and 1988. After meta-analysis, it was found that cover letters, questionnaires of four pages or less, a return envelope with postage stamp and a small monetary reward—all tend to ensure and enhance the return of mail questionnaire.

(iii) *Telephone survey:* It can be treated as a compromise between interview and questionnaire. In this type of survey, a trained interviewer asks questions from respondent on telephone and records answers. This is a very popular survey method because about 95% population can be reached by telephone. However, telephone survey sacrifices the visual feedback, which is readily available in a face-to-face interview. Many researchers today are using *computer-assisted telephone interviewing (CATI)*. CATI is a telephone surveying technique where the interviewer follows a script provided by a software application, that is, here a computerized questionnaire is administered to respondent over telephone. With CATI, the interviewer with headset and microphone, sits before a computer and commands to computer to make a telephone call to respondent. When the contact is made, the interviewer reads the questions posed on the screen and records the respondent's answer directly into the computer. Once he enters an answer, the computer readily shows the next question on the screen. *Interactive voice response (IVR)* is another innovation in the field of telephone survey. IVR includes several computer-automated systems through phone technology (Tourangeau, 2004). With IVR, a respondent listens question as well as responses options over the telephone and the responses of the respondents are recorded by voice recognition software or touch-tone entry. All computer-based interviewing has obvious advantages of being fast and showing a few errors only.

(iv) *Panel survey:* In panel survey, the same sample is measured two or more times. The first survey of the sample either by interview or by questionnaire is called *first wave* of the panel. The second survey of the same sample after some time in future is called *second wave* and so on. The waves in a panel study can be spaced either closely together or far apart in time. The sample of the individuals used is called the *panel*. The sample can represent either a general population or a specific population. Panel survey is a variation of longitudinal study. In panel survey, the researcher not only measures the net change but also identifies the source of change in terms of specific individuals, who are themselves changing. Panel study also provides information regarding a natural temporal ordering of variables, which usually provides an insight when interpreting the results in terms of cause and effect because an effect cannot precede its cause. (However, ordering does not necessarily establish cause and effect. It merely indicates whether or not a cause and effect relationship is possible.) The primary objective of panel survey is to determine whether or not the various outcomes experienced by the respondents at later waves (the time of resurvey) are determined by their experiences, attitudes, etc. at the earlier points in time or waves.

To prove as a successful research technique, survey method must meet at least the following two criteria:

(i) The sample must be representative of the population. It means that the issue of sampling in survey research is important. Usually, for ensuring representativeness in the sample, the researcher uses two types of systematic samples—*simple random sample* and *stratified random sample*. In simple random sample, the researcher selects the individuals in such a way that every individual has an equal probability of being included in the sample. For this, the researcher needs a complete list of members of population. In stratified random sample, the researcher classifies the population into different groups or strata according to important characteristics like sex, education, region, socio-economic status or SES, etc., and then selects a random sample of groups and draws a sample of individuals within each selected group.

(ii) The way in which questions are worded exerts strong impact upon the outcomes of the survey. For example, if the question asked is—Do you think that multiple murderers should be executed? Many people will say 'yes' because the person has committed not one nor two rather multiple murders. But if the question asked is reworded like this—Are you in favour of capital punishment for a murder?, then comparatively, small percentage may say 'yes'.

Survey method has strengths and weaknesses. Important *strengths* may be enumerated as under:

(i) At moderate cost, survey can provide an accurate and precise description of the characteristics of the population. If used properly by fulfilling all the requirements honestly, survey can produce a very clear portrait of attitude and social characteristics of a population (Delamater and Myers, 2009).

(ii) Surveys are considered as an effective means to provide an inference about the incidence of various social behaviours. This is especially true for those behaviours of the individuals that occur infrequently or in private settings.

(iii) Social psychological researchers frequently use surveys for testing predictions (such as predictions about impact on personal identity and self-esteem) from theory like symbolic interaction theory. Survey methods are also used to test hypotheses about structure and function of attitudes, which are based on cognitive theories.

There are some *weaknesses* of the survey method, which mainly uses questionnaire and interviews for collecting data from the respondents. Both these techniques depend on self-reports by the respondents. Some researchers are having a view that these self-reports remain no longer a valid source in many conditions such as

(i) When respondents are asked to recall from memory about their past experiences, they may give a wrong information due to poor memory.

(ii) Sometimes respondents deliberately do not respond to the questions asked about themselves in an honest way. This is especially done when the survey questions are highly personal, illegal or otherwise embarrassing to reveal.

(iii) Some respondents, while answering survey questions, fall prey to various kinds of response set. For example, they may answer all questions by marking either 'agree' or 'disagree' option or they may give extreme answers too frequently. In either of the response set, the validity of the survey becomes questionable because such response set introduces various kinds of response biases (Singh, 2011).

Despite these weaknesses, survey methods are frequently used by social scientists, particularly social psychologists and sociologists, for studying various types of social behaviour and social thoughts.

7. *Archival research*

Although social psychologists, in general, prefer to collect original data for testing their hypotheses, sometimes they have to depend on using data that already exist and were collected for another purpose. Archival research provides a good platform for such work. In fact, the researcher in archival research avoids both the laboratory and the field. In archival research, the existing records or documents are analysed or reanalysed in an attempt to test a hypothesis. For example, if a researcher hypothesises that the phases of moon are related to various kinds of criminal activities, he may consult meteorological office for a period of, say three years to document when changes in moon's phases occurred, and then, may look at daily crime data printed in newspapers and magazine for the same three-year period. By using such pre-existing records, the researcher can be able to confirm the hypothesis framed earlier. Researchers are, in general, having a view that when archival data of high quality exist, the researcher may decide that analysing such data is preferable, rather than collecting and analysing fresh data. In such a situation, archival research may cost less than any alternative method.

There are many sources of archival data. Of these sources, the primary ones are census data, various types of data banks, formal organisations like insurance companies and banks, newspaper and magazines, etc.

There are some strengths and weaknesses of archival research. Important *strengths* are as under:

(i) Archival research has the advantage of being completely *non-reactive*. A non-reactive research is one in which people being studied are unaware that they are a part of the study and they do not know that they are being observed. As such, no participants' or subjects' biases or errors are introduced into the study.

(ii) Archival research usually cost less as compared to the cost of alternative methods because here, the researcher saves the additional cost of collecting data.

(iii) In archival research, the researcher may save time also because he uses data or information, which are in his hand.

(iv) Archival research permits the researcher to test those hypotheses, which are related to behaviours that occur over extended period of time. As we know, in some cases, authority keeps the collected data for decades or even for centuries and this provides a good basis for the researcher for investigating various types of questions and inferences.

Archival research has following *weaknesses*:

(i) In archival research, the researcher has no control over the type and quality of information and he has to keep himself satisfied with whatever is available to him.

(ii) Archival researcher may not find all types of data that he wishes to study.
(iii) Archival researcher has most of the time doubt regarding originality of the available data. He has a little idea about the research design used or the procedures followed in collecting data.
(iv) In archival research, it is difficult for the researcher to create a reliable and valid analysis scheme, especially when the records or documents are complex in nature.
(v) Sometimes, the researcher has to face a very peculiar situation because some sets of record contain several kinds of inconsistencies apart from some missing information. In such a situation, the researcher fails to draw any conclusion in a meaningful way.

Despite these limitations, archival research is the only cheaper and economical means for studying those phenomena, which are related to such behaviour that have already occurred in pretty past.

8. *Content analysis or document analysis*

Content analysis as a method in social psychological research was first defined by Berelson (1952), who pointed out that it is a collection of techniques for coding written or spoken information into a set of descriptive categories systematically and reliably. Thus, *content analysis* is a systematic technique for gathering and analysing the content of a text. The terms *content* and *text* need further explanation here. The *content* refers to words, pictures, symbols, ideas, themes or any message that can be communicated. Whereas, the *text* is anything written, visual or spoken that basically serves as a medium of communication. It may include books, newspaper, magazine, article, advertisements, official documents, filing or video-tapes, photographs, musical lyrics, article of clothing or work of art. Thus, content analysis basically involves undertaking examination of documents or messages to locate specific characteristics and then making an inference based on their occurrences. For example, if news magazine serve as a source, the researcher can use content analysis to code the reportage of news articles into a form suitable for statistical analysis.

Content analysis is a non-reactive measure because the process of placing words, symbols, messages, etc. in text to communicate to a reader or receiver occurs without any type of influence from the investigator, who actually analyses the content.

A researcher who is using content analysis usually follows some steps as under:

(i) The first step is to identify the informational unit to be studied. It may be a word, sentence, paragraph, etc.
(ii) The second step is to identify the categories into which the units will be sorted.
(iii) The third step is to code the units in each document into the categories. In coding, the researcher systematically converts the symbolic content from text into quantitative data. As the researcher gathers data, he analyses them with statistical technique in the same way that an experimenter or survey researcher does.
(iv) At the final step, the researcher looks for a relation within the obtained categorised data.

Content analysis has been successfully used for various types of topics. For example, some studies have addressed issues like relationship between the mortality rates associated with AIDS and newspaper coverage of that disease (Adelman and Verbrugge, 2000), relationship between rhetorical forms of speech and applause from the audience (Heritage and Greatbatch, 1986), etc. In other studies, researchers have analysed the content of personal advertisements placed in magazine by gay and lesbian (Bailey et al., 1997).

Content analysis has been found useful for the following three types of research:

(i) In content analysis, the researcher can assess a large amount of texts (such as newspaper articles published over five years) with sampling and multiple coders.
(ii) Content analysis has also proved to be helpful tool when the topic to be studied lie at distance. For example, content analysis has been successfully used to study historical documents, writings of authors who have died and broadcasts of the enemy country, etc.
(iii) Content analysis has also been successfully used to study message in a text that is difficult to see with causal observation. For example, content analysis done by Aries (1977) revealed that although not aware of it, in the same sex groups, men talk more about achievement and aggressive themes, whereas women talk more about interpersonal matters and social relationship.

Content analysis has some strengths and weaknesses. Content analysis can be easily used to examine the effect of experimental manipulation upon dependent variable. If, for example, an investigator wants to study the effect of practice upon improvement of handwriting of children, content analysis will be of no less importance than any other experimental measure. In social psychological research, content analysis has been found to be especially useful for the explanation of consensual beliefs, values, etc. of the societies and their cultural products. However, content analysis does have some inherent *weaknesses*. First, generalisation on the basis of content analysis is limited to the cultural communication itself. Second, content analysis cannot determine truthfulness of an assertion. It reveals the content in the text, but cannot interpret the significance of the content. Therefore, content analysis should be considered as a supplement and not as a substitute for any subjective examination of documents.

Despite some limitations, content analysis is widely used in social psychological researches for studying topics like attitude, stereotypes, curriculum changes, values, interest, religiosity, college budgets, etc.

9. *Case study method*

Case studies are used frequently in qualitative research. If we trace the history of case study method, it will be obvious that Frederick Le Play (1806–1882) had, for the first time, introduced this method into social science research in his studies of family budgets. Herbert Spencer, an English Sociologist (1820–1903), was first to use case study method in his ethnographic studies. In the field of psychology, exhaustive case studies have been done by Murray and his associates at Harvard Psychological clinic.

Case study is defined as in-depth examination and analysis of an extensive amount of information about one unit or very few units or cases for the period or across multiple periods of time. Therefore, the approach of case study is that of longitudinal studies. Cases may be related to individual, groups, organisations, movements, events or geographic units. The data here are usually more detailed, varied and extensive and are collected through measures like questionnaires, interviews, observations, psychological tests. Data from newspapers, magazines, court, government agencies, etc. are not uncommon. These data may be collected over months, years or across many decades. Thus, in case study, the researcher intensively investigate one or two cases and compare a limited set of cases, focusing on many factors. That way, the researcher uses the logic of analytic induction rather than enumerative induction. Thus, here, the researcher selects one or few important cases to illustrate an issue and analytically study them in detail. In reality, case study helps the researchers in connecting the micro-level or the actions of the individual people to macro-level or large scale social structures and processes (Vaughan, 1992).

In social psychological researches, the following two types of case studies are commonly used:

(i) **Observational case study:** Observational case study is one in which the researcher studies the current phenomena for which the observation could be used to supplement documents and interviews. Jobe and Pope (2002) conducted a famous observational case study for the purpose of identifying the degree to which teachers used various principles from their university-based methods class in student's teaching in English.

(ii) **Historical organisational case study:** As its name implies, such case study aims at studying historical development of an organisation. Here, the data are collected from documents and interviews. A very good example of a historical case study is that of Conroy and Sipple (2001), who studied the merger of two previously separated teacher education programmes—agriculture and math/science. Documents were reviewed and these two groups of teachers were interviewed. It was found that two groups of teachers were having different ideas about what should be emphasised in teacher education programme. The merger programme caused both agriculture and science educators to work with each other. Old assumptions were dropped and an integrated programme for teacher education was framed.

When the researcher makes extension of a single case to make the field broader one, it is called *multicase study*. A multicase study is one which begins as a single case study and subsequently expands to two or more cases (Bogdan & Biklen, 2003). The added cases intend to enhance the generalisability of the multicase study. Besides, such case studies also provide good ground for making comparisons so that the results of the two or more cases may be compared and contrasted. In social psychology, researchers sometimes use multicase study for making a better prediction about social behaviour being studied.

The major strength of case study is that it provides an in-depth observation and analysis of the social unit. This yields so much valuable information for the researcher that he otherwise may not be getting. Such analysis also helps in providing sufficient base facts for developing a suitable hypothesis regarding the social unit being studied. The most serious limitation is that the obtained results lack generalisability. Besides, such method is also costly in terms of time and money. Another limitation of case study is that it suffers from the danger of subjectivity on the part of researcher, who may be biased by the knowledge of what he or she is looking for. This may result in some ambiguous behaviour being interpreted to confirm the hypothesis.

10. Meta-analysis

Social psychologists have been doing empirical researches for the last several decades. Unfortunately, the results of these studies relating to the same topic or issue do not agree. For example, some studies show that the presence of others facilitate the performance of the individual, whereas some studies show that the presence of others retards the performance of the individual. Likewise, some studies in social psychology have demonstrated that contact with members of a group reduces a prejudice and produces more favourable attitude, whereas some other studies have shown that such contact has not any impact upon prejudice, and therefore, not upon the existing attitude too. Meta-analysis is a special research technique that allows an investigator to establish some order out of this chaos.

The term *meta-analysis* essentially means analysis after or beyond the original analysis. Thus, meta-analysis is the analysis of analyses completed usually as a rather large collection of quantitative studies. Therefore, *meta-analysis* may be defined as a statistical technique, which allows the researcher to combine the results of all available previous studies relating to a question or topic to determine what, collectively, they tell us (Rosenthal, 1991). Here, the researcher gathers the details about a large number of aspects of research such as sample size, when published, size of the effects of variables, etc. and then analyses this set of information in quantitative ways that permit statistical analysis of relationships, central tendency and other interesting quantitative features. In conducting meta-analysis, the researcher performs essentially the following three steps:

(i) The researcher typically locates all previous studies on the question. This task is made easy by using computerised researches of libraries and databases. Moreover, these previous studies are selected on the basis of criteria framed by the researcher.

(ii) For each study, the effect size (ES), as suggested by Glass (1977), is calculated. The *effect size* is a common measure for expressing the results across previous studies. Some researchers call *ES* as *d statistic*, which is a standard score (z-score) of the mean of one group referenced in the distribution of another group. Thus, an effect size is a score expressed in standard deviation units when the results are being summarised across studies involving experimental group and control group. The formula for statistic is as under:

$$\text{ES or } d = \left| \frac{\overline{X}_E - \overline{X}_C}{S_C} \right|$$

where,

$\overline{X}_E$ = Mean of experimental group
$\overline{X}_C$ = Mean of control group
S_C = Standard deviation of the control group

Not in all meta-analyses, standard deviation of one group is used in computing *d* statistic. Some meta-analyses compute the *d* statistic by subtracting the mean difference and dividing it by a *pooled standard deviation*, which is the average of the standard deviations of two groups.

(iii) Finally, the researcher averages all the values of *d* of each selected study. The average *d* value tells us about the direction of difference between the two groups and how larger the difference is for all the studies combined together. A general guide rule is that a *d* of 0.20 tells us about small difference, a *d* of 0.50 tells us about moderate difference and a *d* of 0.80 tells about large difference.

There are several examples of meta-analysis done in social psychological researches. Cox and Davidson (1995) conducted meta-analysis to study findings on whether alternative education programmes help juvenile delinquents in improving their school performance. They searched all such research articles that utilised alternative education programmes for youth and found 241 studies on the basis of following three criteria:

(a) Studies mentioned a separate curriculum.
(b) Studies were held in a separate building.
(c) Studies included quantitative measures of programme.

Based on these three criteria, only 87 studies were selected. Subsequently, the researchers checked whether these studies used statistical tool and it was found that 57 studies had used statistics. After making meta-analysis of these 57 studies, the researcher finally concluded that alternative education programmes slightly improved the self-esteem and school performance. However, they did not directly reduce the delinquent behaviour of adolescents. Likewise, Yammarino et al. (1991) conducted another important meta-analysis in which they selected 115 research articles on mail survey. All these articles were selected from 25 journals. After meta-analysis, it was reported that various materials like a return envelope with postage stamp, short questionnaire, cover letter and a small monetary reward tend to improve the safe return of mail questionnaire.

Generally meta-analysis summarises quantitative research, but some researchers like Hodson (1998) have conducted meta-analysis of qualitative field research case studies on workplace setting.

Meta-analysis has some strengths and weaknesses. Important *strengths* are as under:

(i) Social psychologists are having a view that meta-analysis is a very useful way for summarising results and comparing the conditions of the studies, which are reviewed by the researcher.

(ii) Meta-analysis sometimes also bring organisation and meaning to the results, which are mixed and apparently contradictory.

However, meta-analysis is not without weaknesses. Its important *weaknesses* are as follows:

(i) In meta-analysis often a tendency is found on the part of researcher to exclude studies that do not support the conclusions of interest. This introduces a bias in meta-analysis.

(ii) Meta-analysis requires a substantial effort because this is not done by including six to seven studies, rather a large number of studies such as sixty, eighty or even more than it are included. This takes a lot of time and puts hurdle in maintaining an even spirit on the part of researcher.

Despite these limitations, meta-analysis is a good statistical procedure on the part of social psychologists for synthesising the results across numerous independently conducted research studies.

11. Internet research

This is a new method of research, which is being used by social psychologists. In this type of research, information about social behaviour from the participants is collected by means of computer using Internet. Internet is the world's largest computer network, which links many of scientific research and educational computers as well as commercial networks. Internet uses Transmission Control Protocol (TCP)/Internet Protocol (IP). Internet research has some strengths and weaknesses. Its important *strengths* are as under:

(i) Internet makes it very easier to recruit participants, who are not college students and who come from distant geographical areas having diverse backgrounds.

(ii) When the participants complete the research task on line, it saves much time of the researcher. Not only that, it also increases the efficiency of data collection.

(iii) Internet research provides an online forum, which makes the study of many topics including prejudice, communication as well as the spread of new ideas easier one (Kraut et al., 2004).

(iv) Internet research is less expensive and is more comprehensive than the traditional methods of research.

However, Internet research is not without pitfalls. Important *weaknesses* are as under:
(i) Some biases in Internet sample may creep into. For example, some individuals may participate in the study more than once. Likewise, some may present a fake identity or respond in a malicious manner. Such biases in the sample may invalidate the results.
(ii) Internet research also suffers from a problem in data collecting setting. When participants are studied in laboratory setting, the research exercises a better control over their behaviour. But when participants respond by using a computer at their home or at work, it is impossible to monitor their behaviour or to control some undesirable distractions.

Despite these limitations, the use of Internet research is increasing day by day. Researchers are also striving to find ways to minimise the problems associated with Internet research.

VALIDITY OF EXPERIMENT

There are three major types of validity of experiments in psychology—*internal validity*, *external validity* and *ecological validity*.

Internal validity is one of the main criteria of evaluation of the experiments in social psychology. An experiment is said to have internal validity if the results (or measures of the dependent variable or DV) can be very obviously and quite confidently attributed to the manipulations of independent variable (IV). In other words, internal validity is the extent to which results can be interpreted accurately to the manipulation of the independent variable. Sometimes, variables (other than independent variables) that are not controlled by the experimenter do affect the results. Such variables are called *extraneous variables* or *confounding variables*. An experiment with confounding variables has low internal validity. Experimenters try to adapt a design, which could maximally control the confounded variable.

Campbell and Stanley (1966) outlined several threats to internal validity of an experiment. The experimenter must eliminate all those threats if he really hopes to draw a valid conclusion. Such important threats are *familiarity or testing, maturation, selection bias, experimental mortality*, etc. *Testing* means the impact of pre-testing upon the performance of subjects during post-testing. The pre-testing may make the participants or subjects more familiar or skilled and proficient on subsequent testing or post-testing and this may enhance the performance on the post-testing. *Maturation* poses another threat to validity. When the experiment continues for a longer period of time, the participants may became more mature and wise since the beginning of the experiment and this may unnecessarily enhance the performance of the participants. For example, suppose children of 5 years age are tested for their coordination skills and then are given training for developing various types of coordination skills. After six months, they are tested again and are found to exhibit better performance. This improves performance may be due to training, the variable which the experimenter is testing but it may also be due to maturation occurring within six months. Another threat to internal validity is the *selection bias*, which occurs when due to one reason or the other, the control group is not equated to the experimental group, and consequently, these two groups may differ in terms of motivation, interest and even in ability. These differences may cause change in the results of the experiment. *Experimental mortality* means loss of subjects during the period of experimentation. Those participants who remain present during the entire period of experimentation are generally more motivated, more interested and more attentive than those who either drop out in the middle or forcefully remain present. This produces a confounding effect in the sense that it causes an imbalance among the subjects.

External validity is another important aspect of experiment. It refers to the generalisability of results from one specific experiment to the other experiment, people and measures (Pennington, Gillen and Hill, 1999). If different experiments using different methods, participants, tests, instruments, produce results similar to that of the original experiment, then it can be safely said that this original experiment has external validity. A very important threat to external validity of the experiment comes from what has been called *Hawthorne effect*, which refers to the enhancement in performance prompted by the participants' awareness of participation in an experiment. When participants demonstrate Hawthorne effect in any experiment, the results of the experiment are likely to differ from the results of those experiments, where no such effects are being demonstrated. The conclusion thus reached become difficult to be generalised.

External validity is helpful in providing more confidence in theory because if several different experiments rather than one or two experiments provide support to theory, then naturally, we place more confidence in it. Internal and external validities may stand opposite of each other because an internally valid experiment means a very high control over extraneous variable. However, a very high control in experiment may make it so unique that its results may be difficult to be generalised to the other experiments or situations.

Ecological validity means generalisability of the results of the experiment to the real-life situation. Broadly, this is one form of external validity. A laboratory or field experiment is said to have ecological validity if the results are relevant and apply to more or less similar situation of day-to-day life. For example, if knowing about the different patterns of non-verbal behaviour occurring between different people making conversation in a laboratory really improves the social skills of the participant in real life situation, then this is an example of ecological validity. Figure 2.1 presents these three different type of validity.

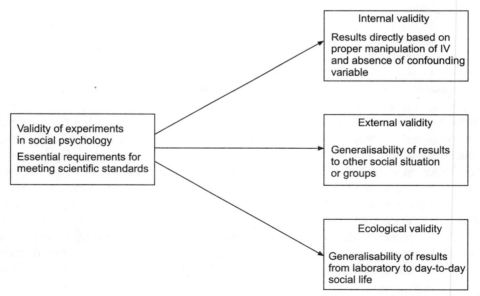

Figure 2.1 Three types of validity needed to be considered in the evaluation of experiments in social psychology.

Experiments done in the area of social psychology are unlikely to be valid in all these three ways, that is, with respect to internal, external and ecological validities. Of these, internal validity enjoys the superiority in the sense that without an internal validity, experiment is futile and meaningless (Campbell and Stanley, 1966).

SOCIAL PSYCHOLOGY OF EXPERIMENT

The intensive study of factors that limit internal validity and external validity of the experiments has led to a variable called *social psychology of psychological experiment* (Adair, 1973; Gergen, 1978). This line of investigation is concerned with all the factors, processes and conditions that enter into the complex interaction of participant, experimenter and laboratory. Social psychology of experiment is itself a social situation because its subject matter is other people who interact with the experimenter. Such situation has attracted many researches in attempts to identify sources of biases and errors. Social psychological experiments have identified three main sources of such bias or error—*demand characteristics, experimenter effect* and *participant effect*.

Demand characteristics refer to the implicit and explicit cues that may communicate the behaviour expected in the experimental setting. According to Orne (1962), the major demand characteristic of social psychology experiment is that of being a good subject or participant. This automatically means cooperating with the experimenter and providing him with the results he wants. While this may seem harmless, but it is really very harmful when the participants try to puzzle out for themselves about what the experiment is and act out accordingly to confirm the hypothesis of the experiment. If this really happens, the validity of the whole experiment is undermined. Really, the participants should behave in the experimental conditions in a natural and spontaneous way, ignoring what the experiment is actually about. For controlling such demand characteristics, the experimenter may conduct pilot studies to find out if there are any cues which are being picked up by the participants. If such cues are found, they can be eradicated.

Experimenter effect is another important source of bias in social psychology experiment. *Experimenter effect* refers to a condition when the results of the experiment are distorted either intentionally or unintentionally by the characteristics or behaviour of the experimenter. This is called *Rosenthal effect* after the name of Rosenthal (1969), who had for the first time demonstrated it. In fact, such errors of observation may make the results consistent with the hypothesis of the experiment. Rosenthal (1969) identified three types of experimenter effects—*biosocial effect, psychological effect* and *situational effect*.

Biosocial effect refers to the effect created due to the various aspects of experimenter such as sex, race, age, physical appearance, status, warmth, anxiety level and so on. For example, an attractive female experimenter may obtain responses from the participant different from those obtained by an unattractive female experimenter. Likewise, a high-status experimenter such as a doctor or a professor or an engineer may elicit more conforming responses from the participant than does a low-status experimenter such as a compounder or a student or a contractor.

Psychological effect refers to those factors, which are concerned with the general attitude and personality traits of the experimenter. This is concerned with question like—Is the experimenter extrovert or introvert? Does the experimenter give instruction in a cold or friendly way? Questions like these have an obvious impact upon the participant's behaviour and thinking and prone them to behave accordingly rather than behaving in accordance with the demand of the experimental situation.

Situational effect has also been extensively researched by the social psychologists. Situational factors mainly revolve around the issue of knowing the hypothesis, which is going to be tested through experiment. Rosenthal (1969) reported that frequently a tendency is found to produce such results, which should be consistent with the hypothesis, but in reality, this does not happen. Moreover, the expectations of the experimenter are also communicated thorough facial expression, tone of voice, etc. Such experimenter's expectancy affects and distorts the results to a greater extent. Rosenthal and Fode (1963) demonstrated the effects of experimenter's expectancy in one experiment in which some students trained rats to run a maze. One group of students was told that the rats were bright and intelligent, whereas the other group of students was told that the rats were dull and slow. But the reality was that all rats were equally capable, and therefore, they were neither dull nor bright. Results revealed that the students who had expectation and belief that rats were bright, produced results showing better and improved performance as compared to the students who had expectation about their rats to be dull ones. One solution for controlling the effects of experimenter bias, according to Rosenthal, is to use blind experimenters, that is, experimenters who do not know (and therefore, blind) the hypothesis under study or who are not aware of all the conditions of the experiment.

Participant (or subject) *effect* is another major concern. Sometimes, participants become unnecessarily too helpful and this causes problem. But even more dangerous is the situation when the participants adopt a negative or hostile attitude and try to disrupt the normal flow of the experimental situation. This is called *evaluation apprehension*. Such apprehension may force the participant to present himself apparently in a good mood such as in happy mood and fully understanding the experimenter's instruction. But the reality may be that the participants are not clear on most of the points. Such situation falsifies the results and affects the external validity of the experiment too.

All these social psychological aspects of the experiment must be properly handled or overcome so that the validity of the experiments may be enhanced. Figure 2.2 presents the summary of these three effects as discussed above.

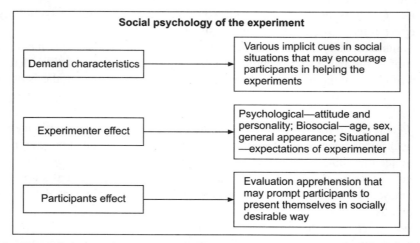

Figure 2.2 Demand characteristics, experimenter effect and participant effect as potential sources of errors in the experiments of social psychology.

Research in social psychology must conform to high moral and ethical standards set up by the different associations of psychologists. Ethical principles developed by the American Psychological

Association (2002), the Canadian Psychological Association (2000) and the British Psychological Society (2000) are very important ones and urge the researchers to do the following:

1. Participants should make informed consent: The principle of informed consent clearly specifies that the people who are to act as participant in the social psychological research have a right to know about their participation in the activity and have also a right to make a free choice regarding participation. Thus, by informed consent is meant consent voluntarily given by a potential participant who decides to participate in the research *after* being told what will be involved in participation. Potential participants must be told of any possible unpleasant or harmful effects of the research being conducted. Following six elements are essential to informed consent:

(i) The researchers must give the potential participants an explanation of the purposes of the research as well as brief description of the procedures to be employed. However, they do not and need not tell anything about the hypotheses of the research.
(ii) The researchers should clearly inform the potential participants about any foreseeable risk in participation.
(iii) The researchers should provide information about the likely medical or psychological resources available in case the participants are adversely affected as a consequence of participation.
(iv) The researchers should provide a description of benefits to the participants.
(v) The researchers should provide answers to the questions, if asked, about the research.
(vi) The researchers should clearly inform the potential participants that they can terminate their participation, if they feel so, at any time. In other words, option of withdrawal always lies with the potential participant and pressure should not be used for continuation.

2. Deception should be avoided as far as possible: This principle cautions the researcher to be truthful and use deception only if essential and justified by a significant purpose (Myers, 2005). In social psychological researches, particularly in experimental researches, the researchers are forced to use deception to combat demand characteristics and social desirability biases while gathering data about socially important topics. Suppose that the researcher straightforward tells the participant that we are going to study how failure at the important task affect people's self-esteem. It is very much expected that no participant will be ready to participate in this study because nobody would like to take pain of failure and that too on important task. Even if the participant agrees to participate, he would not be able to prevent his responses to be affected by the knowledge of the research topic. Here, the participant will try to help in confirming the researcher's expectation or the participant may try to behave in the most sociable acceptable way. Either condition arises because the researcher did not use deception and either condition would easily invalidate the findings of the research.

Most researchers agree to the fact that many social-psychological areas such as altruistic behaviour, aggression, racial and gender prejudice and conformity are so sensitive that deception is necessary for producing valid results. The famous study of obedience to authority by Stanley Milgram provided an example of stressful consequences of deception. In this study, researcher misled the participants by letting them believe that they were giving increasingly strong electric shocks to another person who was crying in pain and going to fell unconscious. Of course, none of the condition mentioned above was true, but because participants believed it, the entire experience was painful, stressful, and therefore, unethical too. Likewise, experiment by Hardy and Latane (1986) provided another example of harmful consequence of deception. In this experiment, the researchers intended to compare the participant's effort on a task when they thought they were working alone as compared to when they thought they were working in the presence of others. The researchers misled the participants by telling them that the study intended to examine the effects of sensory deprivation on noise production. When the participants were requested to yell and clap as loudly as they could, it was found that they made less noise when they thought that another person was performing with them than when they thought they were performing alone. In this experiment, deception was used, but its consequences were minor. Researchers have shown that about one-third of studies done in the field of social psychology have used deception in their search for truth (Korn and Nicks, 1993).

Researchers have shown that most deceptions can have serious consequences (Eisner, 1977). It may cause embarrassment and lowered self-esteem in participants. It can also damage a trusting relationship between the participants and the researcher. Deception globally helps society in negatively perceiving the social research. Therefore, deception should be used where it is absolutely necessary and that too with proper caution.

3. Participants should be debriefed at the end of the study: Today, the researchers in the field of social psychology agree that deception should be kept at minimum because of its negative consequences. Not only that, they are interested in informing the participants regarding deception as soon as possible after completion of their participation in research. This is called *debriefing*. Thus, *debriefing* is broadly defined as the process of informing the research participants as soon as possible after completion of their participation in the research regarding the purposes, procedures, scientific value of the research as well as discussing any questions raised by the participants. Debriefing becomes important when the deception has been used. Debriefing has the following important goals:

(i) The researcher can explain any necessary or unavoidable deception in a better way.
(ii) The participant can raise questions and concerns about the different aspects of research and the researcher can easily address them.
(iii) Both the researcher and the participant can discuss the overall purpose, procedures and methods of the study. This may enhance the scientific value of the study.
(iv) The process of debriefing also allows the researcher for detecting and dealing with any possible negative effects of the research.

Thus, it is obvious that debriefing at the end of research allows social psychological researcher to explain to the participant what the research is all about and why deception, if employed, was essential. Fortunately, most of the researches have shown that debriefing can provide deceived participants with more favourable and positive attitude towards both themselves as well as towards the research (Thompson, Cowan and Rosenhan, 1980). For doing so, it is essential that the debriefing must be thorough and must emphasise the importance of research and treat participants with maximum respect and regards.

4. Confidentiality regarding participants should be ensured: Researchers should guarantee confidentiality and anonymity to the participants in their researches. This means that the participants should not be identified unless this was the part of the research and also consented by the participants. Right to confidentiality and anonymity is considered important because some researches done in social psychology invades the privacy of the participants. Researches done in the areas like intimate relationship, sexual behaviour, political and religious belief generally pry into participants' lives, and thus, make an invasion of privacy. Therefore, researcher must maintain confidentiality and anonymity to the participants while studying such sensitive issues.

These are the major ethical issues and values, which should be considered by social psychologists while conducting researches relating to social behaviour. Besides these ethical considerations, the researchers should also avoid practices that may subject the participants to physical or mental stress. The study of social behaviour involves stressful situations, which often produce negative emotional reactions such as fear, shock, or sometimes, a sense of inadequacy too. The worth mentioning point here is that the researchers should attempt to achieve the objectives of the research with less and less stressful experiences to the participants. Different methods of research raise differential degree of ethical issues. For example, field experiments, in general, pose more ethical problems of social psychology than laboratory experiments do. Field experiments generally raise important issues like issue of deception, invasion of privacy and informed consents. Figure 2.3 presents the summary of all these ethical principles.

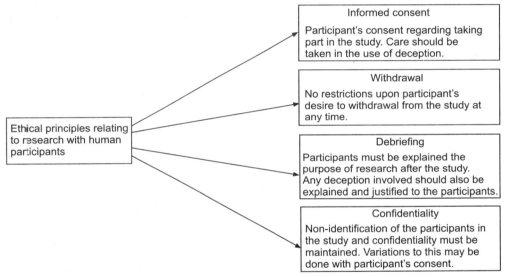

Figure 2.3 Summary of ethical principles of informed consent, withdrawal, debriefing and confidentiality commonly required in the experiments of social psychology.

ROLE OF THEORY IN SOCIAL PSYCHOLOGICAL RESEARCH

Social psychologists not only describe social behaviour but also explain the reason behind this. For example, social psychologists not only describe the prevalent caste prejudice in India but also want to exhibit why people of one caste is negatively prejudiced against the people of the other caste. Likewise, social psychologists not only describe aggressive behaviour of the people but also explain why people become more aggressive in one situation as compared to the other situation. Such explanation obviously involves *construction of theories*, which are defined as an integrated set of principles that explain and predict observed events (Myers, 2005). In simple words, theories are frameworks for explaining the various types of social behaviour. Before explaining the process of developing a theory, it is essential that we should discuss the following three essential requirements of a good scientific theory:

1. Theories are the statements about constructs: Theories are about constructs, which are abstract concepts because we cannot see and touch them. For example, aggression, anxiety, self-esteem, prejudice, attitudes—all are the examples of construct. Theories are the statements about these constructs. For example well-known social comparison theory contains two important constructs—knowledge about others attitude and evaluation of one's own attitudes.

2. Theories describe causal relations: Theories describe causal relationship among various constructs. Theories state clearly that change in one construct (cause) tends to produce corresponding changes in the other construct (effect). Since theories offer reasons to explain why events occur, they are considered very powerful by the researcher. Social comparison theory provides a good explanation of cause and effect; our knowledge of other people's performance, opinion, etc. causes change in how we evaluate our own performance and opinion.

3. Theories are general in scope: Theories are intended to be general in scope, applying to many people in different types of settings. However, theories may differ in their range of applicability. For example, social comparison theory has very wider applicability because it is basically a statement about how people evaluate many aspects of their life. Other theories have, however, limited scope because they focus on either male or female or people of a particular tribe or people of a particular culture. In general, greater the generality of a theory, the more it is useful in explaining the behaviour of the people in different settings.

Now, the question is how does a theory develop? Following Baron, Byrne and Branscombe (2008), five-stage procedure is involved in developing a theory, which is described below:

1. Researchers collect the existing evidences regarding a social behaviour. On the basis of these evidences, a theory, which basically reflects the evidence, is proposed.
2. The formulated theory consists of basic facts and statements about the constructs and their relationship. Not only that, the theory also makes certain prediction about observable events. For example, the theory might predict the conditions under which people exhibit more caste prejudice or more aggression.
3. The predictions, which are technically called *hypothesis*, are tested by actual research. Hypothesis serves many purposes. First, hypothesis allows researcher to test a theory by suggesting how one may try to falsify it. Second, hypothesis gives direction to research. Third, predictive nature of a good theory also makes it more practical. Kurt Lewin, one of the modern social psychology founders, has rightly said, "There is nothing so practical as a good theory".
4. If the researcher obtains results, which are consistent with the theory, then the theory is taken to be more accurate. However, if the results do not support the theory, theory goes under modification and further tests are done.
5. At the last stage, either the theory is accepted as accurate or rejected as invalid and inaccurate. Even after being accepted, the theory goes on further refinement with the help of new researches.

Let us take an example to illustrate what has been said in the five-stage process. Suppose a social psychologist formulates a theory, which reveals that people prefer to engage themselves in behaviour that is rewarding or reinforcing. Since social interaction involves both rewards and costs, the persons behave in such a way so as to maximise their rewards and minimise their costs. This theory may lead to specific prediction like the more often a behaviour is rewarded, more likely a person is to perform that behaviour again. If the results of the research are consistent with this prediction as well as with others derived from the theory, confidence in theory is increased. Whereas, if the results of the research do not support the prediction, the theory is modified or perhaps rejected. Thus, the theory about social behaviour ultimately stands or falls on the basis of how well it is supported by valid research. Of course, no theory ultimately stands or falls on the basis of single study because the results of any one study might have been influenced by some ordinary mistakes done by the researcher like use of particular manipulations, poor internal validity, special characteristics of participants, chance variation, etc. (Smith and Mackie, 2007).

The entire process of developing a theory, making prediction, testing it, modifying the theory and again testing it constitutes a part of social psychological research. All these processes have been well illustrated in Figure 2.4.

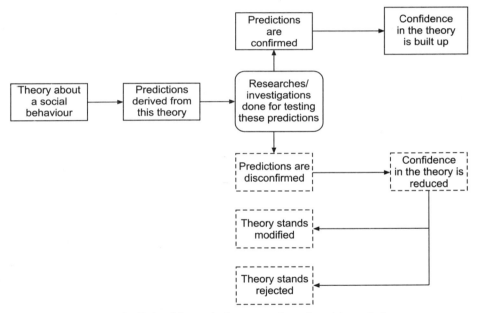

Figure 2.4 Role of theory in the researches of social psychology.

Before closing discussion, it is essential to hint at two points relating to testing of a theory by scientific research. First, no theory is ever proved in any final and ultimate sense. As new researches and concepts do come, the theory needs further modification. Second, researches are not done to prove or verify the theory, rather these are done for providing evidences relevant to the theory under test.

TYPES OF RESEARCH IN SOCIAL PSYCHOLOGY

Six different types of researches are commonly done in social psychology—*descriptive research, correlational research, experimental research, action research, evaluation research* and *cross-cultural research*. All these types are discussed here.

1. Descriptive research

Descriptive research is the most basic type of research in social psychology. In descriptive research, the researcher documents the existing social reality by describing the characteristics and the frequency of occurrence. In other words, here, the researcher documents social reality by looking at what is in social reality. Thus, in descriptive research, the primary purpose is to paint a picture using words or numbers and to present a profile, a classification of types or an outline of steps for answering questions like who, when, where and how. Questions like—who is involved, when did the event took place, how did it happen, where did it happen—are studied by a descriptive researcher. In this way, a descriptive research presents a picture of specific details of the situation, social setting or social relationship. A descriptive researcher generally studies social behaviours like rate of family breakdown, major types of criminal behaviour, frequency of availing health facilities by certain age group, etc.

In descriptive research, the researcher uses methods like observation, survey research, interview, case study content analysis and self-report. Only experimental method is infrequent. For example, a social psychologist might observe the records of police for knowing about the types of criminal behaviour done by adolescents and might also interview them in order to arrive at some meaningful conclusion. Likewise, a social psychologist might observe the records of health care institutions to know about which age group of persons enjoys health facilities the most, etc. A very good example of descriptive research is provided by Cox (1970), who studied stereotypes against blacks and whites. He assessed the occupational role of black and white adults portrayed in the advertisement shown in different magazines. He found out the percentage of blacks and whites shown in the advertisements during 1949–50 and 1967–68. Results revealed that in 1967–68, blacks' role in the advertisement had comparatively enhanced as compared to their own role as well as whites' role in 1949–50. The study provided a support for the general impression that blacks are being readily accepted into higher occupational role.

2. Correlational research

Correlational research is concerned with studying whether or not certain factors or variables are related (or vary together) to another variable. In other words, correlational research goes beyond descriptive research and it not only tells *what is* but also *what comes and goes with what*. If a variable increases (or decreases) and similar trend exists in another variable, that is, other variable also increases (or decreases), a *positive correlation* is said to exist between the two variables. On the other hand, if increases in one variable are followed by decreases in the other variable or vice versa, a *negative correlation* is said to exist. Researchers often use methods of correlation like Pearson r, partial correlation, multiple correlation, factor analysis in correlational research.

One classic but very popular example of correlational research has been conducted by Adorno et al. (1950) in which they examined the correlation between authoritarian personality and ethnic prejudice and political-economic conservatism. *Authoritarian personality* is one which forces others for submission to authority without making any question. Scores on attitudes scales assessing authoritarian personality, ethnic prejudice and political economic conservatism were correlated and they found a position correlation among authoritarian personality, ethnic prejudice and political-economic conservatism. Likewise, in some studies, social psychologists have reported a positive correlation between self-esteem and academic achievement. Children having self-esteem were found to exhibit higher degree of academic achievement.

Although correlational research occurs in real world settings, where the researcher can examine factors like gender, race and social status which cannot be manipulated in the laboratory, such research yields ambiguity of the results. Correlational research allows the researcher in making prediction, but this does not tell whether changing one variable will really cause changes in another. Simply because two variables or conditions vary together does not mean that one causes the other. For example, height and weight of a person are moderately correlated, but one can never say that height causes his weight or weight causes his height. Taking another example, there appears to be positive correlation between cigarette smoking and lung cancer. Can we say that cigarette smoking causes lung cancer? The answer is no. Two variables may be related to each other because both may be related or linked to a third variable. Cigarette smoking and lung cancer may be related because these might be related to a third variable, that is, genetic factor that may predispose a person to cancer, and at the same time, produces a craving for taking nicotine, which is found in cigarette. Likewise, self-esteem of the children may be correlated with achievement because both are linked to underlying intelligence and socio-economic status of the family.

Recent advancement in correlational techniques have, however, made possible to infer cause-effect relationship. To infer causation, the researcher must know the proper time sequence, with the supposed cause preceding the effect. Time-lagged correlations reveal the sequence of events. *Cross-lagged panel correlation* is one such technique, which does indicate causation (Campbell, 1973; Kenny, 1975). We have already earlier cited an example in this chapter showing how a cross-lagged panel correlation reveals the sequence of events (see correlational method of research). Results of correlational research must also be treated with caution because any social behaviour is not determined by one factor, rather there may be multiple causations. Unless all those factors are taken into consideration, the researcher can only arrive at a restricted view.

3. Experimental research

In experimental research, the researcher manipulates the independent variable and examines its impact upon the dependent variable, while keeping all the extraneous variables controlled. The dependent variable is so called because it may depend on manipulations of the independent variable. For eliminating the extraneous variable (also called *controlled variable* or *confounding variable*), random assignment of the participants is done. *Random assignment* is the process of assigning participants to the conditions of an experiment in such a way that all persons have the same chance of being in the given conditions, that is, they have an equal chance of being exposed to each level of independent variable.

One basic feature of experimental research is that it suggests possible cause-effect relationship between the variables. Social psychologists have used experimental research in about three-fourth of their research studies (Higbee et al., 1982) and two out of three experiments represent laboratory research (Adair et al., 1985). There are many laboratory researches, which have vividly shown cause-effect relationship between the variables under study. For example, Berkowitz and Green (1966) in their popular laboratory experiment demonstrated that angered college students, who viewed violent scenes on television acted more aggressively than did similarly angered students, who view non-aggressive films on the television. On the basis of this laboratory experiment, the researchers were able to state that viewing violent films (independent variable) is a cause for enhancing aggressive act (dependent variable) of the participants. Bushman and Anderson (2001) also showed through their laboratory experiment research that exposure to media violence significantly increases aggressive acts among those participants, who were not exposed to such violence.

One of the biggest problems in experimental researches, particularly in laboratory experiment research, is that of generalisability of results. This is because such experimental situation represents a contrived situation. Mundane realism is very low (Aronson et al., 1985). Results obtained in contrived situation of the laboratory experiment research cannot be generalised effectively to real-life behaviour. This concern can, however, be partly offset by incorporating simulations and gaming that represent more of social reality in the experimental situation. A *simulation* is an artificial situation, which is set up to represent a natural situation.

4. Action research

Action research is one form of applied research, which is frequently undertaken by social psychological researchers. Originally conceived by Kurt Lewin in 1940s, action research is carried out with the sole purpose of achieving an understanding of the social behaviour that leads to practical applications and solutions of the real-world problems. Lewin (1948) opined that action research is a kind of comparative research on the conditions and effects of various forms of social action, ultimately leading to an improved social action. In action research, those who are being studied participate in the research and such research tries to raise consciousness or increase awareness of the participants. In action research, the investigators try to equalise power relationship among themselves and the research participants and they always avoid having more control, status and authority than the participants. Action researchers further assume that knowledge grows from the experience and the participants can become more aware of the conditions and learn to take actions that bring about improvement.

In action research, the following five important stages are involved:

(i) **Phase of planning:** This is the first phase of action research, where the researcher makes a detailed and in-depth approach to understand the initial situation that needs improvement.

(ii) **Phase of fact-finding:** This is the second stage, where the researcher collects data regarding the existing problematic situation or social problems. Data collection may be done through interview, questionnaire, survey, etc. Thus, fact-finding stage is the stage of data collection.

(iii) **Phase of action or execution:** This is the third stage of action research, where the researcher formally takes a decision about the actions that should be taken. Such actions generally lead to changed behaviour or the solution of the social problems. Thus, here, the problems are corrected that have been identified in the first stage.

(iv) **Phase of evaluation:** At this stage, after execution of the decision taken or action done, with the help of additional fact-finding, an action is evaluated. Here, the researcher gives emphasis on the fact that whether or not the taken action is supported by some additional facts or data collected thereupon.

(v) **Phase of feedback:** At this stage, the researcher provides a feedback, which is incorporated into subsequent planning and action. Feedback helps in putting confidence not only in the present situation of action being investigated but also in the subsequent planning and action to be undertaken in sequence.

Thus, action research contains five phases in sequence. Figure 2.5 presents the cycle of the phases of action research.

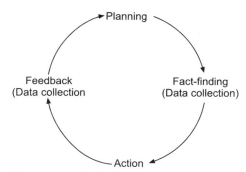

Figure 2.5 Cyclic phase of action research.

There are four common types of action research:

(i) **Participant action research:** In participant action research, the participants assume an active role in formulating, designing and carrying out the research. Here, the researchers and the participants cogenerate knowledge in collaborative process. While fully involving the participants, the researcher assists and provides expertise that guides participants in the entire activities of the research. Here, the researcher plays a role of consultant or collaborator, who assists the participants, but does not have complete control over the research process. The major goal of participant action research is to democratise the knowledge creation process and give focus upon the centrality of social conflict and emphasise upon collective action in improving the social situation.

(ii) **Diagnostic action research:** Such research is basically concerned with identifying the problem situation, analysing it in a way that yields recommendations, which in the long run, may lead to the desired social action.

(iii) **Empirical action research:** In empirical action research, the researcher takes an action following an appropriate decision, and subsequently, keeps a watch over the effects and types of various activities that are carried out for successful execution of social programme or action. Such research involves both methods—participant observation and case study approach for its completion.

(iv) **Experimental action research:** This type of action research is comparatively difficult to conduct. Here, the researcher studies the different action strategies in a controlled research situation, and thus, it allows the researcher to test hypothesis, if any, regarding the action strategies in an empirical way.

Each of these action researches is full of difficulties and problems. Lewin and his coworkers realised that action research was more difficult than laboratory-based research. However, action research has two primary benefits. First, it is problem-focused. The researcher objectively looks for the social problem and the type of problem determines the type of social action. Second, since action research so heavily involves participants in the research, resistance to change is automatically reduced. Once the participants are actively involved in seeking solution of the problems, they become part of the process, and therefore, question of resistance to change does not arise. However, action research has some limitations also. Many of the social problems, which an action researcher confronts, are intractable, that is, they are not easily manageable, since they have to be solved again and again. Therefore, action research makes a very slow progress towards making the progress of society.

Although action research has some limitations, its future is bright. As social psychology is moving towards becoming more and more applied in different fields, the importance of action research is also enhancing.

5. *Evaluation research*

Evaluation research is another applied research that is getting very popular in social psychology. It is defined as a research in which the researcher tries to determine how well a social programme or social policy is working or reaching its goals or fulfilling its objectives. In other words, evaluation research tries to give the answer of this basic question—does a social policy or social programme work? In nutshell, it can be said that evaluation research tries to assess the effectiveness of a programme or a policy by providing reliable and valid data to complement the wide array of information, impressions and values.

Evaluation researchers use different methods for conducting the research. They use survey method, field research and experimental method for judging the effectiveness of a social policy or a social programme. However, evaluation researchers generally take experimental method as one of the most powerful method for the evaluation of a programme or a policy.

Evaluation research is mostly carried out in socio-political systems. It is widely used in large bureaucratic organisations such as business, schools, hospitals, governments, and other large number of non-profit agencies. Most of the social psychologists are having a view that many ethical and political conflicts do often arise in the evaluation research. An evaluation researcher generally poses questions like does a flexitime programme increase employee productivity, does police strictness improves law and order of the town, does a law enforcement programme of mandatory arrest reduce spousal abuse and conflict, is government encouragement regarding intercaste marriage a good means of reducing intercaste conflict, etc. Such questions when answered by an evaluation researchers are affected by various types of ethical and political conflicts because they have opposing interest in the findings about a programme. The findings of the evaluation research can affect the political popularity of a person or promotion of an alternative programme or may open the secrecy of many unsuccessful social programme. Individuals, who are personally displeased with the findings, often try to attack the methods of the research as being biased or inadequate ones. Such people tend to create various types of controversy regarding the researcher as well as regarding his method of research. Not only that, sometimes, the evaluation researchers are subjected to pressure.

As an example of evaluation research, the study conducted by Ball and Bogatz (1971) may be referred here. They attempted to make an assessment of a particular television programme upon conceptual learning among disadvantaged children. In this study, researchers randomly selected some children belonging to the age group of 2 years to 5 years from four different locations and tested their cognitive abilities. Some children, out of these selected ones, were encouraged to watch the television programme. Home visits and discussions with parents and children were arranged to increase their awareness of programme as well as their motivation to watch the programme. Subsequently, these children were compared to another group of children, who were not encouraged to watch the programme (and therefore, they watched the programme less) on the measure of cognitive learning. Results revealed that the encouraged children showed a lot of improvement on the measure of cognitive learning as compared to the non-encouraged children.

Evaluation research is of two general types—*Formative evaluation research* and *summative evaluation research*. In formative evaluation research, the researcher tries to get a continuous feedback on the programme being evaluated. Thus, here, a continuous monitoring is done by the researcher. In summative evaluation research, the researcher looks only at the outcomes of the programme. Evaluation researcher can use qualitative data as well as quantitative data as part of the evaluation programme. Examples of qualitative data are photos, field observation, document study, in-depth interview, etc. Qualitative data allow the researcher to document difficult-to-quantify data. For example, suppose the researcher is evaluating the impact of a particular type of spiritual discourse upon the audience and one person from the audience tells the researcher that the discourse has changed his entire life style. Such qualitative data are difficult to be quantified on any quantitative measure.

Evaluation research is not without limitations. It is commonly found that raw data of the evaluation research are rarely publically available due to various reasons. Not only that, policy makers or those who are directly hit by the evaluation research, can selectively use or ignore evaluation reports.

Despite some limitations, evaluation research is very fascinating and has become one of the major areas of social psychology, especially applied social psychology.

6. Cross-cultural research

Social psychologists often conduct research involving comparisons among various cultures of societies and their members. Culture consists of systems of beliefs, values, norms, artefacts and symbols that are developed by a society and are willingly shared by its members. In such type of research, the researcher studies social behaviour in different cultures and after making a comparative study, he arrives at a certain conclusion. Following Sherif (1963), researches conducted in cultures other than that of own, not only give us a better understanding of people in those cultures but also reveal the general principles underlying social behaviour. Without conducting a cross-cultural research, there is no way of knowing whether the findings based on research using participants in one culture have any importance or relevance for human behaviour in general. In other words, in order to determine the principles underlying human social behaviour, hypotheses must be tested in both our culture as well as in other cultures. For example, one conclusion that high SES (Socio-economic status) parents and middle SES parents differ in child-rearing practices in such a way that have important implications for the development of personality is of moderate interest if it is based on observations made in Indian culture only, but when such SES differences are also reported in other cultures, the findings become relevant and important for studying differences in personality as a function of child-rearing practices.

Basically, there are two approaches which are adopted in cross-cultural research—*emic approach* and *etic approach*. The emic approach to cross-cultural approach studies the behaviour of a particular culture in terms of those things, which are given importance and are only valued by the persons of that culture. The basic assumption of emic approach is that a better understanding of a culture is gained by using indigenous tools, rather than foreign tools used in the other culture. The etic approach, on the other hand, tries to make a comparative study of the social behaviour of persons in one culture to the social behaviours of the persons in the other cultures. This approach tries to establish valid principles of the different cultures and tries to provide such frameworks, which are useful for comparing human social behaviour in various cultures (Berry, 1984). The ideal state for a cross-cultural research is one that combines both these approaches, that is, emic studies should be carried out in order to know position within a culture and for making a comparative study and then etic approach should be adopted (Jing, 2000; Pareek and Rao, 1970).

For betterment, cross-cultural research should be done on equal status collaboration from beginning (that is, from planning) up to the final state (that is, publication state). A few examples of such collaborative research projects in which psychologists of the different countries have worked together are those conducted by Coplan, Tripathi and Naidu (1985); Misra, Knaungo, Rosenstiel and Stuthler (1985), and Tripathi, Coplan and Naidu (1986).

One of the popular classic example of cross-cultural research is the study conducted by Koenig (1971), who did a comparative study of social aspects of the self-concept among American, French and Swedish participants. The researcher tried to obtain consensual responses (that is socially-oriented responses) towards a question—who am I?—by making twenty statements. Higher the proportion or percentage of consensual responses, the more the individual is said to be apparently aware of and concerned about his relations with others individually or collectively. Koenig found in the results that Americans gave more consensual responses than French participants, who in turn, gave more responses than Swedes.

Although cross-cultural researches are very popular means of making a comparative study of variations in social behaviour due to cultural differences, they are beset by several problems as under:

1. There are obvious problems of sampling, reliability of the observation as well as validity of the interpretation of the obtained results. These problems are further aggravated by the researcher's lack of familiarity with culture other than his own.
2. Sometimes, danger of personal bias looms large, especially when the researcher tries to inappropriately apply the values and frame of reference of his own culture to the observation of members of some other culture. One good example of this may come from the basic observation in Indian culture that a child's biological father is wholly and solely responsible for socialising his son or daughter. However, Malinowski (1927) showed that in some cultures, this does not hold true and this role is played by maternal uncle. If the researcher does not know about this cultural difference, it may affect the accuracy of both observation and interpretations in cross-cultural researches.
3. Linguistic differences among the cultures of the societies may also create serious problems of semantic misunderstanding. In cross-cultural researches, errors in communication through language and translation create serious problem in interpretation. Not only psychological variables like intelligence, memory, perception, etc. have been found to be the subject of confounding cultural factors, but even the interpretation of projective tests appears to be similarly affected.

Despite these limitations, social psychologists do cross-cultural researches frequently to widen their scope of the study of various kinds of social behaviour.

Summary and Review

- Social psychology being an empirical science, requires the researchers to use various research methods for collecting data regarding the different aspects of social behaviour. The primary objectives of social psychological research are describing reality, testing existing theories and also developing new ones, discovering causes of some behaviour and providing help in solving social problems.
- Laboratory experimentation involves systematic manipulations of one or more variables (called *independent variables*) in order to determine whether changes in these variables affect some aspect of

behaviour (called *dependent variable*). Experimenter keeps all those variables, other than independent variables, controlled so that they may not affect the outcome of the experiment. Such variables are called *extraneous variables* or *confounding variables*. To ward off artificiality of the laboratory experimentation, simulation and gaming are also usually undertaken.

- Field experiment involves intervention in natural or real-world setting by introducing manipulation into the independent variable and assessing its impact upon the dependent variables.
- *Natural experiment* is one in which the effects of naturally occurring independent variable on the dependent variable are examined.
- Correlational methods require researchers to measure two or more variables to determine whether they are related to one another in any way. Generally, correlation does not provide proof of cause-effect relationship between the variables. However, with advanced statistical techniques such as cross-lagged panel correlation, it is possible to provide such proof.
- *Field studies* are systematic observations about behaviours, as they occur naturally in everyday situation. Since the behaviour is, here, observed in natural settings, it is also called *naturalistic observation*. *Participation observation* is one of the most popular forms of field studies. In this method of research, observer describes a social situation in which he is actively involved. Field studies sometimes use unobtrusive measures, too.
- *Survey research* is a research, which involves sampling a segment of population by asking questions through questionnaires—face-to-face or by mail or by interview. The important process in the survey research is the selection of a representative sample and use of appropriate statistical methods. Although survey research is a very useful tool for collecting information in short time at lower cost, it tends to do so in a relatively superficial manner.
- In archival research, the existing records or documents are analysed or reanalysed in an attempt to test a hypothesis. Social psychologists, in general, are having a view that when archival data of high quality exists, such data are preferable rather than collecting and analysing fresh data. The primary source of archival data may be census data, types of data banks, formal organisations like insurance companies and banks, newspaper and magazines, etc.
- *Content analysis* or also known as *document analysis*, which was popularised by Berelson, is a systematic technique for gathering and analysing the content of the text. Here, the researcher basically undertakes the examination of documents or messages to locate specific characteristics and then makes an inference based on their occurrences. Content analysis is a non-reactive method of research.
- Case study method uses in-depth examination and analysis of an extensive amount of information about one unit or very few units or cases for the period or across multiple period of time. Therefore, the approach of case study is that of longitudinal studies. The data here usually are detailed, varied and extensive and are collected through measures like questionnaires, interviews, observations, and psychological tests. Data from newspapers, magazines, court, government, magazines, government agencies, etc. are not uncommon.
- *Meta-analysis* is the analysis of analyses completed usually on a rather large collection of quantitative studies. Therefore, *meta-analysis* is defined as a statistical technique, which allows the researcher to combine the results of all available previous studies relating to a question or topic to determine what, collectively, they tell us.
- *Internet research* is another method of research in which the researcher collects information about social behaviour of the participants through computer using Internet. Internet is the world's largest computer network, which links many of the scientific research and educational computers as well as commercial network. Internet uses Transmission Control Protocol (TCP)/Internet Protocol (IP).
- There are three types of validity for experiment in social psychology—internal validity, external validity and ecological validity. An experiment in social psychology is said to have *internal validity*

if the researcher is fully confident in stating that the changes in the dependent variable are simply due to the changes introduced in the independent variables because all confounding variables have been controlled. *External validity* refers to generalisability of the results of the experiment from one specific experiment to the other experiment, people and measures. If different experiments using different methods, participants, tests, instrument produce results similar to that of the original experiment, it can be said that this original experiment has external validity. *Ecological validity* means generalisability of the results of the experiment to the real-life situations.

- Social psychology experiment is itself a social situation because its subject matter is other people, who interact with the experimenter. Such situation has attracted much research in order to identify the sources of biases and errors. Social psychology experiments have identified three main sources of such biases or errors—demand characteristics, experimenter effects and participant effects. *Demand characteristics* refer to the implicit and explicit cues that may communicate the behaviour expected in the experimental settings. *Experimenter effect,* also known as *Rosenthal effect*, refer to a condition where the results of the experiment are distorted either intentionally or unintentionally by the characteristics or behaviour of the experimenter. Three types of experimenter effects are biosocial effect, psychological effect and situational effect. *Participant effect* or *subject effect* refers to a condition, where participants may become too helpful or too hostile that disrupt the normal flow of the experimental situation. Due to evaluation apprehension the participant sometimes develop a negative attitude or become too hostile that disrupts the normal flow of the experiment.

- American Psychological Association, Canadian Psychological Association and British Psychological Society have formulated some principles regarding ethical control over the participants in social psychological researches. Important principles are—participants should make informed consent; deception should be avoided as far as possible; participants should be debriefed at the end of the study and confidentiality regarding participants should be ensured.

- Social psychologists not only describe but also explain social behaviour. Such explanation needs construction of theories, which explain and predict observed events. Theories also describe causal relations. Social psychologists adopt a five-stage plan to develop a theory. This five-stage plan of developing a theory constitutes important part of social psychological research.

- Six different types of researches are commonly done in social psychology—descriptive research, correlational research, experimental research, action research, evaluation research and cross-cultural research.

- Descriptive researcher documents the social reality by describing characteristics and their frequency of occurrence. Such researchers prefer reliable and valid measures.

- Correlational research demonstrates how the two variables vary together. Cause and effect relationship between the two variables should be inferred with caution in correlational research.

- Experimental research requires the manipulation of independent variables and control of confounding variables. Here, the researcher examines the impact of such manipulation and control upon dependent variable.

- In action research, the researcher collaborates with participants in identifying a problem, analysing it, engaging in data collection, executing an action to solve the problem, and finally, evaluating the effects of action.

- In evaluation research, the researcher evaluates the application of research methods to assess the effects of a social programme or a policy.

- In cross-cultural research, the researcher tries to make a comparative study of social behaviour of interest in different cultures, including that of own.

Review Questions

1. Discuss the major objectives of social psychological researches. To what extent they have been able to achieve them?
2. How is a laboratory experiment done in social psychology? Discuss the strengths and weaknesses of laboratory experiments.
3. Why are simulation and games used in laboratory experiments?
4. Discuss, with example, the nature of field experiment. Also, discuss the strengths and weaknesses of field experiments.
5. Make distinction between field experiments and natural experiments. What are the advantage and limitations of a natural experiments?
6. Assess the importance of correlation methods in social psychology researches.
7. Discuss the strengths and weaknesses of field studies and naturalistic observation as used by social psychologists.
8. What is survey method? Discuss its strength and weaknesses.
9. Discuss the different types of survey used by social psychologists. Which of them is the most effective in studying attitude and prejudice of the people?
10. What is archival research? Discuss its strengths and weaknesses.
11. What is content analysis? Outline the steps involved in content analysis. Also, discuss its strengths and weaknesses.
12. What is the importance of case study method in social psychological research? Also, discuss the strengths and weaknesses of case study method.
13. What is meta-analysis? When is this done by a researcher? Discuss the need of meta-analysis for social psychological researches.
14. Discuss the different types of validity of experiments of social psychology.
15. Discuss the major sources of biases or errors in social psychological experiments. Suggest some ways to control them.
16. Discuss the major ethical issues and values of social psychological researches. To what extent Indian social psychologists weigh them while conducting a research?
17. Explain the role of a theory in social psychological researches.
18. Citing an example, discuss the role of descriptive research for a social psychologist.
19. Discuss the relevance of correlational research for the discipline of social psychology.
20. Why is experimental research considered as the backbone of the scientific development? To what extent experimental research has made the field of social psychology scientific one?
21. Discuss the major stages involved in an action research. Why is action research considered important for social psychology?
22. Discuss the relevance of evaluation research for the field of social psychology.
23. What is a cross-cultural research? Why do social psychologists consider them effective for their field?
24. Write short notes on the following:
    (i) Participation observation
    (ii) Types of action research
    (iii) Ecological validity
    (iv) Natural experiment
    (v) Role of informed consent, deception and debriefing in experimentations

3. Theoretical Foundations of Modern Social Psychology

Learning Objectives

- Role Theories
- Motivational Theories
- Learning Theories
- Cognitive Theories
- Symbolic Interaction Theories
- Socio-cultural Theories
- Evolutionary Theories

Key Terms

Aesthetic need
Classical conditioning
Cognitive needs
Cognitive structures
Empirical theories
Esteem needs
Evolutionary social psychology
Experiential learning
Interrole conflict

Intrarole conflict
Middle-range theories
Observational conditioning
Operant conditioning
Physiological needs
Role expectation
Role strain/conflict
Schema

Self-actualisation needs
Social exchange theory
Social norms
Social roles
Social values
Symbolic interaction
Theoretical perspectives
Verbal reinforcement

The basic commitment of modern social psychology to the scientific method generally embraces following three types of operations:

1. A careful collection of data or observations
2. Ordered integration of these various observations into hypothesis and theories
3. Testing the accuracy of these hypotheses or theories in terms of the extent to which they can predict future observations or events.

The first operation is referred to as *methodology*, the second operation is called *development of theories* and the third operation is known as *evaluation and prediction* by the social psychologists.

Of these three operations or steps, we shall here concentrate upon the second step, which relates to the development of theories in social psychology.

The term *theory* normally applies to the higher order integration of hypotheses into systematic networks that attempt to describe and predict about the events or behaviour. Social psychologists are committed to develop *empirical theories*, that is, the theories that are based on observation and describe such relationships, which can be verified by the scientific method (Fisher, 1982). In simple words, it can be said that theory is a set of interrelated propositions, which organises and explains a set of behavioural events. Theories, in social psychology, usually do not pertain to some behavioural event, rather to the whole classes of behavioural events. Besides, theories go much beyond mere observable facts postulating causal relationship among variables. If the theory is really valid, it enables the researcher not only to explain the behaviours under consideration but also help him in making predictions about those behavioural events, which were not yet observed.

Social psychologists have developed two types of theories to describe, explain and predict about social behaviour. These are as follows:

1. Middle-range theories
2. Theoretical perspectives

Middle-range theories are those theories, which account for a certain limited range of phenomena such as helping stranger in distress, conforming to group pressures, and developing a positive impression of another person. Middle-range theories are so called because they tend to focus on some specific aspect of social behaviour and don't cover or encompass the whole social life (Taylor, Peplau and Sears, 2006). Thus, middle-range theories are narrow-focus frameworks that tend to identify such conditions, which may produce an explanation of some specific social behaviour. One feature of middle-range theories is that they are developed in terms of cause and effect, that is, they are scientific causal in nature. For example, one middle-range theory of social psychology tries to explain the processes by which persuasion produces change in the attitudes of the people (Petty and Cacioppo, 1986a, 1986b). Still another middle-range theory explains under what conditions frustration leads to aggression (Dollard et al., 1939). Yet another middle-range theory tries to specify the conditions under which contact between the members of different racial and ethnic groups may cause stereotypes to change or disappear (Rothbart and John, 1985).

Another category of theories developed by social psychologists has been properly termed as *theoretical perspectives*, which are broader in scope than the middle-range theories. In other words, theoretical perspectives provide general explanations for a wider array of social behaviours in different types of situations. In fact, these general explanations are rooted in the explicit assumptions about human nature. By making some assumptions about human nature, a theoretical perspective provides the social psychologists a certain platform from where they can examine a wider range of social behaviours. Since generally one theoretical perspective highlights certain features and downplays some other features, it enables the social psychologists to see certain features of social behaviour more clearly than the others. Thus, the importance of theoretical perspective lies in its wider applicability across many different situations as well as it provides a good and scientific framework for interpreting and comparing a wider range of social behaviours occurring in different social situations.

There are different theoretical perspectives, which have been developed by the social psychologists. Important and useful ones are as follows:

1. Role theories
2. Motivational theories
3. Learning theories
4. Cognitive theories
5. Symbolic interaction theories
6. Socio-cultural theories
7. Evolutionary theories

ROLE THEORIES

In day-to-day life, we all perform different types of role. An adult play the role of father in his home, whereas he plays role of an officer in his office. Role theory explains these various roles of an individual in a scientific way.

In fact, *role theory* is a direct transfer from the stage or the world of theatre, where actors do or perform different roles in such a way that may meet the expectations of audience. A *role* can be defined as the pattern of behaviour that a person performs when occupying certain position in social system (Fisher, 1982). The concept of role acts as a bridge between the person and the group and between the levels of personality and culture probably because it is an integrating concept (Secord and Backman, 1974). In fact, it links the person to the complex levels of social functioning such as interpersonal relationship, roles in groups and organisations, etc.

The central idea of role theory is that a substantial proportion of the observable social behaviour is nothing, but simply individuals carrying out their roles just as actors or actresses carry out their roles on the stage. Role theory has some propositions while it tries to explain the observable social behaviour. Those propositions can be briefly described as under:

1. Individuals spend much of their time as members of groups and organisations.
2. these groups and organisations, the individuals occupy some distinct positions.
3. Each of these positions entails a specified role, which means that the individual is expected to perform a set of functions. An individual's role is defined by expectations (held by the other group members) that specify how he or she should perform the set of specified functions. Thus, each role position is associated with some role expectations, which include belief about appropriate behaviours, obligations, rights and privileges that are generally assigned to that role position. According to Secord and Backman (1974), it is expected that a person should behave in a prescribed manner and it is believed that the person would behave that way. In this sense, role expectations act as a conceptual bridge between the role behaviour and the social structure, that is, such expectations link the person to his position in social system (Sarbin and Allen, 1968). Role expectations can be held by a limited number of people or by a very large number of people in society.
4. Group or society often formalises the various expectations, which become norms for the concerned group or society. *Norms* are rules specifying how a person should behave, what rewards will be given for performance and what type of punishment will result for performance.
5. Individuals tend to carry out their roles and perform according to the demands of the prevailing norms. Thus, individuals are primarily conformists and try to meet the expectations of the others. In other words, *role enactment*, a term coined by Sarbin and Allen (1968) and

frequently used in preference to the term *role playing*, is influenced by many factors such as clarity of expectations, degree of consensus on the expectations, skills of the role actor as well as on the degree of compatibility between the self and the role.

6. Members of the society or group finally check the performance of every individual to determine whether it conforms to the expectation of society or group. If the individual meets and justifies the role expectation, he is rewarded in some form like approval, acceptance, praise, money, etc. and if he does not meet or justify the role expectation, he is punished, that is, group members may punish, embarrass or even expel that individual from the group. Social psychologists, in general, are of view that the very anticipation that others will apply sanctions better ensures performance of the person (Delamater and Myers, 2009).

Role theory claims that if the role expectations related to some specified position are known, we can, to a greater extent, predict a significant portion of the behaviour of that individual, who occupies the position. If we want to change the behaviour of the person, it is essential to change or redefine his role. This can be done by changing the role expectations held by the others or by shifting that person to a position, which entirely demands a set of different functions (Allen and Van de Vliert, 1982). For example, if a university shifts Mohan from the position of Deputy Registrar to the position of Controller of Examinations, his behaviour would automatically change to match the role demanded by his new position, although Mohan himself may experience some stress and strain while making adjustment to the new role.

Role theory further explains that the role of a person not only affects his behaviour but also affects his attitude and beliefs. If the role is changed, the person changes his attitude for showing congruence with the expectations that define his roles. A very good example of changes in attitude due to changes in role position is classic study of factory workers by Lieberman (1965). This study examined the effects of role position on the attitudes of the role occupants. In this study, attitudes towards the management and the union of the employees holding different positions were assessed. During the first phase of the study, two groups of workers experienced role changes, that is, some were promoted to the rank of supervisors and some were elected as union stewards. Before and after measurement of attitudes clearly revealed that works promoted to the rank of supervisors held a favourable attitude towards the management and the workers who were elected as stewards tended to exhibit more favourable attitude towards the union. The investigator took the advantage of the period of economic recession, which followed the initial measurement. Due to economic recession, some of the supervisors were demoted to worker positions and some union stewards were not elected to their union positions. Capitalising on these occurrences, the investigator once again assessed the attitudes. Results revealed that the supervisors who were demoted, actually reverted to the attitude they had previously held, and the supervisors who remained in their role maintained their positive attitude towards the management. Results for union stewards were less clear cut. Such results, in general, revealed that the workers' attitude is shifted to fit their new roles, as predicted by the role theory.

Thus, it is clear that the role people occupy not only shapes their behaviour but also shapes their attitude. Social psychologists have also found evidence for the fact that the role can also influence the value that people hold, and therefore, can affect their personal growth and development (DeLamater and Myers, 2009).

Each of us has multiple roles that we enact in our society. The complexity induced by having multiple roles sometimes induces role strain or role conflict. Generally, role conflict is experienced within the individual due to some negative feelings like guilt, embarrassment, shame and so on, and is also observed within the social system as interpersonal conflict between the role partners. There are three types of role conflict—*personal role conflict, interrole conflict, intrarole conflict*. In *personal role conflict*, there is inconsistency or strain between the values and beliefs of the person and the role behaviour expected from him. When a Brahmin having low values and negative beliefs about backwards and *dalits* is expected to start welfare measures for these people, he is likely to suffer from personal role conflict. In *interrole conflict*, a person generally holds two or more such positions that require contradictory role behaviour. As a teacher, a person may give idealistic suggestions to his students, but as a father, he may experience difficulty in fulfilling the same idealistic expectations held by his children or other members of his family. *Intrarole conflict* occurs when different role expectations are held by two or more partners or groups. For example, the parent may expect from his son to study ten hours a day, whereas son may consider it as a very difficult job. How to respond to such conflicting situation is one of the greatest challenge of social life.

For reducing various types of role conflict, role socialisation and role negotiation are the two primary mechanisms. *Role socialisation* refers to learning what is appropriate behaviour in any situation and *role negotiation* is defined as a process of compatibility among expectations through the process of bargaining between the actor and the actor's partners.

It is clear that the role theory is very useful for understanding the substantial part of social behaviour. It is considered very useful for understanding the individual behaviour in social organisations.

Despite its usefulness, role theory has limitations as under:

1. Role theory fails to explain certain kinds of social behaviour. For example, deviant behaviour that violates or contravenes the norms defining a given role is difficult to be explained. Therefore, deviant behaviour poses a challenge for role theory probably because it contradicts the basic assumption that individuals are essentially conformist—deviant behaviour really violates the demands of roles. Of course, some amount of deviant behaviour is explained by the role theory, according to which sometimes people remain ignorant of the norms. Deviance sometimes may also occur when people face conflicting or incompatible expectations from several other persons. In general, it can be said that deviant behaviour is an unexplained exception from the standpoint of the role theory.
2. We know that a substantial portion of social behaviour is explained as conformity to the established role expectations. Role theory fails to explain how role expectations come to be what they are in the first place. Besides, it fails to explain how and when role expectations change. Thus, role theory provides only a partial explanation of the social behaviour.

Despite these limitations, most of social psychologists today consider role theory a good explanation of most of the social behaviour.

MOTIVATIONAL THEORIES

The general approach to explain social behaviour focuses on the individual's own needs or motives. Researches done in the field of social psychology provide many examples of the ways in which our needs influence our attitude and behaviour. Social psychologists try to answer the reason behind the social behaviour in terms of social motives (Taylor, Peplau and Sears, 2006). *Social motives* are the motives, which are related more to the other people than to a particular aspect of environment. Thirst is an example of inborn motive because it is the function of processes within the individual.

Aggression on the other hand, it is an example of a social motive because its expression requires either direct or indirect involvement of the other people. Major social motives studied by social psychologists are affiliation, cooperation, competition, affiliation, achievement, power and altruism.

Early motivational theorists postulated a very limited number of primary drives such as hunger, thirst, sex and pain avoidance. These drives lead to a state of internal excitation, which in turn, leads to behaviour that satisfies the drive and reduces the associated tension. This is the essence of classic drive theory. Freudian or psychoanalytic viewpoints of human motivation emphasise upon such drives, especially those that are associated with sexuality and aggression. But since these early theories do not account for all human behaviour of social life, social psychologists have explored other types of explanatory theories.

Maslow's theory of need hierarchy is one of the important theories for social psychologists. Maslow (1943, 1970) has concentrated upon positive motives, rather than destructive needs such as aggression. He stated a comprehensive set of five basic human needs, which were organised in a hierarchy. He postulated that need at the lower end of the hierarchy must be satisfied before a person can move up to the next level of needs. His hierarchy of needs (Figure 3.1) consists of the following:

1. **Self-actualisation needs:** This is the ultimate motive, which involves the need to fulfil one's unique individual potential.
2. **Esteem needs:** It covers various needs, including need for achievement, competence, mastery, recognition, prestige, fame and status.
3. **Belongingness and love needs:** It covers broadly all those needs that are satisfied by social relationships.
4. **Safety needs:** It includes all those needs that must be met to protect the individual from danger.
5. **Physiological needs:** It covers all those basic internal deficit conditions that must be satisfied for keeping bodily processes maintained. Hunger, thirst, sex needs are good examples of physiological needs.

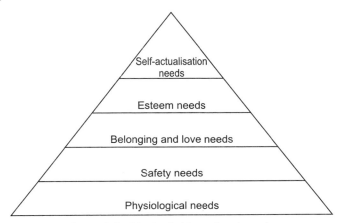

Figure 3.1 Maslow's hierarchy of needs.

Besides these needs, Maslow also talked about *cognitive needs* and *aesthetic needs*. Desire to know, understand and satisfy one's curiosity are included in cognitive needs, whereas cravings for beauty, symmetry and order are included in aesthetic needs. Maslow also coined the term *metamotivation* to refer to the behaviours inspired by growth, needs and values. According to Maslow, this kind of motivation is very common among self-actualisers. Metamotivation often takes the form of devotion to one's own goal or ideal or to something outside oneself. When meta needs are frustrated, it produces *metapathologies*, which are defined as a state showing lack of values, meaningfulness or fulfilment in life. Maslow's need hierarchy is a good attempt to predict what kinds of desires or needs will arise once the old ones are sufficiently satisfied, and therefore, no longer tend to dominate (Frager and Fadiman, 2009). Maslow's model of motivation has been found especially useful for understanding what motivates people to work in an organisation (Fisher, 1982).

Alderfer (1969) further developed and tested Maslow's model and identified three major types of human needs, that is, those related to existence, relatedness and growth. Like Maslow's model, Alderfer's model does not assume that lower level needs must be satisfied before higher level needs emerge.

Another important motivational theory having much relevance to social psychological research is that of McClelland, Atkinson, Clark and Lowell (1953). They proceeded to explain three needs, which were originally postulated by Murray (1938)—*need for achievement* (nAch), *need for affiliation* (nAff) and *need for power* (nPow). The need for achievement involves the desire to accomplish, manipulate and excel at works. The need for affiliation includes desire to interact with others in a way to please them and have their affection. The need for power includes the desire to control other people and influence the social interaction in one's favour. McClelland (1961), in his research, reported many such things, which were considered relevant to social psychology. Important ones are as under:

1. The process of socialising a child is very important for determining one's level of motivation.
2. Degree of independence enjoyed by children during early years of life is central to determine the need for achievement. Higher the degree of independence enjoyed by the children, higher is the level of motivation achievement.
3. People engaged in certain occupations like responsibility, initiation, risk-taking do score high on tests of need for achievement.
4. Measurement of need achievement obtained from children's story books were found to be correlated with the measures of economic production in a number of different countries.

Recently, social psychologists have also started emphasising the ways in which specific situations and social relationships can create and arouse needs and motives. For example, geographical moves often disrupt established social networks of the person and arouse unmet needs for intimacy and a sense of belonging. Such unmet needs for companionship may sometimes lead to seek distractions by abusing alcohol or drugs.

LEARNING THEORIES

The core idea of learning theory is that a person's current behaviour is determined by his past experience. *Learning*, in this context, is defined as the change in behaviour as a result of experience. In any situation, a person learns certain behaviour that is gradually converted into habits. When the person is presented with similar situation, the individual tends to behave in the same habitual way. This approach when applied to explain social behaviour, is called *social learning* (Bandura, 1977).

In fact, learning process includes five central elements—*motivation, association, stimulus, response* and *reinforcement*. Any learning requires a minimal level of motivation on the part of the individual. Besides, it also requires association between stimulus and response. Reinforcement tends to determine what changes in behaviour will occur or what behaviour will be done or both.

Social psychologists have adapted the principles of learning theory for explaining the social behaviour. There are three general principles or mechanisms by which learning occurs. One important learning mechanism is *association* or *classical conditioning*. Pavlov's dog learnt to salivate at the sound of bell because the bell was followed by food every time. After some time, the dog salivated at the mere sound of bell even in the absence of food because the sound of the bell became associated with the food. Human beings learn some social behaviour by association. After a painful visit to a surgeon, the mere mention of the word 'operation' or 'surgery' may evoke anxiety and some erratic behaviour on the part of the person.

Second mechanism is *reinforcement*. The mechanism of reinforcement as applied to the field of learning is the behaviour which is determined primarily by the external events and not by the internal states. A *reinforcement* is defined as any favourable outcome that results from a response. In fact, reinforcement increases the probability of occurrence of a response in future. Responses that are not reinforced tend to disappear because they are not repeated. As early as 1911, Thorndike formulated his famous *law of effect*, which clearly mentioned that the occurrence of the response, if followed by reinforcement, is strengthened, and therefore, such responses are repeated in future. Reinforcement may be positive or negative. *Positive reinforcement* refers to a condition whose presence increases the probability that the behaviour will be repeated. *Negative reinforcement* is a condition or event whose withdrawal tends to increase the probability that the response will be repeated in future. Following Thorndike, Skinner (1953) applied basic principles of learning to social behaviour in what is known as *operant conditioning*. According to the principle of operant conditioning, an individual learns to perform a particular behaviour because it is followed by reinforcement that satisfies the need. He may learn to avoid behaviour that is followed by harmful consequences. A person may learn to help others because his neighbour and members of family praise him for engaging in altruistic behaviour. Skinner's viewpoints regarding learning theory have been especially useful for programme education and in the area of behaviour modification.

One aspect of reinforcement, called *verbal reinforcement*, has also been investigated. The classic study in the field of verbal reinforcement was carried out by Greenspoon (1955). He asked subjects to say all the words that they could think of individually within fifty minutes. For some subjects, the experiment provided verbal reinforcement by saying "mmm-hmm" every time the subject told a plural noun. As predicted by the law of effect, these subjects gave more plural nouns than those subjects who had received no such reinforcement. When this verbal reinforcement was withdrawn, the number of plural nouns decreased. Another study conducted by Cialdini and Insko (1969) showed that verbal reinforcement also tends to affect opinion about different issues and groups, including viewpoints regarding clinical and experimental psychologists.

Third mechanism of learning is *observational learning*, which is most simply defined as learning by watching others. People often learn social attitudes and social behaviours simply by watching other people, technically called *models*. The strongest support to observational learning has come from the researches conducted by Bandura (1977). He believed that much of social learning is *vicarious*, that is, it occurs by way of observation of other people or models. The basic feature of observational learning, also called *imitation* or *modelling*, is that here, the learner neither performs a response nor receives any reinforcement. Many social behaviours are learnt through imitation. For example, adolescents may acquire their political attitude by listening to their parents' conversation during election time. Such learning is called *social learning theory*.

Bandura, a pioneer investigator in the field of social learning theory, pointed out that there are three different effects of exposure to models—*acquisition, inhibition* or *disinhibition* and *response facilitation*. A person who sees a model engaged in novel responses can easily repeat these responses in future, indicating that learning has taken place. For example, when a little child sees his father writing a particular alphabet, say 'A', he may soon start making a similar drawing. Likewise, when a person sees that another person (model) is being punished for a certain behaviour, he is less likely to show that imitative response. This is called *inhibition*. It is due to this inhibition that when a child is punished by the teacher in class for not completing the homework, the other child is less likely to come up with incomplete home task. In response facilitation, the existing response is elicited. This includes responses that have not been previously punished or inhibited. When a model exhibits such behaviour, the people are more likely to imitate him. For example, if one observes the model donating money for some noble cause, he may also voluntarily donate the money for similar causes.

Observation learning, on the whole, has proved very useful for understanding and explaining the acquisition of prejudice, expression of aggression and the effect of mass media on violence in society.

Still another type of learning that has also been found relevant for explaining social behaviour is what has been called *experiential learning* (or *experience-based learning*), which is learning through direct participation. Such learning requires a full awareness of the entire process and context of human learning, including relationship between a learner and another learner as well as between a learner and a teacher. Important key elements in experiential learning are blending of conceptual information with experience and practice, feedback to learners, active learner participation, a supporting climate for learning, and permitting the learners to learn as much as possible from their experience. Social psychologists consider experiential learning very useful for understanding the acquisition of language and reading skills (Fisher, 1982).

Another very important process that is based on the principle of reinforcement and widely researched by social psychologists is social exchange. *Social exchange theory* uses the concept of reinforcement for explaining stability and change in relationship between individuals (Kelley and Thibaut, 1978; Homans, 1974; Cook, 1987). Any behaviour involves some rewards and costs. There may be many types of socially mediated rewards such as money, goods, services, prestige, status, social approval, etc. The theory assumes that human beings are hedonistic and they try to maximise rewards and minimise costs. Therefore, individuals generally prefer to do those behaviours that produce more profit and avoid those behaviours that produce less profit.

According to social exchange theory, the individuals participate in any action or behaviour when they find that they provide profitable outcomes. An individual generally judges the attractiveness of personal relationship by comparing the profits it provides against the profits available in other alternative relationship. Social exchange theories broadly hold that individuals engage in behaviour that is rewarding or reinforcing. Since social interaction involves both rewards and costs, the individuals behave in order to maximise the rewards and minimise the costs. Rewards may be any kind of positive reinforcement, but social approval is the most important reinforcer in social life. Costs include punishment as well as the cost of lost alternatives, that is, the behaviour which could have been done, but somehow it was not done. Profits are the differences between rewards and costs. Besides these, comparison level and the comparison level for the alternatives are also important concepts. *Comparison level* is the simple standard of evaluation. Outcomes above it are pleasing and outcomes below it are annoying. *Comparison level for the alternatives* is defined as the least favourable level of outcome available from an alternative relationship. If a person's outcome (or profit) from a social relationship drops below comparison level for alternative, two things may happen—either the person is motivated to leave the relationship for the one that provides better outcome or he tries to change the behaviour in the relationship in order to enhance the outcomes. A person, however, may stay in an unpleasant relationship (where outcomes are below the comparison level) if there are no better outcomes available in the other relationship. Therefore, the comparison level for alternatives is an important determinant of whether the person will continue in a social relationship. Social exchange theories are also sometimes known as *decision-making theories* because individuals evaluate the costs and benefits of different actions and pick up the best alternative in a fairly logical and reasoned way. They decide to choose the alternative that gives them the greatest rewards at the least cost. Thus, decision-making, here, involves weighing the benefits and costs of possible alternatives and then adopting the best one. The studies of heterosexual relationship show that rewards and costs can explain whether the partners stay in or exist from such relationship (Rusbult, 1983; Rusbult, Johnson and Morrow, 1986). Results of such studies have clearly indicated that partners are more likely to stay and continue such heterosexual relationship as long as one partner finds the other partner as physically attractive and when such relationship does not entail undue hassles like high monetary cost, broken promises, lack of involvement, irritating argument, etc. as well as when such romantic relationship with other attractive alternatives are not readily available. In nutshell, it can be said that in such a relationship, the person is more likely to stay only when rewards are high, costs are low and alternatives are not up to the mark.

The basic principles of social exchange theories help us in understanding a variety of social processes, including small group processes. People join groups and conform to the group norms for obtaining rewards. If the person somehow chooses to deviate from the group norms, he does so either because a deviant behaviour becomes more profitable or because he joins a different group if his profit drops below the comparison level for the alternatives.

Social exchange theory also tries to predict the conditions under which the individuals restructure or change the personal relationship. In such prediction, the central concept involved is equity (Adams, 1983; Walster, Walster and Berscheid, 1978). Equity is said to exist in relationship when participants or partners feel that rewards that they receive are proportional to the costs they incur. A supervisor getting less money than a manager may feel that the relationship is equitable because the manager has to take more responsibility and also has a higher level of education. However, when the participant somehow feels that the relationship is inequitable, due to inappropriate allocation of rewards and costs, the relationship becomes unstable. Participants feel inequity difficult to tolerate and may also become aggressive. Social exchange theory predicts ways to modify the inequitable relationship. In such situations, people, according to the prediction of the theory, try to reallocate costs and rewards so that equity is restored. Waster et al. (1978) had suggested that equity perspective has a potential to become a general theory of social psychology that is applicable to numerous social relationships. It has been successfully applied to the field of interpersonal attraction and employee satisfaction in work organisation.

If we pay attention to the learning theories, it becomes obvious that they, on the whole, are concerned with the past experiences and somewhat less concerned with the present situation. One of the major elements of learning theories is reinforcement and the reinforcement mechanism characterises social behaviour as hedonistic with the individual trying to maximise profits from outcomes. Therefore, this cannot easily explain some selfless behaviour such as altruism and martyrdom.

COGNITIVE THEORIES

The core of cognitive theories is that cognitive processes are the basic determinants of social behaviour. The cognitive processes include several types of mental processes such as perception, memory, judgment, problem solving, decision-making, etc. Cognitive theories do not deny the existence of external stimulus, but they maintain that the link between the stimulus and the response is not automatic, rather cognitive processes intervene between the stimulus and the response. As a consequence, the persons not only meaningfully interpret the meaning of the events/stimuli but also select appropriate behaviour/actions as response.

Making a historical trace, it can be said that cognitive theories in social psychology have seen influenced by gestaltistic movement of Kohler and Koffka. One of the major principles of gestalt psychology is that people generally respond to the configuration of stimuli, rather than responding to single and discrete stimulus. In simple words, it can be said that people try to understand the meaning of the stimulus only by viewing it in the entire context of system of elements of which that stimulus is one part. Cognitive approach further emphasises upon the fact that an individual's behaviour depends on the way social situation is perceived by the individual. Lewin (1951) applied the ideas of gestalt psychology to social psychology by emphasising the importance of social environment as perceived by the person. In fact, he developed field theory as one means of representing the psychological and social forces that interact to determine the behaviour of the individual. According to Lewin, the behaviour of the individual is affected by both the individual's personal characteristics such as abilities, personality and genetic dispositions as well as by the social environment perceived by the individual.

According to some modern cognitive theorists such as Wyer and Srull (1984), Markus and Zajonce (1985), and Fiske and Taylor (1991), human beings are more active in selecting and interpreting the stimuli. In other words, human beings actively structure the environment in a cognitive way because of the following two reasons:

1. Since it is not possible to attend to all stimuli available in the environment, the individual selects only those stimuli, which are useful to them, and thus, ignores the other.
2. Individuals actively control which categories or concepts can be used to interpret the stimuli in the environment. Perhaps due to this, several individuals can form different impressions of the same complex stimulus.

Cognitive theories emphasise upon a concept called *cognitive structure* for explaining the social behaviour. The term *cognitive structure* refers to any form of organisation in cognition. Since individual cognitions are interrelated, cognitive theory gives special emphasis upon studying how they are related to memory and how they affect a person's judgement. Social psychologists are of opinion that the persons use specific cognitive structures called *schemas* (or also called *schemata*) to make sense of complete information about the other persons, groups, roles and situations. The term *schema* refers to the basic sketch or framework of what we know about people, things, roles, etc. Thus, schema is a mental framework, which contains information relevant to self, other people, specific situations or events. Schemas are formed on the basis of previous experience, cultural and social norms. Once schemas are established, they help us in guiding over behaviour and interpreting new situations (Fiske and Taylor, 1991). For example, our schema for a professor may be the set of traits, which are thought to be the characteristics of a professor, that is, intelligent, logical, analytic, thorough, research-minded, etc. When we hold this schema, it does not mean that we believe that every person with this set of characteristics is a professor or that every professor has all these characteristics.

Schemas are considered important in social situations because they help the person in interpreting them efficiently. Whenever we meet with a stranger, we usually form impression on the basis of what characteristics he is showing. While doing so, we not only observe the person's behaviour but also use our knowledge of similar persons we have met in our lives. In other words, we use schemas to form an impression about that person. These schemas help the person in processing the information by enabling him to recognise which personal characteristics are important and which are not. Schemas, thus, structure and organise the various information about the person and they also help us in remembering and process the information quickly in a better way. Sometimes, they fill the gaps in knowledge and enable the person to make judgement and prediction about the others. However, schemas are not always perfect as predictive devices (DeLamater and Myers, 2009).

Social psychologists have developed several ways to study cognitive structure. One very common way is to observe changes that occur in the cognitions of the person when they are challenged or attacked. In fact, these changes make revelation about the undying structure or organisation of the person's cognition. A very important idea emerging from this approach is the *principle of cognitive consistency* (Heider, 1958; Newcomb, 1968). Heider explained that an individual is motivated to keep a balanced state of consistent relationship in his perceptions and knowledge of other people and social objects. The perceived bonds or connections may be positive or negative and balance exists when the bonds are in agreement. Newcomb extended Heider's theory and focused on interpersonal attraction or rejection between two persons (say A and B) in relation to a third person or some other object (say X) that can be liked or disliked. If a person holds ideas that are inconsistent (A and B both like X but not each other, say for example), he will experience internal conflict. In reaction, he is likely to change idea, thereby making the idea consistent and resolving the conflict. As an example, suppose Mohan holds the following cognitions about Shyam:

1. Shyam has been his good friend for the last ten years.
2. Mohan dislikes taking hard drugs and all those who are habitual drug abusers.
3. Shyam has recently run into a bad habit of taking hard drugs.

These cognitions of Mohan are obviously interrelated, but they are obviously incongruent with each other. In such a situation, following the principle of cognitive consistency, a change in cognition is predicted. In other words, Mohan may change either his negative attitude towards drug abusers or his positive attitude towards Shyam, or probably, he may intervene and try to change Shyam's behaviour.

In the field of social psychology, cognitive theory has made several contributions. It has explained several diverse behaviours such as self-concept, perceptions of persons and attribution of causes, impression management, attitude change and group stereotypes, etc. In all these contexts, cognitive theorists have produced many insights and striking predictions about social behaviour.

Cognitive theories differ from learning theories in the following two ways:

1. Cognitive theories give emphasis upon the present perceptions and related processes, whereas learning theories emphasise the past or prior experiences.

2. Cognitive theories emphasise the importance of the individual's perception or interpretation of the situation, whereas learning theories emphasise objective reality of the situation, where previous experience of the person has a substantial impact.

Despite a wider applicability of the cognitive theories, there are some limitations as under:

1. Cognitive theories over simplify the way in which people process a complex information. Due to this over-simplification, the theories loose the scientific outlook.
2. Since cognitive phenomena are not directly observable and can be inferred only from what people say or do, definitive tests of various predictions from cognitive theory are very difficult to conduct.

Despite these limitations, cognitive theories have proved a boon for social psychologists for studying the various types of social behaviour.

SYMBOLIC INTERACTION THEORIES

Symbolic interaction theory emerged in the early part of 1900 and it has its roots in philosophy, psychology and sociology. G. Herbart Mead (1934) was the most influential person in this field and is known as the founder of symbolic interactionism.

Symbolic interaction theories are very important theories developed for the purpose of explaining social behaviour (Charon, 1995; Stryker, 1980). This theory, like cognitive theories, places emphasis upon cognitive processes like perceiving, thinking, reasoning, etc., but it places more emphasis upon interaction taking place between the individual and society for understanding the social behaviour.

The theory has both psychological as well as sociological base. The major focus of the theory is upon human social interaction, which can best be understood by studying humans because they clearly possess the ability to perform the process of thinking, reasoning and planning. Thus, the theory makes reference to cognitive processes, and therefore, has a psychological base. The theory has a sociological base in the sense that one of the major concerns is to understand the human cooperative behaviour, which was considered as the essence of society in Mead's view. Animal cooperative behaviour is different in the sense that it is controlled by instincts. Human cooperative behaviour is made possible because humans possess the higher mental process, and therefore, live in a symbolic world as well as in physical world. Different from animals which respond to the stimuli directly, human beings respond to stimuli, which are mediated by their symbolic world. The stimuli impinging upon the individuals are given meaning through cognitive processes, and subsequently, are responded to according to the attached meaning.

One of the basic premises of symbolic interaction theory is that human nature and social order are nothing but the products of symbolic communication among people. Here, human behaviour is neither considered as a response to stimulus or stimuli nor as an expression of biological drives or conformity to the roles and norms, rather it is thought to emerge continually through communication and interaction with others.

Symbolic interaction theory views human beings as goal-seeking and proactive. For achieving goals, people generally formulate various plans of actions. Many such plans can easily be accomplished through making cooperation with others. To establish cooperation with others, the meanings of things or situation must be shared and consensual. Any social interaction in terms of symbolic interaction theory, is considered tentative and such interaction has always some degree of unpredictability and indeterminacy. People, who are interacting with each other, must fit their actions together and achieve consensus. Not only that, they must continually negotiate new meanings of their actions or reform old meanings. Thus, people making interaction formulate plan for the actions, try them and then adjust them in light of others' responses.

Symbolic interaction theory further emphasises that a person can not only act towards others but he can also act towards self. Self is composed of two elements— *I* and *Me*. The 'I' is the impulsive tendency of the person, whereas 'Me' is the generalised others and provides direction to the propulsion. Every behaviour begins with 'I' and then is directed by 'Me'. In other words, it can be said that 'I' suggests an action and 'Me' restricts it by saying 'let us examine the alternatives'. In fact, the generalised others part of one is nothing but a set of roles, which a person uses for comparative self-evaluation. This may involve simultaneously taking the role of a group of others such as all the members of the family or all members of a friendship group, etc. This, in fact, allows the person to view himself from collective perspective of the group or society. In this sense, self may be considered as the reflection of a group or a society. As we know, one very important component of self is *identity,* that is, an individual's understanding of who he or she is. People who are making interaction with one another must know answer of the basic questions like who am I and who are these other people? If there occurs a consensus regarding the identity of the persons, the interaction among them is likely to proceed in a smooth way. Sometimes, the identity of an individual becomes very unusual, and as a consequence, the interaction becomes awkward, difficult and even impossible (DeLamater and Myers, 2009). People, who somehow believe that they are superhumanly intelligent, unusually fragile or unusually strong or having direct contact to God or supernatural powers, are the people whose identities are considered unusual. People with such unusual identities create problems in interaction, and in such a situation, consensus is difficult to be achieved. Cooperative actions also become difficult in the absence of such consensus.

Social psychologists are having a view that self occupies a central role in symbolic interaction theory probably because social order is in part, at least, considered to rest upon self-control. Every individual wants a self-respect in his own eyes. To maintain this, it is essential that he must see himself from the point of view of others with whom he is interacting. To have self-respect, he must meet the standards of others at least to some extent. The other persons whose opinions he cares most about are called *significant others*. The significant others are generally those persons who exercise control over rewards/punishments to be given or those who occupy a central position in the group to which he belongs. A person's significant others generally change as one moves through the life cycle. Parents may be replaced by peers as significant others during adolescence.

In nutshell, it can be said that symbolic interaction theory possesses the following major points:

1. It emphasises the central importance of symbolic communication and language in personality and society.
2. It also recognises the importance of self in making social interaction.
3. It also takes into account all those processes, which are involved in achieving consensus and cooperation.
4. It also tries to explain why people avoid embarrassment and maintain face.

The major advantage of symbolic interaction theory is that it gives emphasis upon cognitive process as well as upon the processes of social interaction. The use of the mentalistic concept like self has contributed to the understanding of human behaviour.

Symbolic interaction theory has some limitations also. Important ones are as under:
1. The theory places too much emphasis upon consensus and cooperation, and therefore, neglects the importance of conflict. However, the theory recognises the fact that the interacting people may fail to reach consensus despite their best effort to achieve it.
2. In symbolic interaction theory, the person is simply depicted as a specific personality type, which is directed by another person in interaction and is mainly concerned with maintaining self-respect by meeting others' standard.
3. Some critics point out that the theory overemphasises rational, self-conscious thought of the person and undermines unconscious or various emotional states. The child and the adult are not perceived as ever being influenced by depression, temper tantrums or humourous feelings.
4. The theory does its business well when analysing fluid, developing encounters with significant others. But it does less well when analysing self-interested behaviour or principled action. (DeLamater and Myers, 2009).
5. Propositions derived from the symbolic interaction theory are difficult to be tested because mentalistic phenomena, upon which the theory has given emphasis, cannot be meaningfully observed in a scientific way.

Despite these limitations, the symbolic interaction theory has proved its usefulness in explaining various types of social behaviour in different situations.

SOCIO-CULTURAL THEORIES

Recently, social psychologists have started formulating socio-cultural perspective to better understand and predict about social behaviour in different cultures. They are basically interested in how people's diversified social backgrounds influence their social thoughts and behaviours (Fiske et al., 1998). In seeking to understand such differences, social psychologists have come to recognise the importance of *culture*, which is defined as the shared beliefs, values, norms, traditions and behavioural pattern of the society. Cultural norms, values, beliefs, traditions, etc. are taught by one generation to the next generation through a process called *socialisation*. People learn about their culture not only from parents and friends but also from television programmes and storybooks, etc.

Social norms are considered as the building block of culture. Social norms consist of rules and expectations about how group members should behave in the society. These social norms apply to everyone in the social group, irrespective of his or her position or status. For example, everyone going on the road is expected to obey traffic signs. Professors are supposed to come on time, prepare lectures and lead classroom discussions. Likewise, students are expected to take notes in class, study for tests, pay tuition fee, etc.

Another important aspect emphasised by socio-cultural perspective is *social role*, which is defined as a set of social norms about how a person should behave in a particular social position. In fact, cultures prescribe many pre-established social rules of behaviour. For example, in a marriage, for husband, the traditional social role is to be bread earner, whereas the social role for wife is housekeeping and child rearing.

The socio-cultural perspective is not only useful for understanding the social behaviour within a culture but also for making comparisons of different cultures or social groups. Social psychologists conduct several cross-cultural studies, which clearly show that how social behaviour is affected by the differences in cultural norms, values and roles. Apart from this, such cross-cultural studies are also able to identify important ways in which cultures do differ from each other. A very useful and important distinction that characterises some cultures is individualism versus collectivism (Triandis, 1995). Individualistic culture tends to have loose ties between the individuals. Here, the behaviour of the person is largely guided by the individual goals, rather than by the goals of collectives such as family, work group or organisation. If, at any time, a conflict arises between the personal goal and the group goal, the person puts his self-interest first or pays attention to the personal goal, ignoring the group goal. The identity is very much self-contained and by the stage of adolescence, the individual becomes self-reliant and defines one's personal independent self. The United States and the Great Britain exhibit the individualistic culture. In such culture, autonomy, change, security of the individual and equality are all valued by the individual. On the other hand, in collectivistic culture, right from the birth, people are tied deeply to in-group. Loyalty to the families, adherence to group norms and the care of the family are placed above the care of any other person. The values highly emphasised in such cultures are duty, order, tradition, respect for the elderly, group security, respect for the group status and hierarchy. Here, identity is defined more in relation to others. Such culture nurtures interdependent self (Kitayama and Markus, 1995). People of collectivistic culture are more self-critical and have a less need for positive self-regard (Heine et al., 1999). India, Japan, China, Korea, Mexico, Central America and South America possess collectivistic culture.

Triandis et al. (1988) have shown that sometimes, the same concept has different meanings in individualistic and collectivistic cultures. For example, consider the meaning of self-reliance. Probably, its meaning in individualistic culture (like the United States) is freedom to do what one likes and freedom from constraints of the group, whereas its meaning in collectivistic culture (such as in Asian countries like India, Japan, China, Nepal, etc.) is probably not being a burden to others or not placing excessive demands on one's family or group. Sometimes, a person has opportunity to live in two cultural worlds. Consequently, they often develop conflict about which cultural patterns to follow.

On the whole, we see that socio-cultural perspectives provide a good opportunity to study the impact of cultural patterns on the social behaviour as well as to make a comparative study of the impact of cultural differences upon social behaviour.

EVOLUTIONARY THEORIES

Evolutionary theories have also been applied to study the social behaviour. Popularly known as *evolutionary social psychology*, such theories try to apply the principles of evolution and natural selection for understanding the human social behaviour (Buss and Kenrick, 1998). In fact, evolutionary social psychology rests on the ideas, which were initially advanced by Charles Darwin and later expanded by several biologists to explain the social behaviour of insects, birds and other varieties of animals.

Evolutionary psychology tries to locate the roots of social behaviour in the genes, and thus, intimately links the biological aspects to the social and psychological aspects (Symons, 1992; Buss, 1999; Wilson, 1975). The obvious implication of such efforts is that social behaviour or the predisposition towards certain behaviours is encoded in our genetic material and is passed through the reproductive process. Let us take an example from the area much frequently researched by evolutionary social psychologists. The area is *mate selection*. Buss (1994) showed that men strongly prefer physical attractiveness and youthful appearance in a potential mate (women), whereas women give more value to the male's ability to provide various types of resources to herself and their offspring. From the point of view of evolutionary perspective, the source of such difference lies in the span of fertility. Men can continue to reproduce for a longer period of lives, whereas women have a much more limited period to reproduce children. Therefore, the men, who prefer to mate with women beyond their childbearing years, can no longer produce offspring. Gradually, with lapse of time, a genetic preference for older women is automatically eliminated because such women cannot reproduce. The men, who prefer younger women, tend to produce at a higher rate, and therefore, such social behaviour dominates men's approach to further mating. On the other hand, women are less concerned with mate's age because older men can also reproduce and show more concern about resources necessary for a successful pregnancy and for ensuring proper development of the offspring. According to Buss and Kendrick (1998), the women's solution to this problem is to select such men who can ensure resources and willingness to assist during pregnancy, and thereafter, the women who fail to prefer such men are less likely to have pregnancies and child-rearing experiences. Therefore, women's preference for resource-providing men ultimately dominates in the population.

Evolutionary social psychologists have also provided explanation for different types of social behaviour. For example, altruistic behaviour has been explained from evolutionary perspective. Persons generally assist those to whom they are genetically related (Dawkins, 1982) probably because the persons share genetic materials with all those whom they assist. Thus, they help because of their own genetic code. Likewise, parenting practices are also explained from evolutionary perspective. Males are somewhat less involved in parenting than females because they invest less in offspring production. In other words, males do a single sexual act, whereas females are involved with nine months of gestation and giving birth. Similarly, one common observation is that adults are likely to abuse their stepchildren more than their biological children (Lennington, 1981). According to evolutionary social psychologists, this difference is due to the fact that parents share genetic materials with their biological children and not with their stepchildren (Piliavin and LePore, 1995). Evolutionary perspectives on interpersonal attraction claim that men and women have an evolved disposition to mate with healthy individuals so that they may produce healthy offspring, who will, in turn, successfully pass on their genetic code. According to this perspective, facial and physical attractiveness are basic markers for physical and hormonal health (Thornhill and Grammar, 1999). Thus, the individuals prefer young, attractive partners because they have high reproductive potential.

A close look at the evolutionary perspective clearly reveals that this perspective provides a unifying principle, which ties together many theories of social behaviour having specific focus. Let us take the example of social learning theory and social exchange theory. As we know, the nature of social learning is adaptive. The persons, who have much ability to learn from others, tend to suffer the least from the trial-and-error approach. Therefore, they are more likely to survive and pass that social learning code to their offspring. Likewise, one of the basic notion of the social exchange theory is that individuals are rational and they try to maximise profits. According to evolutionary theory, individuals try to maximise the resources because they help them to survive and perpetuate their genes. Such genetic code is passed on to their offspring.

Keeping in view what has been stated above, it can now be summarised and concluded that evolutionary social psychology has many important central ideas (Brewer, 2004; Buss, 1996). Such important ideas are as under:

1. Many human tendencies and preferences are the result of natural selection. Popularly known as evolved psychological mechanism, they are basically the adaptive responses to specific problems encountered by our ancestors.

2. Many important problems faced by our ancestors were social in nature. Human beings spend their lives in interdependent social groups. Consequently, many evolved psychological mechanisms have to do with relating to the people. These may include a need for belongingness, an ability to cooperate with others and a desire to invest resources for the members of the family.
3. All human behaviours are considered as the product of internal psychological dispositions (including evolved psychological mechanism) and external situational demands. As we know, human beings are biological organisms, who act in specific social contexts. Therefore, both biological and social influences on human behaviour are important.

Despite popularity of the evolutionary perspective, it is not without limitations. One frequently done criticism of the evolutionary perspective is that of its circular reasoning (Kenrick, 1995). In other words, evolutionary psychologists typically observe some characteristics of the social behaviour and then construct an explanation for it based on the presumed contribution to genetic fitness. In such a situation, the logic of the argument then runs like this. Why does a particular behaviour occur? Because it improves the odds of passing on one's gene. But the question arises—how do we know that it occurs? Such an after-the-fact explanation is always easy to construct, but difficult to prove. Therefore, the predictions of the evolutionary social psychology are accepted with considerable risk only.

Summary and Review

- Social psychologists have developed two types of theories—middle-range theories and theoretical perspectives. *Middle-range theories* are those theories, which account for a certain limited range of phenomena such as helping the strangers in distress, conforming to group pressures, etc. On the other hand, *theoretical perspectives*, which are comparatively broader in scope, provide a general explanation for a wider array of social behaviours in different types of social situations. In fact, the explanations provided by theoretical perspective are rooted in the explicit assumptions about human behaviour. Theory of cognitive dissonance by Festinger is an example of theoretical perspective in social psychology.
- *Role theory*, in a wider sense, is a direct transfer from the stage, where actors perform various roles. A *role* is defined as the pattern of the behaviour that an individual performs when occupying a particular position in the social system. The central idea of the role theory is that a substantial portion of observable social behaviour is nothing but simply the individuals carrying out their roles. Each role has some expectations. If the role expectations are known, we can, to a greater extent, predict a significant portion of the behaviour of that individual, who occupies the position. Role theory further explains that the role of a person not only affects his behaviour but also has an impact upon his attitude and beliefs. Since each of us has multiple roles to play in our society, such role enactment sometimes leads to various types of role conflict.
- Motivational perspectives focus on individual's own needs and motives for explaining social behaviour. Early motivational theorists postulated a very limited number of primary drives such as hunger, thirst, sex and pain avoidance. Later on, Maslow postulated five types of needs arranged into a hierarchy, besides cognitive needs and aesthetic needs. Alderfer further developed and tested Maslow's needs and identified three major types of human needs, that is, related to existence, relatedness and growth. Later on, McClelland et al. proceeded to explain three needs such as need for achievement, need for affiliation and need for power.
- Learning theories explain social behaviour in terms of five central elements such as motivation, association, stimulus, response, and reinforcement. Principles of classical conditioning, operant

conditioning, observational learning, experiential learning, reinforcement, including verbal reinforcement, all play a very significant role in learning of social behaviour. Phenomenon like social exchange has been intensively and extensively studied by the principles of learning theories.
- Cognitive theories give more importance to cognitive processes, which intervene between the stimulus and the response. Such theories emphasise cognitive structure for explaining the social behaviour. *Cognitive structure* refers to any form of organisation in cognition. One aspect of cognitive structure considered important in explaining social behaviour is *schema* or *schemata*, which is formed on the basis of previous experiences, cultural and social norms. Once schemas are established, they help us in guiding and understanding the social behaviour.
- Symbolic interaction theories, no doubt, place importance upon cognitive processes such as thinking, perceiving, reasoning, etc. Also, they give more emphasis upon the interaction taking place between the individuals and the society for understanding the social behaviour. In these theories, human beings are viewed as goal-seeking and proactive. The theory argues that a person can not only act towards others but he can also act towards self. Self occupies a very important role in symbolic interaction theory probably because social order, at least, in part, is considered to rest upon self-control.
- Socio-cultural theories give emphasis upon how the behaviour is affected by cultural values, social norms and social roles. Such theories are not only considered important for understanding and explaining social behaviour within a culture but also for making comparison of different cultures or social groups. Cultures differ in their relative emphasis upon individualism and collectivism.
- Evolutionary theories try to apply the principles of evolution and natural selection for understanding the several human social behaviour. Altruism, aggression, parenting practices, etc. are explained in terms of genetic codes. To illustrate the process of genetic code, an example is given here. Males are less involved in parenting than females because they invest less in offspring production. In other words, males do a single sexual act, whereas females are involved with nine months gestation and giving birth.

Review Questions

1. Citing examples, make distinction between middle-range theories and theoretical perspectives in social psychology.
2. Discuss the importance of role theory in explaining the social behaviour. Also, discuss its limitations.
3. Critically explain motivational theories as they are applied to explain social behaviour.
4. Citing examples, discuss how do learning theories explain social behaviour? Also, point out their drawbacks.
5. Discuss the role of cognitive theories in social psychology. How do these theories differ from learning theories?
6. Explain the main features of symbolic interaction theory as used in social psychology.
7. To what extent socio-cultural theories are relevant for understanding the social behaviour in different culture? Cite experimental evidences in support of your answer.
8. How do evolutionary perspectives explain social behaviour? Also, point out the limitations of evolutionary perspectives.
9. Write short notes on the following:
    (i) Experiential learning
    (ii) Self in symbolic interaction theory
    (iii) Vicarious learning
    (iv) Evolutionary social psychology
    (v) Social learning

4 SELF AND IDENTITY

Learning Objectives

- Meaning and Nature of Self
- Development (or sources) of Social Self
- Self and Culture
- Effects of Self upon Thoughts, Behaviour and Emotions: Process of Self-regulation
- Identity: The Self We Interact
- Self-esteem
- Self-serving Bias
- Self as an Object of Prejudice

KEY TERMS

Above-average effect	Reflected appraisal	Self-discrepancy
Actual selfs	Role identity	Self-esteem
Collectivistic culture	Role playing	Self-knowledge
Ideal self	Role taking	Self-reference effect
Independent self	Salience hierarchy	Self-schema
Individualistic culture	Schema	Social comparison
Interdependent self	Self	Social identity
Look-glass self	Self-awareness	Social self
Material self	Self-comfort	Stereotype effect
Ought self	Self-competence	Terror management theory
Personal-social identity	Self-concept	

In this chapter, focus has been given to what social psychologists have learnt about the nature of self. Some social psychologists have pointed out that the self is the heart of social psychology because our thinking about ourselves not only influences our choices and behaviours but also it serves as a reference point for how we perceive and interact with others. In this chapter, we shall focus on the development of social self, and how it influences our thinking, behaviour and emotions. One aspect of self, that is, self-esteem has been widely focused to answer several questions related to self. Subsequently, we shall discuss how we evaluate ourselves—a process of social comparison. Finally, we shall discuss self as an object or target of prejudice. Here, we shall examine the effects of being a target of prejudice for a number of self-related processes, including cognitive, emotional and performance consequences.

MEANING AND NATURE OF SELF

Self is commonly understood as the collection of beliefs that we hold about ourselves. It organises our thoughts, feelings and actions. It enables us to recall and remember our past, assesses our present and projects our future. For these reasons, no topic in psychology is more researched than the topic of self. According to one estimate in 2002, the word *self* appeared in 10,343 books and articles summarised in Psychological Abstracts. Now, how do social scientists define the term *self*?

There are four components of self: *self-knowledge*, *self-comfort*, *impression management* and *self-esteem*. This entire self-world bears analogy with a German term *Eigenwelt*, more popular in existentialism, broadly refers to the relationship between the person and himself or herself. The meaning is more appreciated when compared with its two comparison terms *Mitwelt* and *Unwelt*. Mitwelt refers to the person's relationship with other persons preferably with his contemporaries and unwelt refers to the individuals relationship with environment. Due to the subjective nature of self, several definitions of self have been given. According to Ausubel (1952, p. 13), *self* is defined as the combination of one's physical appearance, personal memories and sensory images. Yinger (1971, p. 158) defined *self* as the mental images of *who I am* or *what I want to be*. Taylor, Peplau and Sears (2006, p. 131) defined *self* as the collection of beliefs we hold about ourselves. The contents of these beliefs are called *self-concept*. Self concepts include not only our self-schemas about who we are at present, but also they include who we might become, that is, our possible selves, which involve our vision of the self we dream of becoming in future. Self-schemas consist of beliefs about self that organise and guide the process of self-relevant information. The evaluation we make of those beliefs is called *self-esteem*. Individuals with high self-esteem have a very clear sense of what their personal qualities or characteristics are. Such persons set appropriate goal for themselves, use feedback in self-enhancing ways and strengthen their positive feelings and memories (Wood, Heimpel and Michela, 2003, Christensen, Wood and Barrett, 2003). Persons with low self-esteem have generally less clear self-conceptions and often select unrealistic goals, tend to be very pessimistic about future, remember their past negatively and often exhibit the negative moods (Heimpel et al., 2002). Indian researches have also shown that self-esteem influences different affective and cognitive processes. Among college students, self-esteem is found to be positively related to internal locus of control (Pandey, 1993) and negatively related to the fear of success (Kumari, 1995). Likewise, girls with higher level of self-esteem show better interpersonal communication and higher level of self-disclosure as compared to boys (Priscilla and Karunanidhi, 1996). Kumar and Shankhdhar (1998) likewise demonstrated that rural Scheduled Caste girls possessed a stronger self-concept in comparison to their urban counterparts while both groups were highly frustrated. Two dimensions of self-esteem are central—*self-competence*, that is, evaluations of ourselves as capable and *self-liking*, that is, personal fondness for the self (Tafarodi, Marshall and Maline, 2003).

Researchers have frequently and largely studied people's explicit self-esteem, that is, concrete positive and negative evaluations they make of themselves. But recently, researchers have also started paying attention to implicit self-esteem (Greenwald and Farnham, 2000). *Implicit self-esteem*, as its name implies, refers to less conscious evaluations the person makes of himself. Sometimes, studies of implicit self-esteem reveal such things, which are not revealed by the studies of explicit self-esteem. For example, sometimes, implicit self-esteem appears to be more sensitive than explicit self-esteem for a specific situation in which the person finds himself (Egloft and Schmukle, 2002; Woike, Mcleod and Goggin, 2003). How a person feels about himself in a context in a given moment in known as *state self-esteam*.

Some researchers have differentiated different components of self. Mead (1934) divided self into 'I' and 'Me'. According to Mead, 'I' includes the impulsive tendencies of the person, that is, drives, needs and instincts are included in the 'I' component. All these impulses are unorganised and spontaneous. 'Me' is considered as the social dimension of the self. 'Me' gives some specific direction to the impulses. As a consequence, 'I' component does the socially acceptable behaviour. Every act starts with the 'I' and ends with 'Me'. 'I' and 'Me' work together in cooperative spirit for satisfying the initial impulse in socially acceptable way. The components of self most frequently identified by some other social psychologists are material self and social self. The *material self* generally includes the perceptions the individual has of his own body, but it is frequently extended beyond the individual's own body to include the other people as well as the objects. Brothers, sisters, parents, spouse, children, work, school, house, community or car may become part of an individual's material self. In this sense, attack of any of these is considered attack on self and achievement by any of them is considered achievement of the self. Material self can probably be placed at the personal end of what Baron, Byrne and Branscombe (2006) had called *personal-social identity continuum*. The descriptions of the self at the personal level are intragroup in nature, where judgements are based on the comparison between the individuals, who are the members of the same group.

The *social self* refers to the perception an individual has of the social roles he occupies and how these roles are performed. It is just possible that an individual may have several social selves, one for each of the major social role occupied by him in the society. Parental, family, marital, occupational and recreational roles are a few examples of the major roles around which people generally develop a social role. The social self probably lies on the social identity end of personal-social identity continuum. The descriptions of the self at the social identity level are intergroup in nature, that is, they involve contrasts and comparison between one group and the other group. Self-descriptions are generally stable over time, but different aspects of the self may be more salient as the person shifts from one social role to another. Shibutani (1961) expressed the view that the conceptions of the self may vary on five dimensions, as the person performs different social roles:

1. **Degree of integration:** Integration is one of the major dimensions. It refers to the consistency of the elements of the self and its manifestation in behaviour. Individuals, who have integrated self, exhibit predictable behaviour. Such people do not feel and act hostile at one moment and placid and calm at the next moment unless the social conditions have changed to some extreme.

2. **Extent of conscious awareness:** Some people may have highly integrated selves, but they may lack the conscious awareness of their selves. In other words, they are not very much aware of what they think and how this affects their behaviour and actions. Thus, the self of the person seems to vary in degree to which they are consciously aware of their selves.

3. **Degree of stability:** Although self seems to be stable over time, changes in it occur as people shift their social roles and the reference group. Usually, the adolescents and the young adults

experience greater degree of change in self as they take on new roles such as entering into college, getting married, starting a new business, becoming a parent, or joining a new job.

4. Nature of evaluation: People also vary in how they evaluate themselves. Researches done in the field of self-esteem bear testimony to the fact that some people evaluate their selves in positive way, whereas some other people evaluate their selves in negative way. Positive evaluation helps in setting realistic goal, whereas negative evaluation helps in setting unrealistic goal.

5. Social consensus: This refers to consensus between the individuals' perception of their selves and how other people perceive them. Self may vary in the degree of social consensus. There are people who feel that they are something special, although others may perceive them very ordinary. Likewise, there are people who are really very competent and good, but they have a negative concept of the self. Although such exceptions do exist, generally reaction of others towards us results in a fairly high degree of consensus.

Thus, it is obvious that social psychologists have a very objective meaning of the term *self*, which includes both self-concept and self-esteem. In fact, how we think about ourselves varies, to a greater extent, according to where we are on personal-social identity continuum.

DEVELOPMENT (OR SOURCES) OF SOCIAL SELF

The origin of the self is social. Our self-schema, the organised structured set of cognition about something, is really produced in our social relationship. Throughout the life, an individual meets new people and enters new groups. The constant feedback from the new people and group modifies the self to a greater extent because we interpret others' responses in order to figure out how we appear to them. Researches done in this field have revealed that social self is shaped by many types of influences. These influences are as follows:

1. Role taking and role playing
2. Social identity
3. Social comparison
4. Success and failure
5. Other people's judgement or reflected appraisals

These may be discussed as under:

1. Role taking and role playing: *Role* refers to the actions expected from those who occupy a particular social position. Roles may be taken or they may be played. *Role taking* refers to the process of imaginatively occupying the position of others and viewing the self and the situation accordingly (Hewitt, 1997). Researches have revealed that the genesis of self is role taking because through it, the children learn to respond in a reflexive way. When a child imagines the other's responses to the self, he acquires the capacity to look at oneself from other's perspective. This gradually shapes his self. Researches have revealed that a child develops the ability to infer the thoughts and expectations of others between the age of 4 and 6 years (Higgins, 1989).

Apart from role taking, role playing also lies at the genesis of social self. When we enact new social roles in our lives, we may, at first, feel phony. But gradually, uneasiness becomes over because what begins as role playing gets absorbed into our sense of self. Thus, role playing gradually becomes a reality. The deeper lesson of role playing studies has very clearly shown that what is unreal, can easily evolve into reality, paving the way for the development of a social self (Myers, 2005).

For dramatising the idea that the origin of the self is social, Cooley (2002), a well-known sociologist, coined the term *looking-glass self*, where emphasis has been given upon our habit of using how we imagine another's perception as a mirror for perceiving ourselves. The most important looking glass for children are their parents and family, and later, their playmates. They are considered as the children's significant others, which constitute the people, whose reflected views have the greatest influence on the development of self-concept. As the individual grows, the widening circle of friends, relatives, teachers and colleagues become his significant others. The changing image of self acquired throughout the lives depends on the social relationship a person develops.

Mead (1968) refining the viewpoints of Cooley, emphasised upon the idea that the self arises out of and is manipulated through social interaction. According to Mead, a child progresses through two stages in the development of self through role taking and role playing. The first stage is the *play stage* and the second stage is the *game stage*. Each stage is characterised by its own form of role taking. In *play stage*, the young children imitate the activities of those around them. Through such play, children learn to organise different activities into meaningful roles (nurse, doctor, teacher, and so forth). Usually, this involves other children and one who plays, for example, the role of doctor, has an opportunity to view other's child behaviour from the perspective of a doctor. At this stage, children learn to take the role of other one at a time. The second stage is the *game stage*. The term *game* here indicates that now the child can simultaneously take a number of roles relevant to a particular behaviour. Here, the child does the organised activities such as the complex games of school, house and team sports. Role taking, at the game stage, requires the child to imagine the viewpoint of several others at the same time. Repeated involvement in organised activities allows children to realise that their own actions are part of a pattern of interdependent activities of the group. With this realisation of new knowledge, children construct *generalised other*, which refers to the attitude and expectations held in common by the members of the organised groups with which they do interact. When the child imagines what the group expects from him, he takes the role of generalised other. As the child grows older, he controls his own behaviour more and more from the perspectives of generalised other. Gradually, the children learn to internalise the attitude and expectations of other by incorporating them into self. Our own views that we perceive from others generally imply positive or negative evaluation. These evaluations also become part of the self we develop. Those behaviours that others judge favourably contribute to the positive self-concept. On the other hand, when others criticise or punish our actions, the self-concept we develop, becomes negative.

2. Social identity: An individual becomes the member of the different social groups based on the criteria such as gender, caste, class, nationality or political affiliation. A definition of the self in terms of the defining characteristics of a social group is called *social identity* (Hogg, Terry and White, 1995). According to Tajfel (1981), *social identity* is defined as the part of the individual self-concept, which is derived from the membership in social group (or groups) together with the value and emotional significance attached to the membership. Social identity exerts influence on the development of the social self. If a person defines himself as a member of the group, these characteristics become standards for his thoughts, feelings and actions. If a person's interaction with others, whether members or not, tends to confirm the importance of these attributes, they become part of the self, one knows. Researches have shown that the cognitive representation of the self and the groups to which an individual belongs are closely interrelated (Smith and Henry, 1996). Social identity tends to exhibit the influence of social structure on self via consensually defined social groupings (Deaux and Martin, 2003). Madnawat and Thakur (1986) compared the self-concept of Scheduled Caste and Brahmin children (6–11 years) studying in a central school. They reported that Scheduled Caste children due to their own social identity, were having lower self-esteem and higher marginality. Lal (1987) also reported that social class was a significant determinant of self-image and self-concept.

3. Social comparison: Much of our lives revolve around social comparison. A person generally feels handsome when he perceives others as homely. Likewise, he feels smart when others seem to him are dull. The hypothesis that people learn about and based on which, evaluate their personal qualities by comparing themselves to the others is called *social comparison theory*, which was initially proposed by Festinger (1954). In this theory, he claimed that people want to evaluate themselves accurately, and therefore, they seek out similar others for comparison. According to social comparison theory, self-concept is shaped by comparisons between ourselves and others. By knowing what physical or social attributes distinguish us from similar or similar others, social comparison enables us to construct a sense of our own uniqueness. In fact, those attributes or characteristics which distinguish us from most of the similar others often become the defining features of the self. In fact, many motives lead people to compare themselves to the others (Suls, Martin and Wheeler, 2002). These motives may include desire for accurate self-evaluation, desire for empathy and connectedness, inspiration from other's outstanding performances (Lockwood and Kunda, 1997) or desire for the positive feelings about themselves from making comparison to the others, who are inferior (Helgeson and Mickeleson, 1995). These motives influence us whom we choose for comparison, since we make many social comparisons in our lives; we ultimately summarise them and this summary enables us to know in what ways we differ from the others. Not only that, this summary permits us to construct a self-concept that gives us a strong sense of being unique and distinctive from the others.

4. Success and failure: Our daily experiences coming from success and failure also help shape our self-concept. The common observation has been that after experiencing academic success, students tend to develop high self-confidence and higher appraisal of their academic ability, which often encourage them to work harder and achieve more and more (Felson, 1984; Marsh and Young, 1997). Likewise, Ozer and Bandura (1990) reported that after mastering physical skills essential for repelling a sexual assault, a woman feel less vulnerable, less anxious and more winning and in control. Gill et al. (1988) conducted a study on the students of physical education and reported that those students, who were physically more fit and strong, were having high self-concept. Likewise, several other researches have revealed that in comparison to those people, who are having low self-esteem, people with high self-esteem are happier, less neurotic, less troubled by pathological syndromes, less prone to drug and alcohol addictions and more persistent after failure (Brockner and Hutton, 1978; Tafarodi and Vu, 1997).

5. Other people's judgement or reflected appraisals: The self-concept of a person is shaped by what he receives from the others in the form of their judgement about his own behaviour. The idea according to which a person bases his self-concept or self-schema on the judgement he receives from the others during social interaction is called *reflected appraisal*. Various researches have been conducted in which people's self-ratings on traits like self-confidence, intelligence, physical attractiveness, etc. have been compared, with the views of themselves that they receive from others. Some studies have also compared self-ratings with actual views of others. Results of these studies have widely supported the hypothesis that the perceived reactions of others rather than their actual reactions are considered important for the development of self-concept (Felson, 1989). Some researches have been conducted to examine the impact of various significant others on one's appraisal of the self in some selected domains or areas. Felson (1985) as well as Felson and Read (1986) conducted studies in which relative influence of parents and peers on the self-perceptions of 4th through 8th grade children about their academic ability, athletic ability and physical attractiveness was examined. Results were interesting and supporting to expectations; parents affected self-appraisals in the areas of academic and athletic ability; whereas peers were found to have an impact upon perceived attractiveness. According to their impact upon self-appraisal, they were found to develop self-concept. Mead (1968) expanding upon the concept of looking-glass self as enunciated by Cooley (1902) also supported the view that what matters for the development of self-concepts is not what others actually think of us, but what we perceive them as thinking about us.

Thus, we see that there are different sources for the development of self in our society. Social psychologists must pay attention to these various sources for the understanding of proper development of self.

SELF AND CULTURE

Cross-cultural researches done by social psychologists have revealed that the concept of self vary greatly in light of the different cultural perspectives (Rhee, Uleman, Lee and Roman, 1995). In the pioneer study conducted by Markus and Kitayama (1991) in which Western cultures were contrasted with Eastern cultures, two types of dimensions were identified—*individualism* and *collectivism*. In individualistic culture, the person gives priority to his own goal over the group's goal, and he defines one's identity in terms of personal attributes rather than in terms of group identifications (Myers, 2005). The United States of America, Australia, and Great Britain have individualistic culture. In such culture autonomy, change, security of the individual and equality are highly valued. Such culture gives birth to what is called *independent self*, which is defined as the sense of oneself as autonomous bounded, unique, unitary and separate from social context (Geertz, 1974). Such perspective can be called *decontextualised theory of self* (Mishra, Akoijam and Mishra, 2009). It is often referred to as *mechanical and individualistic view*. The people of individualistic culture like that of the Unites States, Great Britain, etc. not only construe the self as an independent unit but also they actually define independence as a fundamental task of socialisation. Western culture teaches people how to be independent. Therefore, independent self is largely composed of individual attributes such as ambition, good humour or extroversion. This set of characteristics is considered distinctively one's own, even when they are shared by the others. According to Mishra (2001), decontextualised perspective of self has the following major assumptions:

1. Self is rational and governed by self-interest. It has an inherent tendency to influence the objects.
2. For optional functioning, it is healthy practice to exercise control over other, while lack of it is considered pathological and harmful.
3. A fully functioning person must have control over the other on his/her own terms and conditions.

4. Being a causal agent, self constitutes the irreducible ultimate reality and a repository of all potential abilities and skills.
5. Persons are intrinsically free to choose whatever they want to be and it is a free action.

Collectivism is another cultural dimension in which people give priority to one's group, often to one's extended family or work group and define one's identity accordingly. Cultures of China, Japan, India, Africa as well as Central and South America give emphasis upon collectivism. In such culture, people generally value duty, order, tradition, respect for the elderly, group security, respect for the group status, etc. Such culture gives rise to what is called *interdependent self*. People having interdependent self are more self-critical and have less need for positive self-regard. Interdependent self also possesses a set of internal qualities like abilities, thoughts, feeling, traits, etc. Such people define identity more in relation to the others. In their culture, self becomes meaningful and complete largely in the context of social roles and relationship, rather than in terms of independent, autonomous action. This is called *contextualised theory of self*. Thus, with an interdependent self, persons have a stronger sense of belonging. In fact, such persons have not one self, rather many selves such as self-with-parents, self-at-work, self-with-friends, etc. Therefore, interdependent self is embedded in social relationships. Here, the goal of social life is to harmonise the social relationship and provide support to one's communities. Here, conversation among persons is more polite and less direct (Holtgraves, 1997). However, interdependent self, in fact, is no longer a bounded whole, but reality is that it changes its structure with the nature of social context (Kanagawa, Cross and Markus, 2001).

Making review of the Indian studies on individualism-collectivism variable, Sinha and Verma (1987) reported that individualism is often associated with modernity and it is also correlated with social pathology. Likewise, collectivism is associated with low economic development and it is correlated with mental health and social harmony. Sinha and Verma further noted that Indians are collectivistic, and from this angle, the low economic growth of the Indian society is, at least, partly due to this collectivistic orientation. Indian studies have further shown that most Indians identified the in-group into which they were born, that is, their family, whereas Americans preferred in-group that they could choose from their own such friends. In another very interesting study, J.B.P. Sinha, J.N. Sinha, J. Verma and R.B.N. Sinha (2001) analysed the choice of collectivist/individualist behaviour and intentions. Their findings revealed that concerns for family or family members tended to evoke a purely collectivist behaviour. However, in the case of compelling and urgent personal needs and the goals coming in direct confrontation with the interests of family or friends, a mix of both individualist and collectivist behaviours and intentions were reported. Individualist behaviour intended to serve the interest of collectivist behaviour was the third opted choice and the respondent's (or participants) education emerged as a significant moderator of the choices expressed.

Nisbett (2003) made a comparative study of Japanese and Americans. Both types of participants were shown an animated underwater scene. Subsequently, they recalled what they saw. Results revealed that Japanese recalled 60% more background features than what was recalled by Americans. Not only that, Japanese spoke more of relationship among the organisms seen such as frog swimming in group, etc. and Americans attended more to some focal object such as big fish and attended less to the surroundings. Likewise, Kitayama et al. (2003) showed that when Japanese were asked to draw in a smaller empty box (say 90 mm^2) a shown proportioned line (say 30 mm, which is one third of the height of square), they did so accurately than Americans. On the other hand, when Americans were asked to draw a line of the same absolute length, they more accurately ignored the context and drew an identical line. On the basis of these studies and similar other, Nisbett finally concluded that Japanese's thinking is more holistic, that is, they perceive and think about objects and people in context of their environment.

In another cross-cultural research, Dhawan et al. (1995) reported that while defining themselves, Indian respondents (participants) made a large number of references to social identities. In other words, they preferred to describe themselves more in terms of roles, groups, caste, class, gender, etc. On the other hand, American participants made a large number of references to self-identity. This clearly indicated that self in India is less individualistic than what is generally observed in America. Although there is a salience of interdependent self-concept amongst Indians, there are studies that have not reported such clear polarisation. For example, Mishra and Giri (1995) observed that though individual differences exist, the self-construal, a mix pattern of both independent self and interdependent self is often reflected. Likewise, Srivastava and Misra (1997) reported that descriptions showing social identity were more predominant than autonomous descriptions. Not only that, independent and interdependent life goals were found positively related in moderate fashion.

In another significant study conducted by Kitayama and Markus (2000), it was demonstrated that Japanese students and American students differ on the source of origin of positive emotions like happiness and elation. Their findings revealed that for Japanese students, happiness originates with positive social engagement, that is, with feeling close, friendly and respectful. However, for American students, happiness generally comes more from disengaged emotions, that is, with feeling effective, superior and proud. Triandis (2000) further showed that when there occurs conflict in collectivistic culture, it is usually between two groups. On the other hand, individualistic culture breeds more conflicts between two or more than two individuals, leading to crime and divorce.

Markus and Kitayama (1994) compared self-concept in independent culture and interdependent culture and reported the following major differences:

1. Independent culture defines self in terms of unique individual separated from social context. On the other hand in interdependent culture, the self is defined as something connected with the others in terms of social roles and relationship. This can be easily seen in Figure 4.1.

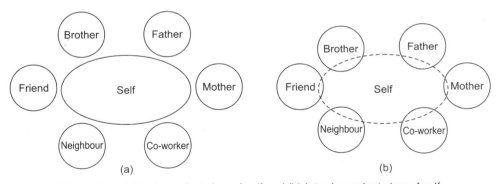

Figure 4.1 (a) Independent view of self and (b) Interdependent view of self.

2. In independent culture, self is unitary and remains more or less stable and constant across different situations and relationships. But in interdependent culture, self is fluid and variable and changes from situation to situation or from one relationship to another.

3. In independent culture, self disapproves conformity, whereas in interdependent culture, self disapproves egotism.
4. In independent culture, self is primarily considered internal and private having abilities, thoughts, feelings, traits, etc., whereas in interdependent culture, self is considered external and public having statuses, roles and relationships.
5. In independent culture, self is unique, expressing oneself clearly and always promoting one's own goals, whereas in interdependent culture, self is belongings, acting appropriately, expressing in indirect way and promoting group's goals.
6. Independent self is supported by the individualistic western culture, whereas interdependent self is supported by the collectivistic Asian and third world cultures.

Oyserman et al., (2002) had, however, made the observation that pigeonholing cultures as individualist or collectivist oversimplifies the issue because within any culture, individualism may vary from individual to individual. Researches have shown that it also varies across the different regions of the country. Despite this, the conception of self in independent culture and interdependent culture is fundamentally important. It influences how persons think about themselves, how people relate to others, what emotions are experienced in different situations and what motivates people to do a certain kind of behaviour.

EFFECTS OF SELF UPON THOUGHTS, BEHAVIOUR AND EMOTIONS: PROCESS OF SELF-REGULATION

Why do we develop self? What is the fundamental purpose of having a self? According to social psychologists, the answer is that self regulates many aspects of our lives, that is, self helps in controlling and governing many aspect of social life, including our thoughts and feelings, emotions and behaviour. In this section, we shall examine these three types of impact of self.

Self influences thoughts and feelings through self-schemas. *Schema* is defined as an organised structured set of cognitions about something. Just as people hold schema about other people or events, they have also schemas about themselves. Self-schema describes the dimensions along which people think about themselves. There are three components of self-schema—self as one is (*actual*), as one would like to be (*ideal*) and as one ought to be (*ought*). Self-schema influences cognitive processes in different ways (Markus and Wurf, 1987). Self-schema also influences the processing of incoming information. Those sets of information are readily processed by the persons that are in accord with self-schema. Self-schema also influences the way we interpret the feedback. As we know, the feedback that the person receives from other is most of the time vague, incomplete, and sometimes, inconsistent too. It is the self-schema, which determines how a person processes such feedback information. Generally, in such a situation, the person pays more attention to the relevant and important information and selectively focus on the information that strengthens the self-concept. It is also because of self-schema that a person typically perceives more confirmation of his self-concept than actually exists.

Self-schema also influences the retention and memory of the person. Sanitioso, Kunda and Fong (1990) conducted one study to confirm this. In their study, the participants were made to believe that either extroversion or introversion was a desirable trait. Subsequently, they were asked to remember information about themselves relevant to the trait. Results clearly showed that participants remembered those information quickly that were related to the trait. This result clearly bear evidence to the fact that when information or events are related to the self, they are retained and recalled better.

Another way through which self affects our thoughts, feelings and behaviour is *self-awareness*, where we take the self as the object of our attention and focus on our own actions and thoughts. Broadly, this corresponds to 'Me' aspect of action (Mead, 1934). There are many situations such as mirrors, focus of cameras, public speech, recordings of our own voice, which cause self-awareness because these situations directly present the self to us as an object. Researches have shown that when people are self-aware, it influences their behaviour. Gibbons et al. (1985) had shown that when people are highly self-aware, they are likely to behave in an honest way, accurately report about their moods, psychiatric problems and hospitalisation. People with higher degree of self-awareness act in a way that is more consistent with their personal and social standards. In fact, their behaviour is controlled and regulated by self. When people are not self-aware, their behaviour becomes more habitual or automatic. A widely accepted theory to explain such effects of self-awareness assumes that when people pay attention to self, it activates the self-schema, which in turn, leads to self-evaluation at any of the three levels—experiential, behavioural and global (Gibbons, 1990; Wicklund, 1975). All these evaluations force the persons to think and behave according to the standards contained in the self.

Still another way of knowing about the impact of self upon thoughts and feelings is *self-discrepancy*, which is defined as the condition in which three components of self-schema, that is, self as one is (actual self), self as one would like to be (ideal self) and self as one ought to be (ought self) differ (Higgins, 1989). When a person evaluates one self, he uses ideal self or ought self as the reference point. According to Higgins' self-discrepancy theory, discrepancy between actual self and ideal self as well as between actual self and ought self influence our emotional well-being, and ultimately, our self-esteem. Thus, here, self is compared with some internal standards. This entire process is called *self-regulation*. Outcome of such comparison motivates us to behave in a certain way. When the actual self matches with the ideal self, the person experiences satisfaction, but when this does not match, he experiences discomfort (Higgins, 1989). In fact, when discrepancy occurs between actual self and ideal self, the person experiences disappointment, dissatisfaction or sadness, which together are called *dejection-related emotions*. Such condition also produces a reduction in the self-esteem. In fact, ideal self represents positive outcomes towards which people strive. Higgins (1998) had called them *promotion goals*. When these promotion goals are achieved, the persons feel joy or elation, but when these goals are not achieved, causing discrepancy from ideal self, then it produces sadness and dejection. On the other hand, when there occurs discrepancy between our actual self and the ought self, *agitation-related emotions* such as fear or anxiety is produced (Boldero and Francis, 2000). Ought self generally involves negative outcomes, which people try to avoid. Higgins had called them *prevention goals*. When these goals are not accomplished, there occurs discrepancy from ought self and it causes emotions of anxiety and agitation. However, when these prevention goals are accomplished, they produce feelings of relaxation and relief. One study was conducted by Higgins, Klein and Strauman (1985) to test the two types of predictions mentioned above. They asked students to list up to 10 attributes each regarding the actual self, ideal self and ought self. Discrepancy was noted by comparing the two lists—an attribute listed in both lists (say actual and ideal state) was a match, whereas an attribute listed in one state with its opposite in other state was considered as a mismatch. Self-discrepancy score was the total number of mismatches minus the total number of matches. The researchers measured the discomfort experienced by the participants with the help of questionnaire. Results demonstrated that as the actual self-ideal self discrepancy increased, the frequency and the intensity of dejection-related emotions increased. Likewise, as the actual self-ought self discrepancy increased, agitation-related emotions such as fear, anxiety, irritability increased.

Further researches have shown that concerns about ideal self or the ought self generally emerge from temperament as well as from early socialisation, that is, we are disposed and may be taught by the society to think in terms of ideal self or ought self. Manian, Strauman and Denney (1998) reported that the people, who are more concerned with their ideal self, are generally those people who have been raised by their parents in warm and supportive way, whereas those who exhibit more concern about ought self are the people who have been raised by a parenting style marked by rejection. Cultural differences also affect ideal self or ought self orientation. People raised with independent sense of self (individualistic culture) are more likely to motivate with discrepancy between actual self and ideal self, whereas people with interdependent sense of self (collectivistic culture) exhibit more concern to the demands of others (Lee, Aaker and Gardner, 2000).

Thus, we see that self-discrepancy, no doubt, motivates us to meet our personal goals and standards, but at a likely cost. In some cases, self-discrepancy triggers negative emotions that lead to a cycle of dejection, sadness, anxiety, and lower self-esteem (Pyszczynski and Greenberg, 1987).

Overall, it can be concluded that self affects thoughts, feelings and behaviours of the persons through self-schema, self-awareness and self-discrepancy.

IDENTITY: THE SELF WE INTERACT

In this section, we shall concentrate on one important question—how does self influence the planning, control and regulation of our behaviour? Of course, the most general answer to this question would be that an individual is motivated to plan and regulate that which conforms to and reinforces the identities that he claim for himself. However, related to this, the following three questions remain unanswered:

1. How are behaviours linked to a particular identity?
2. Of the different identities, what determines which one will be chosen for enactment in a particular situation?
3. How does identity produce consistency and unity in behaviour?
   These three questions are being discussed here.

1. How are behaviours linked to a particular identity?

Identities are defined as the meanings attached to the self by one's self as well as by others (Geccas and Burke, 1995). Identity is definitely the condition of being identified in feeling, interest and the like (Paranjpe, 1998). In fact, when a person thinks of his identities, he is actually thinking of the various plans of actions that he is expecting to execute. Identities have two major sources—one source of identities is membership in social categories or groups called *social identities* and another source is the specific social roles that a person enacts, popularly called *role identities*. We know that self-schemas include both identities as well as some associated personal qualities. Some people emphasise the identities, whereas some people emphasise the personal attributes. For example, in response to the question of 'Who am I?', the former type of people may say father, mother, principal, etc., whereas the latter type of people may say easy-going, intelligent, peace-loving, etc. Researches have revealed that behavioural preferences of these two types of people may differ. Levy, Wheeler and Jenkins (1986) pointed out that in the area of game, the people emphasising the social aspect of the self would tend to prefer team sports such as football, volleyball, basketball, etc., whereas the people emphasising personal qualities would prefer individual sports such as swimming, running, etc. Likewise, the persons, whose self-concept is predominantly social, would tend to prefer such occupations that offer social rewards such as good friendship and status, whereas the persons, whose self-concept is predominantly personal, would prefer job that offers rewards such as opportunities for self-expression, personal growth, etc.

Social psychologists have shown that the link between identities and behaviours is established through the common meanings (Burke and Reitzes, 1981). Members of group who agree on the meanings of the particular identities and behaviours can easily regulate their own behaviours for establishing the identities they want. If, somehow, members do not agree on the meanings of the particular identities and behaviours, they may experience difficulty in establishing their preferred identities. Following *identity control theory* (Burke, 2004), it is predicted that an actor uses social meaning of his identity as a reference point for evaluating the situation. The behaviour of other person and the situational elements are evaluated by the actor in accordance with whether or not they maintain his identity. The actor subsequently selects and enacts behaviour for maintaining one's identity in the situation.

Social identities, which are based on group membership, have also powerful impact upon the behaviour. We know that there are widely held meanings or stereotypes associated with many groups. A person may willingly adopt behaviour associated with some positive stereotypes such as adopting certain food preferences associated with vegetarianism. Persons' behaviour may also be influenced by negative stereotypes. For example, a tribal student in India may perform poor in an academic testing situation because he may believe that others stereotype him as being less intelligent and creative, which ultimately produces anxiety and disrupt his academic performance.

2. Which identities will be chosen for enactment in a particular situation?

There are different types of identities and each identity suggests a separate and independent line of action. Sometimes, these lines of actions are not compatible too. In such a situation, the person has to choose any one identity and act in the situation accordingly. The following factors influence the decision to enact one rather than another identity:

(i) **Hierarchy of identities:** Some identities do not have equal importance to the person. Therefore, the persons organise all the identities in terms of their salience, that is, in terms of their relative importance to the self-schema. This hierarchy exerts a major impact on the person's decision to enact one or another identity (McCall and Simmons, 1978; Stryker, 1980). Generally, if the identity is more salient, the person perceives that the concerned situation is more appropriate for enacting the identity as well as such salient identity is also frequently chosen for performing the concerned activities (Stryker and Serpe, 1981). Now, the question arises—what determines whether a particular identity lies in central or peripheral position in the salience hierarchy? In order to provide an honourable answer to this question, social psychologists have identified certain factors (mentioned below), which play a significant role in locating the position of the identity in salience hierarchy.

(a) How much resources such as time, energy, effort, money, etc. have been invested in constructing the identity directly determines the position of identity in salience hierarchy. If much resources have been invested, the identity may occupy a central position in the hierarchy.

(b) The extrinsic reward and intrinsic satisfaction derived from enacting the identity have also an impact. Higher reward and satisfaction of such types are considered instrumental in getting an identity at a central position.

(c) To what extent the self-esteem has been put on stake while enacting the identity well also determines the position of the identity. If the person feels that he has no danger of losing the self-esteem in enacting the identity, it is very likely that such identity may be kept in the central position in the hierarchy.

One basic characteristic of salience of identity is that it shifts as the person goes on engaging in various types of interaction and experiences higher degree of success or failure.

(ii) **Need for identity support:** A person is likely to enact those identities that need support. For example, if a student has spent several hours continuously in solitary study, he may have a need for having a relaxed social contact, and therefore, he may prefer to go to a club or friend circle to find someone to chat in a relaxed way.

(iii) **Social networks:** Every person is a part of a network of social relationship. Researches have shown that if numerous and significant relationships depend upon enactment of a certain identity, the person feels more committed to that identity. For example, take the role of a professor. Chances are that many of the relationships such as with fellow professors, university officials, local governments, etc. depend upon the continued occupancy of professor role. If he leaves the university, he would be losing all such relationships. In such a situation, where high level of commitment exists, leaving the university will definitely produce a traumatic experience. Researches have further shown that if the person has higher degree of commitment for a given role identity, then that identity will be more important in the salience hierarchy. For example, if the person considers participating in religious activities is very important and crucial for maintaining social relationship, he keeps his religious identity more salient and important as compared to his parents, friends and worker identities (Stryker and Serpe, 1981).

(iv) **Situational opportunities:** The nature of social situation is restrictive in the sense that it allows only some identities to be enacted in a profitable way. As a consequence, in any particular situation, the person chooses an identity considering whether the situation offers opportunities for profitable enactment. For example, suppose that Mohan is a very good singer. Therefore, the salience of his identity as a singer is established. Despite this salience of the identity, if the situation is such that nobody wants to listen his song, there will be no opportunity to enact the identity. Thus, situational opportunity also determines that to what extent, the role identity will be enacted. Kenrick et al. (1990) conducted a series of studies in which students were asked to rate the extent to which various personal qualities or traits like adjustment, intellectual ability, dominance, likableness, social control and social inclination could be displayed in each of the six different situations. Results revealed that the students agreed that intellectual ability can be shown in academic setting, but not in recreational setting. Likewise, dominance can be exhibited in athletic and business settings, but not in religious settings. Similarly, adjustment and social inclination can be displayed in recreational setting, but not in religious setting.

3. How does identity produce consistency and unity in behaviour?

In the self, many types of identities called *multiple identities* are included. A person might consider himself studious in academic situation, hard-working at the office and fun-loving when relaxing with a group of friends. Despite these multiple identities, he experiences himself in a unified entity. Following are the two reasons for such unity and consistency:

(i) **Salience hierarchy:** Salient identities provide consistency and unity to behaviour. In fact, salience hierarchy helps the person in developing a unified and consistent self despite the multiple identities. This is done in three ways mentioned below:

  (a) Salience hierarchy provides us with a basis for choosing which situation the person should enter and which situation he should avoid. Social psychologists have reported that students tend to choose those interactions clearly, which are consistent with their salient identity and avoid those interactions in their daily lives that are not consistent with their salient hierarchy (Emmons, Diener and Larsen, 1986).

  (b) Salience hierarchy also influences the consistency of behaviour across different situations. This has been confirmed in a study conducted by Emmons and Diener (1986). The investigators asked the students to report the extent to which ten affective states and ten behavioural responses occurred in different situations over a month period. Subsequently, they analysed the results for findings out consistency across the different situations. Sufficient degree of consistency was shown across the situations.

  (c) Salience hierarchy also influences consistency in behaviour across time. This fact has also been confirmed by Serpe (1987), who had taken data from a sample of 310 students at three points during their first semester in college. In this study, the salience of five identities such as academic ability, athletic/recreational involvement, friendship, extracurricular involvement and dating was measured at each of three points. Results revealed a general pattern of stability in salience.

Social psychologists further express the opinion that although self-concept exhibits consistency over time, it may change due to the fact that the life transitions may change the role one plays and the varying situation one encounters (Demo, 1992). This naturally produces a need to come out from one social role and adopt new role and bring a change in salience hierarchy.

(ii) **Self-verification strategies:** Our self is consistent and unified over time because we adopt certain strategies that verify our self-perception. One set of strategies comprises behaviours that lead to self-confirming feedback from others. Such self-confirming feedback from others may come from the following three situations:

  (a) Generally, we engage in selective interaction with friends, roommates and others who share our viewpoints.

  (b) Sometimes, people display identity that tends to produce identity confirming behaviour from others. At a railway platform in India, most of the people treat a man bearing white full pant and black coat as ticket examiner.

  (c) Persons tend to behave in ways that may enhance the identity claims, especially when those claims have been put to challenge. An unprejudiced Brahmin when led to believe he is prejudiced towards Dalit, may offer more help to a Dalit than when his egalitarian identity has not been threatened.

Another set of strategies involve the processing of the feedback information in such a way that they fully support these self-concepts. Social psychologists, however, feel that all there self-verifying strategies can be employed to some limited extent only. At some occasions, we want accurate feedback regarding our abilities. In such a situation, we tend to evaluate feedback from others by comparing it with our self-representations (Swann and Schroeder, 1995) and such evaluation may lead to some kind of changes in our behaviour or a changes in our self-representation.

Thus, we see that our identities are not only related to some particular behaviour and we select some identities out of many for enactment in a particular situation according to some criteria. These identities also produce consistency and unity in behaviour of the person.

SELF-ESTEEM

The *self-concept* is what we think about the self, whereas *self-esteem* is the positive or negative evaluation of the self. Thus, self-esteem is the evaluative component of the self-concept (Gecas and Burke, 1995). In simple words, it can be said that self-esteem is the overall attitude towards self. It ranges from positive to negative.

In this section, we shall concentrate upon the following six areas which are related to self-esteem:

1. Sources of self-esteem
2. Measurement of self-esteem
3. Self-esteem and behaviour
4. Dark side of self-esteem
5. Protecting self-esteem
6. Sex and self-esteem.

Discussion of each of these six areas is presented below:

1. Sources of self-esteem

People differ in the level of self-esteem. Some people enjoy high self-esteem and some people display low self-esteem. What can be the reason? Social psychologists have answered this question in terms of sources of self-esteem from which self-esteem originates. These sources are mainly three—family experience, social comparison and performance feedback.

(i) **Family experience:** Family experiences play a significant role in the development of self-esteem. Here, particularly, the parent–child relationship is considered important for the development of self-esteem. Coopersmith (1967) showed that the following four types of parental behaviours promote higher self-esteem:

  (a) Parental behaviour showing love, affection and involvement in children's affairs
  (b) Parental behaviour imposing a well-defined and clear limits on children's behaviour
  (c) Parental behaviour which allows children latitude within these limits and respects their initiativeness such as participating in making family plans, etc.
  (d) Parental behaviour that favours non-coercive form of discipline and avoids physical punishment

Researches have been also shown that the self-esteem is promoted by the reciprocal influence of parents and their children on each other (Felson and Zielinski, 1986). Children who exhibit self-esteem also display more self-confidence, self-control, self-knowledge and the sense of competence. Such children are loved, accepted and trusted by their parents. Consequently, their self-esteem is further promoted. A longitudinal study of adolescents has clearly shown that when parents frequently resort to criticism, negligence and shaming, it tends to lower the self-esteem and produces depression (Robertson and Simons, 1989)

(ii) **Social comparison:** Social comparison is considered crucial for the development of self-esteem. In social comparison, the person tries to compare his abilities, performance, etc. with others and accordingly, he takes a decision about the self. Why do people compare themselves with others? According to Festinger's social comparison theory, people compare themselves to others because for many attributes, domain, etc., there is no objective standard yardstick against which comparison can be done. Since these other people are highly informative, they provide a better evaluative standard. Social comparison may be of two types—upward social comparison and downward social comparison. In *upward social comparison*, the person compares his performance, attributes, etc. with such a person's performance, attributes who does better than the self. In *downward social comparison*, the person's performance is compared with those person who is less capable to perform in comparison to the self. Researches have supported the fact that downward social comparison boots the self-esteem (Gibbons et al., 2002), whereas upward social comparison lowers the self-esteem and may lead to the feeling of incompetence, shame and inadequacy (Patrick, Neighbors and Knee, 2004). Generally, desire for self-improvement leads to the upward social comparison with the persons who are more successful. The danger, of course, here is that such comparison with successful people may produce a low self-esteem, with feelings of incompetence, jealousy, shame or inadequacy. A desire for self-enhancement can lead people to make downward social comparison with others, who are less successful or less happy or poor performer (Wills, 1981; Lockwood, 2002). Downward social comparison has favourable impact upon self-esteem of the person.

Two very important perspectives on self, that is, self-evaluation maintenance model of Tesser (1988) and social identity theory of Tajfel (1972), both based upon Festinger's (1954) original social comparison theory, describe the consequences of social comparison in different social situations. Tasser's model applies when the person categorises the self at personal level and he compares oneself as an individual with the other individual. Tajfel's model applies when the person categorises the self at group level and he compares oneself with the category or group to which the other also belongs. According to self-evaluation maintenance model, for maintaining a positive view of the self, we maintain distance from others who perform better than ourselves on the given dimension, but remain closer to others who perform worse. Doing so in both cases protects our self-esteem from being lowered. Social identity theory emphasises that our group identity is salient. The theory further suggests that we shall move close to all those with whom we share an identity and maintain distance from all those in-group members who perform poorly or otherwise make our social identity negative and ridiculous. Such psychological movement towards and away from a comparison with others doing better or worse is a good means by which positive self-evaluations or high self-esteem is maintained. Pleban and Tesser (1981) had confirmed such effect from their study.

(iii) **Performance feedback:** Performance feedback directly hits the level of self-esteem. When people get feedback about the success or failure of their performance, their self-esteem is accordingly shaped. When we attain goals and overcome obstacles, a high level of self-esteem is derived from it (Franks and Marolla, 1976). In other words, self-esteem is partly determined by our sense of efficacy of competence and power to control events effectively (Bandura, 1982). Even people with lower positions in the society such as clerks, unskilled workers, etc., who have a very limited opportunity to develop efficacy-based self-esteem strive for converting almost any kind of activity into a standard task against which they may test their efficiency and prove their competence (Gecas and Schwabe, 1983). Despite some cultural variations, self-esteem is pushed by success and good performances and is pulled down by failure, bad performances and negative feedback (Smith and Mackie, 2007).

Obviously, self-esteem is built up from the information we obtain from the different sources of society.

2. Measurement of self-esteem

In day-to-day life, we have several types of evaluations of the characteristics of the self or categories of outcome upon which we stake our self-esteem. Such characteristics or categories are technically called *contingencies* of self-esteem (Crocker and Wolfe, 2001). The person weigh and combine the evaluations of his specific contingencies. For example, he may say "I am the most intelligent boy in the class, but an incompetent cricket player." Such personal evaluations are weighed and combined in making the overall evaluation of the self-esteem. If a person weighs his positively identities and traits as important ones, he maintains a high level of overall self-esteem, while still admitting some limitations or weaknesses. On the other hand, if he weighs his negatively evaluated identities, he may have a low overall level of self-esteem though he may have some good qualities or characteristics regarding the self.

Some social psychologists try to assess the global self-esteem with the help of agreement or disagreement with direct statements. Rosenberg (1965) developed one such verbal scale, named as *Rosenberg self-esteem scale*, for assessing the self-esteem of a person. The scale consists of 10 items to be answered by the respondents on 5-point scale—5 indicating *very true of me* and 1 indicating *not very true of me*. One sample item from Rosenberg scale is '*On the whole, I am satisfied with myself*'. Higher score on the scale indicates higher level of self-esteem and lower score indicates lower level of self-esteem.

In India, Rajini (1985) had developed one such scale called *self-concept scale*, which has been standardised on Indian clinical and normal populations. This scale consists of 80 items, which have been grouped into four subscales—*personal self-esteem, family self-esteem, social self-esteem* and *self-confidence*. Each subscale has 20 items. Both positive and negative items have been included in the scale. Respondents give responses on a 5-point scale, ranging from strongly agree to strongly disagree on Likert pattern. Higher scores indicate higher self-esteem and self-confidence and lower scores indicate lower self-esteem and self-confidence.

All these explicit measure of self-esteem, including Rosenberg scale are susceptible to bias due to people's self-presentation concerns, that is, their desire to present themselves in the best possible ways (Robins, Hendin and Trzesniewski, 2001). Therefore, some social psychologists have recommended for unconscious assessment procedures. In such unconscious procedure, attitudes towards self may be better revealed. An evidence for this logic comes indirectly from *self-reference effect* in which people display a preference for objects owned by self or for something which is reflective of self.

For example, people generally prefer to name a new shop on his own name, showing a self-reference effect. Gray et al. (2004) conducted one study in which they measured event-related potentials or ERPs(brain responses) of the participants while they were observing self-relevant words and non-self-relevant words. It was found that the participants automatically (without making any conscious effort) paid more attention to self-relevant words than the non-self-relevant words. Since such important process appears to be involved in the self-reference effect, it can be concluded that any attempt designed to improve self-esteem in this way might be effective when administered at the unconscious level.

Social psychologists have also paid attention to the assessment of short-term increases in the state of self-esteem. When a person achieves a very important goal of his life, his self-esteem may, for the short time, be enhanced. Investigators have tried to study how a person feels about the self in such short period laboratory settings. Greenberg et al. (1992) observed that when participants are given false positive feedback about their score on a task, their self-esteem is raised. Likewise, positive feedback for being accepted by others also raise the self-esteem (Leary, 1999). Even when participants' thinking is directed towards desirable aspects of their selves, self-esteem is enhanced (McGuire and McGuire, 1996).

Social psychologists, thus, have tried to assess the self-esteem both explicitly as well as implicitly.

3. Self-esteem and behaviour

Self-esteem has a direct influence on human behaviour. There are two types of people—people with high self-esteem and people with low self-esteem. The behavioural pattern of both these two types of people differ.

People with high self-esteem behave in a different way as compared to the people with low self-esteem. Adults, adolescents and children having high self-esteem are more social and popular among their friends. Not only that, they are more confident of their opinions and judgements and their self-perception is more distinct and sharper (Campbell, 1990). Such people are academically more successful and ambitious. They are also found to be more assertive in their social relations. Rosenberg et al. (1995) showed that the persons with high self-esteem score higher on the measure of psychological well-being. As per the research done, during their school years, such persons had participated more in extracurricular activities and were frequently elected to various leadership positions. It has also been found that the persons with high self-esteem experience less stress following the death of beloved ones and cope with the resulting problems more effectively (Johnson, Lund and Diamond, 1986). In fact, people with high self-esteem roll out an arsenal of weapons to defend against the various types of threats. For example, they fight stress or negative feedback with the use of self-enhancing biases and problem-focused coping. (Epstein, 1992; Josephs et al., 1992). In fact, they make a social comparison with others who are worse and poor performers and make a self-enhancing attributions for their failures. Finally, a very strong sense of control makes people with high self-esteem tackle any problem head-on. Thus, the successful use of the self-serving biases and coping strategies restores high self-esteem so that the whole cycle can restart.

People with low self-esteem behave in a different way. Such people tend to be socially ineffective and anxious. Their interpersonal relationship is threatening. Their approach towards others is less positive and suspicious. They are easily hurt by the criticism done by others. Not only that, they have little faith in their ability. The strength of their self-efficacy is poor. They frequently expect that their ideas and principles would be rejected by the others. During school years, such persons frequently used to set low academic standard, and were less popular among their classmates. They were also less active in classroom and in extracurricular activities. People with low self-esteem often show anxiety, depression and discouragement. Their overall adjustment is very poor.

Thus, we see that self-esteem, whether high or low, causes different and contrasting behaviour. However, some social psychologists have expressed their doubt whether high or low self-esteem causes specific types of behaviour or vice versa. A high self-esteem may enable a person to express his opinions and views more forcefully for the obvious purpose of convincing others. But the experience of influencing and convincing others may, in turn, cause enhancement in the self-esteem. Thus, reciprocal influence, rather than self-esteem causing a particular behaviour, is also a common phenomenon (Rosenberg, Schooler and Schoenbach, 1989).

4. *Dark side of self-esteem*

People have sometimes high self-esteem and sometimes low self-esteem. High self-esteem fosters pleasant feelings, resilience, whereas low self-esteem fosters anxiety, depression, drug abuse and some types of delinquent behaviour (Baumeister et al., 2003). The dark side of the low self-esteem is exhibited in tension, with the findings that people expressing low self-esteem are somewhat more vulnerable to clinical problems like anxiety, depression, loneliness and other kinds of eating disorders. With these feelings, they are susceptible to view everything through dark glasses, that is, they view others' worst behaviours as something lacking warmth, love and affection (Murray et al., 2002; Ybarra, 1999). Crocker and Park (2004) also reported that persons with low self-esteem and worth experience more stress, relationship problems, drug and alcohol use, anger and eating disorders. Such persons are most contingent upon external sources of self-esteem. On the other hand, those who pursue self-esteem rely more on internal source such as personal qualities and virtues. But such persons who pursue self-esteem seem ironically to lose sight of what really makes for quality of life because their primary goal remains feeling good about themselves. They may become less open to eye-opening criticisms and they are more likely to blame others, rather than sympathise and empathise others. They also feel pressurised to succeed, rather than enjoying the activities of life. In future, such pursuit for high self-esteem may fail to enhance and satisfy one's strong needs for competence, relationship and autonomy. Besides these effects, when a person with high self-esteem is somehow threatened, he reacts by putting others lower, and sometimes, he becomes aggressive and violent. Heatherton and Vohs (2000) conducted one study in which this effect was confirmed. They threatened some undergraduate students with a failure experience on an aptitude test. There was also a control group of subjects, who did not have such failure experience. Results revealed that the high self-esteem subjects became more aggressive and antagonistic as well as rude and unfriendly with the failure experience.

Thus, we see that there is obviously some dark sides of both low and high self-esteems. Low self-esteem directly arouses very negative feelings and pathological states of anxiety, depression, drug abuse, and some forms of delinquency. Striving for higher self-esteem gradually robs the quality and enjoyment of life because this inclination pressurises a person to succeed and succeed at any cost.

5. *Protecting self-esteem:*

People want to protect their self-esteem. People with high self-esteem expect to perform better and they usually do the same. People with low self-esteem expect to perform poorly and they also usually do it. In fact, people want to protect their self-esteem whether that is high or low. In other words, they want to experience self-verification in the feedback received by them. People with high self-esteem want self-enhancing feedback, whereas people with low self-esteem want self-derogating feedback.

There are several techniques through which a person protects his self-esteem. Important ones are as under:

(i) **Making selective social comparison:** According to Festinger (1954), people make social comparison with other persons due to the lack of any objective standards for evaluation. In general, people compare themselves with others who are similar in several respects such as age, sex, economic status, occupational abilities and aptitudes (Suls and Miller, 1977; Walsh and Taylor, 1982). Generally, the person makes comparison with those others who are a bit inferior to oneself so that one can rate oneself favourably and can protect the self-esteem. Persons tend to avoid comparison with those others who are far superior to themselves. Researches have further shown that once the persons make a social comparison, they usually tend to overrate their relative position (Felson, 1981). This was proved in one study conducted by Heiss and Owens (1972), who obtained self-ratings from a large number of American adults, who were mostly the people with low self-esteem. Results revealed that 98% adults rated above average as spouses, parents, sons or daughters or in the attributes of trustworthiness, intelligence and willingness to work and 2% rated below average on the same dimensions.

(ii) **Manipulating appraisals:** We can protect the self-esteem by manipulating the appraisals from others. Persons can interpret others' appraisals as more favourable or unfavourable than they actually are. Jussim, Coleman and Nassau (1987) conducted one study in which some college students performed an analogy test and subsequently, they were given positive, negative or no feedback about their performance. Each student, then, completed a questionnaire. Results revealed that the students with high self-esteem perceived the feedback, whether positive or negative, as more positive than the students who were having low self-esteem. Generally, persons choose to associate with those people who can share their view regarding self, and avoid those who do not share their view. Secord and Backman (1964) found that women tend to associate most frequently with those women whom they believe saw them as they saw themselves. Likewise, Swann and Predmore (1985) found that the people who are having negative self-esteem tend to associate with the people who think poorly of themselves.

(iii) **Selective information processing:** People protect their self-esteem by attending to those occurrences or events, which are consistent with their self-evaluation. Our memory also acts to protect our self-esteem. People showing high self-esteem recall good, and successful activities more often, whereas those people with low self-esteem are more likely to recall bad, irresponsible and unsuccessful activities. Schlenker, Weigold and Hallan (1990) conducted one study in which both types of participants showing high and low self-esteem performed a task. Subsequently, the investigators told some that they had failed and to some that they had succeeded. Later, self-ratings done by these participants demonstrated biased ratings. High self-esteem participants who succeeded, tended to increase their ratings, whereas low self-esteem participants did not. Not only that, low self-esteem unsuccessful participants gave themselves lower ratings, whereas high self-esteem successful participants did not. Thus, both high and low self-esteem participants by resorting to the selective information processing protected their self-esteem.

(iv) **Selective commitment to identities and personal qualities:** We also protect our self-esteem by committing ourselves to those self-concepts that may provide feedback consistent with our self-evaluation and giving little or no weight to all those that provide feedback, which challenges them. Several studies have provided support for this contention. Hoelter (1983) reported that people tend to enhance their self-esteem by assigning more weight to all those identities and personal qualities, which they consider particularly admirable and praiseworthy. Tesser and Campbell (1983) showed that people tend to increase or decrease identification with a social group when the concerned group becomes a greater or lesser potential source of self-esteem. Cialdini et al. (1976) conducted a study in which they demonstrated that students identify more with their school when they describe their victories (we won) than defeats (they lost). Such identities not only protect their self-esteem but also enhance them. Brown, Collins and Schmidt (1988) further showed that low self-esteem participants belonging to successful group downplayed their connection to the group and also minimised their contributions to success. Such participants were more likely to link themselves to the successful group when they were not the members of it.

These techniques protect the self-esteem of a person. The description of these techniques very clearly shows that human beings actively process the social events or modify the meanings of social events actively in order to protect and enhance the self-esteem.

6. Sex and self-esteem

Does sex of a person affect the self-esteem? Is there difference between the level of self-esteem of a woman and the level of a self-esteem of a man? The answer is yes. Researches bear clearly testimony to the fact that the level of self-esteem of a woman, in general, is lower than the level of the self-esteem of a man. The obvious reason is that in our society, women frequently are ascribed lower status and are also subjected to various kinds of prejudices, stereotypes and biases. Their lowered social structural position have negative consequences for their self-esteem. The famous sociologist, George Herbert Mead (1934) had very clearly mentioned that our self-esteem, to a large extent, develops from the feedback we receive from the others in our society. Women in comparison to men have lower self-esteem because they, most of the time, receive devalued feedback from society.

Some researches have been conducted to test the above viewpoint. Williams and Best (1990) conducted a cross-nation research in which participants from fourteen countries were selected for the study. After analysis of their results, they have concluded that in countries like India and Malaysia, most of the women have negative self-esteem probably because they are expected to remain in their home to spend time as housewife or mother. In countries like England and Finland, where women are most active outside their home by making valued participation, they never perceive themselves inferior to men in any respect. The essence of this research is that when women are deprived of participation from outside their homes, they feel devalued and then they are forced to develop a negative self-esteem. Major et al. (1999) had done a meta-analysis of studies, comparing self-esteem of men and women in 226 samples taken from Canada and the United States of America and reached to the conclusion that men have significantly higher self-esteem than women. They also reported that such difference in self-esteem of men and women was far less in professional class and was the greatest among those in middle and lower classes. Likewise, those women, who have attained culturally advanced positions in the society, also tend to show lesser self-esteem loss.

Thus, we finally conclude that women, in general, do have lower level of self-esteem as compared to men. The greater the devaluation, discrimination, prejudice and biases the women suffer in society, higher is their self-esteem loss.

SELF-SERVING BIAS

Self-serving bias refers to the tendency to perceive oneself in favourable way. This is one of the ways through which self-concept is favourably built and self-esteem is strengthened. People want to make a positive assessment of themselves and most of the people manage to see themselves favourably. Most of the people show what has been called *above-average effect* in which they think that they are better than an average person on almost all major dimensions. Even when the person is presented with negative social feedback about his performance, the person shows his ignorance as if he knows nothing and again emphasises only information, which supports the self favourably (Sanitioso and Wlodarski, 2004).

Self-serving bias is frequently shown while people tend to explain their personal outcome. If the outcome is positive, we accept all those information, which suggest that we are responsible for that. Several experiments have found that people accept credit when they get success. They attribute the success to internal factors like their ability, intelligence, efforts. However, they attribute negative outcome or failure to external factors like bad luck, others' hindrances, etc. (Campbell and Sedikides, 1999). Attributing positive outcomes to internal factors like ability and negative outcomes to external factors like chance or bad luck is especially found in those people, who have high self-esteem (Schlenker, Weigold and Hallam, 1990). Researches have shown that people not only show self-serving biases for their personal outcomes but they also do so for their group's achievements. For example, supporters of cricket team often believe that their presence and cheering are responsible for the victory of the team. However, some cultural limits on people's willingness to grab credit have been reported. For example, among Chinese people, modesty is one of the important component of self-esteem. Accordingly, the students of Chinese school attribute their success primarily to teachers, whereas the students of American school attribute it more to their own abilities and skills. Conversely, when faced with negative outcomes, Chinese students blame themselves and explain their failure as stemming from their own mistakes or flaws, whereas American students tend to explain their failure or negative outcome in terms of faults of others.

Self-serving bias is adaptive most of the time. When good outcomes occur, high self-esteem people, as compared to low self-esteem people, tend to savour and sustain good thoughts and feelings (Wood et al., 2003). Researches have confirmed that self-serving biases also help protect people from depression and physiological cost of stress (Taylor et al., 2003). In *terror management theory* developed by Greenberg, Solomon and Pyszczynski (1997), it has been proposed that the positive self-esteem is adaptive because it buffers anxiety, including anxiety related to death. Such positive self-esteem protects us from feeling terror over our eventual death. Thus, increased self-esteem nourished by self-serving biases obviously leads to decreased anxiety.

Self-serving bias may become, sometimes, maladaptive too (Myers, 2005). The persons, who blame others for their own failure, are often more unhappy and tense from within than the people who readily acknowledge their mistakes and failures (Anderson et al., 1983; Newman and Langer, 1981; Peterson et al., 1981). Researches have also shown that self-serving biases can also poison a group performance (Schlenker and Miller, 1977).

SELF AS AN OBJECT OF PREJUDICE

What happens when a person finds that he is getting prejudice treatment in the group or gets such treatment due to being a member of devalued group? How does he feel when he gets prejudice-based negative treatment stemming from his own group membership? In other words, what happens when self of the person gets a prejudice treatment from members of his own group? Researches have shown that three types of consequences occur in such cases:

1. emotional consequences,
2. cognitive consequences and
3. behavioural consequences.

These are described as follows:

1. Emotional consequences

Perceived prejudice affects our psychological well-being. Emotional responses to a negative outcome depend on the attribution made for it. Schmitt and Branscombe (2002) conducted one experiment in which they compared the internal component of attributions to prejudice against one's group (self at group level) with that of external component of attribution. When negative outcomes are attributed to the prejudice against the membership of group, this reflects an internal and relatively stable cause. When compared with another important internal and stable feature of the self such as lack of intelligence or social skills, etc., an attribution to the prejudice against the group might be proved to be self-protective. When negative outcomes are compared with the actual external attribution (something that is not related to the self of the participant), then attribution made to prejudice against the group membership may prove to be harmful for well-being. Researches have clearly shown that the worst attribution that a person can make for the psychological well-being is that there is something unique about the self (perceiving oneself as uniquely stupid and less intelligent), which is stable and applicable to many situations. On the other hand, the best attribution for the psychological well-being is that where negative outcome is perceived to be due to entirely something that is unstable and is unlikely to be met in many situations. Thus, when attribution for the negative outcomes reflects external causes rather than prejudice against the membership of the group, psychological well-being is protected (Baron, Byrne and Branscombe, 2006).

2. Cognitive consequences

Perceived prejudice against the membership of a group, particularly devalued or disadvantaged group, also affects our ability to learn, memorise and acquire skills. It means that such prejudice has obvious cognitive consequences too. Researches have shown that when people are afraid of the fact that they may be found out as the member of a devalued group or of a group which is socially disadvantaged or banned, then such fear tends to negatively affect the cognitive abilities like learning and memory (Lord and Saenz, 1985; Frable, Blackstone and Scherbaum 1990). Performance of such persons suffers because their cognitive abilities are impaired. Researches have further revealed that what is considered a devalued social identity in one culture is not necessarily considered as the same in the other culture. Therefore, the cognitive deficits may be found only in the devalued social identity. Levy and Langer (1994) confirmed this from their study in which they reported that senior citizens (older citizens) of the United States of America showed deficit in memory, while their counterparts in China did not. This difference was due to the fact that in the United States, elderly people are negatively stereotyped in terms of poor memory, and therefore, they are considered as negative aspect of social identity, whereas in China, elderly people are considered as affectionate social category and are viewed with veneration.

3. Behavioural consequences

Perceived prejudice can also have some behavioural consequences. One of such consequences extensively researched is what is generally called *stereotype effect*, which is defined as the belief of a person that he might be judged in terms of negative stereotype since he belongs to a particular group or his performance confirms the negative stereotype of that group. When people value their ability in certain domain, but in the concerned domain, the group is stereotyped as performing very poorly, then the stereotype effect is likely to occur. Suppose a tribal woman has good knowledge in the field of subjects like Physics and Chemistry. But since she belongs to a tribal group, which is stereotyped for performing poorly, her performance in the concerned domain (Physics and Chemistry) may suffer due to stereotype effect. Likewise, women, in general, have poor knowledge of Mathematics. But a woman having good knowledge of Mathematics, may do worse in Mathematics test when she is told about the stereotype that men do better in Mathematics than women. Such stereotype effect has been clearly found in a study conducted by Spencer, Steele and Quinn (1999). Inzlicht and Ben-Zeev (2000) further showed that poor performance occurs only in stereotype-relevant dimension (Mathematics) and it is not that all types of performance do suffer.

Since such stereotype threats are difficult to control or eliminate all together, social psychologists have considered three response options that are available to the devalued group members when they experience stereotype threat. One response option is that people can cope with the stereotype threat by distancing themselves from the performance domain (such as Mathematics). Still another option may be that people can distance from their group as a whole (women group). Both these types of response options are, however, costly. The third response option, which is preferable, is that people may distance from only the stereotypic dimensions relevant to high performance in the domain, but do not do so in stereotypic dimensions that are irrelevant to success in the domain. In other words, in this third response option, people show preference for disidentifying only the negative parts of their group's stereotype.

Now, the question is—why does stereotype threat reduce the performance of the people? Researches have revealed that stereotype threat creates anxiety and stress among people. As a result of such anxiety and stress, their performance suffers a lot. Although verbal measures of anxiety (self-report measure) have failed to reveal the important role of anxiety in stereotype threat effects, the non-verbal measure of anxiety has clearly established the role that anxiety plays in stereotype threat effects.

Researches have also revealed that stereotype threat can also undermine the performance in advantaged or valued or dominant group also. Thus, the performance deficit due to stereotype threat is not limited to only historically devalued or disadvantaged group. Men, who are stereotyped as being less emotional than women, when reminded regarding their emotional deficit status, perform poorly on a task requiring identification of emotions. Aronson et al. (1999) conducted one study in which whites were compared with Asians in terms of performance deficit due to stereotype threats. Whites, regarding whom although no stereotype existed that they perform poorly in Mathematics, when threatened by potentially negative comparison with Asians, who were stereotyped as showing better performance in Mathematics than whites, tended to exhibit poor performance in the concerned domain (Mathematics).

Thus, we see that when self of a person is made prejudiced, it has obvious consequences like emotional consequences taxing psychological well-being, cognitive consequences producing performance deficits and behavioural consequences producing stereotype threat.

Summary and Review

- *Self* refers to the collection of beliefs we hold about ourselves. The answers of the basic questions *who am I?* and *what do I want to be?* are embedded in self. The contents of these beliefs are called *self-concept* and the evaluation we make of those beliefs is called *self-esteem*. Material self and social self are two most important components of self.
- There are different sources of development of social self. Five such sources are role taking and role playing, social identity, social comparison, success and failures and reflected appraisals.
- Cross-cultural researches have shown that self vary greatly in light of different cultural perspectives. There are two basic dimensions of cultural variations—individualistic culture having dominance in Western countries and collectivistic culture having dominance in Eastern countries, including India. Individualistic culture gives rise to independent self, whereas collectivistic culture gives rise to interdependent self.
- Self regulates our thoughts, feelings, emotions and behaviour. Self influences thoughts and feelings through *self-schema*, which is defined as an organised structure of set of cognition about something. There are three components of self-schema—self as one is (actual self), self as one would like to be (ideal self) and self as one ought to be (ought self). Another ways through which self affects our behaviour are self-awareness and self-discrepancy.
- Self also influences the planning, control and regulation of our behaviour. Behaviours are linked to a particular identity. Of the different types of identities available before the person in any situation, he selects a particular identity for enactment, keeping in view the various criteria. The selected and enacted identity produces consistency and unity in the behaviour.
- *Self-esteem* is the evaluative component of self. It is the positive or negative evaluation of the self. Thus, it is the overall attitude towards self. Social psychologists have identified three sources of self-esteem—family experience, social comparison and performance feedback. Self-esteem has been measured with the help of various self-report measures. Self-esteem has a direct impact upon human behaviour. The behavioural pattern of people with high self-esteem and low self-esteem does differ. Social psychologists have also reported about the dark side of self-esteem. People with low self-esteem suffers from a lot of problems, including depression, anxiety, relationship problems, drug and alcohol use, eating disorders, etc. People with high self-esteem generally feel pressurised to succeed more and more, and they are, therefore, devoid of enjoying the activities of life. Self-esteem is protected by adopting various techniques like making social comparison, manipulating appraisals, as well as through selective information processing, selective commitment to identities and personal qualities. Researches have also revealed that men, on the whole, have higher level of self-esteem than women.
- Many self-serving biases are shown by the persons for explaining their personal outcomes. A positive outcome is explained by the above-average effect, whereas the negative outcome is explained by luck or some external causes. Researches have shown that there are examples, which show that self-serving biases can both be adaptive as well as maladaptive.
- Perceived prejudice regarding the self may have three types of consequences—emotional consequences, cognitive consequences and behavioural consequences. Emotional consequences tax psychological well-being, cognitive consequences produce performance deficits and behavioural consequences produce stereotype threat.

Review Questions

1. Give the meaning and nature of self.
2. Discuss the important sources of development of social self.
3. Citing evidences, discuss the impact of culture upon the development of self.
4. Make a comparative study of independent self and interdependent self.
5. Discuss the impact of self upon thoughts, behaviour and emotions of a person.
6. How does our identity affect our behaviour? Does identity produce consistency and unity in behaviour?
7. Discuss the different sources of development of self-esteem. How is self-esteem measured?
8. How is behaviour influenced by self-esteem? Outline a plan for protecting self-esteem.
9. Point out the dark side of the self-esteem. Does sex of a person influence the level of self-esteem?
10. Discuss self as an object of prejudice. Also, discuss the important consequences of perceived prejudiced status of self.
11. Write short notes on the following:
    (i) Self-serving biases
    (ii) Measurement of self-esteem
    (iii) Material self and social self
    (iv) Independent self and interdependent self

5. Social Cognition, Social Perception and Attribution

Learning Objectives

- Meaning and Nature of Social Cognition
- Components of Social Cognition: Schema and Prototypes
- Impact of Schema upon Social Cognition: Schematic Processing
- Self-fulfilling Nature of Schema
- Cognitive Heuristics: Mental Shortcuts for Reducing our Efforts in Social Cognition
- Potential Sources of Errors in Social Cognition
- Cognition and Affect: A Reciprocal Relationship
- Field of Interpersonal Perception: Social Perception and Person Perception
- Role of Non-verbal Cues in Person Perception
- Recognising Deception in Non-verbal Cues
- Impression Formation
- Integrating Information about Others
- Impression Management
- Self-perception
- Attribution: Understanding the Causes of Others' Behaviour
- Theories of Attribution
- Bias and Error in Attribution
- Applications of Attribution Theory
- Cultural Basis of Attribution

Key Terms

Actor-observer effect	Bottom-up processing	Deliberate attribution
Additive model	Categorisation	Dispositional
Anchoring and adjustment heuristics	Category-based process	Emic culture
Attribute-focused process	Change of meaning	Etic culture
Automatic monitoring	Cognitive heuristics	Event schema
Automatic priming	Cognitive load	Exemplars
Availability heuristics	Continuum model	External attribution
Averaging model	Correspondence bias	False consensus effect
Base-rate fallacy	Counterfactual thinking	Focus of attention

Group schema	Overconfidence	Self-promotion techniques
Halo effect	Parallel-constraint	Self-schema
Implicit personality	Perseverance effect	Simulation heuristics
Impression formation	Person perception	Situational
Impression management	Personal schema	Slime effect
Internal attribution	Planning fallacy barrier	Social cognition
Interperson perception	Positivity bias	Social desirability
Mood congruence memory	Priming	Social perception
Mood-dependent	Prototypes	Spontaneous
Negativity bias	Rebound effect	Subtractive rule
Negativity effect	Representativeness	Tactical impression
Non-common effect	Role schema	Thought suppression process
Operating process	Schema	Top-down processing
Optimistic bias	Self-fulfilling prophecy	Trait centrality
Other-enhancement	Self-perception	Weighted averaging model

Our thinking about social world is important. The ways we interpret, analyse, remember and use the various types of information about the social world broadly represent our social cognition. In other words, how we think about other people, our various relations with them and social environments in which we live are important in making decisions about others. There are several aspects of social cognitions, which are important for understanding the behaviours of others with whom we interact. Various components of social cognition such as schemas and humanistic are especially important for examining the basic principles underlying social thoughts. In this connection, a look at the interplay between social cognition and affect has also been considered very useful. In the present chapter, we shall concentrate upon the components of social cognition, cognitive heuristics, potential sources of errors in social cognition, interplay of cognition and affect, social perception, impression formation and impression management. Besides these topics, the related concept of attribution, theories of attribution and applications of attribution theory will also be highlighted.

MEANING AND NATURE OF SOCIAL COGNITION

According to Neisser (1967), *cognition* is a wider term, which encompasses all processes by which the sensory input is transformed, reduced, elaborated, stored, recorded and finally used. Thus, cognition includes a wide range of mental processes like perception, attention, memory, thinking and decision-making, etc. The central components of cognitive psychology are perception, attention, memory, thought and language (Eysenck and Keane, 1995). The word *social* added to *cognition* has more than one meaning (McGuire, 2003) such as cognitions representing social realities or cognitions shared by the members of the society. If we pay a look towards past, it will be obvious that the study of role of cognitive process in social behaviour received impetus with the publication of Heider's (1944) paper *Social Perception and Phenomenal Causality*. In fact, social psychologists, in general, take publication of Fiske and Taylor's book *Social Cognition* in 1984 and its second revised edition done in 1991 as a marker in the field and as one of the basic momentums for establishing the field of social cognition. Social cognition is broadly concerned with the above said areas like attention, memory, etc., but in a social context, it includes what people attend to, perceive, think and remember about themselves and other people. Basically, it takes into account how different social contexts and situations tend to influence these processes within the people. Keeping these basic facts into consideration, *social cognition* can be defined as a process by which we interpret, analyse, remember and use information about the social world (Baron, Byrne and Branscombe, 2008). In other words, in social cognition, we think about other people, our relations with them, and finally, about social worlds or environments in which we live. That is the reason why Taylor, Peplau and Sears (2006) had defined social cognition as the study of how people form inference from the social information in the environment. Likewise, Higgins (2000) defined social cognition as the study of how people make sense of other people and themselves, that is, learning about what matters in the social world. In a nutshell, social cognition is such an area of social psychology that explores how a person selects, interprets, remembers and uses social information.

Analysing these definitions of social cognition, we arrive at the following major characteristics of the social cognition:

1. In social cognition, people interpret, analyse and remember the information they get from other people.
2. In social cognition, information is not only remembered and analysed, rather it is also used by the persons in different social contexts or social settings. This helps in understanding the social world.
3. In social cognition, people arrive at certain conclusion after using the information in their social world. Thus, social cognition also helps in making decisions about the behaviours and actions of others as well as those of ourselves.

If we go into the depth of the process of social cognition, we get some important hints about the important aspects of social cognition. First, our social thought is not always rational, rather it is subjected to some kinds of errors such as our tendency to remain stick to the views and beliefs even in the presence of evidences that those views and beliefs are wrong. We do this probably because thinking about social world involves hard and strenuous efforts. Therefore, we avoid it or at least minimise it to the possible extent and remain intact and feel safe with our earlier held views and beliefs. Second, the processing of social information appears to be completed in automatic manner due to some kinds of stereotype prevalent in the society. For example, if we hear the news of a woman doing the job of a truck driver, we immediately conclude that this information may be wrong because the job of a truck driver involves very hard and strenuous work, which ordinarily cannot be done by a woman. Moreover, temperamentally women are not fit for this job. Thus, the information is automatically processed with the help of stereotype. We never care to think and examine the information carefully and systematically. Third, if the viewpoints of other person are challenged, he becomes emotional, which in turn, makes him behave in more unreasonable way than ever. This means that there is an obvious link between the cognition and affect, both reciprocally influence each other. Such interplay between cognition and affect is also a very important aspect of social cognition.

COMPONENTS OF SOCIAL COGNITION: SCHEMA AND PROTOTYPE

Human mind is capable of processing information in a very sophisticated manner. One of our most basic mental processes is *categorisation*, which is defined as our tendency to perceive stimuli as the members of groups or classes, rather than perceiving them as something isolated, differentiated and unique entities. In other words, categorisation refers to how a person identifies the stimuli and groups them together as the members of a particular category. Categorisation occurs automatically with a little mental effort. For example, we can easily categorise a book, tree, or animal. A person also categorises himself according to age, sex, marital status, etc.

Rosch and Mervis (1975) pointed out that some members of a category are somehow more representative than the other members. They are called *prototypes*. Thus, prototype is an abstraction that represents typical or quintessential resistance of a class or group. For example, sparrows and robins are more representative of category birds than penguin because one important distinguishing feature of birds is that they can fly. Cantor and Mischel (1979) pointed out that *prototypicality* is defined in terms of the number of attributes that a category member shares with the other members of the same category and the fewer attributes that he shares with the members of another category. We have prototype of many people like lawyers, doctors, engineers, officers, psychologists, etc. Since prototype is an ideal type, what we do when we meet a specific person is simply categorising that person according to salient features or attributes, which may fit one or more of prototypes we hold in our mind. Researches have revealed that prototypes are strongly determined by societal, cultural and developmental factors (Pennington, Gillen and Hill, 1999).

Although it seems easier to categorise people, events, situations and even self according to some fundamental attributes, the reality is otherwise probably because the categories we use are not isolated from one another, rather they are linked together and form a structure. For example, we may think of a woman not only having various attributes such as being intelligent, physically attractive, fluent in Hindi and English language but also bearing certain relations to other persons or entities (like sister of my friend, taller than my wife, and owner of a business firm). These other persons or entities may have relations with still other persons and entities. In this way, people build a cognitive structure consisting of persons, attributes and relations.

Social psychologists prefer to use the term *schema* or *schemata* to denote the said type of well-organised structure of cognitions about social entity like a person, group, role or event. Schemas generally include information about an entity's attributes and its relation with other entities. Thus, schema refers to a mental structure containing information relevant to self, other people, specific events or situations. More specifically and scientifically, *schemas* are defined as the mental frameworks around a specific theme that help us in organising social information and guiding the processing of such information (Baron, Byrne and Branscombe, 2006). Schemas are established on the basis of previous experience, cultural and social norms or perceived understanding and provide a good framework for organising, interpreting and processing social information. Once schemas are established, they help us in interpreting new situations and in guiding our behaviour.

Fiske and Taylor (1991) had classified schema into four major types—self-schema, person schema, role schema and event schema. All these four types of schema serve vital functions in processing, organising and using social information. A brief description of these types is as follows:

1. Self-schemas

Self-schemas are defined as cognitive generalisations about the self based upon the experiences of the past. In fact, self-schemas are the structures that tend to organise our conception of our own characteristics (Markus, 1977). Self-schemas form the cognitive component of the self-concept and are organised around the specific traits or features (called *schematic traits*), which we generally think of as most central to our self-image. For example, if a person thinks about the self as being independent one (opposed to dependent one), he may see himself as assertive and individualistic one. If he behaves consistently with this self-schema, he may refuse to take money from parents, refuse to ask others to help him and will try to lead a discussion, etc.

2. Person schemas

Person schemas are the mental structures, which represent knowledge about the traits of specific personalities (such as Mrs. Indira Gandhi, Dr. Rajendra Prasad, President Bill Clinton, etc.) or the types of individuals (such as introvert, psychopath, manic-depressive, extrovert, etc.). Person schema organise the person's conception of others' personalities and enable him to develop expectations about others' behaviour.

3. Role schemas

Role schemas are defined in terms of various attributes and behaviours, which are typical of the persons who occupy a particular role in the society. In other words, role schemas indicate which behaviours and attributes are typical of persons occupying a particular position or role in the group. These roles can be either achieved or ascribed. *Achieved roles* are acquired through effort and training. Examples are various occupational roles such as those of a bank manager, a team captain, a nurse, etc. *Ascribed roles* refer to those over which we have no control. Examples are age, gender, race, caste, etc. In our society, the role of a female is different from the role of a male. Role schemas are often considered as stereotype, especially when considered in relation to ascribed roles of gender and race (Fiske and Taylor, 1991).

4. Event schemas

Event schemas are defined as the mental frameworks which relate to some specific events or situations. In other words, event schemas are the schemas regarding important recurring events of our society (Hue and Erickson, 1991). Event schemas are scripts, which indicate what is expected to happen in a given situation (Abelson, 1981). These scripts or event schemas help us in anticipating how to behave in the given situation. In our society, we have event schemas for wedding, birthday party, funerals and eating at restaurant. For example, event schema for wedding helps us in deciding what type of dress we should put on, how we should interact with groom and bridegroom, what and how we should eat, etc. Likewise, there are honeymoon scripts for married couples, which dictate what type of behaviour a groom expects from a bridegroom and a bridegroom from the groom. As long as both act according to the honeymoon script, things go well. However, if any one person does not behave according to the script, subsequent disturbances in their married life are likely to start.

Besides these four types of schemas enunciated by Fiske and Taylor (1991), some other social psychologists also added one more schema called *group schema* (Eckes, 1995; Taylor and Crocker, 1981). *Group schemas*, also known as *stereotypes*, are defined as the schemas regarding the members of a particular social group or category (Hamilton, 1981). Stereotypes, in fact, tend to indicate such attributes or behaviours, which are typical of members of that group or category. In Indian culture, wide varieties of stereotypes are used about different social groups or categories. For example, females are religious-minded and of low intelligence; husbands are like god for wives, teachers are idealistic and politicians are opportunistic.

In this section, we have especially emphasised the four plus one type of schema, which show how we process various types of social and other information about people. Figure 5.1 summarises each of the five types of schemas and their functioning regarding social information processing.

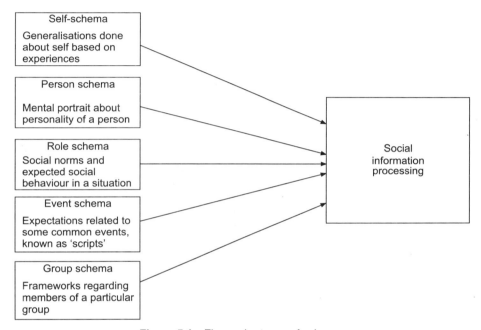

Figure 5.1 Five major types of schema.

IMPACT OF SCHEMA UPON SOCIAL COGNITION: SCHEMATIC PROCESSING

Schematic processing requires three cognitive processes like attention, encoding and retrieval involved in social cognition (Wyer and Srull, 1984), and because of this, it has an influence upon our social cognition. Therefore, schema, especially schematic processing, influences our cognition as cognitive processes of attention, encoding and retrieval are involved in it.

Attention refers to what we notice selectively. It is impossible to pay attention to every event stimulus present in our environment. Therefore, we have to be selective. We are most likely to attend to some aspects of the situation or event or people more often than others, and schemas provide us with the criteria for being selective one. Information regarding stimulus or person, which is consistent with the schema, is likely to be noticed and entered into the consciousness. Information that is inconsistent with schemas is often ignored (Fiske, 1993) unless it is extraordinary in some sense.

Encoding refers to matching one's existing schema with the incoming information. Once schemas are formed, information consistent with them is easier to encode, rather than encoding inconsistent information. However, it has been shown that the inconsistent information sometimes more readily noticed and encoded. In fact, such inconsistent information is so unexpected that it forces our attention to mind to catch it and make a note of it. (Stangor and Ruble, 1989; Stangor and McMillan, 1992). For example, students have a well-established schema for a professor and they expect him to teach in class and answer the questions raised by them. But suppose that a professor instead of teaching, starts showing magic tricks in the class and cutting jokes. Students who are present in his class, luckily or unluckily, will always remember this experience because the experience is highly inconsistent with the schema for a professor.

Retrieval from memory is the third process. The information which is readily retrieved or recalled is of two types—schema-consistent information or schema-inconsistent information. Researchers have shown that overall, schema-consistent information is better recalled than schema-inconsistent information. This was supported by Cohen (1981) in his experimental research. Participants in this study were provided with a videotape of a couple having dinner. Half the participants were told that the wife was librarian and the other half were told that she was waitress. Results revealed that the participants recalled more prototypical features associated with the concerned schema role. This shows that schema-consistent information is better retrieved than schema-inconsistent information. Researches have also shown that schema-consistent information is processed automatically with a little mental effort, but schema-inconsistent information receives more in-depth processing (Devine and Ostrom, 1988). Perhaps due to this, in-depth processing information inconsistent with schemas may be strongly present in the memory, or even more strongly than the information consistent with schemas (Baron, Byrne and Branscombe, 2006).

Researches done by Stangor and McMillian (1992), Tice et al. (2000) showed that the effects of schemas upon social cognition are also influenced by some other factors. Such effects are found to be stronger when schemas are themselves well-developed and strong, and also such effects are stronger when cognitive load is high rather than low (Kunda, 1999). *Cognitive load* here means how much mental efforts we are expending at a given time. When a person tries to handle so much information at a time, he relies more on schemas because they permit us to process these information with least mental effort.

Although schemas provide certain advantages because they are very helpful in processing information in easy way, they have also some disadvantages, which are discussed below:

1. Schemas may produce some distortions in understanding our social relationship. Schemas play a very important role in developing prejudice by strengthening stereotypes about a social group. It is due to schema produced prejudice that we see any politician as opportunist and corrupt, although the reality may be otherwise. Unfortunately, schemas, once formed, are difficult to change. Researches have shown that schemas, once formed, show *perseverance effect*, remaining unchanged even when some concrete contradictory evidences are provided (Kunda and Oleson, 1995). For example, when a person receives inconsistent information with schema of a doctor, that is, he is told that the doctor is a good cook and dancer, the person does not alter schema of doctor, but puts such doctor in a special category, comprising persons who do not confirm the schema or stereotype. However, such forced misapplication of a schema may lead to incorrect characterisations and influences, and this, in turn, may produce inappropriate responses towards other persons, groups or events.
2. Schema can be self-fulfilling. People generally accept information that fits consistently with a schema. In fact, there are experimental evidences, which show that persons show a

confirmatory bias when collecting new information relevant to schemas (Higgins and Bargh, 1987; Snyder and Swann, 1978).
3. It has been found that when people face missing information, they fill the gaps with knowledge by adding such elements that are consistent with their schemas. Sometimes, these newly added elements are factually incorrect. Such situation creates inaccurate interpretation or influence about people, events or groups.

Keeping in view these disadvantages, any impact of schema upon cognition has to be treated with caution.

SELF-FULFILLING NATURE OF SCHEMA

As we have seen, schemas can sometimes be self-fulfilling or self-confirming because they influence the social world in a way to become consistent with themselves. Schemas can lock us into perceiving the social world in a way that may not be accurate. Experimental evidences have shown that schemas not only influence the type of information we seek from a person and subsequent inferences we make, but also affect the person's actual behaviour and self-image. When a person's wrong expectations about another person lead that person to adopt those expected attributes and behaviour, it is called *self-fulfilling prophecy*. Self-fulfilling nature of schema has been shown in several studies. Snyder, Tanke and Berscheid (1977) conducted one study in which they gave some male college students a folder of information about a woman on the campus. The folder included a picture that represented a woman as either highly attractive or highly unattractive. Reality was that the photos were fake and were randomly assigned to women, irrespective of their true looks. Each student was then allowed to talk with the woman (whose folder they had read) on phone for 10 minutes. The investigators tape-recorded the conversations done. Results indicated that the participants who believed that they were talking with a beautiful and attractive woman behaved more warmly on phone than the participants who believed that they were talking with an unattractive woman. Not only that, the women who had been wrongly presented as highly attractive were perceived by the other students who judged the tape to be more likable, friendly and sociable in their interactions as compared to those who were miscast as unattractive. Results clearly confirmed the self-fulfilling nature of schema. Earlier to this study, Rosenthal and Jacobson (1968) had conducted another study in which also there occurred confirmation of the self-fulfilling nature of schema. During early 1960s, there was a strong belief in the United States that the teachers' schema (belief) about the minority students was causing them (teachers) to behave less favourably than majority group students. As a result, the academic performance of minority group of children was falling rapidly. The investigators, administering intelligence test to the students of school in San Francisco, told teachers that some of the students are intellectually very superior and they are about to bloom academically. In reality, this was not true. The investigator's hypothesis was that such information might change the teachers' schema (belief) about these students, and hence, their behaviour towards them would also change. There was also a control group of students about whom teachers were not given any type of information. After eight months, the investigators again tested both groups of students. Results revealed that those students who had been identified as bloomers to their teachers really showed a significant gain on their intelligence test score as compared to the students of control group. The reason was that the bloomers were given more attention, more challenging tasks, better feedback and more opportunity to respond in their class by the teachers in comparison to the students of control group. In sum, the teachers' schema about the students had operated in self-fulfilling manner—the students about whom the teachers believed that they would bloom actually academically did better. Sadker and Sadker (1994) reported that teachers' lower expectation for success by minority students actually pulled down the confidence level of these students and that had contributed to very dismal performance by them.

Conclusively, it can be said that schemas are like a two-edged weapon. On one hand, they help us in processing information regarding social world quickly with minimal mental effort, and on the other hand, they encourage us to perceive the social world in a way that may not be accurate one.

COGNITIVE HEURISTICS: MENTAL SHORTCUTS FOR REDUCING OUR EFFORTS IN SOCIAL COGNITION

At one time, we are capable of handling only a certain amount of information. But generally, we have to handle a large number of information at any time. Consequently, we often experience what is called *information overload*. It is a condition in which our ability to process the given information is exceeded. An example of information overload is shown in Figure 5.2, where a driver is driving the car on a busy road and talking on cell phone. To deal with such a situation, we adopt some strategies. One very popular strategy is *heuristics*, which are simple rules or mental shortcuts for making complex decisions or drawing inferences rapidly and in seemingly effortless manner (Baron, Byrne and Branscombe, 2006). The early work on heuristics was done by Trensky and Kahneman in 1970s and in early 1980s. Based on these research works, four most important heuristics were identified—representativeness heuristic, availability heuristic, anchoring and adjustment heuristic, and simulation heuristic. These are discussed below:

Figure 5.2 Information overload as driver is talking on cellphone while driving in heavy traffic.

1. *Representativeness heuristic*

In representativeness heuristic, a judgement is made about a person, event or object based on how similar or representative it is thought to be of a category or prototype. In other words, in this heuristics, we take a few characteristics or attributes that we know about a person, event or object and select a schema that matches those characteristics (Dawes, 1998). The representative heuristic, thus, helps us in deciding if a particular person or event is an example of a particular schema. Tversky and Kahneman (1974) demonstrated this in one of their early studies. In this study, the participants were told that an imaginary man had been selected from a group of 100 persons and they were asked to estimate the probability that he was engineer. There were three groups of participants—one control group and two experimental groups. Some participants of the experimental groups were told that 30% of men were engineer, whereas the others were told that 70% of men were engineer. Members of the control group were not provided with any additional information. Members of the experimental groups were also provided with a personal description of the man which either resembled or did not resembled the common role schema of an engineer. Results were in expected direction. It was found that the participants of the control group, who were given information only about frequencies, estimated the probability of being an engineer on this basis. In other words, they thought that the imaginary man was more likely to be an engineer when the frequency or base rate was 70% than when it was 30%. But the members of the experimental groups, who were given personal details, tended to overlook the frequency or base rate and took the decision in terms of representativeness, that is, if the personal description of the man was representative of an engineer, he (imaginary person) was categorised as engineer, irrespective of the base rate information. This tendency to ignore the base rate information is called *base rate fallacy*. Due to tendency to ignore the base rate that indicates the frequency with which the given events or pattern occur in total population, decision or judgement based on representativeness heuristic is likely to become wrong.

2. *Availability heuristic*

Availability heuristic refers to a strategy in which a person makes judgement about the social world on the basis of how easily specific kinds of information are available or can be brought to mind. In other words, when we are to judge the likelihood of an event, we are more likely to base our judgement on the availability of relevant information. For example, a person might rate divorce rate higher than what it is in reality if his social network, which includes his family and friend circle, has frequently witnessed divorce. Tversky and Kahneman (1982) had provided a strong support for this heuristic. In English language, there are more than twice as many words with 'K' as third letter as there are with 'K' as first letter. Irrespective of this, when the investigators asked the participants some questions about the relative frequency of 'K', most of the participants responded that there are more words beginning with 'K', rather than having 'K' as the third letter. This happened because it is easier to think of such words, and therefore, they are readily available from memory. Thus, availability heuristic enables the person to answer questions concerning quantity and frequency on the basis of how quickly or easily the person can retrieve examples from memory. The ease with which the volume of information is retrieved, in fact, determines the answer (Macleod and Campbell, 1992).

Researches have revealed that the use of availability heuristic is likely to cause bias in social cognition due to several factors as under:

(i) This heuristic does not control for idiosyncratic or eccentric exposure or unusual samples or instances. Such idiosyncratic instances leave a strong impression on mind, and therefore, they are readily available and influence social cognition.

(ii) The storage and retrieval of information can also produce some availability biases. For example, when a person works in a group, he may believe that he has contributed far more than the other members of the group because his own cognitive efforts and attention are readily available in the memory.

A concept which is closely related to availability heuristic and widely studied by social psychologists is priming. *Priming* is defined as a process whereby exposure to stimuli or events that strengthen the availability of certain types or categories of information causes them to come more readily to mind. Due to priming, the availability of specific types of information held in memory is enhanced. In our day-to-day life, we have numerous examples of priming effect. When Psychology Honours students for the first time are told by their teachers regarding the different types of mental diseases and their accompanying symptoms in human, even very minor problems like not having good sleep at night, not concentrating on studies properly, experiencing fear from spider, may force them to think that he is suffering from some kind of mental disorder. Why does this so-called *psychology student syndrome* occur? It occurs due to priming effect, that is, due to the fact students are exposed to the description of diseases day after day in their classes by teachers and this leads them to think in an exaggerated manner when faced with mild symptoms. Likewise, a person after seeing a horror film may perceive a shadow as a potential monster or something, which is highly dreadful.

Researches have further shown that priming effect may also occur even when the individuals are unaware of priming stimuli. Such effect is known as *automatic priming* (Bargh and Pietromonaco, 1982). Thus, automatic priming indicates that availability of certain types of information can be enhanced by priming stimuli even when we are not aware of having been exposed to such stimuli. Erdley and D'Agostino (1989) supported such automatic priming effect from their study. In this study, a group of participants had traits of personality related to honesty. This group of participants was flashed upon the screen very briefly some personality traits that were related to honesty. Another group of participants which was a control group, was similarly exposed to some neutral words that were not related to honesty trait. After this, participants of both groups were asked to read a description of an imaginary person depicted in a vague manner. After reading the description, they were asked to rate the hypothetical person on a number of dimensions, including honesty. Results demonstrated that those participants who were briefly exposed to honesty-related words, although with no conscious awareness of them, rated the imaginary person higher on the honesty trait as compared to those participants who were exposed to neutral words. Results confirmed what has been called automatic priming.

3. Anchoring and adjustment heuristic

When people try to form judgement from the ambiguous information, they often reduce their ambiguity by starting with a reference point called *anchor* and then making an adjustment with it. Let us take an example. Suppose a person is asked to make an estimate of how many people attended the National Book Fair held at New Delhi last month. The person has no idea about this, but he has heard that a very large number of people used to visit the book fair. He has come to know that about 3 lakh people visited such book fair held in Lucknow five months back. Assuming that a very large number of people visited the National Book Fair, he may guess that about 5 lakh people might have attended this fair. In this example, the person has no information about the specific event in question, but he is using the information about a similar event as a reference point or anchor to which he adjusts reference information to arrive at a certain conclusion.

Social judgements are no exception because the information about the social situation is also vague most of the time. Anchors can be of great help when people try to derive meaning from ambiguous information and behaviour. Sometimes, people use self as an anchor point. For example, suppose someone asks you whether Mohan, one of your classmates, is intelligent. For you, it is easier to answer this question by trying to decide whether or not Mohan is intelligent than you. If Mohan seems to be more intelligent than you, you decide that he is intelligent. But if Mohan seems to be less intelligent than you, you decide that he is not intelligent. Your judgement about the intelligence of Mohan is not based on his absolute standing on any intelligence test, but is based on whether he seems to be more intelligent or less intelligent than you (or the anchor). Thus, in social judgement tasks, the self happens to be a common anchor.

4. Simulation heuristic

Simulation is defined as the ease with which a hypothetical scenario can be constructed. Suppose you have borrowed a car from your friend for family excursion trip. The car runs into accident and is badly damaged. Now, several things come to your mind as an answer to this question—what would happen when my friend will come to know that his car is badly damaged in an accident? You think through what you know about your friend and several possibilities are generated. You may think that he will ask to pay for the car or he is a rich person, and therefore, will ignore the whole thing or he may start quarrelling with me and damaging my household property, etc. Despite all these, it is easiest to imagine that he will most probably ask to make payment for the damaged car. Such inferential technique is known as *simulation heuristic* (Kohneman and Tversky, 1982). Researches have shown that simulation heuristic can be used for a wide variety of tasks such as doing prediction, explaining causality and doing affective responses (Mandel and Lehman, 1996; Kahneman and Miller, 1986).

These are the important heuristics that we often use for making judgement about social world. The reason of why we allow our thinking to be influenced by these heuristics to such an extent is that they save our mental effort in making judgement about social world.

POTENTIAL SOURCES OF ERRORS IN SOCIAL COGNITION

In our efforts to understand others and make sense out of the social world, we are subjected to several kinds of tendencies that lead us to some serious errors. In this section, we have considered several of these errors or tilts in social cognition.

1. Negativity bias

Negativity bias refers to the enhanced sensitivity to negative information or negative stimuli. In other words, negativity bias shows greater sensitivity to negative information in comparison to the positive information. If someone describes the positive traits like being intelligent, social, resourceful, good-looking, etc. about an unknown person, and he also mentions a negative information that he (the unknown person) is a veteran criminal, then in such a situation, what one is likely to remember the most? According to the researches done in social psychology, one is very likely to remember his negative trait of being a veteran criminal because this negative information stands out in memory.

If we pay attention to the negativity bias, it will be clear that such bias, in a way, reflects features of the external world that tend to threaten our well-being or safety. Due to this, it is especially important that the person must be sensitive to such stimuli and must readily respond it. Such reasoning has been supported by many researches. Ohman, Lundqvist and Esteves (2001) conducted one study in which participants were asked to search for neutral, friendly or threatening faces from other faces showing discrepant expressions. Results revealed that irrespective of the background faces, the participants identified the threatening faces more accurately and readily as compared to neutral or friendly faces. Several other studies have also shown that the participants are faster and more accurate in identifying threatening faces as compared to non-threatening faces.

2. Optimistic bias

When we make judgement about the social world, optimistic bias also occurs. *Optimistic bias* is opposite of negativity bias and it refers to the person's predisposition to expect things, events to turn out overall well. Research findings by Shepherd, Ouellette and Fernandez (1996) provided support that there are several people who strongly believe that they are more likely to experience positive events and less likely to experience negative events in comparison to the others. There are two common aspects of optimistic bias—overconfidence barrier and planning fallacy. In *overconfidence barrier*, the person shows greater confidence in his beliefs, thoughts and judgements than what is justified. This leads to error in our social cognition.

There are many people who strongly believe that they are more likely to get a good job and lead a happy married life but less likely to believe that they will have negative experience like becoming seriously ill and losing his job and status, etc. *Planning fallacy* is another aspect of optimistic bias and it refers to the tendency to do various types of optimistic predictions concerning how long a given task will take for final completion. Often it has been found that the government frequently exhibits planning fallacy by announcing optimistic schedule for completion of public works like new railway lines, new aerodromes or new bridges or new roads, etc.

Social psychologists have conducted researches to provide answer to the question—why do we fall prey to planning fallacy? They have reported that there are three major factors, which account for planning fallacy:

(i) When a person makes an announcement regarding what time it will take in completing the work, he enters into narrative mode of thought in which he mainly concentrates upon the future and how the task will be performed. The natural consequence of such narrative mode of thought is to prevent him from acknowledging the past showing how much time similar project took in its completion. As a result, the check that might prevent him from being highly optimistic about the completion of work is ignored (Buehler, Griffin and Ross, 1994).

(ii) When a person looks into past to acknowledge how much time the similar project took in its completion and finds that it took longer time than expected, he generally attributes such delay to the factors lying outside his control. As a result, the real obstacles in the final completion of the project are overlooked and the person falls prey to planning fallacy.

(iii) Strong motivation to complete a task also contributes to the planning fallacy. When predicting what will happen, a person, due to strong motivation, often predicts that what will happen will be what they want to happen. Therefore, they make very optimistic predictions regarding when the desired project will be completed. Thus, we see that planning fallacy is also influenced by our hopes, desires or motivatives (Buehler, Griffin and McDonald, 1997).

The optimistic bias is also clearly evident when the person compares his past and his future. Although the person perceives the past mixed in terms of highs and lows, that is, in terms of success and failure, he tends to perceive the future to be rosy or golden having more and more positive events and showing only a few negative events. This tendency is so strong that it occurs even when the person has just experienced some negative events (Newby-Clark and Ross, 2003). Explaining this, social psychologists have said that looking towards past no doubt reminds us of our failures and related disappointments, but looking towards the future, we must always think about happy goal and personal happiness. Since our cognition is most likely to be dominated by these positive thinking about the future rather than by the negative feeling of the past, we become overly more optimistic and display optimistic bias. Not only that, when a person thinks about future, particularly about far-off future, he thinks about it in a more abstract rather than concrete terms. This, in turn, enhances our level of creativity too (Forster, Friedman and Liberman, 2004).

Researches have shown that there is exception to a general rule of optimism, and in some situation, the optimistic bias may be reversed and turned to pessimism. This usually occurs when people expect to receive information that may be negative having important consequences for them. In such a situation, they brace for the loss and show a reversal of the optimistic pattern. In fact, people tend to be pessimistic showing a strong tendency to anticipate the negative outcomes (Taylor and Sheppard, 1998). Researches have further shown that this occurs due to the people's desire to be ready for facing the worst or loss.

3. Counterfactual thinking

Imagined alternative version of actual events is known as *counterfactual thinking*. In many situations, when people imagine might-have-been, they provide evidence to engage in counterfactual thinking. For example, suppose a student fails in examination, and subsequently, if he thinks that if he had done hard labour in his study, he would not have failed. This illustrates the use of counterfactual thinking. We often use counterfactual thinking to mitigate the bitterness of disappointments. For example, after the death of our loved one, we simply often say that the death was inevitable and nothing could be done against the wish of God. People adjust their view concerning the inevitability of death and tend to make such events more bearable (Tykocinski, 2001). If we develop different counterfactual thought such as 'if we had taken to her to the hospital quickly, his life would have saved', then the suffering is likely to be enhanced. Thus, by thinking that negative events or disappointments are inevitable, we tend to make these events more acceptable and bearable.

Researches have shown that counterfactual thinking seems to occur automatically in many situations and their effects can be reduced only through hard cognitive work in which they are either suppressed or discounted (Goldinger et al., 2003).

Why do people engage in counterfactual thinking? Researches suggest that counterfactual thinking about might-have-been serves any of the several motives. First, in some circumstances, counterfactual thinking may help people to feel better. For example, a person who met with a car accident may focus less on the damage caused to the car than on the fact that he would have been killed if he had sat on the front seat by the side of the driver. Imagining how much worse things could have been makes the person feel better in the present unpleasant situation. Second, counterfactual thinking may sometimes serve a preparatory function for the future. When a person imagines that how easily he could have avoided the problem that produced negative effect, the strong motivation to change and improve is increased (McMullen and Markman, 2000). For example, if a person realises that his car would not have been taken under control of police if he had not tried to proceed ahead despite red traffic signal, he probably will not be doing that again. Likewise, if the persons compare their current outcomes with less favourable ones, they may experience positive feelings of satisfaction or hopefulness. Common example of this we often see among those Olympic athletes who win bronze medal and often found saying that this is like to have winning no medal whatsoever. Alternatively, counterfactual thinking done in upward direction, where current outcomes are compared with more favourable ones than the person actually experienced, a strong feeling of disappointment, despair and envy may ensue (Sanna, 1997). For example, Olympic athletes who won silver medal, but actually had imagined to win gold medal, may experience such disappointment due to upward counterfactual thinking. Thus, counterfactual thinking strongly influences the affective states or mood of the persons.

4. Thought suppression

As its name implies, *thought suppression* means active efforts to prevent certain thoughts from entering into consciousness. Thus, in thought suppression, the person really avoids thinking about things or events he does not want to think about. A newly appointed college lecturer who is afraid of facing a big crowd of students in the class does try to avoid thinking about all ways in which he could fail at the task (see Figure 5.3). Although the person succeeds sometimes in driving such thinking from mind, most of the time it proves to be a very difficult task.

Figure 5.3 A newly appointed teacher is nervous in the classroom.

Wegner (1992) studied thought process in detail and came to the conclusion that thought suppression basically involves two types of processes—automatic monitoring process and operating process. The first process in thought suppression is *automatic monitoring process*, where the person researches for evidences that unwanted or unpleasant thoughts are about to intrude. After this, the second process called the *operating process*, which is more effortful and less automatic (therefore, more controlled) starts. In this second process, the person makes a very effortful and conscious attempt to distract himself by finding something else to think about. Thus, the first process acts as an *early-warning system*, which signals that some unpleasant or unwanted thoughts are present and the second process acts like a *prevention system* that actively ties to keep thoughts out of consciousness by way of distraction.

In normal condition, the above two processes of thought suppression do their job in a satisfactory manner. But there occurs a deviation from this normal condition such as when the person faces information overload or he is fatigued, the second process, that is, operating process does not work well, whereas the first process, that is, monitoring process continues to signal about the unwanted or unpleasant thoughts. In such a situation, the person experiences what is called *rebound effect* in which the unwanted thoughts occur at even a higher rate in comparison to the stage before efforts to suppress them had started.

Now, a question arises here—what effects do we observe when we engage (or fail to engage) ourselves in thought suppression? Researches have confirmed the view that people resort to thought suppression only as a means of influencing their own behaviours and feeling. For example, if person wants to avoid the feeling of depression, it will be very useful to avoid thinking about all those events and experiences that have made him depressed. But sometimes people may fail in their efforts at thought suppression. Kelly and Nauta (1997) showed that people who are high in reactance, that is, people who react very negatively to the perceived threats to their personal autonomy and freedom, generally fail in thought suppression. Since such people generally reject advices from others because they want to do things in their own way, they may find any instruction to suppress certain thoughts a very difficult task.

5. Limits of person's ability to think about social world

Researches done by social psychologists have shown that there are some limits on our ability to think rationally about the social world. One of the limitations is perhaps due to what is called *magical thinking* (Rozin and Nemeroff, 1990). In such thinking, people make assumptions that do not held up to rational scrutiny, but are very compelling. For example, a person's belief that the things which are similar to each other share fundamental properties, well illustrates magical thinking. People would not like to eat a chocolate which has been made similar in shape and colour to a lizard even though they know, rationally, that its shape and colour has nothing to do with its taste and quality. There are many social situations in which our thinking is influenced by such magical thinking. People of the advanced society generally make fun of the popular superstitious belief that a cat when crossed the path before a person going on the same path is an indication of some misfortune. A person may not accept this particular belief, but his own thinking cannot be said to be totally free of such magical thinking.

Another limitation involves the person's inability to take into account the moderating variables in many situations (Baron, Byrne and Branscombe, 2006). We have to take decision in many such social situations in which the effect that seems to stem from one factor can, in fact, stem from another. In such a situation, our limited processing capacity works against the rationality. Fiedler et al. (2003) conducted one study in which the participants were given some information about 32 women and 32 men, who had applied for admission into two separate universities. Among women, 13 were accepted and 19 were rejected by the university and among men, the opposite was true, that is, 19 men were accepted and 13 were rejected by the university. Additional information, however, suggested that this difference was due to the fact that women had applied to such university whose rejection rate was higher due to higher standards of selection, whereas most of the men had applied to such university whose rejection rate was lower due to not so high standard of selection. Since participants were not able to apprehend the effect of this moderator variable (university selectivity), they assume that women were kept at disadvantage simply because they were women and not because they chose to apply to a university with higher rejection rate. This type of error in social processing occurred among participants even when they were told and shown evidence for higher rejection rate.

Conclusively, it can be said that despite being flooded by various types of errors such as negativity bias, optimistic bias, counterfactual thinking, magical thinking, thought suppression and failure to take into moderator variable, we are able to manage to sort, store and use a large number of social information in a meaningful and efficient way.

COGNITION AND AFFECT: A RECIPROCAL RELATIONSHIP

Researches bear testimony to the fact that there is a complex interplay between cognition and affect. Our feelings and moods influence many aspects of cognition, that is, the way we process and use social information. Likewise, cognition also exerts strong influence upon the several aspects of affect. Thus, a reciprocal relationship exists between cognition and affect.

How is cognition influenced by affect?

Historically, affect has been considered as a disturbing factor or force that disrupts normal thinking and reasoning. However, current investigations have shown that affect do not always work as a disrupting force, rather it is viewed as a facilitating mechanism which not only provides information but also helps in goal attainment. Sinha and Jain (2004) reported that positive attitude towards life is a common predictor of sense of high accomplishment. Affect influences cognition of a person in several ways. In general, it has been reported that when the person is in good or positive mood, he tends to be more sociable, more altruistic and show other positive actions. On the other hand, when he is in bad mood, he keeps himself withdrawn and engages less in any positive actions.

Apart from these general influences of affect on behaviour, social psychologists have shown that affect influences several important aspects of cognition such as memory, judgement, perception of risk, creativity, etc.

Affect influences mood of a person through two mechanism—mood-dependent memory and mood-congruence memory. *Mood-dependent memory* refers to a state where what we remember while in a given mood is determined, in part, by what we learned when we were previously in that mood. For example, if a person has stored some information in his memory in good mood, he is more likely to remember that information when he is in similar mood. Eich (1995) had confirmed the existence of mood-dependent memory. He had pointed out that such memory may prove to be very important for understanding many social behaviours. For example, mood-dependent memory clearly explains why depressed persons have difficulty in remembering times when they were in happy mental state (Schachter and Kihlstrom, 1989). When they are in negative depressed mood, they are unable to recall information stored previously when they were in positive or good mood. *Mood congruence memory* refers to the fact that a person is more likely to store or remember positive information when in positive mood and negative information in negative mood. It means that the person tends to notice or remember information that is congruent with his current moods. Lyubomirsky, Caldwell and Nolen-Hoeksema (1998) showed that the people, who are depressed, recall more negative material when they were in negative mood—a fact that confirms mood congruence memory.

Affect also influences judgements. People who are in good mood judge everything such as their health, other people, future and their belongings such as car, house, etc. in a better condition (Fiske and Taylor, 1991). So far as the impact of negative mood is concerned, the evidence is mixed because negative mood has a less reliable impact upon judgements as compared to positive mood. Mood is also found to influence prediction that people make about future. (Desteno et al., 2000). Depressed individuals tend to be accurate in making pessimistic predictions, but they are less accurate in making predictions about positive events. Mood influences not only our judgements but also how we make judgements. People with good moods are expansive, inclusive and impulsive in their decision-making. They take decisions quickly, make more unusual connections among the things about which they think, and they think in a more stereotyped way (Park and Banaji, 2000). On the other hand, persons in negative mood generally slow down the information processing—they make decision slowly, work slowly and make more complex causal attribution and they are methodical and precise (Ruder and Bless, 2003).

Researches have also shown that the current mood of a person also influences his creativity, which is another important component of cognition. When the person is in happy mood, a wider and stimulating range of ideas of association does occur in his mind as compared to when he is in negative mood. As a consequence of such stimulation, the person is likely to combine these associations into a new pattern, providing evidence for creativity (Estrada, Isen and Young, 1995).

How is affect influenced by cognition?

Cognition is not only influenced by affect but it also influences our affect. One common way by which cognition influences affect is through our interpretation of emotion-provoking events. The famous cognitive arousal theory propounded by Schachter and Singer (1962) provides a good support for this. The theory clearly mentions that as a person makes cognitive interpretation of the physical arousal, he experiences emotion. For example, if a man experiences pleasant arousal in the presence of a physically attractive woman, it may be concluded that he is in love with her. Likewise, if a person feels increased arousal when his car is pushed from behind by some youngster's' motor cycle, then it may be concluded that what he felt is anger. In both examples, the cognitive interpretation of the arousal produces an emotion.

Another way in which cognition can influence emotions is by activating schemas containing a strong affective component. For example, suppose we label a person as politician. In such a situation, the schema for the category of politician suggests two things to us—first, what traits probably he possesses, and second, how we feel about the politician. If we have positive traits about the politician in our schema, we shall have positive feelings about the politician and if we have negative traits about the politician in schema, we shall be showing negative feelings about the politician.

Still another way in which cognition influences our affect involves our efforts to regulate emotions and feelings. One common technique of regulating our emotions or feelings is our *counterfactual thinking* in which we adjust our thoughts about the probability of negative events. As a consequence of this adjustment, negative events seem unavailable, and therefore, less distressing (Medvec and Savitsky, 1997). If a person compares his disappointing outcomes with something less favourable one or if he contemplates various ways in which the present disappointing results could have been avoided and positive ones could have been attained, he may experience a positive feelings of satisfaction or hopefulness. For example, if an Olympic athlete wins bronze medal and thinks that this is equivalent to have won no medal whatsoever, his level of dissatisfaction or negative feelings may be reduced and the positive feelings may be enhanced to some extent.

Another cognitive mechanism used for regulating feelings and emotions is to give into temptation. When we are distressed, we consciously choose to engage in activities that, while damaging in the long run, make us feel better in short run. A student failed in the examination, may accompany several negative thoughts and to ward off such feelings, he may resort to excessive smoking and drinking. Tice et al. (2000) explaining such a situation had pointed out that cognitive factors play an important role in such behaviour. Their explanation is that a person often consciously choose to yield to temptation at times when he experiences negative affect. This happens not in automatic manner or can be considered as a sign of weakness. In fact, it is a strategic choice made by the person. A person yields to temptation because in face of intense negative affect, he changes his priorities. Reducing the impact of negative outcomes comes on first priority or becomes the primary goal, and therefore, he does whatever it takes to achieve this goal. Tice et al. (2000) testified this explanation with the help of study in which they clearly found that the persons in bad mood caused by negative outcomes tended to procrastinate more but only when they believed that doing so would enhance their moods.

Conclusively, it can be said that our feelings and moods influence several aspects of cognition as well as cognition also influences our feelings and moods. The relationship between these two variables is two-way street (McDonald and Hirt, 1997).

FIELD OF INTERPERSONAL PERCEPTION: SOCIAL PERCEPTION AND PERSON PERCEPTION

Interpersonal perception is a new area of social psychology related to how people view one another. Studying interpersonal perception required an observation of at least two actual people. It examines the various types of judgements people make about others using both verbal and non-verbal cues. In a nutshell, interpersonal perception involves judgements that the perceiver makes about the target where target is a real person. Ordinarily, the perceiver and the target have a relational history (Kenny, 1994).

Social psychologists have paid attention to two major related areas of interpersonal perception—social perception and person perception. *Social perception*, which is more general than person perception, involves perception of social processes. The objects of social perception are the person's relations with others, including his perception of groups and social institution. In social perception, the objects are the person's social relations with others. In this way, social perception is broadly used to refer to the role of socially generated influences on the basic processes of perception. In nutshell, *social perception* refers to the processes through which a person seeks to know and understand other persons (Baron, Byrne and Branscombe, 2006). Since long social perception has been regarded as the base of understanding social thought and social behaviour.

Person perception refers to the manner in which impressions, opinions or feelings about other persons are formed. (Secord and Beckman, 1964). The basic assumption of person perception is that the perceiver may exist apart from and outside the world of the person being judged.

Thus, a person may judge the other person not through the direct sensory information, but on the basis of the statement given by others or based on the knowledge of who he is or on the basis of clues contained in a photograph in a film or through a sample of handwriting. He need not interact with others in order to make his judgement. Thus, in person perception, which is different from object perception, the perceiver focuses on specific traits to form an overall impression of others (Feldman, 1985).

Researches done in the field of person perception have revealed that there are following four fundamental points about person perception:

1. Persons are perceived at different levels of complexity, which vary from one person to another. For example, Mohan (perceiver) may classify Sohan in terms of his superficial characteristics, whereas Shyam may classify Sohan in terms of his less readily observable traits of personality.
2. Every perceiver has certain central traits or characteristics that he or she emphasises while perceiving others. The other person is always perceived and sized up with respect to the degree to which he possesses or lacks those central traits.
3. The centrality of traits in forming impression about others is probably a function of the perceiver's own personality.
4. Others are often described in relational terms, rather than in terms of abstract traits. It means that others are perceived in a way how other relates to the perceiver as well as to the other persons.

Researches have further shown that there are different modes of perceiving others. Important modes of person perception are as under:

1. A person is generally described in terms of outward appearance such as his body build-up, mannerisms, facial features, etc.
2. A person is described mostly in terms of central trait and its immediate implications. (Watkins and Pegnircioglu, 1984) For example, an extrovert person may be described as social, happy-go-lucky, caring for others, outspoken, taking interest in wider range of activities, etc. In fact, central traits serve to organise the impression and provide a general framework for interpreting information, which is received subsequently. In fact, Asch (1946), who first conceived of the notion of central traits, had pointed out that the meaning of additional descriptive terms is altered under the influence of central traits.
3. A person is generally perceived and described in terms of a cluster of congruous traits, that is, traits which seem to belong together. For example, a person having tall and muscular body build-up may be described as being aggressive, forceful and self-confident.
4. A person is also described in terms of varieties of traits, including some incongruous traits only. *Incongruous traits* are the traits which seem not to belong together. For example, a person may be described as being hard-working, honest and kind, but aggressive, suspicious and introverted.

Of these modes of person perception, most adults use less complex modes on some occasions and immature persons frequently fail to use the complex mode of person perception.

ROLE OF NON-VERBAL CUES IN PERSON PERCEPTION: FORMING IMPRESSION OF OTHERS

In social interaction, persons are often faced with situations having minimal information, minimal interaction and lack of defined and structured relations. In such a situation, they form impression about others on the basis of non-verbal cues provided by changes in facial expressions, eye contact, posture, body movements, and touching. The salient movement of body parts such as smiles, scowls, nods, gazing, gestures, leg movements, postural shifts, caressing, slapping, etc. all constitute *body language*. Since body language entails movements, it is also known as *kinesics* (from Greek word *kinein*, which means to move). The information converged by such cues and the person's efforts to interpret these inputs are technically called *non-verbal communication*.

Social psychologists have identified three primary reasons why person perception is formed on the basis of non-verbal cues:

1. In a face-to-face situation, where verbal behaviour of a person is readily observed, persons sometimes try to conceal true feelings or characteristics. Sometimes, non-verbal cues or behaviour may reveal these feelings and characteristics because such behaviour is irrepressible or difficult to control and even when the person tries to conceal their feelings, they often leak out their feelings in many ways through non-verbal cues (DePaulo et al., 2003).
2. In day-to-day situations, where stimulus information is very limited, non-verbal cues are used as a scientific basis of making judgement. In the absence of these non-verbal cues, the perceiver may draw erroneous conclusion. Geidt (1955) had conducted one study in which interview behaviour of the patient depicted in a silent film (that is, in the presence of non-verbal cues) was judged very differently as when the same behaviour was judged from sound film, where both verbal and non-verbal cues were present.
3. Forming information of others in limited situation with minimal interaction enables the investigators to identify those variables, which are generally obscured by the complexity of face-to-face situation.

Researches have revealed that six important non-verbal cues are generally most salient in person perception. These are being discussed here.

1. Facial expression

Many hundred years ago, Cicero, a Roman Orator, rightly remarked that the face is the image of the soul. Obviously, he meant by this statement that human emotions and feelings are often reflected by the face. Modern researches have confirmed the basic meaning of this statement of Cicero. Researches have revealed that six basic emotions such as fear, anger, happiness, sadness, surprise and disgust are clearly observed from the face of the persons (Izard, 1991, Rozin, Lowery and Ebert, 1994). However, regarding contempt, the agreement on what specific facial expression represents it, there is not much consistency. Figure 5.4 clearly reflects that six different types of emotions can be displayed from six different types of facial expressions.

Researches have also shown that emotions can occur in some combinations such as joy may be mixed with sorrow and surprise may be combined with fear. Evidences have provided support to the fact that facial expressions of fear, anger, disgust, sadness and happiness are universal, and therefore, recognised around the world (Ekman and Friesen, 1975). Contempt, surprise and interest may also be universal, but the investigators are less certain of these expressions (Ekman, 1993). Recent research findings have indicated that while facial expressions indeed reveal much about the emotions of a person, our judgement in such a situation also depends on the social context in which the facial expressions occur as well as on the various situational cues (Russell, 1994; Carroll and Russell, 1996). For example, among Chinese, sticking out the tongue is a gesture of surprise and not that of disrespect or teasing. If a person comes from Indian social context, he may easily misunderstand his or her facial expression. Likewise, Carroll and Russell (1996) conducted a study in which the participants were shown a photo of a face showing what would normally be judged as fear, but at the same time, they also read a story suggesting that the concerned person was really showing anger. Results revealed that in such situation, most of the participants described the face showing anger.

Figure 5.4 Six faces each showing six different types of emotions.

Besides these, cultural differences also exist in providing precise meaning of facial expressions. For example, in India, linguistic, religious, geographical and other factors are so diversified that it is very difficult to generalise the true meaning of facial expressions. Expression of emotion like *lajja* can vastly differ among various situation because *lajja* can be associated with different emotional experiences like shyness, shame, guilt, bliss, happiness, etc.

Physiognomy, the art of reading the faces, is really based on the important assumption that personality traits can be inferred from the facial features as well as from the expressions. For example, one study conducted by Secord and Muthard (1955) very clearly demonstrated that facial photographs of women who had narrowed eyes, a relax mouth, a smooth skin and considerable lipstick were perceived as more feminine and sexually attractive than the women who lacked such facial features. Likewise, Secord, Dukes and Bevan (1954) showed in their study that a man with a coarse oily skin, a dark complexion, heavy eyebrows as well as with straight mouth was perceived as quick-tempered, sly, hostile and conceited.

2. Eye contact

Generally, it is said that eyes are windows to the soul. This is really true when people interact with someone in a face-to-face situation, with gazes and stares. At the minimum, eye contact indicates interest or lack of it. We often learn more about the feelings and emotions of others from their eyes. For example, a high level of gazing from another person is taken to be a sign of positive feelings, friendliness or liking (Kleinke, 1986) and if someone avoids direct eye contact in the social interaction, it is generally concluded that he is shy, or unfriendly or has a little liking (see Figure 5.5).

Figure 5.5 Eye contact that displays liking.

Another form of eye contact is *staring*, where another person gazes upon us continuously and keeps on gazing regardless of what we do. A stare is often regarded as a sign of hostility or anger. When another person stares at us, it is very likely that we would terminate social interaction and also prefer to leave the place (Greenbaum and Rosenfield, 1978).

3. Gesture, posture and bodily movements

Gestures provide important information about the feelings and emotions of others. Many bodily gestures are widely accepted and convey specific information. Gestures for 'stop', 'come'. 'sit down', 'yes', 'no', 'go away' and 'good bye' are widely known. Gestures have meaning only when the perceivers and the participants understand the contexts, especially when they understand the culture. In Indian culture, when a person provides a gesture of simultaneously raised index figure and middle finger, it conveys the meaning of victory. Sweeping and expansive gesture may suggest force and vigour. Such gestures are called *emblems*, that is, body movements carrying specific meanings in a given culture. Figure 5.6 presents two gestures, which convey specific meanings in Indian culture, but their meanings may be nothing in some other culture or they may convey some different meanings in different culture. One study conducted by Schubert (2004) revealed that same gesture can have different meaning for women and men. For example, those gestures, which are associated with bodily force such as clenching action like clenched fist, indicate increased power or desire to obtain power, whereas for women such clenching action seems to indicate loss of power or much reduced hope to regain it. In sum, the meaning of gestures depends on the contest, on the person doing the action, on the culture as well as on the recipient of the communications.

Body posture also reveals feelings and emotions of the persons. Commonsense psychology suggests that a person with a slumped posture, who moves very slowly, may be perceived as dull, lifeless and depressed. Erratic movements may indicate nervousness. Sarbin (1954) conducted a very popular experiment in which body postures were represented by stick figures. These were such figures in which the neck, hands, limbs, trunk and feet were each represented by a single line and the head was represented by an oval shape. Results revealed that the participants demonstrated wider consensus in choosing terms representing some feeling, attitude or trait that seemed to be clearly suggested by the posture. Researches conducted by Ekman (1964) indicated that the body posture provides very useful cues for the judgement of the extent to which a person is relaxed or tense, whereas head provides cues about the pleasantness or unpleasantness of the feelings of the participants.

Figure 5.6 One person showing index and middle finger raised and another showing only thumb raised.

Body movements in which one part of the body does something to another part (such as rubbing, scratching, etc.) tend to suggest emotional arousal. Greater frequency of such behaviour indicates higher level of arousal. Researches have also shown that postures involving the whole body can also be informative. Tagiuri (1960) had conducted an experiment in which movement of the entire person along some particular path was investigated. Participants were presented line figures together with the information that they represented the path through which the person moved. They are asked to describe what kinds of person the line figure represented. In this experiment, one figure was a straight line, another was a regular curve and still another was a very erratic path. Results revealed that for many paths, the participants agreed upon the type of a person who might display such movement. For example, a straight and direct path was often described as a representative of a direct, straightforward and honest persons. A zigzag path was described as a characteristic of a vacillating, undependable and wavering person. Recently study conducted by Aronoff, Woike and Hyman (1992) also supported the fact that body postures provide important information about others' emotions and feelings. In their study, two groups of characters in classic ballet were identified. One group of character played dangerous or threatening role such as Macbeth, etc. and another group played warm, loving and sympathetic roles such as Romeo, Juliet, etc. Subsequently, the investigators proceeded to examine the examples of dancing by these characters in actual ballets to see if they adopted the same postures or different postures. Results revealed that characters playing dangerous or threatening roles tended to adopt angular or diagonal postures in their dances, whereas characters playing warm, affectionate and sympathetic roles exhibited rounded postures in their dances. Results confirmed the hypothesis that different body postures convey different types of emotions and feelings.

4. Body-build and physical appearance

Impression about the personality of others is also formed on the basis of body-build and physical appearances, although the validity of such inferences is questionable. Kretschmer (1925) had suggested that tall, lean and thin persons are usually sensitive, withdrawn and reserved, whereas short, and fat persons are sociable and forceful. He had based this suggestion on the observation that schizophrenics tended to be tall and thin, whereas manic-depressives tended to be short and fat. Sheldon, Stevens and Tucker (1940) as well as Sheldon and Stevens (1942) provided a different system of body-build and related it to personality. They suggested that there are three basic types of body-build—ectomorphic, mesomorphic and endomorphic and each is associated with different types of temperamental characteristics. For example, *endomorphs* (heavy and fat persons) were characterised as relaxed, slow to react and loving physical comfort; *mesomorphs* (persons with strong muscles and athletic build) were associated with energetic, enjoying exercise and assertive of some postures and movements and loving physical adventure. The *ectomorphs* (tall and thin persons) were imaginative, self-directed, introvert and disliking social activities.

Thus, some impression about other's personality is formed on the basis of his body-build and physical appearance, although there are psychologists who are very much apprehensive to such wider generalisations based on body-build.

5. Voice quality and dress

Variations in speech other than the actual verbal content, that is, words are called *paralanguage* and tend to carry great emotional meaning (Banse and Scherer, 1996). Certain qualities of voice have been found to be very much helpful in person perception. Vocal behaviour includes pitch, loudness, speed, emphasis, inflection, breathiness, stretching or clipping of words, pauses, etc. Voice qualities of loudness, pitch and stress usually express the emotional side of the communicator. Emotions have also been judged from the tonal qualities present in the pronunciation of letters of alphabet. (Dusenberry and Knower, 1939). Some researches have revealed that voice alone is enough to produce high degree of agreement among judges on the personality traits of the stimulus persons (Fay and Middleton, 1941). How a person is perceived depends also much upon in what ways he has dressed himself. Researches done by Stone (1959, 1962) clearly showed that a person is readily and variably perceived according to the clothing he wears.

6. Touching

Touching is also one of the important non-verbal cues through which we form impression about others. During conversation when one person touches the other person, what information will this behaviour convey to the person who has been touched? Its answer usually depends on three factors—first, *who did the touching* (a strange, a friend, same sex member, or opposite sex member, etc.); second, *the nature of the physical touching* (gentle or rough, brief or prolonged as well as what part of the body touched, etc.) and third, *context* in which touching took place (a social setting, doctor's room, etc.). Keeping in view all these factors, if touching is considered appropriate and justified, it produces positive feelings in person who has been touched (Smith, Gier and Willis, 1982). In most of the cases, if opposite sex friend touches for long in a situation considered appropriate, it indicates love and sexual interest of the person who is touching.

One of the most common form of touching prevalent in most cultures is handshaking. Varieties of beliefs exist about the meaning of handshake, depending on whether it is firm or limp, dry or damp. Chaplin et al., (2000) conducted a very interesting experiment. The study involved four trained coders (two women and two men). Each coder shook hands twice with 112 men and women and rated the participants on four different measures of personality. Results revealed that men or women with a firm handshake were rated by the coders as extroverted and also emotionally expressive. They were also given low ratings on shyness. Women who shook hands firmly were also rated as very open to new experience.

In sum, it can be said that in person perception, where one forms impression about others, various non-verbal cues are very much *helpful*, especially in those situations in which minimal information and minimal interaction take place.

RECOGNISING DECEPTIONS IN NON-VERBAL CUES

The common observation has been that the persons who are using non-verbal cues for conveying their feelings and emotions, sometimes use some deceptions. If we pay attention to certain non-verbal cues, we can easily recognise efforts at deception by others even in those situations, where these persons belong to the culture other than their own. Researches conducted by DePaulo et al., (2003) revealed that deception by others can, to a greater extent, be detected with the help of the following information:

1. Eye contact: Certain aspects of eye contact can easily reveal lying or some kind of deception on the part of communicator. For example, the persons who are lying often blink more and display more dilated pupils than the persons who are telling the truth. Generally, such persons avoid direct eye contact with the receiver of the communication, and sometimes quite surprisingly, they try to maintain high level of eye contact in order to make an attempt to take for showing honesty in the eyes of others.

2. Microexpressions: When emotion-provoking events occur, fleeting facial expression, which are difficult to suppress, are ordinarily reflected on the face of the communicators. Such expressions are called *microexpressions* and reveal communicator's true feelings or emotions. For example, if Shyam asks Mohan whether he likes his newly purchased car and after watching closely Mohan's face, he finds one *microexpression* such as frowning immediately followed by another microexpression such as smiling, it becomes an enough sign for the fact that Mohan is lying because he is expressing one opinion, whereas, in fact, he really has another.

3. Interchannel discrepancies: *Interchannel discrepancies* refer to inconsistencies among different channels or types of non-verbal cues. For example, if discrepancy occurs between facial expression (one channel) and body movements (another channel), it is assumed that the concerned person is showing deception or lying. For example, if someone showing facial expression for happiness for your work, has difficulty in looking straightforward into your eye (that is, unable to make eye contact), it means that he is telling lie. Likewise, someone attempting to convey the impression of warmth may smile and make eye contact, but leans away, rather than leaning toward the person with whom he is conversing (DePaulo, 1992). This obviously indicates that he is acting to show warmth, indicating a condition of deception.

4. Exaggerated facial expressions: Exaggerated facial expressions such as laughing more than usual in the situation or showing higher degree of sorrow in a given situation is a typical indication of the fact that the person is lying. For example, on the death of husband if a neighbour starts weeping and showing sorrow more than his wife or his members of the family, this becomes a sign of the fact that the neighbour is pretending to show sorrow, and therefore, he is using deception through his exaggerated facial expressions and related bodily movements.

Besides these non-verbal cues, linguistic style of the person also reveals deception. It has been commonly observed that when people are highly motivated to lie, pitches of their voice often rise. Likewise, they often take longer to respond to a question or describe any situation or event. Liars hesitate more and make more errors while speaking probably because they are all arousing to lie. Such persons are more likely to feel guilty and this explains why liars fidget more, speak more hesitatingly and less fluidly and make more negative statements than those who speak truth (Vrij, Edward and Bull, 2001). The voice tone of liars often seems negative. Not only that, they exhibit a strong tendency to start the sentences, stop them and again begin them. Besides, it has also been observed that when people are lying, they use different words as compared to when they are telling the truth (Vriz. et al., 2001). For example, when people are lying, they avoid using personal pronouns such as I, me, etc. Since such people have feeling of guilt, they prefer to use words that may reflect negative emotions. Words relating to simple actions such as go, walk, talk, etc. are used more frequently to describe the story, rather than more specific words like without, except, alternatively, but. Researches have further shown that women as compared to men seem to have an important edge with respect to non-verbal cues. In fact, they are better at both sending and interpreting such cues (Mayo and Henley, 1981; Rosenthal and DePaulo, 1979). This gives them important advantage in several situations and may account for our widespread belief in what is called *women's intuition*.

In day-to-day life, we have plenty of examples that show that lying is not only ethically wrong but also undermines the quality of social relations because it tends to spread from one person to another. Such effects may be a contributing factor to some kinds of scandals in various corporate sectors. Lying by top management in corporate sector may encourage unethical behaviour by many other, often with disastrous impact. In India, *Satyam scandal* is well-known in which the company's founder and chairman, Shri Ramalinga Raju resorted to overt lying, which threw the company into a big crisis.

IMPRESSION FORMATION

We get information about other people from various sources. We may read some facts about someone. We may get some information from third party. We have several occasion to observe and know about the behaviour of others. Irrespective of how we get information about others, we, as perceivers, try to find way for integrating these diverse facts into a coherent picture. The process of organising diverse information into a unified and gestalt impression of the other person is called *impression formation* (Delamater and Myers, 2009). It is considered fundamental to person perception.

In a classic experiment, Asch (1946), while developing a configural model, demonstrated that some traits have more impact than the others on the impressions we form about others. Such traits are said to have trait centrality. Asch, like other social psychologists of that time, was strongly influenced by gestalt psychology. One of the basic principles of gestalt psychology states that the whole is often greater than the sum of its parts, which obviously means that what we perceive is often more than the sum of the individual sensations. Applying this principle to the understanding of impression formation, Asch pointed out that a person does not form impressions simply by adding together all the traits he observes in other persons, rather he perceives these traits in relation to one another so that these traits cease to function individually and instead become the part of an integrated, dynamic whole. In this study, two groups of undergraduate students were given identical lists of seven traits describing about a stranger. Those traits were

First group: Intelligent, skillful, industrious, warm, determined, practical, cautious
Second group: Intelligent, skillful, industrious, cold, determined, practical, cautious

Obviously both groups received the list of same traits except that the trait *warm* was replaced by *cold* for the second group. All participants were then requested to write a brief paragraph indicating their impressions and completed a checklist to rate the stimulus person (stranger) on other characteristics such as wise, generous, happy, good-natured, humorous, sociable, popular, humane, altruistic and imaginative. Results revealed several interesting points, which are as under:

1. The participants experienced no difficulty in performing the task. They were able to arrange the trait information into a coherent whole and to construct a composite frame or sketch about the stimulus person.
2. Substituting the trait *warm* for the trait *cold* produced a larger difference in the overall impression formed by the participants. When the stranger was warm, the participants typically described him as happy, successful, popular and humorous. But when he was cold, they described the stranger as unsociable, unhappy and self-centered.
3. The words *warm* and *cold* had a larger impact than the other traits on the overall impression formed about the stranger or stimulus person. This was clearly demonstrated, for instance, by a variation in which Asch repeated the basic procedure of the previous experiment, but substituted the word *polite* and *blunt* in place of *warm* and *cold*, respectively. A comparison of the results showed that whereas describing the stimulus person as warm rather than as cold made a great difference in forming the overall impression about the stimulus person, describing the stimulus person as polite and blunt produced a little difference. Thus, in this study, the warm/cold trait displayed more centrality than the polite/blunt trait because the former produced larger differences in the participant ratings.

A follow-up study by Kelley (1950) confirmed Asch's findings. He replicated warm/cold findings in a realistic situation. Participants (students) in the class of Psychology course received trait description of a guest lecturer before he spoke in the class. The trait descriptions were similar to those used by Asch (that is, industrious, practical, skillful, intelligent, etc.), but differed regarding the warm/cold variable. Half of the students received trait descriptions that contained the word *warm* and the remaining half of the students received trait descriptions that contained the word *cold*.

Subsequently, the lecturer came to the class and led the discussion for about 20 minutes. Afterwards, the students (participants) were asked to report about their impression of the lecturer. Results revealed that those who had read the lecture as cold rated him as less considerate, popular, sociable, good-natured, humorous and humane than those who had read him as warm. Since all participants had seen the guest lecturer in the classroom, the differences in their overall impressions could stem only from the use of warm or cold in the profile they had read.

Several theories are available to account for why a single trait embedded in profile has such an impact in forming impression about others. One such theory is *implicit personality theory*, which refers to the beliefs of the person regarding what traits or characteristics tend to go together. In fact, these theories are a kind of specific schema (or mental map) and clearly suggest that when the person possesses some traits, they are likely to possess other traits as well. In the studies of Asch (1946) and Kelley (1950), the participants had a clear schema regarding what traits go with being warm and what traits go with being cold. Such schemas are commonly observed in many contexts of our life. For example, we expect the first-borns to be high achievers, and therefore, also intelligent, ambitious, independent and dominant. Likewise, we expect middle-borns to be friendly, outgoing, thoughtful and caring. The strength of these implicit beliefs about the effects of birth order has been well-illustrated in a study conducted by Herrera et al. (2003). The investigators asked participants to rate first-born, middle-born, last-born and only child as well as themselves on different trait dimensions such as bold-timid, agreeable-disagreeable, emotional-unemotional, creative-uncreative, extroverted-introverted, responsible-irresponsible, and so on. Results indicated that the first-borns were seen as being more intelligent, responsible, unemotional and stable ones; middle-borns were perceived as least bold and envious ones; last-borns were perceived as disobedient, emotional, irresponsible but creative ones and the only child was seen as being the most disagreeable and careless ones. Results clearly indicated that there existed a link between implicit beliefs and the important traits.

Implicit personality theories are clearly shaped by cultural variations. For example, in our culture, there is a prevalent implicit belief that physically attractive persons are also intelligent, and possess good social skills. Such beliefs may not be found in other culture.

INTEGRATING INFORMATION ABOUT OTHERS

In day-to-day life, we often receive a lot of information. New experiences with others typically add information to the impression we already have in our mind. In general, when forming impression of other, perceivers try to integrate information about many seemingly contradictory characteristics to create a unified and coherent impression of that individual (Asch and Zukier, 1984). How is this done? Social psychologists are of opinion that the various information are integrated in many ways that are described below:

1. Models of information integration

There are several models to explain how perceivers combine information about the stimulus person or the stranger. Asch's configural model, Anderson's cognitive algebra model, and Fiske and Nenberg's continuum model are the important ones. We have already discussed Asch's configural model. All these models are based on a key assumption—the most important aspect of a perceiver's impression of stranger or stimulus person is the overall positive or negative evaluation of that person. Two different models, that is, additive model and averaging model have emerged out of the large body of researches, concerning how several units of information are integrated into an overall impression (Anderson, 1968).

(i) **Additive model:** Additive model maintains that each unit of information is assigned a value and added in with others to produce an overall impression of the other person. For example, in order to apply additive model to predict how you feel towards a stranger, you may be asked to rate the value or importance of certain characteristics of the stranger. Using a scale of ±1 to ±10 (the scale is arbitrary), say for example, the perceiver gives the value to such traits like tolerant (+6), responsible (+7) and friendly (+5); so, his overall impression score will be equal to 6+7+5=18 (see Table 5.1; column I). When one more favourable trait, say sincere (+2) is added, his total overall impression score is enhanced to 20 (column II). Likewise, if some negative traits such as dishonest (–6) and stubborn (–4) are added, his overall total score comes down to –8 (column III) and if one more negative trait such as unimaginative (–2) is added, his total score is further reduced to –10 (column IV). Table 5.1 presents the additive model with four different combinations of traits. A very important feature of the additive model is that when we add traits with positive value, we tend to increase the favourableness of our overall impression, whereas when we add the traits with negative values, we decrease its favourableness.

Table 5.1 A Comparison of Additive Model and Averaging Model for Forming Impressions

	I	II	III	IV
Additive model	Tolerant (+6) Responsible (+7) Friendly (+5)	Tolerant (+6) Responsible (+7) Friendly (+5) Sincere (+2)	Attractive (+2) Stubborn (–4) Dishonest (–6)	Attractive (+2) Stubborn (–4) Dishonest (–6) Unimaginative (–2)
Overall impression score	+18	+20	–8	–10
Averaging model	Tolerant (+6) Responsible (+7) Friendly (+5)	Tolerant (+6) Responsible (+7) Friendly (+5) Sincere (+2)	Attractive (+2) Stubborn (–4) Dishonest (–6)	Attractive (+2) Stubborn (–4) Dishonest (–6) Unimaginative (–2)
Overall impression score	+6	+5	–2.67	–2.50

(ii) **Averaging model:** This model proposes that the ratings of the traits are averaged rather than summed. In averaging model, the impact of new information depends on whether this new information is more favourable or less favourable than the overall impression we already have in our mind. Consequently, incorporating a new, mildly positive trait (like sincere) into a strongly positive or favourable impression makes the resulting impression less positive (column I versus column II), whereas including a mildly negative trait (like unimaginative) to a strongly negative impression makes the resulting impression less negative (column III versus column IV).

Although the research evidences strongly indicate that people integrate information according to the demands of averaging model, there are a few studies that have reported support for the averaging model (Anderson, 1962; Fishbein and Hunter, 1964). Anderson (1974) made a review of a number of studies which compared and contrasted additive model and averaging model. Most of the studies have provided support for the averaging model. Thus, it seems that as an individual receives additional number of information about another, the units of information are averaged together to form an overall impression.

Although both additive model and averaging model make a definitive appeal, many empirical studies of impression formation today supports a third model, which is the refinement of averaging model and known as *weighted averaging model* (Anderson, 1981). According to this new model, perceivers no doubt average value of traits to form impression of others; they also give more weight to some information and less weight to some other information depending on the context in which impression is being formed. For example, if the stimulus person or the stranger is described as attractive, sincere, honest, armed and dangerous, it is very likely that the last two traits may overshadow the remaining traits and receive more weight in comparison to the other traits in the perceiver's evaluation of the stimulus person. Now, the question arises—what factors influence the weight assigning process done by the perceiver? Researches have revealed that the following six factors tend to influence the weight assigning process:

(i) Perceivers give more weight to those units of information which are received from credible sources and less weight to the information received from incredible sources.
(ii) Perceivers tend to give weight to those attributes or traits that pertain to the purpose or judgement at hand.
(iii) Perceivers give more weight to negative traits than to the positive traits because negative information is distinctive where individuals generally present socially desirable selves (Coovert and Reeder, 1990).
(iv) Perceivers tend to focus more on those elements or traits that stand out from the background and less in elements that mixes up with the overall situation.
(v) Perceivers give less weight to the information that is very inconsistent with past impressions or is superfluous with already known impressions.
(vi) Perceivers give weight to the first impression more heavily than the subsequent impressions.

Both the configural model of Asch (1946) and the cognitive algebra model of Anderson assume that the entire range of information about an individual is integrated in forming an impression about a person. However, they differ in how this integration is done. Asch, using a gestaltic perspective, proposed that in order to get a coherent whole, some aspects of the person have to be modified during the process of impression formation. He, therefore, emphasised that the meaning of individual features and their interrelationship with each other must be taken into account. In other words, this holistic model of Asch assumed that a global impression is formed about a person, and verbal evaluation influences how specific characteristics of the person are interpreted. Thus, Asch's interpretation constitutes *top-down information processing*. Anderson, on the other hand, proposed that the perceiver/observer assesses the implications of each known piece of information about the target person separately. Subsequently, the perceiver combines them algebraically into an impression. In other words, Anderson emphasised that the impression of an individual is formed by a mathematical integration of evaluative ratings of each trait associated with the target person. Anderson, thus, applied a *bottom-up processing*.

Asch's model and Anderson's model, though utilise a different process of information integration, are not conflicting rather complimentary (Pavelchak, 1989). This conclusion was based on a study especially designed to include both processes. In the first part of the study, participants were asked to rate 50 personality traits and 35 subjects (such as Economics,

Mathematics, English, and so on) on a scale of likeability. In fact, these were used for the purpose of comparison for the second part of the experiment, which was carried out a few days later. Subsequently, two groups of the same participants were formed—*piecemeal group* and *category group*. Participants of the piecemeal group were asked to rate their likeability for a target person described as studious, precise, bright and methodical (four traits), and then, were requested to suggest what subjects of study he (or she) might be taking. In category group, participants were asked to guess the subjects of the study first, and then, they were asked to make evaluation of likeability of the target person. The investigator's hypothesis was that if the participants make categorical-based judgement (based on Asch), the likeability of the ratings for the target person will match the likeability of the suggested subject study made in the first part of the experiment. On the other hand, if the participants make their piecemeal-based judgement (based on Anderson), then the evaluation of the person will match the average scores for those four traits used in the second part of the experiment. Results revealed that both these two different processes of information formation were operated in the experiment depending on the instructions received from the experimenter.

Fiske and Neuberg (1990) developed another model of information formation, named as *continuum model*. They developed this model believing that both Asch's model and Anderson's model could be complimentary to each other, depending on the context in which the impression is formed. According to continuum model, we initially categorise a person on the basis of information we have about him. For example, we may categorise a person on the basis of his gender, occupation, education, caste, etc. If we have no involvement with that person or the person is of little importance to us, the process of information process is unlikely to continue ahead. But if the person is relevant to us and we enter into social interaction with him, we pay more attention to the information we have got so far. This is then checked against the initial categorisation, and if found consistent, the confirmation of the initial impression is made.

If, however, the additional information is found inconsistent with the initial category level used, an alternative category is sought using a specific process of categorisation. If no suitable categories are available, a typical process of impression formation, that is, an attribute-focused piecemeal process starts. In continuum model, at the one end lies category-based processes (the initial categorisation) and at the other end lies attribute-focused processes (impression formed following additional information). In between these two ends of the continuum, there are category confirmation, recategorisation and piecemeal integration depending on the situational requirements (see Figure 5.7).

When the observer has little time or motivation to attend further information, category-based impression takes priority. On the other hand, when the observer has sufficient time as well motivation to attend further available information, or when situation demands accurate impression, a piecemeal-based process is started because in such situation, inconsistent information may be present. Here, a balanced view and variable weightings attached to a particular trait are needed to make an accurate judgement. From Figure 5.7, it is obvious that after getting information about the target person, the observer makes initial categorisation such as male, female, American or African, etc. According to the model, the person always proceed in terms of serial step-by-step manner with category-based process first in an automatic way. But if he applies attribute-based processing because he is either highly motivated or nature of attributes or traits is such that it resists recategorisation of the individual as belonging to any particular group, the process of forming impression about the target person proceeds ahead. A piecemeal integration of all available information is ultimately done if the information meant for recategorisation fails to identify appropriate category. If the analysis of other available information is found consistent with the category label, initial categorisation is upheld.

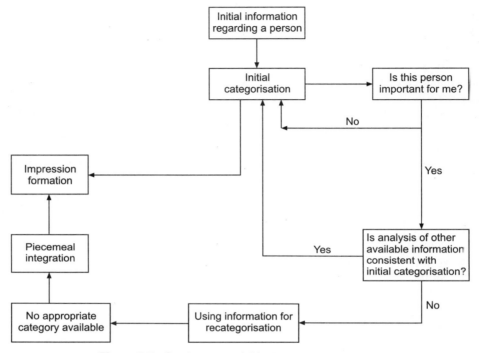

Figure 5.7 Continuum model for impression formation.

Making use of further developments in cognitive processing, Kunda and Thagard (1996) developed an alternative model, named as *parallel-constraint-satisfaction model*. According to this model, in forming impression instead of serial processing, both category-based or stereotypical information and individuating information are processed simultaneously and both have more or less equal impact upon the final impression. Kunda and Thagard had based this interpretation on an earlier research done by Duncan (1976), who had examined the effects of stereotypes by interpreting the behaviour of the target person observed elbowing another person. He reported that when this behaviour was done by a black person, it was considered as violent push and when this was performed by a white person, it was perceived as a jovial push. How can it be interpreted this with the help of parallel-constraint-satisfaction model? Following this model, Kundra and Thagard argued that when a white person sees that a black person pushes somebody, it tends to activate both violent push as well as jovial push. The stereotypical belief about black people in the minds of whites activates 'aggressive' (attribute), which in turn, activates violent push and deactivates jovial push. On the other hand, if a white person observes another white person pushing somebody, it does not activate 'aggressive', which automatically means that violent push is deactivated and jovial push is activated. Thus, it is obvious that stereotypes do not always dominate impression formation as serial models say, rather both individuating information and stereotypical information operate simultaneously in forming impression.

2. Negativity effect

The observation has been that we tend to pay special attention to negative or potentially threatening information. When we come to form an overall impression of the other person, the negative information is weighed more heavily (Taylor, 1991; Yzerbyt and Leyens, 1991). That is, everything being equal, negative information affects an impression more than the positive trait (Vonk, 1993). The explanation for this negativity effect is that such units of information are more unusual and distinctive.

3. Positivity bias

People tend to perceive other people more often positively than negatively. This is called *positivity bias*. Sears (1983) conducted a study in which students rated 97% of their professors as favourable, despite the fact that they had mixed experiences in their classes.

Positivity bias and negativity effect work together in forming the overall impression. People generally act in a good way towards each other. Negative information, which initially attracts attention, often leads us to ignore people. People who are optimistic display a stronger attentional bias for positive stimuli relative to negative stimuli, and in forming the overall impression, they exhibit more positivity bias.

4. Imputing consistency

In forming the overall impression, even in the situation where the observer has a very few pieces of information, he tends to impute consistency in the characterisation of others. Due to this tendency, we tend to categorise people as good or bad, social or unsocial, etc. We then go on to perceive other traits consistent with this basic evaluation. Such tendency towards evaluative consistency is known as *halo effect*. For example, if the person is categorised as good, he is also perceived as intelligent, social, generous, etc. If he is categorised as bad, he may be perceived as ugly, dull, inept, etc.

5. Resolving inconsistencies

Sometimes, we have internally inconsistent information about the other. In such a situation, we try to resolve inconsistencies while forming the overall impression about the other. Let us take an example. You may be told that Amitabh is a kind, social and sincere person. But at the same time, one of your friends may tell you that Amitabh is unsocial, irresponsible and conceited. How are these internally incongruent units of information incorporated into the overall impression?

Negative information causing incongruency is not soon forgotten, rather such impressions are often remembered. This happens because for integrating incongruent information into the overall impressions, the person has to do a lot of cognitive exercises. He has to think about why incongruent information occurred, whether friend's report is trustworthy, whether Amitabh really behave that way, etc. Thus, for understanding incongruent information, people has to go through the complicated process. As a result of this complicated process, it comes to play a more important role in forming the overall impression in comparison to the units of information consistent with the already held information (Hastie and Kumar, 1979). When the person is made cognitively too busy with the other tasks to make inconsistent information more comprehensible, the bias for remembering inconsistent information is eliminated (Macrae et al., 1999). Researches have further shown that when traits or items of information are only mildly incongruent with each other, they are easy to integrate in forming the overall information (Hampson, 1998) and when they are extremely incongruent, and therefore, difficult to reconcile with each other, people sometimes leave them unintegrated and that way, recognise the incongruency (Casselden and Hampson, 1990).

The relative impact of positive and negative information was also explored in Singh and Teoh's (2000) study. Participants were required to make judgements about the intellectual and social attractiveness of the target person from a pair of moderate as well as extreme intellectual and social traits. Results revealed that positive intellectual and negative social traits received more weight in the intellectual and social attractive responses, but the negative moderate traits received more weight in social attraction.

Researches have revealed that when we receive contradictory and inconsistent information about others, it provides challenges to two basic social motives—our sense of mastery and understanding is threatened by the unexpected information (particularly by negative information) and our ability to maintain social relationship with the person is thrown into doubt. When we try to reconcile the inconsistent and contradictory information, it has several impacts on our cognitive processes, including memory (Smith and Mackie, 2007), which are mentioned below:

(i) People generally take more time for thinking about negative information than about the positive information.
(ii) People try to explain negative information so that some meaning may be derived.
(iii) Extra processing and time improves people's ability to recall inconsistent or contradictory information.

6. First impression versus latter impressions

The common belief is that the first impression is comparatively more important and has an enduring impact in forming the impression of other. In fact, this belief has been supported by many empirical researches. Observers who form an impression of others give more weight to the information received early in sequence than to the information received later in sequence. This is called *primacy effect* (Luchins, 1957a). In one pioneer classic study conducted by Asch (1946), the primacy effect was tested and confirmed. In this study, a set of six descriptive traits was presented to a group of participants with positive traits first like this—intelligent, industrious, impulsive, critical, stubborn and envious. The participants of second group received the same set of traits in the reversed order—envious, stubborn, critical, impulsive, industrious and intelligent.

All participants then wrote a brief description of the concerned person and checked a list of personality traits for the ones they believed the person possessed. Results indicated that when the positive traits were given first (as was done in case of first group), a more favourable impression was formed as compared to when the negative traits were given first (as was done in case of second group). Thus, primacy effect clearly occurred in Asch's experiment.

The primacy effect in real life is very obvious, as careful management of initial information can readily influence people to form and maintain particular impression of another. Researches have revealed that the primacy effect has been found to occur even when the later information is contradictory or inconsistent with the early information. Luchins (1957b) conducted one study in which the participants were given two paragraphs describing about a young adult. One paragraph described the adult with extroverted traits like being friendly, social, outgoing and confident man. Another paragraph described the same young adult with introverted traits like preferring loneliness, being unfriendly availing social encounter, etc. Half of the participants were first given extroverted paragraph, and then, were given introverted paragraph. Remaining half of the participants were first given introverted paragraph, and then, were given the extroverted paragraph. After reading the two paragraphs, the participants were asked to describe the adult using both sets of information. Results revealed that those participants who were exposed to the extroverted paragraph first described the young adult as friendly, social, likable and outgoing in spite of latter information being contradictory one. Likewise, an introverted description emerged from the participants who had gone through the introverted paragraph first. Results provided support for the emergence of primacy effect despite the latter information being contradictory one.

What accounts for primacy effect? There are several explanations available. One explanation of the primacy effect is Asch's *change of meaning theory*, which states that the first information creates an initial impression, which has an impact upon the interpretation of latter information in such a way that it makes it consistent with our initial impression. Another explanation is that we attend very carefully to the first units of information we get about the other, but we pay less attention to the latter additional information. We consider the first units of information sufficient enough for making a judgement. It is not that we interpret latter information differently, rather we simply use it less. The basic assumption behind such explanation is that whatever information we attend first has the biggest impact on our impressions (Dreben, Fiske and Hastie, 1979).

Although primacy effect is a common phenomenon, sometimes, it does not occur and rather its opposite state occurs. There are conditions or situations in which the most recent information that we acquire, exerts the biggest and the strongest influence upon the overall impression formation. This is technically called *recency effect* (Steiner and Rain, 1989). A recency effect generally occurs when pretty time has passed and the person has forgotten his first impression or when the person judges characteristics like moods or attitudes that have changed over the time. Some attempts have been made by social psychologists to induce recency effect in laboratory setting by asking participants to make a separate evaluation after each new unit of information is received (Stewart, 1965).

Researches have revealed that if both primacy effect and recency effect become the basis of forming impression of others, it is the primacy effect which is especially important both in real life situation as well as in laboratory settings. Jones et al., (1968) conducted one study in which the relative impact of primacy effect and recency effect on impression formation was examined. In this study, participants observed the performance of a confederate in a SAT-type aptitude test. Half of the participants observed a confederate solving the first few puzzles, thus suggesting intelligence, but facing difficulty in solving the latter puzzles. The other half of the participants witnessed another confederate doing poor while solving the first few puzzles, thereby suggesting poor intelligence, but solving the latter puzzles in a better way. Reality was that in both conditions the confederate had solved exactly the same number of puzzles. The only difference was that in one case, success was at the start and in other case, the success came at the end. Despite these, participants rated the confederate as more intelligent when he started well and then tailed off than when he started poorly and then did well. Clearly, the participants gave more weight to the confederate's performance on the first few puzzles—a primacy effect.

7. Schemas

Generally, we process and form impression about others using stereotypes or preconceptions we hold about the categories that define the people. Technically, these stereotypes are called *schema* (plural-schemata or schemas), which is an organised, structured set of mental framework, including some knowledge about the category, which helps us in organising social information and processing such information. Several types of schemas have been considered important in person perception, that is, in forming impression of others.

Person schemas are one popular type. These are cognitive structures that describe the personalities of other individuals. One type of person schemas focuses on one particular type of a person such as Mrs. Indira Gandhi, Dr. Rajendra Prasad, etc. The schemas about such personalities may include as being honest, serious about duties and responsibilities, concerned for the welfare of the people, etc. Some person schemas focus on the other types of people. One schema for the introvert might include elements like preferring loneliness, avoiding social contact, preferring imaginative thinking, self-centered, etc. All these schemas help us in gathering information and forming an overall information about the others.

There are other schemas which focus on groups. The most common is *group stereotype*, which is defined as a set of characteristics attributed to all members of some specified group or social category (McCauley, Stitt and Segal, 1980). Just like the other types of schemas, stereotypes also tend to simplify the complexities of the social world. Rather than treating every member of the group individually, stereotypes encourage the person to think about and treat all doctors, engineers, politicians, etc. in the same way. Thus, stereotypes help us in forming impression about another and in predicting his/her behaviour with minimal information that he or she belongs to a particular category or group.

8. *Prototypes*

When we form impression about others, we often utilise prototype of the schema. The *prototype* is defined as an abstract ideal of the schema (Taylor, Peplau and Sears, 2006). Usually, prototypes are specified in terms of a set of attributes or characteristics. In forming impression of others, these abstractions are brought to mind and are used as a basis for the decision. For example, we have some ideal abstractions about a police officer—type of physical characteristics a police officer possesses and the typical ways of behaving by a police officer, etc. When we categorise a new person as police officer, we bring all these abstractions in our mind and compare his attributes with these abstractions and then take a decision.

9. *Exemplars*

Most social psychologists today agree that forming impression of others involves not only prototypes or ideal abstractions but also the *exemplars*—concrete examples of behaviours that they have performed and we have actually encountered. For example, if you are evaluating a new person as police officer, you compare the person not only with the prototype for an ideal police officer but also with a particular past police officer who had put you in trouble or had protected you from the trouble. Keeping in view the exemplars, you form an impression about that new person.

Researches have revealed that when the person has very little information, he is most likely to use prototype in forming impression of others. When we have a little more information, the person generally uses both prototypes and exemplars in forming impression (Linville, Fisher and Salovey, 1989). For categories or persons about which we have plenty of information, we are likely to use our more well-developed and formed schemas (Sherman and Klein, 1994).

Social Cognition, Social Perception and Attribution

Thus, we see that in forming impression of others, we tend to integrate different types of information about categories or persons with the help of various factors.

IMPRESSION MANAGEMENT

Impression management (or also known as *self-presentation*) is something in which we keep ourselves engaged throughout the lives. It can be defined as a deliberate effort to make a good impression on others. Here, the person deliberately makes an attempt to act in such ways that may create good impression of the self on others. Such persons who successfully do impression management, tend to gain advantages in many situations (Wayne and Linden, 1995; Sharp and Getz, 1996).

Perhaps the most common motive of self-presentation or impression management is to make a good impression (Schlenker, 1980). This is done by adopting several tactics of successful impression management (Fiske and Taylor, 1991). Social psychologists have called this *tactical impression management*, where the persons try to present themselves in such a way so as to create a false, exaggerated or misleading images in the minds of others. Such important tactics or techniques are as under:

1. Self-promotion

Self-promotion refers to conveying positive information about oneself to others either through one's actions or through telling some positive things about the self. This technique is also known as *self-enhancement technique* (Baumeister, 1998). In such technique, a person makes efforts to increase his appeal to others. He may try to boost his physical appearance through style of dress, personal grooming and bearing particular type of eye glasses that tend to enhance impression of being an intelligent person. He may also describe himself in positive terms.

However, self-enhancement can sometimes be tricky. Telling about one's achievement can enhance the impression management, but it can also backfire and may create impression that one is conceited (Cialdini and De Nicholas, 1989; Jones and Pittman, 1982). The chief reason is that the observers often evaluate a person on more than one dimension at the same time. The self-promoter may convince others that he is intelligent and competent, but may also display egotism. Still another technique of self-enhancement is the careful use of modesty (Cialdini and De Nicholas, 1989). For example, the captain of cricket team, whose brilliant plays have just saved the team from losing championship, may describe his performance as better one and emphasise that he could not have done it without the true support of the entire team.

Researches have shown that people engage in self-promotion not only by the act they do but also by associating with the people who are successful, powerful or very famous. In fact, such people bask in the reflected glory of others. Cialdini and De Nicholas (1989) have used the term *birging* to refer to such tendency of the people. People enhance their individual self-presentation by highlighting their associations with the powerful or famous person, even when their associations may be trivial ones. For example, if a person tells us that he comes from the same village to which the first Indian President Dr. Rajendra Prasad belonged, then he is definitely trying to impress us by his indirect association with this famous and powerful personality.

The cases of successful impression management through which marginalised person gained position of power in Indian context are a few cases of *eunuchs* (popularly called as *hijras*), who rose to good political position. *Hijras* are considered as social parihas in India and are stigmatised on the basis of their apparently transgressive gender identification. History of Indian politics shows that in the past decades or so, some *hijras,* through successful impression management by presenting themselves as people who can rise above the caste, religion, corruption and nepotism typical of Indian politicians, have been elected to public office at the local or state level, defeating candidates from national political parties like Congress (I) and Bharatiya Janata Party (BJP). Besides, there have also been examples where total votes obtained by eunuchs were greater than the total combined votes obtained by Congress (I) and BJP. In fact, starting phase of putting *hijras* as the electoral rolls as in case of Sohagpur constituency in Madhya Pradesh was simply regarded as joke by politicians. But later on, they were themselves surprised by the trend of voting. A recent film *Welcome to Sajjanpur* portrays eunuch character of *Munnibai,* who contests elections and wins from a male-dominated village in India, also shows how can a marginalised person gains position of power through successful impression management.

Researches bear testimony to the fact that an important factor in self-enhancement is the context in which people talk about themselves. In fact, the context of the conversation makes a crucial difference in how the observers interpret self-promoting statements. Holtgraves and Srull (1989) conducted an experiment in which they compared the impression of people who made positive statements about their intellectual ability under different conditions. People who mentioned their intellectual accomplishment in response to some specific questions raised by the observers were able to create a more favourable impression in comparison to those people who talked about their intellectual accomplishment without being asked anything regarding it. In contrast, such people who went out of their way to tell about their intellectual accomplishment were perceived as less considerate, less likeable, and more egotistical.

2. Other-enhancement

Other-enhancement is the opposite of self-enhancement or self-promotion. Here, efforts are made by the person to make the observer or target person feel good in various ways. Thus, here, a person tries to create positive mood or reactions in others.

One common technique of other-enhancement is *ingratiation*, where the person tells all positive things about the listeners (Kilduff and Day, 1994) and attempts to increase target person's liking for himself (Wortman and Linsenmeir, 1977). Certain preconditions tend to increase ingratiation. Persons may try to ingratiate themselves when they somehow depend on the target person for certain benefits and somehow assume that the target person is more likely to grant those benefit to the others whom he likes. Researches have shown that people are more likely to use ingratiation tactics when the target person is perceived to exercise his discretion in distributing rewards or benefits (Jones et al., 1965).

Flattery is one of the popular techniques of ingratiation. In order to be effective, flattery should not be careless or indiscriminate. The popular belief is that people are best flattered in those areas, where they wish to excel and are not sure about this. This hypothesis was tested by Michener, Plazewski and Vaske (1979) in their study in which female participants were told that their supervisor valued either efficiency or sociability. The supervisor was the target of ingratiation because his positive evaluations might increase the earnings of the participants. Before their supervisor made the evaluations, participants were given opportunity to flatter him. In other words, the experimenters asked the participants to rate the supervisor's efficiency and sociability and told them that supervisor would see these ratings. Results revealed that those who believed that the supervisor valued efficiency publicly rated him high on efficiency than on sociability, whereas those who believed that the supervisor values sociability publicly rated him higher on sociability than on efficiency. Results confirmed the hypothesis formed in the beginning.

Gordon (1996) showed through his study that the targets of flattery are more likely to believe it and to like the flatterer than the observers. Several experiments were conducted to know about the plausible reasons. That is, vanity of the target, reduced ability to make accurate attributions or the desire to show liking for others account for the reactions of the target person. Results showed that it is the target's vanity which counts much more than the other factor, that is, people like to be evaluated positively (Vonk, 2002).

Other enhancement technique also incorporates several different types such as expressing agreement with the view of the target person (opinion conformity), doing small favour for him, asking for his advice and feedback in some manner (Morrison and Bies, 1991) and convincing the target that he is needy and deserving (supplicate). Wayne and Ferris (1990) had also reported that when the person tries to express liking for the target person through high level of eye contact, nodding in agreement, and smiling, this also helps in creating positive moods and reactions in the target person. In supplication, the person tries to convince the target person that he is really needy and deserving (Baumeister, 1998). This tactic is often used by roadside beggars. By dressing in ragged clothes, they convey to the passer-by that they are in need for money. While some people choose to use this tactic, others are forced to do so to get benefit from government and non-governmental organisations. Students sometimes use this tactic in order to influence the teacher for changing their grade, and therefore, they are often found saying, "But I did really hard labour and I know a lot more than what was asked in the examination."

Downside of Impression Management

Researches have shown that these techniques of impression management work effectively, provided they are used carefully (Witt and Ferris, 2003). However, use of tactics of impression management is accompanied by some limitations as under:

1. If the techniques of impression management are overused or are not used with caution, or used ineffectively, it can boomerang adversely and may create negative opinions rather than positive ones in the target person. Vonk (1998) reported that such persons in work setting, who show tendency to lick upward but kick downward, that is, who praises their superiors but treat their subordinates with contempt and disdain, produce negative rather positive opinions in others. She has termed this tendency as *slime effect*.
2. Impression management involves both verbal and non-verbal behaviour. In general, impression management becomes less convincing when there occurs discrepancy in verbal and non-verbal behaviour. For example, a person who says he is very happy in a depressed and glum tone of voice is not very convincing and credible.
3. Impression management or self-presentation may be dangerous to the physical health. In fact, many risky behaviours result, in part, from the desire to make a favourable impression on others. In order to look slim and physically attractive, people often resort to dieting, which may be hazardous to our health. Likewise, taking alcohol, tobacco and drug use as well as excessive use of steroids by athletes are commonly done in our society to impress others. All these practices prove hazardous to health in the long run. Numerous adolescents die

every year as a result of showing off whether by driving recklessly or diving into water. Take the example of teenage pregnancy, which is being rampant in the so-called modern society. Such pregnancy can be easily prevented by the use of condoms. Why don't such sexually active young people use condom? Researches have indicated that self-presentational concerns are major cause (Leary et al., 1994). Some young males and females are afraid to buy condom because others may infer that they are sexually active. Likewise, some males and females are afraid to suggest condom use because they fear that it might suggest that their partners are unfaithful.

4. Tactical self-presentation may also be hazardous to our social relationship. Generally, it has been found that we tend to engage in what is called selective self-presentation, that is, we tend to enhance our positive features and withhold information that may create negative impression. This happens most frequently in romantic relationship. This is done for the obvious purpose of preserving the romantic relationship. Cole (2001) conducted a study on 128 heterosexual couples and found that many males and females made such selective self-presentations, that is, misleading communication (such as lying) with their partners for such purposes. These behaviours are also guided by norm of reciprocity in withholding information and intentionally using misleading communication in romantic relationship. These behaviours, motivated by a wish to preserve the relationship, may lead to downward spiral and eventual dissolution of the much desired romantic relationship.

Thus, tactical self-presentation concerns can also tax us in varieties of ways.

SELF-PERCEPTION

Schachter's work on emotions had very clearly revealed that a person can use the combination of internal arousal and situational cues to make inference about the nature of emotional state. What other sources of information can be used to come to the conclusion that what we are like? One possible answer is our own behaviour. This is called *process of self-perception*, where one perceives and reacts to oneself. The very idea that one perceives oneself in very much the same fashion that he perceives other is by no means a new idea. William James (1890) had written extensively about self as an object of knowledge. Later on, Charles Cooley (1902) propounded several ideas about how the perception of oneself arose out of the social origins. He suggested that one perceives oneself as he might perceive his image in a mirror and he named this conception as *looking-glass self*. George Mead (1934) later on modified and developed the idea of looking-glass self by proposing that one manages this reflexive look at oneself basically by taking the role of others. Thus, in stepping into the shoes of another person, a person is enabled to look back upon himself in the same way as he might regard any other person as a social object.

Although these early ideas of Cooley and Mead had been formulated in most general terms and were not submitted directly for experimental verification, they definitely provided an important foundation for later expansion of scientific knowledge about self-perception. Bem (1972) had proposed a theory of self-perception, which clearly relates to the attributions people make about the meaning of their own behaviour. According to Bem, the individuals become aware of their own attitudes, emotions, dispositions and other internal states in the same way they learn about other people, that is through the observation of behaviour. The theory very clearly suggests that if situational cues or past experiences are irrelevant or weak to a greater extent, after viewing one's own behaviour, a person applies the same attributional principles which are used in the attributions of others to identify the causes of the behaviour done by himself. Let us take an example to illustrate this fact. Suppose you observe that a person is helping a pretty old person in crossing a very busy road. This observation leads you to reasonably conclude that the person (or helper) is altruistic or at least very favourably disposed to that old person. Now, suppose further that person is no one but you yourself and helping the old man in crossing the busy road. When you try to analyse your own behaviour, Bem's theory would tend to predict that you would be making the same kind of attribution about your own behaviour and also, that you are altruistic and display positive attitude towards that old person.

In a nutshell, Bem's theory of self-perception definitely indicates that people tend to apply the same kind of attribution to their own behaviour that they use for others. Through such process, they are able to understand and infer about how they feel and why they have carried out certain actions.

ATTRIBUTION: UNDERSTANDING THE CAUSES OF OTHERS' BEHAVIOUR

The term *attribution* refers to the process through which the observer infers the causes of another's behaviour (Delameter and Myers, 2009). More formally, attribution means our efforts to understand the causes of others' behaviour, and on some occasion, the causes of our own behaviour as well (Baron, Byrne and Branscombe, 2006). Generally, in attribution, a person observes another's behaviour and goes backward to locate its causes in terms of intentions, abilities, traits, motives and situational pressures. When the observer attributes others' behaviour in terms of internal state of the person who did it, it is called *dispositional attribution*. On the other hand, when the observer attributes others' behaviour in terms of person's situation or environment, it is called *situational attribution*. Let us take an example. Suppose an observer comes to know that his friend is still unemployed. The observer might judge that his friend is unemployed because he is lazy, irresponsible and lacks proper aptitude and abilities. This is an example of dispositional attribution. On the other hand, he might judge that his friend is unemployed because there is lesser employment opportunities in his line of work as well as due to the depressed economy of the country. This is an example of situational attribution. Likewise, a teacher in the class may wonder whether a child's poor academic performance is due to lack of motivation and ability (a dispositional attribution) or due to physical and social situations (a situational attribution).

Now, one important question is—what determines whether an observer attributes the behaviour of others in terms of disposition or in terms of situation? Social psychologists agree that in an attempt to answer this question, one has to consider the strength of situational pressures on the person. These pressures may include role pressures as well as rewards and punishments applied to the persons by others in the given environment. For instance, suppose we observe that a judge awards death penalty to a criminal. The observer might infer that the judge is tough and hard-hearted (dispositional attribution). However, suppose the observer come to learn that state law requires that for the crime done, death penalty should be imposed. Now, the observer would see the judge as not tough as responding to the role pressures (situational disposition). Nowadays, this logic has been formalised in terms of a *subtractive rule*, which mentions that when making attributions about personal dispositions, the observer subtracts the perceived impact of situational forces from the personal disposition implied by the behaviour itself (Trope and Cohen, 1989). In the above example, following subtractive rule, the observer must subtract the effect of situational pressures (state law) from the disposition conveyed by the behaviour itself. After during this, he may conclude that the judge is not especially tough or very much inclined to impose death penalty.

THEORIES OF ATTRIBUTION

Attribution theories focus on the processes we use to infer causes of another's behaviour and its sources (Lipe, 1991). In other words, *attribution theory* is the study of processes a person employs in linking the events (behaviour) with their underlying conditions (causes) (Heider, 1958). The person links the behaviour of another person to the underlying conditions in an effort to understand why that person has acted in a particular way and to predict how he or she will act in future. The underlying causes may be either the personal characteristics (dispositional attribution) or the environmental conditions (situational attribution). Behaviour caused by personal characteristic is perceived as internally caused and behaviour linked to the environmental conditions is seen as being externally caused.

Before going to the details of theories of attribution, it is important to give a look at the underlying fundamental concepts, when we are most likely to make attribution and when attributions are made either spontaneously or after deliberations. In fact, the conceptual foundation on which theories of attribution were developed, was provided by Heider (1944). He had offered three basic principles, which underlies all theories of attributions. These are as follows:

1. Behaviour is perceived as being caused.
2. Perceptions regarding causation are important.
3. Locus of cause(s) of behaviour is perceived to be with the person, the situation or a combination of both.

Regarding the first point, we attribute causes to virtually all behaviour. Everything that others do or are done by ourselves is believed to be caused by one or a number of specific causes. The second point relates to how behaviour is perceived to be caused rather than how it is actually caused. This is of great interest to the attribution theorists. As we know that different people with different perspectives may offer different causal attributions for the same behaviour. Attribution researchers are concerned to find out if there are distinct patterns in the different ways in which people, from different perspectives, attribute causes to behaviour. The third point relates to the fact that people attribute causes to person or situation or a combination of both. When causes are attributed in terms of personality traits, motives, interactions (all internal over which the person has some control), it is called *internal attribution*. When causes are attributed in terms of situation or environment over which person has a little control or no control, it is called *external attribution*. Theories have been developed to predict when people make internal attributions and when they make external attributions. However, the internal-external distinction is relative and not absolute one (Ross, 1977). Let us take an example to illustrate this relative distinction. Suppose Abhishek has bought a house. One person may say that he has bought the house because it (house) was so secluded or isolated. It means that he has bought the house because there was something about the house itself, which attracted him to purchase it (external attribution). Another person may say that he has bought the house because he liked privacy, which automatically emphasises that Abhishek's need for seclusion caused him to buy the house (internal attribution). Here, the point to be noted is that external attribution implies that the house is secluded, whereas the internal attribution implies that Abhishek likes privacy. Thus, an internal attribution may then have external implications and vice versa. Researchers in the field of attribution theories are facing the problem of locating when people prefer internal attributions and when they prefer external attribution. This problem gets further augmented due to the fact that in some context, they use both types of attributions.

Another fundamental concept in attribution theories relates to the basic question—when are attributions made? Weiner (1985) examined this problem in detail and came to the conclusion that there are two main conditions under which people are most likely to make attributions.

1. When something unexpected or surprising happens, we are most likely to make attribution. For example, when a person finds that his best and most dependable friend starts behaving like an enemy, this will naturally surprise him and he will make attribution for such behaviour of his friend.
2. When the person fails to get the desired outcome (such as fails to pass an examination), he is likely to make attribution.

Besides these conditions, a person is also likely to make attribution when he is in bad mood or experiencing negative emotion (Bohner et al., 1988)

Still another fundamental concept in attribution theories relates to spontaneous attribution versus deliberate attribution. The common observation has been that at times, we may offer spontaneous causal attributions, whereas at other times, attributions are made after proper deliberation, thought and gathering of information. Gilbert (1989) did extensive research in these two general types of attributions and developed what is popularly called *two-stage model*. According to Gilbert's two stage model, spontaneous and initial reactions are distinguished from the responses resulting from deliberation. In the *spontaneous stage*, the behaviour, person and situation are categorised and identified and whatever immediate information are available, they are used for making an attribution. For example, if Mohan is showing a very irritable behaviour at work and is in bad mood, one can attribute this to either the stressful work (external attribution) or to his moody and emotional nature (internal attribution). This example clearly shows that we try to interpret ambiguity to make an external or internal attribution. When one engages in unambiguous behaviour such as making overt aggressive behaviour, usually here, internal attribution is made. Jones (1990) showed that spontaneous attributions, most of the time, are dispositional (rather than situational).

When situation does not permit spontaneous attribution as is the case when behaviour done by the target person is vague, ambiguous and unexpected, the *deliberate stage* starts. Here, at this stage, same additional units of information about the vague behaviour are collected such as how that person behaves at different times, how some other people behave in that situation, etc. All such additional units of information are used to adjust the initial and spontaneous attribution made earlier.

There are different models or theories of attribution. Important ones are as under:

1. Heider's naive psychology attribution theory
2. Jones and Davis' correspondent inference attribution theory
3. Kelley's model of causal attribution
4. Shaver's attribution model
5. Weiner's attribution model

Heider's naive psychology attribution theory

The earliest formulation of attribution theory emerged from the work of Fritz Heider (1958). His proposition was that the persons are naive psychologist, who always try to understand and seek causation to the behaviour of others in order to make prediction about others' behaviour. According to Heider's theory, most of the persons apply one of the following three possible explanations to the causes of the behaviour of others:

1. They may explain that other person's behaviour or the behaviour of the target person is caused by the surrounding situation. In other words, the person does a particular behaviour under situational pressure and constraints.
2. The second explanation may be that the behaviour done by the target person is unintentional, and probably, it will not be occurring in future.
3. The third explanation may be that the target person has done the behaviour intentionally due to his personal attribute. Once the personal attribute has been identified about the target person, prediction about his future behaviour becomes easy.

Thus, this theory tries to explain attribution on the basis of simple naive explanations done by the common people. Therefore, it cannot be regarded as fully scientific one.

Jones and Davis' correspondent inference attribution theory

Jones and Davis (1965) modified the original formulation of attribution process and focused on the consequences of the behaviour on which attributions are made. The correspondent inference model of Jones and Davis attempts to discover conditions under which an individual's behaviour corresponds to their dispositions such as personality traits, intention, attitude, temperament, etc. This model attempts to account for how behaviour corresponds to the enduring and stable aspects of personality. This type of attributions serve the functions of reducing uncertainty and enhancing the predictions to be done about future behaviour.

Jones and McGills (1976) had pointed out that we generally utilise five types of information when making correspondent inference—free choice, non-common effects, social desirability, hedonic relevance and personalism. Figure 5.8 summarises these five types of information that are used in making correspondent inference.

Of these five types of information, two types of information have received the greatest attention, *that is*, uncommon or non-common effect of behaviour and social desirability. Let us take an example to illustrate these two factors. Suppose Priya wants to pursue postgraduate study in Sociology and for this purpose, she targets three universities—X, Y and Z. Related to each of these three universities, she focused on five factors—academic status, location of the campus, distance from home, security for women students and sports facilities. She makes enquiries and obtains the information, as summarised in Table 5.2.

All these three universities are common with respect to four factors. However, with respect to a factor, that is, the location of the campus, they differ—university X is located in small town, university Y is located in isolated village and university Z is located in large city. The non-common effect with respect to choosing these three universities is that university Y is located in isolated village. By contrast, if she chooses to go to university Z, here the non-common effect is its location in larger city. Suppose further that university Z is not socially desirable, that is, not popular because

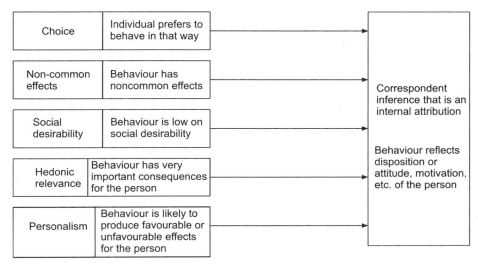

Figure 5.8 Major factors determining whether or not a correspondent influence is made.

Table 5.2 Common and Non-common Effects Arising from Choosing which of The Three Universities to Attend

Factors	University X	University Y	University Z
Academic status	High	High	High
Location of campus	In small town	In isolated village	In large city
Distance from home	Distant	Distant	Distant
Security for women students	Sufficient	Sufficient	Sufficient
Sports facilities	Good	Good	Good

very few students want to go to that university. In such a situation, it can be attributed that Priya possesses the trait of gregariousness. If every student wants to go to university Z, nothing can be said about Priya. From this example, it is obvious that correspondent inference is made when a behaviour has few non-common effects and is low in social desirability. Thus, the theory argues that the uncommon effects of an action permit inferences about behavioural dispositions. It also shows that a correspondent inference between behaviour and personality as dictated by Jones and Davis requires deliberation and thought about numerous social and personal information.

In a nutshell, it can be said that Jones and Davis (1965) emphasised the importance of uncommon behaviour and their unique effects. According to them, a culturally defined role behaviour is not considered much suitable for attributional consideration because personality traits are not much expressed. They had also suggested that attribution process becomes even more complex when the involvement of the person making the attribution is kept in mind. The common observation has been that the normal attribution process gets biased if the individual attempting to ascertain the attributes of other is benefited by the behaviour being observed.

Kelley's model of causal attribution

Kelley (1967, 1972) proposed a system of attributing behaviour done by others. In many everyday social situations, we make attribution about the cause of behaviour based on no more than single observation of the person. To make such an attribution, we generally rely on our existing knowledge or schema of how people behave in general. This has been termed as *causal schemata* by Kelley (1972), who had defined it as a general conception the person has about how certain kinds of causes interact to produce a specific kind of effect. This viewpoint of Kelley is called *causal schemata model*. Take an example to illustrate this. You observe that a stranger on the railway platform has suddenly collapsed. Since you do not know about the stranger, you cannot think back as to how he behaved in the past. Therefore, for making attribution, you will rely on your existing knowledge or schema of how people behave in general. As such you infer that the stranger might have collapsed due to excessive alcohol consumption or there may be heart attack. This shows that making attribution based on single act or behaviour of the target person requires heavy dependence on the stereotypes, implicit personality theory or cultural or societal norms, etc. Further, deliberations are now needed to arrive at a particular cause of the observed behaviour. In doing so, Kelley suggested that two types of principles are generally adopted—discounting principle and augmentation principle. In *discounting principle*, other causes of behaviour are discounted if one is known to be present. Thus, this principle demonstrates the tendency people have towards simplicity in social perception. *Augmentation principle* is the opposite of discounting principle, where adjustment is made towards situational attribution.

To describe the general process people often use to explain behaviour, Kelley (1967) introduced the principle of covariation. Kelley was of opinion that there are many possible cause-and-effect relationship present in any situation and we try to analyse the relationship in order to pinpoint a particular cause for a behaviour. The *principle of covariation* clearly states that the cause, which we choose to explain an effect, is a cause that is present when the effect is present, and absent when the effect is also absent.

Following the principle of covariation, an observer can use one of the three specific types of causes to explain an effect:

1. The dispositions or stable characteristics of the actor or individual who is demonstrating the behaviour
2. The entity, that is, the target person at which the behaviour is directed
3. The situation or circumstances in which behaviour occurs

Let us take an example. Suppose Sita got angry with Ranjeeta and slapped her face in a party. In this example, the observer may think that Sita slapped Ranjeeta probably because Sita, by nature, is cruel and aggressive (something lies with the actor itself), or it had been caused because Ranjeeta might have done very insulting and derogatory behaviour (something about the target person) or it might be caused by the situation (something happened at the party).

But one basic question that arises here is—how do we know which explanation is appropriate and correct? According to Kelley, in order to arrive at a correct answer, we consider three kinds of information as under:

1. Consensus information: It refers to the degree to which other people react similarly in the same situation. For example, suppose Rajesh behaves aggressively towards Shyam. In this example, high consensus will be that most of the other people behave in an aggressive way towards Shyam and low consensus will be that other people do not behave in an aggressive way towards Shyam.

2. Distinctiveness information: It indicates the extent to which the same behaviour occurs in relation to the other people or stimuli. For example, if Rajesh only gets angry at Shyam and does not get angry with anyone else, the behaviour is considered to have high distinctiveness. But if Rajesh frequently gets angry with Shyam as well as with others, the behaviour is said to have low distinctiveness.

3. Consistency information: It indicates the extent to which the actor behaves the same way in other situations. If Rajesh often gets angry with Shyam, the behaviour is said to have high consistency. On the other hand, if Rajesh rarely gets angry with Shyam, the behaviour is said to have low consistency.

By using these three kinds of information, Kelley suggested that we make attributions either to the dispositional factors (something about the actor or person), or to the situational factor (something about the target person or the circumstances). Kelley's model is called *covariation model* because the attribution of a person or situation cause depends on how three types of information covary to produce an overall judgement. In general, when consensus and distinctiveness are low and consistency is high, we tend to make dispositional attribution. But when consensus, consistency and distinctiveness are all high, we tend to make attributions to the external, situational factors. Table 5.3 shows the details when an internal (person or actor), external (situation) or circumstance attribution will be made. A *circumstance attribution* is one, where there are a combination of special factors that are operating at that time only.

Table 5.3 Kelley's Covariation Model Showing Types of Attributions with Examples

Attribution	Type and Category of Information	Examples
Internal disposition (Rajesh is an aggressive person.)	High consistency	Rajesh is always aggressive towards Shyam.
	Low distinctiveness	Rajesh is aggressive towards most of the other people.
	Low consensus	Nobody else acts aggressively towards Shyam.
External or situational (Shyam causes Rajesh to behave aggressively.)	High consistency	Rajesh is always aggressive towards Shyam.
	High distinctiveness	Rajesh is not aggressive towards most of the other people.
	High consensus	Most other people act aggressively towards Shyam.
Circumstance attribution (Rajesh was in bad mood because he had lost his purse containing many valuables.)	Low consistency	Rajesh has never been aggressive towards Shyam before.
	High distinctiveness	Rajesh is not aggressive to most of the other people.
	High consensus	Most of the other people act aggressively towards Shyam.

Kelley's model has been experimentally tested. McArthur (1972) conducted one experiment for investigating Kelley's model. He gave participants different combinations of three types of information. Overall, McArthur found a clear-cut support for the combinations of information mentioned by Kelley's model for making internal, external and circumstance attributions. McArthur also reported that overall, people make more internal attribution than external attribution. Besides, distinctiveness information was perceived to be the most important type of information, consistency the second most important and consensus the least important. Hewstone and Jaspars (1987) as well as Pruitt and Insko (1980) also provided support for Kelley's covariation model.

The covariation model has also some negative points, which are as follows:

1. This model misleadingly suggests that people use only said three types of information. Garland et al. (1975) reported that when people were permitted to ask for any information they wanted, only 23% of requests were made for consistency, distinctiveness and consensus information. Some 29% of requests were for other types of information relating to personality traits.
2. The covariation model emphasises that people use all three types of information equally, but some research evidences suggest that this is not the case. Research done by Alloy and Tabachnik (1984) suggested that people are not good at assessing and using covariation formation in predicted manner.
3. Many researches done on covariation model have used short descriptions of the behaviour, and therefore, the findings cannot be generalised to the complex situation representing the real behaviour.

Despite these limitations, Kelley's covariation model is an elaborate theory, which intends to explain how people perceive the causes of behaviour. The model clearly attempts to predict when we will make internal, external and circumstantial attributions.

Shaver's attribution model

Shaver (1975) developed a general theory of attribution by combining major elements of the theories of Heider, Jones and Davis as well as that of Kelley. His theory had formulated three clear assumptions about human nature upon which attribution theory is based. These are as follows:

1. Shaver's theory assumes that behaviour does not occur by chance, rather it is determined, and thus, can be predicted.
2. Another assumption about human nature is that people have a desire to understand, explain and predict the behaviour of others.
3. Another assumption is that observable behaviour does not always permit valid inferences about its underlying causes, that is, personality attribution. It means that inferences of a personality characteristic on the basis of observations of a limited number of behaviours are somewhat questionable.

Taking these three assumptions into consideration, Shaver (1975) developed a model of attribution. In attribution process, the first step is to determine whether the person really committed behaviour. For example, it is to determine here whether Rajesh really did aggressive behaviour towards Shyam. At the second step, it is determined whether the behaviour done was intentional. For example, whether Rajesh intentionally showed aggressive behaviour towards Shyam. At the third step, it is determined whether the behaviour was coerced, that is, whether Rajesh showed aggression towards Shyam under coercion. If the observer finds answer at steps 1 and 2 in yes and at step 3, in no, disposition attribution (trait of aggression) is made. On the other hand, if the observer finds answer at steps 1, 2 and 3 in yes, attribution to environment or situation is made (Rajesh might have shown aggression towards Shyam because he was forced to do so by others).

Weiner's attribution model

Weiner (1979, 1986) developed an attribution model for success and failure. For explaining success or failure, Weiner opined that we attribute it to one (or more) of four basic causes—ability, effort, task difficulty and luck. Now, the question is—how does the person arrive at one of these four causal attributions? The answer is that attribution depends on the categorisation on each of these three dimensions—internal-external, stable-unstable and controllable-uncontrollable.

Internal-external dimension is concerned with the locus of cause, that is, something about the person or actor or observer (internal) or about the situation (external). *Stable-unstable dimension* refers to whether the internal cause is changeable (unstable) or enduring and permanent (stable). Personality traits and temperament are internal stable causes (Miles and Carey, 1997), whereas motives, health, fatigue, mood are internal unstable causes. The same is true in case of external causes. Some external causes such as laws or social norms that enforce consistency in behaviour are stable causes, whereas some other external causes such as bad luck are unstable external causes.

Controllable-uncontrollable dimension indicates whether internal causes can be controlled or will remain uncontrollable. Persons can learn to hold their tempers in check. This illustrates controllable internal causes. Disabilities or chronic illnesses are not fully controllable, and therefore, illustrate uncontrollable internal cause. Likewise, effort put into revising a task is controllable, whereas facing a difficult examination question paper is really uncontrollable. Table 5.4 summarises how four basic causes are categorised according to each of these three dimensions.

Table 5.4 Weiner's Model for Attribution of Success and Failure Displaying Possible Causes Related to Each of Three Dimensions

	Internal		External	
	Stable	Unstable	Stable	Unstable
Controllable	Typical effort	Unusual effort	Help from friends	Help from unknown
Uncontrollable	Ability or aptitude	Mood	Task difficulty	Luck or chance

From Table 5.4, it is obvious that ability is usually considered internal and stable. In other words, observers usually construe ability or aptitude as the property of the individual (not of the environment) and they consider it stable because it does not change from moment to moment. Likewise, task difficulty is external and stable because it depends on objective task characteristics. Luck or chance is external and unstable.

Researches have shown that whether the observers attribute the performance to internal or external causes depends on how the person's performance is compared with that of others. This model has received considerable attention in the field of education and sports. It has been reported that the adults and children, who tend to attribute failure on a task to any internal and stable cause such as unhealthy habit, are not likely to persist on the task. On the other hand, making external attribution for failure tends to protect a person's self-esteem. Frieze and Weiner (1971) conducted another important study to demonstrate the major predictions of the model. They gave participants information about an individual's performance (success or failure) at a given task. Participants were also provided information about the person's past success rate on the same as well as similar task. Not only that, they were also provided information about others' success rate on the same task. These data enabled the participants to view the actor's performance as consistent or inconsistent with his past performance. Subsequently, participants reported their judgements which showed that

1. Success was more likely to be attributed to internal factors such as ability, aptitude, and effort than was failure.
2. Performance similar to that of others was attributed to external factors such as task difficulty, whereas performance different from that of others such as success, where others failed, or failure, where others succeeded, was attributed to internal factors like ability, effort, aptitude etc.
3. Performance consistent with one's own previous records was attributed to stable factors like ability, task difficulty, whereas performance inconsistent with one's past record was attributed to unstable factors like luck, chance and effort.

Although Weiner's model has much popularity and has wider experimental support, there are concerns among some quarters whether people actually use these three dimensions and if they really use it, whether they adopt such a logical and detailed approach. Krantz and Rude (1984) reported in their study only a few participants actually classify the four common causes (ability, effort, task difficulty and luck) along each of Weiner's three dimensions. In fact, individuals perceive human attributes differently. For example, intelligence (ability factor) is perceived as stable by some participants and unstable (that is, likely to change) by others.

Despite these, Weiner's model enjoys popularity among social psychologists for attribution of success and failure. Recently, it has also been extended to the analysis of how we judge responsibility and blame (Weiner, 1995).

BIAS AND ERROR IN ATTRIBUTION

In attribution, the observers carefully scrutinise the environment, form impressions and interpret the causes of the behaviour in rational way. In reality, however, they often deviate from logical steps/methods described by attribution theory and fall prey to various types of biases and errors. Common biases and errors in attribution as reported by most of the social psychologists are discussed here.

1. Correspondence bias: Overattribution to dispositions

Correspondence bias is an important error that occurs in the process of attribution. In correspondence bias, the observer overestimates the role of dispositional factors (personality traits) in attribution. *Correspondence bias* is defined as the tendency to explain the causes of other's behaviour as stemming from (corresponding to) dispositions even when the observer is provided with clear evidences for situational causes (Jones, 1979; Gilbert and Malone, 1995). This bias seems to be so common that it has been called *fundamental attribution error* (Higgins and Bryant, 1982; Small and Peterson, 1981). Such error results from the failure by the observer to fully apply the subtractive rule. This tendency was first identified by Heider (1944), who had clearly observed that many observers ignore or minimise the impact of situational constraints and role pressures on others and simply interpret behaviour as caused by the person's motives, traits, attitudes, intentions, etc.

Researches have revealed that although correspondence bias occurs in several situations, it has been found to be strongest in those situations where both distinctiveness and consensus (to use Kelley's terms) are low (Van Overwalle, 1997). Similarly, such bias has also been found to be higher when we try to predict others' behaviour in distant future rather than in the immediate future (Nussbaum, Trope and Liberman, 2003). The reason is that when we think about distant future, we simply do so in abstract terms and think in terms of global traits. As a result, we ignore the likely external causes of behaviour.

Social psychologists have provided several explanations for correspondence bias. First, when we observe the behaviours of others, we focus on his/her behaviour and situational causes run into background. As a consequence, the dispositional causes (internal causes) become more salient and easier to notice as compared to the situational causes, which might have also caused the behaviour, but are less salient. Second, even when we notice some situational causes in other's behaviour, we generally give them insufficient weight in our attributions. Third, when we observe other's behaviour, we assume that the behaviour reflect his traits or dispositions. Subsequently, we try to correct this by taking into account the possibilities of the effect of current situations. This is similar to the mental shortcuts called *anchoring and adjustment*. But generally, this correction is insufficient and the external factors are not given as much weight as they should receive. The result is that we tend to attribute in terms of dispositional factors and ignore the situational factors.

Gilbert and Malone (1995) suggested the following four main reasons for explaining the correspondence bias:

(i) When people make attribution of other's behaviour, they assume that what a person does or says, is consistent with his attitudes, beliefs and intentions.
(ii) While making attribution, people do not take sufficient account of situational constraints.
(iii) The link between the person and behaviour is overemphasised because people have tendency to make spontaneous trait attributions.
(iv) Spontaneous attributions are treated at face value and are not adjusted sufficiently against situational causes when further deliberations are made.

Correspondence bias is also influenced by cultural factors. Such error appears to be more common or stranger in those cultures, which emphasise individual freedom, that is, in individualistic culture, which is found in the United States of America, Canada and Western Europe. However, this error is very weak or less common in the cultures, which emphasise interdependence, group membership and conformity, all characteristics of collectivistic culture as we find in Eastern countries like India, Japan, China, etc. This difference obviously reflects that in individualistic culture, there is a *norm of internality*, which clearly specifies that the individuals should accept the responsibility of the outcomes of their own behaviour. In collectivistic culture, this norm is either weaker or absent.

Researches have also reported that correspondence bias can also occur for attribution of groups. Why do sometimes Hindus seem to dislike Muslims and Muslims seem to dislike Hindus to the extent that Hindu-Muslim riot erupts? Of the many causes, one cause is correspondence bias that occurs while attributing the behaviours of Muslims or Hindus. Hindus attribute the behaviours of Muslims more in terms of dispositional causes (beliefs, attitudes, traits, etc.). Likewise, Muslims also attribute the behaviours of Hindus more in terms of dispositional causes, ignoring the impact of situational causes. Doosje and Branscombe (2003) provided one support for correspondence bias occurring in group attribution. Participants (both Germans and Jewish) visited museum showing events during the Holocaust displaying German atrocities against Jews during World War II. They were asked to rate the extent to which these atrocities were due to the aggressive nature of Germans (internal cause) or to the situational context in which these actions occurred (external factors). Results revealed that Jewish people, whose group had been badly harmed, attributed German atrocities to internal causes than German themselves had attributed. This study clearly shows that attribution can be affected by group membership.

2. Actor-observer effect

While explaining fundamental attribution error or correspondence bias, we see that situational factors tend to be ignored. This applies when we make attribution about other's behaviour. However, when we attribute causes to our own behaviour, situational factors tend to be overemphasised. This is known as *actor-observer difference* (Jones and Nisbett, 1972). Here, the actor (or self) is the individual attributing causes (mainly external or situational) to his own behaviour, whereas the observer is the other person attributing causes (mainly internal or dispositional) to another's behaviour. Observers tend to attribute the actors' behaviour to the internal characteristics of actors, whereas actors see their own behaviour as more due to the characteristics of the external situation. In a nutshell, actor-observer effect involves our tendency to attribute our own behaviour to the external or situational causes, but that of others to the dispositional or internal causes (Watson, 1982).

Nisbett et al., (1973) conducted one study, which has provided evidences for actor-observer difference. In this study, male students were asked to write descriptions explaining why they liked their girlfriends and why they chose their majors. This was their actor's role. Now, as observers, they were requested to explain why their best friend liked his girlfriend and chose his major. Results revealed that when explaining their own actions, the students emphasised external characteristics like beauty and attractive qualities of their girlfriends and interesting aspects of their majors. However, when they were explaining their friends' behaviour, they downplayed external characteristics and gave emphasis upon their friends' internal dispositions like personality traits, attitude and preferences.

Social psychologists have provided the following three explanations for actor-observer effect:

(i) Actor-observer difference may be due to simply the fact that we have more privileged information when we explain our own behaviour rather than another's behaviour. This is because that we know a lot more about we have acted or behaved in past in comparison to how another person has acted in the past.

(ii) Salience or focus of attention of casual factors is different for actors and observers. This is called *focus of attention bias*. The observer perceives the individual (actor) more salient since attention is focused more on that person than the surrounding situation. Conversely, the individual is more alert and attentive to the forces in the environment than his own personality when making self-attribution. A very striking demonstration of focus of attention bias had been made by Taylor and Fiske (1978). The study involved six participants and two speakers (speaker 1 and speaker 2). All participants observed the conversation between the two persons (speaker 1 and speaker 2). Two observers sat behind speaker 1, thus facing directly speaker 2, two observers sat behind speaker 2, facing directly speaker 1 and two sat on the sides equally focused on both speakers (see Figure 5.9).

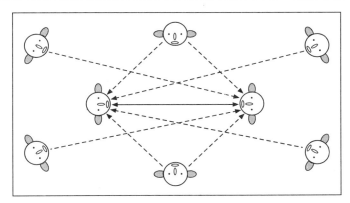

Figure 5.9 Focus of attention bias.

Analysis of the measures taken after the conversation showed that the observers thought that the speaker they faced not only had more influence on content and tone of conversation but also had greater impact on other speaker's behaviour. Observers who sat on sides paid attention to both speakers equally, and therefore, they attributed both speakers showing equal influence to them. The study clearly reveals the fact that we perceive the stimuli, which are more salient in the environment or which attract our attention most as casually influential ones.

If the above line of argument is correct, it can be predicted that any technique which changes salience for the actor and observer should result in the corresponding change in the attributions made. Storms (1973) conducted a study in which it was demonstrated that actor-observer attribution could be reversed by showing the actor a videotape of himself. In his experiment, there were two participants who took part in conversation. Also, there were two observers—each observer watched one of the participants during conversation. Storms videotaped the conversation and played it back to the participants in one of the two ways. There were two conditions in the experiment—same orientation condition and opposite orientation condition. In the *same orientation condition* of the experiment, half the participants saw the same videotape which they had seen live. In other words, the actor saw the videotape of the person with whom he was in conversation and the observer saw the person he was assigned to watch originally. In *opposite orientation condition*, the situation was a bit different. In this condition, the remaining half of the participants saw the videotape from opposite orientation, that is, actors watched themselves in conversation and the observers watched the person whom they had not watched initially in the live conversation. Besides these two groups, there was also a control group of participants, who watched only the live conversation and was not allowed to watch videotape playback. Subsequently, all participants were asked to rate the extent to which friendliness, nervousness and dominance, etc. of the persons they watched initially was due to either dispositional factors or situational factors. Results revealed that actor-observer effect was present in the control group as expected. Participants who witnessed the videotape in the same orientation condition produced even greater actor-observer effect. The most interesting part of the results was that the participants who were in the opposite orientation of the videotape playback reversed the actor-observer difference. Actors perceived their behaviour strongly in dispositional terms and observers perceived their behaviour in situational terms.

Still the third explanation for actor-observer effect has been provided in terms of *false consensus effect*, which refers to an obvious tendency to view our own attitudes, choices and behaviours as more common than they actually are (Marks and Miller, 1987). It is due to the false consensus effect that we see our friends' acquaintances as more alike ourselves in terms of behaviour, attitude and traits. Ross, Greene and House (1977) conducted a study to demonstrate false consensus effect. In this study, students were asked to walk around the campus with a board on which a word 'REPENT' was written. The students, who agreed, estimated that about 60% of other people asked would also agree, whereas the students, who refused, estimated that over 75% of other people asked would also refuse. This study clearly showed that in attributing causes to others, people think their own choices and preferences as much more common than they actually are and underestimate the situational constraints and pressures.

3. Self-serving bias

Self-serving bias in attribution is very common. It refers to the tendency to attribute positive outcomes to internal causes, that is, one's own traits or characteristics, but negative outcomes to external causes, that is, luck, chance or task difficulty. People tend to take credit for acts that yield positive outcomes, whereas they tend to blame others for bad outcomes and attribute them to external causes (Ross and Fletcher, 1985; Campbell and Sedikides, 1999). In Weiner's model (1985) of attribution, we have seen that attribution of success is done in terms of internal, stable and controllable causes, and failure is attributed in terms of external factors such as task difficulty and bad luck. It clearly means that in the former case, a person tells that he is responsible for the success, but in the latter case, he tells that failure was not occurred due to his fault.

Support for self-serving bias in attribution has been provided by many studies. One very important study was conducted by Bernstein, Stephan and Davis (1979). In this study, students were asked to explain the various grades they received in three examinations. Results revealed that students receiving grades A's and B's attributed their grades to their abilities and efforts than to good luck or easy tests. Students who received grades C's, D's and E's attributed their grades largely to bad luck and difficulty of the tests. Other studies have also confirmed self-serving bias in attribution (Johnson et al., 1964; Reifenberg, 1986). Self-serving bias is also found when athletes report the results of their games (Lau and Russell, 1980). The members of the winning team take credit for winning (we won), whereas the members of the losing team are more likely to attribute the outcome to the external causes like strategies of their opponent, etc.

Why does self-serving bias occur in attribution? There are two possible explanations—cognitive explanation and motivational explanation. According to *cognitive explanation*, self-serving bias occurs because we expect to get success and have a tendency to attribute the expected outcomes to the internal causes more than to the external causes (Miller and Ross, 1975). According to *motivational explanation*, the self-serving bias occurs due to our need to protect and enhance our self-esteem or desire to look good to others (Greenberg, Pyszczynski and Solomon, 1982; Zukerman, 1979). Subsequent research has reported difficulties in making a clear distinction between these two factors or explanations (Tetlock and Manstead, 1985). However, of these two explanations, research reports favour more to the motivational explanation (Brown and Rogers, 1991).

Some research studies have further indicated that the strength of self-serving bias varies across different cultures (Oettingen, 1995). Such bias is stronger in those cultures, which emphasise individual accomplishments such as the United States and other Western societies. However, this bias is weaker in those cultures, which emphasise group outcomes and group harmony such as in Asian countries like China, India, Japan, etc.

Despite these errors and biases in attributing the causes of other behaviours, we generally arrive at accurate conclusion about others' traits, motives, and intentions by observing their behaviours.

APPLICATIONS OF ATTRIBUTION THEORY

Social psychologists have successfully applied attribution theory to the three areas, that is, depression, education and workplace. These are discussed below:

1. Attribution and depression

Attribution theory has been applied to depression, particularly to unipolar depression (not to the bipolar depression). *Bipolar depression* is one where the individual alternates between depression and mania, whereas *unipolar depression* is one where the individual has only depressive episodes, with no history of mania. Although many factors play a role in depression, one factor that has been paid due attention is the self-defeating pattern of attribution. Depressed people generally adopt a negative attributional style, which is the opposite of self-serving bias. They attribute negative outcomes to stable internal causes such as lack of ability or own personality traits, but attribute positive outcomes to unstable external causes such as good luck or some special factors. As a consequence, such persons feel that they have a little or no control over what happens to them. As such, their depression further deepens.

Application of Weiner's model for success and failure to depression has maintained two dimensions of internal-external, and stable-unstable and introduced a third dimension of global-specific. A *global attribution* is one where the person perceives the cause of a behaviour to be related to many different behaviours in his life, whereas in *specific attribution*, the person pinpoints on any specific behaviour for causation. A person who is depressed would make an internal, stable and global attribution. Such negative attributional style also lowers the self-esteem of a person. Sweeney et al., (1986) reviewed a large number of studies and found a resemble correlation between the attributional style and depression.

Attributional retraining for the depressed has been launched and such retraining aims at changing the negative attributional style, that is, to take personal credit for successful outcomes, to stop blaming themselves for negative consequences and to view at least some failures resulting from the external factors beyond their control. Seligman et al., (1979) developed a questionnaire to assess a person's attributional style. Abramson and Martin (1981) suggested four ways in which depressives should change their perception of causes of their own behaviour as well as that of others. These are as follows:

(i) Attributional retainer or therapist should reverse the attributional style from, for example, internal, stable and global for negative outcomes to external, unstable and specific. As a consequence, the person perceives control over the outcomes of his behaviour. This change from helplessness to believing one can help oneself is becoming very crucial for the cure of depressive symptoms.

(ii) Depressives should set realistic rather than unrealistic and unattainable goals in their lives.

(iii) The therapist should try to help the person find attainable goals rather than unattainable goals that are attractive and desirable.

(iv) Depressives' feeling of being helpless and having no control over what is happening should be changed to a balanced position where they should have the same degree of control as others' have on the situation.

The application of attribution model, particularly Weiner's model, for understanding and treating depression, has proved valuable for clinical psychologists. Of three dimensions of the model, the internal-external dimension is seen as the most important one because it directly relates to the controllability of behaviour. According to Forsterling (1988), reversing attributions for positive outcomes from external to internal and for negative outcomes, from internal to external has proved to be the most effective way of raising self-esteem and alleviating depression.

2. Attribution and education

Attribution has also successfully applied to changing the negative attributional style of the underachievers. The observation is that underachievers generally attribute their failures to lack of ability, and therefore, show little persistence when given a new task. When this attributional style is changed through training, the academic performance of underachievers is likely to be improved. Dweck (1975) conducted a field experiment to prove this fact. She identified some elementary school-age children, who were underachievers and were showing a negative attributional style. She provided a retraining programme that lasted for twenty-five sessions during which these children were given a series of success and failure experiences on mathematics problems. Whenever they were unsuccessful because they had made errors, they were taught to attribute this failure to lack of effort rather than to their poor abilities. There was also a control group of children, who were not retrained and had experienced unmitigated success. Results revealed that children, who were retrained, improved their performance and put greater effort even after the programme was over. However, the children of the control group, who had not been retrained, performed poorly. Andrews and Debus (1978) had later provided support for Dweck's findings.

3. Attribution in workplaces

Whether it is government office or non-governmental organisation, an all too common occurrence that the employees, especially female employees, face is that of *sexual harassment*, which is defined as unwanted contact or communication of sexual nature. At workplace, a male employee may view comment on a woman's dress or appearance as an inoffensive compliment, but women may view it as an attempt of sexual harassment. If this is the reality, it automatically implies that the causes of the same behaviour are perceived differently by two sexes. Here comes the role of attribution theory and several studies have confirmed this. A study conducted by Smirles (2004) may be relevant here in shedding important light and providing insight.

Smirles (2004) conducted one study in two parts. In this study, male and female students acted as participants, who were provided a brief description of an employer, who had threatened the career of an employee if the person did not consent to have a sex relationship with the employer. The sex of both employee and employer was varied in such a way that different groups of participants may be exposed to all possible combinations such as a male harassing a female, a male harassing a male, a female harassing a male and a female harassing a female. After reading the descriptions, participants were asked to rate the extent to which the employer and the victim were responsible for what happened. Results from the first part of the study indicated that female participants, as compared to the male participants, held the victim less responsible and employer more responsible for what happened, regardless of the sex of the victim. This happened probably because of *defensive attribution*, which refers to the attribution that occurs when we see that we are similar to someone who had faced negative outcomes (here, victim of sexual harassment). When we perceive ourselves similar to the victim, we may experience these negative outcomes. Because women are the frequent victims of sexual harassment than men; women perceive greater similarity with the victim (regardless of victim's gender), and therefore, they blame the victim less for the negative outcomes. To reduce these negative outcomes, we attribute blame to the external causes (employer) while minimising blame for the victim.

In the second part of the study, the participants were provided with the description of the victim's response to sexual harassment. Responses were acquiescence (surrender before the employer for meeting his demands) and resistance (threatening the employer for making the matter public). There was also a control group, which did not receive any information on victim's reaction. Attribution theory, here, predicts that a victim who yields to the demand of the employer will be perceived as more responsible for sexual harassment than a victim who resisted. This is so probably because the victims can resist but if they fail to resist, this shows at least, in part, that victims possess some internal factors like weakness or a lack of strong determination on their part. These predictions were confirmed in this study because it was reported that the victims who agreed to the demands of the employer were held as responsible for sexual harassment by both men and women than the ones who had actually resisted. This result, overall, suggests that attribution theory can provide an in-depth insight into the causes and also into the prevention of sexual harassment.

Thus, we find that attribution theories have wider applicability in different fields. Their applications in the field of depression has been remarkably applauded by social psychologists.

CULTURAL BASIS OF ATTRIBUTION

Culture plays a significant role in attribution process and in producing bias and error in attribution. This is probably so because our attributions are linked to the schemas and the schemas often contain and reflect cultural element.

Social psychologists have widely studied the use of fundamental attribution error across different cultures. For several years, fundamental attribution error was thought to be fundamental in the sense that all people, regardless of the culture, were thought to exhibit a strong tendency towards dispositional attribution. However, recently, a number of researchers have investigated the fact whether the attribution biases and errors are consistent across different cultures. Researches have, today, confirmed the fact that attribution errors, including fundamental attribution errors, vary across culture and the major difference relates to the fact that whether there is individualist or collectivist culture. As we know, individualist culture emphasises the individual, and therefore, its members are predisposed to use individualist or dispositional attribution in terms of traits, attitudes, intentions, interest, etc. In collectivist cultures, the emphasis is more on context in which the groups and interindividual relationship are emphasised. As a consequence, members of collectivist culture are likely to include situational elements in their attribution.

Singh et al. (2003) studied the role of culture in blame attribution. In a series of three cross-cultural experiments, they successfully demonstrated that in Western culture like the United States and Europe, a person is considered blameworthy for not meeting an expectation. Participants from Western culture blamed the individual more than the group, whereas participants from Eastern culture like China, India, Japan, etc. blamed the group more than the individual. Higgins and Bhatt (2001) explored the emic (culture specific) and the etic (universal) features of causal attributions in India and Canada. In this study, a comparison of causal attributions about positive and negative life events between the Indian participants and the Canadian participants were made. It was found that Indian participants displayed more contextual causes and a stronger self-serving bias more than their Canadian counterparts. The study further revealed that although both groups of participants distinguished clearly between achievement and interpersonal events, this distinction was stronger among Canadian participants. Cross-cultural differences have also been reported in the attribution of success and failure (Fry and Ghosh, 1980). They took matched groups of White Canadian and Asian-Indian Canadian children aged between 8 to 10 years. It was observed that the self-serving bias was present in White Canadian children, who attributed success to the internal factors like ability and efforts and failure to bad luck and other external factors. On the other hand, Asian-Indian children attributed success more in terms of external factors like luck and failure mainly in terms of internal factors like lack of ability.

Thus, we see that there are clear cultural variations, biases and errors in attribution process.

Summary and Review

- *Social cognition* is the study of how people form inferences from the social information in the environment. In other words, social cognition is the study of how people make sense of other people and themselves and learn about what matters in the social world.
- Schema and prototypes are the two important components of social cognition. *Prototypes* are abstractions that represent typical or quintessential of a class or group. *Schemas* refer to the mental structure containing information relevant to self, other people, specific events or situations. Schemas are of four types—self-schema, person schema, role schema and event schema. Both prototypes and schemas help us in organising social information and guiding the processing of such information.
- Schematic processing requires three cognitive processes of attention, encoding and retrieval involved in social cognition. Our social cognition, that is, understanding of the social world, are influenced by these processes of attention, encoding and retrieval.
- There is self-fulfilling or self-confirming nature of schema. When a person's wrong expectations about another person lead that person to adopt those expected attributes and behaviours, it is called *self-fulfilling prophecy*. Self-fulfilling nature of the schema has been shown in several studies.
- Persons utilise various mental shortcuts, called *cognitive heuristics*, in an attempt to reduce effort in social cognition. These heuristics mainly include representativeness heuristics, availability heuristics, anchoring and adjustment heuristics and simulation heuristic.
- There are potential sources of errors in social cognition. Among these sources of errors or biases, negativity bias, optimistic bias, counterfactual thinking, thought suppression, limits of person's ability to think about social world, etc. are also there.
- Social psychologists have reported a reciprocal relationship between cognition and affect. There are ample evidences to show that affect, that is, our moods, feelings and emotions has a substantial impact upon cognition. In general, it has been reported that when the person is in good or positive mood, he tends to be more altruistic, sociable and show other positive actions. On the other hand, when he is in bad mood, he keeps himself withdrawn and does less altruistic behaviour. Affect tends to influence the mood of a person through two mechanism—mood-dependent memory and mood-congruence

memory. Researches support the fact that cognition also influences the affect. Most common ways through cognition influences our affect, including mood, are counterfactual thinking and by activating schemas containing a strong affective component.

- Recently, social psychologists have become more directly interested into interpersonal perception. They have classified the field of interpersonal perception into two major areas—social perception and person perception. *Social perception* involves perception of social processes. The objects of social perception are the person's relations with others, including his perception of groups and social institution. *Person perception* refers to the process in which impressions, opinions or feelings about other persons are formed. The basic assumption of the person perception is that the perceiver may exist apart from and outside the world of the person being judged.

- Non-verbal cues have important roles to play in person perception. Non-verbal cues from facial expression, eye contact, gesture, posture and bodily movements, body-builds and physical appearance, voice quality and dress as well as touching are found to be very helpful in person perception. Deception is commonly involved in expressing feelings and emotions through these non-verbal means of communication. Therefore, social psychologists have also devised various means for detecting these deceptions. Interchannel discrepancies and exaggerated facial expressions are common means of such detection.

- *Impression formation*, which is regarded as fundamental to person perception, refers to the process of organising diverse information into a unified and gestalt impression of other person. In a classic experiment, Asch, who developed a configural model, had demonstrated that some traits have more impact than the others on the impressions we form about others. Such traits are said to have trait centrality.

- For integrating information about others, some models have been developed by social psychologists. Additive model, averaging model, weighted averaging model are the popular models (Anderson, 1981). Besides, continuum model and parallel-constraint-satisfaction models are used for information integration. Besides these models, other factors such as negativity effect, positivity bias, imputing consistency, resolving inconsistencies, first impression versus last impression, schemas, prototypes, exemplars—positive and negative examples help and influence information integration.

- *Impression* (also known as *self-presentation*) is something in which we keep ourselves engaged throughout our lives. *Impression management* is defined as deliberate efforts to make a good impression on others. This is commonly done by adopting several tactics of successful impression management. This is known as *tactical impression management*. Important techniques are self-promotion, other-enhancement techniques, including ingratiation, supplication, etc.

- There is downside of the impression management. Techniques of impression management works well, provided they are used carefully. Sometimes, tactical self-presentation can prove hazardous to the existing social relationship.

- *Self-perception* is a process where one perceives and reacts to oneself. Being partly satisfied by early explanation of self-perception, Bem (1972) developed a theory called *self-perception theory*, which clearly relates to the attributions people make about the meaning of their own behaviour. According to this theory, people become aware of their own attitudes, emotions, dispositions and other internal states in the same way they learn about other people, that is, through the observation of behaviour.

- *Attribution* is a process through which we make efforts to understand others' behaviour, and on some occasion, the causes of our own behaviour as well. The most common attribution are dispositional attribution and situational attribution. In *dispositional attribution*, we attribute the behaviours of others in terms of personality traits, attitudes, interests, intention, etc. In *situational attribution*, we attribute the causes of others' behaviour in terms of external factors such as the situation in which the behaviour has occurred.

- There are five major models/theories which have been developed to account for attribution—Heider's naive psychology attribution theory, Jones and Davis's correspondent inference attribution theory, Kelley's model of causal attribution, Shaver's attribution model and Weiner's attribution model. Of these five models, Kelley's model, particularly his covariation model, has been the most influential one. Weiner's model is especially useful for explaining attribution for success and failure.
- Social psychologists have reported some biases and errors in attribution. Such important biases are—correspondence bias, actor-observer effect and self-serving bias. Due to these biases or errors, we fail to arrive at an appropriate cause of others' behaviour.
- Attribution theory has been widely applied to different fields. Of these fields, its applications in the areas like depression, education and in workplaces have been widely appreciated.
- The process of attribution as well as biases and errors have also cultural bases. Two types of culture, that is, individualist culture and collectivist culture clearly reveal differential types of biases and errors in attribution. People of individualistic culture like the United States of America, Canada, Europe, etc. utilise dispositional attribution, whereas the people of collectivist culture as we find in Asian countries, emphasise situational attribution.

REVIEW QUESTIONS

1. Define social cognition. Also, discuss the important elements or components of social cognition.
2. What is schematic processing? How does schema influence cognition?
3. Citing examples, explain the self-fulfilling nature of schema.
4. What do you mean by cognitive heuristics? Discuss various cognitive heuristics applied by a person while understanding the social world.
5. Discuss the potential source of errors in social cognition. To what extent those errors tend to invalidate the process of social cognition?
6. Does cognition influence affect? Cite experimental evidences.
7. Does affect influence cognition? Support your answer with evidences.
8. Make difference between social perception and person perception. Also, discuss the important modes of person perception.
9. Discuss the role of various non-verbal cues in person perception.
10. What types of deceptions occur in non-verbal cues? To what extent they influence person perception?
11. Define impression formation. Citing experimental evidences, discuss the different models of information integration.
12. Citing relevant studies, discuss the factors that play important roles in information integration.
13. What do you mean by impression management? Discuss various techniques of impression management.
14. Define attribution. Citing examples, make distinction between dispositional attribution and situational attribution. When are attributions made?
15. Discuss Jones and Davis's correspondent inference attribution theory.
16. Examine critically Kelley's model of attribution.
17. Examine critically Weiner's attribution model.
18. Discuss the important types of biases and errors made in attribution.
19. Citing evidences, discuss the various applications of attribution theories.
20. Write short notes on the followings:
    (i) Cultural basis of attribution
    (ii) Shaver's model of attribution
    (iii) Correspondence bias
    (iv) Self-serving bias

6 SOCIALISATION

Learning Objectives

- Meaning and Nature of Socialisation
- Theoretical Perspectives of Socialisation
- Agents of Socialisation
- Process of Socialisation
- Outcomes of Socialisation
- Concept of Adult Socialisation

Key Terms

Anaclitic identification	Ego integrity	Observational learning
Anticipatory socialisation	Epigenetic principle	Permissive style
Authoritarian style	Eriksonian perspective	Psychoanalytic perspective
Authoritative style	Fidelity	Psychosocial development
Cognitive competence	Gender role	Role acquisition
Cognitive development	Hope	Role discontinuity
Competence	Internalisation	Self-regulation
Critical period	Linguistic competence	Socialisation
Ego identity	Neglectful style	

We know that social psychology concerns itself with the study of interplay between the individual and social structure. As one of the subsets of social psychology, socialisation directly focuses upon this interplay. In other words, here, we emphasise general questions like—how does a human infant become social, how does a child come to believe that he should show respect to his teachers and parents, should learn to read, and should get marks in the examination, how does he come to know about the moral standards of society, etc. The process by which all these things take place is known as *socialisation*. The important agents in socialisation are other persons most prominently the parents, teachers, siblings, playmates and others, who are considered significant to him. Formerly, the term *socialisation* was applied to the child learning and it did not cover adult learning experiences. In fact, this view was synonymous with the day-to-day phrase 'bringing up the child'. But recently, the meaning of socialisation has been broadened to include learning of adult behaviour as well. In fact, socialisation process becomes active each time a person occupies a new position in his life. Therefore, socialisation does not stop at any age and continues throughout life. In this chapter, we shall focus on the agents of socialisation, theoretical perspectives of socialisation as well as on the process and outcomes of socialisation.

MEANING AND NATURE OF SOCIALISATION

Socialisation is a term used by social psychologists, sociologists, anthropologists and educationists to refer to broadly a process that makes human beings the true social actors, and this process includes learning of skills, habits, knowledge, motivations, and identities that enables us to interact with the social environment. In fact, it is a life long process of inheriting and disseminating values, norms, customs, and idealogies providing individuals necessary skills and habits for making smooth and healthy interaction within the society. Thus socialisation provides a means by which social and cultural continuity is maintained.

There have been several attempts to define socialisation. *Socialisation* may be defined as the process by which a person learns the ways of a society or social group so that he can adequately function within it (Elkin and Handel, 1978). Still a more broad view about the meaning of socialisation had been provided by Secord and Backman (1964). According to them, socialisation is an interactional process in which a person's behaviour is modified to conform with the expectations held by the members of the groups or society of which he is a member. This inclusive viewpoint very clearly points out that socialisation does not stop at a certain age, instead it continues throughout the life. In fact, socialisation process becomes active each time a person occupies a new position in his life. Similarly, Albrecht, Thomas and Chadwick (1980) opined that the socialisation can best be understood as such learning processes and resultant products that allow an individual to become an adequately functioning member of the society. The person internalises the normative dimensions of the social group and these internalised social norms, in turn, govern the behaviour of the person.

Analysing these viewpoints, we get several important facts about the concept of socialisation, which are discussed below:

1. Socialisation is a subset of learning in the sense that in order for socialisation to occur, learning must take place. However, not all learning is included in socialisation. Socialisation includes only those learnings that are necessary for sustained social interaction.
2. Two aspects of socialisation make socialisation distinct from the other processes of change. First, only attitudinal and behavioural changes occurring through learning are relevant. It means automatically that other changes such as those resulting from growth are not considered as the part of socialisation. Second, only those changes in behaviour and attitude, which have their origins in the social interaction, that is, interaction with the others are considered as the products of socialisation. Thus, a child may engage in repeated social interactions with his parents involving talking, instructing, holding, toilet training and so on. Over the time, the child develops the required behaviour to become an adult member not only of that family but also of the large society within which the family has developed.

3. In socialisation, the person is seen as conforming to the normative expectations found in the existing social order. It does not call attention to deviant or other non-normative behaviour.
4. Socialisation is not considered as something which moulds a person to standard social pattern. In fact, persons are subjected to different combinations of socialisation pressures and they tend to react differently to them. As a consequence, socialisation process can produce differences and similarities among persons.

Thus, we find out socialisation, which is a process of social learning, does not stop at any age and continues throughout the life. It makes the person a responsible person of the society.

THEORETICAL PERSPECTIVES OF SOCIALISATION

There are four important theoretical perspectives to socialisation. These perspectives tend to shed light upon the different aspects of social learning that are considered central to the process of socialisation. Those four theoretical perspectives are psychoanalytic perspective, Eriksonian perspective, social learning perspective and symbolic cognitive perspective.

1. Psychoanalytic perspective

Psychoanalytic perspective to socialisation has been formulated by Sigmund Freud. This approach basically emphasises upon the importance of the quality of parent-child relationship in socialisation. The psychoanalytic perspective postulates a developmental view of the emerging socialised being.

As we know, the Freudian approach to personality development has delineated five psychosexual stages of development—*oral stage, anal stage, phallic stage, latency stage* and *genital stage*. He was of view that during these stages of development, different processes of interaction take place within the family and those interaction processes are considered as basic to the child being socialised. For example, how mother interacts with child during toilet-training, feeding, sleeping, bathing, etc., or how father interacts with child when asking him to read the books and write alphabets. The ways parents interact with their child are seen as foundation stone for developing various types of personality characteristics. Different families interact with children in different ways and this is perhaps responsible for variation in socialisation from person of one family to person of another family (Zigler and Child, 1973).

As the child moves through the stages of psychosexual development, considerable emphasis is placed upon the source of energy, that is, *id*, which is often referred to as the *reservoir of psychological energy*. Id operates by the pleasure principle, that is, it tries to obtain pleasure and avoid pain. For id, pleasure means a state of low energy levels or inactivity and pain means tension that is brought about by excitation or increases in energy. Thus, when stimuli create tension, id tries to reduce tension and to return the organism to a low level of energy. Two mechanisms are employed by id to reduce tension—reflex action and primary process. In *reflex action*, id responds automatically to the sources of irritation. Examples of such reflex mechanism are sneezing, coughing and blinking. In the *primary process*, the individual reduces tension by forming a mental image of an object previously associated with satisfaction of basic drives. For example, the hungry baby may reduce hunger tension by forming an image of food or his mother's nipple.

As the child develops, other dimensions of intellectual processes, namely, *ego* and a little later, *superego* begins to develop. In fact, ego evolves out of id to enable the organism to deal with the reality of the situation. In contrast to id's pleasure-seeking nature, the ego follows the *reality principle*, which aims to preserve the integrity of the organism by suspending instinctual gratification until either an appropriate object or environmental condition that will satisfy the need has been found. Thus, ego temporarily suspends the pleasure principle that demands immediate action and by means of the secondary process, that is, by realistic thinking delays action until a need-satisfying object is found. Unlike the id, ego makes a distinction between fact and fiction, tolerates a moderate amount of tension, changes as a result of new experiences and develops cognitive perceptual skills.

Superego evolves out of the ego and is the last major system of personality to be developed. In fact, superego represents an internalised version of society's norms and standards of behaviour. In order for an individual to function constructively in society, he must acquire a system of values, norms, ethics, attitudes that the society approves. This is acquired through the process of socialisation and in terms of psychoanalytic perspectives through the development of superego, which is guided by morality principle. There are two subsystems of superego—the *conscience* and the *ego ideal*. Conscience is acquired through the use of punishment by the parents and the ego-ideal is learned through the use of rewards by parents. When an organism (or a child) does something wrong, his conscience makes him feel guilty, but when he obeys his parents and wins his approval, he feels proud. The major functions of superego are to inhibit the urges of id, to persuade ego to substitute moralistic goal for realistic goal and to strive for perfection. Once the superego is said to have been developed, the child is considered to be fully *socialised*.

In psychoanalytic perspective, the first important social object in the child's world is his parents. Social psychologists are of view that as the child moves through the different stages of psychosexual development, he is said to be identifying with his parents. Thus, identification is the central concept in psychoanalytic perspectives. In the process of identification, the person incorporates the qualities of another person into his own personality. Parents seem to be perceived as central figures in identification process. That is the reason why a child comes to resemble his parents by assimilating their major characteristics (Hall, 1954). By *anaclitic identification*, the child tends to incorporate the characteristics of a person who is very loving, affectionate and warm to him. By *identification with aggressor*, the child adopts the characteristics of a powerful or aggressive person.

Thus, the psychoanalytic perspective of socialisation emphasises that the people, in order to attain ideal character and to become properly socialised, must relinquish the passivity of early childhood days when love, security and physical comfort (all gratifications) were unconditionally given and nothing was expected in return. They must learn to work, postpone immediate gratification, become responsible and play roles in accordance with the social norms.

The psychoanalytic perspective, however, adopts a negative or passive view of the organism because this perspective sees tension in the organism as inherently unpleasant and emphasises the fact that the child engages in activity until a state of complete balance is achieved. Much of the contemporary work in ego psychology has rejected this passive view of the organism (White, 1963) and investigates intrinsic pleasure attributed to the various activities like play, manipulation, exploration and expression of curiosity.

2. Eriksonian perspective

Erik Homburger Erikson's viewpoints represent a systematic extension and liberalisation of Freud's view of the role of ego in personality functioning. Popularly known as *ego psychologist*, Erikson (1963) proposed that ego often functions independently of id impulses, emotions and motivations. In his view, ego is neither defensive in nature nor concerned with the control of biological urges, instead ego often functions in a manner to help individuals adapt positively to the challenges presented by their surroundings. This new perspective examines ego function in relation to society. It paints a positive view of personality attributing to the ego organising and synthesising functions.

Erikson (1963) postulated that human development is governed by the epigenetic principle of maturation, which occurs in a series of stages universal to humankind. In his farmers book, *Childhood and Society* (1963) he outlined a sequence of eight separate stages of psychosocial ego development. He posited that these eight stages are the result of epigenetic principles. According to *epigenetic conception of development*, each stage in the life cycle has on optimal time, called *critical period*, in which it remains dominant and when all the eight stages have been unfolded according to plan, a fully functioning personality comes into existence. Furthermore, Erikson also hypothesised that each psychosocial stage is accompanied by crisis, that is, turning point in the life of a person. The crisis arises from physiological maturation and social demands made upon the person at that stage. Positive resolution of each crisis creates positive components such as basic trust, autonomy, etc., which are absorbed into the emerging ego and further healthy development is assured. Conversely, if the conflict persists or is resolved in unsatisfactory way, the negative components such as mistrust, doubt, shame are incorporated into the ego. In such condition, ego is damaged to a greater extent and unhealthy personality develops. A positive resolution of conflict at one stage also increases the chances that the individuals will succeed in resolving crises at other stages. Thus, stages are interrelated and dependent on one another (Erikson, 1963).

Erikson's analysis of socialisation can best be presented by describing the distinctive features of the eight stages of psychosocial development as follows:

(i) **Infacy–trust versus mistrust–hope:** This is the first stage of psychosocial development and corresponds closely to the Freud's oral stage and occurs during the first year of life. If the mother acts in loving and consistent way, the infant is likely to develop a sense of basic trust. The basic trust that develops between the mother and the child is truly an interpersonal experience. Not only do the mother's dependability and love foster trust in the infant but the infant, too, begins to act in a trustworthy way. On the other hand, if the mother acts in an unreliable, aloof and rejecting way, a sense of mistrust develops. In such a situation, the mother is likely to frustrate, anger and enrage the infant. If the interpersonal experiences with the mother are more positive than negative, the child develops an attitude towards others, which is more trusting than mistrusting. If the child successfully resolves the crisis of trust versus mistrust conflict, a psychosocial strength or virtue called *hope* develops within the child that serves to maintain the individual's belief in the meaning and trustworthiness of the cultural world.

(ii) **Early childhood–autonomy versus shame and doubt–will power:** This is the second stage of psychosocial development and coincides with the Freud's anal stage, covering roughly the periods of second and third years of life. Acquisition of sense of basic trust sets the stage for attainment of a sense of autonomy and self-control in the children. During this stage, the child's muscle begin to mature and he starts to learn how to exercise control over them. At this stage, if the parents guide their child's behaviour gradually and firmly, a sense of autonomy and self-control develops. Here, autonomy does not mean giving the child unrestricted freedom, rather it means that parents must maintain or keep degree of freedom over the child's growing ability to exercise choice. If the parents are either too permissive or too harsh and demanding, the child is likely to experience a sense of defeat that can lead to shame and doubt, concerning his ability to make effective judgements and to exercise control over his life. In such a situation, a psychosocial attitude of self-doubt, ineptitude and powerlessness generally develops among children.

(iii) **Play stage–initiative versus guilt–purpose:** This stage of development, arising in the age of 4 to 5 years, bears some resemblance to Freud's phallic stage. Here, the preschool child passes through what Erikson has called *play stage*. During this stage, the child is challenged by his social world to be active, to master new skills, and to win approval by being productive. He starts taking initiative for assuring additional responsibility for himself as well as for others. This is the stage, where the children begin to feel that they are counted as persons and their life has a goal or purpose. If the children are punished for their new and initiative advances, they develop a sense of guilt. Erikson pointed out that persistent sense of guilt may evolve into a variety of adult forms of abnormality such as generalised passivity, sexual impotence, psychopathic acting out, etc. If the parents behave in an understanding way and guide their children's motives and desires into socially acceptable activities, they develop a sense of purpose, which involves identifying with parents and setting major goals of life.

(iv) **School age–industry versus inferiority–competency:** This is the fourth stage of psychosocial development and loosely parallels Freud's latency period and occurs in the 6 to 12-year children. Here, for the first time, a child turns to school life and is expected to learn the rudimentary skills of the culture via formal education such as reading, writing, etc. According to Erikson, children develop a sense of industry when they begin to understand the technology of their culture through attending school. *Industry* means that the children are busy in learning how to complete jobs. Teachers play important role in their lives because they prepare the children for future as well as for careers by introducing them to the technology of the culture. The major danger of this period is that the children may fail to learn new things and develop feelings of inferiority. The result becomes that the children may lose confidence in their ability to take part in the working world. However, this feeling of inferiority or incompetence may be minimised by the parents by gradually preparing children for the rigours of the school environment and by encouraging them to trust their teachers. Erikson believed that a positive identification with their teachers goes a long way in minimising these conflicts and in developing a strong ego. The overall result of such treatment by parents and teachers is that the children develop the virtue of competence that provides them a healthy preparation for their roles in later life.

(v) **Adolescence–ego identity versus role confusion–fidelity:** This is the fifth stage of psychosocial development, which occurs from ages 13 to 19 or 20. The individuals, who have properly resolved the conflicts inherent in the prior stages, bring into adolescence a growing sense, called *ego identity,* at the positive end and a sense of *role confusion* at the negative end. *Ego identity* refers to the totality of self-perceptions and various self-images that have been integrated and show awareness of both past and future. Erikson had stressed the psychosocial nature of ego identity. Here, emphasis is placed upon the ego and the way it is affected by society, particularly by peer groups. However, *adolescence* is such period during which an identity crisis is normative. In fact, Erikson considers adolescence as a moratorium between childhood and adulthood in which individuals attempt to solve several kinds of problems. These identity crises experienced by adolescence generally stem from *role confusion*, concerning who they are and what they will become. Many such adolescents experience a profound sense of aimlessness, disorganisation and futility. They feel inadequate, depersonalised, alienated, and sometimes, also seek even a *negative identity*, which is defined as the identity that is opposite to the one prescribed for them by society, particularly by parents and peers.

When the adolescents are able to resolve the ego identity-role confusion crisis, a virtue, called *fidelity*, emerges. Erikson (1964) defined *fidelity* as the ability to sustain loyalties freely pledged in spite of inevitable contradictions of value system. Adolescents are now much more honest with themselves as well as with significant others. In fact, fidelity represents a young person's capacity to perceive and abide by the social moves, ethics and ideologies of the society.

(vi) **Young adulthood–intimacy versus isolation–love:** This is the sixth stage which spans the ages of 20 to 24. At this stage, the person is genuinely ready for social as well as sexual intimacy with another person. *Intimacy* is defined as the ability to establish close relationship with others. Erikson was of opinion that a truly intimate relationship is possible only between partners, who have clearly established identities and loyalties. Young adults, who fail to develop intimacy, develop a sense of *isolation*, which is defined as the inability to take chances with one's identity by sharing true intimacy. Such persons are self-absorbed and engage in such interpersonal relationship, which are purely formal and superficial. Such people have also attitude of futility and alienation about their vacations.

Healthy resolution of the intimacy-versus-isolation crisis produces a virtue called *love*, which includes, in addition to romantic qualities, ability to commit oneself to others and abide by such commitments. This type of love is shown through the attitude of care, respect and responsibility towards others.

(vii) **Middle adulthood–generativity versus stagnation–care:** This seventh stage corresponds to the middle years of life covering 25 to 65 years. This stage encompasses generativity or stagnation. Generativity encompasses not only the production and rearing of children but also includes the creation of products, ideas, art and so forth, which can be easily and appropriately used for the benefit of others. *Generativity* is said to have occurred when a person begins to show concern not only for the welfare of next generation but also for the whole society in which the next generation will live and establishes and guides those who will replace them. It resides not only in the parents but also in those who contribute to the betterment of young people. Those who fail to establish generativity slip into *stagnation*, which is defined as a state of self-absorption in which the individual's personal needs are of central concern. Such persons cease to function as productive members of the society and are interpersonally impoverished. If the capacity of generativity exceeds their sense of stagnation, a virtue of care emerges. As a consequence, older generation shows concern for helping the younger generation to develop in constructive ways as far as possible.

(viii) **Maturity–ego integrity versus despair–wisdom:** This is the final stage of psychosocial development that lasts from 65 years to death. Practically, in all cultures, this stage signals the onset of old age. At this stage, a true maturity comes and practical sense of 'wisdom of the ages' comes into being, provided the person is 'gifted'. This stage encompasses intense reflection, involving reminiscence, recollection of memories, and attempts to reconstrue the meaning of life while welcoming the impending death. Healthy people, at this stage, are able to look back at their lives and conclude that they were special and had meaning. They gladly accept the inevitability of death as a necessary part of the life cycle and do not fear it. Thus, elderly people, who function well, see a unity and clear meaning in their lives. In Erikson's terminology, such people have ego integrity.

At the other extreme are the individuals who are unable to accept the inevitable failures in their lives and who have led a selfish and uncaring lives' experiences. This is called the *stage of despair* because in the sunset years, they realise that life is now short and there is no time to start a new life or try out a new path to integrity (Erikson, 1964). If the capacity of ego integrity exceeds the sense of despair, a virtue, called *wisdom*, emerges. Wisdom allows a person to envisage human problems in their entirety and to communicate to the younger generation a constructive example of the life of a unique human being.

Thus, in Erikson theory of socialisation, roles of society as well as the roles of the persons themselves are accorded equal emphasis with respect to the development and organisation of personality. Besides, Erikson was sensitive to the stage of adolescence and had considered this stage as pivotal in the formation of an individual's psychological and social being. On the whole, the major thrust of Erikson's theory is that the way we approach and resolve issues at one stage of psychosocial stage influences the way we approach and resolve issues at the next stage of psychosocial stage. A positive outcome at any one stage results in ego strength and a sense of control along with the positive feelings of self-work and mastery. Negative outcomes at any stage not only damages the chances of successful negotiation but also leads to the psychosocial problems and poor social functioning in late life.

3. Social learning perspective

Social learning perspective emphasises that socialisation is primarily a process of children learning the shared meaning of the groups to which they belong (Shibutani, 1961). In the simplest form, social learning perspective sees a child as learning what behaviour is appropriate and inappropriate in any social situation because he is rewarded for some behaviour and not rewarded for the others. Here, learning is seen basically as establishing links between stimulus and reinforcer. Reward and punishment are considered important in the stamping in or stamping out the processes of connecting specific stimulus with specific reinforcer. In fact, successful socialisation demands that the child must acquire considerable information about the world. He must learn about the social environment. He must also learn language to communicate his ideas or needs to others. He needs to learn to identify persons encountered in his immediate environment. Above all, he must also learn about the physical or natural realities such as what things are dangerous and what things are not dangerous.

The social learning perspective tends to undermine internalisation process because it is a state of organisms, which cannot be measured, and therefore, does not make important contribution to the study of socialisation.

The process through which social learning takes place are universal, although the content, that is, what is learned varies from group to group. In social learning perspective, there is an emphasis upon the adaptive nature of socialisation. It means that the child learns the verbal and interpersonal skills, which are considered necessary to interact successfully with others. After properly acquiring these skills, a child is able to distinguish his own groups from the other and even add or modify the meanings by introducing some new kinds of ideas.

Researches in the field of socialisation have shown that both the developmental processes and the social learning are important for socialisation. The developmental age, for example, determines that what type of behaviour a child can learn. However, the developmental processes are not enough in themselves for the learning of complex social behaviour. Besides appropriate developmental age, social interaction is necessary for socialisation. Davis (1947) illustrated the interplay of developmental readiness and social learning by citing a case of *Isabelle*, who had to live alone with her deaf-mute mother until the age of 6½ years. When she was found, she was not making any sound other than a croak. When she entered formal schooling, only after two years, her vocabulary enhanced more than 1500 words and she had fully acquired the linguistic skills of a 60-year old. The case is a typical illustrative of the fact that for socialisation, both developmental readiness and social interaction are necessary.

Although social learning perspective explains well the acquisition of social behaviour and demonstrates the external or stimulus control over the behaviour, it has some inherent difficulties, which are mentioned below:

(i) The most important weakness of social learning perspective is its difficulty in handling observational learning. If a child simply observes other people being rewarded or punished for their behaviour, why should he is expected to learn appropriate or inappropriate behaviour from that? Without reference to some internal cognitive processes, no easy answer can be given. Albert Bandura, a pioneer in the field of social learning, by formulating vicarious, symbolic and self-regulatory processes in human learning and rejecting the mechanistic modal of earlier period, was able to find an answer to this question. According to Bandura, social learning perspective rejects the traditional passive view of the human beings and replaces it with a cognitively operative and action-initiating organism. He emphasised the cognitive and social side of human behaviour by formulating the term *self-regulation*. By this, he referred to a process in which a person enhances and maintains his own behaviour by rewarding himself (positive reinforcer) and withdrawing rewards (negative reinforcer) whenever he fails to attain self-prescribed standards. Thus, the presence of an internalised standard of conduct is created in the social situation and this internalised standard makes possible to control one's own behaviour.

(ii) Why should a child repeat a given behaviour for which he has not been rewarded? Explanation of such maintenance of acquired behaviour pattern over time poses a problem. However, this problem is usually discussed in terms of what is called *intermittent reinforcement schedule*. If the observer finds that there is no reward for the behaviour being done, the explanation offered is that if the observer remains present long enough, he would observe a reward.

4. Symbolic cognitive perspective

This perspective is the outgrowth of two different but related bodies of literature. One comes from the more sociological sources of symbolic interaction and another from the discipline of child psychology. The symbolic cognitive perspective tends to highlight the individual as an actor, who continuously constructs his own meaning system. However, socialisation outcome must also be seen as a person's cognitive development as it takes place during the cognitive developmental period. This perspective gives emphasis upon a number of processes that are considered as basic to socialisation. Among others, it clearly emphasises that self and society should not be understood as distinct entities. Society consists of interrelated social institutions and each such institution consists of interrelated sets of roles. These roles are the society expected behaviour. A person who adopts a given role also internalises the expected behaviour and acts accordingly. Once a person accepts the role and adopts as personally appropriate those behaviours which the society expects, then it is said that he has become socialised. In symbolic interaction approach, the individual is considered both as an actor as well as a reactor. The self is said to exist when the person initiates action towards himself as social object, being the initiator of the action. Such view has been strongly supported by cognitive development approach, which was championed by Kohlberg (1973). He pointed out that social cognition always involves role-taking, that is, the very awareness that the other is in some way like the self the other knows it well, and therefore, responsive to the self in a system of complementary expectations. Social development, as explained by him, is the restructuring of the concept of self in its relationship to the concepts of other people.

From such conceptualisation, there emerges a basic fact of socialisation, which emphasises the interactional nature of the organism and the social order. The emerging self or a child is seen as progressing through the related steps of development. The child is seen as selectively and actively processing information according to his own age of cognitive development.

In a nutshell, this perspective places emphasis upon the outcome of action initiated by the person in selecting and giving meaning to the stimuli, which is always dependent on the person's cognitive development stage. For highlighting cognitive development, Kohlberg (1973) developed a model consisting of three levels of moral development. Each level of moral development has two stages. The first level is called *preconventional level*. Ten-year old children are at this level. At stage 1 of this level, the children's behaviour is largely controlled by punishment and children make every effort to avoid punishment. As the child matures, he enters stage 2, where he becomes aware of rewards. However, at this level (preconventional level), child shows no internalisation of moral values. Moral reasoning is entirely controlled by reward and punishment. By internalisation, here, we mean the developmental changes from the behaviour that is externally controlled to the behaviour that is internally controlled. The second level is that of *conventional level*, where the child's internalisation is intermediate in the sense that the children abide by certain standards (internal), but there are essentially the standards of others (external). At stage 3 of this level, the child conforms to the rules and norms of the society for meeting the expectations of others. At stage 4 of this level, the child internalises general standard of behaviour, irrespective of the role partner. At this stage, moral judgements are based on understanding and the social order, law and duty. Most of the children go through this second stage in between the ages of 13 and 15. The third level is that of *postconventional level*, which is characterised by full internalisation. This is the highest level of moral development, and here, moral development is internalised and moral reasoning is self-generated. At stage 5 of this level, the individual behaves according to rational, agreed-upon standards. Here, the person recognises that laws are important for society, but at the same time, he knows that law can be changed. At stage 6 of this level, the person accepts the abstract moral principles such as justice, freedom, honesty, etc. When the person is faced with dilemma between law and conscience, a personal, individualised conscience is followed. By the age of 16, about 20% children enter stage 5 and less than 10% enter stage 6.

This cognitive development view, thus, sees the person as selector of available stimuli in an effort to give them accurate meaning, which might be related to the underlying cognitive structure. This view has special significance for symbolic cognitive approach, which considers human organism as an actor forming his own cognitive and symbolic view of the society as he becomes a functioning member of it.

PROCESS OF SOCIALISATION

The *process of socialisation* means the way the socialisation occurs. Researches done by social psychologists have shown that there are three processes through which socialisation takes place—instrumental conditioning, observational learning or modelling and internalisation.

1. Instrumental conditioning

Instrumental conditioning is one of the important processes of socialisation. It is a process through which an individual learns what response to make in any situation for obtaining a positive reward and avoiding a negative reinforcement. Here, the individual's behaviour is instrumental in the sense that it tends to determine whether he is rewarded or punished.

The most important process in learning of many skills is a type of instrumental learning called *shaping*, which refers to a series of successive approximations in which the learner's behaviour gradually comes closer and closer to the specific response desired by the reinforcing agent. Shaping is interactive in character because in socialisation, the degree of similarity between the desired and observed responses required by the socialising agent partly depends on the learner's past experience.

Researches have shown that when shaping behaviour, a socialising agent can use either positive reinforcement or negative reinforcement. Examples of positive reinforcer are food, water, money, high grades because their presence strengthens the learner's response. Negative reinforcer are those stimuli whose withdrawal strengthens response. Examples of negative reinforce are pain, electric shock, loud noise, etc.

There are several possible schedules of reinforcement such as fixed ratio schedule, variable ratio schedule, fixed interval schedule and variable interval schedule, which are considered important for the process of socialisation. The *fixed ratio schedule* tends to provide reinforcement following a specified number of correct but non-reinforced responses. Paying a worker on a piece rate such as ₹100 for every five items produced, is an example of fixed ratio schedule. The *variable ratio schedule* provides reinforcement after several non-rewarded responses, with the number of responses between reinforcements varying. Researches have shown that this schedule produces the highest and the most stable rates of response. In *fixed interval schedule*, the first correct response is reinforced after a specified period has elapsed. If the learner is somehow aware of the length of the time, he generally tends to respond only at the beginning of the interval. Many schools, for example, arrange examinations at fixed intervals such as at the middle or at the end of the semester or session. That is the reason why some students study only just before the examination. In *variable interval schedule*, the first correct response is reinforced after a variable period. Since in this type schedule, the person cannot guess at what time the reinforcement will be given, he responds at a regular rate.

Punishment means presentation of a painful stimulus or such stimulus by socialising agent that may cause discomfort and tends to decrease the probability of the preceding behaviour done by the learner. Researches have found that punishment is a common practice used by parents in child rearing. Corporal or physical punishment such as pinching, slapping, sparking or hitting are commonly used by parents and tend to vary by the age of child. With increasing age, it tends to decline (Straus and Filed, 2003). In other words, parents use less and less physical punishment as the age of the child advances. The use of psychological techniques such as shouting, threatening, name-calling, etc. has been reported by more than 85% of the parents of children of all ages. The use of corporal punishment during child rearing is more common among low-income parents as well as among African-American parents (Straus and Stewart, 1999), whereas the use of psychological techniques did not vary much by sociodemographic characteristics or by race (Straus and Field, 2003). There are several factors that determine the effectiveness of punishment. First, when punishment is given in proximity to the behaviour, it becomes effective. If it is given in terms of forewarning or following the action or behaviour, it is less effective as compared to when it is given as the behaviour occurred (Aronfreed and Reber, 1965). Second, punishment becomes effective when it is accompanied by reason (Parke, 1969). Third, since punishment is usually administered by a particular person, it becomes effective only when that person is present. That is the reason why it has been found that when parents are absent, children may engage in activities for which their parents had punished them earlier (Parke, 1970).

Researches have revealed that corporal punishment has some long-term consequences. Therefore, parents and caregivers have to be very cautious in delivering such punishment during child-rearing practices. Straus, Sugarman and Giles-Sims (1997) reported that mothers (of 6 to 9 years children) who reported spanking the child, produced antisocial behaviour in their children. Also, the use of psychological punishment was found to be clearly associated with such problematic behaviours like running away, being suspended from school, etc. in adolescence.

Researchers have further shown that children learn several types of behaviours through instrumental learning. Performance of some of these behaviours is extrinsically motivated and performance of some other activities are intrinsically motivated. When extrinsically motivated, behaviours are dependent on whether someone else will reward appropriate behaviours or punish inappropriate ones. When intrinsically rewarded, the behaviours are performed to achieve an internal state that the persons finds rewarding. Lepper, Greene and Nisbett (1973) reported that the external rewards do not always improve performance. Rather providing reward for behaviour that is intrinsically motivated, in fact, reduces the frequency or quality of the activity.

Closely related to the concept of intrinsic motivation is the concept of self-reinforcement. With the growing standards of socialisation, children not only learn specific behaviours but also learn to perform some standards. For example, children not only try to learn to write, rather they try to learn to write neatly and accurately. These standards become a part of the self and having learned them, a child frequently uses them for judging his own behaviour. In this way, he becomes capable of self-reinforcement. Bandura (1982) opined that repeated successful experience with an activity over time creates a sense of competence in the concerned area of activity. This is called *self-efficacy*. Self-efficacy reinforces a person to seek opportunities to engage in that activity. On the other hand, experiences of repeated failure to perform the task tends to create perception that one is not efficacious and this state is likely to lead to avoidance of the task. A student, who perceives himself as poor at delivering speech, will probably not enter the school debate.

2. Observational learning

Observational learning, also called *modelling*, refers to the acquisition of behaviour based on the observation of another person's behaviour and its consequences for that person. Children learn many behaviours through modelling or observational learning. By observing another person who is called a *model*, performing certain skill or behaviour, a child can increase his own skills.

Bandura (1982) pointed out that when models are observed being reinforced for certain behaviours, the observer is more likely to perform those behaviours. The interpretation of this finding is that the observer experiences the model's reinforcements vicariously. In fact, Bandura carried out an experiment to test the hypothesis that rewarding the model increases the probability that the observer will learn some of his behaviours. In one experiment, three groups of nursery school children were taken and these groups observed child models under three different conditions—an aggressive model was rewarded, an aggressive model was punished and a non-aggressive model was neither punished nor rewarded. There was also a fourth group of children, who acted as a control group, and therefore, had no exposure to models. Results revealed that the model, who had been observed being rewarded, was copied by the children to a greater extent.

Whether or not the children learn from observing a model also depends on the important characteristics of model. Children generally tend to initiate high status and nurturant models than those models who are low in status and nurturance (Bandura, 1969). Lewis and Brooks-Gum (1979) conducted a study in which it was shown that the preschool children, who were given dolls representing peers, older children and adults consistently chose adult dolls as people they would go to for help and older children as people they would prefer for teaching. It was also found that children liked more to model themselves after nurturant persons than after cold and impersonal ones. It obviously meant that socialisation is likely to be effective when a child has nurturant and loving parents or caregiver.

3. Internalisation

Internalisation is an important socialisation process. In internalisation, initially, external behavioural standards (for example, those held by father, mother, teacher, etc.) become internal, and subsequently, guide the person's behaviour. In other words, *internalisation* is defined as the process in which one adopts the values, attitudes, behaviour of those who are significant others. Any behaviour or action is said to be based on internalised standards when the person engages in it without considering possible rewards and punishments. There are various types of explanations that have been offered to the process by which internalisation occurs, but all of them agree that the children are likely to internalise those behaviours, which are held by powerful or nurturant adult caregivers.

Researches have shown that all important theories of internalisations such as psychoanalytic, social learning or cognitive accept that socialisation occurs through the process of internalisation. In fact, internalisation results in the exercise of self-control. Individuals tend to conform to the internal standards even when there is no surveillance of their behaviours or acting by others, and therefore, no rewards are given for their conformity. Political leaders and religious saints, who are widely admired for their actions that are often unpopular, frequently do so because their beliefs are internalised.

Thus, we see that socialisation takes places due to various processes underlying it. For understanding how socialisation works, these processes must be taken into consideration.

AGENTS OF SOCIALISATION

As we know, socialisation means all those learning processes that allow a person to become an adequately functioning member of the society. Most of the social psychologists are of view that socialisation has the following four major components:

1. Socialisation is a learning process.

2. Socialisation has a target person, that is, a person who will be socialised.
3. Socialisation involves an agent, that is, someone who acts as a source for providing social learning.
4. Socialisation has an outcome, that is, the persons being socialised acquire new skills, knowledge and behaviour.

In the present section, we shall deal with the agents of socialisation only. Social psychologists have identified some important factors, which act like agents of socialisation only. Important agents of socialisation are as under:

1. Family

Family is the first important and typical social group into which one child is socialised. Researches have revealed that although the form of family organisation and the specific functions it does may vary from culture to culture, families in the entire world have one common denominator—adult caretakers interact with the child, out of which the first learning of appropriate or inappropriate behaviour comes out. In the families, there are different practices that affect the socialisation. Some of these major practices are given below:

(i) **Parental support and control:** Parental supportive or emotional relationship between parent and offspring directly affects the socialisation of the children. Supportive interpersonal relationship fosters those characteristics in children that are valued in society. Such relationship includes love, support and warmth. Such supportive relationship tends to develop high self-esteem and sufficient cognitive abilities. Relationship of this kind also helps in exhibiting moral attitudes and behaviour and in adopting the dominant values of the society (Bronfenbrenner, 1977). Rollins and Thomas (1979) reported that parental emotional support is associated with high self-esteem, enhanced creativity, advanced cognitive development, instrumental competence, conformity to societal norms and acceptance of societal moral values among children. On the other hand, absence of parental emotional support is related to the behaviours like delinquency, aggression, learning disabilities and mental illness.

Like parental support, parental control or discipline also affect the process of socialisation. Different techniques of parental control or discipline affects the child behaviour and attitude in different way. Researches have revealed that there are two main types of discipline or control used by parents—induction and coercion. In *inductive-control method*, direct contest of will between parents and child is avoided and parents reason to induce voluntary behaviour in the child. In other words, here, the parents reason by giving information to the child about possible consequences of behaviour for the child or others. In *coercion method*, parents directly use their status, control of resources and physical methods in attempting to induce an appropriate behaviour. Rolling and Thomas (1979) conducted studies in which children from homes characterised by inductive parental discipline were compared to the children from homes characterised by coercive parental discipline. It was found that children from homes characterised by parental inductive discipline had developed many socially approved attributes like social competence, self-esteem, conformity, social insight, adequate sense of morality, ability to control the environment, etc. On the other hand, children raised in homes with parental coercion discipline were lacking these said social attributes.

When the effects of parental support and parental control were combined, the results were still more clear and distinguishing. Emotionally supportive homes with inductive method of discipline produced children having distinct advantages from the viewpoints of socialisation. Such children tended to be more creative, showing high level of moral behaviour and demonstrated relatively high level of self-esteem. Likewise, children raised in non-supportive home with coercive parental discipline tended to exhibit many socially inappropriate behaviours like aggression, drug abuse, etc.

(ii) **Child-rearing practices:** Many studies of socialisation have focused upon child-rearing techniques (or parenting style) and their likely impact upon social and cognitive development. There are four types of parenting style—authoritarian parenting, neglectful parenting, authoritative parenting and permissive parenting (Baumrind, 1971; Maccoby and Martin, 1983). In *authoritarian style*, parents show strictness, punish misdemeanours and set a standard of behaviour, which the child is expected to attain. In *permissive style*, parents are highly involved with their children and place a very few rules of strict discipline and permit their children complete freedom of behaviour. Such permissive or indulgent parents are tolerant and warm but exercise little authority. It is also known as *indulgent style*. *Authoritative style* is one which is intermediate between authoritarian style and permissive style—a style where parents tend to be liberal, granting considerable behavioural freedom and latitude to their children. Parents belonging to authoritative style are very reasonable and consistent in their relationship with children and gradually increase the child's level of responsibility in accordance with the level of child's competencies and also encourage their independence. In *neglectful style*, parents are not at all involved with their children lives and they spend little time with their children. Of these four styles, the first three were suggested by Baumrind and the fourth one, that is, neglectful style was suggested by Maccoby and Martin. These four parenting styles have differential impact upon the socialisation of the children. The four parenting styles and children behaviour were found to be correlated. Major findings revealed that children reared under authoritarian style adopted by parents are more shy, withdrawn, unfriendly and very slow to trust others. Those reared under indulgent style are immature, unruly, and likely to be bored soon on a task when faced with difficulty and have little control over their own behaviour. Children reared under authoritative style are found to be friendly, happy, showing conformity to social norms and independent individuals. Children reared under neglectful parenting style are found to be socially incompetent, showing poor self-control and are not achievement-oriented. The four parenting styles are summarised in Figure 6.1.

Although Baumrind's study clearly shows a differential impact of parenting style upon socialisation of children, it has been criticised on the following three important points:

(a) She used correlations between parenting styles and children behaviour in arriving at the said conclusions. Critics have pointed out that correlation can prove mere link or relation between two variables and it cannot show causation.
(b) Some children raised in indulgent parenting style were found to display none of the unpleasant behaviours usually found associated with this parenting style.

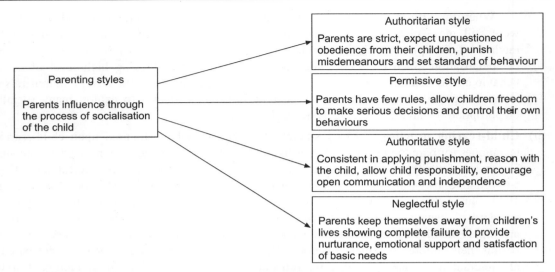

Figure 6.1 Four parenting styles suggested by Baumrind (1971), Maccoby and Martin (1983).

(c) Some psychologists emphatically have said that it is not the parenting styles themselves, which socialise children in different ways, rather the way the children themselves perceive and evaluate the care they receive from the parents (Dunn and Plomin, 1990) does have an impact upon socialisation.

In some cultures, particularly in Western culture, child-rearing practices have been found to differ among different socioeconomic status (SES) group. *SES* is defined as grouping of people according to similar occupational, educational and economic characteristics. Researches have revealed that parents from low SES families often place a high value on external characteristics such as obedience and neatness. They are more likely to use physical punishment and frequently criticise their children (Hoff-Ginsberg and Tardif, 1995). On the other hand, parents of middle SES families place a high value on internal characteristics such as self-control and delay of gratification. Such parents are more prone to praise, accompany their children with reasoning, and frequently ask questions to their children.

2. Peers

Peers also play a powerful role in the socialisation. Peers are commonly understood as the children of about the same age and the same level of maturation, who feel and act together. One of the major functions of peer group is to provide source of information and comparison about something outside the family. For proper socialisation, good peer relationship is considered important. Social isolation or poor peer relationship is associated with many problems like delinquency, depression and drug abuses. Roff, Sells and Golden (1972) reported that poor peer relationship in childhood is associated with dropping out of school and various kinds of delinquent behaviours in adolescence. Likewise, Hightower (1990) reported that satisfactory and harmonious peer relationship in adolescence is related to positive mental health during midlife.

Some studies have identified behaviours associated with five types of peer social status (Wentzel and Asher, 1995; Wentzel and Battle, 2001). These five types of peer social status are—popular children, average children, neglected children, rejected children and controversial children. *Popular children* as those children who are frequently considered as best friends and are rarely disliked by peers. Such children are happy, show enthusiasm and concern for others, listen carefully, maintain open lines of communication and are self-confident (Hartup, 1983). Such children engage more in prosocial behaviour and are rarely aggressive. They also help set the rules and norms for the group. *Average children* are those who receive both positive and negative nominations from their peers. *Neglected children* are infrequently nominated as best friends, but are not disliked by peers. *Rejected children* are those who are infrequently nominated as best friend and are very much disliked by their peers. *Controversial children* are those who are frequently nominated as someone's best friend and are also disliked. Of these various types of children, from the point of view of socialisation, popular children are considered the best and rejected children and neglected children suffer the most. Rejected children often have more serious adjustment problems than do neglected children (Buhs and Ladd, 2001). Majority of rejected children is characterised by aggression, impulsiveness and disruptiveness.

Havighurst (1972) pointed out that there are four ways through which peer group helps children in becoming socialised. These are discussed below:

(i) Peer group helps children to learn to get along with the age-mates and to behave in such a way that is socially acceptable to them.
(ii) Peer group can promote children's personal independence by providing them emotional satisfaction from friendship with peers.
(iii) Peer group provides opportunity for the children to learn appropriate social attitudes like how to enjoy social life and group activities and how to like people.
(iv) Peer group also helps children in developing a rational conscience and a scale of values to supplement or replace the values of authoritarian conscience.

3. School

School is another important agent of socialisation. School is the child's first experience with formal and public evaluation of performance. In school, the behaviour and work of the children are evaluated by the same standards and judgements and are made public to the others in class as well as to the parents. In school, children tend to develop those traits which facilitate social interaction throughout life. In this sense, schools civilise children.

Researches have revealed that there are different aspects of schools, which have an impact upon children's socialisation. Both class size and pupil's location in the class determine the extent to which the pupil participates in the classroom activities. While participation is higher in smaller classrooms, pupils seated in the front and centre of the class, popularly called *action zone*, participate more than pupils seated in the remaining parts of the room (Gump and Ross, 1977). Researches have also revealed that with the increase in class size (that is, with forty and above pupils), the total amount of discussion decreases. However, a smaller percentage of children do participate frequently in such situation. Apart from this, in small class, there are greater group activities, more individualisation, more positive student attitudes, less misbehaviour and teachers are also more satisfied (Minuchin and Shapiro, 1983).

Teacher's role is another important aspect of school that affects the socialisation process. Teachers play a variety of roles in school, that is, evaluators, disciplinaries and models. Teachers' impressions and expectations concerning pupil's probable success has been found to affect children's academic progress. Rosenthal and Jacobsen (1968) found that pupils succeeded when teachers believed that they would do well and pupils did less well when there was expectation on the part of teachers that they (pupils) would not succeed much. The type of evaluation conditions introduced by teachers also affect pupil's performance and anxious children have been found to improve their performance under optimal test-taking conditions (Hill and Eaton, 1977).

Researches have shown that social comparison has an important influence on the behaviour of school children. Since teachers make public evaluations of the pupil's work, each pupil can judge his performance in comparison to the others' work. Such consistent evaluations help pupil in building and modifying his image of self.

Besides, textbooks or reading material also serve important socialising functions. Many of the attitudes and cultural values that slowly emerge during early school years are the product of contents and themes of textbooks pupils go through. Good textbooks and reading materials having moral implications in real life act as booster for moral development of pupils.

4. Neighbours

Neighbours also act as important agent of socialisation. They directly affect the social and emotional development of children. Neighbours influence the socialisation process in different ways. Children are readily influenced by the behaviour of the neighbours. If they are friendly, cooperative, sympathetic and social, it is likely that children's social development will be positive and it will accelerate the process of socialisation. On the other hand, if the neighbours are quarrelsome, aggressive, egocentric, prejudiced, it is likely that children may develop some unsocial behaviour patterns. Such neighbours tend to retard the socialisation process.

5. Caste and class

Caste and class are also important agents of socialisation. In India, caste is a very popular means of recognising the strength of a person. Caste is determined by birth. It provides the norms that a man or woman should marry another woman or man of his or her own caste, what type of occupations he will probably undertake and to whom he or she will develop intimacy. All these rules and norms force the persons of a particular caste to behave accordingly. Although with the recent advancement in technology and culture, earlier restrictions imposed by caste have, to a greater extent, relaxed. That is the reason why today intercaste marriages are frequently being done, and later on, society has to approve such marriages.

Social class also influences socialisation. Indian society, like many others of world, has three layers—high, middle and low. All these three classes of people have their own features and have different levels of socio-economic status. Such features allow their members to develop their own viewpoints regarding the various social problems and issues. As a consequence, they are socialised accordingly. It is due to this social class difference that we find that a person of high social class thinks and behaves in a different way from a person of low social class, despite the fact that both of them are in the same social situation.

6. Language

Language has been described as one of the greatest intellectual feats (Bloomfield, 1933). Language is a tool through which socialisation is done from early stages of life. The child, who develops a strong linguistic capacity, generally shows a better social development than a child who has somehow not been able to develop his linguistic capacity or has developed a poor linguistic capacity. With enriched linguistic capacity, a person is able to convey his ideas, views and thinking to others as well as understand the meaning of others speech. This facilitates various types of social learning, which in turn, strengthens the socialisation process. Those who are deprived of opportunity to develop adequate linguistic capacity, are also not able to learn the significance of various social norms of the society. The classic case of *The Wild Boy of Aveyron* in France and *The Wolf Children of Bengal* in India are good examples of how due to deprivation of human society even the human children behave like animals and their languages were more like animals than like human beings. Deprived of human language, when they were placed in human society to learn something, they took a lot of time, and later on, they failed to be socialised properly. Recently, Davis (1949) reported the case of two children—*Anna* and *Isabelle*. Isabelle, who had some human company during her early childhood, was able to develop adequate language skills, while Anna, deprived of such company, did not. Accordingly, Isabelle became more readily socialised as compared to Anna often when they joined human company.

7. Political, economic and religious institutions

Various institutions in the society also exert important impact upon socialisation. Political parties and leaders do frequently influence the minds of people, who are suggested and sometimes forced to behave in a particular way. Such practice strengthens the existing way of behaving and prepares a particular kind of social norms. Gradually, persons learn to behave according to those social norms.

Economic institutions also exert some influence upon socialisation. In order to meet their needs, people frequently join various institutions located in public and private sector. In these various institutions, people have to interact with others. As a consequence, they learn some new social behaviours. Not only that, their behaviour, attitude and thinking are also modified by those interactions. The whole situation that way allows persons to learn to behave according to the social values and norms.

Religious institutions also affect socialisation. Every such institution tends to elicit new and unique belief and values in its followers. For example, Hindu religion clearly mentions that after death, a person gets a place in heaven if he has done good things in his life and he goes into hell if he has done wrong and sinful acts in his life. This belief fosters many types of social and ethical behaviour and influences the social interaction of the person.

Thus, we find that there are different types of agents of socialisation. Each agent tends to promote socialisation from his own unique viewpoint.

OUTCOMES OF SOCIALISATION

Individuals who are socialised tend to acquire new skills, knowledge, attitudes and behaviour. This is known as *outcomes of socialisation*. Such important outcomes are being discussed in this section.

1. Linguistic competence

Linguistic competence is one of the important outcomes of a socialised child. A child's acquisition of speech reflects both the development of necessary perceptual and motor skills as well as the impact of social learning.

Language acquisition, which is the outcome of socialising a child through first three years of life, passes through four stages (Bates et al., 1987). The first stage called *prespeech stage* lasts for about first 10 months and involves speech perception, speech production, and some intentional communication. The infants perceives all of the speech sounds during first few weeks of life. At the age of 2 to 3 months, they begin producing sound and at 4 to 7 months, they start producing sounds specific to their parent's languages. In doing so, they initiate the sounds they hear. So far as the intentional communication is concerned, data indicate that vocal exchanges involving 4 months old infants and their mothers are patterned. In other words, vocalisation by either infant or mother was followed by silence, allowing the other person to respond.

The second stage starts at 10 to 14 months, and at this stage, the infant for the first time recognises that things or objects have names. This ability to use names reflects the proof for cognitive as well as linguistic development. The first word produced are usually nouns that name specific object. The third stage starts at about 18 months, where there is vocabulary burst and the child almost doubles the number of words that are correctly used. It obviously reflects the maturation of some cognitive abilities. This is followed by an increase in the complexity of vocalisation, leading to occurrence of the first full sentence which happens at the stage of 22 months. Such speech such as 'Give chocolate, Mommy' is definitely telegraphic, that is, the number of words is greatly reduced in comparison to adult speech (Brown and Fraser, 1963). The fourth stage is a stage of grammaticisation, which occur at the age of 24 to 30 months. At this stage, the child's use of language reflects the fundamentals of grammar. In his attempt to learn to make grammatically correct sentences, there occurs speech expansion. In other words, here, at this stage, an adult often responds to children's speech by repeating it in expanded form. Such speech expansion contributes to language acquisition by providing children such a model, which helps them in conveying more effectively the meanings they intend to.

The next stage of language development during socialisation is marked by occurrence of private talk or speech in which the child talks loudly to himself often for extended periods. Such private speech generally begins at about 3 years of age, which increases in frequency until 5 years of age and disappears by about 7 years of age. Such private speech serves mainly two major functions—first, private talk contributes to the development of the sense of self because such speech is addressed to the self as an object and includes application of meaning to self such as 'I am boy', and second, private talk helps children in developing awareness of the environment because they repeatedly name the aspects of physical and social environment.

Leaper, Anderson and Sanders (1998) conducted a meta-analysis of observational studies of parents' use of language in interaction with their children. Such analysis have revealed several differences in the types of communication between fathers and mothers. For example, mothers are found to be more supportive and less directive as compared to fathers. Not only that, parents also differ in the way they talk to their daughters and sons. In this way, children are socialised to gender differences in language use as they interact with their parents.

2. Cognitive competence

Quite closely related to the language competence is what has been called *cognitive competence*. For a child (or even for adult), it is not possible to remember each object, animal and person as a distinct entity. Therefore, things must be categorised into inclusive groupings such as cats, dogs, boys, girls, houses, etc. A category of objects and the cognitions which the individual has about the members of that category, say for example, dog make up a schema, which permits us to make sense of the world around us.

During socialisation, children learn various types of schemas. For this, language learning is essential because language provides the names around which schemas generally develop. In the beginning, children use a very general schema only. For example, some children learn the word 'cow' at the age of 10–12 months and then apply it to all animals such as dogs, cats, goats, etc. With maturation, however, they develop some abstract schema 'animal' to discriminate among cows, dogs and goats. Researches have shown that with the advancement in age, children become increasingly skilled at classifying diverse objects and treating them as equivalent. For example, by the ages of 6 to 8 years, children learn to sort objects based on the visual features and by the age of 10 to 12 years, they learn to use functional or superordinate categories like food and sort objects into groups (Rigney, 1962). By the age of 2 to 3 years, children correctly differentiate between babies and adult by seeing photographs. Likewise, by the age of 5, the children employ four categories—little children, big children, parents and grandparents. As children learn to group objects into meaningful schemas, they also learn how others feel about the categories. Social psychologists have considered these skills very important in determining the social interactions. Only by having the ability to group objects, persons and situations, children can readily determine how to behave towards them.

3. Gender role

One very specific outcome of socialisation that is seen in almost all cultures is the gender role of the person. Male role and female role are clearly expelled out because every society has differential expectations regarding the characteristics and behaviour of men and women. In our society, men are expected to be more extroverted, competitive, logical, ambitious and able to make decision quickly. Likewise, females are expected to be high in warmth and expressiveness, that is, gentle, tactful and sensitive. Parents utilise differential treatment at birth to male and female child. Generally, male child is handled vigorously and roughly, whereas female child is given more cuddling during socialisation. Not only that, male and female child are dressed differently from infancy and are also given different types of toys to play with. Mothers and fathers also behave differently while interacting with infants. Fathers are generally found to engage the child in rough and tumble and physically stimulating activities (Walters and Walters, 1980), whereas mothers generally engage in behaviour oriented towards fulfilling the child's physical and emotional needs and wishes (Baumrind, 1980).

Researches have also revealed that generally, by the age of 2 years, child's concept of self as male or female, that is, gender identity develops. Likewise, by the ages of 2 and 3 years, differences in aggressiveness become evident, with boys showing more physical and verbal aggressive acts than girls. By the age of 3, the children frequently choose same gender-peers as playmates. This enhances the opportunities to learn gender-appropriate behaviour via modelling (Lewis and Brooks-Gunn, 1979). Children also learn gender-appropriate behaviour by observing the parents' interaction. Parents reward the behaviour of children associated with the gender roles and punish behaviour inconsistent with these roles.

The definitions of gender role vary from culture to culture. For example, Asian cultures are patriarchal and parents may socialise female children to follow the restrictive norms designed to serve the family rather than express individuality (Root, 1995). In Indian culture, qualities that are prized are nurturance and affiliation and not autonomy and self-assertion that are predominant pathways of Western culture (Vindhya, 2011). This practice is not seen in cultures such as in America, where families have more individualistic views of behaviour and decision-making.

Another major influences on gender role socialisation are those of school and mass media. Teachers tend to reward appropriate gender role behaviour among children. They often reinforce aggressive behaviour in boys and submissive behaviour and dependency in girls (Serbin and O'Leavy, 1995). The contents of the books that are read and told to primary school students portray men and women different and this facilitates them in learning of appropriate gender roles. Mass media also play a significant role in socialising the children in appropriate gender roles. Researches have analysed the contents of various television programmes, television advertising, feature films as well as other media reports showing different portrayals. Thompson and Zerbinos (1995) did content analysis of 175 episodes of 41 animated television series and reported that male characters were portrayed as independent, ambitious, athletic and aggressive, whereas female characters were shown as emotional, defendant, domestic and romantic. Sommers-Flanagan, Sommers-Flanagan and Davis (1993) analysed 40 music videos and reported that men generally tended to engage in more dominant, aggressive behaviour, whereas women engaged in subservient behaviour and were frequently shown as object of aggressive sexual advances.

4. *Moral development*

One obvious outcome of proper socialisation is moral development of children and adolescence. In moral development, two aspects are considered important—one aspect is the acquisition of knowledge of social rules and another aspect is the process through which children become capable of making moral judgements.

(i) **Acquisition of knowledge of social rules:** Each society, organisation and group has some rules governing behaviour. These rules are called *norms* that state whether the behaviour is acceptable, unacceptable for a person in specific situation.

Now, the question is—what influences which norms the children will acquire or learn? Social psychologists have identified some factors that directly influence the acquisition of norms by children. Some of these factors are discussed as under:

(a) *Culture of the society:* The culture of the society directly affects the acquisition norms. In Indian culture, the children learn to honour the elders by touching their foot and women learn to cover their private parts of body properly with clothing in public. Parents often have norms that they apply distinctively to their own children. Mothers and fathers expect certain behaviours from their own sons or daughters, but may show different expectations for others' children. For example, they may expect their own children to be more polite, friendly and cooperative than other children in interaction with adults. Not only that, they also expect better performance in school from a child, who had done well in the past in comparison to those who had problems in schools. Likewise, parents expect greater politeness from a 12-year old child than from a 6-year old. In all of these ways, each child is socialised to somewhat different norms and the outcome is a young person having his own uniqueness in personality.

(b) *Normative pressure from peers:* When children engage in cooperative play at the age of 5–6 years, they begin to experience some normative pressure from peers. Children bring different norms from their separate families, and therefore, they tend to introduce new expectations. Sometimes, peers' expectations are found to be in conflict with those of parents. For example, many parents do not allow their children to play with toy gun or swords. However, children, through involvement with their peers, may come to know that other children routinely play with such toys. As a consequence, some children may experience normative conflict and may try to find out strategies for resolving such conflicts. Moreover, the norms of peer group emphasise participation in group activities, which are impulsive and spontaneous, whereas parental norms emphasise behaviour directed towards long-term outcomes as well as homework and other educational activities that ultimately contribute to academic achievement.

(c) *School:* School is another influencing factor for acquisition of knowledge of social rules. In school, children are exposed to *universalistic norms* or the rules that apply equally to all children. At school, children learn to wait their turn, to control their impulsive behaviour and work without much support and supervision. Thus, school becomes the first place, where a child is treated primarily as a member of the group rather than a unique individual.

(ii) **Capability to make moral judgement:** Children not only learn norms of their social groups but also they develop an ability to evaluate behaviour in some specific situation by applying certain standards. The process through which children become capable of making moral judgements is called *moral development*, which has basically two components— reasons one adheres to social rules and the important bases used to evaluate actions by self or others as good or bad.

Piaget (1965), a famous Swiss psychologist, was the first person to explain bases for moral judgement and found three important bases for moral judgements—amount of benefit/harm, actor's intentions and application of agreed-upon rules or norms. Kohlberg (1969) further extended Piaget's work by analysing the reasoning by which people reach moral judgements. By analysing the various stories involving conflict between human needs and social norms or laws, Kohlberg proposed a developmental model, with three levels of moral reasoning, each level having two stages. The first level is that of *preconventional morality* having stage 1 of obedience and punishment orientation, where rules are obeyed by children in order to avoid punishment and other troubles. Stage 2 of this level is that of hedonistic orientation, where rules are obeyed in order to obtain rewards for the self. The second level is the level of *conventional morality*, which has again two stages, that is, stage 3 and stage 4. The third stage is the good boy/nice girl orientation, where rules are obeyed by children to please others and avoid disapproval. The fourth stage is that of authority and social-order maintaining orientation, where rules are obeyed to display respect for authorities and maintain social order. The third level is that of *postconventional morality*, which has stage 5 and stage 6. The fifth stage is that of social contract orientation, where rules are obeyed because they represent the desire of majority and also to avoid the violation of rights of others. The sixth stage is that of universal ethical principles, where rules are obeyed in order to adhere to one's principles. Kohlberg opined that the progression from stage 1 to stage 6 is universal in nature and all children starting from stage 1 progress through stages in order. Few people reach at the stage of 5 or 6. He has further opined that attaining higher levels is better or more appreciable.

5. Orientation towards work

Work is of central importance in social life of human beings. Adults employed in different occupations develop different orientations towards work, and their orientations, in fact, influence how they socialise their children. Kohn (1969) had conducted extensive research to examine the influence of the differences between social classes in values transmitted through socialisation. In this study, fathers were submitted a list of traits, including success, self-control, obedience, responsibility and good manners and were asked to show how much they value each for their sons and daughters. In fact, underlying these specific characteristics, a general dimension of self-direction versus conformity is usually found. Analysis of data obtained from 3 to 15-year old children indicated that emphasis on self-direction and reliance on internal standards increased as the level of social class went up. The relationship between values and social class was found not only in the samples of American fathers but was also observed in Japanese and Polish fathers (Kohn et al., 1990). Such differences in the evaluations of particular traits reflect differences in the conditions of works. In general, middle-class occupations involve the manipulation of people and symbols, and here, the work is not closely supervised. They require workers who are self-directing and can make judgements based on the knowledge and internal standards. Working-class occupations are more routinised and more closely supervised. They require workers with a conformist orientation. A study conducted by Morgan, Alwin and Griffin (1979) found that differences in values parents place on self-direction influence the kinds of activities in which they encourage their children to participate. For example, parents who value self-direction tend to encourage their children to take college-preparatory courses because without college education, jobs providing higher level of autonomy could not be achieved. By the age of 16, many adolescents develop expectations about jobs that they will hold as adults. These adolescents' expectations have provided a clear basis for educational and career choices.

Thus, we find that socialisation has clear impact upon human beings. Persons being socialised acquire new skills, knowledge and behaviour through some specific outcomes of the socialisation itself.

CONCEPT OF ADULT SOCIALISATION

We know that the process of socialisation does not stop at any point. In fact, such process occurs not only in childhood and continues throughout the life. In childhood, the socialisation is directed at some basic outcomes such as gender roles, acquisition of language and various types of social norms for making healthy interaction. In adulthood, the socialisation focuses at some different points and it basically aims at strengthening the adult roles. Researches have shown that there are three processes considered important for adult socialisation—role acquisition, anticipatory socialisation and role discontinuity.

1. Role acquisition

Throughout the life, a person has to learn some new roles. During adulthood, the major roles learned by a person are those of intimate partner or spouse' work roles, parent, grandparent, and finally, the role of retiree. Each of these roles requires role acquisition, learning the expectations and skills associated with the new role.

It has been reported that in recognition of the need to train people for new roles, many groups, governmental and non-governmental organisations provide socialisation opportunities through formal training. These groups and organisations are given responsibility to train the new role occupants for developing necessary skills. Often such training occurs on the job. The various refresher courses as well as orientation courses arranged for college teachers by different Indian universities in collaboration with the University Grants Commission are good examples of such formal training, which aim at developing necessary skills in them. Recently, the Government of Bihar has proposed to set up State Training Council for training the state government staffs from class 4 to class 1 for equipping them to meet the challenges of new roles after being promoted to the next post (Hindustan Times, Patna, October 26, 2011)

Apart from these, there may be a separate period of formal training outside the organisation before the person is allowed to occupy a new role. In fact, this alternative measure is the basis for many junior or technical college training programmes. Various training programmes for dental technicians, paramedical activities, truck drivers, beauticians are a few examples of such type of socialisation.

2. Anticipatory socialisation

Anticipatory socialisation is another important process seen in adult socialisation. It is the learning of those behaviours or activities that provide people with the knowledge and skills about those roles that they have not yet assumed. For example, the aspiring politicians or students, who want to adapt political career, attend closely the behaviour and activities of ministers and members of Parliament. Observation has been that the successful anticipatory socialisation entails goal setting, planning and sound preparation for future roles. Such preparation may occur through part-time jobs, special courses, reading and conversing with the individuals who are considered significant. People also prepare from future roles by trying out elements of their anticipated roles. The best example of this is found in a couple, who is planning marriage and who generally tends to share purchases and take joint outing.

Anticipatory socialisation is distinct from explicit learning because such socialisation does not intend to role preparation by socialisation agents (Heiss, 1990). It eases the transition into new roles to be undertaken. However, it is more effective for some roles than the others. Anticipatory socialisation works well for those future roles that are highly visible. For example, parent roles are directly observed by children, and therefore, they easily learn parent role to be enacted in future. Anticipatory socialisation also earns role transition if the future roles are presented accurately. If some aspects of future roles are kept deliberately in dark to hide some negative feelings and conflict, it may result in poor anticipatory socialisation.

3. Role discontinuity

Despite anticipatory socialisation, the acquisition of a new role does not always proceed smoothly because changing role can produce stress due to new expectations and performing new tasks and interacting with new types of people. Social psychologists are of view that entering a new role becomes especially difficult where there is found role discontinuity. By role discontinuity, we mean a state where values, identities and expectations associated with a new role contradict those of earlier roles. When a person enters into a discontinuous role, he must revise his earlier expectations and aspirations. One of the best examples of role discontinuity is retirement, which requires that the retiree must shed his earlier expectations and aspirations and must assume a new and completely different expectations. During working years, career-oriented adults are expected to strive for autonomy and productivity and to build their identities mainly around their job or work. However, after retirement, they have to enter into some new and contradictory roles, that is, they have to play now less productive roles and rebuild their identities around new personal and social activities.

Thus, we find that adult socialisation incorporates processes like role acquisition, anticipatory socialisation and role discontinuity, which together make the field more explicit.

Summary and Review

- Socialisation is a subset of social learning. It is an interactional process in which a person's behaviour is modified to conform with the expectations held by the members of the group or society of which he is member.
- There are four important theoretical perspectives of socialisation—psychoanalytic perspective, Eriksonian perspective, social learning perspective and symbolic cognitive perspective. *Psychoanalytic perspective*, formulated by Sigmund Freud, basically emphasises the importance of parent-child relationship in socialisation. Such perspective postulates a developmental view of the emerging socialised being. *Eriksonian perspective*, developed by Erik Erikson, emphasises among others, that ego often functions in a manner to help individuals adapt positively to the challenges presented by their surroundings. This perspective examines ego function in relation to society. Erikson's analysis of socialisation has been presented by the distinctive features of the eight stages of psychosocial development starting from infancy and ending with maturity. Each psychosocial stage is accompanied by *crisis*, that is, turning point in the life of the person. The positive resolution of crisis creates positive components, that is, basic trust, autonomy, etc., which are absorbed into the emerging ego, and further, healthy development is assured. Conversely, if the conflict persists and gets resolved in unsatisfactory way, the negative components such as mistrust, doubt, shame, etc. are incorporated into the ego. *Social learning perspective* emphasises that socialisation is basically a process of children learning, that is, shared meaning of groups to which they belong. In other words, social learning perspective sees a child as learning what behaviour is appropriate and inappropriate in any social situation because he is rewarded for some behaviour and punished for some other behaviour. *Symbolic cognitive perspective* tends to highlight the individual as an actor, who continually constructs his own meaning system. The perspective further holds that any socialisation outcome must also be seen as the person's cognitive development as it takes place during cognitive developmental period.
- Socialisation takes place with the help of different types of agents. Important agents of socialisation are family, peers, school, neighbours, caste and class, language, political, economic and religious institutions. All these agents play a significant role in both childhood socialisation and adult socialisation.
- Socialisation takes place through some processes. Social psychologists have outlined three such processes—instrumental conditioning, observational learning and internalisation. *Instrumental learning* is a process through which an individual learns what response to make in any situation for obtaining a positive reward and avoiding a negative reinforcement. *Observational learning*, also called *modelling*, is another process where children or adults learn many social behaviours through making observation of another person, who is called *model*. Bandura was a pioneer psychologist, who provided a sound experimental base for validity of observational learning. In *internalisation*, the person adopts initially external behavioural standards (for example, those held by father, mother, teacher, etc.), internalises them and subsequently, the person's behaviour is guided by them. In other words, through internalisation, the person adopts as one's own values, attitudes, and behaviours of those who are significant others.
- Outcomes of socialisation result in acquiring new skills, knowledge, attitudes and behaviours. Such important outcomes that are commonly observed are linguistic competence, cognitive competence, gender roles, moral development and some specific work orientation.

- Adult socialisation is also important and distinct from childhood socialisation in its function and aims. Three processes considered important for such socialisation are role acquisition, anticipatory socialisation and role discontinuity. In *role acquisition*, an individual learns new roles. Such roles are learnt through on-the-job training or through training before he undertakes a job or work. *Anticipatory socialisation* prepares the individual for future roles to be enacted. *Role discontinuity* is a state where values, identities and expectations associated with a new role contradict those of earlier roles.

Review Questions

1. Define socialisation. How is socialisation explained from psychoanalytic perspective?
2. Examine critically Eriksonian perspective to socialisation.
3. Discuss social learning perspective for explaining socialisation of child.
4. Describe the role of symbolic cognitive perspective in explaining the nature of socialisation.
5. Citing relevant studies and examples, discuss the role of important agents or factors that influence socialisation of a child.
6. Discuss the important processes underlying socialisation.
7. Describe the important outcomes of socialisation.

7 SOCIAL ATTITUDES AND PERSUASION

Learning Objectives

- Brief Historical Review
- Defining Attitude and Its Components
- Functions of Attitude
- Attitude and Behaviour
- How Do Attitudes Guide Behaviour?
- Formation and Maintenance of Attitudes
- Attitude Change and Persuasion
- Theories of Attitude Organisation and Change
- When Do Attitude Change and Persuasion Become Difficult?
- Dimensions of Attitudes
- Measurement of Attitudes

Key Terms

Affective component
Attitude-to-behaviour process model
Behavioural component
Bogardus scale
Bogus pipeline technique
Chance conditioning
Cognitive component
Cognitive dissonance
Compliance
Concept of congruity
Dimensions of attitude
Discrepant message
Ego-defensive function
Error-choice technique
Explicit attitude
Forewarning
Guttman scale
Heuristic function
Identification
Implicit attitude
Information-motivation function
Inoculation against counter attitudinal
Internalisation
Knowledge function
Likert scale
Persuasion
Primacy effect
Reactance
Reasoned-action model
Recency effect
Scale discrimination technique
Selective avoidance
Semantic differential scale
Sleeper effect
Theory of planned behaviour
Thurstone scale
Two-step flow of communication
Value-expressive

Attitude occupies one of the central positions in the field of social psychology. Nearly about at least half a century, it has been a primary point of focus for both sociologists and psychologists. In 1918, the sociologist, W.I. Thomas referred attitude as the subject matter of par excellence of the discipline and the psychologist, G. Allport in 1935 referred attitude as the keystone in edifice of the field of social psychology. In fact, many early social psychologists defined their field as the scientific study of attitudes (Allport, 1935). Due to several reasons, the study of attitudes is considered central to the field of social psychology. First, attitudes represent a very basic aspect of social cognition, and therefore, they influence our thoughts even if they are not reflected in the overt behaviour of the person. Second, attitudes often affect our behaviour and this is especially found in those situations where attitudes are strong, well-established and clearly accessible. This chapter, among others, focusses on attitude formation, how attitudes are changed—the process of persuasion, the measurement of attitudes. When the attitude change and persuasion become difficult is also highlighted in the chapter.

BRIEF HISTORICAL REVIEW

If we trace the history, it will be obvious that the use of the concept of attitude in the social science literature dates back to the writings of Herbart Spencer and Alexander Bain during 1862 to 1868. They had suggested that a person's mind would tend to fall into a set pattern or attitude that would colour his perception of the situation. A few years later, important experimental advances were made by German scientists, who regarded attitude as a mental set or preparedness that could significantly influence physical reaction time.

The introduction of the concept of attitude into sociology is usually attributed to Thomas and Znaniecki in 1918 in their famous work *The Polish Peasant*. Allport expressed the idea that prior to publication of this book, the term *attitude* was very *infrequently* used in sociological literature. After publication of this book, however, the term was used with greater enthusiasm by a number of writers.

History bears testimony to the fact that the rise of popularity of the concept of attitude could easily be seen in the conjunction with the demise of the concept of instinct. During twentieth century, the term *instinct* had received a good deal of attention from both psychologists and sociologists. However, it shortly came under devastating attack from several corners. The primary impetus that made the term *attitude* more popular was from many early social psychologists, who assumed that attitudes were simply behaviours in miniature. If one really wants to predict behaviour, then one has to determine the person's attitude towards the object, events or persons. This marked the beginning of a large number of research articles during 1930s dealing with the measurement of attitudes.

Today, social psychologists use the term *attitude* to refer to the individuals' evaluation of virtually any aspect of their social world because it is capable of colouring every aspect of experience (Petty, Wheeler and Tormala, 2003).

DEFINING ATTITUDE AND ITS COMPONENTS

Attitude is a mental state because it exists in a person's mind. Allport (1968) noted that the concept of attitude is probably the most distinctive and indispensable concept in contemporary American social psychology. The fact that attitudes are of greater interest to social psychologists is due to their key role in directing and channelling the various kinds of social behaviour.

Attempt has been made by psychologists to define attitudes in concrete way. A few important definitions are as under:

An *attitude* is defined as an individual's tendency or predisposition to evaluate an object or a symbol of that object in a certain way (Katz and Stotland, 1959).

The term *attitude* refers to certain regularities of an individual's feeling, thoughts and predispositions to act towards some aspect of his environment (Secord and Backman, 1964).

An *attitude* is defined as an enduring system of three components centring about a single object, the beliefs about the object—the cognitive component, the affect connected with objects—the feeling component and the disposition to take action with respect to the object—the action tendency component (Krech, Crutchfield and Ballachey, 1962).

Analysing these definitions, we get some basic points about the nature of attitude.

In fact, attitudes are the evaluations of objects, issues or persons. In other words, attitude is cognitive representation that summarises our evaluation of an attitude object (Smith and Mackie, 2007). Attitude objects may be the self, other people, things, actions or idea (McGuire, 1985; Zanna and Rempel, 1988). Any attitude has three components—affective, behavioural and cognitive, popularly called *ABC model of attitude* or *tripartite model of attitude*. (see Figure 7.1). Affect is used in psychology to mean emotion or feeling. So, *affective component* of an attitude is the way a person feels towards objects, events or other persons. In other words, the affective component of attitude consists of person's emotions and affect towards any object or event or person, especially positive or negative evaluations. The *behavioural* component of an attitude is the action that the person takes with respect to object, person or situation. In other words, behavioural component consists of how the individual tends to act towards the stimulus. The *cognitive component* of attitude refers to the way the person thinks about another person, object or situation. These are the thoughts or broadly cognitions, which include beliefs and ideas about the object of attitude.

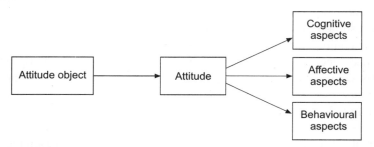

Figure 7.1 Relationship between attitude, attitude object and ABC components of attitude.

The three components of attitude may be illustrated by an individual's unfavourable attitude towards sex education.

1. The affective component of the attitude is his vigorous emotional feeling against sex education. This component is inferred from the fact that he becomes emotionally disturbed and his blood pressures arises as he hears about sex education or it is inferred from his angry behaviour when he argues with a proponent of sex education.
2. The cognitive component of his attitude may consist of his ideas about sex education. This component is inferred from what he says he believes. For example, he may say that

sex education is against morality and it may enhance sex-related problems among persons, especially the adolescents.
3. The behavioural component consists of action tendencies. These are inferred from what he will do or what he actually does. For example, he may write to Education Minister for banning sex education. He may also read articles written by persons who are against sex education. He may himself write in print media such articles that advocate ban on sex education.

Since cognitive, affective and behavioural components all have the same object, it is expected that they would all form a single and relatively consistent whole. Researches have shown that the degree of consistency among components is related to other characteristics of the attitude. Higher degree of consistency between cognitive and affective components is associated with greater degree of stability in attitude and higher resistance to persuasion (Chaiken and Yates, 1985). Greater consistency is also associated with stronger relationship between attitude and behaviour of the person.

Attitude may be positive (positive reaction high and negative reaction low), negative (positive reaction low and negative reaction high), indifferent (positive reaction low and negative reaction low) and ambivalent (positive reaction high and negative reaction high).

It is proper to make here a brief mention about a distinction commonly made between attitude and opinion. An *opinion* may be defined as a belief that a person holds about some object in his environment. It differs from attitude in the sense that it is relatively free of emotion. In other words, it lacks affective component, which is important for attitude. In opinion, the cognitive component is prominent. It may be expressed in terms of a factual statement. For example, a person may believe that a woman worker is less effective and capable than men. If this is a matter of fact for him, it may be regarded as his opinion.

Likewise, another relevant distinction may be made between attitude and value system. Attitude is thought of pertaining to a single object even though that object may be abstract one. But value system is the orientation towards whole classes of objects. Values represent how we feel morally and ethically about the world in which we live. Individual attitudes are frequently organised into a value system. For example, an individual, whose value system has humanitarianism as a central value, may have a positive attitude towards social welfare, democratic practice, and equitable distribution of wealth and negative attitude towards capital punishment, war, dictatorship, and so on.

Why are attitudes viewed important? Social psychologists have answered this question and reported that there are some obvious reasons, which are as follows:

1. Attitude can affect our thoughts. Attitude may be conscious and reportable, called *explicit attitude*, or it may be uncontrollable or not consciously available to us, called *implicit attitude*. Either attitude affects our thoughts. Social psychologists directly learn about explicit attitude towards attitude objects as the persons report about their thoughts and feelings they have. Implicit attitude can be assessed through *Implicit Association Test* (*IAT*) (Greenwald, McGhee and Schwartz, 1998), which is based on establishing degree of readiness with which we can associate various social objects with positive or negative descriptive words. For example, if one immediately says 'lazy' after listening the name of a particular social group, one can easily conclude that the person has negative implicit attitude towards that social group. However, it is not a good predictor of behavior and does not correlate with other attitude measures.

2. Since attitude can affect our behaviour, it is considered important for social psychologists. When attitude is strong, it forcefully affects our behaviour (Bizer et al., 2006). If, for example, a person has strong positive attitude towards megastar Amitabh Bachchan, he will prefer to watch his films and enjoy hearing about the various events of his life on TV or through other means.
3. Since attitude influence behaviour, we can predict about behaviour of an individual if we know about his attitude. For example, if a person has a strong positive attitude towards reality show on TV, it can be predicted that he will like to watch Big Boss, Nach Baliye, etc.

FUNCTIONS OF ATTITUDE

After forming attitudes towards the object, person or situation, we generally retain it at least for some time. But the question is—why do we retain them? One answer is that this serves some functions for us (Katz, 1960; Pratkanis and Greenwald, 1989; Shavitt, 1990). In fact, we form attitude because they are useful for us. Important functions served by attitudes are as under:

1. Instrumental or heuristic function: Individuals develop favourable attitude towards objects that are rewarding and unfavourable attitude towards objects that thwart or punish them. Once attitudes are formed, they provide a simple means of evaluating the objects. Favourable attitude produces positive evaluation and unfavourable attitude produces negative evaluation. Such function of attitude is also known as *adjustive or ulitarain function* because it enables a person to achieve a desired goal and avoid what is distasteful. In brief, this function is hedonistic in nature because it serves the purpose of increasing pleasure or satisfaction and avoiding pain or punishment (Ennis and Zanna, 2000).

2. Knowledge or schematic function: Attitudes serve to rapidly make sense of our social world, which is highly complex. We generally group people, objects or events into some categories or schemas and simplify attitudes that allow us to understand about them. For example, when we come to know that the person is doctor, we develop a certain kind of attitude, which enables us to know something from him about health guide. Researches have further shown that individuals view new information that provides support for their attitudes as more convincing and accurate whereas those information are not perceived as convincing that contradict their existing attitudes (Munro and Ditto, 1997). Likewise, even weak information is perceived as strong one if it is consistent with the existing attitude, and conversely, even strong information is perceived as weak one if it is found inconsistent with the existing attitude (Chaiken and Maheswaran, 1994). In brief, the knowledge function is concerned with how a person organises and processes information about his social world. This function allows us to see the social world as a more familiar, predictable and less uncertain place.

3. Self-esteem function: By holding certain attitude, the self-esteem function of attitude defines self well and maintains or enhances self-worth. A person may obtain satisfaction by expressing himself in terms of attitudes that are appropriate to his personal values and self-concept. By doing so he, in fact, enhances his self-worth. For example, a person with strong religious and moral values may receive much satisfaction by engaging in all those actions that foster such values. By doing so, he would definitely enhance and strengthen his self-worth. Such acts become self-validating and act on those attitudes. Such function is also called *value-expressive function* or *social identity function* (Smith and Mackie, 2007).

4. Ego-defensive function: The ego-defensive function acknowledges that attitudes can serve to protect people from themselves and other people. Sometimes, attitudes, in fact, serve as ego-defensive function, where a person tend to protect himself from the acknowledgement of unpleasant truths about himself or of the harsh realities of his environment by holding a particular attitude. A Brahmin, who is prejudiced against Dalit, may hold the view that he is against such prejudice and discrimination. In fact, by holding such attitude, he protects himself from recognising that he is prejudiced against Dalit. A corrupt official may hold the view that he is against corruption. In fact, in all such situations, the persons want to be like most others and accepted by others by holding a positive and socially desirable attitude towards the issues. Such attitude, in fact, protects him from being criticised.

5. Impression motivation function: Researches have shown that our attitudes can be easily used to lead others to develop a positive view of ourselves. When really motivated to do so, we can shift our attitudes in order to create the desired impression on others. This is known as *impression motivation or management function* (Smith and Mackie, 2007). It has been reported that the more attitudes served an impression motivation function, the more they led people to formulate arguments favouring the existing attitudes. Not only that, such strong impression motivation function also tends to have a clear impact upon how information is processed about social world. This has been clearly demonstrated in a study conducted by Nienhuis, Manstead and Spears (2001). The researchers hypothesised that when attitudes produce stronger motivation to impress others, the persons tend to generate more arguments to support their attitudes. In this study, there were three conditions of impression motivations—*high motivation condition, moderate motivation condition* and *low motivation condition*. Participants in these various conditions were required to generate arguments in favour of the legalisation of hard drugs. It was found that in high motivation condition, participants generated more new arguments and they also reported that they used those arguments in convincing the other person.

Thus, we find that attitudes serve many different functions, which shape their likely influence on processing the varieties of social information.

ATTITUDE AND BEHAVIOUR

On many occasions, we find that behaviour affect our attitude, and sometimes, people change their attitudes when they find that their behaviour contradicts them. However, most of the people generally think of the attitude as being the primary source of behaviour. In other words, knowing about the attitudes of a person, we can predict about his behaviour, thereby assuming consistency between attitude and behaviour. For example, if we know that the attitude of a person towards premarital sex is unfavourable, we can predict that such person will oppose such sexual relationship and will advocate for punishment for all those who engage in such relationship. Social psychologists have, however, pointed out that there are situations in which behaviour does not follow from the attitude. In fact, degree of the influence of attitudes over behaviour has been one of the most important controversies in attitude research (Taylor, Peplau and Sears, 2006).

In 1930, La Piere, a White Professor, toured around the United States by car with a young Chinese student and his wife. At that time, people in the United States were prejudiced against the Chinese. These three travellers stopped at 66 hotels and motels and ate at 184 restaurants. They kept a detailed record of how they were treated. They were given service at all places, except one. Six months later, La Piere sent a questionnaire to each place asking whether they would accept Chinese couple as guests. He received responses from 128 and 92% of those who replied, indicated that they would not serve Chinese guests (LaPiere, 1934). LaPiere and some psychologists after him interpreted such findings as indicative of major inconsistency between attitude and behaviour (Wicker, 1969). Our behaviour and expressed attitudes do differ because both are subjected to other influences. One social psychologist counted 40 separate factors that tend to complicate their relationship (Triandis, 1982).

However, some psychologists have criticised such conclusion as underestimating attitude-behaviour consistency. Some studies done later on have reported higher degree of consistency between attitude and behaviour (Kraus, 1995). As a consequence, in recent years, there has been serious attempts by social psychologists for determining the conditions or factors that yield higher or lesser degree of consistency between attitudes and behaviour. These factors that tend to influence the degree of consistency between attitude and behaviour also attempt to answer the question—when and why do attitudes influence behaviour? It is discussed as follows:

1. Activation of the attitude

At any moment, we have thousands of attitudes in our mind. Most of the time, a particular attitude is not within our conscious awareness and we act without considering our attitudes. If any attitude is to influence behaviour, it must be activated, that is, brought from memory into the present consciousness (Zanna and Fazio, 1982). Researches have shown that an attitude is usually activated by exposure of the person to its object, particularly if the concerned attitude is originally developed through direct experience with that object. Thus, a very easy way to activate the attitude is to arrange the situations in which the persons are directly exposed to the objects. In a well-furnished room, soft lighting and semi-nude dresses by a girl may act as cues for activating the partner's positive attitude towards romantic and sexual activity.

Researches have further shown that some attitudes such as stereotypes are activated automatically by the presentation of the object (Devine, 1989), whereas some others attitudes are slow to be activated (Fazio et al., 1986). Attitudes which are activated automatically by the presentation of the objects are highly accessible. Greater the accessibility of the attitude, greater is the influence on categorising and judging objects. Attitude accessibility means the ease with which a specific attitude can be remembered and brought into conscious awareness. Evidences also indicate that the more accessible an attitude is, the more it is likely to guide and influence behaviour (Fazio and Williams, 1986). An important factor that determines whether an attitude is accessible in memory is how frequently it is expressed. Suppose a person frequently raises voice against unfair means adopted by students in the examination hall. These frequent opportunities to express this attitude are likely to change the behaviour of that person towards the authority, who controls the examination. Easily accessible attitudes also come to be viewed as important (Roese and Olson, 1994). The more the opportunities the person has to express an attitude, the more he is likely to regard that attitude as important for himself. Attitude accessibility also tends to influence how people process persuasive messages. The greater accessibility of attitude tends to force the person to elaborate more on the persuasive messages as oppose to processing them.

2. Characteristics of attitude

There are some features of the attitude themselves that influence the attitude-behaviour relationship. Some of these features are discussed below:

(i) **Strength of attitude:** Attitude may be strong and clear or it may also be weak and vague one. Strong attitudes are stable and have personal implications. Strong attitudes are generally held about important issues and about those which one feels extreme and certain. Such attitudes are often formed through direct experience, and therefore, become highly accessible (Bizer and Krosnick, 2001). Strong attitudes produce some definite and obvious behaviour and account for higher consistency between attitudes and behaviour. For example, if one has strongly favourable attitude towards the policies of the present government, he will do all those behaviours that will promote the successful execution of the government plans. He will show a higher degree of attitude-behaviour consistency. On the other hand, when we observe inconsistency between attitude and behaviour, it is all because of the fact that attitudes are weak and vague.

Several factors tend to contribute to strong attitude and thereby, to the higher attitude-behaviour consistency. One factor is amount of information the person has about the object of attitude. More information about the object makes the attitude stronger, and thus, brings more consistency between attitude and behaviour. Another factor that strengthens attitudes is rehearsing and practicing them. When people frequently think about and express their attitudes, attitude-behaviour consistency becomes high. Strong attitudes are often embedded attitudes. In other words, such attitudes are tied to the various beliefs of the persons. Therefore, they can predict behaviour better as compared to those attitudes, which are less embedded ones.

A concept closely related to the strength of attitude is the importance of the attitude. If the attitudes are important and relevant ones, they directly reflect fundamental values and strong self-interest. Such important and relevant attitudes are not only highly resistant to change but also show a strong relationship with behaviour (Zuwerink and Devine, 1996). Social psychologists have called such state as *vested interest* of the persons, that is, the extent to which attitudes are relevant to the persons who hold it. The results of many studies have shown that if the person has greater such vested interest, his behaviour is likely to be more influenced by such attitudes (Sivacek and Crano, 1982).

(ii) **Stability of attitude:** Stable attitudes are easily accessible, and therefore, more likely to predict behaviour as compared to the attitudes that are less stable and not accessible in memory (Kraus, 1995). When the person's attitudes become unstable due to some reasons, their current attitude predict behaviour more than the attitudes that they held some time back, say a few months back. Researches have shown that consistency between attitudes and behaviour is at a maximum when they are assessed at the same time. Longer time intervals tend to diminish attitude-behaviour consistency because not only attitude changes over time but also people and situations do change. For example, when a girl of 14 years says that she does not want to have a son or daughter does not necessarily reflect her behaviour at the age of 28. The longer the time between assessing the attitude and behaviour, the more such unforeseen factors may arise.

(iii) **Direct personal experience:** Evidences suggest that the attitudes formed on the basis of direct experience with the object, about which a particular attitude is held, tend to exert stronger effects on the behaviour than those attitudes which are formed indirectly. Regan and Fazio (1977) confirmed such effect in their study in which there were two groups of participants placed under two different conditions. One group was placed in direct-experience condition in which the participants played with sample puzzles and the other group was placed in indirect-experience condition where the participants were given only description about the puzzles. Researchers then measured the attitude of the participants and later gave them opportunity to play with the puzzles. Results revealed that correlation between attitude and behaviour was higher for participants who had direct experience with puzzle than those who were having indirect experience.

Social psychologists have further claimed that the attitudes based on direct personal experience are more predictive of subsequent behaviour for several reasons. In fact, attitude is broadly a summary of a person's past experiences. Therefore, an attitude grounded in direct experience predicts future behaviour more accurately. Not only that, direct experience makes more information available about the object of attitude itself (Kelman, 1974). Both amount of information and direct experience taken together enhances the relationship between attitude and behaviour.

(iv) **Affective-cognitive aspects of attitude:** In some attitudes, cognitive component, that is, belief about the attitude object is dominant, whereas in some other attitudes, affective component, that is, emotion or feeling (positive or negative) is more dominant. In the first case, cognitive component is the stronger determinant of behaviour (Millar and Tesser, 1986), whereas in the latter case, the affective component is the stronger determinant of behaviour. However, when cognitive and affective components of attitude are consistent with each other, it does not matter which is made dominant or salient. Both are highly correlated with the behaviour where either one is made dominant (Miller and Tesser, 1989). Researches have shown that the greater the consistency between cognition and evaluation, greater is the strength of attitude-behaviour relationship. Chaiken and Yates (1985) conducted one experiment in which this relationship was confirmed. In this study, participants' beliefs and evaluations regarding capital punishment were measured by questionnaire. Subsequently, participants who were either high or low in consistency (between beliefs and evaluations) were asked to write two essays—one on death penalty and one on unrelated topic. Results revealed that essays on death penalty written by high consistency group were more internally consistent than those written by low consistency group. This happened because their attitudes were part of an internally consistent structure.

3. Situational constraints

In fact, how a person behaves is frequently the interaction of his attitudes and the constraints present in the situation (Klein, Snyder and Livingston, 2004). *Situational constraints or pressures* refer to an influence on behaviour due to the probability that other persons will come to know about the behaviour and respond positively or negatively to it. Such constraint often determines whether our behaviour is consistent with our attitudes. When situational constraint on the person is strong, there would be a weaker relationship between attitude and behaviour. For example, a student in the presence of his teacher may treat his fellow student in a friendly manner, although he may be holding an unfavourable attitude towards him. Sometimes, the influence of situational constraints is so strong that people develop completely different attitudes towards the same attitude object in different situations. For example, Minrad (1952) observed that how white coal miners in the actual workplace of coal field treated black coal miners as equal, but as socially inferior when they met them in the outside world. It means that we often develop a context-dependent attitude towards a single social target that brings discrepancies in attitude and behaviour. Impact of strong situational constraint can also be seen in the classic La Piere (1934) study in which well-drafted and presenting a respectable and gentleman look, a Chinese couple who was asking for rooms was hard to refuse despite feelings of prejudice and unfavourable attitude towards their ethnic group (Chinese).

HOW DO ATTITUDES GUIDE BEHAVIOUR?

Next important question in which social psychologists are seen interested in finding out answer is—how do attitudes guide or shape behaviour? Social psychologists are of opinion that there are some mechanisms through which attitudes guide the behaviour. In this section, we shall consider two such mechanisms. One mechanism considers behaviour that are driven by attitudes based on reason action and other mechanism examines the role of attitudes in more spontaneous and automatic behavioural responses.

Reasoned action model

In the preceding pages, we have discussed several factors that influence the relationship between a single attitude and a behaviour. However, in our daily lives, there are many occasions where the attitude object or situation tends to elicit multiple attitudes. In such situations, to make prediction about what the person will do becomes more difficult. Researchers have shown that when the attitude object evolves several attitudes, the person often engages in deliberations and processes the various information carefully (Fazio, 1990). In fact, in such a situation, we generally consider the attributes of the object, the relevant attitudes and the likely costs and benefits of the potential behaviour. One important attempt to take this entire process into consideration is *theory of reasoned action or thought* developed by Fishbein and Ajzen (1975; Ajzen and Fishbein, 1980). The theory is based on the assumption that the behaviour is rational and it incorporates several factors that tend to affect consistency between attitude and behaviour.

Theory of reasoned action is basically an attempt to specify all those factors that determine attitude-behaviour consistency. The theory or model is summarised in Figure 7.2.

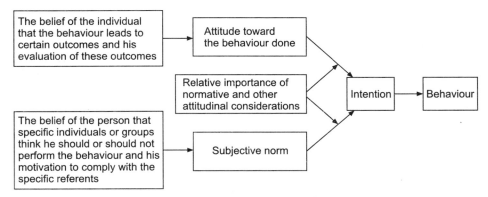

Figure 7.2 Key components in the theory of reasoned action.

The central idea of the theory of reasoned action is that the individual's behaviour can be predicted from behavioural intention. For example, if a woman expresses her intentions to use contraceptive devices to avoid pregnancy, she is more likely to do so than another woman who has no such behavioural intention. As shown in Figure 7.2, behavioural intentions themselves can be predicted from two variables—the person's attitude towards the behaviour and the subjective social norms. For example, does the woman think that using a contraceptive device is positive for her? This represents attitude towards the behaviour. *Subjective social norm* is the person's perception of others' belief about whether a behaviour is appropriate or not. In other words, subjective social norm provides one form of situational constraint. In this example, woman's perception of what others think she should do—does her husband want her to do, is it her ethical or moral behaviour, what will her parents think, etc. A person's attitude about his or her own behaviour is influenced by the person's beliefs about likely consequences or outcomes of the behaviour and the person's evaluation—positive or negative—of each consequence or outcome (see Figure 7.2). In fact, the desirability of each possible outcome is weighted by the likelihood of that outcome (contraceptive measure for this woman is likely to prevent pregnancy and such measure does not have any obvious side effects). Subjective social norm is influenced by the individual's beliefs about the reactions of the significant others to the behaviour and his or her motivation to comply with those expectations. In other words, subjective social norm is predicted by the perceived expectations of significant others weighted by motivation to comply with those expectations (her husband may strongly desire her to use the contraceptive and she wants to please him; her mother may oppose it, but she may think that mother's views are outdated today).

The theory of reason action has been widely used and appreciated because it makes people seem reasonable and takes attitudes as one of the important determinants of behaviour. Another cause of its popularity is its simplicity, that is, it explains a wide range of behaviours using a small number of variables. A good example is the study by Manstead, Proffitt and Smart (1983), who examined whether a pregnant woman would bottle-feed or breast-feed their babies. Through prenatal questionnaires, the researchers measured behaviour intentions (whether or not the woman intended to breast-feed), attitude towards behaviour (whether she believed that breast-feed establishes a closer mother-baby relationship) and subjective social norms (what did close female friend, mother, doctor prefer and to what extent the woman was motivated to follow their advices). The researchers finally reported that the correlation between these various attitudes and actual post birth breast feeding was 0.77, which was quite high. This theory or model has also been used successfully to predict other behaviours. For example, Fishbein et al. (1980) reported substantially a high correlation between voting intentions and how people actually voted in both an American presidential election and referendum on nuclear power. It has also been found that when this model is combined with quantitative measures of the components of attitudes, it can predict a specific behaviour and specific situation. For example, one study attempted to predict weight loss among college women (Schifter and Ajzen, 1985). In this study, the participant's attitude, behavioural intentions, and subjective norms about losing weight were measured. Some other variables, including whether or not the participants had detailed plan for losing weight, were assessed. About one and half month later, the amount of weight actually lost was measured. In final analysis, it was reported that the amount of weight loss was substantially related with the intention and having a detailed plan regarding weight loss. In fact, intention to lose the weight was found to be determined by attitude and subjective norm.

The theory of reasoned action has been criticised on some grounds. First, the model assumes that our behaviour is determined mainly by our intentions. This is not always correct because there are some situations in our life where past behaviours may be even more influential than our present intentions. For instance, whether one has donated blood in the past is a much better predictor of the fact that he may donate blood in the next few days than the statement that he intends to donate the blood. In fact, the impact of past behaviour becomes particularly strong when the stated intention is not compatible with the person's self-identity (Granberg and Holmberg, 1990). Second, the model does not take into account whether the behaviour is under control of the person. In other words, our behaviour may be affected not only by intentions but also by whether we have ability or resources needed to carry out the intention. A student may intend to have high marks in the examination, but there may be many factors outside his control (such as non-availability of book, time, etc.).

Keeping in view this second criticism, Ajzen (1989) modified the theory of reasoned action to incorporate a person's perceived behavioural control. This revised model is known as *theory of planned behaviour*. Perceived behavioural control means people's appraisals of their ability to perform a particular behaviour. Perceived behavioural control influences both behavioural intention and behaviour itself. These two theoretical perspectives, that is, theory of reasoned action and theory of planned behaviour have been successfully applied to predict behaviour in many different types of situation. Research suggests that these theories are successful in predicting whether 403 undergraduates, whose attitude were analysed towards engaging in safer sex, were able to do so more when the perception of one's ability to use condoms was added to the analysis (Wulfert and Wan, 1995).

Attitudes in spontaneous and automatic behaviour reactions

There are many such situations in which people tend to act quickly without much deliberations and their reactions are automatic and more spontaneous. In such a situation, which is mostly emergent and surprising, attitude seems to influence behaviour directly and in seemingly automatic manner, and here, behavioural intention has a little role to play. Fazio (1989) had proposed a theoretical approach called *attitude-to-behaviour process model* to deal with this. According to this model, events trigger our attitudes which influence how we should perceive the attitude object. At the same time, our understanding of how people are expected to behave or our knowledge regarding what is appropriate in such situation is also activated. Both these together, that is, our attitudes and what is appropriate in the given situation determine our overt behaviour. Let us illustrate attitude-to-behaviour process model with an example. Suppose on the highway, you are driving a car. Suddenly another person cuts his vehicle before you and with much difficulty you avoid the accident. This event would activate an attitude towards such person who has done such dangerous behaviour and at the same time, it would activate your past knowledge or experience that such action is non-normative or unexpected. Both these actions together determine your behaviour in such a situation. You may report the matter with police or you may think that the person must be in hurry due to some personal reasons.

In a nutshell, we can say that attitudes guide or shape our behaviour through two mechanisms, which operate under somewhat different and contrasting conditions. When the person has time to engage in careful and reasoned actions, he tends to weigh each available alternative and then decides how he should go ahead. But in situation, which is hectic and emergent in nature, such deliberate or reasoned thought processes fail to occur and the person has no time to think over the alternatives. In such cases, our attitudes seem to instantly shape our perceptions of the different events, and thereby, our immediate behaviour to them (Bargh, 1997).

FORMATION AND MAINTENANCE OF ATTITUDES

How are attitudes formed? From where do they come? Social psychologists have tried to answer these questions. Important sources that contribute to the formation and development of attitudes are discussed here.

1. Genetic factors: Although formation of attitude is largely influenced by learning factors, some recent researches done by Waller et al. (1990) and Keller et al. (1992) have produced evidences for the fact that genetic factors tend to play some role in the formation and development of attitudes. There researches have vividly shown that the attitudes of the identical twins correlated more highly than the attitudes of non-identical twins towards many social issues ranging from religious matters to job satisfaction. This was found in both conditions, that is, when identical twins were reared apart and were reared together.

2. Classical conditioning–Learning based on association: Most social psychologists today agree that the process of social learning or socialisation plays an important role in the formation of attitude. One process of social learning is classical conditioning learning, which is based on association of stimulus and responses. As we know, in classical conditions, the stimulus gradually elicits a response through repeated association with other stimuli.

Early studies have demonstrated that when initially neutral words are paired with stimulus like electric shock that elicits a strong negative response from the person, the neutral words soon comes to elicit the negative response on its own, providing evidence for the formation of unfavourable attitude (Staats et al., 1962). The use of classical condition in developing attitude may be illustrated from some common experiences of the life. If a child in the classroom frequently finds that the teacher calls his one of the class fellow as 'lazy', 'dirty', 'stupid', etc., indicating an unfavourable attitude of the teacher, he also develops similar negative attitude towards that fellow. Initially, the child was neutral towards his fellow. Several experiments have shown that classical conditioning can produce unfavourable attitude towards groups (Lohr and Staats, 1973; Staats and Staats, 1958). More recently, Krosnick et al. (1992) demonstrated that conditioning may also occur subliminally (that is, below the level of consciousness of an individual). In this study, photos of strangers engaged in different routine activities were shown to some students, who were the participants. Interspersed with these pictures, some other pictures were presented for brief period of time to induce either positive or negative feelings. The purpose of presenting the other photos for such a brief period of time was that the participants may not be aware of them, hence that was subliminal. Results revealed that the participants who were shown such positive photos subliminally evaluated the stranger more positively than the participants who were exposed to the negative photos. The findings clearly indicate that attitudes can be formed by subliminal conditioning, that is, by a classical conditioning of attitudes by exposing to such stimuli, which are below person's threshold of conscious awareness.

3. Instrumental conditioning–Learning based on consequences: Another way in which social attitudes are acquired is through instrumental conditioning in which learning is based upon direct experience with the attitude object. If a person experiences rewards to attitude object, he develops a favourable attitude. On the other hand, if the person experiences punishment after interacting with attitude object, he may develop a negative or unfavourable attitude towards the attitude object. By rewarding children with smiles or approval, parents play an active role in shaping the attitudes of their children. It is because of this reason the attitudes of the most of the children towards religions, social and caste issues are found very similar to their parents (Sinclair, Dunn and Lowrey, 2005).

However, only a small portion of our attitudes are based on direct experiences. We have attitudes towards many political and filmy personalities to whom we have never met. Likewise, we develop attitudes towards members of certain religious groups, although we have never been in the direct contact with the member of those groups. In fact, such types of attitudes are learnt through the interaction with third parties and in developing such attitude, instrumental conditioning definitely plays a significant role.

4. Observational learning–Learning based on illustrations: Observational learning also plays an important role in developing an attitude. In fact, observational learning or modelling is a social learning theory (Bandura, 1973) and in this approach, attitudes are learnt through observing the behaviour of significant others, and crucially, how a particular behaviour is rewarded or punished. Many children develop attitudes by what they observe their parents or significant others are doing. Children learn to smoke by observing that his seniors or parents do so. Even when children are asked not to do what they (parents) are doing, they do it and develop a similar attitude.

Besides, children as well as adults are exposed to mass media, especially television, films, magazines, newspaper and so on. These media provide an ample opportunity for observational learning because they present interpretative packages or frames about an object that tend to influence the attitudes of viewers or readers. By portraying actors and events in certain ways, TV serials, newspapers, and magazines can produce a certain type of image of any social group as being volatile, dangerous and highly unreasonable, which in turn, can produce negative attitude. The opposite may also be true, that is, by presenting a positive image of social groups these media can be instrumental in shaping positive attitude of the persons. Gunther (1995) observed that when the person views violent actions or pornographic materials through media, he thinks it is the other people who will be affected most through such actions or materials and they will not be affected by these things. This has been termed as *third-party effect* of media exposure, where, in fact, impact on others' attitudes and behaviours is overestimated and the impact on self is underestimated.

5. Social comparison: Social comparison also contributes to the formation of attitude. In social comparison, we compare ourselves with another person or group of people and develop attitude as we think it to be proper. In fact, as a result of social comparison with attitudes held by others with whom we identify, new attitudes can be formed. Researches have shown that hearing others whom we like and respect, expressing negative views about a group with whom we have never met, may lead to adopt similar attitudes (Terry, Hogg and Duck, 1999). In such situations, attitudes are developed as a result of social information, coupled with our desire to be similar to the people whom we like and respect.

6. Miscellaneous factors: Apart from the important factors mentioned above, there are some other factors that influence attitude development. One such factor is *group membership*. In most of the groups, there is pressure to show conformity. Such pressure to conform shapes our attitudes just as they do shape our behaviour. Another factor is *child rearing* in which parental values, beliefs and practices affect attitudes of the children. If the parents have joined a certain political party and have strong positive attitude towards it, it is very likely that their sons or daughters will also be expressing similar positive attitudes because parental values and beliefs will have direct influence upon their cognition. Researchers have shown that some attitudes are formed through chance conditioning (Olson and Zanna, 1993). In *chance conditioning*, learning takes place by chance or by mere coincidence. Let us take an example to illustrate it. Suppose you had four encounters in your lifetime with a homeopath physician or doctor. If all the four were negative, you may develop a negative view regarding homeopathy. Likewise, people often develop strong attitude towards certain city or food on the basis of one or two unusually good or bad experiences. Attitudes are also formed through *direct instruction* either by parents or by significant other. For example, parents may tell their children that cigarette smoking is dangerous and injurious to health. As a consequence, some children may form unfavourable attitude towards cigarette smoking. Still another factor is *interaction with others*. Sometimes, attitudes are developed because the person is surrounded by other people with that attitude. For example, if a person's friends hold the attitude that non-vegetarian foods are not good for health, the person is more likely to develop an unfavourable attitude towards non-vegetarian foods. Likewise, if most of the friends think that smoking is cool, the person is also most likely to have a similar view taking smoking as cool one (Eddy et al., 2000).

In a nutshell, formation or development of attitude is influenced by a host of factors, which must properly be understood in order to know about the entire story.

ATTITUDE CHANGE AND PERSUASION

Today, social psychologists agree with the view that perhaps no other area of social psychology has aroused as much interest as the phenomenon of attitude change (McGuire, 1969). They have made efforts to change the attitudes of the people through the use of various kinds of messages. This process is technically known as *persuasion*. In most cases, efforts at persuasion involve some elements—some source directs some type of message (communication) through some means to some persons or group of persons. Thus, there are four primary elements of persuasion—*the communicator, the message, the means through which the message is communicated* and *the audience*. In other words, who says what by what means to whom? When changes in attitude takes place in the already existing direction, that is, from favourable to still more favourable or unfavourable to still more unfavourable, it is called *congruent change*. On the other hand, when changes in attitude take place in the opposite direction, that is, from favourable to unfavourable or vice versa, it is called *incongruent change*. Other things being equal, congruent changes are easy to introduce than incongruent changes.

Before explaining the role of persuasive message in attitude change, it is essential to discuss the meaning of the term *persuasibility* and the other two related terms, that is, *conformity* and *suggestibility*. *Persuasibility* refers to the tendency of the person to accept or reject the persuasive communications. We know that some persons are more susceptible to persuasive communication than others. Hence, they differ in the trait of persuasibility. *Conformity* refers to the acceptance or non-acceptance of some norm or standard. As we have seen, persuasibility relates to the acceptance or rejection of persuasive communication of any kind, but conformity is limited to the tendency of a person to conform to the group norms or standards. Moreover, persuasibility is concerned with any kind of influence attempted by the source of the communication, whether or not his position is normative. Thus, persuasibility is more general than conformity. Group norms or standards generally give pressure on conformity of the behaviour if the individual's behaviour deviates from the norms.

There may be individual difference in response to such pressures. Some persons may yield easily to such pressure, whereas some may oppose such pressure. *Suggestibility* is a broader term than persuasibility. It refers not only to a person's susceptibility to persuasive communications but also includes tendency to respond to various communications or towards actions of the other persons who have no persuasive intention. Suggestibility is also often applied to those situations where the subject is unaware that the various behaviours that he is performing have been suggested by others or where he is totally unaware of the behaviours themselves.

How do those four factors affect attitude change? In fact, how easily a person can be influenced is, to a great extent, related to the way people tend to process information. In the *elaboration likelihood model (ELM)* of persuasion, it is assumed that people either elaborate on what they hear (that is, on the basis of the fact of message) or they do not elaborate at all and prefer to pay attention to the surface characteristics of the message (Petty and Cacioppo, 1986). Two types of processing are recommended in this model—*central route processing* and *peripheral route processing*. Generally, attitude change may take place either through central or peripheral route to persuasion. When people are motivated and able to think in a systematic manner about the issue, they are likely to adapt *central route* to persuasion. Thus, central route to persuasion occurs when interested people focus on arguments and make systematic processing of information presented in persuasive messages. On the other hand, when issues do not involve systematic thinking, persuasion may occur through a much faster route, called *peripheral route*, where people use heuristic or incidental cues such as speaker's attractiveness to make snap judgement they are using as peripheral route. Researches have shown that central route to persuasion being more thoughtful and less superficial brings more durable change in the attitudes of the people (Myers, 2005).

1. Who says?: The characteristics of the communicator

Social psychologists have reported that who is saying affects the audience's attitude. There are some characteristics of this communicator, which directly affects the audience and brings a change in attitude. Such important characteristics are as under:

(i) **Credibility of the communicator:** In most persuasion attempts done for the purpose of bringing attitude change, a highly credible communicator is preferable to one with poor or low credibility. Hovland and Weiss (1951) were first to study the impact of credibility of the communicator on the change of attitude. Expertise and trustworthiness make the source credible one. In their study, participants received identical communications on several topics. However, the source of the communication was made to seem of either high or low credibility. Results revealed that on immediate basis, the highly credible source was more effective in bringing changes in the attitudes and opinions than was the communicator with low credibility. When compared to the attitudes of the same subjects one week prior to the start of the experiment, the highly credible communicator produced significantly greater attitude changes. However, it was also found that the immediate impact of the communicator's credibility did not appear to last very long. After four weeks, such impact diminished. It was clearly observed that not only did the large amount of attitude change produced by credible source or communicator decreased over time, but the degree of attitude change produced by the message given by the low credible communication also increased.

The effect of message from the low credible communicator did not immediately reach full strength apparently due to its association with low credibility, but after some time, it seemed to have a greater effect. This delayed persuasion after the audience forgets the source or its connection with message is called *sleeper effect*.

What accounts for sleeper effect? How has it been explained? Explaining the effect, researchers have said that the audience tends to dissociate the communication from the communicator as the time passes. In other words, participants in the high credibility condition, immediately after listening about the message, were influenced partly by the content of what they heard and partly by the fact that the communicator was an expert. As time passed, the part of the communication associated with the credibility of the source tended to disappear, since the participants had dissociated the message from the communication. Likewise, participant in the low credibility condition expressed the attitude that reflected the content of message minus the effect associated with the communicator's low credibility. As time elapsed, the inhibitory effect of the communicator's low credibility tended to disappear. Some researchers have confirmed such explanation from their study (Kelman and Hovland, 1953). However, this study also showed that the sleeper effect was eliminated by reinstating the association between the communicator and communication. Some social psychologists have expressed doubt over the validity of the sleeper effect. Gillig and Greenwald (1974) failed to replicate the findings of Hovland and Weiss regarding sleeper effect in their seven experiments, and therefore, argued that the social psychologists should lay the sleeper effect to rest. As stated above, perceived expertise and perceived trustworthiness together make the source credible one. Social psychologists have also studied the impact of these two upon attitude change by separating them. Expert is a person who is knowledgeable on the topic. Researches have shown that the message about tooth brushing from recognised dental association was much more convincing than the same message from a group of students who have completed their project on dental hygiene (Olson and Cal, 1984). Moreover, Bochner and Insko (1966) provided sufficient evidences that show that with controlled trustworthiness, expertise in itself tends to raise credibility and persuasiveness.

Trustworthiness, which is a bit more difficult to test, also enhances persuasiveness and brings significant attitude change. In general, trustworthiness is treated as the characteristic of being able to establish confidence in other's intent. Trustworthiness is higher if the audience believes that the communicator is not trying to persuade them (Walster and Festinger, 1962). We also perceive them as sincere and trustworthy, who argue against their own interest. Walster, Aroson and Abrahams (1966) conducted one study to confirm this. In this study, some subjects heard that a convicted criminal was arguing in favour of increase in the rights of individuals and decrease in the power of police. Some other subjects heard that the convict was arguing in favour of increasing the power of police and decreasing the rights of the individuals. Results showed that when the subjects' attitude about the strengthening of police powers at the cost of individual liberties was assessed, no attitude change occurred in those who had heard that the convict was arguing consistently with his self-interest. However, it produced significant changes in the attitude of the listeners when they heard that the convict had argued in favour of greater police power. This happened because in the latter case the listeners held the convicts more sincere and trustworthy than in the former case.

Likewise, when a Chief Minister states that he should be put under the purview of Lokpal, he is perceived as more trustworthy by the public than a Chief Minister who argues that Chief Minister should be kept out of the purview of the Lokpal. Accordingly, any message from the former category of Chief Minister would be more persuasive and would likely to bring more attitude change than the same message coming from the latter category of Chief Minister. It has also been shown that the communicator who speaks rapidly is often more persuasive than a communicator who speaks more slowly (Miller et al., 1976). This probably works by influencing the perceived credibility of the communicator.

In nutshell, it can be said that a highly credible source/communicator is more effective than a low credible source in producing attitude change. Credibility seems to be the function of at least expertise and trustworthiness. However, researches on sleeper effect have indicated that the impact of credibility is short-lived. It is because the enhancing effect of the high credibility communicator may be diminished over time and the attitude change produced by the low credibility communicator may increase over time.

(ii) **Attractiveness and likableness:** Attractive communicator produces more attitude change in audiences than those who are less attractive. One important aspect of attractiveness is the *physical appeal.* Researches have shown that the messages, especially emotional ones, are often more influential when they come from beautiful and attractive people (Chaiken, 1979; Pallak et al., 1983). In general, an attractive communicator is also likable. An attractive and likable communicator tends to have more effect on audience than those who are disliked or have produced hostility (Mills and Aronson, 1965). The salesman, who dresses neatly, and therefore, become more likable, pleasant and attractive, is more likely to enhance sale by affecting the changes in attitude among the customers in the desired direction.

(iii) **Power of the communicator:** There are some instances, which show that we are likely to be more influenced by those communicators who have power than those who do not have such power (Raven and French, 1958). This is partly true because the attribute of power usually affords the communicator with the power to impose sanctions if the person fails to comply with the request. That is the reason, why a person is more influenced by boss than from someone who ranks below him in the hierarchy. To bring effective change in the attitude, however, the powerful source must be visible or must have the ability to monitor the degree of compliance.

(iv) **Similarity:** Similarity of the communicator is another important factor that influences persuasibility and attitude change (Nesbitt, 1972). We tend to like people who are alike us. Not only that, we are also much influenced by them. Dembroski, Lasater and Ramirez (1978) conducted one study in which African-American junior high school students were given a taped dental appeal for cleaning the teeth. Next day, dentist assessed the cleanliness of their teeth. It was found that those students who heard the appeal from an African-American dentist had cleaned their teeth better than who had received the same appeal from non-African-American dentist. This shows that when the people find similarity with the communicator, they are more influenced and bring change in their attitude. As a general rule, people respond better to the message that comes from someone who belongs to their own group (Wilder, 1990).

2. What is said? The characteristics of the content of message

What the person or the communicator says is also an important factor for bringing changes in the attitude. Social psychologists have pinpointed upon certain characteristics of the message, which tend to bring changes in attitude. Such important characteristics are as under:

(i) **Rational versus emotional appeals:** The basic question arises here—is a purely logical, rational and reasonable message most effective in producing attitude change or one that arouses emotional appeal? The answer depends on two basic factors. First factor is how people's attitude is initially formed. When the people's initial attitude is formed primarily through emotion, they are persuaded most by emotional appeals, that is, emotional appeals in their case become more effective in producing attitude change. On the other hand, when people's initial attitude is formed through reasonable, logical and rational appeal, they are more persuaded later on by logical and reasonable arguments (Edwards, 1990; Fabrigar and Petty, 1999). Researches have further shown that an emotion-based attitude can be changed by new emotions and to change an information-based attitude, new information must be added. Another factor is the nature of audience. When the audience is well-educated and analytical in nature, the people are more responsive to rational appeals in comparison to less educated or less analytical audience (Cacioppo et al., 1983, 1996). This happens because well-educated and analytical people process information through central route, whereas less educated, less analytical and disinterested audience processes information through peripheral route.

Emotional appeal of the message may be producing either good feelings or bad feelings (negative emotions such as fear). Research evidences have shown that when messages are associated with good feelings, they become more persuasive, and therefore, more effective in bringing attitude change. Good feelings generally enhance persuasion partly because people are motivated to think positively and partly because they link good feelings with the message (Petty et al., 1993). People in good mood and with positive feelings see the world through rose-coloured glasses and generally make faster and impulsive decision. In fact, they adopt a peripheral route, rather central route of processing the information. As a consequence, they are easily swayed even by weak arguments. Thus, a clever communicator tries to create good mood and feeling in the audiences so that his message may prove more persuasive for them because they will not think too much about it.

Messages can also be effective by evoking fear or negative emotion. Fear-arousing communications are helpful in changing attitude of the people towards various issues like smoking, driving carefully, brushing their teeth more often, and so on. The effectiveness of fear-arousing communications has also been shown in risky sexual behaviours and drinking. The early research conducted by Janis and Feshbach (1953) tried to examine the relationship between fear and attitude change. In this study, they persuaded people to brush their teeth more carefully and to use better oral hygiene practices under three conditions—low fear condition, moderate fear condition and high fear condition. Results revealed that lower levels of fear were the most effective in producing attitude change. Only 8% participants changed their attitude in high fear condition. The explanation is that high level of fear raised subjects' defence mechanisms, and basically, they were not responsive to the message.

Later work, however, showed opposite results; high fear appeals led to a greater attitude change. In a series of investigations, Leventhal and his colleagues reported greater influence when participants/subjects were made highly fearful (Leventhal and Niles, 1965; Leventhal, Singer and Jones, 1965; Leventhal, Watts and Pagano, 1967). Direct relationship between fear-arousing communication and attitude change has been reported in several other studies conducted on advisability of taking injections for tetanus (Dabbs and Leventhal, 1966) and adhering to safe driving recommendations (Leventhal and Niles, 1965).

However, playing on fear does not always make a message more potent. For example, many people who are afraid of deadly disease like AIDS are not found abstaining from sex or using condoms. Not only that, many individuals, who have been made to fear from an early death from smoking, continue to smoke. In fact, fear-arousing messages are found to be more effective only when the individuals are shown solutions and are allowed to feel capable of implementing it (Ruiter et al., 2001; Devos-Comby and Salovey, 2002). Reality is that the persons may engage in denial because when they are not told how to get rid of danger, frightening messages can be naturally overwhelming (Leventhal, 1970; Rogers and Mewborn, 1976).

Janis and Feshbach's study and Leventhal and his colleagues' study provide conflicting results if both are taken to be valid. How can the difference be reconciled? Some social psychologists have shown an inverted U-shaped relationship between degree of fear and attitude change (see Figure 7.3) (Worchel and Cooper, 1979). According to this viewpoint, some degree of arousal is necessary for maximal attitude change (Cohen, 1957). In this view, attitude change increases as the degree of fear increases from low to moderate. However, as degree of fear rises from moderate to high level, and therefore, becomes intense, it interferes with an individual's ability to cope with the problem. In such a situation, the person avoids or denies the information. He definitely comprehends what is presented, but he refuses to believe that it applies to him. This resists further change in attitude.

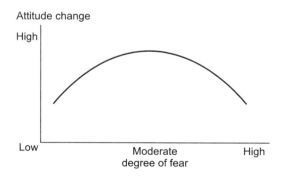

Figure 7.3 Inverted U relationship between degree of fear and attitude change.

(ii) **Discrepant message:** A message which is different or with which the audiences do not expressed agreement is called *discrepant message*. As we know disagreement produces discomfort, which prompts people to change their attitudes and opinions. Some early data regarding this was collected in study conducted by Hovland and Pritzker (1957), who provided messages, which were deviated slightly, moderately or extremely from the opinions expressed by the subjects. Data regarding their attitude status were collected both before and after the message. Results revealed that attitude change was a direct function of discrepancy—the greater the difference between message provided by the communicator and the opinions held by the subjects, the greater is the attitude change.

Subsequent researches have shown that the relationship between discrepancy and attitude change is a function of discrepancy and the perceived expertise of the communicator. It means discrepancy and credibility interact, that is, the effect of large versus small discrepancy depends on whether the communicator is credible. This has been confirmed in one popular study conducted by Aronson, Turner and Carlsmith (1963). They presented subjects to rate stanzas taken from some obscure poetry. Subsequently, subjects were presented with a communication/message, which advocate ratings that were either wildly, moderately or narrowly discrepant from the ratings done by the subjects. The communications were attributed to either a credible source like T.S. Eliot or a very poor credible source like the name of a college teacher. Subjects were then given another opportunity to rerate the stanzas. Rerating, in fact, served as a measure of the degree to which their attitude was influenced by the communication. Results revealed that attitude change among the subjects was high if discrepancy was generated by the credible source. When the communicator was lacking expertise, the moderate level of discrepancy was a bit effective.

(iii) **One-sided appeal versus two-sided appeal:** The communicator may present one side of the message (that is, positive aspect) or he may present both sides of the message, (that is, both positive and negative aspects) for bringing change in the attitude of audience. The relative effectiveness of one-sided communication versus two-sided communication was studied in a classic research done by Hovland, Lumsdaine and Sheffield (1949). The study used several hundred soldiers in US army. After Germany's defeat in World War II, the US army did not want soldier to relax and the army wanted to motivate the soldiers to pursue the ongoing war with Japan and convince them that the war would not end quickly or easily. One group of soldiers was presented with a 15-minute radio broadcast arguing that it would take at least two more years to conclude the war with Japan. A second group was presented the identical communication except that a few minutes of contradictory arguments were included in the broadcast. At the end of the study, the attitudes of both groups and a control group of soldiers, who did not hear the communication, were measured. Results revealed that soldiers of both experimental groups believed more strongly that the war could continue for at least two or more years than did the control group and there was no significant difference in attitude change between the group that heard one-sided communication and the group that heard two-sided communication. However, some interesting findings emerged when the researchers took the initial attitudes of the soldiers into consideration. It was revealed that one-sided communication was far more effective in strengthening the belief of those soldiers who had initially agreed with the communication. On the other hand, two-sided communication was more effective among those soldiers who had initially opposed the point of view of the communication. Lumsdaine and Janis (1953) also reported similar findings. In their study, half of the subjects listened to one-sided communication and other half of the subjects listened to two-sided communication. It was found that both types of communications were equally effective in producing attitude change. However, it was only two-sided communication that was capable of producing changes that could withstand a counterattack.

Jones and Brehm (1970), later on, tried to refine the analysis of one-sided and two-sided communications. They presented the argument that two-sided communications are effective only to the extent that audiences have realisation that there are two tenable positions. One-sided communication is effective because such communication does not raise contradictions. On the other hand, people who know that there is second side of an issue also feel that their freedom to adopt a position is threatened by a communication which insists on only one correct instance. To maintain their freedom, such persons resist persuasion. Thus, if people are (or will be) aware of opposing arguments, a two-sided communication will prove to be more persuasive and enduring. Apparently, a one-sided communication stimulates an informed audience or awarded audience to think of counterarguments and to view the communicator as biased one. Therefore, a direct lesson is that if the audience is to be exposed to opposing views, try to present a two-sided communication. Geers et al. (2003) further showed that for those people, who are optimists, positive appeal works best, whereas for those, who are pessimists, negative appeal becomes more effective.

(iv) **Primary effect versus recency effect:** When both sides of the argument, that is, both pro and con arguments about an issue are to be presented, then it must be decided which argument should be presented first in order to be more persuasive. The effect of information presented early is called *primacy effect* and the effect of information presented later is called *recency effect*. There are arguments in favour of both effects. Information presented early is most persuasive because first impressions are important. Not only that, the first speaker has also better chance to make his or her points with sufficient impact to decrease the attention the audience is likely to pay to the arguments presented by the opponent. It is also argued that there is increased probability of retention of the later arguments (that is, in favour of recency effect).

The key to the argument presented above lies in the timing relating to both the amount of time between the presentation of the two arguments and the amount of time between the second presentation and the point at which the audience has to take a decision. Researches have shown that if there is very little time between two presentations, that is, when two messages or communications are back to back, with a little time gap, the primacy effect usually occurs, that is, the advantage seems to go to the first speaker's message (assuming that both speakers are equally credible and their arguments are equally organised and rational). This is especially true when the first presentation stimulates thinking (Haugtvedt and Wegener, 1994). On the other hand, if there is a gap between two presentations and if the decision must be made immediately after the second presentation, recency effect will occur with greater influence (Miller and Campbell, 1959).

(v) **Drawing conclusion from the message:** Researches have shown that the importance of drawing a conclusion by the communicator or not drawing a conclusion and leaving it to be drawn by the audience is also a potent factor. Hovland and Mandell (1952) were of view that the desirability of drawing explicit conclusion would lend upon the level of intelligence of the audience. If the level of intelligence of the audience is high, it would be more persuaded for drawing conclusion for itself. On the other hand, less intelligent audience might not prove successful at drawing proper conclusions. In their study, Hovland and Mandell prepared two communications advocating the devaluations of US dollar. The only difference between the two communications was that one came to the clear conclusion that the dollar should be devaluated and other communication allowed the subjects (audience) to draw their own conclusion from the facts presented. Results revealed that more than twice the number of subjects changed their attitude in the direction advocated in the message when the conclusion was clearly and explicitly drawn by the communicator for audience than when it was left to the audience for drawing conclusion. However, the level of the intelligence of the audience did not produce any significant differences. One of the dangers associated with allowing audience to draw its own conclusion was that it might not draw the desired implications.

In nutshell, it can be said that the communication or messages whose conclusions are explicitly drawn are more persuasive, and hence, effective in bringing attitude change than the messages whose conclusions are left to the audience. However, the messages of the latter type can prove to be more effective if they can be understood well and if the audience is sufficiently motivated to undertake the effort of arriving at the conclusions (Linder and Worchel, 1970).

3. How is it said?: The channel of communication

The way a message is delivered to the audience also affects the persuasibility or likelihood of bringing changes in attitude. The message can be communicated in writing, in face-to-face situation, on film or in some other way. Social psychologists' attempt to use various channels of communication in making the message more persuasive can be described as under:

(i) **Actively received appeal versus passively received appeal:** An active persuasive not only delivers message that attracts the attention of the audience but also makes it understandable, convincing, memorable and compelling. Such message involves the audience actively, and therefore, becomes more persuasive and effective in bringing changes in the attitude. Passively received appeals are not so effective. In fact, such appeals are sometimes effective and sometimes not effective. On minor issues such as which brand of milk supply to buy, passively received appeals through newspaper, radio or TV may prove to be effective. But on more familiar and important issues like attitude towards intercaste marriage persuading people through passive appeals may prove to be a herculean task.

(ii) **Face-to-face influence versus media influence:** There seems to be almost an universal agreement that face-to-face influence or personal influence is more effective than the influence of various mass media such as television, radio, newspaper, mails, etc. in changing attitudes. In an early study conducted by Lazarsfeld, Berelson and Gaudel (1948), it was found that personal influence proved much more effective in inducing changes in attitude towards voting for a particular candidate than the mass media. They suggested that the greater effectiveness of the face-to-face influence was due to the greater flexibility of the personal persuasion. There are some field experiments too, which support the effectiveness of personal influence over the influence of mass media. Eldersveld and Dodge (1954) conducted one field experiment in which participants were divided into three groups. All participants were exposed to a political persuasion intending not to vote for the revision of city charter. It was found that in the group, whose participants were exposed only to what they saw and heard in the mass media, only 19% changed their mind and voted for the revision. In the group, whose members received some mails in support of the revision, 45% participants voted for it. Among the participants of the third group who were contacted personally and given the appeal on face-to-face basis, 75% changed their attitude in favour of revision. The study clearly bears a testimony to the fact that personal influence is much more effective than mass media. In another field experiment conducted by Farquhar et al. (1977), it was found that those participants who received personal contacts as well as media appeals regarding reducing coronary heart disease changed most, whereas those participants who were exposed only to multimedia campaign such as TV, radio, newspapers and direct mail, slightly improved their health habits to decrease the risk of coronary heart disease. Once again this field experiment established the supremacy of personal influence over media influence in changing attitude.

Although the findings support the personal influence more than media influence, the power of media should not be underestimated. In fact, those who personally influence us in a face-to-face contact, actually get their ideas often from various sources of media themselves. In fact, many of the media's effects operate in a *two-step flow of communication* (Katz, 1957), which states that the flow of the communication is from media to some leaders (or persons) and from leaders to the ordinary rank-and-file members. The two-step flow model of communication very clearly demonstrates that even if the media has little effect on the people's attitude, it penetrates our culture in many subtle ways and has a big indirect effect.

Social psychologists have also compared the impact of different media upon the attitude change. They have come to the conclusion that of the different media, the lifelike medium tends to be more persuasive than the others. The order of persuasiveness of the message is *live mode, videotaped mode, audiotaped mode* and *written mode*. Many evidences support the fact that videotaped message is more persuasive than audiotaped message in producing attitude and opinion change (Fransden, 1963), and some studies have demonstrated the superiority of audiotaped messages over the printed mode (Wilke, 1934). Chaiken and Eagly (1976) suggested that the complexity of the communication/message and modes of communication interact to produce persuasion. They argued that simple message can probably be comprehended on any modes of communication and greater yielding for videotaped messages may result in increased persuasion. On the other hand, the complex messages may prove to be more effective if they are presented in written form. Chaiken and Eagly conducted study in which the participants (students) were asked to read, listen to or watch a persuasive message. Half of the time, the message was simple and half of the time, it was difficult and complex. Results indicated that the participants were persuaded by simple messages when they were presented in videotaped form, but were more persuaded by the complex messages when they were presented in written form.

Related to the mode of communication is another factor, called *communication's style* that affects persuasiveness, and therefore, attitude change too. Factors like the physical distance between the communicator and the audience (Albert and Dabbs, 1970), the eye contact (Mehrabian and Williams, 1969) between the communicator and the audience also tend to contribute to the effectiveness of message in producing attitude change. McGinley, LeFevre and McGinley (1975) reported that body postures also affect persuasiveness of the message. They showed their participants two types of body postures of the communicator— open body posture (leaning backward, hand held outward, legs stretched out and elbows away from the body) and a closed body picture (arms crossed, hand folded in lap and elbows next to the body). Results revealed that participants who saw open body posture of the communicator were more persuaded than were the subjects who saw the closed body posture of the communicator. Likewise, researchers have shown that the communication delivered at a high rate of speech makes the communicator seem more expert and credible in the eye of audience, and therefore, is proved to be more persuasive than the communication delivered at a slow rate (Miller et al., 1976).

4. To whom is it said?: Factors related to the audience

Finally, there are some factors which are either characteristics of the audience or are related to the audience, and tend to affect persuasiveness of the message and bring a desired change in the attitude. Such important factors are as follows:

(i) **Intelligence level of the audience:** It is widely understood that highly intelligent people are less susceptible to persuasive communications than the people with low intelligence. The explanation is that highly intelligent people would be more critical of the message; they are usually more informed and have a better understanding of the logic of the argument. Yet early researches up to 1937 showed almost a zero correlation between intelligence level and resistance to persuasive communications (Murphy, Murphy and Newcomb, 1937).

(ii) However, a review of studies done later by Hovland, Janis and Kelley (1953) indicated that for some types of the communications such as those having impressive logical arguments, intelligence is positively associated with persuasive communication and for other types such as communications having illogical and irrelevant argumentation, intelligence is negatively correlated. Hovland, Lumsdaine and Sheffield (1949) also failed to confirm a predicted relationship between the level of intelligence and the effectiveness of one-sided or two-sided communications. Likewise, Hovland and Mandell (1952) were not able to support the fact that intelligence would be related to the drawing of some explicit conclusions in communications. McGuire (1968) provided an explanation for the lack of consistent finding relating to intelligence and persuasibility. As it is known, any persuasion process includes at least two subprocesses—comprehension of message and yielding to the message. Highly intelligent people may be better able to resist any persuasive attempt and to comprehend the message. On the other hand, less intelligent people might yield, provided they have comprehended the message. In the process of attitude change, the highly intelligent people may easily comprehend the message and may, therefore, be easily persuaded by it. Likewise, they may also be more confident about their own position and opinion, and therefore, they are in the position to provide more counterarguments, and in general, more resident to persuasive attempt. The entire process operates in opposite directions and may offset each other. In much similar way, less intelligent people may be more influenced by the message because of their poor ability to define their own point of view, but their poor ability to comprehend the content of the message may render that message less effective. In this way, the offsetting processes for people at different levels of intelligence may result in the appearance of no significant difference in the final attitude change (Eagly and Warren, 1976).

Self-esteem of the audience: Self-esteem of the audience also affects the persuability of the message. People with low self-esteem are perusable than the people with high self-esteem.

The explanation is that people with low self-esteem are more concerned about their personal ability and adequacy, they think negatively about themselves and are also less confident and happy. Therefore, they easily go by what is said to them. Cohen (1959) conducted a study in which he found that people with low self-esteem were more persuaded by the message than were the people with high self-esteem. Not only that, some studies have shown that people with high and low self-esteem differ in the way in which they handle the threatening message (Cohen, 1959; Silverman, 1964). Persons with low self-esteem are very sensitive to the negative information about themselves. But people with high self-esteem tend to deny or repress such information about themselves. As a consequence, they are not much persuaded by the message.

However, some recent studies do not fully support the above explanation. Rhodes and Wood (1992) showed that people with moderate self-esteem are very easily influenced by the message. People with low self-esteem are often very slow to comprehend the message, and therefore, are hard to be persuaded. Those with high self-esteem, no doubt, comprehend the message, but remain confident of their view and opinion. Therefore, they are also hard to be persuaded.

(iii) **Personality of the audience:** Are some people more susceptible to attitude change efforts or to persuasive efforts? Answer seems to be 'yes', although it is more complex. Some social psychologists are of view that persuasibility may be a personality trait. If so, it can be easily found that some people are easily persuaded for bringing change in attitude, irrespective of the type of message used, content of the message and the source of the message. Hovland and Janis (1959) conducted a series of investigations and they were able to identify some perusable personalities, who were easily influenced by any type of message given from any type of source. They concluded that indeed there is a personality characteristic, which can be called *persuasibility*, although the effect is weak. Therefore, efforts to find a personality correlate of persuasion have shifted from looking to a global personality type (persuasibility) to looking for a particular aspect of personality.

Persons who have aggressive personalities are less likely to be persuaded by the message. Aggression may coexist with dogmatism or close-mindedness. A person who is fully convinced with the rightness of his position (closed-minded) is less likely to be persuaded to bring a change in his attitude. Likewise, persons who have had a history of success are also less likely to be persuaded because they are more self-confident and less reliant upon the message.

(iv) **Age of the audience:** Depending on their age, people tend to develop different types of social and political attitudes. One explanation for this is the life cycle explanation and another explanation is a generational explanation. The *life cycle explanation* states that attitude change becomes difficult as people grow older because with the advancement in age, they become more and more conservative. The *generational explanation* states that attitudes of the older people adopted when they were young, go largely unchanged because these attitudes are different from those being adopted by young people today.

Of these two explanations, research evidences mostly favour the generational explanation. In various attitude surveys in which attitudes of younger and older people over several years were examined, it was reported that older people usually shows less change in their attitude as compared to the attitudes of younger children (Sears, 1986). However, towards the end of the life cycle, older people may again become susceptible to attitude change probably due to decline in the strength of their attitudes whatsoever it may be.

(v) **Thoughtfulness of the audience:** Our thinking and need for cognition also affect the changes in attitude. In fact, human mind is not like a sponge, which soaks whatever is poured over it. If the message induces favourable thought, it definitely persuades us. If it provokes us to think of unfavourable or contrary arguments, it fails to persuade us. In fact, what we think in response to a message, is very crucial for attitude. For example, if we think that source of the message is trustworthy and expert, we generally follow the peripheral route. In such a situation, we have favourable thoughts and are less likely to make counterarguments. On the other hand, when we mistrust the source, we follow the central route and think by putting many counterarguments. Researches have shown that as the person mentally elaborates on an important issue, the strength of the arguments as well as our thoughts tend to determine our attitudes. But if the issue is unimportant, peripheral routes such as expertise and attractiveness of the source, rather than strength of the message arguments, tend to have more effect upon our attitude (Petty, Cacioppo and Goldman, 1981).

Likewise, it has also been reported that when the people are warned that someone is going to persuade them, the people generally think so many counterarguments to make persuasion less effective. Thus, forewarned becomes forearmed. Freedman and Sears (1965) conducted a study in which it was demonstrated that persuasion becomes difficult in the situation of forewarning. They warned one group of adolescents that they would hear a talk over why a ban on driving by teenagers should be imposed. Other group of adolescents did not hear such talk. Results revealed that those adolescents who had been forewarned did not change their attitude, whereas those who had not heard the talk, changed their attitude.

Some researches have shown that persuasion is enhanced by distracting people with something that attracts their attention just strong enough to inhibit counterargument (Festinger and Maccoby, 1964; Keating and Brock, 1974). Regan and Cheng (1973), however, found that distraction is facilitative of attitude change only when the message is simple. Harkins and Petty (1981) also confirmed Regan and Cheng's conclusion.

(vi) **Role playing by the audience:** One important way to induce changes in attitude is to have a person play the role of someone who has a position contrary to his own position. Originally, Moreno (1953) developed the technique of role playing, which proved to be an important adjunct to psychotherapy. However, the first social psychological study utilising the technique of role playing was conducted by Janis and King (1954). In this study, participants came to the sessions in groups of three. Each subject was given a topic as well as an outline, with a request to develop one persuasive communication that may prove to the contrary to his true beliefs and attitudes. Subsequently, one subject gave the attitude-discrepant communication to the other two participants in his groups. Thus, each subject actively role-played an attitude-discrepant position on one issue and passively listened to counterattitudinal position regarding the other two issues. After the session was over, the attitudes of the participants were assessed. It was found that greater attitude change occurred in the role playing situation than in the situation in which subjects only passively heard the information.

(vii) **Group factors:** Since most of our attitudes are founded in the groups in which we hold membership, it is important to consider group factors, especially when we try to evaluate our efforts to bring changes in attitudes. For example, if a person is supported by a group of which he is a member for holding an attitude similar to that of the group, he does not get persuaded easily and show resistance to change the attitude. On the other hand, when the membership of the group has been terminated, he becomes much more amenable to the persuasive appeals. Thus, when group factors change, attitudes are more amenable to change (Cantril, 1963; Toch, 1965). In fact, groups become important because they provide reminder to the person that who he or she is and how he or she should behave and believe.

Thus, we find that attitude change through persuasion has many dimensions. If one is to make one's persuasion more effective for inducing attitude change, one has to be very careful in considering these various dimensions satisfactorily.

THEORIES OF ATTITUDE ORGANISATION AND CHANGE

Today, social psychologists assume that an attitude is a multidimensional concept because it has three components, namely, affective component, behavioural component and cognitive component (popularly called *ABC components*). Here, important questions are how these components organised and related, and how different attitudes are related to each other. To explain these questions, several theories of attitude organisation have been developed. All these theories assume that the persons attempt to maximise internal consistency and avoid cognitive inconsistency, which is frequently referred to as *dissonance, imbalance, incongruence,* and so forth. These theories also assume that greater the degree of cognitive inconsistency, higher is the probability that the person would reorganise and change his attitude because such inconsistency creates discomfort in the person.

Major theories of attitude organisation and change can be classified under three general categories:

1. Cognitive consistency theories of attitude change
2. Social learning theories of attitude change
3. Other theories of attitude change

These theories of attitude change incorporate several theories, which are discussed as follows:

Cognitive Consistency Theories of Attitude Change

The central idea of cognitive consistency is based on the assumption that a person always tries to maximise consistency among the various components of attitude or between two or more than two attitudes, which are related to each other. In other words, the affective response towards an attitude object should be consistent with our belief and knowledge about that object and both should be consistent with our behaviour towards that object. For example, if a person believes that smoking is harmful for both physical health as well as mental health, then the person should express a negative emotional response towards smoking and on behavioural level, he should abstain from smoking. Likewise, if a person holds two attitudes which are related to each other, they should be consistent with each other. For example, if a person has favourable attitude towards Muslims, he should also have a favourable attitude towards Islam religion. In each of these examples, if the components of attitudes are not consistent, then according to the demands of the theory, the person will experience psychological stress, popularly called *dissonance* or *inconsistency*. To ward off such feeling, the person will try to induce some kind of changes in his attitude.

In this section, four cognitive consistency theories—Heider's P-O-X model, Newcomb's A-B-X model, Festinger's cognitive dissonance theory and Osgood and Tannenbaum's congruity theory—are discussed.

1. Heider's theory: Heider's P-O-X model or popularly known as *balance theory* is the grandfather of all the cognitive consistency theories (Heider, 1946, 1958). The theory is concerned with how we make attitudes regarding people and the attitudinal object consistent. The major element in the model is the person notated by 'P' and the other two elements in the model are 'O', notation for other person and 'X', notation for another entity, which may be a person or an object. In fact, Heider's model considers consistency among beliefs and affects held by an individual and is usually described in terms of person (P), another person (O) and an attitude object (X). In this way, there are three relevant evaluations—(i) the first person's (P) evaluation of other person (O) (ii) the first person's (P) evaluation of other person or object (X), and (iii) other's person's (O) evaluation of the attitude object (X).

Among these three elements, Heider differentiated between two different types of relationship—unit relationship and affective relationship. *Unit relationship* indicates the degree to which the elements are perceived to belong together due to some kind of similarity. *Affective relationship* indicates nature of liking among the elements and the nature of liking may be positive (+) or negative (–). Since nature of prediction of the model is same for both relationship, we shall concentrate only upon the affective relationship for explaining attitude changes.

According to model, there can be eight different possible P-O-X combinations of relationship, as shown in Figure 7.4.

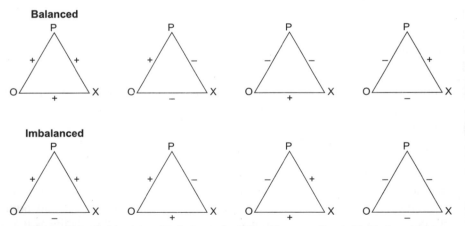

Figure 7.4 Balanced and imbalanced relationship according to Heider's model.

According to the model, if one takes the signs of three relationship and multiplies them together, a balanced state is said to exist if the outcome is positive and an imbalanced state is said to exist if the outcome is negative. Putting the same in other words, it can be said that a system with one positive and two negative relations or three positive relations produces a balanced state, whereas a system with a negative or two positive relations or three negative relations produces imbalanced state.

Two terms *balance* and *imbalance* are very important in this theory. Therefore, they need to be defined. According to Heider, *balance* is defined as a stable cognitive state, which is comfortable to the person or perceiver, whereas *imbalance* is unstable cognitive state, which motivates a person to change the nature of one of the relationships to achieve a balanced state. Let us take an example to illustrate it. Suppose Amitabh (as P) holds Sohan (as O) in high regard and esteem. It means that the affective relationship is positive. Further, suppose that Amitabh also likes Alok (as X), thus making another positive relationship. But suppose that Amitabh perceives that Sohan does not like Alok (a negative affective relationship). According to Heider's balance theory, this entire episode would create an imbalanced state (two positive and one negative relation). This will motivate Amitabh to change the imbalanced state into balanced one by changing his view either about Sohan or about Alok or the nature of relationship between Sohan and Alok. These modes of resolving imbalance involve a change in Amitabh's attitude.

Heider's balance theory has some drawbacks. Important drawbacks are as under:

(i) The theory does not take into consideration the various degrees of affect in a relationship. In this model, the relationship is either balanced or imbalanced and no provision for the degree of relationship is made. For example, it is completely possible that Amitabh has a very strong, intimate and important relationship with Sohan, while only vaguely knowing Alok. Consequently, it would not matter much for Amitabh whether Sohan does not like Alok. In such a situation, a state of imbalance may not be created in Amitabh.

(ii) Another drawback of the theory is that it does not predict which of the several ways of restoring balance will occur. Following Leventhal (1974), there are three possible ways for reducing imbalance. First and the most direct way is to affect a change in the attitude. For example, Amitabh does not really like Sohan after all.

The second way is simply to deny that the relationship even exists. For example, Sohan does not really mean it when he told Amitabh that he does not like Alok. A third possible way is to modify and differentiate the attitudinal object to include attributes that would be consistent with a balanced relationship. For example, Sohan is right; there is something on the part of Alok which Amitabh does not like, although Amitabh likes Alok most of the time. Balance theory does not predict which of these three ways of reducing imbalance will be chosen by the person.

(iii) In the model, there is no provision for handling complex cases. In fact, the model assumes greater isolation or independence in the decision-making process than is usually found. In most of the situations, P must be considered more than O and X. There are many situations in which the basic balance model is of little help due to its relative simplicity. Take an example of strained relationship between husband and wife. The wife, due to the strained relationship over years, has developed a deep hatred for her husband. The husband, however, has a plenty of wealth, which he has got from his parents. The wife feels that because her marital relationship has suffered a lot, she deserves access to wealth of her husband. The only way she can fulfil her desire is to stay married and outlive him. What will happen in such case? This states an imbalance relationship for which resolution is difficult to predict. Here, other objects become important and other relationships need to be considered.

Despite these drawbacks, the balance theory has a marked influence on the attitude, and with some exceptions, the major predictions of the model have been held to be satisfactory and well-established (Rodrigues, 1967). Therefore, the theory remains an important cognitive consistency model.

2. **Newcomb's A-B-X model:** Newcomb (1953, 1961) proposed a model which can be considered more a theory of interpersonal attraction than a theory of attitude change. However, it draws so heavily upon Heider's P-O-X model that it becomes important to consider it here. The Heider and Newcomb's models have many common features. Both models emphasise a kind of *cognitive homeostasis*, that is, tendency for attitudes to develop and change in such a way that a state of consistency balance is developed.

Newcomb (1963) stated that as the members of group interact with one another, each member selects and processes information about objects of common interests, about other members in terms of their attitude towards the object as well as in terms of their attitudes towards one another. This information is selected and processed in order to avoid inconsistencies and conflicts involved in imbalance relationship. According to Price, Harburg and Newcomb (1966), imbalance relationship, which is avoided because of painful nature, involves a conflict between the preference for consistent world and the confrontation of the reality that is less consistent, likely anxiety regarding the fact that anxiety may eventuate or both.

Newcomb stated that there may actually be three kinds of situations—states in which balance has been achieved, non-balanced state in which the person feels indifference, and imbalanced states in which the person takes steps to restore balance.

Like in Heider's model, three kinds of states can be identified in Newcomb's theory— a normal state or a state of rest or balance, intrusion of certain forces or events that disturbs this state of balance, and operational mechanisms that bring the system back to the state of balance. Figure 7.5 deals with the same core features with which Newcomb's A-B-X model deals. Sohan (A) likes Anil (B), who has positive feelings about Ashok (X). However, Sohan dislikes Ashok (X). In such a situation, it is predicted, in general, that the situation would be unstable and would create pressure for change in one of the connecting links. However, Newcomb's model, at this point, proposes another consideration that must be taken into account. According to Newcomb, Sohan's liking towards Anil and disliking towards Ashok are not independent of each other, but in reality, are highly interdependent. In other words, one of these two relationships cannot be considered without considering the other. Now, consider a situation in which Sohan and Anil, who are highly attracted towards each other, disagree about worth of Ashok. Such disagreement, as per Newcomb's theory, tends to create a strain towards symmetry, where individual concern is forced to change some of the elements in the relationship (Newcomb preferred to use the word *symmetry* instead of balance). The amount of such strain would be the function of the following three factors:

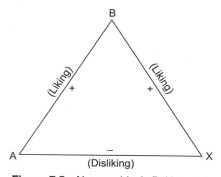

Figure 7.5 Newcomb's A–B–X model.

(i) Degree of Sohan's (A's) attraction or liking towards Anil (B)
(ii) Intensity of Sohan's attitude towards Ashok (X)
(iii) Sohan's perception of the discrepancy between his opinion of Ashok (X) and Anil's opinion of Ashok

Newcomb proposed in his model that the state of created imbalance would be resolved through the process of communication. For example, Sohan may communicate with Anil regarding Ashok, presumably to change his (Anil's) attitude towards Ashok and restore balance. The amount of communication from Sohan to Anil regarding Ashok will be directly affected by the above three factors. Thus, strain is reduced through communication, where Sohan convinces Anil about the worthlessness of Ashok or Anil may convince Sohan about the worth of Ashok. Such increased communication, however, does not continue indefinitely (Schachter, 1951). Schachter (1951) conducted one study in which three new members were added to establish social groups. Out of these three, one played the role of *conformist*, another played the role of *slider* and third played the role of *deviant*. The conformist member accepted and went along the position of the group; the slider in the beginning played a deviant role, but subsequently, he was more towards accepting the position of the group and the deviant member played a non-conformist role throughout the experiment. As predicted from Newcomb's model, the conformist member was the focus of little group's communication. In fact, in such member, there was found no strain towards symmetry because he had already accepted the position of the group. The slider was definitely the focus of group communication that increased as his attitude started showing shift towards the group. In this case, effort to reduce imbalance was quite obvious and as that effort started meeting the success, it increased in intensity. In the beginning, the deviant too was the focus of high level of communication, but since he displayed no change, he was internally rejected by the social group. Results clearly showed an orientation towards symmetry or balance, but of slightly different nature. The social group comes to dislike and reject the deviant, who continues to hold a position discrepant from his own despite his efforts to change it. Thus, here, balance is achieved with two negative and one positive relationship.

Another way in which P (Sohan) can reduce strain in perceptual system is by perceiving X (Ashok) inaccurately (Newcomb, 1961). Such distortions are basically the results of P's decision to maintain balance at all costs because of its importance to his psychological adjustment rather than to accept the truth irrespective of its costs.

Newcomb's balance theory, as stated above, is concerned more with the problem of interpersonal attraction than with the attitude change. However, his emphasis upon the interdependence of A's attitudes towards both B and X as well as his introduction of increased communication as one means of resolving the imbalance serves to resolve some of the ambiguities of the basic balance model proposed by Heider. Moreover, Newcomb's idea that the negative relationship between person (P) and another individual may lead to a non-balanced state characterised by P's apathy has been challenged by researchers, who have shown that there are some activities which are likely to occur that may lead to an attempt to restore balance. Therefore, three-way situations are likely to be either balanced or imbalanced, with an attempt on the part of P to restore balance.

3. Festinger's theory of cognitive dissonance: The theory of cognitive dissonance was developed by Festinger (1957). It is the most widely researched cognitive consistency theory, as it offers a general theory of human social motivation. A cognition, for the purpose of this theory, may be thought of as a piece of knowledge about an attitude, an emotion, a behaviour, a value, and so on.

Two cognitions may be in the state of consonance or in the state of dissonance. Two cognitions are *consonant* if one cognition follows or fit with the other. For example, the cognition that it is about 1600 km from Patna to Jammu fits well with the cognition that you decide to travel by air to go there. The state of consonance does not produce any tension in the person. Two cognitions are said to be *dissonant* if one cognition follows the opposite of other. *Dissonance* has been defined by Festinger as a negative drive state, which is produced when a person holds two cognitions, which are psychologically inconsistent. For example, a smoker who knows that smoking produces lung cancer illustrates two dissonant or discrepant cognitions. The cognition 'I am smoker' does not fit with cognition that 'smoking causes lung cancer' and creates a state of dissonance. A person who has dissonant cognition is said to be in the psychological state of dissonance that is experienced as unpleasant psychological tension. This tension has a drive-like properties which a person wishes to change towards feeling comfortable, thus brings a change in the attitude.

Festinger's original view was that any inconsistency could cause tension, and hence, dissonance. However, Cooper and Fazio (1984), after reviewing two decades of research on dissonance, outlined the following four conditions necessary for actions to produce dissonance and for that dissonance to produce attitude change:

(i) The first condition is that the individual must be aware of the fact that an inconsistency between an attitude and a behaviour would have negative consequences. When a person, somehow, sees no problem or undesirable effect arising between an attitude and a behaviour, dissonance would not be occurring and there will not be any change in the attitude. For example, if the smoker believes that smoking will not cause lung cancer or will not produce any ill-health effect, there will be no dissonance, and therefore, no change in the attitude of the smoker.

(ii) The second condition is that the individual must take responsibility for the behaviour. In terms of attribution, the person must make internal attribution in which he may feel that the behaviour (smoking) is under his control and he can stop it whenever he wishes to do so. A smoker freely chooses to smoke and the dissonance may not occur if he regards smoking behaviour to be the result of being forced to smoke (an external attribution).

(iii) The third condition is that the individual must feel physiological arousal. When the individuals are placed in a dissonant condition, they show some kinds of physiological arousal, which must be felt as an unpleasant and discomfort state (Losch and Cacioppo, 1990). If this is not the case, there will be no drive in the person to bring a change in his attitude. Elliot and Devine (1994) provided evidence to this effect. They conducted an experiment in which the participants in one condition were asked to write an essay counter to their own attitude, that is, in favour of enhancement in tuition fees. In other condition, the students were asked to write essay in consistent with their attitude, that is, against the enhancement in tuition fees. Results revealed that participants in counter-attitude condition demonstrated significantly higher ratings of unpleasant feelings than the participants who were asked to write essay consistent with their attitudes.

(iv) The fourth condition is that the individual must attribute the felt dissonance to the inconsistency between their attitude and behaviour. When an individual attributes the physiological arousal to something other than his own behaviour (such as to some external factors), dissonance does not occur, and therefore, there is no attitude change.

Table 7.1 provides the summary of the above four conditions using general example of smoking as instances of producing dissonance.

Table 7.1 Conditions Leading to The Emergence of Cognitive Dissonance

Condition	Dissonance Present
Attitude behaviour inconsistency perceived to have negative consequence	Smoking causes lung cancer.
Individual takes responsibility for his behaviour	I chose to smoke.
Negative physiological arousal experienced by the person	Feeling of discomfort is experienced about consequences of smoking.
Discomfort arousal is attributed to inconsistency	I feel concerned about smoking.

Researches have shown that there are certain factors that affect the magnitude of dissonance arousal. Such important factors are as under:

(i) The magnitude of dissonance increases as the degree of discrepancy among cognitions increases. A person who delivers a speech against pre-marital sex has more discrepancy between his cognitions if his attitude is extremely favourable to pre-marital sex than if it is only marginally favourable.

(ii) The magnitude of dissonance directly increases as the number of discrepant cognitions and degree of discrepancy among them increase. In other words, as number and degree increase, so does the dissonance. For example, a person taking ice-cream will feel dissonance if he believes that he should not take it because he suffers from tonsillitis. But he will experience more dissonance if he also has these cognitions—he is allergic to cold, the taste of ice-cream is not liked by him, or he has also vowed before doctors for never taking the ice-cream.

(iii) The magnitude of dissonance is inversely proportional to the number of consonant cognitions held by the person. It means that greater the number of consonant cognitions, lesser is the magnitude of dissonance. In some life situations such cognitions exist and they tend to support certain aspects of an otherwise discrepant cognition or situation.

(iv) For estimating the magnitude of dissonance from factors listed above, the importance of various cognitions should also be taken into account. The magnitude of dissonance may be expressed in terms of the following ratio:

$$\text{Dissonance} = \frac{\text{Importance} \times \text{Number of dissonant cognitions}}{\text{Importance} \times \text{Number of consonant cognitions}}$$

From the above equation, it becomes clear that more nearly equal the relative proportions of consonant and dissonant cognitions, the greater will be the magnitude of the dissonance. On the other hand, if there are only few dissonant cognitions and many consonant cognitions, the magnitude of dissonance will be relatively low. The number of dissonant cognitions can never exceed the number of consonant cognition because this would produce change and the dissonance would be removed. Hence, the maximum value that dissonance can reach is one which is found when the proportions of dissonant and consonant cognitions are equal.

Festinger had propounded some propositions of the theory as under:

(i) The dissonance is a psychologically uncomfortable state and it motivates the individual to reduce the dissonance and achieve consonance.
(ii) When dissonance is experienced by the individual, he not only tries to reduce it but also actively avoids situations and information, which may increase dissonance.
(iii) The strength of the pressure to reduce dissonance is the function of the amount of dissonance.

Since dissonance is experienced as an unpleasant drive state, the person is motivated to reduce it. There are four ways of reducing distance, which are as follows:

(i) *Changing a behavioural cognitive element*: When the knowledge of an individual's own behaviour becomes dissonant with his cognition (or belief), it is easier to change his behaviour and reduce dissonance. For example, if Mohan smokes, but thinks it is bad for his health, he may stop smoking and reduce dissonance.

(ii) *Changing an environmental cognitive element:* Sometimes, it is found that the behaviour of a person is dissonant with some environmental factor, which can be changed. The easiest aspect of environmental factor, which can be changed, is the social and interpersonal environment. Thus, a smoker, who is disturbed by dissonance, may tend to seek support from all those smokers, who can present arguments against the view that lung cancer is caused by smoking. He may, for example, point to the fact that many doctors also smoke.

(iii) *Adding new cognitive elements:* Sometimes, it becomes difficult to bring a change in any of the cognitions in dissonance. In such situations, the person can reduce dissonance by adding new cognition elements to outweigh the dissonant ones. For example, a smoker anxious of developing lung cancer may convince himself that smoking is relaxing, and thus, tones up health. In fact, smokers may think that the benefits of smoking (that is, reduced tension, improved weight control, feeling of euphoria) outweigh the costs of smoking (Lipkus et al., 2001). Likewise, a person, who faces dissonance due to purchasing of a costly car which he cannot afford, may convince himself by adding a new cognition that he is very likely to get a substantial enhancement in his pay or he is likely to get soon his pay arrears.

(iv) *Engaging in trivialisation:* For reducing dissonance, the person can engage in trivialisation in which he can conclude that attitudes or behaviours in question are trivial or not important. In such a situation, he does not pay much attention to either attitudes or behaviours. Therefore, any inconsistency between them no longer remains important one (Simon, Greenberg and Brehm, 1995).

Besides these direct means, dissonance can also be reduced by indirect means, where the basic discrepancy between attitude and behaviour remains unaffected, but the underlying unpleasant feelings produced by dissonance are reduced. Such method is commonly applied when dissonance is produced by important attitude or self-belief. When the attitude-behaviour discrepancy is related to important attitude, the person does not focus much upon reducing the gap between attitude and behaviour. Instead, he focuses upon other things such as self-affirmation that allows the person to feel good about the self despite the gap. In fact, in self-affirmation, the person restores positive self-evaluations that are threatened by discrepancy between attitude and behaviour and this is done by focusing on good things about self or on positive self-attributes (Tesser, Martin and Cornell, 1996).

Implications of dissonance theory: What is the usefulness of the theory in predicting attitude change? In fact, from the theory the following two hypotheses may be derived:

(i) If an individual is forced to say or do something opposite to his private attitude, he would try to modify or bring a change in his attitude so as to make it consonant with the cognition of what he has said or done.

(ii) The pressure used to elicit the behaviour contrary to one's private attitude beyond the minimum needed to elicit it, will tend to produce less changes in attitude. It means greater the pressure beyond minimum needed, lesser is the change in attitude.

Festinger and Carlsmith (1959) conducted an experiment to verify these hypotheses. The experiment was interesting and important because predictions from dissonance theory were borne out opposite to that of common sense. In this study, college students were asked to spend an hour doing the most boring tasks, that is, turning 48 pegs a quarter-turn consecutively and placing spools on a tray, then emptying it and filling it again. When the participants completed these boring and tedious tasks, the experimenter (E) told them to tell before other persons who had to act as subjects that the task was, in fact, very interesting, exciting and full of fun. Then came the experimental manipulation. Some participants were promised a reward of $1 and some participants were promised a reward of $20 for telling lie. Finally, all participants were asked to indicate their actual attitude towards the task. According to the dissonance theory, the participants who were paid $1 for advocating a counterattitudinal position should experience more dissonance, and consequently, greater attitude change than the participants who were paid $20. Results of the experiment confirmed this prediction. The condition of $1 provided insufficient justification for telling lie, and therefore, it produced more dissonance, and hence, participants, to ward off the feeling of dissonance, changed their attitude and said that the task was really interesting. In other words, participants who were paid only $1 experienced distressed for thinking that they would lie to someone for only $1. Therefore, they decided not to lie that the task really was really interesting and full of fun. Therefore, these participants had to change their attitude towards task so that they would not be really lying, and therefore, could maintain their self-image of honesty. Social psychologists have termed this surprising effect as the *less-leads-to-move effect*. In such effect, offering persons smaller rewards for engaging in counterattitudinal behaviour often produces more dissonance or attitude-behaviour discrepancy and so more attitude change than when they are offered larger rewards. Such effect has also been confirmed by Leippe and Eisenstadt (1994). The condition of $20 provided a sufficient justification for telling lie, and hence, there was a lesser dissonance but more pressure for advocating counterattitudinal position. Therefore, they did not change their attitude much. The relative amounts of dissonance in the two experimental conditions may be illustrated by the following ratios:

$$\text{Greater dissonance} = \frac{\text{Feeling that task is dull and insignificant}}{\text{Pressure by E + Payment of \$1}}$$

$$\text{Lesser dissonance} = \frac{\text{Feeling that task is dull and insignificant}}{\text{Pressure by E + Payment of \$20}}$$

The numerators of these two ratios are the cognitions associated with private attitude—the feeling that the task is dull and insignificant. These cognitions are dissonant with engaging in the behaviour. The denominators are the cognitions consonant with engaging in the behaviour. These cognitions are derived from the pressure to conform to the experimenter's request and the desire for the monetary payment (refer the explanation given under applications of dissonance theory—forced compliance behaviour).

Applications of dissonance theory: Cognitive dissonance theory has been incorporated into different areas of applications. The breadth of application of dissonance theory is the primary reason that social psychologists have conducted researches on Festinger's original theory for over 40 years. The major areas where the theory has been applied are decision-making, forced compliance behaviour and justification of effort.

(i) *Decision-making:* A person who makes a decision in which the alternatives considered have both positive and negative consequences generally experiences what is called *post-decisional dissonance*. Such dissonance is experienced only after a decision has been made. The dissonance is experienced because both chosen alternative and rejected alternative have positive and negative features, and rejected alternatives may have positive features, which are absent in the selected alternative as well as the selected or chosen alternative may possess some negative features. This can be illustrated through an example.

Suppose you are trying to decide which car (that is car A or car B) to buy. The most direct way to assist decision-making would be to draw up a checklist of the important features you are looking for in both cars and compare the two cars. Suppose that you have isolated six features, which are equally important for you. Those features are price, petrol, spares, comfort, servicing and outlook. Table 7.2 presents these features of the car A and B along with your valuation.

Table 7.2 Features of Car A and Car B with Valuation of the Buyer

Features	Car A	Value	Car B	Value
Price	Relatively cheap	+	Expensive	−
Petrol	Economical	+	Economical	+
Spares	Hard to get and expensive too	−	Available and cheap	+
Comfort	Smooth and quiet	+	Hard and noisy	−
Servicing	Frequent and cheap	+	Infrequent and expensive	−
Outlook	Unattractive	−	Attractive	+

Implementing a simple decisive rule you will probably buy car A. After buying car A, you will experience dissonance because you have made a choice in which there are negative features (such as outlook being unattractive and spare parts are expensive and hard to get) and rejected a choice with some positive features (such as outlook being attractive, spare parts are cheap and easy to get).

Such post-decisional dissonance can be reduced by two ways—one is by *bolstering* the chosen alternative, which means that the consonant information will be selectively collected to make the selected alternative even more attractive and rejected alternative less attractive (Ehrlich et al., 1957). The negative features of rejected alternatives may also be exaggerated for reducing the post-decisional dissonance (Brehm, 1956). Generally, it has been found that people who had just bought a car or some expensive article look at magazine articles and advertisements, which praise their choice of purchase and ignore or read reports criticising rejected alternatives. Another way of reducing such post-decisional dissonance is to trivialise the positive features of the alternative rejected (Simon et al., 1995).

(ii) *Induced or forced compliance behaviour:* Findings from several forced compliance experiments are explained in terms of justification. This was first investigated in the classic experiment by Festinger and Carlsmith (1959), which we have already discussed. The idea was that when there was sufficient external justification ($20 in Festinger and Carlsmith experiment), there was a little dissonance among the participants, and hence, they did not change their attitudes. However, when the external justification for telling lie was insufficient ($1 payment), participants experienced more cognitive dissonance. Dissonance can be reduced by changing one of the cognitions—the participant has already done or said something against his view (he is forced or requested to comply with the experimenter's request), so this cannot change. The consequence is that the participant's own view or attitude changes should be consonant (or less dissonant) with his behaviour. Since low reward condition ($1) offers insufficient external justification for the behaviour, internal justification is sought and the internal justification is to view the experimental task as interesting (providing evidence for changes in attitude), and thus, dissonance is reduced or eliminated. Such surprising effect has been called by social psychologists as *less-leads-to-more effect*, which shows that fewer reasons or smaller rewards for an action often lead to higher degree of attitude change. In order to occur less-leads-to-more effect clearly, the following conditions must be kept in view:

(a) Less-leads-to-more effect occurs only in those conditions in which an individual believes that he has an option to do or not to do the attitude-discrepant behaviour. A higher degree of coercion may undermine dissonance.
(b) Small rewards or fewer reasons lead to greater attitude change only when the individual believes that he is personally neither responsible for chosen course of action nor for negative effects it tends to produce. For example, when the authority asks one to do certain behaviour, he may not feel responsible for his action or dissonance, if produced.
(c) Less-leads-to-more effect fails to occur when the individual views that payment received by him is a kind of bribe rather than a deserved payment for rendering the services. To the extent the person believes that he is being bribed, the effect gets reduced.

Keeping these conditions in view, to induce the person to say or do contrary to his attitudes can be an effective technique for bringing attitude change.

(iii) *Justifying effort:* Before getting a membership to a group, a party, or a society or an association, there are often what are called *initiation rites* to go through. The general prediction is that the more effort a person puts into achieving the goal, more important, attractive and worthwhile it is finally perceived to be after the goal is achieved. Dissonance theory claims that regardless of how attractive and worthwhile the goal is, it is initiation rites as what a person goes through to achieve it that determines its worth. If the person has put a lot of time and effort for gaining membership of a society, group or club, and subsequently, discovers that the society is worthless or useless for his purpose, then dissonance arises. It is because the cognition 'I have put a lot of effort and time for gaining membership' and 'the group, club or society is dull and worthless for my purpose' are dissonant. Normally, a person does not put much effort and time for something that is useless and worthless. To reduce the dissonance, the person could leave the society or club or group to which he has just joined. But this is unlikely to occur because in such a condition, he will have to acknowledge indirectly that he has wasted his time and effort. However, he may change his attitude towards the club or society, as Festinger and Carlsmith had predicted, and may consider it worthwhile and purposeful. This would justify the time, effort and energy expended. Aronson and Mills (1959) conducted an experiment to test this prediction. The researchers asked some women participants to join a group discussing the psychology of sex. Before joining group, the participants were told to go through a screening test, which acted like initiation rites. Participants were randomly allocated to one of three screening test conditions—severe initiation condition, where the participants had to recite aloud obscene words and sexually explicit passages in the presence of a male; mild initiation condition, where the participants recited aloud sexual but not obscene words; and no initiation condition, where the participants were admitted to the discussion group without any initiation or screening. After this, participants in each condition listened to a live discussion of the psychology of sex. In fact, participants in each condition listened the same tape recording of a discussion, which was deliberately made dull and boring. After listening to this boring discussion, participants were asked to tell how much they liked it and found it interesting, worthwhile and entertaining. Results revealed that the participants who had gone through the condition of severe initiation found the discussion interesting and worthwhile. The participants of mild initiation condition reported that discussion was only slightly interesting and worthwhile, and the participants who were admitted to the discussion without any initiation reported that discussion was dull and boring. These results were in accord with the prediction of dissonance theory of Festinger. The participants who were admitted to the discussion group after severe initiation condition had experienced higher degree of dissonance, and therefore, to reduce it, they changed their attitude towards the boring and dull discussion by telling it to be more interesting and worthwhile. Axsom and cooper (1985) further demonstrated that whatever the person puts effort into may result in dissonance and attitude change. They further showed that the attitude change resulting from attempts to reduce dissonance may last for a year or more.

Criticisms of dissonance theory: Although dissonance theory has been extremely stimulating force within and beyond social psychology, there are some exceptions to the theory. Important points of criticism are as under:

(i) Some social psychologists like Chapanis and Chapanis (1964) suggested that there were methodological flaws in the original experiment conducted by Festinger and Carlsmith (1959). For example, one common argument is centred on the concept of evaluation apprehension, that is, the participants were concerned with the fact that the experimenter in the study would evaluate them positively (Rosenberg, 1965). According to this view, $20 payment offered to the participants was pretty large and might have led to the suspicion on the part of the participants that the experimenter was in reality trying to buy attitude change. For being evaluated positively by the experimenter, the participants might have resisted attitude change in that condition.

(ii) Another criticism of dissonance theory of attitude change was from Bem (1967, 1972), who proposed a self-perception or self-judgement theory. Bem argued that dissonance experiment such as the experiment done by Festinger and Carlsmith (1959) does not really reflect individual attitude change as a dissonance-reducing procedure. Since the outcomes of the experiment can be explained and predicted without reliance on internal motivational state of dissonance, something quite different such as self-judgement may be happening and the outcomes can be easily explained in terms of self-judgement. Applying this principle to the outcomes of Festinger and Carlsmith's (1959) experiment, Bem argued that it is not necessary to look at internal motivational state of dissonance to explain the behaviour of the participants. The behaviour of the participants can be entirely explained if we view the situation from their point of view. A participant who is paid $20 may perceive that there is a clear external reason for his behaviour—the $20 justification. Likewise, the participant who is paid $1, perceives his behaviour much in the same way as others would do, and reasons that making a positive statement for so little external incentive must imply that really the task was interesting and he enjoyed it. The end result would be the same as in the dissonance theory of attitude change (a positive attitude in lesser incentive condition), but the mechanism of explanation would be different.

(iii) The cognitive dissonance theory apparently contradicts reinforcement-based learning theories as well as common sense explanation since it maintains that the participants put forth effort or express changes in attitude in negative relationship to the amount of reward. According to reinforcement-based learning theories as well as common sense explanation, greater reward ($20) should have produced more changes in the attitude than the smaller reward ($1), but in reality, the case was opposite.

(iv) Some social psychologists have begun to investigate the physiological aspects of dissonance (Croyle and Cooper, 1983) and have shown that dissonance reduction may occur in ways other than modifying relevant cognitive elements. For example, Steele, Southwick and Critchlow (1981) found in their study that social drinkers, who got opportunity to drink alcohol following the arousal of dissonance, demonstrated less attitude change than those who did not drink. Apparently alcohol tended to reduce the aversive impact of dissonance allowing dissonant cognitive elements to be held without having the experience of unpleasant feeling.

(v) Another alternative explanation of dissonance which is similar to that of Festinger and Carlsmith was provided by Tedeschi, Schlenker and Bonoma's (1971) *theory of impression management*. The basic contention of this theory is that we are all socialised to appear consistent. Others in the social world reward us for seeming to be consistent and they punish us for showing inconsistency. Consequently, we learn to manage the impressions that we give to others for producing consistency in behaviour. The crux of theory of impression management is that we do not have an internal need for consistency. It rules out intrapsychic tension as motivation for changing the attitude. The findings of the dissonance theory can be explained within the framework of impression management. In $20 condition, there was less attitude change because for such a high external incentive, the participants felt satisfied for telling a lie and they thought that their behaviour was quite consistent with their feeling of satisfaction. That is why the participants were quite successful in leaving the impression that they were rational and had a clear need to be consistent in beliefs and behaviour.

Despite these limitations, dissonance theory has been a very stimulating force within social psychology. The basic theme of the theory has motivated research, which has greatly advanced the understanding of human cognition.

Comparison between balance theory and cognitive dissonance theory: Balance theory and cognitive dissonance theory both rest upon the common assumption that a person's behaviour is, to some extent, motivated by a drive to maintain consistency or consonance among cognitive elements. However, there are some basic differences between them as under:

(i) Balance theories are mainly concerned with describing balance systems and how they are maintained by the persons, whereas cognitive dissonance theories, in general, try to predict what happens when somehow balance is not maintained due to the intervention of some unexpected cognitive elements.

(ii) Most of the researches in balance theories appear to be largely concerned with the person's attitudes towards others with respect to his attitudes towards the third element, which may be other person or issue or some form of behaviour. Researches with cognitive dissonance are more action-oriented because they are concerned with a sequence of events in which a person makes a decision which is inconsistent with his previous behaviour and affects the consequent behaviour, presumably the attitude. Here, the person feels free to make a decision for resolving the conflict (called *dissonance*) due to inconsistency.

If we pay attention to these differences, it becomes obvious that they are not very sharp and distinctive. Keeping this in view, it can be concluded that these two types of theory do not contradict each other, but actually serve to complement each other.

4. Congruity theory: This theory was propounded by Osgood and Tannenbaum (1955). The theory is based on the assumption that it is simpler to hold congruent attitudes towards two related objects than to have varying attitudes towards them. The congruity theory goes a step ahead than the principle of balance because it makes quantitative prediction explicit about what will happen if the two related objects are not in a state of congruity. Suppose, for example, a favourite cinema star (or a filmy hero) endorses a concept we oppose. In such a situation, the theory predicts that we would feel less favourable towards the cinema star but more favourable towards the concept; thus, attitudes towards both cinema star and concept are likely to change. In this way, our support for cinema star would likely to go down and our feelings to all those who took the same position would become somewhat negative. Likewise, if a person has a lukewarm attitude towards the captain of Indian cricket team, Shri Mahendra Singh Dhoni, but is enthusiastic about cricket, then he will become more favourable towards Shri Dhoni and perhaps slightly less enthusiastic about cricket so that the intensities of the two attitudes shift together. In fact, congruity is said to exist when two related objects are evaluated with equal intensity. According to congruity theory, if two attitude objects that are located at different points on the continuum are linked by what Osgood and Tannenbaum (1955) called an *associative assertion*, the attitude that we hold least strongly would change the most and more strongly held attitude will change the least. In other words, strongly held attitudes are less amenable to change and weakly held attitudes are more likely to change because they are more likely to be influenced by contrary opinion or information.

Thus, congruity theory not only makes prediction about the direction of attitude change but also specifies the amount. In this way, it is more precise than other cognitive-consistency models. Though experimental evidence, no doubt, supports the congruity principle, there are limitations to the scope of its operations. The very precision of the theory has created many contrary findings, which cannot be explained by the initial model. Besides, the utility of congruity theory in bringing out large scale attitude change remains questionable.

Social Learning Theories of Attitude Change

Social learning theories of attitude change grew out of the application of the reinforcement principles of classical conditioning model and operant conditioning model.

As we know, the classical conditioning model grew out of the experimental work of Pavlov (1928). In his famous experiment, Pavlov presented a dog with an unconditioned stimulus (meat powder) that elicited a natural response (salivation). The unconditioned stimulus was then paired with a conditional stimulus (ringing a bell) which, after several paired presentations, elicited the same response, that is, salivation.

Several studies conducted by Staats and Staats (1958) are the typical representation of the work employing the classical conditioning model to the problem of attitude change. In one of their studies Staats and Staats proceeded to determine whether or not attitudes towards national names could be changed by pairing these names with stimulus words that produced either positive or negative responses. They found that words like 'gift', 'beauty', 'sweet' produced positive response and words like 'ugly', 'sad', 'sour' produced negative responses. The positive words were paired with names like 'Swede' and negative words were paired with names like 'Dutch'. After several such presentations, it was found by researchers that the name 'Dutch' produced more negative responses in the participants and the national name like 'Swede' elicited a positive response. Other researches indicated that the same results could be accomplished using individual names also. Olson and Fazio (2001) also observed that if positive events are frequently and repeatedly associated with attitude object, they soon come to elicit the feelings associated with those events, thus providing evidence for attitude change. In their study, they asked some female students to watch a series of slides that included pairings of novel objects with either positive or negative words or images. Results revealed that objects earlier paired with positive images or words were then eliciting positive attitudes and objects earlier paired with negative images or words were then eliciting negative attitudes.

In our day-to-day life, we find numerous applications of this method. Television advertisements that pair products with well-known and liked personalities from films or games are the common example. When such personalities are shown to recommend the use of a particular product, our attitudes are formed and changed accordingly. We also become ready to use the products towards which we were having a neutral attitude. Examples showing consequences of negative pairings need to be considered also. During the time of general election in the country, the politicians who face critical charges against their character or face trials in the court of law are urged to stay out of their constituency probably because their negatively evaluated personality could lead to a transfer of negative responses or feelings among the public.

The conditioning model provides another theoretical framework for explaining attitude change. This model assumes that the behaviour is the result of its consequences. In other words, if the response is rewarded, the person is likely to continue that response. On the other hand, if the response is followed by punishment or negative reinforcement, the person may discontinue the response.

There are four essential steps that must be completed for changing attitude in the desired direction in terms of principles of operant or instrumental conditioning:

1. It must be established by the researcher that what type of attitude the participants should hold at the conclusion of the experiment.

2. The present attitude held by the participant must be assessed for determining the amount and type of change to be elicited.
3. Appropriate primary or secondary reinforcement or punishment must be provided.
4. A schedule of reinforcement must be followed. Generally, a continuous reinforcement schedule is used to establish a new attitude, but changes in attitude will be most effectively induced if an intermittent schedule is employed.

Scott (1957) conducted an experiment to demonstrate the effectiveness of operant conditioning model in attitude change. He used a debate situation to examine the effect of reinforcement on attitude change. Participants were requested to defend the assigned positions on some important issues. At the conclusion of debate, some participants (debaters) were declared as winners and some others as losers. Results indicated that those who were declared winners changed their attitudes towards favouring the position advocated and those who were declared losers did not change their attitudes. Likewise, Singer (1961) also conducted an experiment to demonstrate the application of operant conditioning model in attitude change. He reinforced his experimental subjects by the saying *good* and *right* when their responses indicated a prodemocratic attitude in the form of F-scale (used to assess authoritarianism). There was also a control group of subjects who were not reinforced. All subjects were, then, presented E-scale (a different form of the scale to assess authoritarianism). Results indicated that the subjects of the experimental group had significantly changed their attitudes and took a more prodemocratic position, whereas the subjects of the control group had shown a very little change in their attitude.

Another most interesting study showing the importance of reinforcement in attitude change is Newcomb's Bennington College research. Newcomb (1958), during each of the four consecutive years, made a comparison of the attitude of junior and senior students with those of freshmen and sophomores towards several issues of the day. At that time, majority of the students attending Bennington College came from well-to-do, conservative, republic families. However, the situation at the college was different. Moreover, they came into contact with a situation, where faculty was liberal and the expression of non-conservative attitudes came to be associated with greater prestige and higher status. Results revealed that a significant change in attitude occurred during the four years period. Majority of students who were conservative, republic as freshmen demonstrated attitudes typical of rather liberal democrats by the end of the fourth year in the college. According to Newcomb, the change in attitude from conservative to liberal was largely a function of reward system at Bennington. Holding liberal attitude was rewarded both by the faculty as well as by the older students, who had already shown much change.

Thus, changes in attitude obviously take place when we are rewarded or reinforced or when new positions are more personally satisfying, thus providing the support for application of operant conditioning model in attitude change.

Other Theories of Attitude Change

Under this section, two important theories of attitude change—Kelman's three process theory and assimilation-contrast theory—are discussed.

1. Kelman's theory: Kelman (1961) proposed a theory of attitude change, which specifies the conditions under which attitude changes are manifested and the conditions under which they are not manifested. Moreover, the theory also specifies that conditions under which temporary changes in attitude take place or some permanent changes in attitude take place.

Kelman had identified three distinct processes of social influence that are instrumental in bringing changes in attitude. *Social influence* is defined as a change in the person's attitude or behaviour that is produced by the influencing agent (Raven, 1974; Tedeschi, 1974). The influence can be either intentional or unintentional. The three processes of social influence following Kelman are—compliance, identification and internalisation. These are being discussed here.

(i) **Compliance:** *Compliance* may be defined as a change in overt or public behaviour after exposure to others' opinions (Hewstone et al., 1996). It is said to occur when a person accepts influence from another person or group because he or she hopes to achieve a favourable reaction from the other. In such a situation, the expression of opinion, even though a person privately disagrees with what is being expressed, becomes instrumental in gaining reward or avoiding some punishment. This, in turn, brings a change in attitude. For example, when a person finds that his boss becomes happy and feels proud of jokes he tells, the person may laugh whole heartedly at the boss's joke even when he thinks that the jokes are boring. Such behaviour of the employee may help in pleasing the boss and changing his attitude favourably.

The compliance is likely to occur when the influencing agent has strong control over rewards and punishment that the person might receive. For example, a little child often complies with the order of a strict teacher even though the private feelings of the child are in other direction. Here, the influencing agent (teacher) has strong degree of control over the reward and punishment to be awarded to the child. Likewise, researchers have shown that when the influencing agent somehow lies in a position to closely observe the behaviour of the person, compliance is most likely to occur. For example, a child in the classroom behaves well when a strict teacher is watching him. Despite all these, an attitude adopted through compliance is very likely to be abandoned if the influencing agent loses control over the person. Not only that, such attitude stands isolated from other attitudes and values.

(ii) **Identification:** Identification is said to occur when a person tends to adopt certain actions or attitudes because they are associated with a satisfying relation to another individuals or group. Identification, thus, becomes a means of establishing a good and desirable relation with another person as well as supporting the self-definition, which is a part of that relation. There can be several forms of identification. One popular form is often shown in an attempt to be like the other person. This is commonly shown by the children who copy the behaviours of others or some model that has impressed them. Another form of identification is one, where a person forms a relation with another person, which demands a behaviour different from that of his own. Here, the person behaves in accordance with the expectations of the other person. For example, a person adopts the suggestions of a doctor and behaves according to the expectations of the doctor. A third form of the identification is one, where the person maintains his relation to a group in which his self-definition is tagged. For example, an engineer adopts the attitude and behaviour expected of him by his other fellow engineers.

Whatever may be the form of identification, it occurs because the person has satisfying relations with another person or group and also requires activation of the relation in order to make it occur. A daughter having good and affectionate relation with her mother tends to adopt many of her behaviours and attitudes. Thus, identification clearly requires that there must be a good relation between the person and the influencing agent. Changes in attitude are maintained only so long as the relation to the influencing agent remains satisfying one and so long as the agent himself or herself retains the attitude.

(iii) **Internalisation:** *Internalisation* refers to the acceptance or adoption of beliefs, values, attitudes, etc., as one's own. In other words, internalisation involves acceptance of externally imposed rules as internal standards, which in turn, guide our behaviour. Internalisation is said to occur when a person accepts influence since the induced behaviour is congruent with his value system. The attitude or behaviour is, in fact, demanded by the values of the individual and becomes instrumental in solving the problem. For example, a person with social and liberal attitude will appreciate the programmes of the government for providing free medical care to the poor and aged people because one of his values is that the government should promote the public welfare programme. Internalisation is likely to occur in the situation, where the influencing agent is highly credible or believable. Changes in attitudes as a function of internalisation are likely to persist so long as values relevant to their adoption are maintained. In internalisation, unlike compliance and identification, the attitude or behaviour is intrinsically rewarding to the person. Hence, attitude changes comparatively last longer.

Thus, Kelman had tried to explain changes in attitude through these three processes of attitude change. A point of importance is that any particular situation is not the pure example of any one of these three processes. Often two or even all the three processes may occur simultaneously. For example, if the influencing agent has a strong and powerful control over a person, compliance is likely to occur. But if there is also a good and satisfying relation with the influencing agent, both compliance and identification may occur together. In addition, if the attitudes or behaviours required are also congruent with the attitude held by the person or the value system of the person, internalisation is also likely to occur.

Social psychologists have considered Kelman's theory as important one because it takes into account the conditions that control the three influence processes along with their permanence of the attitude. Kelman's theory also takes into account the principles of learning to some extent.

2. Assimilation-contrast theory: Assimilation-contrast theory of attitude change was developed largely from the work of Sherif and Hovland and its roots of growth can be traced to two older traditions in social psychology.

The first tradition from which assimilation-contrast theory grew was the critical analyses done by the authors of Thurstone techniques for assessing attitudes. As we know, in developing Thurstone attitude scale, a number of judges evaluate various attitude statements in terms of their favourability or unfavourability towards the attitude object, and the assumption of Thurstone was that the judges' evaluations of the statements are independent of their own attitudes towards the object of the attitude. Many researches have provided support to this assumption (Ferguson, 1935), but the researches done by Hovland and Sherif (1952) and Sherif and Hovland (1953) strongly criticised the earlier findings related to Thurstone's scale. These researchers observed that it was a common practice in constructing such scales to eliminate those judges who sorted thirty or more attitude statements into a single pile due to their carelessness. They proposed that rather than being careless, such judges might be having extreme attitudes towards attitude object, and therefore, they might be bunching statements in one or two categories at the end of the scale opposite their own position. Sherif and Hovland reported in their study that, in fact, both black and white judges, with favourable attitudes, tended to place several statements in two or three piles at the unfavourable end of the scale. They termed such phenomenon as *contrast effect*, which states that all statements or items that contrast with the position of the person on the issue tend to be grouped or clustered together and a very little discrimination, if any, is made among them.

The second tradition from which assimilation-contrast theory grew was judgement scales in which Sherif conducted a long series of experiments. Such judgement scales have been readily exemplified by his early work on autokinetic effect. Sherif's observation was that in case of physical ambiguity, the persons tended to develop reference scales to act as anchors of judgement. In case of such ambiguity, the judgement of any single person tended to converge towards group mean, which in future trials, acted as baseline against which other events or items could be assessed.

The major assumption of assimilation-contrast theory is that to what extent any communication done for the purpose of bringing changes in attitude will be effective depends on the way the recipient characterises it. This involves a two-state process, which is mentioned below:

(i) The recipient is likely to take a decision regarding the position advocated by the message or communication relative to his or her own position regarding attitude object.

(ii) Basing his or her view on this judgement, the recipient will tend to either assimilate the information by changing his attitude in the direction advocated by the communication (or message) or reject the communication by bringing no change in attitude (contrast effect).

While considering judgemental process, Sherif and Hovland proposed that communication or message done for bringing changes in attitude can fall within any of the following three latitudes or ranges depending on the position advocated by the communication relative to the recipient's own attitude on the issues:

(i) **Latitude of acceptance:** It contains those positions around the recipient's attitude that he or she judges as acceptable, and therefore, he agrees or accepts it.

(ii) **Latitude of non-commitment:** Under this latitude, those communications or messages are kept, which are sufficiently different from the recipient's position, and therefore, are not readily assimilated, neither are automatically rejected. Thus, this latitude acts as a residual category.

(iii) **Latitude of rejection:** It contains those messages, which are judged to be unacceptable. Since they fall outside the range of acceptance, they do not bring any change in attitude.

The basic fact in predicting attitude change, following assimilation-contrast theory, is to determine the amount of discrepancy between the current position or attitude of the recipient (called *internal anchor point*) of the message and the position or the attitude advocated by the message. The prediction of the theory is that if the persuasive message falls within the latitude of acceptance, attitude change will occur. On the other hand, if the message falls outside the latitude of acceptance, especially if it falls within the latitude of rejection, attitude change will not occur. Rather if any persuasive message falls within the latitude of rejection, it may produce a boomerang effect, and thus, may tend to reinforce the initial position of the recipient (see Figure 7.6).

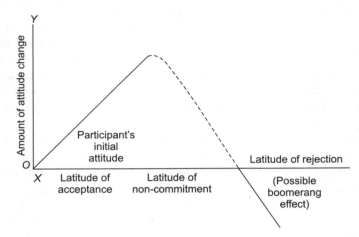

Figure 7.6   Relationship between persuasive communication and attitude change.

Sherif and Hovland also pointed out that the amount of changes in attitude induced by persuasive message would be an increasing function of the discrepancy between initial position and that of the position advocated by the message so long as the message falls within the latitude of acceptance (refer Figure 7.6).

The assimilation-contrast effect that lies behind the changes in attitude can be exemplified as—so long as the persuasive communication or message falls within the latitude of acceptance, actual discrepancy between individual's own position and the position advocated by the message is underestimated as an increasing function of the discrepancy. On the other hand, if the persuasive communication falls within the latitude of rejection, actual discrepancy between individual's own position and the position advocated by the message is overestimated as decreasing function of the amount or magnitude of discrepancy. Explaining the latter point further, it can be said that an individual, who holds an extreme attitude regarding attitude object, is likely to have a relatively narrow latitude of acceptance. Consequently, neutral items will fall outside that latitude and it would be perceived by the recipient as advocating a more extreme position than they actually do (contrast effect) and would be ultimately rejected.

In a nutshell, it can be said that the usefulness of this theory in predicting attitude change is obviously dependent on the ability of the investigator to identify the present position (called *internal anchor point*) of the participant to determine the breadth of the latitude of acceptance and devise a persuasive message, which falls near the border (but not outside the margin) of that latitude.

Conclusion Regarding Theories of Attitude Change

The theories discussed above are only a sample chosen from a larger number of theories that have many points of similarity and dissimilarity. As a group, they make major contribution to the problems of attitude organisation and change. However, the very existence of so many theories in itself suggests that many problems relating to attitude organisation and change remain to be solved.

WHEN DO ATTITUDE CHANGE AND PERSUASION BECOME DIFFICULT?

In our day-to-day life, we are constantly bombarded by persuasive attempts to change our attitudes. Generally, such attempts do come from friends, relatives, colleagues at work, the media, etc. If we are really susceptible to all persuasive communications, our attitudes would be changing constantly. This may cause problem of adjustment. Therefore, some resistance to persuasive communication is required. The common observation has been that strongly held attitudes are resistant to change and social psychologists have explored five main ways in which we resist attitude change—reactance, forewarning, selective avoidance, making counterargument actively, inoculation against counterattitudinal views. A discussion follows here.

1. Reactance: Reactance is one way to resist persuasive communication, and therefore, changes in attitude too. *Reactance* refers to negative reactions to persuasive communication done by others for the purpose of reducing our freedom by getting us to do what they want us to do. Reactance often increases resistance to persuasion and researchers have indicated that in reactance, we often change our attitude and behaviour in the opposite of what we are being urged to believe or to do (Brehm, 1966; Rhodewalt and Davison, 1983). Such effect is known as *negative attitude change*. Fuegen and Brehm (2004) showed that in case of reactance experienced by the person, strong arguments in favour of attitude tend to produce greater opposition to the advocated position than when a moderate or weaker argument is presented.

2. Forewarning: *Forewarning* means advance knowledge about the fact that someone will attempt to bring a change in our attitude through some persuasive message. It has been shown that forewarning often increases resistance to persuasion that follows (Johnson, 1994; Baron, Byrne and Branscombe, 2006). Forewarning resists persuasion because we can develop counterarguments and think more about our attitude in advance. In addition, forewarning also provides us with pretty time for collecting and recall some relevant facts and information that help in refuting the persuasive attempt. Pennington, Gillen and Hill (1999) reported a study in which two groups of participants were presented with a persuasive communication. One group had been given advance warning regarding the persuasion attempt, whereas the other group was not given such warning in advance. Results indicated that the latter group displayed more attitude change than the former group. This way of forewarning has been found to be particularly effective in inoculating young children (four to eight years old) against television advertisement (Feshback, 1980).

Social psychologists have expressed the view that those, who want to persuade others as well as want to counter the effects of forewarning, should try to distract the persons in between the time of forewarning and the receipt of the persuasive message. In fact, such distraction is found to prevent participants from counterarguing. Wood and Quinn (2003) reported that the forewarning is generally effective in increasing resistance and simply expecting a persuasive message (without actually receiving it) also tends to influence attitude in the resistant direction. Krosnick (1989) showed that the benefits of forewarning in producing resistance to attitude change are most likely to occur when we consider the attitudes to be important and relevant one. However, when the attitudes are less relevant or trivial, resistance seems to occur in smaller degree. Thus, in many situations, forewarned is really to be forearmed in so far as the persuasive message is concerned.

3. Selective avoidance: Selective avoidance is another strategy to resist the impact of persuasive message. It refers to a tendency to focus attention away from information that challenges our attitudes. Such avoidance generally increases resistance to persuasive message. Television viewing provides one of the best example of selective avoidance. People do not simply see all those programmes, which are being shown on television, rather they select some specific events, programmes that suit their views and mute or turnout the programmes that contradict their viewpoints. Thus, to resist attempts to persuade, the people tend to adopt a strategy that results in selective exposure to information. Sometimes, opposite effects are likely to occur. Generally, we tend to give full attention to all those items of information that support our own view and ignore information that contradicts our viewpoint. Such phenomenon, called *selective exposure*, ensures that our attitude remains intact for a longer period of time because attitudes are maintained, even though objectively there is sufficient evidence to justify the change. Selective avoidance, therefore, may not be a very rational strategy for dealing with attitude relevant information.

4. Making counterargument actively: Selective avoidance is a persuasive mode of resisting the persuasive attempts. In addition to this, the individuals also tend to actively defend the existing attitude by providing counterarguments against the views that are contrary to the existing attitude (Eagly et al., 1999). A study conducted by Eagly et al. (2000) has provided a clear evidence for this. Two groups of participants (students) were selected for the purpose. One group was having pro-attitude towards abortion and the other group was having attitudes against abortion. Both groups of students were exposed to persuasive messages delivered by a female communicator. For one group, the message was consistent with the existing attitude (pro-attitudinal message) and for the other group, it was contrary to the existing attitude (counterattitudinal message). After hearing the messages, participants reported their attitudes towards abortion. They also listed the various thoughts that were indeed coming to their mind while listening the message. Results revealed that for participants, both counterattitudinal message and pro-attitudinal message were equally memorable. But the participants reported more systematic thoughts about the counterattitudinal message and also reported more contrary thoughts about it. It obviously meant that they were actively counterarguing against the message. On the other hand, participants reported more supportive thought regarding pro-attitudinal message. Keeping all this in view, we can say that we are really so good at resisting persuasion that we not only ignore or avoid the information, which is inconsistent with our views, but also very actively process counterattitudinal message.

5. Inoculation against counterattitudinal views: Social psychologists are of view that an individual can be inoculated against persuasion if he is first presented with views that oppose his own views, along with the arguments that tend to refuse these counterattitudinal positions presented by persuasive message (McGuire, 1961). The logic is that when a person is presented with counterarguments against the opposing view, he tends to generate additional counterarguments of his own and this makes him more resistant to changes in attitude. McGuire and Papageorgis (1961) conducted a study to confirm this effect. In their study, the participants received attitude statements (such as every person should brush his or her teeth after every meal), along with one of the two types of arguments. One type of argument supported the statement and the other type of argument refuted the statement. The former was called *supportive defence condition* and the other was called *refutational defence condition*. About two days later, the participants were given additional messages that attacked the original statements with new sets of arguments. After this, the attitudes of the participants were assessed. Results revealed that refutational defence condition proved to be more effective in resisting the persuasive message. In other words, it can be said that exposure to arguments opposed to the person's original attitude serve to strengthen the views he already holds, making him more resistant to subsequent efforts to change them.

Thus, there are some strategies, which can be adopted to make the persuasive message resistant for bringing a desired change in the existing attitudes.

DIMENSIONS OF ATTITUDE

Attitude has several dimensions, which are important to the problem of measurement. Such important dimensions are as under:

1. **Direction:** *Direction* refers to positive or negative, for or against the object, person or event. On any attitude scale, direction may be indicated on like-dislike response option or agree-disagree response option. A person way have a favourable or positive attitude or unfavourable or negative attitude towards, say pre-marital sex.
2. **Degree:** *Degree* refers to the amount of favourableness or unfavourableness of attitude. For example, do we like equality of women in all situations or do we like to restrict this equality to only a limited areas of life and work?
3. **Intensity:** *Intensity* refers to the strength of feeling that may accompany an attitude. Does the person feel strongly about the target of the attitude or his feelings are weak or ambivalent? Intensity of attitude can be assessed by checking a greater or lesser number of options weighted in certain direction or by selecting a response option from an array whose intensity ranges from weak to strong.

   Both dimensions, namely, direction and intensity are loaded with affective component of attitudes. Direction indicates feelings for or against the attitude object, and intensity refers to the strength of feelings involved in the attitude.
4. **Centrality:** Another dimension of attitude is centrality. *Centrality* refers to the extent to which it is held close to the centre of a system of attitudes and values, which are considered significant for the person. Does attitude occupy a key position or is it simply peripheral? Centrality has implications for affective, cognitive and behavioural aspects. Attitudes that are strongly held and valued are likely to be central and supported by a set of beliefs and are also likely to provide sufficient motives for doing some actions. The attitudes held with reference to the self are good examples of centrality. Individuals feel more strongly about themselves than about any other person or object. Not only that, their beliefs about themselves are also likely to be held strongly and they are also ready to go on defensive if both attitude and supporting belief are questioned.

5. **Salience:** *Salience* refers to the extent to which an attitude is given prominence by the person. In other words, it can be said that salience indicates the extent of freedom with which one expresses one's attitudes. Some teachers might have strong anti-feeling for the present vice-chancellor of the university, but may not be ready to come out openly with their denunciations regarding the vice-chancellor. They may not be giving any particular prominence to such attitudes and beliefs in their day-to-day interaction with others.
6. **Consistency:** *Consistency* implies integration of attitudes. For example, if a person has a pro-feeling towards the women, does he show similar feelings towards all women, irrespective of their class and official position? If he really shows a pro-feeling towards all women, it means his pro-attitude towards women has a greater degree of consistency.

All these six dimensions of attitude are highly relevant when one is going to assess the attitude.

MEASUREMENT OF ATTITUDE

Before going into the details of measurement techniques of attitude, it is essential to emphasise that attitude is a hypothetical construct. In other words, the attitude itself cannot be directly observed, rather it must be inferred from the behaviour of the persons. One cannot simply remove the cover of human brain and point to various attitude.

Attitudes are assessed through the behaviours of the person. There are two general techniques of assessing attitudes—indirect measures and direct measures. A discussion follows here.

Indirect measures

Indirect measures of attitude are the measures in which persons are not asked about their attitudes directly. They are asked to do something or give their reactions to stimulus situation. On the basis of those reactions or behaviours, an estimate about their attitude is made. Such concealed or disguised approaches are attempted to assess attitude through measurement of cognitions and feelings, which are subtly connected with the object in question. Important indirect measures of attitude are as under:

1. Physiological techniques: Physiological techniques such as galvanic skin response or GSR, heart rate and pupillary dilation are commonly used to assess attitude. Here, assumption is that the affective component of attitudes correlates with the activities of autonomic nervous system. Rankin and Campbell (1955) used GSR as measure of attitude. Likewise, Katz et al. (1965) used heart rate as the measure of attitude. Hess (1965) used pupil size as the measure of attitude. According to Hess' findings, if a person's pupils were dilated (that is, increase in pupil size), a favourable attitude was indicated. If there was pupil's constriction (decrease in pupil size), it was indicative of unfavourable attitude. However, such approach met with only limited success.

Cacioppo and Tissinary (1990) tried to assess both the direction and intensity of the attitude of a person through the measurement of the person's facial muscles. Measurement of facial muscles is done through facial electromyography (or EMG), which captures minute facial muscle movements or electrical activity, not normally visible to human eye. In their study, they showed that a favourable attitude is indicated by the increased activities of the zygomatic muscles (see Figure 7.7). Unfavourable attitude is indicated by the increased activities of the corrugator muscles. Electrical activities can be measured even when the changes in facial expressions are not visible and reported evidences suggest that these measurements can accurately assess people's attitude towards social groups (Vanman et al., 1997). Apart from these, it is also proposed that the degree of activities of the either set of muscles is an indicator of strength with which a person holds the attitude. However, approach (EMG) requires specialised equipment, a carefully controlled environment and extremely helpful and cooperative research participants.

Another attitude measure based on facial EMG tries to assess the modulation of eye blink reflexes during the exposure to an object. Lang el al; (1990) found that the exposure to the positively evaluated images or stimuli was associated with eye blink inhibition whereas negatively evaluated images or stimuli were associated with amplification of eye blink reflexes. Physiological measures of attitude are also based upon assessment of brain activities through the Positron Emission Tomography (PET) and Functional Magnetic Resonance Imagery (FMRI). It has been reported that activity in amygdala, a part of lymbic system, is linked to the processing of negatively evaluated stimuli (Lesoux, 1996). Recently, Phelps el al. (2000) recorded the activities of amygdala for white participants while they were observing the images of African American faces and White faces. They found a difference in activities of amygdala in these two instances, with enhanced activities in observation of the faces of African American.

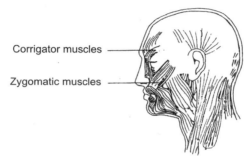

Figure 7.7 Facial movement activities and attitude change (based on suggestions by Cacioppo and Petty, 1981).

There are some problems with the physiological measures. Unfortunately, the technology is not yet at a stage where such measurements can be accepted with great reliability. Two specific problems with such measures are worth mentioning. First, most physiological techniques have been successful in examining the extent of the intensity of attitude of a person, but they do not assess the direction, that is, whether the attitude held is positive or negative (Cacioppo and Petty, 1981). A second problem with physiological measurement is the great variation in the way a person's physiologies respond to stimuli. For example, Mohan may respond to stimuli, which make him angry with an increased heart rate. Sohan's heart rate may not change when he is angry but his pupils may contract and Abhishek may display anger by an increase in blood pressure. It is also accepted that most of the physiological measures are sensitive to other variables also.

2. Projective techniques: Projective techniques, originally developed to assess wants and other personality variables, have also been successfully used to assess the attitudes of the person. Such techniques take advantage of the fact that people often project their own attitudes on to others. Figure 7.8 illustrates the use of projective techniques.

In Figure 7.8, the person may be asked to fill in the balloons. Examples are intended to investigate a person's attitude towards the parents. From the answers, it may be easily inferred whether a person has a submissive or disrespectful attitude towards his parents. Haire (1950) successfully used projective technique in assessing attitudes of the housewives towards coffee.

Figure 7.8 Example of projective technique for measuring the attitude of a person.

3. Error-choice technique: Error-choice technique was developed by Hammond (1948) for assessing the attitudes towards labour management. In this technique, the persons, whose attitudes are to be assessed, are forced to choose between two alternative answers to questions, each of which is made equally wrong, but in the opposite direction from the correct answer. One illustrative item from the labour management test is mentioned below:

Average weekly wage of war worker in 1945 was

- (i) $37.00
- (ii) $57.00

If the subject chooses $57.00 from both wrong alternatives, it presents a more favourable picture of the labour that may be assumed to reflect an underlying pro-labour attitude.

4. Lost-letter technique: In this technique the attitude is assessed through unobtrusive behaviour observation. In Milgram's classic lost-letter technique, the ostensibly lost letters are placed in public places (Milgram el al., 1965). The addresses in the envelopes are manipulated. Here assumption is that the person with more positive attitude towards the addresses are likely to pick up the envelope and put it in the mailbox. The rate and speed of returning for these letters is taken as indicator of attitude towards the addressee.

5. Implicit association test: The implicit association test (IAT) has been proposed by Greenwald, McGee and Schwartz (1998). In this technique, the implicit attitude is measured by pairing the object of the attitude with pleasant and unpleasant words. Such test intends to measure the associative strength between each target concept and a particular attribute. For example, for assessing implicit attitude towards *eunuch* (Hijira), the participant may be presented with the images of eunuch with images of normal person interspersed with pleasant word such as *happy*, *attractive*, *intelligent*, *good manners*, etc. and same unpleasant words such as *ugly*, *rotten*, *dull*, etc. In one phase of the test, the participant's task would be to react as quickly as possible by pressing the key whenever a picture of eunuch or unpleasant word is presented and a different key whenever a picture of normal or pleasant word is presented. In the second phase the pairing would be reversed so that the participant is required to press one key for a eunuch pleasant word and different key for a normal person or an unpleasant word. Thus the first phase would be a congruent phase and the second phase would be that of an incongruent phase. The participant with unfavourable implicit attitude towards the eunuch would find the first phase easier than the second phase. The difference between the average latencies between the two phases provides a measure of implicit attitude.

Since IAT is an unobtrusive and non-reactive measure of implicit attitude, it is a very popular method of assessing socially stigmatized attitudes. It has also been successfully used to test theories in social psychology.

6. Bogus pipeline technique: Some studies have been conducted in which a form of deception has been used in order to know about the true attitudes of the people. Jones and Sigall (1971) had called this technique *bogus pipeline technique*. In this technique, the participants are convinced that the researchers already know their true attitudes. An elaborate-looking electronic machine is attached for measuring their attitudes towards an issue or object. Subsequently, the investigators ask the participants to indicate verbally or in written form what they believe the machine has disclosed. Thus, the participants tend not to inhibit their true attitudes, since they have been forced to believe that their true attitudes have already been recorded by the machine. Sigall and Page (1971) for the first time used this bogus pipeline technique in their study of racial stereotyping. They asked one half of white American students to rate on the questionnaire the extent to which the various stereotypical terms such as lazy, dull, etc. were applied to black Americans. The other half of the participants were attached to a bogus pipeline and were asked the same question. Results were dramatic. For example, while students using questionnaire technique indicated that they did not think that the stereotypical terms like lazy, dull, etc. were really applied to black American students. However, the participants who believed that the researchers had already got an accurate reading of their attitudes and opinions by means of bogus pipeline technique, admitted that the stereotypical terms were applied to black American to some degree.

Thus, in some situations, the bogus pipeline technique is undoubtedly a useful technique in ascertaining attitudes. Ostrom (1973), however, cautioned that research evidences were not yet fully sufficient to hail the bogus pipeline technique as panacea for difficult attitude measurement. Moreover, it does not always work.

In contrast to bogus pipeline, there is another technique called **bona fide pipeline**, where the implicit attitude or prejudice may be automatically elicited through priming, that is, through the exposure to some stimuli or events that prime various types of information stored in memory, making it easier to influence the on-going reactions (Towles-Schwen and Fazio, 2001). In this technique, the participants are usually shown a list of adjectives and they are requested to indicate whether they have experienced good or bad feeling by pushing a button. Before seeing the adjective, they are, however, exposed to the faces of persons from different ethnic or racial groups (such as tribals, blacks, Asians, etc). Here, assumption is that implicit attitude will be revealed by how quickly the participants respond to the words. If a negative attitude is triggered by the exposed face (or prime), the participant will respond faster towards having negative meanings. However, they will respond slowly to the words with positive meanings because this meaning will be inconsistent with the negative attitudes produced by the priming stimulus (or face). Researches done using this procedure have revealed, that people's implicit attitudes are automatically elicited by the members of racial or ethnic groups, and this ultimately, affect their important forms of behaviour such as decision-making, friendliness, etc.

There are advantages and disadvantages of disguised or indirect measure. Principal advantages are as under:

(i) Indirect measures are less likely to produce socially desirable responses. Therefore, a true measurement of attitude is likely to occur.
(ii) Under certain conditions, indirect measures have higher validity than direct measures such as rating scales. This advantage applies particularly to the attitudes, which tend to violate group norms, and hence, are not publicly revealed by the individual as well as to the attitudes, which are unacceptable to the self-concept of the person.
(iii) In indirect measures, individuals are unlikely to know about what attitude is being measured.
(iv) In indirect measures, the indication of the strength with which the attitude held is also readily obtained.
(v) Indirect measures enable the investigator to measure attitude without producing an impact upon attitude itself.

Major disadvantages are as under:

(i) Indirect measures do not allow the investigators to measure attitude directly.
(ii) In indirect measures, attitudes are inferred. Inference sometimes does not come to the expectation.
(iii) Indirect measures are not as reliable as one would desire. If we pinpoint the physiological measures, there have been reported conflicting evidences regarding their validity and reliability.

Direct measures

Direct measures of attitude are those in which direct statements about the attitude object are presented before the person who expresses his views in terms of given response options. Attitude scales in the form of ratings and questionnaires are popular direct measures of attitudes. An *attitude scale* may be defined as a series of questions that provide precise and reliable information about the extent to which the people like or dislike the attitude object (Dawes and Smith, 1985). In this section, several direct measures—Thurstone scale, Likert scale, Bogardus scale, Guttman scale, scale discrimination technique and semantic differential scale—are discussed.

1. Thurstone scale: The first major attempt to assess social attitude through the development of attitude scale was done by Thurstone and Chave (1929). Thurstone (1931) constructed several scaling techniques. The most widely used is *equal-appearing interval method*. Thurstone's method consists of statements (about 70 to 75 statements) towards the attitude object. The statements are then given to a group of about two hundred judges (individuals), who are asked to place it on a scale having eleven categories that appear to cover equal portions of scale. One end of this eleven-category scale is designated to mean that the statement is strongly favourable towards the attitude object and the other end of the scale is designated to mean that the statement is strongly unfavourable towards the attitude. The middle point of the scale (F) is designated as neutral (see Figure 7.9).

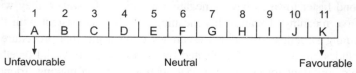

Figure 7.9 Thurstone equal appearing interval scale.

These categories, ranging from A to K, are commonly assigned the value from 1 to 11, respectively. Each judge places the statement in any one of the eleven categories, which he considers appropriate to the extremity and direction of the statement. One of the fundamental assumptions here is that the judges do not express their attitudes in sorting the statement. They simply decide the degree to which the item is favourable, unfavourable or neutral. For example, suppose the given statement is 'Nationalisation improves the economy of the country'. A judge might decide that this statement expresses favourable attitude towards nationalisation, and therefore, he might place it in category J. The final scale value for a statement is determined from the values assigned by all the judges. The median of all judgements becomes the scale value of the statement. Another measure, called *Q-value*, is determined for each statement by calculating semi-interquartile range of the distribution of judgements obtained for that statement. Q-value becomes the measure of ambiguity; a high Q-value indicates lack of agreement regarding sorting of statement by judges and a low Q-value indicates high consensus among the judges. Finally, on the basis of scale value, Q-value and the desire to have statements that cover the range of eleven-point scale, approximately fifteen to twenty statements are selected. In other words, final statements are selected from the larger pool according to the following two criteria:

(i) Statements having the greatest agreement among judges (that is, with lower Q-values) regarding scale values are selected.
(ii) Statements are selected so that their scale values may range in approximately equal intervals all the way along the eleven-point scale.

After the scale has been constructed, it is used to assess a person's attitude. The person simply selects those statements with which he agrees. His attitude score becomes the average of the scale values of the statement with which he agrees. For example, suppose that he agrees with five statements having scale values 3.2, 3.6, 4.7, 4.9 and 5.8. Then, his attitude score will be a sum of these five ratings divided by the number of items, that is 22.2/5 = 4.44 indicating that he is slightly unfavourable towards the attitude object, since 6 is the midpoint of the eleven-point scale. If a person agrees with the statements having widely varying scale values, then his median or average score is looked with suspicion. In Thurstone scale, since the statements are very carefully scaled, a person should agree only with those statements which are fairly close to his position. A situation in which a person agrees with the items having widely varying scale values tends to indicate carelessness in marking statements, a failure to understand instruction or a defined and definite position towards the attitude object.

Some difficulties have been found in Thurstone attitude scaling. Such important difficulties are as under:

(i) Thurstone assumed that judges' own attitude did not affect the sorting of the statements. But contrary evidences were reported. Hovland and Sherif (1952), Sherif and Hovland (1953) found that judges with extreme personal attitudes sorted a higher percentage of the statements into one particular category, and thus, they biased the scale. These findings indicate that the attitudes of judges tended to bias the sorting of the statements.
(ii) Thurstone scale takes much time and effort in its construction. Hence, the scale does not appear to be useful one from the point of view of construction.
(iii) Thurstone and Chave had not provided any objective basis for selecting the most discriminating statements from among the statements having approximately the same scale values. It may

just be possible that the statements having approximately the same scale values differ in their discriminatory power.

2. Likert scale: Shortly after publication of Thurstone scale, Likert (1932) developed a scaling method that has come to be known as the *method of summated ratings*. This method is one of the most popular and widely used techniques for attitude measurement. Like Thurstone scaling technique, the investigator begins with a large number of statements about the attitude object. These statements are administered to a group of subjects (judges), who indicate their own attitudes by responding to one of the five response options like strongly agree, agree, neutral, disagree and strongly disagree. Weights of 1, 2, 3, 4 and 5 are, respectively, assigned to these response options for favourable statements, whereas for unfavourable items, weights are given in the reversed order. An example related to attitude towards nationalisation is provided below:

(i) Public sector organisations are earning higher profit than private sector organisations.

Strongly agree	Agree	Neutral	Disagree	Strongly disagree
5	4	3	2	1

(ii) Employees of public sector organisation do not take much enthusiasm and initiativeness in discharging their duties.

Strongly agree	Agree	Neutral	Disagree	Strongly disagree
1	2	3	4	5

In the above example, the first statement shows a pro-attitude towards nationalisation (a favourable statement), whereas the second statement shows an anti-attitude towards nationalisation (an unfavourable statement). Accordingly, the first statement has been weighted as 5, 4, 3, 2 and 1 for strongly agree, agree, neutral, disagree and strongly disagree, respectively, and the second statement has been weighted in the reversed order.

After scoring or giving weight to individual item, the total score for each subject or judge is determined by adding their individual scores. Finally, an internal consistency analysis or item analysis is done. This is done by determining the extent to which the response of the persons in the standardisation group to a particular item are consistent with their total scores. This last step may be accomplished by computing correlation between scores on an item and the total scores on all the items. Then, those items yielding higher correlations are retained for the final scale. In fact, it is the use of item analysis in the Likert's method that clearly distinguishes it from Thurstone's scaling method. Usually, a set of about twenty items is selected for the final scale.

One of the basic problems with Likert scale is that the interpretation of the meaning of the minimum and maximum possible scores is clear, but the scores falling in between these two limits are difficult to be interpreted. Maximum score indicates favourable attitude and minimum score indicates unfavourable attitude. But scores falling in between the minimum and the maximum possible scores are difficult to be interpreted because the scores corresponding to the neutral point is not known (Krech, Crutchfield and Ballachey, 1962). Obviously, it will be illegitimate to assume that the neutral region in Likert scale corresponds to the midpoint of the possible range of scores. Another difficulty with Likert scale is the very assumption that each statement has identical weight in relation to every other statement. This is not necessarily a valid assumption. In reality, different individuals may show a given attitude to the same degree, yet they may respond differently to different statements of the scale. Therefore, it is difficult, if not impossible, to ensure that each statement counts the same as every other item.

3. Bogardus scale: Bogardus (1925) had developed a scale for the purpose of measuring and comparing attitudes towards different nationalities. His scale is popularly known as *social distance scale*. This scale consists of a number of statements, which are selected, on a prior basis to elicit responses that could be treated as the subject's degree of acceptance for any nationality group. For assessing attitude towards each nationality, seven classifications are offered as under:

   (i) To close kinship by marriage
  (ii) To my club as personal friend
 (iii) To my street as neighbour
 (iv) To employment in my occupation
  (v) To citizenship of my country
 (vi) To accept as visitors in my country
(vii) Would exclude from my country

If we pay attention to these classifications, it would be obvious that classifications progress in an orderly way from one implying a willingness to establish a close degree of relationship with the nationality to one implying willingness to accept only a remote relationship or none at all.

With Bogardus's social distance scale, it is possible to compare different people's attitudes towards the same nationality or to compare a single person's attitudes towards various nationalities. This scale has been widely used for these purposes in social-psychological researches. Social psychologists are of view that with some appropriate modifications, this type of scale may be adapted to measure attitudes towards any category of persons. One such adaptation of Bogardus scale was done by Crepsi (1945) and he named it as *social rejection thermometer*, which is frequently used for the measurement of attitudes towards conscientious objectors.

4. Guttman scale: While studying American soldiers during World War-II, Guttman (1950) developed a scaling technique, called *cumulative scaling* or *scalogram analysis* that tends to develop a set of items for attitude measurement, which will be unidimensional. Guttman proceeded to develop such a scale in which response to any single item could be determined by a total score on the whole set of items. In other words, if the scale has properties emphasised by Guttman, a person with higher rank or score than another person on the same set of statements will get a ranking just as higher on every statement in the set as the other individual. Explaining the Guttman scale in non-technical sense, it can be said that an attitude scale is considered unidimensional if on every item, a person, with a more favourable attitude, gives a response which is more favourable than what is obtained from a person with less favourable attitude. In such a situation, his response to every item will be perfectly consistent with his overall position on the dimension of the attitude.

The nature of a unidimensional scale can be illustrated with a hypothetical illustration. Suppose that an attitude scale consists of three items and each item can yield four possible scores—3, 2, 1 and 0, representing an agreement with all three items on one end and disagreement with all three on the other end. If eight subjects are to take this scale (considering it as a unidimensional scale), the scores and the pattern of responses would be something like those presented in Table 7.3.

Table 7.3 Hypothetical Illustration of a Unidimensional Scale

Subject	Score	Agrees with Item		
		1	2	3
1	3	×	×	×
2	3	×	×	×
3	3	×	×	×
4	3	×	×	×
5	2	×	×	
6	2	×	×	
7	1	×		
8	0			

A look at Table 7.3 reveals that items are perfectly consistent. Scores of 3 are made by agreeing with items 1, 2 and 3. Likewise, scores of 2 are made only by agreeing items 1 and 2 and disagreeing with item 3, which is apparently a more extreme statement. None of the subjects makes a score of 2 by agreeing with items 1 and 3 or with 2 and 3. Likewise, a score of 1 is made by agreeing with item 1 and not with 2 or 3. Still another sign of consistency is picked up by the observation that everyone who agrees with item 3 also agrees with items 2 and 1 and everyone who agrees with item 2, agrees with item 1.

One essential characteristics of unidimensional scale is that its pattern of responses is reproducible from the knowledge of the scale score. In the above example, we find that the subject, who has made a score of 3, agrees with items 1, 2 and 3 and the subject, who has made a score of 2, agrees with items 1 and 2, but disagrees with item 3. In this way, for every other score, pattern of responses can be reproduced. In practice, however, such perfect consistency (or reproducibility or unidimensionality) is seldom achieved. Therefore, Guttman (1950) opined that a certain measure of error is allowed and he suggested that the pattern of responses must be at least 90% reproducible in order for the scale to be treated as unidimensional one. Clearly, then, 10% of responses may fall outside the range of unidimensionality.

Guttman cumulative scaling has been criticised on the basis of selecting the initial set of statements. According to him, selection of a sample of statements is simply a matter of intuition and experience. Therefore, the content validity of cumulative scale is difficult to estimate. Another problem with unidimensional scale is that this is not fit for measuring complex attitude, which is generally multidimensional. Still another problem is that a scale may be reproducible when taken by one group of individuals, but not when taken by another group of individuals.

5. Scale discrimination technique: This technique was developed by Edwards and Kilpatrick (1948). In fact, this technique is an attempt to synthesise the methods of scale construction developed by Thurstone, Likert and Guttman. The basic steps involved in this technique are as under:

A large set of dichotomous statements are prepared or selected. As in Thurstone's scaling method, these statements are given to the judges, with the request to sort these statements into categories according to the degree of favourableness. Those items which are not sorted consistently by the judges are treated as vague or ambiguous. Therefore, they are rejected. The remaining statements or items are constructed in multiple-choice format, with six response categories such as strongly agree, agree, mildly agree, mildly disagree, disagree and strongly disagree. These statements with six response options are now given to a group of new subjects, who respond to each item by choosing the alternative that best describes his own viewpoint. Each statement is then scored to derive a total score for the subject. Subsequently, like Likert scale, each item is subjected to item analysis and the items, which are found to be non-discriminating ones, are rejected. The remaining items are, then, dichotomised and subjected to cumulative scaling.

Scale discrimination technique, thus, represents a blend of Thurstone, Likert and Guttmann's techniques for scaling. But this approach, however, needs to be tested by various researchers for determining its strengths and weaknesses.

6. Semantic differential scale: The semantic differential scale is a tool of measuring attitude developed by Osgood, Suci and Tannenbaum (1957) as a part of their effort to study the measurement of meaning.

All objects have both denotative and connotative meanings. The *denotative* meaning refers to the pointing to aspect of the object. Concrete objects such as table, chair, mobile phone are easy to define because we can point to the object and clear up any confusion, if any. *Connotative* meaning, on the other hand, refers to emotive meaning or emotional response produced in the person by that concrete object.

The semantic differential scale is a technique for assessing connotative meaning. Connotative meaning is more important for understanding the concept because it generates emotional or emotive response. According to Osgood, Suci and Tannenbaum, connotative meanings are multidimensional. They identified three dimensions—*evaluative* characterised by adjective pairs like good-bad; *potency* characterised by adjective pairs like weak-strong and *activity* characterised by adjective pairs like fast-slow.

In using the semantic differential scale, the researcher presents the respondents with a series of bipolar adjective scales. Each scale has two ends, with two adjectives having opposite meanings (see Table 7.4). The respondent's task is to put a mark in the space at the appropriate point between two adjectives. For example, if he considers an IAS officer to be 'good' one, he would put a mark in the space nearest to 'good', if he considers a IAS officer to be neither 'good' or 'bad', he would put a mark halfway between the two extremes and so on. In the semantic differential scale, the concept is usually rated on seven-point scale having bipolar adjectives at two extremes with opposite meaning. Some have used nine-point scale also, but seven-point scale is more common.

Table 7.4 A Semantic Differential Scale to Measure Connotative Meaning to Concept of an I.A.S. Officer

Good	└─┴─┴─┴─┴─┴─┴─┘	Bad
Sincere	└─┴─┴─┴─┴─┴─┴─┘	Insincere
Worthless	└─┴─┴─┴─┴─┴─┴─┘	Valuable
Dishonest	└─┴─┴─┴─┴─┴─┴─┘	Honest
Strong	└─┴─┴─┴─┴─┴─┴─┘	Weak
Fast	└─┴─┴─┴─┴─┴─┴─┘	Slow
Cold	└─┴─┴─┴─┴─┴─┴─┘	Warm
Dirty	└─┴─┴─┴─┴─┴─┴─┘	Clean

After the data have been collected, the investigator analyses them by using various statistical techniques.

The semantic differential scale has advantages and disadvantages. Major advantages are as under:

(i) Since the semantic differential scale measures the connotative meaning, it can be used with any concept or object, from a specific person to the entire nation.

(ii) In such scale, the investigator can compare the person's attitudes on three dimensions, permitting a more complex differentiation among the respondents.
(iii) The scale has also been successfully used for assessing the meaning of role identities (father, engineer) and role behaviour (love, building construction) (Heiss, 1979; Smith-Lovin, 1990).
(iv) The scale permits the study of sub-cultural differences in attitudes. It may be found that emotive response to the concept 'I.A.S. Officer' varies significantly between the different groups such as Indian tribal culture and Indian non-tribal culture.
(v) The scale also allows studying sex-typed differences. Male and female respondents may display different connotative responses to the concept or object.

However, there are some disadvantages with semantic differential scale. The major disadvantages are as under:

(i) The scale does not possess the trait of practicality because it requires more time to administer and score.
(ii) In the scale, the appropriateness of pairs of adjectives remains often questionable and little consensus exists among the experts regarding the suitability of the pairs selected.

Despite these disadvantages, the semantic differential scale has been frequently used as a measure of attitude.

Conclusion Regarding Attitude Measurement

Social psychologists have attempted to assess attitude through both indirect and direct measures. Of these measures, direct measures of attitudes through attitude scales are most popular. Among the various attitude scales, Likert scaling technique of attitude measurement is the most popular choice of the researchers.

Summary and Review

- The use of the concept of attitude is not new. It dates back to the writing of Herbart Spencer and Alexander Bain during 1862 to 1868. A few years later, some further experimental advances were made by German scientists, who regarded attitude as a mental set or preparedness. Today, social psychologists use the term *attitude* to refer to the individual's evaluation of virtually all aspects of their social world.
- *Attitudes* are defined as enduring systems of affective component, behavioural component and cognitive component. It is called *ABC model of attitude*. Affective component is the feeling part, behavioural component is the motivation for doing some actions or behaviour and cognitive component is the belief part of the attitude.
- Attitude serve five important functions—instrumental or heuristic function, knowledge or schematic function, self-esteem function or value expressive function, ego-defensive function and impression motivation or management function.
- There is interconnectedness between attitude and behaviour. Generally, we behave according to our existing attitude. So, it can be said that attitude determines our behaviour. The behaviour of the person can be predicted if we know his attitude, although sometimes there is discrepancy between what people do and what their attitudes are. Social psychologists have identified four variables that tend to affect the relationship between the attitudes and behaviour—activation of attitude, characteristics of attitude, correspondence between attitude and behaviour, and situational constraints.

- How do attitudes guide behaviour? Attitudes guide our behaviour through two mechanisms, which operate under somewhat different and contrasting conditions. One mechanism operated through what is called *reasoned action model*, which states that when a person has time to engage in careful reasoned actions, he tries to weigh each alternative available, and then, decides how he should go ahead. But in the situation which is hectic and emergent in nature, such deliberate and reasoned thought processes fail to occur and the person has no time to think over the alternatives. Here, our behaviour is governed by what is called *attitude-to-behaviour process model*.
- There are several factors that influence the formation and maintenance of attitudes. Such important factors are genetic factors, classical conditioning learning, instrumental conditioning learning, observational learning, social comparison and several other miscellaneous factors.
- Social psychologists have studied attitude changes through persuasion. There are four primary elements to persuasion—the communicator, the message, how the message is communicated, and the audience. In other words, who says what by what means to whom is important for persuasion, and therefore, for attitude change. There are certain characteristics of the communicator such as credibility, attractiveness and likeableness, power and similarity with audiences, which enhance persuasiveness, and therefore, favour attitude change in the direction advocated. Various characteristics of the message content also influence attitude change. In some situations, rational and reasonable message becomes more effective in bringing changes in the attitude, whereas in some situations, emotional appeal of the message becomes more effective in doing so. Likewise, discrepant message is more instrumental in bringing attitude change, though the relationship between discrepancy and attitude change is a function of discrepancy and perceived expertise of the communicator. For making the message more persuasive, one-sided and two-sided communications are presented time to time. In general, if the audience is to be exposed to opposing views, two-sided communication is more effective. Likewise, information presented first (primacy effect) becomes more effective in persuasion than the same information presented later on (recency effect). How the message is said or the channel of communication is also an important factor in making a message more effective. Actively received appeal versus passively received appeal has been studied by the social psychologists. In general, actively received appeal is found to be more persuasive and effective in bringing attitude change than passively received appeal. Likewise, information or communication given under face-to-face influence is more persuasive and effective than the information given through various mass media. Factors related to the audience also influence persuasion. In general, intelligence, self-esteem, personality, age, truthfulness of the audience are directly related to the persuasion of the communication. Role playing done by audience has also direct bearing on the persuasive nature of communication.
- Social psychologists have propounded several theories for explaining attitude organisation and change. Important cognitive consistency theories are Heider P-O-X model, Newcomb's A-B-X model, Festinger's cognitive dissonance theory and Osgood and Tannenbaum's congruity theory. Besides, social learning theories of attitude change that include classical conditioning model and operant conditioning model have also been considered important. Apart from these, Kelman's three process theory and Assimilation-contrast theory are relevant for the explanation of attitude change.
- Under certain conditions, attitude change and persuasion becomes difficult. Social psychologists have proposed that under the condition of reactance, forewarning, selective avoidance, making counterargument actively and inoculation against counterattitudinal views, attitude change becomes difficult because persuasion does not work well.
- There are some dimensions of attitude, which are considered important for the measurement of attitude. Such important dimensions are direction (feeling for or against the attitude objects), degree (amount of favourableness or unfavourableness), intensity (strength of feeling of being for or against), centrality (that is, supported by beliefs, highly valued and having sufficient motives for some actions), salience (prominence) and consistency (integration of attitudes).

- Social attitudes can be assessed through both indirect and direct measures. In indirect measures, the person is not aware of the fact that his attitudes are being assessed. Important indirect measures are physiological techniques, projective techniques and the bogus pipeline technique. Direct measures are those where the person is aware that his attitudes are being assessed. This includes various questionnaire and attitude scales. Important attitude scales are Thurstone scale, Likert scale, Bogardus scale, Guttman scale, scale discrimination technique and semantic differential scale. Of these various scales, Likert scale followed by Thurstone scale is very popular among the investigators.

REVIEW QUESTIONS

1. Present a brief historical background of the study of attitude.
2. Define ABC model of attitude. Also, discuss the various functions of attitude.
3. Discuss the factors that influence attitude-behaviour consistency.
4. How do attitude guide behaviour? Cite experimental evidences in favour of your answer.
5. Discuss the implication of the reasoned action model.
6. Discuss the factors that influence formation and maintenance of social attitude. Cite experimental evidences in support of your answer.
7. Explain the concept of persuasion. Briefly explain the relevance of different elements of persuasion for attitude change.
8. Discuss the characteristics of the communicator that influence attitude change.
9. Discuss the various characteristics of the message that has implication for attitude change.
10. Discuss the impact of different channels of communication upon attitude change.
11. What are the characteristics of audience that influence persuasion and attitude change?
12. Examine critically Heider's P-O-X model of attitude change.
13. Make a comparative study of P-O-X model and A-B-X model of attitude change.
14. Examine critically Festinger's dissonance theory of attitude change.
15. Define cognitive dissonance. What are the conditions under which cognitive dissonance can arise?
16. Make a comparative study of balance theory and cognitive dissonance theory.
17. Examine critically congruity theory of attitude change.
18. How do social learning theories explain attitude change? Do they provide satisfactory explanation?
19. Examine critically Kelman's three process theory of change.
20. How does assimilation-contrast theory explain attitude change? What improvement can you suggest over the explanation provided by the theory?
21. Make a comparative study of Thurstone scale and Likert scale of attitude measurement.
22. Discuss the various indirect measures of attitudes. Are they satisfactory?
23. Write short notes on the following:
    (i) Dimensions of attitude
    (ii) Guttman scale of attitude measurement
    (iii) Reasoned action model
    (iv) Concept of cognitive dissonance
    (v) Congruity theory
    (vi) Attitude-to-behaviour process model
24. Under what conditions attitude change and persuasion become difficult? Cite experimental evidences in favour of your answer.

8. Stereotyping, Prejudice and Discrimination

Learning Objectives

- Nature and Contents of Stereotypes
- Why Do People Form and Use Stereotypes?
- Activation of Stereotypes
- Impact of Stereotypes on Judgements and Actions
- Changing Stereotypes and Barriers to Stereotype Change
- Gender Stereotypes
- Shifting Standards: Does No Difference in Evaluations or Ratings Mean Absence of Stereotypic Thinking?
- Stereotypes Associated with Single and Married Persons
- Concept of Prejudice and Discrimination
- Forms of Prejudice and Discrimination
- Origin, Development and Maintenance of Prejudice and Discrimination
- Reduction of Prejudice and Discrimination
- Measurement of Prejudice

Key Terms

Assumed similarity effect
Attribution
Authoritarian personality
Benevolent sexism
Categorisation
Collective guilt
Contact hypothesis
Differential respect
Discrimination
Distinctiveness
Fundamental attribution error
Gender stereotype

Glass ceiling effect
Hostile sexism
In-group homogeneity
Jigsaw classroom
Objective scales
Out-group homogeneity
Prejudice
Racism
Realistic group conflict theory
Recategorisation
Relative deprivation
Scapegoat theory

Sexism
Social identity theory
Social inequalities
Socialisation
Stereotype
Subjective scales
Superordinate goals
Threats to self-esteem
Tokenism
Ultimate attribution error
Women are wonderful effect

Prejudice can prove to be one of the most destructive aspects of human social behaviour. It often produces chilling acts of violence. Muslims and Hindus frequently engage in violence against each other due to one or the other kinds of prejudice. More than 6 million European Jews were killed by Nazis in 1940s in the name of purifying the European racial stock. In the United States of America, perhaps the most severe prejudice has been against African Americans.

Prejudice is not limited to ethnic and racial groups. It may also be religious and sexual. For example, gay men and lesbians are subject to such intense prejudice by the heterosexual majority. Overweight persons often become targets of prejudice. Likewise, elderly people are often assumed to have poor physical and mental energy.

Since generally, there is a link between attitude and behaviour, an attempt is made to explore how prejudicial attitudes can be manifested in discrimination or discriminatory behaviour. In this chapter, we will examine the nature of stereotyping and will also consider how it is related to discrimination. Why people form and use stereotypes is also highlighted. Then, the focus of the chapter is turned to the perspectives on origin and nature of prejudice. Lastly, various strategies for reducing prejudice and discrimination as well as some important measures for assessing it are explored.

NATURE AND CONTENTS OF STEREOTYPES

In our day-to-day life, we often find ourselves having only limited and categorical information about an individual. For example, we know that he is a professor, a doctor, an engineer or a policeman. In such a situation, where other information about a person is minimal, such knowledge is likely to have an impact upon our perception of that person. The process of assigning attributes to a person solely on the basis of the class or category to which he or she belongs is called *stereotyping* and a *stereotype* is a schema or set of beliefs about a certain group of people. Stereotypes are, in fact, the cognitive frameworks that directly influence the way the persons process the various social information. In fact, stereotypes are the cognitions and expectations assigned to the members of the groups simply on the basis of their membership in the groups (Weber and Crocker, 1983). In other words, stereotypes are the impressions that individuals form about groups by associating the groups with particular traits or characteristics that they are deemed to share (Eagly and Mladinic, 1989; Hamilton, 1981). Thus, stereotypes involve gross generalisations that are acquired through misinformation and that ignore individual differences and are resistant to change even in the light of new evidences (Fisher, 1982) Walter Lippman, a journalist, introduced the current meaning of stereotypes in 1922 and saw stereotypes as pictures in head (simplified mental images of how group looks like and what it does). Stereotypes often incorporate more than just traits, physical appearance, typical interest and goals, preferred activities, occupations, likely behaviours and similar characteristics. (Brewer, 1988; Deaux and LaFrance, 1998; Twenge, 1999; Biernat and Thompson, 2002). Thus, a stereotype is a rigid, oversimplified or biased perception of individuals or groups. It is usually derogatory but need not always be so. The common stereotypes are—Tribals are superstitious and ignorant, Marwaris are stingy and miserly, Bengalis are religious and sentimental, businessman are penny pinchers, professors are idealistic and absent-minded, politicians are shrewd, opportunist and liars, Negroes are niggers, dirty and mean-minded and Punjabis are hardy and assertive, British are reserved and Americans are outgoing. All these examples show that stereotype is to generalise.

The major characteristics of stereotype may be enumerated as under:

1. Individuals are categorised according to certain identifying attributes. In other words, individuals have many attributes differing greatly in distinctiveness. Society selects certain attributes as means of identifying various categories of person, and generally, ignores others. These attributes may be physical, may involve membership in the group or organisation or may even be based upon certain distinctive behaviour patterns. For example, a doctor is expected to be polite, kind, human-loving, intelligent, grasping, progressive, etc. As soon as we know that a person is doctor, we assume that the person must be possessing these attributes. The example clearly shows that the stereotype is special form of categorical response and membership in the category automatically evokes the judgement that the individual possesses all the attributes belonging to that category (Secord, 1959).

2. Perceivers agree regarding the attributes that the persons in the category possess. In stereotype, there is found consensus regarding attributed traits. The class of individuals having some form of common identification is assumed to share certain personal attributes. For example, elderly persons may be viewed as old fashioned, conservative, passive, cantankerous and unsociable; women may be considered as weak, submissive, warm, dependent and relationship-oriented and men may be considered as dominant, independent, aggressive and task-oriented. Likewise, Negroes may be perceived as superstitious, lazy and dishonest and professors may be considered as idealistic, impractical and absent-minded. An early study conducted by Katz and Braly (1933) and repeated twice by Gilbert (1951) and Karlins, Coffman and Walters (1969) illustrates such consensus for various ethnic stereotypes.

   However, consensus on stereotypes even for the most definite stereotypes is sometimes partial. Secord and Backman (1964) reported that about Negro, although stereotypes are definite, some subjects differed even in assigning physical attributes. About 94% subjects told that dark skin is the very characteristic of Negroes, whereas 6% said that it is only somewhat characteristic. Likewise, with respect to the characteristic of wide nose, 71% subjects said it is very characteristic, but 27% said it is only somewhat characteristics.

3. Discrepancy exists between the attributed traits and the actual traits. In stereotype, there exists discrepancy between the attributed traits and the actual traits. In this sense, they are thought of as at least partly false because traits attributed are almost always an oversimplification of the true characteristics of the stereotyped individuals. In fact, inaccuracy of social stereotypes is derived from one of the elements of its definition, namely, all individuals of a particular category or class possess the traits assigned to that category or class. As we know, the individuals vary universally in the kinds of traits that make up a social stereotype, it is very clear that stereotyped traits do not apply in the same degree to each and every member of the class. In such situation, when the person attributes exactly the same characteristics to each person of the category, his stereotype is necessarily a departure from reality. For example, if one considers every Indian woman as weak and dependent, it would be wrong one because it does not apply to some Indian women like Rani Lakshmi Bai, Kiran Bedi, etc. However, if the perceiver believes that the traits he knows are possessed by the average member of a class of persons and at the same time, recognises the fact of individual differences, there would be nothing necessarily inaccurate about his judgements.

4. Stereotypes are ready-made frames of reference for interpreting objects and events about which our knowledge is not adequate. They are rigid and fixed ways of thinking about a class of persons and every individual we meet who belongs to that class is perceived in that fixed and rigid way. We perceive a politician as an opportunist and shrewd one, although he may not be so.
5. Stereotypes are fixed and standardised beliefs that are passed on from one generation to another, and in the course of time, they may be given the status of axiom. In fact, stereotypes are not rationally analysed and no attempt is made to find about their truth. They are blindly accepted and if any one questions their validity, he is totally ignored. In case, there comes any contradictory fact, then it is considered as an exception.
6. Stereotypes are based on feelings, bias and prejudice. They are hasty generalisations, which are emotionally toned or they may be analogies wrongly arrived at, but they provide us relief from the strain of thinking and analysing. For example, if we see a person with Gandhi cap, we immediately think that he has the qualities of Congressman. If we see that the person is doctor, we assume that he must be possessing all the qualities of a doctor.
7. Stereotypes persist partly because through their constant use, they have become a part of our mental make-up and partly because they strengthen our association with our own group. Persons tend to perceive their stereotypes so intimate part of themselves that they take steps to defend them when they are threatened by contradictory examples.
8. Stereotypes are oversimplied statements, which work as a substitute for accurate facts or individual experience. They are expressed as group accepted images, ideas or beliefs and are usually verbalised. Punjabis are hardy and assertive is an oversimplied statement that characterises all those who are Punjabis. Reality is that not all Punjabis are hardy and assertive.
9. Stereotypes are resistant to new information. We do not accept any information, which contradicts the existing stereotypes. We are not ready to accept that tribals are science-minded and intelligent because the stereotype is that tribals are dull and of poor intelligence.

Contents of stereotypes

The contents of stereotypes are of many different types. These can be discussed as under:

1. Stereotypes include many types of characteristics: Stereotypes include not only traits but also many other things such as physical appearance, typical interest and goal, preferred activities and occupations (Anderson and Klatzky, 1987). Early research on stereotypes done by Katz and Braly (1933) showed that American college students held well-developed beliefs (stereotypes) about the traits characterising various ethnic groups such as Negroes, Chinese, Germans and Americans. Results showed a commonly agreed-upon stereotype. Negroes were perceived as superstitions (84%), lazy (75%) and ignorant (38%); Germans were described as science-minded (78%) and industrious (44%); Chinese as superstitious (48%) and intelligent (47%). What is particularly significant about Katz and Braly (1933) study was that it had been replicated twice in the years following its publication, once in 1951 and again in 1967. This permits us to trace the changes in stereotypes over time (Karlins, Coffman and Walters, 1969). One change that was significantly noticed was the nature of specific adjectives chosen over the years. Obviously, there was a trend among the American college students to attribute more positive characteristics to most racial and ethnic groups in later years.

Gender stereotypes are also held even more strongly and confidently than racial and ethnic stereotypes (Jackman and Senter, 1981). *Gender stereotypes* are the stereotypes which are conceived with traits possessed by females and males and that make a distinction between the two gender from each other. Many persons describe women as sensitive, warm, soft-hearted, dependent and people-oriented, whereas men are described as independent, dominant, task-oriented and aggressive (Spence, Deaux and Helmreich, 1985). Gender stereotypes should not be confused with the term *sexism*, which refers to biases and negative responses towards females.

Age stereotypes are also held by people. The common stereotypes regarding elderly are that of passivity, unsociability and senility (Rodin and Langer, 1980). In fact, such views are manifestations of what is called *ageism* (Butler, 1980). According to Butler, ageism involves negative attitude towards older people as well as towards aging process and discrimination against older people and policies that sustain stereotypes about aged.

There are also group stereotypes. A person may perceive members of one group with feeling of disgust and repulsion, a second group with feeling of fear and apprehension and a third group with feeling of respect and admiration (Smith and Mackie, 2007). Consequently, the first group may be thought of as disgusting, the second as hostile and the third as admirable.

2. Stereotypes can be either positive or negative: Stereotypes can include positive as well as negative characteristics. We have cited several examples that show this. Take example of women stereotypes. Women are considered sensitive and warm, apart from being dependent and weaker. Sensitivity and warmness are the positive stereotypes that the group members themselves value and take pride in claiming. Positive stereotypes, however, may have negative consequences. For example, a common set of beliefs about women includes the idea that they are purely moral, delicate and in need of men's protection. This type of pattern is termed as *benevolent sexism* (Glick and Fiske, 1996) because observation has been that despite its apparent positive tone, people who hold such beliefs also tend to hold more hostile beliefs about women. Glick et al. (2000) conducted one study in which subjects from 19 nations participated and it was found that nations with higher average benevolent sexism score also tended to have more gender inequality such as poor representation of women in powerful and well-paying jobs.

3. Stereotypes can be accurate or inaccurate: Many stereotypes do indeed have a grain of truth. Many researchers have found some aspects of stereotypes to be true and accurate in the direction, if not in degree (Jussim, 2005). This is not much surprising since people join a class such as political party, club, professional associations and other groups precisely because they share attitudes, beliefs and feelings. Social customs also help in creating accurate stereotypes by prescribing what adolescents and retiree, men and women and different groups should think, feel and do. Eagly (1987), Eagly and Johnson (1990) conducted meta-analysis, which showed that gender stereotypes reflect actual direction of gender differences. In their study, they reported that males are aggressive, whereas females are soft-hearted (on aggressiveness); males are independent, whereas females are submissive and dependent (on influenceability); males are strong and tough, whereas females are affectionate, emotional, sensitive, sentimental (on emotionality), and males are autocratic and dominant, whereas females are sensitive and emotional (on leadership style). Likewise, the generalisation that men are, on an average, taller and stronger than women is correct (Deaux and LaFrance, 1998).

Despite all these, stereotypes can also be inaccurate. Many people hold the stereotype that males are more effective leaders than females. Eagly, Karau and Makhijani (1995) did a meta-analysis of the researches and reported no sex differences or even small differences favouring men being effective leader in business, educational or governmental organisations. Likewise, the belief that men are intelligent than women is inaccurate and has been refuted by scientific researches. In fact, blanket stereotypes about groups, even when they have a grain of truth, usually contain inaccuracy because they are overgenerations about many different individuals. As a consequence, they can be destructive because they are applied to those individual group members whom they may not fit at all. For example, not every woman is dependent or emotional, not every American is industrious and intelligent and not every Negro is lazy and superstitious.

Conclusively, it can be said that whatever be their content—positive or negative, accurate or inaccurate —stereotypes are the real part of our daily lives. Each of us use several types of stereotypes for arriving at a conclusion about the perceived person or a class.

WHY DO PEOPLE FORM AND USE STEREOTYPES?

As we know, stereotypes, whether negative or positive, are only approximations and as such do not tell us the whole truth about any group or individual. The question arises—why do we form and use them, if they are so patently inaccurate?

The reality is that stereotypes are indispensable in almost every type of social interaction. People form and use stereotypes because they serve some obvious purposes discussed below:

1. Stereotypes conserve mental effort and improve efficiency: Human beings are cognitive misers. In other words, they invest the least amount of cognitive effort possible in many different situations. People use stereotypes because they (stereotypes) save considerable cognitive effort. In fact, stereotypes are short-cut way of abstracting a number of characteristics about another person or group of persons, organising them into a pattern of expectations and responding to the individual or individuals as though they were that pattern. It would be impossible to interact with or respond effectively to the other people if we do not use stereotypes in our interaction. When we use stereotypes, we do not bother much about careful and systematic processing because they (stereotypes) help us in knowing what members of this group are like. Many studies have supported this function of stereotypes (Macrae, Milne and Bodenhausen, 1994; Bodenhausen, 1993).

2. Stereotypes help us in maintaining our pre-existing beliefs: In some human beings there is found tendency to seek and interpret information that confirms the existing beliefs. This is known as *confirmation bias* and it is found both in some social situations when information that disconfirms the existing beliefs are either ignored or discarded as well as in cognitive tasks where hypotheses are tested to confirm the already existing beliefs rather than entertain such hypotheses, which would disconfirm the existing beliefs. Stereotypes also provide people information about the typical or model characteristics that are supposed to possess by the persons belonging to a particular group. They act as theories, which guide our attention and exert strong effects on how we process social information (Yzerbyt, Rocher and Schradron, 1997). When we face the information relevant to an activated stereotype, such information is readily and quickly processed and remembered better than the information, which are said to be inconsistent with stereotypes. Researches have shown that when information inconsistent with the stereotypes somehow enters the consciousness, we actively refute or change in subtle ways so that it may seem consistent with the stereotypes (Kunda and Oleson, 1995). In fact, stereotypes produce what Dunning and Sherman (1997) had called *inferential prison* in the sense that once stereotypes are formed, they shape perceptions of the people in such a way that new information about the members of the stereotyped groups is interpreted as confirming our own stereotypes, despite the reality being opposite to it. In this way, we tend to keep our pre-existing stereotype intact. Researches have also shown that when we encounter with a person who belongs to a particular group about whom we have a stereotype, and the characteristics of this person does not fit the stereotype, (say a tribal person being highly active, intelligent and cultured one), we do not change our stereotypes, rather in such a situation, we place such person into a special category or subtype, which consists of a person that does not confirm the stereotypes (Queller and Smith, 2002). Once again, we find a clear evidence for the fact that stereotypes help us in maintaining our pre-existing beliefs as well as in processing social information in a set order.

3. Stereotypes help us in feeling positive about our own group identity in comparison to other social groups: Stereotypes motivate us to feel positive about our own group by developing the feeling of *in-group homogeneity*, where in-group members are perceived as more similar to each other than the out-group members. Stereotypes also lead us to conclude that the members of another group (out-group) are all alike. The tendency to perceive individuals belonging to the groups other than one's own as all the same is known as *out-group homogeneity effect* (Linville et al., 1989). The mirror image of out-group homogeneity effect is *in-group differentiation*, where the persons tend to perceive the members of their own group as being different from one another, that is, as being more heterogeneous than those of the out-groups.

Now, the question is what accounts for out-group homogeneity effect and the tendency to perceive members of the in-group as similarly united and homogeneous? Two common explanations have been provided. One explanation is that we generally have less exposure and experiences with the individual differences of members of the out-group, whereas we have a great deal of frequent exposure and experiences with the members of the our own group (Linville, Fisher and Salovney, 1989). Another explanation is that depending on perceiver's needs and purposes in the given situations, either the in-group or the out-group can be perceived as relatively more homogeneous. If the person develops a sense of insecurity and injustice, in-group homogeneity will be emphasised and if he wants to attribute negative characteristics, out-group homogeneity may be liked.

4. Stereotypes are formed and used for justifying inequalities: Stereotypes prevalent in a society are often used to justify the existing social inequalities. They do so by portraying groups as deserving their social roles and positions on the basis of their own characteristics. Every society maintains inequalities that benefit some groups and harm others. For example, gaps in income and opportunity between men and women and between tribal and non-tribal persist in India. Likewise, there exists gap in income and opportunity between whites and blacks in the United States of America. Researches have shown that as stereotypes reflecting these differences have been developed, they have justified and rationalised the underlying inequalities (Pettigrew, 1980). For example, historically, women have been viewed in ways that justify their treatment as unintelligent, weak and dependent. Moreover, stereotypes often incorporate emotions we associate with groups. We perceive some groups not only as hostile, stubborn, aggressive, and deviant but also as frightening, frustrating, threatening and impulsive. Once the beliefs and feelings are firmly established in stereotypes, they provoke prejudiced judgements and provide a justification for various types of inequalities and discriminating behaviour.

5. Stereotypes can be strongly formed through the process of social communication: Researches have shown that stereotypes can be formed and strengthened through the process of social communication. When we form impression about a group by being told about it (second-hand experience), their impressions are more stereotypic than what is formed through first-hand experience (Thompson, Judd and Park, 2000). These second-hand impressions, once formed, remain highly stereotypic even after direct experience with the members of the group itself. Social psychologists have further reported that discussion of group members' behaviours among several people also tends to make their impressions more stereotypic (Brauer, Judd and Jacqueline, 2001).

Thus, we see that there are several factors which account for the formation and use of stereotypes. All these factors must be taken into account when one has to understand the reasons behind the development of stereotypes.

ACTIVATION OF STEREOTYPES

As we know, a stereotype can influence our judgements or behaviours only when it comes to mind. The very first thing that we notice about other people is often their group membership and once a category is activated, the related stereotype comes to mind as well. Reality is that some categories seem so important that we use them to classify people even when they appear irrelevant to the social situation. For example, the first thing that most of the people ask from the parents of a newborn is—is it a girl or boy? Researches have shown that in almost every social interaction, people tend to note general categories like gender, age, race, etc. (Stangor, Lynch, Duan and Glass, 1992). In India, general category like caste and community, likewise, is also very common, which is noted by people.

Now, the question is what activates stereotypes? Researches have shown that once established, a stereotype can be activated by obvious cues. The more obvious and salient the cues to category membership, the more likely it is that the category and its related stereotypes will be readily coming to mind. For example, women with a highly feminine physical appearance and dress are perceived as also having highly feminine nature and qualities (Deaux and Levis, 1984). Researches have further shown that a category often becomes salient when only a single member of the group is present. Let us take an example. Suppose a woman is hired as a member of a group in which all other members are males or its reverse, a male joins all-female member group or a Negro student joins a class of all white students. Such solo appearances, because of their salience, attract more attention and this extra attention usually leads to particularly stereotypic perceptions. A solo female seems to be more feminine and a solo male, likewise, seems to be more masculine (Taylor, 1981). Thus, such solo appearance due to its salience is likely to increase the stereotypic thinking. Kanter (1977) also recorded the similar effects in his field studies.

Stereotypes can also be activated automatically. Stereotypes sometimes become so well-learned and so often used that its activation becomes automatic. Cues that relate to group membership can easily bring stereotypic information to mind even when the perceiver does not consciously notice the group membership at all. One study conducted by Wittenbrink, Judd and Park (2001) supported the view that the stereotypes can be automatically activated. In this study, each trial student (participant) saw XXXXX on a computer screen and this was followed by either a word or a non-sense letter string. In fact, some of the words were related to black or white stereotypes. Participants had to press one of the two keys to indicate whether or not the letters seen on the screen made an English word. Quite unknown to the participants, on some trials, the word *black* or *white* was also flashed on the screen before XXXXX for such a brief time that it could not be consciously registered. In fact, such words were acting as prime. Results revealed that the participants readily reacted to negative black stereotypic words such as poor, dishonest, lazy and violent on those trials, where the word *black* had been flashed as a prime. The same was true for positive stereotypic words such as intelligent, ambitious, progressive, wealthy, etc. on trials, with white primes. Results clearly showed that group labels automatically activate group stereotypes.

Researches have also shown that feelings about groups as well as specific traits information contained in stereotypes can also be activated automatically. Petty and Cacioppo (1986) using facial electromyography (EMG) demonstrated such possibility. EMG measures electrical activity of the facial muscles that create expressions such as smile or frown. Evidences obtained from the study have shown that these measurements can accurately assess a person's automatically activated positive or negative feelings about social groups (Vanman et al., 1997). Another study conducted by Fazio et al. (1995) also provided some evidences to this effect. They used a priming technique in which participants saw images of black or white faces on a computer screen and it was followed by words that were clearly positive or negative, but were not related to racial prejudice, for example, sky, disease, rape, sunshine, etc. Participants were requested to press one of two keys as rapidly as possible to indicate whether the word is positive or negative. Results revealed that after exposure of white's person face, most of the participants' responses to positive words were faster and following the exposure of black's person face, the responses to negative words were faster. Results revealed that feelings about groups can be activated readily and automatically.

Various kinds of evidences have vividly supported the fact that the stereotypes can be activated easily if appropriate cues are available. Not only that, feelings about the group can also be activated automatically.

IMPACT OF STEREOTYPES ON JUDGEMENTS AND ACTIONS

Stereotypes directly affect our judgements and actions towards another group. Such stereotypes can affect our interpretation of behaviours done by the members of the groups. Stereotypes seem to have greater effect when the judgements are to be made under time pressure, when emotions are intense and when people hold powerful positions. The following points discuss it further:

1. Stereotypes affect judgements and actions: Stereotypes, once activated, easily serve as a basis for making judgements or guiding actions towards a group. Stereotypes can change people's interpretation of behaviours done by different groups. For example, suppose both a man and a woman complete a very difficult and complex task successfully. Now, for a person, who is observing this and has stereotypic ideas about gender differences in abilities, the success in case of male might be attributed to man's great skills and abilities, but in case of female, it might be attributed to woman's luck or chance. Evidences for such type of interpretation have been provided by Deaux and Emswiller (1974). Stereotypes also affect consequential judgements about others. For example, suppose a police officer is patrolling in a riot-hit area or in naxal area. If a stranger suddenly appears on the road holding a metal object in his hand, the police officer may immediately decide that the held object must be a weapon. This occurs probably because the police officer has a stereotypic thinking.

2. Stereotypes tend to have greater effects when the judgements are to be made under time pressure: Social psychologists are of view that time pressure or other similar conditions which limit people's cognitive capacity generally tend to increase the effects of stereotypes on their judgements. Researches have shown that people who are to make decision about others, under time pressure, are more likely to rely on stereotypes than those who have sufficient time for taking decision (Freund et al., 1985). One study conducted by Bechtold, Naccarato and Zanna (1986) revealed that if the participants were given less time for deciding about male and female job candidates, they relied more on gender stereotypes. Likewise, Payne, Lambert and Jacoby (2002) reported that the participants' tendency to misidentify tools as weapons when primed by black faces was enhanced by time pressure.

Related to time pressure is the factor of complexity involved in information. Complex information is too difficult to be processed adequately. In such a situation, people generally rely on stereotypes for making judgements (Bodenhausen and Lichtenstein, 1987).

3. Stereotypes have greater effect upon judgements when emotions are intense: Experimental evidences have shown that stronger emotions compel the person to depend more on stereotyping by disrupting careful processing and short-circuiting attention (Dijker, 1987). Wilder and Shapiro (1984) showed that fear, anxiety and sadness generally tend to increase the impact of stereotypic expectations on perceptions of the members of the group, and not only that, they also tend to decrease the recognition of differences among the group members. Bodenhausen (1993) conducted one study in which the investigators examined the impact of anger on stereotyping. In this study, students (participants), who acted as mock jurors, were asked to decide the guilt or ignorance of a defendant whom some believed to be a Latino and others believed that the defendant was ethically non-descript. Results revealed that the participants, who were made angry by the investigator through experimental manipulation before reading the evidence, were found to deliver guiltier verdict against the Latino defendant as compared to the verdict delivered against the other defendant. In contrast, those participants, who were not made angered, treated the two defendants the same.

4. Stereotypes have greater effect upon judgements when people hold powerful position: Social psychologists have shown that those persons, who hold powerful position, generally tend to stereotype others. Persons with more power are inclined to attend the information which is consistent with negative stereotypes about the members of subordinate groups (Goodwin et al., 2000). On the other hand, members of subordinate group, because they need to be accurate and individuate members of powerful group, tend to exhibit lesser degree of stereotype. Such stereotypes of subordinate or less powerful group reflect their negative experiences with the members of those groups. For example, black Americans are most likely to stereotype whites as greedy and selfish (Johnson and Lecci, 2003). Researches have shown that power leads to stereotyping for two general reasons. (Goodwin et al., 2000). First, those holding powerful positions are in lesser need than powerless people to perceive others accurately. In fact, powerful persons can be cognitively lazy and simply apply stereotypes. Second, many stereotypes tend to support the social position of powerful and the boarder systems that provide groups differential access to power (Glick and Fiske, 2001). The common observation reveals that when a boss interacts with a subordinate, he (boss) tends to develop more stereotypic thinking than what the subordinate may think about the boss.

In this way, stereotypes tend to have wider impact upon the judgements and actions. This impact is enhanced when strong emotions, power position and time pressure are associated with the person, who stereotypes the members of the other group.

CHANGING STEREOTYPES AND BARRIERS TO STEREOTYPE CHANGE

Many social psychologists are of view that stereotypes remain stable as long as the nature of intergroup relationship between the two groups is stable (Tajfel, 1981; Oakes et al., 1995). However, when the relationship between the group changes, stereotypes do also change. Sometimes, we like to think that stereotypes originate from ignorance. As a consequence, learning more about a group can change a stereotype. For example, suppose a member of group who is regarded as hostile and clannish comes to live with you as tenant in your home. After many interactions with you, he turns out to be unobjectionable and even loving. Thus, as a consequence of intimate contact, you are able to know many things that remove the ignorance and change the stereotype. This simple idea that contact with a group member, who isolates the group stereotype, brings its downfall is the basis of one of the most researched theories of stereotype change. This is known as *contact hypothesis*, which suggests that under some conditions, direct contact between the members of different groups tends to reduce intergroup stereotyping and related prejudice and discrimination. The hypothesis further states that after knowing about group members on a one-to-one basis, it becomes just possible to say that they do not fit with the stereotypes associated with that group.

Moreover, social psychologists have identified some specific situations in which stereotypes can be changed. For example, it is easier to disconfirm stereotypical traits when the behaviour that reflects the trait is clear rather than ambiguous (Rothbart and John, 1985). Take an example to illustrate this. It is easier to disconfirm the stereotype that a woman is talkative rather than to disconfirm the stereotype that a woman is emotional because it is easier to observe the trait of talkativeness rather than that of emotionality. Rothbart and John (1985) further showed that it is easier to disconfirm positive traits than negative traits. For example, it is easier to change the perceiver's belief that a woman is kind than to change his belief that a woman nags. Rothbart and John (1985, p. 85) had rightly commented, "Favourable traits are difficult to acquire but easy to change, whereas unfavourable traits are easy to acquire difficult to lose". Another condition in which disconfirmation of a stereotype is more likely to occur is one in which the target person otherwise closely matches the category. In other words, the persons are more likely to change a feature of stereotype if the disconfirming behaviour is somehow in the context of the behaviour that fits a stereotype or specific category.

Some barriers to stereotype change

As it has been described above, stereotype can be changed by a single inconsistent experience and this process is called *conversion* (Rothbart, 1981), which apparently appears to be appealing. But the question is—does true conversion occur so easily? The answer is probably no. It has been found that even when people obtain information that is clearly inconsistent with a stereotype, the stereotype may remain unchanged. Social psychologists, in general, have isolated the following three major barriers to stereotype change:

1. People tend to explain away the inconsistent information: One popular barrier to stereotype change is the tendency of the persons to explain away the inconsistent information. Information which is in some way discrepant with stereotype about group members often makes us hard for its causes, and generally, in such a situation, we tend to find some special circumstances to explain it. For example, the women, who succeed in very difficult, complex and even dangerous tasks that are typical of man's world, are often viewed as very lucky or highly motivated, rather than very capable and meritorious. Heilman and Stopek (1985) confirmed this from their study. Thus, encountering a few successful women. who violate the stereotype of their group, does not change the perceiver's stereotypes.

2. People tend to create a new category for exceptions to rule: Even when inconsistent information are numerous and difficult to be explained away, people tend to defend their stereotypes by compartmentalising the information into specific subtypes, which are the categories narrower than broad groups. Subtype is a subset of a group, which is not consistent with the stereotype of the group as a whole (Baron, Byrne and Branscombe, 2006). Such special differentiated category protects stereotyped beliefs from change. For example, we can maintain our belief that outstanding physical feats are the realm of the young adults if we compartmentalise the stereotype—inconsistent pretty older people (who are equally successful) in special subtypes, which is exception-to-the-rule category. Examples are people like Lew Hollander (80 years old) who competed the grueling Annual Fort Ironman World championship in Kona Hawaii, USA in 2012 and Olga Kotello, a 92-year old track-and-field champion from Canada to be the world's greatest athlete. Rothbart and John (1985) showed that female business executives, who work along competent and successful male colleagues, can form a subtype of carrier woman, and thus, it allows male executives to maintain a more general belief that most women cannot succeed in business.

3. People tend to see the behaviour of unusual group members as being irrelevant to the group stereotype: Another way to resist stereotype change is to differentiate a typical group member, popularly called *contrast effect*. If the people cannot explain away inconsistent information or compartmentalise such information by creating new subtypes, they may defend their stereotypes by perceiving stereotype disconfirming individuals as remarkable or exceptional ones. In fact, people, who do not behave as expected and seem even more different, tend to create what is termed as *contrast effect*. Through contrast effect, members who deviate from expectations of their group seem even different from the rest of the group than they really are. Consequently, the observers or perceivers can easily decide that these deviant and unusual people are not true group members at all. In fact, this difference makes them exceptions to the rule. As such, they have a very little impact on perceiver's impressions of the group as a whole. In the study conducted by Manis, Nelson and Shedler (1988), the impact of contrast effect in defending the change in stereotype was demonstrated. In their study, the researchers deliberately created a certain type of stereotype of patients in mental hospital among the participants, that is, the college students. Subsequently, the participants were required to read statements that were supposed to be written by the hospital patients. The statements revealed that the patients were either severely disturbed or only mildly disturbed. These college students, then, read statements prepared by the other patients, who showed a moderate level of pathology. Results revealed that those participants, who had been led to expect severe disturbance, judged these new patients to be only mildly ill and those, who had been led to expect only mild disturbance, judged the new patients to be extremely ill. All this happened because of contrast effect. Likewise, such effect also explains why our stereotypes of an employed women are quite different from those found for a typical woman and similar to an employed man.

Obviously, then, there are some barriers to stereotype change, and therefore, the contact hypothesis, has only limited importance for the phenomenon of stereotype change.

GENDER STEREOTYPES

Although men and women do differ in various aspects of their behaviour, gender stereotypes exaggerate such differences. *Gender stereotypes* are defined as the stereotypes or beliefs concerning the traits possessed by males and females and they distinguish male and female from each other (Deaux and Kite, 1993). Such traits include both positive and negative traits. For example, on the positive side of female, gender stereotypes are that they are viewed as warm, kind/polite, considerate and nurturant. On the negative side, they are viewed as dependent, weak and emotional. Our collective impression of women is that they are high on warmth, but low on competence. In Indian society, traditionally, women are stereotyped to have an inferior status, and thus, are excluded from the benefits of development process. Researches done by Indian psychologists have shown that the older generation, young males and those from lower socio-economic status tend to have more traditional views about women than the other groups (Das, Sharma and Sinha, 1994; Jai Prakash and Suvarna, 1996). Dani (1995), however, showed that females tend to show greater female stereotypes than males.

Males are also assumed to have both positive and negative stereotypic traits. For example, on the positive side, males are viewed as competent, stable, self-confident and assertive, whereas on the negative side, they are viewed as aggressive, insensitive and arrogant. Our collective portrait of a male stereotype is that males are high on competence, but low on communal traits. Such collective portrait becomes indicative of relatively high status of male in comparison to female. However, due to strong emphasis on warmth and being considerate, people, in general, tend to feel somewhat more positively about women on the whole as compared to men. Eagly and Mladinic (1994) had called this *women are wonderful effect*.

Despite such effect and greater likeability for women, they had to face some problems. Traits supposedly possessed by the women in comparison to male traits are viewed as less appropriate for high status position. Women's traits make them more appropriate for their supportive roles as frequently reflected in working women's role like clinical, nursing, etc. Several studies have confirmed the fact that women generally experience less favourable outcomes in their careers, and therefore, are prevented as a group from reaching top position because of their gender (Stroh et al., 2004). This is known as *glass ceiling effect* (Baron, Byrne and Branscombe, 2008). Not only that, when females violate stereotypic expectancies concerning warmth, nurturance and being considerate, and instead, act according to the portrait of a leader, particularly in male domains, they are likely to be outright rejected.

Despite glass ceiling, a few women manage to reach the top position enjoying high status. A few examples are Mrs. Pratibha Patil, Mrs. Meera Kumar, Mrs. Indira Gandhi, Mrs. Kiran Bedi, Mrs. Sarojini Naidu, etc. from India and Mrs. Benazir Bhutto, Mrs. Margaret Thatcher Mrs. Bidhya Devi Bhandari and Mrs. S. Bandarnaike from foreign countries, who have managed to break through the glass ceiling effect. The success of such token high-status women is taken as evidence that gender no longer matters and discrimination is no longer an appropriate explanation for women's lack of success. Tokenism has, however, some negative consequences. Those women, who somehow do not achieve position like a few successful token women, may come to believe that they have only themselves to blame. Not only that, tokenism may harm the token's self-esteem as well as how they are viewed by others. Evidences provide support for the fact that the persons, who are hired as token representative of their groups, are viewed negatively by the other members (Yoder and Berendsen, 2001). It has also been observed that the people's confidence in their own role is diminished by awareness of tokenism. Brown et al. (2000) conducted a study in which this fact was confirmed. In their study, the investigators gave impression to some women that they had been selected to lead the group because there was a quota for women, whereas some other women were led to believe that they had been selected on the basis of their qualifications. Results revealed that in the former case, women's performance was undermined as compared to that of the women in the latter case.

Researches have further shown that women agree with the view that their group has distinctively positive attributes than do men. In a major study involving more than 1500 participants from different countries, Glick et al. (2000) had shown that beliefs regarding positive distinctiveness of women's finer qualities such as they are more moral, pure and are truly, necessary for men's happiness, etc. are often agreed with more by females than by males, whereas males uniformly show higher degree of hostile sexism than do women. The former beliefs are termed as *benevolent sexism*. Hostile sexism is the view held by males that women are a sort of threat to men's position (such as they seek special favour they generally do not deserve). Generally, men display hostile sexism more strongly towards women, but this difference is often reversed with respect to benevolent sexism (Glick et al., 2000).

Gender inequality present in the society also contributes to the development of both benevolent sexism and hostile sexism. If in the society, women are rarely found in high-status jobs, have poor educational opportunities and poor living conditions as compared to men, a gender inequality is said to exist. Such gender inequality tends to enhance both forms of sexism. However, only hostile sexism predicts negative stereotyping of women.

Besides sexism and glass ceiling, women's experiences especially at workplace are affected by what has been termed by social psychologists as *differential respect*, which is considered as critical for woman of being her high-status position. Since men occupy positions of greater power and higher status than women, people seem to believe that men deserve greater respect than women. Jackson, Esses and Burris (2001) conducted a series of studies for determining whether differential respect actually does play role in discrimination against women. In these studies, male and female participants rated applicants (both men and women) for relatively high status or low status jobs. Besides rating the applicants in terms of whether they should be hired, both male and female also completed a standard measure of masculine and feminine stereotyping. At last, they also indicated their level of respect for both male and female applicants. Results revealed that men received higher rating of respect than women, and therefore, it was confirmed that the factor of differential respect played an important role in at least some form of discrimination against women.

Now, the next question that haunts the mind is—are gender stereotypes really accurate? Although male and females differ with respect to various aspects of behaviour, the magnitude of such differences is much smaller than what is supposed by gender stereotypes (Plant et al., 2000). In fact, gender stereotypes seem to be an exaggeration of the behaviours typical of male and female role. Gender stereotypes are said to be an exaggeration in the sense that they do not take into consideration any overlap between men and women. Reality is that not all men are independent and not all women are emotional. Some women are more independent than an average man, and likewise, some men are more emotional than an average woman. Deaux and Lewis (1983) conducted a study in which men and women participants were asked to estimate the probability that a male and a female possessed a behaviour, a trait or a physical feature. Results revealed numerous sex differences. However, participants did not perceive that all men and no women possessed masculine attributes. Participants rated men to be independent than women, but still, they thought that women had 58% chances of being independent. Likewise, participants perceived that women were more likely than men to nurse the children, but men had 50% likelihood of taking care of children. The study clearly showed that our beliefs about men and women are not mutually exclusive. In the modern days, moreover, the gender roles have shifted, and accordingly, there has been change in the behaviours associated with both the genders (Eagly and Wood, 1999).

What activates gender stereotypes? Social psychologists have isolated the following three factors that tend to activate gender stereotypes:

1. Amount of information available about the person: If we have less information about a person, it is very likely that we perceive and react to him or her on the basis of stereotypes. Condry and Condry (1976) conducted a study in which adults watched videotape of a baby. Half of the total adults were told that they were watching a boy and the remaining half were told that they were watching a girl. Results revealed that the adults who thought that they were watching a boy, they perceived the child as significantly more active and forceful than did the adults who thought that they were watching a girl. In another study conducted by Vogel et al. (1991), children (aged 5, 9 and 15), college students and mothers observed the videotapes of infants labelled as male or female. Results revealed that college students as well as children viewed the female infant as softer, nicer, smaller and more beautiful than the male infants. Mother's evaluations were not affected by gender labels probably because their personal experiences with babies made them less dependent on gender stereotypes.

2. Salience of person's group membership: Another factor that activates the use of gender stereotype is the salience of the person's group membership. Here, by salience, we mean that the person's gender stands out and is a very prominent characteristic. For example, when we meet a woman personally, her gender becomes more salient and prominent than when we read her article. Another factor affecting gender salience is the percentage of women to men in a given group. A person's gender become more salient when he or she is in numerical minority such as being the only woman in all-male working group or being the only man in all-female working group. In fact, such solo or token status calls special attention to the person's distinctive social category and makes role vulnerable to stereotyping. Cohen and Swim (1995) conducted a study in which it was found that college male and female students tended to have different reactions to the prospect of being lone person of their gender in group. College students, who anticipated being the only man or the only woman in the group, expected to be treated in a stereotyped way by the other group members. For men, the prospect of being stereotyped was positive because it was expected that the male would take a leadership role in the all-female group. But for female, the prospect of being stereotyped was negative. It was expected that such woman would feel less comfortable in the all-male group and would show preference to switch to different group. One study conducted by Taylor (1981) also illustrated how solo status enhances gender stereotyping. The participants, who were all students, evaluated the members of six-person tape-recorded discussion group. Some groups had a solo woman or a solo man, whereas some others had equal number of men and women. After listening the tape, the participants rated the group members. Solos were perceived as playing gender-stereotyped roles. Solo women were seen as motherly, nurturant type or group secretary, whereas solo men were perceived as leader, father-figure or macho type. Results clearly supported the view that group composition enhanced the solo's gender and contributed to the stereotyped perceptions of the solo's behaviour.

3. Balance of power: Balance of power also affects the tendency of stereotyping. Fiske (1993) reported that in work situation, boss has more power and control over subordinates. Powerful person is more likely to form stereotyped impression of their subordinates probably because they do not pay much attention to their subordinates nor do they want to be bothered. The subordinates who are relatively powerless will attend carefully to the more powerful boss. Paying attention to the behaviour of the boss helps the subordinates in predicting what their boss is likely to do and it leads to the formation of usually less stereotypical impressions of the boss, who has more power and control. This analysis applies well to understanding the gender stereotypes because women are often found in the position of lower power relative to men. This is often found in a relationship, where boss is male and his secretary is female. Boss often perceives his secretary as dependent, soft and sexy.

SHIFTING STANDARDS: DOES NO DIFFERENCE IN EVALUATIONS OR RATINGS MEAN ABSENCE OF STEREOTYPIC THINKING?

In the modern days, overt discrimination on the basis of caste, class, religion, language, gender, etc. is considered illegal. Therefore, overt discrimination based on these indices has been substantially reduced. Despite this, social psychologists are able to show that there are some subtle forces, which continue to support such discrimination.

When people evaluate or rate members of two different groups in a similar way, what does this indicate? Does it mean that stereotypes are not operating? The common sense theory says that yes, in such situation, there is no discrimination, and therefore, no stereotypic thinking is operating. But on the basis of the experimental evidences, social psychologists have been able to demonstrate that even when ratings or evaluations for the two groups are similar, stereotypes do continue to affect our behaviour.

The research works on shifting standards have shown that, in fact, stereotypes do continue to operate even when the two groups are evaluated similarly (Biernat and Vescio, 2002). The idea of shifting standard is that the people might have one standard for defining a behaviour for one group but another standard for defining the behaviour for the other group. In other words, shifting standards convey the view that we use one group as standard but shift to another group as comparison standard while judging the members of a different group. The idea of shifting standards clearly indicate that identical evaluation ratings do not translate into the same behavioural expectations nor do the fact that stereotypes are not operating in such a situation. Researches have provided support to shifting standards. Biernat and Vescio (2002) conducted a study in which the idea of shifting standards was confirmed. In this study, the college students enacted the role of baseball manager and rated the athletic abilities of some male and female photographs. Results revealed that among the set of male and female photographs rated equal in athletic ability, the students expected the male players to have better batting averages than the female players. The researchers concluded that the same judgement of athletic ability was interpreted differently for male and female players. Bridges et al. (2002) also conducted a study in which college students rated men and women, who stayed at home to take care of children and the men and women, who went outside home to work full time. In results, it was found that although students perceived men and women homemakers equally communal (and also more communal than full time working men and women), women homemakers were perceived to be more affectionate, taking part in children care activities and comfort providing than male homemakers. Once again, the study showed that the same trait that is being communal is associated with differential expectations regarding females and males. Let us take some practical examples. Suppose you come to know that a woman travels across the country alone. You may classify that behaviour as highly independent. However, the same behaviour displayed by a male may be classified as less noteworthy. Since we presume that men are more independent than women, it may take more independent behaviour done by male to be judged as equally independent as a woman. Likewise, a woman may be rated as earning a lot and a male may also be rated as earning a lot. But both these ratings may not mean the same thing. For a male, earning a lot means earning really many times a female is earning because in society, males are expected to earn more than females. Since women generally tend to compare themselves with other women and because they are known to earn less than men, women may conclude that they are earning a lot. Further, suppose you gave a woman executive a score of 10 on a scale ranging from 1 to 10 in which high score meant extremely good executive. Similarly, you gave a score of 10 to a male executive on the same scale. Does this mean that these two executives would tend to exhibit similar overall performances? Following Biernat and Vescio (2002), the identical scores on the subjective scales can take on different meanings depending on the group membership of the person being rated or evaluated. The subjective scales are response measurements, which are open to different interpretation and lack an externally grounded referent. In fact, the case of shifting the meaning of subjective standards becomes the basis for real stereotyping effects, despite the fact that same ratings have been given to two quite different targets. But there are also other standards available that always mean the same thing, irrespective of what is being referred to. These standards are called *objective scales*, where the meaning is same, no matter to whom they are applied. In such scales, measurement units are tied to external reality so that they mean the same things regardless of different group membership. For example, money in terms of Rupees, Dollars, Pounds, etc. per year are measurement units tied to external reality. Thus, male and female executive may be rated as extremely good executive on subjective scales which, in fact, conceal the presence of stereotypical judgements. But male executives may be rated to do higher turnover in terms of Rupees per year as compared to female executive. Such ratings on objective scales definitely expose the presence of stereotypical judgements. Thus, the same ratings on subjective scales do not compulsorily mean equality on objectives scales or show absence of stereotyping.

STEREOTYPES ASSOCIATED WITH SINGLE AND MARRIED PERSONS

In recent years, the concept of singalism has attracted the attention of social psychologists. The concept of *singalism* refers to the negative stereotyping and discrimination directed towards the people who are single as against those who are married. The common stereotypic traits associated with the single persons are being lonely, insecure, self-centred, unhappy, independent, and immature, whereas the common stereotypic traits associated with the married persons are being loving, happy, stable, matured, honest, giving, kind, etc. DePaulo and Morris (2006) conducted a study in which they measured how single and married people are perceived. Results revealed that single persons were mostly perceived with negative characteristics like those mentioned above, whereas married people were characterised with positive characteristics, as mentioned. Not only that, 50% of time, married people were perceived as kind, caring and giving, whereas only 2% single persons were perceived with these traits. This difference in stereotypes between married and single persons was enhanced when the targets were described as forty years old than when they were described as only 25 years old.

Research done by Depaulo and Morrie further showed that single people are themselves not aware of the discrimination being done against them. They reported that singles were asked to tell if they were victim of any group that had been the target of discrimination, only 4% mentioned that single was such a category. Likewise, when asked directly if singles might be victimised, only 30% said this might be possible. All this shows that singles themselves fail to acknowledge the singalism and this is one of the reason of lack of awareness of the negative stereotyping and discrimination they usually face. In others words, singles are not aware of the negative stereotyping and discrimination done against them. Depaulo and Morris (2006) further pointed out that the negative stereotyping and discrimination against singles serve to glorify an important social system, called *marriage*, and perhaps, this is one of the primary reasons why it is so widespread and legitimised. Apart from all these, singles are also discriminated in many different ways. In their study, when undergraduates were asked to whom they would like to rent property, 70% preferred married couple and only 12% preferred single man and 18% preferred single woman (Depaulo and Morris, 2006).

CONCEPT OF PREJUDICE AND DISCRIMINATION

In fact, there are three interrelated but distinguished components of group antagonism, which is exhibited when the members of in-group display negative attitudes and behaviours towards the members of out-group. They are stereotypes, prejudice and discrimination. *Stereotypes*, which we have already discussed, are cognitive, that is, beliefs about the typical characteristics of group members. *Prejudice* is affective referring to positive or negative feelings towards the target group. *Discrimination* is behavioural referring to the behaviour that puts the target group under disadvantage. In this reaction, we shall concentrate only upon prejudice and discrimination. Prejudice and discrimination are, in fact, more widespread in our society. They influence our social perception and understanding of social world to a greater extent. Therefore, social psychologists have paid special attention to these phenomena.

Prejudice is the evaluation of a group or single individual mainly based on the membership of the group. In other words, prejudice is prejudgement of a group and its individual members. Now, the question is whether the prejudgement is positive or negative. Some definitions of prejudice include both positive prejudgements as well as negative prejudgements. For example, Secord and Backman (1964) defined *prejudice* as an attitude that predisposes a person to think, feel and perceive an act in favourable or unfavourable ways towards a group or its individual members. Likewise, Feldman (1985) defined *prejudice* as positive or negative evaluations or judgements of members of a particular group. For example, sex prejudice is exhibited when an individual is evaluated on the membership in a particular group, that is, as a male and female.

The above definitions show that prejudice includes either positive evaluation or negative evaluation of the members of the group. People may dislike the members of the other group but may also evaluate positively the members of their own group solely on the basis of their group membership. In both cases, the affect or feeling is not related to qualities of the individuals, rather it is obviously due to the group to which the individuals belong.

Despite the fact the prejudice can also be positive, nearly all uses of prejudice refer to negative or unfavourable prejudgement or what Gordon Allport had termed in his famous classic book entitled *The Nature of Prejudice* as an antipathy based on a faculty and inflexible generalisation.

Since prejudice is an attitude, it contains ABC components of attitudes. A prejudiced person may dislike all those who are different from self (affective component), behave in discriminatory manner (behavioural tendency component) and believe them to be dangerous and ill-mannered (cognitive component). Besides, it is based on prejudgement, often reflecting an evaluation made before knowing much about the person's characteristics as an individual. If one is to make distinction between prejudice and attitude, it would be better to tell that in prejudice, the affective component is comparatively more salient.

Discrimination is defined as the behavioural manifestation of prejudice. It is differential to persons considered to belong to a particular group. In other words, discrimination is inequitable treatment of the individuals, who are said to belong to a particular group. Thus, prejudice is negative attitude, whereas discrimination is negative behaviour. Discrimination often has its source in prejudicial attitudes (Dovidio et al., 1996). Discrimination of one group by another group often leads to conflict between the two groups. Since our social norms prevent overt discrimination, prejudicial attitude does not necessarily lead to overt discrimination. Thus, the presence of prejudice does not always lead to discrimination. On the other hand, manifestation of discrimination readily allows to conclude that prejudice is present although even this relationship does not always hold. For example, a person who is not prejudiced towards his distant relative may not like to provide rooms on rent because of his fear of losing privacy in his own home. If one is to make distinction between prejudice and discrimination, one would prefer to say that in the former, the affective component is salient, whereas in the latter, the action tendency component becomes salient.

In India, discrimination based on religion, caste and gender is very common. India presents a picture of multi-ethnic society, with a population of over 121 crore people that speak more than 1600 languages. It has about 3000 communities which are differentiated by different castes. More than 350 tribal communities have also been identified. India has eight major religions of which main religious groups are Hindus (82.64%), Muslims (11.35%), Christians (2.43%) and Sikhs (1.97%) (Pandey, 1988). Despite the overwhelming majority of Hindus in the country, they are outnumbered by Muslims in Jammu and Kashmir (64.19%) by Sikhs in Punjab (60.17%) and by Christians in Nagaland (80.19%) and Mizoram (83.80%). Each of these religious groups has its own belief systems and practices. How to contain these conflicting cultural-religious identities is one of the main challenges before the government. Frequent riots between Hindus and Muslims bear a clear evidence of discrimination that each group does against other. Since 2000 alone, there have been more than 6500 incidents of communal violence in India, with Maharashtra topping the states, where the maximum number of such incidents have taken place (Baron, Branscombe, Byrne and Bhardwaj, 2010).

Discrimination based on caste is also very common because here, caste prejudice is frequently observed. Caste rivalries tend to create caste-based groupings and loyalties. Caste movements are very concerned. Memory of the protests done by anti-reservationists when the Government of India announced reservation of jobs and reserving seats in government educational and professional institutions for backward castes is still very clear. Such practices strengthen caste identities and enhance caste prejudice, leading to discrimination. Despite the fact that our constitution bans any form of discrimination based on caste, atrocities done against Dalits are very common. For example, Ranvir Sena, caste-based paramilitary group in Bihar, is known for its atrocities against Dalits. Likewise, there are also other caste-based organisations, which openly target the other caste by making discrimination.

Discrimination based on gender is also very common. Discrimination begins at the womb and continues throughout the lives of women. Despite various efforts of upliftment of women's position in Indian society, male dominance and ill-treatment of women in the form of rape, abuse, child marriage, child prostitution, low priority on nourishment and education are commonly seen. Many cases of violence against women do not enter the court of law, as they are regarded as private family matters. We clearly remember the case of Bhanwari Devi, a grass-root worker from a remote village in Rajasthan, whose job was to educate women against child marriage. In 1992, she was gang-raped by upper caste people before her husband. The matter came before the court of law, but the court did not found the accused guilty (Virani, 2001). In case of Late Phoolan Devi, extreme discrimination experienced by women also turned the career of even a noble woman, who with a vow to take revenge, had become a hard-core criminal.

The negative evaluations that mark prejudice can stem from emotional associations or from negative beliefs, called *stereotypes*, which we have already discussed in detail. Stereotype means to generalise. To say that professors are absent minded, Americans are outgoing, Indians are religious and married women who keep their own surnames are more assertive and ambitious are some of the popular examples of stereotypes. Thus, stereotypes are beliefs about the personal attributes shared by the people of a particular group or social category. Since stereotypes relate primarily to beliefs, they are cognitive component of group.

Thus, it can be concluded that prejudice, discrimination and stereotypes correspond to affective, behavioural and cognitive components of intergroup antagonism. Prejudices and stereotypes strongly influence an individual's attitude and behaviour in different areas.

FORMS OF PREJUDICE AND DISCRIMINATION

Whenever people put themselves in social groups, prejudice and discrimination often exist. Social psychologists have provided some evidences for their existence in the forms of racism, sexism and tokenism.

Racism is the individual's prejudicial attitudes and discrimination towards the people of a given race or institutional practices that discriminate even when there is no prejudicial intent. Racism is often seen in Western countries, although it has now considerably declined because many countries have introduced laws against such behaviour. However, social psychologists have argued that what exists these days is the modern racism, which is both more subtle and less obvious to detect.

Surin et al. (1995) showed that the modern racism is manifested in the following three ways:

1. Resentment that minority group (say for example, blacks in the United States) may get positive treatment or action
2. Impatience and annoyance over continued demands of minority groups to be treated at par with majority group
3. Denial that minority groups are discriminated in any way

In India, Muslims, Sikhs and Christians are considered as primary minority groups, whereas Hindus enjoy the status of majority group. Members of the majority group are often found to express their prejudicial attitude through the above three ways. Recently, for the reservation given to Muslim backwards within 27% Other Backward Class (OBC) quota by the Government of India for the purpose of bringing them at par with backwards, Hindus have raised much hue and cry. Social psychologists have tried to investigate the modern racism with the help of some unobtrusive measures of behaviour. For example, Franco and Maass (1996) analysed how people talk about characteristics associated with the members of out-groups. They found that people use more general and abstract words about out-group regarded in the negative way than about out-group regarded in the positive way. Gordon (1993) reported that mock jurors set higher bail for a black man accused of committing a crime than a white man accused of exactly the same crime.

Sexism is another form of prejudice and discrimination. Sexism is a prejudice based on gender. Disliking a nurse because he is a male or a woman because he is a truck driver are the examples of sexism. Swim et al. (1995) distinguished between the traditional sexism and the modern sexism. Traditional sexism reflects endorsement of traditional roles for men and women, differential treatments given to men and women and the belief that women are less competent and more dependent than men. Researches done on sex stereotypes have consistently revealed that males are viewed as more competent and independent, whereas females as more warmer and expressive (Deaux, 1985). Modern sexism, by contrast, reflects the denial of any existing discrimination towards women, resentment of any preferential treatment for women and antagonism to women's demand. In the modern time, much has changed and women are viewed as being as successful as men in careers. Eagly and Mladinic (1994) claimed that a more positive stereotype now exists for females in relation to work and they are generally liked more than men. The people, who endorse the modern sexism, tend to underestimate women's difficulties in obtaining jobs traditionally occupied by men.

The above examples show that sexism is typically negative feeling towards women. But sexism, like any affective attitude, may consist of negative or positive feelings. This is clearly reflected in the distinction that Glick and Fiske (1996) made between hostile sexism and benevolent sexism in their Ambivalent Sexism Inventory. Hostile sexism is just as its name sounds—feeling of hostility towards women. It is a negative attitude towards women, especially towards those women who challenge traditional female role. In a nutshell, here, women are perceived as threat to men's position (Baron, Byrne and Branscombe, 2006). Benevolent sexism, by contrast, reflects positive feelings towards women, including a prosocial orientation towards women such as a desire to help women. Thus, benevolent sexism indicates that women are superior to men in different ways, that is, they are more moral, show better taste and play a very important role in men's happiness. Both hostile sexism and benevolent sexism are rooted in patriarchy, gender differentiation and sexual reproduction (Glick and Fiske, 2001). Patriarchy and gender differentiation lead to hostile sexism by enhancing the differences between men and women and justifying the superiority of men. However, men's dependence on women for intimacy, sexual reproduction and gender-differentiated social roles is clearly linked to benevolent sexism. Men generally show hostile sexism more strongly than women, but this difference is often reversed with respect to benevolent sexism (Glick et al., 2000). This reversed relationship is due to the fact that women often agree more strongly with the idea that they possess much positively distinct attributes than do men.

Benevolent sexism, in fact, is also a harmful attitude because it is somewhere rooted in the belief that women are less competent than men and are in acute need of men's help. Glick and Fiske (1999) described the related construct benevolent discrimination as men providing more help to women. Again here, the inherent message is that women are dependent and need help and protection. The behaviour, no doubt, appears prosocial, but really legitimises an inferior position of women.

Tokenism is a form of discrimination. In tokenism, positive action is taken by the individuals, groups or organisations towards a member of the group to whom they are prejudiced. Having made a token benefit, it is subsequently used as an excuse to say that enough has been done to help the discriminated group. In other words, in tokenism, the persons perform very trivial positive action for the members of out-group, and later, these actions are used as an excuse for refusing more beneficial actions for the out-group (Wright, 2001). Summers (1991) conducted a study in which it was shown that people employed as token representatives of a group are perceived negatively by their fellow workers, thus showing discrimination. Yoder and Berendsen (2001) also showed that people who are hired as token representatives of their groups are perceived negatively by the other members of the company.

Thus, we find that prejudice and discrimination are expressed in the form of racism, sexism and tokenism. Out of these three, social psychologists have made an extensive and intensive study of sexism.

ORIGIN, DEVELOPMENT AND MAINTENANCE OF PREJUDICE AND DISCRIMINATION

Social psychologists have put one basic question—from where does prejudice come and why does it persist? To answer this question, we will examine four approaches, which are based on Allport's (1954) outline of theories of prejudice—psychodynamic approach, cognitive approach, historical and socio-cultural approach, and situational approach. These are described below:

1. Psychodynamic approach

Psychodynamic approach, broadly can be called *motivational approach*, emphasises that motivational deficit in the individual's level of psychological functioning can lead to prejudice. In other words, internal dynamics of personality can lead to prejudice. The following factors have been included as explanation of origin of prejudice under this approach:

(i) **Frustration and aggression–Scapegoat theory:** Sigmund Freud was the first person to emphasise and analyse in great detail that when a person is prevented from satisfying his needs, he becomes frustrated and is likely to engage in aggressive behaviour. People who are frustrated normally try to express their aggression towards the source of their unhappiness. However, if the source of frustration cannot be attacked because of fear of retaliation or unavailability, aggression may be displaced towards another target. In such a situation, people look for a scapegoat—someone whom they can blame for their difficulties and whom they can attack. Unemployed youths cannot aggress against the large economic forces that are the real source of their frustration, and therefore, they generally aggress against a more convenient and safer target, that is, the local authority that conducts examinations for appointment to various posts. Several studies have been conducted to test scapegoating theory experimentally. The experiment conducted by Weatherley (1961) is worth-mentioning. In this study, on the basis of an anti-semitism scale, four groups of male college students were formed. Two groups were high in anti-semitism and two groups were low in anti-semitism. One group in each category acted as experimental group, which was subjected to an aggression-arousing situation in which the experimenter made highly insulting remarks during the time subjects were filling out a questionnaire. The control groups in each category—high on anti-semitism and low on anti-semitism—filled out the same questionnaire in a friendly and non-provoking atmosphere. Subsequently, both groups were given picture-story tests, which consisted of eight pencil sketches of different males to whom names, ages and occupations were assigned. Two of the names were Jewish-sounding and two were not. In these tests, subjects were asked to tell story about the sketches. The stories were later analysed to determine the number of aggressive acts done towards the sketches. Results revealed that the highly anti-semitic participants directed more aggressive response to Jewish characters in their stories as compared to the subjects who scored low on anti-semitism. Besides, it was also found that there was no difference between high and low groups in the number of responses assigned to the non-Jewish characters. Thus, a highly anti-semitic individual may have a strong tendency to displace aggression towards Jews, but not necessarily towards the other objects.

Berkowitz and Green (1962) emphasised the stimulus qualities of the scapegoat. In their study, the participants, who worked in pair, were first induced to like or dislike their partner. Later, in half of the subjects, frustration was induced by the experimenter, whereas in the remaining half, a sense of pleasantness was induced. At the end of the study, two pair members, a neutral pair and a confederate of the experimenter were all required to work on a cooperative task. Results revealed that hostility aroused by the experimenter was displaced to the disliked partner rather than to the neutral partner, providing support to the scapegoating theory.

One important source of frustration is intergroup competition. The competition between groups produces conflict, and therefore, prejudice too. Researches have shown that when two groups compete for jobs, housing or social prestige, one group's goal fulfilment may become the other group's frustration. *Realistic group conflict theory* views prejudice as an inevitable consequence of competition among groups for scarce and valued resources or power (Levine and Campbell, 1972; Esses et al., 1998). For example, a competition may arise among the members of upper caste, the members of OBC and Dalits for various government jobs or for admission to the selective colleges. Such competition may prejudice the members of upper castes towards OBC and Dalits because they may not get entry, despite higher rank due to the policy of reservation. A more psychologically related theory called *relative deprivation* suggests that intergroup hostility stems from the perception of deprivation relative to others rather than from absolute levels of deprivation. For example, the economic conditions of the people may be improving but the people, whose conditions may be improving at a slow rate, may feel resentful because they see others increasingly able to afford those things which they cannot. This naturally leads to a feeling of antagonism against the advantaged group.

(ii) **Authoritarian personality:** The most elaborate use of psychodynamic theory is found in authoritarian personality, which suggests that prejudice is the outcome of a particular set of characteristics shared by the term *authoritarian personality* (Adorno et al., 1950). In fact, authoritarian personality appears to relate to certain aspects of family structure and discipline experienced by a person as a child. His parents are generally found to have exercised rigid discipline and affection being conditional upon approval of behaviour. Such personality displays exaggerated submission to authority, extreme levels of conformity to conventional standards of behaviour, self-righteous hostility and punitive attitude towards deviants and members of weaker section and minority. According to Adorno et al. (1950), authoritarians tend to develop hostility towards rigid and demanding parents, but are unable to direct hostility towards parents due to the strong feeling that authority is always right. Instead, authoritarians displace their hostility towards the persons whom they perceive as weak or unconventional.

In order to test this theory, Adorno et al constructed a personality scale to assess authoritarianism and reported after expensive interview that people securing high scores on the scale tended to have the family backgrounds predicted by the theory and also prejudiced towards others, particularly towards the members of a weaker section and minority group. Unfortunately, later researches have provided some difficulties in this direction because it has been shown that not all prejudiced persons share a family background of harsh, demanding parents. Apart from this, even people who score low on the authoritarian scale may be very prejudiced. Thus, the theory of authoritarian personality lacks consistency.

(iii) **Personality needs:** Some personality needs tend to support prejudice. One such need studied frequently is the need of tolerance for ambiguity. As we know, persons differ in their need for tolerance, that is, they differ in the extent to which they are disturbed by confusing or ambiguous situation. At one extreme, there may be persons who want pure clarity and everything in black and white, whereas at the other end, there may be persons who are least disturbed by ambiguous or vague situation, thereby showing a higher degree of tolerance for ambiguity. In general, the persons, who are more intolerant of ambiguity, are also likely to be more prejudiced (Adorno et al., 1950). In such persons, prejudice tend to serve such a need because it clarifies an ambiguous and vague situation. For example, a labourer, who has lost his job and find it difficult to get another, may think that the cause of his unemployment is the influx of many labourers from nearby city, where many organisations have shut down their business.

Similarly, need to achieve a supervisor status may be bolstered and supported by prejudice. Since status is a relative concept, to perceive ourselves as having superior status, we need people below us. Obviously, then, the psychological benefit of prejudice is a feeling of superiority. There are examples from day-to-day lives, where we might have taken secret satisfaction in others' failure or trouble—in school days, we often feel superiority and satisfaction when a classmate fails in the examination. Researches have shown that prejudice is often high among those who are low or slipping on socio-economic ladder and also among those whose positive self-image or self-esteem is threatened (Pettigrew et al., 1998; Thompson and Crocker, 1985). In another study, members of low status sororities were found to be more disparaging of other sororities than were the members of high status sororities (Crocker et al., 1987).

The need for security may be satisfied through the rejection of an out-group. Researches have shown that the conflict between an in-group and an out-group leads to the increased solidarity among the members of the in-group. Such conflict, no doubt, sharpens the boundaries between the groups, labelling each other as enemies and treating the out-group as not even human (Bar-Tal, 2003), but consolidates the identity of in-group (Sherif et al., 1961). Thus prejudice, discrimination and conflict with an out-group are likely to make the person feel more secure in his in-group membership.

(iv) **Threats to self-esteem:** Prejudice clearly develops when people's self-esteem gets threatened. Fein and Spencer (1997) conducted a study in which it was shown that when college students experienced threat to their self-esteem or to their own positive views, they, later on, tended to increase prejudice. Thus, prejudice can play an important role in protecting the person's self-concept. Sinclair and Kunda (1999) conducted an experiment in which white participants received either praise or criticism from a person whom they believed was either a black doctor or a white doctor. Results revealed that when criticisms seemingly came from black doctor, the negative prejudice about blacks were expressed as compared to when praise was received. When they believed that the person was a white doctor, the negative prejudice concerning blacks were not differentially activated. The experiment clearly showed that the threat in the form of criticism from an out-group member can directly encourage expression of prejudice.

2. Cognitive approach

As we know, cognitive processes play a vital role in the perception of other individuals. Such approach is concerned less with the objective reality of the situation and more with the prejudiced person's subjective understanding of the environment and people in it. The central idea of the cognitive approach is that the systematic cognitive biases naturally accompany the perception of others because we need to simplify the surrounding complex world. The cognitive approach, among others, emphasises the following factors:

(i) **Categorisation–In-group versus out-group:** Several studies have shown that the act of categorisation can group people into 'us' (as in-group) and 'them' (as out-group). Sharply contrasting feelings and beliefs are associated with the perception of 'us' (in-group) versus 'them' (out-group). In general, individuals in 'us' category are viewed in more favourable terms, while the persons in 'them' category are viewed more in negative terms. In-group members are seen as possessing positive traits, whereas out-group members are assumed to possess more undesirable traits (Lambert, 1995). Researches have shown that perceiving people as members of 'us' category and 'them' category has three important consequences—in-group favouritism effect, assumed similarity effect and out-group homogeneity effect.

In-group favouritism effect refers to the tendency to give more favourable and positive evaluations and greater rewards to the members of in-group than to the members of out-group (Tajfel et al., 1971). In other words, once people feel that they belong to a group, they tend to favour members of that group at the expense of members of the other groups. People generally evaluate in-group members favourably, reward them more, expect more favourable treatment from them and also find them more persuasive than the out-group members (Brewer and Brown, 1998). One important systematic bias that follows from in-group favouritism is what is called *group-serving bias*. In such bias, members of an in-group make favourable attributions (internal attribution) for the performance of the members of in-group and unfavourable attributions (external attribution) for the performance of the members of out-group.

Second consequence is *assumed similarity effect*, where the members of an in-group assume that the other in-group members share their attitudes and values, and therefore, are more similar to themselves than to the out-group members (Taylor, Peplau and Sears, 2006). In the study conducted by Allen and Wilder (1979), it was shown that even when the group members are arbitrarily or randomly assigned to a group, they tend to perceive the members of their own group as more similar to themselves than are the members of the other group. They randomly assigned some students to two groups on the basis of their artistic preference. They found that even regarding matters wholly unrelated to art, groups tended to perceive other in-group members more similar to them than were the out-group members.

The third consequence is known as *out-group homogeneity effect*, which refers to the perception that the members of out-group are more similar to each other than the members of in-group. In other words, the basic principle here is that they are all alike, whereas we are all diverse persons. Brauer (2001) conducted a study in which the stereotypes held by each of the four different groups of participants, namely, doctors, lawyers, waiters and hair dressers were tested about the other groups. The researcher asked the participants to give the location of the highest and the lowest group member on each trait. Results revealed that the ratings of highest and lowest were highly similar for the out-groups than for the in-groups in almost all cases. Results confirmed the claim of out-group homogeneity effect.

(ii) **Feeling superior to others–Social identity theories:** We have seen above that social categorisation into in-group and out-group is important and in-group favouritism is one of its major effects. Now, the question is—why does the mere act of categorising individuals into an in-group and an out-group produce in-group favouritism? In other words, how does social categorisation results in prejudice? To answer this question at the psychological level, Tajfel and Turner (1986) proposed social identity theory incorporating the following three basic assumptions:

(a) Persons categorise the social world into in-groups and out-groups.
(b) Persons derive a sense of self-esteem from their social identity as members of in-group.
(c) Persons' self-concept partly depends on how they evaluate in-group relative to other groups.

Social identity theory, thus, clearly suggests that the persons seek to feel positively about the in-group and part of their self-esteem depends on identifying with the social groups. Since people, who are identified as members of group, are most likely to express favouritism towards their own group and a bias against the members of out-group, valuing our own group has some obvious implication for prejudice. Researches have shown that an individual wants to maintain a balance between these opposing tendencies in order to be fair-minded and this may somewhat moderate our tendency to boost our own group and put other groups on unfavourable terms (Singh, Choo and Poh, 1998). Despite this tendency to maintain balance, the strong need to enhance our self-esteem wins out and we see other groups unfavourably. According to social identity theory, we are likely to have a high self-esteem if we perceive ourselves as belonging to a superior in-group, and on the other hand, we are likely to have a lower self-esteem if we perceive our in-group as an inferior one. Thus, social identity theory is a mixture of both cognitive and motivational approaches. It is cognitive because mere act of categorising in a group is enough to produce these effects and it is motivational because social identity fulfils self-esteem needs.

(iii) **Distinctiveness:** One of the other ways in which we perceive our world is in terms of distinctiveness. A man in otherwise female group or a female in otherwise men group, a black in otherwise white group or a white in otherwise black group is perceived as more prominent and influential and to have exaggerated good or bad qualities (Crocker and McGraw, 1984). In fact, when someone in the group is made salient or distinctive, we tend to perceive that person as causing whatever happens (Taylor and Fiske, 1978). The extra attention that we pay to the person considered distinctive or salient creates an illusion that he differs from others more than he really does. For example, if people regard you as a man of high talent or creativity, they would probably notice such things in your behaviour, which otherwise go unnoticed. Langer and Imber (1980) conducted a study in which some students were asked to watch a video of a man while reading. Students were led to think that he might be a cancer patient or a homosexual or a millionaire. Results revealed that when students were led to believe that he was a cancer patient, they perceived distinctive facial characteristics and bodily movements, and thus, perceived him to be much more different from the other people.

Researches have shown that how distinctive cases also fuel stereotypes (Rothbart et al., 1978). They asked students to watch 50 slides each showing a man's height. For one group of students, 10 of the men were slightly over 6 feet, that is, up to 6 feet 4 inches. For the other group of students, these 10 men were all well over 6 feet, that is, 6 feet 11 inches. Later on, they asked to report how many men were over 6 feet. Results revealed that those given slightly or moderately tall examples, recalled that 5% were above 6 feet. Those given extremely tall examples recalled 50% were above 6 feet. In a follow-up study, students read themselves the descriptions of the actions of 50 men. Out of these 50 men, 10 men had committed either violent crimes like rape or non-violent crime like forgery. Results showed that those shown the list with violent crimes actually overestimated the number of criminal behaviours. The attention-getting power of distinctive and extreme cases explain why the middle-class people so greatly exaggerate the dissimilarities between themselves and the people of lower class. In fact, the less we know about any group, the more we are influenced by a few distinctive cases (Quattrone and Jones, 1980).

(iv) **Attribution:** Attributional viewpoints for understanding prejudice emphasise the fact that we concentrate on how people tend to form understanding of the reasons behind the behaviour of other person or group. The viewpoints suggest that prejudiced people may systematically bias their attribution in such a way that favourable evaluation is done to the behaviours of in-group and unfavourable evaluation is done to the behaviours of out-group.

Pettigrew (1979) and Jemmott, Pettigrew and Johnson (1983) pointed out that prejudiced people are subjected to what is called *ultimate attribution error*, which is an extension of the fundamental attribution error. As we know, *fundamental attribution error* refers to the tendency of the perceivers to attribute behaviour of other to stable traits and dispositions and attribute their own behaviour as more affected by situational factors. The ultimate attribution error, on the other hand, suggests that a prejudiced person tends to attribute desirable behaviour of his in-group to stable and internal causes (that is, in terms of admirable traits) but attribute desirable behaviours by the members of out-group to external causes or transitory factors. It is called ultimate attribution error because it carries the self-serving bias.

Positive or admirable behaviours by the member of out-group are, in fact, dismissed because they become inconsistent with the negative view regarding the out-group. Pettigrew (1979), in fact, suggested four ways in which the prejudiced person can deal with this problem. First, such positive behaviour of the out-group may be viewed as an exceptional case. Second, such positive behaviour may be due to receiving some kind of special advantage, or simply, due to luck. Third, such act may be caused by situational factors outside their control. Fourth, such positive act may be due to high motivation to succeed and extraordinary effort done by the members of the out-group.

Pettigrew's attributional analysis has been supported by a number of studies. Taylor and Jaggi (1974) conducted one of the most important studies in this regard. They asked a group of Hindu office clerks in Southern India to describe the reasons of the behaviour of a person described in the given short passage. The passage described different types of persons in different situations such as a teacher rewarding or punishing a student, a shopkeeper being either generous or cheating, an individual helping or ignoring an injured or a householder sheltering or ignoring the person caught in rain. The subjects had to choose a reason for the behaviour that represented either an internal attribution or external attribution. Results revealed that when the actor was perceived to belong to his own group (Hindu group), the positive behaviour was attributed to the internal causes and very rarely to the external causes, whereas the negative behaviour was tended to be perceived as due to the external causes. In contrast, when the actor was perceived to be a disliked Muslim group, the positive behaviour was attributed to the external causes and negative behaviour to the internal causes. Results of the experiment provided support to Pettigrew's attributional analysis and further suggested that no matter how exemplary the actions of the out-group member may be, the prejudiced person does not alter his underlying negative views of the out-group to which the member belongs. Thus, ultimate attribution error places the target of prejudice in a clear no-win situation from where any escape appears to be impossible. Pettigrew also said that the ultimate attribution error will be maximum when there is long history of intense conflict and highly negative stereotypes between in-group and out-group.

3. *Historical and socio-cultural approach*

Historical approach to prejudice assumes that various types of intergroup conflicts remain embedded in a long history of deteriorating relations, economic conflict and memories of past injustice and atrocities. An example of historical approach can be seen in case of prejudice against women. Certain occupations can be historically viewed as more appropriate for men than women. For instance, truck driving is historically considered as a masculine profession probably because it needs a lot of physical efforts in driving. However, with the advancement of new technologies such as power steering, power brake, etc., the rationale for discouraging a female to start truck driving no longer holds the truth. Yet today, we have rarely seen a woman doing the job of truck driver partly due to the historical factors.

In India, socio-economically advantaged class often becomes the target of prejudice by socio-economically disadvantaged class. The atrocities and injustice done by the people of advantaged classes towards the people, especially women, of the disadvantaged class since long time back provide one source of negative prejudice towards the people of advantaged class. When the people of disadvantaged class come to know about the history of atrocities, crimes and justice to their ancestral relatives, they become prejudiced against these people. In America, the historical factors contributing to the development of prejudice towards black Americans are its history of slavery, employment discrimination and social and education segregation, which taken together, have produced considerable economic benefits to white Americans (Elkins, 1968).

Historical approach, however, has some limitations and is not able to answer the fundamental questions like why some persons in the advantaged and dominant group become prejudiced, while others do not exhibit such prejudice; why some people of disadvantaged or minorities become the victim of prejudice, while some other prosper and are treated with equal regards.

Socio-cultural approach emphasises the total social context in which prejudice originates and is maintained. Here, sociologists and anthropologists have given emphasis upon several socio-cultural factors that produce prejudice in society. Such important factors are discussed below:

(i) **Social inequalities:** Social inequalities breed prejudice, which justifies the economic and social superiority of those who have wealth and power. Common experience shows that a master views his servant as irresponsible, lazy and lacking interest and ambition—all these justifying his negative prejudice. Researches have shown that even temporary changes in status can affect prejudice. Richeson and Ambady (2003) conducted an experiment in which some white students were led to believe that they were interacting through computer with either a black or white partner as partner's subordinate or supervisor. Results revealed that when the students interacted with a supposed black partner, they were found to display automatic prejudice if they thought that they were acting as supervisor.

Researchers have shown that those people, who are high in social dominance orientation, embrace prejudice and also support political position that justifies dominance. *Social dominance orientation* refers to motivation to make one's own group dominant over the other groups. In fact, such people tend to support those policies of the government, which provide welfare measures for well-off and oppose policies that support downtrodden.

(ii) **Socialisation:** Prejudice is learnt through socialisation—a process of social learning. Prejudice can be learnt inside or outside the home. For example, children may simply imitate the prejudice of adults and friends. Parents, who show prejudice against certain caste or class, readily enforce their children to acquire the same. Children of such parents usually show similar caste prejudice. Two popular complementary studies of Hindu and Muslim children, having prejudiced and unprejudiced parents, were compared. It was found that both Hindu (Rai, 1981) and Muslim (Khan, 1981) children having prejudiced parents showed more prejudice than the children having unprejudiced parents. Clearly, children acquire these prejudice from their parents by the process of socialisation. Hassan (1983), however, reported that there seemed to be no differential impact of father's and mother's prejudice on male child, but female child was found to be influenced more by the prejudice of her mother. Several other Indian psychologists have conducted studies on the development of caste prejudice in children. For example, Singh et al. (1960) conducted a study on caste prejudice in Agra and the neighbouring villages. The sample consisted of children of both sexes belonging to high and low caste groups from rural and urban areas. It was found that there took place earlier and faster development of caste prejudice in the upper caste, rural, male children as compared to lower caste, urban, female children. Prasad (1976) studied caste prejudice in Bihari children with the help of 270 upper caste and 187 backward and schedule caste school students in Patna. The age range was from 5 years to 15 years. The results of the study showed higher caste awareness among low caste children as compared to high caste children. There was no rural-urban difference in caste awareness. Vyas (1973) also studied origins of prejudice in children on a sample of 700 school students in Tamil Nadu. He concluded that prejudice increases with the advancement of age; religions, caste and class prejudice begin by the age of 3, although linguistic prejudice emerges later. He also concluded that the children of high-prejudiced parents demonstrated greater prejudice than the children of low-prejudiced parents. Likewise, religious identity and prejudice were found to be interrelated, with no sex differences in their development (Khan, 1978, 1979).

Researches done in the United States have also shown that conventional prejudices are often learnt very early in life. For example, most urban white children, by the age of 4 or 5, differentiate between white and black and are also aware of prevailing norms about race and exhibit some signs of racial prejudice by the age of 5. The experiences of these early years among children are crucial because prejudice towards highly salient groups does not change much later in an individual's life (Sears and Levy, 2003).

(iii) **Religion:** Religion also plays an important role in the development of prejudice. American researches regarding the impact of Christianity, North America's dominant religion, show that Church members express more racial prejudice than the non-members, and those possessing traditional or fundamentalist Christian beliefs tend to express more prejudice than those possessing less traditional beliefs (Batson et al., 1993; Woodberry and Smith, 1998). In India, religion has still a greater say. Hindus, Muslims, Christians and Sikhs constitute the main religious groups in India. Enayatullah (1981, 1984) examined the relationship of religious affiliation with prejudice and attitudes in Hindu, Muslim and Christian college students. He selected 140 subjects from each of the three religious groups and each religious group included both rural and urban categories. Hindu and Muslim included both low and high castes and Christian included both Protestants and Catholics. Results revealed that on the prejudice scale (having four dimensions such as religious prejudice, caste prejudice, class prejudice and sex prejudice) developed by Singh (1980), Muslim ranked highest, followed by Christians and then Hindus. Hindus, Christians and Muslims tended to exhibit modern attitudes towards religion, caste and social customs. In all three groups, prejudice was positively correlated with anxiety, authoritarianism, rigidity and belief incongruence, whereas it was negatively correlated with attitudinal modernity. In another study conducted by Hassan (1981), it was found that Muslims were more prejudiced than Hindus and also had a higher degree of religiosity and casteism. He also reported a significantly negative correlation between prejudice and religious information.

(iv) **Conformity to the norm of prejudice:** If the prejudice and discrimination against an out-group is well-established in society, the accompanying cognition and feeling regarding the out-group acquires a normative quality. They are shared by the members of the in-group and the members expect each other to hold such attitudes. Pettigrew (1958) provided a strong evidence that social norms and conformity towards them are important factors in prejudice. He studied prejudice against the Negroes in the southern United States and in the Union of South Africa; both regions are characterised by strong prejudice against the Negroes. The study clearly demonstrated that persons who were most likely to conform to the norms of their society were showing prejudice in higher degree. The study confirmed a direct association between conformity and prejudice.

The factors underlying conformity to the norms of prejudice are explained in terms of reward-cost outcomes ensuing from conformity or non-conformity. If prejudice and discrimination against the out-group is the norm, then the overt expression of both prejudice and discrimination is likely to elicit approval from members (Hyman and Sheatslay, 1954). Conversely, expression of friendly and cooperative attitude towards the members of the out-group violates the norm of prejudice and may prove costly in terms of bringing forth disapproval and other kinds of punishment from other in-group members.

(v) **Miscellaneous factors:** Besides the above factors, socio-cultural approaches also include miscellaneous factors like increasing urbanisation, increasing population density, etc., which tend to increase prejudice towards the members of the out-group. Take example of metro cities, where we find the evidences for increasing urbanisation and high population density. Such cities represent environments which can be considered less than an ideal one in many respects. They are perceived as dirty, noisy, unsafe and impersonal. Following sociological analysis, people generally blame the difficulties of urban life for the presence of a group particularly having downtrodden people who come in cities to earn their livelihood.

One general difficulty with socio-cultural approach, as with historical approach also, is that it fails to explain why certain groups are more prejudiced and discriminated than the others, especially when all out-groups are disliked to more or less same degree. Apart from this, prejudice originates even when there is no obvious socio-cultural factors to be identified.

4. Situational approach

The situational approach emphasises all those factors which lie in person's immediate environment and become instrumental in producing prejudice. In a person's immediate environment, peers, parents, neighbour, etc. play significant role. Prejudice is developed through the process of direct reinforcement and vicarious learning. By observing the behaviour of his parents, neighbours and peers, a person develops a similar attitude. That is the reason why there is much similarity between the prejudice of parents and their children. If the parents are negatively prejudiced towards X, children or the members of the family are also likely to develop similar negative prejudice towards the target. In situational approach, social psychologists have also emphasised demographic characteristics as one means to understand prejudice. Researches have shown that three demographic features are systematically related to the origin of the prejudice—geographical region, age and educational level. In South India, people are mere prejudiced against Hindi-speaking people. We frequently hear that MNS people in Maharashtra have beaten people of Bihar and U.P., providing evidence for prejudice and discrimination. Likewise, those who are not much educated, are in general, much prejudiced and older people are more prejudiced than younger people.

The limitation of situational approach is that its explanatory power is limited. The approach does not provide an underlying explanation for acquisition and maintenance of prejudice.

REDUCTION OF PREJUDICE AND DISCRIMINATION

Social psychologists have shown interest in reducing the prejudice and its effect. They have pointed out some means through which prejudice and its effects can be reduced. Such important means are discussed below:

1. Contact–Interacting directly with the target of prejudice: Contact between the prejudiced person and the target person or group has been found to reduce prejudice. First, suggested by Allport (1954), the contact hypothesis puts forward that intergroup contact and cross-group friendship can reduce prejudice if it is planned in an appropriate way. In fact, positive contact, when it reflects increased cooperation and interdependence between groups, can change norms, and thereby, prejudice may be reduced (Van Dick et al., 2004). Contact hypothesis as a means of reducing prejudice is effective, provided the following conditions are met:

(i) Contact becomes effective when there is equal status within a setting for people belonging to both prejudiced person and the target group or person (Norvell and Worchel, 1981). When an officer belonging to Brahmin caste is asked to live in the same double-bed room with a Dalit clerk, the prejudice of the officer is less likely to be reduced. But when the same officer is asked to share the room with equal status Dalit officer, his prejudice, due to equal status is likely to be reduced to a greater extent.

(ii) There must be intimacy and closeness between the members of the two groups, that is, the prejudiced group and the target group. Researches have shown that greater intimacy between the two groups may lead to greater reduction in prejudice. Superficial contact becomes ineffective in reducing prejudice and may even enhance intergroup hostility. Brief, impersonal or occasional contact is not likely to be much helpful (Brewer and Brown, 1998). On the other hand, when there is intimate contact, it helps in individualising the disliked group member, which automatically means that he or she is perceived less in terms of stereotype and more in terms of an individual (Blake and Mouton, 1979).

(iii) Contact has been most effective when two people cooperate in mutually interdependent activity, whose success depends on their joint active contributions. In other words, cooperative interdependence with common goals is an important element in contact hypothesis. The *jigsaw classroom* is one of the examples of such contact requiring cooperative interdependence. It is an educational technique in which each individual is given only part of the information needed to solve a problem, causing other individuals to be forced to work together to find the solution. In doing so, interaction among diverse individuals is increased, making it likely that these individuals will come to perceive each other as partners and form a friendly relationship, rather than labelling others as members of the out-group. The technique works well at the college level as well as at the school level (Lord, 2001).

(iv) Some institutional and societal support for the contact is also needed. If the authority supports the likely contact between the prejudiced group and the target group, the members of the prejudiced group feel encouraged for their efforts and this is likely to reduce their bias and negative attitude towards the members of the target group.

These four conditions and their applications in reducing prejudice are shown in Figure 8.1.

Some experiments have provided support for the validity of contact hypothesis. Cook (1969) conducted a study in which prejudiced white women played a simulation game for a month. In this game, other participants such as white and black confederates were also involved. For playing game, the participants had to cooperate with each other and there was also a fairly good deal of intimate contact in which all participants of more or less equal status were involved. During the breaks, subjects were also holding conversations with each other to enhance intimacy. Results revealed a positive change on the part of about 40% of participants. Clore et al. (1978) also conducted a study in which a situation was provided for intimate, equal status contact over one week period. In fact, interracial attitude and behaviour between each child and one white and one black counsellor during sessions of summer camp had been studied. Results revealed that as a result of intimate contact, interracial attitude had changed a lot.

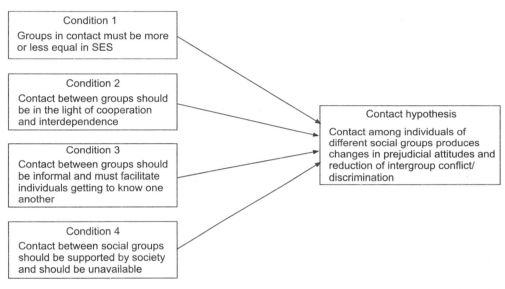

Figure 8.1 Four conditions for making contact between social groups for reducing prejudice and discrimination.

2. Social influence: Stereotypes which are believed to be shared by the members of in-group play an important role in expression of prejudice. When our stereotypic beliefs are endorsed by the members of our in-group, such beliefs become more predictive of prejudice. On the other hand, when we are told that the members of our own group (in-group) have favourable attitude towards the out-group which is the target of prejudice, it is expected that our prejudice may be weakened or reduced (Pettigrew, 1997). It means the social influence created by the views of other members of the in-group has an impact upon the reduction of prejudice. An experimental evidence to this effect has been provided by Stangor, Sechrist and Jost (2001). In this study, the white students were first asked to estimate the percentage of African-Americans (blacks) possessing each of the nineteen stereotypical traits, which included both positive and negative traits. After this, students were told that the other students in the university disagreed with their ratings. In favourable feedback condition, the subjects were told that the other students held more favourable view of African-American, that is, these other students estimated a higher percentage of positive traits and a lower percentage of negative traits in comparison to their ratings. In unfavourable feedback condition, the subjects were told that the other students had less favourable views of African-American than they did, that is, these other students had estimated a higher percentage of negative traits and a lower percentage of positive traits. After receiving this information, the subjects were again allowed to estimate the percentage of African-Americans possessing positive or negative traits. Results revealed that the endorsement of negative stereotypes increased in the unfavourable feedback condition, whereas the endorsement of such stereotypes markedly decreased in the favourable feedback condition. The study clearly supported that the racial prejudice of the white participants was indeed affected by social influence.

3. Recategorisation: *Recategorisation* means shifting and redefining the boundaries between the in-group and the out-group. As a consequence of such recategorisation, the individuals formerly viewed as out-group members may now be perceived as the in-group members. Consequently, the negative prejudice towards the then out-group members may be reduced. Such reduction in prejudice has been explained with the *common in-group identity model* (Dovidio, Gaertner and Validzic, 1998). The model states that the individuals belonging to different social groups come to view themselves as members of a single social entity. Consequently, they develop favourable attitudes towards each other. These favourable attitudes, in turn, enhance positive contacts among the members, and thus, intergroup bias and prejudice are gradually reduced. Now, the basic question that arises here is— how can we induce people of the different social groups to perceive each other as members of a single group? The answer is that when they are allowed to work together in a cooperative spirit towards a shared goal, they come to perceive themselves as belonging to a single entity. (Gaertner et al., 1994). As a consequence, their intergroup prejudice and bias are reduced to a greater extent. Muslims and Hindus may be prejudiced against each other but when they are said that they belong to the same state and have to show their worth by fighting against the people of other state, they may start working in a cooperative spirit, showing evidence of reduction of prejudice against each other. Such things happen because recategorisation is induced.

4. Guilt as prejudice reduction technique: Those persons, who have egalitarian self-image, are generally found to suppress their prejudice. Such persons consider themselves to have given equal treatment to all. Therefore, being faced with the instances of behaving in a prejudiced way and doing discrimination of any sort towards any person or group is likely to produce a feeling of guilt in them. Prejudice will be suppressed to the extent the guilt is induced. Some researches are available to show that the individuals may feel collective guilt if the group, to which they belong, has done some harm to the other group (Branscombe, 2004). In the studies conducted by Powell, Branscombe and Schmitt (2005), they found that the feeling of collective guilt can reduce racial prejudice. In this study, the college white students (participants) were asked to think about the black-white inequality prevalent in the United States. Subsequently, in one condition, participants were asked to pen down all the advantages received because of being white. In another condition, they were asked to pen down all the disadvantages received by blacks because of being black. Such framing simply showed how racial inequality was practiced. Results were in the expected direction. White advantage framing condition produced significantly more collective guilt than did black disadvantage framing condition. Higher the degree of such collective guilt, lower was their racial prejudice. The result of the study clearly suggests that a little collective guilt has the advantage of lowering the racism or prejudice towards the target race.

5. Saying 'no' to stereotypes: Saying 'no' to the stereotype is also one of the promising techniques for reducing prejudice. As we know, stereotypic thinking generates prejudice. When one repeatedly says 'no' to the existing stereotype towards the out-group, it is very likely that it will help in combatting prejudice. Saying repeatedly and frequently in one's mind that women are not dependent and weak, one may gradually reduce one's prejudice against women being dependent and weak one. Kawakami et al. (2000) proved this on the basis of their research. In their study, they first assessed the participants' stereotypic associations. Subsequently, the researchers divided the participants into two groups. One group was placed under what was called *stereotype maintaining condition*, where the participants were instructed to say 'yes' when they saw a photograph of white person and a white stereotype word such as being ambitious, self-confident, etc. or a photograph of a black person and black person stereotype such as poor, dependent, etc. They were also instructed to respond to 'no' when pairings of photograph and words showing stereotype were not consistent, that is, they were required to tell 'no' when the photograph was that of a white person and stereotype words were closely associated with a black person or vice versa. The other group was placed under what was called *stereotype negation condition*, where the participants were instructed to tell 'no' when they were presented with a photo of white person and a word consistent with the stereotype of white person or a photo of black person and a word consistent with the stereotype of black person. On the other hand, they were instructed to respond 'yes' to the photo-word pairings which were inconsistent. In other words, here, the participants practiced negating their implicit racial stereotypes. The practice in both groups continued for several hundred trials. Results showed that prior to negation training, the participants categorised white faces more readily than black faces after seeing white stereotype words but black faces more readily after seeing black stereotype words. After getting the negation training by the participants, these stereotypes were considerably weakened. Thus, it was clear that the stereotypes can be reduced through the process of repeatedly saying 'no' to them.

6. Formation of superordinate goals: Formation of superordinate goals as one means of reducing prejudice and intergroup conflict has been emphasised by Sherif (1966). He conducted a series of experiments in which groups of 11–12-year old boys attending summer school camp in America took part. The field experiments lasted three weeks and were characterised by three stages, each lasting for one week. Stages 1 and 2 were concerned with the development of intergroup conflict between the two groups. Stage 3 dealt with reduction of intergroup conflict and prejudice. Here, we shall concentrate on the third stage.

In the third stage, Sherif made an attempt to reduce the intergroup conflict and prejudice by setting superordinate goals before them. *Superordinate goals* are the goals which could only be achieved by the cooperative act of groups involved. In fact, Sherif stage-managed superordinate goals in the summer camps by causing disruption of water supply and breakdown of the camp lorry (it was not known to the boys in the groups). Results revealed that such superordinate goals increased the cooperation and friendly act among the boys and reduced the intergroup conflict and prejudice. However, Sherif noted that superordinate goals, in order to be effective, must meet the following conditions:

(i) Just setting one superordinate goal was not effective because each group, soon after completing one superordinate task, returned to its hostile way. Therefore, Sherif suggested that the persons must be engaged in a series of superordinate goals.
(ii) Groups must regard the task of superordinate goal as worthwhile.
(iii) There must be equitable participation and contribution from both the groups. Reduction of prejudice is not likely to occur when one group is of higher status or in command and the other group is of lower status or subservient.

Thus, we find that prejudice can be reduced if we follow certain practice suggested above.

MEASUREMENT OF PREJUDICE

The direct way to assess prejudice world is to measure attitudes. However, attitudes towards the target of prejudice are sometimes tricky to tap because there is high degree of social desirability in professing unprejudiced attitudes. Even when the people, who hold prejudice towards the target group, may not be willing to express it because of fear of sanction against them. In view of this, social psychologists have devised some specific methods (mentioned below) for assessing prejudice.

1. **Non-verbal behaviour as one measure of prejudice:** One of the most important and unobtrusive measures of prejudice is to observe carefully the non-verbal behaviour of the prejudiced person. Since verbal behaviour can easily be changed as censored, the non-verbal behaviour is difficult to be controlled or censored. Therefore, it becomes a good measure of prejudice. Feldman and Donohoe (1978) conducted a study in which use of non-verbal behaviour in measuring prejudice was successfully demonstrated. In this study, white subjects, who were either highly prejudiced or little prejudiced, were placed in such a situation in which they were to do the job of teachers to teach third-grade students. In reality, the students were no one but the confederates who were either black or white. The confederates were well-versed and trained persons on the test to be administered by the subject and the subject was encouraged to praise correct responses by saying 'Nice, that's extremely good'. While the subjects were praising these seemingly successful subjects, videotape recordings of their face and shoulders were secretly done. Later, white observers rated these recordings to the degree to which each subject appeared pleased with the student. Results revealed that there were obvious differences in non-verbal behaviour as expressed by their face and shoulders of highly and little prejudiced subjects according to the race of their student. Highly prejudiced subjects acted favourably and more positively at a non-verbal level to the white students in comparison to the black students, although all students had performed equally well on the designed test. The study clearly showed that non-verbal behaviour of the persons can be easily used to infer about the prejudice towards the target person or people with whom they are interacting.

2. **Explicit and obvious behaviours as measures of prejudice:** Apart from non-verbal behaviours, certain explicit and obvious behaviours of the prejudiced persons can also be good indicators of prejudice. For example, if a person helps his neighbour frequently and without any hope of return, he will be said to show a positive prejudice towards his neighbour. On the other hand, if he frequently shows aggressive behaviour towards his neighbour, he will be perceived to exhibit a negative prejudice towards his neighbour. Donnerstein and Donnerstein (1976) as well as Crossby, Bromby and Saxe (1980) showed that differential helping and aggressive behaviours towards whites and blacks provided clear evidence of prejudice of the people who were carrying the behaviours.

Thus, prejudice can be assessed through non-verbal behaviours as well as through some explicit obvious behaviours.

SUMMARY AND REVIEW

- There are three interrelated but distinguished components of group antagonism—stereotype, prejudice and discrimination. Stereotype is cognitive, that is, beliefs about the typical characteristics of group members. In fact, stereotypes are gross generalisation that are acquired through misinformation and that

- ignore individual differences and are resistant even in the light of new evidences provided. Stereotypes can be either positive or negative as well as they can be accurate or inaccurate.
- Persons do form stereotypes because they serve many functions. Stereotypes conserve mental effort and improve efficiency; they help us in feeling positive about our own group identity in comparison to other social groups; they are formed to justify inequalities, and finally, they are also formed through social communication.
- Stereotypes, once activated, can influence our judgements. They can be activated automatically. In fact, sometimes, stereotypes become so well-learned and so often used that their activation becomes automatic.
- Stereotypes directly affect our judgements and actions towards other people. They tend to have greater effects when judgements are to be made under time pressure. When emotions are intense, stereotypes can still have greater effect upon judgement. Researches have also revealed that stereotypes tend to have greater effect upon judgements when people hold powerful position.
- Stereotypes may change if the nature of intergroup relationship between the two groups changes. However, there are some barriers to stereotype change. Generally, stereotypes do change as a result of inconsistent information. But when people tend to explain away the inconsistent information, stereotypes fail to change. Apart from this, people tend to create a new category for exceptions to rule and also tend to see the behaviour of unusual group members as being irrelevant to the stereotype. All these are proved to be effective barriers to stereotype change.
- *Gender stereotypes* are defined as stereotypes or beliefs concerning traits possessed by males and females. Such traits include both positive and negative traits. For example, on positive side, female gender stereotypes are that they are warm, affectionate, nurturant and considerate. On the negative side, female gender stereotypes are that they are dependent, weak and emotional. Likewise, males are also assumed to have both positive and negative traits. Despite the fact that females are generally viewed as low on competence as compared to male, a few women have managed to reach the position of higher status. The success of such token high status women is taken as an evidence that gender no longer matters and discrimination is no longer an appropriate explanation for women's lack of success. However, gender stereotypes are not necessarily accurate because they are said to be exaggeration in the sense that they do not take into consideration any overlap between men and women. Reality is that not all men are independent and not all women are emotional.
- One of the basic questions regarding stereotype is—does no difference in evaluations or ratings mean absence of stereotypic thinking? Although the common sense would answer this question in terms of 'yes', but on the basis of the experimental evidences, social psychologists have been able to demonstrate that even when ratings or evaluations for the two groups are similar, stereotypes do continue to affect our behaviour. The idea of shifting standards clearly indicate that identical evaluation ratings do not translate into the same behavioural expectations nor do the fact that stereotypes are not operating in such a situation.
- Stereotypes associated with single and married person have also been investigated. The common stereotypic traits associated with the single persons are being lonely, insecure, self-centred, unhappy, independent and immature, whereas the common stereotypic traits associated with married persons are being loving, happy, stable, matured, honest, giving, kind, etc. Researches done by Depaulo and Morris, however, showed that single people are themselves not aware of such discrimination.
- Prejudice and discrimination are another elements of group antagonism. *Prejudice* is the positive or negative evaluation of a group or single individual, mainly based on the membership of the group. *Discrimination* is defined as the behavioural manifestation of prejudice. In fact, it is differential treatment to the persons considered to belong to a particular group.
- Prejudice and discrimination often exist and are shown through racism, sexism and tokenism. *Racism* is the person's prejudicial attitudes and discrimination towards people of a given race or institutional

practices that discriminate even when there is no prejudicial intent. *Sexism* is prejudice based on gender. Disliking a nurse because he is a male or a woman because she is a truck driver are the examples of sexism. Sexism exists commonly in two forms—hostile sexism and benevolent sexism. *Hostile sexism* is the feeling of hostility towards women. It is negative attitude towards women, especially towards those women who challenge traditional female job. *Benevolent sexism*, by contrast, reveals positive feelings towards women, including a prosocial orientation towards women such as a desire to help women. Men generally show hostile sexism more strongly than women, but this difference is often reversed with respect to benevolent sexism. In *tokenism*, positive actions are taken by the individuals towards the member of a group to whom they are prejudiced.

- Social psychologists have developed various approaches to explain the origin, development and maintenance of prejudice and discrimination. Following Allport, there are four such theories—psychodynamic approach, cognitive approach, situational approach, and historical and socio-cultural approach.
- Psychodynamic approach, broadly known as *motivational approach*, emphasises that motivational deficit in the individual level of psychological functioning can produce prejudice. In other words, internal dynamics of personality can lead to prejudice. Frustration and aggression, authoritarian personality, personality needs and threats to self-esteem are some of the common psychodynamic factors responsible for origin and development of prejudice.
- Cognitive approach to prejudice emphasises categorisation, that is, in-groups versus out-groups, social identity theory, that is, feeling superior to others, distinctiveness and attribution for explaining the origin and development of prejudice.
- Historical approach to prejudice assumed that various types of intergroup conflicts and memories of past injustice and atrocities induce prejudice. Socio-cultural approach emphasises the total social context in which prejudice originates and is maintained. Here, the factors like social inequalities, socialisation, religion, conformity to the norm of the prejudice and other miscellaneous factors like increasing urbanisation, increasing population density, etc. can cause prejudice.
- Situational approach emphasises all those factors which lie in person's immediate environment and become instrumental in producing prejudice. In a person's immediate environment, peers, parents, neighbours, etc. play a significant role and are responsible for the origin and development of prejudice. Prejudice is developed through the process of direct reinforcement and vicarious learning. Situational approach also emphasises demographic characteristics as one of the means to understand prejudice.
- Prejudice and discrimination can be reduced. Social psychologists have outlined different plans for reducing prejudice and discrimination. Contact between prejudiced person and the target person, social influence, recategorisation, feeling of collective guilt, saying 'no' to stereotypes, and formation of superordinate goals, etc. are some of the means through which prejudice and discrimination can be reduced.
- Prejudice can be assessed through the observation of non-verbal behaviour as well as through more explicit and direct behaviour of the prejudiced persons.

Review Questions

1. Define stereotype. Discuss its characteristics.
2. Point out the major contents of stereotypes.
3. Citing experimental evidences, explain why people form and use stereotypes.
4. How do stereotypes get activated? Provide experimental evidences in favour of your answer.
5. Discuss the important impacts of stereotypes upon judgements and actions.
6. Can stereotypes be changed? Discuss important barriers to stereotype change.

7. Explain the concept of gender stereotype. How are gender stereotypes activated?
8. Does no difference in evaluations or ratings mean absence of stereotypic thinking?
9. Make a comparative study of stereotypes associated with single and married person. Cite experimental evidences.
10. Make distinction between stereotype, prejudice and discrimination. Discuss the different forms of prejudice and discrimination.
11. How does psychoanalytic approach explain the origin, development and maintenance of prejudice? Cite also experimental evidences.
12. Discuss the role of cognitive factors in explaining origin, development and maintenance of prejudice.
13. Explain the role of various socio-cultural factors in origin, development and maintenance of prejudice.
14. Outline a plan for reduction of prejudice and discrimination.
15. Write short notes on the following:
    (i) Measurement of prejudice
    (ii) Collective guilt as one means of prejudice reduction
    (iii) Recategorisation
    (iv) Gender stereotype
    (v) Sexism and tokenism

9
BEHAVIOURS IN GROUP

Learning Objectives

- Meaning and Nature of Social Group
- Group: Some Basic Features and Aspects
- Why Do People Join A Group? Benefits and Costs of Joining
- Types of Groups
- Group Development
- Effects of Presence of Others: Social Facilitation and Social Inhibition
- Social Loafing
- Effects of Being in Crowd: Deindividuation
- Group Decision-making
- Group Polarisation: Risky Shift Beyond Risk Caution Dimension
- Groupthink: Does Group Hinder or Assist Group Decision?
- Biased Use of Information in Groups
- Failure to Share Unique Information from Some Members
- Ways of Improving Group Decisions
- Guidelines for Effective Decision-making
- Group Interaction: Cooperation versus Competition
- Communication Network in Group

Key Terms

Cognitive conflict
Collective effort model
Collectivistic culture
Common knowledge effect
Common-bond group
Common-identity group
Deindividuation
Depolarisation
Devil's advocate
Distraction conflict model
Dominant response
Entitativity
Evaluation apprehension
Group development

Groupthink
Illusion of invulnerability
Illusion of unanimity confirmation bias
Individualistic culture
Normative or social comparison perspective
Persuasive-informative perspective
Primary group
Prisoner's dilemma
Risky shift effect
Schism
Secondary group

Self-categorisation theory
Self-enhancement
Self-transcendence
Social comparison
Social contagion
Social decision schemes
Social inhibition
Social loafing
Social norms
Social roles
Social status
Special interest group
Trucking game

This chapter focuses on social group. Almost at every turn, we are involved in the group. Obviously, there are some reasons for joining a group. A person gets some benefits after joining a group. But sometimes, he has to pay also for joining the group. There are different types of group and each influence us in its own way. Social psychologists have shown that mere presence of others affects our behaviour. In the present chapter, such effect is examined in terms of social facilitation, social loafing and social inhibition. Besides, we shall also discuss some of the effective guidelines for improving group decision. Finally, the basic processes of interaction in groups such as competition versus cooperation are also discussed.

MEANING AND NATURE OF SOCIAL GROUP

The term *social group* or simply *group* is used to characterise a different variety of circumstances. Whenever we see that two or more persons have gathered together, the gathering is called *group*. But this is not the precise use of the term *group* and it may lead to confusion.

To avoid confusion, social psychologists and sociologists have taken pains to define this term. In general, these scientists prefer the term *group* for the people, who are interdependent and have at least the potential for mutual interaction. In other words, a *group* is a collection of two or more persons, who are perceived to be bonded together in coherent unit to some extent (Dasgupta, Banaji and Abelson, 1997). Four specific criteria have been delineated for defining what makes a group (Hare, 1976; Feldman, 1985). These are discussed below:

1. Interaction among members of the groups: The members of an aggregate of people, in order to be called *group*, must be able to make interaction with each other. The interaction need not be physical and face-to-face interaction. Even verbal or written interactions are possible. Group dynamics expert, Shaw (1981) defined group in this sense and said that group consists of two or more people, who interact and influence each other. According to Shaw's viewpoints, students working individually in computer laboratory would not be a group. Although physically together, they are more a collection of persons rather than an interacting group.

2. Perception of belonging together: Another criterion is that people must feel that they belong together. Individuals must view themselves as the members of the group. Turner (1978) rightly said that groups perceive themselves as 'us' in contrast to 'them'. Social psychologists have called this property *entitativity*, which is defined as the extent to which the group is perceived as being a coherent unit (Campbell, 1958). In fact, entitativity varies to a greater extent, ranging from mere collections of people on a particular place at a particular time having little or no feeling of being bonded together to highly intimate groups such as family and friendship groups, where we find a maximum feeling of being bonded together. Such group is called *common-bond group*, which involves both face-to-face interaction among members as well as higher degree of entitativity, that is, the feeling of being bonded together against the common-identity group, whose members are linked through category as a whole with a face-to-face interaction often being entirely absent. Our university, linguistic and gender groups are the examples of common-identity group in which we might not be knowing personally all or even most of the members.

Research have further shown that the size of the group does not matter for entitativity because some small and some large groups tend to exhibit higher degree of entitativity. In fact, some behavioural features like sharing of resources available, reciprocating favours among the members of the group, respecting the group authorities and showing strong adherence to group norms tend to enhance entitativity in the group (Lickel et al., 2006). An assemblage of people waiting at a bus stoppage to board the bus cannot be called group because people waiting would not probably perceive themselves as being associated with one another. On the dimension of entitativity, they are very low.

3. Shared goals and norms: Another criterion is that the persons must share at least one common goal (Shaw, 1976). This automatically suggests that groups are formed to attain goals. One of the major reasons that people belong to groups is to achieve some goal, whose attainment is facilitated by the membership of the group. A related characteristic of the group, especially the formal group, is the existence of shared norms. *Norms* are the rules that govern specific behaviours of the members of the group. In other words, norms refer to the rules of behaviour that are held by the members of the group regarding what is or is not the appropriate behaviour. According to Steiner (1972), norms specify what must or must not be done when. Every member has to respect the norms of the group.

4. Fate interdependence: Another basic criterion regarding the characteristics of the group is the fact that the fate of the members of the group is interdependent. Things or events that affect one group member can also affect the other members of the group, and not only that, it can also affect the ability of the group to meet the goals for which the group has been formed. Thus, the fate of each member in the group is affected by the group's outcomes as a whole and the behaviour of the individuals within the group affects the success of group itself. For example, if a cricket team wins, all members share in the glory. On the other hand, if the team loses, it becomes a loss for the group as a whole. The poor performance of any one member of team may be instrumental in losing the game, and therefore, the fate of that member would affect the fate of other members of the team.

There are varieties of social groupings or categories, which do not meet the criteria for being called group. Crowd is constituted when people are in physical proximity to a common situation or stimulus. This is not a group. People do not interact with each other. All people listening to the speech of the leader are part of the same audience. They also do not interact with each other, and hence, do not qualify to be called group.

GROUP: SOME BASIC FEATURES AND ASPECTS

Before discussing how group affects our behaviour or how our behaviour is affected when we perform in group, it is essential to describe some fundamental aspects of the group and its features. Important aspects are group structure and group cohesiveness, which are discussed below:

1. Group structure

When people interact together in group, they no longer remain entirely undifferentiated. In fact, they develop a defined pattern of behaviour, divide tasks to be done and adopt different roles accordingly. These patterns are called *social structure* of the group (Levine and Moreland, 1998). There are three important elements of the social structure—social roles, social status and social norms. These elements are explained as below:

  (i) ***Social roles:*** In group, different persons perform different tasks and are expected to do different things. In brief, they play different roles. Thus, *roles* are defined as obligations of and expectations for an individual in a particular position (Goffman, 1961). In other words, roles refer to a set of behaviours that the persons with specific positions within the group are expected to perform. Roles are considered normative in the sense that people occupying specific positions are expected to conform to a set of norms associated with the role. Social psychologists have made a tripartite distinction between perceived role, expected role and enacted role (Shaw, 1981). The *perceived role* is defined as the behaviour which the occupant thinks he or she should perform; the *enacted role* is the actual behaviour engaged by the person occupying the role and the *expected role* is the behaviour considered appropriate by others in the group. When these three roles are in accord, there will be little conflict between the occupant of the role and the other members of the group. However, if disparity between any two or all three roles exist, group conflict is likely to occur. If the perceived role and/or enacted role differs greatly from member expectations, the occupant of the role may be asked to vacate the position or put under pressure to conform. There are roles which are assigned by the group. For example, the group may select one person to play the role of leader, another to that of treasurer and still another to the role of bodyguard. On the other hand, there are some roles in the group that are acquired by the members without being formally assigned to them. In such a situation, members often internalise the role and link it to the self-concept. Such internalised role has been found to have very profound effects on the behaviour of the person (Haney, Banks and Zimbardo, 1973). They conducted a famous experiment, called Stanford Prison Experiment in which male college students, who had volunteered for the study of prison life, were confined to simulated prison and were randomly assigned to either the role of guard or prisoner. The major purpose of the experiment was to find out whether as a result of role assignment, the participants would came to behave like real prisoners and real guards. Results revealed that participants really came to act increasingly like actual prisoners and actual guards as the study went ahead. Gradually, the participants in prisoner's role became passive and depressed, whereas those in guard's role became increasingly brutal and were explicitly found to harass the prisoners. In fact, this prison simulation study exerted so powerful influence over the behaviour of the participants that the experiment had to be stopped after only six days. In this study, no external pressure was put on the participants to conform to the role expectations and their perceived and enacted roles were quite consistent with the stereotypical expectations of the guard and prisoner existing in the society.

(ii) ***Social status:*** Another key component of group structure is the status of the members, that is, their position or rank within the group. In most of the groups, some persons have higher status and some persons have lower status. People are generally very sensitive to their status because it is linked to a variety of desirable outcomes, including salary, respect and deference from other group members. That is the reason why groups often use status as one means of influencing the behaviour of their members.

Now, the question arises—how do people acquire high status? According to the expectation states theory of Berger et al. (1986), a person's status in group is affected by specific and diffuse status characteristics. Diffuse status characteristics do not relate directly to the specific ability or skills needed to be successful at a task, but they are general and apply to many tasks across. Examples of diffuse status characteristics are age, gender, ethnicity, wealth, etc. The theory further states that group members want to achieve certain goals and remain willing to assign high status to those members who can help the group in achieving the goal. When group members meet for the first time, they try to assess each person's ability to contribute to the achievement of group goals and these assessments, in turn, prepare the base for each person's status in the group. Researches have shown that height may play a role in determining status. Meta-analyses have shown that taller people are held in higher esteem as compared to shorter people and are perceived as having more skills and are more likely to be nominated as leader of the groups as compared to shorter people (Judge and Cable, 2004). It has also been shown that the people, who possess the group's central attributes, are likely to be accorded a higher status and are most likely to be selected as leader of the group (Haslam and Platow, 2001). Seniority in the group can also result in higher status because it is generally taken to be indicative of wisdom or knowledge of the in-group means (Haslam, 2004). Once people attain a high status in the group, he actually behaves differently than those with lower status. Such persons, in comparison to lower status group members, have been found to be variable and idiosyncratic in their behaviour (Guinote, Judd and Brauer, 2002). The persons, who are having lower status or are junior in group tend to show a stronger need to conform to the group norms.

Status also affects the pattern and content of group communication. Beck et al. (1950) conducted a study in which this fact has been clearly confirmed. In this study, they circulated a rumour in a factory with five statuses of the workers. The investigators were interested in locating who reported the rumour to whom. In the results, they found that the vast majority of reports were in upward direction in the status hierarchy and there were very few communications of rumour between the people of the same status or downwards to the people of lower status. Strodtbeck (1957) conducted a study in which the effect of socio-economic status (SES) of jurors upon leadership, participation and influence was examined. Participants acted as jurors and were requested to reach a verdict as a jury after hearing a tape-recording of a court case. In this investigation, three types of findings finally emerged—(a) high SES jurors were more likely to be elected as chairperson; (b) high status jurors participated more and tried to influence others for accepting their views and (c) high status jurors were better liked than low status jurors. These findings have been explained in terms of expectation states theory, which takes into account status coming from two aspects in the person, that is, specific and diffuse status characteristics. As we know, the diffuse status characteristics are not related to some specific ability or skill for getting a success, rather they are general type of skills, which apply to many tasks across. In the study of Strodtbeck, electing a high status person as foreman of the jury took place because the rest of the jury considered the diffuse characteristics applicable to enacting the role effectively.

(iii) **Social norms:** Social norms are defined as the shared rules and expectations about how the members of a group should behave in a situation (Forsyth, 1998). Among friends, social norms are informal in nature and are created through face-to-face interaction. In other situations, they are, however, predetermined by the structure of the group. In fact, norms function to hold the members of the group together and allow the new members to integrate themselves into the group quickly. In addition, group norms also tend to resolve two types of conflict that may arise in the groups—conflict of interest and cognitive conflict. *Conflict of interest* arises within a group over the status and competitiveness among the members of the group. *Cognitive conflict* refers to differing views, opinions and norms guiding what should be done. Norms also tend to help a group to achieve its goal, maintain itself and define relationship within the group as well as with the members of the other group.

2. Group cohesiveness

Traditionally, *cohesiveness* has been understood as the collection of forces such as individual, interpersonal and intergroup that try to keep members of the group together (Festinger et al., 1950). In fact, today, *cohesiveness* refers to both positive and negative forces that keep members together in the group. It is the characteristic of the group as a whole and is based upon the combined commitment of each individual to the group. When the members of the group like each other and are connected by bonds of friendship, cohesiveness is high (Paxton and Moody, 2003).

Many factors tend to affect cohesiveness of group. Some of the important factors are as under:

(i) One important factor is the extent to which group interacts effectively and harmoniously with minimal conflict. This becomes possible because the members find the group attractive for themselves. Now, the question is—what makes membership of a group attractive to an individual? Early research conducted by Cartwright and Zander (1968) indicated that the major reason of such attractiveness is that the group satisfies individual members' interests. This research further suggested that the factors that enhance interpersonal attraction such as perceived similarity of group members, cooperation and strong acceptance for each other make the group highly cohesive one. Recently, Hogg (1992) while making distinction between personal attraction and social attraction, pointed out that it is the social attraction, which ensures higher degree of cohesiveness in the group. Persons attraction relates to the individual characteristics, personality, etc., which has nothing to do with group cohesiveness. However, social attraction is the liking component of group membership and is based upon self-categorisation theory (Turner et al., 1989). Hogg and Turner (1985) demonstrated that group cohesiveness is displayed irrespective of the fact that the members of a group think whether they like other members or not. Hogg (1992) developed a model, called *interpersonal model* of group cohesiveness and this model demonstrates how cohesiveness results from interpersonal attraction. The model emphasises the importance of cooperation, interdependence and satisfaction along with goals of the group. According to this model, when individual goals cannot be satisfied independently, such persons form a group, become interdependent and cooperate in interaction. This results in mutual satisfaction with the goals of the group. As a consequence, individuals perceive each other as source of reward. This finally results in interpersonal attraction ensuing higher degree of group cohesiveness.

(ii) Group cohesiveness is also affected by forces that discourage members from leaving the group even if they are unsatisfied. Sometimes, people stay in the groups because they have no alternative or the costs of leaving are high.

High degree of cohesiveness is considered beneficial to group functioning. When the members of the group enjoy working together and accept group goals, both motivation and morale become high (Mullen and Cooper, 1994). Highly cohesive groups exert strong influence upon the individual member to behave in accordance with the group norms and expectations (McGrath, 1984). As a consequence, cohesiveness can sometimes enhance productivity and sometimes hamper it. If the norms are strict and require to work hard, cohesiveness will tend to increase productivity. On the other hand, if the group norms are slack off and the members spend more time in talking than completing tasks, high cohesiveness may decrease productivity. Thus, group cohesiveness is important for influencing people, group performance and for producing individual satisfaction.

WHY DO PEOPLE JOIN A GROUP?: BENEFITS AND COSTS OF JOINING

Obviously, people join group because they think they will be benefitted from it. Social psychologists have pointed out some reasons of joining the group. A few important ones are as under:

1. Human being has a fundamental need to belong and he joins a group simply because the group may fulfil the basic need to affiliate (Watson and Johnson, 1972).
2. Groups may be the source of information. Generally, it is impossible for one person to be an expert in all fields. Therefore, we have to depend on others to give us information regarding how to carry out tasks or to complete a task. For example, when a person joins a group having different types of expertise, he may get several useful information, which can be very helpful for him—a member, who is a doctor, can supply several medical information; a member, who is a public prosecutor or advocate in court of law, may provide him legal suggestions; a member, who is an engineer, may give him information relating to the construction of building and its by-laws.
3. A person gains self-knowledge from belonging to different groups (Tajfel and Turner, 1986). His membership to different groups may tell what kind of person he himself is or would like to be. Thus, group membership becomes of central importance to the image of self.
4. Another possible reason for joining a group is that groups provide rewards. Thibaut and Kelly (1959) found that the determinant of whether an individual will remain in one group or go to another is the rewards received by him in that group as compared to the rewards that could be received in other alternative group. If the amount of rewards is low, he will quit the group to join the alternative group. But if he thinks his reward is high enough, he may remain stick to the group.
5. Group often provides a boost to our status. When a person is accepted into prestigious groups such as in a highly selective school or college, political party, club, etc., his status and self-esteem both rise significantly. Research findings, here, indicate that there are two types of persons with respect to status boosting—*persons seeking self-enhancement* and *persons seeking self-transcendence*. By joining a group, the persons seeking self-enhancement boost their own public image and feel that they are somehow superior to others. Whereas the persons seeking self-transcendence emphasise social justice and a strong desire to help others. For the persons seeking self-enhancement, status of the group is important and they more readily identify with it. On the other hand, for the persons seeking self-transcendence, the group status is of less importance. Thus, status is found to be very important to those seeking to boost their own image than to those who are concerned with the goal of providing social justice and helping to others (Roccas, 2003).
6. Another reason for joining a group is that groups tend to facilitate the achievement of goals that an individual could not achieve alone (that is, social change). Examples are plenty to show that oppressed persons like women, downtrodden people, etc. try to attain equal rights by forming a group. Obviously, such goal cannot be achieved by a single woman or by a single downtrodden person. Simon and Klandermans (2001) showed that people who have been the victim of prejudice and discrimination join together to form a group to gain social clout and then, easily succeed in winning better treatment for their group.

Thus, we find that people join a group because they get many benefits—some personal, some collective.

Why does group splinter? Group membership also impose certain costs. In fact, group membership is not always bed of roses. There are some real thorns hidden among benefits. Some of the general costs that group membership has to pay are discussed below:

1. A very common and general cost of group membership is that it often restricts personal freedom. Members of the group are not free to behave according to their own will. They are forced to behave according to the norms of the group in a certain way. If, somehow, they are not able to behave according to the demands and norms of the group, the group may impose strong sanctions or may even expel them from the group. For example, in India, every political party requires that its spokesperson would behave in such a way that credibility and public image of the party may remain positive in the eye of people. The spokesperson has no freedom to express his own view. In case, he violates the norms of the party, he may be criticised or even expelled. In the United States of America, military officers are not allowed to make public statement about politics. Those who do so may be punished. That is the reason why during Korean War, President H.S. Truman sacked an extremely famous General–Douglas McArthur because he had made such public statements.
2. Group members have to pay the cost of the membership in terms of time, energy and resources. If they fail to meet such demands, they have to surrender their membership. For example, there are groups or institutions, which require that members must contribute a certain percentage of income to them. In case, any member fails to make contribution, his membership may be terminated.
3. Sometimes, a member may not like the position and policy that the group has adopted. Such members have to remain silent due to the risk of strong sanctions or withdrawal.

Thus, we find that group members have to pay some costs also for the group membership. The ultimate cost that a member may pay is withdrawing from the group or exiting the group, which they valued much. Why so? The answer to this brief question has been provided by Sani and Todman (2002), who concluded from the study of Church of England that groups splinter or develop *schism*, that is, splintering of the group into distinct factions that could no longer stay together united by any single identity, where the current members feel and perceive that the group has changed so much so that it is no longer the same entity or group they originally joined. In such a situation, the person decides to leave the group and conclude that the others members have changed to the extent that they can no longer be viewed as 'we', that is, falling within the boundaries of their extended self-concept. Such members start feeling that they now no longer possess entitativity. Sani and Todman (2002) suggested that this process is not restricted to the religious groups only, rather similar split may occur in the other groups like political party, social movements and, in fact, to any group based on shared beliefs and values.

TYPES OF GROUPS

The behaviour of the group members is also affected by the type of the group. There are different types of groups over which social psychologists have paid attention. Of those, the major types are given as:

1. Primary group and secondary group: In 1909, Cooley used the terminology of primary group and secondary group. According to him, *primary group* is a group in which interpersonal relationship takes place on face-to-face basis with great frequency. Such relationship is likely to be at more intimate level. The major characteristic of primary groups, according to Cooley is the influence they have in forming the social structure and ideals of the individual. In fact, primary groups are the nursery of human nature because they teach the children the sentiments of loyalty, ambition, sympathy and fellowship, which help in changing an individual into a person.

A primary group is relatively small and its members do have intimate face-to-face contact with the other members. The family is the universal primary group. Apart from this, play-group, neighbourhood, recreational group, working group, and indeed, any type of group in which individuals have some depth of involvement are also placed under primary group.

Secondary groups, on the other hand, are likely to be more impersonal and are characterised by formalised or contractual relationship among members. Here, the relationship among members is indirect and less personal and intimate. One's profession, school, social class, political party, religious bodies, clubs are the examples of secondary groups. Secondary groups tend to satisfy partial and special needs and interests, and therefore, are sometimes described as *special interest groups*. They do not generally involve face-to-face contact and in such groups, even if face-to-face contact occurs, it may not lead to intimacy as it happens in railway compartment. Because of specialised interest, secondary groups are able to chalk out elaborate programmes, frame rules and regulations governing their procedures and set up offices and institutions.

In contrast to secondary groups, primary groups demand and receive more personal involvement and they are likely to allow greater and wider swings in emotional tone. Love, depression, rage, elation, disappointment are more likely to be expressed in case of members of primary group. On the other hand, the expressions of emotions among the members of secondary groups are likely to be more restrained, and sometimes, suppressed altogether. In other words, primary groups provide us opportunity to experience our major satisfactions and dissatisfactions. Thus, primary groups are likely to be more cohesive than the secondary groups because it is within the primary groups that our most pressing social needs such as need for love and attention are satisfied.

2. In-groups and out-groups: In-group and out-group classification is based on intergroup relations. *In-group*, also called *we-group*, is one in which membership and participation are likely to evoke strong feelings of loyalty, sympathy and devotion. There is a feeling of love and sympathy towards the members of one's own group and we are very kind towards the people whom we recognise as belonging to our own group.

Out-group, also known as *they-group*, is others' group and our feelings towards the out-group are that of dislike, opposition, hatred, aggression, avoidance, etc. In fact, out-group is the opposite of in-group and we have no sense of loyalty, cooperation or sympathy with the members of out-group. Rather sometimes, we have prejudice against the members of the out-group.

For every in-group to which a person belongs and for which he has a sense of loyalty, there may be out-groups whose members are, for themselves, the members of in-groups, but the other group may consider them as the members of out-group. For example, Bharatiya Janata Party (BJP) may consider all its members who constitute the party as in-groups, but all members of others' parties like Congress Party, Bahujan Samaj Party, Samajwadi Party as out-groups. The members of out-groups also feel likewise.

There is danger, of course, that exclusiveness of in-groups may lead to their own undoing and historical events related to ruling cliques and oligarchies are full of such examples. A highly intact in-group does not generally permit changes in its members and exclusiveness remains the dominant feature. A study conducted by Ziller, Behringer and Goodchilds (1962) revealed that groups permitting changes in their membership are more effective than those whose membership is stable. Hoffman and Maier (1961) studied problem-solving behaviour of two types of groups—one group was having the members of similar type of personality and the other group was having the members whose personality traits varied. The works of both these groups were observed for a period of two semesters and it was found that heterogeneous group produced higher quality solutions. In fact, exclusiveness, which is implied in in-group, moves towards homogeneity and static complacency, whereas heterogeneity tends to stimulate greater effectiveness.

3. Formal group and informal group: The distinction between formal group and informal group is based on the structure of the group, that is, the type of relations obtaining between the members. A *formal group* is characterised by elaborate and defined rule and regulations. Here, the status of each member is clearly defined and definite rules are prescribed for them. Such definitions and prescriptions are very carefully thought out, and often, there are courses of training for these roles. University, business organisations, government offices are the examples of formal group. Such groups require strict discipline and conformity from its members. Sometimes, conformity is overdone and the members start paying more attention to the rules of procedure than to achievements. This is called *red-tapism*.

An *informal group* is defined as a group that is not hedged in by rigid rules and modes of procedure. Its members tend to enjoy greater freedom of thought and action. Such group emerges naturally in response to the common interests of members. They are formed spontaneously without any formal designation and with common interest. In fact, they exist outside the formal authority system and without any set rigid rules. Coffee-drinking group is a good example of informal group.

4. Exclusive and inclusive groups: *Exclusive groups* are defined as those groups that limit membership to certain class of individuals, who have given qualifications or specifications. For example, association of engineers, association of doctors, association of professors, and association of lawyers are all examples of exclusive groups because their membership is exclusively limited to those persons who are likewise qualified. For example, association of engineers would exclusively include those persons as members who possess professional experiences and qualification of engineer.

Inclusive groups are those groups that open their doors to all comers and may, in fact, very actively solicit membership. Political party and hobby clubs are the examples of inclusive groups. In fact, such group sets no special qualification for membership other than a sharing of interests with the other members, though it is generally observed that such members readily accept the goals and operating rules of the organisations. Inclusive groups are frequently encountered within the context of equalitarian societies.

5. Membership groups and reference groups: *Membership groups* are those groups to which an individual actually belongs such as the family, the play-group, the working group, etc. *Reference groups* are those to which he likes or aspires to belong to gain prestige and material advantage. In fact, this distinction is based on the status needs of the individuals. An assistant professor is a member of college staff, but he may aspire to belong to the university department, academic council, Senate and Syndicate of the university because he will gain more prestige and some material gain also. If a worker of BJP wants to be a member of Congress Party, for him, Congress party would be an example of reference group, whereas BJP would be an example of membership group. Obviously, reference group has a normative effect upon our behaviour. Newcomb's (1943) study of the effect of faculty values on the values of Bennington College students was a classic study showing the effect of reference group upon behaviour. In this study, it was found that liberal values of the faculty members influenced students' value.

GROUP DEVELOPMENT

Groups generally pass through a sequence in their evolution. These sequences are called *stages or phases of group development*. Although some groups go through all five stages described here, many others skip steps, repeat steps and even sometimes dissolve before they reach the later stages (Ilgen et al., 2005). These five stages are as follows:

1. Stage of forming: This is the first stage of group development, where initial process of evaluation and mutual selection are occurring. Members try to understand where other persons stand in the group and what the group as a whole stands for (Moreland, 1987). In fact, this stage is characterised by a lot of uncertainty about the purpose, structure and leadership of the group. All members are here 'testing waters' to determine what types of behaviour are acceptable. For all these reasons, focus is usually given on the leader of the group, who has the highest status in the group and is also expected to strengthen the group's goal (Wheelan, 1994). This stage becomes complete when the members begin to think of themselves as part of the group.

2. Stage of storming: This stage is the stage of intra-group conflict, where conflict among the members are often evident and disagreements can be intense and emotional (Tuckman, 1965). Here, group and individual members are attempting to shape and negotiate the various roles. Furthermore, there is also conflict over who will control the group. Researches have revealed that deciding on group's goals and the best ways to meet them is a common source of conflict among the members. At this stage, conflict may involve interpersonal as well as may relate to the task issues. For example, one member may feel that he has been betrayed by another member's shift of opinion on issue or some members may compete for the leader's attention and favour. Conflict may be listened when a majority forms and persuades the rest of the group to adopt its views. This stage is complete when there emerges a clear hierarchy of leadership within the group.

3. Stage of norming: This stage is characterised by close relationship, harmony and cohesiveness among the group members. A positive group identity develops among the members. In fact, a sense of security and trust emerges as the members' disagreements are resolved into a unified purpose (Wheelan, Davidson and Tilin, 2003). At this stage, group commitment is high (Van Vugt and Hart, 2004). Group members tend to be highly satisfied with the groups and show complete agreement with the purpose of the group as well as with the role and responsibility of individual members. The norming stage is complete when the structure of the group solidifies and the group develops a common set of expectations of what defines correct member behaviour.

4. Stage of performing: At this stage, the group is fully functional. The group moves into the performance. Members cooperate with each other in solving the problems, taking decision and generating output. They easily handle disagreements, if any, and maintain mutual allegiance to the group goals. Researches have shown that the groups which have developed a better and convincing communication pattern and support for task interdependence in the norming stage are better able to adapt to work situation and to the changing task demands in this stage as compared to the groups whose members emphasise independence (Moon et al., 2004).

For permanent groups, the performing is the last stage of development. However, for ad hoc groups like temporary committees, teams, task forces and similar groups that have a limited task to perform, there is an additional stage, called *stage of adjourning*.

5. Stage of adjourning: This is a stage of some ad hoc groups whose members show concern with wrapping up activities rather than task performance. This is the groups' endpoint, where the members often gather to evaluate their work, give feedback to each other and express their feelings about the group (Lundgren and Knight, 1978). It has been found that when the group is cohesive, the psychological impact of adjourning the group can be very similar to that of a break-up of a close relationship, producing the feelings of grief and loneliness. Such stress can be prevented if the members of the group prepare themselves for adjournment by bringing reduction in group cohesion and searching for occasion to join new groups (Mayadas and Glasser, 1985).

Figure 9.1 summarises these five typical stages of group development by pictorial representation.

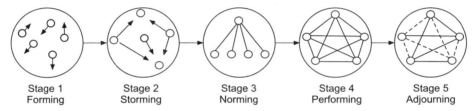

Stage 1 Forming   Stage 2 Storming   Stage 3 Norming   Stage 4 Performing   Stage 5 Adjourning

Figure 9.1 Schematic representation of five stages of group development.

EFFECTS OF PRESENCE OF OTHERS: SOCIAL FACILITATION AND SOCIAL INHIBITION

Social psychological researches have investigated both how individual performance is affected by the presence of other people and how group performance tend to differ from individual performance. Presence of other people sometimes enhances and sometimes retards the performance of the individual (Williams, Harkins and Karau, 2003). A discussion of these two types of effects is given below:

Social facilitation

It has been observed that sometimes people perform better in the presence of others than when they are alone. This is termed as *social facilitation* by social psychologists. A study of social facilitation was conducted by Norman Triplett in 1898. His observation was that cyclists seemed to ride faster when they raced against other cyclists than when they raced alone. To test this observation, he conducted one of the first social psychology experiments on children, who were given the task of winding string on a fisting reel in a group or when they were alone. In the results, it was found that the children worked harder and faster in the presence of other children. Later on, several studies demonstrated this effect. In 1920s, Allport (1920, 1924) conducted some studies in which participants worked on tasks like crossing out all the vowels in newspapers column, doing easy multiplication problems or writing refutations of logical arguments. Results revealed that participants were more productive when there were five other people in the room than when they were alone. Travis (1925) trained participants for several days on eye-hand coordination till a set of standard performance was reached. These trained people then performed on the task in front of passive audience. Performance was compared when they worked alone. Results revealed that eighteen of the twenty participants performed better in front of audience. Social facilitation has been found to occur when the others present actually perform the same task and when they are merely observers. Some studies have also shown that social facilitation occurs when tasks have been well-learnt by the person. Social facilitation has been found to occur among rats, cockroaches and parakeets. Chen (1937) found that the ants dug three times more sand when they were in groups than when they were alone.

However, the presence of others sometimes inhibits the performance of the individual. This is called *social inhibition* or *social impairment* (Aiello and Douthitt, 2001). In early studies done by Allport, it was found that the participants in group setting wrote more refutations of logical argument, but the quality of the work was poor than when they worked alone. Pessin (1933) conducted another study in which the participants learnt a series of seven nonsense syllables either alone or in front of an audience. In the result, it was found that the participants took longer time to learn and committed many more errors in the presence of audience. All these studies confirmed the phenomenon of social inhibition. Processes leading to social facilitation and social inhibition are shown in Figure 9.2.

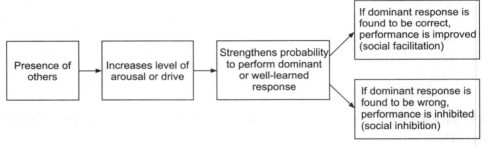

Figure 9.2 Processes leading to social facilitation and social inhibition.

Now, the basic question is—why does the presence of others sometimes improve the performance and some other times retards the quality of performance? Zajonc (1965) provided an answer to this question. He formulated a theory, popularly called *drive theory* that suggests that being in the presence of others increases an individual's level of drive or motivation. Whether the increased level of motivation will facilitate or interfere with performance depends on the responses required by the task. When the task requires a dominant response, increased level of motivation will be helpful. A *dominant response* is defined as the response or behaviour that a person is most able to access, which is well-learnt or innate, simple and highly practical. The presence of others facilitate the performance on simple task such as solving easy arithmetical problems or crossing out vowels or particular consonants, etc. In other words, when dominant response is simple or correct with respect to the task, social facilitation is likely to occur. On the other hand, when the task requires a behaviour that is complex or poorly learnt, the increased level of motivation ensuing from the presence of others tend to impair the performance. Examples of such task would be solving complex arithmetical problem, writing complex logical deductions, and solving new mechanical puzzles, etc. Thus, when dominant response is incorrect with respect to task, social inhibition is likely to occur.

Again, here, one question arises—why does the presence of others motivate us? Several explanations have been provided for this. The first explanation was provided by Zajonc (1965), who claimed that there is fairly simple innate tendency to become aroused by the presence of others. Social facilitation occurs because the presence of others create enough increased arousal to improve performance. Likewise, the presence of others, especially when the task is difficult, produces a level of arousal, which is too high, resulting in social impairment or inhibition (Zajonc et al., 1970). The second explanation was provided by Geen (1991), who had offered two viewpoints—evaluation apprehension and distraction conflict. According to *evaluation apprehension hypothesis*, the presence of others motivate us because we are concerned about the fact that they will evaluate, judge or rate us and we want to make a positive impression. Researches done by Bartis et al. (1988) showed that evaluation hypothesis can increase or enhance the performance for a simple task but impair the performance for a complex task. They conducted an experiment in which participants were asked either to describe different uses of a knife (simple task) or to think of a creative, new ways to use a knife (complex task). In each condition, half of the participants were led to believe that their responses would be evaluated individually and the other half were led to believe that their appropriate responses would be added to a common pool. Results revealed that for simple task, performance of the participant was enhanced, whereas for complex task, their performance was impaired. According to *distraction conflict hypothesis*, the presence of others becomes distracting. For easy tasks, which do not require much attention, the person may compensate for the distraction by concentrating and trying harder. As a consequence, he may perform better. For complex tasks, the distraction created by the presence of the people prove to be harmful. An extension of this explanation is what has been called *distraction conflict model* (Baron, 1986). The model suggests that the presence of others tends to create a conflict between the two basic tendencies—to pay attention to the audience and to pay attention to the task. Such conflict tends to increase arousal which can help or hinder the performance of the task depending on whether the task calls for a dominant response. Individual performance is likely to be impaired if we focus on audience rather than on task.

Recently, a third explanation has been offered by Blascovich et al. (1999). This explanation can be put under the category of biophysiological explanation. They have suggested that the presence of others may evoke one of the two distinctive physiological response patterns—challenge or threat. When the person has sufficient resources to meet the demands of task, a challenge response is likely to occur and when he has insufficient resources to meet the demands of the task, a threat response is likely to occur. The investigators found that the participants who performed a difficult task in front of an audience demonstrated the physiological pattern of threat and showed a poor performance than did the participants who worked alone. On the other hand, the participants who worked on easy task in front of audience showed a physiological pattern of challenge and performed same as those working in alone situation.

Another related problem investigated by social psychologists is to know about how group performance may differ from individual performance. The basic question is—do groups perform better at a task than a person working alone? Social psychologists have spent over more than 50 years exploring this question, and here, due consideration has been given to the technique of brainstorming (Osborn, 1957). *Brainstorming* is a problem solving approach, where each member of a group attempts to solve problems by providing as many novel ideas as possible without evaluation. Subsequently, the ideas provided by the group are pooled, evaluated and some are selected for further consideration. Selected ideas are elaborated by all group members, and finally, a few elaborated ideas are adopted. Osborn (1957) showed that brainstorming would result in improved group performance over individual performance. However, it has also been found that the groups, which use brainstorming, often generate both fewer ideas and ideas of poor quality in comparison to having the same number of individuals working independently on the same task. Social psychologists have provided four main explanations to account for this—evaluation apprehension, social loafing, production blocking and poor group coordination. We have already considered evaluation apprehension. *Social loafing*[1] refers to the tendency to put in least effort when working in group than when working alone. *Production blocking* results from some specific rules in an interacting group (Diehl and Stroebe, 1987). For example, during interaction in the group, rules may be that only one person can speak at a time. As a consequence, some group members may participate less because they cannot get a word in edgeways or may forget what they have to say while waiting for their turn. *Poor group coordination* results from poor shared understanding, less effective methods of working together and ill-defined rules for interaction. All these may result in poor performance of the group at the task.

Group memory is another important related social phenomenon that has attracted the attention of social psychologists. Clark and Stephenson (1995), after a review of literature, showed that groups not only memorise more information than the individuals but also memorise more than the best individual group member. This fact was demonstrated by Clark and Stephenson (1989) in a very popular study in which university students and police officers took part as participants. They were shown a videotape for 5 minutes in which police officer was shown questioning a woman who was alleging being raped. Participants were asked individually or in four-person groups to recall information from this scene. Subsequently, recalled information was categorised according to the correct facts, adding information not given, reconstructions, and meta-statements beyond what was presented in the video. Results revealed that group produced more correct information and made a few meta-statements than the individuals. Later on, the notion of group memory was extended to the small group culture, where groups representing a culture were found to exhibit common memory of norms, rules, friends, relatives, enemies, etc. Thus, shared memory represents a prevailing culture in any small group.

SOCIAL LOAFING

Social psychologists have shown their interest in one related basic question. What would happen if the contribution of each member in the group could not be evaluated individually? For example, if five persons come together to push the stalled car of a woman to the side of the road, there is no way to judge the efforts of any one person. In such a situation, how does the presence of others influence individual performance? This question brings us near to the phenomenon, called *social loafing*.

When a person's contribution to a collective activity cannot be evaluated, he is often found to work less hard and put less effort as compared to when he does the same work in lone situation. This effect has been termed by the social psychologists as *social loafing*. The phenomenon of social loafing was first studied in 1880s by a French agriculture engineer, Max Ringlemann (Kravitz and Martin, 1986). In his study, Ringlemann asked male students to pull a rope as hard as they can. This task was done by them in either lone condition or in a group of 7 or 14 students. With the help of strain gauge, he measured their efforts in kilogrammes of pressure. Results revealed that

---
[1] Social loafing will be considered in detail in the next section.

when pulling alone, the participants averaged about 85 kg per person. However, in group of 7, the total group force was only 65 kg per participant and in group of 14, it was further reduced to 61 kg per participant. This observation confirmed social loafing and it was named as *Ringlemann effect* (Kravitz and Martin, 1986).

More than one hundred studies have confirmed the social loafing effect (Williams, Harkins and Karau, 2003). Latane et al. (1979) conducted one of the most popular experimental studies on social loafing. In this experiment, college students were asked to clap or cheer as loudly as they can in the groups of 2, 4, 6 or alone. Results revealed that the level of clapping or cheering generated per participant decreased as the size of the group increased. Social loafing has been found to occur less often for tasks that are interesting and involving for the participants (Brickner et al., 1986). On the other hand, when tasks do not represent a challenge or individual performance cannot be truly assessed or if the person finds his contribution to the group as of little importance, social loafing does occur frequently. Social loafing has been also found to occur in different tasks like navigating mazes, swimming, writing songs, and evaluating candidates for different job positions.

Now, the basic question is—why does social loafing occur? To answer this question, Karau and Williams (1993) developed a model, called *collective effort model*. Following this model, how hard a person works in a group depends on two factors—the person's belief about his contribution for the success of group and how much the person values the potential outcome of a group success. When the person works in group, it leads to relaxation of effort, especially when he thinks that one will not be able to know how well he performed and he cannot be held responsible for his individual actions.

Researches have also found that sometimes, people work extra hard by increasing their motivation in order to compensate for inept co-workers. This effect is known as *social compensation*. Following Williams and Karau (1991), two conditions are necessary for an individual to show social compensation:

1. The individual must believe that his co-workers are inept and working inadequately.
2. The individual must consider the quality of the group product important.

Recently, Plaks and Higgins (2000) showed that when the individual lacks information about the motivation or ability of his co-worker, he relies on stereotype. In a study, the participants were assigned some mathematical problems to solve and were told that they would be paired with either a male or a female teammate. They were further told that they would receive a joint score based on the performance of their team. In view of the stereotype that men are better performer in mathematics than women, the investigator hypothesised that the participant paired with female teammate would work harder (social compensation effect) than when the participant would be paired with a male teammate (social loafing effect). In results, this hypothesis was confirmed. Thus, it is obvious that when people care about their group's performance and believe that their co-workers are not willing to work hard, unable to do well and also not trustworthy, they work extra to compensate.

Some researches have been done to examine the cross-cultural generality of the social loafing effect (Karau and Williams, 1993). Using the sound production task such as making noise by clapping, some studies have found clear evidence for social loafing in Thailand, Japan, China and India. There is also evidence for cultural differences in social loafing. Karau and Willams (1993) reported that tendency towards social loafing may be high in individualistic culture like that of USA, whereas such tendency may be low in collectivistic culture such as that of Asian cultures. Gabrenya, Wang and Latane (1985) conducted a study on social loafing in which ninth-grade students of Florida and Taiwan participate. In this study, thus, an attempt was made to assess cross-cultural differences in social loafing of American individualistic culture and Chinese collectivistic culture. In this study, the investigators created a sound-tracing test that was described to the participants as a measure of their auditory ability. Both US students and Chinese students were required to work in group as well as alone. Results revealed that US students performed only 88% in group, which was the same when they performed in alone. On the other hand, Chinese students when working in groups performed 108% of their individual level. Another surprising finding was that social loafing was found to occur only in case of boys, whereas girls performed more or less equally well in a group or alone. On the whole, the research provided a support for difference in social loafing in individualistic culture and collectivistic culture. The conclusion clearly states the impact of culture upon social loafing. Later on, seventeen studies done in Asia reported that the people in collectivist culture exhibit less social loafing than do the people in individualistic culture (Kugihara, 2001).

Techniques of reducing social loafing

Social psychologists have outlined some techniques for reducing social loafing. Important ones are as under:

1. Social loafing can be reduced if the contribution of each individual becomes identifiable. If people develop believe that their contribution can be identified and evaluated by the others, social loafing is likely to be eliminated.
2. Providing rewards for high group productivity or performance can also reduce social loafing. Shepperd and Wright (1989) conducted a study in which some participants were told that they could leave the experiment early if their group generated many solutions to the given problems and some other participants were, though, given same problem-solving task, but were not offered the incentive of leaving the experiment earlier. Social loafing occurred to a lesser degree in condition in which the participants were offered incentive.
3. Social loafing can also be reduced by making task more meaningful, difficult, but interesting for the persons. When the task is difficult and challenging, the individuals are less likely to loaf.
4. Social loafing can be reduced by increasing the commitment of the members of the group to a successful task performance.
5. Increasing the apparent value or importance of the task for the participants may also reduce social loafing (Karau and Williams, 1993).
6. If the people working in a group are given some kind of standard of performance such as how much others are doing or their own past performance, they are less likely to loaf (Williams et al., 1981).

All these steps taken together are likely to reduce the tendency for social loafing.

EFFECTS OF BEING IN CROWD: DEINDIVIDUATION

Sometimes, people seem to lose control over themselves in crowd and act differently from how they would if they were alone. In fact, such crowd situations may cause people to lose self-awareness and result in loss of individuality and self-restraint. This phenomenon is called *deindividuation* by social psychologists because it seems to partly stem from the fact that when people are in a large crowd, they tend to submerge their identity and individuality in the crowd (Postmes and Spears, 1998). More formally, *deindividuation* may be defined as a psychological state characterised by reduced self-awareness and social identity brought on by external conditions such as being an anonymous member of a large crowd (Baron, Byrne and Branscombe, 2008).

As far back as 1903, a French Sociologist, Gustave Le Bon observed that people often become lost in crowds and perform acts in crowds that they would not perform if they were alone. He felt that there is a mental homogeneity in crowd and the crowd possesses a collective mind. According to him, in crowd or mob, the emotions of one person spread through the group. In such a situation, when one person does something, others also tend to do it even if it is unacceptable to them. Le Bon called this reaction *social contagion*. As a result, we lose our sense of responsibility and our control system is weakened. Consequently, people do not hesitate in engaging violent and immoral acts.

There was a little formal theorising about the effect of being submerged in crowd until the early 1950s. In fact, Festinger, Pepitone and Newcomb (1952) suggested that people become deindividuated in a group and lose their personal identity. Consequently, they do not assume responsibility for their actions and are more likely to commit acts that they would not be doing alone. Zimbardo (1970) tried to refine the theorising of deindividuation by proposing a model, which states that such factors as anonymity, arousal and being in the large group allow people to shed their own identity. Consequently, they do not assume responsibility for their action nor monitor their own actions. As a result, such people feel inhibition about performing any type of behaviour. Recently, a new factor has also been added. Postmes and Spears (1998) showed that when people are in a large crowd, they are more likely to obey the norms of the group and less likely to behave in accordance with the other norms. For example, in any sporting event, when norm is to boo the member of the opposing team by shouting and throwing bottles and other objects in the field, this is what people generally tend to do. People pay attention to this norm and ignore other norms such as showing respect to other persons and doing polite behaviour.

Does deindividuation occur only in large wild crowd? Social psychologists would say not necessarily. Deindividuation can also occur in smaller groups. Zimbardo (1970) deindividuated some participants by having them wear long coats and hoods over their heads. Other participants were individuated by wearing their own clothes and name tags. Both groups of individuated and deindividuated participants were then placed in a situation in which they were given opportunity to shock the person not in the group (In fact, the shocks were fake and the victim was confederate). Results revealed that deindividuated groups gave shocks of longer duration than did the individuated groups. Likewise, Watson (1973) studied warfare patterns of over 200 cultures. In the results, he reported that in those cultures, where warriors deindividuated themselves by painting and wearing masks, they tortured their captives more than the warriors of those cultures whose warriors were not deindividuated. Diener et al. (1976) also conducted a study, which involved children who were trick-or-treating. The investigators kept themselves in homes in the neighbourhood. When children arrived in this home, some children were asked their names by an adult and others were not. Then, the children were given an opportunity to steal extra candy when the adult was not present in the home. Results revealed that those children who had been asked to tell their names stole less than those who were not asked to tell their names, although the chances of being caught was virtually zero in all cases.

One very important feature in deindividuation is that people feel anonymous here. The next question arises—what exactly happens to the individuals when they feel anonymous? Research conducted by Mullen, Migdal and Rozell (2003) demonstrated that when people feel anonymous, they simultaneously feel reduction in self-awareness and reduction in their social identity. As a consequence, people feel less aware of themselves as individuals and less aware of their social ties to others. Their joint effect confirmed the fact that people in large crowd often demonstrate behaviours which they would never perform under other conditions.

GROUP DECISION-MAKING

Decision-making is an important feature of our life, both at home as well as at work. At home, day-to-day routine decisions are made individually. However, when we are faced with some difficult problems, we generally sat with the members of our family and take a decision. Likewise, at work, routine decisions are usually made at individual level. But for more important decisions, formal decision-making groups are either constituted or already exist. Generally, it is believed that the collective wisdom of a body of people produces a more informed and higher quality of decision as compared to the decision taken by a single person alone.

Psychologists have formulated a set of decision rules that groups use in arriving at decisions. Davis (1973) developed the concept of *social decision schemes* as a simple set of rules for predicting the final decision by a group by knowing the initial views of each group member. He proposed the following four main rules:

1. **Unanimity:** This rule implies that all group members must agree on the decision reached. This is commonly required in legal system, which requires that judges reach unanimous verdicts.

2. **Majority wins:** Under this rule, initial majority position is adopted as final decision of the group. Sometimes the variation on this rule is two-thirds majority and not simple majority only. According to this rule, discussion mainly serves to confirm the most popular initial position of the group.

3. **Truth wins:** This rule states that the correct position or decision will tend to emerge from group discussion, as its correctness is recognised by more and more members.

4. **First-shift rule:** This rule states that the final decision taken by the group will be consistent with the direction of the first shift in opinion shown by the group members.

Researches on these social decision schemes have been conducted both in laboratory and real-life settings and the schemes have been proved remarkably successful in predicting even quite complex decision (Stasser, Taylor and Hauna, 1989). Different rules apply to different types of decision. For example, majority wins rule successfully predicts decision taken for a judgemental or evaluative task, whereas truth wins rule predicts well for the tasks, where there is correct answer (Kirchler and Davis, 1986).

Potential dangers of group decision-making

One important observation has been that the groups do not necessarily make wise decisions. Groups are vulnerable to special forces that not only bias decision-making but also produce disastrous decision (Hinsz, 1995). Four important issues in group decision-making are group polarisation, group-think, biased use of information and failure to share information unique to each member. All these issues are independently dealt with in the subsequent sections.

GROUP POLARISATION: RISKY SHIFT BEYOND RISK-CAUTION DIMENSION

The concept of group polarisation was proposed by French researchers, Moscovici and Fraser (Worchel and Cooper, 1979). *Group polarisation hypothesis* may be defined as the tendency of groups to take decisions that are extreme than the mean of the individual member's initial position (Isenberg, 1986). The concept of group polarisation is so termed because the collective decision tends to move from the average, that is, towards one of the two extreme poles. In fact, polarisation occurs when the members of a group shift their viewpoints towards a position that is similar to but more extreme than their viewpoints before group discussion. For example, if the members of a group like a moderately risky position prior to group discussion, polarisation will be said to occur if they shift towards higher degree of risk after group discussion. Similarly, if the members favour a moderately cautious position, polarisation will be said to occur if they shift in the direction of even greater caution after group discussion.

Researches on group decision-making till early 1960s found that groups were cautious and conservative in taking decision than individuals. In fact, Stoner (1961) studied risk taking by groups and individuals and found, much to his surprise, that group took riskier decisions than an average individual group member. This is called *risky shift effect*. The phenomenon of risky shift has been observed in the studies conducted by many researchers (Cartwright, 1971; Dion, Baron and Miller, 1970). Other studies that also used similar tasks, however, have revealed something opposite to the phenomenon of risky shift. On certain issues regarding which members were cautious or risk avoidant, group discussion actually caused members to become even more cautious than they were in the beginning (Turner, Wetherell and Hogg, 1989). This move away from the risk following the group discussion is known as *cautious shift*. In fact, both risky shift and cautious shift are the forms of underlying phenomenon, called *group polarisation*. Subsequent study done by French researchers, Moscovici and Zavalloni (1969) also demonstrated a decisional shift. They showed that French students, who were holding positive attitude towards De Gaulle and negative attitude towards north American, shifted to be even more positive towards De Gaulle and negative towards north Americans after group discussion. In USA, Myers and Bishop (1970) found that prejudiced high school students shifted towards even more prejudiced attitudes after group discussion, whereas groups of unprejudiced students shifted towards even less prejudiced attitudes. Isozaki (1984) found in his study that university students in Japan gave more pronounced judgements of guilt after discussing a traffic case. Likewise, Brauer (2001) reported that French students' disliking for some people was exacerbated after discussing their negative impressions. All these studies confirm group polarisation.

What is the explanation for group polarisation? Why do groups adopt position that are more exaggerated than the average opinions of their individual members? Researches over last three decades have produced many different explanatory theories, but the following three major perspectives dominate:

1. Normative or social comparison perspective: We are motivated to seek social approval and enhance our self-image. This, in turn, may result in social comparison process in which we become biased towards ourselves, treating ourselves better or more correct than the others. In such a situation, we are generally persuaded by people in our reference group, that is, the groups with which we identify (Abrams et al., 1990; Hogg et al., 1990). In group discussion, if a person finds that others hold view nearer to the valued alternative, he is likely to be more extreme in order to distance himself from the others. Sanders and Baron (1977) supported this viewpoint by showing that if a person is able to know the others' position regarding any issue without having heard their arguments, polarisation effect is likely to occur even without group discussion.

2. Persuasive-information perspective: The central idea, here, is that influence results from accepting evidence about the reality. The perspective holds the view that group discussion produces numerous different arguments. In fact, group discussion elicits a pooling of ideas and most of such ideas favour dominant viewpoint. Those ideas, which provide common knowledge for the group members, are often brought up in discussion and even if somehow they remain unmentioned, may jointly influence the group discussion (Larson et al., 1994). If the ideas in discussion happen to be the same as those a person has already considered, he is very likely to strengthen his own position. Apart from this, some novel ideas may be generated in the discussion and such ideas may support the position held by the person. Consequently, the position of the person may become more extreme. In fact, discussion within group serves to persuade those members who, since they are unaware of arguments, initially choose relatively moderate positions. After discussion, such moderate members shift their opinions in the direction of the most dominant arguments. This produces group polarisation (Burnstein and Vinokur, 1973).

As we know, a person's mind is not a blank tablet for persuaders to write something. What people think in response to the given message is very crucial. Researches have shown that even just expecting to discuss any issue with an equally expert person having opposite viewpoints, can motivate people to marshal their own arguments, and thus, to adapt a more extreme position, thereby providing evidence for polarisation (Fitzpatrick and Eagly, 1981).

Research evidences for either the normative perspective or persuasive-information perspective have been found to be mixed. Isenberg (1986) proposed that both explanations are correct and tend to occur simultaneously in group polarisation. Which explanation would be adopted depends on different circumstances. In fact, social context in which decisions are made, is considered more important than both the different types of arguments produced for a position and the original position a person holds.

3. Self-categorisation theory: *Self-categorisation* refers to the process whereby one identifies with the group and such identification produces conformity within the in-group. The group norm towards which conformity is shown by the members, ideally represents the prototype of the group. That is the reason why the position held by one most prototypical member is adopted as the normative reference. The information provided by such person would be highly persuasive and informative. The position, however, may vary depending on the context of the argument and salience of the out-group. The self-categorisation theory argues that greater group polarisation will occur in the presence of out-group. Hogg, Turner and Davidson (1990) showed that the direction of group polarisation may be reversed if there is a change in the social context. For example, if the in-group has to face a riskier out-group, then the perception of norms of the in-group becomes more cautious. Alternatively, the members of the in-group may perceive an already risky choice to be even more risky when faced by a cautious out-group.

Before closing the discussion on polarisation, one question that is commonly asked is—do group discussions always produce polarisation? The answer is probably no. When the members of the group are more or less evenly split over an issue, group discussion often leads to a compromise between the opposing views of the group members. This process is called *depolarisation* (Burnstein and Vinokur, 1977). Thus, the position reflected in the final group norm is more moderate than the initial views of individual members.

GROUPTHINK: DOES GROUP HINDER OR ASSIST GROUP DECISION?

The common observation has been that sometimes, a seemingly reasonable, considerate and intelligent group also makes a decision that proves to be a disastrous one. To explain such phenomenon, Janis (1982) proposed that this may result from a process called *groupthink*. Janis (1982) defined *groupthink* as deterioration of mental efficiency, reality testing and moral judgement that results from in-group pressures. In groupthink, the group reaches a decision regarding any issue without allowing members to express their doubts and views. The group believes that its decision is unanimous, even when considerable unexpressed dissent may exist. In nutshell, the groupthink is characterised by strong pressures towards unanimity and endorsement of the leader's viewpoint and by attraction to the group as a whole that critical analysis and evaluation of the decision become impossible. Once groupthink sets in, the result is the ill-considered and disastrous decision.

Janis showed that groupthink contributed to several important episodes in USA. He cited the failed invasion of the Bay of Pigs in Cuba in 1960s, the escalation of Vietnam War and President Nixon's attempted Watergate cover-up in the early 1970s. In each of these political episodes, a group of powerful politicians generally led by the President took decision in isolation, ignoring the voices of the dissenters.

Janis proposed a theory of groupthink in which he analysed the antecedents or causes, symptoms and consequences of groupthink (Figure 9.3). These three aspects of groupthink are described below:

Antecedents or causes of groupthink

According to Janis, there are some antecedent factors that cause groupthink. Such important factors are as under:

1. Groupthink often occurs in highly cohesive group. Researches have shown that cohesive group in comparison to non-cohesive group easily develops groupthink (Callaway and Esser, 1984).
2. When the group is sealed off from dissenting opinions, groupthink is likely to develop. In such condition, the group is insulated from its environment, and therefore, gets little critical information (Moorhead and Montanari, 1986).
3. When the group has a strong directive or promotional leader, the groupthink readily develops. Such leader actively and directly provides his or her favoured solution to the problem facing by the group to neglect other alternative solutions. He also argues strongly for it. Group members do not disagree with the leader's viewpoints or consider any alternative actions. Group members may fear of being rejected, and therefore, do not want to raise any voice against the leader.
4. Groupthink develops in those groups, where there is no systematic procedures to evaluate the alternatives.
5. When the group feels high stress or external threat, groupthink is likely to originate. High stress with poor hope for finding a better solution than one favoured by the leader or other influential persons, causes groupthink.

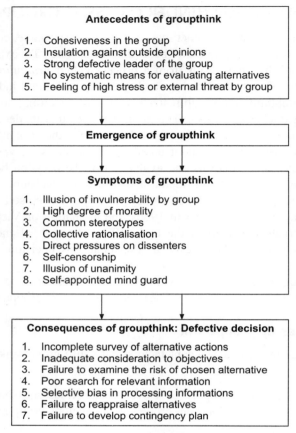

Figure 9.3   Janis's theoretical analysis of groupthink.

Symptoms of groupthink

Janis (1982) outlined some symptoms of groupthink. Important ones are as under:

1. **Illusions of invulnerability:**   Here, members of the group think that they are invulnerable and can never fail. Therefore, they exhibit excessive optimism and excessive risks, which blind them to the warnings of danger. In fact, they become highly euphoric and any possibility of failure hardly crosses their minds.

2. **High degree of morality:**   The members of the group assume inherent superior morality of their group and ignore ethical and related moral issues and their consequences.

   These two symptoms of the groupthink enable the group-members to overestimate their right and might.

3. **Collective rationalisation:**   The group tends to collectively justify their decisions by discounting challenges.

4. **Stereotyped view about opponents:** Group may develop a stereotyped view of opponents or enemy leaders as too evil to negotiate with or too weak and unintelligent to mount some effective counteractions.

   These two symptoms of the groupthink make the members of the group closed-minded.

5. **Conformity pressure:** There are strong group pressures towards conformity and the members of the group become reluctant to express disagreement. The members of the group rebuke those who raise any doubts about group's assumptions, stereotypes, illusions or commitment.

6. **Self-censorship:** The members of the group tend to engage in self-censorship of any deviation from group consensus and each member remains inclined to minimise his own doubts. Since disagreements are often uncomfortable, members tend to withhold their misgivings.

7. **Illusion of unanimity:** Here, each member of the group simply assumes that the other group members hold the same opinions or views and there is no need at all to encourage discussion on issues on which there is disagreement.

8. **Mindguarding:** Some members of the group protect the group from information that may call into question regarding the effectiveness or morality of its decision. Such members, therefore, emerge as self-appointed mindguards, who tend to protect against information that may pull down the effectiveness and morality of the group decisions.

   These four symptoms create pressure towards unanimity among the members of the group.

Consequences of groupthink

Groupthink may sometimes produce disastrous decisions. When the dominant member or a leader promotes an idea and when the group insulates itself from the dissenting views, groupthink is likely to produce, defective decisions (McCauley, 1989) signalled through the following symptoms:

1. Group does not survey alternative actions adequately.
2. Group provides inadequate consideration to objectives.
3. Group does not fully examine the risk of preferred choice.
4. Group does engage in a very poor information search.
5. Group exhibit selective bias in processing information at hand.
6. Group fails to reappraise the alternative choices.
7. Group fails to develop contingency plan.

Combatting groupthink

Janis offered some suggestions for combatting groupthink and enhancing the effectiveness of group decision-making. Important suggestions are as under:

1. The leader of the group should encourage dissenters and call on each member to express his doubts and objections. The leader must show his willingness to accept criticism of his or her ideas.
2. Initially, the leader should remain impartial in discussion. He should not announce his preference for any option or plan. Rather he should state his preference and expectation only after group members have expressed their views.

3. Group should be divided into several independent subgroups, each working on the same problem and making its deliberations independently. Subsequently, they should come together to hammer out the difference in opinion.
4. Experts should be invited to participate occasionally in group discussions and they should be encouraged to challenge the views of the group members.
5. After a tentative consensus has been reached, the group should hold a second meeting, where each member can express any remaining doubts before a final decision is taken.
6. At each meeting, at least one person should be allowed to play devil's advocate to challenge the group ideas.

The net result of these steps would be that the groupthink would be minimised and group effectiveness would be enhanced to a greater extent.

Despite the intuitive appeal of the concept of groupthink, support for Janis's idea is limited. There is a very limited support for Janis's hypothesis that group cohesiveness contributes to groupthink (Michener and Wasserman, 1995; Aldag and Fuller, 1993). Studies conducted by Flowers (1977) and Leana (1985) did not provide support for this hypothesis. Some studies have supported only parts of groupthink theory. For example, Tetlock et al. (1992) conducted a study in which an analysis of the records of 12 different political decisions was done. They concluded that it was possible to make distinction between the groups whose decisions reflected groupthink and the groups whose decision reflected good judgement and vigilance. However, these investigators got mixed success in examining the validity of those factors that were proposed as the causes of groupthink by Janis. Their results confirmed the role of leader in determining the quality of decision-making, but found no support for Janis's hypothesis that groupthink is caused by high group cohesiveness. In fact, many cohesive groups with strong leaders do make excellent decisions.

Now, what is to be concluded about groupthink? Definitely, groupthink provides a valuable insight into potential pitfalls of group decision-making. Supporters of the groupthink concept agree that processes that cause groupthink are more complex than what Janis had originally thought.

BIASED USE OF INFORMATION IN GROUPS

One of the important sources of bias in decision-making group is the tendency of the groups to process available information in a biased manner. In fact, groups, like individual, are motivated to find support for common or shared information, ignoring the unshared one. They rarely engage in systematic sharing of information. Social psychologists have conducted several studies in which biased use of information in group has been shown. Winquist and Larson (1998) conducted a study in which three-person groups of college students were requested to decide which of the professors would be nominated for an award in the field of teaching. Likewise, Larson et al. (1998) conducted another study in which three-person teams of physicians were given some hypothetical cases for making diagnosis. In both studies, members of the group were supplied some shared and some unshared information. Results revealed that the group members spent more time in discussing the shared information than the unshared one. This is known as *common-knowledge effect*. In fact, by devoting so much time to the shared information, groups failed to take advantage of unshared information, which may be still more relevant.

Another similar tendency which influences group decision-making is what social psychologists have called *confirmation bias*. The members of the group often tend to seek and prefer information that supports their initial beliefs. Schultz-Hardt et al. (2000) reported that in decision-making, group's members may use group discussions for confirming their point of views, rather than challenging their initial viewpoints. Thus, the members of the group may use information to justify their own initial decision and they do not use it to learn anything new about what might conflict their own final decision and require them to change their own behaviour.

FAILURE TO SHARE UNIQUE INFORMATION FROM SOME MEMBERS

Another source of bias shown by decision-making group is failure to share information and ideas unique to each member. General observation has been that when the group's members discuss any problem or issue and try to reach a decision about it, they try to concentrate and share only those information, which are shared by most of the members. They tend to ignore the information or idea that is known only to a few members. Thus, the final decision is made on the basis of shared information. This creates no problem if such information is basic for the best decision. But when information related to the best decision is not shared by most of the members, and the members discuss only the information they possesses, the naturally, in such a situation, the group is prevented from reaching the best decision. This tendency is strong in different fields, including medical diagnosis. Researches have shown that when medical students and interns discuss more shared information, they arrive at poor and inaccurate decision. But when they concentrate and pool unshared information, that is, the information known to only some members, they arrive at a more accurate diagnosis (Winquist and Larson, 1998).

WAYS OF IMPROVING GROUP DECISIONS

In the preceding sections, a discussion has been made about several types of biases in group decision-making. These biases such as group polarisation, groupthink, biased processing of information and failure to share information unique to each member tend to produce disastrous decisions. Social psychologists have provided some techniques for improving the quality of group decisions. Such important techniques are as under:

1. **Devil's advocate technique:** In this technique, one member of the group is assigned the task of disagreeing with and criticising the members' viewpoints or decision to be taken. Such member acts as devil to the group. The criticisms done by the so-called devil member become eye-opener for the other members, who are forced to think about the decision they are going to take.

2. **Technique of authentic dissent:** In this technique, some members of one group are assigned to hold differential initial opinions. As a consequence, members of the group are forced to concentrate upon all available information necessary for a healthy and correct decision.

    Some researches have shown that the technique of authentic dissent becomes more effective than the technique of devil's advocate technique probably because of the fact that the former ensures that all available information would be considered in arriving at a decision.

3. **Brainstorming:** Brainstorming technique involves a group of people, usually between five and ten, sitting around a table, generating ideas in the form of free association.

The major focus of the brainstorming technique is more on generation of ideas rather than on evaluation of ideas, the assumption being that if a large number of ideas can be generated, it is likely that some of them may be helpful in arriving at a quality decision. All these ideas are written, pooled, evaluated and some are selected for further elaboration. Those selected are first elaborated by all the members of the group, but without any criticisms. Finally, evaluation of the elaborated ideas allows one or more than one ideas to be adopted. These adopted ideas become instrumental in arriving at a quality decision about the issue. Osborn (1957) showed that adoption of this brainstorming technique results in enhanced group performance and also in good quality decision regarding the issues at hand.

These techniques, if applied successfully, can enhance the quality of group decision.

GUIDELINES FOR EFFECTIVE DECISION-MAKING

Social psychologists have provided some useful guidelines for making group decision more effective. Some of these suggestions are as under:

1. The purpose of the group should be well-defined and clearly understood by the members of the group.
2. The composition of the group should be appropriate so that the members may have necessary skills for discussing and evaluating the problems at hand.
3. The members of the group should communicate freely with each other so that everyone understands each other's aspirations, roles and responsibility.
4. The group must have access to all the necessary resources of information and other supportive elements so as to reach an efficient and fast conclusion.
5. Each member should show commitment to the decision made. Even if some members exhibit different viewpoints prior to reaching the decision, the disagreement and conflict should not be carried over after the decision has been arrived.
6. The group should not be dominated by any member, including leader, so that all group members must be encouraged to give input freely.
7. The size of the group, that is, the number of members in the group should be adequate. Too many members may result in simply waste of time and unnecessary disagreement in opinions and very few members may not be enough to look at a problem from all angles. Usually, for most of the groups, five members are considered to be adequate.

GROUP INTERACTION: COOPERATION VERSUS COMPETITION

People in group generally interact in two ways—by showing cooperation with others or by engaging in competition with others. In the condition of cooperation, they help each other, share information and work together for mutual benefit. Thus, people work here for mutually acceptable goals. The goals of the people in condition of cooperation need not to be identical but achieving them must result in satisfaction for all the concerned persons. In the condition of competition, group members compete with each other. Their own individual goals are given weight and strive to outperform the rest. In such a situation, persons try to secure a greater-than-equal share of rewards available to the members of the group.

Social psychologists have long been interested in understanding both cooperative and competitive behaviour of human beings and their impact upon group performance. In a series of classic studies, the investigators have developed various ingenious ways to study competition and cooperation systematically. One of the classic studies of cooperation and competition was conducted by Mintz (1951). He prepared a special glass jar with an opening at the top and a small opening near the bottom. The top opening contained a number of paper cones. Through the lower opening in the jar, water was added. The subjects were told to extract their cones from jar before water reached the cones. Anyone of the paper cones could be removed from the jar by pulling a string that was tied to its peak. It was not possible for the participants, who were in groups of 15 to 21 persons, to remove more than one cone at a time because they jammed in the neck of jar (see Figure 9.4).

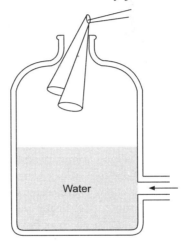

Figure 9.4 A glass jar used in cooperation and competition experiment.

Results revealed that after a few trials, the participants were able to remove all the paper cones by taking turns, that is, by cooperation. The bottom of the glass jar was connected to a source of water, which gradually filled the jar, and therefore, it was imperative to remove the cones before they came into contact with water. It was clearly found that the participants, who had learned to cooperate, performed their tasks efficiently, despite this distraction. Subsequently, the experimenter changed the rule and offered a cash reward for any participant, who was able to get paper cone out of the jar before it got wet. Here, the participants, who had previously got no difficulty in getting their cones out of the jar, now faced many problems. In fact, in 12 out of 16 trials under reward condition, traffic jam developed in the neck of jar due to attempt to draw more than one cone at a time. In the remaining trials in which they had succeeded, they had refused rewards, suggesting the fact that they had not really regarded the situation as competitive one. Several other researchers have also reported that the competition produces higher level of performance in comparison to cooperation. For example, deCharms (1957) conducted a study in which groups of participants were tested under conditions in which they were either rewarded equally (cooperative) or according to their achievement (competitive). Results showed that the performance of each of the competitive groups exceeded groups in comparison to the performance of the cooperative groups. Miller and Hamblin (1963) made a serious attempt to resolve some of the contradictions in results obtained by various studies of cooperation and competition. They reviewed the literature on this subject and conducted their own study. They examined 24 different studies and reported that the system of differential rewards, which is responsible for competition, generally tend to have a detrimental impact upon the performance in studies, where for the completion of the task, interdependence among the group members was essential. In those studies, where there was low interdependence, differential rewards led to an enhanced degree of group productivity. Johnson et al. (1981) reviewed over about 100 studies in which a comparative study of cooperative groups and competitive groups was done and it was found that there were only eight such studies in which competition was superior to cooperation. Shaw (1958) concluded that competitive situations tended to arouse stronger needs for achievement than did cooperative situations, but the stronger needs or motivations might interfere with the performance on certain tasks, resulting into poor scores.

Cooperation and Competition in Two-person Games

Some social psychologists working on competition and cooperation have used laboratory games that simulate key features of everyday interaction. Here, we shall discuss two popular games for the said purpose—the trucking game and the prisoner's dilemma game (PDG).

Trucking game

Deutsch and Krauss (1960) used a simple two-person game, called *trucking game*. Participants were asked to imagine that they were running a trucking company and were required to get a truck from one point to another as quickly as possible. In fact, two trucks were not in competition because they had different starting points and different destinations. There were two routes for destination—the shorter and faster route and circuitous and longer route. The faster and shorter route for both converged at one point to one-lane road and two trucks had to go in opposite directions (see Figure 9.5).

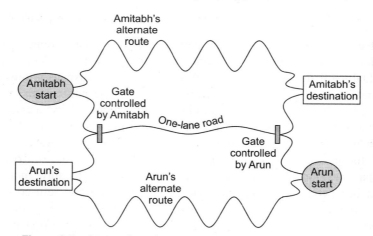

Figure 9.5 A type of road map commonly used in trucking game.

The most optimal way so that both could use this one-lane road would be for one of them to wait until the other had passed through it. If either truck entered the one-lane road, other could not use it. If both entered the lane, neither of them could move until one had backed up. Besides, each participant had a gate (or threat) across direct one-lane road that could be raised by pressing a button.

If the gate was raised, the other participant could not use the lane and he was forced to proceed by alternate route, that is, circuitous route. In fact, the game was set up in such a manner that taking the alternate and circuitous route would mean to lose money, whereas taking the direct and one-lane route would mean to earn money for both sides even if they alternated in this shorter route. This happened because the payoff was determined by the amount of time needed to complete the trip. Deutsch and Krauss found in the results that the participants were more likely to find ways to cooperate and to maximise mutual gains under conditions in which they did not use gates (or threats). However, when the participants possessed potential threats they tended to use gates, thus increasing hostility and competitiveness and making cooperation more and more difficult. In such a situation, there was a little cooperation between the participants and both partners ended up in losing the gains.

Shomer, Davis and Kelley (1966) experimented with Deutsch and Krauss's methodology and gave their participants gates, but no alternative routes. They reported that the availability of threat (or gates) enhanced communication between the participants and facilitated their working out cooperative arrangement. Likewise, Deutsch, Canavan and Rubin (1971) conducted another experiment, which was built upon the early work of Deutsch and Krauss. They manipulated the degree of conflict between the two participants by varying the percentage of direct route that one-lane road covered, making it 20%, 50% or 90%. It was found that greater the proportion of one-lane highway, the greater the conflict between the participants occurred. Moreover, more threats were made by using the gates frequently when one-lane route was proportionately larger than when it was relatively shorter one.

Prisoner's dilemma game (PDG)

The term *prisoner's dilemma* comes from a standard conflict situation, which is used in some of the research studies. It is so called because it is based upon a problem faced by two criminals at a police station. This is also called *non-zero-sum conflict* to distinguish it from zero-sum games. The name *zero-sum* indicates that one party's loss will be other party's gain. The zero-sum conflict represents true competition. Chess is a good example of zero-sum game. The prisoner's dilemma is a non-zero-sum game and illustrates riskiness of cooperation. It is also called *mixed motive situation* because both cooperative and competitive responses (mixed motives) are involved in this type of conflict. In this game, the hypothetical situation concerns two criminals who are arrested and are put into separate rooms by police. Each is told that he has two alternatives—to confess or not to confess. If neither criminal confesses, neither can be convicted of a major crime. However, police tells them that they can still be convicted of minor crime, and therefore, both are likely to get minor punishment. If both confess, both will be convicted for doing major crimes. If one of them confesses and other does not confess, the confessor will be freed for helping the police and the other criminal will get the maximum penalty. The situation is depicted in Figure 9.6.

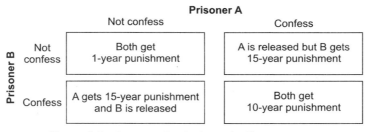

Figure 9.6 An example of prisoner's dilemma game.

The situation obviously contains conflict. If both criminals trust each other, they will not confess and get only light punishment. However, if one criminal is convinced that the other will not confess, he would be doing better to confess because in that case, he may be freed. Because of such conflict, such games are known as *mixed motive games*.

We do not know what the real prisoners or criminals will do in such a situation. But in research on such problem, much of the content of game is removed, but the situation remains basically similar one. In changed situation, the persons do not play for their freedom, but play for the points or money. The exact pattern of payoff varies, but the typical one is shown in Figure 9.7 in which there are say two players Sohan and Mohan.

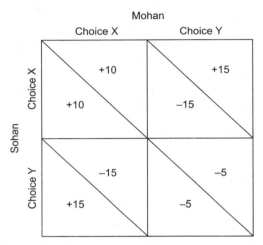

Figure 9.7 Typical prisoner's dilemma payoff matrix.

If both Sohan and Mohan choose option X, each get 10 points. If Mohan chooses Y and Sohan chooses X, Mohan wins 15 points, whereas Sohan loses 15 points. If Sohan chooses Y and Mohan chooses X, Mohan loses 15 points and Sohan gains 15 points. If both choose Y, they both lose 5 points. In other words, it can be said that if both cooperate with each other (choose X), both win 10 points. On the other hand, if they compete (one or both choosing Y) and wish to win even more, say 15 points, they face the risk of losing. In such payoff matrix, the players are told to earn as many points as they can. In such a situation, players know clearly that the best way to earn more and more point is, for both, to select X option, that is, cooperative choice on every trial. However, in typical game situation, only about one-third of the choices are cooperative. As the game progresses, number of cooperative choices goes down. The players tend to choose competitive strategy more and more, despite the fact they know well that they can win more points by showing cooperation. Such effect has also been observed when a group plays against another group (Schopler et al., 2001).

In India, some researches have also been conducted to examine the effect of cooperation and competition. Farooqui (1958) examined the impact of cooperation and competition on group structures in terms of sociometric responses. A qualitative analysis revealed that as compared to the competitive group, the cooperative group had greater emotional expansiveness. The structure of the competitive group was characterised by cleavage and semi closed subgroups. Pareek and Banerjee (1974, 1976) studied cooperative and competitive game behaviour. They took three subcultural groups, namely,

Hindu, *Bohra* and *Tribal* from Delhi and Udaipur. They found that in mixed motive game, the Bohras of Delhi displayed an increase in trust with the advancement of age. In general, participants from Delhi demonstrated the highest and tribals demonstrated the lowest degree of trust in the groups. Pareek (1977) also examined the dynamics of cooperative behaviour among the samples taken from Delhi, Udaipur and Ahmedabad. In the results, it was found that girls were lower in competitive behaviour than boys. Competition was also found to increase with age. Sinha (1968) questioned the usefulness of need for achievement theory in Indian culture, where a different set of situational variables such as the *scarcity of resources* is dominant. His argument was that under limited resource conditions, the members of the group tend to become more cooperative for means, while their enhanced need for achievement may pose as an obstacle in helping each other. Results revealed that although under limited resource condition, the cooperative spirit was found to be better than the competitive spirit, it failed to release extra energy in the persons, whereas the ampleness of resources tended to provide such things. Carment (1974a, 1974b) and Carment and Hodkin (1973) conducted several cross-cultural studies in which impact of cooperation and competition was studied. Carment and Hodkin (1973) studied the effect of presence of others on the performance to contrast the impact of competition motivation on the performance among Indian and Canadian participants. Results indicated that Indians tended to perform much more rapidly than the Canadian and were less responsive to the competitive instructions and to the presence of a co-actor. Alcock (1978) found that Indian males are less competitive than Canadian males in two-person bargaining situations. In another study done by Carment (1974b), the responses of Indian and Canadian male undergraduates in a game of *chicken*, a derivative of prisoner' dilemma game paradigm was analysed. He tried to assess the relative risk-taking tendencies among Indian and Canadian students. His findings revealed that Indians were more competitive than Canadians in maximising difference game (MDG), but this difference was considerably reduced in the chicken game (Pandey, 1988).

Determinants of Cooperation and Competition

Researches done by social psychologists have shown that there are several factors that tend to determine whether we shall behave with other in a cooperative way or in a competitive way in a situation. Some of the important factors are as under:

1. Nature of reward structure: In any social interaction, there can be two types of reward structure—a competitive reward structure and a cooperative reward structure. A *competitive reward structure* is one where one person's gain is another person's loss. Here, the person does his best when others show a very poor performance. In such a situation, the person does his best to compete for obtaining the rewards. Here, the outcomes of the individuals are independent of each other. Individuals are socially independent rather than interdependent in such reward structure. In cooperative reward structure, the outcome of the group members are linked positively with each other. Football team or cricket team represents a cooperative reward structure, where each player tries to put his maximum effort to win the game. In such a situation, every member tries to cooperate well with the other member so that the group may win the game.

Thus, conclusion is that reward structure determines whether a person would engage in cooperative or competitive behaviour. However, sometimes, the reward structure in a situation is mixed or unclear. Individuals may have choices to cooperate or compete as we find in case of trucking game and prisoner's dilemma game.

2. Communication patterns: Communication patterns between the individuals also affect their cooperative or competitive behaviour. According to the study conducted by Orbell, Van de Kragt and Dawes (1988), greater degree of communication ensures more cooperative behaviour (For example, in their study, when three different communication patterns were induced in trucking game, degree of cooperative behaviour varied. In one condition some participants were required to communicate, in another condition some were given opportunity to talk if they need and still in other conditions, others were not allowed to communicate. Results showed that when the participants were required to communicate, cooperation was the greatest, and it was the least when communication was not possible. In fact, communication helped the participants to urge each other to cooperate, to discuss their plans, to learn about each other and to convince each other that they were trustworthy. More or less similar results have been found in prisoner's dilemma game. Wichman (1970) conducted a study in which it was found that when no communication was possible among the participants, the competition was the greatest. When participants were allowed to talk, but not to see each other, somewhat less competition was observed and when the participants could see and talk to each other, there was the least degree of competition. Where there was no communication among the participants, about 40% of responses were cooperative and it was enhanced to about 70% when verbal communication was started among the partners.

3. Individual differences in personal values: The common observation is that every individual differs in his personal values about competition. In general, an individual has three value strategies for interacting with people. These are as follows:

(i) Individuals having competition strategy are oriented towards maximising their own gains in comparison to the partner. They want to do better than the partner.
(ii) Individuals having cooperation strategy are concerned with maximising the joint rewards received by themselves as well as by their partners.
(iii) Individuals are more oriented towards maximising their own gains, with little concern for gains or losses of the partner.

Cooperators prefer cooperative interactions and competitors operate on competitive mode. With lapse of time, an individual may change his own behaviour if he finds that the partner is no longer reciprocating. Researchers have shown that even the most dedicated cooperator may behave in a competitive way if he finds that the partner is emphasising a highly competitive behaviour. This has been commonly observed in the popular trucking game as well as prisoner's dilemma game.

4. Reciprocity: Social psychologists have found that cooperation and competition are influenced by reciprocity. Individuals often feel oblige to return both favours and foe. Research evidences have supported the fact that initial cooperation encourages further cooperation by partner and initial competition provokes further competition by partner. One useful strategy that seems successful in fostering cooperation is reciprocal concession. If one person makes a small concession and waits for other person to do the same, eventually a higher degree of cooperation is done (Esser and Komorita, 1975). However, the concession must be gradual and sequential. The best way is to make reciprocal concession only slightly larger than those made by the other person. This way definitely reinforces the others' cooperation and results in even larger concessions and quick agreement. This strategy generally works well when both sides are willing to cooperate to some extent. If one of the two persons or parties is totally competitive, the only one who argues for cooperation will be exploited and will be held in weaker position than before. Researches have provided sufficient evidences for the fact that cooperative groups are more likely to work successfully when they interact face-to-face in comparison to competitive or individualistic group. Not only that, cooperative groups provide an individual with greater sense of social support from members, enhance self-esteem and foster greater psychological well-being.

5. Culture and cooperation: The culture of the society in which a person is reared also plays a role in determining whether he will engage more in cooperation or in competition. Researches have revealed that collectivistic culture promotes cooperative behaviour, whereas individualistic culture promotes competitive behaviour. Indian culture is an example of collectivistic culture, whereas the culture of USA is an example of individualistic culture. Collectivists view self as interdependent on others and accord priority to relationship, taking the needs of others into account. As such, they exhibit more cooperative behaviour in their social dealings (Sinha and Verma, 1987; Triandis, 1986). Kagan (1977) conducted a cross-cultural study in which eight-year white children from the United States were compared with the Mexican children of the same age while they played a game of marbles. Although the children had the option of cooperating or competing, it was found that the Mexican children cooperated on roughly 7 of 10 trials. On the other hand, children from the United States cooperated on less than 1 trial in 10. It was because of the fact that American culture being individualistic in nature, made more emphasis upon competition than upon cooperation.

6. Social dilemma: Social dilemma is currently an active field of research in social psychology. *Social dilemmas* are the situations in which the action of an individual benefits that individual, but harms the group as a whole. Thus, social dilemmas pit the short-term interests of the individuals against the long-term interests of the group, which also includes the individual. For example, we use car for our benefit, but it produces pollution in cities and contributes to global warming through the greenhouse effect. In fact, as an individual, we are unwilling to change our life style because it is so beneficial to us. Since persons, who are confronted with social dilemmas, sometimes act selfishly and sometimes act cooperatively for the good of collective, the investigators have tried to identify the factors that can tip the balance in one direction or the other. In fact, to overcome social dilemmas, strategies for encouraging cooperation may be more fruitful. However, this requires people to trust each other and not to be selfish. Social dilemmas may also be overcome by restructuring the group task to emphatic interdependence among the people and by focusing on interdependence to increased shared identity and commitment to group rather than individual goals such as introduction of superordinate goal. Besides, reminding people of social norms of cooperation can also reduce social dilemma. Reno, Cialdini and Kallgren (1993) showed that individuals are less likely to litter if they are reminded that there are social norms against littering. The size of the group also makes a difference. In a large group, the effect of one person's selfish behaviour is diluted to a greater extent. A person with cooperative value orientation, as compared to a person with competitive value orientation, is less likely to confront with social dilemma. Better and frequent communication among group members can also increase cooperation. Communication also tends to enhance the feeling of identification with group that ultimately results in better cooperative effort.

In nutshell, we can say that there are many factors which influence cooperation and competition—the two important modes of social interaction.

COMMUNICATION NETWORK IN GROUP

In the late 1940s and in 1950s, several investigators focused their attention on how the communication network influence groups (Bavelas, 1948, 1950; Leavitt, 1951; Shaw, 1954). *Communication network* refers to the typical patterns in which messages are transmitted in the group. All these studies were concerned with the effects of communication networks on group processes and group productivity.

There are two basic types of communication networks—centralised network and decentralised networks (see Figure 9.8).

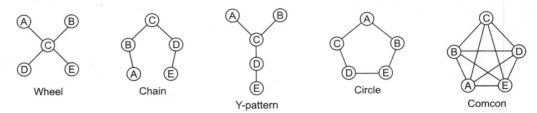

Figure 9.8 Patterns of communication in groups of five persons.

A *centralised network* is one in which one person is the focus of all decision-making and problem solving. The wheel and Y communication patterns are the typical examples of centralised networks. A university in which the heads of the department take their cases for new teaching programmes to the vice-chancellor, who decides on priorities and allocates resources, is an example of a centralised, restricted communication networks that fits into wheel pattern. A *decentralised communication pattern* is one in which the members can communicate freely with one another. For example, a university in which the heads of the department meet together to discuss their needs and vote on allocation of resources is an example of all-connect or completely connected (called comcon), unrestricted pattern.

There are six common types of communication patterns studied by the psychologists—wheel, Y-pattern, circle, chain, all-connect or comcon and grapevine. A brief discussion regarding these patterns is as follows:

1. **Wheel pattern:** In this pattern, only the central person is allowed to communicate with the other members of the group. The person C can communicate with everyone else, but the four peripheral members (A, B, D and E) can only communicate with person C (see Figure 9.8).

2. **Y-pattern:** In this pattern, one person becomes more central than any other. The person C is in central position because D and E can communicate to A and B only through C. Likewise, A and B can communicate to D and E only through C (see Figure 9.8).

3. **Circle pattern:** In this pattern, no one is central and the communication is allowed to flow in all directions.

4. **Chain pattern:** In this pattern, the communication flows up and down the chain, but of course, cannot complete the circle.

5. **All-connect or comcon pattern:** It is a pattern of communication in which all members of the group enjoy complete freedom in making a totally open communication with every other member.

6. **Grapevine:** In this informal pattern of communication, there is found person-to-person network, linking members in all directions. (See Figure 9.9)

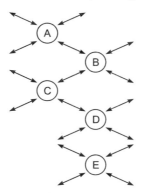

Figure 9.9 Informal patterns of communication in groups of five persons.

Leavitt (1951) experimentally studied the effects of four types of networks (Wheel, Y, Circle and Chain) within a group of five people on performance at problem-solving tasks, member satisfaction and morale. In this experiment, each group used one of the four types of networks. Each member of the group was given a card with six symbols on it. The group task that appeared on every member's card was to identify which of the symbols was a common symbol. Group members were required to communicate to others as dictated by the communication networks. Several measures were taken such as time to solve problems, number of problems solved, number of incorrect solutions, the extent to which group members enjoyed the task and whether a group was perceived to have a leader. In the results, two sets of findings finally emerged. First, on the measure of task performance, the centralised networks solved problems faster and made fewer errors. In other words, groups with a more centralised structure (the wheel and the Y) made fewer errors and required less time to solve the problem than did the decentralised groups (the chain and the circle). Second, the satisfaction of the individual members was highest in the most decentralised network. Those in the circle network expressed the greatest enjoyment in performing the task, whereas the peripheral members of the wheel, chain and Y-pattern enjoyed the task least. In the wheel, chain and Y-pattern, the person C was perceived as group leader. However, no leader was perceived to exist in the circle network. Research works done by subsequent investigators have confirmed these findings relatively for simple tasks. However, for more complex tasks, the more decentralised networks led to better and superior performance. For complex task, the performance of the circle network was the best. Shaw (1981) offered an explanation for such findings. According to him, due to complexity in the task, excessive demand or information overload is placed on the central person in the centralised network. However, the decentralised networks allow a more even distribution of work load among the members of the group. Guetzkow and Simon (1955) reported from their study that the better performance of the centralised networks on simple problems disappeared after about 20 such problems had been solved by a group. In the more decentralised networks, it was found that the members of the group tended to develop their own substructures to compensate for the relative inefficiency of such networks. Business groups usually do well using decentralised networks for solving problems (Tushman, 1978). Burgess (1968) conducted a study in which the efficiency and satisfaction associated with wheel and circle networks were compared. He found that if the errors were punished and reinforcements were introduced, differences in the outcome performance of wheel and circle networks virtually disappeared. Likewise, when the two groups were allowed to arrive at a steady state, there remained no differences between them.

It has been reported that when the formal routes of communication do not serve the group's needs, the members of the group tend to rely upon the grapevine. The members of the group use grapevine to fill in the gaps in information to deal with uncertainty, if any. Researches have shown that sometimes, grapevine can be surprisingly accurate and useful also. Research studies have shown that about 80% grapevine items were work-related rather than personal and about 70% of the details passed through such informal network (grapevine) was accurate (Davis and Newstrom, 1985; Simmonds, 1985).

In recent days, the development of communication and information technology has displaced face-to-face interaction in group communication by fax, e-mail, video conferencing and use of Internet. While these measures are considered very efficient measures of transmitting information, they solely give emphasis upon the task at hand and reduce interpersonal considerations. A study conducted by Kiesler and Sproull (1992) reported that electronically linked group members took longer to reach an all-agreed decision as compared to those interacting face-to-face. Dubrovsky et al. (1991) reported that the group decision-making using e-mail served to reduce differences in status among individual group members.

Summary and Review

- A *group* is defined as a collection of two or more persons, who are perceived to be bonded together in coherent unit to some extent. Interaction among the members of the groups, perception of belonging together, shared goals and norms and fate interdependence are the four major characteristics of any collection of people to be called a group.
- Group structure and group cohesiveness are the two most important features of group. *Group structure* comprises social roles, social status and social norms. *Group cohesiveness* is another feature, which refers to both positive and negative forces that keep members together in the group.
- Social psychologists have tried to provide an answer to one basic question—why do people join a group? People join a group because they get many benefits such as reward given by the group, boosting of social status, facilitation in achievement of goal, etc. At the same time, joining a group may cost people. One popularly observed cost is that it restricts the personal freedom of the members of the group. Sometimes, the members have to pay in terms of time, energy and resources after joining a group.
- There are five major types of group—primary group and secondary group, in-group and out-group, formal group and informal group, exclusive group and inclusive group, membership group and reference group.
- Group develops through a sequence of five stages. Those five stages are stage of forming, stage of storming, stage of norming, stage of performing and stage of adjourning. One last stage of adjourning is found in case of only ad hoc group and not in permanent group.
- The presence of others directly tends to affect the behaviour of the persons. Commonly, such effect is observed in terms of two types of social behaviour—social facilitation and social inhibition. Sometimes, people perform better in the presence of others than when they are alone. This is called

social facilitation. However, the presence of others sometimes inhibits the performance of the individual. This is called *social inhibition*.

- When a person's contribution to a collective activity cannot be evaluated, he is often found to work less hard and put less effort as compared to when he has to do the same work in lone situation. This is called *social loafing*. Social psychologists have developed several techniques to reduce social loafing.
- Sometimes, people tend to lose control over themselves in crowd and act differently from how they would behave if they were alone. Such crowd situation, sometimes, may cause people to lose self-awareness and result in loss of individuality and self-restraint. This phenomenon is called *deindividuation*. One very important feature of deindividuation is that people feel anonymous here.
- Group decision-making is an important feature of our day-to-day life. Generally, it is believed that the collective wisdom of a body of people produces a more informed and higher quality of decision as compared to the decision taken by a single individual. Davis developed the concept of social decision schemes as a simple set of four rules for predicting the final decision by a group. These rules are unanimity, majority wins, truth wins and first-shift rule.
- There are some potential dangers of group decision-making. There are some forces that not only bias decision-making but also produce disastrous decision. Such forces are group polarisation, groupthink, biased use of information and failure to share information unique to each member.
- *Group polarisation* is defined as a tendency of groups to take decisions that are extreme than the mean of the individual member's initial position. This concept is so termed because the collective decision tends to move from the average, that is, towards one of the two extreme poles. The phenomenon of group polarisation has been explained with the help of three major perspectives—normative or social comparison perspective, persuasive-information perspective and self-categorisation theory.
- *Groupthink* refers to deterioration of mental efficiency, reality testing and moral judgement that results from in-group pressures. In other words, in groupthink, the group reaches a decision regarding any issue without allowing members to express their doubts and views. The group somehow believes that its decision is unanimous even when considerable unexpressed dissent may exist. Important systems of groupthink include illusion of invulnerability, high degree of morality, common stereotypes, illusion of unanimity, self-appointed mindguard, direct pressures on dissenters, collective rationalisation, etc.
- Another source of error in group decision-making is biased use of information in groups. When the group shows tendency to process available information in biased manner, it may reach on disastrous and inaccurate decision.
- Failure to share unique information from members is another potential error of group decision-making. The common observation has been that when the group's members discuss any problem or issue and try to reach a decision about it, they try to concentrate and share only those information, which are shared by most of the members. They tend to ignore the information or idea that is known only to a few members. When such information shared only by few members is related to the best decision, and they are ignored at the same time, it is likely that a disastrous decision may be produced.
- Social psychologists have provided some guidelines for improving the effectiveness of group decision-making. Apart from these guidelines, they have evolved some techniques such as devil's advocate technique, technique of authentic dissent and brainstorming for improving the effectiveness of group decision-making.
- When the members of the group do interact with each other, they behave either in a cooperative way or in competitive way with the other members of the group. Both cooperative and competitive behaviour of human beings have been studied by social psychologists in the situation of two-person games. The two popular games are trucking game and prisoner's dilemma. Researches done by social psychologists have revealed that there are several determinants of cooperation and competition. Such important determinants include nature of reward structure, communication patterns, individual differences in personal values, reciprocity, communication patterns, culture and social dilemma.

- There are two basic communication networks in group—centralised network and decentralised network. Wheel and Y-pattern are the examples of centralised network, whereas circle, chain, all-connect or comcon, and grapevine are the examples of decentralised network. For simple task, the performance of groups using centralised networks remains better than the performance of the groups using decentralised network. However, for complex task, the outcome performances of these two types of networks are reversed.

Review Questions

1. Define group. Discuss its characteristics.
2. Discuss the major features and aspects of group.
3. Why do people join a group? Also, discuss the cost of joining a group.
4. What do you mean by group development? Discuss the different stages or phases of group development.
5. How do the presence of others affect the behaviour of persons? In this context, discuss the phenomena of social facilitation and social inhibition.
6. Give the meaning of social loafing. Why does social loafing occur?
7. Discuss the techniques of reducing social loafing.
8. Explain the concept of deindividuation. Does deindividuation occur in large wild crowd?
9. Explain the role of social decision schemes in group decision-making.
10. Discuss some of the major potential dangers of group decision-making. Cite experimental evidences in favour of your answer.
11. Define group polarisation. Discuss the major perspectives that explain group polarisation.
12. Discuss the major causes of groupthink.
13. Discuss the major symptoms and consequences of groupthink.
14. Discuss the major techniques of improving effectiveness of group decision-making. Also, discuss major guidelines provided by social psychologists for improving group decision-making.
15. What light do the trucking game and the prisoner's dilemma game throw upon the nature of cooperative and competitive behaviour of human beings? What is the implication of these studies for understanding human behaviour?
16. Discuss the impact of different types of communication networks upon members of the group.

10 SOCIAL NORMS AND CONFORMITY BEHAVIOUR

Learning Objectives

➢ Concept of Social Norms
➢ Formation of Social Norms
➢ Meaning of Conformity Behaviour
➢ Why Do We Conform?
➢ Factors Influencing Conformity
➢ How Can We Resist Social Pressure To Conform?

KEY TERMS

Autokinetic effect
Collectivist culture
Conformity
Desire for individuation
Descriptive social norms
Dual process hypothesis
Individualistic culture
Informational social influence
Minority influence
Moral realism
Normative social influence
Physical reality
Prescriptive social norms
Private conformity
Public conformity
Reactance
Social norms
Social reality

In every social group, a person wishes to stand well with his fellows, to win their respect and to have relations with them that allows to carry out those activities with which he is concerned. Therefore, he acts in conformity with values, traditions, customs and the like in the society. For example, a Brahmin in an orthodox society must rise early, take his bath and sit on worship. In England, a gentleman must let ladies enter first and must express regret by saying 'sorry' when he brushes past a stranger and the like. Likewise, in some Indian communities, Hindu widows shave their heads, whereas in others, they only cover their heads. Similarly, in the Hopi community, people look down upon all those who strive for personal power and prestige, whereas the Kwakiutl enjoy competition and struggle for status and rank. Thus, each socio-cultural group has some specific characteristics expressed in terms of values, traditions and customs, which represent its social norms or standards.

CONCEPT OF SOCIAL NORMS

Social norm is a very wide term, which includes all types of social expectations and demands in the form of traditions, customs, folkways, rules of conduct, values and the like. In other words, social norm is a widely accepted (often unspoken) standard for appropriate behaviour in a situation. In fact, social norms constitute what is called *ought to definition*—they tend to define the behaviours, which are appropriate for the given situations; they tell us what a person ought to do, and conversely, what he ought not to do. Thus, social norms are generally accepted way of thinking, feeling or behaving that most people in the group agree and accept as right and proper (Thibaut and Kelley, 1959). In this way, social norms are very similar to attitudes in the sense that both are the cognitive representations of the correct and appropriate ways of thinking, feeling and doing/acting in response to any social object or event. However, the two differs because attitudes represent an individual's positive or negative evaluations, whereas norms represent group evaluations of what is appropriate or inappropriate, A father's love for his children is an attitude, whereas the idea that a father should love his children is a social norm. *Descriptive social norms*, that is, what people think, feel and do in a given situation are sometimes contrasted with *prescriptive or injunctive social norms*, that is, what people should or ought to think, feel and do in a given situation. The idea that parents love offspring is a descriptive norms and the idea that parents should love their children is prescriptive social norms. Most social norms contain the qualities of both types of norms because most people think, feel and act in a certain way that we think they should. Although both descriptive and injunctive norms strongly influence our behaviour, in a contain situation like a situation in which antisocial behaviour is likely to occur, injunctive norms tend to exert stronger effects (Brown, 1988; Cialdini el al., 1991). This is because of two reasons. *First*, such norms force people to shift attention from how they are acting in a particular situation to how they should be behaving. *Second*, injunctive norms tend to activate the social motive to do right thing in a situation irrespective of what others are doing or have done. Besides, social norms may also be formal or informal in nature. No cheating in the examination is an example of formal norm whereas informal guidelines such as 'Don't tell lie' is an example of informal social norms.

Social norms are transmitted from one generation to another and can even be traced to many centuries back. For example, folding hands to greet people or taking off shoes before entering temple and kitchen are very ancient social norms in Indian society that are being transmitted from one generation to the next, though they are gradually changing under the impact of foreign culture. Some social norms are short-lived like fashion and fond, whereas others continue for very longer period and become part and parcel of the life of the people. Today, *Dhoti* and *Kurta* have been replaced by shirt and pant, and now, guests are being entertained with coffee or tea instead of milk and curd.

Social norms involve judgements of value. We judge a particular behaviour as either approved or disapproved on the basis of its conformity or non-conformity to a social norm. In other words, social norm denotes patterns of behaviour demanded of members of a group, how they ought to behave and whether they actually behave in expected way or not.

Another feature of social norms is that they have a high emotional tone. For example, Hindus abstain from beef and condemn those who take it. Sikhs hate smoking and Muslims recommend *purdah* for women. All these social norms have emotional tinge and any attempt to violate these norms by the concerned members is strongly resented.

Still another feature of social norms is that it allows a considerable amount of latitude. According to Sherif (1936), social norms rarely specify just one point or one single way of behaviour, and like all concepts, norms encompass a range of behaviour, which is considered tolerable (or permissible) to the behaviour. In fact, this range of tolerable behaviour varies in extent in terms of both importance of the matter and position of a particular member in the hierarchy of the group. In trivial and minor matters, the range of tolerable behaviour is considerably wider, whereas in vital matters, the range is comparatively narrower. In a nutshell, the existence of social norms should not be construed to mean that the behaviour of the social group is rigid. In fact, it allows a good deal of variability and latitude in behaviour.

Social norms of the society are usually not codified, though attempts have been made to do so. *Manu Smriti* is one such best attempt and laws of the state, penal codes, list of religious commandments and the like have codified social norms. If the group does not have written rules, how do we know that it forms the part of social norms? Answering this question, Freedman (1952) had said that by observing the behaviour of the individuals in a group, we can notice striking similarities in the behaviour of the different persons of the group. It is just possible that some of them may express it in words and refer to it as social norm or they may not be able to do so, but still they prefer to conform to these norms. Another thing is that we may find that the group will have certain sanctions, that is, behaviours in conformity to the group norm are rewarded and behaviours not in conformity with the group norms are punished.

Lastly, social norms are in a way social stimulus situations. A person does not react to abstract value or ideal implicit in the norm, but to its concrete forms. For example, a person does not react to law when he stops at red signal, rather he reacts to the danger involved in it and to the policeman who may pull him up. A student salute his teachers because it is done and expected and he learns the social norms of respect for teachers.

FORMATION OF SOCIAL NORMS

The formation of social norms may be studied from two angles—how children come to acquire social norms and how norms arise in group.

How do children come to acquire social norms?

According to social psychologists, norms are revealed through the actions and words of other people. They have studied the growth and development of moral ideas among children. They maintain that moral judgements are clearly not simply assimilated readymade from the previous generation but are reworked in terms of children's needs and their identification with other persons. In 1932, Swiss psychologist, Piaget published his studies relating to the development of children's ideas of right and wrong. He found four stages in the development of response of right and wrong. He studied the way the children learn to play marbles. The little children first began to play the marbles by observing the bigger boys playing them. When asked to tell about who would win, they simply said that everybody would win. Thus, the children were simply enjoying the activities and they were not making any judgement in terms of what was right or wrong. The second stage was characterised by what Piaget called *moral realism*, and children of 4–5 years belong to this stage. At this stage, the rules of game were thought to be strictly enforced. Everything was objectively right or objectively wrong. If any person does wrong, he must be punished irrespective of his motives. If they were told that boys in different localities had different rules, they did not understand it nor cared about this. A little later they entered in the third stage having age groups of 7–8 years. At this stage, they began to realise that the rules are not objective and absolute, but are made by persons and reflect group values. Consequently, they changed the whole conception of what is right and what is wrong. As the child becomes mature by interaction with other people, he grasps the notion of reciprocity. In this process of reciprocity, children realised that the existing rules could be changed by formulating new rules. The fourth stage started around the period of adolescence, where they realised that the reciprocity is not always possible. They started realising that mutual arrangement was not the only criterion of rule-making. Rules could be altered or changed by considerations of justice and equity. If any rule applies to all, this is definitely satisfactory, but there may be cases where rigid universal application of rules may not prove fair. This enabled the children to look upon moral judgement as not something arbitrary, but as something, which was dependent on personal factors.

The above explanation clearly shows that Piaget was explicitly in favour of idea that social norms are not acquired all at once. They develop slowly as a result of interaction, on increasing experience of dealing with different types of people as well as by the personal needs of different individuals.

Although Piaget's explanation has been supported by many others, his idea that early conception of moral rules is rigid and absolute, which is probably due to authoritarian discipline of parents, seems to be too naive. It may be due to lack of understanding of the implication of moral rules and tacit acceptance from the members of the group.

How do norms arise in group?

As we know, social norms are shared norms. They are values or standards of the group and arise in connection with the matters of importance. The conduct, aspirations and the like of the members of the group are regulated by these norms. Such social norms cannot be inferred from the behaviour of a single individual. They emerge from social interactions and can be better known from social situation. Now, one basic question arises—what are the characteristics of social situations in which norms tend to arise?

Social psychologists have identified two types of situations, which are important for emergence of norms—structured situation and unstructured situation. The *structured situation* is one that is compelling, strong, defined and clear, whereas the *unstructured situation* is one that is weak, vague, undefined and ambiguous. In structured situation, the objective factors are strong and compelling enough to determine the behaviour of the person. In such a situation, the behaviour of a person is more or less accurately assessed and definite scales and standards are available to measure its size, speed, etc. Buildings, timetables, objects of definite magnitude, etc. represent structured situation. However, it is the unstructured situation such as birth, death, marriage, illness and the like that give rise to traditions, customs and values. What ceremonies should regulate marriage in any group, what should be done when somebody dies, how we treat intimate friends and strangers, how should we nurse the patient, what type of function should be organised for celebrating birthday of a child are all examples of unstructured situation, which leave room for a number of alternatives for behaviour and experience. That is the reason why such unstructured situation provide ample opportunity for developing customs, traditions, values, etc. The various alternatives are compared and the desirable ones are stabilised or confirmed through the process of social interaction, past experience as well as through established relations and goals. Finally, social norms emerge, and as a consequence, such unstructured situation becomes structured, definite and defined.

Early Experiments on Norm Formation

The formation of a norm as a frame of reference against which perceptual judgements are made can be best illustrated by a well-known laboratory experiment conducted by Sherif (1936). His objective was two-fold—what a person will do when he is called upon to judge a stimulus situation without any external reference and how a group will respond to such stimulus. Each of three participants in this experiment first sat alone in a totally dark room and paid attention to a single point of light. As the participants watched, the light seemed to jump erratically and then disappeared. A little later, the participants again saw the light appeared, moved and disappeared. In fact, the light was stationary. Since the room was totally dark without any point of reference, a stationary point of light appeared to move in jagged circle. This was, in fact, an optical illusion called *autokinetic effect*. Since it was an ambiguous situation, it was not surprising that each participant's estimate of original distance of movement of light differed, ranging from barely an inch to nearly a foot. After a few days, these participants again returned to the laboratory for doing the same task, but this time, they were the members of the three-person groups. In this situation, since they were able to hear one another's estimates of light's movement, group members' response began to converge until they were identical. In other words, three participants in the group demonstrated consensus on some very narrow range of judgements. This agreed-upon range was called *social norms*.

Sherif made two important observations about these laboratory norms. First, if the participants, each forming his norms in individual situation, are later placed in group, they were found to gradually change these individual norms to arrive at a common group norm. Second, if a participant has formed norm in the group situation and on later occasion, tested in alone, he tends to respond in terms of that norm. Thus, group norm was adopted by the individual subjects as their own norm.

This early experiment of Sherif has been criticised on the ground that the experimental situation was ambiguous. Participants could not assess light's movement and they received no feedback about right and wrong responses. The light was really not moving, so any estimate within reason would tend to sound good. Under such circumstances, participants could do nothing much except depending on the responses of others.

Other social psychologists like Secord and Backman (1964) opined that we rely on at least two sources of information to determine the validity of our opinions and actions—*physical reality* and *social reality*. We generally obtain a good deal of information from the physical reality around us, and to some extent, our opinions are evaluated and determined on the basis of this physical reality. Social reality, that is, evaluation and judgement of other persons, often acts as an even more important source of information. The key idea is that the more ambiguous the physical stimuli, the more likely we are to rely on social reality for interpretation of our opinions.

Solomon Asch (1951, 1955) conducted an experiment in which answer to this basic question was sought—what about the decision, which is not ambiguous when physical and other non-social sources of information are available? The answer is that even in such a situation, the persons still have influence of others' viewpoints in arriving at a judgement about the stimulus situation. In his study, the participants gathered in a room and were told that they were participating in an experiment on visual judgement. They were shown a white card with three black lines of differing lengths, followed by another white card with only one line on it (see Figure 10.1). The task before the participant was to determine

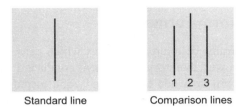

Figure 10.1 Stimuli used in Asch's experiment.

The task before the participant was to determine which line on the first card was most similar to the line shown on the second card. The reality was that in this experiment, only the last person among the participants was the real participant. The others were all confederates, that is, persons following special directions/instructions from the experimenter. The confederates had been secretly instructed by the experimenter to pick the same incorrect line from the three comparison lines. On 12 of the 18 experimental trials, the confederates unanimously selected a wrong answer, responding together that either a shorter or a longer line matched the standard line. The confederates' wrong answer had an obvious impact upon real participants' responses that tended to make them agree with the incorrect answer of the confederates. In fact, the participants agreed with an obviously wrong answer on 6 or more trials.

The obvious results of Sherif and Asch's studies showed that people are influenced by and often adopt the views and opinions of other members of the group. The common observation shows that whether the judgement task is ambiguous or well-defined, whether the group is small or large, the group members typically offer, exchange and accept different points of view until consensus (or norm) evolves.

MEANING OF CONFORMITY BEHAVIOUR

As we know, social influence ranges from simple suggestion to intensive indoctrination such as brainwashing. Our day-to-day behaviour is probably most influenced by the group pressures for conformity, which is simply defined as bringing one's own behaviour into agreement with the social norms or to the behaviour of others (Coon and Mitterer, 2007). In other words, *conformity* refers to the convergence of the person's thinking, feeling and behaviour towards a group norm (Allen, 1965; Kiesler and Kiesler, 1969). In simple words, conformity is the tendency to change one's beliefs or behaviours so that they may match the behaviour of others (Cialdini and Goldstein, 2004).

There are two popular forms of conformity—private conformity and public conformity. *Private conformity* means private acceptance of social norms. When the individuals are truly persuaded that the group is right and when they willingly and privately accept the norms of the group as their own beliefs and values, private conformity is said to occur (Insko et al., 1983). This is also called *internalisation* or *private acceptance*. A good example of private conformity can be seen in Sherif's classic study on conformity towards group norms (discussed earlier), where participants adopted their group's standard opinion regarding the movement of light even though they were never pressurised to do so. This sincere inward conformity is also called *acceptance* (Myers, 2005). *Public conformity* refers to the overt behaviour (consistent with the social norms) done by the individuals, which is not privately accepted. Such public conformity occurs when the individuals respond to some real or imagined pressures and tend to behave consistently with the norms, which they do not accept as true one. In such conformity, the individuals pretend to go along with the demands of the group norms, but privately, they think that the group is not right. Here, individuals conform publicly because they fear of ridicule or rejection. A good example of public conformity can be found in Asch's classic experiment on norm formation, where the participants went along with the incorrect majority view of confederates to avoid being ridiculous. This outward conformity is also called *compliance* (Myers, 2005).

WHY DO WE CONFORM?

To understand why people conform to group pressure, a distinction between the two types of social influence, that is, normative social influence and informational social influence, which was first cited by Deutsch and Gerard (1955), needs to be examined. *Normative social influence* is related to group norms which are the expectations held by group members regarding how to behave. Normative social influence operates because of our attempts to meet the expectations of the group. Here, we have a desire to be liked. We conform because our experience has led us to believe that those who do not respect group norms and behave as dissidents are punished by the other members of the group. In normative pressure to conform, generally, there is public compliance, where somebody publicly conforms to the group norms, but privately maintains a different opinion. *Informational social influence* occurs because we rely on others' perception, experience and knowledge. Here, we conform because we think that other group members have information about the situation, which we are lacking. In informational pressure to conform, generally, there is private acceptance or internalisation, where the person believes the group to be correct. Here, we have a desire to be right. In several situations in which people conform, it is likely that both normative and informational social influence operate. For example, in Asch's experiment on the formation of norm (or conformity behaviours), the participants, who conformed to the responses of the group, probably, were doing so because of a desire to avoid contradicting group norms and potentially being ridiculed or punished in some other way by the group (normative social influence) as well as because they might have thought that the other people had greater experience in the task or know something new which they do not (informational social influence). Generally, in more ambiguous situation, there is greater informational pressure to conform. However, in less ambiguous situation or task, normative pressure is high in producing conformity. This is summarised in Figure 10.2.

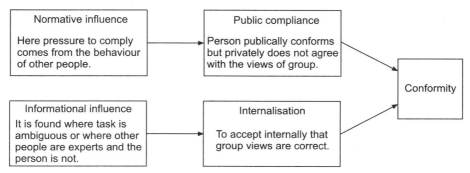

Figure 10.2 Conformity explained in terms of normative and informational social influence.

Social psychologists have studied conformity in the laboratory. Three sets of experiment are generally discussed—*Sherif's experiment, Asch's experiment and Crutchfield's experiment.*

Sherif's (1936) experiment on autokinetic effect clearly reveals how people conform to the established norms. As it has been discussed earlier, autokinetic effect is a kind of optical illusion that occurs when a pinpoint of light is viewed in a totally dark room—a totally stationary light appears to move. In one of his experiments, he brought a group of participants into dark room to observe a pinpoint of light, and then, they were requested to report how far the light moved. After a series of trials, it was found that the range of estimates made by the participants began to converge towards the average and after some more trials, the more extreme estimates tended to become less extreme. Eventually, the group came to establish a norm or a generally agreed-upon estimate of light movement. Participants were found to show conformity to this norm when responding in later trials.

In further study, Sherif reported that the conformity to the norms (or majority judgement) occurs quickly when participants had no prior experience of the task, and therefore, had not developed any frame of reference. In such a situation, when an inexperienced participant sat in a darkened room with two experienced participants and is asked to make an estimate of the movement of the light, he tends to share the same range of movement of the light, showing conformity to the majority judgement. Generally, the more the ambiguous situation and the lesser the experience of the participant, the greater conformity to majority group judgement is likely to occur.

Asch (1951) also conducted a series of experiments to investigate conformity. As discussed earlier, the basic experiment involved presenting a participant with a standard line and a set of three comparison lines. The participants were required to judge which comparison line was closest to the standard line in length. For studying conformity, Asch put a participant in a room, with seven other people who were confederates of the experimenter, but thought to be other participants by the real participant. Arrangement was deliberately made in such a way that the real participant sat at the end of the row. Each person in the room had to state publicly which comparison line was most similar to the standard line. Since the real participant sat at the end of row, he clearly listened to the judgements of confederates before giving his judgement.

There were 18 trials, that is, 18 different lines to be matched. During 12 of these trials, all confederates gave the same wrong answer, which, of course, disturbed the real participant. Varying the experiment with the groups of 2, 3, 4, 8 and 10–15, Asch reported that tendency to conform with majority opinion was in full swing even when there was unanimous majority of only 3 participants. To the utter surprise, the unanimous majority of 15 produced no higher conformity than did that of 3 participants. Asch found that 5% of the total participants conformed to the incorrect, unanimous majority all the time, 70% conformed some of the time, but 25% of the participants remained independent and were never swayed the majority decision. Asch also reported that if just one person voiced a dissenting opinion, the tendency to conform decreased. When just one confederate in the group disagreed with the incorrect majority, the real participant's error dropped from 32% to 10.4%.

Interview conducted after the experiment indicated that most of the participants were quite aware of the differences between the majority's judgement and their own. They felt puzzled. The interview indicated that conformity by participants in this study was of a particular type. To a greater extent, it involved public compliance without private acceptance. Although some participants conformed publicly, they did not accept the majority's judgement privately.

Asch's pioneering research led to many other studies of conformity. Researches have demonstrated similar conformity effects using different types of judgement tasks, including evaluating opinion statements, statement of facts and logical syllogisms.

Crutchfield (1955) devised another method of studying conformity. He was of view that Asch's experimental paradigm was costly in terms of time and number of confederates required as well as this technique demanded a lot of acting from the confederates. In Crutchfield technique, more suitable for large scale research use, five participants sat at a time side by side in the individual booths screened from one another. Each booth had a panel with row of switches that could be used by the participants for responding to the items presented on the slides projected on the wall in front of the group. On this panel, there were also signal lights, which indicated what judgement the other four members gave to the displayed task. The booths were designated by letters A, B, C, D and E and the participants were required to respond in that order. They were asked not to talk during the experimental work. Although this was the way the participants were led to understand, reality was otherwise. In fact, there was really no electrical connection among the five panels and signals were actually delivered by the experimenter with the help of a master control panel in such a way that on all the five individual panels, the light might appear in pre-established order. Moreover, all the five booths were really marked as E so that each participant might be able to see the sequence of judgements allegedly coming from persons A, B, C and D before he came up with his own judgement. In order to introduce greater group pressure, the experimenter made it appear that all four members (that is, A to D) agreed on the answer, which was clearly a deviant to the correct answer. In this way, all five participants were subjected to a conflict between their own judgement and the bogus consensus of the other four participants. Here, the participants might conform by giving the same judgement as that of the group or they might seek their own answer, showing no conformity. The items in the experiment varied widely in content—objective facts, others opinion and attitude, some easy and some difficult items to judge, etc. In fact, Crutchfield conducted several studies using this standard technique and some of his major findings were as under:

1. Substantial amount of conformity was produced by the group pressure and that too in even those situations, where the bogus group consensus, to which the participants showed conformity, was vividly displayed.
2. Conformity was greater in case of difficult items rather than in case of easy items.
3. Even those individuals could be pressurised for conformity towards the tasks who had personal or social relevance to them.
4. There were larger individual differences in conformity. Some individuals demonstrated conformity on all items, some on few and some conform on none. Most individuals conformed on some items and not on others.
5. When participants were privately retested after the experiment session was over, a major part of original conformity to the item disappeared and they reverted to their own private judgement. However, not all conformity effect disappeared.

A comparative study of Asch's experimental procedure and Crutchfield's experimental procedure reveals some similarities and contrast. The similarities are that in both procedures, some forms of deception was used. In Asch's experimental procedure, the confederates spoke lie, whereas in Crutchfield's experimental procedure, the communication between the group members was deliberately falsified and rigged. Despite these similarities, there are certain major differences between the two procedures. In Asch's experimental procedure, the participants were placed in a face-to-face oral communication with group members, whereas in Crutchfield's experimental procedure, the participants were in a way removed from one another and were not allowed to communicate directly and to some degree, they remain anonymous. Researches done by Deutsch and Gerard (1955) and Levy (1960) showed that with identical judgement items used in two types of experimental procedures, the average amount of conformity is higher in case of Asch-type experiment because this situation imposes more powerful group pressure on the individual.

FACTORS INFLUENCING CONFORMITY

When do we conform? To answer this question, social psychologists have studied experimentally the impact of many factors and variables that tend to influence conformity. Such important factors are given as:

1. Size of the group: The size of group influences the conformity. Asch (1956) and early investigators like Rosenberg (1961) and Gerard, Wilhelmy and Conolley (1968) demonstrated that as the size of unanimous majority in the group increases, the amount of conformity by the participants also increases. In Asch-type experiment, when a person is confronted with another person, there will be less conformity and chances are that he will express his opinion independently. However, when confronted by two unanimous individuals, the participant will experience more social pressure to show conformity to their decision. Likewise, confronted with three persons, the participant will tend to exhibit conformity at a still higher rate. In the early studies conducted by Asch (1951), it was found that conformity increases with the size of the group, but only up to three or four members. When the size of the group increases beyond four members, the conformity appears to decline. However, study conducted by Bond and Smith (1996) did not support these early findings regarding group size and conformity and instead, showed that conformity tends to increase with the increase in group size up to eight group members and even beyond that.

2. Group unanimity: Researches have shown that a participant faced with a unanimous majority is under pressure to conform. However, if the group unanimity is broken down, there is striking decrease in conformity. When even one member dissents, the conformity drops to about one-fourth level of the usual level (Taylor, Peplau and Sears, 2006). Researches have shown that irrespective of the status of the dissenter, that is, whether he is a credible or incredible, prestigious expert or someone of low prestige, the conformity is lower substantially (Morris and Miller, 1975) In early study conducted by Asch (1955), the effect of an incorrect, non-unanimous majority on line judging tasks was studied under three different experimental conditions. In one experimental condition, one of the confederates always gave correct judgement (ally); in second experimental condition, a confederate first gave a correct judgement, but later on, defected to incorrect majority view (defector) and in the third experimental condition, one confederate gave even more inaccurate judgement than the other confederates (extreme dissenter). Results revealed that in all the three experimental conditions, the conformity was lower than the condition of unanimous, incorrect majority.

When unanimity of the group breaks down, conformity level goes down. Why? Usually two explanations have been provided by the social psychologists for this:

(i) When any member, even if he is not knowledgeable or less reliable, creates impression on the part of the real participant that majority appears to be wrong, this situation reduces the reliance on majority opinion as an important source of information, and consequently, conformity is reduced.

(ii) When the dissenter endorses a position that the real participant favours, this increases confidence about the judgement and such enhanced confidence tends to reduce conformity.

3. Commitment to the group: Researches have shown that conformity is also affected by the commitment of the members. Commitment includes all the forces, positive and negative, which tend to keep a person in a group. In the group, positive forces like liking for other members of the group, feeling that all group members work together and expecting a gain from belonging to the group, etc. make the group cohesive. Such group becomes more vulnerable to the conformity pressure than the group which is less cohesive. Abrams et al. (1990) reported that conformity is still greater if the sources of influence are perceived as belonging to one's own group. Sometimes, negative forces, which prevent the members from leaving the group, also enhance conformity. Negative forces include factors like having few alternatives or having made huge investment in the group, which may be costly to give up, etc. Such negative forces also increase commitment to the group, and therefore, pressure for conformity to group is also enhanced.

4. Self-esteem and status of the individual: Self-esteem also influences the conformity. Several research studies have shown that the persons with high self-esteem are less likely to conform than the persons with low self-esteem. Stang (1973) found that the individuals with high self-esteem showed less conformity than the individuals with moderate or low self-esteem. Eagly (1987) reported that the people of low status display more conformity to the group standard than those of high status. Milgram (1974) in his experiment on obedience reported that the people of lower status conform to the experimenter's command more readily than the people of higher status.

5. Social norms–descriptive and injunctive type: Social norms affect our conformity behaviour. Some researchers have made distinction between descriptive social norms and injunctive social norms (Reno, Cialdini and Kallgren, 1993). *Descriptive norms*, as the name implies, are the norms that simply describe what most people do in a particular situation. *Injunctive or prescriptive norms*, on the other hand, are the norms that specify what is approved or disapproved behaviour in a given situation. In general, both types of norms influence our behaviour, but injunctive norms may exert somewhat stronger effect, especially in the context of anti-social behaviour. Injunctive norms do influence behaviour because such norms tend to activate the social motive to do what is approved in a given situation. However, people, sometimes, tend to ignore even the injunctive norms. For example, there is an injunctive norm in our society that students should not cheat in the examination hall, but still then, many students ignore this norm and resort to unfair means like cheating. But why do people sometimes ignore even injunctive norms? One answer is provided by *normative focus theory*, which states that norms influence the behaviour of a person to the extent that the person considers them relevant or significant for himself (Cialdini, Kallgren and Reno, 1991). When the person thinks about the norms and views them relevant to his behaviour, norms do influence his behaviour. On the other hand, when the person does not think about norms or views them something not applying to him, the effect of such norms becomes weaker or non-existent, so to say.

6. Culture: The culture of the participant has also been found to affect conformity. Whether the participant belongs to individualistic culture or collectivist culture, has been found to influence conformity behaviour. Members of individualistic culture such as European and North American people define their identity in terms of personal choices and individual attachments. Members of such cultures have friends based on shared interest and activities. Autonomy, change, security of the individual and equality are all highly valued. On the other hand, members of collectivist culture, predominantly Latin American and Asian people, tend to define their identity on the basis of characteristics of collective group to which he or she is permanently attached. In such culture, loyalty to the family is highly valued and the care of the family is placed before the care of the individual. Smith and Harris (1993) in a significant study making review of conformity studies from 1957 to 1985, showed that the level of conformity is higher in collectivist culture as compared to the level of conformity in individualistic culture. Bond and Smith (1996), Kim and Markus (1999) also reported similar findings. In Bond and Smith's (1996) study analysis of 133 studies done in 17 countries confirmed that cultural value has an impact upon conformity. Their analysis vividly showed that as compared to the people of individualistic culture, people of collectivist culture exhibited higher degree of conformity.

7. Competence and skill at particular task: Competence and skill at a certain task also influence conformity behaviour. A competent and skilled participant, in his area of task, is less likely to show conformity. Thus, competence and skill reduce conformity (Weisenthal and Endler, 1976). This is more relevant when understood in context of gender. Eagly and Carli (1981) conducted a study in which results of studies over a 30-year period were reviewed. When statistically combined, the results demonstrated that women were more susceptible to conformity than men. However, on closer and detailed analysis, it was found that women only conformed more than men when the experimental task was sex-typed in favour of males. When such task was used, which showed no sex bias, there was no apparent sex difference (Sistrunk and McDavid, 1971)

8. Desire for individuation: There are people who differ in their desire to do things that publicly differentiate them from others. Some people desire to go along with a group, whereas some others prefer to stand out and maintain a distinctive and independent impression. The latter tendency is called *desire for individuation*. Maslach et al. (1985) studied the impact of desire for individuation upon conformity. They developed a questionnaire for assessing desire for individuation and concluded from their research that in laboratory settings, high-individuation people were less likely to conform, that is, go along with the majority view. In fact, they were creative dissenter by providing some independent judgement. Apart from this, high-individualism subjects were found to be less socially compliant, more critical and less polite. However, low-individuation person were found to conform to the majority opinion frequently.

Thus, we find that there are several factors that do influence conformity.

HOW CAN WE RESIST SOCIAL PRESSURE TO CONFORM?

In general, the pressure towards conformity remains high. Social psychologists have been able to recognise some factors that tend to resist conformity. Such important factors are as under:

1. Reactance: Reaction lowers conformity because it is, in fact, a negative reaction to the efforts done by others to reduce our freedom by getting us to do what they want. In such a situation, we generally change our cognition in the opposite direction of what we are urged to believe or to do. This illustrates a negative attitude change (Rhodewalt and Davison, 1983), and as a consequence, people do not conform to what is suggested by the majority opinion. The theory of reactance is supported by the experiments that have vividly shown that the attempts to restrict a person's freedom often produce an anticonformity boomerang effect (Nail et al., 2000).

2. Need to maintain individuality: People feel pride in being perceived as distinct from others. This need to maintain individuality seems to be a powerful factor that reduces conformity. Greater the desire for individuation, lesser is the conformity. This prediction has been tested in terms of two types of culture—individualistic culture and collectivist culture. In individualistic culture, the desire for individuation is strong, whereas such desire is non-existent in case of collectivist culture. Researches conducted by Bond and Smith (1996) showed that in individualistic culture (such as in European countries and North America), conformity is poor, whereas in collectivist culture (such as in Asian countries), conformity is high.

3. Desire for personal control: The desire to exert control over one's own life also tends to reduce conformity. Some people believe that they should have their own control over the events that occur in their life. When situations demand for yielding towards social pressure, they become disturbed because it runs counter to their desire. They think that if they lose control over their personal events, their personal freedom will also be curtailed. Therefore, such people having a strong desire for personal control tend to resist social pressure to conformity.

4. Persons who cannot conform: In society, there are persons, who cannot conform for psychological, physical and legal reasons. For example, at the time national anthem is being played, a physically handicapped with crippled legs cannot conform to the social norms of being stand up. Likewise, for similar reasons, there are persons in our society, who cannot adhere to the accepted styles of dress. The case of homosexuals is another example. Homosexuals want to conform to social norms, that is, they want to marry but cannot because law inhibits such marriage and restricts to only heterosexual couples. Till today, marriage between homosexual males or homosexual females is fully legal in only one country—the Netherlands. (Baron, Byrne and Branscombe, 2006)

5. Social support: Asch (1955) in his series of experiment clearly showed that even a lone dissenter amongst the confederates destroys the apparent consensus of majority and this little lack of social support encourages the individual to develop alternative to the incorrect majority judgement, thus lowering the conformity. Further researches done by Morris and Miller (1975) and Allen and Levine (1971) showed, respectively, that timing of the support and quality of the support also influence conformity.

Morris and Miller (1975), using Crutchfield's technique, conducted an experiment in which there were two experimental conditions and one control condition. In one of the experimental conditions, the supporter (that is, the confederate giving correct judgement) gave the correct response before the majority gave the same incorrect response. In another experimental condition, the supporter gave the correct response after the majority had expressed its opinion. In control condition, the group of the participants was exposed to an incorrect unanimous majority judgement. In the results, it was found that the conformity was least when the supporter gave his response before (and not after) the majority opinion was expressed. Explaining this finding, Morris and Miller said that this was due to the fact that the support before majority judgement provided the participant with immediate confirmation of his own judgement after viewing the stimulus material on the panel of the display instrument. Obviously, then, timing of support was a factor that reduced conformity.

Allen and Levine (1971) examined the impact of quality of the support, that is, the impact of either credible or non-credible social support. In their experiment, the participants were given a task involving visual perception and the supporter was presented in one of the two ways to the participant. In condition A, the supporter wore glass with thicker lenses and said he had problems in correct vision; in condition B, the supporter did not wear glass and made no reference to his vision. Results revealed that in condition A, where the participants doubted the credibility of the supporter, the conformity was low.

6. Minority influence: Sometimes, a forceful minority influence proves to be more creative with a new idea than the majority influence. As a consequence, minority influence, under the group pressure to conform, does not really change its judgement regarding the task. This situation results in reduced conformity. Researches have shown that to be effective, the minority must be consistent and forceful (Wood et al., 1994). Such consistency and forcefulness are interpreted by the majority as the sign of confidence and certainty in the stand taken by minority. Moscovici, Lage and Naffrechoux (1969) conducted an experiment to show that how sometimes minority influence becomes so forceful that it resists the group pressure created by majority, and thus, conformity is reduced to a greater extent. In this experiment, Ash-type experimental paradigm was used in which there was a majority of naive participants and minority of confederates. There were six persons in the group, who were asked to rate the colour of slides, which were all blue but varied in their luminance. Besides, there was a control group of six naive participants, who described all the slides as blue ones. In the experimental group, both confederates consistently judged the blue slides as green. Results revealed that with this minority influence, about of a third of the participants reported to see at least one green slide and in about 8% of all judgements, slides were perceived as green. These results obviously showed that consistent minority influence had an important effect on the naive majority.

Why does minority influence become too influential? According to Mackie and Hunter (1979), there are some obvious factors that determine the dominant impact of minority influence. First, minority influence becomes more effective when the minorities provide a strong logical arguments for their judgement (Clark, 1990). Second, when the issues or tasks on which judgement or views are required, are not of great importance for the members of the majority group (Trost, Maass and Kenrock, 1992). Third, sometimes, minorities become more effective when they are found to be similar to the majority group in several respects except for the particular behaviour in question (Volpato et al., 1990).

Recently, social psychologists have debated the idea that whether the processes of majority influence (conformity) and minority influence (non-conformity or independence) are same or different (Forgas and Williams, 2001). To settle the issue, one view called *dual-process hypothesis* has been advanced. According to this viewpoint, minority and majority influence tend to induce different cognitive processes in the participants. The minority influence forces the members of the group to think seriously about the task or behaviour in question and also to engage in a systematic processing of information. Consequently, minority influence becomes effective in changing attitudes and opinions of the majority, thus reducing the conformity. On the other hand, majority influence is perceived as a less thoughtful process involved in conformity to group views. Generally, majority influence tends to bring changes in overt behaviour, but not in the private attitudes of the participants.

Thus, it is obvious that people resist conformity due to a lot of factors. All these factors reduce conformity to group pressures.

Summary and Review

- The term *social norm* includes all types of social expectations and demands in the form of traditions, customs, folkways, rules of conduct, values, etc. In other words, social norm is a widely accepted standard for appropriate behaviour in a situation. It tells us what a person ought to do and conversely, what he ought not to do.
- Social norms are developed in the society through the development of moral ideas among children. In 1932, Swiss psychologist, Jean Piaget published his famous studies relating to the development of children's ideas of right and wrong and came to the conclusion that such moral ideas develop through four stages. Social psychologists have also studied the development of norms in groups. Of the two types of situation, that is, structured and unstructured, it is the unstructured situation that gives rise to traditions, customs and values in the society. Early experiments on the formation of norms conducted by Sherif and Ash revealed that social norms develop through social interaction in the group. Whether the judgement task is ambiguous or well-defined, whether the group is large or small, the group's members typically often exchange and accept different points of view until consensus (or norms) evolves.
- *Conformity* refers to convergence of person's thinking, feeling and behaviour towards group norms. There are two popular forms of conformity—public conformity and private conformity. *Public conformity* refers to the overt behaviour done by the persons that are consistent with the social norms, but are not privately accepted. *Private conformity* (or also called *internalisation*) refers to the acceptance of social norms willingly, and here, the persons privately think that the beliefs and values contained in the social norms are those of their own.
- People show conformity due to normative social influence and informational social influence. Normative social influence is related to the group norms and it operates because of our attempts to meet the expectation of the group. Here, we have desires to be liked. In normative pressure to conform, generally there is public compliance (or conformity), where somebody publicly conforms to the group norms and privately maintains a different opinion. Informational social influence occurs because we rely on others' perception, experience and knowledge. Here, we conform because we think that other group members have information about a situation that we are lacking. Here, we make a desire to be right. Generally, in ambiguous situation, greater informational pressure to conform occurs. However, in less ambiguous situation or task, normative influence is high in producing conformity.
- Social psychologists have studied conformity in laboratory. Three noted sets of experiments popularly discussed are Sherif's experiment, Asch's experiment and Crutchfield's experiment. In Sherif's experiment, vague task was used for studying conformity, whereas in Asch's experiment, vivid and clearly defined task was used for studying conformity. Crutchfield developed his technique in order to avoid some difficulties faced with Asch's techniques such as acting of confederates and unnecessary excessive time consumed. A comparative study has revealed that Asch's type of experimental paradigm produces high conformity.
- When do we conform? To answer this question, social psychologists have identified a set of factor that directly influences conformity. Those factors are size of the group, group unanimity, commitment to the group, self-esteem and status of the individual, social norms—descriptive and injunctive type, culture, competence and skill at a particular task and desire for individuation.
- We can resist social pressure to conform. In other words, there are ways to reduce conformity. Reactance, need to maintain individuality, desire for personal control, social support and minority influence are the factors, which tend to reduce conformity. In addition, there are persons who cannot conform.

Review Questions

1. Define social norms. How are social norms developed?
2. What light early studies on norm formation throw on the nature of social norms? Illustrate your answer with examples.
3. Define conformity. Why do people conform to group pressure?
4. Describe the early experimental studies that have been conducted to study conformity behaviour.
5. Discuss the factors that affect conformity to group pressure.
6. Outline a plan to reduce conformity to the group norms.

11. LEADERSHIP AND SOCIAL POWER

Learning Objectives

➢ Defining Leadership
➢ Emergence of Leadership
➢ Functions of Leaders
➢ Transformational and Transactional Leaders: Differential Impact
➢ Personal Characteristics of Leaders
➢ Basic Dimensions of Leader Behaviour
➢ Types of Leaders
➢ How is a Leader Perceived by the Followers?
➢ Theories of Leadership
➢ Meaning and Bases of Social Power
➢ Determinants of Social Power

KEY TERMS

Achievement-oriented leadership	Expert power	Questionnaire
Alternatives	Great man theory	Referent power
Autocratic leader	Informational power	Resource
Behavioural theory	Initiating structure	Reward power
Coercive power	Laissez-faire leader	Selling style
Consideration structure	Least preferred co-workers	Supportive leadership
Contingency theory	Legitimate power	Task specialist
Delegating style	Maintenance specialist	Telling style
Democratic leader	Participating style	Transactional leader
Dependency	Participative leadership	Transformational leader
Directive leadership	Path-goal theory	

Leaders are crucial for the attainment of goal. In fact, leaders decide what is to be done and how things are to be done. In the absence of leaders, no group can be expected to succeed or attain the goal. In fact, people come together in groups to satisfy various types of needs, including task needs and social needs. Their ability to satisfy these needs depends on the effectiveness of a leader.

Apart from this, it also depends on their ability to find a workable kind of structure, which must make clear who shall dominate, direct and influence and who shall occupy the subordinate positions.

In the present chapter, we shall, among others, concentrate upon the various theories of leadership accounting for both emergence and transactional leaders, bases of social power and its determinants so that a complete understanding of the leaders and leadership may be had.

DEFINING LEADERSHIP

Leader is the individual who exercises social power to influence the group members to think, and act in the desired direction. Katz and Kahn (1966) said that the term *leadership* has three major meanings—an attribute of a position, a characteristic of person and a category of behaviour. In most discussions, these three meanings are employed simultaneously. In other words, these three meanings are used to refer to a person, who possesses some attributes or qualities, occupies a certain position and behaves in a certain way. These three meanings are in no sense mutually exclusive.

Another significant attempt to define leader was done by Shaw (1971). According to him, leader is that member of the group who exerts more positive influence over others than they exert over him. The term *positive* here means that the direction of the influence is that chosen by the leader himself. Researches conducted by Forsyth (1999), Reicher, Haslam and Hopkins (2005) revealed that, in fact, leadership is a process in which one or more members of the group are allowed to influence and motivate others to help in attaining group goals. The salient feature of this definition is that it is the group, which grants the leader his or her power.

In a similar tune, Krech, Crutchfield and Ballachey (1962) have defined leader as those members of the group who influence the activities of the group. This viewpoint, along with those of Forsyth, Reicher, Haslam and Hopkins if analysed, reveals the following three important corollaries:

1. All members of the group are, at least to some extent, leaders. This is because every member, to some extent, influences the activities of the other members in the group. The leader differs only in the amount of the influence from the other members of the group. A leader is one who outstandingly influences the activities of the group. The leadership is a quantitative variable and not an all-or-none variable. Thus, this corollary clearly suggests that almost anyone in the group, at one time or another, may be a leader. According to this corollary, since every one is a leader in the group at some time, it is difficult to make clear distinction between leader and follower.
2. Acts of the leadership are instances of interaction or interpersonal behaviour events. Like all forms of interaction, leadership also work in two ways—the leader influences the follower and the follower also influences the leader. Carter, Haythorn and Howell (1950) found that the behaviour of the leader, to a significant degree, reflects the attitudes of the members of the group. They clearly noted that leaders of authoritarian groups tended to behave like authoritarian leaders and the leaders of the equalitarian groups behaved like equalitarian leaders. Brown (1936) also reported that the leader must be perceived as having characteristics similar to those of the followers before being accepted as a leader. In this way, from the follower's point of view, the leader must be seen as one of us, most of us and better than most of us (Krech, Crutchfied and Ballachey, 1962).
3. Third corollary is that we must make a distinction between leader and official head of the group. Gibb (1969) emphasised the distinction between leadership and headship. According

to him, a leader is someone whose authority is spontaneously accorded by his fellow members of the group. On the other hand, a head obtains authority by way of the formal position he holds. Often, it is difficult to determine whether someone, who holds a particular office, is followed voluntarily because he is perceived as a good leader or because of the respectful position of the office. In fact, the person perceived as leader has a significant amount of influence, whereas the official head may have very little influence. That is why, it is said that not all formal leaders (such as heads) are actual leaders.

A reader should keep in mind these three important points while examining the concept of leadership and leaders.

EMERGENCE OF LEADERSHIP

Social psychologists have identified some situations that clearly give rise to leadership. Some of these situations are as under:

1. Group instability: Where there is instability in the group due to internal as well as external threats, there is high probability that new leaders will tend to emerge. In such a situation, there are conflicting forces, which make the members of the group puzzling and the achievement of the group goal becomes difficult. This situation calls for emergence of a powerful leader, who brings the conflicting forces into equilibrium, and thus, he becomes instrumental in achieving a balance-of-power status. Crockett (1955) conducted a study in which it was confirmed that instability within the group gives rise to new leaders. In this study, it was found that the groups in which members held divergent opinions about the group goals and the means through which these goals could be achieved, generated leaders significantly more than the groups, which had a consensus opinion regarding the group goals and its achievement.

2. Group complexity: Group complexity also gives rise to a new leader. As the group becomes large and acquires more and more functions and accessory group goals, its complexity increases. Such group complexity necessitates a number of leaders and provides the obvious conditions for the emergence of many leaders. In large and complex group, a hierarchy of leadership develops. At the top of the hierarchy, there are the main or primary leaders, at the middle of the hierarchy, there are secondary and tertiary leaders and at the bottom levels, there are followers. Researches have shown that as the complexity in the group increases, hierarchical order also increases and at each hierarchy, a new leader emerges.

3. Group crisis: Group crisis has direct impact upon the emergence of the leadership. A crisis in the group is created when the goal of the group is blocked or when the group suffers external threats to its internal security. When crisis is created in the group, the members of the group generally lack understanding as to what steps to be taken for achieving the goal or for warding off the crisis. If at this point, any member of the group or an outside individual is perceived as a means to reach the goal or becomes instrumental in warding off the danger, he is considered as leader.

Social psychologists have expressed the view that crisis in the group influences not only the emergence of leadership but also the distribution of leadership. Historical analysis bears a clear testimony to the fact that in the utter situation of crisis, dictatorship or focused leadership emerges. Leighton (1945) conducted a study in which it was found that during a Japanese relocation camp in

World War II, the individuals were ready to follow any would-be leader if the crisis in the group was created by sudden disruption of established patterns of living within the camp. Not only that, if the intensity of crisis was high because the problems confronting the group were serious, the functions of the leadership were found to be distributed among a number of persons. In case of tasks with lesser difficulty, the leadership became more and more concentrated but with very easy group task, the leadership tended to be distributed. Hamblin (1958) conducted a study in which 12 crisis groups (experimental groups) and 12 control groups (groups having no crisis) were employed. They were to play a game for about 30 minutes by learning special rules. The crisis was created in the experimental (or crisis) groups by sudden unannounced change in the rules of the game. In the results, two things were clear. First, the members of the groups accept leadership when faced with crisis. Second, the members of the groups prefer to select a new leader in place of old leader if the old leader does not quickly meet the crisis. In this experiment, 9 of the 12 crisis groups replaced their old leaders, whereas only 3 of the 12 control groups ever changed their leaders.

4. Failure of the formal leaders or heads: In a group, a formal leader or head generally does many functions. He ordinarily does the function of a policy maker, expert, planner and executive. When official heads fail to discharge these functions or the functions done by the official heads are not satisfactory at all, new leaders are likely to emerge. In an important study conducted by Crockett (1955), it was clearly found that in 83% of the groups whose formal leader or head failed to discharge functions effectively, another person took over those functions and he was perceived as a new leader of the group. As compared to this, in only 39% of the groups in which the functioning of the formal heads was satisfactory, a new leader emerged. Katz et al. (1951) reported similar findings in the study of railroad section gangs. Their results indicated that when the official head of gangs, called *foreman*, failed to function effectively, another person took over functions of the foreman.

5. Satisfaction of wants: The potential leader, like any member, seeks to satisfy his wants by the leadership role. Primary wants to be satisfied by such role are need for power, prestige and material gain. If the group has such potential members, only then it is expected that a leader will emerge. If the group has no potential member having the above wants, no leader will tend to emerge. If the group has several such potential members, distributed leadership is likely to emerge. If the group has a very few such potential members, a highly focused leadership is likely to emerge.

Thus, it is obvious that for understanding the emergence of leadership, not only factors in group situation and perception of the followers should be taken into consideration but the psychology of potential leaders must also be kept in view.

FUNCTIONS OF LEADERS

A leader does many activities in the group. The specific functions of leader vary with the kind of the group being led. For example, leader functioning in an authoritarian group may stress certain specific functions, whereas leader in a democratic group may emphasise other functions. Despite the different nature of the group, a leader must serve, to some extent, a specific set of functions. The common observation has been that a leader primarily functions as executive, planner, policy maker, expert, controller of internal relations, external group representative as well as purveyor of rewards and punishment. According to Bass (1990), a leader does contain necessary functions for successful group performance. Among these functions, planning, organising and controlling the activity of the group members are very important. In formal groups, where roles are clearly organised in status hierarchy, major functions of the leadership are served by high status members. In informal groups, these functions are served by one or several persons, who emerge during the process of social interaction. If we go through the various views expressed by the different social psychologists, we would definitely be concluding that leaders usually do some or all of the following functions:

1. To formulate group goals and communicate them to the members of the group
2. To develop strategies for fulfilment of group goals
3. To specify role assignments and establish standards of performance for the members
4. To facilitate better communication among the members
5. To appoint new members and train them for developing various types of skills such as human skill, conceptual skill, technical skill and personal skill
6. To make healthy interaction with the members of the group so that good relations may be established
7. To provide rewards, punishment and persuasion for encouraging members to do their work satisfactorily
8. To have a watch on the progress of the group and take corrective steps wherever necessary
9. To resolve conflict among the members of the group, if any
10. To serve as the representative of the group
11. To serve as an ideologist, who serves as the source of beliefs, values and norms of the individual members
12. Finally, a leader serves also as a scapegoat, who serves as a target for aggressions of frustrated and disappointed persons (To the extent that a leader assumes responsibility, he may, in the event of failure, be blamed also.)

A close scrutiny of the above functions of a leader makes it clear that leadership is basically a process that involves a tacit exchange between the leader and the followers. When a leader does the functions of planning, organising and controlling, he, in fact, helps the group towards the attainment of its goal. In return of this, a leader gets support from the members for continued control as well as rewards and privileges. This is called *transactional leadership* because it is based on an exchange between the leader and the group members (Hollander, 1985).

In other circumstances, leaders do more than mere mediating rewards and goal attainment for the members of the group in exchange of power, prestige and privilege. They try to convey an extraordinary sense of mission to the group members, stimulate new learnings by the members and arouse new ways of looking at things (Judge and Bono, 2000). In this way, some leaders tend to strengthen group productivity by changing the way the members view their group. In fact, such leaders often create concrete structural changes and foster new practice within the group, thereby strengthening the productivity of the group (Kohl, Steers and Terborg, 1995). Such leadership is termed as *transformational leadership* or also called *charismatic leadership*. Waldman et al. (2001) showed that the transformational leadership is effective in those situations which are volatile and unpredictable because here members are found to show strong commitment for supporting their leader.

Because of the important impact of the transactional and transformational leaders on the followers, we shall discuss it in detail in the next section.

TRANSFORMATIONAL AND TRANSACTIONAL LEADERS: DIFFERENTIAL IMPACT

Transformational leaders and transactional leaders are the two popular forms of leader that do different functions and have differential impact upon the group. As we know, the transformational leaders (also called *charismatic leader*) are the leaders, who exert profound impact upon their followers to the extent that they are supposed to possess some magical power. Such leaders create trust and sense of purpose. They treat followers as individuals and promote self-development of subordinates (Avolio, 2004). Such leaders often create structural changes and institutionalises new practices within the group that tend to strengthen group productivity (Kanungo and Conger, 1992). Kanungo and Conger (1994) further argued that since transformational leaders are proactive, entrepreneurial and change-oriented, they are best suited to the need for change in the developing countries like India. These researchers had also developed questionnaire for assessing various dimensions of transformational leaders. Although followers generally think that transformational leaders do possess some magical power, the researches done by social psychologists have revealed that there is nothing mystical about the impact of such leaders. In fact, their researches have proved that transformational leaders do possess the following four characteristics, which make them appear to have some mystical power:

1. **Inspirational motivation:** Leaders often present visions of glorious future, and thus, inspire people by offering them meaning to their present work as well as to their future work.
2. **Idealised influence:** Followers trust and admire them to the extent that they exert an optimal level of influence upon the followers.
3. **Intellectual stimulation:** Leaders tend to question the existing assumptions of the problem and reframe problems in such way that they are able to induce creativity and innovations in the followers.
4. **Individualised consideration:** Leaders also assume the role of mentors by paying attention to their followers' need for achievement, enhancement and growth.

Researches conducted by Avolio and Bass (2002), Bass et al. (2003) showed that these four characteristics of the leaders make them powerful in the eyes of followers. As a consequence, they are able to boost follower's motivation and performance, to command great respect and force followers to undertake even difficult task. Besides, transformational leaders also possess good communication skills, exciting personal style and high degree of self-confidence (House, Spangler and Woycke, 1991). Above all, such leaders are often master of impression management, which alone has a bigger share in producing the mystical effect on the followers. Some of the examples of transformational leaders are M.K. Gandhi, J.L. Nehru, F.D. Roosevelt and Nelson Mandela (see Figure 11.1).

Researches on transformational leadership in India started with the work of Singh and Bhandarker (1990). These investigators identified the transformational leadership style and their value profiles in Indian organisations. They presented the value profiles of such leaders from both the leaders themselves and their followers (followers' perception). They also recognised the role of Indian socio-cultural context (for example, such role is commonly perceived as *Karta* role in *Kutumb* culture) in developing approach to transformational leader.

Recently, Kark, Shamir and Cohen (2003) showed that transformational leaders tend to produce apparently two contradictory impacts upon the followers; on one hand, they tend to make followers dependent on them and on the other hand, they empower followers by increasing their self-efficacy and self-esteem. This apparently happens because such leaders tend to induce high levels of identification with themselves on personal basis as well as with the group which they lead. As a consequence, the followers feel closer to both the leader and the group. This boosts their self-esteem, personal freedom and self-efficacy.

Figure 11.1 Transformational leaders who truly changed the world.

Moreover, in developing countries like India, transformational leadership role is very important for creation and building of institutions. But the research on the nature of transformational leadership role in institution building has rarely been reported. Only exception is the work of Ganesh and Joshi (1985). They analysed Vikram Sarabhai's transformational leadership style in institution building, which led them to develop several guiding strategies like networking, building and caring that are important for a leader who tries to build an institution.

Transactional leaders, in contrast to the transformational leaders, do also exert powerful influence upon the followers, but in different way. In fact, transactional leadership is based on the exchange between the leader and the group members (Hollander and Julian, 1970; Homans, 1974). Such leaders work largely within the specified system by offering praise, rewards and resources for better group productivity.

By fulfilling the planning, organising and controlling functions in a group, such leaders become instrumental in moving the group towards the attainment of the goal. In return, the leader receives support for the continued control and rewards and privileges. Goodwin, Wofford and Whittington (2001) showed that transactional leaders are able to boost motivation, morale and productivity even in the ordinary work settings, where neither the work nor the goals being sought are highly inspiring.

Social psychologists have attempted to answer one basic question related to these two forms of leadership—which of the two leadership styles is more effective in enhancing the performance of the group? Waldman et al. (2001) conducted a study in which he asked several hundred executives in more than one hundred different companies to rate their leader (CEO) in terms of both transformational as well as transactional style of leadership. Analysis revealed that when the situations were rapidly changing, chaotic, volatile, and unpredictable, transformational leaders outperformed the transactional leaders. On the other hand, when the situation was stable and unchanging, transactional leaders did far better in terms of performance of the group.

PERSONAL CHARACTERISTICS OF LEADERS

Social psychologists have tried to identify some personal characteristics of a leader. The common sense tells us that the most prized quality of leader is experience or time spent in leadership quality. Fiedler (1970) reviewed data from three important experiments and observations of eleven sets of task group supervisors. Finally, he was unable to substantiate the fact that experience has any relationship to the effectiveness of leader. A review of other researches has pinpointed on the following variables:

1. Intelligence: Intelligence is one of the important attributes of a leader. Leaders either appointed, elected or otherwise, generally tend to rate higher in intelligence than the rank and file. Some researches have confirmed this. Mann (1959) did a review of the personality characteristics related to leader behaviour in small group and he found that intelligence was the characteristic quite clearly associated with the leadership. Kiessling and Kalish (1961) conducted another study in which they found a significant and positive correlation between leadership ratings and intelligence test scores. Another study conducted by Lindrgen (1973) also reported a positive correlation between intelligence and leadership.

2. Dominance: Dominance is another major personal characteristic of leader (Mann, 1959). A leader is generally a person who dominates over the other persons in the situation. Megargee (1969) conducted a study in which those university students were selected to act as subjects in two-person experiment, who had scored near the top and bottom of the Dominance scale of California Psychological Inventory. Out of these two persons, one person was to act as leader and the other was to act as follower. The decision as to which of the two would take leader's role was left to the subjects. In the results, it was found that 75% of high dominant men and 70% of high dominant women took the position of the leader in situations in which they were paired with low-dominant individuals of their own sex. When paired with opposite sex, that is, high-dominant women was paired with low-dominant men, the tradition influenced and the women were found to take the follower role in all, but in 22% of the test situations, it was the high-dominant women, who took the decision about who should be in the charge or in the role of the leader.

3. Verbosity or talkativeness: Another important trait of leadership is talkativeness or verbosity. In simple words, the most talkative member of the group is perceived as the leader. This is popularly known as *big mouth theory of leadership*. Riecken (1958), McGrath and Julian (1963) had found support for this theory. Bavelas et al. (1965) conducted a study which demonstrated the relationship between talkativeness and leadership. In this study, the participants first met in a four-person discussion groups and the amount of time that each member spent in talking was recorded. After the first discussion, the participants rated each other on the dimension of leadership. In the next session, each participant had a box in front of him, with a red and green light—green light indicating good performance and red light indicating poor performance. The participant, who had been near the bottom at the verbosity in the first session, was selected to receive positive feedback for talking. In the second session, he received more green signals than any other member in the group. This positive reinforcement for talking enabled him to make his verbal output more than double, and consequently, the group came to perceive him as leader. The conclusion of this study clearly substantiated the importance of verbosity in determining the leadership. Ginter and Lindskold (1975) also substantiated such conclusion. They had groups of four subjects discussing the meaning to be derived from the given paintings. In this experiment, however, one of the four subjects was confederate, who was either most talkative group member or one of the less talkative group members. After the discussion was over, the subjects were asked to nominate a leader from the group. Results revealed that the most talkative member was frequently perceived as the group's leader and as guiding the group discussion. However, the amount of talking had little impact upon participant's perceptions of the expert. Sorrentino and Boutillier (1975) conducted another study in which they manipulated both the quantity and the quality of confederate' talks to the group. It was found that the quality of confederate's talk had a little impact. The more talkative confederate was perceived as having more leadership ability as compared to a less talkative confederate, irrespective of the quality of his talk. Many recent studies have also confirmed the fact that the group members, who talk a lot, tend to be perceived as leaders (Littlepage et al., 1995).

Some researchers have also demonstrated that people respond not only to talkativeness but also to non-verbal signs associated with it. Tiedens and Fragale (2003) conducted a study on groups of business students. They examined how the members of the group respond to the members who assumed either a dominant posture (that is, with an arm dropped on back of an adjacent chair) or submissive posture (that is, with hands in lap). Members with dominant postures influenced the interaction more than the members with submissive postures.

4. Non-conformity: Leaders generally deviate more from the common thinking. Many studies have shown that leaders are non-conformists because they tend to be freer of normative pressures. Harvey and Consalvi (1960) conducted a study in which yielding and non-yielding behaviours of the members of cliques were studied and it was clearly found that the leaders and lower status members tended to conform least, whereas middle status members conformed the most. Wilson (1960) also reported similar findings in his results. Such results and similar others clearly suggest that leaders and low status members do not conform to the group pressures. This happens probably because leaders are able to use their creativity and abilities to think independently for the group, whereas low status persons are not. However, leaders are found to be more concerned about group solidarity. McClintock (1963) conducted a study of small group interaction and found that leaders in order to enhance solidarity, agreed with the other members more and made more generous attempts to reduce tension/conflict then did the other members to the group. It is just possible that leaders tend to keep a reasonable balance between maintaining the cohesiveness as well as solidarity of the group and expressing non-conforming ideas and behaviour.

5. Adjustment: Leaders are generally well-adjusted persons. Therefore, a positive correlation exists between leadership and adjustment. Mann (1959) reviewed several studies and reported that about 30% of studies surveyed demonstrated significant positive relationship between adjustment and leadership. An important study in this regard was conducted by Fitzsimmons and Marcuse (1961).

They selected 50 university students, who were presidents of their fraternities and a matched group of another 50 students, who held neither fraternity nor non-fraternity positions of leadership. This constituted two sharply contrasting group-elected leaders and the no leaders. All these selected students were administered sentence-completion test, which yielded scores in twelve different categories. Results showed that the leaders had higher scores (better adjustment) on eleven categories. Although the leaders and non-leaders exhibited some overlap, the results indicated that the leaders had fewer neurotic traits as compared to non-leaders. Moberg (1953) also reported a positive relationship between leadership and adjustment. He found that those people who had played leadership roles in their churches were better adjusted in old age than those who did not. However, the very fact that the leaders are well-adjusted, does not necessarily mean that they have good insight. One investigator has noted that leaders' perception of their own behaviour are generally not very accurate (Fiedler, 1967).

6. Activities: Those who remain active in any group discussion are perceived as leader by the members of the group. This idea that leaders tend to engage in high degree of participation in group activities is supported by research studies as well. Hayes, Melzer and Bouma (1968) reviewed some studies related to vocal activities in groups and noted that the most active member in the group is one who is often selected as leader enjoying the highest status. Morris and Hackman (1969) conducted another study in which the behaviour of three-person groups working on a variety of tasks was observed. It was found that in two-third of the groups, the members with the highest degree of participation were clearly perceived as the leaders of the group. In one-third of groups, members with the highest degree of participation were, however, not perceived as leaders because their behaviour did not differ significantly from that of high participating leaders except that these non-leaders appeared to engage in more disagreement and spent more time in investigating the task and members' opinion, defining words, etc. In fact, these active non-leaders tended to deemphasise activities that were related to overall performance of the group.

7. Social distance: Although leaders are responsible for maintaining solidarity and cohesion in the group, this does not mean that they favour closeness and intimacy with the group. Several studies have shown that the effective leaders clearly maintain a degree of social or psychological distance between themselves and the other members of the group they supervise. Fiedler (1958) conducted a study of the effectiveness of a variety of task groups and compared successful and unsuccessful groups (or teams). His findings revealed that the psychological distance between the supervisors (leaders) and the subordinates, who are supervised, is positively correlated with various success measures. He concluded that an effective supervisor or leader, who leads the task group, is a person who is able to maintain a degree of psychological distance between himself and the other members of the group. The rationale was that this psychological distance enables the leaders to be more objective, which in turn, prevents them in becoming emotionally involved with the subordinates and permits the establishment of better discipline. Fiedler, however, clarified that these conclusions apply only to work groups. Other types of groups like policy-making groups probably demand leaders with different attitudes towards the other members of the group. Since leaders must also be accepted by the members of the group, social distance in itself will not be a good predictor of group success.

Thus, several important personal attributes together constitute the traits of a successful leader. Here, it would not be fair if a mention is not made of a study conducted by Mann (1959), who made a review of studies carried out from 1900 to 1957. He reported that leaders tended somewhat consistently to be better adjusted, more dominant, more masculine, more extrovert, less conservative and to show greater interpersonal sensitivity than ordinary or rank-and-file members.

BASIC DIMENSIONS OF LEADER BEHAVIOUR

Although different types of leaders tend to share certain traits to some degree, they differ in terms of behaviours they show in their roles. These behavioural styles have been studied by the social psychologists in detail. Although there are probably as many different styles of leadership as there are types of leaders, the researches have shown that most leaders can be placed along a small number of dimensions relating to their overall behaviour done. In very early research on leadership at Ohio State University in USA, the research investigators were able to identify two independent leadership dimensions, which are mentioned below:

1. **Initiating structure (or task role):** This dimension is also known as *production orientation*. The leaders high on this dimension are extremely concerned with getting the job done by the followers. Such leaders define the task, assign the work to be done, establish communication networks, and evaluate work group performance. They urge followers to follow the rules and make subordinate's role explicit. Leaders low on this dimension engage in all such behaviours, but to a lower extent. Leaders high on initiating structure are analogous to task-oriented leadership style.

2. **Consideration (social or people role):** This is another dimension of leadership, which is defined as a behaviour that involves trust, mutual respect, friendship, support and a general concern for the welfare of the followers or subordinates. A leader high on this dimension tends to focus on establishing good relations with their followers. They usually tend to show favour for their followers or subordinates and plan for the welfare of the followers. Leaders low on this dimension do not care well for establishing good relationship with the followers.

Now, the question is—which of the two dimensions of the leadership is superior? It is difficult to answer this. However, the best answer would be neither alone is superior to other. Singh and Srivastava (1979) in their study of 15 first level supervisors and 200 blue-collar workers found that the performance of the subordinates was better under consideration supervision than under production-oriented supervision. However, social psychologists have also expressed the view that the leader high on consideration dimension (showing high concern for welfare of the subordination) produces high group morale no doubt, but because such leaders do not give negative feedback to the subordinates nor give emphasis upon completion of task on urgent basis, performance and efficiency sometimes suffer. On the other hand, when the leaders are high on initiating structure, the work efficiency among the subordinates is definitely high, but they sometimes conclude that the leader is least careful to our welfare. As a consequence, commitment to the group goals tend to suffer. Thus, both dimensions have their own advantages and limitations. Keeping this in view, it can be said that the leaders, who are high on both dimensions, may have an advantage in many situations. In other words, leaders who are concerned with people (consideration) and equally concern with production (initiating) may often prove superior to the leaders showing other patterns of behaviour (see Figure 11.2). Thus a successful leader requires a high level of both consideration and initiating structure. This is called as *Hi-Hi hypothesis* (Miner, 1992).

Besides these dimensions, two other dimensions of leader behaviour have also been uncovered by the researches done by social psychologists. They are as follows:

1. **Autocratic-participative dimension:** This dimension states that whether leaders make all decisions themselves or allow group members to participate in such decisions.
2. **Directive-permissive dimension:** This dimension states that to what extent leaders try to make their presence felt by directing all activities to all members of the group or adopt a permissive approach.

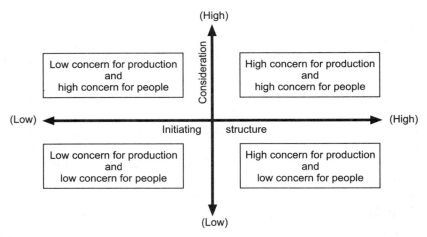

Figure 11.2 Consideration and initiating structure as two basic dimensions of leader behaviour.

In fact, these two newly uncovered leadership dimensions are based on the researches done by Muczyk and Reimann (1987) and Peterson (1997). It has been reported that under emergent situations, where decisions are to be made quickly, an autocratic style of leadership proves helpful and becomes instrumental in raising group performance. On the other hand, where the conditions are normal, stable and relaxed, participative leadership style is preferred by the subordinates. More or less the same is true for the directive-permissive dimension. For example, when the subordinates or followers are new or not much experienced, they prefer directive dimension. On the other hand, when they become experienced, they prefer to work at their own and like that their leaders should now keep their step back.

TYPES OF LEADERS

Social psychologists have variously classified leaders according to the role they play or according to the type of control they exercise. Some of the important and popular types of leaders are discussed here.

One early recognisable attempt to classify leaders was done by Bartlett in 1926, who proposed three types of leaders—institutional leaders, dominant leaders and persuasive leaders. *Institutional leader* is the head of the group such as the executive or the appointed person. The president of the country or the district collector, departmental head in the office or factory are the examples of institutional leaders. In fact, such leaders enjoy prestige attached to their position as the head of the organisation and they exert and maintain authority over the members of the group. Such leaders may be hereditary as we find in case of king or queen of some of the states, or they may be appointed leaders or they may be elected leaders as in case of the President or Prime Minister. The major problem of the institutional leaders is to maintain the status of the organisation and its prestige. Such leaders may or may not have direct face-to-face contact with the followers. *Dominant leaders* are mainly characterised by being extremely aggressive, assertive and extroverted. Such leaders have no patience to think and analyse the situation. They are keen on a series of swift decisions leading the group towards the main goal. The guiding principle of such leaders is that any form of action is better than mere thinking. They show contempt for debate. They are not at all afraid of making mistakes so long as they command men who execute the plans that are placed before them. Napolean, Hitler and Stalin are a few examples of such leaders. Unlike institutional leaders, dominant leaders prefer to take risk of anything to achieve the outcomes affecting a larger number of followers. The *persuasive leaders* are the leaders, who persuade people to accept the common goals. They arise the enthusiasm of the people. They mix with people, understand their problems, needs and feelings. Mahatma Gandhi is a good example of persuasive leader in the history of mankind. Such leader is full of warmth, love and affection to all people. He remains very much sensitive to the ideas and aspirations of the people and develops future plans and programmes of action on the basis of those aspirations of the people.

Leaders have also been classified as task-oriented leaders and social-emotional leaders. *Task-oriented leaders* are the leaders, who believe in getting the work of the group done successfully. Such leader gives suggestions, offers opinion as well as provides relevant information to the group. In fact, he shapes, controls, directs and organises the group in carrying out the task of the group. On the other hand, *social-emotional leader* focuses on the feelings of the group members as well as upon emotional and interpersonal aspects of group interaction. Such leader believes in running the group smoothly and is seriously concerned about the members' feelings. He also sometimes uses human to relieve tension and tries to enhance cohesiveness in the members of the group. In a nutshell, it can be said that a task-oriented leader must be directive, efficient and knowledgeable about the task of the group. Likewise, a social-emotional leader must be agreeable, friendly, conciliatory, showing concern for the feelings of the members as well as socially-oriented. In social group, one person may act as task-oriented leader and another person as a social-emotional leader. Eagly and Karau (1991) reported from their studies that in any social group, men are more likely to emerge as task-oriented leaders, whereas women act generally as social-emotional leader. However, a single person may often serve both functions (Taylor, Peplau and Sears, 2006). Some cross-cultural researches have also confirmed the importance of these two types of leaders (Hui, 1990). Misumi (1995) conducted a study in Japan in which leadership in government, education and industry was examined. He reported four types of leaders in this study—those who were high on task-orientation, but low on social-emotional orientation; those who were high or social-emotional orientation, but low on task-orientation; those who were low on both and those who were high on both. In general, the leaders adopting both these orientations were found to be more effective than the other varieties of leaders.

The other popular types of leaders are those of autocratic leader, democratic leader and laissez-faire. *Autocratic* or *authoritarian type of leader* is characterised by being dogmatic and inflexible. He himself makes all the decision for the group, does not participate in group activities and assigns tasks to the members without specifying any reason and makes changes without any consultation. He alone fully knows the succession of future steps to be taken; he treats himself as the ultimate agent and judge as well as the purveyor of rewards and punishments. Such leader deliberately encourages a segregated group structure in which intercommunication among the members is minimally held and such leader prefers that every communication is routed through him. Since under authoritarian leadership, there is lesser opportunity to develop interpersonal relationship among the members of the group, the attractiveness and cohesiveness of the group deteriorate. The sociometric structure of the group led by the authoritarian leader is likely to be star-shaped (see Figure 11.3).

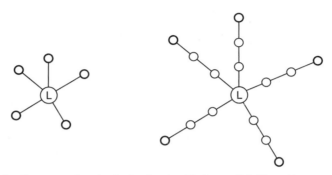

Figure 11.3 Structure of authoritarian leadership in small (left) and large group (right).

A *democratic leader*, on the other hand, exercises his power in a different way. Such leaders prefer maximum participation by the group members in completion of the group task. They seek to spread responsibility rather than to concentrate it. They remain friendly to the members of the group and they make decision only after consultation with the members of the group. Such leaders also try to reduce tension and conflict within the group. They tend to prevent the development of a hierarchical group structure so that special status, privilege and status differential may not predominate. The sociometric structure of the group led by a democratic leader is net-shaped rather than star-shaped (see Figure 11.4).

Figure 11.4 Structure of democrative leadership in small group (left) and large group (right).

Laissez-faire or free-rein leaders are those leaders who play a passive role, do not attempt to direct or coordinate the group, make neither positive nor negative evaluations of the group and follow the rule of minimum exposure to accountability.

A classic study to investigate some aspects of the functioning of the group under these different types of leaders was undertaken by Lewin, Lippitt and White (1939). Groups of 10 to 11-year old boys worked in small groups on a task of mask making and similar other tasks. The adults (experimenters) adapted two different leadership styles—autocratic style and democratic style. Results revealed that under democratic style of leadership, there was highest morale in the group and also members tended to exhibit greatest friendliness and cooperation. However, the performance of the members in the task in terms of quantity was low as compared to the members' performance in the task performed under autocratic style of leadership, although quality-wise, it was better. In democratic style of leadership, boys also kept on working in the absence of leader. However, in autocratic style, boys began to misbehave when the leader was absent. On the whole, under authoritarian leadership, the boys were 30 times as hostile and 8 times as aggressive as they were under democratic leadership. Very poor performance occurred under laissez-faire style of leadership. Here, misbehaviour occurred all the time. However, the boys were found to be friendly towards the leader. In a nutshell, the group performance in terms of quality of work and group cohesiveness were highest with the democratic style of leadership. Experientially induced frustrations proved very disruptive to the group led in authoritarian style, but the democratic-led group tended to meet its difficulties with organised attacks.

Shaw (1955) conducted another study in which the effects of autocratic and democratic types of leaders upon group's satisfaction with its leader and with quality of its products were examined. He assigned leaders to play one of these two roles. Like Lewin, he also found that the group's members were more satisfied with the democratic or non-authoritarian leader. However, he also found that the members of the groups under authoritarian leadership committed fewer errors in their tasks and also required less communication and less time to complete the tasks than did groups led by a democratic leader. This research also finally enabled the investigator to conclude that an autocratic leader facilitates group production no doubt, but it generates a great deal of dissatisfaction among the members of the group. Bailey (1953), however, showed that although a democratic form of leader is generally preferred over autocratic type, sometimes group members may actually resist democratic leadership. According to Krech, Crutchfield and Ballachey (1962), people prefer an autocratic leader over a democratic leader only in those situations in which they have become emotional or find themselves in confusing and ambiguous conditions.

In Indian culture, recently, emphasis has been placed upon a new type of leader, called *nurturant task leader* (Sinha, 1980. 1984). A *nurturant leader* is one who shows proper consideration for his subordinates and a *nurturant task (NT) leader* is one, who makes his nurturance contingent upon the performance of task by the subordinates. Sinha conducted several studies, which linked nurturant task role with the participative and authoritarian style of leadership. However, Sinha (1990) proposed a dynamic developmental perspective to explain the effectiveness of leadership styles in Indian situation. Following this perspective, one of the basic objective of an effective leader is to create a self-controlling autonomous work group. For achieving this objective, leadership roles gradually develop over a period of time from nurturant task at the initial stage to participative at the end (Pandey, 2004).

Thus, we find that there are different varieties of leaders. Among these, democratic leader and autocratic leader are the most popular type. To this set, nurturant-task leader is the new addition.

HOW IS A LEADER PERCEIVED BY THE FOLLOWERS?

Social psychologists have tried to seek the answer of this basic question—how is a leader perceived by his followers? As an answer to this question, they have suggested the following points:

1. Leader must be perceived by the followers as 'one of us': A leader must not be perceived as an outsider by the followers, rather he must be perceived as one of us sharing membership characteristics. Many studies of successful leaders suggest that such leaders tend to share many characteristics with the members of the group. Brown (1936) had rightly commented on this issue that a successful leader must have membership characteristics of the group to which he is attempting to lead.

2. **Leader must also be perceived as 'most of us':** A successful leader must not only be perceived as 'one of us' by the followers but he must also be perceived as incorporating, to a considerable extent, the norms, values, traditions, which are central to the group. One popular conception of leader-group relation is that group is stronger than the leader who must conform to the established norms and values of the group. This view is best illustrated by the story of the French revolutionary leader who, when he observed the mob rush by, said, "*I am their leader. I must follow them*". The role of leader in relation to the established norms of an established group is well-illustrated by several studies (Lionberger, 1953; Marsh and Coleman, 1954). Lionberger found that farm leaders were innovators of new forming methods, and thus, they were perceived as incorporating norms and values of farming operators.

3. **Leader must also be perceived as 'best of us':** A successful leader must be perceived as 'best of us' by the followers. This is because only if he is perceived as 'best of us', that is, outstandingly superior, he can serve as an exemplar as well as father figure of the group. From this, for exercising effective control and coordination of the work of the group, he must also be perceived as outstandingly superior. In case, the leader is not perceived as an expert, he will not be instrumental in achieving the task in an efficient way. Jenkins (1947) did a review of the studies of leadership among military groups and found that leaders were perceived as superior in all those abilities that were relevant to the group task as compared to the rest of the members of the group. Bales (1953) also confirmed from his study on small group that the group perceived that member as leader of the group who had the best ideas in the discussion.

Hollingworth (1942), however, cautioned that leader must be perceived as 'best of us', but apparently, he must not be perceived as 'too much the best of us'. She reported on the basis of study of children that the leader must be more intelligent, but should not be too much intelligent than the average of the group members. Her idea was that if a discrepancy of more than 30 IQ points existed between the leader and the led, the leader-follower relationship either did not develop or quickly disintegrated. For such disintegration, the following reasons were provided:

(i) A too intelligent member of the group may not be perceived by the other members as 'one of us'.
(ii) The interest of too intelligent member may be deviated from the problem to the extent that he may not be motivated to help the group.
(iii) There may not be a proper communication between too intelligent person and other members of the group.
(iv) A too intelligent person may not be perceived as 'most of us' because he may seek to introduce innovations which the group may not be ready to accept, as these innovations may challenge the existing ideology.

4. **Leader must fit the expectations of the followers:** Members of the group have generally a common idea regarding how a leader should behave and what functions should he serve. For example, there are common ideas among the members of the group that the leader must be perceived as father figure and as substitute for individual responsibility. A person who fits in these expectations would definitely be perceived as leader of the group.

Thus, we see that the leaders are perceived by the followers from their own perspectives. A person, who is perceived as fit in terms of these perspectives, is readily perceived as the leader of the group.

THEORIES OF LEADERSHIP

Social psychologists have developed different theories to explain the behaviour of the leaders. Important ones are great man theory or trait theory, behavioural theories participative leadership theory, situational leadership theories, contingency theories, transactional leadership theories and transformational leadership theories, etc. Table 11.1 presents a brief summary of these various theories.

Table 11.1 A brief presentation of different theories of leadership

1. Great man theory / Trait theory
2. Behavioral theories
   - Role theory
   - Leadership grid / Managerial grid model
3. Participative leadership theories
   - McGregor's theory X and theory Y
   - Kurt Lewin's leadership style
   - Renis Likert's leadership style
4. Contingency and situational theories
   - Fiedler's contingency theory
   - Cognitive resource theory
   - Strategic contingencies theory
   - Hersey–Blanchard situational leadership theory
   - House's Path-goal theory of leadership
   - Vroom-Yetton-Jago decision-making model of leadership
5. Transactional leadership theory
   - Leader-Member-Exchange (LMX) theory
6. Transformational leadership theories
   - Bass' transformational leadership theory
   - Burns' transformational leadership theory

In the present book, it is not possible to discuss all theses theories. However, some important select theories will be explained.

1. *Great man theory/Trait theory of leadership*

Some important works in the 19th century started to explore great man theory of length. Thomas Carlyle, a well-known historian once commented that the history of the world is the history of the great men. He identified important talents, skills and physical characteristics of the persons who rose to the power. Likewise, Francis Galton's *Hereditary Genius* in 1869 examined the various leadership qualities in the families of the powerful persons. He had also concluded that the leadership was inherited and therefore, leaders are born and not developed. Most of the social psychologists followed this notion in their early investigations of leadership by examining the personality traits of the successful leaders that distinguished them from their followers. This approach came to be known as *great man theory of leadership*, which evolved into what is now known as trait theory.

According to this theory, a leader is viewed as a person possessing a distinct set of personality traits. This view is encapsulated in the popular slogan—leaders are born and not made. Stogdill (1948) in a review of research pointed out that the characteristics of leaders that make them distinct from the followers are personality traits like alertness, self-confidence, personal integrity, self-assurance, intelligence and dominance needs. Mann (1959) reviewed over 100 studies, seeking to correlate personality characteristics with leadership. His findings revealed that the percentage of positive relationship between intelligence and leadership was 46; between adjustment and leadership, it was 30, between extroversion and leadership, it was 31, between dominance and leadership, it was 38, between masculinity and leadership, it was 16, between conservatism and leadership 5 and between sensitivity and leadership, it was only 15. This provides a weak evidence for supporting the claim that leaders are more intelligent, more extrovert, more dominant and more sensitive than the leaders. Mullen et al. (1989) also added verbosity to this list, but this may be treated as a part of extroversion.

Underlying the great man theory, there are two basic assumptions that have a very little empirical support:

(i) The first assumption is that leadership is a general attribute. A specific person is leader in all situations and all times. Very few studies have supported this assumption. Carter (1953) found that a leader in one task also tends to be a leader in the other tasks. Bell and French (1950) reported that when a leader of one discussion group was transferred to another discussion group, he assumed the role of leadership. Except these meagre supports, many experimental studies have not provided support to this assumption. For example, Carter and Nixon (1949) found that leader in mechanical types of tasks no longer remains a leader when faced with the tasks that require mental or intellectual ability. Merei (1949) studied leadership among groups of nursery school children and found that in all but 26 groups, the leader (older, aggressive and domineering child) was forced to accept group norms and traditions. Despite the fact that the leader was stronger than any member of the groups individually, he could not acquire the position of leadership in most of the groups. This showed that leadership is not a general trait or disposition.

(ii) Another assumption of the great man theory is that the leader has unique background that distinguishes him from his followers. The very fact that good leaders and good followers tend to be the same person definitely suggests that there is nothing different or unique about the leader. For example, Mahatma Gandhi possessed no such traits that were unique to him. He was bright, hardworking, peace-loving and articulate. Thousands of other Indians possessed these same traits and shared similar backgrounds. Why were these Indians not elevated to the position or status of leadership which was attained by Mahatma Gandhi? It means that the second assumption of the trait theory also collapses.

McGrath (1984) pointed out the following five primary reasons of failures of great man theory or trait theory of leadership:

(i) No agreed-upon personality traits exist for comparing leaders from non-leaders.
(ii) There is no common agreed-upon definition of leadership in trait theory. Researchers using different definitions tend to select different people as leaders.

(iii) This theory ignores the relationship between the leaders and the followers. The basic unanswered question is—is relationship good or bad and is different person more or less effective in different situation?
(iv) The theory also assumes that only one leader exists in the group, whereas the reality may be that there may be more than one leader in the group.
(v) The situational factors are completely ignored in this theory.

Despite all these limitations, in the recent years, the picture has changed a lot. With more sophisticated research methods and a scientific understanding of the personality dimensions, many researchers have been forced to conclude that leaders do indeed possess some important traits that make them distinct from non-leaders (Kirkpatrick and Locke, 1991). Researches done by Bennis (2001) and Zaccaro, Forti and Kenny (1991) showed that leaders tend to get higher rating than most of the other members of the group on traits like drive (strong desire for achievement, coupled with high energy), self-confidence, creativity, leadership motivation (need to be in change and exercise dominance over others) and flexibility (ability to recognise appropriate action in the given situation and act accordingly). In addition, some researchers have also demonstrated that some of the *Big Five* dimensions of personality (openness, conscientiousness, extroversion, agreeableness and neuroticism) may tend to determine who will be the leader (Watson and Clark, 1994). For example, Judge et al. (2002) reported that a person high on the dimension of extroversion, agreeableness and openness to experience is more likely to become a leader than those who are low on these dimensions.

In sum, it can be said that traits or attributes of the leader do indeed matter but are only the part of the total picture. What else is important? Most of the social psychologists, today, are of view that different persons showing different patterns of characteristics or attributes can become leader under different situations.

2. *Behavioural theory of leadership*

Behavioural theory does not concentrate on the traits of leaders, rather it emphasises the study of activities of the leaders to diagnose their behavioural patterns. Here the researchers began to study leadership as a set of behavioural patterns evaluating the behaviour of successful leaders and identifying a broad leadership style. The central theme of this theory is that a particular behaviour of a leader provides a greater satisfaction to the followers, and therefore, they recognise him as a good leader. This theory assumes that effective leadership is the result of effective leader role behaviour. Beginning in the early 1940s and continuing through the early 1960s, researches based on the behaviour of leaders were conducted at University of Iowa, Ohio State University and University of Michigan.

Several studies conducted in late 1930s by Lippett and White under the direction of Kurt Lewin at the University of Iowa had a very strong impact. These researchers examined the performance of the groups of 11-year old boys under three different types or styles of leadership: *authoritarian*, *democratic* and *laissez-faire*. Although the outcomes of the performance of the boys under these three leadership styles differed, a sweeping generalisation could not be made. Moreover, from the point of modern research methodology, many of the variables were left uncontrolled. However, they were pioneering and important attempts to show the impact of styles of leadership on the performance of the group and were able to show that the different styles of leadership could produce different reactions from the same or similar group.

Researches conducted at the Ohio State Universities basically aimed at

(i) Identifying the behaviours shown by leaders
(ii) Determining the impact of these behaviours on subordinates' satisfaction and performance.
(iii) Identifying the best leadership style

For identifying the leadership style, questionnaires were developed. The *Leader Behaviour Description Questionnaire (LBDQ)* was developed to assess subordinates' perception of the leaders' behaviour. One another questionnaire, called *Leader Opinion Questionnaire (LOQ)*, measured the leader's perception of his own behavioural style.

After analysing the behaviours of leader in different situations, two important leadership behaviours were identified:

(i) **Initiating structure behaviour (ISB):** In such behavioural style, the roles of leader and followers are clearly defined so that everybody knows what is expected or not expected. Here, formal lines of communication are established and it is clearly decided how the tasks are to be performed.

(ii) **Consideration behaviour (CB):** In this behavioural style, a strong concern for the welfare of the followers is shown and an attempt is made to establish a friendly and supportive work climate based on mutual trust and respect.

Leaders who tended to score high on ISB generally led high-producing groups and were highly rated by their superiors. However, the followers or subordinates of such leaders tended to exhibit lower morale and higher grievances. On the other hand, leaders high on CB generally led groups with higher morale but with lower productivity. In this way, it was found that each of the specific leader behaviours tended to have positive and negative consequences associated with it.

There are two important criticisms of Ohio state studies. First, situational factors and the influence of these factors on the leader's effectiveness were not considered. Second, measurements of initiating/consideration behaviour by the leader and by his or her subordinates were, generally, not found highly related. The leader viewed his behavioural style in one way but the subordinates viewed his behaviour in another way.

Researches conducted at the University of Michigan under the guidance of Rensis Likert revealed two important leader's behavioural styles—*persons-centred* and *production or task-centred*.

(i) **Persons-centred leader behaviour:** Such leader's behaviour gives emphasis upon the persons' well-being. Here, attempt is made by the leader to develop a cohesive work group and ensure the satisfaction of the persons.

(ii) **Task-centred leader behaviour:** In this behavioural style, leader pays a close attention to the employees' work, becomes stricter to the rules, explains work procedures and is deeply interested in standard performance. Thus, the leader behaviour globally emphasises work and how well the employees do the work.

The researchers considered these behaviours as mutually exclusive, and therefore, a leader tends to use one or the other. These researchers further explained that the persons-centred leaders supervised groups with higher morale and productivity, whereas the production-centred leaders tended to supervise the groups with lower productivity and poor group morale.

Critics have made similar comment on Michigan University studies also. First, there are many evidences to support that the behaviour of the leaders changed from situation to situation. For example, a leader might exhibit the person-oriented behaviour under normal and stable situation, but the same leader might change his behavioural style to the task-oriented behaviour in case of critical and emergent situation. Second, there were some other situational factors such as cohesiveness, nature of subordinates' personal characteristics or of the task, which tended to affect the leaders' behaviour and these situational factors were not considered. For example, a leader of non-cohesive group might behave in a different way than a leader of cohesive group, even though they might be working on the similar tasks.

From the Ohio State University studies as well as Michigan University studies, it is obvious that there is duality of leadership and contradictory pressures resulting from the tendency to have concern about both the task and the feelings of the people working on the task. This would seem to convince that a leader could not be an effective leader. It would be an impossible task to perform both functions at the same time. However, Bales and Slater (1955) showed that one person does not generally perform both the functions. Reality is that usually, one person does task-related function and another does the person-oriented function. These researchers studied the groups of 3 to 6 members working on a discussion task. These groups met four times and after each session, the members were asked to rate others on the following three criteria:

(iii) (i) Whom did they like in the group?
(iv) (ii) Who had the best ideas?
(v) (iii) Who, in their opinion, stood not as the leader of the group?

Results revealed that there was an increasing tendency over time for the best liked individual not to be rated as the person with best ideas. Besides, there was a clear tendency to see the individual with best ideas as leader because he provided suggestions for the solutions to the problem. Such person was called *task-specialist* and the best-liked person was called *socio-emotional leader* by these researchers. Thibaut and Kelly (1959) termed socio-emotional leader as *maintenance specialist*, whose chief concern was to create good social climate in the group. Zelditch (1955) studied as many as 56 families and found that in most of the families, there were both a task specialist and a maintenance specialist. Generally, the male members acted as task specialist and the female members acted as the socio-emotional leader. Later on, Stang (1973) also demonstrated that the task specialist (person with best ideas) was not the best-liked person in the group.

Thus, we find that in any group, generally, there are two types of leaders—one leader pushes the members of the group for getting the job done and other leader tries to keep the members of the group happy. It is just also possible that the two types of leaders use different power in their roles. Task leaders tend to use legitimate, expert and coercive power to get the work done by the group members, whereas the socio-emotional leaders prefer to use referent and reward power.

3. *Situational theory of leadership*

Another theory to explain the leadership emergence is the situational theory, which is also called as *time or zeitgeist theory*. Social psychologists have found that trait and behavioural approach to leadership were unsatisfactory because they have failed to identify traits and behaviours common to most leaders. This failure, in itself, suggests that there is indeed a great deal for explaining the emergence of leadership. As a consequence, the emphasis on the study of leadership has shifted from investigating traits of the individuals to the investigation of the characteristics of particular situations that tend to determine who will emerge as the leader. In this way, the situational theory shuns the popular slogan that the leaders are born and not made and the leaders tend to determine the situation. The situational theory or time theory emphasises the fact that it is the particular time or situation that determines who will become the leader (Cooper and McGaugh, 1969).

The situational theory states that a particular person can be a leader in one situation, but not in another because actually, the characteristics of the situation, not the person, lead to the leadership emergence. In an extreme form, the situational theory suggests that anyone can become leader since personality traits and/or behavioural patterns are unimportant (House and Baetz, 1979). In fact, the assumption of the situational theory is that at any particular time, a group of people has certain needs and requires the services of a person who may satisfy these needs. Anyone who fulfils these needs of the people, easily emerges as the leader of the group. Cooper and McGaugh (1969), after careful analysis, pointed out, had Hitler proposed his doctrine in the United States of America rather than in Germany, he would probably have been thrown into jail or shut in some mental institutions. In Germany, however, the time and situation was very appropriate for the people to follow the lead of such an individual.

There are several empirical evidences to support the fact that many situational factors do indeed affect the leadership emergence. Some of these factors are as under:

(i) **Size of the group:** The size of the group has an important bearing on the emergence of the leadership. Several studies have found that if the size of the group is large, it is very likely that leader or leaders will emerge (Carter et al., 1951; Krech et al., 1962). Dyson, Godwin and Hazlewood (1976) reported that leaders were likely to emerge more readily in group having homogeneous membership rather than heterogeneous membership. In a study, it was found that the size of the group determines not only the emergence of the leader but also the type of leadership behaviour (Worchel and Cooper, 1979). In larger groups, the performance or task-type leaders generally tend to emerge, whereas in small groups, emotional leaders tend to frequently emerge.

(ii) **Nature of the situation facing the group:** If the group is facing threat or competition, it is very likely that authoritarian leader is likely to emerge (Worchel et al., 1977). Crisis or competition among the members of the group tends to cause people to rally around a person, who is perceived as individual and who will resolve the crisis (leader). Rabbie and Bekkers (1976) conducted a study on Dutch participants and reported that the leaders, who were aware that they might lose the position of leadership, tried to engage the groups in competitive and threatening situations. Apparently, they thought that they would be less likely to lose their position of leadership in case of external threat to the group.

(iii) **Source of the leader's power:** Group members generally expect more from an elected leader than from an appointed leader (Klein, 1976). Individuals tend to attribute more responsibility for the performance of the group to the elected leader rather than to the appointed leader. In view of this, it can be argued that an elected leader is more insure and more liable to be censured for poor performance than an appointed leader. Apparently, this seems contradictory because elected leader should have popular support for his position.

(iv) **Needs of the members of the group:** The particular needs of the members of the group also determine the emergence of leadership. A person, who is perceived by the members as the best person for satisfying their present needs, is readily perceived as the leader of the group. In fact, the needs of the members of the group enable them to choose an individual, who is fit for satisfying their needs, as the leader of the group. Mulder and Stemerding (1963) conducted a study in which the participants, who owned local grocery stores, were led to believe that many big supermarkets were about to open many stores in their locality. These local grocers met in a discussion groups in which they were told either that there was a good chance that a supermarket would open the stores (high threatening condition) or just a small chance (low-threatening condition). In discussion, two confederates, who supposedly owned a grocery store, played two different roles—one argued for a strong, aggressive course of action and another argued for a light, milder and restrained course of action. The experimenters, then, arranged an election between the two confederates to determine the groups' leadership. Results clearly revealed that the degree of threat affected the grocer's choice. When the threat was intense and high, they chose the aggressive leader and when the threat was low, they chose the milder member as leader. The study clearly showed that needs of the members of the group led them to choose a leader.

Given the fact that leaders are chosen on the basis of how well they satisfy a group's needs, it seems highly probable that if a group's needs vary due to changes in the circumstances, the person chosen as a leader may also change. Support for this notion had been given by Bales (1953), who reported that the person, who supplied the group with the best ideas for solving the problems of the group, was frequently perceived as the leader. This individual was not the best-liked person in the group and different people were perceived as leader as the problem changed. Barnlund (1962) also reported that the changes in the nature of the group tasks as well as shifts in the membership of the group, were instrumental in changing the leadership. In fact, when the requirements of the task changed, leadership tended to shift towards that person who had more appropriate qualifications.

In this way, it is obvious that the situational theory clearly argues that there are no general leadership traits and the traits that make a person leader in one situation may not qualify him to lead in another situation.

Some further researches have shown that the situation plays an important role not only in shaping the emergence of leadership, but also in determining how he will lead. Sanford (1950) found that authoritarian followers did not want that their leader should be group-oriented and egalitarian in his approach. They liked an authoritarian leader. Halpin (1954) conducted another study in which it was found that in low-risk situations followers demanded that the leader should be considerate of the feelings of the group members, whereas in high-risk situations such as in combat zone, the followers expected that the leaders should be task-oriented and authoritarian in their approach.

Thus, the central idea of the situational theory of leadership is that it is the situation that determines who will be the leader. Although this theory has been supported, it has some difficulties. This theory does not explain why some people tend to emerge as leaders more often than the others. In other words, in this theory, we are unable to specify which particular person will be chosen as leader. Thus, a purely situational approach in terms of predicting who is going to emerge as leader is, then, an inadequate explanation.

There are many important situational theories of leadership such as *Hersey and Blanchard situational theory, House's path-goal theory of leadership and Vroom-Yetton-Jago decision-making model of leadership*. A discussion follows.

(i) **Hersey–Blanchard situational leadership theory:** This theory of leadership was developed by Hersey and Blanchard (1969) as life cycle theory of leadership. Later on during mid-1970s, the life cycle theory of leadership was renamed as situational leadership theory (1977). The theory rests on two fundamental concepts: *leadership style* and *individual or group's maturity level*. According to Hersey and Blanchard, the leadership style is understood in terms of *task* behaviour and *relationship behaviour*. Task behaviour consists of one-way communication where leader explains what subordinates are to do and *when, where* and *how* tasks are to be done. Relationship behaviour involves a two-way communication where leaders provide emotional support and help to the subordinates. Clearly, task behaviour and relationship behaviour are two leadership styles that bear similarity to initiating structure and consideration structure emerging out of studies conducted at the Ohio State University.

Now the question is: Which combination of the two leadership styles is appropriate and more effective? According to Hersey and Blanchard, its answer depends upon the task-relevant maturity of the subordinates — the situation. In fact, taking lead from Fidder's theory on situational variables, they incorporated the maturity of the subordinates/followers into their theory. The level of maturity is defined by three features, namely, *degree of achievement motivation, willingness to take responsibility and ability to perform the job as influenced by education and experience*. These features combine to produce four levels of maturity (M_1, M_2 M_3, and M_4) that call for four combinations of task and relationship behaviour on the part of leader such as *Telling style, Selling style, Participating style* and *Delegating style*. Of these, no one style is considered best for all leaders to use all the time. Effective leaders need to be flexible and must be adapting themselves according to the situation.

A brief description of the four levels of maturity M_1 through M_4 is as under.

- **M_1:** Here the subordinates lack the specific skills required for the work and are unable and unwilling to do or to take responsibility for the task.
- **M_2:** The subordinates are not able to take on responsibility for the task assigned. However, they are willing to work at the task. They are novice no doubt but enthusiastic.
- **M_3:** The subordinates are well experienced and able to do the task but somehow lack confidence or willingness for taking responsibility for the task.
- **M_4:** The subordinates are matured from all angles, that is, they are experienced at task, possess the ability to do the task, willing to do the task as well as take responsibility for the task.

In this theory, the key to the effectiveness of the leader is that leader style must match appropriate level of maturity (situation) of the followers. The four styles of the leader that were named by them as S_1 to S_4 are elaborated as under:

1. **Telling style (S_1):** This is characterized by high task behaviour and low relationship behaviour. It proves to be effective when the subordinates are at a very low level of maturity (M_1).
2. **Selling style (S_2):** This is characterized by high task behaviour and high relationship behaviour and is effective when subordinates are on low side of maturity (such as M_2).
3. **Participating style (S_3):** This is characterized by low task behaviour and high relationship behaviour and is effective when subordinates are on high side of maturity (Such as M_3).

4. **Delegating style (S_4):** This is characterized by low task behaviour and low relationship behaviour and is effective when the subordinates are at a very high level of maturity (M_4).

These four leader styles along with four level of maturity have been shown in Figure 11.5.

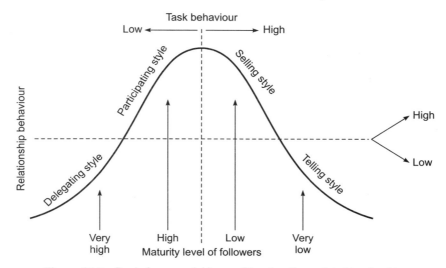

Figure 11.5 Basic framework Hersey-Blanchard's model of leadership.

In a nutshell, it can be said that in this theory leadership behaviour becomes the function not only of the characteristics of leader but also of the characteristics of the followers. The theory further asserts that there is no single *best* style of leadership. Effective leader is one who is task relevant and the most successful leader is one who adapts his style of the leadership to the maturity of the group, he is attempting to lead (Miner, 1992).

The theory has been criticized for its failure to provide a coherent rationale for the hypothesised relationship. Moreover, there is logical inconsistency and ambiguities in the theory. Besides, there has been no empirical test of the theory and there are problems with measurement of instrument used with the theory. Vecchio (1987) conducted a study on more than 300 high school teachers and their principals. He found that newly appointed teachers were more satisfied and performed better under such principals who had structured leadership style but the performance of more experienced and matured teachers was not related to the leadership styles of the principals. Thus his findings, in a way, suggests that in terms of situational leadership, it is quite possible to match a highly structured S_1 style of leadership (Telling style) providing evidence for satisfactory working of the theory, but it is vague in inferring that it would also be good and appropriate to match S_2, S_3 and S_4 respectively with more mature followers. This shows that the theory does not work well at higher level of subordinates' maturity. Later on, Fernandez and Vecchio (1997) also reported similar results. In a nutshell, these researches fail to provide support to the important facts and recommendations of Hersey and Blanchard's theory of situational leadership.

(ii) **Path-goal theory of leader effectiveness:** This theory was advanced by House (1971) and was based on the early work of Evans (1970). The path-goal theory of leader effectiveness was based on the expectancy theory of motivation. According to this theory, the leader's job is to create a work environment through structure, support and rewards that help the subordinates in reaching the goal. The basic idea behind the theory is that a leader can influence the satisfaction, motivation and performance of subordinates mainly by providing subordinates with rewards, (b) making the attainment of these rewards contingent upon the accomplishment of performance goals and helping subordinates in obtaining rewards by clarifying the paths to goals.

Early research on path-goal theory incorporated *initiating structure* and *consideration* as leader behaviour dimensions. Initiating structure provided a mechanism for path-goal clarification and consideration was viewed as making the paths easier to travel. After these initiated research efforts, the theory was revised. Consequently, propositions of the theory was expanded, leader behaviour was redefined, and some additional situational factors were incorporated. The revised theory has the following two basic propositions:

(a) The role of leader is supplemental one. In other words, the leader's behaviour is acceptable and satisfying to the extent that the followers or subordinates perceive such behaviour as a source of satisfaction or as instrumental to satisfaction to be obtained.
(b) The motivational impact of the leader's behaviour is determined by those situations in which the leader functions. Two factors are said to be associated with the situational effectiveness of the leader's behaviour—the characteristics of the followers or subordinates and the characteristics of the work environment.

According to this theory, leader will have to engage in different types of leadership behaviour depending on the demands of the particular situation. Therefore, the basic tenets of the theory can be presented under two general heads—styles of leader behaviour and contingency or situational factors.

(a) **Styles of leader behaviour:** Although the initial researches in path-goal theory utilised two dimensions like initiating structure and consideration as representative of leader's behaviour, the revised current framework includes four distinct styles of leader's behaviour, which are as under:
- *Directive leadership:* Directive leadership is characterised by a leader, who tells subordinates what is expected of them, gives specific guidance regarding what is to be done and how it should be done. Apart from this, such leader also schedules work to be done and encourages the members of the group to follow standard norms of the group.
- *Supportive leadership:* Supportive leadership is characterised by a friendly leader, who exhibits a strong concern for the needs and well-being of subordinates. A supportive leader treats the followers as equal and does things to make the work more pleasant and enjoyable.
- *Participative leadership:* A participative leader is characterised by a leader, who shares the information and emphasises consultation with the followers and uses their suggestions in making decision.
- *Achievement-oriented leadership:* Achievement-oriented leader is one, who constantly emphasises excellence in performance and simultaneously displays confidence that the followers can achieve the set high standards. Generally, such leader sets challenging

performance goals and encourages followers to take personal responsibility for achieving these goals.

Several researches have indicated that these four styles can be exhibited by the same leader in various situations. Such finding is, in fact, not consistent with Fiedler's idea concerning the unidimensionality of leader's behaviour, and therefore, suggests more flexibility.

(b) ***Contingency or situational factors:*** Path-goal theory clearly argues that no single style of leader behaviour will universally result in high level of follower's motivation and satisfaction. Instead, the theory suggests that different types of situations require different styles of leader behaviour. In this theory, two set of factors are considered situational because they can moderate the relationship between leader's style and behaviour of the followers. Two sets of situational factors are the personal characteristics of the subordinates and personal characteristics of the work environment facing subordinates. These are discussed below:

- *Personal characteristics of subordinates or followers:* Several personal characteristics of the followers are thought to influence the extent to which the followers will experience a leader's behaviour as acceptable and satisfying. Important ones are as under:
- *Ability:* An important characteristic is the follower's perception of his or her own ability. When the followers perceive their ability to be low and inadequate, they are likely to find directive leadership acceptable and perceive it to be helpful in future. However, when the followers perceive their ability to be high, directive leadership is perceived to be unacceptable and is unlikely to have any positive effects upon satisfaction or motivation.
- *Locus of control:* Locus of control reforms to the degree to which a subordinate believes that he has control over what happens to him. A person, who believes that he controls his environment and what happens to him occurs because of his behaviour, is said to have an internal locus of control, and the person, who views that what happens to him is determined by circumstances and events outside him and beyond his control, is said to have an external locus of control. Mitchell, Symser and Weed (1975) showed that the internals find a participative leadership style, both acceptable and satisfying, whereas externals tend to respond positively to directive leadership.
- *Needs and motives:* Followers' needs and motives may affect the impact of leader behaviour. In other words, the particular needs, motives and personality characteristics of subordinates tend to influence their acceptance of and satisfaction with different styles of leadership. For example, subordinates or followers with a strong need for achievement may react favourably to achievement-oriented leadership, whereas those having a strong need for affiliation may respond positively to supportive or participative leadership.
- *Characteristics of work environment:* Researches have shown that three important contingency factors in the work environment tend to have positive impact upon subordinate motivation and performance. They are subordinates' tasks, work group and formal authority system.

The subordinate's task may be structured or unstructured with ambiguous requirements and demands. The theory predicts that if subordinates or followers work on a highly ambiguous and unstructured task, the directive leadership style will increase motivation and performance of the followers. On the other hand, if they work on structured tasks, directive leadership will no longer facilitate performance, but simply create frustration among the subordinates. Likewise, the characteristics of work groups also tend to influence acceptance of a particular leader's style. Relationship between leadership style and the behaviour of the work group has been understood through the framework of stages of group development.

Researches have shown that one type of leadership style may be important at a particular stage of group development. For example, during orientation stage of group development, directive style of leadership may be helpful and acceptable. Formal authority system includes various things like norms, procedures, etc. of the group, high pressure or stressful situation as well as situation of high uncertainty. When norms and procedures for achieving the goals are clearly defined, directive leadership may prove to be dissatisfying to the subordinates/followers. Likewise, when tasks are stressful and pressure-packed, directive style may be necessary for task accomplishment, but supportive leadership would result in increased social support and satisfaction. Finally, in a work environment containing a considerable number of uncertainties, directive style of leadership will be comparatively more acceptable.

In a nutshell, it can be said that the theory emphasises that the leader must analyse the nature of situation being faced by the subordinates or followers and then, choose a leadership style, which, in the light of the situational analysis, provides direction and support to the followers.

A number of shortcomings or limitations have been reported. Some of the important ones are as under:

(a) The measurement of leadership style was not clear in the theory. Initially, scales for initiating structure and consideration served as surrogate measures for directive and supportive leadership style. However, it was not clear how participative and achievement-oriented leadership styles could be assessed.

(b) The prediction of path-goal theory regarding individual performance remained vague. Major emphasis had been placed upon motivation and satisfaction. The performance prediction remained unanswered code. For example, leaders of group members, who worked on routine tasks, faced somewhat a paradox. According to path-goal theory, a supportive leadership should be used to increase satisfaction. However, without directive leadership, the members might resort to goofing off, resulting in poor task performance and productivity, thereby creating strong pressure for enhancing productivity from leadership.

Despite these limitations, path-goal theory is considered as a significant contributor to contingency theories because it has identified key leadership styles and situational factors in predicting the effectiveness of any given style of leadership.

(iii) **Vroom-Yetton-Jago decision-making model of leadership:** This theory of leadership was originally developed by Vroom and Yetton (1973) and the name of Arthur Jago was added to theory in 1988. The central theme of the theory is to assess how the nature of the leader, group and situation tend to determine the degree to which the group is to be considered in the decision-making process. Consistent with the contingency outlook, the theory tries to identify those circumstances in which different styles of decision making are the most effective.

In this theory, there are five alternative decision styles that may be used by a leader. These five decision styles are AI, AII, CI, CII and GII. These decision styles are in order of participation from least to most. AI and AI are autocratic decision style where the leader keeps the subordinates in dark regarding the problems he is dealing with. In AI style, the leader takes the decision without any inputs from subordinates whereas in AII, the leader may ask subordinates for some specific information prior to taking a decision. CI and CII are consultative styles where the leaders share the problems with subordinates and ask for their inputs. In CI style, the leader consult with the subordinates individually whereas in CII style, the leader consults with the subordinates in group. However, in all autocratic and consultative styles, it is the leader who takes the final decision. In the fifth style called GII, the leader use a group consensus approach to decision making and shares both authority and responsibility for arising at decision with their subordinates.

In this theory, there are three critical components, which influence the effectiveness of a decision. They are: *quality, acceptance* and *time*. Problem situations differ in the extent to which they possess quality requirement. Some problems that are important and whose alternative design or solutions to the problem may vary from leader to leader, tend to possess quality requirement. On the other hand, there are some simple problem situations where decisions are easy or decisions are concerned with some trivial matter or where all attractive decision styles work equally well, don't possess quality requirement.

Another component in decision is acceptance, which refers to the extent to which the subordinates understand, accept and show commitment to implementing a particular decision. Acceptance is especially critical in those situations where the leader is dependent upon subordinates for implementation. If the leader of the group takes a decision regarding a new policy and send it to his subordinates for implementation and subordinates simply ignores it, then the effectiveness of the decision will be in doubt.

Timeliness is another component. It refers to the extent to which the decisions are to be made within fixed time schedule. It is neither desirable nor effective for leader and subordinates to invest more time in arriving at an acceptable decision of high quality.

In this theory the leader is finally to choose a decision style. The theory views the leader as highly flexible and as capable of adjusting to decision style in light of the demands of the situation. The different types of problem situations require different types of decision styles and an effective leader is one who is capable of diagnosing the problem situation and choosing decision style that results in an effective decision. The theory specifies a set of some diagnostic questions that a leader can employ in determining which decision style is to be adopted. Since the theory states that there are different decision styles of leadership and no one fits all the situations, a leader takes into consideration many things. He may size up the situation, assess the situations facing the group, evaluate the leading support of the group likely to be tendered, and then, effect a style of leading.

The Vroom-Yetton-Jago decision-making model of leadership has been criticized on some grounds. The predictions of the theory have not been tested adequately. Here the process of decision-making is leader-oriented and little attention is paid to leader-led interactions. Although the theory provides a specified procedure of decision-making, there are situations in which there may not be sufficient time to apply the provisions of the theory. For example, when there is emergency or situations that constrain time, the provisions of theory may not be properly applied. Moreover, not each and every leader is capable to handle the decision-making method thrust upon him.

4. *Contingency theory or interactional theory of leadership*

Contingency theory or interactional theory of leadership explains leader's effectiveness rather than leader's emergence, although the two terms are related to each other (Worchel and Cooper, 1979). It is clear from many early researches that neither personality traits nor the situational factors alone fully explain leadership effectively. Therefore, one alternative view that has emerged is what is known as *interactional approach*. This approach holds that under certain situation, one kind of leader will be more effective, while under different situation, an alternative leader will be most effective. Therefore, there is an interaction between the situational factors and personality traits of the leader (Beckhouse et al., 1975; Vroom, 1976).

Here, we shall concentrate upon two interactional approaches to leadership—one approach was developed by Fiedler and another approach was developed by House.

(i) **Fiedler contingency theory of leadership:** The major theoretical model that has been built upon an interactional approach to leadership was developed by Fiedler (1978, 1981),, who propounded a contingency theory of leadership, which focused on both leadership style and the characteristics of the situation. In fact, in this theory, leadership effectiveness is said to be contingent upon the characteristics of the situation as well as upon leadership style. In other words, the effectiveness of leader in achieving high group performance is contingent on the need structure of the leader and the extent to which the leader has control over the particular situation. Four factors that serve as the basic framework for Fiedler's model (see Figure 11.6) are task structure, group atmosphere or leader–member relations, leader's position power, leadership style assessment.

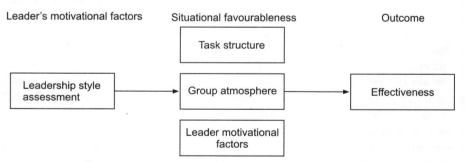

Figure 11.6 Basic framework of Fiedler's model of leadership.

Out of these four factors the first three are related to the characteristics of the situation and the last one signifies the personality of the leader especially the general motivational structure of the leader. These four factors are discussed below:

(a) **Task structure:** The first situational factor, that is, the *task structure*, refers to the degree to which the task goals of the group and the subordinates' roles are clearly defined. A high degree of task structure contributes to a favourable situation for the leader because the leader can more easily monitor and influence subordinates' behaviour on a highly structured task. On the other hand, when the task is unstructured, the leader is not sure about the best way of performing the task and disagreement with subordinates regarding the correct way to do the task tends to exist. Consequently, the leader's ability to control and monitor the subordinates' behaviour is reduced.

(b) ***Leader–member relations:*** Group atmosphere or leader–member relations, a second situational factor, may be either good or poor. When the relationship between leader and followers is good, the leader can count on the loyalty and support of the followers. In such a situation, leader's influence and control are high. When the leader–member relationship is poor, it tends to impair the leader's control and contribute to more unfavourable situation for the leader.

(c) ***Position power:*** This is the third situational factor, which is concerned with the power inherent in the leadership position. It refers to the extent to which the leader possesses, through legitimate, reward or coercive power, the ability to influence the behaviour of the subordinates. The important aspects are the degree to which the leader has power to promote, fire or direct subordinates to the task accomplishment. If the leader possesses greater position power, the leader has greater control over the subordinates and this situation is considered more favourable for the leader. However, poor position power of the leader creates an unfavourable situation for him because here, the leader has very narrow range of rewards and punishments at their disposal.

These three factors can be used to construct a continuum of situational favourability of the group to the leader. The most favourable situation is one in which the relationship between leader and followers is good, the task is highly structured and the power position of the leader is strong, whereas the least favourable situation is one in which the leader–member relationship is poor, the task is unstructured and the power position is weak. Taking the two categories of each of these three variables, Fiedler classified eight distinct (2 × 2 × 2) combinations of situations (or *octants*, as Fiedler had called them) varying from very favourable to very unfavourable situation. Table 11.2 presents eight octants and the overall favourableness rating of each of them.

Table 11.2 Fielder's Typology of Leadership Situations and their Degree of Favourableness

Octants	I	II	III	IV	V	VI	VII	VIII
Leader–follower relations	Good	Good	Good	Good	Poor	Poor	Poor	Poor
Task structure	High	High	Low	Low	High	High	Low	Low
Leader position power	Strong	Weak	Strong	Weak	Strong	Weak	Strong	Weak
Situation	Very Favourable	Favourable	Favourable	Mod. Favourable	Mod. Favourable	Unfavourable	Unfavourable	Very Unfavourable

Table 11.1 obviously shows that Octant I (Good, High, Strong) is highly favourable, Octant IV (Good, Low, Weak) and Octant V (Poor, High and Strong) are moderately favourable and Octant VIII (Poor, Low and Weak) are highly or very unfavourable.

(d) ***Leadership style assessment:*** In order to predict effective leadership in each of these octants, Fiedler emphasised the fact that we must know the leadership style of the person. Based on the research evidences supplied by Bales (1953), Bales and Slater (1955), Fiedler recognised that there are two general styles of leadership. One type is task-oriented and the other type is group-oriented or relations-oriented (social-emotional). Task-oriented leader is mainly interested in getting the job done and relation-oriented leader is comparatively more interested in member's satisfaction and individual members' feelings. Fiedler devised an instrument by which these two styles of leadership can be identified. This is done by asking leaders to cast their mind about all the people with whom they have worked so far in the past and think about the person they liked least—the least preferred co-worker or LPC. With this least preferred co-worker in mind, leader is asked to fill in a set of semantic differential scale containing bipolar items like cooperative–uncooperative, dependable–non–dependable, warm–cold, etc. (see Table 11.3).

Table 11.3 The LPC Scale

Hardworking	|8|7|6|5|4|3|2|1|	Not hardworking
Confident	|8|7|6|5|4|3|2|1|	Not confident
Warm	|8|7|6|5|4|3|2|1|	Cold
Dependable	|8|7|6|5|4|3|2|1|	Not dependable

As per the LPC scale, a favourable attitude towards LPC would attract a high score (high LPC) and an unfavourable attitude towards LPC would attract a low score (low LPC). Leaders securing high LPC score are classified as relation-oriented leader and leaders securing low LPC scores are classified as task-oriented leader. Fiedler reported that relation-oriented leaders are more complimentary, more relaxed and less directive in their behaviour. They are mainly relationship motivated and secondarily task-motivated. Task-oriented leaders are less inclined to tolerate irrelevant comments, demand more from the members of the group and are generally directive in their behaviour.

Fiedler examined the relationship between style of leader, situational favourability and task performance. It was found that the task-oriented leaders turned out to be the most effective in both highly favourable situations and highly unfavourable situations. However, when the favourability of the situation is only moderate, task-oriented leaders are not so effective. The relationship-oriented leaders, on the other hand, exhibit the opposite patterns of results. They are effective in situations of moderate favourability, but less effective in both highly favourable and highly unfavourable situations. Speaking in terms of eight cells of Table 11.2, the task-oriented leaders have proved to be effective in cells I, II, III and VIII, whereas the relationship-oriented leaders have shown their effectiveness in cells IV, V, VI and VII.

The effectiveness of task-oriented leaders in highly unfavourable situations is easily explained because such situation urgently needs directive function of leadership, which a task-oriented leader readily fulfils. Such leaders are also more suitable to highly favourable situations because they would respond very positively to a situation that facilitates the accomplishment of performance goals. The effectiveness of relationship-oriented leaders in moderately favourable situation is less easy to explain. The most plausible explanation is probably that the relationship-oriented leaders may help overcome poor leader-member relation and may facilitate a participative approach to the clarification of ambiguous task demands (House and Baetz, 1979).

Fiedler and other researchers provided a good deal of supportive evidence for this contingency model. In settings as diverse as military, academics, industry and cross-cultural environments, the contingency model has proved to be a good theory, which predicts leadership effectiveness and a meta-analysis of 170 studies showed support for the theory in most of the cases (Strube and Garcia, 1981). In a significant study conducted by Chemers and Skrzypek (1972), three favourable factors in work settings were varied. Their results supported Fiedler's model as high LPC leaders (relationship-oriented leader) were found to be most effective when the situation was moderately favourable, whereas low LPC leaders (task-oriented leaders) were most effective in the very favourable and very unfavourable situations. Hardy (1976) conditioned another study in which fourth-grade children participated as participants and it was found that low LPC leaders were more effective than high LPC leaders when their position power was weak.

Although Fiedler's model had a very wider support, it was criticised and there were some unanswered questions concerning the model. These points are considered below:

(a) A major problem of this model was that there was no completely objective ways to quantify the favourableness of the situation.
(b) classified situations on three dimensions only. But certainly, there were a number of other dimensions on which situations could easily be classified.
(c) Another concern in the theory was that what did LPC really measure? Fiedler's early research indicated that LPC was a measure of the leader's personality. His later research, however, revised the measure of LPC to reflect an individual's motivational structure with respect to social need gratification in groups. Whether LPC measured personality or motivational structure, the link with leader's style remained in uncertain state.
(d) Mitchell et al. (1970) demonstrated that some ambiguity remained as to exactly what behaviours were the characteristic of high and low LPC leaders. As we know, the low LPC leader is task-oriented but some studies have shown that low LPC individual is more socially and emotionally sensitive and less punitive than the high LPC leaders.
(e) Still another problem was concerned with the effects of changing situations on leadership effectiveness. If a low LPC leader entered into a group in which the situation was very unfavourable and he was able to change this situation into a moderately favourable one, would he be less effective under improved situation? The theory predicted that once the situation changes from poor to moderately good, a high LPC individual would tend to be a good leader. This seemed to be very unfortunate prediction.
(f) Fiedler's theory suggested that leaders are either task-oriented or employee-oriented, that is, the leadership style is essentially a unidimensional concept. But behavioural approach to leadership revealed that it is possible for the leaders to be both task-oriented and employee-oriented, varying from a high to low orientation on each factor. Also, in different situations, a leader may be motivated to alter his style from one leadership style to another.

(g) Graen et al. (1970) and Ashour (1973) examined the data of the Fiedler's model and pointed out that many of the correlations between LPC and leadership effectiveness were not significant and each study by itself was not particularly impressive.

Despite these criticisms, Fiedler's contingency model had proven to be a step in right direction to the study of leadership for the following three reasons:

(a) Fiedler's contingency model was one of the first approach to the leadership, which included situational factors within its theoretical framework.
(b) The model clearly claimed that leadership effectiveness is a function of leader's motivational structure and the interaction of the situational factors. The group or organisation may improve the effectiveness of the environment by either modifying the situational factors or attempting to change the style of the leadership.
(c) The model provides a very important implication that one should not speak of leader as being either good or bad. A more realistic viewpoint would be that the leader's style of leading may be effective in one situation but not in another.

Recently, Fiedler has proposed an extended theory, which certainly does not repudiate the earlier contingency theory but builds upon it and extends it into new domains. In this extended theory, due consideration has been given to the situation under which a leader's cognitive resources such as his experience, technical expertise, task-related knowledge, intelligence, etc. relate to the group and its performance. This is known as *cognitive resource theory CRT* (Fiedler and Garcia (1987). In this theory the key consideration is given to the extent to which the leader exhibits the direct behaviour. Leader LPC and the amount of the situational control interact to determine whether the leader is directive. Subsequently, leader's stress, degree of group support and task requirements tend to determine how well group performance is predicted by leader and group member's cognitive abilities. Fiedler linked CRT with LPC theory suggesting that leaders with high LPC scores are the main drivers for the directive behaviour.

CRT rests upon the following two assumptions:

(a) Leaders with high intelligence and competence will make more effective plans, decisions and action strategies than leaders with low intelligence and competence.
(b) Leaders tend to communicate their plans, decisions and action strategies mainly in form of directive behaviour.

The CRT focuses on the impact of leader's intelligence and experience upon his reaction to stress. The theme of the theory is that the stress kills rationality and damages leaders' ability to think logically and analytically. However, the adequate experience and intelligence can lessen the influence of stress on their actions. Intelligence is considered as an important factor in low stress situation, whereas the experience counts heavily during high stress situations. CRT makes the following predictions:

(a) A leader's cognitive resources contribute to the performance of the group only when the leader is directive. When leaders are adept in decision making and planning, as well as in implementing their plans and decisions, they need to tell people what to do rather than expect they agree with them.

(b) Stress affects the relationship between the intelligence and the quality of the decision. High level of stress distracts the leader from the task and it affects the performance negatively. However, when there is low stress, intelligence is fully functional and makes an ideal and optimal contribution.

(c) In high stressful situation, intelligence does not work properly. However, the experience of the similar stressful situations enables the leader to react in appropriate ways and contribute significantly in taking quality decision.

(d) When the task is simple, the intelligence and experience of the leader do not matter much in taking the decision because in such situation, subordinates take their own.

CRT has been criticized. Some of the important criticisms are as under:

(a) The parameters used by the theory regarding the nature of intelligence are not precise. There are many types and degrees of intelligence and the CRT does not account for them properly.

(b) Likewise, many types of stress exist. One should not say simply stress. There are physical stress and psychological stress and each tends to inhibit the performance and has different effect upon different persons. The CRT does not take into account such thing.

(c) Another problem relates to the quantification of stress. We don't find stress scales and even if, we do see, matter may be raised regarding how their quantification has been achieved.

(d) The CRT does not mention task-types and the resources required to complete the task. Simple task requires minimum of leadership but complex and difficult task may require different styles of leader. Moreover, some tasks have phases and for every phase a different approach of leadership is required.

MEANING AND BASES OF SOCIAL POWER

In fact, our life is a game, whose primary goal is power. Any attempt to understand social behaviour must involve examining the meaning of the concept of power (Kipnis, 1976). *Power*, in loose sense, means to make others do something which they normally would prefer not to do. *Social power*, in a scientific vein, refers to the capacity or potential to influence others and to resist influence from them (Michener and Suchner, 1972). From this viewpoint, it is obvious that social power is the property of a relationship between two or more persons and can be best understood in terms of exchange theory. Secord and Backman (1974) defined social power as the power of person A over person B that is joint function of the capacity of person A for affecting the outcomes of the person B relative to his own outcome. Analysing this simple definition, it can be said that if person A has more control over person B's outcomes and has less adverse effect on his own outcomes, then there will be more power of person A over person B.

Social power is often used to influence the behaviour of other persons, but is conceptually different from influence. The major difference between influence and power is that influence involves actually changing the behaviour of the target person, whereas power involves the ability to bring such change. For example, a parent may have a great deal of power (the very potential to change behaviour) over his son and daughter, but some parents exercise this power (influence) more often than the others. Mahatma Gandhi had power to change the thinking, attitudes and behaviour of a large number of people, but influence occurred only when he exercised that power and actually brought about such changes among the mass.

A number of investigators have conducted researches for identifying bases of social power. (French and Raven, 1959; Raven 1974; Michener and Burt, 1974). These researches have revealed six bases of social power—reward power, coercive power, referent power, expert power, legitimate power and informational power. These are discussed below:

Reward power

Reward power refers to a power, which involves giving positive reinforcement to produce changes in behaviour. The reinforcement may be in tangible form such as money, or it may be in terms of intangible form such as praise. In a nutshell, it can be said that reward power exerted by person A over another person B is based upon the perception by person B that person A has capacity to provide rewards for him. A manager has power over an employee because the employee knows that his manager can recommend for promotion or wage increases. A study conducted by Canavan–Gumpert (1977) revealed that reward power (praise) is more effective than coercive power (criticism) in increasing the performance among children.

Although reward power has advantages, it possesses some disadvantages too. Social psychologists are of view that the use of rewards to induce behaviour change is not likely to lead to internalisation in attitudes. This is probably because in such a situation, an individual views himself as performing simply to obtain the reward and it is not internalised in the attitudes of the person. Consequently, if he comes to realise that now, the reward will no longer be given, he ceases to perform the desired behaviour.

Coercive power

Coercive power refers to that power which involves potential to deliver threats and punishment to others so that they may change their behaviour. A supervisor or manager possesses coercive power over his employees because employees know that he has power to punish them in the form of withholding their salary, stopping promotion or even terminating their service. To make coercive power effective, surveillance must be maintained.

There are two important drawbacks that deter the use of coercive power. First, the low-power individual in a coercive relationship is generally motivated to terminate the relationship if he gets the opportunity for doing so. Second, the coercive power requires surveillance of the low-power person. The coercive power may introduce behavioural changes when surveillance is possible but it is unlikely to lead to change in attitudes. Social psychologists have pointed out that there are a number of reasons due to which surveillance becomes a problem. First, generally, despite the best efforts, it is very difficult, if not impossible, to maintain surveillance. Thefts, dacoity, hijacking and other related things continue to occur on public places, despite the fact that the government is expending several crore of rupees on surveillance of airports, railway platforms and other important places of the country. Second, Tedeschi (1974) demonstrated that the use of coercive power by high-power person produces disliking for them as well as they are perceived as hostile. Due to such disliking, it is not possible that a powerful individual will be able to broaden his power base. Third, surveillance fails to produce internalisation. It influences the persons only while they are under surveillance. The primary reason is that in such a situation, the person does not experience dissonance following behaviour done under surveillance because he is found to justify such behaviour by saying that he has done so only to avoid punishment. Finally, surveillance generally leads to distrust and gives birth to conflict (Strickland, 1968).

If we pay attention to reward power and coercive power, there are some similarities between them. In both, the power is limited to that range of behaviour for which person A can reward or punish person B. The strength of both appears to be not only a joint function of the amount of rewards and punishments but also of the perceived probabilities that these will be incurred if one accepts or does not accept the A's attempt to influence. These perceived probabilities are the product of two factors. First, the extent to which B thinks that he is being observed by A. The higher degree of surveillance by A leads B to conclude that his behaviour will be either rewarded or punished. Second, the past relationship of B with A also influences the perceived probabilities. If A has seldom rewarded or punished B for his behaviour in the past, his reward and coercive power is likely to be weak. In this connection, Thibaut and Kelley (1959) had emphasised one distinction between the reward and coercive power. According to them, surveillance is likely to be more difficult in case of coercive power probably because persons display behaviour that is apt to be rewarded, whereas they hide behaviour that may lead to punishment.

Referent power

Individuals gain ability to influence us because we praise and like them. In fact, we want to be similar to the people we admire and praise, and therefore, we often initiate them and try to act as they do. Thus, in case of referent power, a person has power to influence others because they admire him and want to be like them. Referent power is similar to Kelman's concept of identification. One of the major determinants of identification is attraction. The degree to which B is attracted to A, he models himself after A, and thus, B is influenced by A's behaviour. French and Raven (1959) suggested that the strength of the referent power of A over B as well as the range of behaviour to which it applies, tends to vary with the attractiveness of A to B. Referent power is enhanced to the extent that the persons see themselves as similar to the model person. Referent power was one of the strongest bases of our Rashtrapita Mahatma Gandhi. He was admired by millions because of his amazing courage, foresight and charismatic personality. Therefore, many people wanted to be like him and acted as he did.

Referent power may be positive or negative. If the people try to behave like a model person, they admire and are attracted towards him, then it is said to be *positive referent power*. On the other hand, if the people act in a manner opposite to that of a model person whom they dislike, it is called *negative referent power*. A handful of people who disliked Mahatma Gandhi might have conducted a violent campaign because they knew that Mahatma Gandhi preferred a non-violent and peaceful campaign. Regardless of the direction (positive or negative), the model person has referent power in both the cases.

One advantage of referent power is that it does not require surveillance to be effective. People want to be like the model and remain self-motivated to follow the model's behaviours.

Expert power

Expert power is a power to influence others based on one's own expertise or special knowledge. Often people gain power because individuals see them as being knowledgeable about a particular area. This power is based on the famous slogan—knowledge is power. A doctor has expert power over the patient because he is perceived to have special knowledge and insight about the medical problems. If the doctor recommends operation, the patient will probably accept it even when he does not understand why the operation is necessary. The rewards obtained by a person's expert power by others are the feelings of confidence and assurance that the course of action is correct one. Costs that can be avoided by consulting an expert may be the feeling of uncertainty and the feeling of doing wrong things.

Expert power is usually limited to a specific area. Thus, a doctor is able to influence a person on only health-related issues. A person will not follow his advice if he is going to purchase a new car or house. Often people tend to enhance their expert power by the use of diplomas and citations that testify their knowledge in certain area. Expert power may be lost if the expert transmits his knowledge or skill. Continuation of a person's expert power over others is not dependent on the extent to which others' behaviour is subjected to surveillance by him.

Legitimate power

Legitimate power is the power that a person derives from being in a particular role or position. Thus, legitimate power is authority of a person by virtue of certain characteristics such as age, class, or caste or by virtue of his position in some recognised hierarchy. For example, a police officer exercises legitimate power over individuals. Pruitt (1976) demonstrated that legitimate power is based on the norm of *oughtness*, where a person is taught to follow the orders of persons in certain position. For example, a child is taught to follow the words of the parents. Another example of legitimate power is found in the Milgram's studies (1963, 1965), where the participants obeyed the experimenter because of his legitimate power. Besides the norm of oughtness, norms of reciprocity and norms of social responsibility are evoked in legitimate power. *Norm of reciprocity* states that when a person does favour for you, you feel obliged to return it in some way. When a person A evokes this norm requiring person B to repay some of the past social debt, he exerts influence over B. *Norms of social responsibility* states that we should help other persons when they are in need. To the extent B is seen to be dependent on A, A is motivated to exert power over B. This fact has been experimentally confirmed by Berkowitz and Daniels (1964) and Goranson and Berkowitz (1966).

Although sometimes, legitimate power covers a broad area of behaviour, frequently, it is narrow in scope. For example, parents may exert legitimate power over a wide range of their children's behaviour, a university head must restrict his legitimate power to only academic behaviour. Another limitation of legitimate power is that the person, who uses it, must keep himself often aloof from the people whom he wants to influence. That is the reason, why top officers are generally housed separately and have facilities that are separate from all the enlisted men.

Informational power

Informational power has been added as the sixth basis of power to the five types of power suggested by French and Raven (1959). *Informational power* is the power which a person derives because he possesses some specific information or provides logical arguments that may prove helpful to others. It has nothing to do with the source or it is not dependent on the source. As we know, all the above five types of social power are dependent on the source, that is, the bases of power lie on the characteristics of a particular person. An eyewitness to the crime has power to influence the judgement of the Honourable judges because of the information he possesses and not because of his characteristics. This type of independent power is called *informational power*.

Informational power is possessed to the extent that the person does not divulge the needed information. Once the person dispenses the information, his power is reduced. For example, once the eyewitness has been testified, he no longer possesses the power to influence the behaviour of the judge.

These six types of power can be derived from numerous sources. Personal characteristics, skills, material possessions, prestige, information and physical strength are a few of the sources of an individual's power. These various types of powers are associated in everyday situations. For example, parents possess all six types of power over their young children. However, as the children become matured, the expert, reward and coercive powers dwindle. By the time of adolescence, their referent power may disappear, and sometimes, even become negative and the legitimate power is also challenged. These various types of power interact with each other in their effects. One power may augment or reduce the effects of another. However, these various types of social power tend to facilitate ongoing social relationship (Raven and Haley, 1980). These powers are not entirely independent and are seldom found in pure form in real situation.

DETERMINANTS OF SOCIAL POWER

A wide variety of researches done by social psychologists have revealed that there are three interrelated factors, which determine the amount of power the persons are able to exert in a given situation. These factors are resources, dependencies and alternatives. These are discussed below:

Resource

A *resource* is the property or conditional state of a person—a possession, an attribute of personality, a position he holds or a certain way of behaving, which enables him to affect costs and rewards experienced by another person (Secord and Backman, 1974). If he is able to affect reward without having any cost, he is said to exhibit power over others. French and Raven (1959) formulated different types of social powers according to the resources on which they were based. Reward power, coercion power, referent power, expert power and legitimate power are some examples. These powers have already been discussed in the previous section.

Kipnis (1984) clearly pointed out that before power can be used, the person must determine the cost of using it and its effect on the target. The person must also determine what type of influence he wishes and must also know what his resources are. In this way, careful planning and forethought are strictly required in order to decide what type of social power should be utilised in any situation.

Some researches have shown that personality affects the individual's perception of his own power and the way in which that power will be used. Some researchers focus on the person's own attribution of the power that he can exert on a situation. Rotter's distinction between internals and externals is here relevant. Internals find themselves as having power to influence what happens to them, whereas externals see themselves as being affected by luck, chance and forces beyond their control. These two types of views determine power to influence others. Strickland (1965) found that black activists in the civil right movement in USA scored more towards the internal side of internal–external scales than did blacks who were non-activists. It means that internals are more likely to see themselves as possessing power and are more willing to use the power than externals. Christie and Geis (1970) pointed out that there are people who today believe that others can be influenced and manipulated—an interpersonal style recommended by Niccolo Machiavelli in his famous book entitled *The Prince*. They developed Mach scale for measuring people's belief that others can be manipulated and influenced. They reported that individuals scoring high on Mach scale tended to resist influence from others. They tended to be emotionally detached, pragmatic and goal-oriented. On the other hand, individuals with low Mach tended to be cooperative, open and emotionally involved with others. Social psychologists have also shown that high Mach individuals are more effective in using power and influence than low Mach person. Lamm and Myers (1976) found that high Machs were better able than low Machs in determining how other persons would react in group discussion situation. Christe and Geis (1970) further showed that high Machs tended to be males, to come from urban backgrounds and to be comparatively young. High Mach children tended to be more successful in lying and bluffing than did low Mach children.

Dependency

The importance of resource is determined by the dependency of the other person on the resource. Thus, *dependency* refers to the extent to which B is dependent on A for the fulfilment of his needs. A doctor has power over patient to the extent the patient is dependent on that particular doctor for medical help. Such dependencies may have their source in characteristics of a person or the situation or a combination of both. A person with strong need for approval and emotional support (characteristics of the person) will be dependent on those individuals who can readily fulfil his needs. Such characteristics make the resource (the person) especially valuable to the person who is dependent. Sometimes, situation create dependency and call for a particular resource. For example, in an emergency situation, the group may need an expert to solve the problem. Therefore, in such a situation, that person will exercise power over the group who will provide expertise for solving the problem in emergency situation.

Alternatives

Power is also determined by the alternatives available before the person, who is dependent on the resource. In fact, power is determined by the consequence of not complying by B to the request of A. Here, B compares his reward-cost outcome for compliance with that for non-compliance. The greater the disparity between these outcomes, greater will be the A's power over B. In fact, this disparity is a function of alternatives available before B. If B has many alternatives available before him or he may get the resource at a lower cost in relation with person other than A, then, here, the power of A over B will be reduced. This can be illustrated through the example of expert power. Suppose A as a resource person possesses proper expertise in solving a particular problem. B needs to solve that problem. Here, B will be dependent on A and to that extent, A will enjoy power over B. But suppose that there are three others experts (X, Y and Z) available before B for solving the same problem. In such a situation, there are three alternatives before B for seeking expert's help. Such alternative will tend to reduce B's dependencies over A and to that extent, the power of A over B will be reduced.

Thus, we can say that social power is determined by resources, dependencies of other on resource and the alternatives available before the dependent person.

Summary and Review

- Social psychologists have defined *leader* as that member of the group, who influences the activities of the group most. In fact, leader is that member of the group, who exerts more positive influence over others than they exert over him. Thus, acts of the leadership are the instances of interaction or interpersonal behaviour events. Like all forms of behaviour, leadership also works in two ways—the leader influences the followers and the followers also influence the leader.
- Social psychologists have identified several situations that give rise to leadership. Some of these situations are group instability, group complexity, group crisis, failure of former heads or leaders and satisfaction of wants, etc.
- A leader does many functions. Some of the important functions done by a leader are formulation of group goal and communicating them to the members of the group, developing strategies for fulfilment of group goals, facilitating better communication among members to make healthy interaction with the members of the group, providing rewards, punishments and persuasion for encouraging members to do their work satisfactorily, having a watch on the progress of the group, resolving conflict, if any, with the members of the group and serving as representative of the group, etc.
- Transformational leaders and transactional leaders are the two important forms of leader's style and they do different functions and have differential impact upon the group. *Transformational leaders* (also called *charismatic leader*) are the leaders, who exert profound impact upon the followers to the extent that they are supposed to possess some magical powers. Such leaders create trust and sense of purpose. They treat followers as individuals and promote self-development of subordinates. Transactional leaders do also exert powerful influence upon the followers, but in different way. Such leaders work largely within the specified system by offering praise, rewards and resources for better group productivity. Transactional leadership is based on the exchange between the leader and the group members.
- Social psychologists have identified some personal characteristics of leader. Among these, the important ones are intelligence, dominance, verbosity, non-conformity, adjustment, activities, social distance, etc.
- Although different leaders tend to share certain traits to some degree, they differ in terms of behaviour they show in their roles. Important dimensions of leadership are initiating structure, consideration, autocratic-participative dimension and directive-permissive dimension. All these dimensions indicate different types of functions.
- Leaders are of different types. Important types are intuitive leaders, dominant leaders, persuasive leaders, task-oriented leaders, social-emotional leaders, autocratic leaders, democratic leaders, laissez-faire (or free-rein) leaders, etc. Besides these types of leaders, in the recent years in Indian culture, a new type of leader, called *nurturant task* (*NT*) *leader*, has been formulated and also found to be effective one.
- One of the important questions in which social psychologists have shown their interest is how the leader is perceived by the followers. They have opined that leaders must be perceived as 'most of us', 'best of us', and 'as one of us' by the followers.
- Great man theory of leadership is encapsulated in the popular slogan—leaders are born and not made. A person becomes leader because he possesses a set of certain traits like alertness, self-confidence, self-assurance, intelligence, dominance, etc.
- Behavioural theory of leadership does not concentrate upon traits of leaders, rather it emphasises the study of activities of the leaders to diagnose their behavioural patterns. The theme of the behavioural theory of the leadership is that a particular behaviour of a leader provides greater satisfaction to the followers, and therefore, they recognise him as a leader. Social psychologists have outlined two

important leadership behaviour—initiating structure behaviour (ISB) and consideration behaviour (CB). These two behavioural patterns are very popular and are likely to make a person leader.
- *Situational theory of leadership* (also called *time or zeitgeist theory*) is another popular theory, which emphasises the fact that it is the time or situation that determines who will become the leader. Some of the important situational factors that do affect the leadership emergence are the size of the group, nature of situation facing the group, source of the leader's power, needs of the members of the group, etc.
- Contingency theories of leadership such as Fiedler's theory and path-goal theory have been considered. These theories explain leader's effectiveness rather than leader's emergence. Contingency theories, in general, emphasise the fact that leadership effectiveness is said to be contingent upon both the characteristics of the situation and the leadership style.
- *Social power* refers to the capacity or potential to influence others and to resist influence from them. Thus, social power is the property of relationship between two or more persons and can be best understood in terms of exchange theory.
- There are six bases of social power such as reward power, coercive power, referent power, expert power, legitimate power and informational power. The first five powers are dependent on the source, that is, the basis of these power lies on the characteristics of a particular person. Informational power is the independent power because it is based on the particular information that the person possesses.
- Social power is determined by the resources, dependencies and alternatives. *Resource* is the property or conditional state of a person, who influences the other. *Dependency* means to what extent B is dependent on A for the fulfilment of the social needs. Greater the dependences, higher is the power of A over B. *Alternatives* mean how many options are before B that may act as resource-like persons. Greater the number of alternatives before B, lesser is the power of A over B. This is clearly seen in case of expert power.

REVIEW QUESTIONS

1. Define leader. Discuss the functions of a leader.
2. How does a leader emerge in the situation? Discuss the major personal characteristics of a leader.
3. Citing experimental evidences, make distinction between transformational leader and transactional leader.
4. Discuss the different dimensions of leader behaviour.
5. Citing examples, discuss the different types of leader.
6. How is a leader perceived by the followers? Cite experimental evidences in favour of your answer.
7. Examine critically Fiedler's theory of leadership.
8. Citing examples, discuss the behavioural theory of leadership.
9. Examine critically path-goal theory of leadership.
10. Write short notes on the following:
    (i) Great man theory
    (ii) Behavioural theory of leadership
    (iii) Transformational leader
    (iv) Situational theory of leadership
    (v) Laissez-faire leader
11. Examine critically Hersey-Blanchard situational theory of leadership.

12 INTERPERSONAL ATTRACTION AND RELATIONSHIP

Learning Objectives

- Meaning and Nature of Interpersonal Attraction
- Theories of Interpersonal Attraction
- Determinants of Interpersonal Attraction
- Romantic Relationship

KEY TERMS

Amae	Infatuated love	Proximity
Comparison level	Interpersonal attraction	Radiating effect of beauty
Comparison level for alternatives	Intimacy	Reciprocal liking and disliking
Compassionate love	Liking and loving scale	Repeated exposure
Consummate love	Logical love	Romantic love
Decision/commitment	Mere exposure effect	Selfless love
Empty love	Need for affiliation	Similarity
Equality	Passion	Social comparison
Equity	Passionate love	Strain towards symmetry
Fatuous love	Possessive love	Triangular theory of love
Game-playing love		

Aristotle called humans as the social animals. Really, we have intense need to belong, that is, to connect with others in enduring, close relationships. If we pay attention to our ancient historical backgrounds, our ancestors used to form mutual attachments for group survival. When they were hunting or erecting shelter, 12 hands were considered better than 2. For a woman and man, the bonds of attachment and love can lead to children, whose survival depends on the nurturing of two bonded parents, who support each other. In fact, when we find a supporting soul mate in whom we can put faith, we feel accepted and prized. When we fall in love, we feel pleasure and irrepressible joy. For a desire of acceptance and love, we spend huge amount of money on cosmetics, clothes and diets.

Social psychologists have called such phenomenon as *interpersonal attraction*, where one person holds a positive attitude towards the other person. There are many kinds of attraction and also many reasons for people to form attitudes of liking and attraction. In the present chapter, we shall concentrate upon theories of interpersonal attraction, determinants of interpersonal attraction, growth of romantic relationship and love. These topics have been considerably emphasised and researched by social psychologists, who proceed by identifying the various abstract features of interpersonal attraction and examining each of them separately.

MEANING AND NATURE OF INTERPERSONAL ATTRACTION

By attraction, we mean a positive attitude held by one person towards the other person. In interpersonal attraction, a person holds certain attitude towards another person. This attraction is expressed along a scale or dimension, which ranges from strong liking to strong disliking. Thus, *interpersonal attraction* may be defined as a person's evaluation of or the person's attitude about some other person on a dimension ranging from strong liking to strong disliking (Baron, Byrne and Branscombe, 2006). In simple words, interpersonal attraction refers to the extent to which we like or dislike other persons. It means repulsion is also a factor in the process of interpersonal attraction and a person's conception of attraction to another may vary from extreme attraction to extreme repulsion. Depending on the level of feeling of attraction, we categorise the other persons and behave towards them in quite different ways. If the level of liking is strong such as close friend, we try to spend time together and make joint plans for action. Likewise, if the level of liking is mild such as close acquaintance, we enjoy interaction with them when we happen to meet. If there is strong disliking such as an undesirable person or enemy, we actively avoid contact. Social psychologists have tried to do research for identifying such evaluation.

If we pay a close attention to the description given above, it is clear that interpersonal likes and dislikes are determined by person's affective or emotional state. When we experience positive emotions, we make positive evaluations and when we experience negative emotions, we experience negative evaluations. This emotional evaluation is influenced by some factors like physical proximity, repeated exposure to another person, as well as to the observable characteristics that is, how a person looks or sounds. Besides, we also tend to form friendly relationship with those who make us feel comfortable. Social psychologists have been able to demonstrate that the level of attraction is determined, at least in part, by the level of similarity or dissimilarity with respect to attitudes, beliefs, values, interests, etc. If the similarities outweigh dissimilarities, the interpersonal attraction between the two persons is enhanced. On the other hand, if dissimilarities outweigh the similarities, the attraction is considerably reduced. When the interpersonal attraction is accompanied by mutual liking by what they say or what they do, such attraction moves towards a close relationship, as we find mostly in romantic relationship.

THEORIES OF INTERPERSONAL ATTRACTION

Social psychologists have advanced various theories or theoretical models to explain interpersonal attraction. Among these theories, the following four are considered here:

1. Newcomb A-B-X model
2. Learning theory or reinforcement model

3. Exchange theory
4. Equity theory model

These theories are briefly described below:

1. Newcomb's A-B-X model: Newcomb (1956, 1961) developed a theoretical model of explaining some of the issues of interpersonal attraction. This model is based on Heider's balance theory of attitude change. Newcomb's adaptation of Heider's theory focuses mainly on interpersonal attraction or rejection between two people (A and B) in relation to a third person or some other object (X) that can be liked or disliked. In other words, Newcomb's theory takes the perspective of person A along with another person B and an object or issue X. The system considers the positive and negative bonds that exist between the actor, the other person and the attitudinal object. As we know, in Newcomb's model, the attitudinal object X may be a thing such as a brand of motorcycle, or tree or an issue such as television violence, sex education, birth control, etc. or also some another person. Like Heider's model, the system can be either symmetrical (balanced) or asymmetrical (or imbalanced). When all perceived bonds or orientations are positive, a balanced state of symmetry exists. For example, when Shyam (A) and Sohan (B) like each other and both like Sita (X), all the three bonds are positive and a balanced relationship emerges (see Figure 12.1).

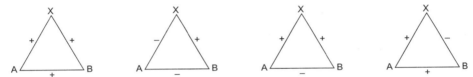

Figure 12.1 Examples of balanced or Imbalanced theory following Newcomb's model.

But symmetry also exists when two bonds one bond is negative and one is positive. For example, Shyam may dislike Sohan and Sita. However, Sohan and Sita may like each other and for this, Shyam has no concern. Imbalance can, however, occur through a number of combinations. A and B both may like X, but they may not like each other. Or A may like both B and X, but B may not like X. In Figure 12.1, the product of three positive sign (+) is positive (+) as well as the product of two negative signs (–) and one positive sign (+) is positive (+), and the system is said to represent a symmetrical relationship. On the other hand, in the imbalanced relationship, the product of two positive signs (+) and negative sign (–) is negative, and it represents an asymmetrical relationship. In Newcomb's terminology, in the imbalanced state, there is a strain towards symmetry such that the perception of asymmetry or imbalance may cause activity on the part of actor (A) to restore symmetry.

Now, the basic question is—why does an actor (A) like symmetrical relationship more than asymmetrical one? Newcomb gave an answer to this question that is different from that of Heider. Newcomb provided two reasons for it. First reason is that human mind always prefers balanced state. Since we have an inherent tendency to prefer to the good form of balance over the bad form of balance, there is strain in perceiving such asymmetrical relationship as balanced or in changing relationships to make them balanced. Second reason behind forming symmetrical relationship is that such relationship helps the person in validating his own opinion about the attitude objects or issue (X). You (A) feel more accurate in your opinion if you come to know that your friend (B) also feels the same way towards an attitude object (X). If you come to know that his friend holds a different opinion about the issue (X), you become less confident of your stand towards the issue.

In such a situation, you react towards the issue by adopting your friend's stance or by getting your friend to adopt your stance. If such situation grows in plenty, you generally tend to decrease your attraction towards your friend (B).

Keeping in view what has been said above, it can be easily predicted that people we like, share our important opinions and people whom we do not like, do not share those opinions. In 1951, Newcomb conducted a study on the students of University of Michigan about their feelings of President Truman's order to dismiss General Douglas MacArthur. Participants in this study were asked how they felt towards dismissal, how their closest friends felt, and how they thought about the people, whom they did not like, felt about the issue. Results revealed that most of the participants felt that their closest friends agreed with them, but the disliked group did not. So, the study clearly revealed that people who are attracted to others feel that these people are close to them and share their important opinions. Considering the other side of the coin, it may be concluded that people are attracted towards those who share their opinions and come to develop friendship with such persons. Newcomb (1961) conducted a study to test this hypothesis. In this study, a group of male students not knowing each other lived together in a house provided by the investigator for over a 16-week period. Elaborate arrangements were made to assess the attitudes of each student on a variety of issues and values. It was clearly found that initially, friendships were not formed on the basis of attitudinal similarity. But as the time elapsed, students knew each other better. Consequently, friendship patterns began to emerge: students having similar values and attitudes began forming friendships with one another. The study clearly showed that the attitudinal similarity served as the basis of choosing friendship groupings.

Now, one basic question arises—how can a person go in restoring symmetry if it does not exist in A-B-X model? For example, your wife (or husband) does not agree with you on issue of having a child, your best friend disagrees with you on voting issue, etc. do represent asymmetrical situations. Therefore, attempt should be made to restore the symmetry because asymmetry produces tension. In such a situation, symmetry can be restored as under:

(i) Husband (A) try to persuade wife (B) to change her attitude towards having a child (X).
(ii) Husband may change his own attitude towards X.
(iii) Husband may change his own attitude towards wife.

Thus, changing any of the sign of A-B-X model would tend to reduce the tension caused by asymmetry. However, there are other possibilities of reducing the strain towards symmetry:

(i) Reducing the importance of topic about which husband and wife disagree
(ii) Reducing the common relevance of the issue

In the first alternative, husband may come to feel that having or not having a child is too trivial to worry. In the second alternative, husband could feel strongly about both wife's view and the issue of having a child, but at the same time, he may conclude that wife's opinion about the issue is irrelevant.

2. Learning theory or reinforcement model: Another model of interpersonal attraction is based upon the principles of learning theory, especially the principles of classical conditioning and vicarious learning. These principles, in general, put forth the idea that the people associated with rewards are liked. Such models were put forth by Lott and Lott (1965, 1974) and Byrne and Clore (1970).

This model suggests that we like those who provide us with rewards and dislike those who punish or annoy us (Byrne 1971; Byrne and Clore, 1970). Through the basic principle of classical conditioning, others become associated with rewarding and punishing circumstances and the person transfers his feelings about the circumstances to the people themselves in a way that is analogous to the dog which learns to salivate at the sound of bell that has been in the past associated with the presence of food (Lott and Lott, 1974). Lott and Lott (1974) applied the idea of conditioning to the development of liking in the following way:

(i) A person receives various rewards such as smiles of approval, praise, enjoyment of a shared activity in the presence of other persons.
(ii) The person reacts to these rewards. For example, a child who is praised, may smile and experience a feeling of pleasure.
(iii) Such responses given by the child or person will become conditioned to all discriminable stimuli that are present at the time when reinforcement was given.
(iv) The person, who is repeatedly present in such circumstance of response-reinforcement sequence, becomes finally able to evoke the responses by his mere presence.

In a nutshell, it can be said that liking for any person is a set of responses that an individual makes in the presence of other persons because these have been previously reinforced in his presence. Such responses may include both overt and covert responses. Examples of overt responses are smiling or talking, whereas the examples of covert responses are feelings.

Various experimental supports have been provided to this conditioning explanation of liking (Lott and Lott, 1960; Lott, Lott and Mathews, 1969). These experiments have used children as participants, generally in game-playing contexts. Many other researchers have also shown that the person, who is associated with a pleasant feeling, will be liked more than a person, who is associated with an unpleasant feeling, irrespective of the fact that whether or not that person was the cause of that feeling. Griffitt and Guay (1969) conducted an experiment in which a bystander was present when one person administered either a reward or a punishment to a subject. It was found that the bystander was liked more when the subject experienced reward than when he experienced a punishment, despite the fact that the bystander had nothing to do with reward and punishment. Griffitt (1970) in another study directly manipulated the pleasantness of a person's experience by varying the temperature and humidity of an experimental room. During such manipulation, a stranger was present in the room. It was found that the stranger was liked more when the room was comfortable than when the room was hot and humid. Likewise, Veitch and Griffitt (1976) found that a stranger, who appeared in the room after listening good news on a radio, was liked more than a stranger, who appeared after the broadcasting of a bad news on the radio. All these experimental findings showed that the stranger's association with pleasantness or unpleasantness of the situation made differences in his ratings of attractiveness, despite the open reality that he had nothing to do with room's temperature or humidity in the former case or with the nature of news report in the latter case.

Lott, Lott and Matthews (1969) expanded learning theory interpretation of interpersonal attraction to imitation and modelling behaviour. They viewed that reward need not be directly experienced rather it is enough for the persons to observe someone else being rewarded for enhancing their liking. They pointed out that the observer, who sees another person being rewarded, may infer or observe certain liking response occurring in that person, and consequently, the observer produces similar responses in himself.

3. Exchange theory: The exchange theory tends to explain interpersonal attraction in terms of exchange processes. (Thibaut and Kelley, 1959). The theory views interpersonal attraction in terms of economic exchange between two people, who assess rewards and costs of maintaining relationship and these are considered useful for explaining on-going, long-term relationship.

Four concepts are basic to the exchange theory—*reward, cost, outcome* and *comparison level*. Each interaction, according to the theory, has some costs that must be paid and certain rewards result. The costs and rewards are defined in broad terms. Any behaviour on the part of one person that contributes to the satisfaction of needs of another is considered as reward. Costs include punishments and deterrents in interacting with another person such as fatigue, anxiety, fear of embarrassment as well as rewards forgone as a consequence of interaction. Foa and Foa (1976) identified six types of interpersonal relationships involving exchange of different kinds of resources—*status* (relationship conferring esteem), *money* (a token with an associated value), *services* (activities done for other person's benefit), *love* (affection, emotional support and warmth), *goods* (objects or products) and *information* (views, information or counsel). For example, suppose A helps B in solving a difficult task. The costs incurred by A are his time and information that he is giving to B and rewards may be the respect and affection he receives in exchange for the help provided.

The *outcome* of an action is represented by simple formula.

$$Outcome = Rewards - Costs$$

According to the theory, any interaction can be viewed at its costs, rewards and outcomes. The theory states that the persons seek out relationship that may maximise their outcomes. One can determine how lasting and satisfying an interaction will be by looking at the outcomes obtained by the participants. In general, if the outcome is positive, the person will be attracted and will want to continue the interaction, but if it is negative, the person may show disliking and will try to end the relationship. A person profits from an interaction with another, however, does not necessarily mean that he likes that person. For attraction to occur, the outcome must be above the minimum level of expectation, which is called *comparison level*. This comparison level is influenced by his past experiences in this type of relation, his past experiences in comparable relations, as well as his judgement of what outcomes others like himself are getting. However, as we know there are relationships in which the participants are very dissatisfied and yet the relationship linger on. To explain this, Thibaut and Kelly (1959) suggested that one must also consider *comparison level for alternatives*, which is defined as the outcomes that an individual feels could be obtained from the best alternative interaction available. In fact, the comparison level for alternatives is the lowest level of outcomes a person will accept in the light of the available alternatives. If the outcome of a given relationship is lower than the comparison level of alternatives, the person is likely to leave the relationship due to disliking. On the other hand, if the outcome is higher than the comparison level for alternatives, the person will remain in the relationship even if he feels dissatisfied. That is the reason, why many unhappy marriages stay because alternative seems even worse. Altman and Haythorn (1965) conducted an experiment to show that the development of attraction in a particular dyad is influenced by the outcomes available in the alternative relations. In this study, they compared the effects of interaction in isolated and non-isolated groups. There were nine pairs of persons, who worked and lived in small room for ten days, with no alternative relationship or outside contact permitted. The pattern of interaction was found to be different in non-isolated or control dyad and isolated dyad. The non-isolated dyads followed a similar schedule with less friendly and sociable behaviour. However, the isolated dyad engaged in more self-disclosure, and depth of disclosure resembled with some close friends. Apart from this, among isolated dyads, much more friendly and social behaviour with proper love and affection is found.

Whether an individual initiates a new relationship or not depends on both the comparison level as well as the comparison level for alternatives. Generally, a person avoids having relationship with others when his anticipated outcomes fall below the comparison level. If such potential relationship appears to yield outcomes above the individual's comparison level, then initiation will depend on the fact that whether the outcomes are expected to exceed the comparison level for alternatives. For example, Amitabh may believe that the relationship with Sita would be very satisfying. He only casually meets with another girl (Sneha) and that relationship is not satisfying. Thus, the potential relationship with Sita is above both the comparison level and the comparison level for alternative, leading Amitabh to initiate contact and friendship with Sita.

A close scrutiny of the exchange theory of interaction reveals that while reinforcement concepts such as reward and punishment have been figured prominently in this theory, this model differs from learning or reinforcement model in the following two basic ways:

(i) In exchange theory of attraction, focus is on the relation between persons rather than on persons themselves. In exchange theory, due emphasis is given on how various characteristics of a relation emerge and how this relationship is changed as a result of reciprocal process of rewards or reinforcement between the individuals.

(ii) Cognitive factors play more important role in exchange theory than in reinforcement theory. Rewards and punishments are considered effective because they are mediated by the expectations and perceived intentions of the interacting persons. These expectations, in turn, are influenced by such normative cognitions as rules of justice and ideas about equivalence in the exchange. That is the reason, why mild but unjust punishment may be felt very severely as compared to a strong but just punishment. Such cognitive elements are lacking in the reinforcement theory of interpersonal attraction.

4. Equity theory: Equity theory explanation of interpersonal attraction moves a step forward than exchange theory by taking into account not only an individual's own outcomes but also the outcomes perceived to be attained by the partner in relationship (Walster, Walster and Berscheid, 1978). The equity theory, first proposed by Adams (1965), suggests that the individuals expect resources to be distributed fairly. Basic to equity theory is the social comparison. Individuals compare their inputs and outcomes with those obtained by others in concern. Equity theory maintains that we seek to emphasise a balance between what we give and what we receive on the one hand and what the partner gives and receives on the other hand. In other words, the theory suggests that we try to maintain a balance between the rewards and costs we experience and those which our partner experiences. In case, it is felt that the partner is receiving more (or less) than his or her just due, the person will experience distress and will try to restore equity by modifying his perception of what he is getting out of the relationship or by modifying his own feelings for the partner. For example, if a working wife feels that her husband leaves a lot of household works for her to be done, she may experience feelings of inequity and revaluate the relationship. During the period of inequity, she may develop a modest feeling of disliking, which may be restored to the liking after the feeling of inequity is reduced and a balance is maintained.

Equity theory is different from equality. In other words, it is not necessary for both partners here to contribute an equal amount of input. If one partner contributes more than the other and also benefits more, the relationship is said to be *equitable*. On the other hand, if one partner receives less benefit than required by his or her contribution level, the person is said to be *underbenefitted*. If a partner, however, receives more benefit compared to his or her contribution level, that person or partner is said to be *overbenefitted*. In either case, the relationship is *inequitable*. According to Adams (1965), under-benefitted partners are less satisfied with their relationship, and therefore, they will be less attracted towards their partners. Equity theory states that the partners will feel comfort in their relationship only when the ratio between their perceived contributions and benefits are equal. The theory can be summarised as under:

$$\frac{\text{Perceived benefits of person A}}{\text{Perceived contributions of person A}} = \frac{\text{Perceived benefits of person B}}{\text{Perceived contributions of person B}}$$

Although these benefits and contributions cannot be easily translated into numerical terms, but suppose for a moment that person A perceives that he gives 20 things to the relationship, while B perceives that he gives only 10 things. Would this be an equitable relationship? Yes, it would be, provided A also perceived 20 benefits from the relationship and B also perceived 10 benefits because the equation would be producing balance.

$$\frac{20}{20} = \frac{10}{10}$$

Here, two important points are important. First, the benefits that two persons receive from one another need not have to be equal, but the ratio between their benefits and contributions must be equal. In fact, a person, who both gives and receives a lot, can be in an equitable relationship with a person, who gives and receives much less. Second, equations emphasise perceived benefits and contribution. The only person who can judge how much he is giving and receiving is the person himself. An outsider might see the relationship as being highly inequitable, whereas the partners themselves may be very happy with it.

If either member of the relationship perceives the relationship to be inequitable, that partner either will take steps to maintain equity or will like to terminate the relationship. A person becomes uncomfortable in relationship either when he feels that he receives too little compared to what he gives or when he perceives too much compared to what he gives. In either case, he is motivated to restore equity by giving more or less or by asking other partner to give more or less.

Some researches have reported gender differences in the salience of equity theory. Prins et al. (1993) reported that in Dutch couples, males, who perceived inequity, neither expressed the desire to have an affair nor reported that they had done so far. However, Dutch women, who perceived inequity in their relationship, both expressed the desire to have an affair and reported more affairs, especially when felt overbenefitted by the relationship. Apart from this, women tend to emphasise that the resources should be distributed according to the norms of equality, whereas males tend to emphasise that they should be distributed according to the norms of equity (Kahn et al., 1980).

DETERMINANTS OF INTERPERSONAL ATTRACTION

Social psychologists have identified three important categories of interpersonal attraction. These are
1. Internal determinants
2. External determinants
3. Interactive determinants

Details of these categories are mentioned below:

1. *Internal determinants of interpersonal attraction*

There are two major internal determinants of interpersonal attraction—need to affiliate and affect. These two are discussed below:

(i) **Need to affiliate:** Human beings are born with the need for affiliation, which is defined as a basic motivation for seeking and maintaining interpersonal relationship. This need is fulfilled through others. In fact, interpersonal attraction is the basis for most voluntary social relationships (Berscheid and Regan, 2005). People do affiliate out of attraction for one another (Coon and Mitterer, 2007). We want to affiliate to persons who are kind and understanding, who have attractive personalities and who like us in return (Sprecher, 1998).

People tend to differ in the strength of their need for affiliation. Some people tend to seek optimal amount of social contact and some prefer to be alone some of the time (O'Connor and Rosenblood, 1996). When affiliation need is not met or when we are ignored, we feel both sad and angry. Such social exclusion may result in less effective cognitive functioning (Baumeister, Twenge and Nuss, 2002). Some situational factors also affect the need for affiliation. For example, in wake of situational catastrophe such as flood, fire, earthquake or blizzard, even the strangers come together and interact with each other in helping manner. Such interactions are described as friendly and cheerful, with people showing maximum liking for helping each other. Schachter (1959) conducted an experiment in which it was shown that anxiety-inducing laboratory experiences tended to arouse the need to affiliate. Now, one of the basic questions arises—why do frightened, anxious people want to interact with other anxious and frightened people? One general answer is that such need for affiliation provides the opportunity for social comparison. In fact in such situations, individuals want to be with others for communicating about what they are experiencing and want to compare their affective reactions and both of these become comforting (Gump and Kulik, 1997).

(ii) **Affect:** *Affect* means the emotional state that has an impact upon perceiving, thinking, motivation, decision-making as well as liking or disliking towards others. Two most important characteristics of affect are intensity and direction. *Intensity* indicates the strength of the emotion and *direction* indicates whether the emotion is positive or negative. Positive intense affect leads to positive evaluations of other people (strong liking), while negative intense affect leads to negative evaluations (disliking) (Byrne, 1997; Dovidio et al., 1995). Positive and negative affective states influence attraction both directly and indirectly. Many experiments have confirmed the idea that a person likes stranger most if the stranger does or says something pleasant as opposed to something unpleasant. McDonald (1962) showed in his experiment that attraction towards other person becomes less if he or she provides punishments in rating the performance on a task rather than rewards. Likewise, our attraction towards a stranger becomes less who invades one's personal space than one who remains at a comfortable distance (Fisher and Byrne, 1975). There is also *indirect effect* or *associated effect* of emotions on attraction. This effect tends to occur when another person is simply present at the same time when one's emotional state has been aroused by something or someone else. For example, if you have just heard the news of being unsuccessful in the examination and met with his neighbour shortly after that, you tend to like that person less than someone you met immediately after winning a lottery of a huge amount of money. Many experiments have demonstrated the associated influences of the affect. For example, May and Hamilton (1980) found that the presence of background music that college students perceived as pleasant produced more liking among them as compared to those background music that were perceived as unpleasant. Social psychologists have explained such effects on attraction with the help of principle of classical conditioning, which clearly states that when a neutral stimulus is paired with a stimulus producing positive affect, it is evaluated more positively and when a neutral stimulus is paired with a stimulus producing negative affect, it is evaluated more negatively even when the person knows nothing about the pairings (Olson and Fazio, 2001).

2. *External determinants of interpersonal attraction*

Interpersonal attraction is determined by some external factors like proximity and observable characteristics such as physical attractiveness, physique, weight, behavioural style, food preferences, names, race, clothing, etc. These are discussed below:

(i) **Proximity:** *Proximity* or *propinquity* means physical closeness between two individuals with respect to where they live and interact, where they sit in a classroom and where they work and so on. There are many studies, which support the fact that proximity leads to attraction. Winerman and Swanson (1952) studied the friendship formations in students in dormitories and found that the highest proportion of friendships occurred among students who lived in rooms that were adjacent to each other. Byrne (1961) reported that in classroom settings, seating patterns do have an important influence on the development of friendships. He varied the seating arrangement for three classes of about 25 students each. In one class, they remained in the same seats for the whole semester of 14 weeks. In second class, they were assigned new seats half way through the semester and in the third class, they were assigned new seats every 3½ weeks. The relationship among students was assessed at the beginning and end of the semester. It was found in results that the students formed closer relationships where seats were not changed and only a few relationship developed among students in the class where seats were changed every 3½ weeks.

Another systematic investigation of proximity and attraction was conducted by Festinger, Schachter and Back (1950) at Westgate West, a housing project for married students. The investigators examined relationship among married couples in a university housing project, which consisted of 17 buildings of 10 apartments spread over two floors. They found that the distance among people on the same floor and on different floors was closely related to the friendship patterns, that is, the closer the two couples lived to each other, the more likely they were to be friends and felt attracted towards each other. Living at different floors reduced the likelihood of forming friendship due to the increased physical distance that led to the reduction in proximity. Those whose apartments were located next to stairs or mailboxes reported a closer friendship than did other couples located elsewhere. The effect is not restricted to location within a building. Newcomb (1961) found that students, who lived as roommates, developed a closer bond of friendship and attraction. Segal (1974) conducted a study on students of police training academy. He asked students to list their three closest friends and found a high correlation between the initial letter of students' surname and those of his friends. The seating arrangements at the academy was done in alphabetical order, placing those with names close in alphabet in close physical proximity.

Now the question is—why does proximity result in attraction? Social psychologists have provided several explanations for this as under:

(a) Proximity provides opportunity to interact with those close to us. This frequent interaction leads to attraction due to three reasons. First, interacting with others provide us with a sense of complete mastery (Smith and Mackie, 1995) by giving us opportunity to solve personal problems (Schachter, 1959). Second, interaction helps in achieving a sense of belongingness by providing warmth, acceptance and stimulation. Finally, interaction leads to attraction because it generates familiarity.

(b) Interacting frequently with someone gives us the opportunity to discover more about him and usually becomes an interesting and rewarding experience.

(c) Proximity leads to attraction because the repeated exposure to someone (or any stimulus) results in increasingly positive evaluation of that person (or stimulus) (Zajonc, 1968). This is termed as *mere exposure effect* (Bernstein et al., 1997). Moreland and Beach (1992) conducted an experiment in which the effects of repeated exposure on attraction were confirmed. In this experiment, four women assistants were recruited, who resembled typical college students. One assistant attended a large psychology lecture course fifteen times during the semester, second assistant attended the class ten times, third assistant attended the class five times and the fourth assistant did not attend the class at all. None of these assistants interacted with any student present in the classroom. At the end of the semester, students were shown slides depicting the photograph of these four assistants and asked to indicate their likings for each. Results revealed that the more times a particular assistant attended that class, the more she was liked by the students even though they had never spoken to the woman. Explaining the effect of repeated exposure, Zajonc (2001) said that with repeated exposure, generally, negative emotions decrease and positive emotions increase. As a consequence, any feeling of uncertainty decreases and the person feels that the stimulus is safe (Lee, 2001).

Some psychologists have demonstrated that the repeated exposure to a stimulus results in likings for that stimulus even when the person is not aware that the exposure has taken place. Monahan, Murphy and Zajonc (2000) showed that the positive affect produced by the repeated exposure to subliminal stimuli generalises to other similar stimuli and even to new stimuli.

But a question also arises—does proximity always have a positive effect? The answer is no. Berscheid and Walster (1978) pointed out that proximity does produce opposite effect too. There are many examples in which we find that most aggravated assaults occur within family units or between neighbours. While neighbours may prove to be our best friends, they may also be the worst enemies. Ebbesen et al. (1975) reported from their study that while most liked people live in proximity, so also the most disliked people. We know that interacting with those who is aggressive, racist and unpleasant leads to more disliking.

(ii) **Observable characteristics:** When we meet with a stranger or unknown person, his several observable characteristics do influence our interpersonal attraction and judgements. Among these observable characteristics, the following are important:

(a) *Physical attractiveness:* One very important factor that affects or influences our initial response to others is physical attractiveness. It has been found that people are most likely to respond positively to those who are physically attractive and negatively to those who are least attractive (Collins and Zebrowitz, 1995). One reason is the common stereotype that attractive people have several other good qualities as well (Eagly et al., 1991). Researches have shown that most people tend to believe that attractive persons are interesting, dominant, social, independent, exciting, well-adjusted, sexy, socially skilled, successful, more masculine (men), more feminine (women) than unattractive persons (Dion and Dion, 1988; Hatfield and Sprecher, 1986a).

The effects of physical attractiveness are very wide-ranging and being attractive definitely brings some advantages. Cash et al. (1977) reported that among a group of supposed candidates for employment (in fact, all confederates of the experimenter), physically attractive applicants were comparatively more preferred. Likewise, Kulka and Kessler (1978) found that in a simulated courtroom situation, physically attractive defendants were treated more leniently. In education too, physical appearance counts. Landy and Sigall (1974) conducted a study in which male students were asked to mark two essays of differing standards. They paired each of the essay with a photo of either attractive female or less attractive female. Results revealed that better grades were given to attractive females. Even in childhood, the impact of physical attractiveness is obvious. Children prefer to have physically attractive playmates and also assume that the less attractive children do possess some unpleasant character traits (Dion et al., 1974). In choosing a sexual partner, the physical attractiveness is considered very important.

Individuals with physical disabilities are often the targets of various types of stereotypes about physical attractiveness. In a study conducted by Silverman and Klees (1989), school students rated a student with a hearing aid as more introverted, afraid, depressed and also insecure as compared to a non-disable student. Likewise, in a study conducted by Fine and Asch (1988), college students associated the general category woman with 'lovable', 'soft', 'married', and 'intelligent', but they termed disable woman as 'ugly', 'lifeless', 'crippled', 'lonely' and 'someone to feel sorry for'.

Social psychologists have also studied what makes some faces more attractive than others. The greatest agreement among persons in judging a face as attractive occurs when men judge the attractiveness of women (Marcus and Miller, 2003). In fact, the study of physical attractiveness has identified some types of women, who are rated as the most attractive. One type is considered cute, having childlike features, large widely spaced eyes and a small nose and chin. Another type of attractiveness is having mature look—high eyebrows, large pupils, prominent cheekbones and a big smile. Still another type is the average face. Such average face is considered more attractive than atypical. People like faces that are symmetrical. Mealey, Bridgstock and Townsend (1999) conducted a study in which some college students rated the attractiveness of photos of the faces of identical twins. Although the identical twins looked very much similar, students assessed the twin with the more symmetrical faces as comparatively more attractive. In fact, beautiful faces seem to be more balanced and well-proportioned, and therefore, more attractive.

Social psychologists have provided several reasons for having an association between physical attractiveness and liking, which are as under:

- There is a common stereotype that good-looking people have several good qualities and this tends to enhance our liking for them.
- When we meet with new people or strangers, we generally pay more attention to physically attractive individuals, especially women than to the other less good-looking persons.
- According to Langlois et al. (2000), the physical attractiveness may be an important clue to good health and reproductive fitness. In other words, a physical attractive face may be a marker of good genes. This explanation is based on the evolutionary principles.
- Still another reason for liking a physically attractive face is the radiating effect of beauty. People, in general, like to be seen with a physically attractive face because they think it will enhance their own public image and popularity.

(b) *Physique:* Physique of a person is also one of the factors that affect liking. Once it was believed that body type provided information about personality (Sheldon, Stevens and Tucker, 1940). But later on, it was realised that it was an inaccurate assumption. Despite this, today people, in general, believe that a round and fat body (endomorphic physique) indicates a sloppy and sad person, a muscular body (mesomorphic physique) indicates good health, but lacking intelligence and a thin and angular body (ectomorphic physique) indicates fearfulness and intelligence (Gardner and Tockerman, 1994). However, as most of the researches have revealed that the least liked physique is the obese person. Crandall and Biernat (1990) found that obese people are often seen negatively. A man sitting with an obese woman is evaluated more negatively than a man sitting with an average weight woman (Hebl and Mannix, 2003). However, some researches have also shown that the stereotypes associated with obesity do not always lead to accurate predictions about how an individual can be expected to behave (Miller et al., 1995).

(c) *Differences in overt behaviour:* Some observable differences in overt behaviour also elicit liking or disliking. For example, a person with a firm handshake is perceived as being extroverted and also emotionally expressive and outgoing (Chaplin et al., 2000). Likewise, individuals respond positively to others who acts modestly rather than arrogantly (Hareli and Weiner, 2000). In initial interactions, persons with a dominant, authoritative and competitive outlook are preferred over those who seem to be submissive, less masculine and non-competitive (Friedman, Riggio and Casella, 1988). However, in subsequent interactions, when additional information becomes available, the preference may change to men who are helpful and sensitive (Jensen-Campbele, West and Giaziano, 1995).

(d) *Miscellaneous factors:* There are a lots of other observable factors, though of little importance, which tend to affect the liking. One such factor is clothing colour. Individuals tend to make an automatic association between brightness and affect, that is, bright generally equals good and dark generally equals bad (Meier, Robinson and Clore, 2004). Likewise, we tend to like less when behaviours of others seem to suggest mental illness (Schumacher, Corrigam and Dejong, 2003) and perceived age (McKelvie, 1993). Some researchers have found that interpersonal attraction is also influenced by what a person eats (Stein and Nemeroff, 1995). A person who eats good food such as apple, orange, rice, roti, salad, chicken is perceived as more likeable than a person who eats bad food like lizard, snake, frog, steak, french fries, doughnuts, etc. A study conducted by Stein and Nemeroff (1995) bears an evidence to this effect. Some evidences are available to support the contention that the first name of the person also influences interpersonal perception and ultimately the liking. Various male and female names elicit different shared positive or negative stereotypes which are then transferred to anyone who happens to have that name (Mehrabian and Piercy, 1993). For example, females having names like Rani Lakshmi Bai, Razia Sultan, and Indira Gandhi and males having names like Bhagat Singh, Bir Chand Patel, Jawahar Lal Nehru, etc. do tend to influence our interpersonal perceptions. Besides, height, especially for males, is considered as a positive factor. This may be one of the reasons for widespread liking and popularity of Megastar, Amitabh Bachchan.

3. *Interactive determinants of interpersonal attraction*

When two people interact with each other, their communication becomes relevant for interpersonal perception. There are two crucial aspects of this communication—degree of similarity of attitudes, beliefs, values and personal characteristics between the interacting persons, and mutual evaluations of liking and disliking. These are briefly described here.

(i) **Similarity:** Perhaps, the maximum researches on interpersonal attraction have been done in the area of relationship between similarity and attraction. Researches suggest that interpersonal attraction and similarity are multidimensional constructs (Lydon et al., 1988) where individuals are attracted to others who are similar to them in attitude, physical characteristics, values, interest, social and cultural background activities, preferences, communication and social skills. However, there are three aspects of similarity that have been investigated in depth—attitude similarity, value similarity and similarity in personal characteristics. These three aspects are discussed below:

(a) *Attitude similarity:* Since early 1900s, the investigators have shown that the persons who like one another tend to share similar attitudes (Schuster and Elderton, 1907). There are two aspects of similarity of attitudes—perceived similarity and actual similarity. Newcomb (1961) conducted a study with experimental college environment which vividly demonstrated the effect of these two types of similarities in attitudes. At the beginning of the study, he found that the perceived similarity in attitudes was strongly correlated with liking amount of the students. At this stage, since students did not know each other's true attitudes, attraction was the only key factor to their interpersonal liking. [In fact, when we are attracted towards another person, we presume that he must be sharing our attitudes (Marks and Miller, 1987). Such perceived similarity of attitudes tend to increase our liking.] As the academic year went ahead, the students could get a chance to know each other well and at this stage, Newcomb found a strong relationship between actual attitude similarity and the liking. Later on, Byrne (1971) underpinned results from Newcomb's study in his research. He conducted his research in two stages. In the first stage, he gave students a questionnaire on attitude to complete. In the second stage, students were given an attitude questionnaire supposedly completed by a fellow student, but in fact, manipulated by the researcher to express similar or dissimilar attitudes to the students' own. Results revealed that the students preferred people who expressed similar attitudes. In other words, they liked similar strangers much better than they liked dissimilar ones. Not only that, the similar strangers were also judged to be comparatively more intelligent, better informed and better adjusted. Many other similar investigations revealed that attraction is determined by the proportion of similarity. According to the law of attraction proposed by Byrne (1971), attraction towards individual is positively related to the proportion of attitude similarity associated with the individual. When there occurs similarity in attitudes, it promotes social interaction (Singh and Ho, 2000). On the other hand, when there occurs dissimilarity in attitude and interest, it provides disliking and avoidance (Singh and Ho, 2000; Tan and Singh, 1995). Higher the proportion of similarity, greater is the liking (Byrne and Nelson, 1965). To illustrate this, you generally tend to like a person, who is perceived to be similar to you on ten out of twenty attitudes (50%), less than the person, who is perceived to agree with you on three out of four attitudes (75%), although in the first case, absolute number of agreements (ten) is greater than in the second case (three). This mathematical relationship between attraction and proportion of perceived attitude similarity forms a straight line when graphed.

The effect of similar attitudes on liking has also been demonstrated in real-life situations. Byrne, Ervin and Lamberth (1970) proved it. They arranged for a computer dating between males and females, who differed either minimally or maximally on responses to fifty-item questionnaire. After introduction of each couple, the partners were asked to spend thirty minutes together on date. Subsequently, they independently completed scale for assessing attraction to each other. Results revealed that attraction was significantly related to similarity in attitude. Such conclusion holds equally true for males and females irrespective of age, educational and cultural differences (Byrne, 1971). Along the lines of Byrne's attraction paradigm, one of the early cross-cultural studies involving participants from four countries, including India, was conducted by Byrne, Gouaux, Griffitt, Lamberth, Murakawa, M.B. Prasad, A. Prasad and Ramirez (1971). Results revealed a significant similarity effect on attraction and lack of its interaction with different cultures indicated that the similarity-attraction function has generality across quite different cultural groups.

The most serious challenge to the effect of attitude similarity on attraction came from the findings of Rosenbaum (1986), who argued that because we find attitudinal dissimilarity so repellent that we seek to avoid it, therefore, dissimilarity is a more important factor of not liking than similarity is of liking. He put forward what was called *repulsion hypothesis*—an alternative to similarity–dissimilarity effect. According to this hypothesis, information about similarity has little or no effect upon attraction—individuals are simply repulsed by information about dissimilarity. But later researches have revealed that this is not a correct view (Smeaton, Byrne and Murnen, 1989). Despite this, some researchers held the view that there is kernel of truth in the repulsion hypothesis because under most situations, dissimilarity in attitude has a slightly stronger effect on attraction than the same amount of information about similarity (Singh and Ho, 2000; Tan and Singh, 1995). Moreover, attitude similarity and attraction are though linearly related, attraction may not contribute significantly to attitude changes (Simons et al., 1970).

(b) *Similarity in values:* Like similarity in attitudes, similarity in values also tends to influence liking. Hill and Stull (1981) conducted a study in which same sex college roommate pairs were studied and it was found that women, who preferred to be roommate, had greater similarity in terms of fundamental values relating to subjects like religion and politics than those who had been assigned to be roommate. The study clearly showed that value similarity enhanced liking. Although the results for male pairs in value similarity were less clear. Results, on the whole, suggested that roommates, who shared basic values about the different subjects, showed more positive relationship than those who did not.

Some significant studies in value similarity and attraction were conducted at Aligarh (Husain and Kureshi, 1979, 1982, 1983a, 1983b; Kureshi and Husain, 1982). Husain and Kureshi (1979) studied the several dimensions of friendship such as best friend roommate, classmate and hostel fellow. They found that values were more important for intimate relationship, liking and attraction than needs, which operate at relatively distant level of relationship. Husain and Kureshi (1983a) also found that attraction between the participants of the same sex and same socio-economic status was more based on the perception of similarity in values.

(c) *Similarity in personal characteristics:* Researches have shown that there is a strong correlation between friends, partners, spouse on variables like age, education, race, religious beliefs, type of background and socio-economic status (Warren, 1966). Newcomb (1961) provided empirical support for this. He allowed male students to live in a college accommodation (rent-free for one semester). The students were assessed on demographic variables such as age and backgrounds, prior to the start of the course. In the results, he found that over the course of time, the attraction and liking among students were strongly related to the pre-existing demographic variables. Similarity in these variables provided important keys for attraction because shared interest gave the students opportunity to interact with each other and those shared interests increased the probability of interaction being positive. However, later research reported a diminution of the effects of demographic similarity because individuals from different races and backgrounds were reported to marry in comparison to previous time (Smolowe, 1993).

Researches have also shown that liking and attraction between people are also associated with personality. We are attracted to those who have personality traits relatively similar to our own. In an early demonstration, Reader and English (1947) administered personality tests to the pairs of friends and found higher correlations among their traits than a control group that consisted of stranger pairs. In India, two studies conducted by Kundu and Biswas (1980) and Kundu and Maiti (1980) are worth mentioning here. Kundu and Biswas (1980) found that increasing chronological age is the primary determinant of stability in friendship relationship. Besides, such stability also depends on the degree of social acceptance and social skills. They clearly found that highly acceptable individuals or groups were able to carry stable friendship relations to a greater extent than the individuals who were relatively less well-accepted. Likewise, Kundu and Maiti (1980) conducted another study on 60 boys in the age range of 9–11 years. Their findings indicated that the age-strength of a child has an impact upon social acceptance, which is a key factor in interpersonal relationship.

Two personality traits—warmth and competence—have also been considered relevant for interpersonal attraction. People appear warm when they show positive attitude towards people and things. On the other hand, people seem cold when they dislike things, disparage them and are generally critical. Folkes and Sears (1977) conducted a study in which the participants read or listened to the interviews in which the interviewees were asked to evaluate different items such as political leaders, cities, college courses and movies. Sometimes, the interviewer expressed positive attitudes, that is, they praised and liked most of cities, politicians, movies, and courses. In other situations, the interviewers expressed negative attitudes. Results revealed that the participants liked the interviewers more when they showed positive attitude (warmth) rather than negative attitude.

Competence is another important aspect. In general, we like people who are competent, that is, who are intelligent and socially skilled. Competent individuals are usually more rewarding to be with than the inept individuals. Leary et al. (1986) showed that we are attracted towards those persons, who are good conversationists. In the first study, they gave college students descriptions of boring versus interesting speakers. Students were reported being bored when the speakers talked too much about themselves or about trivial matters. They also reported being bored by the people, who were tedious, passive and serious in their interactions. In the second study, the students listened to tape conversations designed in such a way that the target speaker was perceived as either boring or interesting. Results revealed that the students liked boring speakers less and they were also rated them as less friendly, less enthusiastic and less impersonal. On the other hand, interesting speakers were perceived as more friendly and likeable.

Researchers have also shown that there is an association between mood and attraction. Locke and Horowitz (1990) conducted a study in which they paired students with others in similar mood states. They found that such pairs showed greater satisfaction in their brief interaction than those pairs whose moods differed. This suggests that being with the people of similar mood enhances the attraction. It is important here to note that the interactions are of brief nature. The long-term interaction with negative mood states, however, does not enhance attraction. McLeod and Eckberg (1993) reported that married couples, where one or both partners are depressed, generally, report reduction in marital satisfaction and attraction towards each other.

There are, however, some limits to the similarity effect. Although similarity usually leads to liking, there are some exceptions to this rule. Sometimes, similarity becomes threatening. For example, if someone similar to us is diagnosed with lung cancer, we may become anxious that we are also vulnerable, and therefore, we may prefer to avoid that person (Novak and Lerner, 1968). Likewise, similarity to ideal-self has a positive effect, but finding that someone closer to your ideal than you yourself really becomes threatening (Herbst, Gaertner and Insko, 2003). Another point is that differences among individuals are sometimes rewarding. Having friends with different abilities, interests and skills becomes advantageous in the sense that it enables us to pool our shared knowledge in mutually beneficial ways (Tayor, Peplau and Sears, 2006).

Explaining the effects of similarity: The question arises—why is similarity so important for interpersonal attraction? Byrne and Clore (1970) argued from the perspective of classical conditioning. According to this perspective, similarity is rewarding to the people because this reassures that there are others, who see the world as we do and share our beliefs. Conversely, dissimilarity is non-rewarding in the sense that it threatens both our perception of the world and self-esteem. Wetzel and Insko (1982) proposed another theory to explain the effect of similarity upon attraction. According to them, the search for similarity actually means search for someone who meets our ideals. They were of view that the individuals tend to prefer those who meet their ideals more than those who are similar to them.

Besides, similarity–dissimilarity effect has been explained by balance theory, social comparison theory as well as by evolutionary perspective as an adaptive response. Balance theory, which was independently proposed by Heider (1958) and Newcomb (1961), states that when people like each other they find that they are similar in some respects. This constitutes a state of balance, which is emotionally pleasant. On the other hand, when two people like each other and find out that they are dissimilar in some respects, a state of imbalance is created. This imbalance is emotionally unpleasant, which forces one of them to store balance by bringing attitudinal change, thus creating similarity. According to social comparison theory of Festinger (1954), the people compare their attitudes and beliefs with those of others because they want to evaluate accuracy and normality by finding that the other people agree with them. When we find that we are not alone in holding a particular belief because others are also holding the similar view, it automatically suggests that our judgement is sound and in accord with reality. Dissimilarity suggests the opposite, and therefore, creates negative effect. Another explanation of similarity–dissimilarity effect rests on an evolutionary perspective as an adaptive response to potential danger. According to Horney (1950), there are three basic alternative reactions to strangers—we move *towards* them with friendly intention, we move *away* from them out of fear with self-protective intention or *against* them with an aggressive intention. Different potential consequences may be associated with different response choice. If we perceive the strangers as good and kind, we move with friendly intention; if the strangers somehow pose threat, then a friendly approach would be dangerous and this least adaptive response could be done. In such situations, we may also aggress against the strangers. Many animals are also genetically programmed to aggress. When male mice finds that a strange mouse has entered their territory and if it is male, he attacks it but if it is female, he seduces it (Wade, 2002).

Following this evolutionary perspective, we are simply programmed to like those who are similar to us and fear and hate those who are different from ourselves, especially if they are males. Likewise, we are automatically vigilant in responding to the cues that alert us to positive and negative consequences, and therefore, we accordingly approach or avoid those cues (Wentura, Rothermund and Bak, 2000).

(ii) **Mutual evaluations—Reciprocal liking or disliking:** Mutual evaluations are another factors that influence interpersonal attraction. In general, we like all those people, whose behaviours or words indicate that they like us. When we like someone, we generally assume that they like us in return (Burleson, 1984).

Dittes and Kelley (1956) examined reciprocity-of-liking principles in series of studies. They asked students to take part in small discussion groups and then gave them written evaluations apparently from other members of the group, but actually prepared by the experimenters. Results revealed that those students, who received negative evaluations disliked the group, while those, who received positive evaluations, liked the group.

Although reciprocity-of-liking rule has much support (Gordon, 1996), there are some exceptions. One exception relates to self-esteem. People with high self-esteem tend to like themselves and people with low self-esteem tend to dislike themselves. People with low self-esteem will not be susceptible to the reciprocity-of-liking rule because they are very likely to dislike people they find liking them, since they do not like themselves (Shraugher, 1975). Moreover, Dittes (1959) also reported that the effect of being liked or disliked varied according to the levels of self-esteem of the participants. Those students, who were high in self-esteem, are not influenced by being liked or disliked by the group. However, for those with low self-esteem, being liked led to very high levels of liking for the group, while being disliked led to high level of dislike for the group. Another exception relates to *ingratiation*, which is defined as a deliberate effort to gain favour often through flattery. If an employee says his boss how much he likes him, the boss might feel that he is being flattered for an ulterior motive. Consequently, the boss may resist and begin to dislike the employee, rather than forming a positive opinion about the employee.

Despite these exceptions, expressing positive feelings about others is apt to produce reciprocated liking.

ROMANTIC RELATIONSHIP

Romantic relationship, a long favourable subject for poet and songwriters, is now a popular topic for scientific research (Berscheid and Regan, 2005). Romantic relationship includes sexual attraction, spending time together, similarity of attitudes and values, and sometimes, also the belief that two people share something special (Baccman, Folkesson and Norlander, 1999). An important and defining characteristic of romantic relationship is some degree of physical intimacy ranging from holding hands to sexual interactions (see Figure 12.2). Depending on the cultural norms of the society, the sexual attraction may or may not lead to some form of sexual behaviour and the physical intimacy may be restricted to holding hands, hugging and kissing or it may include some explicit form of sexual interactions.

Figure 12.2 Physical intimacy in romantic relationship.

A major feature of romantic relationship is the interpretation of one's affect arousal in the presence of partner as strong attraction, which includes at least the potential for love and sex. Besides, both partners in romantic relationship set higher standards for each other than for friends with respect to social status, physical attractiveness, warmth and intelligence (Sprecher and Regan, 2002). Beyond the tone of sexuality, there are some other aspects of romantic relationship that differ from friendly relationship. In friendly relationship, most people prefer a partner who can provide an accurate feedback (Swann et al., 1994). On the other hand, in romantic relationship, at least in the beginning, both partners tend to prefer total approval and acceptance and do not care much for accuracy and truth. In fact, in romantic relationship, the partners want to like and be liked unconditionally and both want to be blessed by compliments, praise and frequently demonstrations of affection.

Social psychologists have tried to explain romantic relationship in terms of three overlapping schemas (Fletcher et al., 1999). The three schemas are *self-schema*, *partner schema*, that is, one's perception of the partner, and schema involving relationship between self and partner or *relationship schema*. Of these three schemas, the schema involving one's partner is often unrealistic and inaccurate because each partner wants to believe that his or her partner is a perfect partner and also wants totally positive feedback from the partner (Katz and Beach, 2000). The partner's virtues are emphasised and any possible faults are not paid attention, and therefore, dismissed (Murray and Holmes, 1999). If the partner is perceived closer to one's ideal, the relationship is considered good and long lasting (Campbell et al., 2001).

The romantic relationship at least partly contains illusions and fantasies, which may be helpful in making relationship crucial and aiding it to survive. In fact, the shared illusions frequently present in the relationship schema are based on a particular belief in romantic destiny, that is, the belief that both partners are made for each other. Such conviction helps in maintaining the relationship lasting (Franiuk, Cohen and Pomerantz, 2002).

Love and loving

In social psychology, extensive literature on attraction has focused upon what is normally called *liking* or *respect* or *high regard*. Love has been the Cinderella sister of liking, being largely ignored by the researchers. Love, in all its richness, its fullness and its power, is such an intense human experience that investigators find it very hard to study. It is almost too personal to be viewed and studied objectively. At the same time, we believe that love is the strongest emotional bond and the most satisfying human experience for those who are fortunate enough to find it.

There are three major problems in studying love. First, the study of any topic requires a measurement tool or technique. Measurement of love is obviously difficult. Second, most of those, who have tried to define love, do not show proper agreement among themselves. Finally, many people think that love is a topic, which should not be studied and to study love is to ruin it.

Despite these problems, Rubin (1973) made a serious effort to define love. He defined *love* as the junction of three important components—caring, attachment and intimacy. *Caring* refers to the feeling that partner's satisfactions are as important to you as your own. *Attachment* means need to be with the partner, to make physical contact and to be approved of. *Intimacy* refers to the bond between two people and usually manifested by close and confidential communication between the partners. Rubin (1973) explored the existence of qualitative difference between liking and loving. Love is something more than intense liking; it is basically the attachment to and caring about another person (Rubin, 1973). He found that people rated intimate partners (loving partners) more highly on certain items (such as I would like to do anything for my partner) than friends, and from this, he developed liking and loving scale to assess the difference between these two types of interpersonal relationship. Later, Berscheid and Hatfield (1974) proposed a psychological theory of love.

In a nutshell, it can be said that love is something more than a close friendship and something different from being sexually or romantically interested in another person. Although the specific details of love may vary from culture to culture (Beall and Sternberg, 1995), it is a universal phenomenon, which combines emotions, cognitions and behaviours.

Most work on the concept of love has been done by social psychologists using survey and questionnaire methods. Most of the social psychologists, today, agree that love takes several different forms (Brehm, 1992). The most common distinction is between passionate love and compassionate love.

Passionate (or *romantic*) *love* is the emotionally charged type of love that sometimes occurs early in romantic relationship. It is defined as a state of intense physiological arousal and intense desire for union with another (Hatfield and Walster, 1978). It often contains unrealistic emotional reaction to another person. Passionate love usually begins as an instant, overwhelming and all-consuming positive reactions that recognise no boundary.

Passionate love has three components—cognitive, emotional and behavioural (Hatfield and Sprecher, 1986b). In *cognitive component*, several things such as preoccupation with the loved objects, an idealisation of person and a desire to know or be known by the other person, are involved. It also contains a desire to see the person as wonderful and perfect in every respect. *Emotional component* includes physiological and emotional arousal, sexual attraction, the strong desire for union and intense need to be loved as much as one loves the other person. In fact, loving and being loved are positive experiences, but they are also accompanied by recurring fear that something can happen that brings end of the relationship. Hatfield and Sprecher (1986b) constructed a passionate love scale for assessing these various positive and negative elements. *Behavioural component* includes active efforts to serve the other and maintaining physical closeness to him or her.

Researches done on passionate love have shown that it increases substantially from early stage of dating to the stage of exclusive relationship. However, it does not increase as the relationship moves from exclusive dating to living together (Hatfield and Sprecher, 1986b). A study on 197 couples conducted by Sprecher and Regan (1998) showed that passionate love declined as the length of relationship increased.

Passionate love is also associated with other intense emotions. The common observation has been that when our love is reciprocated and we experience psychological union with the partner, we tend to experience joy, fulfilment and ecstasy. Thus, positive emotional experiences such as sexual excitement can enhance passionate love. Sprecher and Regan (1998) found that passionate love and sexual desire are positively correlated. However, sexual desire and sexual activity are not related (Regan, 2000). The *unrequited love*, that is, love felt by one person for another, who does not feel love in return, is often associated with jealousy, anxiety or despair. Such one-way love is commonly found among those persons who have conflicted attachment style (Aron, Aron and Allen, 1998). The individual, who loves in vain, feels rejected and the person, who fails to respond, feels guilty (Baumeister, Wotman and Stillwell, 1993).

According to Hatfield and Walster (1981), three factors are necessary for passionate love to occur. First, the person has to learn about love. Persons, generally, are exposed to various love-related images through movies, songs, tales, etc., which motivate them to fall in love (Sternberg, 1986). Second, the appropriate love object such as physically attractive opposite sex person must be present. Third, the person must realise the state of physiological arousal such as sexual excitement, anxiety, fear, etc., which are interpreted as emotion of love.

Compassionate love is another popular type of love researched by social psychologists. As we know, passionate love is too intense and too overwhelming to be maintained on permanent basis. However, compassionate love is different and it is maintained on relatively permanent basis. Such love is based on friendship, mutual attraction, shared interests, respect and proper concern for the welfare of others. Berscheid and Walster (1978) defined *compassionate love* as the affection we feel for those with whom our lives are deeply intertwined. It is a more practical type of love and is a crucial aspect of a satisfying and lasting relationship. Such love emphasises trust, caring and tolerance for partner's mistakes and flaws. Compassionate love develops slowly as two people develop a satisfying relationship. The emotional tone of compassionate love is more moderate. Warmth and affection are more common than the extreme passions. In a nutshell, compassionate love contains such a close friendship in which two persons are sexually attracted, care about each other welfare, express mutual liking and respect and have a great deal in common (Caspi and Herbener, 1990).

Besides these two aspects of love, four other styles of love have been identified (Hendrick and Hendrick, 1986). Those four styles are game-playing love, possessive love, logical love and selfless love. *Game-playing love* is one, where one man or woman in love has two partners at the same time; *possessive love* emphasises the fear of losing one's lover; *logical love* is based upon the suitability of the partner and *selfless love* is one, where a person would prefer to suffer rather than letting his/her lover suffer. Of these various styles of love, people, in general, agree that selfless love and compassionate love are better and desirable, while game-playing love is the worst and least desirable (Hahn and Blass, 1997). Not only that, men more frequently involve themselves in game-playing love than women, whereas women more frequently engage in logical and possessive love than men (Hendrick et al., 1984). Besides all these, there is one special situation of love relationship called *amae*, a Japanese term that denotes a condition in which a person has an extremely positive emotional state where one is a totally passive love object, indulged and taken care of by one's partner. The mother-infant relationship is one example of amae.

Triangular theory of love

Sternberg (1986), whose triarchic theory of intelligence is well-known, proposed a *triangular theory of love*. According to triangular theory of love, there are three basic components of love, that is, intimacy, passion and decision commitment, which combine in different degrees to form several different types of love (Aron and Westbay, 1996), as illustrated in Figure 12.3.

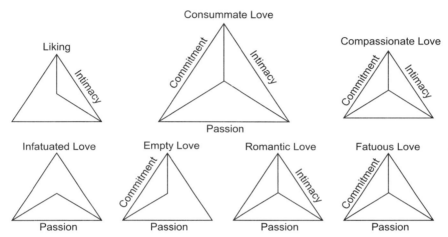

Figure 12.3 Triangular model of love (Based on suggestions by Sternberg, 1986).

Intimacy component refers to those feelings, which promote closeness, bondedness and connectedness. Here, self-disclosure and intimate communication are important. Persons high in intimacy are concerned with each other's welfare and happiness and they value and understand each other. *Passion component* refers to those drives that lead to romance, physical attraction and sexual consummation. In other words, passion is based on romance, physical attraction and sexuality. The *decision/commitment component* consists of a short-term aspect—the decision that one person loves other—and a long-term aspect—a commitment made by the person to maintain that love over time. This is the *cognitive component* of love.

An analysis of these three components led Sternberg to identify the following seven distinct kinds of love, depending on the presence and absence of each component (see Figure 12.3):

1. **Liking:** It has only one of the love components, that is, intimacy. Here, passion and commitment are absent. According to Sternberg, this intimate liking characterises true friendship in which we feel a bondedness, a warmth and a closeness with another person, but with no intense passion or long-term commitment.

2. **Infatuated love:** It is the experience of passion without intimacy or commitment. Therefore, such love may disappear suddenly. This love is often what we feel as love at first sight as we find in puppy love.

3. **Empty love:** This is the experience of commitment without passion and intimacy. Sometimes, a stronger love deteriorates into empty love, that is, commitment remains alive, but intimacy and passion die. In arranged marriages, the relationship often begins as empty love.

4. **Romantic love:** It is the experience of passion and intimacy without commitment as we find in romantic affair. Romantic lovers are bonded emotionally (as in liking) and physically through passionate arousal.

5. **Fatuous love:** It is the experience of passion and commitment without intimacy. This type of love can be exemplified by marriage in which commitment is motivated largely by passion without any stabilising influence of intimacy.

6. **Compassionate love:** Such love consists of intimacy and commitment, but without passion. This type of love is often found in long-term marriage in which passion has gone out of the relationship, but a deep affection and commitment remains alive.

7. **Consummate love:** It is the ultimate experience of love, where all three components, that is, intimacy, passion and commitment remain alive. Such love is the most complete form of love and it represents the ideal love relationship for which many people strive, but very few achieve. Consummate love might be found in an adult love relationship or in some relations between parents and children.

Sternberg's theory is considered as an interesting attempt to pull together many previous concepts. Sternberg stressed the importance of translating the components of love into action. He warned that without expression, even the greatest of love can die (1987, p. 341).

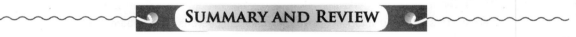

SUMMARY AND REVIEW

- *Interpersonal attraction* is defined as a person's evaluation of or person's attitude about some other person on a dimension ranging from strong liking to strong disliking. In simple words, interpersonal attraction refers to the extent to which we like or dislike other persons.
- Social psychologists have advanced various theories to explain interpersonal attraction. Of these, only four have been discussed. These are Newcomb's A-B-X model, learning theory or reinforcement model, exchange theory and equity theory.
- Newcomb's A-B-X model emphasises balanced or symmetrical relationship. It describes a strain towards symmetry. For example, if A and B like each other, but disagree about the worth of X, then it would tend to create a strain towards symmetry. This model further explains that strain towards symmetry is instrumental in allowing A to predict B's attitudes and behaviours in permitting A to validate his or her opinions or feelings.
- Reinforcement model or learning model explains attraction to be based upon associations with positive rewards. Byrne and Clore as well as Lott and Lott emphasised this model of interpersonal attraction.
- Exchange theory explains interpersonal attraction in terms of economic exchange between two people, who assess rewards and costs of maintaining relationship. For attraction to occur, the outcome, that is, rewards minus cost must be above the minimum level of expectation, called comparison level.
- Equity theory's explanation of interpersonal attraction moves a step forward than exchange theory by taking into account not only a person's own outcomes but also the outcomes perceived to be attained by the partner in relationship. Thus, basic to equity theory is social comparison. The theory suggests that the persons try to maintain a balance between the rewards and costs they experience and those of their partner experiences. Any perceived imbalance is translated into equity by modifying one's perception of what he is getting out of the relationship or by modifying one's own feeling about the partner.
- Internal determinants of interpersonal attraction include factors like need for affiliation and affect.

- External determinants of interpersonal attraction includes proximity (or nearness) and some observable characteristics of the other person. Proximity between two people due to factors like location of residences, working places, classroom seating arrangements, admission within the same course, etc. lead to repeated exposure of the individuals to one another. Repeated exposure often results in positive effect, which enhances the interpersonal attraction—a process called *mere exposure effect* by the social psychologists. Interpersonal attraction is also influenced by various observable characteristics of the strangers we meet. Among these observable characteristics, the physical attractiveness plays a central role. We are, in general, attracted towards a physically attractive person and make several positive attribution. Besides, other observable characteristics such as physique, obesity, behavioural style, food preferences, first names, and clothing colour do influence interpersonal attraction.

Researchers have shown that the persons want to affiliate to those individuals, who are kind and understanding, who have attractive personalities and who are like us. When affiliation need is not met, we feel both sad and angry. Both positive and negative affective states influence attraction directly as well as indirectly. When another person is held responsible for arousing the emotion, it is said to constitute direct effects. But when source of emotion is somewhere else and another person is simply associated with its presence, then indirect effect is said to have occurred.

- Interactive determinants of interpersonal attraction include similarity of attitudes, beliefs, values, interests of the interacting persons and the reciprocal liking and disliking. We are attracted towards those who have similar attitudes, values, interests to us, and develop disliking for those who have dissimilar attitudes, values, interests, etc. In fact, researches have revealed that larger the proportion of similarity information, greater is the attraction. The similarity–dissimilarity effect has been explained by balance theory, social comparison theory as well as by an evolutionary perspective as an adaptive responses to the potential danger. Mutual liking is another factor. We especially like all those people, who indicate in words or deeds that they like and make a positive evaluation of us. We dislike those people, who dislike us and make a negative evaluation of us.
- Romantic relationship includes sexual attraction, spending time together, similarity of attitudes, values and also the belief that two people share something special. A special feature of romantic relationship is some degree of physical intimacy ranging from holding hands to sexual interactions. Love is an important aspect of romantic relationship. *Love* is defined as junction of three important components—caring, attachment and intimacy.
- Social psychologists have made distinction between passionate love and compassionate love. Passionate love is a sudden, overwhelming emotional response to other. It is defined as a state of intense physiological arousal and intense desire for union with other. Compassionate love is based upon friendship, mutual attraction, shared interest, respect and proper concern for the welfare of others. Sternberg's triangular theory of love includes these two components, that is, passion and intimacy plus a third component, namely, decision/commitment, that is, cognitive decision to love and to be committed to a relationship. According to this theory, there are seven forms of love, which combine in different degrees with these three components. Of the seven forms of love, the consummate love is the most complete form of love, where all three components, that is, intimacy, passion and commitment remain alive.

Review Questions

1. Define interpersonal attraction. Discuss its nature.
2. Examine critically Newcomb's A-B-X model of interpersonal attraction.
3. How does reinforcement model explain attraction? Is it satisfactory?

4. Explain interpersonal attraction in terms of exchange theory. What are its limitations?
5. Examine critically equity theory of interpersonal attraction.
6. Citing experimental evidences, discuss the internal determinants of interpersonal attraction.
7. Discuss the role of external determinants in explaining the interpersonal attraction.
8. Discuss the interactive determinants of interpersonal attraction.
9. What do you mean by romantic relationship? How is romantic relationship explained by social psychologists?
10. Define love. Discuss the various forms of love researched by the social psychologists.
11. Write short notes on the following:
    (i) Consummate love
    (ii) Distinction between liking and loving
    (iii) Mere exposure effect
    (iv) Physical attractiveness as determinant of interpersonal attraction.

13 SOCIAL INFLUENCE

Learning Objectives

- Meaning and Nature of Compliance
- Underlying Principles of Compliance
- Techniques of Compliance
- Obedience to Authority
- Factors behind Obedience
- Resisting the Effects of Destructive Obedience

Key Terms

Compliance	Flattery	Obedience to authority
Conformity	Foot-in-the-door technique	Playing hard to get technique
Destructive obedience	Incidental similarity	Proximity of authority
Door-in-the-face technique	Legitimacy of authority	That's-not-all technique
Fast-approaching-deadline technique	Low-ball technique	

Social influence is a common feature of everyday life. It takes place when the actions of an individual or group affect the behaviour of others. In simple words, efforts by one individual or more to change attitudes, beliefs, perceptions or behaviours of one or more others, are termed as *social influence* (Cialdini, 2000, 2006). Social influence may be intentional or unintentional. When a person actively urges a course of action on others, it is said to be *intentional*. On the other hand, a person's anticipation of a negative consequence for not conforming to the group or individual may be enough for changing his attitude and behaviour and if this happens, it is said to be *unintentional*. It may also be called *symbolic social influence* to reflect the fact that it results from our mental representations of other persons rather than their actual presence. There are three forms or types of social influence—*conformity, compliance* and *obedience to authority*. Conformity behaviour has been already discussed in Chapter 10. In the present chapter, therefore, we shall concentrate upon compliance and obedience to authority.

MEANING AND NATURE OF COMPLIANCE

Compliance is one important type of social influence. It refers to getting other people do what we want them to do. Thus, *compliance* is defined as doing what we are asked to do, even though we might prefer not to do (Taylor, Peplau and Sears, 2006). In this way, compliance involves change in overt (public) behaviour after exposure to other people's opinions (Hewstone et al., 1996). The major distinguishing feature of compliance is that it involves responding to a request from another person or group. It does not necessarily involve private acceptance; it may change behaviour that can be observed and measured. In compliance, the expression, opinion, etc., though differ from what is being expressed, become instrumental in gaining some reward or avoiding punishment. For example, an assistant aware of that his boss (officer) is proud of jokes he tells, may laugh heartily at them even though he does not think they are funny. Thus, he avoids the displeasure of his boss.

UNDERLYING PRINCIPLES OF COMPLIANCE

Social psychologists have expressed their view that compliance is based upon some principles. According to Cialdini (1994, 2006), the following are the six main principles:

1. **Liking or friendship:** In general, we are willing to show compliance to the requests from friends or from people towards whom we are attracted or to whom we like. Since we do not like strangers, we do not want to comply with their requests.
2. **Consistency or commitment:** When a person makes a commitment towards an action or position, he is most of the time willing to comply with the requests for behaviour or actions that are consistent with that position or action. On the other hand, requests that are inconsistent with the commitment, are not or little complied.
3. **Reciprocity:** A person is generally willing to comply with a request from someone, who has done a favour or concession in the past than to someone who has not done any favour ever. In simple words, we feel obliged to pay the person back in some way or the other for what he has done so far.
4. **Scarcity:** In general, a person values or makes efforts to secure outcomes or objects that are scarce or decreasing in availability. Consequently, a person is more likely to comply with any request that focuses on scarcity than one that makes no reference to such things.
5. **Social validation:** A person is more willing to comply with any request to those actions which people believe that others similar to him are also doing or thinking in the same way. We want to be always correct and one way to do is to act like others or think like others.
6. **Authority:** In general, a person shows willingness to comply with the requests from someone who holds some legitimate authority than someone who does not hold any such authority.

These various principles underlie many different techniques that are ordinarily used by many people for gaining compliance. These techniques are discussed in the subsequent section.

TECHNIQUES OF COMPLIANCE

There are various techniques of compliance. Based upon different principles, these techniques are discussed here.

1. *Techniques based on reciprocity*

Based upon the principle of reciprocity, where a person feels that he should do favour to those who have done favour to him, there are two popular techniques of compliance—door-in-the face technique and that's-not-all technique.

  (i) **Door-in-the-face technique:** In this technique, for gaining compliance, the requester deliberately puts a large unreasonable request and then, when this is refused, he scales down to a smaller reasonable request (the one he really wants to be fulfilled). This technique is so called because the first refusal seems to slam the door in the face of the person, who makes the request. This technique works well when both unreasonable request and reasonable request are made by the same person and these requests are connected. Cialdini et al. (1975) conducted a study in which the participants were asked to volunteer time for a public cause. Some were asked to give a huge amount of time. When they refused, immediately the researchers requested them to give a much smaller commitment of time. Some other participants were asked to give only smaller amount of time, whereas a third group was given a choice between the two. Results revealed that in the small-request-only condition, only 17% of the participants showed compliance. However, after turning a large request, 50% participants showed compliance.

 (ii) **That's-not-all technique:** This is another technique based on reciprocity principle. In this technique, the requesters offer additional benefits to the target people before they have made any decision whether to comply or reject the specific request. In brief, here, the requesters make a deal and then improve the offer. For example, suppose you go to purchase a television set. The salesman describe the features of the TV and quotes a price. Then, while the customer is mulling over the decision, the salesman adds, this is not all. You will be given a five-piece dinner set at no additional cost if you buy TV today because the extra offer will close tomorrow. The essence of that's-not-all technique is to present a product at a high price, give the customer some time to think about the price and then improve the deal either by adding a product or by lowering the price and making the product more attractive.

Burger (1986) conducted several experiments in which the effectiveness of that's-not-all technique was established. In one of the studies, about half of the people, who stopped at the table of Psychology-club bake sale, were told that they could buy a prepackaged set, including one cupcake and two cookies for 75 cents. There were two conditions in the experiment—control condition and experimental condition. In the *control condition*, 40% of those who enquired actually purchased a cupcake. In the *experimental condition* (that's-not-all condition), the people were told that cupcakes can be bought for 75 cents each. A little later, they were told that they would not only be getting the cupcake but also two cookies for the 75 cents. Results revealed that in this experimental condition, 73% of people purchased a cupcake and this was definitely a higher proportion than in the control condition.

2. Techniques based on commitment or consistency

There are two techniques of compliance, which are based on the principle of consistency or commitment—the foot-in-the-door technique and the low-ball technique.

(i) **Foot-in-the-door technique:** The foot-in-the-door technique is opposite to the door-in-the-face technique. In this technique, the requesters begin with a small request and then, when it is granted, place a larger request—the one they actually desire all along. Thus, one way to increase compliance is to induce a person to agree first to a small request. Once someone has agreed to this small action, he is likely to agree to the comparatively larger or bigger request. Advertisers often use this technique in persuading consumers to do something minor that is connected with the product such as to use money-saving coupons. The advertisers apparently think that any act connected with the product increases the probability that the consumer will buy it in the future. Several studies have indicated that the technique works well, that is, it succeeds in inducing increased compliance (Freedman and Fraser, 1966; Beaman, et al., 1983). In the experiment conducted by Freedman and Fraser, the same women were approached in door-to-door campaign for providing support for safe driving and asked them to sign a petition that would be sent to the state's senators. Several weeks later, different experimenters (confederates) contacted the same women and also other women, who had not been approached before. This time all the women were asked to put in their front portion of the house a large, unattractive sign that read 'Drive carefully'. In the results, it was found that over 55% of women, who had previously endorsed the petition (a small request), agreed to post the sign, whereas only 17% of the other women agreed to post the sign. Thus, we find that getting the women to agree to the initial small request tripled the amount of compliance, showing the effectiveness of the foot-in-the door technique.

Several explanations for the effectiveness of this technique have been offered.

(a) One explanation is the desire to view oneself as acting consistently. Once we have said 'yes' to the small request, we are more likely to say 'yes' to the subsequent and larger ones because refusing these would be inconsistent with our previous behaviours.

(b) Another explanation is based upon self-perception theory. The principle is that whenever a person says 'yes' to the initial request, the individual's self-image changes as a result of the initial act of compliance. In safe driving experiment, a woman might have thought of herself as a kind of person who does not take social action. Once she had agreed to the small request, she may have changed the perception of herself slightly and she was now more likely to comply than she would have been otherwise. This explanation is closer to the explanation based on the principle of consistency.

(c) Another explanation is that the persons, who agree to a small initial request, become involved and committed to the issue itself as well as to the behaviour they perform. These processes may operate simultaneously in determining the person's response to the second request, thus increasing the effectiveness of the foot-in-the-door technique.

Obviously both foot-in-the-door technique and the door-in-the-face technique work well, but we do not know when each of them is most effective. Researches have shown that both seem to work best when the behaviour involved is prosocial, that is, when the requester is to give help to the others. One difference between these two techniques is that the door-in-the-face technique works well when the smaller request follows the larger request immediately and is clearly connected. However, the foot-in-the-door technique works even when the two requests are seemingly unconnected.

(ii) **Low-ball technique:** In this technique, a person is asked to agree to something on the basis of incomplete information and is later told the entire story. In other words, in this technique, for gaining compliance, the initial offer or deal is changed to make it less attractive to the person after he has accepted it. Here, the person is tricked into agreeing to a relatively attractive proposition only to discover later that the terms or conditions are relatively different from those initially expected. According to Burger and Cornelius (2003), the technique works because once an individual has made an initial public commitment to a course of action, he or she is reluctant to withdraw, even when the ground rules are changed. These researchers conducted a study in which there were three conditions—low-ball condition, interrupt condition and control condition. In *low-ball condition,* the caller indicated the participants if they would contribute five dollars to a scholarship fund for underprivileged class of students and those who would do, would receive a coupon for a free drink at the juice bar. After that, when the participants agreed to make a donation, the caller told them that she had just run out of the coupons and could not offer this incentive. The caller then asked if they would still contribute. In *interrupt condition*, the caller made the initial request but without waiting for the participants' answer, she interrupted them and indicated that there were no more coupons for the people, who donated. In *control condition*, the participants were asked to donate five dollars with no mention of any coupons for a free drink at juice bar. Results indicated that in the low-ball condition, 77.6% participants made donation, in the control condition, only 42% participants donated and in interrupt condition, only 16% participants donated. Results indicated that the low-ball technique produced significantly much higher levels of compliance.

3. *Techniques based upon liking*

Compliance is also enhanced through liking or friendship. Here, various impression management techniques for the purpose of ingratiation are used. In ingratiation, we attempt at getting others to like us so that they will be more willing to agree to our requests (Linden and Mitchell, 1988). There are several ingratiation techniques that work well in enhancing the compliance. One technique is *flattery*, that is, praising others in some manner. If we praise others, even not from within the core of heart, it is very likely that they will comply with our request. Another technique is *self-promotion*, that is, informing others about our past accomplishments or positive characteristics. When one comes to know about the high past performance of any person, one is more likely to comply with the request. *Incidental similarity* is another technique for enhancing compliance. In incidental similarity, we call attention to small and slightly surprising similarities between them and us. Such trivial forms of similarity enhance liking or a feeling of affiliation with the requesters, and therefore, increase the tendency to comply with the requester's requests. Burger et al. (2004) conducted a study and reported that the participants were more likely to agree to a small request such as donating to a charity fund from a stranger when this person appeared to have the same first name or birthday as they did than when the stranger did not bear this trivial form of similarity. Besides, some other techniques like improving one's non-appearance, emitting many positive non-verbal cues and doing some small favours for the target people are popularly used for enhancing compliance (Wayen and Liden, 1995).

4. Techniques based on scarcity

We tend to view some objects, things, etc. as scarce, rare and difficult to obtain. These objects or things, in general, are also viewed as more valuable than those which are easy to obtain. Accordingly, we are also ready to expend more as well as to take more pain for obtaining such objects. This what's-scarce-is-valuable principle becomes also the base for some techniques for compliance. Two such techniques are fast-approaching-deadline technique and playing hard to get technique.

In the *fast-approaching-deadline technique*, the compliance is enhanced in such a way that the target people are told that they have only limited time to take advantage of some offer or to obtain some item. In advertisement, this technique is commonly applied. Often through advertisement, the company or business firm announces that a special sale is likely to end on a particular date, which automatically means that after that date, prices will go up. In most of the cases, the time limit is false. In fact, the prices won't go up after the indicated date and may, in fact, continue to drop if the goods remain unsold.

Playing-hard-to-get technique is usually used for enhancing compliance by suggesting that the person or object is rare and hard to get. Keeping in view this thing, whatever is suggested by the rare person is simply complied. This technique is often used by the candidates seeking job for enhancing their attractiveness to the potential employers, and hence, for increasing the probability that the employers will offer a suitable job soon. Job candidates using such technique let the potential employer know that they have other offers too. Researches done by Williams et al. (1993) showed that the technique worked well in the work situation.

In sum, there are different techniques of compliance. The effectiveness of these techniques can vary depending on the theme and the situation.

OBEDIENCE TO AUTHORITY

Obedience involves yielding to the direct orders of a person of higher status or having some authority. Here, *authority* refers to the capacity of one member to issue orders to the others, that is, to direct or regulate the behaviour of other members by involving rights that are vested in the occupied role. Therefore, in obedience, one person orders one or more persons to do something and they do so. This is, in fact, the most direct form of social influence. Obedience to the commands of people, who possess authority, is not surprising because they usually have effective means for enforcing their orders. The surprising thing is that the people, who often lack such power, sometimes also induce high levels of submission from people. Social psychologists have studied obedience to authority in laboratory and the clearest evidence for such effects has been reported by Milgram in a series of famous, but controversial studies (Milgram, 1963, 1965, 1974).

Studies of obedience in laboratory

Milgram (1963, 1965) conducted a study showing the phenomenon of obedience to authority at Yale University. His participants were 20 to 50-year old males; 40% of them had unskilled jobs, 40% had white-collar sales jobs and 20% were professionals. The experimenter informed participants that they were taking part in an investigation into the effects of punishment upon learning. One person in each pair of participants served as a *learner* (who was confederate of the experimenter) and required to supply the second word in pairs of words they had already memorised, after hearing only the first word. Other member of the participants, called *teacher*, would punish if errors were done by the learner by delivering electric shock through a device containing thirty number switches ranging from 15 volts (the first) through 450 volts (thirtieth). During testing, the learner made a number of errors. Errors meant failure to provide the second word in each pair. Each time when the teacher told him that he was wrong, he delivered a shock. Whenever the shock was given, the learner grunted. Teachers were told to enhance the strength of shock each time the learner made error. As the level of shock increased, the learner's reactions became very much dramatic. He yelled and sometimes begged the teacher to stop shocking and even kicked the ball. Despite all these, the experimenter urged the teacher to continue. Results showed that all 40 subjects delivered the 300-volt shock and 65% continued to the final 450-volt level. The teachers showing obedience to the experimenter continued shocking even when the learner screamed for mercy and was apparently experiencing great pain. The reality of the experimental situation was that the learner was a confederate of the experimenter and did not receive any shock. All responses by the learners including errors, grunts, groans, crying, pounding the table had been carefully rehearsed and then tape-recorded to make them identical for all the subjects. The teachers, however, did not know about this reality, that is, the very fact that the situation was staged.

In further experiments, Milgram (1974) reported similar results even in those conditions, which were ordinarily expected to reduce such obedience. The most surprising fact was that many teachers obeyed even when they were asked to grasp victim's hand and force it down on a metal shock plate. Such results were not restricted to any particular culture, rather they were also found in several different countries such as Australia, Germany and Jordan. Similar findings were also reported in case of children (Kilham and Mann, 1974; Shanab and Yahya, 1977).

Milgram's study was criticised on the following three grounds:

1. Critics pointed out that teachers did not really believe that the learner was receiving the electric shock. If this was true, Milgram's results became automatically invalid. However, the conversations which Milgram had with the participants both during and after the experiment provided some evidences that teacher believed he was giving shock to the learner.
2. Some social psychologists considered Milgram's experiment as highly unethical (Baumrind, 1964; Rosnow, 1981) because it involved not only deception but also inflicted severe stress and anxiety on the participants. But Milgram (1992) defended his position and said that there was no evidence of any psychopathology and 83.7% of the participants stated happiness over taking part in the experiment and only 1.3% of the participants were sorry for taking part in the experiment.
3. The generalisation of the obtained results beyond the laboratory to the real world was conditional. Mixon (1972) pointed out that the results could be generalised only if we took the roles (teacher) and rules that operated in a particular social context.

Despite these criticisms and ethical outcry of Milgram's experiments, researchers in at least seven other countries such as Italy, Germany, Australia, UK, Jordan, Spain and Holland attempted to replicate the experiment. Smith and Harris Bond (1993) summarising the results of these studies came to the conclusion that obedience was not isolated to American population in the 1960s.

FACTORS BEHIND OBEDIENCE

One of the basic questions arises here—what factors lie behind obedience even when obedience results in potential harm to others? Milgram (1974) found various situational and social factors affecting people's willingness to show obedience to authority. Using the same teacher–learner paradigm, he conducted several studies and identified some factors like legitimacy of authority, proximity of the learner to the teacher, proximity of the authority figure, sex of the participants, etc. as important ones affecting obedience.

Milgram's studies showed that when the legitimacy of authority was high in the eye of the participants, a higher degree of obedience was maintained. On the other hand, when the legitimacy of authority was low, a poor degree of obedience was reported. That is the reason, why when the study was conducted in Yale University, the participants showed more obedience perceiving higher degree of legitimacy of authority than when the study was conducted using a run-down office in a respectable part of the city that was perceived as having a lower degree of legitimacy of authority. As we know, in Milgram's original experiment, the learner and the teacher were placed in different rooms. But when both were placed in closer proximity, that is, in the same room, fewer teachers were found to administer maximum shock, showing poor degree of obedience. The level of obedience further decreased when the teacher had to take the hand of the learner and put the same on the metal plate for the purpose of delivering shock. The proximity of the authority figure is another factor. When the authority figure (that is, the experimenter dressed in white coat) went away after instructing the teacher regarding giving the shock, only 20% obeyed the initial request of the experimenter for giving increasingly stronger level of shocks. Likewise, two authorities giving conflicting directions to the teacher also resulted in sharp drop of obedience dramatically. Finally, sex of the teachers also influenced the obedience level. When females were used as teachers, only 65% gave shocks to the maximum level and about the same percentage of male participants gave the shocks. However, Milgram reported that females, in general, did experience greater conflict in giving shocks as compared to the male participants. Kilham and Mann (1974) also found similar results.

Besides these, some other factors influencing obedience have also been recognised. First, generally in many situations, the people in authority tend to relieve those who obey the responsibility for their own actions by simply saying that he is only carrying out the orders. In Milgram's experiment, this transfer of responsibility was obvious. In the beginning of experiment, the participants were told that the experimenter (that is, the authority figure) would be responsible for the learner's well-being and the participants themselves would not be held responsible. In day-to-day life, we often find a military or police officer torturing general people by playing the defence that he is only obeying the orders.

Another factor for obedience is the gradual escalation of the authority figure's orders. In a sense, the person in authority use foot-in-door technique asking for small actions first but larger one later. In Milgram's study, the participants were first required to give only mild shock and after this, as the experiment continued, they were found showing obedience to deliver higher intensity of electric shock.

Still another factor enforcing obedience is that people in authority often do bear badges or signs of their status, which automatically signify that such people must be obeyed. In fact, this is a powerful norm and when people are confronted with such authority, they find it difficult to disobey. For example, an officer of the rank of Superintendent of Police has definite badges on his dress and if such officer makes an order or even request, the common people find it difficult to disobey.

Finally, events involving destructive obedience move very quickly and give the person very little time to think over any excuse. For example, in Milgram's experiment, within a few minutes of entering the laboratory, the participants were ordered to deliver the electric shocks to the learner. Such fast pace tended to enhance the obedience on the part of the participants.

In a nutshell, it can be said that obedience is influenced by many psycho-social factors. Evidences within the laboratory as well as in day-to-day life support this. In fact, two important findings from overall programme of Milgram's researches stand out very clearly—first, authority exerts a powerful influence over everybody, perhaps more than we realise and second, destructive obedience may be reduced in the presence of certain factors, but is rarely dominated.

RESISTING THE EFFECTS OF DESTRUCTIVE OBEDIENCE

We have examined the strong influence of obeying the source of authority and its consequences. Social psychologists have raised one basic question here—how can we resist such social influence? In answer, they have suggested some important strategies to resist the effects of destructive obedience. Some of these strategies are discussed as under:

1. Social psychologists have pointed out that the destructive influence of authority can be easily resisted if people raise doubt regarding the expertise and motives of the authority figures. If people are able to know the hidden selfish and beneficial goals of the authority, the power of those in authority is severely weakened.
2. If the persons exposed to the command figures are reminded that they and not the authorities will be held responsible for the harmful consequences, there occurs sharp reduction in the obedience to the commands of the authority figure. Research evidences provided by Kilham and Mann supported this strategy.
3. When individuals are exposed to the actions of disobedient models (that is to the persons who refuse to obey the authority figures), obedience to authority is severely reduced. When a person sees one or more persons refusing to obey the commands of the authority figure, such social support encourages to do the same, with the ultimate consequence that power of the authority is severely weakened. Rochat and Modigliani confirmed this fact from their study. Milgram also found in one of his studies that most naive participants continued to give shocks up to the level of 150 volts. However, when the first confederate rebelled, 80% continued but when the second confederate rebelled, over 60% of the subjects rebelled themselves and refused to obey. Obviously, this result showed that social support decreases a person's tendency to obey authority.
4. When the persons are able to know about the results of social psychological researches regarding blind obedience to the authority figure, they are much inclined to change their behaviour and resolve some plans to resist to the blind obedience.

Thus, there are some strategies through which obedience to authority can be resisted. Although this is true that resisting the commands of the people in authority can sometimes be very dangerous, the history shows the commands of authority figures are resisted.

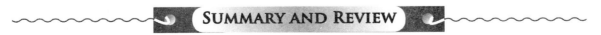

SUMMARY AND REVIEW

- The effects of one or more individuals to change attitudes, beliefs, perceptions or behaviours of one or more others are called *social influence*, which may be intentional or unintentional. There are three forms of social influence—conformity, compliance and obedience to authority.

- *Compliance* is defined as doing what we are asked to do, even though we might prefer not to do. In compliance, expression, opinion, etc. even though differ from what is being expressed, becomes instrumental in gaining some reward or avoiding punishment.
- There are some clear underlying principles of compliance. Social psychologists have maintained that there are six main principles such as liking or friendship, consistency or commitment, reciprocity, scarcity, social validation and anonymity.
- Social psychologists have also discussed some techniques of compliance. Such important techniques are door-in-the-face technique, that's-not-all technique, foot-in-the-door technique, low-ball technique, flattery, incidental similarity, fast-approaching-deadline technique, playing hard to get technique, etc.
- Several factors tend to influence obedience to authorities. Among these factors legitimacy of authority, proximity of the learner to the teacher, proximity of the authority figure, sex of the participants, etc. are important.
- Social psychologists have evolved some strategies to resist the destructive influence of obedience to authority. Four such strategies have been discussed.

Review Questions

1. Define social influence. Discuss the different forms of social influence.
2. Give the meaning of compliance. Discuss the different techniques of compliance.
3. Discuss the major principles underlying compliance.
4. What light the experimental studies of obedience to authority throw upon the nature of obedience?
5. Discuss the factors that influence obedience to authority.
6. Outline a plan for reducing or resisting the destructive influence of obedience

14 AGGRESSION AND SOCIAL VIOLENCE

Learning Objectives

➢ Defining Aggression
➢ Causes of Aggressive Behaviour
➢ Theories of Aggressive Behaviour
➢ Prevention and Control of Aggression
➢ Media Violence

KEY TERMS

Antisocial aggression
Catharsis
Cue theory
Culture of honour
Direct reinforcement
Disinhibtion
Excitation transfer theory
Frustration-aggression hypothesis
General aggression model(GAM)
Hostile aggression
Hostile attributional bias
Hostile expectation bias
Imitation or modelling
Instrumental aggression
Narcissism
Preattribution
Prosocial aggression
Social aggression
TASS model
Weapon effect

Aggression is a human tragedy. The human capacity for aggressive behaviour is staggering. According to an estimate, 58 million humans were killed by the other human beings (an average of nearly one person per minute) during the 125 years period ending with World War II (Coon and Mitterer, 2007). In this chapter, besides defining aggressive behaviour, we shall discuss the major theoretical analysis aggressive behaviour. Subsequently, we shall concentrate upon the determinants of human aggression. Finally, on more optimistic note, we shall examine the various techniques of reducing and controlling aggression. Media violence will also be examined.

DEFINING AGGRESSION

Aggression may be defined as physical or verbal behaviour intended to hurt someone. Accidently injuring someone in a game is not aggression, but cursing out a referee actually shows aggression.

Thus, in aggressive behaviour, the person's intention remains to injure another person physically or psychologically.

The said definition includes distinct types of aggression. Animals exhibit *social aggression* in which they explicitly display rage and silent aggression when one predator stalks its prey. Different brain mechanisms are involved in social and silent aggression. In human beings, mainly two types of aggression have been identified—hostile aggression and instrumental aggression. *Hostile aggression,* also sometimes called *emotional aggression,* involves the wish to hurt the other person and it springs from negative emotions like anger. *Instrumental aggression* aims to hurt only as a means to attain some other end. Such aggression is carried out in order to achieve a specific goal. Hacking into a computer system and robbing a fashionable jacket of others are the examples of instrumental aggression. Most terrorism is instrumental aggression. One important form of instrumental aggression stems from what Levine and Campbell (1972) called *realistic group conflict theory.* According to this theory, aggression between groups arises from real conflict of interest. Sometimes, two groups tend to compete for the same scarce resources. These two groups may aggress against each other as a means of trying to obtain those resources. They may or may not be angry with each other.

At this juncture, a distinction needs to be drawn between anti-social aggression and prosocial aggression. Normally, aggression is considered as bad, but some aggressive acts are good. There are some aggressive acts, which are actually dictated by social norms, and are therefore, prosocial. For example, we appraise the police officer who shoots a terrorist. Likewise, appropriate parental discipline and obeying the orders of the commanders in wartime are actually dictated by social norms, and therefore, they are regarded as necessary. There are some aggressive acts, which fall between prosocial aggression and antisocial aggression and are called *sanctioned aggression.* Such aggressive behaviour includes acts that are not required by the social norms, but they are within their boundary because they do not violate accepted moral standards. For example, a woman, who strikes back at a rapist, shows an example of sanctioned aggression.

Still another distinction needs to be made between aggressive behaviour and aggressive feeling such as anger. Anger is a negative emotional feeling. An individual may be quite angry from inside, but make no effort to hurt another person. The major determinants of anger seem to be attack and frustration, particularly if attributed to an intent to injure.

CAUSES OF AGGRESSIVE BEHAVIOUR

Aggressive behaviour, as per the researches conducted by the social psychologists, seems to stem from a broad range of factors such as personal factors, socio-cultural factors, and situational factors. A discussion of these sets of facts is as follows:

1. *Personal causes of aggressive behaviour*

Social psychologists have identified some personal causes of aggressive behaviour. Important ones are as under:

    (i) **Personality:** Researches have shown that Type A behaviour pattern, which is characterised by extreme sense of competitiveness, overactivity and a sense of time pressure, is associated with high level of aggression and increased levels of coronary heart disease (CHD) (Carver and Glass, 1978; Baron, Russell and Arms, 1985). Besides, some other researches have indicated that people with Type A behaviour pattern are also hostile people. Such people, in comparison to Type B pattern characterised by not being highly competitive nor losing temper readily, show hostile aggression (Strube et. al, 1984). However, as compared to Type B people, Type A people are less likely to engage in instrumental aggression.

Researches have further shown that those with established aggressive behaviour patterns may interpret ambiguous situation as deliberately provoking and this is especially true in case of aggressive children (Dodge and Crick, 1990). It has been frequently found that aggressive children typically interpret accidental events in their playground as intentional, and therefore, may retaliate and behave aggressively. Deficits in social reasoning ability, similar to moral reasoning, tend to produce aggression behaviour. With the advancement of age, social reasoning ability may become more sophisticated. Those people, who have well-developed social reasoning ability, generally think in terms of non-aggressive ways of settling a provoking situation. Therefore, such people tend to show lesser degree of aggression. The children, who fail to provide peaceful potential solutions to the problems, show more aggressive behaviour as compared to those children, who are able to think up in non-aggressive solutions (Dodge and Crick, 1990; Huesmann et al., 1987). Another interesting description of individual personality comes from an extensive study done by Toch (1969, 1975). He used a sample of 77 people, who had been imprisoned and had also a history of unusually violent incidents. With the help of extensive interviews, he developed a set of ten categories into which each of the subjects tell. Among these ten types, there were three major types—self-image promoters, self-image defenders and rep defenders. *Self-image promoters* were those with self-esteem and were always eager to seek out violent situations to promote what they considered to be a more appropriate image. *Self-image defenders* were also having low self-esteem, reacted violently to even the most benign situation or to the slightest in order to ensure that others might not come to similar conclusion about their self-worth. *Rep defenders* were aggressive because of special social roles that they felt were assigned to them. In fact, they were having specific reputation within the social hierarchy and their physical aggressiveness helped them in keeping their image intact as leaders.

In the early 1970s, some evidences began to accumulate that some male individuals, who were born with an extra Y chromosome (XYY), tended to display more aggression and violent behaviour. Such persons are usually taller, but of low intelligence. The study conducted by Jarvik, Klodin and Matsuyama (1973) revealed that prison inmates were fifteen times more likely to have extra Y chromosome than the normal male having only X and Y chromosome. Such findings led some psychologists to conclude that the presence of the additional Y chromosome might account for the violent and aggressive behaviour. However, some alternative explanation began to emerge that cast doubt upon the efficacy of extra Y explanation. For example, Bandura (1973) pointed out that the greater incidence of extra Y males in the prison might be due to their tallness and lower intelligence and these traits, in turn, might be responsible for why they were more engaging in violent and aggressive behaviour in comparison to the males with normal chromosome.

(ii) **Cognitive control and processing—Hostile attributional bias:** The degree of reasoning ability determines aggressive behaviour to some extent and the perception of intention is critical to the decision to retaliate aggressively or not. For example, suppose you are walking on a very busy road and somebody collides sharply with you. At this juncture, you feel annoyed, but when he apologises by saying 'sorry', you perceive this mitigating information indicating the fact that the act was not intentional. Such situation makes you more lenient towards the person and the aggression is less likely to occur. But when your cognitive processing allows you to think that the collision has been done deliberately and with bad intention, you are likely to feel annoyed and may engage in aggressive act also. In other words, our attributions concerning the causes of others' behaviour play an important role in aggression. This gives rise to another important personal characteristic, that is, hostile attributional bias that tends to influence aggression. *Hostile attributional bias* is defined as the tendency to perceive hostile intentions or motives in the behaviour of others, especially when these behaviours are vague one (Dodge et al., 1986). Those who are high on hostile attributional bias rarely give anyone the benefits of doubt; they immediately, without fail, assume that the actions done by others are intentional, and then they accordingly react aggressively. Dodge and Coie (1987) provided support for this fact. Researches have also shown that one of the most potent influences on cognitive control is through alcohol consumption. Alcohol tends to reduce cognitive processing abilities, since it leads people to miss cues that would reduce aggressive behaviour (Steele and Josephs, 1990).

(iii) **Disinhibition:** *Disinhibition* refers to a reduction in the social influences that restrain people from engaging in anti-social behaviour. When a person takes larger doses of alcohol, it leads to complete disinhibition. Disinhibition can occur in three forms—deindividuation dehumanisation and collective aggression.

Deindividuation is produced by several factors like anonymity, diffused responsibility, a novel unstructured situation, arousal due to noise and fatigue. In all these cases, the possibility of punishment for even seriously aggressive behaviour seems a far cry. If people cannot be held accountable for their actions, and thus, can escape punishment, they are more likely to engage in aggressive behaviour. There are evidences that the most serious type of violence in warfare is carried out in societies that use such deindividuating devices such as masks, face and body paints and special garments (Watson, 1973). Dodd (1985) conducted a study in which it was found that when students were asked what they would do if they could be invisible for 24 hours, most of them said that they would rob a bank. A series of studies conducted by Zimbardo (1970) revealed that guaranteed anonymity produces enhanced aggression. Likewise, both men and women behave aggressively at the same level when they become anonymous (Lightdale and Prentice, 1994).

A close companion of deindividuation is *dehumanisation*, which means taking away the human qualities of another person. It has been found that when people are determined to aggress against an individual, for whatever reason, they may dehumanise the victim by attributing different beliefs and values to the target of their aggression (Struch and Schwartz, 1989). Evidences have also shown that deindividuation has also led to the act of collective aggression, including Japanese atrocities against the Chinese and attacks by American troops on women and children in Vietnam.

(iv) **Narcissism:** As we know, Narcissus was an important character in Greek Mythology, who fell in love with his own reflection in the water and got drowned trying to reach it. His name has now become a synonym for excess self-love. In simple words, persons having narcissistic trait tend to have an overinflated view of their own ability or accomplishments. Such persons generally hold the view that they are more capable than others.

Social psychologists are of view that persons high in narcissism tend to show higher degree of aggression even to the slights from others. This happens because such persons have little doubts about the accuracy of their inflated ego and their accomplishments, and therefore, they react very aggressively towards anyone, who undermines them. The study conducted by Bushman and Baumeister (1998) confirmed this.

A related hypothesis investigated by social psychologists is that narcissistic people due to their inflated self-image, perceive themselves as the victims of transgressions more often than non-narcissistic people. McCullough et al. (2003) tested this hypothesis by conducting a study on college students and found that those participants, who scored higher on the measure of narcissism, also reported greater number of transgressions by the others.

Further researches have shown that since narcissists are the people with very high but insecure self-esteem, they are likely to commit more aggression (Donnellan et al., 2005). The self-esteem of these individuals is unstable and fragile and it fluctuates with every event of social praise and rejection (Jordon et al. 2003). Narcissists are more likely to respond to social rejection with aggression, and sometimes, even they lash out against people who are not responsible for the slight (Twenge and Campbell, 2003).

(v) **Traits as situational sensitivities (TASS) model:** TASS model views any social behaviour to be the product of complex interaction between the situational factor and personal traits (Kammarath, Mendoza-Denson and Mischel, 2005). The model points out that many aspects of personality do their functions in a threshold-like manner, that is, only when the situational factors are strong enough to stimulate them, they do influence the behaviour of the persons. When this model is applied to explain aggressive behaviour, it is predicted that the trait aggressiveness influences overt behaviour only when the situational factors are strong enough to activate it. In those people, who are high on the trait aggressiveness, even minor provocation will stimulate an aggressive reaction and its contrast will also be true, where people low on the trait will need higher degree of provocation to trigger aggression. This fact was confirmed in an experiment conducted by Marshall and Brown (2006). They measured the trait aggressiveness of several students and after this, they placed them into three different situations. In one situation, they were exposed to minor provocation from another person; in another situation, they were exposed to strong provocation from another person; and still in another situation, they were not exposed to any provocation from another person. Subsequently, the participants in all these three groups were given opportunity to aggress against the other person. Results revealed that the participants high on the trait aggressiveness displayed higher degree of aggressiveness even after minor provocation from another person, whereas the participants low on the trait aggressiveness showed a little or no reaction to mild provocation, but reacted with strong aggression when they received a powerful provocation. Results clearly provided evidence for the fact that when traits interact with situational factors, they influence aggression.

(vi) **Sensation seeking:** There are persons who seek thrills, excitement and adventures. Such persons are described by the social psychologists as one who are sensation seeking or having a closely related trait, that is, impulsivity (Zuckerman, 1994). Researches have revealed that people high in sensation seeking or impulsiveness tend to experience anger and hostile feelings more often than others. Not only that, their emotions are easily aroused, and therefore, they have very lower threshold for running into angry. They engage in aggressive acts because they crave excitement and thrills. Joireman, Anderson and Strathman (2003) reported that those persons, who are high in sensation seeking or impulsivity, display many tendencies related to aggression. First, such people focus on immediate rather than delayed consequences of behaviour. Second, they are more attracted towards the situations that elicit aggression because they find them thrilling, exciting and appealing. Third, such people are more likely to experience anger and hostility. The overall results of these tendencies is that such persons become more prone to both physical and verbal aggression than others.

(vii) **Gender differences:** In our culture, boys are encouraged to be more aggressive than girls. Social roles cast powerful influences on aggressive behaviour. In general, men are more physically aggressive than woman (Bjorkqvist and Niemela, 1992, Bjorkqvist, 1994; Harris, 1992, 1994) probably because of their greater physical strength. However, in small remote island communities, where tribal people live, this tendency is reversed (Lepowsky, 1994). Researches have shown that as compared to females' aggressive behaviour, males' aggressive behaviour significantly more persists throughout the life span occurring even in the age of seventies and eighties (Walker, Richardson and Green, 2000). However, the size of this gender difference in aggressiveness tends to vary greatly across different situations.

First, in the absence of any provocation by others, males show more aggressive behaviour than females (Bettencourt and Miller, 1996). However, where such provocation is present, the gender difference disappears. In other words, in face of strong provocation, males and females both show aggression more or less equally. Second, the size and direction of gender differences in aggression tend to vary greatly with the type of aggression. Males generally exhibit direct aggression such as physical assaults, pushing, shoving, throwing something at the target, shouting and calling names, etc. (Bjorkqvist, Osterman and Hjelt-Back, 1994). Females, on the other hand, tend to engage more in indirect aggression, which may include spreading rumours about the target person, telling others not to associate with the target person in any way, making up stories to get the person in trouble, etc. Such gender differences with respect to indirect aggression remain present among children as young as eight years old and increase through the age of fifteen and into adulthood (Green, Richardon and Lago, 1996). Such differences have also been reported in several different countries like Sweden, Finland, Poland, Italy and Australia (Owens, Shute and Slee, 2000).

Now, the basic question is—how can these gender differences in aggression be accounted for? One explanation rests upon biological factors, including sex hormones and physique. Male sex hormone, that is, testosterone, while circulates both in male and female, has its higher level among males than in women. Researchers have shown that higher level of testosterone is associated with increased level of aggression. Berman et al. (1993) found that those male students, who were having higher level of testosterone, acted more aggressively on the experimental task. Likewise, Dabbs et al. (1988) reported that both females and males, who were put under imprisonment for violent crime, had higher levels of testosterone than the prisoners, who had not committed such violent crime. Some researchers have shown that social factors also tend to influence the role of testosterone in aggression. For example, Dabbs et al. (1990) reported that high testosterone levels are more strongly associated with the aggressive acts among those people, who came from lower socio-economic status. Male physique having more muscles than female physique accounts for gender differences in aggression. In general, it is less risky and dangerous to be aggressive when a person has muscles and bulk to back up the aggressive actions (Archer, 2004).

2. Socio-cultural factors of aggression

Aggression occurs due to socio-cultural causes. It occurs because the words or deeds of one or more person stimulate aggression in others. These are the social causes of aggression. Besides, there are also some cultural factors, which give rise to aggressive acts. These are discussed below:

(i) **Direct provocation:** Researches have shown that physical or verbal provocation from others is one of the strongest causes of aggression. When we are provoked from others such as when we receive unfair criticism, sarcastic remarks or even physical assaults from others, we tend to return such aggression if we are confirmed that the other person has intended to harm us. There are different types of provocation, which cause anger. One frequently reported provocation is teasing and/or derogatory statements about the members of the family. When a person hears or reads such derogatory statements, he finds it difficult to avoid being aggressive. Researchers have shown that the more a person attributes teasing to hostile motives, the more likely he will respond aggressively (Campos et al., 2007). Cultural differences have also been reported in this regard. For example, people from individualistic culture such as from USA, Western Europe, etc. were found to respond more negatively than the people from collectivist cultures such as from Asian cultures (Campos et al., 2007). This happens because people in individualistic culture are more concerned with uniqueness, whereas people in collectivistic culture show more concern with getting along with others and less concerned with the uniqueness of the person. Another form of provocation is harsh and unjustified criticism, which also provokes the person to show aggressive acts towards the persons who are doing so. Still another form of provocation is condescension, that is, expressions of arrogance or disdain on the part of others is also one potential source of aggression (Harris, 1993). Whatever may be the form of provocation, it breeds aggression.

(ii) **Increased level of arousal:** Researches have confirmed the fact that heightened arousal, whatever its source may be, can enhance aggression in response to provocation, frustration or any other factors. For example, presence of weapons increases aggression more strongly when people are already aroused or angered (Berkowitz, 1993). Likewise, aggressive boys' tendency to see any jostle as an act of aggression is magnified when they are very much anxious (Dodge and Somberg, 1987). Similarly, arousal stemming from such varied sources as participation in any competitive games (Christy, Gelfend and Hartmann, 1971), exercise (Zillmann, 1979) and even some types of music (Rogers and Ketcher, 1979) has been found to increase subsequent aggression.

What explanation is offered. A very good explanation for the fact that arousal produces enhanced subsequent aggression is offered by what social psychologists have called *excitation transfer theory* (Zillmann, 1983, 1988). The theory suggests that the arousal produced in one situation can persist and intensify emotional reactions occurring in later situations. For example, a boss who has quarrelled with his wife, after reaching office may be irritated by the delay done by the personal assistant in putting the file on his table. In fact, the boss may begin to lose temper and mutter, "What is wrong with PA? Can't he get it?". In this example, some portion of arousal persists even when the person (boss) shifts from one situation (home) to another situation (office). When he encounters a minor annoyance, that arousal intensifies the emotional reactions to arousal, making him more aggressive. The excitation transfer theory further suggests that such effects are most likely to occur when the persons involved are not aware of the presence of residual arousal. The theory also suggests that such effects become more obvious when the persons involved recognise their residual arousal, but attribute it to the events occurring in the present situation (Taylor et al., 1991).

(iii) **Frustration:**   Frustration is one of the important causes of aggression. When people do not get what they want or expect, they feel frustrated and this frustration leads to aggression. The relation between frustration and aggression has been widely framed in the famous frustration-aggression hypothesis (Dollard et al., 1939). According to this hypothesis, there are two basic assertions—frustration always lead to some form of aggression and aggression always stems from frustration. In a nutshell, it can be said that the frustrated people always engage in some form of aggression and all aggressive behaviours, in turn, do come from frustration.

These statements may apparently look attractive, but are not necessarily correct. Available evidences suggest that when frustrated, people do not always respond with aggression. Rather, they exhibit many different types of reactions to frustrations varying from despair, depression, etc. to direct attempts to overcome the source of frustration. Therefore, aggression cannot be considered as the automatic response of frustration. Likewise, not all aggressive acts do stem from frustration. People show aggression for many different reasons and in response to many factors. For example, a professional boxer hits his opponent not because of any frustration rather because of his motive to win the prize. A father slaps his child not because of frustration but because of his intention to improve his career or for getting him realised his mistakes. One basic point to be added here is that only when the person perceives the frustration as illegitimate or unjustified, it causes aggression (Folger and Baron, 1996). For example, a person may feel frustrated, and therefore, angry and aggressive, towards his girlfriend when she does not arrive at the appointed time and place. But when he comes to know that she could not come due to the fact that her mother got suddenly ill and was hospitalised, then in that situation, he will not be aggressive towards her girlfriend. Thus, when the cause of frustration is justified or legitimate, we become lenient towards the target.

(iv) **Social status:**   Social status is also a potent cause of aggressive behaviour. Persons belonging to the lower socio-economic status have been found to have link between testosterone levels and aggressive behaviour when compared with the other groups (Dabbs and Morris, 1990). Besides, the social conditions in which people live in also have an impact upon aggressive behaviour. One such factor which has been emphasised by the social psychologists is *relative deprivation,* where a person tends to compare his socio-economic status with that of others in their society and concludes that he lacks as well as has lost those factors assumed to facilitate his growth and adjustment. The theory of relative deprivation clearly states that the feelings of discontent arise from the belief that the other persons or other groups are comparatively better off (Smith and Mackie, 2007). If the person finds impossible to redress the balance by socially approved means, the members of the deprived group may act aggressively. Many historical revolutions and riots were begun in the same way.

Some Indian studies also highlight the impact of social status upon aggressive behaviour. Vig and Nanda (1999) reported that socioeconomic status (SES) and parent–child relationship were the main causative factors of aggressive behaviours in rural and urban adolescents, respectively. Likewise, Tomar (1999) found a significantly higher aggression among adolescent boys as compared to adolescent girls. It was relatively higher amongst those who belonged to lower SES. Likewise, family variables such as poverty and inadequate parental and peer group relationship contributed to aggression among adolescents (Talwar, 1995). Similarly, father's and mother's rejection also contributed towards hostility among adolescents. Violence against children was found to be higher in those families where mother was working outside the home. In fact, among dual-career families, the spillover of work stress into home resulted in aggression and violence against children (Prasad, 2001).

(v) **Exposure to media violence:** Researches have shown that the exposure to violence in films, television and video games increases the tendency to aggress against others because such exposure makes the persons less sensitive to violence and its consequences (Anderson, et al., 2003; Funk et al., 2004). Both short-term laboratory experimental researches and longitudinal researches have supported the idea that exposure to media violence increases aggression among both children and adults. Employing short-term laboratory experiments, some researchers allowed some children or adults to view either violent films and television programmes or non-violent ones. Results, in general, revealed that there was obviously higher levels of aggression among participants, who viewed the violent films or programmes (Bushman and Huesmann, 2001). Some researchers adopted longitudinal procedures to study the impact of exposure to media violence upon aggressive behaviour. In these studies, the participants were studied for many years. Result revealed that as children watched more violent films or television programmes, their level of aggression increased (Anderson and Bushman, 2002; Anderson and Huesmann, 2003; Huesmann and Eron, 1986). This type of finding was replicated in many other countries such as in South Africa, Poland, Australia, Finland, and Israel (Botha, 1990). Thus, the exposure to media violence tended to enhance aggression across different cultures.

Now, the question is—why does the effect of media violence occur? One explanation is that the repeated exposure to media violence strongly affects cognitive relations to aggression and gradually creates what is called *hostile expectation bias*—an expectation that others will behave aggressively. This, in turn, causes persons to be more aggressive (Bushman and Anderson, 2001). In brief, exposure to violent media strengthens beliefs, expectations and other cognitive processes related to aggression. As a consequence, the persons develop strong *knowledge structures* relating to aggression—structures which reflect and combine these beliefs, expectations, schemes and scripts (Baron, Byrne and Branscombe, 2006). When various events in life stimulate these knowledge structures, such persons feel, think and act aggressively because this is what they have learnt. Another explanation is that frequent exposure to media violence reduces an individual's emotional reactions to such events so that he generally perceives them as nothing out of the ordinary.

(vi) **Violent or aggressive pornography:** Pornography means explicit presentation of sexual activity in literatures, films, etc. to stimulate erotic rather than aesthetic feelings. The term *violent* or *aggressive pornography* refers to explicit depictions of sexual activity in which some kind of force is used to coerce a woman to engage in sex. Since pornography often generates high levels of arousal (both negative and positive emotions), it is possible that such effects might even be stronger than what we find in case of media violence. Researchers have shown that violent pornography may indeed have negative effects. Laboratory studies conducted by Linz, Donnestein and Penrod (1988) showed that when men are exposed to violent pornography, their willingness to aggress against women increases. Besides, the repeated exposure to violent pornography appears to produce a desensitising effect in which the emotional reactions to do harm to sexual victims are gradually reduced. Above all, exposure to violent pornography appears to increase the willingness of some persons to engage in similar behaviour and to generate callous attitudes towards various types of sexual violence, including rape. As a consequence, some men and women tend to accept what is generally unacceptable about rape and other forms of sexual violence—for example, the myth that some women unconsciously want to be raped or place deliberately themselves in such a situation in which they are likely to be sexually assaulted.

(vii) **Cultural norms:** There are also norms of aggression. Such norms are pervasive and product of a particular subculture. For example, in Chicago, it is considered wrong to show disrespect by adolescents to youths in the neighbourhood (Smith and Mackie, 2007). The normative response to such disrespect is extreme aggression and violence, including murder (Terry, 1993). Likewise, among boys of the schools, the popularity accorded to aggressive boys provides opportunity to accept violence (Price and Dodge, 1989). Likewise, there is *norm of male aggression,* which is more prevalent in American and European cultures. As compared with Northern European countries, including England, in these cultures, males are praised for being macho (Block, 1973). Still there is another norm called *norm of family privacy,* which condones aggression among the members of the family by excluding violent behaviours done by the family members. That is the reason, why we often remain unwilling to intervene in an altercation between husband and wife, father and son, mother and daughter, etc. Unfortunately, the norm of family privacy ensures that violence within the family is not challenged, which often supports domestic violence (Sherman and Berk, 1984).

In this connection, culture of honour is also very important factor to be considered. According to *culture of honour*, violence and aggression are appropriate only when these are used to protect oneself, one's family or to respond to affronts (Fischer, 1989). In simple words, cultures of honour refers to the cultures in which there are strong norms indicating that violence and aggression are appropriate responses to the insult to one's honour. Historical analysis shows that such norms developed in response to the people's attempt to protect their assets such as cattle, etc. that could easily be stolen. People demonstrated that they would not tolerate such thefts or any other affront to their honour. Therefore, norms condoning violence in response to such insults to one's honour emerged and accepted by the society. Recent findings indicate that culture of honour is still alive today, and operates in different parts of the world (Vandello and Cohen, 2003). However, its impact is especially apparent with respect to sexual jealousy. In culture of honour, women's infidelity— real or imagined—is viewed threatening to male's honour or vice versa and can result in drastic responses—severe physical punishment for both men and women, who is engaged in such informal contact. In cultures of South America as well as in Indian culture, sexual infidelity by a wife or wife's lover is viewed as an insult to male's honour, and so, man takes actions, especially aggressive and punitive action, including murder to restore his honour and it is viewed not merely as justified, but perhaps as actually required. A research evidence to support this fact was provided by Vandello and Cohen (2003), who reasoned that the code of male honour is especially strong in Latin America as well as in the Southern part of the United States. Their hypothesis was that the situations that induce sexual jealousy would also be expected to induce stronger aggressive reactions by jealous people in these cultures as compared to other cultures. In honour-oriented cultures, people should accept such aggression than the people in other cultures (Nisbett and Cohen, 1996). The hypothesis has been confirmed in the studies conducted by Vandello and Cohen (2003) as well as by Puente and Cohen (2003), who clearly indicated that jealousy is really a powerful cause of aggression and the violence stemming from it tends to provide threat to man's honour. Thus, it is clear that cultural factors do play a vital role in the occurrence of aggression.

3. *Situational factors of aggression*

Apart from the personal factors and social factors, situational factors also influence aggressive behaviour. Here, we shall concentrate mainly upon heat, behavioural model, stress, reinforcement, aggression cues and drugs.

(i) **Heat:** Since the time of Hippocrates (460–377 BC), people have theorised about the impact of climate on human behaviour. Temporary climatic variations have been found to affect human behaviour. For example, offensive odours, cigarette smoking, noise, air pollution have all been found to be related to aggressive behaviour (Rotton and Frey, 1985). Likewise, crowding has also been found to be related to the aggressive behaviour. Paulus (1988) showed that crowded conditions in prisons lead to escalation of violence and aggression. However, the most widely studied environmental irritant is heat or temperature (Griffitt, 1970; Griffitt and Veitch, 1971). They conducted studies in which they, having uncomfortable temperature (over 90°F), reported feeling more tired and aggressive as compared to those students who did so in room with normal temperature. Follow-up studies have also revealed that heat triggers retaliative actions (Rule et al., 1987). Studies conducted in six American cities have revealed that when weather is hot, violent crimes are more likely to occur (Harries and Stadler, 1988; Cohn, 1993).

Anderson (1989), Anderson, Bushman and Groom (1997) have examined long-term records of temperatures and police records of various types of aggressive crimes and found, in general, that hotter years indeed produced higher rates of violent crimes. One important question arises here—does this relationship between heat and aggression have any limits? In other words, does aggression increase with heat indefinitely or only up to a certain point? This issue has been well-addressed by several social psychologists like Rotton and Cohn (2000). They have, in general, reported that when temperature rises, people become irritable and may be more likely to lash out at others. But when temperature rises beyond a certain point, people become so uncomfortable that they become lethargic and focus on reducing their discomfort—not on attracting others. Baron (1972) found that the participants showed greater aggression against a confederate when the temperature hovered around a comfortable range of 72°F to 75°F than when it was quite hot (91°F to 95°F). Likewise, Baron and Ransberger (1978) found that rioting tended to escalate when the temperature was between 76°F to 90°F and then dropped off at higher temperatures.

(ii) **Behavioural models:** Another situational factor that promotes aggression is behavioural model, particularly aggressive model. In his earlier researches, Bandura, Ross and Ross (1961) demonstrated that aggressive behaviour can be learnt by observing and then, imitating a model. In fact, the model's aggressive behaviour tends to encourage others to behave in similar ways. We get numerous examples of this in our day-to-day life. Suppose a truck driver dashes a car and the driver of the car dies on the spot. However, luckily, two persons sitting on the back seats of the car go unhurt. The two occupants of the car start beating the driver of the truck. The aggressive act of these two occupants of the car serves as a model for others, who also start behaving aggressively towards the driver of the truck. Researches have shown that aggressive models provide three major types of information that influence the observers. First, models, with the help of their specific actions, demonstrate specific aggressive acts, which are possible in the situation. Second, models give information about the correctness and appropriateness of the aggression, that is, whether they are normatively acceptable in the situation. Third, models also provide information about the outcome to acting aggressively. Observers are more likely to imitate aggressive behaviours, which provide rewards and avoid punishment.

Myer (1972) reported similar effects in his experimental study. The participants in this experiment were first angered and then watched either a real-life incident of aggression or a fictional portrayal of aggression. Subsequently, the participants were given opportunity to aggress against a confederate. Results revealed that those who had seen the actions of aggressive models were more aggressive than the members of a control group, who had not witnessed any film. Turner and Berkowitz (1972) showed that the participants were more likely to imitate a high-status or powerful model than a low-status model and they were more likely to copy the behaviour of a model with whom they could identify than that of a model with whom they could not identify. Children of aggressive parents are more likely to show aggression because they see parents as having power and status. Studies conducted by Walters and Willows (1968) showed that the participants were more likely to initiate aggression when the model was seen as being rewarded rather than punished for acting violently.

Researches have further shown that a successful model clearly conveys information that aggression is acceptable in a particular situation. When the observers are not motivated to do harm, such information or message does not matter. But when the observers feel provoked or are somehow suppressing their inclination to aggress, they often lose their inhibitions after observing the model's aggressive behaviour. That is the reason, why other people, who find that driver of the car has died of his no fault, get provoked and attack the driver of the truck vigorously.

(iii) **Stress:** Various stresses are likely to increase aggressive behaviour and violence. Researches have shown that intimate violence, that is, spousal abuse, child abuse, rape by relatives, and sexual harassment by the members of the family occur due to various kinds of stressors like short relationship duration, misunderstanding of gender role definitions (that is, one has traditional views and the other has modern views), large number of children or dependents in the family. All these are related to domestic or intimate violence, partly through their relationship to more frequent disagreements and more heated disagreement style (DeMaris et al., 2003). Likewise, social stressors like chronic unemployment, experience of discrimination, etc. are related to aggression because of their effects on frustration and anger. Fox et al. (2002) conducted a study in which they found that household income was negatively related to violence, that is, as household income increased, the frequency of physical violence and aggression decreased. However, when either partner wished that the other worked more hours (that is, earned more money), this discrepancy between reality and desire was found to be positively related to physical aggression.

(iv) **Reinforcements:** Rewards or reinforcements also tend to promote aggression. Social psychologists, in general, view that there are three types of rewards such as direct material benefits, social approval and attention, which promote aggressive behaviour directly. Armed robbers, thieves and other young bullies generally get material benefits such as cash, jewelleries and other important and useful goods after their aggressive acts. This naturally reinforces them to do the aggressive acts frequently. Social approval is the second common reward for aggressive acts. We reward soldiers for shooting the enemy in war. We also urge our friends to aggress against those who insult or exploit us. We praise children for showing act of bravery or defending their members of family from attackers. Attention is the third type of reward for aggressive actions. A person, who aggressively breaks social rules in a meeting, gets proper attention of others and this encourages him to repeat the act, as he may be enjoying that others are valuing his acts by paying due attention.

There are obvious experimental evidences to support the fact that the individuals learn aggression through reinforcement. Gean and Stonner (1971) found that the participants increased the degree of aggression when they received verbal reinforcement for violence. Cowan and Walters (1963) found that the schedule of reinforcement is important for determining future aggression. Their findings were that the children, who had been on a partial reinforcement schedule, continued to hit the doll longer than did the children, who had been continuously rewarded. The results of the study clearly showed that the partial reinforcement may be enough to sustain continued aggression even without rewards. In real life, people are not always rewarded after they do aggressive act; in fact, their aggression is successful in bringing reward only some of the time.

(v) **Aggressive cues:** The presence of aggressive cues also promotes aggressive acts. Violence is most likely to occur when aggressive cues pull the cork, releasing pent-up anger. Berkowitz (1981, 1995) found that the presence of weapon is one such cue, especially when it is perceived as an instrument of violence rather than of recreation. Seeing a gun or a violent film tends to arouse a frustrated person and makes him or her more aggressive. Carlson, Marcus-Newhall and Miller (1990) found in their study that the frustrated people tend to respond more aggressively in the presence of gun than in the presence of neutral objects. This is called *weapon effect*. Researches have shown that the effect involves cognitive priming, that is, the sight of weapon primes aggression-related concepts or scripts for behaviour (Anderson, Benjamin and Bartholow, 1998). Thus, guns prime hostile thoughts and punitive judgements (Dienstbier et al., 1998). Researches have also shown that if a member of family becomes angry, the presence of gun in home creates the possibility of weapon effect. Kellermann (1993, 1997) showed that those who kept a gun in the house were 2.7 times more likely to be murdered by the family member or close acquaintance. Still another study found a five-fold increased risk of suicide in homes having guns (Taubes, 1992).

Aggressive cues become effective because they normally reduce inhibitions that prevent aggressive behaviour. Marcus–Newhall et al. (2000) further showed that aggressive cues also affect aggression by a process of ruminative thought. In fact, such cues prime other thoughts and emotions related to aggression and seek new ideas about ways to aggress against the person.

(vi) **Drugs:** Drugs have been found to affect aggressive behaviour, but the direction of effect is dependent on the type of drug and the size of the dose and whether or not the participant is threatened. Taylor and his associates (Taylor and Gammon, 1975; Taylor, Gammon and Capasso, 1976, Taylor et al., 1979) gave the participants drinks that contained either a small dose or large dose of alcohol or marijuana. Subsequently, they were either angered or not angered by a confederate and were given opportunity to aggress against the confederate. Results indicated that the large doses of alcohol increased aggression if the participant was angered or threatened. Indian researchers like Rajendra and Cherian (1992) as well as Thankachan and Kadandaram (1992) also reported that alcoholics show greater degree of anger, hostility and assault behaviour. Marijuana was found to have different impact. The participants, who had consumed large doses of marijuana, were found to be significantly less aggressive than the participants, who had consumed large doses of alcohol.

Subsequent researches done by Bushman and Cooper (1990) as well as Gustafson (1990) showed that when the participants consumed substantial dose of alcohol, they behaved more aggressively and responded to provocation more strongly than those who did not consume alcohol. Now, the question is—why does substantial dose of alcohol makes the participant more aggressive? This issue has been addressed by social psychologists, who have concluded from their researches that alcohol tends to impair cognitive functions of higher order such as capacity to evaluate stimuli as well as memory (Bartholow et al., 2003). Such impairment makes it hard for the individuals to evaluate others' intention (hostile or not hostile) and to evaluate the effects that different forms of behaviour on their part, including aggression, may be produced. There is also an evidence indicating that alcohol can influence aggression simply because it has been associated with such behaviour in the past. It means that since alcohol and aggression are associated with the individuals' lives, any cue associated with alcohol such as picture of bottles in which bear is kept or any advertisement related to it, may be enough to trigger aggression even if the alcohol itself is not consumed. Bartholow and Heinz (2006) supported this fact from their study.

Thus, we see that aggressive behaviour is caused by various personal, socio-cultural and situational factors. One has to focus on these sets of factors if one really wants to understand the causative factors of aggressive behaviour.

THEORIES OF AGGRESSIVE BEHAVIOUR

Social psychologists have formulated several theories to explain aggressive behaviour. Here, we shall mainly concentrate upon four important theories—instinct theory, drive theory, social hearing theory and general aggression model.

1. Instinct theory of aggression: According to instinct theory, aggression represents an innate urge. In other words, this theory attributes human violence to built-in (or inherited urges) to aggress against others. There has been two major proponents of instinct theories—Sigmund Freud and Konrad Lorenz. According to Freud, human beings have an instinct, called *Thanatos* or *death instinct*, which acts in opposition to *Eros* or *life instinct*. The energy of Thanatos is usually directed towards others rather than towards self for avoiding self-destruction. It means that following Freud, aggression is an inevitable and universal outcome of the rechanneling of death instinct.

Freud's view of aggression was shared in many ways by Konrad Lorenz, although the underlying mechanisms differ in major respects because Lorenz saw aggression as adaptive rather than destructive response. As we know, Lorenz is an ethologist. Ethology is the study of the animal behaviour. According to Lorenz, most animals share a fighting instinct, which serves many functions. For example, aggressive behaviour of animals allows them to maintain their own particular territory, which assures a steady supply of food. It also serves to weed out weaker animals and allows only strongest animal to obtain mates and pass their genes on to the next generation. Two extensions of the work of Lorenz are noteworthy here—why human beings kill each other and how instinctual energy builds up and is periodically released.

Lorenz's explanation of why human beings kill each other during some aggressive encounters is based upon the notion that there are two types of basic reactions to danger—fight or flight. Those animals that lack mechanisms to defend themselves such as deer tend to flee during encounter by enemy, whereas those animals that possess the defending mechanisms such as long claws and sharp teeth (like tiger, lion, etc.) tend to fight. Lorenz also pointed out that if the animals have greater fighting abilities, they have also stronger innate inhibitions against aggressing the members of its own species. In case of human beings, as Lorenz argued, the pattern has broken down. Since human beings originally reacted to aggression with flight, as they lacked mechanisms to defend themselves, innate inhibition against aggression towards other persons is comparatively weak. But due to modern technological advances, human beings have obtained great destructive power. Due to the lack of inhibitory impulses, human beings have become relentless killers of each other during aggressive encounters.

Another important outcome of Lorenz's work with animals was his attempt to understand the nature of instinctual aggressive energy. Like Freud, Lorenz suggested that aggressive energy is constantly generated and slowly builds up within the person over the period of time. Such energy continues to build up until it is discharged, usually because of some stimulus present in the environment that elicits the aggression. What will be the amount of aggression that is determined by the amount of energy that has been stored up? If enough energy has been accumulated, it may be released spontaneously even if no overt stimuli eliciting the aggression are present. One implication, here, is that if aggressive energy is discharged through socially desirable means such as sports and games, there would not be left sufficient energy for manifestation through aggression and violence.

Although instinct theory appears to be appealing and sensible, it has been criticised on the following grounds:

(i) The instinct theory lacks the experimental support. In some cases, it is impossible to obtain the support, while in some other cases, testable hypotheses can be formulated, but the obtained evidence does not support the theory. For example, based on the nature of instinctual aggressive energy, one popular hypothesis that can be derived is that participation in aggressive activities should reduce subsequent aggression. Walters and Brown (1963) demonstrated that the participants, who were given reward for hitting an object, were later found to be no less aggressive and sometimes were, in fact, more aggressive than the rewarded participants, who had not hit the object. Likewise, Berkowitz (1973) could not found evidence, where those involved in sports (either as participants or observers) were less likely to show aggression than those who were not exposed to such activities.

(ii) The nature and frequency of human aggressive behaviour varies tremendously across human societies. Consequently, they are much more likely to occur in some than in others. How can aggressive behaviour be explained by the genetic factors if such large differences exist?

However, today with the growth of evolutionary perspective, situation has much changed. It is true that most social psychologists continue to reject the view that human aggressive behaviours stem from innate factors. However, some social psychologists agree with the view that some innate factors do play a role in human aggressive behaviour. In the past, and to some extent, even today, males seeking desirable mates compete with the other males. One obvious way of eliminating such competition is through successful aggression, which drives rivals away or even eliminates sometimes. Such males, thus, become successful in securing mates and transmitting their genes to offspring. This entire episode becomes responsible for the development of a genetically influenced tendency for males to aggress against other males. On the other hand, males do not develop such aggressive tendency towards females because in that case, female would reject him as mate males. In contrast, females might aggress equally against both males and females. Researches done by Hilton, Harris and Rice (2000) provided support to this contention that males behave more aggressively towards the other males than towards females, while similar differences either do not exist or are very weak among females. Such findings have led some social psychologists to conclude that some innate or genetic factors do play a role in human aggressive behaviour.

2. Drive theories of aggression: Almost after rejecting instinct theory of aggression, social psychologists have formulated an alternative explanation in the name of drive theories (Feshbach, 1984; Berkowitz, 1989). Drive theories, in general, suggest that external conditions, particularly frustration, arise a strong motive or drive to harm others. This aggressive drive leads to aggressive behaviour.

One of the best known and popular of the drive theories is *frustration-aggression hypothesis*. This hypothesis was put forward originally by Dollard, Doob, Miller, Mowrer and Sears (1939). According to this hypothesis, frustration produces arousal of drive, whose primary goal is to harm other person or object. This hypothesis makes two bold assertions.

(i) Frustration always leads to aggression of some sort.
(ii) Aggression is always the result of some kind of frustration.

Here, frustration means blocking of some behaviour targeted towards a desired goal. In contrast to the instinct theory of aggression, this hypothesis clearly states that aggression is instigated by the external or environmental events. In an early experiment conducted by Barker, Dembo and Lewin (1941), a line of support was established. They showed a group of children a room full of attractive toys. Some children were allowed to touch and play with the toys immediately, whereas some other children were made to wait for about 20 minutes, looking at the toys before they were allowed to enter the room. Results revealed that those children, who were asked to wait, behaved destructively when given chance to play. In fact, they smashed the toys on the floor. Obviously, here, aggression was the direct response to frustration.

The frustration-aggression hypothesis implies that the nature of frustration influences the intensity of the resulting aggression. Two such factors that intensify the aggression are the strength and arbitrariness of frustration.

According to this hypothesis, stronger frustration leads to increased aggressiveness. An experiment done by Harris (1974) supported this contention. He asked the confederate to cut ahead of people in lines at theatres, restaurants and grocery check-out counters. As directed, the confederate cut in front of either the 2nd or the 12th person in line. The observers recorded the reactions of the person. Results were in hypothesised direction. The people at the front of the line showed high aggressiveness and made more than twice as many as abusive remarks to the intruder (confederate) than the people at the back of the line.

Arbitrariness of frustration is another factor. An individual is apt to feel more hostile when he believes that frustration is arbitrary, illegitimate and unprovoked. On the other hand, when he is able to attribute it to a reasonable, accidental or legitimate cause, there occurs no or little frustration causing no aggression. It means that only arbitrary or illegitimate frustration elicits more aggression. Kulick and Brown (1979) conducted a study in which this fact was confirmed. In this study, the students were frustrated by refusals from the potential donors (in reality, donors were confederates) under two different conditions. In legitimate frustration condition, potential donors offered good and sufficient reasons for refusal, whereas in illegitimate frustration condition, the donors offered weak and arbitrary reasons for refusal. Results revealed that the participants exposed to illegitimate frustration were more aroused than those exposed to legitimate frustration. Not only that, they were also found directing more verbal aggression against the potential donors.

Several decades of researches led to the modifications of the original frustration-aggression hypothesis. There were two important modifications.

(i) Miller (1941), one of its original authors, agreed that frustration does not always lead to aggression and suggested that frustration is only one of the several causes of aggression, and in fact, a relatively weak one. Aggression stems from many causes other than frustration (Zillmann, 1979). Although frustrated people may be motivated to behave aggressively, such persons may restrain themselves due to fear of punishment. Besides, frustration sometimes leads to different responses such as despair, depression or even withdrawal.

(ii) Another modification was done by Berkowitz (1965), who suggested that frustration leads to a readiness to aggress. Actual aggression occurs only when there are appropriate aggression-eliciting cues in the environment. *Aggression cues* are defined as stimuli associated with the source of frustration and with aggressive behaviour, in general. They may be anything such as weapon, names associated with frustrator or a disliked person. Thus, viewpoint of Berkowitz is popularly called *cue theory of aggression*. Berkowitz and his colleagues tested the cue theory of aggression by conducting a number of studies. One representative study was conducted by Berkowitz and Green (1966). In this study, the participants were introduced to a confederate, who either angered them or acted neutrally. After this, the participants were exposed to a violent scene from a movie—a boxing scene—and then, were placed in a position, where it was possible to administer electric shocks to the confederate. For the sake of manipulating the presence of an aggressive cue, the name of the confederate was varied. In one condition, he was named as *Kirk,* which presumably evoked the fighter in the movie played by Kirk Douglas. In the non-aggressive cue condition, the confederate was given a neutral name *Bob,* since it was not associated with the aggressive film. Results revealed that aggression (measured by the number of shocks given to the confederate) was higher when the participants were angered than when they were not. Even more significant finding was that the highest aggression towards the confederate occurred when his name (Kirk) was associated with violent film condition than when it (Bob) was not. These results definitely suggested that the name *Kirk* might have become the aggressive cue because of its association with the boxing films and also further suggested that this aggression cue was instrumental in eliciting aggression from angry participants.

Encouraged by the results of cue theory of aggression, Berkowitz devised a number of weapon effect studies. His hypothesis was that weapons such as guns and knives would be aggression-eliciting cues and the presence of weapons, therefore, might elicit aggression of an angry person. In order to test this hypothesis, Berkowitz and Le Page (1967) conducted a popular study in which confederate angered some participants and did not anger some other. Subsequently, they were then given opportunity to administer shock to the confederate in either weapon condition or non-weapon condition. In weapon condition, a 12-gauge shotgun and a 38-caliber revolver were placed on the table next to the shock apparatus and in non-weapon condition, two badminton rackets were placed next to the shock apparatus. Results indicated that in the weapon condition, when the subjects were angry, they gave more shocks (that is, aggressed more) than in the non-weapon (or badminton) condition. Berkowitz interpreted these results as supporting the hypothesis that weapons elicited aggression from the angry subjects, and thus, served as an aggression cue.

Berkowitz's cue theory of aggression was criticised due to its stand that cues were necessary for aggressive behaviour to occur. Rule and Nesdale (1976) made an extensive review of literature in which it was found that anger alone resulted in aggression. Later Berkowitz (1974) incorporated these criticisms into the amended version of cue theory by postulating that in some cases, anger might have aggression-eliciting properties of its own.

3. Social learning theory of aggression: As we have seen, according to instinct theory's view, aggression is mainly guided by internal processes, while in accordance with the drive theory's view, there is an interplay between the internal motivation of aggressive drives and environmental cues that produce aggression. In contrast, there is another theory of aggression that places little emphasis upon internal processes, and instead, concentrates upon the external environment. This is called *social leaving theory*. The major proponents of social learning theory (Bandura and Walters, 1963, Bandura, 1973) suggest that aggressive behaviours are basically learned behaviours. There are two main mechanisms through which social learning takes place—direct reinforcement/punishment, and imitation or modelling.

Children are often rewarded for acting in aggressive way. The rewards and punishment may not be tangible. Social approval or disapproval can also be effective as reinforcer. When the son beats up a larger or senior boy, the father praises him, and thus, he learns to aggress. The child is also reinforced through the added attention he receives for aggressing. Even when the parents and teachers tend to disapprove of the child's aggressive behaviours, they make the child their focus of attention by scolding him. The child, who is interested in having attention from adults, may be very willing to suffer the negative sanctions that he receives in return for the attention that the aggression brings. In response to check the aggressive behaviour of a child in the classroom, the teacher must halt the class and needs to take him to the principal's room for disciplinary action. During the whole sequence of events, the child lies in the focus of attention, which in itself, may be rewarding to the child. In this way, he learns that attention can be gained by behaving in an aggressive way. The child may also be directly awarded for his aggressive behaviour.

There are experimental evidences to support the fact that the persons learn aggression through verbal reinforcement. For example, Geen and Stonner (1971) found that subjects increased the intensity and amount of aggression when they were reinforced verbally for violence and aggression. Likewise, the children were found to continue to hit the doll longer when they were given partial reinforcement than when they were given continuous reinforcement (Cowan and Walters, 1963).

Another mechanism through which aggression is learnt, according to social learning theory, is imitation or modelling. Children are prone to initiate the behaviours of other persons, especially the persons whom they like or admire. Bandura, Ross and Ross (1961, 1963) conducted a number of studies to illustrate the fact that children learn to aggress by imitation. In their study, nursery school children first observed a model aggressively playing with an inflated plastic clown (a Bobo doll). The model hit the doll, beat it and kicked it. After watching the model, the children were put in a room with several toys—one of the toys being the Bobo doll. The behaviour of the children was carefully observed. Bandura and his associates were able to study different types of model by varying the characteristics of the model. In their study, Bandura, Ross and Ross (1961) clearly demonstrated that the children tended to imitate the same-sex models, that is, boys imitated the male model and the girls imitated the female model. In another study, Bandura, Ross and Ross (1963) had groups of children, who watched a real-life adult, an adult in film or a cartoon figure aggressing against a Bobo doll. Subsequently, the children were intentionally frustrated and put in a room with a Bobo doll. Results revealed that the children, who had watched an aggressive model, whether real life or filmed, showed more aggression against the Bobo doll than did the children who had not. Not only that, the children aggressed in more or less similar way as displayed by the model.

Children also learn aggressive behaviour in their real life. For example, children who are slapped for transgression do, in fact, learn that if someone's behaviour breaks the rule, it is ideal to punish him physically. Lavoie et al. (2002) conducted a longitudinal study in which more than 700 boys took part and found that boys, who experienced harsh parenting practices at the age of 10 to 12, were more likely to be involved in violent dating relationship merely at the age of 16. Intimate violence such as child abuse, spouse abuse, and sibling abuse has also been successfully explained by social learning theory. It has been found that people abusing their spouses and children often themselves grew up in families in which they were the target of such abuses (Gelles and Cornell, 1990).

Social psychologists consider social learning theory of aggression important due to several reasons. These are mentioned below:

(i) Social learning theory complements the frustration-aggression theory because it supplies answers to the questions that cannot be given by frustration-aggression theory. For example, frustration-aggression theory fails to explain why within the same frustrating situation, one person will use gun, another person will lash out with fists and still another will not aggress at all. Social learning theory states that early experiences and learning tend to determine how a person will aggress. If the person expresses his aggression with fist fighting, it means he grew in a family where members often engaged in fist fighting while aggressing. Likewise, if he uses gun for expressing expression, it means that he grew up in a family in which guns were constantly present or shoot-up movies were popularly seen. If the person did not show any aggression, it means he has been grown up in a family where aggression was discouraged.

(ii) Social learning theory is also important because it provides a foundation upon which a programme to reduce aggression can be based. Generally, we find that parents use physical punishment for their children's misdeeds. Such act tends to enhance future aggression. Here, parents tend to act as a model for the children. Outside the home, such children use aggressive response frequently. Sears et al. (1953) found that the children, who had been severely punished for aggression at home, were found to act frequently with aggression outside the home than the children, whose parents had punished them less severally for various aggressive acts. Accordingly, it is argued that aggression can be reduced by developing such programme in which children's aggressive behaviour leads to negative reinforcement in the form of withdrawal of some desired object or love. In such a situation, the children receive no reinforcement or attention for aggression nor do they witness any aggressive model whom they might imitate later. In this way, social learning theory definitely points out that in teaching a child not to aggress, aggression should not be employed as deterrent. This principle was clearly demonstrated in a study in which nursery school teachers rewarded children's cooperative and non-violent behaviour and did not pay any attention to their aggressive behaviour. After two weeks of such treatment, it was found that children reduced their aggressive behaviour significantly.

One general limitation of social learning theory is that the theory focuses on how aggression is learnt and expressed, it does not offer any explanation of why a person aggresses and why he chooses a particular target.

4. General aggression model (GAM): Built on social learning perspective, a newer framework, known as *general aggression model,* has been developed to account for the foundations of human aggression (Anderson, 1997; Anderson and Bushman, 2002a). This is also called *general affective aggression model.* The central idea of the model is that the factors, which increase aggression, do so by increasing aggressive affect, thoughts and arousal. As can be seen from Figure 14.1, GAM tries to integrate about what is known about the origins of aggression. According to GAM, there are two sets of factors that initiate aggressive behaviour—*personal factors* and the *situational factors.* Variables belonging to the first set of factors are certain attitudes and beliefs towards violence, specific skills related to aggression, a tendency to perceive hostile intentions in others, personality traits that favour aggressive behaviour, etc. Variables belonging to the second set of factors include heat, frustration, availability of weapons, some kind of attack from other persons, exposure to aggressive models either in person or in movies or games, etc. These two sets of factors, in turn, lead to overt aggression by way of having their impact upon three important processes—arousal, affective states and cognition. These two sets of factors tend to increase physiological arousal or excitement and enhance hostile feelings with overt signs (affective states) and can also induce persons to think hostile thoughts or may produce beliefs and attitudes about aggression in mind. Depending on the appraisals (or attribution) of the current situation, the person interprets whether the behaviour directed against him or her is intended to harm. This interpretation, in turn, leads to the decision whether to aggress against the other person or restrain their anger.

Bushman and Anderson (2001, 2002) as well as Anderson and Bushman (2002b) have recently expanded their theory to explain why such persons, who are exposed to high levels of aggression either directly or indirectly, tend to become increasingly more aggressive. In fact, repeated exposure to such stimuli tend to strengthen the existing knowledge structures relating to aggression. In other words, their beliefs, attitudes schemes and scripts considered relevant to aggressive behaviour become stronger. Such persons are easily activated by person or situational variables, that is, they are primed for aggressive behaviour.

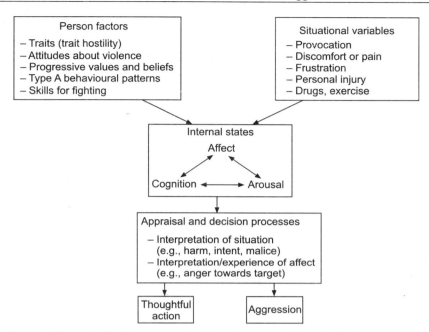

Figure 14.1 Model of General affective aggression (based on suggestions by Bushman and Anderson, 2002).

A close scrutiny of the GAM reveals that it is not a simple rather complex model of aggression. Since the model fully reflects recent progress in the field, it seems much more likely to provide a true view of human aggressive behaviour.

PREVENTION AND CONTROL OF AGGRESSION

Aggressive behaviour is a major problem for all societies in the world. Every society expends much energy to control aggression and violence. Following are some techniques for controlling and reducing aggressive behaviour:

1. Punishment and retaliation: Punishment and/or retaliation is widely used to control aggression. *Punishment* is the procedure in which aversive consequences are delivered to the persons when they engage in aggressive acts. Punishment may come in the form of imposing large fine, putting the person in prison, giving physical punishment for their aggressive actions. In some cases, capital punishment is also given and the persons are executed by legal proceedings.

Social psychologists, here, have concentrated upon two related questions.

(i) Why is punishment used frequently as a means for reducing human aggression?
(ii) Does punishment really work?

So far as the first question is concerned, social psychologists have provided two major grounds for punishing those persons, who engage in various types of aggression. The first is the popular belief in the society that when the persons engage in such aggressive acts, which are not approved by the society, they deserve punishment for mending their behaviour and for causing harm to others. This theory also stresses on the fact that the amount of punishment should match with the amount of harm done by the persons, who have done aggressive acts. Another perspective emphasises the fact that punishment deters persons from engaging in aggressive behaviour in future. Of these two perspectives, the first one is considered more important (Carlsmith, Darley and Robinson, 2002), whereas using punishment as a deterrent to future crimes seems to be comparatively less important.

Does punishment really work? For punishment to be effective in reducing aggression, it is essential that the following four basic requirements must be met:

(i) The punishment must follow the aggressive act promptly.
(ii) It must be strong enough to be highly unpleasant to the potential recipients.
(iii) It must be perceived by the recipients as justified or deserved.
(iv) It must not violate legitimate social norms.

Unfortunately, these requirements are often not met in the criminal justice system. The probability that every single criminal act will be punished is low simply because most criminals are not caught. Even when the criminals are caught, punishment rarely follows the criminal act promptly. Apart from this, very few criminals see punishment as a logical outcome of their criminal act. Finally, criminals often have much to gain through their aggression.

2. Catharsis: *Catharsis* is the reduction of aggressive arousal brought about by performing aggressive acts. The catharsis hypothesis explicitly states that if the persons give vent to their anger and hostility in non-harmful ways, their tendencies to engage in aggressive act decrease in future. Several studies have provided support to the basic catharsis hypothesis. When the person directs aggressive acts against the source of anger, they tend to reduce physiological arousal (Geen and Quanty, 1977). Day-to-day experiences also show that the people, who have been offended or insulted, feel less hostile and become less aggressive after getting a chance to tell someone about it. Dollard et al. (1939) and Freud (1950) also supported the fact that catharsis reduces subsequent aggression. It means that once people have acted aggressively and released their anger, they are less likely to engage in future aggression. But systematic researches done by the social psychologists have shown that performing aggressive acts tend to enhance future aggression rather than reducing it. This has been found to be true (Bushman, 2001; Bushman, Baumeister and Stack, 1999) whether initial aggression is a verbal attack, physical attack or even aggressive play. Recently, Anderson, Carnagey and Eubanks (2003) provided a very clear and strong support to this fact. These researchers hypothesised that the exposure to violent songs or songs with violent lyrics would reduce their level of hostility and aggressive thoughts if catharsis hypothesis was true and if this hypothesis was not true, such exposure would tend to enhance both the feelings of hostility and aggression. Researchers conducted a series of studies in which the participants listened to violent and non-violent songs and their current feeling of hostility and aggressive cognitions were measured. Results of all these studies consistently showed that after listening violent songs, participants showed an increase in both hostile feelings and aggressive cognitions. Geen, Stonner and Shope (1975) also reported similar findings.

Now, the question is—why does initial aggression promotes further aggression? Social psychologists have found out four probable reasons. First, initial aggression tends to produce *disinhibition*, which is defined as the reduction in internal controls against socially disapproved behaviour. Often it is reflected in reports of criminals, who comment that killing is difficult in the beginning but becomes easier thereafter. Second, initial aggression gives us experience of harming others. Third, such initial aggression tends to arouse the anger of the person even further. Finally, after initial aggression, a state of catharsis comes that relieves our tension. Simultaneously, we also get pleasure of blocking the tension and such feeling in itself is rewarding, and in general, we have a natural tendency to repeat the rewarded behaviours frequently.

3. Reducing frustration and attack: As we know, one important cause of aggression is frustration. Therefore, one way to reduce aggression is to reduce the strength and frequency of frustration. Some societies, particularly those who respect socialist philosophies, make a particular effort to reduce the frustration of their citizens by providing more economic equality, individual freedom and other different types of benefits. Many of the frustrations that we experience arise from conflicts with the other people. The resulting anger often encourages persons to make aggressive attacks directed either at the target or at others perceived similar to the target. Thus, one way to reduce aggressive behaviour is to provide persons with alternative means of resolving interpersonal conflicts. Some people may call police, whereas some other may take their conflict with the help of lawyer.

Some societies tend to make provision for collective police protection so that people may not be attacked by bandits or other violent individuals. Such protection helps in reducing chances for widespread violence because people are not themselves goaded into retaliation.

4. Cognitive interventions: Apology is one popular technique of reducing aggression. *Apology* obviously means accepting wrongdoing that includes a request for forgiveness. Such apologies tend to reduce anger (Ohbuchi, Kameda and Agarie, 1989). Likewise, good and clever excuses also have been found to minimise aggression (Weiner et al., 1987).

In anger and resulting aggression, the person's ability to think in proper way, for instance, in evaluating the consequences of his own action, is sharply reduced. Not only that, in such emotional arousal, the person processes the information in a quick and impetuous manner. Results reveal that the person attacks the target or against the persons, who are not the source of annoyance. Researches have shown that when these cognitive deficits are removed, it becomes helpful in reducing aggression. There are two popular techniques of overcoming such cognitive deficits. One technique is called *preattribution,* where a person attributes annoying actions by others to unintentional causes before occurring of provocation. For example, before meeting the target person to whom the person can be annoying and irritating, if the person is reminded that actually, the target person does not mean to make him angry, rather that is just the result of unfortunate personal style, then it is very likely that the aggression towards the target person will be reduced. Another technique is one, where the person may be prevented from thinking previous real or imagined wrongs. Such task can be easily done by engaging one in distracting task such as watching a movie or television programme or working on some complex puzzles or by reading interesting novels, etc. Such distraction produces a cooling-off period during which the anger can dissipate and aggression can be held in check.

5. Observation of non-aggressive models—A social learning approach: Social learning approach to aggression suggests an alternative model of reducing aggression, that is, using non-aggressive model. Just as aggressive model increases aggression, non-aggressive models tend to reduce it. Our Rashtrapita Mahatma Gandhi, while leading the movement to free India from British rule, used pacifist tactics, which have been used by the important leaders of world for maintaining peace. Laboratory experiments have also supported that observation of non-aggressive model can lead to reduction in aggression. Baron and Kepner (1970) conducted a study in which participants observed an aggressive model, who administered more shocks to a confederate than actually required by the task. A group of other participants observed a non-aggressive model, who delivered the minimum number of shocks required. There was also a control group, who observed no model. Results revealed that the participants, who had observed the non-aggressive models, displayed less subsequent aggression than the participants of the control group. In fact, the participants, who had observed the aggressive model, displayed more subsequent aggression than the participants of the control group. Apart from this, research works on modelling effects on prosocial behaviour also supports the conclusion that observation of non-aggressive models may prove to be effective in reducing aggression. Unfortunately, most people in real life are exposed to both aggressive as well as non-aggressive models. In such a situation, the observation of non-aggressive models may not be effective in practical sense.

A more promoting technique for reducing aggression was developed by Huesmann et al. (1983). In this technique, the emphasis is given upon the interpretation of the behaviour made by observer, rather than on the fact that whether the model acts aggressively or non-aggressively. This technique has been frequently used in relation to exposure to media violence, where an active effort is made to change people's attitude towards the meaning of aggression that they often view on television. They are taught that the violence shown on television is unrealistic and the aggressive behaviour does not have the same degree of acceptability in our day-to-day life. Therefore, aggression shown by the television characters is unrealistic and inappropriate. By changing attitudes towards violence by such teaching, it is assumed that the impact of observation of aggression will be considerably reduced. Huesman et al. (1983) conducted a field study in which there were an experimental group and a control group. The experiment group of children received training that emphasised that the behaviour of the characters showing violence on television does not represent the behaviour of most people and camera techniques and special effects provide only illusion that characters are doing aggressive behaviours. The control group of children received training on issues unrelated to aggression. Results revealed that the children of experimental group were rated as exhibiting lower degree of aggression as compared to the children of control group.

Keeping in view the effectiveness of modelling techniques, Indian researchers have also developed training programmes for reducing aggression. One such programme for reducing aggression in delinquent boys was developed through modelling techniques. Vidyasagar and Mishra (1993) reported that teacher and therapist ratings indicated decrease in aggression both during and the follow-up study after modelling exposure. Also, the efficacy of behaviour therapy techniques in reducing aggression of delinquent males using relaxation therapy and systematic desensitisation was examined. Kaliappan and Kaliappan (1993) reported significantly less aggression in these two therapy groups as compared to the control group.

In a nutshell, social psychological approach to aggression provides some obvious ways for preventing and reducing its occurrence.

6. Forgiveness: Forgiveness is another technique for reducing aggression. *Forgiveness* means giving up desire to punish all those who have hurt us, and instead, act in prosocial way towards them. Obviously, forgiveness then contains two goals. The first goal is to give up the desire for taking revenge and the second goal is to forgive the persons to the extent that we actually start behaving towards them in helpful way. McCullough, Fincham and Tsang (2003) experimentally confirmed the fact that the first goal is easier to attain than the second goal. Forgiveness, particularly giving up the desire for taking revenge, tends to enhance our psychological well-being apart from reducing aggression. Karremans et al. (2003) demonstrated this fact in their research. Their results revealed that those participants, who had been led to believe that they had forgiven the offender (forgiveness condition), exhibited higher degree of self-esteem as well as lower levels of negative affect than those in the no-forgiveness condition. Further researches have shown that the benefits of forgiveness are more obvious and stronger for committed relationship than for the ones to which they are less committed.

How does forgiveness work? One process that underlie forgiveness is *empathy,* where people engaged in forgiveness try to understand the feelings and emotions that caused the offending person to harm them, and at the same time, they make generous attributions about the causes of the offenders' behaviour. Above all, people showing forgiveness avoid ruminating about post transgressions and concentrate on other things, thus shutting the door for negative thoughts.

Thus, we find that any attempt to reduce aggression involves a careful planning of keeping several factors in view.

MEDIA VIOLENCE

The term *mass media* is cliché abbreviation of mass media of communication, which refers to the entire family of technological devices that permit communication among masses. Mass media have existed ever since man carved hieroglyphics on stone or clay tablets, permitting the communication of ideas over both time and space. From stone tablets to the printing press, to daily newspapers, to telephone and telegraph, to radio, and ultimately, to TV, the mass media have progressed towards permitting increasingly immediate and close communication to mass audiences.

Social psychologists have studied impact of mass media upon aggressive behaviour in detail. Television is one of the most popular media and has become a member of everyone's household (Unnikrishnan and Bajpai, 1996). According to a survey done, by the age of five, a child watches television for almost two and three hours each day (Siegel, 1969), and by the age of ten, the child watches television for four to six hours daily. Adults too see television programmes giving sufficient time. In a study, it was found that about 61% of television programmes depicted aggression and violence (Anderson et al., 2003). Exploring the impact of TV and TV advertising on children, Unnikrishnan and Bajpai (1996) showed that children's understanding of the social world is largely influenced by what they view on TV screen. Now, the question is—is there a causal link between viewing aggressive acts and violence and committing them? Two major theories about human aggression (that is, frustration-aggression theory and social learning theory) make different predictions for the effects of television violence. The catharsis hypothesis of frustration-aggression theory states that the participation in aggressive act will tend to lessen the aggressive behaviour. This suggests that if the people are allowed to play aggressively or if they vicariously experience aggression by watching violence on television, they will be less instigated to aggress. By witnessing violence, viewers can reduce their own needs to act aggressively because the vicarious experience of violence can lead to catharsis. The social learning theory as well as Berkowitz's cue theory suggest that viewing aggression on television would lead to more aggression, rather than reducing aggression through catharsis. Displayed aggression serves as a model for the viewer to imitate and it can provide aggression cues that are enough to release the viewer's aggressive behaviour.

Results of the various research studies on relationship between witnessed violence and aggressive behaviour reflect a conflicting view. Some studies reported an actual decline in aggressive behaviour after witnessing television violence (Feshbach, 1961; Feshbach and Singer, 1971; Freedman, 1984; Milavsky et al., 1982). In Feshbach's (1961) study, angry or non-angry participants watched either an aggressive film or a non-aggressive film. He found that when opportunity to aggress was given, the angry subjects, who had witnessed the aggressive film, were less aggressive than were the participants who had seen the non-aggressive film. Feshbach and Singer (1971) conducted a field study involving 625 boys between the ages of 10 and 17. These boys were assigned to watch either aggressive programmes or non-aggressive programmes for six weeks. Subsequently, they were given opportunity to aggress. Results revealed that the boys, who watched the aggressive movies, were less aggressive and engaged in only half as many fights as were in the case of boys, who had watched the non-violent programmes. Although Feshbach and Singer's study has been criticised on several grounds, it still provides the strongest support for catharsis hypothesis. Kapoor and Verma (1997) also found that highly aggressive adolescents watched TV for a longer period of time with high degree of concentration.

However, the later researches have contradicted these findings. It has been shown by many researches that exposure to media violence tend to increase aggressive behaviour by strengthening beliefs and other cognitive processes related to aggression (Anderson and Bushman, 2001). In fact, there are five processes that explain why exposure to media violence enhances aggressive behaviour (Huesmann and Moise, 1996). Those processes are as under:

1. **Imitation:** Social learning through imitation of aggressive media models helps the viewers in learning various techniques of aggression.
2. **Cognitive priming:** Exposure to media violence activates aggressive thoughts and pro-aggression attitudes. Such thoughts and attitudes are later expressed in terms of behaviour.
3. **Desensitisation:** After being exposed to violent media repeatedly, viewers become desensitised (lesser sensitive) to aggression. This makes them less reluctant to hurt people.
4. **Legitimation/Justification:** Exposure to such violence media that successfully attains goals and has positive results legitimises aggression and makes it more pleading and acceptable.
5. **Arousal:** Exposure to media violence repeatedly produces excitement and physiological arousal, which may amplify aggressive responses to even those situation, which are usually considered milder.

Murray and Kippax (1979) showed that all these processes clearly operate in linking media violence to aggression. To investigate these processes, researches have been conducted in several laboratories as well as field experiments on children, adolescents and adults have also been conducted using portrayals of aggression, both live and film. Wells (1973) replicated the Feshbach and Singer's study and reported that the television violence caused an increase in aggressive behaviour of the viewers. Friedrich and Stein (1973) conducted experiments on nursery school children, who watched aggressive, neutral or prosocial programmes for a four-week period. The behaviour of the children was observed before, during and after the television viewing. Results revealed that aggressive programmes increased aggressive behaviour in children, who were in above average category of aggressive behaviour before viewing the programmes. Some other studies viewed that people, who viewed more hours of violent television (Singer and Singer, 1981), listened to music with violent lyrics (Anderson, Carnagey and Eubanks, 2003) or played violent video games (Anderson and Dill, 2000), showed more aggressive behaviour. A study conducted by Viemero and Paajanen (1992) in Finland revealed that if the children were allowed to watch more TV violence, they were later found to show more aggressive fantasies and engage in aggression. A review of 28 studies examining the effects of media violence on children and adolescents demonstrated that the media violence enhanced their aggression in interactions with strangers, classmates and friends. Bushman and Geen (1990) also showed that media violence may lead to aggression by activating information related to aggression in memory. Parke et al. (1977) also conducted three extensive studies (two in the United States and one in the Belgium) showing the impact of television on aggressive behaviour. In this study, participants were juvenile delinquents whose behaviour was observed for a three-week period for establishing a baseline measure of general aggressiveness. Subsequently, they were randomly assigned to two groups for a week. Half of the subjects watched aggressive movies each night and the other half watched non-aggressive movies. During the final three-week phase, these participants were carefully observed and evaluated on aggressiveness dimension. Results revealed that in each case, the participants, who had watched the aggressive movies, behaved more aggressively than the participants, who had viewed the neutral movies. The Belgium study uncovered a particular provocative effect, that is, immediately after the participants watched aggressive movies, their physical aggression had increased. The long-term effect of watching aggressive films was the greatest for verbal aggression. Another study conducted by Johnson et al. (2002) took 707 family with children between the ages of 1 and 10. Data were collected regarding television-viewing behaviour by the children during 1991–1993 and on aggressive behaviour through the year 2000. It was found that the time spent at the age 14 for watching television was positively correlated to the aggressive acts against others at the age of 16 and 22.

Now, the question remains—why does exposure to the media violence encourage aggressive behaviour? Berkowitz (1984) provided a neo-associationist analysis of such phenomenon. His theory is based on the belief that as we process information, we automatically react to its content (that is, here aggression) and later tend to translate those thoughts elicited by viewing violence into anti-social acts. This theory is based upon cognitive psychological theory and emphasises that memory consists of series of nodes linked via associated pathways. As the person thinks, various nodes associated with the thoughts are activated. For example, suppose you are watching a film showing violent murder. As you go on watching, related thoughts about events, guns, knives, blood, etc. are likely to be activated automatically, leading to physiological arousal. Consequently, the probability to commit an aggressive act is elevated (Phillips, 1986) (see Figure 14.2). However, not every person, who has watched such movie, behaves aggressively; so, obviously, some other factors do play roles.

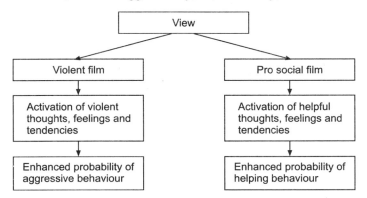

Figure 14.2 A neo-associationist analysis of exposure to media violence.

Conclusively, it can be said that both field study and laboratory study indicate that under most conditions, viewing violent programmes would increase the aggressive behaviour of the viewers. In other words, exposure to violent television programmes, movies, video games and music increases the likelihood of aggressive and violent behaviour by the viewers. Such effects are both short-term and long-term in nature. In fact, growing body of evidence suggests a circular relationship between aggression and television viewing (Friedrich–Cofer and Huston, 1986). Since aggressive children are not much popular among their peers, they spend more time in watching television. This exposes such children to more violence and teaches them aggressive behaviour by reassuring that their behaviour is completely right.

Summary and Review

- *Aggression* may be defined as physical or verbal behaviour intended to hurt someone. Among human beings, two main types of aggression have been identified—hostile aggression and instrumental aggression. *Hostile aggression*, also called *emotional aggression*, involves the wish to hurt the other persons and it springs from negative emotions like anger. *Instrumental aggression* aims to hurt only as a means to attain some other end. Thus, such aggression is carried out in order to achieve a specific goal.
- There are three sets of causes or factors of aggression—personal causes, socio-cultural causes and situational causes. *Personal causes* include personality, hostile attributional bias, disinhibition, narcissism, TASS model, sensation seeking and gender differences. *Socio-cultural factors* include direct provocation, increased level of arousal, frustration, social status, exposure to media violence, violent or aggressive pornography and cultural norms. *Situational factors* include factors like heat, behaviour models, stress, reinforcement, aggressive cues, drugs, etc.
- Various theories have been formulated to explain aggressive behaviour. Important ones are instinct theory, drive theories, social learning theory and general aggression model. According to instinct theory, aggression represents an innate or inherited urge. Freud and Lorenz made a significant contributions here. Drive theories, in general, suggest that external conditions, particularly frustration, arouse a strong motive or drive to harm others. Frustration-aggression theory and cue theory of aggression are better examples of drive theory. Social learning theory of aggression emphasises the fact that aggressive behaviours are basically learnt behaviours. Such behaviours are learnt through direct reinforcement and imitation and/or modelling. General aggression model (GAM) states that factors that increase aggression do so by increasing aggressive affect, thoughts and arousal. There are two sets of factors that imitate aggressive behaviours—personal factors and situational factors. *Personal factors* include factors like certain attitudes and beliefs about violence, specific skills related to aggression, personality traits that favour aggressive behaviours, etc. *Situational factors* include factors like heat, frustration, availability of weapons, exposure to aggressive models, etc.
- There are various means of preventing and controlling aggression. Such important means are punishment and retaliation, catharsis, reducing frustration and attack, observation of non-aggressive models, forgiveness, etc.
- Special attention has also been given to media violence. Of the various types of media violence, the impact of television violence has been particularly discussed. Some evidences do provide support to the fact that exposure to the television violence and aggression reduces aggressive behaviour in actual life, whereas the majority of studies do provide support to the fact that such exposure enhances the aggressive behaviours in real life of the persons.

Review Questions

1. Define aggression. Discuss the major personal causes of aggressive behaviour.
2. Citing relevant studies, discuss the socio-cultural causes of aggressive behaviour.
3. Discuss the major factors of aggression.
4. Examine critically instinct theory of aggressive behaviour.
5. Examine critically drive theory of aggressive behaviour.
6. How does social learning approach explain aggressive behaviour? Cite experimental evidences in favour of your answer.
7. Outline a plan for preventing and controlling aggressive behaviour.
8. Write shot notes on the following:
    (i) General aggression model (GAM)
    (ii) Media violence
    (iii) TASS model

15 PROSOCIAL BEHAVIOUR: ALTRUISTIC AND HELPING BEHAVIOUR

Learning Objectives

- Defining Prosocial Behaviour and Altruism
- Five Steps of Bystander Intervention: A Decision Tree Analysis
- Determinants of Prosocial Behaviour
- Basic Motivation behind Prosocial Acts: Theories
- How Can Helping Behaviour be Increased?

KEY TERMS

Altruism	Diffusion of responsibility	Norms of reciprocity
Arousal-cost-reward model	Egoism	Norms of social responsibility
Audience inhibition	Implicit bystander effect	Pluralistic ignorance
Competitive altruism approach	Just world hypothesis	Psychological distance
Decision tree	Kinship selection theory	Selective altruism
Diffusion of responsibility	Negative-state relief hypothesis	Tit-for-tat effect

We are social beings and as a social being, we often act alone or in groups to benefit other people. Some of these acts of kindness are quite ordinary such as helping an elderly person in crossing a busy road or in shopping, etc. However, at other times, we make a generous effort and devote energy to help others such as helping a battered women or people with cancer, AIDS, spending hours to help the victim of earthquakes, tsunamis, hurricanes, etc. Social psychologists have termed such behaviours of everyday life as *prosocial behaviour*—a behaviour whose immediate goal is to help or benefit others.

In the present chapter, after defining prosocial behaviour, we shall discuss about the determinants of prosocial behaviour and then its motivational theories. Next, we shall concentrate on basic question—how can prosocial behaviour be increased?

DEFINING PROSOCIAL BEHAVIOUR AND ALTURISM

Prosocial behaviour and altruism are quite related terms in meaning. Therefore, we should first clear the meanings of these two terms.

Altruism means an unselfish concern for the benefit and welfare of others. In other words, altruism means performing an act voluntarily to help someone else when there is no expectation of reward in any form, except the feeling of having done a good and positive dead (Schroeder et al., 1995). This simple definition implies that whether an act is altruistic or not, it depends on the intention of the helper. Suppose you want to help homeless people, but at the same time, you also want to impress your friends. Since your action involves an intention to help, it is definitely an example of prosocial behaviour. However, you have a specific motive to impress your friend. Therefore, this behaviour cannot be counted as an example of altruistic behaviour. Thus, altruism is motivated by a desire to help someone else rather than yourself (Batson and Coke, 1981). In fact, it is a subcategory of helping behaviour which involves an intentional act of providing benefit to others (Hogg and Vaughan, 1995).

Prosocial behaviour is much a broader category (Batson, 1998). It is defined as any helpful action that benefits other people without necessarily providing any direct benefit to the helper and it may even involve risk for the helper. In simple words, prosocial behaviour includes any act that helps or is designed to help others, regardless of the helper's motives. Many prosocial acts are not altruistic. If a young person volunteers to work without salary for building up his resume for future job opportunity, this behaviour is not altruistic, rather it is a prosocial behaviour. It is because he is working (or extending help) without any salary. But behind this, there is an ulterior motive to make his resume stronger. Therefore, his behaviour cannot be regarded as altruistic in true sense of the term.

Altruism must also be distinguished from egoism and heroism. *Egoism* is the opposite of altruism. It is characterised by a refusal to become concerned about anything except oneself and one's own interests. *Heroism* refers to the actions that involve courageous risk-taking behaviour to obtain a socially valued goal. A good example is a dangerous act undertaken to save the life of somebody else. In this way, here, both aspects are involved. A person, who engages in risky behaviour for fun, is not a hero and saving one's own life is definitely valuable, but not heroic.

FIVE STEPS OF BYSTANDER INTERVENTION: A DECISION TREE ANALYSIS

In any emergency situation, altruistic behaviour tends to involve committing an action that would help the person in need. Latane and Darley (1970) pointed out that engaging in prosocial act involves not just one decision, but a series of separate decisions. Only if the person makes an appropriate decision quickly at each decision point, he or she will be intervened in an emergency. These decisions points are together called *decision tree*. At each point, the branches are available, which cause the bystander to go about his business with or without prosocial intervention (see Figure 15.1). A discussion of these five decision points is given as:

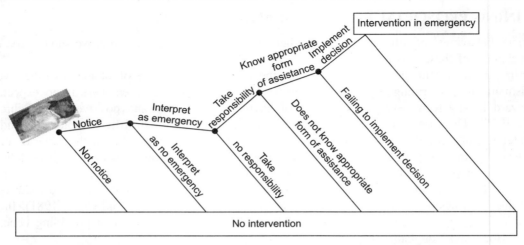

Figure 15.1 Decision tree analysis of bystander intervention in emergency.

Step 1: Notice or fail to notice the critical incident

The first step of bystander intervention in emergency is to notice the critical incident clearly. At this decision point, the bystander must notice the incident with full mind and only then, he can decide about the prosocial act. It has been found that when the person is preoccupied by personal concerns, he pays less attention to such critical event. As a result, prosocial act is less likely to occur and the person is driven to no intervention side (see Figure 15.1). Darley and Batson (1973) conducted a crucial experiment to test the importance of this first step in the decision process. This study was conducted with the students, who had been placed under training for clergy, that is, the individuals who are likely to help a stranger in need. The investigators instructed the participants of the groups to walk to nearby building for speech assignment. Some participants were told that they had plenty of time to reach the designated building, participants of other group were told that they were right on schedule with just enough time to get there and the third group's participants were told that they were late for the speaking assignment and needed to be in hurry. The first group was the least preoccupied group, the third group was the most occupied and the second group was intermediately preoccupied. The question was that whether or not this varying degree of preoccupation would influence the participants engaged in prosocial behaviour. Along the route to the building where speech was to be delivered, an emergency was staged, that is, a stranger (actually a research assistant) was slumped in doorway, coughing and groaning. Would the participants notice this apparently sick or injured person? Results revealed that out of those participants who had spared time, 63% provided help. Of group that was on schedule, 45% provided help. In hurried or the most preoccupied group, only 9% provided help to the stranger. Some of the preoccupied participants, in fact, stepped over the stranger and continued their way. Results obviously provided support to the fact that a busy or preoccupied person fails to provide little help because he is not aware that an emergency actually exists.

Step 2: Interpreting an event as emergency

The second step of bystander intervention for providing help is to correctly interpret an event as emergency. The common observation has been that the presence of multiple witnesses generally tends to inhibit helping behaviour not only because of the diffusion of responsibility but also because it is embarrassing to misinterpret the situation and act accordingly. This tendency for an individual surrounded by a group of strangers in hesitating and doing nothing to the stranger is based on what social psychologists have called *pluralistic ignorance* (Baron, Branscombe, Byrne and Bhardwaj (2010). Pluralistic ignorance refers to the fact that since none of the bystanders responds to an emergency (in which stranger is), no one knows for sure what is happening and each depends on others to provide cues. This becomes a situation where each individual is less likely to respond if others fail to respond. Latane and Darley (1968) experimentally proved this fact. In their experiments, students were placed in a room either alone or with two other students, with a request to fill the questionnaires. After several minutes, the experimenter secretly and quietly pumped smoke into the research room through a vent. Results revealed that when the students were working alone, 75% stopped when smoke appeared and went to report about the problem. When three students were in room, only 38% reacted to smoke. When the smoke became thick, creating difficulty in seeing, 62% continued their work in the smoke-filled room. Rutkowski, Gruder and Romer (1983) further showed that such inhibiting effect is much less if the members of the group are friends probably because friends are likely to acquaint each other with what is happening in the situation.

One basic question arises here—what cues do people use in deciding if an emergency really exists? Shotland and Huston (1979) diagnosed through their researches that there are five important characteristics, which may lead us to perceive an event as emergency:

(i) Something suddenly and unexpectedly happens
(ii) Harm to the victim is likely to increase in future unless someone intervenes.
(iii) There is clear threat of harm to the victim
(iv) The victim is helpless and needs outside assistance
(v) Some types of intervention are possible.

In this way, our interpretation of a situation is a vital factor in offering help to the strangers. Shotland and Straw (1976) conducted a study in this regard. In this study, participants came to the department of psychology individually in the evening to fill out a questionnaire. While working alone on the task, they heard a loud fight started in the corridor (actually staged by drama students). In a stranger condition, where a woman was heard to tell, "I do not know you", 65% of the participants intervened either directly or by calling police, whereas in marriage condition, where woman was heard telling, "I do not know why I have ever married you", only 19% of the participants intervened. This result showed that even though the fights were identical in all respects, the participants perceived the situation as more serious and woman as more eager for help in stranger condition.

Step 3: *Deciding about personal responsibility to provide help*

Even when the emergency is perceived and interpreted correctly, a bystander may not still offer help to the victim because he may not be sure whether or not it is his responsibility to provide help. When several bystanders or potential helpers are present, each of them may think that others will take responsibility to provide help to the victim. This is known as *diffusion of responsibility*. When there is only one bystander, he or she usually assumes responsibility to help because there is no alternative.

One important demonstration of taking personal responsibility comes from a field study conducted by Maruyama, Fraser and Miller (1982). In this study, there were groups of children, who visited certain house while trick-or-treating and were asked to donate candies for hospitalised children. Investigators manipulated children's perception of responsibility by introducing three experimental conditions. In one experimental condition, the woman who greeted the children made each one personally responsible for donating candies by putting the child's name on a bag for the candies. In another experimental condition, they made one child responsible for the entire group. In the third experimental condition, no one was given responsibility. Results showed that when each child was made individually responsible, the average donation was five candies; when one child was made responsible, the average donation came down to three and when no one was responsible, an average of only two candies per child was given. Thus, results clearly supported the idea that the more personal responsibility a child was given, the more generously the child donated to help the hospitalised children. Wegner and Schaefer (1978) reported that the presence of large number of victims and a small number of potential helpers tend to increase prosocial behaviour. Researches have further shown that two factors tend to enhance the likelihood of bystander helping—one is reduction in the psychological distance between victim and bystander and reduction in the psychological distance among the bystanders themselves. For example, if the bystander and victim know each other or are somehow related, probability of rendering help by the bystander is increased. Likewise, people who know each other, for example, workmates, are more likely to act as helpful bystanders than the groups of strangers (Rutkowski et al., 1983).

Step 4: Deciding about the knowledge or skills to help

The next step of providing bystander's help is to decide whether or not he possesses the necessary competence or skills to do so. In fact, people feel a greater sense of obligation to intervene if they have skills to help effectively. Clark and Word (1974) conducted a study in which the participants witnessed to person (actually a researcher) pass out from an electric shock due to malfunctioning of the equipment. It was found that out of the participants, who were having formal training experience in working with electrical equipment, 90% intervened to provide help. Those who had no electrical skills, only 58% intervened. Likewise, in medical emergency, only a doctor or registered nurse can more likely to be helpful than a professor of psychology. Similarly, only good swimmers can provide help to a person, who is drowning in deep river.

Step 5: Taking a final decision to help

After passing through the first four stages, the help by bystander may not occur unless he or she makes ultimate decision to do the helpful act. Here, at this stage, the potential helpers engage in cognitive algebra because they weigh the positive versus negative aspects of helping act (Fritzsche, Finkelstein and Penner, 2000). A person acts prosocially if the perceived profits (that is, rewards minus cost of helping), outweigh the profits of not helping. Rewards for being helpful are mainly provided by the emotions and beliefs of the helper but there are many types of potential costs. For example, you might be drowned while helping a person, who is himself drowning. A person may be asking to have a lift in your car simply as a trick leading to robbery or some worse event. Not helping a person in need may lead you to feel guilty. Such thoughts may influence whether or not you offer help. Dovidio et al. (1991) successfully tested these cost-benefit considerations that influence helping behaviour.

Piliavin et al. (1981) showed that decision to help is based on the following three considerations:

(vi) (i) Becoming physiologically aroused by the distress of the victim
(vii) (ii) Labelling the arousal as personal distress in oneself
(viii) (iii) Calculating the benefits and costs of helping and not helping

This is technically known as *arousal-cost-reward model*. The greater the level of arousal, the more likely the person will show readiness to help (Piliavin et al., 1981). The greater the potential rewards in comparison to potential costs to both the helper and the victim, the more likely is that the victim will be helped (Dovidio et al., 1991).

Thus, it is clear that to provide help in emergency situation is not a one-time decision, rather it involves a number of steps or decisions, and only if all of these decisions are positive, actual helping behaviour occur.

Although most of the helping behaviour occurs in the prescribed steps, there are some altruistic behaviours that occur quickly and perhaps even impulsively. For example, a person who jumps into an icy lake to save a drowning child is unlikely to have gone through these various steps. Rather such acts may be motivated by basic emotions and values having to do with human life and personal courage.

DETERMINANTS OF PROSOCIAL BEHAVIOUR

Helping behaviour is influenced by different sets of factors. Some of these factors are situational (external) and some are personal (or internal). Let us examine these factors in light of the researches done by social psychologists.

Situational (external) determinants of prosocial behaviour

There are some external or situational factors upon which social psychologists have given due attention. Important ones are as follows:

1. Modelling and prosocial behaviour: An important factor that promotes helping behaviour is *behavioural model,* where the person observes someone else who is providing help. In other words, the presence of helpful bystander provides a strong social model and the result is an increase in helping behaviour among the other bystanders, who are present there. Bryan and Test (1967) conducted an early field experiment to provide support for such observation. In this field experiment, a young woman (research assistant) with a flat tire parked her car near the road. It was observed that those persons were much more inclined to help that woman, who had previously occasioned a staged scene in which another woman with car trouble was observed receiving help. Another study found that the presence of a model increased adults' willingness to donate blood (Rushton and Campbell, 1977). Macaulay (1970) gave an additional support to Byran and Test's findings. She reported that contributions to a Salvation Army Collection Box increased considerably when a model was observed making a contribution.

Hornstein (1970) added a provision of usefulness of a model in inducing greater altruistic behaviour. In his study, participants observed a model returning a wallet. The model appeared either very pleased with being able to return the wallet or annoyed while doing so. When the participants were later put in a position to return a wallet, it was found that those, who had seen a pleased model, were more likely to provide help than those who had seen an unhappy model. Obviously then, it is not sufficient to observe someone helping; the model must enjoy his or her altruistic behaviour.

Modelling effects hold for children as well. Studies have consistently shown that when children are exposed to generous and helpful models, they behave more generously towards others than when they are exposed to selfish model (Lipscomb et al., 1982). In another study conducted by Lipscomb, McAllister and Bregman (1985), it was found that the children exposed to models, who behaved inconsistently (sometimes generously and sometimes selfishly), donated less than the children exposed to a consistently generous model, but more than the children exposed to consistently selfish model.

Researches have also shown that helpful models in media also enhance prosocial behaviour (Sprafkin, Liebert and Poulous, 1975). In a study conducted by Forge and Phemister (1987), the influence of positive models has been confirmed. In this research study, it was found that preschool children, who watched such prosocial shows as *Sesame Street* or *Barney and Friends,* were found to respond more in prosocial way than those children, who did not watch such shows.

The presence of a social model tends to increase helping behaviour due to the following reasons:

(i) A model opens eyes for the appropriate kind of acting that is possible or effective in the situation. Those who do not know how to help, can emulate the model.
(ii) A model provides information about the costs and risks involved in helping. By providing help under the condition of danger, a model demonstrates others that risks incurred are justified.
(iii) A model conveys message that offering help is appropriate in a particular situation. In fact, a helping model may enhance the salience of social responsibility norm. If the observer becomes aware of this norm, others may decide to help.

Models can also inhibit helping behaviour. If the models appear disinterested or unresponsive to a person, who is in the need of help, others are less likely to provide help (Smith et al., 1973). In fact, unresponsive models can produce an effect known as *audience inhibition,* where others fail to help because they fear of embarrassment (Latane et al., 1981).

2. Liking and prosocial behaviour: Liking also influences prosocial behaviour. When we like a person, and therefore, we are attracted towards him or her, chances of doing prosocial behaviour increases. In fact, any characteristic that promotes attraction also increases prosocial behaviour (Clark et al., 1987). When the victim is similar in age, sex, race, political ideologies, etc., we readily provide help to him or her (Dovidio, 1984). Likewise, physically attractive victim receives more help than a physically unattractive one (Piliavin and Unger, 1985). It has been shown with respect to race that whites are more likely to help other whites than blacks, even in the situations where refusing to help may be justified on non-racist grounds (Dovidio and Gaertner, 1981). Hornstein (1978) showed in the series of field studies that similarity of political ideologies and opinions promote helping behaviour. Researches have further shown that even superficial similarity such as similarity in mode of dress tend to enhance prosocial behaviour. Emswiller et al. (1971) found in their study that students (participants) complied with the requests more often when the confederate's mode of dress was similar to their own than when it was different.

3. Mimicry and prosocial behaviour: Mimicry also influences the helping behaviour. *Mimicry* means automatic tendency to imitate the behaviour of persons with whom interaction is done. Persons are found to mimic tone of the voice, rate of speech, postures, mannerisms and also mood of others

(Van Barren et al., 2004). Since mimicry enhances liking, empathy and rapport, it plays a key role in promoting prosocial behaviour. Van Barren et al. (2003) conducted a study, which substantiated the fact that mimicry increases prosocial behaviour. In this experiment, students were or were not mimicked while making interaction for six minutes with the experimenter. Subsequently, the experimenter accidentally dropped several pens on the floor. In another condition, a different person entered the room and dropped pens on the floor. Still in another condition following interaction, each student was paid two euros and later given option of keeping the money or donating some or all for a charity that would help hospitalised children. Results revealed that in each of these three experimental conditions, those who had been mimicked, were found to provide more help than those who were not mimicked.

4. Being rewarded in the past and prosocial behaviour: Tendency to engage in prosocial behaviour may depend on the way in which similar helping has been rewarded in the past. In our day-to-day life, we often find that when we are rewarded for doing helping behaviour (such as helping pretty old person in crossing a busy road and getting blessings from him), we tend to do so in future. Moss and Page (1972) conducted a study to find out a relationship between rewarded helping and subsequent helping. In this study, a passer-by was approached by a stranger (confederate) and asked direction for going to a particular place of the town. The request was complied. The stranger, who was actually an experimental confederate, responded by saying something positive such as 'thank you' or by grumbling, "I fail to understand what you are telling. I will have to ask someone else" or by saying something neutral such as 'OK'. Subsequently, the passer-by next saw a woman, who dropped a small bag on the ground and apparently failed to notice it. It was found that the people, who had been rewarded positively earlier (thank you condition), were much more likely to provide help in taking the lady her bag than were the people, who had been negatively reinforced (grumbling condition) last time when they had offered help. Results confirmed the fact that being rewarded in the past enhances helping behaviour.

5. Norms and prosocial behaviour: Almost every society has a norm that looking after others is valued and praised. One could, therefore, argue that helping behaviour is normative and behaving prosocially is rewarded in the society. Prosocial behaviour can be increased when the rules or norms of the situation allow the activity, which is consistent with helping victim. Staub (1970) conducted a study to substantiate the fact. They asked some children to sit alone in small room for drawing a picture. Each child made to believe that another child was sitting in the next room and was also drawing a picture. In one condition, the children were instructed to stay in their respective room. In another condition, the children were specially permitted to go into other room because there were extra pencils there. In both conditions, children heard a crash coming from the next room followed by a cry of girl, who supposedly sitting there. Results revealed that in the condition in which they were allowed to use the nearby room, about 50% provided help. In the condition, in which they had been asked to stay in their respective room, only 15% of the children broke the rule in an attempt to provide help to the victim. Staub's study was replicated with adult subjects by Ashton and Severy (1976) and similar results were reported.

Researches done by social psychologists have, in fact, proposed two main types of norms, which tend to determine helping behaviour—reciprocity and social responsibility. According to the *norm of reciprocity*, we should help all those who help us (Gross and Latane, 1974), that is, *tit-for-tat effect*. An experiment was conducted by Goranson and Berkowitz (1966) in which a favour was done by the experimenter, who was acting either voluntarily or was compelled to do so, for the participants. Later, the participants had a chance to help the experimenter. Results revealed that even when the subjects did not expect to see the experimenter again, they showed readiness to do a favour for him as he had previously done a favour for them. This effect was much more obvious and pronounced when the experimenter had done the favour voluntarily.

One important factor that limits the reciprocation of a favour is concerned with synchronisation of favour with the recipient's needs (Schopler, 1970). When a person offers help, which is in accord with the recipient's specific needs, then such favour is most likely to be reciprocated. But if the favour is a general one such as donation of money, it is looked up with suspicion by the recipient. Similarly, if the magnitude of the favour far exceeds the requirements of the situation, it is most likely to be attributed to donor's needs and is not likely to be reciprocated.

Another norm is the *norm of social responsibility*, which specifies that we should always offer help to those in need, irrespective of the possibility of future repayment (Schwartz, 1975). Fiske (1991) reported that in western societies, even very valuable resources such as land and water are given to those in need. Miller et al. (1990) made a comparative study of the norm of social responsibility in Hindu Indians and Americans. It was found that Americans were much less likely to believe in moral obligation to help other with a moderate need, whereas Hindu Indians do have a strong feeling of such type of moral obligation to help others with a moderate need.

In contrast to social norms, moral norms have also been found to influence the prosocial behaviour. Van der Linden (2011) found that moral norms were the single most important predictor of the desire to donate to charity. The researches further argue that the prosocial behaviour such as charitable givings are often guided by personal feeling of what is right thing to do in a given situation. When prosocial behaviour like charitable giving takes place in a private setting (that is, in absence of any social pressure) such behaviour is likely to be guided by internal moral considerations.

6. Responsibility for the problem (deservingness) and prosocial behaviour: In general, we are less likely to provide help to the strangers if we come to believe that by their own misdeeds or faults, the strangers have been trapped (Higgins and Shaw, 1999; Weiner, 1980). However, if we have clear reason to believe that the stranger is an innocent person and there is no fault of his, we are readily inclined to help him. The study conducted by Weiner, Perry and Magnusson (1988) showed that students were less sympathetic and were less likely to provide help to a person, who developed deadly disease AIDS through promiscuous sexual contact than through a blood transfusion. The common observation has been that the need viewed as stemming from illegitimate sources undermines the prosocial behaviour by blocking empathic concern, blocking our sense of normative obligation and increasing the possibility of condemnation. Thus, the attribution we make about the people in need is an important determinant and this supports what is called *just world hypothesis*, which clearly states that people get what they deserve, that is, bad things happen to only those people who deserve misfortune and good people face only happy encounter or events. Sometimes, this belief becomes so powerful that it adversely affect judgement about innocent victims of rape and sexual assault. If a person has a strong faith in just world hypothesis, he tends to refuse to help others. Miller (1977) substantiated this fact in his study. In this study, students were asked to donate payments meant for their research participants to needy families. The study was started just before Christmas and some students were told that the department of psychology was raising money for families in need of help over Christmas, whereas some other students were raising fund for families having year-round needs.

Results revealed that students with a weak just world hypothesis gave the same amount, regardless of the information they had been given about the participants. In fact, those participants, who were having a strong faith in just world hypothesis, donated more for the temporary specific needs of the poor families at Christmas and much less for those, who were always in the need of financial assistance year-round. Recently, Warren and Walker (1991) also reported similar findings from their study by showing that those with a strong belief are much less likely to give in cases of continuous needs because they feel that such people are themselves responsible for their fate or condition.

7. Time pressures and prosocial behaviour: Time pressure also affects prosocial behaviour. In general, people, who are in hurry for attending their business or work, are less likely to help someone in need than the people who are not in a hurry. Darley and Batson (1973) conducted a study in which individual male students were asked to go to the other nearby building, where they were to give a short talk. Some students were told to hurry because they were already late and the researcher was waiting there. Some other students were told that they can take time as they like and talk would not begin for next several minutes. As the students went from one building to other nearby building, they encountered a man slumped in doorway coughing and groaning. The experimenters were interested in seeing whether the students would offer help to the slumped man. Results showed that only 10% of those in hurry helped the slumped man, whereas 63% of those, who were not in hurry, provided help. Obviously then, time pressure had an impact upon helping behaviour. In fact, time pressures caused some participants to overlook the needs of victim. Another factor that might have influenced was conflict about whom to help—the victim or the experimenter. The possibility that conflict might have affected the helping behaviour was supported by another study conducted by Batson et al. (1978) using a similar design. In this study, some male students were sent individually to another nearby building for interacting with computer. Some were told to hurry and some others were not. Besides, some were led to believe that their participation was of vital importance for the researcher, whereas others were told that their participation data was not essential. As student walked to the nearby building, he encountered a male slumped on the stairs, coughing and groaning. Then, the question was—would the subject help this victim? Results showed that only 40% of those students, who were in hurry, provided help to the victim, whereas 65% of those, who had no time pressures, provided help. This result was for those students, who considered research participation important and essential one. On the other hand, when the research participation was not considered important, the subjects in hurry were as likely to help (70%) as those not in hurry (80%). The results clearly showed that subjects also weighed the costs and benefits to both experimenter and victim before arriving at a final decision.

8. Environmental conditions: Environmental conditions, particularly weather and city size, are found to influence helping behaviour. Cunningham (1979) studied the effect of weather on helping behaviour in two popular field studies. In the first field study, some pedestrians were approached outdoors with a request to complete a questionnaire. It was found that the pedestrians were found to provide more help when the day was sunny and temperature was comfortable. In the second field study, it was found that in climate-controlled restaurant, customers left more helpful and generous tips when the sun was shining. Likewise, Ahmed (1979) reported that when the weather was sunny rather than rainy, people provided more help to a stranded motorist.

City size has also been found to affect helping behaviour. Levine et al. (1994) showed that strangers were more likely to be helped in small towns than in large towns. Amato (1983) studied helping behaviour in 55 Australian communities ranging from small villages to major cities. In this study, five different types of helping behaviour were studied—a student asking pedestrians for writing their favourite colour (colour request), a pedestrian inadvertently dropping an envelope on the road (dropped envelope), a man requesting for donating money to the multiple sclerosis society (donation for society), a salesman, obviously giving wrong directions to someone (correcting inaccurate directions) and man with bandaged leg crying out in pain (hurt leg). Results revealed that in the four out of the five measures of help, the percentage of people who helped was significantly greater in small towns as compared to the larger cities.

9. Number of bystanders and prosocial behaviour: Prosocial behaviour is also influenced by the number of bystanders (potential helpers). Researches have shown that as the number of bystander increases, the likelihood that any one bystander will help a victim decreases (Latane and Darley, 1970; Latane and Nida, 1981). Such effect has been termed by the social psychologists as *bystander effect*. In the experiment conducted by Latane and Rodin (1969), the participants heard a loud crash from the next door followed by a woman screaming and crying for help due to pain in her ankle. In the experiment conducted by Darley and Latane (1968), the individuals participating in a discussion over an intercom suddenly heard someone in their group choking, gasping and calling for help, apparently affected by an epileptic seizure. In both these experiments, similar findings emerged. As the number of bystanders increased, the likelihood that anyone would help the victim sharply decreased. In fact, bystanders were found to help most often and most quickly when they were alone with the victim. When many other potential helpers were present, it inhibited the intervention in the emergency.

Now, the question—why does the presence of other potential helpers inhibit the helping behaviour? Social psychologists have provided three different types of explanations (mentioned below) for explaining bystander effect.

(i) ***Diffusion of responsibility:*** One explanation is in terms of diffusion of responsibility, which is created by the presence of several potential helpers. When only one bystander is present and witnesses an emergency, the responsibility to intervene is focused wholly on that individual. But when there are many bystanders, the responsibility to intervene is shared. Here, obligation to help and potential costs of failing to help are also shared. Experiments have supported the idea that it is not simply the number of people present that is important, rather the lessened feelings of personal responsibility that result from being in the group is also important (Ross, 1971). Researches have further shown that the diffusion of responsibility occurs only when a bystander believes that the other persons or witnesses are capable of providing help. A person diffuses responsibility in lesser degree to the witnesses, who are too far away to take effective action or too young to cope with the emergency (Bickman, 1971). Despite the presence of others having a strong effect on helping, bystander effect can also be enhanced merely by thinking about the presence of other people even if they are not there. This effect is known as *implicit bystander effect* (Gracia et al., 2002). In such cases, if the persons are primed to think about themselves as part of a group of friends, and subsequently, confront a situation that calls for their help, they are less likely to provide help than if they have not been primed. Thus, implicit bystander effect points out clearly that each person's individual contribution in helping situation is important.

(ii) ***Interpreting the situation:*** A second explanation for the bystander effect is in terms of ambiguity in the interpretation of the situation. Bystanders are sometimes uncertain if a particular situation is actually an emergent one. If others ignore the situation or act as if nothing is happening, we, too, may assume that no emergency exists and do not show any readiness for helping the victim. In fact, bystanders often try to appear calm and avoid overt signs of worry until they see whether others are alarmed or not. Through such behaviour, they unintentionally encourage each other to define the situation as not problematic. Thus, they inhibit each other from helping. The impact of bystanders on interpreting a situation was demonstrated by Latane and Darley (1970). In this experiment, college students started completing a questionnaire. After a few minutes, smoke began to enter the room through the air vent. Soon, the smoke became so thick that it was difficult to see anything and breathe normally. In the condition, where the subjects were alone, they usually walked around the room to investigate the smoke and about 75% reported the smoke to the researcher within 5 minutes. In another condition, where the real subject was present in the room with two other confederates, who had been instructed to ignore the smoke, only 10% reported about the smoke. There are researches, however, showing the fact that increasing the number of bystanders does not inhibit individual helping behaviour under certain conditions such as when observation shows that others are indeed alarmed (Darley, Teger and Lewis, 1973) and when the need for help is so vague that others' reactions are unnecessary to define the situation (Clark and Word, 1972).

(iii) *Evaluation apprehension:* This refers to the concern about what others expect of them and how others will evaluate their behaviour. Researches have shown that evaluation apprehension can either inhibit or promote helping behaviour. Evaluation apprehension inhibits helping behaviour when the bystanders feel that the others may view their intervention as foolish or wrong one. When the bystanders find that the others see no need to intervene or even oppose intervention, intervention by them will be a foolish act. On the other hand, when there are no cues suggesting that other witnesses are opposing intervention, evaluation apprehension promotes helping. In such a situation, bystanders tend to assume that others are approving intervention. In laboratory study demonstrating such effect, bystanders witnessed a convulsive nervous seizure or a violent assault (Schwartz and Goftlieb, 1980). In such a situation, the knowledge that others are watching tend to increase our tendency to help the victim.

Personal (internal) determinants of prosocial behaviour

There are some internal or personal determinants of prosocial behaviour. Several such factors have already been discussed while discussing the steps of bystander intervention. Besides, other internal factors to be discussed include genetic factor, emotional states, empathy and some personality factors. These are discussed below:

1. Genetic factors: Sociobiological approach emphasises that we have an innate tendency to help others, possibly as an evolutionary survival tactic (Barath, 1977). Although it is true that altruistic behaviour will not have a survival value for an individual, altruistic acts can increase the survival of one's genes if those altruistic behaviours are directed toward others, who tend to share the same genes or helping blood relatives. This is known as *kinship selection theory* (Meyer, 2000; Cialdini et al., 1995; Pinker, 1998). In fact, kinship selection helps some of our own genes to survive and Burnstein et al. (1994) found that intention to help in situations of serious danger is stronger between kinsmen. As the blood relatives share many genes with altruistic individual, the reproduction of these relatives passes many of own altruistic genes to the next generation (Krebs and Miller, 1985). Many studies, in general, have supported the fact that we are more likely to help others, who are closely related to us than the people who are not related (Neyer and Lang, 2003). In this regard, a series of studies was conducted by Burnstein, Crandall and Kitayama (1994). In these studies, the participants were asked to whom they would help in emergency. As predicted on the basis of genetic similarity, the participants were found to express the view that they would help a close relative than either a distant relative or stranger. Not only that, they further expressed the view that they would provide help to younger relatives who have many years of reproductive life ahead than those who are old ones. Thus, an innate biological drive for helping behaviour has evolutionary value (Dawkins, 1985). But sometimes, blood relatives do not help each other and they often help those who are not related to them at all. How is it explained by genetic factor? Sociobiologists explain helping unrelated people by proposing that helping involves reciprocity. If I help you, you will help me, and thus, both of us increase our chances of surviving long enough for reproducing our genes.

2. Emotional states: Emotional states of the potential helper may be positive or negative. Positive emotional state creates good mood and negative emotional state creates bad mood. A body of research has shown that people in good mood tend to display higher level of prosocial behaviour. Good mood promotes both spontaneous helping and compliance requests for help. In a study conducted by Isen (1970), it was found that suburban school teachers, who got feedback that they scored well on the tests, donated more to school library fund than the teachers, who received no feedback on their performance. Likewise, Isen and Levin (1972) reported that people showed more readiness to help a stranded caller, who had dialled a wrong number from a pay phone, if they had just received a gift than if they had received no gift. Some other mood-enhancing experiences that are generally found to increase helping behaviour include hearing good news from radio or someone else, recalling happy experiences, reading statements describing pleasant feelings, listening to good music and enjoying good weather.

There are some obvious reasons why being in good mood increase the probability to do prosocial behaviour. First, since people in good mood are less concerned with their problems and are less preoccupied with themselves, they concentrate more on needs and problems of others. Such attention generally creates empathy, which often leads to helping. Second, people in good mood tend to view the world in positive light and tend to maintain the glow of happiness. By offering help to others, they maintain and even increase this happiness. Third, people in good mood often feel more fortunate as compared to others, who are deprived of good mood. They recognise that their good fortune is out of balance with others' need and to maintain this balance, they use their resources more and more for helping others (Rosenhan, Salovey and Hargis, 1981).

However, there are evidences where positive moods can decrease prosocial responding (Isen, 1984). A person in positive mood, when encounters an ambiguous emergency situation, tends to view the situation as non-emergent one. Even if he perceives the situation emergent one, the positive mood tends to resist prosocial behaviour as it would involve something unpleasant and difficult actions, which may reduce his pleasant feelings (Baron, Branscombe, Byrne and Bhardwaj, 2010).

Negative emotional states create negative mood and this is likely to reduce helping behaviour. A person in negative mood focuses on his or her problems, and therefore, is less likely to engage in prosocial behaviour (Amato, 1986). Those in bad moods like feeling sad or depressed, focus inwards on their difficulties and anxieties (Berkowitz, 1970) and they are less concerned with other's distress, and therefore, are less inclined to help others (Weyant, 1978). However, one exception to this phenomenon is the feeling of guilt. Researches have shown that when guilt is induced within the person, it increases the likelihood of guilty person helping more and more. Regan et al. (1972) conducted a study in which the participants were led to think that they had broken an expensive camera, and then, they were given an opportunity to help someone, who had dropped a pile of groceries. Results revealed that those, who had experienced guilt, provided help, while only 15% of the participants among whom no guilt was induced (control group participants) stopped to help. Such effect has been replicated in many other studies (Salovey et al., 1991). Explaining why guilty people help more, Baumeister et al., (1994) said that guilt functions to knit together interpersonal relationship. If the person feels guilty about something, he always seeks an opportunity to strengthen any social relationship he comes across ever.

Negative mood sometimes promotes helping behaviour. If the person is in bad mood, but the act of helping allows him to feel better, a prosocial behaviour is most likely to occur (Cialdini, Kendrick and Bauman, 1982). Likewise, if negative feelings are not intense, the emergency is clearly visible and if the helping behaviour is interesting and satisfying rather than dull and unrewarding, the person is likely to help others (Cunningham et al., 1990). To explain how bad mood promotes helping act, Cialdini et al. (1973, 1987) formulated the *negative-state relief hypothesis*. This hypothesis rests upon two basic assumptions—first, people experiencing negative mood such as depression or sadness are motivated to reduce them and second, many persons have learned from childhood that helping others improve their own mood through receiving thanks and praise. The hypothesis predicts that when person of this type goes in bad mood, they try to help others primarily as a means of boosting their own spirits. In reality, this is an egoistic motive for helping rather than an altruistic motive because persons are trying to provide help mainly to relieve themselves of sadness or depression rather than reducing others' sufferings.

3. Empathy: *Empathy* refers to the vicarious experience of an emotion, which is congruent with or possibly identical to the emotion that another person is experiencing (Eisenberg and Miller, 1987). In other words, *empathy* can be defined as an emotional response and understanding of another person's distress. A person in empathy feels what another person is feeling and also understands why that person feels as he or she does (Darley, 1993; Duan, 2000).

Empathy is enhanced by various situational factors. Believing that victim is similar to oneself whether in race, attitude and personality, promotes empathy, which in turn, promotes helping behaviour. Empathy can also be heightened by role expectations that expressly induce role-taking (Shott, 1979). Researches have shown that when the observers actively try to imagine how another person feels rather than simply observing how that person reacts, both empathy and helping behaviour increase (Toi and Batson, 1982). Several studies have shown that higher level of empathy produces greater help-giving behaviour (Batson et al., 1983; Dovidio, Allen and Schroeder, 1990; Eisenberg and Miller, 1987).

Empathy consists of two components—affective component and cognitive component. *Affective component* means to feel distress in response to the distress of others as well as feeling sympathetic. Researchers have shown that affective component of empathy is found among infants, (Brothers, 1990) among primates (Ungerer et al., 1990) as well as among dogs and dolphins (Azar, 1997). The *cognitive component* of empathy is comparatively a unique human quality that develops after we progress infancy. The cognitive component includes ability to consider the viewpoint of another person. It is also called *perspective taking*. Altruistic behaviour much depends on this perspective taking because this leads to empathetic concern for the person in need. If the perspective of the victim is not taken into account, personal distress is produced, and then, motive for helping becomes egoistic, since helping is offered purely as a means to reduce one's own personal distress (Batson and Oleson; 1991). Batson's model has been outlined in Figure 15.2.

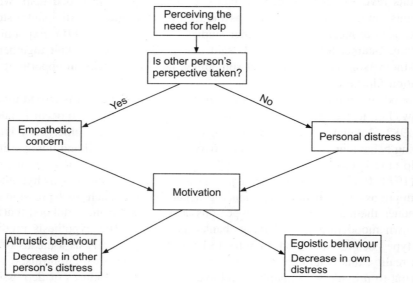

Figure 15.2 Empathy-altruism model based on suggestions by Batson (1991).

Empathy-altruism model developed by Batson attempts to address the motivational link between empathy and prosocial behaviour. The model proposes that a person can experience two distinct states of emotional arousal after seeing the victim—personal distress and empathy. *Personal distress* incorporates unpleasant emotions such as worry, alarm and being shocked when seeing the victim, whereas *empathy* involves emotions like compassion, warmth and tenderness towards the other (Batson and Coke, 1981). These two emotional states give rise to two different motivations (see Figure 15.2). Suppose the bystander experiences personal distress at the sight of victim's condition. He may be motivated to reduce this unpleasant emotion and offer help to the victim. Here, he provides help to the victim no doubt, but the fundamental motive is to reduce his own distress (that is, an egoistic motive and not an altruistic motive). On the other hand, suppose the situation is such where bystander experiences empathy after seeing the condition of victim. Because of such empathic feeling which contains compassion, tenderness, sympathy and like, he may be motivated to offer help to the victim. Here, he is providing help to the victim and this act is fundamentally being motivated by the desire to reduce the other's distress (that is, an altruistic motive and not an egoistic motive). Thus, arousal states of personal distress and empathy give rise to different motives and either one encourages helping behaviour. Batson et al. (1983) conducted an experiment to test this prediction. In this experiment, the participants served as observers, who watched another participant (who did the role of worker) over closed-circuit television. The worker performed a sequence of 10-digit recall trials and was administered electric shocks at random intervals. When these shocks were applied, the worker reacted with expression of pain. There were two conditions in the experiment—easy escape condition and difficult escape condition. In the *easy escape condition,* the participants were instructed that they need to watch only the first two trials, and then, were free to leave if they liked. In the *difficult escape condition,* the participants were instructed to stay and watch all 10 trials. After the second trial, all participants completed a questionnaire that contained adjective scales measuring their feelings towards the worker. Some of these adjectives reflected personal distress (such as worried, disturbed, upset, etc.), whereas other adjectives reflected empathy (such as sympathetic, compassionate, moved, etc.). After completing the questionnaire, the participants were told that since the worker had now an unbearable traumatic experience, they may help the worker by taking the remaining shock trials in their place. Results revealed that the participants' willingness to take the shocks depended on the predominant emotional response (empathy or distress) and on the ease of escape (easy or difficult). It was clearly found that when empathy was high, the frequency of helping behaviour was high, irrespective of whether the escape was easy or difficult. However, when the level of distress was high, the frequency of helping behaviour dropped off substantially and the escape was easy, that is, the participants left the situation rather than taking the shocks themselves. Such results confirmed the prediction of empathy-altruism model.

Feeling of empathy sometimes complicates the situation when there are multiple victims, who need help at the same time. In such a situation, we resort to what is called *selective altruism,* where we help only one and ignore the others (Batson et al., 1999). For example, when several children, with their sad appearance, ask for help, we generally resort to selective altruism, where any one or two is selected for help and others are ignored.

4. Personality factors: Researches have shown that there are certain personality factors/variables, which are associated with prosocial behaviour. People, who possess high degree of interpersonal trust, engage in more prosocial behaviour than the people, who have low degree of interpersonal trust, and therefore, mistrust others (Cadenhead and Richman, 1996). Likewise, McHoskey (1999) reported that the people, who are high on Machiavellianism dimension of personality, engage in lesser degree of prosocial behaviour as compared to the people, who are low on this dimension. Machiavellianism is a composite name for being distrustful, cynical, egocentric, manipulative and controlling. Based on the findings of various researches, social psychologists have developed a concept of altruistic personality, which includes several dispositional variables associated with prosocial act (Eisenberg et al., 2002; Graziano et al., 2004). These variables are as under:

(i) *Empathy:* Persons engaged in prosocial behaviour are high on the dimension of empathy. In other words, such persons are self-controlled, tolerant, socialised, conforming and motivated to make a good impression before others. People, who are more empathetic, naturally tend to be more emotionally moved by others' sufferings, and therefore, more motivated to help others.

(ii) *Social responsibility:* People, who frequently engage in prosocial act, have belief that each and every person has responsibility for doing his best to help others in need.

(iii) *Internal locus of control:* People, who provide help to others, have internal locus of control and a belief that a person can easily choose to behave in such a way that tends to maximise good outcomes and minimise bad ones. On the other hand, the people, who do not provide help, tend to have external locus of control, with belief that behaviours are controlled by luck, fate and other uncontrollable factors.

(iv) **Belief in just world:** People, who do prosocial acts, perceive the world as a fair and predictable place in which good behaviour is rewarded and bad behaviour is punished. Such belief leads to the conclusion that helping those who are in need is a good deed and it will actually benefit the people, who help.

(v) **Low egocentrism:** People, who do prosocial act, do have lower degree of egocentrism and are less self-absorbed and competitive.

(vi) **Self-efficacy:** Self-efficacy is the belief that one's actions are likely to be successful (Granziano and Eisenberg, 1997). Once empathetic feelings are aroused, the belief that one can effectively help becomes crucial in setting helping behaviour in motion. Colby and Damon (1995) demonstrated that like empathy, self-efficacy is also related to small and short-term forms of help as well as long-term forms of help.

Conclusively, it can be said that prosocial behaviour is influenced by a host of external and internal factors.

BASIC MOTIVATION BEHIND PROSOCIAL ACTS: THEORIES

Based on the various researches, some explanations of the motivation underlying prosocial behaviour have been outlined by the social psychologists. To answer the question why anyone would ever be motivated to engage in prosocial behaviour, several psychological theories have been proposed. Here, we shall concentrate on the following five major explanations:

1. Empathy-altruism model: As discussed earlier too, this model was developed by Batson et al. (1981). According to this model, at least, some prosocial acts are solely motivated by the desire to help someone in need. When people observe emergency, empathy is aroused and they provide help simply because the victim needs help and they feel good to provide help. Motivation aroused by empathy can be so strong that the helper is willing to engage in unpleasant, dangerous and even in life-threatening behaviour (Batson et al., 1995). In fact, compassion for someone in need outweighs all other considerations (Batson et al., 1995). (For detailed discussion of this model, see previous section.)

2. Negative-state relief model: Sometimes, we help because the person in need or distress makes us feel so bad, producing negative emotions that we are, in a way, forced to reduce our negative emotions. This explanation of prosocial behaviour is called *negative-state relief model* (Cialdini, Baumann and Kenrick, 1981). Thus, according to this model, when we see someone in trouble such as mangled bodies of victim in plane crash, whose son or daughter has disappeared, a personal distress is created in us. *Personal distress* means our own emotional reaction to the plight of others such as our feelings of shock, horror, alarm or helplessness. Such personal distress upsets us and produces anxiety. People help the victim in order to improve their mood by reducing negative emotions through offering help (Dietrich and Berkowitz, 1997). Various other researches have shown that negative emotions increase the occurrence of helpful behaviour (Fultz, Schaller and Cialdini, 1988).

However, it is also said that there is no necessary connection between personal distress and prosocial behaviour. Helping behaviour motivated by our desire to reduce our own personal distress and discomfort is egoistic and not altruistic.

3. Empathetic joy hypothesis: This hypothesis states that the prosocial behaviour is motivated by the positive emotion a helper expects as a result of having a beneficial impact on the person in need. Here, helping behaviour is primarily motivated because helper is interested in producing positive impact upon the life of victim. Obviously, one implication of empathetic joy hypothesis is that it is crucial for the helper to know that his or her actions had a positive impact on the victim. If, however, helping is entirely based upon empathy, feedback about its effects would carry no meaning. To test such prediction of empathy joy hypothesis, Smith, Keating and Stotland (1989) conducted a study. In this study, research participants watched a videotape in which a female student was found saying that she might drop out of college because she felt isolated and distressed. She was described as either very similar to the participants (condition of high sympathy) or very dissimilar to the participants (condition of low sympathy). After watching the videotape, the participants were given opportunity to offer some helpful advice. Some participants were told that they would be provided feedback regarding the effectiveness of their advice, while others were told that they would not be able to know what the female student actually decided to do. Results revealed that empathy alone was not enough to elicit prosocial behaviour. Participants were found to be helpful only if there was higher empathy and feedback about the impact of their advice. Results of the study confirmed the reality of empathic joy hypothesis.

It is worthy to note that all these three theoretical models explaining motivation behind prosocial acts rest on the assumption that people engage in prosocial behaviour either because they feel good or because it makes them feel less bad or experience less negative emotion.

4. Competitive altruism approach: Carrying the above general idea a step ahead, some investigators have pointed out that prosocial behaviour can sometimes be motivated by self-interest, that is, people help others with an expectation of reciprocation from persons being helped, along with various possible rewards. Such perspective on prosocial behaviour is called *competitive altruism approach*, which states that helping others boosts the own status and reputation of the helper and it brings him large benefits, which generally offset the costs of engaging in prosocial behaviour. Such people, who help others substantially, are not only respected by others but also are conferred high status, which in future, brings many advantages. There are many examples of people, who donate large amount to the universities and are treated like VVIP when they visit their alma mater, and sometimes, the buildings are even named after him. In the University of Delhi, Ratan Tata Library is one such popular example.

Explanations provided by the competitive altruism approach were supported by the research study conducted by Hardy and Van Vugt (2006). In this study, the high school students were the participants. These students participated in a game in which players could earn money for themselves or for the entire group. At the start, participants were given one hundred pence and were told that they could contribute any amount from zero to one hundred pence to private fund, which they would be keeping as individual and any amount they wished to the group or public fund. There were two conditions—reputation condition and no reputation condition. In *reputation condition*, participants were given information regarding other players' contribution to both public and private funds and were told that information about their contributions would also be provided to the other players. Thus, in this condition, donating to the group fund could bring enhanced status and reputation to the donors. In *no reputation condition*, the participants received no information on other players' choice, and therefore, donating to the group would not necessarily boost the donor's reputation and status. Results revealed that in the reputation condition, the more each one donated, the higher was his or her status. In the no reputation condition, the prosocial behaviour, that is, donating to the group fund, had no impact upon status. Results provided support for the competitive altruism approach. Researches done by Flynn et al. (2006) also showed that most of the time people engaged in prosocial behaviour as a way of boosting their status and reputations.

Conclusively, it can be said that one important motive behind engaging in prosocial behaviour is the desire to boost one's own status and reputation.

5. Genetic determinism model: This model explains prosocial behaviour in terms of our genes. Some light has already been thrown on this explanation in previous section of this chapter. The central idea of this model is that we are, in general, more likely to help others to whom we are biologically related in comparison to those people to whom we are not related (Neyer and Lang, 2003). This is called *kin selection theory*. Burnstein, Crandall and Kitayama (1994) conducted a series of studies in which the participants were asked whom they would choose to help in emergency. It was found that the participants, on the basis of genetic similarly, told that they would help those who were their close relative than either a distant relative or non-relative. Not only that, it was also found that the participants expressed a view that they were more likely to help young relatives, who have many years of reproductive life ahead than the older ones, who have crossed their productive period. This is because of the fact that the key goal of human beings is getting their genes transmitted to the next generation.

One trouble with genetic determinism model is that we do not just help our biological relatives, rather we also help people who are not biologically related to us. Why do we do so? According to genetic determinism model, this cannot be considered as adaptive behaviour because it no longer helps us in transmitting our genes to the next generations. However, answer to this question is provided by *reciprocal determination theory*, which states that we help others who are not related to us because helping is usually reciprocated. If we help others, they will also help us; so, we ultimately get benefitted and chances of our survival are increased.

Thus, we find that there are different factors and different types of motivation that contribute to the prosocial behaviour.

HOW CAN HELPING BEHAVIOUR BE INCREASED?

Social psychologists have given a serious thought over the issue of enhancing helping behaviour in society. Helping is essential for the group life and social functioning and insights from various researches have shown us how to increase both the giving help and our chances of receiving it when we are actually in need. Some of the important ways through which prosocial behaviour can be enhanced are as under:

1. Reducing ambiguity—Making the need for help and cooperation clear: Ambiguous situation generally reduces prosocial behaviour because the helper fails to understand the need of the victim. Thus, when you are in trouble and need the help of others, do not expect that passer-by can see and automatically provide help. Therefore, the wise step would be to make your need obvious by shouting 'help me'. Thus, when there remains no ambiguity, it is very likely that the potential helper or passer-by will provide help. The benefits of making the need for help clear has been demonstrated in a series of studies of why people report crimes (Bickman, 1979; Bickman and Rosenbaum, 1977). In this series, the participants witnessed a staged shoplifting, which an experimental confederate interpreted for one group of participants by saying "Look at her, she is shoplifting. She put that in her purse". However, with another group of participants, he remained silent. Results revealed that the participants, who had the events interpreted for them, were more likely to report the crime than those who did not.

2. Teaching norms that support helping and cooperation: Norms that support helping and cooperation can be taught in the society. Families and schools can teach norms supporting social responsibility and helping behaviour. They can also enhance helping behaviour by personal examples or models (Rushton, 1975). Children can learn to be altruistic, friendly and self-controlled by looking at television programmes depicting such behaviour patterns because seeing promotes doing (Johnston and Ettema, 1986). In a popular study conducted by Stein and Friedrich (1972), it was found that pre-schoolers, who watched such episodes that promoted compassion and cooperative social values, were found to be more helpful than the children, who witnessed neutral or aggressive programmes. In another significant study, Hearold (1986) statistically combined 18 comparisons of prosocial programmes with neutral programmes. She found that on an average, if the viewer witnessed prosocial programmes instead of neutral programmes, he was found to be elevated from the 50th to the 74th percentile in prosocial behaviour. Likewise, models like the heroic rescuers providing help to others in emergency situations as portrayed in various TV shows were also found to increase the accessibility of norms supporting helping and displaying various ways to help and make clear the good consequences of helping (Krebs, 1970).

3. Increasing internal attributions for helping and cooperation: Another way to increase helping and friendly behaviour is to foster helpful self-concept so that the motivation would remain internal rather than external. Researches have shown that such internal attribution tends to increase prosocial behaviour. Batson et al. (1978) and Batson et al. (1987) vividly showed that people doing good deeds for their own sake rather than for external rewards do engage themselves more in prosocial behaviour and they often get themselves booked for helping behaviour. In these series of researches, the investigators led people to attribute to a helpful act either to the external factors or to their own compassion. When they were asked to help on unrelated task, the participants, who had labelled themselves as compassionate, provided more help than those, who had attributed the helpful act to some external factors. Piliavin et al. (1982), likewise, showed that people, who thought of themselves as helpful, were more likely to help again when the time came. Thus, if internal attribution for helping and cooperation is enhanced, it is very likely that the prosocial behaviour will also be increased.

4. Activating prosocial norms: Social norms that support helping need to be activated or brought to mind before they can guide behaviour. One such norm is social responsibility norm, which is the belief that people should help those who need help without thinking of future exchange (Schwartz, 1975). In India, where there is relatively collectivist culture, the people support the social responsibility norm more strongly than the people of individualist culture of west (Baron and Miller, 2000). Researches have shown that activating norms like 'everyone should do his share' or 'every individual makes a difference' tend to enhance prosocial behaviour for collective rather than individual good. When people are made self-aware, these norms are activated and people show readiness towards helping. A study conducted by Duval, Duval and Neely (1979) showed that the women, who had just seen their own image on a television monitor, were more likely to volunteer their time, money and efforts for a needy cause than the others.

5. Increasing responsibility: Researches have confirmed the fact that focusing responsibility on specific people makes normative pressures to provide more and more help just as diffusing responsibility among many people lessens one's feelings to help others. Therefore, if one is interested in getting help, it should be made clear the person who wants help (Moriarty, 1975). Social psychologists are of view that a personal approach makes one feel less anonymous and more responsible. Jason et al. (1984) conducted a study in which it was found that personal appeals for blood donation are much more effective than posters and media announcements provided such personal appeals come from friends. Non-verbal appeals have also been found to be effective when they are personalised (Omoto and Synder, 2002).

6. Promoting identification to those who need help and cooperation: A feeling of identification and connectedness with the person in need breeds empathy, which in turn, increases helping behaviour. The obvious principle that we help others to whom we are connected works clearly with kin, friends and in-groups. The connectedness is what motivates helping as an end in itself, and therefore, can sustain helping even if no personal rewards are involved. This is the reason, why the various kinds of religious faith, which promote connectedness among all humankind, do act as a powerful motivator for providing help to those, who are in need for getting help.

Thus, we find that there are various ways through which helping behaviour can be increased.

Summary and Review

- *Altruism* means an unselfish concern for the benefit and welfare of others. In other words, altruism means performing an act voluntarily to help someone else when there is no expectation of rewards in any form, except the feeling of having done a good and positive deed. Altruism is distinct and opposite of egoism, which is characterised by a refusal to become concerned about anything except oneself and one's own interest. All prosocial behaviour may or may not be altruistic. In fact, some are altruistic and some are egoistic.
- Following a decision-tree analysis, there are five steps of bystander intervention. The first is to notice or fail to notice the critical incident, the second step is interpreting an event as emergency, the third step is deciding about personal responsibility to provide help, the fourth step is deciding about the knowledge or skills to help and the fifth step is taking a final decision to help.
- There are two sets of factors that influence prosocial behaviour. One set of factors contains situational or external factors and other set of factors contains personal or internal factors. Situational or external factors include modelling, liking, mimicry, being rewarded in the past, social norms, responsibility, time pressures, environmental conditions, number of bystanders, etc. Internal or personal factors include genetic factors, emotional states, empathy, personality factors, etc.
- Social psychologists have provided some motivational explanations for prosocial behaviour. Five such explanations have been provided—empathy-altruism model, negative-state relief model, empathetic joy hypothesis, competitive altruism approach and genetic determinism model.
- Social psychologists have also concentrated on ways to increase helping behaviour. Some of the preferred ways to increase helping behaviour are reducing ambiguity, teaching norms that support helping and cooperation, increasing internal attributions for helping, activating prosocial norms, increasing responsibility and providing identification to those, who need help and cooperation.

Review Questions

1. Define altruism. Make distinction between altruism, egoism and heroism.
2. With example, discuss the major steps involved in bystander intervention.
3. Citing relevant studies, discuss the major situational determinants of helping behaviour.
4. Citing relevant studies, discuss the major internal factors that influence helping behaviour.
5. Outline a plan for increasing helping behaviour.
6. Write short notes on the following:
    (i) Empathy altruism model
    (ii) Negative-state relief model
7. Discuss the major motivational theories that account for helping behaviour.

16 LANGUAGE AND COMMUNICATION

Learning Objectives

- Language: Properties and Structure
- Functions of Language
- Critical Period Hypothesis
- Linguistic Hierarchy
- Theories of Language Development
- Language and Thought
- Diversity in Language Acquisition among Indian Children
- Language Acquisition and Theory of Mind
- Bilingualism/Multilingualism in Indian Society
- Reading Acquisition among Indian Children
- Gender Differences in Verbal Communication
- Barriers to Verbal Communication
- Nature and Purpose of Communication
- Models of Communication
- Communication Network
- Non-verbal Communication
- Combining Verbal and Non-verbal Communication
- Gender Differences in Non-verbal Communication
- Communication and Social Structure

Key Terms

Bilingualism
Chain network
Circle network
Code mixing
Code switching
Comcon network
Communication network
Critical period hypothesis
Deep structure
Encoder-decoder model
Enculturation model
Face structure
First language learning
Hollow organism
Inconsistent information
Intentionalist model
Intersubjectivity
Kinesics
Language acquisition device (LAD)
Language mixing
Linguistic hierarchy
Linguistic intergroup bias
Linguistic relativity hypothesis
Mand responses

Morphemes	Pre-intellectual language	Stage of orthographic
Multilingualism	Prelinguistic vocalisation	Syntax
Non-verbal communication	Proxemics	Tact responses
Paralanguage	Second language learning	Theory of mind (ToM)
Perspective-taking model	Semantics	Transformational rule
Phonemes	Socio-linguistic competence	Verbal communication
Phrase structure rule	Stage of alphabetic	Wheel network
Pragmatics	Stage of logographic	Y-shaped network

Human beings are talking animals. In fact, they have built a world of words and live in this world as they live in the world of things and persons. They use words as tools to control the behaviour of others as well as that of themselves. The most important characteristic of this speech tool is its social nature because it is through speech and language that human beings communicate their thoughts, desires and feelings to one another. In fact, communication which consists of ways in which persons transmit intended or unintended messages to others is the heart of human social interaction. One of the major characteristics that distinguishes human beings from other species is the ability to communicate on a structured, symbolic level through the use of language. But communication also occurs through a host of non-verbal behaviours such as facial expressions, body movements, gestures and tone of voice.

This chapter considers the important components of language, and then, theories of language development. Besides, the importance of critical period hypothesis in language development are also examined. Subsequently, diversity in language acquisition among Indian children, relationship among language acquisition and theory of mind, bilingualism/multilingualism in Indian society and reading acquisition among Indian children are discussed. An attempt is made to discuss the nature and purpose of communication, various useful models of communication, particularly encoder-decoder model, intentionalist model and perspective-taking model. Besides concentrating upon different communication networks, the various types of non-verbal communication, social psychologists' most preferred area, are also discussed. Finally, the chapter concentrates upon the reciprocal nature of communication and social structure because there are ample evidences to suggest that social relationship shapes communication and is also shaped by the communication.

LANGUAGE: PROPERTIES AND STRUCTURE

Language is the structured system of sound patterns (words and sentences) that have socially standardised meaning. It provides a set of symbols that thoroughly catalogues the objects, events, and processes in the human environment (De Vito, 1970). In simple words, language involves the use of arbitrary sounds that have accepted referents and that can be rearranged in different ways to have different meanings (Lefrancois, 1980). This definition points out three characteristics of language as described by Brown (1973)—*displacement, meaningfulness* and *productiveness*. Language involves displacement in that it permits the representation of objects and events that are not immediate. In other words, it employs symbols as arbitrary representations of objects and events that are or were real or abstract and hypothetical. Language must also be organised semantically since the communication of meaning is one of the major functions of language. Finally, productiveness implies that given a set of speech sounds and system of rules necessary for pairing sounds with meaning, we can produce an infinite number of communications. With a mere hundred words, some people can talk forever (Lefrancois, 1983).

Greene (1990) identified the following four ways in which language was investigated:

1. As a universal social context, something that we acquire throughout our lives
2. In terms of the knowledge individuals have of the language they use
3. In terms of how it is understood by people who share a common language
4. In terms of how it is used to communicate in social contents

Kellogg (1995) defined *language* as a system of symbols, which allows communication of ideas among two or more individuals. This definition of Kellogg makes a distinction between communication and language according to which language tends to provide a vehicle for communication to take place.

Hockett (1960) identified sixteen major characteristics of language. Some of the most important ones are summarised in Table 16.1.

Table 16.1 Characteristics of Language

Characteristics of Language	Meaning
Semanticity	Words have meaning.
Arbitrariness	Words and symbols used are abstract because they do not look like the objects they stand.
Openness	Language can be used to produce new and unique message.
Displacement	Language can be used to refer to the objects which are not present.
Tradition	Language can be learnt and taught.
Prevarication	Language can be used to lie and deceive.
Reflectiveness	One can communicate about the communication system itself.
Learnability	Speaker of one language can learn another one.
Duality of patterning	Combinations of words, sentences and sounds are meaningless unless they are appropriately put together.

Following Gleitman (1981), there are five important properties of all human languages. These five properties are discussed as under:

1. Language is creative (or novel): Early associationists and modern behaviour theorists such as Skinner pointed out that language, in principle, is no different from any other kind of learned task that humans can master. In their viewpoints, all such skills are based on a strong network of associations. Many of these psychologists have clearly emphasised associative connections between sounds and mental images (such as having a mental picture of a cat after hearing the word 'cat'), whereas others have stressed the association between certain stimuli and responses (saying 'you are most welcome' after hearing 'thanks'). With the help of such associations, we effortlessly create and interpret new sentences on the spot. Except a very few such sentences as how are you, what is new and surprising, etc., all the rest are at least partly new. Therefore, it can be argued that memorisation cannot explain how a person learns a language.

2. Language is structured: Individuals construct sentences in lawful ways. Speakers construct their sentences in accordance with the rules of grammar. Every person learns organising principles or rules of grammar and that of meaning. These rules tell us how to create and understand boundless new instances. Sentences that are ungrammatical (or not well-formed) are rarely uttered, not even they are understood or remembered. Several studies have confirmed this. In these studies, the participants listened to the sequences of words that varied in meaningfulness and in grammaticality. In an experiment conducted by Marks and Miller (1964), the participants were required to detect those varied sequences in the presence of a loud background noise. In another experiment conducted by Miller and Isard (1963), the participants were asked to memorise and recall such sentences. In both these studies, similar results were obtained. The well-formed meaningful sentences were easiest to detect and memorise, whereas the meaningless and scrambled sentences were hardest to detect and memorise.

3. Language is meaningful: Each word in language expresses a meaningful idea. In other words, the used word indicates about something (such as dog or table), action (run or hit), abstraction (fun or justice), relation (greater or smaller), quality (red or altruistic), and so on. The purpose of human language is to express all these meanings, and therefore, we have no choice except to learn a word for each. Our memory for all these words is really amazing. We not only string these meaningful words in row but also put them in word patterns (grammatical sentences). Every human language possesses the property that it can express simple meanings with words and complicated meanings with sentences.

4. Language is referential: Language users know well which words refer to which objects, events and scenes in the world. For example, if a child says, "That is a dog", after seeing a dog, here, he is referring to dog by using the uttered sentence. But if he speaks this sentence by pointing to a cat, we would say that he has not learnt English very effectively. Thus, one basic problem in the use of language is how to use language for describing the world of real things and events. In other words, the basic question is—how does a person learn to relate each word to its correct referent? Theory of associativism has provided a very simplistic explanation by asserting that various events in the world act as direct stimuli to speech responses. According to this explanation, word learning would go like this. Suppose an adult sees a dog and says it 'dog'. On hearing the adult, a child may form an association between the sight of a dog and the sound 'dog'. Therefore, when this child next sees a dog, he too says 'dog' in response. But in real-life use of language, this explanation may not always be true. Here, we often cannot even identify a particular stimulus that evokes some sentences from a speaker.

5. Language is interpersonal: Another property of language is that it is interpersonal. Language helps in cutting cross from one individual to another. For this, the speakers and listeners must know not only a language but also the rules for using language appropriately in successful communication. Such rules are called *conversational rules*. In fact, what a person says about an object or situation, it is not simply a description of that situation. What one says depend on a person's knowledge, beliefs and wishes about the listener. It means that to speak appropriately, one must built a correct mental picture of the other to whom the speech is addressed (Clark and Clark, 1977). Speakers have also a variety of abilities to adjust their speech styles in response to the ways they tend to perceive their listeners. For example, Freed (1980) and Newport (1977) conducted studies in which it was shown that speech was simplified to foreigners and to young children, who were perceived as not understanding the language satisfactorily.

Psychologistics, as we know, is the study of how language is acquired, produced and used as well as how the sounds and symbols of language are translated into meaning. Researchers have devoted much time and effort to study the structure of language and rules governing its use. According to some researches, the structure and rules governing language involve five different components—phonemes, morphemes, syntax, semantics and pragmatics. Phonemes and morphemes belong to phonology, which describes the system of sound for a language. These five components are discussed below:

1. Phonemes: The elementary sounds of language are phonemes. In fact, phonemes are the smallest units of sound in spoken language. They are the basic building blocks of a spoken language. For example, the word 'rat' is made of three phoneme 'R', 'a', and 't'. Phonemes do not sound like the single letter of alphabet such as 'a', 'b', 'c', 'd', but like the sounds of the letters as they are used in words like 'c' in cat and 'b' in boy. Letters that are combined to form sounds are also phonemes such as 'ch' in child and 'th' in the. The same phoneme (sound) may be represented by different letters in different words as 'o' in story and 'ei' in height. The same letter can also serve as different phonemes. For example, letter *a* can be sounded as four different phonemes as in day, watch, cadet, law.

How many phonemes are there? English uses 45 phonemes, but some languages have as few as 15 and others have as many as 85 phonemes (Solso, 1991). Although phonemes are the basic building blocks of language, they alone, with a few exceptions, do not provide language with the meanings.

2. Morphemes: Phonemes generally combine into larger units called *morphemes*, which are defined as the smallest meaningful units of language. A morpheme may be a word (mat, pig, etc.) or it may be part of a word such as prefix or suffix (*sub, ed., ing,* etc.). Many words in English are single morphemes such as learn, reason, book, etc. The single morpheme 'reason' becomes the two-morpheme 'reasonable'. The letter 's' makes a word plural, and thus, it is a morpheme. The morpheme dog (singular) becomes two-morpheme when 's' is added to become dogs (plural).

3. Syntax: Syntax describes the structure of language and the ways words are put together to form sentences. In other words, syntax is the aspect of grammar that specifies the rules for combining and arranging words to form phrases and sentences. Each language has its own set of rules for creating sentences from words and for expressing grammatical relations among words. An important rule of syntax in English is that adjectives usually come before noun. So, we say 'black dog' and not 'dog black'.

4. Semantics: *Semantics* refers to the study of the meaning of words and sentences. In simple words, semantics refers to the meaning one derives from morphemes, words and sentences. Experiences with words and an understanding of how words represent external objects and events are the basic raw materials for the acquisition of language. The same word can have different meanings depending on how it is used in sentences. For example, 'I pen below a few lines regarding your brother', 'Give me my pen'; 'I do not mind', 'He has lost his mind'. In the former two sentences, the word 'pen' has two different meanings. Likewise, in the last two sentences, the word 'mind' has two different meanings.

Syntax and semantics are not fully separable structure of a sentence and their meanings are inherently related. Recently, there has been an increased effort to combine the study of sentences and syntax and to clearly specify the relationship between structure and meaning.

5. Pragmatics: *Pragmatics* can be defined as the rules governing the use of language in context of speakers and listeners in the real world (Shatz, 1983). For example, when a child learns to use a polite language, and why a child talks differently before teachers and before peers are the field of the study of pragmatics. In fact, this subfield of language has basically emerged out of the recognition that much of child language as well as that of adult cannot be understood without the knowledge of context in which it occurs. Finally, pragmatics is also concerned with how a child learns conversational rules, and therefore, provides a clear link between language development and one of the basic purpose of language, that is, communication.

Thus, the structure of language has varied components. There are about 6000 spoken languages throughout the world (Berreby, 1994) and whether the language is spoken, written, signed and otherwise used, it remains one of the most complex human capabilities.

FUNCTIONS OF LANGUAGE

Language plays important functions in all aspects of our daily life. In fact, it serves as a vast variety of purposes. Halliday (1975) described the following important functions of language:

1. **Instrumental function:** Language permits us to satisfy our needs and express our wishes and desires. This is *I want* function.
2. **Regulatory function:** This function of the language allows us to control the behaviour of others by issuing demands and requests. It is described as *do that* function.
3. **Interpersonal function:** This function facilitates our encounters with others in social situations. This is the *me and you* function.
4. **Personal function:** This function allows our personal identity, our expressions of unique views, feelings and attitudes.
5. **Heuristic function:** This function allows to explore and understand our environment. Halliday termed this functioning as *tell me why* function of language.
6. **Imaginative function:** This function facilitates us in escaping from reality into a universe of our own making. This is *let's pretend* or be *poetic* function of language.
7. **Informative function:** Finally, language permits us to communicate new information. This is the *I have got something to tell you* function.

As the list suggests, language serves a wide range of purposes for us. Of the various purposes, language makes two vital contributions to human condition. First, it enables people to communicate with each other (interindividual communication) and second, it facilitates thinking (intraindividual communication). The first contribution, that is, *interindividual communication* is the process by which people transmit information, ideas, and attitudes to one another. This feature of language allows us to coordinate the complex group activities. As such, the language provides us with the foundation for family, economic, political, religious and educational institutions. The second contribution of language is that it facilitates thought and other cognitive processes. Language enables us to encode our experiences by assigning some names to them. In this way, language helps us to do partition of the environment into manageable units and areas that are relevant to us.

CRITICAL PERIOD HYPOTHESIS

The concept of critical period has been given due attention by psychologists. It refers to certain period in life during which both favourable and unfavourable circumstances can have lasting and irreversible consequences upon later development. This notion has received impetus from the research work of Konrad Lorenz, a Nobel Prize winning ethologist. Lorenz (1935) demonstrated that there is short period of time early in the lives of goslings and ducklings during which they begin to slavishly follow the first moving object that they see—their mother, a human being, a bull or whatever. This is called *imprinting* and once this has occurred, it is irreversible. The object becomes 'mother' for the birds so that thereafter, they prefer it over all others, and indeed, will follow no other. Imprinting is different from other forms of learning in two ways. First, imprinting can take place only during a relatively short period of time, which is termed as *critical period*. Second, imprinting is irreversible, that is, it is highly resistant to change so that the behaviour appears to be inborn.

The common observation is that language learning is very much easier in children than in adults. This is regarded as an evidence for the fact that there is a critical period for language learning. This period is thought to extend roughly from three months to puberty. According to critical period hypothesis, some characteristics of the brain do change as the critical period comes to its closure so that language learning (both of the first language and of later ones) becomes very difficult (Lenneberg, 1967).

Critical periods tend to govern the acquisition of a number of important behaviour patterns in human beings as well as in some animal beings. One good example is the attachment of the infant to its mother that can generally be formed in early childhood. Another example is bird song. Male birds of many species learn a song that is characteristic of their own kind. They learn this song by listening to adult males of their own species. But such exposure remains effective only if it occurs at a certain period in the life of the bird. This has been well-documented for white-crowned sparrow (Marler, 1970). In this study, the critical period for learning of the song was between seventh and sixtieth day of their life. To make the white-crowned sparrow learn the song with full glory, the baby birds must hear adult's song during the said critical period. The next forty days are marginal periods during which if the baby birds hear the song, but have not heard it before, they learn some limited basis of the sparrow song without full elaborations heard in normal adults. If the exposure comes still later, it has no effect at all. The bird will never sing.

Evidence for the critical period in language learning comes from three primary sources, which are discussed below:

1. First language learning: The direct test of critical period hypothesis is first language learning. Can one learn to speak a language after childhood has passed? The appropriate answer comes from examining the cases of such children, who grew up in the wild or who were isolated from language contact by insane parents. Some of these cases were carefully analysed and studied by Brown (1958). In 1920, some Indian villagers found a wolf mother in her den with two baby wolves and two were human children, subsequently named as *Kamala* and *Amala*. At that time, Kamala was about eight years old and Amala was only one and a half years old. They were thoroughly wolfish in appearance and behaviour. Within a year, Amala died but Kamala lived to be eighteen years old. In time, Kamala learned to walk erect, to wear clothing and even to speak a few words.

Kamala and Amala had been removed from all human society. There are, however, some other children who have been raised by humans, but under inhumane conditions in which their both parents had deprived the baby of all human contacts. *Isabelle* and *Genie* are the examples of two such isolated children. Isabelle, from her early infancy, was given only the minimal attention to sustain her life. Apparently, no one spoke to her. She was six-year old when discovered. She had no language and her cognitive development was very poor. But within a year, the girl learned to speak. Her tested intelligence was normal (Brown, 1958). But Genie was discovered at the age of fourteen years. She had lived tied to chair, was frequently beaten and never spoken to. Since her discovery, she had been constantly taught by psychologists and linguists (Fromkin et al., 1974). But Genie did not become a normal language user. Ever after many years of instruction, she could not learn the little function words, pronouns and auxiliary verbs nor could she combine propositions together in elaborate sentences (Curtiss, 1977). Maximally, she was using some words, but with vague meaningful organisation.

Now, the basic question is—why was Genie not progressing to full language learning while Isabelle did? Why did Kamala learn to speak a few words? The best answer is that the crucial factor was age at which language learning generally begins. Genie was found and given language training after she has reached puberty, while Isabelle was only six. The age of Kamala at the time of discovery was also eight years. It is tempting to suppose that when Isabelle and Kamala were discovered, they were in the midst of critical period of language learning, and therefore, they could develop into a normal language user. But Genie had just entered puberty, and therefore, was at the margin of the critical period. That is the reason, why she was only able to learn the language basics and never acquired its elaborations or details.

2. Second language learning: Learning of second language also confirms the role of critical period hypothesis. It is a common observation that children pick up a foreign language very rapidly and soon start speaking it like natives. This is much less found in adults. This happens because adults have crossed the cutting line, which lies at puberty. This is more clearly found among immigrants from another country, who tend to learn the language of their new home. Many such immigrants continue to speak this language with an accent and have occasional lapses at certain point of grammar. Once again, such events give suggestions for a critical period of language learning that ordinarily continues till puberty. If that period is passed, the language learning becomes difficult at least from the point of view of language elaborations.

3. Recovery from aphasia: Studies done in the field of aphasia also provide support for the critical period hypothesis. In aphasia, there is a marked disturbances of language functions and this occurs as a function of damage to certain regions of the left cerebral hemisphere. Now, the question is—do aphasia patients tend to recover? The answer to this basic question depends on the age of the person. If the aphasia has occurred due to the damage to the brain in childhood, the recovery is much better, but if that has occurred in adulthood, the recovery will rarely be completed. It means that language use is not regained when the damage has occurred in adulthood, but it is regained when it has occurred in childhood. This means that a child can relearn language even after he has lost most of it, but an adult cannot. This clearly supports the hypothesis that there is a critical period for language learning.

Taken as a whole, it can be said that there is found a critical period in language learning. All the three evidences discussed above have provided full support for this. The possibility of critical period for language acquisition is also supported by research on adults, who communicate via sign language. Adults, who acquire sign language early in life, seem to be more proficient and efficient than those, who learn such language late in life (Baron, 2005).

LINGUISTIC HIERARCHY

Language is organised in a hierarchy of its various structure. At the bottom of the hierarchy, language comprises little snippets of sound and at the apex end, it consists of sentences and conversations (see Figure 16.1).

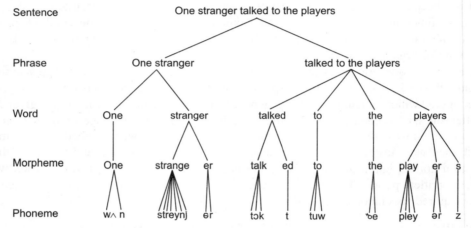

Figure 16.1 Hierarchy of linguistic structure.

A close look at Figure 16.1 reveals that at each level of linguistic hierarchy, the units of the language are tightly organised into a structure. These units are explained as follows:

1. Phonemes–Units of sound: Speech sounds that are perceived to make distinction in meaning are called *phonemes*. In English language, there are forty five phonemes, which are written by twenty-six symbols (letters) of the English alphabet. In fact, they are the perceptual units of which different speech sequences are composed. For example, consider the word 'den', which begins with a sound that is different from the word 'pen' but is more or less the same as the sound that ends 'bed'. The common element is the phoneme which is designated by the symbol 'd'. Hearing an utterance as a sequence of phonemes partly depends on the extent to which the spoken language is known. Once the learners have acquired the system of sounds used in their mother tongue, they usually become rigid in their phonemic ways. Therefore, it becomes hard for them to utter or perceive any others. As a speaker of the language, the person not only learns the phonemes that constitute its sound elements but also learns the ways in which these phonemes can be combined into words. Every language has some phonological rules that specify which phonemes can and which cannot go together. Consider, for example, that a company wants to name its food product as *Tlitos*. Although this new arrangement of phonemes can be pronounced, it seems somehow un-English like because English speakers may sense intuitively that English word rarely starts with 'tl' even though this sequence of phonemes is acceptable in the middle of the word as we find in 'battling'. Thus, the product cannot be named meaningfully as *Tlitos*. This shows that there is phonological rule, which puts some restriction on combination of phonemes.

2. Morphemes and words—Units of meaning: At the next of linguistic hierarchy are morphemes, where fixed sequences of phonemes are joined. We know that *morphemes* are the smaller language units that carry bits of meaning. We usually call such morphemes as prefixes, suffixes, roots and stems. Some morpheme stands alone such as 'strange', which means 'odd'. Some morphemes cannot stand alone as word, but can be easily combined with other morphemes to make complex words. For example, 'er' (meaning 'one who') and 's' (meaning more than one) cannot stand alone, but when they are combined, a complex word such as strange + er + s = strangers is derived.

Another characteristics of morphemes is that their patterns in language are restricted in precise ways. It means that we cannot record or rearrange the morpheme to get 'erstrangers' in place of 'strangers' and 'splayer' in place of 'players'. It means that morphemes have fixed position in English words.

3. Phrases and sentences: At the next level of language hierarchy lie phrases and sentences, which are formed by organising the words into patterned sequences. The number of sentence units in any language is very large. At this level of language hierarchy too, there exist rules of combination. For example, it is appropriate to tie words into sentences like 'That is a dog'; 'Mohan works hard', etc., but it is inappropriate to tie words into sequence like 'A that is dog' or 'Hard Mohan works', etc. Speakers and listeners quite effortlessly recognise whether or not sentences have well-formed sequences.

Thus, we find that with the help of phonemes and morphemes, a boundless number of sentences are formed. The question is—how does human mind deal with this ever expanding number or items? The best possible answer to this question is that a person does not learn billions of sentences, rather he learns about the general rules, which tell us how to construct any sentence. Thus, it is obvious that linguistic rules exist at each level of hierarchy and without such rules, we will never be able to learn, understand and speak any language.

THEORIES OF LANGUAGE DEVELOPMENT

In 1799, a nude boy was observed running in woods of France. The boy, who was 11 years old, was captured by three hunters when he climbed into a tree in an attempt to escape from them. He was called *Wild Boy of Aveyron* and was believed to have lived alone in the woods for six years (Itard, 1976). When he was captured by the psychologists, he made no effort to communicate. Rather even after several years, he remained unable to communicate effectively. This case of wild boy raises questions about how people acquire language. Is the ability to acquire language product of biological factors? Or is language learnt or influenced by the environment? Precisely, when and how does language ability develop? In this section, we shall try to answer these questions by taking into consideration various perspectives of language acquisition.

Language development is often divided into two major stages—*prelinguistic and linguistic*. During the prelinguistic stage which ranges approximately from birth to twelve months, the infant produces a number of different types of vocalisation such as cooing, chuckling and babbling. When the child enters the linguistic stage at about 12 months of age, he begins to use individual words. Psychologists and psycholinguistics interested in developing a theoretical framework have studied both these stages in support of their model. The area of language development has been influenced heavily by theoretical views. There are three such important views—nativist perspective, environmentalist perspective and interactionist perspective. A discussion of these three perspectives is as follows:

1. *Nativist perspective*

According to this theoretical view, language acquisition is an innate ability. According to nativists such as Chomsky (1968), McNeill (1970), Morley (1957) and Lenneberg (1967, 1969), human beings are endowed with a biological capacity for language. Historically, our understanding of the biological basis of language appears to be clearly rooted in the study of language disorders resulting from brain damage (Geschwind, 1972). For example a person suffering from expressive aphasia shows difficulty in expressing thoughts in speech and writing. Likewise, when the person suffers from receptive aphasia, he has trouble in understanding written or spoken language.

Chomsky's (1968) contribution to nativist perspective has been very influential. He proposed that human nervous system is equipped with what he called *language acquisition device* (*LAD*) or an *acquisition model* (*AM*), which is a neurological system prewired in such a way that the individual is able to process and receive language. In fact, LAD is not a structure in the brain, but the innate capacity to learn grammar. In view of Chomsky, the basic structure of language is biologically channelled. In the process of language acquisition, children merely learn the peculiarities of language of their society and not the basic structure of language. In support of his view, Chomsky cited data on linguistic universals. He pointed out that while languages of the world differ in their surface characteristics, which he called *surface structure*, they have some basic similarities in their composition, which he called *deep structure*. In simple words, Chomsky described the sound or word sequence in a verbal expression as its surface structure and its meaning, including grammatical relations, as deep structure. The surface structure and deep structure are not identical. The problem in understanding language is essentially one of deriving deep structure from the surface structure. Chomsky (1965) pointed out that there were three situations, where surface structure might be misleading. These are given below:

(i) Sometimes, different surface structures, that is, different order of words have identical meanings, that is, identical deep structure. For example, 'Mohan ate the food' is semantically equivalent to 'The food was eaten by Mohan', in spite of very different surface structures of the two sentences.

(ii) There are situations where sentences with identical surface structures (in terms of order) tend to have different meanings. For example, consider the following sentences:

> They (are eating) (apples).
>
> They (are) (eating apples).

The surface structure of the two sentences are identical, but the first sentence means that some people are eating apples, whereas the second sentence means that apples are for eating, not for cooking or other purpose.

(iii) There are situations where a single sentence can have two or more meanings. For example, consider the following sentence:

They are racing horses.

The sentence may mean that a group of horses are racing horses and not ploughing horses. The sentence also means that a group of people are racing horses.

Chomsky suggested that through preverbal, intuitive rules, the individuals turn surface structure into deep structure and vice versa. These rules with phrase structure rules and transformational rules taken together are called *transformational grammar*. Thus, transformational grammar is a set of highly precise rules for generating acceptable sentences. Such transformational grammar is biologically built into the functioning of human organism. Chomsky did not put the claim that a child is endowed with specific language such as English, Hindi, Bengali, etc. Rather, he simply suggested that the children possess an inborn capacity for generating productive rules (grammar).

In support of Chomsky, McNeill (1966a, 1966b) asserted that a child has innate predisposition for language acquisition. He further argued that any attempt to explain language from point of view of innate predisposition for acquisition must focus on the innate capacities of the child and subsequently, identify how these (capacities) interact with experience to bring about effortless and extremely rapid acquisition of the native language of the young child.

The most thorough and precise advocacy for biological determinants of language acquisition was presented by Lenneberg (1967). Lenneberg considered language acquisition to be a function of biological maturation and species-specific phenomenon. He argued that non-humans cannot be trained to use language in human manner because in underlying speech, there are a number of anatomical and physiological features that do not exist in species below the level of human beings. According to him, ability to understand and generate a language is uniquely human and inherited as species-specific characteristic. The inherited biological determinants include primarily the structure of the articulatory apparatus, including mouth and larynx, specific brain counters that process language and a specialised auditory system. Lenneberg, Rebelsky and Nichols (1965) conducted a study in which the prelinguistic sound making of both deaf and hearing infants was studied. It was found that the deaf infants not only went through the same sequence of vocalisations as the hearing infants but also they produced much more noise. Results suggested that the emergence of prelinguistic behaviour does not depend on social factors such as training and reinforcement, but instead, is a function of maturational factors.

Lenneberg further pointed out that despite vast cultural variations, the children around the world acquire language in a strikingly similar order. The observation has been that everywhere children begin to babble at six months of age, use two-word combinations near the end of the second year and tend to learn and master basic syntax about the age of four or five. He (Lenneberg) found that 450 out of 500 children were able, at thirty nine months, to name a large number of objects in their houses, to comprehend spoken instructions and produce structurally very complex sentences spontaneously. These overall similarities in language acquisition for different children and different languages are so great that it is very much convincing to assume that human brain is inherently programmed for language acquisition.

The idea of language acquisition as an innate ability is also supported by the fact that individuals learn language for more quickly and easily during certain period of biological maturation, especially from infancy to puberty technically called *critical period for language learning*. Researches have shown that before puberty, a child can achieve the fluency of a native speaker in any language without much training. Later, language learning becomes difficult. That is the reason, why when family moves to a foreign country, children learn the language much more quickly than their parents.

Some of the most striking evidences for the possibility of an innate predisposition for language learning come from the work on children, who speak creole language (Bickerton, 1983). It was found by Bickerton that when adults of different cultures such as Japanese, Chinese, Koreans, Portuguese and Filipinos came together, they developed a *pidgin language*—a simplified linguistic system created when two or more than two languages come into contact. Thus, pidgin is a hybrid language that takes the vocabulary of dominant language, but lacks grammatical complexity and tend to vary from speaker to speaker. He further observed that children of these pidgin speakers did not speak pidgin, but they tended to develop a different language, called *creole*. In sharp contrast to pidgin, creole is a developed linguistic system and the structure of language is more or less similar among all the children in the whole community, irrespective of the parents' language. The most remarkable fact is that the first generation of creole-speaking children don't differ from subsequent generations of speakers, which automatically suggests that the acquisition of creole happens very rapidly and automatically. The most direct implication of this observation, according to Bickerton, is that the first language acquisition is mediated by an innate device, which provides children with a single and fairly specific grammatical model.

Although we are probably biologically predisposed for language acquisition, it is unlikely that biological principles alone account for all aspects of language development. Moreover, it is important to note that Chomsky's theory dealt only with syntax (that is, rules for joining words together to form phrases and sentences). Critics pointed out that he failed to provide a model for understanding crucial aspects of meaning or semantics (Grice, 1968; Searle, 1969).

2. Environmentalist perspective

Supporters of this perspective suggest that language acquisition can be explained by learning principles. Some theorists stress reinforcement principles (Skinner, 1957; Miller and Dollard, 1941; Mowrer, 1960), while others give more weight to imitation (Bijou, 1976; Bullock, 1983; Whitehurst, 1980). An explanation of language acquisition from principles of classical and operant conditioning asserts that at first, the child tends to emit a variety of sounds, none of which have any meaning to either child himself or to the adults belonging to the child's environment. Eventually, the child produces sound that are similar to the sounds in adult language and the adults respond positively to those utterances of the child. In this way, through systematic recognition and rewarding by the parents or other adults, the child begins to learn the meanings that are attached to each such type of sound (phonological development). In that, the sounds or utterances become conditioned responses to the rewarding stimuli emitted by the parents through their reactions. Thus, the child first learns to put sounds together to form words (called *morphological development*), and subsequently, on the basis of adult reactions to those words, he begins to put words together to form larger meaning system (called *systematic development*). Making the entire episode still more clear, Skinner made it obvious that during the language acquisition, parents first selectively reinforce those parts of child's babbling sounds, which are most similar to the adult speech. Such reinforcement tends to increase the frequency of vocalisation of those sounds of the child. Thus, parental reinforcement gradually shapes the child's language behaviour through successive approximation until it becomes more and more like adult speech. The fundamental notion in Skinner's theory of language acquisition is that a child learns language because he or she is shaped into it. For example, sounds like 'Ma' may be reinforced with a smile from mother and 'da' with a smile from daddy.

In his famous book *Verbal behaviour*, Skinner (1957) vividly tried to show that language is acquired by children in three obvious ways, which are as under:

(i) There are *mand responses*, a term which was coined by Skinner from words such as 'command' and 'demand'. According to Skinner, parents react differently to the random babbling utterances produced by children. If, by chance, a child emits a 'wa' sound, parents generally conclude that child is asking for water and respond by providing it. Such sequence, if repeated, tends to increase the probability that 'wa-wa' will be uttered whenever the baby wants water.

(ii) There are *tact responses*, a term suggested by Skinner from the word 'contact'. While the child is making random babbling, he may utter 'wa-wa' sound when playing with water or being bathed. Although the child never associates 'wa-wa' with water, the parents tend to make the association and in one way or another, reward the child with linguistic acquisition. When such sequence is repeated, the child learns to make a 'wa-wa' sound whenever he comes into contact with stimulus, that is, water.

(iii) Skinner was of view that children tend to acquire language through *echoic responses* in which they echo the sounds made by adults in the context of a particular stimulus. For example, a child may, time and again, hear the parents telling the clear liquid as water. In turn, he may echo the response 'wa-wa'. The parents may, subsequently, reinforce the utterances by providing child with water.

Skinner also made it clear that the children learn grammatical constructions in much the same way that they learn words. In fact, they learn specific sentence frames into which they substitute words by means of generalisation.

In series of publications done by Staats (1961, 1968), Staats and Staats (1958), social learning approach to language development was extended. Staats focused upon the concept of discrimination learning and also on stimulus generalisations to allow for acquisition of words as well as for combining the words into novel formulations. Following Mowrer (1960), Staats emphasised the fact that the vocalisations of the parents in association with positive reinforcement (such as food, water, etc.) produce secondary reinforcing qualities for the parents' voices. Additional stimulus generations from parents' vocalisations to the child's own vocalisations quickly lead to the child's own productions acquiring secondary reinforcing quality. In this way, the child's own vocalisations tend to become reinforcing in and of themselves. In sum, then, direct reinforcement provided by parents for the production of sounds of their own is replaced by self-reward of the child's own vocalisations.

There is no trouble from environmentalist perspective to show that children initiate adult speech patterns. According to the researches done by Bijou (1976), Bullock (1983) and Whitehurst (1980), a child picks up words, phrases and sentences directly through imitation, and then, through reinforcement and generalisation, the child learns when it is appropriate and meaningful to use them in different context. Rosenthal, Zimmerman and Durning (1970) also showed that certain aspects of verbal behaviour can be modified by imitation. They reported that the types of questions produced by an adult model were found to affect the types of questions subsequently produced by sixth-grade children. This obviously indicated the impact of imitation upon the acquisition of verbal behaviour. Likewise, a combination of imitation and reinforcement has been found in both natural and laboratory experiments to be a more effective method than simple modelling for teaching complex grammatical constructions (Whitehurst, 1980). In recent past, some programmes for parents based on learning principles have also developed. These programmes have been found to be effective for encouraging children, who are delayed in their language development for catching up their peers (Zelazo, Kearsley and Ungerer, 1984).

Bernstein (1964), a sociolinguistic, also provided support to environmentalist perspective by way of giving proper attention to how the child learns the social uses of language. In accordance with the researches done by Bernstein (1964) and his other associates like Hess and Shipman (1965), our knowledge of role of social factors in language development will be vastly improved as a detailed analysis of child–adult interactions is carried out. These investigators were of view that in addition to the child's acquisition of structural rules for language, he must also learn another set of rules, which refers to when he should speak, when he should remain silent, which linguistic code he should use and to whom (Hymes, 1967).

Following are the criticisms faced by environmentalist perspective:

(i) Environmentalist perspective emphasises the role of imitation and reinforcement without taking into consideration the unique contribution of the child to the language development. For example, we know that the children extract simple rules from speech they hear and subsequently, use them in their language. Gradually, these rules help the child in approximating the speech of the adults. We also know that most children tend to practice their language and try out new grammatical rules when they are alone. According to social learning theory perspective, the child is regarded as a hollow organism, who responds only to the external stimulation, that is, reinforcement.

(ii) (ii)　Environmentalist perspective emphasises the fact that children learn language because they are rewarded for speaking correctly and not rewarded for violating the rules of speech. But observational studies done on children and parents together have shown that parents are just as likely to reward their children for incorrect statements as they are to reward them for correct ones. Brown and Hanlon (1970) examined whether parents approved or disapproved their children's errors in verb forms, plurals and subject-verb agreement. Their findings showed that the parents responded to the child's meaning of sentences rather than to the grammar. The findings obviously showed the fact that reinforcement alone cannot explain the child's learning of correct grammar. In fact, children do pass at their own rate through the principal stages of syntactic and semantic development, irrespective of the pattern of reinforcement. Later, Brown (1973) studied the child's acquisition of morpheme words and correlated this to the frequency with which the parents use these words. A very low correlation was found and this led him to conclude that the order of word acquisition apparently is influenced by the factors other than modelling the language of the parents.

Cazden (1965) also reported similar findings. In this experiment, there were two groups of children. In one group, the experimenter took care not to repeat the children's words. In another group, the experiment carefully repeated the children's utterances and in addition, placed them into correct grammatical form. Results showed that the group that was corrected did not score higher on various linguistic measures. In fact, the opposite was true, that is, the children that were left to converse with each other without having their words repeated seemed to develop faster than those whose utterances were repeated with corrections.

Although there is not much support for environmentalist perspective of language acquisition, our common sense still leads us to assume that adult spoken language does have significant impact upon what the child acquires. Children compile specific information from what they hear and formulate hypotheses concerning the nature of the language they proceed to acquire.

Integration of nativist and environmentalist perspectives: The nativist position as exemplified by the work of Chomsky (1965), Lenneberg (1967) and McNeill (1966a) focuses on the fact that prelinguistic behaviour and early linguistic behaviour unfold under the influence of the process of biological maturation and are relatively independent of experiential influences. The environmentalist position as explained by the work of Skinner (1957), Mowrer (1960), Bijou (1976), Miller and Dollard (1941), in sharp contrast to the nativists, assumes that environmental factors exert considerable influence on language development. Given that the environmentalist and the nativist perspectives seem to be radically different, the question is whether there is any common ground between them.

One point of common ground or convergence between the two perspectives is that both agree that language is acquired in a social context. Another point of convergence or agreement is on the existence of the individual and group differences in linguistic performance. Lenneberg's interpretation of these differences is that they result from complex interactions between social and biological factors in development. On the environmentalist side, there is much literature related to the role of environmental factors in determining individual and group differences (Cazden, 1966).

Still another point of convergence between the two perspectives is concerned with appropriate methods to study child language. Nativist like Chomsky (1965) and environmentalist like Bijou (1976), Bullock (1983)—all would agree that a broad spectrum of tasks, situations and linguistic analytic procedures are necessary for assessing the child's language capabilities.

As we know, in explaining language acquisition, the nativists stress upon the internal mechanisms of speaker–listener himself, whereas environmentalists stress upon the role of external forces acting upon the child. These two viewpoints are in conflict, but they can be conceded. It is possible to integrate these two models so that the coexistence of both social factors and biological factors in determining linguistic behaviour would be admitted. For example, it is possible to hold the view that all humans are, by their nature, equal with respect to language competence, and simultaneously, to accept the existence of differences (both individual and group differences) in language performance.

Evidences provided so far by the studies of language acquisition have revealed that neither nativist perspective nor environmentalist perspective can explain all developmental language phenomena. In fact, there are four kinds of phenomena (mentioned below) for which we need explanations in the context of language acquisition.

(i) Development of prelinguistic vocalisation
(ii) Acquisition of basic language structure
(iii) Acquisition of elaborated language sequences
(iv) Acquisition of different modes of communication, that is, ability to use different styles of speech considered appropriate in a particular social situation

It is quite possible that social factors play a lesser role in the development of the skills represented in first and second points, but a greater role in those skills defined in third and fourth points At present, there is very little evidence on the precise role of either biological or social factors in language acquisition.

3. Interactionist perspective

Some social psychologists are of view that language acquisition cannot be understood by examining learning or genetic factors in isolation from one another. Rather, dynamic and complex interactions take place between biochemical processes, maturational factors, learning strategies and the social environment (Blount, 1975; Nelson, 1977).

The most important assumption of the interactionist perspective is that although we know that basic language abilities are governed by biological factors, environmental factors are also important in language acquisition. Clearly, certain biological factors predispose us to acquire language, but at the same time, our environment contributes to how and how well this innate potential is realised. In other words, while the pattern of language development may reflect certain ways in which the information is processed by the brain, the rate and speed with which children pass through the stages of language development may be more susceptible to the effects of family and environment (Bloom, Rocissano and Hood, 1976). In addition, the interactionist stresses the importance of the role of the child in language mastery.

Thus, the interactionist perspective represents basically an attempt to combine biological heritage with a number of different environmental determinants. Currently, it offers the most encompassing explanation of language acquisition. Bruner (1983) proposed the term Language Acquisition Support System (LASS) for representing factors in the social environment that facilitate the learning of a language. One could, then, say that when LAD and LASS interact in mutually supportive way, a normal language development occurs.

LANGUAGE AND THOUGHT

One of the important issues debated by the linguists and the social psychologists is the relationship between language and thought. The traditional view on the relationship between language and thought is that language we use is determined by thought or by our thinking. This idea can be traced back to ancient Greek philosopher, Aristotle, who had pointed out that language has been developed for the purpose of expressing the thoughts of the people (Garnham and Oakhill, 1994). But in the twentieth century, the following three alternative views on the relationship between language and thought were developed:

1. Thinking depends on language (Whorf, 1956).
2. Language depends on thinking (Piaget, 1968).
3. Language and thought develop independently among children until they are approximately two years old. At this age, they become interdependent and develop together (Vygotsky, 1962).

A discussion of these three views is given here.

1. Whorf's view: Thinking depends upon language

Whorf (1956) proposed that the language we use determines the structure of our thought processes. The work of Whorf was closely associated with the work of his teacher, Edward Sapir, and as a consequence, the view that language determines thought is usually referred to as the *Sapir–Whorf hypothesis*. The idea that language determines thought is known as *linguistic determinism* or *linguistic relativity hypothesis*. According to this hypothesis, people who speak different languages tend to perceive the world in different ways because their thinking is determined, at least partly, by words available to them. Whorf's ideas concerning this type of relationship between language and thought were developed through the studies of Native American languages such as Apache and Hopi. He claimed that different languages impose different ways of thinking and viewing the world by the speakers. For example, Whorf (1956) argued that because Hopi has no words that refer to time, it must have a different conception of time as compared to others who have. Another widely cited proof by Whorf referred to the languages used by Eskimo. Languages of Eskimo people have a number of different words for 'snow' such as 'apikak' for first snow falling, 'aniv' for snow spread out and 'pukak' for snow for drinking water, whereas the English-speaking people have only one word 'snow' (Restak, 1968). Whorf claimed that such a rich and varied selection of words for snow enabled Eskimos to think differently about it than did the English speaking people, whose language lacked specific words for different snow conditions. Unfortunately, this anecdote evidence proved to be false being more myth than reality (Pullum, 1991). In fact, English speaking people also have many different words for snow (slush, sleet, powder, dusting to name a few).

A close scrutiny of the research work reveals that neither Sapir nor Whorf provided any scientific studies to support their hypothesis. However, there have been many studies by other investigators. In an early study conducted by Brown and Lenneberg (1954) for Sapir–Whorf hypothesis, the names for colours apparently influenced the cognitive task of recalling the colour. In another study, the researchers assumed that in a language, colour name would influence the ability of the people, who grew up with that language, to make better perceptual discrimination of colours. Lucy and Shweder (1979) found that basic colour terms, in fact, directly influenced colour recognition memory. But an earlier series of study on perception of colours conducted by Rosch–Heider (1972) and Rosch-Heider and Oliver (1972) found opposite effects. According to their hypothesis, if language determines thinking, then the people, whose language contains many names for colours, should be better at thinking and making discrimination among colours than those whose language has only a few colour names. The participants were English-speaking Americans and the Dani, members of remote tribe in New Guinea, whose language had only two names for colours—*mili* for dark, cool colours and *mole* for bright, warm colours.

The researchers showed participants from both groups single-colour chips of 11 colours—black, white, red, green, blue, brown, yellow, purple, pink, orange and grey for 5 seconds each. Subsequently, they, after 30 seconds, were requested to select 11 colours they had viewed from a larger group of 40 colour chips. Results revealed no significant differences in the performance of the Dani and the American subjects in discriminating or thinking about the 11 basic colours. Thus, Rosch–Heider's study did not support the linguistic relativity hypothesis. More recent researches done by Davies et al. (1998a, 1998b), Laws et al. (1995)also supported Rosch–Heider's findings and the idea of *cognitive universalism*—a theory according to which concepts are universal and they influence the development of language.

2. Piaget's view: Language depends upon thinking

Piaget's views are more or less opposite of those taken by Whorf. In fact, Piaget opposed the idea that language is responsible for thought (Greene, 1990). His argument in support of the fact that thought precedes language came from one important observation of the way in which use of language develops in children. According to Piagetian view, a child's way of thinking changes first and this is followed by a change in language used by a child so that he may be able to express new ideas and a new way of thinking (Garnham and Oakhil, 1994). Piaget (1968) pointed out that a young child uses speech to express his thoughts rather than to communicate with the other people. He called such use of language *egocentric speech*. A young child uses language in the presence of his parents no doubt, but his speech is not directed towards them, rather his speech is merely a reflection of their own thoughts and intentions. However, with the advancement of age, the egocentric speech disappears and the child becomes capable to consider thoughts and feelings of others. Harley (1995) pointed out that one important way of testing Piagetian view would be to examine the language skills of children with some form of cognitive impairment. The rationale here would be that if thinking was necessary for language, then the children, whose cognitive development was impaired, should also display poor language skills. Yamada (1990) presented a case study of a participation named 'Laura' and found that although the general cognitive ability of Laura was very poor, she was capable of producing complex sentences. Thus, the result of Yamada case study does not support Piagetian view that thought precedes language. In fact, there is a very little support to Piagetian view. He underestimated the fact that children can use language to ask questions and learn about the world from other people (Hartland, 1991). In simple words, he underestimated the social function of language and there is a very little research response to Piagetian view of language (Harley, 1995).

3. *Vygotsky's view on the relationship between language and thought*

Vygotsky, a Russian psychologist (1962), pointed out that language and thought develop independently in young children (that is, up to about two years of age), but with the advancement of age, language and thought become interdependent. Vygotsky (1986) used the term *pre-intellectual language* to refer to the crying and babbling used by children of ages up to two. During this stage, the children use words to name objects in terms of their properties. For example, a child of this age may refer the cats as 'meaau-meaau' because of the sound a cat makes. During this stage of development, thought remains non-verbal and relies on images and perceptions. However, at some point, language and thought become connected and this enables a child to use verbal thought. With the advancement of age, children start using language for describing their actions. Gradually, verbal descriptions begin to be expressed before the child completes an action, rather than following it. For example, rather than a child saying 'hit ball' after he has hit the ball, it will occur before the action takes place. Vygotsky (1962) interpreted this as an evidence for the fact that language and thought are gradually becoming interdependent. Thus, following Vygotsky, language has now two different functions for the child—language becomes one internal means of thinking and problem solving and another function, which is external, is that it involves engaging in social interaction and communicating with other people.

Vygotsky's viewpoint regarding relationship between language and thinking appears to be more plausible than Piaget's viewpoint (Garnham and Oakhill, 1994).

DIVERSITY IN LANGUAGE ACQUISITION AMONG INDIAN CHILDREN

Language acquisition by a child is a dynamic rather than static process. No doubt that it follows some degree of uniformity, yet it is characterised by many diversities and individual differences due to various socio-cultural contexts. Several researches have been conducted by Indian psychologists and psycholinguistics on different aspects of language development in India during the past decades. These researches have thrown light upon the fact that although acquisition of different Indian languages proceeds uniformly, there is a wide range of individual differences.

Chengappa and Devi (2002) studied language acquisition in Kannada and Hindi. The age range of children, who participated in this study, was from birth to five years. The investigators collected a large corpus of speech samples by recording children's spontaneous utterances, utterances produced in natural interaction with others, narrative speech in the form of strong telling and picture completion. Subsequently, in-depth analysis of all these data in terms of phonological, morphological and syntactic aspects was done by the investigators. Results revealed that the course of language acquisition in Hindi and Kannada was more or less similar with some differences in the sequence and the age of acquisition. The primary differences in language acquisition of Hindi and Kannada were as under:

1. Inflection of verb for number was found in 42–48 month group for Kannada knowing children, while among Hindi knowing children it was found at the age of 24–30 months.
2. Aspirated consonants were found in Hindi-knowing children at the age of 36–42 months, whereas Kannada-knowing children did not display this aspirated-non-aspirated consonants even at the age of 54–60 months. This difference was attributed to the fact that phonemic contrast between aspirated and non-aspirated consonants is merged in spoken Kannada.

Some other Indian researchers have also done studies on specific linguistic features of various Indian languages. For example, Khokle (1994) studied the acquisition of aspirated segment in Marathi. Sailaja (1994) studied the role of syntax in acquisition of Telugu and Devaki (1994) studied the development of past tense in Kannada knowing children.

Lakshmi Bai (2000) studied speech development of her own children, who acquired Tamil and Telugu simultaneously. In this study, an attempt was made to provide a descriptive account of the development of phonology and lexicon in young bilingual children. The study provided support for the view that the development of phonology cannot be studied in a meaningful way without simultaneously considering the lexical items that contain the speech segments, which are highly affected by phonological processes operating at particular stages of development. This study also revealed that there are two distinct stages in phonological development. In the first stage of development, the children pay attention to the whole word in an undifferentiated manner. In the second stage, the children pay attention to articulatory details of the sound system that makes up the lexical items. However, these stages are not distinct, as they may overlap.

Some investigators have studied the influence of environmental input on language acquisition. Narasimhan (1998) wrote a very interesting book on language acquisition. Shukla and Mohanty (1995) investigated the impact of maternal influence on children's speech style. In their study, a positive correlation between mother's speech and child's speech was found. Particular orientation in mothers' speech could explain the individual differences in the style of children's speech to some extent. Misra (1994) analysed thirty mother–child interactions and found that children's use of specific dimensions of a pragmatic system was clearly affected by mother's language, and thus, the study provided support for motherese hypothesis.

LANGUAGE ACQUISITION AND THEORY OF MIND

Researches have been conducted to find a relation between language ability and theory of mind (commonly abbreviated as ToM). The term *ToM* is a somewhat odd phrase to refer to the individual's recognition of the concept of mental activity in others. This term is used with regard to children. A child with a theory of mind is a child, who recognises that people have beliefs, desires and mental lives as well as has an explanatory framework to account for the others' action. Psychologists believe that a child first develops theory of mind when his age ranges from 2½–5 years (Reber, Allen and Reber, 2009; Padakannaya, 2009). During this period, rapid growth in children's mental state vocabulary (such as think, guess, know, see, want, talk, etc.) is taken as an indicator of ToM development. Babu and Misra (2000) found a significant relationship between ToM and children›s acquisition of mental state words. Children's schooling, parents' literary level and mother's knowledge of vocabulary have been found to be significant contributors in the development of ToM and the acquisition of mental state vocabulary in children. Differences in ToM acquisition is generally explained by the language practice at home. Therefore, presence of sibling, joint family, pre-schooling experience tends to contribute towards a rapid development of ToM. During this said period, the major development in language also takes place. Hence, attempt has been made by the investigators to focus on the nature and extent of the relationship between language acquisition and ToM.

Investigators like Babu (1989), Babu and Mishra (2000), Missal (1995), Panda (1991) and Pattnaik (1997) Pattnaik and Babu (2004) conducted a series of studies to examine the relationship between ToM and various aspects of language development in the Indian social context of Orissa. They reported that children do not start to make distinction between verbs on the basis of their presupposition until 4–5 years, which is also the period of development of ToM. Some investigators have examined the impact of parents' literacy in meta-language skill, which includes the development of ToM (Acharya, 1997; Babu and Nanda, 1994). It was found that those children, who came from literate parents, were able to make distinction between 'say-mean' than those children, whose parents were illiterate.

Synthesising these various studies and also some similar studies reported in western culture, Babu and Mohanty (2001) pointed out that language facilitates the development of ToM because it provides a means to encode the various experiences and social interactions. On the whole, this in turn, contributes to a better development of language and cognition. Thus, the development of ToM and language become interdependent and correlated. Babu and Mohanty (2001) further reported that beyond the prelinguistic phase of development, theory of mind including meta-representations, attitudes, cognition and linguistic or communicative processes become mutually overlapping and synergistic social acts.

BILINGUALISM/MULTILINGUALISM IN INDIAN SOCIETY

In today's world, bilingualism/multilingualism has become a norm. *Bilingualism* means ability to speak as well as understand two languages and *multilingualism* means ability to speak and understand more than two languages. Bhatia and Ritchie (2004) wrote a very important book entitled *The Handbook of Bilingualism* in which bilingualism and multilingualism in India as well as in the world have been discussed in detail. The world's estimated 5000 languages are believed to be spoken in about 200 nations. It is estimated that 41% of the English speakers are estimated to be bilingual. The spread of bilingualism and multilingualism is likely to increase in future. Consequently, psychologists have started paying more and more attention to this field. As a result of their efforts, two major international journals have been launched during the last decades—*The International Journal of Bilingualism* was started in 1997 and another journal entitled *Bilingualism: Language and Cognition* was started in 1998.

In India, Mohanty (1994a, 1994b, 2000, 2001 and 2003) is working continuously in the field of psychology of bilingualism and multilingualism. His theoretical framework is based upon the *Vygotskian model*, which emphasises that all cognitive processes are rooted in socialisation and are influenced by a variety of cultural tools that include language, art, architecture, number system, etc. Mohanty has given much emphasis upon the developmental and educational implications of multilingualism in the Indian socio-cultural system. According to him, acquisition of language and its use overlaps with the acquisition of the major requirements of culture. He has provided a good place for the proper growth of bilingualism and through his researches, he has highlighted the positive aspects of bilingualism for Indian society, where cultural pluralism and multilingualism are accepted norms.

Mohanty et al. (1999) and Mohanty and Perregaux (1996) extensively studied the process and developmental stages of multilingual socialisation in Indian children. Based on studies conducted in Uttar Pradesh, Haryana and Odisha, Mohanty and his colleagues identified three stages of the development of language socialisation in the multilingual Indian society. The sample included in this study was children in the age range of two to nine years. The pattern of development of language socialisation was explained in terms of three developmental periods, each period having two stages. These three stages were *the period of language differentiation,* which continues up to about four years of age, *the period of awareness of language,* which continues from four to five years of age and the *period of multilingual functioning,* which continues from six to seven plus years of age.

Mohanty (1994a) also tried to explain bilingualism in Indian society in the light of Berry's enculturation model. Based on two dimensions, Berry (1999) tried to explain the interactions between two cultures in terms of acculturation attitude of the individuals. These two dimensions are maintenance of one's own identity and establishing a relationship with people of other culture. According to Berry, in such a situation, there can be four outcomes—assimilation, integration separation and marginalisation. When applied to bilingualism, the corresponding outcomes of these four outcomes would be transitional bilingualism, language integration, linguistic nationalism and double semilingualism. In fact, such analysis has also received an echo in Hamers and Blanc's differentiation of bicultural language I, monocultural language II, accultural and decultured kinds of bilingualism as cited by Bhatia and Ritchie (2004). On the basis of several studies conducted by Mohanty (1994b, 1998), it was concluded that when socio-economic status or SES, IQ and school-climate related variables were controlled, the children of mother tongue-medium schools performed better than L2 (English) medium school children. Such results obviously advocates the supremacy of education through the mother tongue. Thus, following Mohanty, mother tongue should alone be the medium of instructions up to the primary level, and later, at the appropriate stages, regional, national and English languages should be introduced.

In the context of study of bilingualism and multilingualism, code mixing and code switching are very interesting. *Code mixing* means mixing of various linguistic units such as morphemes, words, modifiers, phrases, etc. mainly from two participating grammatical systems within a sentence. Therefore, it is intrasentential. *Code switching* is one which operates across sentences of two language system. Therefore, it is intersentential. Bhatia and Ritchie (2004) used the term *language mixing* for covering both code mixing and code switching. Their researches showed that language mixing is not random, but systematic and complex because social variables such as class, religion, gender and age can influence language-mixing behaviour. According to them, sanctioning people express a negative attitude towards Hindi-English language mixing, but still they might reflect a positive attitude unconsciously, which could be reflected by their liberal language mixing in day-to-day communication. This kind of analysis of language mixing emphasises basically social-psychological factors. Besides, there is matrix language analysis of language mixing, which provides an analysis based upon psycholinguistic dimension. The matrix language model tends to describe language mixing on the basis of the hierarchical relationship between the matrix language and the embedded language. *Embedded language* is one that contributes to the imported material (Bhat and Chengappa, 2004). *Matrix language* is a base language that provides the sentence with its basic character. Bhat and Chengappa conducted researches in which the matrix language model was tested on normal Kannada–English bilinguals and results revealed an underlying matrix language system for Kannada–English language mixing (Padakannaya, 2009).

READING ACQUISITION AMONG INDIAN CHILDREN

Reading is a fascinating subject of scientific enquiry. *Reading* may be defined as a process of deriving meaning from the written form of language. In fact, reading is a complex neuro-psycholinguistic process having perceptual, cognitive, linguistic, motivational and neurobiological components. Previously, reading was viewed basically as a process involving two basic components, that is, decoding and comprehension, but nowadays, besides these two, another important component, called *decoding speed*, has also been added (Joshi and Aaron, 2000).

Reading acquisition undoubtedly involves universal future. Indian studies conducted in this field have suggested that there are script-specific components in literary acquisition. Frith (1985) formulated a model of reading acquisition, which has generated a lot of researches. According to this model, children go through three successive stages of reading acquisition—stage of logographic, stage of alphabetic and stage of orthographic. In *logographic stage*, children read certain commonly seen words—the holistic process without deciphering their constituent unit. Here, often the first letter of the word plays a vital role. In the next stage, that is, in the *stage of alphabetic,* children learn grapheme to phoneme correspondence rules and use that knowledge for writing and reading. This is a slow process because alphabetic strategy implies successive conversion of letter strings to their corresponding sound units. In *orthographic stage*, children go back to the visual strategy of processing print at the morphemic level without any phonemic mediation by considering letter order (Padakannaya, 2009). Karanth and Prakash (1996) conducted a longitudinal study of normal children's ($N = 48$) learning to read Kannada from UKG through grades 1 and 2 for testing the validity of Frith's model. Their study failed to find any evidence for logographic-like stage of reading among children. Wimmer and Hummer (1990) also doubted the existence of this state in reading acquisition of German.

Some investigators have studied reading acquisition in other languages. For example, Vasanta (1999) studied knowledge of phonological and orthographic properties of Telugu words. His study led him to conclude that younger children tended to pay greater attention to the phonological aspects of words, whereas older children of grade five tended to pay more attention to the orthographic properties of the words they read. Swain and Sahu (2002) studied reading acquisition among Oriya children, who were studying in grades 2–5. Their findings revealed that the children's scores on the measures of short-term memory, long-term memory and Raven's Coloured Progressive Matrices (RCPM) determined their performance in oral reading test. Iyer (2000) studied developmental pattern of Malayalam reading and its relationship with meta-phonological skills.

All these studies and several others done by Indian researchers (Sahu, 2003) have revealed that western models of reading acquisition are not adequate to explain the phenomenon. This automatically implies the significance of indigenous models of reading acquisition. Keeping in view these various studies, Padakannaya and Mohanty (2004) suggested that in Indian languages, the normal course of reading acquisition follows a fixed sequence, as shown in Figure 16.2.

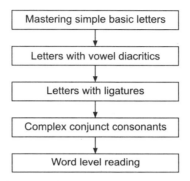

Figure 16.2 Sequence for normal course of reading acquisition.

In this context, the research work of Patel (2004) is also worth mentioning. He presented an exhaustive description of the design of Brahmi script as well as an in-depth linguistic analysis of aksara in both spoken and written form. Patel's work is considered important partly because he provided a comprehensive analysis of aksara, which is the basic unit of graphemic symbol in the Indian writing system and partly because he emphasised the cultural and social inputs to reading acquisition. Padakannaya and Mohanty (2004) extended the work of Patel on aksara and suggested an aksara-based model of reading for Indian scripts. The basic feature of this model is that it has emphasised the dual routes of lexical and non-lexical processing in reading. The transparent and orthographic syllable nature of aksara tends to favour the phonological/non-lexical strategy of reading. Researches on Indian scripts have, in general, suggested that non-lexical strategy is a very common strategy employed in reading Indian languages. Following Padakannaya and Mohanty (2004), the common pathway before reading aloud is shown in Figure 16.3.

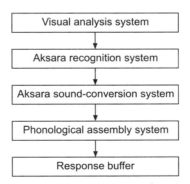

Figure 16.3 Common pathway before reading aloud.

Patel's work is considered important because he had demonstrated the importance of Indian oral tradition for various theories and models of reading acquisition. In fact, he emphasised the phonetic wisdom as represented in various *Patha*, *Pada* and *Vikruti* of *Veda* citation and successfully linked it to the emergence of literacy (Padakannaya, 2009).

GENDER DIFFERENCES IN VERBAL COMMUNICATION

The common stereotype is that women talk more than men. Does such stereotype has a real base? In order to answer this question, James and Drakich (1993) did a review of literature relating to talking among adults. Their finding did not provide support to the stereotype because they reported that out of the 56 studies reviewed, 24 showed that men talked more than women, 10 studies showed that men talked more on some measures and 4 studies revealed mixed findings and 2 studies revealed that women talked more than men.

Now the question is—why do men talk more than women? The classical explanation is based upon status theory. Since men have higher status than women in society, they are more dominant force in communication. However, James and Drakich (1993) provided a different explanation. According to them, the nature of men's task behaviour is such that it is likely to involve more talking than women's socio-emotional behaviour. For example, giving advice to someone (usually men's task behaviour) is likely to take longer than agreeing with someone. Moreover, setting in which talking is done, is also important. James and Darkich (1993) found that as compared to women, men are especially more likely to talk in structured or formal setting. On the other hand, when the setting or situation is informal or unstructured, where socio-emotional behaviour dominates rather than task behaviour, women talk more than men.

Apart from general amount of talking, some researchers have revealed that there are some specific differences in language used by men and women. Here, the research work of Mulac (1998) is worth-mentioning. He reviewed literature on sex differences in language use and concluded that

1. Women were more likely to use intensive adverbs (such as so, really), refer to emotions in language, ask questions, use longer sentences and also use hedges (that is, may be, kind of, etc.).
2. Men, in comparison to women, were more likely to refer to quantity in language (that is, I walked four times as far to office as my colleague does), use directives and make reference to themselves.

These differences in the use of language by men and women are considered to reflect different types of relationships. Often women seem to talk in ways that maintain relationship (Maltz and Broker, 1982) and they encourage others to communicate by putting some questions and making responses that further encourage conversation. Thus, throughout the conversation, women use minimal response (such as saying OK, uh-uh, etc.), which encourages others to continue their speech. On the other hand, men's language is less facilitative of relationship. Men interrupt others, tend to challenge others, ignore others' comment and make declaration of facts and new opinion (Maltz and Broker, 1982).

For holistic understanding of verbal communication of men and women, Mulac, Bradac and Gibbons (2001) provided a three-dimensional classification given as under:

1. First, use of language is *direct* or *indirect*. Women's language is more indirect because they ask questions and use hedges. On the other hand, men's language is more direct because they use directives.
2. Second, language can be *elaboration* or *succinct*. Since women use longer sentences and also take help of intensive adverbs, their language is comparatively more elaborative.
3. Third, language can be *affective* or *instrumental*. Since women's socio-emotional behaviour is more dominant, their use of emotional words is more affective. On the other hand, men's reference to quantity in language is instrumental.

There are several qualifiers to the above discussed sex differences in language. For example, one important factor that influences the use of language by men and women is the sex of the person with whom one is talking. Women's greater use of polite language may take place only when they are talking with men. Carli (1990) found that women used more disclaimers, tag questions and hedges when talking with men rather than with women. The common belief that men interrupt more than women during conversation is actually not consistent and depends on the context. Zimmerman and West (1975) conducted a study in this regard and reported that in other sex dyads, men accounted for 96% of the interruptions but in the same sex-dyads, men and women interrupted each other equally often. Further researches have shown that men and women tend to interrupt. Maltz and Broker (1982) found in their study that men interrupt to assert themselves and win the floor, whereas women interrupt to request elaboration or clarification from the communicator. Aries (1996) found that setting or situation also influences interruptive behaviour. During informal conversations, women interrupt more than men. However, during formal conversation, men interrupt more than women. Also, it has been reported that women often talk at the same time as one another, completing each other's sentences and agreeing with one another. Such interruptions tend to show enthusiasm and involvement in the conversation rather than any kind of dominance.

Another important reason for sex differences in verbal communication is concerned with the topic of conversation. Men and women speak about different topics that require different languages. It has been found that male same-sex dyads talked more about women, sports, being trapped in relationship and drinking, whereas female same-sex dyads talked more about men, relationship, clothes and feelings (Martin, 1997).

BARRIERS TO VERBAL COMMUNICATION

According to Gordon (1970), there are some obvious barriers to effective verbal communication. Important ones are as under:

1. **Criticising:** When someone criticises others or makes a harsh, negative evaluations of another person, it generally reduces further communication. For example, when a teacher says to his student that it is due to his own fault that he has failed in the examination. Such criticism is liking to produce a barrier in communication between teacher and student.
2. **Name-calling and labelling:** When one engages in name-calling and labelling, it generally results in reducing communication. One person might say another person, "you are stupid, thief and dirty". Often when a person is very much emotionally hurt by the behaviour of other, he resorts to name-calling and labelling.

3. **Threatening:** Threatening is another barrier which disrupts the communication. Threats are intended to control the behaviour of other person by force. For example, a person may tell to another person, "If you do not do what I am telling you, your life will be spoiled." Such threats obviously produce a barrier in further communication.

4. **Advising:** *Advising* means talking down to other while giving them a solution to the problem. For example, a teacher may say to the student, "This arithmetical problem is so easy to solve. I do not understand why you were not able to solve it?" Such advice may irritate the student, who may decide to maintain distance from the teacher.

5. **Ordering:** *Ordering* means commanding another person to do what you want. Such direction does not always prove to be effective because it creates resistance. For example, father may tell his son, "Write this essay, right now!" Likewise, a teacher may say to the student in the class," Stand up on the bench." Such ordering being very distasteful and disrespectful to the listener is likely to reduce further communication.

6. **Moralising:** This means preaching somebody what he should do or he should not do. Such moralising generally increases guilt and anxiety on the part of the listeners and tends to reduce verbal communication. For example, when a boss says to one of his subordinates," you should have done homework for the meeting which is going to be held today. You should feel sorry for this."

Thus, we find that there are several factors which tend to create barriers in verbal communication between speakers and listeners. In order to avoid such barriers, the speakers should place the things verbally in a much soft and guarded language.

NATURE AND PURPOSE OF COMMUNICATION

Communication is the heart of human social interaction. Indeed, one of the major characteristics that make distinction between human beings and other species is the ability to communicate on a structured, symbol level through the formal use of language. Communication consists of ways through which individuals transmit intended or unintended messages to others. Since it is necessary for people to be able to communicate their thoughts, feelings and attitudes for carrying out their social activities, communication is uniquely a social process.

The term *communication*, in psychological sense, refers to the exchange of ideas, thoughts and experiences between the individuals. In simple words, communication may be broadly defined as the process of meaningful interaction among human beings. More specifically, it is a process by which meanings are perceived and understandings are reached among human beings. Thus, communication is a simple process of passing information, ideas or even emotions from one person to another. There are four important characteristics of communication, which are given below:

1. The nature of communication is dynamic because it involves a constant process of change. As the attitudes, feelings, emotions and expectations of the persons, who are in communicative interaction, changes, the nature of their communication also changes.
2. Communication is irreversible because once the message is sent, it cannot be taken back. For example, once we have engaged in an emotional outburst or have made a slip of tongue, we cannot erase it. Our apologies can make it light but cannot erase what was communicated.

3. Communication is a continuous process because it never stops, whether we are awake or asleep, we are continuously processing ideas or thoughts, since brain remains active.
4. Communication is interactive because we are constantly interacting with other people or with other ideas. Others tend to react to our speech and we react to our own speech and then react to those reactions. In this way, a cycle of action or reaction forms the basis of the communication.

The basic purposes of communication are as under:
1. To develop understanding among the interacting persons
2. To foster any attitude that is necessary for motivation and cooperation
3. To discourage the spread of misinformation, ambiguity and rumours, which can produce stress and tension among interacting persons
4. To improve the relations between interacting persons by keeping communication channels open and accessible
5. To encourage social relations between interacting persons by encouraging intercommunication (This tends to satisfy the basic human need for a sense of belonging and for friendship.)

There are two general types of communication—*verbal communication* and *non-verbal communication*. Verbal communication uses language that is spoken. Spoken language includes sounds, words, meanings and grammatical rules. In fact, it is socially acquired system of sound patterns with meanings agreed on by speakers and listeners. To understand the meaning of sounds of speakers and to produce an appropriate response, the listeners must recognise the following components:

1. Distinct sounds which compose the language (phonetic component)
2. Combination of sounds into words (morphologic component)
3. Meaning of words (semantic component)
4. Conventions for putting words together built into language (Syntactic component or grammar)

Unspoken languages such as sign languages and computer language lack sounds (or phonetic component), but they include the remaining components of spoken language. For example, people use sign language such as a particular body movements to signal words (morphology) with shared meanings (semantics) and they also combine these words into sentences according to the grammatical rules (syntax). Social psychologists' main focus has been on how language fits in social interaction and influences it (Giles et al., 1981).

MODELS OF COMMUNICATION

Social psychologists have formulated three models of communication—encoder–decoder model, intentionalist model and perspective-taking model.

1. *Encoder–decoder model*

According to this model, the communication originates in the speaker's desire to convey some ideas or feelings. He encodes the message into a set of symbols and transmits it to the listeners. The listener decodes the message. In other words, the encoder–decoder model simply views communication as a process in which an idea or feeling is encoded into symbols by the speakers, transmitted to the listeners and decoded into the original idea or meaning (Krauss and Fussell, 1996). The entire process is shown in Figure 16.4.

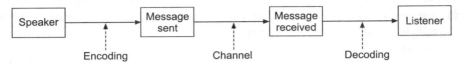

Figure 16.4 Encoder–decoder model.

According to the encoder–decoder model, the basic unit of communication is the message, which has its origin in the desire of the speaker to communicate. When the speaker encodes the information, which he wants to communicate, into a combination of verbal or non-verbal symbols, a message is said to be constructed. The message can be sent by face-to-face interaction, telephone, electronic means or in writing. The listener has to decode the message in order to arrive at the meaning of the message that speaker wants to communicate.

As we know, the goal of the communication is to transfer the message content accurately from speaker to listener. The more codable the idea or feeling in the language, the more accurate will be the communication. In fact, the accuracy of communication depends on the extent to which the message inferred by the listener clearly matches the message intended by the speaker. According to this model, the primary influence on communication accuracy is that of *codability*, which can be defined as the extent of interpersonal agreement about what something is called. Codability is partly the function of language. In general, the messages, which are easily coded, are more accurately transmitted to the listeners (Delamater and Myers, 2009). Codability also involves an agreement between the speaker and the listener about what something is to be called. It also depends on the way to which the speaker and the listener define symbols such as words and gestures in the same way. That is the reason, why two persons of the same religion, class, caste, etc. and using same language, when interact with each other, do not experience any difficulty in coding–decoding. But with a person of different religion, caste, class, etc. and using different language, when we converse, we realize difficulty in coding–decoding the message. However, sometimes, the processes of encoding and decoding are very deliberate or mindful (Giles and Coupland, 1991). This is particularly true when we listen to a speaker, who communicates on a novel topic.

Communication is not always a conscious process. Rather, it also occurs without any self-conscious planning. For example, in very familiar or routine situation, a person often relies on a conversational script, that is, an organised series of utterances that occur with a little or no conscious thoughts. Researches have shown that communication accuracy is typically high in the situations governed by conversational scripts. On the other hand, if the conversation is scripted, listeners do pay attention to only the generic content of message and not to its idiosyncratic features. Kitayama and Burnstein (1988) tested this prediction in a field study in which students were approached by a stranger, who asked for a piece of paper. Prior to the request, some students (participants) were asked to pay attention to it and some other students were not forewarned. Results revealed that forewarned students were more likely to remember the specific words used in the request than those who were unprepared.

2. Intentionalist model

We have just seen that the encoder–decoder model emphasises messages, which consist of symbols and whose meaning can be widely and clearly understood. In fact, it tends to direct our attention to the literal meaning of verbal messages. But, in reality, messages are not interpreted directly, rather in terms of intention of the speakers. According to the intentionalist model, the communication involves the exchange of communicative intentions and messages only serve as means to ends (Krauss and Fussell, 1996). The speaker selects the message, which he or she believes is most likely to accomplish his or her intention.

In this model, the communication originates with the intention of speaker to achieve some goals or objectives or to have some impact upon the behaviour of the listener. However, there is no fixed, one-to-one relation between words and the intended effects. Therefore, the speaker can use different types of utterances or messages to achieve his intended effect. For example, suppose you are lying in your room and want your roommate to bring Sprite for you to drink. Exhibit 16.1 presents some of the utterances that you would like to make.

EXHIBIT 16.1

1. Give me a glass of Sprite.
2. Can you give me some Sprite?
3. Would you give me something to drink?
4. Would you give me some Sprite?
5. Would you mind if I ask you to give some Sprite?
6. I am thirsty.
7. Have you bought some Sprite from the shop?
8. How is that Sprite we bought?

According to the intentionalist model, decoding the literal meaning of the message is only a part of the communication. To be successful, the listener must correctly infer the speaker's underlying intention. For example, to the question—*how is that Sprite we bought?*—an appropriate response to that literal message would be 'good'. But if the communication is really to be successful, your roommate must infer your intention, that is, you really want to drink Sprite. As we know, utterances state something as well as do something (Searle, 1979). For example, in Exhibit 16.1, utterances number 1 to 6 clearly state the speaker's desire to drink sprite, whereas utterances number 7 and 8 do not. But all eight utterances perform an action and each has a force of request. Reality is that the utterances are not significant because of their literal meaning, but they are significant because they contribute to the work of interaction in which they occur (Geis, 1995). According to this model, when inferring the speaker's intention, the listener must take into account the context, especially the status or role relationship between the speaker and the listener and the social context in which the message is provided. For example, if you and your roommate are intimate friends, you might choose a less polite form of utterance such as option 2. But in the presence of your father-in-law and mother-in-law your request to them most probably would be different and may take a different form such as option 4.

For knowing whether the message has achieved the intended effect, speaker generally relies on the feedback provided by the listener's reactions. If the feedback indicates that the listener has interpreted the message accurately, the speaker may elaborate, change the topic or end the interaction. On the other hand, if the speaker finds that the listener has inferred a different meaning from that intended, he will often attempt to send the same message using different words and gestures.

In order to be successful for any communication, it is essential that the speaker must cooperate with the listener by formulating the content of message in a manner that reflects the listener's way of thinking about the events, objects, etc. In turn, the listener should also cooperate by trying to actively understand the message. He must go beyond the literal meanings of the words for inferring the correct meaning of the speaker. According to Grice (1975), listeners tend to assume that most talk is based on the *cooperative principle*, which means that the listeners generally assume that the speaker is behaving cooperatively by trying to be informative, truthful, clear and relevant to the interactions being made.

3. *Perspective-taking model*

Perspective-taking model is based upon symbolic interaction theory. According to this model, the communication involves exchange of messages using symbols, whose meaning varies across different situations. In fact, the model views the process of communication as both creating and reflecting a shared context between the speaker and the listener. The model specifies that the communication involves both verbal and non-verbal symbols, whose meaning depends on the shared context created by both the speaker and the listener. The development of this shared text requires reciprocal role-taking, where both the speaker and the listener place themselves in the role of each other so that they may understand the perspective of each other. In fact, the context created by the ongoing interaction changes from time to time and both the speaker and the listener must be attentive to these changes for making communication successful.

In this model, the accuracy of communication depends on shared meanings. Both speakers and listeners must select and discover the meanings of words through their context. When the meanings of message are not clear, speakers and listeners must jointly work out their meanings as they go along. In order to be successful, communication depends on what social psychologists have called *intersubjectivity*, where both the speaker and the listener need information about other's status, plan and intentions. When both are known to each other, they can share their past experiences with each other as the basis for effective communication. On the other hand, when they are not known to each other, and are therefore, strangers, listener uses stereotypes as a basis for making inferences about the plans and intentions of the speaker and vice versa.

This model specifies that both the production and interpretation of communication are influenced by the interpersonal context in which it occurs (Giles and Coupland, 1991). There are three basic elements in the context that influence communication—*norms, representations of prior similar situations* and *emotional arousal*.

As we know, every social situation has a norm regarding the way of communication. These norms tend to specify what language is to be used, what topics are appropriate or inappropriate and how persons of varying status should be addressed. Depending on these norms, we communicate the message that vary in words, tone, etc. For example, suppose a person wants another person to bring a glass of water. To his son in his home, he may say, "Bring a glass of water". To an employee, he would say, "Would you bring a glass of water?". To his son at work, "Please bring a glass of water, Monu". These examples show that these different ways of making a request reflect differences in speech rules depending on the setting as well as on the relationship between the listener and the speaker.

Each situation, particularly a new situation, tends to evoke the representations of prior similar situations or the language once used or heard in those situations (Chapman et al., 1992). These conversational histories provide the people with the contents of speech repertoires. When we meet with a stranger in the party, we generally speak in a manner which proves to be effective in facilitating conversation in similar situation.

Listeners also interpret messages in light of emotions elicited in them. If the situation is such that evokes the same representations and emotions in both the speakers and listeners, the communication becomes generally effective and accurate.

Researches have shown that the members of group tend to share a *linguistic intergroup bias* (Maass and Arcuri, 1992). Such bias indicates that there are some subtle and systematic differences in the language we use to describe events as a function of our group membership. We generally describe other members of our own group behaving in a proper way and the members of out-groups behaving in an improper way at the very abstract levels. This automatically encourages positive stereotypes regarding the members of own group and negative stereotypes about the members of other group. This technique tends to encourage an attribution to the individual rather than to the group. Wigboldus, Semin and Spears (2000) conducted a study in which these processes were examined. In this study, the participants were asked to write some message regarding a male or female, who behaved in a way consistent or inconsistent with the gender stereotypes. It was found that stereotype-consistent behaviours were described abstractly and stereotype-inconsistent behaviours were described concretely. These messages were then provided to the other participants, who answered questions about the incidents. As predicted, the stereotype-consistent behaviours were attributed to the group membership, whereas stereotype-inconsistent behaviours were clearly attributed to the individuals.

The model also requires that to attain mutual understanding and facilitate communication, language performance must be appropriate to the social and cultural context. If it is not appropriate to the social and cultural context, even grammatically acceptable sentence will make no sense. For example, a sentence like 'my brother eats raw lizard' is grammatically correct but in Indian culture, the listeners would have difficulty in interpreting it. But in lizard-eating culture, this utterance would be quite meaningful and sensible. This example shows that the successful communication clearly requires sociolinguistic competence. Sentences or utterances that are in accord with sociolinguistic competence make sense to the listeners because they fit with the listeners' social knowledge (Hymes, 1974). The utterances that clash with what is known about the social relationship to which it refers, suggest that a speaker is not sociolinguistically competent (Grimshaw, 1990).

Conclusively, it can be said that according to the perspective-taking model, the speaker must produce a message that has not only an appropriate literal meaning but also an intention appropriate to the relationship and social setting. The message must reflect appropriate degree of intersubjectivity between the speaker and the listener, consistent with the interaction context, including sociolinguistic competence.

COMMUNICATION NETWORK

A *communication network* is the pattern of direction in which information flows in a group or an organisation. In simple words, who talks to whom in the group involves the study of communication network. Researches have created different types of communication networks in laboratory groups and have studied the impact of these structures on satisfaction, efficiency and perceptions of leadership. Leavitt (1951) conducted some early researches for examining different types of communication netwcrks and their impact upon the satisfaction level of group members. He used four types of communication networks—*wheel*, *chain*, *circle* and *Y-shaped network*. Later on, Shaw (1964) added one more communication network, that is, *comcon*. He used networks of five-person groups. These five types of communication network of five-person groups are represented in Figure 16.5.

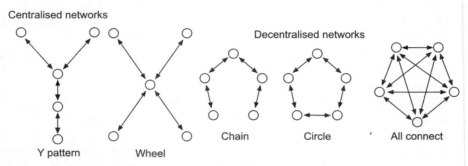

Figure 16.5 Communication networks of five-person groups.

A discussion of these five communication networks is presented here.

1. **Wheel network:** In this network, there is obviously one member of the group who has very centralised position. Therefore, in this pattern, only the central person is allowed to communicate with the other members of the group. Thus, in this network, the information flows to and from a single person, who is at centralised position. Members in the group communicate mainly with that person rather than with each other. Such a communication network is a fast means of getting information from the members, since the person at centralised place can do so directly and efficiently.

2. **Chain network:** In the chain network, members may only communicate with the person adjacent to them. Here, the communication information can flow up and down the chain, but of course, cannot complete the entire circle.

3. **Y-shaped network:** In this type of communication network, one person becomes more central in the communication than any other. In this network, the member at the fork of the 'Y' usually becomes the central person in the network.

4. **Circle network:** In this network of communication, no one is central and the communication is allowed to flow in all directions. Here, the members can communicate with their immediate neighbour, but not with others in the group.

5. **Comcon network:** The word *comcon* is short for *completely connected*. Comcon pattern is one that totally allows open communication among all the members of the group.

Of these various communication networks, the wheel pattern is more restricted than the circle pattern and 'Y' pattern is more centralised than the comcon pattern.

Using these various communication patterns, researchers have tried to find their impact upon group performance both in terms of achieving the goals and its ability to satisfy the members of the group (Leavitt, 1951). It was found that the communication pattern such as circle is characterised by slow flow of communication and inefficiency in terms of problem solving, but it produces greater satisfaction for the group members, who participate almost equally in the communication flow. The highly centralised patterns such as wheel pattern and Y-shaped pattern are characterised by higher efficiency, but less satisfaction for the outlying members. Leavitt also reported that although highly centralised patterns tended to be efficient in terms of task-oriented behaviour, they perpetuated errors made by the people in those highly centralised positions. For example, circle network permits for greater correction of errors by the other members of the group than does the wheel or Y-shaped pattern.

Subsequent researches have shown that communication patterns are related to other dimensions of the group. Shaw (1954a, 1954b) demonstrated that when any information is distributed unequally among the members of the group, highly centralised groups were found to be less efficient in terms of problem solving in comparison to the groups in circle or chain. Although centralised networks appear to work better for simple tasks, the more complex tasks such as solutions of mathematical problems are completed more efficiently with decentralised networks (Shaw, 1954a). Shaw also showed that if the nature of the problem was such that it required thinking and innovation, it was better solved by the less centralised networks. Shaw (1964) also revealed that when the problem solving dimension was unusually high with respect to the task to be done by the group, the person occupying the centralised position in highly centralised network, might become frustrated and overloaded with unmanageable amount of communication.

Similar researches in the real-world organisations have shown the effects of different communication networks on morals and performance. For example, Mears (1974) reported a case study in which management in business corporation tried out a series of different communication networks. Initially, a group consisting of the chief executive and heads of the several divisions was organised in a circle network, with free communication among all the members. It was found that although in such network, morale was high, but performance suffered because no work was done due to spending time in baseless debate and discussion. Subsequently, the group was rearranged in wheel network, with the chief executive at the centre. Such communication pattern reduced motivation and produced errors in relaying information, and thus, both performance and morale suffered. Lastly, a modified circle network was arranged and this allowed each member to communicate only with others, who were directly involved in the decision at hand. Such arrangement resulted in greater satisfaction and productivity. Results clearly send a message that communication networks are very important in real-life situation too.

NON-VERBAL COMMUNICATION

A person does not communicate with words alone. He uses a variety of other behaviours to have a full meaning of his message across other people. These behaviours include such elements like facial expression, body posture, tone of voice, etc. The communication done through these various elements is called *non-verbal communication* (Danziger, 1976; Mehrabian, 1972).

Experimental researches have concentrated upon three general types of non-verbal communications—kinesics (body language), proxemics and paralanguage.

1. Kinesics (body language)

The silent movement of the body parts such as smiles, nods, scowls, gazing, gestures, leg movements, postural shifts, caressing, slapping, and so on constitute *body language*. Since body language entails movement, it is known as *kinesics*. Different types of body language convey different meanings in communication. Usually, when a communicator leans towards the receiver and takes a direct orientation, it is perceived as having a positive attitude towards the receiver. The study conducted by Mehrabian (1968) confirmed it. In this study, some subjects viewed pictures of a seated communicator and were requested to rate how much they thought the communicator liked them (subjects). The shown picture varied in various dimensions such as in terms of degree of leaning (forward or backward), the openness of the posture and the amount of relaxation. It was found in the results that when the communicator leaned slightly forward, adopted an open posture and appeared to be relaxed, he was perceived to be expressing a positive attitude. In day-to-day conversation, we often gesture with our hands to show our inherent desire. Handshake is one such very popular gesture. Depending on whether handshake is firm or limp, dry or damp, its meaning varies. In fact, handshake can make a strong first impression and influence future interactions. The research conducted by Chaplin et al. (2000) confirmed this fact. In this study, there were four trained coders (two men and two women) and each of them shook hands twice with 112 men and women and rated the participants on four measures of personality. Results revealed that the man or woman, who shook hand firmly, was rated by the coders as extroverted and emotionally expressive and was given very low ratings on shyness. Not only that, the women, who shook hand firmly, were also rated as open to new experience. Similarly, nodding one's head, folding one's arms and pointing can convey emotional feelings, status and responsiveness or attention. Likewise, when two people get together, the one who has more relaxed posture is usually a person who has higher status. For a lower-status person to adopt a more relaxed posture is usually seen as being disrespectful or defiant (Mehrabian, 1969). The erect position with the head thrown back tends to communicate aloofness and the more relaxed position inclining towards the other person tends to communicate friendliness and interest (Mehrabian, 1972).

In addition to posture, the way in which a person moves from one place to another is often expressive of self-confidence and status. A person who walks stiffly or hesitantly tends to give a very different impression than that person who strides briskly and effortlessly.

Facial expressions usually indicate the degree of affiliation and warmth in the relationship. Generally, we pay attention to the face of the persons with whom we are communicating. Moreover, the face is capable of producing many different types of behaviours. One dictionary points out 98 behaviours of which 25 involve face (Rashotte, 2002). Some of the common examples of behaviour involving face are closing one's eyes, barring the teeth, licking the lips, frowning, grinning, raising one's eyebrows and smiling. The physical features of the face combined with these various movements convey a variety of messages, including information about social identity. Various personality traits can be inferred from the facial features and physiognomy, that is, the study of reading faces, is based on this fact. Hassin and Trope (2000) conducted a very important study in this regard. In this study, participants were given photographs and descriptions of a target person. These photographs had been selected based on high and low ratings by the other participants on the confidence, charisma and dominance of the person in the photo. Participants were asked to rate the target person on 13 personality scales. Results revealed that when the verbal description was vague, the characteristics of the photo significantly affected the ratings. The results obviously show that people tend to make inferences about personality on facial features.

Eye contact and eye movement (in facial expression) tend to reflect the closeness of the relationship. Positive eye contact indicates attraction and respect. People tend to engage in mutual glances if they like each other, but they try to avoid looking at other if they dislike (Exline and Winters, 1965). Extending this study a bit further, Rubin (1970) studied the eye-contact patterns of heterosexual couples, who were waiting together to participate in an experiment of psychology. It was observed that those couples, who were in love, were more likely to gaze into each other's eyes than those, who were not in love. Although the implication of these two studies is that eye contact reflects a positive relationship, this is not always true. Commenting on this point, Ellsworth and Carlsmith (1968) pointed out that eye contact serves to intensify the ongoing verbal content of the relationship, whether it is positive or negative. In general, research on eye contact seems to show that a limited amount of eye contact communicates liking (Exline and Winters, 1965), whereas excessive eye contact communicates threat. Success and failure experiences also seem to be related to the amount of eye contact—eye contact drops after a failure experience and increases after a success experience (Modigliani, 1971). Argyle and Dean's (1965) *affiliative conflict theory* indicates that eye contact is related to our need to affiliate with others, and approach and avoidance forces produce an equilibrium among proximity, eye contact and other elements of intimacy. People maintain a level of eye contact with others in relations to their interpersonal distance that produces degree of intimacy they desire. If the people's distance becomes closer, they tend to reduce the frequency and duration of eye contact to maintain the same degree of intimacy. If the people are further away, they increase eye contact.

Studies conducted by Schlosberg (1952, 1954) found that facial expressions demonstrated high accuracy and agreement in their judgements of basic simple emotions like fear, surprise, happiness, anger, sadness, disgust and interest, and such agreement is cross-cultural (Ekman, Sorenson and Friesen, 1969). The research seems to demonstrate that so long as the response patterns are in fairly broad, general categories such as sadness, there is evidence of the existence of universals. However, finer distinctions do not appear to be universal insofar as their modes of expressions are concerned. For example, it does not appear to be universal what gestures tend to accompany fear as opposed to distress in general. Various researchers have led to the conclusion that there is no universal language of gestures, but some broad and general expressions such as fear, sadness or happiness appear to carry same gestural components across many cultures.

2. *Proxemics*

Proxemics focuses on spatial distance between the people communicating with each other as well as on their orientation towards each other. Until 1960s, social psychologists had a little interest in the area of proxemics, but with the publication of work of anthropologist, Hall (1959), they started taking interest in it. Hall was impressed by the cultural variation that occurred in what was considered to be the proper distance between the two people interacting with each other. Researches have indicated that the distance between people is an indication of perceived attitude created through previous interpersonal relations, which subsequently exist among the people. People tend to increase the distance between themselves when they dislike or do not know each other. Individuals trying to be friendly try to sit closer in comparison to the people who attempt to convey negative feelings (Heshka and Nelson, 1972). People who stand close together also generally perceive that the other person likes them more than does someone who stands further away (Mehrabian, 1968). When people are completely strangers, the physical distance between them is increased as much as possible (Becker, 1973). For the Arabs, the proper distance between two interacting persons is a few inches between each person's nose, and for Americans, a distance between two and three feet is most preferred. This invisible boundary for Latin Americans is smaller than that of North Americans. If a Latin American and North American starts communicating with each other, the Latin American tends to more closer in an attempt to maintain proper distance, whereas North American will start to back away. Indians prefer a distance between two to three feet (depending on the degree of intimacy) while communicating with each other.

Apart from the body language, people also communicate non-verbally through the personal effects that they select. For example, their hairstyle, choices of clothing, make-up, eyewear (contact lenses) and the like do convey many message. Joseph and Alex (1972) showed that a uniform tends to communicate political opinion, lifestyle, social status and occupation, depending on how its wearer behaves.

3. *Paralanguage*

Paralanguage focuses on vocal behaviour, which includes pitch, loudness, speed, emphasis, inflection, breathiness, stretching of word, pauses, and so on. All vocal aspects of speech other than words are called *paralanguage*. Paralanguage includes laughing, crying, sighing, moaning, and so on. Scherer (1979) showed that shrillness of voice and rapid delivery tend to communicate tension and excitement in most situations.

Now, one basic question arises—what is the significance of non-verbal communications for interpersonal relations? It has been shown that non-verbal communications tend to indicate five basic qualities of the relationship—trust, closeness, power, attraction and status. Verbal communication fails to focus on these critical dimensions (Fisher, 1982). Non-verbal behaviour may also be useful in detecting deception on the part of the speakers (Zuckerman et al., 1979).

Mehrabian (1972) conducted several studies looking at the relative contributions that verbal, vocal and facial channels make to the overall attitude formed by the listeners. The effect of communication on the sender was assessed by a 6-point scale of liking varying from +3 to −3. Mehrabian's analysis indicated a relative contributions that each of three variables made to the overall assessment of liking and was expressed in terms of the following formula:

$$\text{Total liking} = 55\% \text{ facial} + 38\% \text{ vocal} + 7\% \text{ verbal}$$

This formula clearly indicates that non-verbal components (facial and vocal elements) carry much more weight (93%) in communication than the verbal content (7%). But we should not overgeneralise from this result. What is really required is more integrated study of how verbal and non-verbal elements combine to determine the overall effect of communication (Firestone, 1977).

COMBINING VERBAL AND NON-VERBAL COMMUNICATION

As we know, the communication is multichannelled. Information is converged to us simultaneously through several channels such as verbal, paralinguistic, kinesic and proxemic cues. Thus, communication is the function of many stimuli being emitted at the same time.

Now, one basic question here arises—what is gained and what problems are caused when different communication channels are combined? There can be two types of situation—one situation may be where different channels appear to convey consistent information and another situation may be where different channels appear to convey inconsistent information. In the former situation, different channels reinforce each other and communication becomes more accurate. But in the latter situation, the message given by different channels may produce confusion or even arouse a suspicion of deception. Both these outcomes are discussed below:

1. When different channels of communication are consistent: We receive multiple cues at the same time and these cues often seem redundant because each carries the same message. For example, a warm tone of voice accompanying a smile convey the same thing, that is, positive attitude or liking. But reality is that multiple cues are seldom redundant and they are better judged as complementary (Poyatos, 1983). In fact, the warm tone and the smile convey that the complement is sincere. In this way, multiple cues tend to convey some added information, reduce vagueness and increase the accuracy of communication (Krauss, Morrel–Samuels and Colasante, 1991).

When any one channel of communication is taken alone, it does not carry much weight for accuracy of message exchanged during conversation. For example, by itself, verbal aspect of language is insufficient for accurate communication. In fact, paralinguistic cues and kinesic cues tend to supplement verbal cues by supporting and emphasising them. Grayshon (1980) conducted a study in which the importance of paralinguistic cues was clearly demonstrated. In this study, 251 Nigerian students taken from secondary school and college were the participants. These participants knew English language well, but they did not know the paralinguistic cues of British native speakers. Then, the participants listened to two British recordings with identical verbal content. In one recording, paralinguistic cues hinted that the speaker was giving the listeners a brush-off, whereas in other recording, the paralinguistic cues indicated that the speaker was apologising. Results revealed that about 97% participants failed to make distinction in the meaning that the speaker was conveying, that is, they failed to make distinction between brush-off and apology behaviour. This happened obviously because of the fact that these participants had no idea of paralinguistic cues of British native speakers. Archer and Akert (1977) conducted another study in which supremacy of multiple communication cues information alone in determining the accuracy of communication was established. In this study, the participants (students) were required to observe scenes of social interaction that were either displayed in a video broadcast or described verbally in a video broadcast transcript. Thus, the participants received either full multichannel communication or verbal cues alone. Subsequently, these participants were asked questions relating to what was going in the scene. Results revealed that those participants, who were exposed to multichannel communication (both verbal and non-verbal cues during watching the video broadcast), were more accurate in interpreting social interactions by giving correct answers to the questions asked than those, who were given only the verbal cues. The findings clearly show that we gain accuracy in communication due to consistency in multichannel cues.

2. When different channels of communications are inconsistent: Sometimes, the messages sent by different channels of communications are inconsistent with one another. Such situation makes interaction during communication difficult and problematic one. For example, what would you do if your boss welcomes you during office hours with warm words, a frowning face followed by an annoyed voice? In such a situation, it is very likely that you will react with uncertainty and caution and you will try to infer why the boss is sending such confusing cues. In such a situation, people adopt some strategies to resolve apparently inconsistent cues. Such strategies depend on the likely inference about the reasons for apparent inconsistency (Zuckerman, DePaulo and Rosenthal, 1981). There can be several reasons for inconsistent cues such as the communicator's ambivalent feelings, poor communication skills or an intention to deceive. Researches have been conducted in which a comparison of the relative weight we generally attach to messages from different channels (when we do not suspect suspicion) is done. Mehrabian (1972) conducted a set of studies in which the participants judged the emotions expressed by actors, who posed contradictory verbal, paralinguistic and facial cues. These studies vividly showed that the facial cues were found most important in determining which feelings were correct, next important cues were those of paralinguistic and last in importance were the verbal cues. In later researches, participants were exposed to more complete combinations of visual and auditory cues and it was found that they depended on facial cues rather than paralinguistic cues when these two were inconsistent. Participants also exhibited a preference for facial cues that was found to increase with the advancement of age, indicating the fact that it is, in fact, a learned strategy (De Paulo et al., 1978). Some researches have argued that people tend to use social context in judging which channel is more credible (Bugenthal, 1974). They tend to think over the fact that whether or not different channels such as verbal content, facial expression or tone of voice is appropriate to a particular social situation. For example, if a person recognises that the situation is stressful and tensed, he relies more on those cues that seem consistent with such situational context (such as strained tone of voice) and less on cues that tend to contradict them (such as a happy face or verbal statements of calmness). On the other hand, if the emotional expression is vague, the situational cues tend to determine the emotion that the observers attribute to the person. For example, an individual in a frightening situation displaying an expression of moderate level of anger is judged to be afraid. Thus, persons tend to resolve apparent inconsistencies among different channels of communications in favour of the channel, whose message seems to be the most appropriate for the social context or situation.

GENDER DIFFERENCES IN NON-VERBAL COMMUNICATION

In general, women are better than men in decoding or reading non-verbal behaviour. Women seem to be comparatively more sensitive than men to non-verbal cues, thereby they can more accurately interpret the meaning of non-verbal behaviour (Hall, 1998). Females are better able to understand the real meaning behind various non-verbal cues such as facial expression, vocal intonation and body position. Psychologists have studied the accuracy of gender difference in non-verbal communication. In a typical study, the participants watched a videotape of a person expressing a series of emotions. After being exposed to each segment of film, the participants indicated which of the several emotions such as happiness, disgust or fear, they thought was being displayed. In some other studies, the participants listened to the recording of voices that were content-filtered, that is, altered so that the words were garbled and only the tone of voice was distinct. More than a hundred studies regarding accuracy in decoding the non-verbal behaviour have been conducted and they more or less consistently have reported that women perform better than men. The female advantage is the greatest in reading facial expression, followed by reading body cues and the poorest in decoding voice tone. Such finding seems to be generalised in several countries like Malaysia, Japan, India, Mexico, New Zealand, Hong Kong, Israel (Hall et al., 2000). It is also generalised to infants, children and adolescents (McClure, 2000). In fact, Hall et al. (2000) conducted a meta-analytic review of literature on non-verbal behaviour. They emphatically concluded that women smile and gaze more than men; women stand closer to others, face others more directly and are more likely to touch other people; women have less expansive body movement than men; and women are more accurate in interpreting others' emotional expressions and are better able to convey emotions than men.

Several possible explanations for such gender difference have been proposed. One explanation is that women are expected to be expert in emotional matters because in growing up, they are trained to be skillful in non-verbal behaviour. A second explanation is that women have genetically programmed sensitivity to non-verbal cues because of their role in caring for infants. A third explanation is that women are generally more relationship-oriented than men, and therefore, are strongly motivated to know and understand what others are feeling. Finally, women are generally in position of lesser power as compared to men, and according to subordination hypothesis, people in subordinate roles pay more attention to the feelings of those, who are in power. Therefore, women pay more attention to men's non-verbal behaviour, and thus, their decoding ability excels.

Researches have also shown that the sex of target does not make a difference in decoding accuracy of non-verbal communication. In simple words, it can be said that women are more accurate than men in decoding both men's and women's emotions. One exception is deception. Researches have shown that women are not more accurate than men in judging deception, unless a language is involved where they are better than men in judging deception (Forrest and Feldman, 2000).

COMMUNICATION AND SOCIAL STRUCTURE

Social psychologists have shown reciprocal concern about the impacts of social structure and communication. The basic questions here are—how does social relationship shape communication and how does communication modify or maintain social relationship? In this section, we shall concentrate upon the following three related issues

1. Gender differences in communication
2. Link between communicative styles and position in social stratification system
3. Communicating status and intimacy

1. *Gender differences in communication*

Researches have revealed that there are systematic gender differences in communication and this is how social structure influences communication. Since 1970, many studies intending to establish gender differences in communication have been conducted. In these studies, men and women have been compared using interruptions. Zimmerman and West (1975) studied the casual conversation of mixed gender dyads, where they reported that men interrupted women more frequently than the reverse. Other researches have shown that women's verbal communication make more frequent use of tag questions (It's really very cold, isn't it?), disclaimers (I may be wrong but…) and hedges (In my opinion…). In non-verbal behaviour such as smiling, gazing, decoding, sending, touching and flirting, there also exist gender differences. Several meta-analyses have indicated that females smile more than males (Hall et al., 2000; LaFrance, Hecht and Paluck, 2003) and this gender difference appears to be the largest among teenagers (LaFrance et al., 2003). When the situation is friendly, women tend to engage in gazing more than men (Helgeson, 2005). In decoding or reading the meaning of non-verbal cues of facial expression, vocal intonation and body language, females are better than males. Sending indicates the capacity to convey one's own emotions without intentionally doing so. Since female's emotional responsiveness is central to gender role of female, it is not surprising to know that women are better senders than men (Hall et al., 2000). Researches conducted by Major (1981) and Stier and Hall (1984) revealed that men initiate touch more than women and these researches further agreed that women received more touch than men and there were more touching in female–female interactions than male–male interactions. Flirting or courtship signalling is another class of non-verbal facial expression and behaviour exhibited by women that tends to attract men for approaching them. It is widely believed that male initiates contact, and therefore, relationship with female. Often male physically approaches and initiates verbal interaction. But some researches have shown that women take initiative, using non-verbal signals, in encouraging males to initiate verbal interactions (Moore, 1985).

Some researchers have studied how gender and contextual variables such as type of relationship, group task or authority structure tend to interact to influence communication. For example, Fishman (1983) reviewed the studies conducted in 1970s and 1980s and found that when men attempted to change the topic of conversation, they succeeded 96% of time, whereas when women attempted to change the topic of conversation, they succeeded only 36% of time. This indicated difference in status of men and women. However, a recent study conducted by Okamoto and Smith–Lovin (2001) revealed that the topic shifts were more related to the internal status structure of the group than to the gender.

On the whole, it can be said that men and women differ with respect to different communicative styles.

2. *Link between communicative styles and position in social stratification*

Speech style is associated with social status in most of the countries (Giles and Coupland, 1991). The use of standard speech is associated with high socio-economic status and high power, whereas the use of non-standard speech is associated with low socio-economic status and low power. *Standard speech* is one which is characterised by proper pronunciation, diverse vocabulary, correct grammar and abstract content. *Non-standard speech* is one which is characterised by improper pronunciation, limited vocabulary, incorrect grammar and directness. That is the reason, why we find that persons of high socio-economic status and in high political power are usually very articulate and grammatically correct while making public statements. Some analyses have pointed out that those, who use non-standard speech, are less capable of abstract and complex thought. These so-called deficit theories make the assertion that this restricted language makes the persons, who are generally of lower socio-economic status and disadvantaged class, cognitively inferior.

Speech style has also been found to be influenced by interpersonal context. In informal conservation such as in parties or clubs, people tend to use non-standard speech with the other persons, regardless of their socio-economic status. However, when we switch to formal settings such as in classroom or at some public platform, we use standard speech. Studies have also reported systematic differences in how listeners evaluate speakers, who are using either standard or non-standard speech. Luhman (1990) conducted one such study in which students heard the tape recordings of young men and women describing themselves. Four of the recordings, two by men and two by women, were in standard speech with proper accents, and four others were identical in content, but were in non-standard speech with Kentucky accents. It was found that the listeners gave the speakers with standard speech, high rating on status and the speakers with non-standard speech, received low ratings on status.

Thus, we find that speech style clearly reflects a broad social stratification of the speakers. We judge the status of the speakers on the basis of their speech styles.

3. *Communicating status and intimacy*

In social relationship, two central dimensions are status and intimacy. *Status* is associated with exercise of power and control, whereas *intimacy* is concerned with the expressions of affiliation and affection that create social solidarity (Kemper, 1973). In the present section, we shall discuss how a specific communication expresses, maintains and changes status and intimacy in social relationship.

As we know, forms of address directly tell the relative status in social relationship. Superiors address inferiors or juniors with familiar forms (such as by first name or nickname, for example, Mohan or Mohi) and inferiors use formal address (title and last name) for their superiors. When status between the two is equal, they use the same form of address with one another. When status differences are vague, the individuals tend to avoid addressing each other. They, in fact, shy away in choosing an address form thinking that it might grant too much or too little status. In case, there is clear status difference between people, the right to initiate the use of the more familiar or equal forms of address belongs to superior. In fact, it is the high status person, who usually initiate changes towards familiar behaviours like greater eye contact, physical proximity, touching or self-disclosure. Not only that, the choice of language to be used with the other people expresses the view of relative status and tends to influence our social relationship. People generally make language uses smoothly, easily expressing differences in status appropriate to the situation (Stiles et al., 1984). For example, it is often found that teachers tend to communicate to the students in standard speech showing their high status. But when they want to encourage their students, they switch to some local or informal language reducing their status differences. Johnson (1994) conducted a study in which the impact of authority and gender on verbal and non-verbal communication was examined. In this study, group consisted of a manager and two workers. The investigator created a simulated retail store, where manager gave instructions to the subordinates and monitored their work. It was found that the authority (manager) affected verbal communication—subordinates talked less, were less directive and also provided less feedback as compared to superior (manager). Gender also affected non-verbal behaviours of smiling and laughing. Female in all-female groups smiled and laughed more than men in all-male groups. Alkire et al. (1968) conducted a very important study in which it was found that status influenced communicative efficiency. In this study, some female students were organised in dyads in which one student was designated as the sender and was given the task of describing a series of abstract designs to the other subject designated as the receiver, who could neither see the receiver nor the design being described. In this study, there were two stages. During the first stage of the study, no mention was made about the status of the subjects and no significant difference in the performance of the group was found. In the second stage of the study, the researcher made a particular point of announcement regarding high status and low status of the subjects. Such announcement had significant impact. An analysis of the tape recordings of interchange between the partners suggested that the low status receivers characteristically displayed more submissive behaviour by reducing the number of queries directed at the sender, whereas high status receivers, when interacting with low status senders, increased the number of their queries. Moreover, high status senders, in communicating with low status receivers, tended to use more abstract and technical language in describing the abstract designs. The results provided support for the fact that status influence communicative efficiency.

Researches have shown that paralinguistic cues also communicate status in social relationship. Persons of higher status interrupt their partners more during conversations and talk more themselves. Inferiors grant status to their superiors by not interrupting and responding with 'mm-hmm' from time to time during the conversation. When the status is equal, these paralinguistic cues are distributed more equally (Krauss and Chiu, 1998). Body language also serves to communicate status. People of high status tend to exhibit relatively relaxed posture with their arms and legs in asymmetrical positions. Those, who belong to low status, tend to stand and sit in more tense and symmetrical position. Superiors speak more when speaking than listening, whereas inferiors look more when listening than when speaking. Not only that, superiors are comparatively more likely to intrude physically on inferiors by touching or pointing at them (Leffler, Gillespie and Conaty, 1982).

Communication also expresses intimacy, which is another dimension of social relationship. Often we find that people use formal version of language with strangers and they use local dialect with friends and intimate. The use of slang gives impression to in-group intimacy and solidarity. The content of conversation indicates the intimacy of social relationship. As relationship becomes more intimate, we disclose more personal information about ourselves. Intimacy is also indicated by conversational style. Hornstein (1985) conducted a study in which telephone conversations between strangers, acquaintances and friends were analysed. It was found that friends, as compared to strangers, used more implicit openings, raised more topics and were more responsive. Conversations of acquaintances were more or less similar to those of strangers.

People also accommodate verbal and paralinguistic behaviour to express intimacy and liking. According to the theory of speech accommodation, people express or reject intimacy by accommodating or adjusting their speech behaviour during conversation to converge with or diverge from the listener. To express liking or intimacy, they try to make their own speech similar to that of the listener. To reject intimacy or communicate disapproval, they emphasise the differences in speech between their own and that of the listener. Likewise, by the adjustment of paralinguistic behaviour during conversation, intimacy is expressed or rejected (Thakerar, Giles and Cheshire, 1982). Speakers, who want to express liking, tend to shift their own pronunciation, speech rate, pause lengths, vocal intensity, etc. during conversation to match those of the listeners. On the other hand, the speakers, who wish to communicate disapproval, modify these paralinguistic behaviours in ways that make them diverge more from the listener's paralinguistic behaviour. Researches have also revealed that among bilinguals, speech accommodation tends to determine the choice of language (Bourhis et al., 1979). To show intimacy, bilinguals change to the language they believe the listeners would prefer to speak. To reject intimacy, they choose such language which is the listener's less preferred language. We also express intimacy through body language and interpersonal spacing. Those, who like each other and are intimate, gaze into each other's eye (Rubin, 1970). We also communicate liking by assuming moderately relaxed postures, moving closer and leaning towards others, orienting ourselves face-to-face and also touching them (Mehrabian, 1972). In increased emotional intimacy, we increase body engagement from an arm around shoulder to full embrace (Gurevitch, 1990).

Thus, we find that there is a reciprocal impact of social structure and communication. Social relationship tends to shape communication and communication tends to maintain and modify social relationship.

Summary and Review

- Language is the structured system of sound patterns. Therefore, it involves the use of arbitrary sounds that have accepted referents and that can be rearranged in different ways to convey different meanings. There are three distinctive features of language—displacement, meaningfulness and productiveness.
- There are five important properties of language—language is creative; language is structured; language is meaningful; language is referential and language is interpersonal.
- There are five major components of language—phonemes, morphemes, syntax, semantics and pragmatics.
- Language serves many functions. Following Halliday, it serves instrumental function, regulatory function, interpersonal function, personal function, heuristic function, imaginative function, and informative function.
- The concept of critical period refers to certain period in life during which both favourable and unfavourable circumstances can have lasting and irreversible consequences upon the later development. Researches have revealed that there is a critical period for language learning. This period is thought to extend roughly from three months to puberty. According to critical period hypothesis, some characteristics of the brain do change as the critical period comes to its closure so that later language learning becomes very difficult.
- Language is organised as a hierarchy of its various structures. At the bottom of the hierarchy, language comprises little snippets of sound and at the apex end, it consists of sentences and conversations.
- There are three major theoretical views, which explain language development—nativist perspective, environmentalist perspective and interactionist perspective. According to the supporters of nativist perspective such as Chomsky, McNeill, Morley and Lenneberg, language acquisition is an innate ability. Human beings are endowed with a biological capacity for language. According to environmentalist perspective, language acquisition can be explained through learning principles and other social factors. Some psychologists in doing so more emphasise reinforcement principles, whereas some other emphasise imitation. Skinner, Miller and Dollard, Bijou, Bullock and Whitehurst are the popular supporters of environmentalist view. Interactionist perspective emphasises that language acquisition is the function of dynamics and complex interactions taking place among biochemical processes, maturational factors, learning principles and the social environment.
- The relationship between language and thought has been studied by presenting the viewpoints of Whorf, Piaget and Vygotsky. Comparatively, Vygotsky's viewpoints have been preferred.
- Language acquisition among children no doubt follows some degree of uniformity, it is basically characterised by many diversities and individual differences due to various socio-cultural contexts. Researches done by Indian psychologists have pinpointed that although language acquisition of different Indian languages proceeds uniformly, there is a wide range of individual differences. Important Indian contributors to this field are Chengappa and Devi, Khokle, Lakshmi Bai, Devaki, and so on.
- Researches have shown a relation between language ability and theory of mind (ToM). Psychologists believe that a child first develops a theory of mind in the age range of 2½ to 5 years. During this period, rapid growth in children's mental state vocabulary is taken as an indicative of ToM development.
- In today's world, bilingualism/multilingualism has become a norm. In this field, the work of Mohanty is very important. Based on his own researches, he identified three stages of development of language socialisation in the multilingual Indian society—period of language differentiation, period of awareness of language and period of multilingual functioning. Mohanty tried to successfully explain bilingualism in Indian society in the light of Berry's enculturation model.

- Indian psychologists have also studied the process of reading acquisition. Previously, reading was viewed as basically a process involving two basic components, that is, decoding and comprehension. Nowadays, another component, called *decoding speed,* has also been added. Researches have further shown that there are script-specific components in literacy acquisition.
- Communication is the heart of human social interaction. Communication means exchange of ideas, thoughts and experiences between individuals. In simple words, it is a process of meaningful interaction among human beings. The major characteristics of communication include its dynamic, irreversible, continuous and interactive nature.
- There are three basic models of communication—encoder–decoder model, intentionalist model and perspective-taking model.
- A communication network is the pattern of direction in which information flows in a group or organisation. In simple words, who talks to whom in the group involves the study of communication network. Five important communication networks have been identified—wheel network, chain network Y-shaped network, circle network and comcon network. Of these five networks, the wheel pattern is more restricted than the circle pattern and Y-shaped pattern is more centralised than the comcon pattern.
- Non-verbal communication has been intensively studied by the social psychologists. There are three major types of non-verbal communication—kinesics (body language), proxemics and paralanguage. Kinesics includes silent movement of the body such as smiles, nods, scowls, gazing, gestures, leg movements, postural shifts, caressing, slapping, facial expression, and so on. Proxemics focuses on spatial distance between the people communicating with each other as well as on their orientation towards each other. Paralanguage focuses on vocal behaviour, which includes pitch, loudness, speech, emphasis on inflection, breathiness, stretching of words, pauses, and so on. Making the relative importance of verbal and non-verbal communication, Mehrabian pointed out that non-verbal communication carry much more weight, that is, 93% and verbal communication carries only 7% weight in the overall assessment.
- There has been found gender differences in non-verbal communication. In general, women are better than men in decoding or reading non-verbal behaviour. Females can comparatively better understand the real meaning behind various non-verbal cues such as facial expression, vocal intonation and body position. Researches have also shown that women are more accurate than men in decoding both men's and women's emotions. One exception is deception.
- Researches have shown that when both verbal and non-verbal channels of communication are consistent, a meaningful conversation does emerge. But when they are inconsistent, the interaction during communication becomes difficult and problematic one.
- Social psychologists have shown that here is a reciprocal relationship between communication and social structure. This fact has been substantiated by studying gender differences in communication, exploring link between communicative styles and position in social stratification system as well as by communicating status and intimacy with the listeners.

Review Questions

1. Define language. Discuss its major properties.
2. Discuss the importance of various components of language.
3. Discuss the nature of language. Discuss its major functions.
4. Describe the importance of critical period hypothesis in acquisition of language.
5. Critically examine the nativist perspective of language development.

6. Critically examine environmentalist perspective of language development.
7. Outline a plan for integration of nativist perspective and environmentalist perspective.
8. Discuss the importance of interactionist perspective in language development.
9. Discuss the process of diversity in language acquisition among Indian children.
10. Citing relevant studies, discuss the relation between language acquisition and theory of mind.
11. Discuss the importance of bilingualism/multilingualism in Indian society.
12. Discuss the process of reading acquisition among Indian children.
13. Citing relevant studies, discuss the gender differences in verbal communication.
14. Discuss the nature and purpose of communication.
15. Critically examine the different models of communication. Which of them is more useful and why?
16. Citing relevant studies, discuss the various types of non-verbal communication.
17. Citing relevant studies, discuss the outcomes of the combination of verbal and non-verbal communications.
18. Discuss the reciprocal nature of communication and social structure.
19. Write notes on the following:
    (i) Linguistic hierarchy
    (ii) Gender differences in non-verbal communication
    (iii) Communication network
    (iv) Theory of mind
    (v) Language and thought

17 APPLICATIONS OF SOCIAL PSYCHOLOGY

Learning Objectives

- Social Psychology: Education
- Social Psychology: Personal Health
- Social Psychology: Legal System
- Social Psychology: Entrepreneurship
- Social Psychology: Sports

Key Terms

Assimilation	Frustration-aggression	Overwriting hypothesis
Audience effect	hypothesis	Personal standards perfectionism
Auditorium classroom style	Geographical playing position	Planning fallacy
Bracketed morality	Helping relationship	Self-critical perfectionism
Buffering effect hypothesis	Home ground advantage	Seminar classroom style
Closed classroom climate	Integration	Separation
Cluster classroom style	Lie detection	Sequential line up
Direct effect hypothesis	Marginalisation	Simultaneous line up
Eyewitness identification	Minimisation	Source monitoring theory
Eyewitness testimony	Off-set classroom style	Team cohesion
Face-to-face classroom style	Open classroom climate	Team performance
False confession	Optimistic bias	
Forgetting hypothesis		

Social psychology is an applied science. The various principles, theories and concepts of social psychology have been applied in different fields such as education, health care, legal system, entrepreneurship, sports, etc. In the present chapter, applications of the principles of social psychology are discussed in each of these five areas. First, the application of its principles are discussed in the field of education. Teacher variable and various types of classroom climate are discussed in the light of their impact upon educational performance. A discussion is made in the chapter for improving the outcome of education.

Social psychology, as applied in health care, is the next topic of discussion. Here, various social and personal causes of stress, ways to cope with stress, impact of stress upon health and well-being, and ways for promoting healthy lifestyles are discussed in light of both indigenous findings as well the findings by foreign nationals.

Social psychology as applied in legal system is discussed next. Here, especially ways of police interrogation, eyewitness identification and testimony, issues related to criminal defendants are selected for discussion in light of the relevance of the principles of social psychology.

Social psychology of entrepreneurship is the next topic of discussion. Here, basically, an attempt is made to discuss the answer of two basic questions—why do only some persons become entrepreneur? Why are some entrepreneurs more effective and successful than others?

Finally, the usefulness of the principles of social psychology for sport psychology is discussed. Here, mainly, sport aggression, audience effect, team cohesion and leadership issues in sport particularly issues relating to coach-athlete compatibility and geographical playing position are highlighted.

SOCIAL PSYCHOLOGY: EDUCATION

We spend the largest part of our waking hours in various educational settings such as in play schools, primary schools, secondary schools, colleges and universities. During all this time in educational settings, we are involved in many important processes. We learn facts through education, which is essentially a process of social learning in which one individual who has gained an accumulation of skill or information attempts to communicate these various skills and ideas to others. In fact, during this time, we interact with our teachers. We develop interpersonal relationship with others and we become members of many groups. Due to the importance of these various social interactions, social psychologists have shown their interest in examining the impact of these interactions, which shape our future in a variety of subtle and pervasive ways.

If we look at the history, in the late 1940s, social psychologists showed interest in studying only social-psychological variables. The few early studies that gave attention to social variable in educational settings emphasised teaching and evaluation of the performance of the students (Lindgren, 1978). However, by 1970s, this trend changed and social psychologists were then ready to study social processes and structures in educational settings and contributed to the understanding and improvement of educational institutions. Getzels (1969) developed a good framework for the social psychology of education in which several issues and empirical work relating to these various issues were reviewed. His viewpoint mainly emphasised that social psychology of education should deal with the behaviour in educational settings that are conceived as *social system*—a system that provides settings for interpersonal and group behaviour.

Before proceeding ahead, two related concepts—*social psychology for education* and *social psychology of education*—should be made distinct. Social psychology for education takes cognisance of those basic socio-psychological principles, which have been derived from laboratory experiments on students for explaining problems in educational settings. While this may acquaint the teachers with social-psychological thinking, it definitely lacks the relevance to educational issues (Bar–Tal and Saxe, 1978). On the other hand, social psychology of education emphasises the social-psychological issues that are concerned with the social functioning of individuals and groups in educational settings. Here, various issues and problems are studied in educational settings using conceptual and methodological tools of social psychology. This, in turn, may prove useful for social psychology because unique educational problems may force the discipline to develop new theories and methods, which may have general applicability and relevance.

School as a Social System

School as a social organisation is full of human interactions that constitute the school climate. In the early studies, school climate was organised under six types—*open, autonomous, controlled, familiar, paternal* and *closed*. Thus, climate varies from extreme closed to open type. Later on, three studies conducted by Darji (1975) Dekhtawala (1978) and Shelat (1974) at the Centre of Advanced Study in Education, M.S. University, Baroda led to the development of twelve dimensions of school climate instead of 8 dimensions as proposed by Halpin (1966) and these dimensions were assessed by Organisational Climate Development Questionnaire (OCDQ). The new four dimensions were organisational hierarchy, communication, human relations, freedom and democratisation. In these three studies, categories of school climate were simplified and made easier by restricting them to only three major ones—*open, closed* and *intermediate groups*. Closed climate schools were more similar to the classical bureaucratic model of impersonalised standardised procedures, distribution of authority, power and role conflict (Bhogle, 1971). Climate studies have been conducted on samples drawn from schools of Gujarat, Rajasthan, Tamil Nadu, Punjab and Maharashtra. These studies have invariably categorised school climate as closed one (Shelat, 1979; Sharma, 1973; Pillai, 1973; Gupta, 1976 and Mehare, 1976).

Researches have shown that a school as a social system contributes to the academic achievement of students. Sharma (1971) found a higher level of academic achievement of pupils in those schools, where teachers had a higher level of need satisfaction. Schools under control of government were found to have a more homogeneous environment than the schools that run under private sectors. Teachers' behaviours, within this system were also found to change due to school organisational climate. Kumar (1972, 1975) examined the impacts of six types of social climate of school upon students' behaviour in terms of four variables—personal-social adjustment, value orientations, attitudes towards certain educational objects and scholastic achievement. Results revealed that open climate emerged as the most effective for personal-social adjustment followed by closed, paternal, autonomous controlled and familiar type, but it was not related to variables like attitude towards school and scholastic performance. Open organisational schools climate was found to be good for pupil's achievement and teacher satisfaction (Rao, 1976). Some researchers examined the relationship between closeness of the school climate and work alienation experienced by teacher and have found a difference between work alienation in open climate and closed climate schools, but not between open climate and intermediate schools. Desai and Dekhtawala (1979) conducted a study in which teachers from 100 secondary schools were selected and organisational climate, leadership behaviour, teacher morale and academic motivation were examined. Results revealed that in most of the cases, the climates of the schools were found to be closed type. Region, size of the school and types of school were found not to have any impact upon school climate. However, location of school (rural-urban) and academic achievement of schools were found to have a significant relation with school climate.

Classroom as a Group

One important constituent of school is classroom, and therefore, considerable attention has been paid to the functioning, processes and outcomes of the class. Every classroom is a unique and distinct social unit with its own set of norms, its own psychological atmosphere, its own set of role relationships and its own special blend of behavioural expectancies. The social climate of one classroom may be different from the social climate of the other classroom because one classroom may be charged with excitement and enthusiasm, whereas other classroom may be tensed and depressed and still other bordering on anarchy. Such differences have an impact.

There are two aspects of classroom, which do have an impact—spatial arrangement of pupils in the classroom and organisation of the classrooms itself. A classroom consists of many pupils, usually 20 to 40 pupils. Pupils sit at different places in classroom. Does a pupil's location within the classroom make a difference? Are pupils in front more active than those in the rear? Researches have shown that location does make a difference. The participation is highest among pupils seated across the front and down the middle of the room (Gump and Ross, 1977). Not only this, the size of the classroom also affects the classroom achievement. Researches have revealed that in small classes, there is greater group activity, more individualisation, more positive student attitude, less misbehaviour and above all, the teachers are more satisfied with such classes (Minuchin and Shapiro, 1983). However, the size of the classroom produces a little difference in the achievement of the pupil within the usual range of twenty to forty, although the smaller size of the classes may be advantageous to mathematics and reading in early stages and may aid the academic progress of disadvantaged and handicapped pupils (Rutter, 1983).

The teacher may organise and structure the classroom in different ways. For example, he can organise the class into small groups; he can arrange the class in such a way that the students maximally participate in decision-making; he can arrange for students to help each other; he can arrange classroom activities in the traditional manner or he can arrange for the open classroom, where all pupils rarely engage in the same activity and in which they do not dutifully listen to their teacher, rather they tend to be scattered around room. Some researchers have made a comparative attempt to evaluate the effects of open versus traditional classrooms and have reported that pupils in open classrooms engage in more prosocial behaviour and in more imaginative play, although they are also more aggressive than the pupils in traditional structured classroom (Huston–Stein et al., 1977).

Renne (1997) proposed five different types of classroom arrangement styles—auditorium style, face-to-face style, off-set style, seminar style and cluster style. All these classroom arrangement styles have differential impact upon social interaction. In *auditorium style*, all students sit facing the teacher. This arrangement tends to inhibit face-to-face student contacts and the teacher is free to move anywhere in the room and make social interaction. In *face-to-face style*, students sit facing each other. Distraction from other students is higher in this arrangement. In *off-set style*, small number of students (usually three or four) sit at table, but they do not sit directly across from one another. This produces less distraction than face-to-face style and has been found to be effective for cooperative learning activities. In *seminar style*, generally, ten or more students sit in circular, square or U-shaped arrangement. In *cluster style*, small number of students (usually four to eight) work in small, closely bunched groups. This arrangement has been found effective for collaborative learning activities.

Teacher Variable

By far the most significant variable in educational institutions is teacher. The expectation of the teacher has a direct bearing on academic success. Such expectations are formed from a variety of sources such as pupils' post academic record, achievement test scores, family background, appearance and classroom conduct history. Teachers often develop more positive expectations for high ability students than for low ability students and these expectations are likely to influence their behaviour towards them. Researches done by Brophy (1985, 1998) showed that teachers require high ability students to work harder, wait longer for them to respond to questions, criticise them less often, praise them more often, are more friendly to them, call on them more often and seat them closer to the teacher's desks than they do for the students with low ability. Researchers have also reported that with support, teachers can adapt and raise their expectations for students with poor abilities (Santrock, 2006). Rosenthal and Jacobson (1968) conducted a very popular study in which the impact of expectation of teachers on the pupil's actual scholastic success or failure was examined. In this study, in several school classes, teachers were informed that 20% of their students were intellectually bloomers. In fact, these 20% were randomly chosen. For asserting the impact of teacher's expectations, the pupils were administered intelligence test before the experiment commenced and again after about eight months of additional classroom experience with the expectant teacher. Results showed that those pupils, for whom the teachers had been led to expect greater intellectual gain, demonstrated a significantly greater increase in IQ scores than did the non-labelled control children. Further analysis revealed that one important area of academic performance, that is, reading was also affected. The intellectual bloomers did far better than the rest of their classmates in reading. Not only that, these bloomers were also rated as higher in the intellectual curiosity than the control children.

Besides, teachers also act as an evaluator, as a disciplinarian and as a social model. The way the teachers organise evaluation procedures makes an important difference in pupil's attitudes, motivation and performance. Researches have shown that anxious pupils tend to improve their performance under optimal test-taking conditions rather than in time pressure conditions. Hill and Eaton (1977) tested the impact of two types of evaluation procedures on pupil's arithmetic performance—time pressure condition and optimising condition. Under *time pressure condition*, time limits were imposed so that children could complete two-thirds of the problems they attempted and would fail to complete the remaining third. In *optimising condition*, there was no such time limit, and therefore, failure experience was minimised. Results revealed that the performance of the anxious pupils under optimised condition was better and more satisfactory than their performance under time pressure condition. Thus, the type of evaluation procedures adapted by teachers definitely had an impact upon the pupil's performance.

Teacher also act as a disciplinarian. Here, the basic question is—how effective are different teacher control techniques for achieving and maintaining classroom order and pupil's motivation? According to the researches done by Kazdin (1982), operant reinforcement principles to classroom control have been very successful. In some cases, social reinforcement in the form of verbal approval is used, whereby teachers are taught to praise appropriate behaviour and ignore disruptive behaviour in a systematic way. Still another technique that has found to be effective in establishing classroom control is the combination of materials or token rewards and social reinforcement. In token rewards, pupils accumulate points or tokens for good behaviour, which they can, later on, exchange for material rewards such as candy, comics or toys. Several studies have demonstrated the impact of token rewards upon the effectiveness of controlling children in classrooms. But token rewards should be used with caution because under some circumstances, they may undermine pupil's interest in academic activities. There are many activities in school that are intrinsically interesting for pupils. What would happen if the children are rewarded for already interesting activities? Researches have shown that activities that are intrinsically interesting may lose their appeal if rewards are provided (Lepper, Greene and Nisbett, 1973).

Besides, teacher's behaviour, in general, has been found to produce a different psychological environment for different students in the same classroom. Kakkar (1982) studied teacher's behaviour using praise and reproof scales in two classrooms on two occasions separated by a four-week interval. It was found that students in praise-dominant environment and those living in a predominantly reproof-laden condition showed a marked and significant differences in academic achievement, intelligence, total personality, self-concept and social self-scores.

Classroom Climate

Classroom climate is another important variable that has a direct impact upon pupil's academic achievement. Rao (1976) defined classroom climate as a general academic and psychological atmosphere prevailing in the classroom as a function of outcomes of the behaviours of teachers, pupils and their interactions. Thus, *classroom climate* is explained in terms of interactive processes that occur in a classroom between teachers and pupils on one hand and among pupils on the other. Pupils' perception of teachers and teachers' perception of pupil influence each other reciprocally and tend to build classroom climate. There can be two general types of classroom climate—open classroom climate and closed classroom climate. *Open classroom climate* tends to show better personal social adjustment, value formation and attitude development among pupils. On the other hand, *closed classroom climate*, in general, tends to encourage custodial attitude of teachers towards pupils (Gandhi, 1977; Mehta, 1977; Sahasrabudhe, 1977).

In classroom, the nature of interaction between teachers and pupils determines the extent to which the climate is congenial or otherwise. The climate may fall at any point along a continuum ranging from congenial to non-congenial. A *congenial climate* is one where both pupils and teachers perceive themselves in a positive and coordinating way. Researches have shown that in congenial classroom climate, teachers are supportive, integrative and democratic, whereas in non-congenial classroom climate, teachers are defensive, dominating and authoritarian.

Teachers' classroom behaviour is considered important in classroom climate, which has a direct bearing on learning outcomes and achievement. Pareek and Rao (1970) conducted a study in which classroom behaviour of school teachers in Delhi using Flanders' interaction analysis technique was studied. It was found that authoritative behaviour of the teachers had a deteriorating impact upon pupil's achievement.

Some researches have shown that openness of the classroom climate tends to facilitate the capacity of the school to adapt to new educational facilities in a shorter time. Pillai (1973) reported a positive correlation ($r = 0.65$, $P<0.01$) between openness of classroom climate and innovativeness. However, the findings of Buch (1973) and Gupta (1976) showed that the organisational climate of school and colleges did not affect innovativeness.

Social Factors, Social Motivation and Academic Achievement

Various researches have shown that there are several such social factors that do have a direct impact upon academic achievement and social motivation of students. Lower value orientations, child-rearing values, social class membership, family atmosphere, peer group influence, social deprivation and social disadvantage do make a lot of difference in academic achievement and motivation of the students. A thorough discussion of some of the factors is as follows:

1. Child-rearing practices: Child-rearing practices do have an impact upon academic achievement and social motivation of the students (Eccles, Wigfield and Schiefele, 1998). When parents provide a positive emotional climate during their rearing practices, it motivates children to internalise their parents' values and goals. Panda (1983) also reported that parental lifestyle and child-rearing practices have a significant effect on the academic achievement and other cognitive learning of elementary school children.

2. Family pattern: A family pattern in which parents provide specific experiences at home to help children tends to produce high motivation and academic achievement among students. Wigfield and Asher (1984) found that reading to one's preschool children and providing reading materials in the home are positively related to students' later reading achievement and motivation. Some other researchers have found that the children's skills and work habits when they enter kindergarten are the best predictors of academic motivation and achievement at both elementary and secondary schools (Entwisle and Alexander, 1993). Within the family pattern, birth order has also a direct impact on the academic achievement (Singh and Sharma, 1978), the middle one having a supremacy in the achievement over the others.

3. Peer group: Peer group tends to affect academic achievement and motivation through social comparison, social competence, peer co-learning and peer group influences (Eccles, Wigfield and Schiefele, 1998). Students do compare themselves with their peers on their standing from the point of view of social and academic performance (Ruble, 1983). Adolescents are more prone to make social comparison than younger ones (Harter, 1990). Positive social comparisons usually result in higher self-esteem, and negative comparisons produce lower self-esteem. Generally, students make comparison with those students who are most similar to them in age, ability and interests. Likewise, the students, who are more popular because they are more accepted by their peers and who have good social skills, often excel in school and tend to develop positive academic achievement motivation (Wentzel, 1996). Bal (1974) also reported satisfactory relationship between popularity and academic attainment partially out the contribution of intelligence. However, rejected students, especially those with aggressive tendency, display several problems relating to the motivation and achievement, including getting low grades and also dropping out of school.

4. Socioeconomic status (SES), Social deprivation and Social disadvantage: SES has also been found to influence academic performance, adjustment and social motivation. Studies conducted by Ahluwalia and Deo (1975), Raj and Krishnan (1980) and Venkataih (1980) reported a positive relationship between SES and academic performance. Obviously, the students belonging to upper SES also exhibit better academic performance. Social deprivation has also been found to affect educational performance and mental development of pupils. Nair (1981) observed that underachievement among students of secondary schools was significantly high when father's occupation, income, education, mother's education and caste were low and the family size was large. Likewise, social disadvantage has also been found to have negative impact upon academic and scholastic achievement. Various studies have reported that scholastic achievement of disadvantaged children was lower than that of advantaged children.

5. Labelling and expectancy: The way a student is labelled either on the basis of socio-psychological disability or physical disability tends to determine pupil's classroom performance and teacher's behaviour. Negative labelling tends to bring down the motivation and academic achievement of students in the classroom. Teacher's expectancy from certain pupils in terms of their caste and class affects pupil's achievement. A positive expectancy on the part of teachers boosts the morale of students and has favourable impact upon their academic performance (Mathur and Singh, 1975; Panda and Dash, 1980).

Conclusively, it can be said that there are various social factors that influence classroom achievement and motivation of the students. In order to understand them well, it is essential to have a look on those factors in a global way.

Improving the Outcome of Education

The role of social psychology, especially the applied social psychology, is to help document the existing reality of the education, including its deficiencies, and to suggest a range of possible methods to improve the educational outcomes for both teachers and students. There are three major applications of theory and practice for improving such educational outcomes—teacher–student relationship, use of small group methods in teaching and application of organisational development (OD) to educational systems.

1. Teacher–student relationship: A good teacher–student relationship is a helping relationship, where teacher neither directs nor instructs, but stimulates initiativeness and facilitates learning. A teacher, who presents himself as a real and genuine person, is likely to elicit a more genuine and active involvement by the students in various academic activities. A teacher should actively understand the thoughts and feelings of students so that they may be drawn into a climate of self-initiated learning, where motivation and achievement flourish. A teacher should also accept, trust, and prize students in a non-responsive way so that the capacity for growth and learning may be developed properly. There are several studies which have shown that how some basic qualities of genuineness, empathetic understanding, and non-possessive warmth have improved the educational outcomes from primary schools to the university and college level. Aspy (1969) found that basic qualities of the teachers like genuineness, respect and empatic understanding in the classroom are positively related to the students' achievement. Gordon (1974) pointed out that by increasing teachers' interpersonal effectiveness, teacher can experience greater satisfaction and accomplishment for themselves as well as for their students. Some experts believe that those teachers, who share responsibility with students for making classroom decisions, increase student' commitment to the decisions that ultimately improves the final educational outcomes (Eggleton, 2001; Lewis, 2001).

Some other researchers have tried to analyse the effect of student–teacher classroom interaction on the educational performance of students (Mohanty and Pani, 1979). In this study, four levels of teacher–student relations were introduced in the classroom following Flanders interaction analysis tool. In Flanders interaction analysis tool, there are ten categories of teacher–student interaction such as accepts feelings, praises or encourages, accepts or uses ideas of pupils, ask questions, lecturing, giving directions, criticising and justifying authority, pupil-talk (response), pupil-take (initiation) and silence. Teacher's initiatives or direct attempts to influence consist of behaviours such as lecturing, criticising, justifying authority and giving directions. Indirect attempts to influence consist of teacher responses to students' communication such as accepting ideas or feelings, and giving praise and encouragement. These two sets of categories bear some resemblance to directive versus non-directive or client-centred approach to helping relationship. The various classroom interactions were found to have a significant impact upon academic achievement of class 7th students. Rao and Pareek (1976) also reported a similar study in which a more comprehensive measure of achievement was used. In this study also, Flanders interaction analysis tool was used. They found that when the behaviour of the teacher was indirect during interaction in the classroom, it led to well-adjusted, more intelligent, initiative-taking, less need persistent, and more defensive patterns among pupils in their reaction to frustrations as compared to when the behaviour of the teacher was direct. Low teacher–student ratio also produced more or less the same set of characteristics as those observed in case of indirect teacher behaviour.

Researches have shown that certain emotional needs of the pupils can be fulfilled by a joint interaction of teachers, parents and pupils (Marfatia, 1973). It has been found that non-authoritarian teachers are more liked by the students (Jha, 1973). Likewise, Singh (1974) found that the academic performance of teachers seems to be a significant determinant of their classroom verbal behaviour.

2. Use of small group methods in teaching: Social psychologists have developed significant knowledge about the important small group process such as communication, status and role, decision-making, group dynamics norms and leadership and this conceptual knowledge has proved to be very useful for analysing classroom behaviour as well as for suggesting more effective methods for teaching (Schmuck and Schmuck, 1975). Not only that, the emphasis upon human relation training has also given rise to the development of numerous methods and techniques for experiential set up (Stanford, 1977). These conceptual developments have been in accord with the principles of experimental learning fostered in the field of adult education (Knowles, 1975). In all these various approaches, one common and important point has been that pupils have been involved as an active, participating and experiencing whole person in group learning situation.

According to Fisher (1982), the first step in adopting to the group process to the various types of teaching is to accept that the class is indeed a group of people with shared expectations, norms values and goals. It is never a collection of separate teacher–student relationships. Schmuck and Schmuck (1975) analysed classroom behaviour in terms of various group processes and subsequently, developed implications for possible actions for teacher and taught. For example, they were of opinion that pupils' peer group norms on appropriate behaviour of the classroom would, most of the time, be in opposition to the goals of the teacher and school authorities.

On the topic of classroom leadership, it is argued that although the teacher is handed over main leadership role in the classroom, other leaders are also present. The extent to which the teacher is authoritarian or democratic sets the tone for norm formation in the classroom. But once the school has been in session for a few weeks, student leaders begin to emerge. Again, this time, it is the teacher, who, to a greater extent, may determine which students attain leadership position. The teacher can encourage and even reinforce the leadership behaviour of one student and withhold reinforcement when the same leadership behaviour is exhibited by another student. As we know, an influential leader must have the esteem of everyone in the group (Homans, 1961). This automatically means that students can exert considerable pressure on a teacher by giving or withholding their esteem, and thus, by this, they can shape the behaviour of the teacher. It also explains why a given teacher would be a successful leader with one group of students and not so successful within a different group.

Group dynamics in the classroom has also been investigated and successfully applied in improving classroom behaviour of teacher and students that ultimately has favourable impact upon improving the outcome of the education. In fact, the classroom is the collection of interdependent individuals. The dynamics of their interrelationships depend on the roles that have been established through interaction. Whenever there is a change in the expected behaviour of any group member, the dynamic interrelationships of the entire group must necessarily change. If a group has certain expectations about an individual's behaviour, then, usually, the pressure on the role behaviour becomes so great, that the individual tends to respond in a way consistent with those expectations. Take an example of a small group or two-person group in which the expectations of the superordinate member clearly determine the behaviour of the subordinate member. Suppose a high school student complaints that his mother treats him as if he were a child. An objective analysis of the behaviour of students may reveal that he indeed does not let his mother down—he behaves like a child. The dynamic relationship between the interacting people can exist only if both the members play their expected roles. If the student, who is being treated like a child, stops behaving like a child, his mother would change her expectations, and ultimately, her behaviour towards him.

3. **Organisation development in educational institutions:** The practice of organisation development (OD) has also been successfully applied to the educational institutions with beneficial outcomes. *Organisation development* is a systematic long-range effort to improve an organisation's problem solving and effectiveness through a more effective and collaborative management of organisation culture. Any OD programme has two major goals.

(i) (i) To improve the functioning of the individuals, teams and total organisation
(ii) (ii) To teach organisation members how to continuously improve their own functioning

In an overview of organisation development in schools, Schmuck and Miles (1971) provided a comprehensive collection of strategies for improving educational outcomes. These include the improvement of classroom group processes and problem-solving procedures, the use of change agent teams, the use of survey data feedback and the facilitation of student advocacy. In fact, Schmuck et al. (1972) and Schmuck et al. (1977) produced two handbooks of organisation development in schools that presented a detailed discussion regarding how different training and consultation activities are adapted to educational institutions in which methods of clarifying communication, establishing goals, managing conflict, solving problems and making decisions are involved. Let us take an example in which OD is demonstrated to have beneficial outcome for the educational settings.

Suppose a new higher secondary school is to be opened in the district. The principal, vice-principal, twenty teachers, three peons, one librarian, one gatekeeper and one sweeper are there and these persons have never worked together before. The principal decides to use OD technique for improvement of school and its employees. He calls an organisational consultant to help form the staff into an interdependent team. A fortnight-long workshop is held to help the staff get acquainted to improve interpersonal communication skills, to develop psychological contract between individual staff and the school and to prescribe methods of leadership and decision-making. At the end of the workshop, the members feel closer to each other, develop communication skills and have a clear sense of how to approach organisational problems in collaborative manner. Further meetings and workshops are held. Then, the members feel well in working together and enjoy the favourable climate of the organisation. Consequently, the new higher secondary school may experience a very poor absenteeism of the employees, a low turnover of the staff and is perceived as a model school in the district. Keys and Bartunek (1979) conducted a study in which an attempt was made to demonstrate the impact of organisation development upon school functioning. In this study, training workshops for teachers of seven experimental schools were organised in which the principal and seven teacher from each school participated. The participants were trained in communication skills, participative problem solving, and conflict management. Subsequently, these participants were requested to provide similar training to the remaining teachers back in schools. In the following year, the teachers in schools met to identify common goals that would form the basis of the educational change. Questionnaires from all teachers and interview from two teachers from each school were used to assess the extent of agreement on goals and use of human relation skills. Similar data were collected from teachers of seven other schools that had not received such training. Results revealed that the teachers from the seven experimental schools showed greater gain in goal agreement than the control schools. Teachers from the experimental schools (the trained group) reported greater participation in discussions and decision-making and resorted to more use of management skills than the teachers from control schools. Not only that, such favourable effects transferred to new teachers, who had joined these experimental groups. On the basis of this study conducted by Keys and Bartunek, it can be safely concluded that organisation training can enhance the effectiveness of member participation in problem solving and decision-making. The intervention in this study was found to be successful even though the entire faculty members of the schools had not received training from external consultants.

Thus, we see that social psychology of education has various facets and each can contribute significantly to the improvement of existing educational systems.

SOCIAL PSYCHOLOGY: PERSONAL HEALTH

Social psychology has much to contribute to our understanding of those factors that affect health and personal well-being. Growing evidences suggest that health is a biopsychosocial process because it is governed by a complex interaction among genetic, psychological and social factors (Taylor, 2002). Biological factors such as genetic predisposition to a particular disease, psychological factors such as the experience of stress and social factors such as the amount of social support one receives from family and friends tend to interact with each other and have an impact upon the health of a person. Various researches have suggested that there is a very strong link between the lifestyles a person adopts and his health and illness. A *healthy lifestyle* is one in which we avoid behaviour potentially harmful to health and seek early detection and effective treatment of illness (Glanz et al., 2002). Since social psychology studies topics which are related to lifestyles of a person such as attitudes and beliefs, different ways of coping with stress and personal characteristics that have an important role to play in the health of the person as well as its principles and theories have been widely applied for understanding health and illness of the people.

Health Behaviour and Health Attitude

What is health? Health is frequently described and explained in various discourses that are socially constructed. The word *health* is derived from Old High German and Anglo-Saxon words meaning whole, holy and hale. Culturally as well as historically, there are strong associations of health with concepts such as wholeness, hygiene, holiness, cleanliness, etc.

As we know, the concept of health and illness are embodied in day-to-day talk and in thought of people of all cultures and religions. One early Greek physician, Galen (BC 200–129) followed the Hippocratic tradition and pointed out that *hygieia* (health) or *euexia* (soundness) occurred when there was proper balance between the hot, cold, dry and wet components of the body. The four bodily humours were blood, phlegm, yellow bile and black bile. Blood was considered as hot and wet; phlegm was considered as cold and wet; yellow bile was considered as hot and dry and black bile was considered as cold and dry. Any disease was thought to occur by external pathogens, which tended to disturb the balance of the body's four elements—hot, dry, cold and wet. Galen believed that body's state could be put out of equilibrium by excessive heat, cold, dryness or wetness. Such disequilibrium or imbalance might be caused by anxiety, distress, fatigue, insomnia, etc.

Today, the meaning of health is different and broad one. The World Health Organisation (WHO) published a definition in 1946. This definition states that *health* is the state of complete physical, social and spiritual well-being, not simply the absence of illness. According to WHO definition, *health* is seen as well-being in its broadest sense and well-being is the product of a complex interplay of biological, socio-cultural and spiritual factors. However, the WHO definition overlooked some key elements of well-being. For example, the economic factors cannot be ignored. Likewise, the psychological aspect of well-being cannot be fully ignored in any meaningful definition of health. Therefore, a complete and meaningful definition would be—*Health* is a state of well-being with physical, psychosocial, cultural, economic and spiritual attributes and not simply the absence of illness (Marks et al., 2008).

In classical Indian traditions, health is understood as a state of delight or a feeling of spiritual, physical and mental well-being (*prasannatnmendriyamanah*), and in fact, this explanation is very similar to the WHO definition of health/well-being (Dalal, 2001; Sinha, 1990). Based upon the teachings of *Bhagvadgita*, Verma (1998) pointed out that human well-being unfolds at three levels, namely, *cognitive, conative* and *affective*. Well-being at the cognitive level demands self-examination leading to freedom from desires and attachment called *anasakti* (Naidu and Pande, 1999). At the conative level, well-being requires the performance of one's duty or *Karma* (Verma, 1994, 1998; Ram, 2000). Finally, at the affective level, the well-being lies in the attainment of freedom from I and mine. In sum, then, the Indian traditional perspective provides an ideal state of human functioning and constitutes health and well-being as a state of mind that is quiet, peaceful and free from various kinds of conflicts and desires.

Health behaviours are all those behaviours undertaken by people who are healthy to enhance or maintain their good health (Taylor, Peplau and Sears, 2006). These behaviour, among others, include consuming healthy diet, getting regular exercise, getting sufficient sleep, controlling weight and making use of health-screening programmes. Researches have shown that the more healthy behaviours people practised, the fewer illnesses of all kinds they reported and the more energy they are said to possess (Belloc and Breslow, 1972).

Since good health behaviours are essential to good health, it is very important to understand attitudes, which force people to practise good health behaviours or continue to practise the faulty ones. Researches done by Bandura (1986) Rogers (1984) and Weinstein (1993) showed that practising health behaviours rested upon five sets of beliefs presented as below:

1. General health values, which include interest in health and concern about health
2. A belief in personal vulnerability to certain disease or disorder
3. Realisation that the threat to health posed by a disorder or disease is severe
4. Belief of self-efficacy relating to performing the necessary response for reducing the threat
5. Belief regarding response efficacy, which means that the response will be effective in overcoming the threat

These health beliefs generally predict health behaviours quite well. Another attitudinal component that predicts health behaviour was added by Fishbein and Ajzen's (1980) *reasoned action model*, which states that behaviour is a direct result of a behavioural intention. Knowing an individual's intention, we are able to predict whether, for example, he or she will use preventing screening programmes, use contraceptives, and do physical exercise among other health behaviours. However, some factors are not fully incorporated into this attitude model. For example, among adolescents, many risky behaviours are not planned; rather they happen as a result of circumstances, which lead them to engage in smoking, drinking, unprotected sexual behaviour and other risky behaviours. Besides, some health behaviours are controlled by positive or negative consequences and these factors are also not explained by attitude models. Moreover, attitude models assume that people use extensive cognitive capabilities for making health behaviour decisions. But sometimes, we make inferences or decision very rapidly using highly salient or heuristic processes. In general, when a health issue is perceived to be very important and relevant, it is likely to be processed systematically through central attitude change routes, but when the issue is perceived to be less relevant for self, people are likely to use heuristically based judgement strategies (Rothman and Schwarz, 1998).

Thus, we see that the attitudes we hold about health, in general, and about our own health, in particular, are important determinants of our health behaviour. Levy et al. (2002) conducted a longitudinal research in which this fact was more vividly established. In this study, the researchers tried to assess individual's self-perceptions of aging—that is, their beliefs that what would happen to them as they would become older. After this assessment, they divided the participants into those who had mainly positive perceptions about their own aging and those who had negative perceptions. These two categories of the participants were followed over more than twenty years. A surprising result was obtained. Those having positive attitude and perceptions were more likely to continue living almost seven-and-a-half years longer than those with negative beliefs and perceptions. According to these researchers, such difference was attributed to the will to live. In other words, people with positive beliefs and self-perception of aging tended to perceive their lives as hopeful, fulfilling and worth-living, while those with negative beliefs and negative self-perceptions of aging tended to perceive their lives as hopeless, worthless and empty. People with positive self-perceptions took better care of themselves to live a healthier lifestyle. Consequently, they lived longer. The study clearly confirmed the link between healthy attitudes and healthy behavioural practices.

Health behaviour is also influenced by health-related cognitions, especially the dimension of their awareness. Parasher (2002) considered awareness studies important because they provide information about current status of knowledge of people as well as information about their lifestyles. Latha and Suresh (2002) reported that knowledge and health behaviours or lifestyles are significantly related to each other in coronary heart disease patients. Likewise, Biswas and Daftuar (2000) conducted another study in which out-of-school slum adolescents of Anand district of Gujarat participated as subjects. Their findings revealed gender variation in awareness and concerns about reproductive and sexual health. Males were found to be more aware than females. Collumbien and Hawkes (2000) observed that slum, rural and tribal people lacked basic knowledge in the area of fertility, maternal health and sexually transmitted diseases (STDs). Sachdeva (1998) also observed that female university students were not in favour of the repressive traditional Indian sexual standards relating to pre-marital and non-procreative sex. Likewise, some Indian researchers have reported a varying degree of awareness about HIV/AIDS (Veeraraghavan and Singh, 1999; Agarwal and Kumar, 1996). Recently, Chatterjee et al. (2001) reported a very low degree of awareness about HIV/AIDS among both school boys and their teachers. About half of such teachers and school boys reported that such patients should be kept in isolation for preventing the spread of shameful disease. Bharat (2000) conducted another study in which he examined how HIV/AIDS patients are perceived and interpreted in low income communities of Mumbai. His observation revealed many misconceptions and fears despite high familiarity with this disease. Men were found to convey not only greater awareness but also more misconceptions about HIV/AIDS.

Stress, Health and Illness

Stressful life experience and the ways people cope with those stressful events have an impact on health and illness (Taylor, 2002). *Stress* is defined as a negative emotional experience accompanied by predictable physiological, biochemical and behavioural changes, which are designed to reduce or adapt to the stressors. Generally, we think stress as originating from particular event such as being stuck in traffic, being late for an appointment, getting poor marks in the examination, etc. Although there is some commonalities in experience of stress, not everyone perceives the same event as stressful. For example, one person may experience job interview as stressful, whereas another person may welcome it and consider it as a challenge. It means that to some extent, stress lies in the eye of beholder, and this fact makes stress a psychological process. Therefore, any event is stressful when that is regarded as stressful and not otherwise (Lazarus and Folkman, 1984).

Now, the question is—what makes events stressful? Social psychologists have identified some characteristics of events that help in being appraised them as stressful. Generally, negative or unpleasant events produce more psychological distress and produce more physical symptoms in comparison to positive stressful events (Sarason, Johnson and Siegel, 1978). Likewise, unpredictable or uncontrollable events cause more stress than controllable or predictable ones (Bandura et al., 1988; Suls and Mullen, 1981). This happens because uncontrollable events do not allow the people to develop ways to cope with the problem. For example, excess sound from your own TV may be less distressing than the similar sound from neighbour because you can turn off or lessen the volume of your own TV. Similarly, social psychologists have pointed out that ambiguous events generally cause more stress than what is caused by clear-cut defined events. This is because of the fact that when events are clear, people are more inclined to find solutions and they are not left stuck at the problem-solving stage (Billings and Moos, 1984). Likewise, events may be unresolvable or resolvable. In general, unresolvable events are perceived as more stressful than those which can be resolved.

Causes of Stress

There are several factors that contribute to health. Social psychologists have concentrated upon some factors that add to our total stress quotient. Among the most important of these are major stressful live events, hassles of daily life and various dispositional factors, and social factors, etc. These are described below:

1. Major stressful live events: Social psychologists in their earlier researches have tried to demonstrate the relation of stress to health by recognising the role of major stressful life events in the onset of illness and health. Major stressful life events include death of spouse, jail term, marital separation, divorce, death of members of family, personal injury or illness, and so on. Working earlier in this field, Holmes and Rahe (1967) pointed out that any life event requiring people to change or adopt their lifestyles would result in stress. Like Selye, they basically assumed that both negative events and positive events demand that a person must adjust in some way, and therefore, both kinds of events are associated with stress. Holmes and Rahe (1967) developed a scale, called *social readjustment rating scale* (*SRRS*), to measure the amount of stress in person's life in terms of *life change unit* (*LCU*), which is the numerical value assigned to each life event. For example, in SRRS, the critical live events such as death of spouse, divorce and death of a closed family member were given LCU of 119, 98 and 92, respectively. After administering the scale, LCUs for all live events experienced by the person are added. If the added value is in between 0–150, no significant problems are said to exist; if the value is in between 150–199, mild life crisis indicating 33% chances of illness is said exist; if the value lies between 200–299, moderate life crisis indicating 50% chances of illness exists and if the added value is more than 300, major life crisis indicating 80% chances of illness exists. In a study conducted by Kendler and Prescott (1999), it was found that stressful life events of the kind listed in SRRS were excellent predictors of the onset of depression. The SRRS was later revised by Miller and Rahe (1997) to reflect the changes in the ratios of events in the 30 intervening years since its inception in 1967.

Since the SRRS tends to be more appropriate for older and the established adults, it does not suit much for college students, who are affected by stressful events such as entering college, changing majors or the breakup of a steady relationship (Crandall, Preisler and Aussprung, 1992). Therefore, for assessing stress experienced by college students, one of its recent versions named as college undergraduate stress scale (CUSS) has been developed (Renner and Mackin, 1998).

Indian psychologists have also remained very active in associating stressful live events to illness and health. Across different categories of people based on occupation, gender, age and habitat, people who experience stress are found to be more susceptible to unhealthy lifestyles, illness and lower well-being (Dalal, 2001; Naidu, 2001). Subsequent researches have further shown that people who are exposed to life-event stress are at a greater risk of psychological distress (Agrawal and Dalal, 1994; Banerjee and Vyas, 1992; Jagdish and Reddy, 2000; Rastogi and Kashyap, 2001; Sharma et al., 2004). These researchers further showed that the number/frequency of critical life events is not much important. What appears to be significant is the perceived negative impact either directly or through a maladaptive coping (Sharma, 2003; Sharma et al., 2004).

2. Hassles of daily life: The bulk of stresses that we experience daily actually come from little frustrations, delays, irritations, minor disagreements and similar annoyances. These daily annoyances are termed as *hassles* (Lazarus, 1988; Kazarus and Folman, 1984; Delongis, Folkman and Lazarus,

1988). These researchers suggested that daily hassles like too many responsibilities, problems with works, inconsiderate neighbours, trouble making decision, separation from family, misplacing or losing things, etc. are important cause of stress. High positive correlation was found between scores of hassle scales and reports of psychological symptoms. Thus, the more stress people reported due to daily hassles, the poorer was their psychological well-being. Whereas the major life events of Holmes and Rahe's scale (1967) tend to have a long-term effect upon person's chronic physical and mental health, the day-to-day hassles have impact upon immediate health and well-being and are considered as better predictors of short-term illnesses such as headache, cold, and similar other symptoms (Delongis et al., 1988). In a study conducted by Fernandez and Sheffield (1996), it was found that among 261 participants who experienced headaches, the scores of hassle scale were significantly better predictors of headaches than were the scores on life events scale.

3. Dispositional factors: *Disposition* refers to personal resources that reside within a person. Dispositional factors work directly through their association with health and illness. Many personality traits/types have been found to demonstrate a closer link with greater stress and dysfunctional well-being. For example, Type A personality, who is competitive, ambitious, hates to waste time and is easily annoyed, is associated with enhanced physiological reactivity to stress, which is one of the mechanisms that initiate and hasten the development of coronary heart disease (CHD) (Contrada et al., 1985; Krantz and Manuck, 1984). Researches have linked various other dispositional factors such as locus of control, ego strength, field dependence, optimism, extraversion, future orientation, etc. with various indicators of mental health (Shrivastava, 2004; Mukherjee and Mukhopadhyay, 1998). Indian researchers have further tried to establish relationship between various indigenous dispositional concepts like *tamasic* disposition and *anasakti* (means non-attachment) disposition. Pandey and Naidu (1992) reported that when faced with stressors, those persons who practice *anasakti* were found to be less distressed and exhibited fewer symptoms of ill-health. Likewise, Daftuar and Anjali (1997) found that *tamasic* disposition tended to generate occupational stress, with severe psychological psychosomatic and behavioural consequences. Some researchers have studied the role of trait anger (a component of type A personality) and trait anxiety in cardiovascular disease (CVD). According to the research done by Ghosh and Sharma (1998) and Sharma (2003), higher trait anger was found to be associated with hypertension or peptic ulcer. (These patients resorted to greater anger suppression and control of their angry feelings. Such patients also reported higher trait anxiety (Pradhan and Shrivastava, 2003).

4. Socio-cultural factors: The importance of socio-cultural factors in causing stress is emerging as a significant focus of research. Here, important factors that are considered are poverty, job stress, acculturative stress, family structure, residential density and environmental hazards.

  (i) ***Poverty:*** Poverty is stressful for several reasons. Poor people lack sufficient money for meeting the basic necessities of life. Such condition can produce too many stressors for both adults as well as children. Researches done by Park et al. (2002), Aligne et al. (2000) and Schmitz et al. (2001) revealed that poverty often leads to poor medical care, increased rates of disabilities due to improper prenatal care, noisy and overcrowding environments, violence, substance abuse, etc. All these conditions generate stress and have a taxing impact upon personal health of the person.

(ii) **Job stress:** Stress resulting from the conditions of job is also very common. Even if the person has high salary, there are some stresses associated with workplace. Some of the important sources of stress in the workplace include workload, lack of control over decisions, long working hours, poor physical work condition and lack of job security (Murphy, 1995). Researchers have further shown that stress from workplace results in more or less same symptoms as stress from any other sources. Such important symptoms are high blood pressure, indigestion, headache, anxiety, irritability, anger, depression, etc. and some behaviour symptoms such as overeating, poor job performance, drug abuse, changes in family relationship (Anschuetz, 1999). Besides, one serious effect of workplace stress is *burnout*, which is defined as negative emotions, thoughts and behaviour as a consequence of prolonged stress (Miller and Smith, 1993). The common symptoms of burnout are extreme dissatisfaction, lowered job satisfaction, pessimism and a strong desire to quit.

(iii) **Acculturative stress:** Culture also affects stress. *Acculturation* refers to a process of adapting to a new or different culture often the majority culture. When a person from one culture comes to live in another culture, that person may experience some stress. The stress resulting from the need to change and adapt to the dominant or majority culture is known as *acculturative stress* (Berry and Kim, 1998). According to Berry and Kim (1998), there are four methods that a person chooses to enter into dominant culture and these methods tend to produce differential degree of stress in the person who enter into dominant culture. The four methods are integration, assimilation, separation and marginalisation. In *integration*, a person tries to maintain the identity of his original culture and to form a positive relationship with the members of new and dominant culture. Integration produces a lower degree of acculturation stress (Ward and Rana–Deuba, 1999). In *assimilation*, the person gives up his original cultural identity and completely adopts the ways of new dominant culture. Assimilation produces a moderate level of acculturative stress due to loss of cultural patterns and rejection by the other members of his original culture, who have not preferred assimilation (Lay and Nguyen, 1998). In *separation*, the person rejects the majority cultural pattern and ways and tries to maintain his original culture identity. People opting for such method refuse to learn the language of the majority culture and they live where others from their own original culture live. Separation results in higher degree of stress and if separation is forced, rather than voluntary, the degree of stress would still be higher. In *marginalisation*, the people neither maintain contact with their original culture nor join the dominant culture. They live on the margins of both cultures without becoming part of either culture. Consequently, marginalised people have little in the way of social support to help them deal with various stressful life events. As such, the level of acculturative stress is high among marginalised persons.

(iv) **Family structure:** Several domains of our behaviour are regulated more directly at family level than at individual level. We find a strong tradition of understanding the various psychosomatic illness from the perspective of family. Some studies have highlighted the impact of nuclear and joint families upon health and illness, though the results have not been consistent (Dastidar and Kapoor, 1996; Jagdish and Yadav, 1999). It has been pointed out that the functional content of family relations does have an impact of health and illness. For example, if a conflict frequently occurs between the members of family, the personal, physical and mental health of the members are adversely affected and their members succumb to various types of illnesses (Evans et al., 1998).

(v) ***Residential density and environmental hazards:*** Residential crowding and the resulting environmental pollution also cause stress and affect the health and well-being in the long-term time. Living in such crowded homes is likely to have negative consequences for human physical and psychological health (Arora and Sinha, 1998; Pandey, 2003). In an important study conducted by Evans et al. (1998) on 10 to 12 years old children of Pune city, it was found that chronic residential crowding was associated with elevated blood pressure, learned helplessness, impaired parent–child relationship, and poor adjustment in schools. All these have adverse impact upon physical and mental health of the dwellers.

Nowadays, environmental hazards particularly biological pathogens, physical hazards, chemical pollutants and shortage of specific natural resources are posing serious problems for the personal health. Researches have revealed that the incidence of water-borne diseases, tuberculosis, respiratory infections, etc. have provided ample evidence for the concerned fact (Singh and Misra, 2004).

How Does Stress Affect Health and Well-Being?

Stress plays a very important role in personal health. It affects both our physical and mental health. But how do exactly such effects occur? Growing research evidences suggest that stress affects our health by draining our resources, producing negative affect, disturbing our physiological balance and ultimately disturbing our internal chemistry. In fact, it disturbs our internal chemistry by interfering with efficient operation of our immune system, which helps in recognising and destroying potentially harmful substances such as bacteria, viruses and cancerous cells. The main cells of immune system are leucocytes, usually known as *white blood cells*. Three important types of leucocytes are granulocytic leucocytes that engulf and destroy bacteria and antigen-antibody complexes, monocytes which generally recognise carbohydrates on surfaces of microorganisms and lymphocytes that are subdivided into B cells, NK or natural killer cells and T cells and tend to attack specific targets such as virus-infected and tumour cells. B cells produces antibodies that control infection. A fairly consistent finding has been that chronic stress is associated with down regulation of immune systems with changes found particularly in the number of NK cells, the total number of T cells and the proportion of T helper cells to T suppressor cells (Marks et al., 2008). Some studies have shown that anticipated stressors, that is, those that have not yet occurred but which were expected, are found to be related to the decreased percentage of T helper cells, which enhance immune responses. Another variety of T cell is T suppressor cells that inhibit immune responses.

Baum (1994) gave some suggestions for a model that tends to explain how stress can affect our health and well-being. This model states that stress produces both direct and indirect effects upon us (see Figure 17.1). Direct effect includes higher blood pressure, increased amount of fat in the body cells, etc.

Indirect effect involves influences on our health-related behaviour such as delay in seeking medical assistance, less effort to engage in preventive behaviour and so on as well as influences upon our fitness-related behaviour such as choosing less nutritional food, sleeping less, increase in smoking and consumption of alcohol.

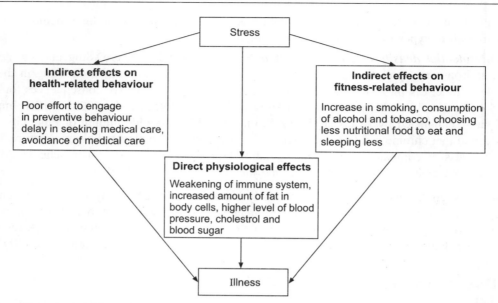

Figure 17.1 A model that relates stress, illness and health (based on suggestions given by Baum, 1994).

Although this model is very effective and useful in explaining several ways in which stress affect our health, it does not include all the ways in which stress may affect our health.

How to Cope with Stress?

Coping is considered as a cognitive and behavioural effort, which may help people in psychosocial adaptation with various stressful events. Thus, coping strategies are the activities that people can take to reduce or minimise the effects of stressors and they can include both psychological strategies and behavioural strategies. In very simple words, *coping* is a process of attempting to manage demands, which are viewed as taxing or exceeding the resources (Lazarus and Folkman, 1984). There are three major coping strategies commonly followed by a person for reducing the adverse effects—*emotion-focused coping,* where the person makes efforts to replace the negative emotions produced by stress with more positive ones; *problem-focused coping,* where the person makes efforts to alter the situation itself, that is, the cause of stress and *seeking social support,* where the person tries to draw on maximally the emotional task resources provided by others for reducing the adverse effect of stress.

As said above, in *emotion-focused coping*, the person engages in all those activities that reduce the negative feelings and emotions produced by stress (Lazarus, 1993). Thus, in emotion-focused coping strategies, an attempt is made to change the way a person feels or emotionally reacts to stressor. This tends to reduce the emotional impact of stressors and makes it possible to deal with the problem effectively. Some of the common emotion-focused strategies are trying to perceive the situation in positive way (positive reappraisal), positive self-task, positive statements about self, writing about one's feeling and emotions in diary and so on. For example, if a person loses his job, he may decide that it is not a major tragedy because he will soon get still a better job or view it as a challenge—an opportunity to get a better job with higher salary.

Problem-focused coping strategies are one, where people try to eliminate the source of stress or reduce its impact through their own actions (Lazarus, 1993). In simple words, problem-focused strategies are the attempts to do something constructive about the stressful conditions that are harming, threatening or challenging an individual. Therefore, such strategies are direct and consists of reducing, modifying or eliminating the source of stress itself. For example, if a student is getting a poor grade in mathematics and appraises this as a threat, he may decide to study harder, get a tutor or drop the course and select some other subject.

Well-functioning persons generally use a combination of problem-focused and emotion-focused coping strategies in almost every stressful situation. Folkman and Lazarus (1980) conducted a study in which coping patterns of 100 subjects over a 12-month period were studied and they found that both types of coping strategies were used in 98% of 1300 stressful events that they had confronted. It was further revealed that problem-focused coping strategies increased in situations, where subjects were appraised as changeable and emotion-focused coping strategies increased in those situations that were appraised as not changeable and uncontrollable. In using these two types of strategies, gender variations were observed because males used both problem-focused coping strategies and emotion-focused coping strategies, but female counterparts preferred to use emotion-focus coping strategies (Sahu and Misra, 1995; Sharda and Raju, 2001).

Recently, Minhas (2003) studied the coping strategies adopted by Kashmiri migrant children in Jammu due to the militancy of their native land. They were found to resort to strategies, which included daydreaming, withdrawal and compensation. All these children, thus, largely used emotion-focused coping strategies rather than problem-focused coping strategies.

Some researchers have revealed that emotion-focused coping strategies may be effective in short run, but they may be ineffective or even dangerous in the long term. For example, researches done by Goeders (2004) revealed that after having the experience of being stressed, some people drink alcohol or take drugs. Although this makes them feel better for some time, it leaves the cause of stress largely unchanged and even may damage their health.

Seeking social support is another popular strategy for reducing the impact of stressors because we know that health and happiness are influenced not only by social cognition but also by social relationship. Social support is conceptualised as support provided usually in time of need, by a spouse, or other members of the family, or by friends, neighbours, colleagues, or others. Social support can involve tangible support, information and advice as well as emotional support. Social support either elicited or provided spontaneously plays an important role in dealing with life's challenges and threats (Sharma and Misra, 2010). Social support has been found to encourage health-providing behaviours and reduce the impact of stress so that people will be less likely to resort to unhealthy ways of coping such as smoking or drinking (Adler and Matthews, 1994). Further, social support has also been found to reduce the impact of stress from unemployment, long-term illness, retirement and bereavement (Krantz et al., 1985). Individuals with proper social support have been found to recover more quickly from illnesses and lower their risk of deaths from specific diseases (House et al., 1988). Social support has been found to help moderate the surviving heart attack and increase the longevity of surviving the cancer patient (Turner, 1983). Berkman and Syme (1979) conducted a study on 44775 individuals over a 9-year period and found that people with low social support were twice as likely to die as those high in social support. Indian researchers were also found that a reliable social support of kin and friends often reduces the risk of diseases and enhances quick recovery from mental and physical illness (Pal et al., 2002; Dalal, 2001; Pradhan and Misra, 1995).

Sharma (1999) analysed the role of family as support system. There have been found two mechanisms that explain how social support lessens the impact of stressors and promotes health and well-being. They are direct effect hypothesis and buffering effect hypothesis. Emotional support is more likely to produce a stress-buffering effect. Moreover, the efficacy of social support is likely to be dependent on the following five factors (Sharma, 1989):

1. Who is providing support?
2. What kind of support is provided?
3. To whom is the support provided?
4. When and for how long is the support produced?
5. What is the issue/problem for which the support is provided?

Recent findings have indicated that having a pet can also reduce the negative impact of stress (Allen, 2003). A study conducted by Allen, Shykoff and Izzo (2001) showed that the stockbrokers, who had described their work as stressful and usually had high blood pressure, when were allowed to be with a pet, it provided an excellent source of social support. One reason of pets being effective in reducing the negative impact of stress is that they provide non-judgemental social support, that is, they love their owners in all situations.

One recent finding has suggested that providing social support rather than receiving social support is very important. Brown et al. (2003) conducted a study in which they compared the impact of giving and receiving social support on mortality in a group of 846 elderly married people. It was found that those participants, who provided high levels of support to others, were significantly less likely to die over a five-year period as compared to the participants, who had provided little or no support to others. However, receiving social support from others, including spouse, did not appear to influence mortality among participants. The study provided a hint that it is better to give than to receive social support, especially when it comes to relate to the illness and personal health.

Personal Factors, Health and Illness

All of us know that there is a large difference between personal health and illness. Some persons are rarely ill and go to doctor, while others suffer from frequent illnesses. Although there can be money factors, which are responsible for this, personal characteristics play an important role in promoting health and well-being. Some of these personal factors are hostility and anger, perfectionism, optimism and pessimism, psychological hardiness, social support and socio-economic status. We have already considered social support. Therefore, we shall concentrate upon the remaining ones.

1. Hostility and anger: Researches have supported the view that the individuals rated high on hostility and anger have been found to be at higher risk for heart disease than those who are rated low on anger and hostility. A study conducted by Niaura et al. (2002) revealed that high level of hostility is a better predictor of heart disease in older men. Smith (2003) reported that medical students showing high level of anger while under stress were more than three times more likely to develop premature heart disease and five times more likely to have an early heart attack, than those who were rated low on anger. Suarez (1998) conducted a study in which it was found that a person with higher level of hostility when angered by another person tended to display higher blood pressure, higher heart rate and other related physiological signs of high levels of stress in comparison to the persons, who were having a low level of hostility.

2. **Perfectionism:** *Perfectionism* means a person's tendency to be perfect or nearly perfect in everything he does. Social psychologists have identified two different patterns of perfectionism—personal standards perfectionism and self-critical perfectionism. In *personal standards perfectionism*, the person sets extremely and often unrealistically high standards for himself. In *self-critical perfectionism*, the person constantly engages in harsh criticism of their own actions, expresses an inability to derive satisfaction from successful performance and chronic concerns about other's criticism and expectation (Blankstein and Dunkley, 2002). Of these two patterns of perfectionism, self-critical perfectionism damages personal health and well-being. Persons characterised by self-critical perfectionism

   (i) Constantly blame themselves for everything
   (ii) Perceive that they cannot get social support from others when needed
   (iii) Perceive that other people are highly critical of them
   (iv) Always have doubt about their own ability to deal with the stressful live events

Due to these various characteristics, persons having the pattern of self-critical perfectionism generally experience negative feelings as well as feeling of helplessness. Consequently among them, the level of stress becomes high that affects their personal health.

3. **Optimism and pessimism:** People who are optimistic do have happy thoughts and generally cope more effectively with stress. Apparently, happy thoughts become healthy thoughts. Since optimistic people generally expect good outcomes, such positive expectations help in making them more stress-resistant than pessimists, who generally expect bad outcomes. Researches have shown that optimists are more likely to use problem-focused coping strategy, seek social support and find positive aspects of a stressful situation (Carver et al., 1993; Sheier and Carver, 1992). On the other hand, pessimists generally use denial or tend to focus on their stressful feelings (Sheier et al., 1986). In a study conducted by Sheier and Carver (1985), it was found that optimistic students reported fewer physical symptoms at the end of semester examination than those who were pessimistic. Thus, we find that being optimist one can have good personal health, whereas being pessimist one can damage his personal health.

Further researches have shown that optimists tend to live longer and have improved functioning of their immune system. Maruta et al. (2002) conducted a longitudinal study of optimists and pessimists over a period of 30 years. The results for pessimists were discouraging. Such people had much higher death rate than did the optimists and those who were still living had more problems with physical and emotional health than optimists. The optimists had a 50% lower risk of premature death and were calmer, peaceful and were leading a happy life than the pessimists. An earlier study conducted by Segerstorm et al. (1998) revealed that optimists were having higher level of helper T cells and higher levels of natural killer cells. Seligman (2002), a social learning psychologist, outlined the following four important ways in which optimism may affect longevity of a person:

   (i) Optimists are more likely than pessimists to take care of their personal health by preventive measures such as going to the doctor regularly and eating only right things.
   (ii) Optimists are less likely to develop learned helplessness—a tendency to stop trying to achieve a goal that has been blocked in the past.
   (iii) Optimists are less likely to become depressed than pessimists. Depression lowers the proper functioning of immune system.

(iv) Since optimists experience less psychological stress, they have more effectively functioning immune systems than pessimists.

4. Psychological hardiness: Our common observation has been that some people under great stress succumb to illness, while others do not. Why so? Probably the answer lies in one unique characteristic of the people that is *psychological hardiness*, which is defined as a combination of three psychological qualities or attitudes, namely, commitment, challenge and control (three C's) shared by people, who can undergo high level of stress yet keep themselves healthy one. Kobasa (1979) did pioneer study in this field. She studied 670 male executives, who had symptoms of illness due to stressful life events in the preceding three years. She then administered personality questionnaires to 200 executives, who had high rank on both stress and illness and to 126, who had equally experienced stressful life events, but were having few symptoms of illness. In results, she found that high stress/low illness male subjects were more immersed in their social lives and work. They enjoyed challenge and had a better control over events than their high stress/high illness counterparts. Three years later, Kobasa et al. (1982) looked at the same executives. This time, their observation was that the high stress/low illness group remain healthy and retained their attitudes of commitment, challenge and control—three basic characteristics that Kobasa collectively called *hardiness*. The author has also developed a scale for assessing psychological hardiness named Singh Psychological Hardiness Scale (SPHS) published by National Psychological Corporation, Agra.

Now, the question is—why would these three characteristics lessen the negative impact of stress? Commitment forces the person to willingly make sacrifices and deal with hardships. Control empowers the person to look at stressful events not much harming as they can be put on hold. People with a sense of personal control typically cope more successfully with stressful events, even with those stressful events that are largely uncontrollable (Helgeson, 1992). Seeing events as challenges rather than as problems also tend to change the level of stress experienced (Ciccarelli and Meyer, 2006). Following Roth et al. (1989), a person having the characteristics of commitment, challenge and control generally possesses a cognitive style such that stressful life events are interpreted less negatively, and therefore, they are rendered less harmful.

5. Socio-economic status: Researchers have shown that there is an obvious link between socio-economic status and personal health. Overall, if a person belongs to higher level of socio-economic status, his personal health is better (Steenland, Henley and Thun, 2002). Indian researchers have also shown that persons in lower socio-economic status tend to display poor physical and mental health/well-being as indexed by various measures (Chaturvedi and Michael, 1993; Misra and Agrawal, 2003; Panjiyar and Rout, 1999; Srivastava and Bhatnagar, 2000). The reason for having better health in case of people of higher socio-economic status is that they have greater material resources than the persons lower in socio-economic status. Recent findings, however, raise another possibility that one important factor which may underline such difference is general intelligence. Persons belonging to the upper socio-economic status having higher intelligence know better about what it takes to be healthy and are more likely to put this knowledge to practical use than the persons who belong to lower socio-economic status. However, this conclusion awaits research support.

In this way, we find that several personal factors do have a direct impact upon health and illness of the person.

Promoting Healthy Lifestyles

In determining how long we live, many factors do play important roles. According to Perls and Silver (1999), some genetic factors do play a role in determining such longevity. They reported that a group of genes found on a single human chromosome tends to determine the life span of a person. But recent researches have shown that environmental factors, especially our lifestyle, are more significant factors in determining the longevity of the person. A healthy lifestyle promotes personal health and well-being. Social psychologists are of view that a healthy lifestyle is one in which an individual avoids all those behaviours that are considered potentially harmful to his health (that is, excessive use of alcohol, smoking, unprotected sex and unprotected exposure to burning sun) and seeks early detection and effective treatment of illness when it occurs. Researches done by Powell et al. (1986) revealed that the first factor leading to premature death is unhealthy lifestyle, that is, about 53.5% of death occurs due to unhealthy lifestyle. The role of healthy and unhealthy lifestyles in promoting health as well as illness was shown in one famous study conducted by Levy et al. (2002). These investigators conducted a longitudinal study stretching across more than twenty two years. In this study, based upon assessment of the participant's self-perception of aging, two groups were formed. One group of participants had mainly positive perceptions about their own aging and the other group of participants had negative perceptions about their own aging. After about two decades, it was found that the participants with positive beliefs about aging lived on the average 7.5 years longer than those with negative beliefs. The major reason for this difference was that the persons with positive self-perceptions of aging perceived their lives as hopeful, fulfilling and worth living, that is, they had a healthy lifestyles. On the other hand, those with negative self-perceptions tended to perceive their lives as hopeless, full of helplessness, empty and worthless, that is, they had unhealthy lifestyle.

Researches have revealed that in unhealthy lifestyle, many factors have their significant contributions. Among these, unhealthy diet, overeating, lack of exercise, alcohol or drug abuse, too little sleep are important ones. But the most dangerous behaviour of all are smoking and drug abuse.

Exercise is considered as the best means of keeping fit and healthy. Several studies have shown that regular aerobic exercise pays rich dividends in the form of improved physical and mental health as well as fitness. *Aerobic exercise* refers to the exercise which uses large muscle groups in continuous, repetitive action and requires increased oxygen intakes, increasing breathing and heart rates. Some of the examples of aerobic exercise are running, swimming, brisk walking, cycling, rowing and jumping rope. To improve cardiovascular fitness and endurance and to lessen the risk of heart attack, aerobic exercise should be performed regularly. Regular aerobic exercise has been considered beneficial for people of all age groups. Even pre-schoolers have been shown to receive cardiovascular benefits from planned regular aerobic exercise (Alpert et al., 1990). In case of older people, regular and planned aerobic exercise yields dramatic increases in muscles and bone strength. Researchers have established the following benefits of exercise:

1. It moderates the effect of stress.
2. It benefits the immune system by improving the functioning of natural killer and activity (Fiatarone et al., 1988).
3. It burns up extra calories, enabling the person to lose weight or maintain the correct weight.
4. It increases the functioning of heart, enabling it to pump more blood with each beat, and thus, improves circulation of blood.

5. It makes bone denser and stronger, helping to prevent osteoporosis among women.
6. It raises high density lipoprotein or HDL (good blood cholesterol) level, which helps the body in reducing low density lipoprotein or LDL (bad cholesterol) level which helps in removing plaques being built up on the artery walls.

SOCIAL PSYCHOLOGY: LEGAL SYSTEM

As we know, in social psychology, a wide range of topics related to social behaviour and thoughts are studied. Therefore, it is not surprising that social psychologists have conducted researches on several legally relevant topics. Among these, effects of police interrogation, eyewitness identification and testimony and criminal defendants are the most important ones.

Aspects of Police Interrogation

Police makes interrogation of the witnesses and suspects before a case reaches the courtroom. Here, the following two factors have been found to be important ones:
1. The way police makes interrogation from witnesses and suspects
2. How media presents the information about the case

The way police makes interrogation from suspects is very important. Generally, police resorts to *inquisitorial approach*, that is, a way through which search for truth is established. Even if the police does so, serious forms of bias enter the process of interrogation. When interrogated by police, suspects generally find themselves in a highly stressful and emotion-changed setting. As a result, they become confused and they confess to even those crimes, which they have not committed. To make the matter worse, the judges of court tend to accept these confession true one and then innocent people are convicted.

Now, the question is—how can such distortions be avoided? One way to solve this problem is that interrogations by the police should be videotaped. Such videotaping is likely to prevent the police using strong-arm tactics. Not only that, it also helps the judges in making accurate judgement about the validity of the confessions. However, the videotaping also involves one problem, which results from our basic tendency to perceive whatever is in the focus of our attention as being more important and central to those events, which are not focused of our attention. In videotaping of police interrogation, generally what happens is that defendant becomes the focus of attention. As a consequence, the illusory correlation may occur and the judges are likely to view any confessions obtained as true and voluntary. Lassiter et al. (2002) conducted several studies in which participants viewed videotapes of police interrogations in which the suspects had made confessions. There were two conditions—in one condition, the camera was focused entirely on the suspect and in other condition, the camera was focused both on the suspect and the interrogator. All other factors such as the suspect's answers and the interrogator's questions, etc. were held constant. Results were in expected direction. The participants rated the confessions in suspect-focus condition as more voluntary and suspects were rated as more guilty as well as fit for harsher sentences in comparison to the condition, where suspects and interrogators both were focused. This happens probably because of the fact that whatever serves as the focus of our attention becomes the centre of our initial thoughts and this, in turn, determines later judgements. The study conducted by Lassiter et al. (2002)

had obvious implication that if videotaping done during the police interrogations was likely to be effective and beneficial, the camera should be focused more or less equally on both the defendant and the interrogator.

Another factor that tends to influence the outcome of police interrogations is the location of the interrogation. There may be two types of location—*threatening location* such as police headquarters and *non-threatening location* such as defendant's home or place of work. Researchers have revealed that the police interrogations done in threatening or intimidating location are more purposeful and worthy than the police interrogations done in non-threatening locations.

There are some other aspects of police interrogations, which cast social influence. One such factor is the use of minimisation approach, where the interrogator minimises the crime by blaming the victim rather than the suspect or defendant for what happened. This creates a false sense of security as well as a belief in defendants that the interrogator will minimise the strength of the evidence and the seriousness of the charge with the implicit promise that the punishment will be very mild. Although this approach seems to be non-coercive, it is less obvious way to illicit compliance. Another tactics of social influence is one in which the police interrogators show the suspects with false fingerprint data, inaccurate eyewitness identifications, bogus polygraph results and false confession of a fellow suspect for persuading them to confess (Kassin and Kiechel, 1996).

Media converge is also important factor. Often it is found that a lot of information regarding suspects in various newspapers and on virtually every news programme on television about the suspects creates a strong tendency to form a negative impression about the suspect. People also tend to believe various assertions and disclosures done by media (Gilbert, Tafarodi and Malone, 1993). As a consequence, suspects or dependants are often viewed as guilty by the public even before the trial begins. From such effect of pre-trial publicity, the prosecution is benefitted and there occurs substantial harm to the defence. Moran and Culter (1991) substantiated this fact from their study. The government officials take advantage of such effect by providing as much crime information as possible to the newspapers and various TV channels so that a strong negative impression may be created in public regarding the suspect, in general. The greater the amount of publicity about the crime, the greater is the tendency on the part of judges to convict the person who has been accused of committing the crime. Thus, the media effects tend to influence both pre-trial judgement of the public as well as post-trial judgement done by the judges of the court.

Eyewitness Identification and Testimony

Eyewitness testimony plays a very important role in many trials. *Eyewitness testimony* means the evidences provided by the individuals who have witnessed the crime. Apparently, nothing can be more convincing than eyewitness testimony. But the reality is otherwise. Eyewitness testimony depends on human perception, thought and memory. These cognitive processes are far from perfect. Therefore, eyewitness testing often becomes inaccurate. Researches have revealed that eyewitnesses sometimes falsely identify innocent persons as criminals (Wells, 1993), tend to make mistakes about important details concerning a crime (Loftus, 2003), and sometimes, also tend to report or remember about those events that did not actually take place (Zaragoza et al., 2000). Now, the question is what makes eyewitnesses inaccurate? How can a person, who is actually present when crime occurred, make such serious errors? Social psychologists have distinguished between two groups of factors that influence eyewitness identification—estimator variables system variables.

1. Estimator variables

Estimator variables incorporate those factors that are related to eyewitness or the situation in which the event was witnessed. Important estimator variables are as under:

(i) **Proper opportunity to view the event:** For acquiring a complete and accurate information about an event, it is essential that witness must be able to see and/or hear it clearly. In general, a person, who witnesses an event that happens 20 yards away on a clear day, is able to provide a better and accurate information than a person who witnesses an event that occurs 100 yards away on a sight. Shapiro and Penrod (1986) pointed out that witnesses are more likely to identify faces correctly when they look at them at larger and devote a greater degree of attention to the faces during the acquisition phase.

(ii) **Weapon focus:** *Weapon focus effect* is an effect where eyewitnesses tend to remember more information about the weapon used to commit a crime than about the criminal, who was using the weapon. Such effect has been demonstrated in many studies (Steblay, 1992). Such effect occurs because witnesses, who try to evaluate the degree of level, may find it useful to keep their eyes on the weapons held by the criminals. Sometimes, novelty of the weapons also draw people's attention (Pickel, 1999). Researchers have shown that weapon focus effect is more likely to occur in those situations where weapons are unexpected or surprising (Pickel, 1999). For example, witnesses are more likely to focus on weapons in a temple, mosque or in a church, where they are unexpected than at a shooting place, where they are expected.

(iii) **Stress and anger:** Witnesses often experience negative emotions or stress. They may be angry that a crime is taking place as well as much worried about a person who is being victimised. They may also be fearful because they may also be harmed. All these negative emotions affect the memories of eyewitnesses. Christianson (1992) conducted a study in which it was found that the individuals, who witnessed a negative emotional event, tended to have a very accurate memory of the event itself but less accurate memories of what happened before and after the event. For example, an individual, who has witnessed a violent attack of pistol shot on a victim, is likely to have the accurate memories of pistol attack, but less accurate memories of what attacker did after the attacks. In fact, witnesses very often make mistakes partly because intense emotions tend to exert effects on the information processing. Such effects often occur when witness is also the victim of a crime. Loftus (1992) cited a case in which a rape victim identified a wrong man as rapist. This wrong man, though was innocent, was convicted and eventually, released when the actual rapist was caught and confessed the crime. Several other studies have confirmed the fact that strong emotions often contribute to such distortions (Wells, Luus and Windschitl, 1994).

(iv) **Retention interval and intervening information:** The amount of time that passes between witnessing an event and making identification or providing testimony is a significant factor that affects the accuracy of eyewitness. Researches have shown that with the lapse of time, the accuracy of eyewitness identification decreases (Loftus, 1992; Wells, 2002). One obvious reason of why accuracy decreases over the time is forgetting with the lapse of time. People forget details that could help them to make accurate identifications. Wells (2002) pointed out that accuracy drops dramatically soon after an event and then diminishes more slowly. Still another reason of loss in accuracy is the misleading post-event information from several sources such as news stories, statement given by other witnesses, police sources, etc. All these information blend together as a part of what seems to be remembered. The major reason of inaccuracy, here, becomes the failure of eyewitness to distinguish between what is actually remembered and what has been learned later on.

There are three major explanations of the impact of post-event information upon memory. The first is *overwriting hypothesis*, which states that the post-event information actually replaces the information that witnesses registered about an event in their mind, and thus, changes the existing memories permanently (Loftus, 1979). Thus, according to overwriting hypothesis, memory is very similar to something written on a chalkboard, where it can be easily erased and replaced with something else. The second is *forgetting hypothesis*, which posits that with the lapse of time, people simply forget details of a witnessed event. When the persons are asked questions about material they have forgotten, they tend to use other available information, including post-event information for answering the question. It means that post-event information, according to forgetting hypothesis, does not change the existing memories, rather it just fills up the gap created by forgetting (McCloskey and Zaragosa, 1985). A third explanation has been provided by *source monitoring theory*, which states that the people retain memories of both original event and post-event information. The trouble is that witnesses show difficulty in *source monitoring*, which is defined as a process in which individuals tend to determine from where they have acquired various pieces of information. As a consequence, witnesses may mistakenly conclude that post-event information has actually come from their observations of the original event (Johnson, Hashtroudi and Lindsay, 1993). Of these three explanations, the explanation put forward by the source monitoring theory is considered as the best explanation.

(v) **Memory distortion and construction:** Our memory that stores unlimited moments of information for years and decades is far from being perfect and is subjected to many kinds of error. The most important of such errors is *memory construction*, that is, formation and development of memories for events that the person had never experienced. One basic question here is—from where these false memories, that is, the memories for events that were never experienced, do come from? The most common answer is that such memories are somehow planted unintentionally in our minds by the words or actions of others. In some situations, such memories may also be the result of deliberate efforts to create them.

There are several ways through which false memories can be created. One obvious way is to simply imagining about an event. One recent research has shown that simply imagining about an event can generate false memories about it (Mazzoni and Memon, 2003). Another factor that generates false memories is actively making up information about some event while trying to answer a question about it (Ackil and Zaragoza, 1998). When the persons make up information about an event or experience that never took place, they somehow come to believe it. The surprising fact here is that the person comes to believe it or accept it as true even when he is forced to confabulate or told to make up answers to the questions about things or events that have never occurred (Zaragoza et al., 2001).

2. System variables

System variables include those factors which are under the direct control of criminal justice or legal system. Suggestive questioning by police or attorneys and biases in police line ups are the examples of system variables. A discussion of these factors is as follows:

(i) **Suggestive questioning:** Eyewitness identification is also influenced by the questioning techniques used by criminal investigators. Researches have shown that the way witnesses are questioned influences not only the response they provide but also their memories of the events (Wells, 2002; Roebers and Schneider, 2000). Some questions are suggestive even though they are not misleading. Even minor changes in the wording of a question can influence the way people respond to it. This has been clearly shown in a classic study conducted by Loftus and Palmer (1974). In their study, the participants watched a video of a car accident. Subsequently, they were asked to estimate the speed of the cars at the time of accident. Here, words were changed to describe the accident. The participants estimated the speed at which the cars contacted, hit, bumped, collided or smashed. The questions was framed like this— 'about how fast were the cars going when they...'. Results revealed that the participants, who were asked about the speed at which the cars contacted, gave estimate of 31.8 miles per hour, whereas those participants, who were asked about the speed at which the cars smashed, gave the estimate of 40.8 miles per hour, that is, 9 miles per hour higher than the participants, who were asked about the speed at which the cars contacted. Thus, witnesses' interpretation of the events was influenced by the way the question was framed and asked.

    Sometimes, the criminal investigators deliberately ask misleading questions. Investigators may ask witnesses about questions that contain misleading *post-event information*, that is, information about non-existent events or events that did not actually happen. Such post-event information makes us believe that we remember something that did not actually exist. Loftus (1975) conducted another study in which such role of post-event information was confirmed. In this study, the participants were shown a video of car accident. Subsequently, the participants were asked one of the two questions—'how fast the white car going while travelling along the country road?' and 'how fast was the white car going when it passed the barn while travelling along the country road?' Reality was that there was no barn in the video. Results revealed that 17% of the participants, who were put the second question, later reported that they had seen a barn, whereas only 3% of the participants, who were asked the first question, did report about the barn. The results clearly showed that the post-event information, when included in the question, made us believe that we remembered something that did not exist originally.

(ii) **Line up biases:** Criminal investigators often ask witnesses to identify a suspect as the perpetrator of crime. This is done from either photo spread or a live presentation of one or more possible suspects. In photo spread, the witnesses identify the perpetrator from a group of police photographs. In identification based upon live presentation, one or more suspects are presented. This in-person identification procedure contains two things—*show up* and *line up*. A *show up* is defined as a procedure in which a witness is asked to decide whether or not a single suspect is the perpetrator. For example, a police inspector, who catches someone running away from a crime place, may bring him to the witness and ask, "Is this the person who threw acid on you?" In line up, the witnesses are shown several individuals for identifying the perpetrator. A meta-analysis conducted by Steblay et al. (2003) showed that the rate of correct eyewitness identifications is more or less same between the show up and line up. Moreover, when the perpetrator is actually not present either in show up or line up, witnesses may actually be less likely to commit error or make false identification in the show up rather than in line up. Thus, show ups are more suggestive than line ups because presenting a single person to the witness may strongly implies that the concerned person is the actual criminal.

Line ups are of two types—simultaneous line ups and sequential line ups. In *simultaneous line ups,* several potential suspects are shown at a time and the witness is asked to identify the perpetrator. In *sequential line ups*, the potential perpetrators are shown one at a time and witnesses are asked to identify whether the person is the perpetrator before being exposed to the next person. Of these two types of line ups, simultaneous line ups are more troublesome because they encourage relative rather than absolute judgements, that is, decision about which person looks most like the perpetrator rather than decisions about whether the perpetrator is really present in the line up (Wells, 1984).

Researches have shown that the instructions given during line ups also influence the accuracy of eyewitness identification. For example, when the police officer asks the question, "Which person is the one who threw acid upon you?", it implies that the real perpetrator is actually present in the line up and this is likely to help the witness in identifying the perpetrator (Steblay, 1997).

Methods of Assessing Eyewitness Accuracy

Several approaches have been developed for assessing the accuracy of eyewitnesses. One popular approach is relying upon the confidence of eyewitness. Several studies have shown that the police is more likely to trust a witness who claims to be very confident about his identification than one who expresses less confidence in making identification (Brewer and Burke; 2002, Potter and Brewer, 1999). But the relationship between eyewitness confidence and accuracy, in general, tends to be very poor (Sporer et al., 1995). Another approach of assessing the eyewitness accuracy is the length of time that witnesses take in making identification. The witnesses, who identify the suspect quickly, are likely to be more accurate than the witnesses, who take longer time in making their decisions (Dunning and Perretta, 2002). In their study, these investigators reported that witnesses, who identified a perpetrator in 10 or fewer seconds, were accurate 87.1% of the time, whereas the witnesses, who took longer than 10 seconds, were found to be accurate only 46.3% of the time. Still another approach requires witnesses to separately identify the different features of the suspect. For example, the witness might identify perpetrator's face from a given sets of photographs, identify his voice from a set of audio recordings and finally select his body from a set of photographs. Researches have shown that the witnesses, who consistently identify the same individual from different types of features, are likely to be more accurate than the witnesses, who select different persons for different features.

How to Increase the Accuracy of Eyewitnesses?

The accuracy of eyewitness testimony can be improved with the help of improved interviews and better line up procedures. In *improved interview*, eyewitnesses are encouraged to report everything they can remember. Such procedures provide them with multiple retrieval cues and can easily increase accuracy of the recall. Sometimes, witnesses are also asked to describe events from different perspectives and in several different orders. These steps seem to enhance the accuracy of eyewitness testimony. *Improving police line ups* is another method of enhancing the accuracy of eyewitnesses. Wells and Luss (1990) suggested that line up is analogous to a social psychological experiment and based on this analogy, the police can improve the accuracy of line ups by using the common experimental procedures such as using a control group. For example, police may use a blank line up control group, where the witness is shown only a line up containing all innocent people or non-suspects. If the witness fails to identify any of them as perpetrator, it is concluded that there is some accuracy in his identification. On the other hand, if any person, here any innocent, is identified, the witness is informed and then, cautioned about the danger of making false identification. This whole procedure improves the accuracy of the eyewitnesses when actual line ups are constructed. Besides these techniques, there are also other methods through which eyewitness accuracy can be enhanced. Such methods include the presentation of the pictures of crime scene as well as the victim before identification is made, showing one member of the line-up at a time rather than the entire group and increasing witnesses to give their first impressions. All these methods have also been found to enhance the accuracy of eyewitness testimony (Leary, 1988; Culter, Penrod and Martens, 1987; Dunning and Stern, 1994).

Criminal Defendants

Besides the eyewitnesses, social psychologists have also studied the various experiences of criminal defendants. There are two important issues, which are related to criminal defendants—false confessions and lie detection.

False confessions do occur during the police interrogations. When police officers question criminal suspects, they try to get those suspects confess that they are guilty of committing a crime. Such false confessions are of three types (Kassin and Wrightsman, 1985)—voluntary false confessions, coerced-complaint false confessions and coerced-internalised false confession. In *voluntary false confession*, a person willingly confesses to a crime that he or she has not committed. For example, a father may falsely confess to commit a crime in order to keep his son away from going to jail. In *coerced-complaint false confession,* people are pressurised to admit guilt, but privately continue to believe in their own innocence. In order to avoid police coercions or stopping police to resort to coercive tactics, sometimes people falsely confess to have committed the crime. *Coerced-internalised false confession* occurs when people actually come to believe that they committed crimes, which they did not commit (Taylor, Peplau and Sears, 2006). A study conducted by Ofshe and Watters (1994) reported that a man was arrested after his adult daughters recovered memories of sexual abuse. The man initially claimed to be innocent. However, after numerous questioning sessions in which he was hypnotised and was asked leading questions, he came to believe that he, in fact, had abused his daughters. Although no physical evidence of the abuse was ever found, the man pleaded guilty to several counts of third-degree rape. Researches have shown that false confessions seem to be especially occur among those teenagers and individuals, who are highly suggestible (Redlich and Goodman, 2003). Apart from this, certain techniques of questioning also tend to increase the rate of false confessions. There are two popular techniques of questioning—one is minimisation and the other is deal, that is, explicit offer of leniency in exchange for confession. In *minimisation*, the interrogators downplay the significance of crime so that confession by the defendant or suspect may seem to be less serious (Kassin and McNall, 1991). An interrogating officer, for example, using the technique of minimisation might say, "I understand that mistake has taken place. Why don't you just tell me about that mistake?"

In the technique of *deal*, there is an obvious offer for leniency in exchange for confession. Social psychologists are of view that when both minimisation and deal are used in combination, the likelihood of false confession is increased.

The likely consequences of false confessions in legal contexts is that the suspect is likely to be charged with the crime and indicted because confession is considered as the most powerful evidence that can be presented in the court. In a study conducted by Kassin and Neumann (1997), mock jurors were presented with a simulated murder trial. There were two conditions. In one condition, the jurors heard that the defendant had confessed the crime, but later on retraced his confession. In other condition, jurors heard that an eyewitness had identified the defendant in the line up. In former condition, about 62% of the jurors voted to convict the man, whereas in the latter condition, only 27% of the jurors voted to convict the defendant. The results obviously suggested that false confessions could lead to wrongful conviction of innocent individuals.

Lie detection is another critical issue related to criminal defendants. How can the police officer determine whether the suspect is lying about his or her involvement in the crime? In general, it is believed that the persons who are lying often give off some non-verbal cues such as blinking or tilting their heads. But the researchers have provided evidence for the fact that these non-verbal cues are not sufficient and the observers are unable to detect lies with the help of these cues much above the level of chance (DePaulo, 1994; Frank and Ekman, 1997). Despite their training and experiences, the police officers may not be better in detecting lies with the help of these non-verbal cues. Mann, Vrij and Bull (2004) confirmed this fact in one investigation in which British police officers watched video segments from police interrogations of actual criminal suspects. Some suspects were telling the truth and some suspects were lying. It was found that officers correctly recognised truth-telling suspects 66% of the time and lies-telling suspects 64% of the time, with somewhat higher levels of accuracy among trained and experienced officers. Likewise, in another study conducted by Ekman and O'Sullivan (1991), the law enforcement officials watched the videotapes of 10 individuals who told the truth or lied about their reactions to a film. It was found that only very trained and experienced members were able to detect lying at above the chance level (50%) and even they were accurate only 64% of the time. Both these studies showed that there was no correlation between participants' judgement and their lie detection ability. The questions here arises—why are not even trained police officers or criminal investigators better at lie detecting task? Social psychologists have pointed out two primary reasons for such failure. One reason is that the police officers or criminal investigators often have mistaken beliefs about their physical cues that may indicate deception. For example, such investigating officers often indicate that looking away during an interview indicates that the suspect is lying, but this has not been confirmed in the researches done by social psychologists (Stromwall and Granhag, 2003). Still another reason is that such officers often expect deception from suspects, and therefore, tend to overestimate the likelihood that any given individual is telling a lie. Due to such expectation of deceit, the investigating officers have lower standards for deciding about lying.

If the criminal investigating officers cannot reliably tell whether the suspects are telling truth or telling lie, how can one be sure that innocent suspects are not being convicted or arrested and the guilty persons are not being released? To remove this deadlock, the police officers or criminal investigating officers are being helped with polygraph or lie detector tests. Such test is designed to pick up changes in the heart rate, blood pressure, respiration rate, and galvanic skin response, which commonly accompany the anxiety that occurs when a person lies. The common version of the polygraph test is the *control question test*, where the suspect is asked questions about his or her involvement in the crime (such as did you embezzle two lac rupees from the treasury?) as well as control questions about unrelated wrongdoings (such as did you ever steal anything?). The assumption in this line of questioning is that an innocent person should become more aroused when answering control questions about previous wrongdoings (which he or she did not commit) than when answering questions about the crime (which he or she did not commit). On the other hand, the guilty person should become more aroused when answering questions about the crime.

But polygraph is really not a lie detector. It detects only physiological changes associated with the various types of emotional arousal. It fails to distinguish lying from fear, sexual arousal, anxiety, anger or general emotional arousal. The assumption is that when people lie, they feel anxious and their anxiety causes physiological changes in blood pressure, heart rate, breathing, perspiration, etc.

Now, the question is—how accurate is the polygraph? Saxe et al. (1985) conducted a series of studies of actual criminal suspects and they found that 20% of the innocent suspects were pronounced guilty of lying on the polygraph test. Researches done by Kleinmuntz and Szucko (1984) revealed that the percentage of innocent people being falsely accused of lying is pretty higher with as many as one out of three innocent people. What about the guilty persons? It has been found that one out of four persons, who lied on the polygraph test, were judged to be telling the truth. Therefore, it can be concluded that even with polygraph testing, the police officers or criminal investigating officers may not be able to determine consistently and accurately whether the suspects are telling the truth.

SOCIAL PSYCHOLOGY: ENTREPRENEURSHIP

The principles of social psychology have also been successfully applied to the field of entrepreneurship. An *entrepreneur* is a person who recognises an opportunity for a new business and actually starts one (Baron, Byrne and Branscombe, 2008). Entrepreneurs play a very important role in the economies of their states or even of the entire country. Such persons do not simply create wealth and opportunity for growth for themselves, rather they provide new jobs and increase prosperity for the large number of other persons. Such people are, in fact, unique in the sense that they create something (new businesses, etc.) out of what was initially nothing. Various theories and principles of social psychology have shed light upon various issues related to the entrepreneur's behaviour. Some important issues are as follows:

1. Why do only some persons become entrepreneur?
2. Why are some entrepreneurs more effective and successful than the others?

Let us discuss these two issues in detail.

Why do only some persons become entrepreneur?

Several concepts and findings of social psychology have provided insight into why some persons, but not others, become entrepreneurs. In this context, the following concepts, findings and principles have been found to be relevant:

1. Modelling or observational learning: Social influence from modelling or observational learning is a very important factor in deciding to become an entrepreneur. When a person is exposed to other persons, who are entrepreneurs, it provides him with the knowledge and skill he needs to become an entrepreneur. That is the reason, why we find that when one member of the family has started a business, other members are also lured to start a new business. This happens obviously because of observational learning. Some research studies have vividly reported that having entrepreneurs in one's family does play a significant role in making decision about becoming an entrepreneur (Shane, 2003).

2. Personality factors: Researches have shown that Big Five dimensions of personality play a significant role in deciding to become an entrepreneur. For example, persons high on the dimension of extraversion are more likely to become an entrepreneur than the persons who are low on this dimension (Baron and Markman, 2004). Likewise, persons high on the dimension of openness to experience are less likely to start a new business than the persons who are low on this dimension. This happens probably because such persons tend to enjoy new and innovative activities and like to jump from one activity to another. They find new business, which requires to focus intensely, very much unattractive and unappealing.

3. Cognitive processes: Some cognitive processes are directly related to the decision to become an entrepreneur, and therefore, have a direct impact upon such decision. Optimistic bias and planning fallacy are two such important cognitive factors. *Optimistic bias* means tendency to expect more favourable outcomes in almost any situation than can be rationally expected. Simon, Houghton and Aquino (2000) showed that entrepreneurs were more influenced by such bias than the other persons. Likewise, *planning fallacy,* which refers to the tendency to believe that we can accomplish more in a given period of time than we actually can, is also high among the entrepreneurs than among the other persons. Both these biases are likely to influence the decision to start a new business.

4. Perception of risk factors: Perception of risk is another cognitive factor. Researches have shown that entrepreneurs, in general, are not prone to take risks, but they do perceive lower level of risk in any situation (Stewart and Roth, 2001). Such perception, in turn, leads them to be more willing to take the plunge and start a new business.

Thus, we find that there are several factors that account for why some persons become entrepreneur.

Why are some entrepreneurs effective and successful than the others?

Why do some entrepreneurs become a multimillionaire, whereas some other entrepreneurs become the bankrupt and frequently described as 'living dead'? In simple words, why do some entrepreneur become successful, whereas some others prove to be highly unsuccessful? Social psychologists have tried to answer these questions in terms of some social, cognitive and individual factors that account for the success or failure.

Among social factors, the social skills of the entrepreneur is very important. Social skills, being an umbrella term, include various competencies like skill at social perception, being persuasive and ability to make good first impression, play a significant role in making any entrepreneur successful or unsuccessful. Baron and Markman (2003) conducted a study in which a formal support was established. They administered questionnaire for assessing several types of social skills of the entrepreneurs working in two different institutions—cosmetics and high-tech. They also obtained information on the entrepreneurs' financial success, that is, information about total earnings from their new businesses. Results were in expected direction. One social skill, that is, accuracy in perceiving others was positively related to the financial success for entrepreneurs of both institutions. However, social adaptability, that is, ability to adapt quickly and well to new social situations was highly correlated with the financial success of cosmetics industry. Still another social skill, that is, expressiveness which is closely related to extraversion, was found to be positively correlated with the financial success of the entrepreneurs of high-tech industry.

Now, the question is—why are entrepreneurs' social skills considered so important for their success? The answer is that an entrepreneur has to face a highly unstructured and uncertain situations, where he has to form new social relationships with many different types of persons such as customers, suppliers, employees, etc. In such a situation, the entrepreneur with better social skills is likely to be benefitted.

Some cognitive factors are also responsible for making some entrepreneurs more successful than the others. Researchers have examined the potential role of counterfactual thinking in entrepreneurs' success. *Counterfactual thinking* is the thinking where the person tends to imagine different outcomes in any given situation than the ones actually occurred, that is, here, the person thinks about might-have-beens (Roese, 1997). Researches done by Roese (1997) revealed that counterfactual thinking tends to produce a mixed bag of positive and negative reactions in business settings. On the positive side, by engaging in counterfactual thinking, entrepreneurs tend to consider past events from the perspective of constructing still more effective strategies, which may generate more positive outcomes in future. On the negative side, engaging in such counterfactual thinking, the entrepreneurs tend to develop the feelings of regret about actions taken or actions that were done but produced negative results. Baron (2000) conducted another study in which he compared the impact of counterfactual thinking of entrepreneurs with those of the non-entrepreneurs such as government employees, school teachers, etc. Both groups of participants, who were matched on a wide range of socio-economic variables such as age, income, education, etc., were asked to indicate the frequency with which they have engaged in counterfactual thinking, following some disappointing outcomes. Results revealed that entrepreneurs engaged themselves in counterfactual thinking less frequently than the non-entrepreneurs. Thus, it is clear that entrepreneurs, though engaged in counterfactual thinking less frequently, tend to use such thoughts to develop improved task strategies in future, and thus, it ultimately helps them in getting success. Some cognitive biases or tilts such as optimistic biases, planning fallacy and affect infusions tend to operate least among successful entrepreneurs. In fact, such biases tend to distort information processing and produce a less optimal decision (Baron, 1998; Busenitz and Barney, 1997). Still another cognitive bias that may be relevant to the entrepreneurs' success is the sunk cost or also known as *escalation of commitment*. *Sunk cost* means tendency to stick with those decisions that had initially generated negative outcomes (Ross and Staw, 1993). If an entrepreneur falls prey to this cognitive tilt, it is likely that his survival in the new business is put under question mark. On the other hand, it is also true that any new business rarely produces positive results immediately, and therefore, to get the ultimate success in the business, he has to stay with the course even in the face of negative results.

Brockner, Higgins and Low (2004) tried to relate the bias of sunk cost to regulatory focus theory for explaining entrepreneurs' success. The theory states that in regulating their own behaviour for achieving the most desired states, the persons generally adopt one of the two contrasting perspectives—a *promotion focus* in which they focus mainly on attaining positive outcomes or a *prevention focus* in which they concentrate mainly on avoiding negative outcomes, and here, the ultimate goal sought is safety (Camacho, Higgins and Luger, 2003). When the person adopts the regulatory goal of promotion focus, he tries to achieve positive outcomes and when, on the other hand, the person adopts the regulatory goal of prevention focus, he heavily concentrates on avoiding mistakes or avoiding those decisions that may produce negative outcomes. Which of the two regulatory focuses is more effective from the point of view of helping entrepreneurs in avoiding the danger of sunk costs? The answer is that it all depends on how the entrepreneurs interpret initial negative results. If these initial negative results are seen as a better option than those which are currently available, but that is not being pursued by them, the entrepreneurs with a promotion focus will have an advantage because such persons are interested in attaining positive results and the best way to attain such result is to switch to the new and better course of action that is currently available. On the other hand, the persons with prevention focus are primarily concerned with avoiding losses and any attempt to give up the present course of actions would mean that they are bound to experience such negative outcomes (or losses). If somehow the better option is not available, the persons with the preventive focus have an advantage, that is, they find it easier to come out of the trap of sunk costs.

In a nutshell, it can be clearly pointed out that the various theories and principles of social psychology tend to provide in-depth insights into how entrepreneurs think and guide their future course of actions.

SOCIAL PSYCHOLOGY: SPORTS

As we know, sport psychology is an exciting discipline dedicated to both the performance of athletes and social-psychological aspects of human enrichment. *Sport psychology* is broadly defined as a science in which the principles of psychology are applied in sport setting or exercise setting. Griffith established the first laboratory of sport psychology at the University of Illinois in 1925. In recent years, several scholarly societies have merged to represent the discipline and application of sport psychology. In the United States of America, the North America Society for Psychology of Sport and Physical Activity (NASPSPA) and the Association for the Advancement of Applied Sport Psychology (AAASP) are the most prominent ones.

Social psychology of sport deals with the psychological issues related to groups. Here, in this section, we shall concentrate upon sport aggression, audience effect on sports, team cohesion and leadership in sport.

1. *Sport aggression*

Aggression is any form of behaviour directed to the goal of harming or injuring another person. There are two types of aggression—hostile aggression and instrumental aggression. In *hostile aggression*, the primary goal is the injury of another human being. Here, intent is to make the victim suffer. In football, when a player directly kicks in the legs of the running opponent player from behind, it constitutes an act of hostile aggression. In *instrumental aggression*, the intent to harm another is present, but the purpose is to realise some external goal such as money, victory or prestige. Here, the aggressor views the aggression act as instrumental in obtaining the major goal. In baseball, the manager may order the pitcher to hit a batter in retaliation for some earlier infraction. Here, the pitcher is not necessarily angry at the batter, but somehow sees hitting the batter as instrumental in achieving the goal of victory. One important category of behaviour that is often confused with aggression is *assertiveness* or *assertive behaviour*. Generally, we find that coaches encourage their athletes to be more aggressive. In such a situation, what they really mean is that they should be more assertive, which involves the use of legitimate physical or verbal force to achieve one's goal. However, there is no intention to harm the opponent. Thus, assertiveness requires the expenditure of energy and effort and there is no intent to harm. Therefore, any resultant harm is just incidental to the game. Whatever the types of aggression may be, most sports make provision for penalties if the aggressive behaviour is perceived to be intentional and/or dangerous.

Various theories of aggressive behaviour have been proposed. Of these various theories, four are worth mentioning in the context of sport aggression. These are instinct theory, social learning theory, Bredemeier's theory of moral reasoning and Berkowiz's frustration-aggression hypothesis.

Instinct theory is based upon the work of Freud and Lorenz. Freud pointed out that aggression is unavoidable since it is innate like hunger, thirst and sexual desire. A very important corollary of the instinct theory is that aggression results in purging or releasing of the aggression drive. The release of the pent-up aggression is called *catharsis*. According to this theory, striking an opposing player in the game serves as a catharsis of pent-up aggression.

Social learning theory states that aggression is a function of learning. Bandura (1977), a leading advocate of social learning theory, argued that catharsis has no place in social learning theory, and in fact, aggression has a circular effect, which means that one act of aggression leads to further aggression and this pattern is continued till the circle is broken by some type of reinforcement—positive or negative. Smith (1980) pointed out that violence in the game of the hockey is due to social learning or modelling. Youngsters learn aggression by watching their role models, professionals and/or persons on television.

Bredemeier's theory of aggression, based on Jean Piaget's theory of cognitive development, posits that a person's willingness to engage in aggression is related to his state of moral reasoning (Bredemeier, 1994). He pointed out that there is a relationship between level of moral reasoning and overt acts of athletic aggression, since human aggression is basically considered as unethical. The common observation is that the level of morality necessary for everyday life is often suspended during athletic competition. This suspended ethical morality is known as *bracketed morality* (Bredemeier, 1994). Moreover, researches done by Stephens and Bredemeier (1996) showed that athletic teams tend to create a moral atmosphere that may be conducive to the willingness to aggress.

Frustration-aggression theory, originally presented by Dollard et al. (1939), posits that aggression stems from frustration and the aggressive acts provide catharsis of the anger associated with the frustration. Berkowitz (1958, 1993) reformulated this frustration-aggression theory by stating that frustration, in fact, does not necessarily result in aggression and proposed that frustration simply creates a readiness for aggression. In reality, for aggression to occur, certain stimuli or cues associated with aggression must be present. These cues are associated by the frustrated people with aggression. For example, the poor condition of pitch may evoke anger among frustrated cricket players, who are somehow sure of their defeat by the opponents. Thus, according to Berkowitz's theory, a frustrating event creates readiness for aggression.

Various situational factors have been found to be associated with sport aggression. For example, it has been found that as environmental temperature increases, the players tend to show more aggression. The perception of the opponent's intention is another factor. If the athlete perceives that an opponent's intention is to inflict harm, it is very likely that such athletes will respond with aggression against the opponent. A study conducted by Harrell (1980) showed that basketball players, who perceived that their opponents' rough playing was intentional and mainly aimed to inflict harm to them, were more likely to be aggressive than when they perceived that roughness was incidental in nature. Thus, the players, who perceived that the opponent was trying to inflict harm, would tend to respond in the same way. Besides this, several other factors related to the structure of game also contribute to the aggression in sport setting. For example, generally, we find that the lowest number of acts of aggression occurs in the beginning hours of the play. But as the game proceeds, the acts of aggression also tend to increase. Likewise, if the players find that the outcome of the participation in the game will not be in their favour, that is, they are going to lose, they are more likely to engage in aggressive behaviours than the members of the winning team. Similarly, playing at home or away also determines aggressive behaviour. Researchers have found that soccer teams tend to be more aggressive when playing away from home, whereas aggression is almost equal for home and visiting ice hockey teams.

What is the impact of aggression on the performance of the athletes? The common wisdom suggests that acts of aggression on the part of the athletes tend to distract them and result in decrement in performance. Aggressive acts are not only distracting to the individuals but they are likely to be distracting to the team as a whole. Aggression tends to enhance the level of physiological arousal that may be interfering to the good performance because of the fact that such arousal may be above an athlete's zone of optimal functioning.

Aggression in sport setting can be curtailed or minimised. Aggression in sport setting can be curtailed by both athletes as well as spectators. Utilising the basic principles of social psychology, sport psychologists have provided the following suggestions for curtailing aggression by athletes:

(i) Athletes should be provided with non-aggressive models.
(ii) Athletes engaged in aggressive act or violence of any sort must be penalised or faced to leave the ground.
(iii) Any external stimulus or cue that may provoke aggression in the field of play should be immediately removed.
(iv) The coaches, who allow their athletes to engage in aggressive acts, should be fined or suspended from their duties.
(v) Coaches should be encouraged to attend workshops/seminar, etc. for dealing with the aggression shown by athletes.
(vi) Various strategies and coping skills aimed at curtailing aggression should be practised by the athletes.

Some suggestions have also been made for curtailing aggression by the spectators:

(i) All athletic events should be promoted as one of the family affairs.
(ii) The sale and distribution of alcoholic beverages in sport should be banned.
(iii) Interaction between the members of the opposing teams should be encouraged by the coaches and managers.
(iv) The media should in no way encourage the perception of hatred between the members of the two teams.

2. Audience effects on sports

Audience effect is a very important factor for athletic performance. There are many variables, which are related to audience and can affect the athletic performance. In this section, we shall concentrate upon two such major variables—social facilitation and home-ground advantage.

Social facilitation means enhancement of task performance caused by the mere presence of other people (Baron and Byrne, 2000). The use of the phrase *mere presence of others*, indicates that other people may be audience or co-actors. Over more than 115 years age, Triplett in 1898 published one of the first experiments in social psychology. His finding was that the competing cyclists produced faster times when racing with another cyclist than simply when cycling alone. Later on, Triplett in 1898, devised a laboratory task to investigate whether or not the performance could be enhanced in the presence of other people (co-actors) performing the same task. Participants were required to wind in line on a fishing reel as quickly as they could. Following a practice period, participants performed the task both alone as well as in pairs. Results revealed that performance was faster when the task was done in pair, rather when did it alone. Travis (1925) also conducted researches in which the effect of being observed by other people on the performance of a pursuit-rotor task was examined. In this study, the participants were first trained to use a pursuit-rotor that involved holding a pen or stylus and following a moving target. Travis found that the participants made fewer errors in the presence of audience than when they performed the task alone.

Several other studies have been conducted investigating the impact of social facilitation and have reported contradictory results. Allport (1924) conducted several studies, where the participants worked alone in cubicles or sitting around a table together. His findings revealed that when the participants worked on simple task such as crossing out certain letters in words in the presence of others, their performance was better. However, with more complex task such as solving some complex puzzles, the performance was better when the participants worked alone. Dashiell (1930) reported that the number of multiplications done by the participants increased in the presence of others, but so did the number of errors made. Schmitt et al. (1986) reported that the participants did better in typing their names in the presence of audience, but when they were asked to type their name backwards, performance was better when they worked alone. Zajonc et al. (1966) reported that even animals tended to learn simple mazes faster in the presence of other animals, whereas the complex mazes are learnt faster when the animal is left alone.

Zajonc (1965) put forward a theory to explain these apparently contradictory findings. Zajonc's basic observation was that performance is facilitated and learning is impaired by the presence of others. In other words, his basic rule was that the performance of well-learned or well-practised tasks is enhanced by the presence of other people, whereas the performance of new or complex task is inhibited by the presence of others. He used the term *dominant response* to refer to the behaviours we are most likely to perform in a given situation. When a person has learned a behaviour or is highly skilled at any sport such as balling or batting in a cricket game, then this is his dominant response. Likewise, a basketball player, who is skilled at throwing the ball through the hoop, can be regarded as having this as a dominant response. The player would have practised this behaviour time and again. Therefore, in the match, the presence of others, including other players and audience, enhances or facilitates the dominant response. On the other hand, when a person is learning a new skill, error or poor performance becomes the dominant response. When such person performs in the presence of others, the audience causes the person to make more errors showing poor performance.

For example, a person, who has rarely played basketball ever before, will get fewer balls through the hoop in front of audience than when practising alone.

Several studies have been conducted to test the prediction that the presence of audience would facilitate well-learned behaviours and inhibit poorly-learnt behaviours. Michaels et al. (1982) reported that the presence of an audience affected the performance as predicted by the Zajonc's theory of dominant response. The dominant response of skilled players was to pot balls and the dominant response of unskilled players was to miss shots or not to pot balls. Audience facilitated both these dominant responses. Similar findings were reported by MacCracken and Studulis (1985). They found that the children skilled at balancing tasks showed better performance in the presence of audience, whereas children poor at balancing task showed poor performance in front of audience. Geen (1989) also reported similar findings supporting the idea of facilitation of the dominant response in the presence of audience.

To explain such effect of social facilitation, three theories have been put forward—drive theory, attention-conflict theory and apprehension-conflict theory. According to *drive theory of social facilitation* proposed by Zajonc (1965), the presence of other people tends to increase the general arousal level of a person, and this in turn, increases the tendency to perform the dominant responses. When the level of arousal is low, the performance suffers. Likewise, when the level of arousal is too high, that is, exceeding the optimum level, performance again is likely to suffer due to signs of panic and disorganisation. This theory suggests that the presence of others, when dominant responses are performed by the athletes, increases arousal to an optimum level for performance. But when the person works alone, his arousal does not reach the optimal level. In this way, the presence of others increases arousal level to the optimal level, causing better performance of the dominant response. Researches have revealed that optimal level of arousal is different for new and well-learned tasks. This is applied well to the context of sport. Suppose, for example, one is playing golf. If the person has never or rarely played golf, he is likely to perform better alone than when other people are watching him. In fact, playing golf requires concentration on many things such as ball, fairway and swing, and therefore, results in quite a high level of arousal in the first place. The presence of others may push the level of arousal too high. Therefore, the performance will suffer than when the person has played the golf alone. This principle applies equally to other sports such as tennis, ice skating, etc. With team sports, the situation may be a little different, but generally, a team that has played together on different occasions is likely to perform better in the presence of audience than a team that is quite newly formed.

Saunders (1983) proposed a different explanation of social facilitation based on the idea that the presence of other people creates a distraction to the person, who is performing the task. Such distraction interferes with the amount of attention the person is likely to give on the task. As a consequence, the person experiences conflict between whether to attend the task or the audience. Such conflict increases the arousal level in the person. This increased arousal level facilitates performance on simple task and interferes performance on the complex task. This view of Saunders is called *distraction-conflict theory*. Saunders et al. (1978) conducted a study to examine the impact of distraction conflict on the performance of the task. Participants were presented with either a simple or difficult task to perform in the presence of others performing either the same or different task. Results revealed that the participants in high distraction condition (same task with co-actors) did perform at a higher level on the simple task, but committed many errors, showing poor performance on the complex task.

The *apprehension-conflict model of social facilitation* states that when the person performs on a task in the presence of others, he is also concerned with the idea that the others are evaluating his performance (Cottrell, 1972; Cottrell et al., 1968). When a person is playing a game or a sport in the presence of others, then according to Cottrell, he experiences evaluation apprehension, which produces arousal on simple or well-learnt task. Such arousal is likely to facilitate the performance. However, for a new or complex task, the evaluation apprehension tends to increase arousal to too high level, with the consequence that the performance is inhibited or interfered.

Figure 17.2 summarises the different models used to explain social facilitation.

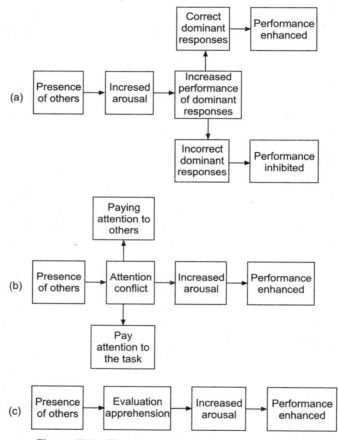

Figure 17.2 Three explanations for social facilitation.

Home ground advantage is another important variable in social facilitation. Sometimes, games are played at home ground, and sometimes, the players have to go to other countries for playing the game. When the games are played in own country, there are some advantages to the players. Such advantages are called *home ground advantage*. Courneya and Carron (1992) defined home ground advantage as the consistent finding that home teams in sports competitions win over 50% of the games played under a balanced home-and-away schedule.

The fact that home ground advantage in some team sports such as basketball, baseball, football, ice-hockey and soccer is well-documented. Edwards and Archambault (1989) reported that media made more reference to home advantage than any other factor. Such effect has been shown to be consistent over time. Pollard (1986), using archive and historical data, reported the evidence for home ground advantage from 1888 to 1984. Other researchers using similar data have provided support for home ground advantage. For example Schwartz and Barsky (1997) and Edwards (1979) reported findings using statistical analysis of matches across different sports. Their findings clearly supported the fact that home ground advantage exists, but the magnitude varies from sport to sport. Their analyses revealed that football (soccer) players enjoyed the greatest home advantage at about 70%, while the baseball players enjoyed only 50% level. Pollard (1986) reported that high level of home ground advantage for soccer remained around 70% for over 100 years. According to Bray and Carron (1993), home ground advantage is present in both amateur and professional sports and such advantage applies equally to team and individual sports. Courneya and Carron (1992) reported that home ground advantage is present in sports played by both males and females.

What is the explanation for home ground advantage? Home ground advantage has been explained in terms of five factors—travel for the visiting team, familiarity, psychological factors, audience and official (referees, etc.). It is found that if the visiting team has to travel across time zones, the players get little rest between the games, and then, they are put at a disadvantage in comparison to the home team. In fact, travelling to country with a different climate and culture may also put the visiting team at a disadvantage (Pace and Carron, 1992). Familiarity with the playground is another factor that gives advantage to the home team. Officials (referees, etc.) also tend to influence home ground advantage, although results are not consistent. Carron and Hausenblas (1998) reported no home ground advantage tendered by officials. However, Nevill and Holder (1999) conducted a study on football referees in England and Scotland and found that these referees favoured home-side players. This effect has been found to increase as the size of audience increases, perhaps reflecting the sheer number of home-side supporters as compared to the number of supporters to the visiting team. Likewise, audience has also some impact upon home team as well as upon the visiting team. Generally, among audiences, there are more people who support the home team and home team fans generally show some hostility towards the players of the visiting team. Thus, home team advantage is strongly influenced by the presence of supportive and interactive fans and the number of such fans. Schwartz and Barsky (1977) demonstrated that the winning percentage of home teams increased as the size of the audience increased. Their observation was that the players of sports such as basketball and ice hockey enjoyed greater home advantage than those of baseball and football. Likewise, audience hostility is also a factor. Researches done by Greer (1983) showed that sustained hostile spectator protests have a negative impact upon the performance of the visiting team, but it leads to some improvement in the performance of the home team. Psychological factors resulting from crowd density also affect home ground advantage. In fact, in bigger size of the crowd (high crowd density), more home team fans are present. These factors create volume of noise shown in support and such high volume has a favourable psychological impact upon the players. A small number of fans in visiting team tends to create low volume of noise for support, and thus, fails to create any psychological impact upon the players.

Figure 17.3 shows these five factors used to explain home ground advantage.

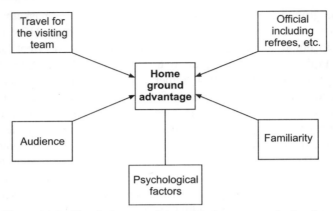

Figure 17.3 Five factors used to explain home ground advantage.

Now, the question is—is playing at home always an advantage or can it be sometimes a disadvantage also? The answer is home ground does not always provide advantage. There are also some home disadvantages due to several reasons. One reason may be that fans may expect the home players to win at any cost and this can result in additional pressure to play well. Another reason may be that playing in the presence of a very vocal and supportive audience generally raises the arousal level to such an extent that it interferes with the performance (Wright et al., 1995). Baumeister and Steinhilber (1984) also showed that performing in front of home supporters on home ground sometimes possesses disadvantage effect. According to their research, the more important the game, the less likely home team is to win on its home ground.

3. *Team cohesion*

Here, it is first essential to make distinction between group and team. Social psychologists have defined *group* as a collection of individuals, who have relations to one another and are interdependent for achieving the goal. Obviously, this definition suggests that the persons in the group interact with each other and develop interpersonal relationship for proper functioning and achieving the goal. A team differs from the group and is, in fact, a special kind of a group. Morris and Summers (1995) defined *team* as a group of players, who have a well-developed collective identity and who work together to achieve a specific goal or set of goals.

The most important distinguishing feature of a team is that it has an obvious goal such as to win the game it plays. Groups, especially workgroups, have goal and objectives, but often these are not about competing, but about achieving.

Team cohesion is one property of the team and is similar to group cohesion. Because an athletic team is a group, the meaning of group cohesion applies equally well for team cohesion. Carron (1982) has defined *team cohesion* as a dynamic process that is commonly reflected in the tendency for the group to stick together and remain united in the pursuit of its goals. In fact, team cohesion is the elusive ingredient that changes a disorganised collection of persons into a team. In other words, team cohesion is the glue or cement, which binds together the individuals in a group (Schachter, 1951). However, psychologists tend to prefer greater precision and have proceeded to define this glue or cement as the extent to which members of the team identify with the goals and aspirations and tend to like each other (Hogg, 1992). This way of defining reflects two key dimensions of cohesion—

task cohesion and social cohesion. *Task cohesion* means the extent to which the members of the team work together to achieve the task (in case of sport, winning the game). *Social cohesion* means the extent to which the members of the team are attracted to each other. Task cohesion and social cohesion are the two dimensions, each of which may vary from high to low (Cota et al., 1995).

There are two sets of factors or determinants, which contribute to the development of team cohesion—external factors and internal factors. *External factors* are those factors which are external to the team such as geographical and social environments. *Internal factors* are those factors which are internal to the team such as individual characteristics of the team and leadership qualities.

Geographical factors are important determinants. These factors relate to the availability of a particular sporting facility in the area and the environment in which a team gets a chance for playing their sport against other teams. If the player finds the various geographical factors, including the climatic conditions, favourable and familiar, the cohesion is likely to enhance. Social factors such as pear pressure, family expectations, early socialisation of children, etc. also play an important role in determining team cohesion. Due to the pressure of his peers, a player in football team may feel more committed to the team and team cohesion. Still other external factors are the competition with another team and intergroup conflict. A classic study conducted by Sherif et al. (1961) demonstrated how competition between two teams for the same resources produced hostility and aggression between the teams and served to strengthen and faster cooperation and cohesion among the members of the team. This research is relevant in the context of teams in two ways. First, cooperation among members of the team leads to cohesiveness, especially when competition and winning are the main goals for the team. Second, coaches must set tasks, which require members of the team to cooperate and work together in order to be successful.

Internal factors that are mainly related to the characteristics of team leadership qualities also tend to determine the cohesiveness of the team. Team homogeneity has been found to be one of the important factor of team cohesion. *Team homogeneity* means the idea that individuals in the team are similar on one or more personal factors such as commitment to the sport and team, socio-economic status, etc. Cox (1990) reported that when the team lacks homogeneity, that is, where team is heterogeneous, and therefore, differ on one or more personal factors, then it shows lower level of team cohesion. Likewise, the stability of the team has also been found to be related to team cohesion (Forsyth, 1990). Teams that have been together both in terms of the existence of the team and the length of the time a player has been with the team, generally tend to exhibit higher degree of team cohesiveness. On the other hand, newly formed teams exhibit lesser degree of team cohesiveness. The size of the team also affects cohesiveness (Schultz and Schultz, 1994). Sport psychologists have shown that as rise of the team (that is, number of members in the team) increases, cohesiveness in the team decreases. In such a situation, players should be put into subgroups at times so that a sense of cohesiveness may be enhanced. Likewise, initiation of a new player to a team has an important influence on the commitment of that player, and consequently, on the cohesiveness of the team. Generally, it has been found that higher initiation rites to join a team can lead to greater subsequent team cohesion. On the other hand, the players, who become a member of the team with little or no effort, generally show lesser commitment to the team, and consequently, the cohesiveness in the team is reduced (Aronson and Mills, 1959).

Researches have shown that leadership is an important factor in determining cohesiveness within a team (Westre and Weiss, 1991). Leaders such as coaches, captains, managers, etc. should give consistent and clear directions with respect to team goals and interpersonal relationship. They should alone involve members of the team in taking decision. All such efforts of the team leader tend to foster the team cohesiveness. Researches have further shown that a democratic style of leadership fosters team cohesiveness, except when the situation is highly unfavourable.

Sport psychologists have also tried to assess team cohesiveness. Carron et al. (1985) developed a very popular and widely used measure of team cohesiveness, called *Group Environment Questionnaire (GEQ)*. This questionnaire was developed from a conceptual model of team cohesion based on two dimensions—team perception and group orientation. *Team perception* is the individual players' perception of the team that is subdivided into two components—group integration and individual attraction. *Group integration* is concerned with the individual's perception of the group as a whole, that is, how well or poorly the members of the group work together. *Individual attraction* means the team players' personal attraction to the group, that is, how much a player likes being in the group. Another dimension, that is, *group orientation* is also divided into two components—social cohesion and task cohesion. *Social cohesion* means the extent to which each player is attached or bonded to the team as a unit to satisfy various social needs. *Task cohesion* is concerned with how well the players are in agreement and are bonded to the team as a unit to satisfy task completion needs. Thus, in GEQ, team cohesiveness is assessed by four separate measures, as shown in Figure 17.4. GI-S means attachment to the team for satisfying social needs; GI-T means attachment to the team for satisfying task completion needs; IA-S means attraction to the team for satisfying social needs and IA-T means attraction to the team for satisfying task completion needs.

		Group Interaction (GI)	Individual attraction (IA)
Group Orientation	Social (S)	GI-S	IA-S
	Task (T)	GI-T	IA-T

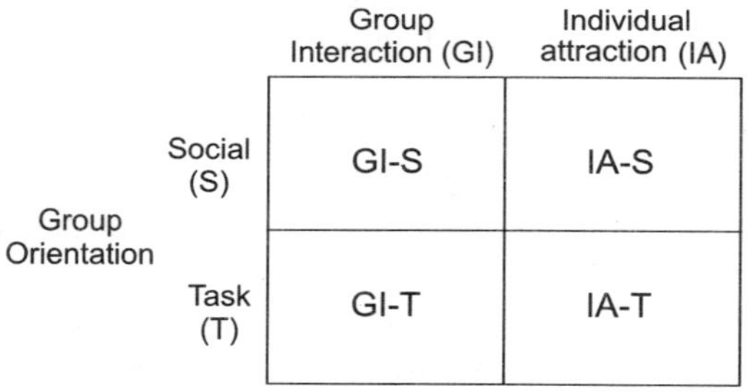

Figure 17.4 Conceptual model of team cohesiveness.

GEQ contains 18 Likert-scale type items representing each of four measures. One side of the scale indicates the position of 'strongly agree' and the other side of the scale indicates the position of 'strongly disagree'. Obtaining four measures of team cohesion in this way allows to identify specific areas, where team cohesion is high and low. This further permits time and attention to be focused on the areas that need to be improved and where cohesion needs to be raised. Suppose a cricket team is found to score high on three measures, but low on IA-S (that is, attraction to the team to satisfy social needs). This obviously indicates that fulfilling of social needs of the individual players is not forthcoming. Accordingly, action is needed to change perception or changing what the team can provide in this respect.

There are some obvious consequences of team cohesiveness. These are team satisfaction and team performance. High levels of team cohesion result in high level of team satisfaction. Martens and Peterson (1971) confirmed this relationship and proposed a circular model of linking team cohesion to satisfaction and performance. According to this model, the following assertions have been made:

(i) High level of team cohesion leads to high level of team performance.
(ii) Successful performance of team leads to high level of satisfaction among team players.
(iii) High level of satisfaction among players of team leads to enhanced level of team cohesiveness.

The above facts are illustrated in Figure 17.5.

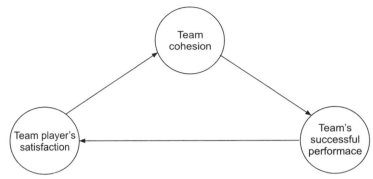

Figure 17.5 Circular relationship between team cohesion, team successful performance and team satisfaction.

William and Hacker (1982) proposed a slightly different model, which is based on successful or high level of performance as a consequence of both team cohesion and satisfaction of the team members. According to this model, it is the successful or unsuccessful performance of the team that affects both cohesion and satisfaction. Researchers have clearly shown that team players or members gain satisfaction and enjoyment if they become part of the cohesive team (Carron et al., 1997). Further, if the members of the team perceive their team as highly cohesive, they want to continue with that team (Spink, 1995).

Several researches have been done to explore the nature of correlation between the level of team cohesion and level of team performance and success. Widmeyer et al. (1993) did a review of studies conducted on cohesion-performance limits. They reported that 80% of the researches reported positive correlation, which meant that high team cohesion was associated with poor performance and low team cohesion was associated with good successful performance. Remaining 3% of empirical studies reported no significant correlation between the team cohesion and the team performance. A study conducted by Slater and Sewell (1994) showed that high team cohesion was a strong causal factor in good team performance.

Other researchers have identified some other factors for explaining and understanding the complex relationship between team cohesion and team performance. One such factor is self-efficacy. Teams that have developed high level of team cohesion tend to exhibit high level of group efficacy as well. Team homogeneity is another factor. Spink (1992) showed that successful volleyball teams were characterised by high level of team cohesion on the part of both starters and non-starters. On the other hand, less successful teams were characterised by a lack of team homogeneity or agreement in team cohesion between starters and non-starters. This finding had obvious implication for the coach, who must develop high team cohesion among all members of the team and not just starters. Another factor is *group norms,* which refer to the values, standards and rules that the members are expected to adhere to. Newly formed sports teams are unlikely to have established set of norms. But long-standing sports teams usually have a well-established set of norm. When a new player joins a sport team having well-established norms, he is expected to conform or adhere to the prevailing norms of the team. In fact, norms function to hold the group together, and hence, considered as an important factor in determining the level of team cohesion that exists. The relationship between team cohesion and team norms is circular, that is, one reinforces the other. In simple words, high cohesiveness leads to high degree of conformity to the team norms and vice versa.

It is obvious from the above discussion that team cohesion plays an important role in keeping the performance of the team to a satisfactory level. Therefore, we must know the technique to build a team. What is team building? *Team building* is defined as a process normally carried out by coaches, captains and managers for enhancing social and task cohesion (Carron and Dennis, 1998). Cox (1998) suggested some principles considered useful for team building. Such important principles are as under:

(i) Each player must be aware of the responsibilities of the other players in the team.
(ii) Formation of cliques within the team should be avoided.
(iii) The head coach or manager must take time to learn personal matters about each team player.
(iv) Routine and practice games/matches should be arranged to encourage cooperation.
(v) Emphasis upon good performance should be done even when a team may lose a game or match.
(vi) Coaches should try to develop the feeling of 'we' amongst the players.
(vii) Emphasis should be given upon developing a sense of pride within the team and subgroups of large teams.
(viii) Coaches should set goals for the team and get the players be proud of successes.
(ix) Coach must ensure that each player understands the importance of his role in the team and that it is enacted.
(x) Captains and coaches should also sometimes expect tension and conflict within the team and they should address them as soon as possible.

Leadership in sport is another major dimension. Various theories of leadership have important applications in sport leadership. One early theory of leadership is the *trait theory*, which states that persons born with certain traits can only be a successful leader, that is, a successful coach or captain in sports. But this viewpoint was not much preferred. Another theory is *universal behaviour theories of leadership* that has turned the focus of attention from universal traits to universal behaviour of successful leaders. Unlike trait theory, the belief was that leaders are made, not born. Thus, it pointed out that consideration and initiating structure are the two most important factors characterising the behaviours of the leaders. *Consideration* refers to a certain pattern of behaviour that is characterised by friendship, mutual trust, respect, and warmth between the leaders (that is, coaches or captains) and subordinates (athletes). It is characterised by a leadership style, which is democratic, egalitarian, employee-oriented and relationship-motivated. Conversely, *initiating structure* refers to the leader's behaviour that is task-motivated, autocratic, authoritarian and production-oriented. These two types of behaviour are considered relatively independent, but not necessarily incompatible. The obvious application of universal behaviour theory is that the coaches and leaders of sport teams should strive to establish well-defined pattern of organisation and communication, while at the same time, they must display the behaviours of friendship, trust, respect and warmth. *Fiedler's contingency theory* is another popular theory of leadership that suggests that leader effectiveness is somehow situation-specific and leader behaviours that are effective in one situation may not be effective in another. The obvious implication is that effective leadership depends on specific environmental situations. In fact, according to this theory, leaders are endowed with a disposition towards task-orientation or relationship-orientation. The obvious application of this theory is that captains or coaches should learn to recognise their own personality dispositions and should try to work for compensating their weaknesses through personal adjustments or with the help of assistant coaches. If head coach is a task-oriented leader, a relationship-oriented assistant coach must be hired to provide a better personal touch. Another set of theory is *situation-specific theories* of leadership, according to which leadership is a function of interaction between the leader's behaviour in a specific situation and the situation itself. Path-goal theory is one example of this category of theories. In this theory, the emphasis is given upon needs or goals of the subordinates or athletes. In fact, here, leader is perceived as facilitator. The coach or leader helps the athlete in achieving the goal and the success of leader is judged in terms of whether or not the athletes (subordinates) achieve their goals. The obvious application of this theory is that the captain or coach must help the athletes in selecting the worthwhile goals and point out the path to successfully reach the goal.

One important factor linked with leader effectiveness is coach-athlete compatibility or the quality of the relationship between the coach and the athlete. Coach-athlete compatibility has proved to be an important determinant of team success and team satisfaction. In studying coach-athlete compatibility, the researchers tend to compare the behaviour of effective coach-athlete dyads with behaviour of those of less effective coach-athlete dyads. Dyads are compared with the help of an instrument, called *Fundamental Interpersonal Relations Orientation Behaviour Questionnaire (FIRO-BQ)* developed by Schutz (1966). This questionnaire measures the level of affection, control and inclusion existing between coach and athlete in the dyad. *Affection* means closed personal emotional feelings between the members of the pairs, *control* means the perception of power, authority and dominance and *inclusion* means positive association among the members and is related to communication openness and two-way interaction. Researches have, in general, revealed that compatible coach-athlete dyads are characterised by good communication and presence of rewarding behaviour coming from coach to athlete. There is a feeling of mental respect and desire to communicate honest feelings. Such dyads are also characterised by coaches, who consistently reward athletes for effort and performance (Weiss and Friedrichs, 1986). On the other hand, incompatible coach-athlete dyads are characterised by lack of communication and any rewarding behaviour. There is a feeling of detachment and isolation from each other. The obvious application of coach-athlete compatibility is that the coaches must encourage two-way communication between themselves and their athletes. If the athletes feel that their coaches value their feelings and viewpoints, they will be comfortable in a two-way interaction.

Further researches on coach-athlete compatibility have suggested that the relationship between coach and athlete has a plenty of opportunities for improvement. When the quality in interaction between coach and athlete is lacking, the coaches can be provided assertiveness training to help them relate to athletes (Miller, 1982). *Assertiveness* involves appropriate expression of feeling and thoughts on the part of coach so that self-esteem of athlete is not damaged.

Geographical playing position is also an important factor in studying leadership in sport. The playing position appears to be highly related to the leadership opportunity. Grusky (1963) hypothesised that the player's position in baseball was related to leadership opportunity. His main contention was that the critical factor in player's location was the opportunity for player's interaction. He further pointed out that opportunity for high interaction of the players was associated with centrality (that is, specific location of the athletes), communication and nature of the task. In Grusky's design, the infielders and the catchers were recognised as high interactors, whereas the outfielders and pitchers were considered to be low interactors. According to his analysis, about 77% of the managers were from high interaction group and only 23% were from low interaction group. Loy and Sage (1970) also reported similar results in baseball game. Chelladurai and Carron (1971) proposed a geographical model based on the dimensions of propinquity and task dependence. Propinquity dimension is associated with the observability and visibility of an athlete by teammates, whereas the task dependence is associated with the level of interaction required to successfully complete a task. Clearly, certain position in athlete team enjoys greater propinquity and dependence and these positions are often associated with greater leadership potential. Chelladurai and Carron's two-dimensional model has been applied to baseball by most of the researchers and it has also been successfully applied to football (Bivens and Leonard, 1994), basketball and volleyball with similar results.

Summary and Review

- The theories and principles of social psychology have been applied in different areas such as education, health care, law, entrepreneurship, sports, etc.
- The principles of social psychology have been successfully applied in education. The field of education is actively applying social-psychological concepts, especially studying the social functioning of educational system at different levels of analysis. School as a social system provides useful insight into understanding the impact of different types of school climate upon social interaction. Classroom climate, teacher variable, social motivation and other social factors do have an impact upon academic achievement. Various principles of social psychology have also been found useful in improving the outcome of education.
- Social psychology is also very useful for personal health behaviour and health attitude. A good health behaviour is found in those people, who hold good and positive health attitude towards stressful life experiences and the ways people cope with those stressful events have an impact upon health and illness. Apart from these factors, there are various social factors that have an impact upon health behaviour and well-being of the people. Social psychologists have also focused upon those concepts that promote healthy lifestyles among people.
- Social psychology has also an impact upon legal system. The way police makes interrogation, eyewitness identification and testimony, false confession by criminal defendants, lie detection have been found to be influenced by the principles of social psychology.
- Social psychology has also its impact upon entrepreneurship. As a consequence of applying the principles of social psychology, researchers have been able to find answer to two basic questions—why do only some persons become entrepreneurs? Why are some entrepreneurs more effective and successful than the others?
- The principles of social psychology have also been found useful for sport psychology. Various theories and principles of social psychology have been successfully applied to explain sport aggression, social facilitation, home ground advantage, team cohesion and its impact upon team performance and team satisfaction, leadership in sport, including coach-athlete compatibility as well as geographical playing position.

Review Questions

1. Citing examples, explain school as a social system.
2. Explain the impact of classroom and teacher variable upon the academic performance of the students.
3. Examine the impact of different social factors upon academic achievement of the students.
4. Outline a plan for improving the outcome of education.
5. Discuss the major causes of stress.
6. Citing relevant studies, explain how stress affects health and well-being.
7. Write short notes on the following:
    (i) Health behaviour and health attitude
    (ii) Classroom climate
    (iii) Coping with stress
8. Discuss the personal factors which influence health and well-being of a person.
9. Outline a plan for promoting healthy lifestyles.
10. Discuss the different aspects of police interrogation and their relevance for understanding the behaviour of witnesses and suspects.
11. What makes an eyewitness accurate? Cite experimental evidences in favour of your answer.
12. Discuss the various methods of assessing eyewitness accuracy.
13. Discuss the relevance of false confessions and lie detection in understanding the behaviour of criminal defendants.
14. Write an essay on the social psychology of entrepreneurship.
15. Discuss some of the relevant variables related to audience that have an impact upon athletic performance.
16. Discuss the impact of team cohesion upon team performance and team satisfaction.
17. Write short notes on the following:
    (i) Home ground advantage
    (ii) Coach-athlete compatibility
    (iii) Consequences of team cohesion

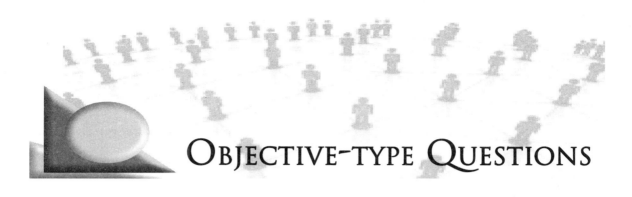

OBJECTIVE-TYPE QUESTIONS

CHAPTER 1 INTRODUCING SOCIAL PSYCHOLOGY

1. Social psychology is scientific in nature because it adopts some core values. Which of the following is not included in those core values?
   - (a) Skepticism
   - (b) Objectivity
   - (c) Open-mindedness
   - (d) Morality

2. The first laboratory experiment in social psychology was conducted in the field of
   - (a) Social loafing
   - (b) Social attitude
   - (c) Social facilitation
   - (d) None of these

3. The scientific study of new thoughts, feelings and behaviour of one person being influenced by the real, imagined or implied behaviour of other people is known as
   - (a) Experimental psychology
   - (b) Social psychology
   - (c) General psychology
   - (d) Social work

4. The first book on social psychology was written by
   - (a) E.A. Ross
   - (b) William McDougall
   - (c) C.H. Cooley
   - (d) G.W. Allport

5. The parent's disciplines of social psychology are
   - (a) Sociology and anthropology
   - (b) Sociology and psychology
   - (c) Psychology and anthropology
   - (d) None of these

6. The famous book entitled *The Nature of Prejudice* was written by
   - (a) R.F. Bales
   - (b) G. Allport
   - (c) F. Heiden
   - (d) K. Lewin

7. The period covered by the fifth ICSSR Survey in Psychology is
   - (a) 1993–2003
   - (b) 1993–2005
   - (c) 2003–2013
   - (d) 2005–2010

8. Who emphasised upon the statement that person and society are in a state of symbiotic relationship where one cannot be separated from other?
   - (a) A.K. Dalal
   - (b) D. Sinha
   - (c) G. Misra
   - (d) S.K. Mitra

9. Who defined social psychology as the science of the behaviour of individual in society?
   - (a) Secord and Backman
   - (b) Ketch, Crutchfield and Ballachey
   - (c) Ross and McDougall
   - (d) None of these

10. Who concluded the famous *Summer Camp Study* in which teenage boys had participated and had demonstrated that how conflicts develop between groups?
    - (a) Cartwright
    - (b) Sherif
    - (c) Festinger
    - (d) Hovland

11. Who had opposed the McClelland's idea that the important cause of India's under development was the low achievement of people?
    - (a) J.B.P. Sinha
    - (b) M.M. Sinha
    - (c) D. Sinha
    - (d) None of these

12. An Indian psychologist who was trained in experimental psychology under Bartlett but later shifted to social psychology and proved to be one of the most important researchers in studying various social behaviours. Identify that psychologist among the following:
    - (a) S.K. Mitra
    - (b) D. Sinha
    - (c) J. Pandey
    - (d) J.B.P. Sinha

13. Who proposed NT (Nurturant–Task) model of leadership in India?
    - (a) Purnima Singh
    - (b) A.K. Dalal
    - (c) S.K. Mitra
    - (d) J.B.P. Sinha

14. Who visited India for studying social psychological consequences of Hindu-Muslim hatred and social violence under UNESCO Plan?
    - (a) G. Murphy
    - (b) R. Rosenthal
    - (c) G.W. Allport
    - (d) E. Erikson

15. What do KAP studies stand for in social psychology?
    - (a) Knowledge, attribution and practice studies
    - (b) Knowledge, attribution and prosocial behaviour studies
    - (c) Kinesics, attitude and prosocial behaviour studies
    - (d) Knowledge, attitude and practice studies.

16. Around which two goals our social behaviour revolves?
    - (a) Survival and production
    - (b) Production and culture
    - (c) Cooperation and competition
    - (d) Prejudice and discrimination

17. Who is often called the father of modern social Psychology?
    - (a) Gordon Allport
    - (b) Kurt Lewin
    - (c) David McClelland
    - (d) Theodore Newcomb

Answers

1. (d) **2.** (c) **3.** (b) **4.** (a) **5.** (b) **6.** (b) **7.** (a) **8.** (b) **9.** (b) **10.** (b)
11. (a) **12.** (b) **13.** (d) **14.** (a) **15.** (d) **16.** (a) **17.** (b)

CHAPTER 2 RESEARCH METHODS IN SOCIAL PSYCHOLOGY

1. Which of the following is not the objective of social psychology course?
   (a) Identifying correlation between variables
   (b) Discovering causes of some behaviour or event
   (c) Testing existing theories and also developing new ones
   (d) Discovering psychological principles under duress

2. Which of the following increases the credibility of laboratory experiments done in the field of social psychology?
   (a) Internal validity
   (b) Experimental realism
   (c) Control of extraneous variables
   (d) All of the above

3. Which design is frequently used in the field experiment?
   (a) Before-and-after design
   (b) Reverse counterbalancing design
   (c) Quasi-experimental design
   (d) None of these

4. Which one can provide a causational explanation of social behaviour?
   (a) Cross-lagged panel correlation study
   (b) Cross-sectional study
   (c) Simple correlational study
   (d) None of these

5. Which one is the systematic observation about behaviours as they occur naturally in everyday life situation?
   (a) Field experiment
   (b) Field study
   (c) Field observation
   (d) Field tour

6. Interactive Voice Response (IVR) is one form of
   (a) Panel survey
   (b) Telephone survey
   (c) Interview study
   (d) None of these

7. Which is not a necessary condition for any interview survey to be successful?
   (a) Accessibility
   (b) Cognition
   (c) Motivation
   (d) Training

8. Which of the following is considered as a complete nonreactive research?
   (a) Archival research
   (b) Survey research
   (c) Content analysis
   (d) None of these

9. Which type of research is generally not undertaken by social psychologists?
   (a) Correlational research
   (b) Action research
   (c) Evaluative research
   (d) In-depth research

10. Which is not the essential characteristic of a good scientific theory?
    (a) Theories are statement about construct.
    (b) Theories describe causal relation.
    (c) Theories are general in scope.
    (d) Theories help in reducing self-serving bias.

11. Which one has the higher degree of internal validity but poor degree of external validity?
    (a) Field study
    (b) Field experiment
    (c) Laboratory experiment
    (d) Cross-sectional study

12. When performance is enhanced due to subjects' awareness in participation in an experiment, it is known as:
    (a) Halo effect
    (b) Howthrone effect
    (c) Hard-easy effect
    (d) Endowment effect

13. Match List I with List II and answer on the basis of codes given.

    List I
    1. Debriefing
    2. Informed consent
    3. Withdrawal
    4. Confidentiality

    List II
    A. Non-identification of the participants in study
    B. No restriction upon participant's desire to keep away from the study at any time
    C. Participant's permission regarding taking part in the study.
    D. Participants must be explained the purpose of the research after study.

    Codes :

	A	B	C	D
(a)	2	4	3	1
(b)	3	4	1	2
(c)	4	2	3	1
(d)	4	3	2	1

14. Indigenous concepts and tools are better for understanding a culture than some foreign tools and concepts is much emphasised in which of the following approaches:
    (a) Etic approach
    (b) Emic approach
    (c) Mitwelt approach
    (d) Unwelt approach

15. Who originally conceived the idea of action research?
    (a) E. Aronson
    (b) A. Bandura
    (c) K. Lewin
    (d) D. Bem

Answers

1. (d) **2.** (d) **3.** (b) **4.** (a) **5.** (b) **6.** (b) **7.** (d) **8.** (a) **9.** (d) **10.** (d)
11. (c) **12.** (b) **13.** (d) **14.** (b) **15.** (c)

CHAPTER 3 THEORETICAL FOUNDATIONS OF MODERN SOCIAL PSYCHOLOGY

1. In social psychology, there are theories that focus upon the specific aspect of social behaviour and do not cover the whole social life. Such theories are called:
   (a) Theoretical perspectives
   (b) Middle-range theories
   (c) Theory of specificity
   (d) None of these

2. Which is a mechanism for reducing role conflict?
   (a) Role enactment
   (b) Role socialisation
   (c) Role diversity
   (d) All of the above
3. According to Maslow, which is the second level of needs from lower end of hierarchy?
   (a) Esteem needs
   (b) Physiological needs
   (c) Safety needs
   (d) Self-actualisation
4. Who considered need for achievement, need for affiliation and need for power jointly as one of the powerful motivational behaviour for social development?
   (a) Murray
   (b) Alderfer
   (c) Maslow
   (d) None of the above
5. Which is not the effect of exposure to models?
   (a) Acquisition
   (b) Inhibition
   (c) Response facilitation
   (d) Discrimination
6. In explaining social behaviour, cognitive theories basically emphasise
   (a) Schemas
   (b) Cognitive map
   (c) Cognitive structure
   (d) Cognitive consistency
7. In light of symbolic-interaction theory, which of the following is not correct?
   (a) The theory views human beings as goal seeking and proactive.
   (b) The theory emphasises that the person can also act towards self.
   (c) The theory focuses on the fact that behaviour continually emerges through communication and interaction with others.
   (d) The theory does its business well even when analysing self-interested behaviour or principled action.
8. Indians are characterised by the spirit of
   (a) Collectivistic culture
   (b) Individualistic culture
   (c) Materialistic culture
   (d) None of these
9. Which theory emphasises the principle of natural selection in explaining social behaviour?
   (a) Learning theories
   (b) Motivational theories
   (c) Evolutionary theories
   (d) Cognitive theories
10. Whose research work is based upon the concept of ERG need?
    (a) Maslow
    (b) Murray
    (c) Bandura
    (d) Alderfer
11. Social behaviours inspired by growth, needs and values are known as:
    (a) Metagrowth
    (b) Metamotivation
    (c) Metaneeds
    (d) None of these
12. Learning through direct participation is called
    (a) Observational learning
    (b) Social learning
    (c) Experiential learning
    (d) None of these
13. Which one is not an effect of exposure to models?
    (a) Response facilitation
    (b) Acquisition
    (c) Inhibition
    (d) Individuation

14. Parent may expect from his son to study ten hours a day where as son may find it a very difficult job. This illustrates:
    (a) Intrarole conflict
    (b) Interrole conflict
    (c) Personal role conflict
    (d) None of these
15. A theory in social psychology, which explains only a specific social behaviour is known as:
    (a) Empirical theory
    (b) Objective theory
    (c) Middle-range theory
    (d) Specific theory

Answers

1. (b) 2. (b) 3. (c) 4. (a) 5. (d) 6. (c) 7. (d) 8. (a) 9. (c) 10. (d)
11. (b) 12. (c) 13. (d) 14. (a) 15. (c)

CHAPTER 4   SELF AND IDENTITY

1. The collection of beliefs we hold about ourselves is known as
    (a) Self-liking
    (b) Self-competence
    (c) Self-esteem
    (d) Self-concept
2. According to Mead, which is the correct division of self?
    (a) Material self and social self.
    (b) I and me
    (c) Inter self and Intra self
    (d) None of these
3. Who coined the term *looking glass self*?
    (a) Myers
    (b) Cooley
    (c) Mead
    (d) Higgins
4. Which of the following has no role in shaping social self?
    (a) Social comparison
    (b) Social identity
    (c) Reflected appraisals
    (d) Self-regulation
5. Which statement in not correct?
    (a) In independent culture, self disapproves conformity, whereas in interdependent culture, self disapproves egoism.
    (b) Independent self is supported by the individualistic western culture, whereas interdependent self is supported by the collectivistic Asian and Third world cultures.
    (c) In independent cultures, self is unique and always promoting one's own goals, whereas in interdependent culture, self is belongings expressing in indirect way and promoting group goals.
    (d) In independent culture, self is fluid, variable and changing from situation to situation, whereas in interdependent culture, self is unique and separate from social context.
6. Self influences thought and feeling of the persons through various ways. Which of the following is not the correct way?
    (a) Self-schemas
    (b) Self-awareness
    (c) Self-discrepancy
    (d) Self-control

7. Which is not the correct source of self-esteem?
   - (a) Reward and punishment
   - (b) Social comparison
   - (c) Family experience
   - (d) Performance feedback
8. The self-serving bias refers to the tendency to attribute success to _____ causes and failure to _____ causes.
   - (a) Stable, unstable
   - (b) Controllable, uncontrollable
   - (c) Specific, ambiguous
   - (d) Internal, external
9. Which is not the component of self-schema?
   - (a) Self as one is
   - (b) Self as one would like to be
   - (c) Self as one ought to be
   - (d) Self as perceived by ones
10. The positive and negative evaluation of self is technically known as
    - (a) Self-esteem
    - (b) Self-evaluation
    - (c) Global self
    - (d) Self-liking
11. Which one of the following is not a component of self?
    - (a) Self-control
    - (b) Impression management
    - (c) Self-esteem
    - (d) Self-perception
12. The ways individuals define themselves in terms of their group membership is known as
    - (a) Groupthink
    - (b) Social identity
    - (c) Consensual validation
    - (d) Social comparison
13. Self-esteem develops from different sources. Which one is not a source of development of self-esteem?
    - (a) Family experience
    - (b) Social comparison
    - (c) Performance feedback
    - (d) Self-objectification
14. Match List I and List II and answer on the basis of codes given below:

    List I
    - (A) Self-schema
    - (B) Self-esteem
    - (C) Self-presentation
    - (D) Self-handicapping

    List II
    1. A generalised evaluation of self
    2. When a person develops doubt regarding his abilities to do a task
    3. Organisation of information about self
    4. The way one presents oneself before public

    Codes :

	A	B	C	D
(a)	3	4	1	2
(b)	2	3	1	4
(c)	3	1	4	2
(d)	1	3	2	4

15. Which one of the following are correct regarding self-concept?
    1. Self-concept follows the general laws and principles of perception established in experimental psychology.
    2. Self-concept incorporates not only one's perceptions of what one is like but also what one thinks one ought to be.

3. Self-concept represents an organised, coherent and integrated pattern of self-related perceptions.
4. Development of self-concept follows a specific time table of critical stages.

Codes:
(a) 2, 3 and 4
(b) 1, 3 and 4
(c) 1, 2 and 3
(d) 1, 4 and 2

16. Match the List I and List II and answer on the basis of codes given:

List I		List II
A.	Mitwelt	1. A person exists in given place at a particular time. Being conscious of it, he can choose the direction of his life.
B.	Dasein	2. Experience and meaning we share with others through our relationship.
C.	Unwelt	3. Unique presence of human beings of self-awareness and self-relatedness.
D.	Eigenwelt	4. The biological and natural environment for humans as well as animals including biological needs, instincts and drives.

Codes:

	A	B	C	D
(a)	2	1	4	3
(b)	2	1	3	4
(c)	2	4	1	3
(d)	1	2	3	4

Answers

1. (d) 2. (b) 3. (b) 4. (d) 5. (d) 6. (d) 7. (a) 8. (d) 9. (d) 10. (a)
11. (d) 12. (b) 13. (d) 14. (c) 15. (a) 16. (a)

CHAPTER 5 SOCIAL COGNITION, SOCIAL PERCEPTION AND ATTRIBUTION

1. Mental structures that represent knowledge about the traits of specific personalities or to the types of the individuals are called of
    (a) Event schema
    (b) Role schema
    (c) Person schema
    (d) None of these

2. A strategy in which the person making a judgement about the social world on the basis of how easily specific kinds of information are brought to mind is known as
    (a) Representativeness heuristics
    (b) Adjustment heuristics
    (c) Availability heuristics
    (d) Simulation heuristics

3. The opposite of optimistic bias is
    (a) Counterfactual thinking
    (b) Thought suppression
    (c) Negativity bias
    (d) Pessimistic bias

4. A tendency to make various types of optimistic predictions concerning how long a given task will take for a final completion is known as
   (a) Planning fallacy
   (b) Overconfidence barrier
   (c) Counterfactual thinking
   (d) None of these
5. The overestimation of the frequency of airplane accidents involves
   (a) Consensus heuristics
   (b) Representativeness heuristics
   (c) Availability heuristics
   (d) None of these
6. When a person's expectation of another influences how the other person acts, the result is
   (a) A self-serving bias
   (b) A self-fulfilling prophecy
   (c) Primacy effect
   (d) Fundamental attribution error
7. Physiognomy refers to
   (a) art of reading the faces
   (b) making influence through eye contact
   (c) making influence through gesture and posture
   (d) None of these
8. Attribution is concerned with the question of
   (a) Who our best choice for friends is
   (b) How we can best achieve our goals
   (c) Why a person and others act the way both do
   (d) How a person can best achieve his goals
9. The fundamental attribution error refers to the tendency to explain the behaviour of others in terms of
   (a) Stable causes
   (b) Unstable causes
   (c) External cause
   (d) Internal causes
10. A person tends to attribute behaviour to external causes if consistency is ………., distinctiveness is ……….. and consensus is …………
    (a) Low, high, high
    (b) Low, low, low
    (c) High, low, low
    (d) High, high, high
11. Which is not correct about first impression?
    (a) First impression often serves as self-fulfilling prophecies.
    (b) First impression forms a framework through which other information is interpreted.
    (c) A person usually pays close attention to early information than to later information he receives about a person.
    (d) The importance of first impressions is greatly overrated.
12. The tendency of the person to overemphasise dispositional causes and underemphasise situational causes when he explains the behaviour of others is known as
    (a) Self-serving bias
    (b) External bias error
    (c) Grouping error
    (d) Fundamental attribution error
13. A person usually tends to make _____ attribution to explain his own successful behaviour and _____ attributions to explain the successful behaviour of others.
    (a) Dispositional, situational
    (b) Biased, dispositional
    (c) Situational, dispositional
    (d) Situational, biased

14. Following Kelley, if a person reacts the same way to a number of stimuli, it is said to be
    (a) High consistency
    (b) High consensus
    (c) Low convariation
    (d) Low distinctiveness
15. Following Kelley, if a person acts the same way to a stimulus overtime, there is found to be
    (a) High consistency
    (b) High covariation
    (c) Low distinctiveness
    (d) High consensus
16. Which one is not used in making judgement about social world?
    (a) Negativity heuristic
    (b) Availability heuristic
    (c) Representativeness heuristic
    (d) Simulation heuristic
17. Which of the following are the sources of error in social cognition?
    (1) Negativity bias
    (2) Counterfactual thinking
    (3) Thought suppression
    (4) Person perception
    Codes :
    (a) 1 and 4
    (b) 2 and 4
    (c) 1, 2 and 3
    (d) 2, 3 and 4
18. The process by which we use social stimuli to form impressions of others is known as
    (a) Self-perception
    (b) Person perception
    (c) False consensus effect
    (d) Positive illusion
19. When we tend to decide that a person's behaviour was caused by a relatively enduring tendency to think, feel or act in a certain way, it is referred to as:
    (a) Situational attribution
    (b) Causal attribution
    (c) Dispositional attribution
    (d) None of these
20. Tendency to make a disproportional attribution even when a person's behaviour was caused by the situation is called as:
    (a) Self-fulfilling prophecy
    (b) Correspondence bias
    (c) Confrontational bias
    (d) Fixed mindset

Answers

1. (c) 2. (c) 3. (c) 4. (a) 5. (c) 6. (b) 7. (a) 8. (c) 9. (d) 10. (d)
11. (d) 12. (d) 13. (a) 14. (d) 15. (a) 16. (a) 17. (c) 18. (b) 19. (c) 20. (b)

CHAPTER 6 SOCIALISATION

1. Socialisation is considered as subject of
    (a) Learning
    (b) Thinking
    (c) Personality
    (d) Perception
2. Which one is considered as reservoir of psychological energy?
    (a) Id
    (b) Ego
    (c) Superego
    (d) None of these

3. In which stage role confusion is created among person during socialisation?
   (a) School age
   (b) Adolescence
   (c) Play stage
   (d) Young adulthood

4. During early socialisation, children develop a sense of purpose, which helps in setting major goals of life. This occurs in
   (a) School age
   (b) Early childhood
   (c) Play stage
   (d) Infancy

5. According to Kohlberg, a sense of full internalisation develops among children during socialisation. In which one of the following stage such internalisation occurs?
   (a) Conventional level
   (b) Post-conventional level
   (c) Pre-conventional level
   (d) At none of the levels

6. Which of the following is not a component of socialisation?
   (a) Socialisation has an outcome.
   (b) Socialisation has a target.
   (c) Socialisation involves an agent.
   (d) Socialisation involves an adult caretaker.

7. There are children who receive both positive and negative nominations from their peers. Such children belong to the category of
   (a) Controversial children
   (b) Rejected children
   (c) Average children
   (d) Neglected children

8. The process of adopting as one's own values, attitudes, behaviour of those who are significant others is called
   (a) Cognitive competence
   (b) Internalisation
   (c) Observational learning
   (d) None of these

9. When a person learns those behaviour or activities that provide him with the knowledge of skills about which he has not yet assumed, it is called:
   (a) Role acquisition
   (b) Role discontinuity
   (c) Anticipatory socialisation
   (d) None of these

10. Which is not the correct statement about socialisation?
    (a) Socialisation involves social interaction.
    (b) In socialisation, the person conforms to the normative expectations of the society.
    (c) Socialisation generally stops at the end of adolescence.
    (d) Socialisation involves attitudinal and behavioural changes.

11. According to Erikson, adequate training, sufficient education and good models during age range 6 to 11 years will lead to:
    (a) Identity
    (b) Imitativeness
    (c) Industriousness
    (d) Autonomy

12. Match List I and List II and answer on the basis of codes given:

    List I
    A. Love
    B. Fidelity
    C. Hope
    D. Wisdom

    List II
    1. Ego integrity vs. Despair
    2. Trust vs. Mistrust
    3. Ego Identity vs. Role Confusion
    4. Intimacy vs. Isolation

Code :

	A	B	C	D
(a)	2	3	4	1
(b)	4	2	3	1
(c)	4	3	2	1
(d)	4	3	1	2

Answers

1. (a)   2. (a)   3. (b)   4. (c)   5. (b)   6. (d)   7. (c)   8. (b)   9. (c)   10. (c)
11. (c)   12. (c)

CHAPTER 7   SOCIAL ATTITUDES AND PERSUASION

1. Three components of an attitude are
   (a) Opinion, belief and knowledge
   (b) Cognitive, emotional and behavioural
   (c) Source, message and medium
   (d) Positive, negative and neutral

2. Researches done in the field of attitude have revealed that an attitude has all except which of the following components?
   (a) Cognitive component
   (b) Behavioural component
   (c) Emotional component
   (d) Biochemical component

3. Which is not a function of attitude?
   (a) Social identity function
   (b) Schematic function
   (c) Heuristic function
   (d) Convergent function

4. Who proposed the theory of reasoned action model?
   (a) Allport
   (b) Fishbein and Ajzen
   (c) Minrad
   (d) None of these

5. Individual's behaviour can be predicated from behavioural intention. This has been emphasised by
   (a) Reasoned action model
   (b) Cognitive consistency model
   (c) Balance model
   (d) None of these

6. Which one is not the component of persuasion?
   (a) Medium
   (b) Message
   (c) Source
   (d) Norm

7. Delayed persuasion after the audience forgets the source or its connection with message is known as
   (a) Halo effect
   (b) Sleeper effect
   (c) Confounding effect
   (d) Modality effect

8. Match List I with List II and answer on the basis of the code given:

List I	List II
1. Heider	A. Congruity theory
2. Osgood	B. Cognitive dissonance theory
3. Festinger	C. P-O-X model
4. Newcomb	D. A-B-X model

   Codes:
   (a) A B C D
       1 3 2 4
   (b) A B C D
       2 3 4 1
   (c) A B C D
       2 3 1 4
   (d) A B C D
       1 2 3 4

9. Which of the following attitude scaling method/s has/have been proposed by L.L.Thurstone?
   1. Summated ratings
   2. Paired comparison
   3. Scalogram
   4. Equal-appearing intervals

   Codes:
   (a) Only 4
   (b) Only 2
   (c) 2 and 4
   (d) 3 and 4

10. Following Kelman, three processes of social influence instrumental in bringing changes in attitude are:
    (a) Compliance, identification and internalisation.
    (b) Compliance, obedience and internalisation.
    (c) Obedience, conformity and compliance.
    (d) Conformity, internalisation and compliance.

11. Which of the following makes changes in attitude easily?
    (a) Reactance
    (b) Dissonance
    (c) Forewarning
    (d) Selective audience

12. Which is not a dimension of attitude?
    (a) Centrality
    (b) Consistency
    (c) Salience
    (d) Expectancy

13. Read each of the following two statements—Assertion (A) and Reason (R)—and indicate your answer using the codes given below:
    Assertion (A): Dissonance is a negative drive.
    Reason (R): The magnitude of dissonance is inversely proportional to the number of consonant cognitions.

    Codes:
    (a) Both A and R are true and R is the correct explanation of A.
    (b) Both A and R are true but R is not the correct explanation of A.
    (c) A is true but R is false.
    (d) A is false but R is true.

14. Which is not true?
    (a) The magnitude of dissonance decreases as the degree of discrepancy among cognition increases.
    (b) The magnitude of dissonance directly increases as the number of dissonant cognition and degree of discrepancy among them increases.

(c) The magnitude of dissonance is inversely proportional to the number of consonant cognitions held by the person.
(d) A person can reduce dissonance by adding new cognitive elements to outweigh the dissonant ones.

15. In which area cognitive dissonance theory of Festigner is not correctly applied ?
    (a) Forced compliance behaviour
    (b) Justification of efforts
    (c) Decision-making
    (d) Self-judgement

16. Read each of the following two statements—Assertion (A) and Reason (R) and indicate your answer using the codes given below:
    Assertion (R): Likert scaling technique is based on the method of summated ratings.
    Reason (R): Due to summated ratings Likert scale yields a poor degree of internal consistency.
    Codes:
    (a) Both A and R are true and R is the correct explanation of A.
    (b) Both A and R are true but R is not the correct explanation of A.
    (c) A is true but R is false.
    (d) A is false but R is true.

17. Match List I with List II and answer on the basis of the codes given

List I	List II
A. Social distance	1. Osgood, Suci and Tannenbaum
B. Cumulative scaling	2. Edwards and Kilpatrik
C. Scale discrimination technique	3. Bogardus
D. Semantic differential scale	4. Guttman

    Codes:
    (a) A B C D   (b) A B C D
        4 2 3 1   3 4 1 2
    (c) A B C D   (d) A B C D
        4 3 2 1   3 4 2 1

18. Which of the following would create the most cognitive dissonance?
    (a) I am Indian. I do not like Indian food.
    (b) I am an honest person. I cheated him badly.
    (c) I should have gotten that job. I was not hired.
    (d) I bought Maruti 800 car. I wish I had a Wagon R.

19. What would be the total number of pairs in a study scaling the twelve attitude items by the method of paired comparison?
    (a) 162
    (b) 72
    (c) 60
    (d) 66

20. Which function of attitude is hedonistic in nature?
    (a) Heuristic function
    (b) Schematic function
    (c) Ego-defensive function
    (d) Self-esteem function

Answers

1. (b) 2. (d) 3. (d) 4. (b) 5. (a) 6. (d) 7. (b) 8. (c) 9. (c) 10. (a)
11. (b) 12. (d) 13. (b) 14. (a) 15. (d) 16. (b) 17. (d) 18. (b) 19. (d) 20. (a)

CHAPTER 8 STEREOTYPING, PREJUDICE AND DISCRIMINATION

1. Which of the following is not a correct statement?
   (a) Stereotypes are based on feelings, bias and prejudice.
   (b) Stereotypes are over-simplied statements.
   (c) Stereotypes are ready-made frames of reference.
   (d) Stereotypes mould according to new information arrived.

2. Which of the following is not correct in light of formation of stereotypes?
   (a) Stereotypes conserve mental effort and improve efficiency.
   (b) Stereotypes uproot our pre-existing beliefs.
   (c) Stereotypes are formed and used for justifying inequalities.
   (d) Stereotypes can be formed through the process of social communication.

3. Which is not the correct impact of stereotype upon our judgement?
   (a) Stereotypes have greater effects upon our judgements when emotions are intense.
   (b) Stereotypes have greater effects upon our judgement when we work under time pressure.
   (c) Stereotypes have greater effect upon our judgements when people hold position of power.
   (d) Stereotypes have greater effect upon our judgements when there is no one to consult.

4. Traits supposedly possessed by the women in comparison to male traits are viewed as less appropriate for high-status position. The truth of this statement has given rise to
   (a) Glass ceiling effect   (b) Sleeper effect
   (c) Halo effect   (d) Modality effect

5. Read each of the following two statements—Assertion (A) and Reason (R) and indicate your answer using the codes given below:
   Assertion (A): Powerful person is more likely to form stereotyped impression.
   Reason (R): Glass ceiling effect generates stereotypes.
   Codes:
   (a) Both A and R are true and R is the correct explanation of A.
   (b) Both A and R are true but R is not the correct explanation of A.
   (c) A is true but R is false.
   (d) A is false but R is true.

6. Prejudice is to _____ as discrimination is to _____.
   (a) Thought, competition   (b) In-group, out-group
   (c) Stereotypes, conflict   (d) Attitudes, behaviours

7. According to the realistic group conflict theory, many prejudices develop because
   (a) Human beings are genetically programmed for competition with other persons
   (b) Of competition over scarce resources
   (c) Realistic trait differences exist between advantaged and disadvantaged
   (d) The persons model their prejudice as exhibited by their members of family

8. The bias that plays a role in stereotyping and prejudice is
   (a) Motivation   (b) Priming
   (c) Illusory correlation   (d) Confirmation

9. Dissonance is often reduced by changing
   (a) Behaviour   (b) Evaluation
   (c) Motivation   (d) Attitude

10. Disliking a nurse because he is a male or a woman because she is truck driver constitutes the example of
    (a) Racism
    (b) Sexual anomaly
    (c) Sexism
    (d) Sexual deviation

11. Read each of the following two statements—Assertion (A) and Reason (R) and indicate your answer using the codes given below:
    Assertion (A): Social categorisation results in prejudice.
    Reason (R): Persons derive a sense of self-esteem from their social identity as members of in-group
    Codes:
    (a) Both A and R are true and R is the correct explanation of A.
    (b) Both A and R are true but R is not the correct explanation of A.
    (c) A is true but R is false.
    (d) A is false but R is true.

12. Read each of the following two statements—Assertion (A) and Reason (R) and indicate your answer using the codes below:
    Assertion (A): Prejudiced person tends to attribute desirable behaviour of his in-group in terms of admirable traits, but attribute desirable behaviours by members of out-group to external causes or transitory factors.
    Reason (R): Ultimate attribution error carries the self-serving bias.
    Codes:
    (a) Both A and R are true and R is the correct explanation of A.
    (b) Both A and R are true but R is not the correct explanation of A.
    (c) A is true but R is false.
    (d) A is false but R is true.

13. Which one does not cause prejudice ?
    (a) Social inequalities
    (b) Socialisation
    (c) Religion
    (d) Globalisation

14. Match List I with List II and answer on the basis of the codes provided.

List I	List II
A. Hostile sexism	1. Positive action taken by individuals towards members of the group to whom they are prejudiced
B. Benevolent sexism	2. Negative attitude towards women especially those women who challenge traditional female role
C. Glass ceiling effect	3. Positive feelings towards women, including a prosocial orientation towards women
D. Tokenism	4. Women, in general, experience less favourable outcomes in their carriers because of gender

Codes:

(a) A B C D
    2 1 3 4

(b) A B C D
    2 3 1 4

(c) A B C D
    3 4 1 2

(d) A B C D
    2 3 4 1

15. Recent researchers indicating the role of social conditions playing a role in the formation of prejudice and discrimination suggest that the prejudice may originate from
    (a) In-group, out-group conflict.
    (b) Realistic group conflict theory.
    (c) Competition among competing social groups.
    (d) Our own thinking process.

16. Mohan really likes Sunita. When asked why, he responds, "Because she gives as much to our relationship as she takes." Mohan's comment about Sunita illustrates:
    (a) Social identity theory
    (b) Balance theory
    (c) Equity theory
    (d) Elaboration likelihood model

17. If a person believes in saying 'First impression count', he agrees with the principle of
    (a) Primacy effect
    (b) Glass ceiling effect
    (c) Halo effect
    (d) Decency effect

18. Which explanation of prejudice assumed that the same processes that help others in forming attitude, also help in forming prejudiced attitudes?
    (a) Social inequality
    (b) Frustration and aggression
    (c) Authoritarianism
    (d) Social cognition

19. In which of the following situations prejudice and discrimination are least likely to develop?
    (a) Two different groups of immigrants competing for jobs
    (b) Two different religious groups each giving weight to one's own religion
    (c) Two different groups, with one group being blamed for the economic backwardness of the other
    (d) Two groups dealing with the aftermath of an earthquake

20. The self-fulfilling prophecy is the negative outcome of
    (a) Urbanisation
    (b) Social identity
    (c) Referencing grouping
    (d) Stereotype vulnerability

21. Which one of the following is incorrect regarding the causes of the origin of prejudice?
    (a) Competition for scarce resources
    (b) Perception of threat to self-esteem and/or group interest
    (c) Categorising ourselves as a member of a group and others as members of a different group.
    (d) Unfavourable or negative actions directed towards members of other group.

22. Which is not a correct way of reducing prejudice and discrimination?
    (a) Recategorisation
    (b) Superordinate goal
    (c) Social influence
    (d) Attribution

23. Match List I with List II and answer on the basis of codes given below:

List I	List II
A. Planning fallacy	1. Tendency to adhere to bad decisions even if losses increase

B. Confirmation bias
C. Counterfactual thinking
D. Escalation of commitment

2. Tendency to evaluate events by thinking about some alternatives
3. Tendency to underestimate the resources needed to achieve a goal.
4. Tendency to pay attention mainly to information that confirms existing view.

Codes :
(a) A B C D
    3 4 2 1
(b) A B C D
    2 4 3 1
(c) A B C D
    3 2 4 1
(d) A B C D
    2 1 3 4

Answers

1. (d) 2. (b) 3. (d) 4. (a) 5. (c) 6. (d) 7. (b) 8. (c) 9. (d) 10. (c)
11. (a) 12. (a) 13. (d) 14. (d) 15. (d) 16. (c) 17. (a) 18. (d) 19. (d) 20. (d)
21. (d) 22. (d) 23. (a)

CHAPTER 9   BEHAVIOURS IN GROUP

1. Which is not an element of social structure of group?
   (a) Social roles
   (b) Social status
   (c) Social norms
   (d) Social cohesion

2. Which is not the reason for joining a group?
   (a) Group provides a boost to the status of a person.
   (b) Group provides reward.
   (c) Self-knowledge of a person is enhanced after joining a group.
   (d) Group enhances personal freedom of a person.

3. What does entitativity mean?
   (a) Having common goals
   (b) Having physical closeness
   (c) Having psychological commodity
   (d) All of the above

4. Family is an example of
   (a) Formal group
   (b) Primary group
   (c) Reference group
   (d) None of these

5. In which stage of group development a sense of security, harmony and cohesiveness develop among members of the group?
   (a) Stage of storming
   (b) Stage of forming
   (c) Stage of norming
   (d) Stage of performing

6. The term *social facilitation* refers to
   (a) Negative effects on the performance due to the absence of others.
   (b) Negative effects on the performance due to the presence of others.
   (c) Positive effects on the performance due to the presence of others.
   (d) Both positive and negative effects on the performance due to the presence of others.

7. Read each of the following two statements—Assertion (A) and Reason (R) and indicate your answer using the codes given below:
   Assertion (A): Fully satiated chickens will eat if placed among chickens who are eating hungrily.
   Reason (R): Being in presence of others increases the organism's level of drive.
   Codes:
   (a) Both A and R are true and R is the correct explanation of A.
   (b) Both A and R are true but R is not the correct explanation of A.
   (c) A is true but R is false.
   (d) A is false but R is true.
8. Social loafing is likely to occur when
   (a) Individual's output is to be evaluated.
   (b) Individual's output is to be monitored.
   (c) A task is very challenging.
   (d) Individual output is difficult to be identified.
9. Match List I with List II and answer on the basis of codes provided.

List I	List II
A. Social facilitation	1. Any process whereby a person's attitudes, opinions, beliefs or behaviour are changed
B. Social influence	2. The term refers to the audience effect and coaction effects
C. Social cognitive theory	3. An approach to social learning incorporating findings from the field of learning
D. Social identity	4. Part of the self-concept that derives from group membership

   Codes:
   (a) A B C D   (b) A B C D
        2 1 3 4   2 1 4 3
   (c) A B C D   (d) A B C D
        1 2 3 4   3 1 2 4

10. The people with whom a person identifies most strongly are known as
    (a) Reference group   (b) Out-group
    (c) In-group   (d) Them-group
11. Match List I with List II and answer on the basis of codes provided.

List I	List II
A. Moscovici and Fraser	1. Groupthink
B. Janis	2. Group polarisation
C. Karan and Williams	3. Collective effort model
D. Allport	4. Social facilitation

    Codes:
    (a) A B C D   (b) A B C D
         1 2 3 4   2 1 4 3
    (c) A B C D   (d) A B C D
         2 1 3 4   1 2 4 3

12. Which of the following does not reduce social loafing?
    (a) Making contribution of each individual identifiable.
    (b) Making task meaningful and interesting.
    (c) Providing punishment for high group productivity or performance.
    (d) Increasing commitment of the members to successful task performance.
13. In social decision schemes, which of the following is not included?
    (a) First-shift rule
    (b) Truth wins
    (c) Majority wins
    (d) Win-win
14. When the group takes decision that are extreme than the mean of the individual member's initial position, the phenomenon is known as
    (a) Risky shift effect
    (b) Group polarisation
    (c) Cautious shift
    (d) None of them
15. Which of the following is not correct statement?
    (a) Groupthink occurs in non-cohesive group.
    (b) Groupthink develops in a group having a strong or promotional leader.
    (c) When the group is sealed off from dissenting opinions, groupthink is likely to develop.
    (d) Groupthink develops in a group having high stress or external threat.
16. Which method/technique does not improve group decisions?
    (a) Technique of authentic dissent
    (b) Devil's advocate technique
    (c) Brain storming
    (d) Technique of reciprocity
17. Which pair can be placed under centralised communication networks?
    (a) Wheel pattern and Y-pattern
    (b) Chain pattern and circle pattern
    (c) Wheel pattern and chain pattern
    (d) Y-pattern and circle pattern
18. The earliest demonstration that mere presence of other has an impact on individual behaviour was an experiment in the field of
    (a) Conformity
    (b) Prejudice
    (c) Social facilitation
    (d) Groupthink
19. The prisoner's dilemma game (PDG) is an example of
    (a) Zero-sum game
    (b) Non-zero sum game
    (c) A true competitive game
    (d) None of these
20. Grapevine refers to
    (a) A formal communication
    (b) An informal communication
    (c) All-connect communication
    (d) None of these
21. The first experimental study on social facilitation was conducted by
    (a) Allport
    (b) Triplett
    (c) Heider
    (d) NewComb
22. Which of the following does not reflect groupthink?
    (a) Collective rationalisation
    (b) Self-censorship
    (c) Deindividualisation
    (d) Mindguarding
23. Which one illustrates riskiness of cooperation?
    (a) Prisoner's dilemma
    (b) Mindguarding
    (c) Both a and b
    (d) Neither a nor b

24. Match List I with List II and answer on the basis of codes given:

List I	List II
1. Devil's advocate technique	A. A process whereby identification with group produces conformity in the group
2. Brainstorming	B. A group of people generating ideal in form of free association.
3. Illusion of invulnerability	C. Members of the group showing excessive optimism, euphoria and any possibility of failure hardly crosses their minds.
4. Self-categorization	D. Any one member of the group is assigned the task of disagreeing with group decision.

Codes :
(a) A B C D
    1 2 3 4
(b) A B C D
    4 3 2 1
(c) A B C D
    4 2 3 1
(d) A B C D
    2 4 3 1

25. When each member of the group assumes that the other group members hold the same opinions or views regarding any issue, and therefore, there is no need for any discussion, it is called as
(a) Self-censorship
(b) Illusion of unanimity
(c) Conformity pressure
(d) Mindguarding.

Answers

1. (c)   2. (d)   3. (d)   4. (b)   5. (c)   6. (d)   7. (a)   8. (d)   9. (a)   10. (c)
11. (c) 12. (c) 13. (d) 14. (b) 15. (a) 16. (d) 17. (a) 18. (c) 19. (b) 20. (b)
21. (b) 22. (c) 23. (a) 24. (c) 25. (b)

CHAPTER 10   SOCIAL NORMS AND CONFORMITY

1. A father's love for his offspring is an example of
(a) Social norm
(b) Attitude
(c) Opinion
(d) None of these

2. According to Piaget, how many stages are in developing a sense of right and wrong among children?
(a) Three
(b) Four
(c) Two
(d) Five

3. Which is not a correct statement?
(a) Social norms involve judgement of value.
(b) Social norms have a high emotional tone.
(c) Social norms allow for a considerable amount of latitude.
(d) Social norms apply to a limited section of society.

4. Auto-kinetic effect is
   (a) An optical illusion
   (b) Auditory illusion
   (c) Tactual illusion
   (d) None of these

5. Various studies have shown that the degree of conformity is greater in
   (a) Tribal culture
   (b) Individualistic culture
   (c) Collectivistic culture
   (d) All cultures

6. A pattern of conformity in which even when conditions are not ambiguous, an unanimous group majority influences individual's judgement is known as
   (a) Informational influence
   (b) Asch effect
   (c) Auto-kinetic effect
   (d) Normative influence

7. Read each of the following two statements—Assertion (A) and Reason (R) and indicate your answer using the codes below:
   Assertion (A): Normative social norms are related to group norms.
   Reason (R): Normative social norms generally produces public compliance.
   Codes:
   (a) Both A and R are true and R is not the correct explanation of A.
   (b) Both A and R are true and R is the correct explanation of A.
   (c) A is true but R is false.
   (d) A is false but R is true.

8. Which of the following factors does not affect conformity?
   (a) Group unanimity
   (b) Size of the group
   (c) Culture
   (d) Minority influence

9. Norms that specify what is approved or disapproved behaviour in a given situation are called
   (a) Injunctive norms
   (b) Descriptive social norms
   (c) Perscriptive social norms
   (d) None of these

10. Match List I with List II and answer on the basis of the codes provided.

List I	List II
A. Individuation	1. A negative reaction to efforts done by others to reduce our freedom
B. Reactance	2. Desire to do something that publicly differentiates a person from others
C. Normative social	3. Expectations held by group members regarding how to behave
D. Informational social	4. Tendency of a person to rely on others' perception, experience and knowledge

    Codes:
    (a) A B C D
        2 3 4 1
    (b) A B C D
        2 1 4 3
    (c) A B C D
        2 1 3 4
    (d) A B C D
        1 2 4 3

11. 'A father should love his children' is an example of:
    (a) Attitude
    (b) Social norms
    (c) Social cognition
    (d) None of these

12. Which type of social norms do influence the behaviour most in the situation in which antisocial behaviour is likely to occur?
    (a) Descriptive norms
    (b) Injunctive norms
    (c) Both 'a' and 'b'
    (d) Neither 'a' nor 'b'
13. Which of the following does not resist conformity?
    (a) Reactance
    (b) Social support
    (c) Desire for personal control
    (d) Social contagion

Answers

1. (b) 2. (b) 3. (d) 4. (a) 5. (c) 6. (b) 7. (b) 8. (d) 9. (a) 10. (c)
11. (b) 12. (b) 13. (d)

CHAPTER 11 LEADERSHIP AND SOCIAL POWER

1. According to Katz and Kahn, which is not related to the meaning of leadership?
   (a) Leader as a category of behaviour
   (b) Leader as an attribute of position
   (c) Leader as a characteristic of person
   (d) Leader as a powerful role
2. Which one does not help in the emergence of leadership?
   (a) Group complexity
   (b) Group instability
   (c) Group crisis
   (d) Dissatisfaction of wants
3. When the leadership style encourages a proper exchange of various activities between the leader and the group members, it is known as
   (a) Transformational leader
   (b) Transactional leader
   (c) Democrative leader
   (d) Authoritarian leader
4. Which is not the characteristic of transformational leader?
   (a) Intellectual stimulation
   (b) Idealised influence
   (c) Individualised consideration
   (d) Dominance
5. Leaders who strongly believe in getting the work done by the subordinates are classified as originating from
   (a) Consideration structure
   (b) Initiating structure
   (c) Participative dimension
   (d) None of these
6. In which of the following leadership styles the star-shaped structure of the group is likely to emerge?
   (a) Free-rein leadership
   (b) Democratic leadership
   (c) Autocratic leadership
   (d) None of these
7. The statement that leaders are born and not made fits with the claim of
   (a) Greatman theory
   (b) Behavioural theory
   (c) Zeitgeist theory
   (d) None of these

8. According to Fiedler's model, which factor is not considered important for leader's behaviour?
   (a) Leader-member relations
   (b) Task structure
   (c) Leadership style assessment
   (d) Cooperation of leaders

9. Match List I with List II and answer on the basis of the codes provided.

List I	List II
A. Task-oriented leader	1. Creates concrete structural changes and fosters new practice
B. Transformational leader	2. Believes in exchange of views/activities between leaders and following
C. Transactional leader	3. High LPC score
D. Relation-oriented leader	4. Low LPC score

   Codes:
   (a) A B C D
       4 1 2 3
   (b) A B C D
       4 3 2 1
   (c) A B C D
       4 2 1 3
   (d) A B C D
       2 1 3 4

10. Read each of the following two statements—Assertion (A) and Reason (R) and indicate your answer using the codes below:
    Assertion (A): Relation-oriented leaders are more directive and more aggressive in their behaviour.
    Reason (R): Leaders often create concrete structural changes and foster new practice within the group.
    Codes:
    (a) Both A and R are true and R is the correct explanation of A.
    (b) Both A and R are true but R is not the correct explanation of A.
    (c) A is true but R is false.
    (d) A is false but R is true.

11. Leaders who are successful in exerting profound effects on their followers and who establish special types of relationships with their followers are usually called
    (a) Democratic leaders
    (b) Transformational leaders
    (c) Normative leaders
    (d) Consultative leaders

12. Path-goal theory of leadership does not emphasise
    (a) Directive leadership
    (b) Supportive leadership
    (c) Participative leadership
    (d) Free-rein leadership

13. A doctor influences patient because he (doctor) is perceived to have special knowledge. This illustrates the concept of
    (a) Reward power
    (b) Informational power
    (c) Expert power
    (d) Knowledge power

14. Which of the following factors has no impact upon determination of social power?
    (a) Resource
    (b) Dependency
    (c) Alternative
    (d) Message

15. Match List I with List II and answer on the basis of codes provided.

    List I
    A. Cognitive resource theory
    B. Situational leadership theory
    C. Path-goal theory
    D. Normative decision theory

    List II
    1. Hersey and Blanchard
    2. Robert House
    3. Fiedler and Gracia
    4. Vroom, Yetton and Jago

    Codes:

    (a) A B C D
        3 4 2 1
    (b) A B C D
        1 3 2 4
    (c) A B C D
        3 1 2 4
    (d) A B C D
        4 2 1 3

16. Which of the following two styles of leadership were identified in Ohio State leadership studies?
    (a) Authoritarian and democratic
    (b) Employees-centred and production-centred
    (c) Initiating structure and people-oriented
    (d) Initiating structure and consideration for relationship.

17. Researches conducted at the University of Michigan under the guidance of Rensis Likert revealed two important behavioural styles of leader. What were those two styles?
    (a) Person-centred leader behaviour and task-centered leader behaviour
    (b) Person-centred leader behaviour and initiating-structure behaviour
    (c) Task-centred leader behaviour and consideration behaviour
    (d) Initiating structure behaviour and consideration behaviour

18. A patient is deeply influenced by the advice of a doctor. This illustrates:
    (a) Informational power (b) Expert power
    (c) Legitimate power   (d) None of these

19. In famous Milgram's studies on obedience, the participants obeyed the experimenter. This illustrates
    (a) Coercive power   (b) Referent power
    (c) Reward power   (d) Informational power

20. In legitimate power which of the following norm(s) are evoked?
    (a) Norm of reciprocity   (b) Norms of social responsibility
    (c) Norm of oughtiness   (d) All these three norms

21. Which of the following best describes Hi-Hi hypothesis?
    (a) High consideration structure and high initiating structure
    (b) High autocratic structure and high participative structure
    (c) High directive structure and high permissive structure
    (d) High social structure and high emotional structure.

Answers

1. (d) 2. (d) 3. (b) 4. (d) 5. (b) 6. (c) 7. (a) 8. (d) 9. (a) 10. (d)
11. (b) 12. (d) 13. (c) 14. (d) 15. (c) 16. (d) 17. (a) 18. (b) 19. (d) 20. (d)
21. (a)

CHAPTER 12 INTERPERSONAL ATTRACTION AND RELATIONSHIP

1. A person is most likely to be attracted to someone who is _____ and with whom he had _____ contact.
   (a) Similar, much
   (b) Dissimilar, little
   (c) Similar, little
   (d) Dissimilar, much

2. Which does not seem to be related to increased attraction?
   (a) Similarity
   (b) Propinquity
   (c) Physical attractiveness
   (d) Complementarity

3. Which is best supported by the researches on interpersonal attraction?
   (a) Opposite attracts
   (b) Familiarity breeds contempt
   (c) Similarities attract
   (d) Absence makes one grow fonder

4. Match List I with List II and answer on the basis of the codes given.

List I	List II
A. Equity theory of interpersonal attraction	1. Adams
B. A-B-X model of interpersonal attraction	2. Thibaut and Kelley
C. Exchange theory of interpersonal attraction	3. Lotts and Lotts
D. Learning theory of interpersonal attraction	4. Newcomb

   Codes:
   (a) A B C D
       2 4 3 1
   (b) A B C D
       1 4 3 2
   (c) A B C D
       1 4 2 3
   (d) A B C D
       2 4 1 3

5. Read each of the following two statements—Assertion (A) and Reason (R) and indicate your answer using the codes below:
   Assertion (A): According to Newcomb's A-B-X model, symmetrical relationship between two persons exist only when the perceived bonds are positive.
   Reason (R): The model considers positive and negative bonds that exist among the actor, the other person and the attitudinal object.
   Codes:
   (a) Both A and R are true and R is the correct explanation of A.
   (b) Both A and R are true but R is not the correct explanation of A.
   (c) A is true but R is false.
   (d) A is false but R is true.

6. Which is/are causes of interpersonal attraction?
   (a) Proximity
   (b) Clothing colour
   (c) Attitude similarity
   (d) All of them

7. Following Rubin, which is not a component of love?
   (a) Intimacy
   (b) Attachment
   (c) Caring
   (d) Passion

8. Of the following physical features, which one increases physical attractiveness ratings more when possessed by a male than by a female?
   (a) Sex drive
   (b) Physical stamina
   (c) Sexual activity
   (d) Height of the body

9. Which is the complete form of love according to Sternberg?
    (a) Consummate love
    (b) Romantic love
    (c) Infatuated love
    (d) Compassionate love
10. Following Sternberg's triangular theory, which is not one of the central components of love?
    (a) Intimacy
    (b) Compatibility
    (c) Commitment
    (d) Passion
11. Which one of the following proposed the ABX theory of dyadic attraction?
    (a) Heider
    (b) Fiedler
    (c) Newcomb
    (d) Jones
12. The feeling of intimacy and attention we have for someone that are not accompanied by passion or physiological arousal is known as
    (a) Fatuous love
    (b) Infatuated love
    (c) Compassionate love
    (d) None of these
13. The mother-infant love relationship is an example of
    (a) Amae
    (b) Logical love
    (c) Self-less love
    (d) Child-playing love
14. A love felt by one person for another who does not feel love in return is known as
    (a) Empty love
    (b) Liking
    (c) Unrequited love
    (d) Fatuous love
15. Romantic relationship has been generally explained through different schemas by social psychologists. Which of the following schema is not included in those set of schemas?
    (a) Partner schema
    (b) Self schema
    (c) Relationship schema
    (d) Ideal schema
16. According to Byrne's law of attraction which one of the following is the correct statement?
    (a) Attraction towards the person is positively related to the proportion of attitude similarity associated with the person.
    (b) Attraction toward the person is positively related to the proportion of similarity in values associated with the person.
    (c) Attraction towards the person is positively related to the proportion of similarity in personal characteristics associated with the person.
    (d) Attraction towards the person is related to the degree of propinquity between that person and one who likes him or her.
17. Compassionate love is characterised by
    1. Intimacy
    2. Commitment
    3. Passion
    Codes:
    (a) 1 only
    (b) 1 and 2 only
    (c) 1 and 3 only
    (d) 1, 2 and 3
18. Interpersonal attraction includes
    1. Liking
    2. Disliking
    3. Praise

Codes:
(a) 1 and 3 only
(b) 1, 2 and 3
(c) 1 and 2 only
(d) 2 and 3 only

Answers

1. (a) 2. (d) 3. (c) 4. (c) 5. (d) 6. (d) 7. (d) 8. (b) 9. (a) 10. (d)
11. (c) 12. (c) 13. (a) 14. (c) 15. (d) 16. (a) 17. (b) 18. (c)

CHAPTER 13 SOCIAL INFLUENCE

1. Which is not a form of social influence?
   (a) Compliance
   (b) Obedience to authority
   (c) Conformity
   (d) Dominance

2. The technique of starting with a large request and then switching to a small one is known as
   (a) Foot-in-the-face
   (b) Face-in-the-door
   (c) Door-in-the-face
   (d) Foot-in-the-door

3. The foot-in-the-door technique becomes effective because it produces changes in
   (a) Attitude
   (b) Behaviour
   (c) Self-perception
   (d) Self-confidence

4. The door-in-the-face technique is found to be most effective if
   (a) The second request is unreasonable.
   (b) There is little time between the two requests.
   (c) Both requests are large.
   (d) The attempt of influence is recognised.

5. What percentage of the subjects in Milgram's original obedience experiment administered what they thought was the maximum of 450 volt shock?
   (a) 75%
   (b) 45%
   (c) 25%
   (d) 65%

6. A very attractive initial offer is made to get people to commit themselves to an action and subsequently, the terms are made less favourable. This statement fits well with
   (a) Door-in-the-face technique
   (b) Low ball technique
   (c) Foot-in-the-door technique
   (d) Fast-approaching deadline technique

7. Which is not a technique for enhancing compliance?
   (a) Self-promotion
   (b) Incidental similarity
   (c) Flattery
   (d) Lexicographic choice

8. We feel obliged to pay the person back in some way or the other for what he has done so far. This illustrates
   (a) Principle of consistency
   (b) Principle of liking
   (c) Principle of social validation
   (d) None of these

9. Which technique is based upon the principle of commitment or consistency?
   (a) Door-in-the-face technique
   (b) That's-not-all technique
   (c) Foot-in-the-door technique
   (d) Approaching deadline technique

10. The technique of starting with a small request, and then, when it is granted, placing a longer request is called
    (a) Foot-in-the-door technique
    (b) Door-in-the-face technique
    (c) That's-not-all technique
    (d) None of these
11. Robert Cialdini is well- known for his researches in the field of
    (a) Social attitude
    (b) Attribution
    (c) Social influence
    (d) Social norms.
12. The compliance does not honour the principle of
    (a) Consistency
    (b) Reciprocity
    (c) Scarcity
    (d) Consensual validation
13. Which of the following cannot be considered as a technique of ingratiation?
    (a) Self-promotion
    (b) Flattery
    (c) Incidental similarity
    (d) Friendship
14. When the initial offer of deal is changed to make it less attractive to the person after he has accepted it in order to gain compliance, it illustrates
    (a) Low-ball technique
    (b) Fast-approaching-deadline technique
    (c) Playing-hard-to-get technique
    (d) None of these.
15. Which of the following group of techniques is based upon the principle of reciprocity?
    (a) Door-in-the-face technique and foot-in-the-low technique
    (b) Foot-in-the-door technique and low-ball technique
    (c) Low-ball technique and fast-approaching-deadline technique
    (d) Door-in-the-face technique and that's – not-all technique

Answers

1. (d) 2. (c) 3. (c) 4. (b) 5. (d) 6. (b) 7. (d) 8. (d) 9. (c) 10. (a)
11. (c) 12. (d) 13. (d) 14. (a) 15. (d)

CHAPTER 14 AGGRESSION AND SOCIAL VIOLENCE

1. The concept of aggression as a basic human instinct forcing people to destructive acts was part of early _____ theory.
    (a) Humanistic
    (b) Instinct
    (c) Psychoanalytic
    (d) Behavioural
2. Which neurotransmitter seems to be most involved in aggression?
    (a) Dopamine
    (b) Testosterone
    (c) Serotonin
    (d) None of these
3. Which one has not been studied as a cause of aggressive behaviour?
    (a) Marijuana
    (b) Alcohol
    (c) Frustration
    (d) Pain
4. Which area of brain is most involved in aggressive behaviour?
    (a) Cerebellum
    (b) Cerebrum
    (c) Amygdala
    (d) Cortex

5. A women who strikes back at a rapist shows
   (a) Instrumental aggression
   (b) Hostile aggression
   (c) Prosocial aggression
   (d) Sanctioned aggression

6. A police officer shoots a terrorist. This is an example of
   (a) Sanctioned aggression
   (b) Prosocial aggression
   (c) Anti-social aggression
   (d) None of these

7. Match List I with List II and answer on the basis of codes given.

List I	List II
A. Disinhibition	1. Tendency to perceive aggressive motives in others' vague behaviours
B. Deindividuation	2. Overinflated view of own ability or accomplishments.
C. Narcissism	3. Reduction in social influences that usually restrain people from engaging in anti-social behaviour
D. Hostile attributional bias	4. Complete anonymity of person.

   Codes:
   (a) A B C D
       3 4 2 1
   (b) A B C D
       3 1 2 4
   (c) A B C D
       3 4 1 2
   (d) A B C D
       4 3 2 1

8. Match List I with List II and answer on the basis of the codes given.

List I	List II
1. Zuckerman	A. Sensation seeking
2. Bandura	B. Social learning theory
3. Anderson and Bushman	C. General aggression model
4. Dollard et al.	D. Frustration-aggression hypothesis

   Codes:
   (a) A B C D
       2 3 1 4
   (b) A B C D
       1 2 3 4
   (c) A B C D
       1 2 4 3
   (d) A B C D
       2 3 4 1

9. Read each of the following two statements—Assertion (A) and Reason (R) and indicate your answer using the codes given below:
   Assertion (A): Frustration always leads to aggression of some sort.
   Reason (R): Anger and cues are instrumental in manifestation of aggressive behaviour.
   Codes:
   (a) Both A and R are true and R is the correct explanation of A.
   (b) Both A and R are true but R is not the correct explanation of A.
   (c) A is true but R is false.
   (d) A is false but R is true.

10. According to GAM model of aggression, aggressive behaviour occurs by affecting some important processes. Which is not included in those processes?
    (a) Observation
    (b) Arousal
    (c) Affective stages
    (d) Cognition

11. Which of the following factors does not help in reducing aggression?
    (a) Retaliation
    (b) Catharsis
    (c) Cognitive intervention
    (d) Sensation seeking

12. Who will show more aggressive and violent behaviour?
    (a) Person born with XY chromosome
    (b) Person born with XYY chromosome
    (c) Person born with XX chromosome
    (d) Person born with XXY chromosome

13. Read each of the following two statements—Assertion (A) and Reason (R) and indicate your answer using the codes below:
    Assertion (A): Aggressive behaviour is the product of complex interaction between situational factors and personal traits.
    Reason (R): TASS model of aggression states that the situational factors activate the aggressive behaviour if such trait inclination exists within the person.
    Codes:
    (a) Both A and R are true and R is the correct explanation of A.
    (b) Both A and R are true but R is not the correct explanation of A.
    (c) A is true but R is false.
    (d) A is false but R is true.

14. 'Aggression is always the result of some sort of frustration' was claimed by
    (a) Dollard
    (b) Sears
    (c) Mower
    (d) All these three

15. According to General Aggression model, which of the following does not initiate aggressive behaviour?
    (a) Type B behavioural pattern
    (b) Progressive values
    (c) Skills for fighting
    (d) Personal injury

16. Which of the following does not encourage media violence?
    (a) Cognitive priming
    (b) Imitation
    (c) Desensitisation
    (d) Social contagion

17. Presence of weapon such as gun, pistol, etc increases aggression more than the presence of some neutral objects. This occurs mainly due to
    (a) Cognitive priming
    (b) Increased level of arousal
    (c) Frustration
    (d) Direct provocation

Answers

1. (c)   2. (b)   3. (a)   4. (c)   5. (d)   6. (b)   7. (a)   8. (b)   9. (d)   10. (a)
11. (d)   12. (b)   13. (a)   14. (d)   15. (a)   16. (d)   17. (a)

CHAPTER 15 PROSOCIAL BEHAVIOUR: ALTRUISTIC AND HELPING BEHAVIOUR

1. Which does not affect the bystander effect?
   - (a) Whether the situation is ambiguous
   - (b) Whether the bystander appears calm
   - (c) Personalities of the bystander
   - (d) Number of bystander

2. According to bystander effect, Mohan is more likely to get help if there is (are)
   - (a) Crowd of people standing nearby
   - (b) No other people standing nearby
   - (c) Several people standing nearby
   - (d) Only one other person standing nearby

3. In famous Latane and Darley experiment, subjects were most likely to help when
   - (a) They were with a friend
   - (b) There was one stranger in the room
   - (c) They were alone in the room
   - (d) They were four other people in the room

4. According to researches on prosocial behaviours, the best prediction of bystander intervention is
   - (a) Situational variable of the victim appearance
   - (b) Situational variable of the size of the group
   - (c) A person's score on the scale of altruism
   - (d) Individual's belief in religious value

5. Mohan helps Sohan in the hope of being favoured one day by Sohan in the coming election. This behaviour of Mohan is an example of
   - (a) Altruistic behaviour
   - (b) Egoistic behaviour
   - (c) Partial behaviour
   - (d) None of these

6. When none of the bystanders responds to an emergency situation in which the victim is lying and no one knows what is happening and each depends on the other to provide cues, it is referred to as:
   - (a) Diffusion of responsibility
   - (b) Implicit bystander effect
   - (c) Pluralistic ignorance
   - (d) Audience inhibition

7. According to arousal-cost-reward model, which statement is not correct?
   - (a) Becoming physiologically aroused by the distress of the victim.
   - (b) Labelling the arousal as personal distress in one-self.
   - (c) Calculating the benefits and costs of helping and not helping.
   - (d) Asking from friends/relatives about exact cost to be paid in helping.

8. Read each of the following two statements—Assertion (A) and Reason (R) and indicate your answer using the codes given below:
   Assertion (A): We should help all those who help us.
   Reason (R): People get what they deserve, that is, bad things to bad people and good things to good people.
   Codes:
   - (a) Both A and R are true and R is the correct explanation of A.
   - (b) Both A and R are true but R is not the correct explanation of A.
   - (c) A is true but R is false.
   - (d) A is false but R is true.

9. Match List I with List II and answer on the basis of the codes given.

List I	List II
A. Tit-for-tat effect	1. Strong faith in norms of reciprocity

B. Just world hypothesis
C. Bystander effect
D. Pluralistic ignorance

2. None of the potential helpers responding because no one knows what is happening
3. People get what they desire
4. Helping behaviour decreases with the increase in potential helper

Codes:

(a) A B C D
    1 3 2 4
(c) A B C D
    2 1 3 4

(b) A B C D
    1 3 4 2
(d) A B C D
    2 1 4 3

10. When helping behaviour is reducing simply because of a thinking that so many potential helpers might be present in the situation, this is known as
    (a) Diffusion of responsibility
    (b) Implicit bystander effect
    (c) Explicit bystander effect
    (d) Negative state relief hypothesis

11. The explanation provided by negative state relief hypothesis supports
    (a) Altruistic behaviour
    (b) Egoistic behaviour
    (c) Both of them
    (d) None of these

12. Match List I with List II and answer on the basis of the codes given below:

    List I
    A. Empathy altruism model
    B. Negative state relief model
    C. Competitive altruism approach
    D. Kin selection theory

    List II
    1. Motivated to help those who are biologically related than those who are not
    2. We help others in the hope of being helped long with other rewards
    3. Sometimes we help others for reducing our undesirable feelings
    4. We help the victim because victim really needs help

    Codes:

    (a) A B C D
        4 3 2 1
    (c) A B C D
        2 4 3 1

    (b) A B C D
        4 2 3 1
    (d) A B C D
        1 2 3 4

13. The opposite of altruism is:
    (a) Heroism
    (b) Egoism
    (c) Idealism
    (d) Egocentrism

14. Bad things happen to those who deserve misfortune and good things happen to those who are happy and lucky. Which of the following hypothesis supports this statement:
    (a) Just world hypothesis
    (b) Thought suppression hypothesis
    (c) Reciprocal altruism hypothesis
    (d) Hypothesis of external justification

15. According to Piliavin et al. (1981), decision to help is based on some considerations. Which of the following is not included in those considerations?
    (a) Becoming physiologically aroused by the victim
    (b) Labelling the arousal as personal distress in oneself
    (c) Calculating the costs and benefits of helping and not helping
    (d) Deciding about knowledge or skills to help.

Answers

1. (c)   **2.** (d)   **3.** (c)   **4.** (b)   **5.** (b)   **6.** (c)   **7.** (d)   **8.** (b)   **9.** (b)   **10.** (b)
11. (b)   **12.** (a)   **13.** (b)   **14.** (a)   **15.** (d)

CHAPTER 16   LANGUAGE AND COMMUNICATION

1. According to Gleitman, which is not the property of human language?
   - (a) Language is creative
   - (b) Language is referential
   - (c) Real-life language is unstructured
   - (d) Language is interpersonal
2. Which is not a component of language?
   - (a) Pragmatics
   - (b) Phonemes
   - (c) Morphemes
   - (d) Productiveness
3. Which of the following is 'do that' function of the language?
   - (a) Informative function
   - (b) Heuristic function
   - (c) Regulatory function
   - (d) Interpersonal function
4. Which cannot be considered as evidence for the role of critical period in language learning?
   - (a) First language learning
   - (b) Second language learning
   - (c) Recovery from aphasia
   - (d) Third language learning
5. Who is the supporter of nativist perspective of language development?
   - (a) Lenneberg
   - (b) Skinner
   - (c) Mowrer
   - (d) Whitehurst
6. Match List I with List II and answer on the basis of the codes given below:

List I	List II
A. Linguistic relativity hypothesis	1. A neurologically-based system that helps in processing and receiving language
B. Critical period	2. A pidgin language
C. Creole language	3. Both favourable and unfavourable experiment of life during a certain time frame having an impact upon later development
D. Language acquisition device	4. Thinking depends on language

   Codes:
   - (a) A B C D
         4   3   1   2
   - (b) A B C D
         4   1   2   3
   - (c) A B C D
         4   3   2   1
   - (d) A B C D
         2   1   3   4
7. Who championed the view that thinking determines the language?
   - (a) Vygotsky
   - (b) Piaget
   - (c) Sapir
   - (d) Lennberg

8. Till the age of 2 years, language and thinking develop independently, but with the advancement of age, language and thought become interdependent. This view is supported by
   (a) Piaget
   (b) Vygotsky
   (c) Harley
   (d) Yamada

9. Theory of mind first develops in which of the following periods?
   (a) 2.5 to 5 years old
   (b) 1.5 to 2.5 years old
   (c) 2.5 to 3.5 years old
   (d) 4.5 to 6.5 years old

10. Which is not a stage of reading acquisition according to Frith model?
    (a) Stage of orthographic
    (b) Stage of alphabetic
    (c) Stage of logographic
    (d) Stage of visual analysis

11. Which is not a characteristic of communication?
    (a) Communication is a dynamic process.
    (b) Communication is a reversible process.
    (c) Communication is a continuous process.
    (d) Communication is an interactive process.

12. A communication network that totally allows open communication among all members of the group is technically known as
    (a) Circle network
    (b) Chain network
    (c) Comcon network
    (d) None of these

13. When a person tries to communicate something through laughing and crying, he is using
    (a) Proximics
    (b) Paralanguage
    (c) Kinesics
    (d) None of these

14. Read each of the following two statements—Assertion (A) and Reason (R) and indicate your answer using the codes given below:

    Assertion (A): The use of standard speech is associated with high socio-economic status and with high power.
    Reason (R): Socioeconomic status always determines the quality of speech standard.

    Codes:
    (a) Both A and R are true and R is the correct explanation of A.
    (b) Both A and R are true but R is not the correct explanation of A.
    (c) A is true but R is false.
    (d) A is false but R is true.

15. According to encoder-decoder model of communication, the basic unit of communication is:
    (a) Message
    (b) Medium
    (c) Speaker
    (d) Listener

16. Perspective-taking model is based upon:
    (a) Role theory
    (b) Social learning theory
    (c) Symbolic interaction theory
    (d) Cognitive theory

17. Which of the following elements in context does not influence communication?
    (a) Norms
    (b) Representation of prior similar situations
    (c) Emotional arousal
    (d) Self-persuasion

18. A theory stating that concepts are universal and they influence the development of language is known as
    (a) Cognitive universalism
    (b) Linguistic universalism
    (c) Conceptual universalism
    (d) None of these

19. According to the researches of Mehrabian (1972), the relative contributions that verbal, vocal and facial channels make to overall liking by the listeners is
    (a) 55% facial, 38% vocal, 7% verbal
    (b) 50% facial, 40% vocal, 10% verbal
    (c) 55% facial, 40% vocal, 5% verbal
    (d) 50% facial, 37% vocal, 13% verbal
20. Which of the following communication network is more centralised?
    (a) Circle network
    (b) 'Y' shaped network
    (c) Chain network
    (d) Common network

Answers

1. (c) 2. (d) 3. (c) 4. (d) 5. (a) 6. (c) 7. (b) 8. (b) 9. (a) 10. (d)
11. (b) 12. (c) 13. (b) 14. (c) 15. (a) 16. (c) 17. (d) 18. (a) 19. (a) 20. (b)

CHAPTER 17   APPLICATIONS OF SOCIAL PSYCHOLOGY

1. A classroom style in which all students sit facing the teacher is called
    (a) Cluster style
    (b) Seminar style
    (c) Auditorium style
    (d) Face-to-face style
2. Which type of classroom climate encourages custodial attitude of teachers towards pupils?
    (a) Open classroom climate
    (b) Closed classroom climate
    (c) Both of these
    (d) None of these
3. Behaviour is a direct result of a behavioural intention. This statement is associated with
    (a) Reaction action model
    (b) Reason action model
    (c) Behaviour control theory
    (d) None of these
4. Social readjustment rating scale measures
    (a) Adjustment problems of the individual
    (b) Amount of stress in life of the individual
    (c) Amount of psychological distress only in the life of the individual
    (d) None of these
5. In which of the following a person experiences maximum stress during acculturation?
    (a) Integration
    (b) Assimilation
    (c) Separation
    (d) Marginalisation
6. When a student gets a very poor marks in Mathematics, and therefore, decides to replace it by Biology, he is using
    (a) Emotion-focused coping strategy
    (b) Problem-focused coping strategy
    (c) Seeking social support
    (d) None of these
7. The three C's, that is, commitment, challenge and control together constitute
    (a) Psychological hardiness
    (b) Psychological boldness
    (c) Psychological health
    (d) None of these

8. Which of the following does not belong to estimator variables of eyewitness identification?
   (a) Weapon focus
   (b) Memory distortion
   (c) Lineup biases
   (d) Retention interval and intervening information
9. When a police officer shows the potential perpetrators one at a time and asks the witness to identify whether the person is a real perpetrator, the procedure is called
   (a) Simultaneous lineups
   (b) Sequential lineups
   (c) Blank lineups
   (d) None of these
10. Match List I with List II and answer on the basis of the codes given.

    List I
    A. Deal
    B. Minimisation
    C. Regulatory focus theory
    D. Apprehension conflict theory

    List II
    1. Explicit offer of leniency in exchange for confession.
    2. Downplaying the significance of crime so that confession by the suspect may seem to be less serious.
    3. When performing in presence of others, the very realisation that others are also evaluating his performance.
    4. A strategy where for achieving the most desired states, a person concentrates some perspectives either positive or negative.

    Codes:
    (a) A B C D
        1 2 3 4
    (b) A B C D
        2 1 3 4
    (c) A B C D
        1 2 4 3
    (d) A B C D
        2 1 4 3

11. If a person loses his job, he may decide that it is not a major tragedy because he will soon get a better job. This illustrates the use of
    (a) Problem focus strategy
    (b) Emotion focus strategy
    (c) Seeking a social support
    (d) None of these.

Answers

1. (c) 2. (b) 3. (a) 4. (b) 5. (c) 6. (b) 7. (a) 8. (c) 9. (b) 10. (c)
11. (b)

GLOSSARY

A-B-X model: A model that involves the relationship of two persons and an attitude object. The model posits that the relationship between the persons and attitude object will strain to become symmetrical.

Action research: A type of applied research developed by Kurt Lewin in which the scientist collaborates with a group or organisation, which is experiencing difficulty, collects data that is interpreted and transformed into appropriate action, which is then evaluated by collecting further data.

Actor-observer effect: A tendency to attribute own behaviour mainly to situational causes, but the behaviour of others to internal or dispositional causes.

Additive principle: In impression formation, additive principle is an idea that pieces of information about a person are processed in terms of their evaluative implications and are then added together to form an overall impression.

Aggression cues: These refer to stimuli that are associated with the source of frustration and with aggressive behaviour. When paired with frustration, such cues may elicit aggression.

Aggression: It is the behaviour that is intended to inflict harm or injury on another person or object.

Altruism: This is unselfish desire for the welfare of other people.

Altruistic personality: A personality having dispositional variables like empathy, belief in just world, acceptance of social responsibility, internal locus of control and not being egocentric.

Ambivalent sexism: It is the mixture of benevolent attitude towards women and hostile attitudes.

Anchoring and adjustment heuristic: Such heuristic involves the tendency to use a number or value as a starting point to which the person subsequently makes adjustment.

Anger: It is intense emotional response of disliking which accompanies some types of aggression.

Antisocial aggression: This refers to aggressive acts such as rape or murder that commonly violate social norms.

Applied social psychology: As an applied science, the social psychology deals with those practices and social psychological researches done in the real-world settings that aim at understanding human social behaviour and providing appropriate solutions to the various important social problems.

Applying social psychology: Here, psychologists attempt to explain real-world social behaviour by using theories developed mainly from laboratory research.

Arbitrary frustration: This refers to thwarting that is perceived as unreasonable or unwarranted.

Attitude inoculation: It is exposing people to weak attacks upon their attitudes so that they would be able to refute when strong attack is done.

Attitude-to-behaviour process model: A model of how attitude guides behaviour that emphasises the influence of attitudes and stored knowledge regarding its appropriateness in a given situation. This, in turn, influences the overt behaviour.
Attribution theory: It is a theory describing how people explain the behaviour of others; for example, by attributing to external situations or to internal dispositions such as traits, attitudes, motives, etc.
Authoritarian personality: A personality type that is characterised by extreme conformity to conventional standards, exaggerated submission to authority, ethnocentrism and self-righteous hostility.
Autokinetic phenomenon: *Auto* means self and *kinetic* means movement. In social psychology, autokinetic phenomenon is the apparent movement of a stationary point of light in the darkness.
Availability heuristic: A heuristic in which the judgements are made on the basis of how easily some specific information can be brought to mind.
Averaging principle: In impression formation, averaging principle is an idea that the pieces of information about a person are processed in terms of their evaluative implications and are then averaged together to form an overall attitude.

Balance theory: This theory was proposed by Heider, which posits that we maintain consistency among our sentiment and relations. People are motivated to those with whom they are connected by physical proximity or other links. We like others with whom we agree and dislike those with whom we disagree.
Behaviour component: It is a component found in an attitude that consists of a person's tendencies to act towards the attitude object.
Behavioural confirmation: It is a type of self-fulfilling prophecy whereby people's social expectations lead them in such a way that cause others to confirm their expectations.
Benevolent sexism: This refers to positive attitudes and willingness to help women, who are perceived as virtuous and who embrace traditional women's roles.
Big five dimensions of personality: Big five dimensions of personality include basic dimensions of personality. These five dimensions are Extraversion or E, Agreeableness or A, Openness to experience or O, Neuroticism or N and Conscientiousness or C, which is commonly encoded as 'OCEAN' for better recall.
Black sheep effect: Such effect occurs when a member of the in-group behaves in a way that threatens the value of group identity.
Body language: This refers to the information transmitted about attitudes, emotions, etc. by the position, gesture, posture and movement of one's body.
Bogus pipeline: It is a procedure that befools people into disclosing their attitudes. Here, the participants are first convinced that a machine can use their psychological responses for measuring their private attitudes. Then, they are asked to predict the machine's reading, thus providing information about their attitudes.
Bona fide pipeline: It is a technique, which is used to measure subtle form of prejudice or attitude through priming where exposure to certain events primes information stored in memory making it easier to influence our on-going reactions.
Brainstorming: A technique for coming up with new and creative solutions to the problems. Here, the members of the group discuss the problem and generate as many different solutions as possible, withholding criticism until all possibilities have been presented.
Bystander effect: It is a type of special effect that states that when other people are present, it is less likely that any one person will engage in helping the stranger in distress. The diffusion of responsibility created by the presence of other people is one popular explanation for the effect.

Case history: It is the information about a particular person or event. Such information often has more persuasive impact on people's judgement than others.
Categorisation: It is a process by which we perceive people or other stimuli in groups or categories rather than perceiving each person as a distinct individual.

Category-based processing: It is a cognitive processing that is based upon the fact that the perceivers attend individuals mainly in terms of groups or social category to which they belong.

Catharsis hypothesis: It is a view that by expressing aggression, a person tends to reduce his or her aggressive roles.

Central route (to persuasion): It refers to attitude change that results from systematic processing of information presented in persuasive messages.

Coerced-complaint false confession: This refers to a confession by an individual, who is pressurised to confess a crime, but who privately believes that he or she is innocent.

Coerced-internalised false confession: This refers to a confession by an innocent person, who is pressurised to confess a crime and then comes to believe privately that he has actually committed the crime.

Cognitive component: It is a component of attitude that consists of person's beliefs, knowledge and fact about the object of the attitude.

Cognitive consistency: It is taken as the major determinant of attitude formation and change. Here, people exhibit tendency to seek consistency among their attitudes.

Cognitive dissonance: It is an internal state that results when the individuals notice inconsistency among two or more attitudes or between their behaviour and attitudes.

Cohesiveness: In group dynamics, cohesiveness refers to both positive and negative forces that cause members to remain in the group. In fact, cohesiveness is the characteristic of a group as a whole and generally, results from the degree of commitment of each individual to the group.

Collective guilt: It refers to an emotion that can be experienced when individuals are confronted with the harmful actions done by their in-group against an out-group. Such guilts are usually experienced when harmful actions are perceived as illegitimate.

Common knowledge effect: According to this, members of the group spend more time in discussing shared rather than unshared information.

Comparison level for alternatives: It is a level or standard that is used to evaluate the quality of our social relationships. Our comparison level for alternatives is our evaluation of one particular relationship against other relationships that are currently available.

Comparison level: This is a level or standard that we use to evaluate the quality of our social relationship. In fact, the comparison level of the person is the level of outcomes (benefits and costs) he expects.

Compassionate love: A practical type of love that emphasises trust, caring and tolerance of the partner's flaws. Such love generally develops slowly as the partners become interdependent.

Compliance: In compliance, an act is performed at the request of others.

Conformity: It is the voluntary performance of an act because others are doing it.

Conformation bias: It refers to tendency to pay attention to information that confirm the existing beliefs and ignore the information that disconfirms such beliefs.

Consideration: It is an important dimension of leader behaviour that makes an emphasis on establishing good relations with their subordinates and on being liked by them.

Consummate love: It is a type of love that combines intimacy, passion and commitment/decision.

Contact hypothesis: This hypothesis states that the increased contact between the members of various social groups can be effective in reducing prejudice against each other.

Correspondence bias (fundamental attribution error): Tendency on the part of the persons to explain others' behaviour as stemming from disposition even in the presence of clear situational evidences.

Counterfactual thinking: This refers to imagined alternative versions of actual event; these are people's 'what' or 'If only' thoughts about past or present consequences ('what might have been').

Culture of honour: This refers to the culture in which the most prevalent norms is that aggression is an appropriate response to insults to one's honour.

Culture: It depicts the shared beliefs, values, traditions and behaviour patterns of a particular group.

Deadline technique: A technique for enhancing compliance in which the target persons are told that they have only limited time to take advantage of some offer or concession.

Debriefing: It is a feature of research in which after the subjects' participation is over, the purposes and procedures of the research are explained to the subjects, their questions are answered and the scientific value of the research is also discussed.

Deception: A deception is said to occur in research when the participants are misinformed or misled about the study's methods and purposes.

Decision-making theories: According to decision-making theories, people calculate the costs and benefits of various behaviours and select the best behaviour in a logical way.

Dehumanisation: It is the process of taking away the personhood or human qualities of another person or group through one's actions. Dehumanising another person often facilitates aggression against that person.

Deindividuation: It is a psychological state characterised by reduced self-awareness and reduced social identity, brought by an external condition such as anonymity in a large crowd. The behavioural consequences of deindividuation depend on the norms of the situation, which can be either prosocial or antisocial.

Demand characteristics: These depict the aspects of the research study that make subjects more aware of their participation in the research, and thus, bias their behaviour. For example, subjects may try to avoid negative evaluation from the experimenter or may try to cooperate with the experimenter for substantiating the hypothesis.

Devil's advocate technique: It is a technique for improving the quality of group decision in which one member of the group disagrees with and criticises whatever plan or decision is under consideration.

Diffusion of responsibility: It is a process whereby the presence of other people makes each individual feel less responsible for causing events or solving problems. It tends to decrease the likelihood that a person will provide help to a stranger in distress.

Displaced aggression: It depicts aggression against someone, who is not the source of provocation. Such aggression occurs because the person, who does this, is unwilling to aggress against the initial source of provocation.

Dispositional attribution: This refers to perceiving the cause of a person's action as stemming from his or her disposition such as attitudes, ability or personality.

Dissonance: It is a state of aversive arousal that results when a person holds two beliefs that contradict each other.

Distraction-conflict theory: This theory posits that social facilitation stems from the conflict produced when individuals simultaneously pay attention to other persons and to the task being performed.

Distributive justice: This concept refers to people's judgement about whether they are receiving a fair share of available rewards or of any social relationship.

Door-in-the-face technique: It is a technique for compliance in which the person first makes a larger request and then after refusal, the person is more likely to agree with a second, real, smaller request.

Downward social comparison: This depicts the comparison of one's ability or trait with those of someone, who is perceived as worse off than oneself.

Drive theory of aggression: It is a theory of aggression that suggests that aggression stems from external conditions, which arouse motive to harm or injure others.

Drive theory of social facilitation: It is a theory that posits that mere presence of others arouses and tends to increase the likelihood to perform the dominant responses.

Dual-processing model: It is a model that states that a person can process information in a careful, systematic fashion or in a more rapid, efficient fashion. Different aspects of a person or situation predict which mode of processing a person will use.

Ego-involvement: In attitude change, it is the subjective linking of an attitude to strong ego needs that makes attitudes more emotionally-laden, and therefore, resistant to change.

Egoism: It is a motive to increase one's own welfare. The opposite is *altruism*, which aims to enhance another's welfare.

Elaboration-likelihood model: It is a theory of persuasion and attitude change in which the important variable is the amount of careful thought given to the arguments (elaboration or cognitive effort). With more careful processing, attitude change depends more on the central processing and less on peripheral processing.

Emotion-focused coping: It is a technique of coping with stress in which a person engages in activities that reduce or counter negative feelings produced by stress.

Empathic joy hypothesis: It is a hypothesis that states that prosocial behaviour is motivated by the positive feeling and emotion a helper anticipates experiencing as a result of having a beneficial impact on the life of the person being helped.

Empathy: This refers to the vicarious experience of another's feeling by putting oneself in another shoes.

Empathy-altruism hypothesis: This hypothesis states that prosocial behaviour is solely motivated by the desire to help someone in need and by the fact that it feels pleasant to help.

Entitativity: It refers to the extent to which a group is perceived as being a coherent entity.

Entrepreneurs: These are the persons, who recognise an opportunity for a new business and actually start it.

Equal-status contact: It refers to contact on an equal basis. For example, to reduce prejudice, inter-religion contact should be established between the persons equal in status.

Equity: It is a condition in which the outcomes people receive from a relationship are proportional to what they contribute to it.

Ethnocentric: It is the belief in the superiority of one's own ethnic and cultural group and having a corresponding disdain for all other groups.

Evaluation apprehension: This refers to a person's concern about how others evaluate him or her. It is often a concern about making a good impression in public.

Expectancy value theory: This theory states that decisions are based on the combination of two factors the value of the various possible outcomes of the decision and the likelihood or probability that each outcome will actually occur.

Expectation status theory: This theory states that the status of the person in the group may be affected by various diffused state characteristics such as age, wealth, ethnicity, etc.

Experimental realism: It is the extent to which an experiment absorbs and involves its participants.

External validity: The extent to which the results of an experiment can be generalised to real-life social situations and to the persons different from those participated in the study.

Eyewitness testimony: This refers to the evidences given by the persons who have witnessed a crime.

False consensus effect: It is a tendency to overestimate the commonality of one's abilities and one's desirable behaviours.

Fearful-avoidant attachment style: It is a style in which the person exhibits low self-esteem and low interpersonal trust. This is considered as the most insecure and the least adaptive attachment style.

Field research: This refers to a research done in natural field or real-life setting outside the laboratory.

Foot-in-the-door technique: It is a technique for gaining compliance in which the requester first makes a small request and then, when this is granted, proceeds to a larger real request.

Frustration: It is a mental condition resulting from blocking the goal-directed behaviour.

Frustration-aggression theory: This theory states that frustration is a very powerful determinant of aggression and aggression is always caused by frustration.

Fundamental attribution error: It is the tendency of observers to overestimate the causal importance of a person's dispositions and underestimate the importance of the situation when they explain the person's behaviour.

Gender role: It is a set of behaviour expectations or norms for males and females.

Gender stereotypes: These are the stereotypes regarding the traits possessed by males and females that distinguish the two genders from each other.

Gender: It includes characteristics that are socially influenced by which one defines male and female.

General aggression model: It is the theory of aggression, which suggests that aggression is triggered by a wide range of input variables, which tend to influence arousal, affective stages and cognitions.

Glass ceiling: These are the barriers created by attitudinal bias, which prevent able and efficient women from advancing to top-level positions.

Great person theory of leadership: This theory views leaders as possessing certain traits, which set them apart from other persons. Such traits are possessed by all leaders, no matter where and when they are born and lived.

Group polarisation: Sometimes, groups take more extreme decision than do the individuals alone. Polarisation may lead to a risky shift or a cautious shift depending on the initial views of the group members.

Group serving bias: It is the tendency of the members of the group to hold favourable attributions for the performance of members of we-group (internal attribution for success and external attribution for failure) and unfavourable attributions for the performance of members of they-group.

Group: A group comprises two or more people, who are interdependent and have at least the potential for mutual interaction.

Groupthink: It is the tendency of members of highly cohesive groups to assume that their decisions cannot be wrong, and an information contrary to these decisions should be ignored.

Halo effect: In this effect, the liked person is assumed to possess good qualities of many kinds, whether or not the observer has any correct information about those qualities.

Hardiness: It is a personality dimension having three C's—a sense of *commitment*, a positive response to *challenge* and an internal sense of *control* that seem to help people cope effectively with stress.

Health behaviour: This refers to the actions taken by a person, who is healthy, to enhance or maintain good health.

Health psychology: It is the branch of psychology that studies the relation between psychological variables and health.

Heuristic processing: It is the processing of information in a persuasive message, which involves mental shortcuts or rules of thumb for reducing complex problems into simple ones.

Heuristics: It refers to a shortcut for problem solving that reduces complex or vague information into more simple judgemental operations.

Hi–Hi hypothesis: This relates to the fact that successful leader requires a high level of both consideration and initiating structure.

Hostile aggression: It is a type of aggression, whose major objective is to inflict some kind of harm or injury on the victim.

Hostile attributional bias: It is a tendency to perceive hostile motives in others' actions, especially when these actions are vague.

Hostile sexism: In hostile sexism, there is a view that women are threat to men's superior position or there are some negative attitudes towards women, who challenge men's power or reject traditional gender roles.

Hypocrisy: This involves advocating some attitudes or behaviour and then acting in a way that is inconsistent with these attitudes or behaviours.

Hypothesis: It is a testable proposition that describes a relationship that may exist between at least two variables.

Illusion of control: This refers to the perception of uncontrollable events as subject to one's own control.

Illusion of transparency: It is the illusion that our concealed emotions may leak out and can be easily read out by others.

Illusory correlation: It is the perception of stranger association between two variables than really exists.
Implicit bystander effect: It is the tendency of people in group to help less to the stranger when simply thinking about being in a group.
Implicit personality theories: These include beliefs about what traits or characteristics tend to go together such as 'weak' goes with 'cowardly' and 'calm' goes with 'decisive'.
Implicit stereotypes: These are the stereotypes that are expressed outside the person's awareness and are also not under the control of the person.
Induced compliance: It is a compliance in which persons are somehow induced to say or do things inconsistent with their true attitudes.
Information overload: This refers to the instances in which the ability to process information is exceeded.
Informational influence: It is the conformity that occurs when the person accepts evidence about reality provided by others.
Informational social influence: It is the social influence that is based upon the desire to be correct or to possess accurate perceptions of the social world.
Informed consent: It is an ethical principle requiring that the participants should be told enough so that they may decide about their participation in the research.
Ingratiation: It involves the use of strategies such as flattery by which people seek to gain the favour of others.
In-group favouritism effect: It is the tendency to give more favourable evaluations and greater rewards to the members of in-group than to the members of out-groups.
In-group: It is the group to which a person belongs.
Initiating structure: It is an important dimension of leader's behaviour that motivates the leader for getting the job done anyhow.
Inoculation defense: This refers to a view in attitude change developed by McGuire that a person becomes more resistant to the effects of persuasive communications when he is exposed to weak counterarguments.
Instrumental aggression: In this type of aggression, the primary objective is not to harm the victim, but to attain some other goal, for example, depriving the victim of promoting to the next rank, or getting some benefit, etc.
Insufficient justification effect: It is the reduction in dissonance by internally justifying one's behaviour when external justification is insufficient.
Interdependent self-concept: It is a self-concept developed in terms of one's connections or relationship with others. Women generally are more expected to have an interdependent self-concept than men.
Internal validity: It is the extent to which a conclusion can be validly drawn from the research.
Interpersonal attraction: It is a person's attitude about another person that is expressed on a dimension ranging from strong liking to strong feelings of disliking.
Intimacy: It is the closeness felt by two people. In Sternberg's triangular model of love, it is an important element.

Jealousy: It is the emotion produced when a person perceives a real or potential attraction between his or her partner and a rival. As a result, there are feelings of anger, anxiety and depression.
Job satisfaction: This includes the attitudes held by the persons towards their job.
Just world phenomenon: It is the tendency of the people to believe that the world is just and the people, therefore, get what they deserve and deserve what they get.

Kin selection: It is a concept that evolution has selected altruism towards one's close relatives so that the survival of mutually shared genes may be enhanced.
Knowledge function: This function of attitude provides aid in interpreting new stimuli and influences our rapid responding to attitude-relevant information. This is also called *schematic function*.

Leadership: It is a process through which one member of the group influences the attainment of shared group goal more than any other member of the group.

Leading questions: These are the questions that are put by investigating officer and are designed to generate specific responses.

Learned helplessness: It refers to the hopelessness learned when a human or animal perceives no control over repeated undesirable and bad events.

Less-leads-to-more effect: It is an effect in which providing individuals to small rewards for engaging in counterattitudinal behaviour often produces high dissonance, and therefore, more attitude change than when they are provided larger rewards.

Locus of control: It is the extent to which a person perceives the outcomes as internally controllable by his own efforts and actions or as externally controlled by chance or some outside forces.

Low-ball technique: It is a technique for gaining compliance, where an offer is changed to make it less attractive to the target person, especially when the person has accepted it.

Media violence: This refers to depictions of violence in mass media such as television, radio, newspaper, etc.

Mere exposure effect: It is the effect by which simply being exposed frequently to a person or object tends to increase the liking for that person or object. Such repeated exposure most often enhances liking when our initial reaction is either positive or neutral.

Meta-analysis: It is a quantitative approach that summarises and synthesises the results of many earlier studies on a topic. Statistics are used to estimate the overall size of the effect.

Microexpressions: These are the fleeting facial expressions generally lasting for a few tenths of a second.

Middle-range theories: These theories account for major categories of behaviour, but do not attempt to cover all human behaviour in general. These theories might try to explain attribution, prosocial behaviour and aggression, but not all three at once.

Mimicry: It is the automatic tendency to imitate those with whom we frequently interact. Being mimicked is likely to increase one's prosocial tendencies.

Minimisation: It is an interrogation technique of legal system, where the investigator downplays the significance of crime to make a confession seem less serious.

Modelling: Modelling is said to occur when a person not only observes but actually copies the behaviour of a model. Modelling is also known as *imitation* or *observational learning*.

Mood-congruent memory: It is a tendency of people to remember material whose valence fits with their current mood state. For example, a person in bad mood is more likely to remember negative materials/ thoughts, etc.

Mood-dependent memory: It is an effect, which states that what a person remembers in a given mood may be determined, at least in part, by what he learned when he was previously in that mood.

Mundane realism: It is the extent to which an experiment is superficially similar to day-to-day situations.

Narcissism: It is a personality disposition mainly characterised by high self-esteem, feeling of superiority, sensitivity to criticism, need for admiration, lack of empathy and exploitative behaviour.

Natural selection: It is an evolutionary process by which nature selects traits that enable organisms to survive and reproduce in a particular environment.

Naturalistic fallacy: This refers to an error of defining what is good in terms of what is observable. For example, what is typical is normal and what is normal is good.

Need for affiliation: It is the basic motive to seek and maintain interpersonal relationship.

Need to belong: It refers to a need, which binds with others in relationships that provide positive interactions.

Negative-state relief mode: It is an idea that prosocial behaviour is done by the bystander's desire to reduce his or her own uncomfortable negative emotions.

Negativity bias: This refers to a sensitivity to negative information than to positive information.

Non-common effects: These are the effects produced by a particular cause that could not be produced by any other cause.
Non-verbal communication: It is the communication between two individuals that fails to involve content of spoken or written language. It depends on facial expression, gestures, postures, etc.
Non-zero-sum games: In these games, the outcomes need not sum to zero. With cooperation, both parties can win and with competition, both parties can lose. It is also called *mixed-motive situation*.
Norms of reciprocity: These social norms dictate that we should reward those who reward us.
Norms of social justice: These norms dictate fairness and the just distribution of resources. Such norms promote prosocial behaviour.
Norms of social responsibility: These social norms dictate that we should help all those who depend upon us. This may also contribute to emergence of prosocial behaviour.

Obedience: It is a form of social influence in which one person orders another to perform some action and that person simply comply.
Observational learning: It is a form of learning in which individuals learn or acquire new behaviour as a result of observing the behaviour of others.
Optimistic bias: It is a bias where the person is predisposed to expect something to happen well overall.
Out-group homogeneity: It is a tendency to perceive the members of out-group as all alike or similar than the members of the in-group.
Overconfidence phenomenon: It is the tendency to be more confident than correct, that is, to overestimate the accuracy of one's beliefs.
Overjustification effect: It is an effect that results from bribing people to do what they already like doing. As a consequence, they may then see their actions as externally controlled rather than intrinsically appealing.
Own-race bias: It is a bias exhibited by people when they more accurately recognise faces of their own race.

Paralanguage: This refers to the information conveyed by variations in speech due to pitch, loudness and hesitation.
Passionate love: It is the emotionally charged type of love that sometimes characterises the early stages of romantic relationship.
Peripheral route to persuasion: These are the aspects of communication, where people are influenced by incidental cues such as speaker's attractiveness.
Perseverance effect: It is a tendency for beliefs and schemas to remain unchanged, though some contradictory evidences have been provided.
Personal space: It refers to a buffer zone that a person likes to maintain around his bodies during social interaction. Its size depends on our familiarity with whoever is near us.
Personal-social identity continuum: Self can be categorised in two distinct ways, that is, at personal level and at social identity level. At personal level, the self can be thought of as a unique individual, whereas at the social identity level, the self is considered as a member of the group.
Persuasion: It is a process by which a message induces change in beliefs, attitudes or behaviours.
Planning fallacy: It is a tendency to do optimistic prediction concerning what time a given task will take for completion.
Pluralistic ignorance: It is a tendency of the bystanders in an emergency situation to depend on what other bystanders do and say, although the reality is that none of the bystander is sure about what is happening or what to do about it.
Positive illusion: It depicts mild false positive self-enhancing perceptions of one's personal qualities.
Possible selves: These are the schemas that a person holds concerning what they want to become in future.
Prejudice: It is usually a negative attitude towards the members of a social group.
Pretrial publicity: This involves media coverage about criminal investigations for a particular trial. Such publicity may influence the judgement to be delivered by the judges.

Primacy: It is a tendency to use an initial impression to organise and interpret the subsequent event.
Priming effect: It is a tendency of current thoughts about materials/events to influence the interpretation of subsequent information.
Prisoner's dilemma: It is a laboratory game used by social psychologists in study of cooperation and competition. The game provides the fundamental dilemma of whether to compete with the hope of attaining large rewards at the expense of other person or to cooperate with the hope of receiving lesser personal rewards, but greater joint rewards.
Problem-focused coping: It is a coping strategy in which attempt is made to cope with stress by altering the cause of stress.
Prosocial aggression: This involves aggressive acts that support the accepted social norms such as a woman slapping her rapist.
Prosocial behaviour: It is the behaviour that helps or is intended to provide help to others regardless of helper's motives.
Prototype: It is a schema that is defined by the specific features of a particular type of person or situation such as librarian or marriage party.
Proximity: This refers to physical closeness between two persons in terms of where they live, where they work and where they sit in the office/classroom.
Punishment: It is a method in which aversive consequences are delivered to the person after he has engaged in specific actions.

Random assignment: It involves placing subjects in experimental conditions in a manner that guarantees that assignment is made entirely by chance such as by using random numbers table, etc.
Rape: This is forced sexual activity without the consent of the partner.
Reactance theory: This theory refers to Brehm's idea that a person attempts to maintain his freedom of action. When somehow this freedom is threatened, he does whatever he can to restore it such as by refusing to comply with a request.
Realistic group conflict theory: This theory states that prejudice arises from competition between the groups or from real conflicts of interest between the groups and the frustration produced by those conflicts.
Reasoned action model: This model explains the link between attitude and behaviour displayed by people. The model assumes that the behaviour is ultimately the result of behavioural intentions, which are the end product of an interpretation of attitudes towards specific behaviours, subjective perception of norms regarding specific behaviour and the perceived amount of control that a person has over specific behaviour. It is also known as *theory of planned behaviour*.
Recency effect: According to this, the information presented last sometimes has the most influence upon the person.
Reflected appraisal: It is the self-evaluation based on the perceptions and evaluation of others.
Relative deprivation: This refers to the perception that a person is less well off than the others to whom he compares himself.
Representative heuristic: According to this, sometimes, despite contrary odds, a person presumes that something or someone belongs to a particular group if representing a typical number.
Risky shift: After taking part in a group discussion, people are sometimes willing to support riskier decisions than they were holding before the group discussion. In fact, this is part of the process of group polarisation, which can lead to either riskier or more cautious decisions, depending on the initial views of group members.
Role: It is a set of responsibilities that define how people in a given social position ought to behave.

Sanctioned aggression: This type of aggression is permissible by the norms of the individual's social groups.
Schema: It is an organised cognitive framework developed through experience and it affects the processing of new social information.

Selective altruism: When a large group of individuals is in need and only one or two selected individuals are helped, then it is said to be selected altruism.
Self-efficacy: It is the belief that one can achieve a goal as a result of one' own behaviour and planning.
Self-esteem: It is the self-evaluation made by the person. It includes one's attitude towards oneself along a positive-negative dimension.
Self-evaluation maintenance model: The model points out that for keeping a positive view of the personal self, a person distance himself from all those, who perform better and move closer to others, who perform worse. By doing so, he tends to protect self-esteem of the person.
Self-fulfilling prophecy: It refers to a belief that, in a sense, itself comes true.
Self-monitoring: It is the monitoring by people of their own behaviour in response to others' expectancies. High self-monitors are effective not only in monitoring their behaviour but also in adjusting their actions according to others' expectations.
Self-serving bias: It is a bias or tendency where the person attributes positive outcomes to internal causes (such as one's own traits, abilities etc.) and negative outcomes to external causes (chance, difficulty level of the task).
Sexism: It is a prejudice in which men typically show negative responses towards women.
Shifting standard: Here, a person uses one group as the standard, but shift to another group as comparison standard when judging the members of different group.
Show up: It is a police line up in which specific suspect is presented to an eyewitness, who must determine whether that person is the perpetrator.
Similarity-dissimilarity effect: It is an effect which states that people respond favourably to indications that another person is similar to themselves and unfavourably to indications that another person is dissimilar from themselves.
Simultaneous line up: It is a police line up in which several potential suspects are shown at a time and the witness is asked to identify the perpetrator.
Sleeper effect: This refers to the delayed attitude changes that are not immediately perceivable after exposure to the communication.
Slime effect: It is a tendency to form negative impression of others, who give regards to the superiors, but who treat subordinates with disdain.
Social cognition: This refers to the way in which people interpret, analyse, remember and use information about the social world.
Social comparison theory: This theory was proposed by Festinger for evaluating themselves. In the absence of objective non-social criteria, people evaluate themselves by comparing themselves with the other people. Implicit in this theory is that individuals tend to choose those with similar abilities and attitudes as comparison group.
Social density: This refers to the objective number of people in a given space such as the number of person residing in dormitory room.
Social dilemma: It is a situation in which the short-term choice that is most rewarding for an individual will ultimately lead to negative outcomes for all concerned.
Social exchange theory: This theory analyses the interaction between people in terms of outcomes (rewards minus cost), which the persons exchange with each other.
Social facilitation: It is a tendency of persons to perform better on simple task in the presence of others.
Social identity: In the study of self, social identity is that part of the person or individual's self-concept that derives from his or her membership in social group with the value and emotional significance attached to his membership.
Social impact theory: In this theory, either positive or negative influence of an audience on a target individual depends on three factors—number of observers, strength of audience and immediacy of audience in time or space.

Social influence: This involves efforts by one or more individuals for changing attitudes, beliefs, perceptions or behaviours of the target person.

Social learning theory: This theory emphasises that a person learns social behaviour by observing and imitating and by being rewarded and punished.

Social loafing: It is a reduced motivation and effort to work when individuals work collectively in a group as compared to when they work individually.

Social norms: These refer to rules in a social group concerning what actions and attitudes are appropriate.

Social perception: It is a process through which the person seeks to understand and know the other persons.

Social psychology: It is the branch of psychology that studies any or all aspects of human behaviour that involves persons and their relationship with other persons or groups, society as a whole.

Social responsibility norms: These norms dictate that people will provide help to those who are dependent on them.

Social roles: It is a set of social norms about how a person in a particular social position is expected to behave.

Social status: It is a person's rank in a group based on characteristics such as age, gender or position in a business.

Social support: This is a means of coping with stress, where a person draws on the support of emotional and task resources.

Source monitoring: It is a process of identifying the source of a piece of information stored in memory. According to this theory, eyewitnesses sometimes tend to include post-event information in their descriptions of any event simply because they do not correctly identify the source of that information.

Spotlight effect: This involves a belief that others are paying more attention to one's appearance and behaviour than they really are.

Stereotype threat: The threat that targets of stereotypes feel in situations in which stereotype is salient. This threat can harm their performance in the ways consistent with the stereotype.

Stereotypes: These are the beliefs about the typical characteristics of members of a group or social category.

Stress: It is a process in which a person appraises environmental events as harmful or threatening and responds to that appraisal with physiological, emotional, cognitive and behavioural changes.

Stressful life event: Any event in a person's life that requires him to make changes; negative, ambiguous and uncontrollable events are most likely to be perceived as stressful.

Subliminal conditioning: It is the classical conditioning of attitudes by exposure to stimuli that are below individual's threshold of conscious awareness.

Superordinate goals: These are the goals that can be attained by cooperation among many individuals. For example, peace in any group is an example of superordinate goal.

System variables: These refer to a set of factors that affect eyewitness identification. Such factors are under the direct control of criminal justice. Line up construction is an example of system variable.

Systematic processing: This refers to a very careful scrutiny of the arguments in persuasive communication that gives argument strength, induces counterarguing and makes attitude change more enduring.

Task leadership: A task leader is one who directs and organises the group in carrying out specific task.

Terror management theory: Terror management theory is one which suggests ways that a person attempts to deal with threat to the self when his own mortality is salient.

That's-not-all technique: It is a technique for gaining compliance in which the influencer first offers one deal and subsequently, while the person is considering this possibility, improves the offer.

Theory of planned behaviour: This theory is the extension of theory of reasoned action. It suggests that besides certain attitudes towards the given behaviour and subjective norms about it, people also consider their ability to perform the behaviour.

Third-person effect: Such effect is said to occur when the influence of media exposure on others' attitudes and behaviours is overestimated and the influence on self is somehow underestimated.

Transactional leader: It is a leader, who prefers to direct the members of the group by reminding them for desired behaviour and by taking action for correcting mistakes of the members.

Transformational leader: It is also known as *charismatic leader*. Such leader stimulates others to transcend their own needs and interests for a common goal. This type of leader can continue to the full range from most horrific (that is, Adolf Hitler) to the most progressive situation (that is, Nelson Mandela).

Transsexual: This refers to an individual, whose psychological gender identity tends to differ from his biological sex. For example, someone who is anatomically a female, but believes that he is really a male trapped in a female body.

Triangular theory of love: This theory makes use of Sternberg's theory of love that consists of three basic components—intimacy, passion and decision/commitment.

Trivialisation: It is a technique through which dissonance is reduced, since the attitudes or behaviours that are inconsistent with each other are cognitively reduced.

Type A behaviour pattern: It is a personality pattern that is characterised by high levels of the sense of competitiveness, time urgency and hostility.

Type B behaviour pattern: It is a personality pattern characterised by the absence of those characteristics that are associated with Type A behaviour pattern.

Typicality effect: It is an effect, where the person behaves towards an out-group member who is seen as the most typical of that group in ways consistent with one's stereotypes about the out-group.

Ultimate attribution error: It is a tendency to make more favourable attributions to the members of in-group than about the members of out-group.

Unrequited love: It is a condition in which A loves B, but B does not love A in return.

Upward social comparison: It is the comparison of one's traits or abilities with those who are better off than oneself.

Value analysis: It is a category of content analysis that focuses on the tabulation of the frequency with which a particular value is expressed in a message.

Vicarious learning: It involves learing by observing or behaviour or action.

Voluntary false confession: When a person willingly confesses a crime that he or she had not committed, then it is said to be voluntary false confession.

Weapon focus effect: It is a special kind of phenomenon in which eyewitnesses remember more information about the weapon used in crime rather than about the criminal, who was holding the weapon.

Within-group comparison: It is a comparison that is made between the target and the other members of the same class or category only.

Working self-concept: It involves the aspect of the self that is salient in particular situational context.

Workplace aggression: This refers to any type of behaviour through which a person seeks to harm his colleagues at workplace.

Yerkes–Dodson law: The law generalises that task difficulty and arousal interact such that on difficult tasks, the performance is improved by low levels of arousal but on easy tasks, high arousal level facilitates performance relative to the low levels.

REFERENCES

Abelson, R.P. (1968), *Simulation of social behaviour*, In G. Lindzey and E. Aronson (Eds.), *The Handbook of Social Psychology*, 2nd edn., Vol. 2, Reading, Mass: Addison-Wesley.
Abelson, R.P. (1981), The psychological status of the script concept, *American Psychologist*, **36**: 715–729.
Abrams, D., Wetherell, M., and Cocharne, S. (1990), Knowing what to think by knowing who you are, self–categorization and the nature of norm formation conformity and group polarization, *British Journal of Psychology*, **29**: 97–119.
Abramson, L.Y. and Martin, D.J. (1981), Depression and the causal inference process, In J.M. Harvey, W. Ickes, and R.F. Kidd (Eds.), *New Directions in Attribution Research*, Vol. 3, Hillsdale, NJ: Erlbaum.
Acharya, B. (1997), Role of literacy environment in children's acquisition of meta-language, literacy and meta-representation, In G. Misra (Ed.), *Psychology in India*, 5th ICSSR Survey, Delhi: Longman/Pearson.
Ackil, J.K. and Zaragoza, M.S. (1998), Memorial consequences of forced confabulation: Age differences in susceptibility to fake memories, *Developmental Psychology*, **34**: 1358–1372.
Adair, J.G. (1973), *The Human Subject: The Social Psychology of the Psychological Experiment*, Boston: Little Brown.
Adair, J.G., Dushenko, T.W., and Lindsay, R.C.L. (1985), Ethical regulations and their impact on research practice, *American Psychologists*, **40**: 59–72.
Adams, J.S. (1965), Inequity in social exchange, In L. Berkowitz (Ed.), *Advances in Experimental Social Psychology*, **2**: 267–229, NY: Academic Press.
Adams, J.S. (1983), Towards an understanding of in-equity, *Journal of Abnormal and Social Psychology*, **69**: 19–25.
Adelman, R. and Verbrugge, L. (2000), Death makes news: The social impact of disease on newspaper coverage, *Journal of Health and Social Behaviour*, **41**: 347–367.
Adinarayan, S.P. (1941), A research in colour prejudice, *British Journal of Psychology,* **31**: 217–229.
Adinarayan, S.P. (1953), Before and after independence – A study of racial and communal attitudes in India, *British Journal of Psychology,* **44**: 108–115.
Adinarayan, S.P. (1957), A study of racial attitudes in India, *Journal of Social Psychology*, **45**: 211–216.
Adinarayan, S.P. (1958), Case in India: A psychological approach, *Religion and Society*, **5**.
Adinarayan, S.P. (1964), *The Case for Colour*, Bombay: Asia Publishing House.
Adler, N. and Matthews, K. (1994), Why some people are sick and some stay well?, *Annual Review of Psychology*, **45**: 229–259.

Adorno, T.W., Frenkel-Brunswik, E., Levinson, D.J., and Sanford, R.N. (1950), *The Authoritarian Personality*, NY: Harper.
Agarwal, A.K. and Kumar, R. (1996), Awareness of AIDS among children in Haryana, *Indian Journal of Public Health*, **40**: 38–45.
Agrawal, M. and Dalal, A.K. (1994), Patients in Indian hospitals: Environmental stresses and affective reactions, *The Indian Journal of Social Work*, **55**: 41–46.
Agrawal, R. and Misra, G. (1986), A factor analytic study of achievement goals and means: An Indian view, *International Journal of Psychology*, **21**: 717–731.
Ahluwalia, S.P. and Deo, S.A. (1975), Study of relationship between socio-economic status and academic achievement of high school students, *Journal of Educational Research and Extension*, **12**: 1–5.
Ahmed, S.M.S. (1979), Helping behaviour as predicated by diffusion of responsibility, exchange theory and transitional sex norms, *Journal of Social Psychology*, **74**: 939–954.
Aiello, J.R. and Douthitt, E.A. (2001), Social facilitation from triplett to electronic performance monitoring, *Group Dynamics: Theory, Research and Practice*, **5**: 163–180.
Ajzen, I. (1989), Attitude structure and behaviour, In A.R. Pratkanis, S.J. Breckler and A.G. Greenwood (Eds.), *Attitude, Structure and Function*, Hillsdale, N.J.L: Erlbaum.
Ajzen, J. and Fishbein, M. (1980), *Understanding Attitudes and Predicting Social Behaviour*, Upper Saddle River, NJ: Erlbaum.
Albert, S. and Dabbs, J.M., Jr. (1970), Physical distance and persuasion, *Journal of Personality and Social Psychology*, **15**: 265–270.
Albrecht, S.L., Thomas, D.L., and Chadwick, B.A. (1980), *Social Psychology*, NJ: Prentice-Hall.
Alcock, J.E. (1978), A cross-cultural study of bargaining behaviour. In J. Pandey's (Ed.), *Psychology in India*, Vol. 2 (3rd ICSSR Survey) New Delhi: Sage Publications.
Aldag, R.J. and Fuller, S.F. (1993), Beyond fiasco: A reappraisal of the groupthink phenomenon and a new model of group decision processes, *Psychological Bulletin*, **113**: 533–552.
Alderfer, C.P. (1969), An empirical test of a new theory of human needs, *Organizational Behaviour and Human Performance*, **4**: 142–175.
Aligne, C.A., Auinger, P., Byrd, R.S., and Weitzman, M. (2000), Risk factors for pediatric asthma contributions of poverty, race and urban residence, *American Journal of Respiratory Critical Care Medicine*, **162**(3): 837–877.
Alkire, A.A., Collum, H.E., Keswan, J., and Love, L. (1968), Information exchange and accuracy of verbal communication under social power conditions, *Journal of Personality and Social Psychology*, **9**: 301–308.
Allen, K. (2003), Are pets a healthy pleasure? The influence of pets on blood pressure, *Current Directions in Cognitive Science*, **12**: 236–239.
Allen, K., Shykoff, B.E., and Izzo, J.L. (2001), Pet ownership but not ACE inhibitor therapy, blunts home blood pressure responses to mental stress, *Hypertension*, **38**: 815–820.
Allen, V.L. (1965), Situational factors in conformity, In L. Berkowitz (Ed.), *Advances in Experimental Social Psychology*, **8**: 133–175, NY: Academic Press.
Allen, V.L. and Levine, J.M. (1971), Social pressure and personal influence, *Journal of Experimental Social Psychology*, **7**: 122–124.
Allen, V.L. and Van de Vliert E. (1982), A role theoretical perspective on transitional process, In V.L. Allen and E. Van de Vliert (Eds.), *Role Transitions: Exploration and Explanations*, NY: Plenum.
Allen, V.L. and Wilder, D.A. (1979), Group categorization and attribution of brief similarity, *Small Group Behaviour*, **10**: 73–80.
Alloy, L.B. and Tabachnik, N. (1984), Assessment of covariation by humans and animals: The joint influence of prior expectations and current situational information, *Psychological Review*, **91**: 112–149.
Allport, F.H. (1920), The influence of the group upon association and thought, *Journal of Experimental Psychology*, **5**: 159–182.
Allport, F.H. (1924), *Social Psychology*, Boston: Houghton Mifflin.

Allport, G.W. (1935), Attitudes, In C. Murchinson (Ed.), *A Handbook of Social Psychology*, Worcaste Mass: Clark University Press.
Allport, G.W. (1954), *The Nature of Prejudice*, Reading: Addison–Wesley.
Allport, G.W. (1965), *The Nature of Prejudice*, Cambridge, M.A.: Addison-Wesley.
Allport, G.W. (1968), The historical background of modern social psychology, In G. Lindzey and E. Aronson (Eds.), *The Handbook of Social Psychology*, 2nd edn., Vol. I, Reading, Mass: Addison-Wesley.
Allport, G.W. (1985*)*, The historical background of social psychology, In G. Lindzey and E. Aronson (Eds.), *The Handbook of Social Psychology*, 3rd edn., Vol. I, NY: Random House.
Alpert, B., Field, T., Goldstein, S., and Perry, S. (1990), Aerobics enhances cardiovascular fitness and agility in preschoolers, *Health Psychology*, **9**: 48–56.
Altman, L. and Haythorn, W.W. (1965), Interpersonal exchange in isolation, *Sociometry*, **28**: 411–426.
Amato, P.R. (1983), Helping behaviour in urban and rural environment: Field studies based on taxonomic organization of helping episodes, *Journal of Personality and Social Psychology*, **45**: 947–961.
Amato, P.R. (1986), Emotional arousal and helping behaviour in real-life emergency, *Journal of Applied Social Psychology*, **16**: 633–641.
American Psychological Association (2002), *Ethical Principles of Psychologists and Code of Conduct*, p. 32, Washington, DC: APA.
Anant, S.S. (1970), Caste prejudices and its perception by Harijans, *Journal of Social Psychology,* **82**: 271–278.
Anderson, C. and Dill, K. (2000), Video games and aggressive thoughts, feelings and behaviour in the laboratory and in life, *Journal of Personality and Social Psychology*, **78**: 772–790.
Anderson, C.A. (1989), Temperature and aggression: Effects on quarterly, yearly and city rates of violent and nonviolent crime, *Journal of Personality and Social Psychology*, **52**: 1161–1173.
Anderson, C.A. (1997), Effects of violent movies and traits hostility on hostile feelings and aggressive thoughts, *Aggressive Behaviour*, **23**: 161–178.
Anderson, C.A. and Bushman, B.J. (2001), Effects of violent video games on aggressive behaviour, aggressive cognition, aggressive affect, psychological arousal and prosocial behaviour: A meta-analytic review of the scientific literature, *Psychological Science*, **12**: 353–359
Anderson, C.A. and Bushman, B.J. (2002a), Human aggression, *Annual Review of Psychology*, **53**: 27–57.
Anderson, C.A. and Bushman, B.J. (2002b), Media violence and the American public revisited, *American Psychologist*, **57**: 448–450.
Anderson, C.A. and Huesmann, L.R. (2003), Human aggression: A social cognitive view, In M.A. Hogg and J. Cooper (Eds.), *The Sage Handbook of Social Psychology*, London: Sage.
Anderson, C.A., Benjamin, A.J.J., and Bartholow, B.D. (1998), Does the gun pull the trigger? Automatic priming effects of weapon pictures and weapon names, *Psychological Science*, **9**: 308–314.
Anderson, C.A., Bushman, B.J., and Groom, R.W. (1997), Hot years and serious deadly assault: Empirical tests of the heat hypothesis, *Journal of Personality and Social Psychology*, **73**: 1213–1223.
Anderson, C.A., Carnagey, N.L., and Eubanks, J. (2003), Exposure to violent media: The effects of songs with violent lyrics on aggressive thoughts and feelings, *Journal of Personality and Social Psychology*, **84**: 960–971.
Anderson, M.H. (1962), Application of an additive model of impression formation, *Science*, **138**: 817–818.
Anderson, N.H. (1968), Likeableness ratings of 555 personality traits words, *Journal of Personality and Social Psychology*, **9**: 272–297.
Anderson, N.H. (1974), Cognitive algebra: Integration theory applied to social attribution, In L. Berkowitz (Ed.), *Advances in Experimental Social Psychology*, **63**: 346–350, NY: Academic Press.
Anderson, N.H. (1981), *Foundations of Information Integration Theory*, NY: Academic Press.
Anderson, S.M. and Klatzky, R.L. (1987), Traits and social stereotypes: Levels of categorization in person perception, *Journal of Personality and Social Psychology*, **53**: 235–246.
Andrews, C.R. and Debus, R.L. (1978), Persistence and causal perception of failure: Modifying cognitive attributions, *Journal of Educational Psychology*, **70**: 154–166.

Anschuetz, B.L. (1999), The high cost of caring: Coping with workplace stress, *The Journal Newsletter of the Ontario Association of Children's Aid Societies*, **43**(3).

Archer, D. and Akert, R. (1977), Words and everything else: Verbal and nonverbal cues in social interpretation, *Journal of Personality and Social Psychology*, **35**: 443–449.

Archer, J. (2004), Sex differences in aggression in real-world settings: A meta-analytic review, *Review of General Psychology*, **8**: 291–322.

Argyle, M. and Dean, J. (1965), Eye contact, distance and affiliation, *Sociometry*, **28**: 289–304.

Aries, E. (1977), Male-female interpersonal styles in all males, all females and mixed groups, In A. Sargent (Ed.), *Beyond Sex Roles*, 292–299, Boulder Co: West.

Aries, E. (1996), *Men and Women in Interaction: Reconsidering the Differences*, NY: Oxford University Press.

Aron, A. and Westbay, L. (1996), Dimensions of prototype of love. *Journal of Personality and Social Psychology*, **70**: 535–551.

Aron, A., Aron, E.M., and Allen, J. (1998), Motivations for unreciprocated love, *Personality and Social Psychology Bulletin*, **24**: 787–796.

Aronfreed, J. and Reber, A. (1965), Internalized behaviour suppression and the timing of social punishment, *Journal of Personality and Social Psychology*, **1**: 3–16.

Aronoff, J., Woike, B.A., and Hyman, L.M. (1992), Which are the stimuli in facial displays of anger and happiness? Configurational bases of emotion recognition, *Journal of Personality and Social Psychology*, **62**: 1050–1066.

Aronson, E. and Mills, J. (1959), The effects of severity of initiation on liking for a group, *Journal of Abnormal and Social Psychology*, **59**: 177–181.

Aronson, E., Brewer, M., and Carlsmith, J.M. (1985), Experimentation in social psychology, In G. Lindzey and E. Aronson (Eds.), *The Handbook of Social Psychology*, Vol. I, Hillsdale: Erlbaum.

Aronson, E., Turner, J.A., and Carlsmith, J.M. (1963), Communicator credibility and communicator discrepancy as determinants of opinion change, *Journal of Abnormal and Social Psychology*, **67**: 31–36.

Aronson, J., Lustina, M.J., Good, C., Keough, K., Steele, C.M., and Brown, J. (1999), When white men cannot do math: Necessary and sufficient factors in stereotype threat, *Journal of Experimental Social Psychology*, **35**: 29–46.

Arora, P. and Sinha, P. (1998), A study of the relationship between perception of residential crowding, personality characteristics and need patterns among adolescents, *Social Science International*, **14**: 46–59.

Asch, S. (1951), Effects of group pressure upon the modification and distortion of judgement, In H. Guetzkow (Ed.), *Groups, Leadership and Men*, Pittsburgh: Carnegie Press.

Asch, S. (1955), Opinions and social pressure, *Scientific American*, **11**: 32.

Asch, S.E. (1946), Forming impressions of personality, *Journal of Abnormal and Social Psychology*, **41**: 258–290.

Asch, S.E. (1952), *Social Psychology*, Englewood Cliffs, NJ: Prentice-Hall.

Asch, S.E. (1956), Studies of independence and conformity: A minority of one against a unanimous majority, *Psychological Monographs*, **70**: 1–70.

Asch, S.E. and Zukier, H. (1984), Thinking about persons, *Journal of Personality and Social Psychology*, **46**: 1230–1240.

Ashour, A.S. (1973), Further discussion of Fiedler's contingency model of leadership effectiveness: An evaluation, *Organisational Behaviour and Human Performance*, **9**: 369–376.

Ashton, N.L. and Severy, L.J. (1976), Arousal and costs in bystander intervention, *Personality and Social Psychology Bulletin*, **2**: 268–272.

Aspy, D.N. (1969), The effect of teacher-offered conditions of empathy, congruence and positive regard upon student achievement, *Florida Journal of Educational Research*, **11**: 39–48.

Augomcha, A.B. (1999), *Secessionism: A Psychological Study*, unpublished doctoral dissertation, University of Delhi, Delhi.

Ausubel, D.P. (1952), *Ego-involvement and Personality Disorders*, NY: Grune and Stratton.

Avolio, B.J. (2004), In G.R. Goethals, G.J. Sorensen, and J.M. Burnes (Eds.), *Encyclopedia of Leadership*, **4**: 1558–1566, Thousand Oaks, CA: Sage.

Avolio, B.J. and Bass, B.M. (Eds.) (2002), *Developing Potential Across Full Range of Leadership*, Mahwah, NJ: Erlbaum.

Axsom, D. and Cooper, J. (1985), Cognitive dissonance and psychotherapy: The role of effort justification in inducing weight loss, *Journal of Experimental Psychology*, **21**: 149–160.

Azar, B. (1997), Defining the trait that makes us human, *APA Monitor*, **1**: 15.

Babu, N. (1989), Development of narratives and theory of mind, In G. Misra (Ed.), *Psychology in India*, Vol. I, 5th ICSSR Survey, Delhi: Pearson.

Babu, N. and Misra, S. (2000), Development of mental state words among Oriya speaking children: Pragmatics or Semantics?, *Psychological Studies*, **45**: 24–29.

Babu, N. and Mohanty, A.K. (2001), Language, theory of mind, and cultural construction of knowledge: A review, *Indian Psychological Abstracts and Reviews*, **8**: 3–47.

Babu, N. and Nanda, S. (1994), Acquisition of text-interpretation distinction as a consequence of literacy, *Indian Education Review*, **36**: 39–50.

Baccman, C., Folkesson, P., and Norlander, T. (1999), Expectations of romantic relationships: A comparison between homosexual and heterosexual men with regard to Baxter's criteria, *Social Behaviour and Personality*, **27**: 363–374.

Bailey, J.C. (1953), A classroom evaluation of the case method, In K.R. Andrews (Ed.), *Case Method of Teaching Human Relations and Administration*, Cambridge, Mass: Harvard University Press.

Bailey, J.M., Kim, P., Hills, A., and Linsenmeier, J. (1997), Butch, femme, or straight acting? Partner preferences of gay men and lesbians, *Journal of Personality and Social Psychology*, **73**: 960–973.

Bal, N.S. (1974), Relationship between popularity among pears and academic over-under achievement, *Indian Journal of Psychology*, **49**: 33–48.

Bales, R.F. (1950), A set of categories for the analysis of small group interaction, *American Sociological Review*, **15**: 257–263.

Bales, R.F. (1953), The equilibrium problem in small groups, In T. Parsons, R.F. Bales, and E.A. Shils (Eds.), *Working Papers in the Theory of Action*, Glencoe, Illinois: Free Press.

Bales, R.F. and Slater, P. (1955), Role differentiation in small decision-making groups, In T. Parsons and R.F. Bales (Eds.), *Family Socialization and Interaction Processes*, Glencoe, Illinios: Free Press.

Ball, S. and Bogatz, G.A. (1971), *The First Year of Sesame Street: An Evaluation*, Princeton, NJ: Educational Testing Service.

Bandura, A. (1969), Social learning theory of identificatory processes, In D. Goslin (Ed.), *Handbook of Socialization Theory and Research*, Chicago: Rand McNally.

Bandura, A. (1973), *Aggression: A Social Learning Analysis*, Englewood Cliffs, NJ: Prentice-Hall.

Bandura, A. (1977), *Social Learning Theory*, Upper Saddle River, NJ: Prentice-Hall.

Bandura, A. (1982), Self-efficacy mechanism in human agency, *American Psychologist*, **37**: 747–735.

Bandura, A. (1982), The self and the mechanism of agency, In J. Suls (Ed.), *Psychological Perspectives on the Self*, Vol. 1. Hillsdale, New Jersey: Erlbaum.

Bandura, A. (1986), *Social Foundations of Thought and Action: A Social Cognitive Theory*, Upper Saddle River, NJ: Prentice-Hall.

Bandura, A. and Walters, R.H. (1963), *Social Learning and Personality Development*, NY: Holt, Rinehart and Winston.

Bandura, A., Coiffi, D., Taylor, C.B., and Brouillard, M.E. (1988), Perceived self-efficacy in coping with cognitive stressors and opioid activation, *Journal of Personality and Social Psychology*, **55**: 479–488.

Bandura, A., Ross, D., and Ross, S. (1961), Transmission of aggression through imitation of aggressive models, *Journal of Abnormal and Social Psychology*, **63**: 575–582.

Bandura, A., Ross, D., and Ross, S.A. (1963), Imitation of film-mediated aggressive models, *Journal of Abnormal and Social Psychology*, **66**: 3–11.

Banerjee, S. and Vyas, T.N. (1992), A study of alexithymia and life events in patients with peptic ulcer, *Journal of Personality and Clinical Studies*, **8**: 63–66.

Banse, R. and Scherer, K.R. (1996), Acoustic profiles in vocal emotion expression, *Journal of Personality and Social Psychology*, **70**: 614–636.

Barath, D.P. (1977), *Sociobiology of Behaviour*, NY: Elsevier.

Barelas, A., Hastorf, A.H., Gross, A.E., and Kite, W.R. (1965), Experiments on the alteration of group structure, *Journal of Experimental Social Psychology*, **1**: 55–71.

Bargh, J.A. (1997), The automaticity of everyday life, In R.S. Wyer (Ed.), *Advances in Social Cognition*, Vol. 10, Mahwat and NJ: Erlbaum.

Bargh, J.A. and Pietromonaco, P. (1982), Automatic information processing and social perception: The influence of trait information presented outside of conscious awareness on impression formation, *Journal of Personality and Social Psychology*, **43**: 437–449.

Barker, R., Dembo, T., and Lewin, K. (1941), Frustration and aggression: An experiment with young children, *University of Iowa Studies in Child Welfare*, **18**: 1–314.

Barnlund, D.C. (1962), Consistency of emergent leadership in groups with changing tasks and members, *Speech Monographs*, **29**: 45–52.

Baron, A., Byrne, D., and Branscombe, N.A. (2008), *Social Psychology*, New Delhi: Prentice-Hall of India.

Baron, B.A. and Markman, G.D. (2004), Towards a process of entrepreneurship: The changing impact of individual level variables across phases of new venture development, In M.A. Rahim, R.T. Golembieweki, and K.D. Mackenzie (Eds.), *Current Topics in Management*, Vol. 9, New Brunswik, NJ: Transaction Publishers.

Baron, J. and Miller, J.G. (2000), Limiting the scope of moral obligations to help: A cross-cultural investigation, *Journal of Cross-cultural Psychology*, **31**: 703–725.

Baron, R. and Ransberger, V. (1978), Ambient temperature and the occurrence of collective violence: The long, hot summer revisited, *Journal of Personality and Social Psychology*, **36**: 351–360.

Baron, R.A., Branscombe, N.R., Byrne, D., and Bhardwaj, G. (2010), *Social Psychology,* Delhi: Pearson.

Baron, R.A. (1972), Aggression as a function of ambient temperature and prior anger arousal, *Journal of Personality and Social Psychology*, **21**: 183–189.

Baron, R.A. (1998), Cognitive mechanisms in entrepreneurship: Why and when entrepreneurs think differently than other persons, *Journal of Business Venturing*, **13**: 275–294.

Baron, R.A. (2000), Counterfactual thinking and venture formation: The potential effects of thinking about 'What might have been', *Journal of Business Venturing*, **15**: 79–92.

Baron, R.A. (2005), *Psychology*, Delhi: Pearson/Prentice-Hall.

Baron, R.A. and Byrne, D. (2000), *Social Psychology*, Boston, MA: Allyn and Bacon.

Baron, R.A. and Kepner, C.R. (1970), Model's behaviour and attraction toward the model as determinants of adult aggressive behaviour, *Journal of Personality and Social Psychology*, **14**: 335–344.

Baron, R.A. and Markman, G.D. (2003), Beyond social capital: The role of entrepreneurs' social competence in their financial success, *Journal of Business Venturing*, **18**: 41–60.

Baron, R.A., Russell, G.W., and Arms, R.L. (1985), Negative ions and behaviour: Impact on mood, memory and aggression among Type A and Type B persons, *Journal of Personality and Social Psychology*, **48**: 746–754.

Baron, R.S. (1986), Distraction-conflict theory: Progress and problems, In L. Berkowitz (Ed.), *Advances in Experimental Social Psychology*, **19**: 1–40, NY: Academic Press.

Bar-Tal, D. (2003), Collective memory of physical violence: Its contribution to the culture of violence, In E. Cairns and M.D. Roe (Eds.), *The Role of Memory in Ethnic Conflict*, NY: Palgrave MacMillan.

Bar-Tal, D. and Saxe, L. (1978), *Social Psychology of Education: Theory and Research*, Washington, DC: Hemisphere.

Bartholow, B.D. and Heinz, A. (2006), Alcohol and aggression without consumption: Alcohol cues, aggressive thoughts and hostile perception bias, *Psychological Science*, **17**: 30–37.

Bartholow, B.D., Pearson, H.A., Gratton, G., and Fabiani, M. (2003), Effects of alcohol on person perception: A social cognitive neuroscience approach, *Journal of Personality and Social Psychology*, **85**: 627–638.

Bartlett, F.C. (1932), *Remembering: A Study in Experimental and Social Psychology*, Cambridge: Cambridge University Press.

Bartis, S., Szymanski, K., and Harkins, S.G. (1988), Evaluation and performance: A two-edged knife, *Personality and Social Psychology Bulletin*, **14**: 242–251.
Bass, B.M. (1990), *Bass and Stogdill's Handbook of Leadership: Theory, Research and Managerial Applications*, 3rd edn., NY: Free Press.
Bass, B.M., Avolio, B.J., Jung, D.I., and Berson, Y. (2003), Predicting unit performance by assessing transformational and transactional leadership, *Journal of Applied Psychology*, **88**: 207–218.
Bates, E., O'Connell, B., and Shore, C. (1987), Language and communication in infancy. In J. Osofsky (Ed.), *Handbook of Infant Competence*, 2nd ed., NY: Wiley.
Batron, C.D., Schoenrade, P., and Ventis, W.L. (1993), *Religion and the Individual: A Social-Psychological Perspective*, NY: Oxford University Press.
Batson, C.D. (1998), Altruism and prosocial behaviour, In D.T. Gilbert, S.T. Fiske, and G. Lindzley (Eds.), *The Handbook of Social Psychology*, 4th edn., **2**: 282–315, NY: McGraw-Hill.
Batson, C.D. and Coke, J.S. (1981), Empathy: A source of altruistic motivation for helping?, In J.P. Rushton and R.M. Sorrentino (Eds.), *Altruism and Helping Behaviour*, Hillsdale, NJ: Erlbaum.
Batson, C.D. and Oleson, K.C. (1991), Current status of empathy-altruism hypothesis, In M.S. Clark (Ed.), *Prosocial Behaviour*, 62–85, Newbury Park, C.A., Sage.
Batson, C.D., Ahmed, N., Yin, J., Bedell, S.J., Johnson, J.W., Templin, C.M., and Whitside, A. (1999), Two threats to the common good: Self-interested egoism and empathy induced altruism, *Personality and Social Psychology Bulletin*, **25**: 3–16.
Batson, C.D., Cochran, P.J., Biederman, M.F., Blosser, J.L., Ryan, M.J., and Vogt, B. (1978), Failure to help when in hurry: Callousness or Conflict?, *Personality and Social Psychology Bulletin*, **4**: 97–101.
Batson, C.D., Coke, J.S., Jasnoski, M.L., and Hanson, M. (1978), Buying kindness: Effect of an extrinsic incentive for helping on perceived altruism, *Personality and Social Psychology Bulletin*, **4**: 86–91.
Batson, C.D., Duncan, B.D., Ackerman, P., Buckley, T., and Birch, K. (1981), Is empathic emotion a source of altruistic motivation?, *Journal of Personality and Social Psychology*, **40**: 290–302.
Batson, C.D., Fultz, J., Schoenvade, P.A., and Paduano, A. (1987), Critical self-reflection and self-perceived altruism: When self-reward fails, *Journal of Personality and Social Psychology*, **53**: 594–602.
Batson, C.D., Klein, T.R., Highberger, L., and Shaw, L.L. (1995), Immorality from empathy-induced altruism: When compassion and justice conflict, *Journal of Personality and Social Psychology*, **68**: 1042–1054.
Batson, C.D., O'Quin, K., Fultz, J., Vanderplas, M., and Isen, A.M. (1983), Influence of self-reported distress and empathy on egoistic versus altruistic motivation to help, *Journal of Personality and Social Psychology*, **45**: 706–718.
Baum, A. (1994), Behavioural, biological and environmental interactions in disease processes, In S. Blumenthal, K. Matthews, and S. Weiss (Eds.), *New Research Frontiers in Behavioural Medicine: Proceedings of National Conference*, Washington, DC: NIH Publications.
Baumeister, R.F. (1998), The self, In D.T. Gilbert, S.T. Fiske, and G. Lindzey (Eds.), *The Handbook of Social Psychology*, 4th edn., **1**: 680–740, NY: McGraw-Hill.
Baumeister, R.F. and Steinhilber, A. (1984), Paradoxical effects of supportive audiences in performance under pressure: The home field advantage in sports championships, *Journal of Personality and Social Psychology*, **47**: 85–93.
Baumeister, R.F., Campbell, J.D., Krueger, J.I., and Vohs, K.D. (2003), Does high self-esteem cause better performance, interpersonal success, happiness or healthier lifestyles?, *Psychological Science in Public Interest*, **4**(1): 1–44.
Baumeister, R.F., Campbell, J.D., Krueger, J.I., and Vols, K.D. (2005), Exploding the self-esteem myth, *Scientific American*, **292**: 84–92.
Baumeister, R.F., Twenge, J.M., and Nuss, C.K. (2002), Effects of social exclusion on cognitive processes: Anticipated aloneness reduces intelligent thought, *Journal of Personality and Social Psychology*, **83**: 817–827.
Baumeister, R.F., Wotman, S.R., and Stillwell, A.M. (1993), Unrequited love: On heartbreak, anger, guilt, scriptlessness and humiliation, *Journal of Personality and Social Psychology*, **83**: 817–827.

Baumiester, R.F., Stillwell, A.M., and Heatherton, T.F. (1994), Guilt: An interpersonal approach, *Psychological Bulletin*, **115**: 243–267.
Baumrind, D. (1964), Some thoughts on ethics in research: After reading Milgram's behavioural study of obedience, *American Psychologist*, **19**: 421–423.
Baumrind, D. (1971), Current patterns of parental authority, *Developmental Psychology Monographs*. 4(1): Part 2.
Baumrind, D. (1980), New directions in socialization research, *American Psychologist*, **35**: 639–652.
Bavelas, A. (1948), Some problems of organisational change, *Journal of Social Issues*, **3**: 48–52.
Bavelas, A. (1948), Some problems of organizational change, *Journal of Social Issues*, **3**: 48–52.
Bavelas, A. (1950), Communication patterns in task-oriented groups, *Journal of Acoustical Society of America*, **22**: 735–730.
Beall, A.E. and Sternberg, R.J. (1995), The social construction of love, *Journal of Social and Personal Relationship*, **12**: 417–438.
Beaman, A.I., Cole, M., Preston, M., Klentz, B., and Steblay, N.M. (1983), Fifteen years of the foot-in-the-door research: A meta-analysis, *Personality and Social Psychology Bulletin*, **9**: 181–186.
Bechtold, A., Naccarato, M.E., and Zanna, M.P. (1986), Need for structure and the prejudice–discrimination link, In E.R. Smith and D.M. Mackie, *Social Psychology*, 3rd edn., NY: Psychology Press.
Beck, K.W., Festinger, L., Hyomovitach, B., Kelley, H.H., Schachter, S., and Thaibaut, J.W. (1950), The methodology of studying rumour transition, *Human Relations*, **3**: 307–312.
Becker, F.D. (1973), Study of spatial markers, *Journal of Personality and Social Psychology*, **26**: 439–445.
Beckhouse, L., Tanur, J., Weiler, J., and Weinstein, E. (1975), And some men have leadership thrust upon them, *Journal of Personality and Social Psychology*, **61**: 76–82.
Bell, G. and French, R. (1950), Consistency of individual leadership position in small groups of varying membership, *Journal of Abnormal and Social Psychology*, **45**: 764–767.
Belloc, N.B. and Breslow, L. (1972), Relationship of physical health status and health practices, *Preventive Medicine*, **3**: 409–421.
Bem, D.J. (1967), Self-perception: An alternative explanation of cognitive dissonance phenomena, *Psychological Review*, **74**: 183–200.
Bem, D.J. (1972), Self-perception theory, In L. Berkowitz (Ed.), *Advances in Experimental Social Psychology*, **6**: 1–62, NY: Academic Press.
Bennis, W. (2001), Leading in unnerving times, *MIT Sloan Management Review*, **42**: 97–102.
Berelson, B. (1952), *Content Analysis in Communication Research*, NY: Free Press.
Berger, J., Webster, M., Ridgeway, C., and Rosenholtz, S.J. (1986), Status cues, expectations, and behaviour, In E.J. Lawler (Ed.), *Advances in Group Processes*, **3**: 1–22, Greenwich: JAI Press.
Berkman, L.F. and Syme, S.L. (1979), Social networks, host resistance, and mortality: A nine–year followup study of Alameda country residents, *American Journal of Epidemiology*, **109**: 184–204.
Berkowitz, L. (1958), The expression and reduction of hostility, *Psychological Bulletin*, **55**: 257–283.
Berkowitz, L. (1965), The concept of aggressive drive: Some additional considerations, In L. Berkowitz (Ed.), *Advances in Experimental Social Psychology*, **2**: NY: Academic Press.
Berkowitz, L. (1970), The self, selfishness and altruism, In J. McCauley and L. Berkowitz (Eds.), *Altruism and Helping Behaviour*, NY: Academic Press.
Berkowitz, L. (1973), Control of aggression, In B.M. Coldwell and H.M. Ricciutti (Eds.), *Review of Child Development Research*, Vol. 3, Chicago: Chicago University Press.
Berkowitz, L. (1974), Some determinants of impulsive aggression: Role of mediated associations with reinforcements for aggression, *Psychological Review*, **81**: 165–176.
Berkowitz, L. (1981), How guns control us, *Psychology Today*, 11–12.
Berkowitz, L. (1984), Some effects of thoughts on anti and prosocial influences of media events: A cognitive neo-associationist analysis, *Psychological Bulletin*, **95**: 410–427.
Berkowitz, L. (1989), Frustration–aggression hypothesis: Examination and reformulation, *Psychological Bulletin*, **106**: 59–73.

Berkowitz, L. (1993), *Aggression: Its Causes, Consequences and Control,* Philadelphia: Temple University Press.
Berkotwitz, L. (1993), *Aggression: Its Causes, Consequences and Control,* NY: McGraw-Hill.
Berkowitz, L. (1995), A career on aggression, In G.G. Brannigan and M.R. Merrens (Eds.), *The Social Psychologists: Research Adventures,* NY: McGraw-Hill.
Berkowitz, L. and Daniels, L.R. (1964), Affecting the salience of the social responsibility norm: Effects of past help on the response to dependency relationship, *Journal of Abnormal and Social Psychology,* **68**: 275–281.
Berkowitz, L. and Geen, R.G. (1966), Film violence and cue properties of available targets, *Journal of Personality and Social Psychology,* **3**: 525–530.
Berkowitz, L. and Green, J.A. (1962), The stimulus qualities of the scapegoat, *Journal of Abnormal and Social Psychology,* **64**: 293–301.
Berkowitz, L. and Le Page, A. (1967), Weapons as aggression-eliciting stimuli, *Journal of Personality and Social Psychology,* **7**: 202–207.
Berman, M., Glande, B., and Taylor, S. (1993), The effects of hormones, Type-A behaviour patterns and provocation on aggression in men, *Motivation and Emotion,* **17**: 125–138.
Bernstein, B. (1964), Elaborated and restricted codes: Their social origins and some consequences, In J.J. Gemperz and D. Hymes (Eds.), *The Ethnography of Communication, American Anthropologists,* **66**(6): Part II, 55–69.
Bernstein, D.A., Clarke–Stewart, A., Roy, E.J., and Wickens, C.D. (1997), *Psychology,* 4th edn., NY: Houghton Mifflin.
Bernstein, W.M., Stephan, W.G., and Davis, M.H. (1979), Explaining attributions for achievement: A path analytic approach, *Journal of Personality and Social Psychology,* **37**: 1810–1821.
Berreby, D. (1994), Figures of speech: The rise and fall and rise of Chomsky's linguistics, *The Sciences,* 44–49.
Berry, J.W. (1984), Toward a universal psychology of cognitive competence, *International Journal of Psychology,* **6**: 193–197.
Berry, J.W. (1999), *Cultures in Contact: Acculturation and Change,* Allahabad: Pant Social Science Institute.
Berry, J.W. and Kim, U. (1998), Acculturation and mental health, In P.R. Dasen, J.W. Berry, and N. Sartorius (Eds.), *Health and Cross-Cultural Psychology: Towards Applications,* Newbury Park, CA: Sage Publications.
Berscheid, E. and Regan, P. (2005), *The Psychology of Interpersonal Relationship,* Englewood Cliffs, NJ: Prentice-Hall.
Berscheid, E. and Reis, H.T. (1998), A little bit about love, In T.L. Houston (Ed.), *Foundations of Interpersonal Attraction,* 335–381, NY Academic Press.
Berscheid, E. and Walster, E. (1974), Physical attractiveness, In L. Berkowitz (Ed.), *Advances in Experimental Social Psychology,* **7**: 157–215, NY: Academic Press.
Berscheid, E. and Walster, E. (1978), *Interpersonal Attraction,* 2nd edn., Reading, MA: Addison–Wesley.
Bettencourt, B.A. and Miller, M. (1996), Gender differences in aggression as a function of provocation: A meta-analysis, *Psychological Bulletin,* **119**: 422–447.
Bharat, S. (2000), Perception of AIDS in Mumbai: A study of low income communities, *Psychology and Developing Societies,* **12**: 43–65.
Bhat, S. and Chengappa, S. (2004), Matrix language: Listeners' perspective, International conference on cognitive science, University of Allahabad, Allahabad, India, 16–18 December.
Bhatia, T.K. and Ritchie, W.C. (Eds.), (2004), *The Handbook of Bilingualism,* Oxford: Blackwell Publishing.
Bhogle, S. (1971), Role conflict in teachers, *Indian Journal of Psychology,* **46**: 399–404.
Bickerton, D. (1983), Creole languages, *Scientific American,* **249**: 116–122.
Bickman, L. (1971), The effect of another bystander's ability to help on bystander intervention in an emergency, *Journal of Experimental Social Psychology,* **7**: 367–379.
Bickman, L. (1976), Observational methods, In C. Sellitz, L.S. Wrightsman and S.W. Cook (Eds.), *Research Methods in Social Relations,* NY: Holt, Rinehart and Winston.
Bickman, L. (1979), Interpersonal influence and reporting of a crime, *Personality and Social Psychology Bulletin,* **5**: 32–35.

Bickman, L. and Rosenbaum, D.P. (1977), Crime reporting as a function of bystander encouragement, surveillance and credibility, *Journal of Personality and Social Psychology*, **35**: 577–586.

Biernat, M. and Thompson, E.R. (2002), Shifting standards and contextual variation in stereotyping, *European Review of Social Psychology*, **12**: 103–137.

Biernat, M. and Vescio, T.K. (2002), She swings, she hits, she's great, she's benched: Implications of gender-based shifting standards for judgement and behaviour, *Personality and Social Psychology Bulletin*, **28**: 66–77.

Bijou, S. (1976), *Child Development: The Basic Stage of Early Childhood*, Englewood Cliffs, NJ: Prentice-Hall.

Billings, A.G. and Moos, R.H. (1984), Coping, stress and social resources among adults with unipolar depression, *Journal of Personality and Social Psychology*, **46**: 877–891.

Biswas, U.N. and Daffuar, C.N. (2000), Adolescence, sexuality and health: Awareness and perceived constraints among out-of-school slum children, In U. Vidhya (Ed.), *Psychology in India: Intersecting Cross-roads*, 176–201, ND: Concept.

Bivens, S. and Leonard, W.M. (1994), Race, centrality and educational attainment: An NFL perspective, *Journal of Sports Behaviour*, **17**: 24–42.

Bizer, G.Y. and Krosnick, J.A. (2001), Exploring the structure of strength-related attitude features: The relation between attitude importance and attitude accessibility, *Journal of Personality and Social Psychology*, **81**: 566–586.

Bizer, G.Y., Tormala, Z.L., Rucker, D.D., and Petty, R.E. (2006), Memory-based versus on-line processing, implications for attitude strength, *Journal of Experimental Social Psychology*, **42**: 646–653.

Bjorkqvist, K. (1994), Sex differences in physical, verbal and indirect aggression: A review of recent research, *Sex Roles*, **30**: 177–188.

Bjorkqvist, K. and Niemela, P. (1992), New trends in the study of female aggression, In K. Bjorkqvist and P. Niemela (Eds.), *Of Mice and Women: Aspects of Female Aggression*, 3–16, San Diego: Academic Press.

Bjorkqvist, K., Osterman, K., and Hjelt–Back, M. (1994), Aggression among university employees, *Aggressive Behaviour*, **20**: 173–184.

Blake, R.R. and Mouton, J.S. (1979), Intergroup problem solving in organizations: From theory to practice, In W.G. Austin and S. Worchel (Eds.), *The Social Psychology of Intergroup Relations*, Monterey: Brooks/Cole.

Blankstein, K.R. and Dunkley, D.M. (2002), Evaluative concerns, self-critical and personal standards perfectionism: A structural equation modeling strategy, In G.L. Flatt and P.L. Hewitt (Eds.), *Perfectionism: Theory, Research and Treatment*, Washington, DC: American Psychological Association.

Blascovich, J., Mendes, W.B., Hunter, S.B.G., and Salomon, K. (1999), Social facilitation as challenge and threat, *Journal of Personality and Social Psychology*, **77**: 68–77.

Block, J. (1973), Conceptions of sex roles: Some cross-cultural and longitudinal perspectives, *American Psychologist*, **28**: 512–526.

Bloom, L., Rocissano, M., and Hood, L. (1976), Adult-child discourse: Developmental interaction behaviour information processing and linguistic knowledge, *Cognitive Psychology*, **8**: 521–528.

Bloomfield, L. (1933), *Language,* NY: Henry Holt and Company.

Blount, B.G. (1975), Studies in child language, *American Anthropologist*, **77**: 580–600.

Bochner, S. and Insko, C.A. (1966), Communicator discrepancy, source credibility and opinion change, *Journal of Personality and Social Psychology*, **4**: 614–621.

Bodenhausen, G.F. (1993), Emotion, arousal and stereotypic judgement: A heuristic model of affect and stereotyping, In D. Mackie and D. Hamilton (Eds.), *Affect, Cognition and Stereotyping: Intergroup Processes in Intergroup Perception*, 13–37, San Diego, CA: Academic Press.

Bodenhausen, G.V. (1993), Emotions, arousal and stereotyping judgements: A heuristic model of effect and stereotyping, In D.M. Mackie and D.L. Hamilton (Eds.), *Affect, Cognition and Stereotyping: Interactive Processes in Group Perception*, San Diego: Academic Press.

Bodenhausen, G.V. and Lichtenstein, M. (1987), Social stereotypes and information processing strategies: The impact of task complexity, *Journal of Personality and Social Psychology*, **52**: 871–880.

Bogardus, E.S. (1925), Measuring social distances, *Journal of Applied Psychology*, **9**: 299–308.

Bogdon, R.C. and Biklen, S.K. (2003), *Qualitative Research in Education: An Introduction to Theories and Methods,* Boston: Allyn and Bacon.

Bohner, G., Bless, H., Schwartz, N., and Strack, F. (1988), What triggers causal attributions? The impact of subjective probability, *European Journal of Social Psychology,* **18**: 335–346.

Boldero, J. and Francis, J. (2000), The relation between self-discrepancies and emotion: The moderating roles of self-guide importance, location relevance, and social self-domain centrality, *Journal of Personality and Social Psychology,* **78**: 38–52.

Bond, R. and Smith, P.B. (1996), Culture and conformity: A meta-analysis of studies using Asch's line judgement task, *Psychological Bulletin,* **119**: 111–137.

Bose, G. (1939), Progress of psychology in India during the past twenty five years, In B. Prasad (Ed.), *The Progress of Science in India During the Past Twenty Five Years,* Calcutta: Indian Science Congress Association.

Botha, M. (1990), Television exposure and aggression among adolescents: A follow-up study over 5 years, *Aggressive Behaviour,* **16**: 361–380.

Bourhis, R.Y., Giles, H., Leyens, J.P., and Tajfel, H. (1979), Psycholinguistic distinctiveness: Language diversity in Belgium, In H. Giles and R.N. St. Clair (Eds.), *Language and Social Psychology,* Oxford, UK: Blackwell.

Branscombe, M.R. (2004), A social psychological process perspective on collective guilt, In N.R. Branscombe and B. Doosje (Eds.), *Collective Guilt: International Perspective,* NY: Cambridge University Press.

Brauer, M. (2001), Intergroup perception in the social context: The effects of social status and group membership on perceived outgroup homogeneity and ethnocentrism, *Journal of Experimental Social Psychology,* **37**: 15–31.

Brauer, M., Judd, C.M., and Jacqueline, V. (2001), The communication of social stereotypes: The effects of group discussion and information distribution on stereotypic appraisals, *Journal of Personality and Social Psychology,* **81**: 463–475.

Bray, S. and Carron, A.V. (1993), The home advantage in alpine Skiing, *The Australian Journal of Science and Medicine in Sport,* **25**: 76–81.

Bredemeier, B.J. (1994), Children's moral reasoning and their assertiveness, aggressive and submissive tendencies in sport and daily life, *Journal of Sport and Exercise Psychology,* **16**: 1–14.

Brehm, J.W. (1956), Post-decisional changes in desirability of alternatives, *Journal of Abnormal and Social Psychology,* **52**: 384–389.

Brehm, J.W. (1966), *A Theory of Psychological Reactance,* NY: Academic Press.

Brehm, S.S. (1992), *Intimate Relationships,* 2nd edn., NY: McGraw-Hill.

Brewer, M.B. (1988), A dual process model of impression formation, In T. Srull and R. Wyer (Eds.), *Advances in Social Cognition,* **1**: 177–183, Hillsdale, NJ: Lawrence Erlbaum Associates.

Brewer, M.B. (2004), Taking the social origins of human nature seriously: Toward a more imperialist social psychology, *Personality and Social Psychology Review,* **8**: 107–113.

Brewer, M.B. and Brown, R.J. (1998), Intergroup relations, In D.T. Gilbert, S.T. Fiske, and G. Lindzey (Eds.), *The Handbook of Social Psychology,* 4th ed., NY: McGraw-Hill.

Brewer, N. and Burke, A. (2002), Effects of testimonial inconsistencies and eyewitness confidence on mock-juror judgements, *Law and Human Behaviour,* **26**: 353–364.

Brickner, M.A., Harkins, S.G., and Ostrom, T.M. (1986), Effects of personal development: thought provoking implications for social loafing, *Journal of Personality and Social Psychology,* **51**: 763–770.

Bridges, J.S., Etaugh, C., and Barnes–Farrell, J. (2002), Trait judgements of stay–at–home and employed parents: A function of social role and/or shifting standards?, *Psychology of Women Quarterly,* **26**: 140–150.

British Psychological Society (2000), *Code of Conduct, Ethical Principles and Guidelines,* p. 32, Leicester: England.

Brockner, A.J., Higgins, E.J., and Low, M.B. (2004), Regulatory focus theory and entrepreneurial process, *Journal of Business Venturing,* **19**: 203–220.

Brockner, J. and Hutton, A.J.B. (1978), How to reverse cycle of low self-esteem: The importance of attentional focus, *Journal of Experimental and Social Psychology,* **14**: 564–578.

Bronfenbrenner, U. (1977), Who cares for America's children? *6th Annual Family Research Conference*, Brigham Young University, Provo, Utah.
Brophy, J. (1985), *Teacher–student interaction*, In J.B. Duseck (Ed.), *Teacher Expectancies*, Mahwah, NJ: Erlbaum.
Brophy, J. (1998), *Motivating Students to Learn*, NY: McGraw-Hill.
Brothers, L. (1990), The neural basis of primate social communications, *Motivation and Emotion*, **14**: 81–91.
Brown, J.D. and Rogers, R.J. (1991), Self-serving attributions: The role of physiological arousal, *Personality and Social Psychology Bulletin*, **17**: 501–506.
Brown, J.D., Collins, R.L., and Schmidt, G.W. (1988), Self-esteem and direct versus indirect forms of self-enhancement, *Journal of Personality and Social Psychology*, **55**: 445–453.
Brown, J.F. (1936), *Psychology and The Social Order*, NY: McGraw-Hill.
Brown, R. (1958), *Words and Things*, NY: Free Press, Macmillan.
Brown, R. (1973), *A First Language*, Cambridge, Mass: Harvard University Press.
Brown, R. and Fraser, C. (1963), The acquisition of syntax, In C. Cofer and B. Musgrave (Eds.), *Verbal Behaviour and Learning*, NY: McGraw-Hill.
Brown, R. and Hanlon, C. (1970), Derivational complexity and order of acquisition in child speech, In J.R. Hyes (Ed.), *Cognition and the Development of Language*, 11–53, NY: Wiley.
Brown, R. and Lennenberg, E.H. (1954), A study in language and cognition, *Journal of Abnormal and Social Psychology*, **49**: 454–462.
Brown, R.P., Charnsangravej, T., Keough, K.A., Newman, H.L., and Rentfrow, P.J. (2000), Putting the 'affirm' into affirmative action: Preferential selection and academic performance, *Journal of Personality and Social Psychology*, **6**: 400–407.
Brown, S.C., Nesse, R.M., Vinokur, A.D., and Smith, D.M. (2003), Providing social support may be more beneficial than receiving it, *Psychological Science*, **14**: 320–327.
Brown, L.M. (1998), Ethnic stigma as a conceptual experience: A Possible selves perspectives, *Personality and Social Psychology Bulletin*, **24**: 165–172.
Brune, J. (1983) *Child's talk*, New York; Norton.
Bryan, J.H. and Test, M. (1967), Models and helping: Naturalistic studies in aiding behaviour, *Journal of Personality and Social Psychology*, **6**: 400–407.
Buch, P.M. (1973), An inquiry into conditions promoting adaptability in Indian schools, In J. Pandey (Ed.), *Psychology in India*, ND: Sage Publication.
Buehler, R., Griffin, D., and Mac Donald, H. (1997), The role of motivated reasoning in optimistic time predictions, *Personality and Social Psychology Bulletin*, **23**: 238–247.
Buehler, R., Griffin, D., and Ross, N. (1994), Exploring the planning fallacy: Why people underestimate their task completion times, *Journal of Personality and Social Psychology*, **67**: 366–381.
Bugenthal, D.E. (1974), Interpretations of naturally occurring discrepancies between words and intonation, Modes of inconsistency resolution, *Journal of Personality and Social Psychology*, **30**: 125–133.
Buhs, E.S. and Ladd, G.W. (2001), Peer rejection as antecedent of young children's school adjustment: An examination of mediating processes, *Development Psychology*, **37**: 550–560.
Bullock, D. (1983), Seeking relations between cognitive and social-interactive transitions, In K.W. Fischer (Ed.), *Levels and Transitions in Children's Development: New Directions in Child Development*, San Francisco: Jossey–Bass.
Burger, J.M. (1986), Increasing compliance by improving the deal: The That's-not-all technique, *Journal of Personality and Social Psychology*, **51**: 277–283.
Burger, J.M. and Cornelius, T. (2003), Raising the price of agreement: Public commitment and the law-ball compliance procedure, *Journal of Applied Social Psychology*, **33**: 923–934.
Burger, J.M., Messian, N., Patel, S., del Parlo, A., and Anderson, C. (2004), What a coincidence! The effects of incidental similarity on compliance, *Personality and Social Psychology Bulletin*, **30**: 35–43.

Burgess, R.L. (1968), Communication networks: An experimental revaluation, *Journal of Experimental and Social Psychology*, **4**: 324–337.

Burke, P. (2004), Identities and social structure: The 2003 cooley-mead award address, *Social Psychology Quarterly*, **67**: 5–15.

Burke, P.J. and Reitzes, D. (1981), The link between identity and role performance, *Social Psychology Quarterly*, **44**: 83–92.

Burleson, J.A. (1984), Reciprocity of interpersonal attraction within acquainted versus unacquainted small groups, In R.S. Feldman (Ed.), *Social Psychology*, International student edition, ND: McGraw-Hill.

Burnstein, E. and Vinokur, A. (1973), Testing two classes of theories about group induced shifts in individual choice, *Journal of Experimental Social Psychology*, **9**: 123–137.

Burnstein, E. and Vinokur, A. (1977), Persuasive argumentation and social comparison as determinants of attitude polarization, *Journal of Experimental Social Psychology*, **13**: 315–332.

Burnstein, E., Crandall, C., and Kitayama, S. (1994), Some neo-Darwinian decision rules for altruism: Weighing cues for inclusive fitness as a function of the biological importance of the decision, *Journal of Personality and Social Psychology*, **67**: 217–234.

Busenitz, L.W. and Barney, J.B. (1997), Differences between entrepreneurs and managers in large organizations: Biases and heuristics in strategic decision making, *Journal of Business Venturing*, **12**: 9–30.

Bushman, B.J. (2001), Does venting anger feed or extinguished the flame? Catharsis, rumination, distraction, anger and aggressive responding, In R.A. Baron, D. Byrne, and N.R. Branscombe, *Social Psychology*, 11th edn., ND: Prentice-Hall of India.

Bushman, B.J. and Anderson, C.A. (2001), Media violence and the American public: Scientific facts versus media misinformation, *American Psychologist*, **56**: 477–489.

Bushman, B.J. and Anderson, C.A. (2002), Violent video games and hostile expectations: A test of the general aggression model, *Personality and Social Psychology Bulletin*, **28**: 1679–1686.

Bushman, B.J. and Baumeister, R.F. (1998), Threatened egotism, narcissism, self-esteem and direct and displaced aggression: Does self-love or self-hate lead to violence?, *Journal of Personality and Social Psychology*, **75**: 219–229.

Bushman, B.J. and Cooper, H.M. (1990), Effects of alcohol on human aggression: An integrative research review, *Psychological Bulletin*, **107**: 341–354.

Bushman, B.J. and Geen, R.G. (1990), Role of cognitive–emotional mediators and individual differences in the effects of media violence on aggression, *Journal of Personality and Social Psychology*, **58**: 156–163.

Bushman, B.J. and Huesmann, L.R. (2001), Effects of televised violence on aggression, In D. Singer and J. Singer (Eds.), *Handbook of Children and Media*, 223–254, Thousands Oaks: Sage.

Bushman, B.J., Baumeister, R.F., and Stack, A.D. (1999), Catharsis, aggression, and persuasive influence: Self-fulfilling or self-defecting prophecies?, *Journal of Personality and Social Psychology*, **84**: 1027–1040.

Buss, D.M. (1994), *The Evolution of desire: Strategies of Human Mating*, NY: Basic Books.

Buss, D.M. (1996), The evolutionary psychology of human social strategies, In E.T. Higgens and A.W. Krughlanski (Eds.), *Social Psychology: Handbook of Basic Principles*, New York: Guilford.

Buss, D.M. (1999), *Evolutionary Psychology*, Boston: Allyn and Bacon.

Buss, D.M. and Kenrick, D.T. (1998), Evolutionary social psychology, In D.T. Gilbert, S.T. Fiske, and G. Lindzey (Eds.). *The Handbook of Social Psychology*, 4th edn., Boston: Allyn and Bacon.

Buss, D.M. and Shackelford, T.K. (1997), From vigilance to violence: Mate retention tactics in married couples, *Journal of Personality and Social Psychology*, **72**: 346–361.

Butler, R.N. (1980), Ageism: A foreward. *Journal of Social Issues*, **36**: 8–29.

Byrne, D. (1961), Interpersonal attraction and attitude similarity, *Journal of Abnormal and Social Psychology*, **62**: 713–715.

Byrne, D. (1971), *The Attraction Paradigm*, NY: Academic Press.

Byrne, D. (1997), An overview (and underview) of research and theory within the attraction paradigm, *Journal of Social and Personal Relationships*, **14**: 417–431.

Byrne, D. and Clore, G.L. (1970), A reinforcement model of evaluative responses, *Personality: An International Journal*, **1**: 103–128.

Byrne, D. and Nelson, D. (1965), Attraction as a linear function of proportion of positive reinforcements, *Journal of Personality and Social Psychology*, **1**: 659–663.

Byrne, D., Ervin, C., and Lamberth, J. (1970), Continuity between the experimental study of attraction and real-life computer dating, *Journal of Personality and Social Psychology*, **16**: 157–165.

Byrne, D., Gouaux, C., Griffitt W., Lamberth, J., Murkava, Prasad, M.B., Prasad, A., and Ramitez (1971), The ubiquitous relationship: Attitude similarity and attraction, *Human Relations*, **24**: 204–207.

Cacioppo, J.T. and Petty, R.F. (1981), Electromyograms as measures of extent and affectivity of information processing, *American Psychologist*, **36**: 441–456.

Cacioppo, J.T. and Tassinary, L.G. (1990), Inferring psychological significance from physiological signals, *Scientific American*, **45**: 16–28.

Cacioppo, J.T., Petty, R.E., and Morris, K.J. (1983), Effects of need for cognition on message evaluation, recall and persuasion, *Journal of Personality and Social Psychology*, **45**: 805–818.

Cacioppo, J.T., Petty, R.E., Feinltein, J.A., and Jarvis, W.B.G. (1996), Dispositional differences in cognitive motivation: The life and times of individuals varying in need for cognition, *Psychological Bulletin*, **119**: 197–253.

Cadenhead, A.C. and Richman, C.L. (1996), The effects of interpersonal trust and group status on prosocial and aggression behaviours, *Social Behaviour and Personality*, **24**: 167–184.

Callaway, M.R. and Esser, J.K. (1984), Groupthink: Effects of cohesiveness and problem-solving procedures on group decision-making, *Social Behaviour and Personality*, **12**: 157–164.

Camacho, J., Higgins, E.T., and Luger, L. (2003), Moral value transfer from regulatory fit: What feels right is right and what feels wrong is wrong, *Journal of Personality and Social Psychology*, **84**: 498–510.

Campbell, D.T. (1958), Common fate, similarity and other indices of the status of aggregates of persons as social entities, *Behavioural Science*, **4**: 14–25.

Campbell, D.T. (1973), The social scientist as methodological servant of the experimenting society, *Policy Studies Journal*, **2**: 72–95.

Campbell, D.T. and Stanley, J.C. (1966), *Experimental and Quasi-experimental Designs for Research*, Chicago: Rand McNally.

Campbell, J.D. (1990), Self-esteem and clarity of self-concept, *Journal of Personality and Social Psychology*, **59**: 538–549.

Campbell, L., Simpson, J.A., Kashy, D.A., and Fletcher, G.J.O. (2001), Ideal standards, the self, and flexibility of ideas in close relationships, *Personality and Social Psychology Bulletin*, **27**: 447–462.

Campbell, W.K. and Sedikides, C. (1999), Self-threat magnifies the self-serving bias: A meta-analysis integration, *Review of General Psychology*, **3**: 23–43.

Campos, B., Keltner, D., Beck, J.M., Gonzaga, G.C., and John, O.P. (2007), Culture and teasing: The relational benefits of reduced desire for positive self-differentiation, *Personality and Social Psychology Bulleting*, **33**: 3–16.

Canadian Psychological Association (2000), *Canadian Code of Ethics for Psychologists*, p. 32, Ottawa: Canadian Psychological Association (www.cpa.ca/ethics2000.html).

Canavan–Gumpert, D. (1977), Generating reward and cost orientations through praise and criticism, *Journal of Personality and Social Psychology*, **35**: 501–514.

Cantor, N. and Mischel, W. (1979), Prototypes in person perception, In L. Berkowitz (Ed.), *Advances in Experimental Social Psychology*, **12**: 3–52, NY: Academic Press..

Cantril, H. (1963), *The Psychology of Social Movements*, NY: Wiley.

Carli, L.L. (1990), Gender, language and influence, *Journal of Personality and Social Psychology*, **59**: 941–951.

Carlsmith, K.M., Darley, J.M., and Robinson, P.H. (2002), Why do we punish? Deterrence and just deserts as motives for punishment, *Journal of Personality and Social Psychology*, **83**: 284–299.

Carlson, M., Marcus–Newhall, A., and Miller, N. (1990), Effects of situational aggression cues: A quantitative review, *Journal of Personality and Social Psychology*, **58**: 622–633.
Carment, D.W. (1974a), Indian and Canadian choice behaviour in a maximizing difference game and in a game of chicken, *International Journal of Psychology*, **9**: 213–221.
Carment, D.W. (1974b), Indian and Canadian choice behaviour in a mixed-motive game, *International Journal of Psychology,* **9**: 303–316.
Carment, D.W. and Hodkin, B. (1973), Coaction and competition in India and Canada, *Journal of Cross-Cultural Psychology,* **4**: 459–469.
Carroll, D., Smith, G., and Bennett, P. (1994), Health and socio-economic status, *The Psychologist*, 122–125.
Carroll, J.M. and Russell, J.A. (1996), Do facial expressions signal specific emotions? Judging emotion from the face in context, *Journal of Personality and Social Psychology*, **70**: 205–218.
Carron, A.V. (1982), Cohesiveness in sport groups: Interpretations and considerations, *Journal of Sport Psychology*, **4**: 123–138.
Carron, A.V. and Dennis, P.W. (1998), The sport team as an effective group, In J.M. Williams (Ed.), *Applied Sport Psychology: Personal Growth and Peak Performance*, Mountain view, CA: Mayfield Publishing Company.
Carron, A.V. and Hausenblas, H.A. (1998), *Group Dynamics in Sport*, Morgantown, WV: Fitness Information Technology.
Carron, A.V., Spink, K.S., and Prapavessis, H. (1997), Team building and cohesiveness in sport and exercise setting, *Journal of Applied Sport Psychology*, **9**: 61–72.
Carron, A.V., Widmeyer, W.N., and Brawley, L.R. (1985), The development of an instrument to assess team cohesion in sport teams: The group environment questionnaire, *Journal of Sports Psychology*, **7**: 244–266.
Carter, L. (1953), Leadership and small group behaviour, In M. Sherif and M. Wilson (Eds.), *Group Relations at the Crossroads*, NY: Harper.
Carter, L. and Nixon, M. (1949), Ability, perceptual, personality and interest factors associated with different criteria of leadership, *Journal of Psychology*, **27**: 377–388.
Carter, L., Haythorn, W., Shriver, B., and Lanzetta, J. (1951), The behaviour of leaders and other group members, *Journal Abnormal and Social Psychology*, **46**: 589–595.
Carter, L.F., Haythorn, W., and Howell, M.A. (1950), A further investigation of the criteria of leadership, *Journal of Abnormal and Social Psychology*, **45**: 350–358.
Cartwright, D. (1971), Risk taking by individuals and groups: An assessment of research employing choice dilemmas, *Journal of Personality and Social Psychology*, **20**: 361–378.
Cartwright, D. (1979), Contemporary social psychology in historical perspective, *Social Psychology Quarterly*, **42**: 82–93.
Cartwright, D. and Zander, A. (1968), *Group Dynamics: Theory and Research*, NY: Harper and Row.
Carver, C.S. and Glass, D.C. (1978), Coronary-prone behaviour pattern and interpersonal aggression, *Journal of Personality and Social Psychology*, **376**: 361–366.
Carver, C.S., Pozo, C., Harris, S.D., Noriega, V., Scheier, M.F., Rabinson, D.S., Ketcham, A.S., Moffat, F.L., and Clark, K.C. (1993), How coping mediates the effect of optimism on distress: A study of women with early stage breast cancer, *Journal of Personality and Social Psychology*, **65**: 375–390.
Cash, T.F., Kehr, J.A., Polyson, J., and Freeman, V. (1977), Role of physical attractiveness in peer attribution of psychological disturbance, *Journal of Consulting and Clinical Psychology*, **45**: 987–993.
Caspi, A. and Herbener, E.S. (1990), Continuity and Change: Assortative marriage and consistency of personality in adulthood, *Journal of Personality and Social Psychology*, **58**: 250–258.
Casselden, P.A. and Hampson, S.E. (1990), Forming impression from incongruent traits, *Journal of Personality and Social Psychology*, **59**: 353–372.
Cazden, C.B. (1965), Environmental assistance to the child's acquisition of grammar, In S.L. Albrecht, D.L. Thomas, and B.A. Chadwick, *Social Psychology*, Prentice-Hall.
Cazden, C.B. (1966), Subcultural difference in child language: An interdisciplinary review, *Merrill-Palmer Quarterly*, **12**: 185–219.

Chaiken, S. (1979), Communicator physical attractiveness and persuasion, *Journal of Personality and Social Psychology*, **37**: 1387–1397.

Chaiken, S. and Eagly, A.H. (1976), Communication modality as a determinant of message persuasiveness and message comprehensibility, *Journal of Personality and Social Psychology*, **34**: 605–614.

Chaiken, S. and Maheswaran, D. (1994), Heuristic processing can bias systematic processing: Effects of source credibility, argument ambiguity and task importance on attitude judgement, *Journal of Personality and Social Psychology*, **66**: 460–473.

Chaiken, S. and Yates, S. (1985), Affective cognitive consistency and thoughts-induced polarization, *Journal of Personality and Social Psychology*, **49**: 1470–1481.

Chapanis, N.P. and Chapanis, A.C. (1964), Cognitive dissonance: Five years later, *Psychological Bulletin*, **61**: 1–22.

Chaplin, W., Phillips, J., Brown, J., Clanton, N., and Stein, J. (2000), Handshake gender, personality and first impressions, *Journal of Personality and Social Psychology*, **79**: 110–117.

Chaplin, W.F., Phillips, J.B., Brown, J.D., Clanton, N.R., and Stein, J.L. (2000), Handshaking, gender personality and first impressions, *Journal of Personality and Social Psychology*, **76**: 893–910.

Chapman, R.S., Strein, N.W., Crais, E.R., Salmon, D., Strand, E.A., and Negri, N.A. (1992), Child talk: Assumptions of a developmental process model for early language learning, In R.S. Chapman (Ed.), *Processes in Language Acquisition and Disorder*, Chicago: Mosby/Year Book.

Charon, J.M. (1995), *Symbolic Interactionism: An Introduction, Interpretation and Integration*, Englewood Cliffs, NJ: Prentice Hall.

Chatterjee, C., Baur, B., Ram, R., Dhar, G., Sandhukhan, S., and Dan, A. (2001), A study of awareness of AIDS among school students and teachers of higher schools in north Calcutta, *Indian Journal of Public Health*, **45**: 27–30.

Chaturvedi, S.K. and Michael, A. (1993), Do social and demographic factors influence the nature and localization of somatic complaints?, *Psychotherapy*, **26**: 255–260.

Chelladurai, P. and Carron, A.V. (1971), A reanalysis of formal structure in sport, *Canadian Journal of Applied Sport Sciences*, **2**: 9–14.

Chemers, M.M. and Skrzypek, G.J. (1972), Experimental test of the contingency model of leadership effectiveness, *Journal of Personality and Social Psychology*, **24**: 172–177.

Chen, S.C. (1937), Social modification of the activity of ants in nest building, *Physiological Zoology*, **10**: 420–436.

Chengappa, S. and Devi, B. (2002), Developmental milestones of language acquisition in Indian languages: Kannada and Hindi, In G. Mishra (Ed.), *Psychology in India*, **1**: 111–150.

Chomsky, N. (1965), *Aspects of Theory of Syntax*, Cambridge, Massachusetts: MIT Press.

Chomsky, N. (1968), *Language and Mind*, NY: Harcourt Brace Jovanovich.

Christensen, T.C., Wood, J.V., and Barrett, L.F. (2003), Remembering experience through the prism of self-esteem, *Personality and Social Psychology Bulletin*, **29**: 51–62.

Christianson, S. (1992), Emotional stress and eyewitness memory: A critical review, *Psychological Bulletin*, **112**: 284–390.

Christie, R. and Geis, F. (1970), (Eds.), *Studies in Machiavellianism*, NY: Academic Press.

Christy, P.R., Gelfand, D.M., and Hartmann, D.P. (1971), Effects of competition-induced frustration on two classes of modeled behaviour, *Developmental Psychology*, **5**: 104–111.

Cialdini, R.B. (1994), *Influence: Science and Practice*, 3rd edn., NY: Harper Collins.

Cialdini, R.B. (2000), *Influence: Science and Practice*, 4th edn., Boston: Allyn and Bacon.

Cialdini R.B. (2006), *Influence: The Psychology of Persuasion*, NY: Collins.

Cialdini, R.B. and Baumann, D.J. and Kenrick, D.T. (1981), Insights from sadness: A three-step model of development of altruism as hedonism, *Developmental Review*, **1**: 207–223.

Cialdini, R.B. and De Nicholas, M.E. (1989), Self-presentation by association, *Journal of Personality and Social Psychology*, **57**: 626–631.

Cialdini, R.B. and Goldstein, N.J. (2004), Social influence: Compliance and conformity, *Annual Review of Psychology*, **55**: 591–621.
Cialdini, R.B. and Insko, C.A. (1969), Attitudinal verbal reinforcement as a function of informational consistency: A further test of two factor theory, *Journal of Personality and Social Psychology*, **12**: 342–350.
Cialdini, R.B., Borden, R., Thorne, A., Walker, A., and Freeman, S. (1976), Basking in reflected glory: Three (football), field studies, *Journal of Personality and Social Psychology*, **34**: 366–375.
Cialdini, R.B., Darby, B.L., and Vincent, J.E. (1973), Transgression and altruism: A case for hedonism, *Journal of Experimental Social Psychology*, **9**: 502–516.
Cialdini, R.B., Kallgren, C.A., and Reno, R.R. (1991), A focus theory of normative conduct, *Advances in Experimental Social Psychology*, **24**: 201–234.
Cialdini, R.B., Kendrick, D.T., and Baumann, D.J. (1982), Effects of mood on prosocial behaviour in children and adults, In N. Eisenberg (Ed.), *The Development of Prosocial Behaviour*, 339–359, NY: Academic Press.
Cialdini, R.B., Schaller, M., Houlainham, D., Arps, K., Fultz, J., and Beaman, A.L. (1987), Empathy-based helping: Is it selflessly or selfishly motivated?, *Journal of Personality and Social Psychology*, **52**: 749–758.
Cialdini, R.B., Trost, M.R., and Newson, J.T. (1995), Preference for consistency: The development of a valid measure and the discovery of surprising behavioural implications, *Journal of Personality and Social Psychology*, **69**: 318–328.
Cialdini, R.B., Vincent, J.E., Lewis, S.K., Catalan, J., Wheeler, D., and Darby, B.L. (1975), Reciprocal concessions procedure for inducing compliance: The door-in-the-face technique, *Journal of Personality and Social Psychology*, **31**: 206–215.
Ciccarelli, S.K. and Meyer, G.E. (2006), *Psychology*, ND: Pearson Education.
Clark, H.H. and Clark, E.V. (1977), *Psychology and Language: An Introduction to Psycholinguistics*, NY: Harcourt Brace Javanovich.
Clark, M.S., Ouellette, R., Powel, M.C., and Milberg, S. (1987), Recipient's mood, relationship type and helping, *Journal of Personality and Social Psychology*, **53**: 94–103.
Clark, N.K. and Stephenson, G.M. (1989), Group remembering: Individual and collaborative memory, In P.B. Paulus (Ed.), *Psychology of Group Influence*, 2nd edn., Hillsdale, NJ: Erlbaum.
Clark, N.K. and Stephenson, G.M. (1995), Social remembering: Individual and collaborative memory for social information, *European Review of Social Psychology*, **6**: 127–160.
Clark, R.D. (1990), Minority influence: The role of argument refutation of the minority position and social support for the minority position, *European Journal of Social Psychology*, **20**: 489–497.
Clark, R.D. and Word, L.E. (1972), Why don't bystanders help? Because of ambiguity, *Journal of Personality and Social Psychology*, **24**: 392–400.
Clark, R.D. and Word, L.E. (1974), Where is the apathetic bystander? Situational characteristics of the emergency, *Journal of Personality and Social Psychology*, **29**: 279–287.
Clore, G.L., Bray, R.M., Itkin, S.M., and Murphy, P. (1978), Interracial attitudes and behaviour of summer camp, *Journal of Personality and Social Psychology*, **36**: 107–116.
Cohen, A.R. (1957), Need for cognition and order of communication of determinants of opinion change, In C.I. Hovland (Ed.), *The Order of Presentation is Persuasion*, NH, Conn: Yale University Press.
Cohen, A.R. (1959), Some implications of self-esteem for social influence, In C.I. Hovland and I.L. Janis (Eds.), *Personality and Persuasibility*, NH, Conn: Yale University Press.
Cohen, C.E. (1981), Person categories and social perception: Testing some boundaries of the processing effects of prior knowledge, *Journal of Personality and Social Psychology*, **40**: 441–452.
Cohen, L.L. and Swim, J.K. (1995), The differential impact of gender ratios on women and men: Tokenism, self-confidence and expectations, *Personality and Social Psychology Bulletin*, **21**: 876–884.
Cohn, E.G. (1993), The prediction of police calls for service: The influence of weather and temporal variables on rape and domestic violence, *Environmental Psychology*, **13**: 71–83.
Colby, A. and Damon, W. (1995), The development of extraordinary moral commitment, In M. Killen and D. Hart (Eds.), *Morality in Everyday Life: Developmental Perspectives*, 342–370, NY: Cambridge University Press.

Cole, T. (2001), Lying to the one you love: The use of deception in romantic relationships, *Journal of Social and Personal Relationships*, **18**: 107–129.
Collins, M.A. and Zebrowitz, L.A. (1995), The contributions of appearance to occupational outcomes in civilian and military settings, *Journal of Applied Social Psychology*, **25**: 129–163.
Collumbien, M. and Hawkes, S. (2000), Missing men's messages: Does the reproductive health approach respond to men's sexual health needs?, *Culture, Health and Sexuality*, **20**: 135–150.
Condry, J. and Condry, S. (1976), Sex differences: A study in the eye of beholder, *Child Development*, **47**: 812–819.
Conroy, C.A. and Sipple, J.W. (2001), A case study in reform: Integration of teacher education in agriculture with teacher education in mathematics and science, *Journal of Vocational Educational Research*, **26** (2): 206–243.
Contrada, R.J., Wright, R.A., and Glass, D.C. (1985), Psychophysiological correlates of Type A behaviour: Comments on Houston (1983), and Holmes (1983), *Journal of Research in Personality*, **19**: 12–30.
Cook, K. (Ed.) (1987), *Social Exchange Theory*, Newbury Park, CA: Sage.
Cook, S.W. (1969), Motives in a conceptual analysis of attitude-related behaviour, In W.J. Arnold and D. Levine (Eds.), *Nebraska Symposium on Motivation*, Vol. 17, Lincoln: University of Nebraska Press.
Cooley, C.H. (2002), *Human Nature and the Social Order*, NY: Charles Scribner's Sons.
Coon, D. and Mitterer, J.O. (2007), *Introduction to Psychology*, Delhi: Thomson Wadsworth.
Cooper, J. and Fazio, R.H. (1984), A new look at dissonance theory, In L. Berkowitz (Ed.), *Advances in Experimental Social Psychology*, **57**: 229–233, NY: Academic Press.
Cooper, J. and McGaugh, J.L. (1969), Leadership: Integrating principles of social psychology, In C.A. Gibb (Ed.), *Leadership*, Baltimore: Penguin Books.
Coopersmith, S. (1967), *The Antecedents of Self-esteem*, San Francisco: Freeman.
Coovert, M.D. and Reeder, G.D. (1990), Negativity effects in impression formation: The role of unit formation and schematic expectations, *Journal of Experimental Social Psychology*, **26**: 49–62.
Coplan, R.D., Tripathi, R.C., and Naidu, R.K. (1985), Subjective past, present and future fit: Effects on anxiety, depression and other indicators of well-being, *Journal of Personality and Social Psychology*, **48**: 180–197.
Corbin, J. and Strauss, A. (1990), Grounded theory method: Procedures, canons and evaluative criteria, *Qualitative Sociology*, **13**: 3–21.
Cota, A.A., Evans, C.R., Dion, K.L., Kilik, L., and Longaman, R.S. (1995), The structure of group cohesion, *Personality and Social Psychology Bulleting*, **21**: 512–580.
Cottrell, N.B. (1972), Social facilitation, In C. McClintock (Ed.), *Experimental Social Psychology*, NY: Holt, Rinehart and Wilson.
Cottrell, N.B., Wack, D.L., Sekerat, G.J., and Rittle, R.H. (1968), Social facilitation of dominant responses by the presence of others, *Journal of Personality and Social Psychology*, **9**: 245–250.
Courneya, K.S. and Carron, A.V. (1992), The home advantages of sports competition: A literature review, *Journal of Sports and Exercise Psychology*, **14**: 13–27.
Cowan, P.A. and Walters, R.H. (1963), Studies of reinforcement of aggression: Effects of scheduling, *Child Development*, **34**: 543–551.
Cox, K.K. (1970), Changes in stereotyping of Negroes and Whites in magazine advertisements, *Public Opinion Quarterly*, **33**: 603–606.
Cox, R.H. (1990), *Sport Psychology: Concepts and Applications*, Dubuque, DA: William C. Brown.
Cox, R.H. (1998), *Sports Psychology: Concepts and Applications*, Boston: McGraw-Hill.
Cox, S. and Davidson, W. (1995), A meta-analysis of alternative education programmes, *Crime and Delinquency*, **41**: 219–230.
Crandall, C.S. and Biernat, M. (1990), The ideology of anti-fat attitudes, *Journal of Applied Social Psychology*, **20**: 227–243.
Crandall, C.S., Preisler, J.J., and Aussprung, J. (1992), Meaning life events stress in the lives of college students: The undergraduate stress questionnaire (USQ), *Journal of Behavioural Medicine*, **15**: 627–662.
Crano, W.D. and Brewer, M.B. (1973), *Principles of Research in Social Psychology*, NY: McGraw-Hill.

Crespi, L.P. (1945), Public opinion towards conscientious objectors: III. Intensity of social rejection in stereotype and attitude, *Journal of Psychology*, **19**: 251–276.
Crocker, J. and McGraw, K.M. (1984), What's good for the goose is not good for the gender: Solo status as an obstacle to occupational achievement for males and females, *American Behavioural Scientist*, **27**: 357–370.
Crocker, J. and Park, L.E. (2004), The costly pursuit of self-esteem, *Psychological Bulletin*, **130**: 392–414.
Crocker, J. and Wolfe, C. (2001), Contingencies of self-worth, *Psychological Review*, **108**: 593–623.
Crocker, J., Thompson, L.L., McGraw, K.M., and Ingerman, C. (1987), Downward comparison, prejudice and evaluation of others: Effects of self-esteem and threat, *Journal of Personality and Social Psychology*, **52**: 907–916.
Crockett, W.H. (1955), Emergent leadership in small decision-making groups, *Journal of Abnormal and Social Psychology*, **51**: 378–383.
Crossby, F., Bromley, S., and Saxe, L. (1980), Recent unobtrusive studies of black and white discrimination and prejudice: A literature review, *Psychological Bulletin*, **87**: 546–563.
Croyle, R.J. and Cooper, J. (1983), Dissonance arousal: Physiological evidence, *Journal of Personality and Social Psychology*, **45**: 782–791.
Crutchfield, R.S. (1955), Conformity and character, *American Psychology*, **10**: 191–198.
Culter, B.L., Penrod, S.D. and Martens, T.K. (1987), Improving the reliability of eyewitness identification: Putting content into context, *Journal of Applied Psychology*, **72**: 629–637.
Cunningham, H.R., Barbee, A.P., and Pilkingham, C.C. (1990), What do women want? Facial-metric assessments of multiple motives in the perception of male physical attractiveness, *Journal of Personality and Social Psychology*, **59**: 61–72.
Cunningham, M.R. (1979), Weather, mood, and helping behaviour: Quasi-experiments with the sunshine Samartian, *Journal of Personality and Social Psychology*, **37**: 1947–1956.
Curtiss, S. (1977), *Genie: A Linguistic Study of Modern Day 'Wild-child'*, NY: Academic Press.
Dabbs, J.M. and Leventhal, H. (1966), Effects of varying the recommendations in a fear-arousing communication, *Journal of Personality and Social Psychology*, **4**: 525–531.
Dabbs, J.M. and Morris, R. (1990), Testosterone, social class and antisocial behaviour in a sample of 4462 men, *Psychological Science*, **1**: 209–211.
Dabbs, J.M., Hopper, C.H., and Jurkovic, G.J. (1990), Testosterone and personality among college students and military veterans, *Personality and Individual Differences,* **11**: 1263–1269.
Dabbs, J.N., Ruback, R.B., Fraday, R.L., Hopper, C.H., and Sgoutas, D.S. (1988), Saliva, testosterone and criminal violence against women, *Personality and Individual Differences*, **9**: 269–275.
Daftuar, C.N. and Anjali, A. (1997), Occupational stress, organizational commitment and job involvement in *Sattva*, *Rajas* and *Tamas* personality types, *Journal of Indian Psychology*, **15**: 44–52.
Dalal, A.K. (2001), Health psychology, In J. Pandey (Ed.), *Psychology in India Revisited: Developments in the Discipline*, Vol. 2, ND: Sage.
Dani, V. (1995), Female stereotypes of adolescents as a function of gender, coeducation and mother's employment, *Praachi Journal of Psycho-cultural Dimensions*, **11**(1–2): 23–26.
Dankekar, V.M. and Rath, M. (1971), *Poverty in India*, Poona: Indian School of Political Economy.
Danziger, K. (1976), *Nonverbal Communication*, NY: Pengamon.
Darby, J.M. and Batson, C.D. (1968), From jerusalem to jericho: A study of situational and dispositional variables in helping behaviour, *Journal of Personality and Social Psychology*, **8**: 377–383.
Darji, D.R. (1975), A study of leadership behaviour and its correlates in the schools of Panchmahal district, *Doctoral Dissertation*, Baroda: MS University.
Darley, J.M. (1993), Research on morality: Possible approaches, actual approaches, *Psychological Science*, **4**: 353–357.
Darley, J.M. and Batson, C.D. (1973), From jerusalem to jericho: A study of situational and dispositional variables in helping behaviour, *Journal of Personality and Social Psychology*, **27**: 100–108.

Darley, J.M. and Latane, B. (1968), Bystander intervention in emergencies: Diffusion of responsibility, *Journal of Personality and Social Psychology*, **8**: 867–881.

Darley, J.M., Teger, A.I. and Lewis, L.D. (1973), Do groups always inhibit individuals' response to potential emergencies?, *Journal of Personality and Social Psychology*, **26**: 395–399.

Das, I., Sharma, A., and Sinha, S.P. (1994), Effect of gender and economic status upon attitude towards status of women, *Journal of Indian Academy of Applied Psychology*, **20**(2): 193–196.

Dasgupta, N., Banaji, M.R., and Abelson, R.P. (1997), Beliefs and attitudes toward cohesive groups, In E.R. Smith and D.M. Mackie, *Social Psychology*, 3rd edn., NY: Psychology Press.

Dashiell, J.E. (1930), An experimental analysis of some group effects, *Journal of Abnormal and Social Psychology*, **63**: 180–187.

Dastidar, P.G. and Kapoor, S. (1996), Fractured versus intact families differential impact on children, *Journal of the Indian Academy of Applied Psychology*, **22**: 35–41.

Davies, I.R.L., Laws, G., Corbett, G.G., and Jerrett, D.J. (1998a), Cross-cultural differences in colour vision: Acquired 'colour blindness' in Africa, *Personality and Individual Differences*, **25**: 1153–1162.

Davies, I.R.L., Sowden, P., Jerrett, D.T., Jerrett, T., and Corbett, G.G. (1998b), A cross-cultural study of English and Setswana speakers on a colour triads task: A test of Sapir-Whorf hypothesis, *British Journal of Psychology*, **89**: 1–15.

Davis, J.H. (1973), Group decision and social interaction: A theory of social decision schemes, *Psychological Review*, **80**: 97–125.

Davis, K. (1947), Final note on a case of extreme isolation, *American Journal of Sociology*, **52**: 432–437.

Davis, K. (1949), *Human Society*, NY: Macmillan.

Davis, K. and Newstrom, J.W. (1985), *Human Behaviour at Work: Organizational Behaviour*, 7th edn., NY: McGraw-Hill.

Dawes, R.M. (1998), Behavioural decision-making and judgement, In D. Gilbert, S. Fiske, and G. Lindzey (Eds.), *The Handbook of Social Psychology*, 4th edn., **1**: 479–548, NY: McGraw-Hill.

Dawes, R.M. and Smith, T.L. (1985), Attitude and opinion measurement, In G. Lindzey and E. Arouson (Eds.), *The Handbook of Social Psychology*, **3**: NY: Random House.

Dawkins, R. (1982), *The Extended Phenotype*, San Francisco: Freeman.

Dawkins, R. (1985), *The Selfish Gene*, Oxford: Oxford University Press.

De Paulo, B.M. (1994), Spotting lies: Can humans learn to do better?, *Current Directions in Psychological Science*, **3**: 83–86.

De Paulo, B.M., Rosenthal, R., Eisenstat, R.A., Rogers, D.L., and Finkelstein, S. (1978), Decoding discrepant nonverbal cues, *Journal of Personality and Social Psychology*, **36**: 313–323.

De Vito, J.A. (1970), *The Psychology of Speech and Language*, NY: Random House.

Deaux, K. (1985), Sex and gender, *Annual Review of Psychology*, **36**: 49–81.

Deaux, K. and Kite, M. (1993), Gender stereotypes, In F.L. Denmark and M.A. Paludi (Eds.), *Psychology of Women: A Handbook of Issues and Theories*, 107–139, Westport, OCT: Greenwood Press.

Deaux, K. and LaFrance, M. (1998), Gender, In D.T. Gilbert, S.T. Fiske, and G. Lindzey (Eds.), *The Handbook of Social Psychology*, 4th edn., **1**: 788–827, NY: McGraw-Hill.

Deaux, K. and Martin, D. (2003), Interpersonal networks and social categories: Specifying levels of contexts in identity process, *Social Psychology Quarterly*, **66**: 101–117.

Deaux, K.K. and Emswiller, T. (1974), Explanations of successful performance on sex-linked tasks: What is skill for the male is luck for female, *Journal of Personality and Social Psychology*, **29**: 80–85.

Deaux, K.K. and Levis, L.L. (1984), Structure of gender stereotypes: Interrelationships among components and gender label, *Journal of Personality and Social Psychology*, **46**: 991–1004.

Deaux, K.K. and Lewis, L.L. (1983), Components of gender stereotypes, *Psychological Documents*, **13**: 25–34.

deCharms, R. (1957), Affiliation motivation and productivity in small groups, *Journal of Abnormal and Social Psychology*, **55**: 222–226.

Dekhtawala, P.B. (1978), A study of organizational climate, leadership behaviour, teacher morale and pupils' academic motivation in secondary schools of Gujarat state, *Research report*, Baroda: Centre for Advanced study in Education, MS University.

Delamater, J.D. and Myers, D.J. (2009), *Textbook of Social Psychology*, Australia: Cengage Learning.

Delongis, A., Lazarus, R.S., and Folkman, S. (1988), The impact of daily stress on health and mood: Psychological and social resources as mediators, *Journal of Personality and Social Psychology*, **54**(3): 486–495.

DeMaris, A., Benson, M.L., Fox, G., Hill, T., and Van Wyk, J. (2003), Distal and proximal factors in domestic violence: A test of an integrated model, *Journal of Marriage and Family*, **65**: 652–667.

Dembroski, T.M., Lasater, T.M., and Ramires, A. (1978), Communicator similarity, fear-arousing communications and compliance with health care recommendations, *Journal of Applied Social Psychology*, **8**: 254–269.

Demo, D.H. (1992), The self-concept over time: Research issues and directions, *Annual Review of Sociology*, **18**: 303–326.

DePaulo, B.M. (1992), Non-verbal behaviour and self-presentation, *Psychological Bulletin*, **111**: 203–243.

DePaulo, B.M. and Morris, W.L. (2006), The unrecognized stereotyping and discrimination against singles, *Current Directions in Psychological Science*, **15**: 251–254.

DePaulo, B.M., Lindsay, J.J., Mahone, B.F., Muhlenbruck, L., Chandler, K., and Cooper, H. (2003), Cues to deception, *Psychological Bulletin*, **129**: 74–118.

Desai, D.B. and Dekhtawala, P.B. (1979), Teacher morale: Concept and researches, In D.B. Desai, D.C. Joshi, N. Shelat and P. Buch (Eds.), *School Management and Change*, Baroda: Center for Advanced Study in Education.

Desteno, D., Petty, R.E., Wegener, D.T., and Rucker D.D. (2000), Beyond valence in the perception of likelihood: The role of emotion specificity, *Journal of Personality and Social Psychology*, **78**: 397–416.

Deutsch, M. and Gerard, A.B. (1955), A study of normative and informational social influences upon individual judgement, *Journal of Abnormal and Social Psychology*, 51, 629–636.

Deutsch, M. and Krauss, R.M. (1960), The effect of threat upon interpersonal bargaining, *Journal of Abnormal and Social Psychology*, **61**: 181–189.

Deutsch, M., Canavan, D., and Rubin, J. (1971), The effect of size of conflict and sex of the experimenter upon interpersonal bargaining, *Journal of Experimental Social Psychology*, **7**: 258–267.

Deutsh, M. and Gerard, H.B. (1955), A study of narrative and informational social influence upon individual judgement, *Journal of Abnormal and Social Psychology*, **61**: 181–189.

Devaki, L. (1994), Development of past tense in Kannada children, In B. Lakshmi Bai and D. Vaserta (Eds.), *Language Development and Language Disorders: Perspective From Indian Languages*, 53–62, ND: Bahri Publications.

Devine, P.C. (1989), Stereotypes and prejudice: This automatic and controlled components, *Journal of Personality and Social Psychology*, **56**: 5–18.

Devine, P.G. and Ostrom, T. (1988), *Dimension versus information processing apparatus to social knowledge: The case of inconsistency management*, In Bar-tel D. and Kruglanski, A.W. (Eds.), *The Social Psychology of Knowledge*, 231–261, Cambridge: Cambridge University Press.

Devos-Comby, L. and Salovey, P. (2002), Applying persuasion strategies to alter HIV relevant thoughts and behaviour, *Review of General Psychology*, **6**: 287–304.

Dhawan, N., Rosenman, J.J., Naidu, R.K., Thapa, K., and Rettek, S.I. (1995), Self-concepts across two cultures: India and the United States, *Journal of Cross-Cultural Psychology*, **20**: 606–21.

Diehl, M. and Strobe, W. (1987), Productivity loss in brainstorming groups: Towards the solution of a riddle, *Journal of Personality and Social Psychology*, **53**: 497–509.

Diener, E., Fraser, S.C., Beaman, A.L., and Kelem, Z.R.T. (1976), Effects of deindividuation variables on stealing among Halloween trick-or-treaters, *Journal of Personality and Social Psychology*, **33**: 178–183.

Dienstbier, R.A., Roesch, S.C., Mizumoto, A., Hemenover, S.H., Lott, R.C., and Carlo, G. (1998), Effects of weapons on guilt judgements and sentencing recommendations for criminals, *Basic and Applied Social Psychology*, **20**: 93–102.

Dietrich, D.M. and Berkowitz, L. (1997), Alleviation of dissonance by engaging in prosocial behaviour or receiving ego-enhancing feedback, *Journal of Social Behaviour and Personality*, **12**: 557–566.

Dijker, A.J.M. (1987), Emotional reactions to ethnic minorities, *European Journal of Social Psychology*, **47**: 1105–1117.

Dion, K., Baron, R., and Miller, N. (1970), Why do group makes riskier decision than individuals?, In L. Berkowitz (Ed.), *Advances in Experimental Social Psychology*, Vol. 5, NY: Academic Press.

Dion, K.L. and Dion, K.K. (1988), Romantic love: Individual and cultural perspectives, In R.J. Sternberg and M.L. Barnes, *The Psychology of Love*, NH, CJ: Yale University Press.

Dion, K.L., Berscheid, and Walster, E. (1974), What is beautiful is good, *Journal of Personality and Social Psychology*, **2**: 285–290.

Dittes, J.E. (1959), Attractiveness of group as function of self-esteem and acceptance by group, *Journal of Abnormal and Social Psychology*, **59**: 77–82.

Dittes, J.E. and Kelley, H.H. (1956), Effects of different conditions of acceptance upon conformity to group norms, *Journal of Abnormal and Social Psychology*, **53**: 100–107.

Dodd, D.K. (1985), Robbers in classroom: A deindividuation exercise, *Teaching in Psychology*, **12**: 89–91.

Dodge, K.A. and Coie, J.D. (1987), Social-information-processing factors in reactive and proactive aggression in children's peer groups, *Journal of Personality and Social Psychology*, **53**: 1146–1158.

Dodge, K.A. and Crick, N.R. (1990), Social information processing bases of aggressive behaviour in children. Special issue: Illustrating the value of basic research, *Personality and Social Psychology Bulletin*, **16**: 8–22.

Dodge, K.A. and Somberg, D.R. (1987), Hostile attributional biases among aggressive boys are exacerbated under conditions of threat to self, *Child Development*, **58**: 213–224.

Dodge, K.A., Pettit, G.S., McClaskey, C.C., and Brown, M.M. (1986), Social competence in children, *Monographs of the Society for Research in Child Development*, **51**(2): 1–85.

Doise, W. (1978), *Groups and Individuals: Explanations in Social Psychology*, United Kingdom: Cambridge University Press.

Dollard, J., Doob J., Miller, N., Mowrer, O., and Sears, R. (1939), *Frustration and Aggression*, NH: Yale University Press.

Donnellan, M.B., Trzesniewski, K.H., Robins, R.W., Moffitt, T.E., and Caspi, A. (2005), Low self-esteem is related to aggression, anti-social behaviour and delinquency, *Psychological Science*, **16**: 328–335.

Donnerstein, M. and Donnerstein, E. (1976), Modeling in control of interracial aggressions: The problem of generality, *Journal of Personality*, **45**: 100–116.

Doosje, B. and Branscombe, N.R. (2003), Attributions for the negative historical actions of groups, *European Journal of Social Psychology*, **33**: 235–248.

Dovidio, J.E., Gaerther, S.L., Isen, A.M., and Lawrance, R. (1995), Group representations and intergroup bias: Positive affect, similarity and group size, *Personality and Social Psychology Bulletin*, **21**: 856–865.

Dovidio, J.F. (1984), Helping behaviour and altruism: An empirical and conceptual overview, In L. Berkowitz (Ed.), *Advances in Experimental Social Psychology*, **17**: 362–427, NY: Academic Press.

Dovidio, J.F. and Gaertner, S.L. (1981), The effects of race, status and ability on helping behaviour, *Social Psychology Quarterly*, **44**: 192–203.

Dovidio, J.F., Allen, J.L., and Schroeder, D.A. (1990), Specificity of empathy-induced helping: Evidence for altruistic motivation, *Journal of Personality and Social Psychology*, **59**: 249–260.

Dovidio, J.F., Brigham, J.C., Johnson, B.T., and Gaertner, S.L. (1996), Stereotyping prejudice and discrimination: Another look, In C.N. Macrae, C. Stangor and M. Hewstone (Eds.), *Stereotypes and Stereotyping*, NY: The Guilford Press.

Dovidio, J.F., Gaertner, S.L., and Validzic, A. (1998), Intergroup bias: Status, differentiation and a common in-group identity, *Journal of Personality and Social Psychology*, **75**: 109–120.

Dovidio, J.F., Piliavin, J.A., Gaertner, S.L., Schroeder, D.A., and Clark, R.D. (1991), The arousal cost reward model and the process of intervention, In M.S. Clark (Ed.), *Review of Personality and Social Psychology, Prosocial Behaviour,* 86–116 Newbury Park, CA: Sage.

Dreben, E.K., Fieske, S.T., and Hastie, R. (1979), The independence of evaluative and item information: Impression and recall order effects in behaviour-based impression formation, *Journal of Personality and Social Psychology*, **37**: 1758–1768.

Duan, C. (2000), Being empathic: The role of motivation to empathize and the nature of target emotions, *Motivation and Emotions*, **24**: 29–49.

Dube, S. and Sachdev, P.S. (1983), *Mental Health Problems of Socially disadvantaged*, New Delhi: Tata McGraw-Hill.

Dubrovsky, V.J., Kiesler, S., and Sethna, B.M. (1991), The equalization phenomena: Status effects in computer-mediated and face-to-face decision-making groups, *Human Computer Interaction*, **6**: 119–146.

Duncan, B.L. (1976), Differential social perception and attribution of intergroup violence: Testing the lower limits of stereotyping blacks, *Journal of Personality and Social Psychology*, **34**: 590–598.

Dunn, J.F. and Plomin, R. (1990), *Separate Lives: Why Siblings are so Different*, NY: Basic Books.

Dunning, D. and Perretta, S. (2002), Automaticity and eyewitness accuracy: A 10–12 second rule for distinguishing accurate from inaccurate positive identifications, *Journal of Applied Psychology*, **87**: 951–962.

Dunning, D. and Sherman, D.A. (1997), Stereotypes and facit inference, *Journal of Personality and Social Psychology*, **73**: 459–471.

Dunning, D. and Stern, LB. (1994), Distinguishing accurate and inaccurate eyewitness identification via inquiries about decision processes, *Journal of Personality and Social Psychology*, **30**: 510–517.

Dusenberry, D. and Knower, F.H. (1939), Experimental studies of symbolism of action and voice II: A study of specificity of meaning in abstract tonal symbols, *Quarterly Journal of Speech*, **25**: 67–75.

Duval, S., Duval, V.H., and Neely, R. (1979), Self-focus, felt responsibility and helping behaviour, *Journal of Personality and Social Psychology*, **37**: 1769–1778.

Dweck, C.S. (1975), The role of expectations and attributions in the alleviation of learned helplessness, *Journal of Personality and Social Psychology*, **31**: 647–685.

Dyson, J.W., Godwin, P.H. and Hazlewood, L.A. (1976), Group composition, leadership orientation and decisional outcomes, *Small Group Behaviour*, **7**: 114–128.

Eagly, A.H. (1987), *Sex Differences in Social Behaviour: A Social Role Interpretation*, Hillsdale, NJ: Lawrence Erlbaum Associates.

Eagly, A.H. and Carli, L. (1981), Sex of researcher and sex-typed communications as determinants of sex differences and influenceability: A meta-analysis of social influence studies, *Psychological Bulletin*, **90**: 1–20.

Eagly, A.H. and Johnson, B.T. (1990), Gender and leadership style: A meta-analysis, *Psychological Bulletin*, **108**: 233–256.

Eagly, A.H. and Karau, S.J. (1991), Gender and emergence of leaders: A meta-analysis, *Journal of Personality and Social Psychology*, **60**: 685–710.

Eagly, A.H. and Mladinic, A. (1989), Gender stereotypes and attitudes towards women and men, *Personality and Social Psychology Bulletin*, **15**: 543–558.

Eagly, A.H. and Mladinic, A. (1994), Are people prejudiced against women? Some answers from research on attitudes, gender stereotypes and judgement of competence, In W. Stroebe and M. Newstone (Eds.), *European Review of Social Psychology*, **5**: 1–35, NY: Wiley.

Eagly, A.H. and Warren, R. (1976), Intelligence, comprehension and opinion change, *Journal of Personality*, **44**: 226–242.

Eagly, A.H. and Wood, W. (1999), The origins of sex differences in human behaviour: Evolved dispositions versus social roles, *American Psychologist*, **54**: 408–423.

Eagly, A.H., Ashmore, R.D., Makhijani, M.G., and Longo, L.C. (1991), What is beautiful is good but...: a meta-analytic review of research on the physical attractiveness stereotype, *Psychology Bulletin*, **110**: 107–128.

Eagly, A.H., Chen, S., Chaiken, S., and Shaw–Barnes, K. (1999), The impact of attitudes on memory: An affair to remember, *Psychological Bulletin*, **124**: 64–89.

Eagly, A.H., Karau, S.J., and Makhijani, M.G. (1995), Gender and effectiveness of leaders: A meta-analysis, *Psychological Bulletin*, **117**: 125–145.

Eagly, A.H., Kulasa, P., Brannon, L.A., Shaw, K., and Hutson-Comeaux, S. (2000), Why counterattitudinal messages are as memorable as proattitudinal messages: The importance of active defence against attack, *Personality and Social Psychology Bulletin*, **26**: 1392–1408.

Ebbesen, E.B., Duncan, B., and Konecvi, V.J. (1975), Effects of contents of verbal aggression on future verbal aggression: A field experiment, *Journal of Experimental Social Psychology*, **11**: 192–204.

Eccles, J.S., Wigfield, A., and Schiefele, V. (1998), Motivation to succeed. In W. Damon (Ed.) *Handbook of Child Psychology*, 5th ed., Vol. 13, NY: Wiley.

Eccles, J.S., Wigfield, A., Harold, R., and Blumenfeld, P.B. (1993), Age and gender differences in children's self and task perceptions during elementary school, *Child Development*, **64**: 830–847.

Eckes, T. (1995), Features of situations: A two-mode clustering study of situation prototypes, *Personality and Social Psychology Bulletin*, **21**: 366–374.

Eddy, J., Fitzhugh, E., and Wang, M. (2000), Smoking acquisition: Peer influence and self-selection, *Psychological Reports*, **86**: 1241–1246.

Edwards, A.L. and Kilpatrick, F.P. (1948), A technique for the construction of attitude scales, *Journal of Applied Psychology*, **32**: 374–384.

Edwards, J. (1979), The home field advantage, In J.H. Goldstein (Ed.), *Sports, Games and Play: Social and Psychological Viewpoints*, Hillsdale, NJ: Erlbaum.

Edwards, J. and Archambault, D. (1989), The home field advantage, In J.H. Goldstein (Ed.), *Sports, Games and Play: Social and Psychological Viewpoints*, Hillsade, NJ: Erlbaum.

Edwards, K. (1990), The interplay of affect and cognition in attitude formation and change, *Journal of Personality and Social Psychology*, **59**: 202–216.

Eggleton, T. (2001), *Children's Literacy Development*, Boston: Allyn and Bacon.

Egloff, B. and Schmukle, S.C. (2002), Predictive validity of an implicit association test for assessing anxiety, *Journal of Personality and Social Psychology*, **83**: 1441–1455.

Ehrlich, D., Guttman, I., Schonback, P., and Mills, J. (1957), Post-decision exposure to relevant information, *Journal of Abnormal and Social Psychology*, **54**: 98–102.

Eich, E. (1995), Searching for mood dependent memory, *Psychological Sciences*, **6**: 67–75.

Eisenberg, N. and Miller, P.A. (1987), The relation of empathy to prosocial and related behaviour, *Psychological Bulletin*, **101**: 91–119.

Eisenberg, N., Guthrie, I.K., Cumberland, A., Murphy, B.C., Shepard, S.A., Zhou, Q., and Carlo, G. (2002), Prosocial development in early childhood: A longitudinal study, *Journal of Personality and Social Psychology*, **82**: 993–1006.

Eisner, M.S. (1977), Ethical problems in social psychological experimentation in the laboratory, *Canadian Psychological Review*, **18**: 233–241.

Ekman, P. (1964), Body positions, facial expression and verbal behaviour during interviews, *Journal of Abnormal and Social Psychology*, **68**: 295–301.

Ekman, P. and O'Sullivan, M. (1991), Who can catch a liar?, *American Psychologist*, **46**: 913–920.

Ekman, P., Sorenson, E.R., and Friesen, W.V. (1969), Pan cultural elements in facial displays of emotions, *Science*, **164**: 86–88.

Ekman, S. (1993), Facial expression and emotion, *American Psychologist*, **48**: 384–392.

Ekman, S. and Friesen, M.V. (1975), *Unmarking the Face*, Englewood Cliffs, NJ: Prentice-Hall.

Eldersveld, S.J. and Dodge, R.W. (1954), Personal contact or mail propaganda? An experiment in voting turn out and attitude change, In D. Katz, D. Cartwright, S. Eldersveld and A.M. Lee (Eds.), *Public Opinion and Propaganda*, NY: Dryden Press.

Elkin, F. and Handel, G. (1978), *The Child and Society: The Process of Socialization*, NY: Random House.

Elkins, S.M. (1968), *Slavery: A Problem in American Institutional and Intellectual Life*, Chicago: University of Chicago Press.

Elliot, A.J. and Devine, P.G. (1994), On the motivational nature of cognitive dissonance as psychological comfort, *Journal of Personality and Social Psychology*, **67**: 382–394.

Ellsworth, P.C. and Carlsmith, J.M. (1968), Effects of eye contact and verbal contact on affective response to a dyadic interaction, *Journal of Personality and Social Psychology*, **10**: 15–20.
Emmons, R.A. and Diener, E. (1986), Situation selection as moderator of response consistency and stability, *Journal of Personality and Social Psychology*, **51**: 1013–1019.
Emmons, R.A., Diener, E., and Larsen, R.J. (1986), Choice and avoidance of everyday situations and affect congruence: Two models of reciprocal interactionism, *Journal of Personality and Social Psychology*, **51**: 815–826.
Emswiller, T., Deaux, K., and Wills, J.E. (1971), Similarity, sex and requests for small favours, *Journal of Applied Social Psychology*, **1**: 284–291.
Enayatullah (1981), Religious affiliation and attitudes of students in an Indian university, *Unpublished Doctoral Dissertation*, Ranchi: Ranchi University.
Enayatullah (1984), Religious affiliation and prejudice, *National Seminar on Psychology and Secularism in India*, Ranchi: Bihar Psychological Association and P.G. Department of Psychology, Ranchi University.
Ennis, R. and Zanna, M.D. (2000), Attitude function and the automobile, In G.R. Maio and J.M. Olson (Eds.), *Why We Evaluate: Functions of Attitudes*, 1–36, Mahwah, NJ: Lawrence Erlbaum Associates.
Entwisle, D.R. and Alexander, K.L. (1993), Entry into the school: The beginning school transition and educational stratification in the United States, *Annual Review of Sociology*, **19**: 401–423.
Epstein, S. (1992), Coping ability, negative self-evaluation, and overgeneralization: Experiment and theory, *Journal of Personality and Social Psychology*, **62**: 826–836.
Erdley, C.A. and D'Agostino, P.R. (1989), Cognitive and affective components automatic priming effects, *Journal of Personality and Social Psychology*, **54**: 741–747.
Erikson, E.H. (1963), *Childhood and Society*, NY: Horton.
Erikson, E.H. (1964), Notes on the Sociology of Deviance, In H. Becker (Ed.), *The Other Side*, NY: Free Press.
Esser, J.K. and Komorita, S.S. (1975), Reciprocity and concession-making in bargaining, *Journal of Personality and Social Psychology*, **31**: 864–872.
Esses, V.M., Jackson, L.M., and Armstrong, T.L. (1998), Intergroup competition and attitudes towards immigrants and immigration: An instrumental model of group conflict, *Journal of Social Issues*, **54**: 699–724.
Estrada, C.A., Isen, A.M., and Young, M.J. (1995), Positive affect improves creative problem solving and influences reported source of practice satisfaction in physicians, *Motivation and Emotion*, **18**: 285–300.
Evans, G.W., Lepore, S.I., Shejwal, B.R., and Palsane, M.N. (1998), Chronic residential crowding and children's well-being: An ecological perspective, *Child Development*, **69**: 1514–1523.
Evans, M.G. (1970), The effects of supervisory behaviour on the path-goal relationship, *Organizational Behaviour and Human Performance*, **5**: 277–298.
Exline, R.V. and Winters, L. (1965), Affective relations and mutual glances in dyads, In S. Tomkins and C. Izard (Eds.), *Affect, Cognition and Personality*, NY: Springer.
Eysenck, M.W. and Keane, M.T. (1995), *Cognitive Psychology: A Students' Handbook*, Hove: Erlbaum.
Fabrigar, L.R. and Petty, R.E. (1999), The role of affective and cognitive bases of attitudes in susceptibility to affectively and cognitively-based persuasion, *Personality and Social Psychology Bulletin*, **25**: 363–381.
Faizo, R.H. (1990), Multiple processes by which attitudes guide behaviour: The MODE model as an integrative framework. In L. Berkowitz (Ed.), *Advances in Experimental Social Psychology,* **23**: 75–109. NY: Academic Press.
Fao, E. and Foa, V. (1976), Resource theory of social exchange, In J. Thibout J. Spence and R. Carson (Eds.), *Contemporary Trends in Social Psychology*, Morristown, NJ: General Learning Press.
Farooqui, M.A (1958), Cooperation, competition and group structure. *Journal of Psychological Researches,* **2**: 60–70.
Farquhar, J.W., Maccoby, N., Wood, P.D., Alexander, J.K., Breitrose, H., Brown, B.W., Haskell, W.L., McAlister, A.L., Meyer, A.J., Nash, J.D., and Stern, M.P. (1977), *Community Education for Cardiovascular Health*, 1192–1195, Lancet.

Fay, P.J. and Middleton, W.C. (1941), The ability to judge sociability from voice as transmitted over a public address system, *Character and Personality*, **13**: 303–309.

Fazio, R.H. (1989), On the power and functionality of attitudes: The role of attitude accessibility, In A.R. Pratkanis, S.J. Breckler and A.G. Greenwald (Eds.), *Attitude Structure and Function*, 153–179, Hillsdale: NJ: Erlbaum.

Fazio, R.H. and Williams, C.J. (1986), Attitude accessibility as a moderator of the attitude-perception and attitude behaviour relations: An investigation of the 1984 presidential election, *Journal of Personality and Social Psychology*, **51**: 505–514.

Fazio, R.H., Jackson, J.R., Dunton, B.C., and Williams, C.J. (1995), Variability in automatic activation as an unobstrusive measure of racial attitudes: A bonafide pipeline?, *Journal of Personality and Social Psychology*, **69**: 1013–1027.

Fazio, R.H., Sanbonmastu, D.M., Powell, M.C., and Kardes, F.R. (1986), On the automatic activation of attitudes, *Journal of Personality and Social Psychology*, **50**: 229–238.

Fein, S. and Spencer, S.J. (1997), Prejudice as self-image maintenance: Affirming the self through derogating others, *Journal of Personality and Social Psychology*, **73**: 31–34.

Feldman, R.S. (1985), *Social Psychology*, NY: McGraw-Hill.

Feldman, R.S. and Donohoe, L.F. (1978), Non-verbal communication of affect in interracial dyads, *Journal of Educational Psychology*, **70**: 979–987.

Felson, R.B. (1981), Ambiguity and bias in the self-concept, *Social Psychology Quarterly*, **44**: 66–69.

Felson, R.B. (1984), The effect of self-appraisals of ability on academic performance, *Journal of Personality and Social Psychology*, **47**: 944–952.

Felson, R.B. (1985), Reflected appraisal and the development of self, *Social Psychology Quarterly*, **48**: 71–78.

Felson, R.B. (1989), Parents and the reflected appraisal process: A longitudinal analysis, *Journal of Personality and Social Psychology*, **56**: 965–971.

Felson, R.B. and Reed, M. (1986), The effects of parents on the self-appraisal of children, *Social Psychology Quarterly*, **49**: 302–308.

Felson, R.B. and Zeilinski, M. (1986), Children's self-esteem and parental support, *Journal of Marriage and the Family*, **51**: 727–735.

Ferguson, L.W. (1935), The influence of individual attitude on construction of an attitude scale, *Journal of Social Psychology*, **6**: 115–117.

Fernandez, E. and Sheffield, J. (1996), Relative contributions of life events versus deity hassles to the frequency and intensity of headaches, *Headache*, **36**(10): 595–602.

Fernandez, C.F. and Vecchio, R.P. (1997), Situational leadership theory revisited: A test of an across-jobs perspective, *Leadership Quarterly*, **8**(1): 67–84.

Feschback, N. (1980), The child as 'psychologist' and 'economist', In D.L. Pennington, K. Cillen, and P.S. Hill, *Social Psychology*, London: Arnold.

Feshbach, S. (1961), The stimulating versus cathartic effects of a vicarious aggressive activity, *Journal of Abnormal and Social Psychology*, **63**: 381–385.

Feshbach, S. (1984), The catharsis hypothesis, aggression drive and the reduction of aggression, *Aggressive Behaviour*, **10**: 91–101.

Feshbach, S. and Singer, R.D. (1971), *Television and Aggression*, San Francisco: Jossey-Bass.

Festinger, L. (1954), A theory of social comparison processes, *Human Relations*, **7**: 117–140.

Festinger, L. (1957), *A Theory of Cognitive Dissonance*, Stanford, CA: Stanford University Press.

Festinger, L. and Carlsmith, J.M. (1959), Cognitive consequences of forced compliance, *Journal of Abnormal and Social Psychology*, **58**: 203–210.

Festinger, L. and Maccoby, M. (1964), On resistance to persuasive communications, *Journal of Abnormal and Social Psychology*, **47**: 382–389.

Festinger, L., Peptone, A., and Newcomb, T. (1952), Some consequences of deindividuation in a group, *Journal of Abnormal and Social Psychology*, **47**: 382–389.

Festinger, L., Schachter, S., and Back, K. (1950), *Social Pressures in Informal Groups: A Study of Human Factors in Housing*, Stanford, CA: Stanford University Press.

Fiatarone, M.A., Morley, J.E., Bloom, E.T., Benton, D., Makinoden, T., and Solomon, G.F. (1988), Endogenous opioids and the exercised-induced augmentation of natural killer cell activity, *Journal of Laboratory and Clinical Medicine*, **112**: 544–552.

Fiedler, F.E. and Gracia, J.E. (1987), *New approaches to Effective Leadership: Cognitive resources and effective performance*, New York: John Wiley.

Fiedler, F.E. (1958), Interpersonal perception and group effectiveness, In Tagiuri and Petrullo (Eds.), *Person Perception and Interpersonal Behaviour*, Stanford: Stanford University Press.

Fiedler, F.E. (1967), *Theory of Leadership Effectiveness*, NY: McGraw-Hill.

Fiedler, F.E. (1978), The contingency model and the dynamics of leadership process, In L. Berkowitz (Ed.), *Advances in Experimental Social Psychology*, Vol. II, NY: Academic Press.

Fiedler, F.E. (1981), Leadership effectiveness, *American Behavioural Scientist*, **24**: 619–632.

Fiedler, K., Walther, E., Freytag, P., and Nickel, S. (2003), Inductive reasoning and judgement interference: Experiments on Simpson's paradox, *Personality and Social Psychology Bulletin*, **29**: 14–27.

Fine, M. and Asch, A. (Eds.), 1988, *Women with Disabilities*, Philadelphia: Temple University Press.

Firestone, I.J. (1977), Reconciling verbal and nonverbal models of dyadic communication, *Environmental Psychology* and *Nonverbal Behaviour*, **2**: 30–44.

Fischer, D. (1989), *Albion's Seed: Four British Folkways in America*, NY: Oxford University Press.

Fishbein, M. and Ajzaen, I. (1975), *Belief, Attitude, Intention, and Behaviour: An Introduction to Theory and Research*, Reading, MA: Addison-Wesley.

Fishbein, M. and Ajzen, I. (1980), *Understanding Attitudes and Predicting Social Behaviour*, Upper Saddle River, NJ: Prentice-Hall.

Fishbein, M. and Hunter R. (1964), Summations versus balance in attitudinal organizations and change, *Journal of Abnormal and Social Psychology*, **69**: 505–510.

Fishbein, M., Ajzen, I., and Hindle, R. (1980), Predicting and understanding voting in American elections: Effects of external variables, In I. Ajzen, and M. Fishbein (Eds.), *Understanding Attitudes and Predicting Behaviour*, Englewood Cliffs, NJ: Prentice-Hall.

Fisher, J.D. and Byrne, D. (1975), Too close for comfort: Sex differences in response to invasions of personal space, *Journal of Personality and Social Psychology*, **32**: 15–21.

Fisher, R.J. (1982), *Social Psychology: An Applied Approach*, NY: St. Martin's Press.

Fishman, P. (1983), Interaction: The work women do, In B. Thorne, C. Kramerae and N. Henley (Eds.), *Language, Gender and Society*, Rowley, MA: Newbury House.

Fiske, A.P. (1991), The cultural relativity of selfish individualism: Anthropological evidence that humans are inherently sociable, In M.S. Clark (Ed.), *Review of Personality and Social Psychology*, **12**: 176–214, Newbury Park, CA: Sage.

Fiske, A.P., Kitayama, S., Markus, H.R., and Nisbett, R.E. (1998), The cultural matrix of social psychology, In D.T. Gilbert, S.T. Fiske, and G. Lindzey (Eds.), *The Handbook of Social Psychology*, **2**: 915–981, Boston: McGraw-Hill.

Fiske, S.T. (1993), Social cognition and social perception, In L.W. Porsen and M.R. Rosenzweig (Eds.), *Annual Review of Psychology*, **44**: 155–194.

Fiske, S.T. and Neuberg, S.L. (1990), A continuum of impression formation, from category based to individualling processes: Influences of information and motivation on attention and interpretation, In M. Zanna (Ed.), *Advances in Experimental Social Psychology*, **23**: 1–74, San Diego, CA: Academic Press.

Fiske, S.T. and Taylor, S.E. (1991), *Social Cognition*, NY: McGraw-Hill.

Fitzpatrick, A.R. and Eagly, A.H. (1981), Anticipatory belief polarization as a function of the expertise of a discussion partner, *Personality and Social Psychology Bulletin*, **1**: 636–642.

Fitzsimmons, S.J. and Marcuse, F.L. (1961), Adjustment in leaders and non-leaders as measured by the sentence completion project technique, *Journal of Clinical Psychology*, **17**: 380–381.

Flanders, N.A. (1970), *Analyzing Teaching Behaviour*, Reading, Mass: Addison-Wesley.
Fletcher, G.J.O. and Haig, B. (1990), The layperson as naïve scientists: An appropriate model for personality and social psychology, In E.R. Smith and D.M. Mackie, *Social Psychology*, 3rd edn., Hove: Psychological Press.
Fletcher, G.J.O., Simpson, J.A., Thomas, G., and Giles, L. (1999), Ideal in intimate relationships, *Journal of Personality and Social Psychology*, **76**: 72–89.
Flowers, M.L. (1977), A laboratory test of some implications of Janis' groupthink hypothesis, *Journal of Personality and Social Psychology*, **35**: 888–896.
Flynn, F.J., Reagans, R.E., Amanatullah, E.J., and Ames, D.R. (2006), Helping one's way to the top: Self-monitors achieve status by helping others and knowing who helps them, *Journal of Personality and Social Psychology*, **91**: 1123–1137.
Folger, R. and Baron, R.A. (1996), Violence and hostility at work: A model of reactions to perceived injustice, In G.R. Vanden Bos and E.Q. Bulato (Eds.), *Violence on the Job: Identifying Risks and Developing Solutions*, 51–85, Washington, D.C.: American Psychological Association.
Folkes, V.S. and Sears, D.O (1977), Does everybody like a liker?, *Journal of Experimental Psychology*, **13**: 505–519.
Folkman, S. and Lazarus, R.S. (1980), An analysis of coping in a middle-aged community sample, *Journal of Health and Social Behaviour*, **21**(3): 219–239.
Forgas, J.P. and Williams, K.D. (2001), *Social Influence: Direct and Indirect Processes*, Philadelphia: Psychology Press.
Forge, K.L. and Phemister, S. (1987), The effects of prosocial cartoons on preschool children, *Child Study Journal*, **17**: 83–88.
Forrest, J.A. and Feldman, R.S. (2000), Detecting deception and judge's involvement: Lower task involvement leads to better lie detection, *Personality and Social Psychology Bulletin*, **20**: 118–125.
Forster, J., Friedman, R.S., and Liberman, N. (2004), Temporal construal effects on abstract and concrete thinking: Consequence for insight and creative cognition, *Journal of Personality and Social Psychology*, **87**: 177–189.
Forsterling, F. (1988), *Attribution Theory in Clinical Depression*, Chichester: Wiley.
Forsysh, D.R. (1999), *Group Dynamics*, Belmount, CA: Wadsworth.
Forsyth, D.R. (1990), *Group Dynamics*, Pacific Grove, CA: Brooks/Cole.
Forsyth, D.R. (1998), *Group Dynamics*, 3rd edn., Pacific Grove, CA: Books/Cole.
Fox, G.L., Benson, M.L., Demorris, A.A. and Van Wyk J. (2002), Economic distress and intimate violence: Testing family stress and resource theories, *Journal of Marriage and Family*, **64**: 793–807.
Frable, D.E., Blackstone, J., and Scherbaum, C. (1990), Marginal and mindful: Deviants in social interactions, *Journal of Personality and Social Psychology*, **59**: 140–149.
Frager, R. and Fadiman, J. (2009), *Personality and Personal Growth*, ND: Pearson.
Franco, F.M. and Maass, A. (1996), Implicit versus explicit strategies of out-group discrimination: The role of intentional control in biased language use and reward allocation, *Journal of Language and Social Psychology*, **15**: 335–359.
Franiuk, R., Cohen, D. and Pomerantz, E.M. (2002), Implicit theories of relationships: Implications for relationship satisfaction and longevity, *Personal Relationships*, **9**: 345–367.
Frank, M.G. and Ekman, P. (1997), The ability to detect deceit generalizes across different types of high-stake lies, *Journal of Personality and Social Psychology*, **72**: 1429–1439.
Franks, D. and Marolla, J. (1976), Efficacious action and social approval as interacting dimensions of self-esteem, *Sociometry*, **39**: 324–341.
Fransden, K.D. (1963), Effects of threat appears and media transmission, *Speech Monographs*, **30**: 101–104.
Freed, B. (1980), Foreigner talk, baby talk and native talk, *International Journal of Sociology of Language*, **28**: 2.
Freedman, A. (1952), *Principles of Sociology*, NY: Holt.
Freedman, J.L. (1984), Effect of television violence on aggressiveness, *Psychological Bulletin*, **96**: 227–246.
Freedman, J.L. and Fraser, S.C. (1966), Compliance without pressure: The foot-in-the-door technique, *Journal of Personality and Social Psychology*, **4**: 195–202.

Freedman, J.L. and Sears, D.O. (1965), Warming, distraction and resistance to influence, *Journal of Personality and Social Psychology*, **1**: 262–266.

French, J.R.P. and Raven, B.H. (1959), The bases of social power, In D. Cartwright (Ed.), *Studies in Social Power*, Ann Arbor: University of Michigan.

Freud, S. (1950), Why war?, In J. Strachey (Ed.), *In Collected Papers*, Vol. 3, NY: Basic Books.

Freund, T., Kruglauski, A.W., and Shpitzajzen, A. (1985), The freezing and unfreezing of impression primacy: Effects of need for structure and fear of invalidity, *Personality and Social Psychology Bulletin*, **11**: 479–487.

Friedman, H.S., Riggio, R.E., and Casella, D.F (1988), Non-verbal skill, personal charisma and initial attraction, *Personality and Social Psychology Bulletin*, **14**: 203–211.

Friedrich, L.K. and Stein, A.H. (1973), Aggressive and prosocial television programmes and the natural behaviour of preschool children, *Monograhs of the Society for Research in Child Development*, **38**(4): Whole No. 151.

Friedrich–Cofer, L. and Huston, A.C. (1986), Television violence and aggression: The debate continues, *Psychological Bulletin*, **100**: 364–371.

Frieze, L. and Weiner, B. (1971), Cue utilization and attributional judgements for success and failure, *Journal of Personality*, **39**: 591–605.

Frith, U. (1985), Beneath the surface of developmental dyslexia, In K.E. Patterson, J.C. Marshall, and H. Coltheart (Eds.), *Surface Dyslexia Neuropsychological and Cognitive Studies in Phonological Reading*, 301–310, London: Erbium.

Fritzsche, B.A., Finkelstein, M.A. and Penner, L.A. (2000), To help or not to help: Capturing individuals decision policies, *Social Behaviour and Personality*, **28**: 561–578.

Fromkin, V., Krashen, S., Curtiss, S., Rigler, D., and Rigler, M. (1974), The development of language in genie: A case of language acquisition beyond the critical period, *Brain and Language*, **1**: 81–107.

Fry, P.S. and Ghosh, R. (1980), Attributions of success and failure: Comparison of cultural differences between Asian and Caucasian children, *Journal of Cross-Cultural Psychology*, **11**: 343–363.

Fuegen, K. and Brehm, J.W. (2004), The intensity of affect and resistance to social influence, In E.S. Knowles and J.A. Linn (Eds.), *Resistance and Persuasion*, 39–63, Mahwah. NJ: Erlbaum.

Fultz, J., Shaller, H., and Cialdini, R.B. (1988), Empathy, sadness and distress: Three related but distant vicarious affective responses to author's sufferings, *Personality and Social Psychology Bulletin*, **14**: 312–325.

Funk, J.B., Bechtoldt–Baldacci, H., Pasold, T. and Baumgartner, J. (2004), Violence exposure in real life, videogames, television, movies, and the internet: Is there desensitization?, *Journal of Adolescence*, **27**: 23–39.

Gabrenya, W.K., Wang, Y., and Latane, B. (1985), Social loafing on an optimizing task: Cross-cultural differences among Chinese and Americans, *Journal of Cross-cultural Psychology*, **16**: 223–242.

Gaertner, S.L., Rust, M.C., Dovidio, J.F., Bachman, B.A. and Anastasio, P.A. (1994), The contact hypothesis: The role of common ingroup identity on reducing intergroup bias, *Small Group Research*, **25**: 224–249.

Galton, M. (1987), An ORACLE Chronicle: A decade of classroom research, *Teaching and Teacher Education*, **3**: 299–313.

Gandhi, K.A. (1977), A study of school climate as a function of personality of school personnel and pupils' control ideology, In J. Pandey's (Ed.), *Psychology in India*, Vol. II, ND: Sage.

Ganesh, S.R and Joshi, P. (1985), Institution building: Lessons from Vikram Sarabhai's leadership, *Vikalpa*, **10**: 399–413.

Ganguli, H.C. (1971), Psychological Research in India: 1920–67, *International Journal of Psychology*, **6**: 165–177.

Gardner, R.M. and Tockerman, Y.R. (1994), A computer-TV methodology for investigating the influence of somato-type on perceived personality traits, *Journal of Social Behaviour and Personality*, **9**: 555–563.

Garland, H.A., Hardy, A., and Stephenson, L. (1975), Information search as affected by attribution type and response category, *Personality and Social Psychology Bulletin*, **1**: 612–615.

Garnham, A. and Oakhill, J. (1994), *Thinking and Reasoning*, Oxford: Blackwell.

Gecas, V. and Burke, P.J. (1995), Self and Identity, In K.S. Cook, G.A. Fine and J.S. House (Eds.), *Sociological Perspectives on Social Psychology*, Needham Heights: Allyn and Bacon.

Gecas, V. and Schwalbe, M. (1983), Beyond the looking glass self: Social structure and efficacy base self-esteem, *Social Psychology Quartely*, **46**: 77–88.

Geen, R.G. (1989), Alternative conceptions of social facilitation, In P.B. Paulus (Ed.), *Psychology of Group Influence*, NY: Academic Press.

Geen, R.G. (1991), Social motivation, *Annual Review of Psychology*, **42**: 377–391.

Geen, R.G. and Quanty, M. (1977), The catharsis of aggression: An evaluation of a hypothesis, In L. Berkowitz (Ed.), *Advances in Experimental Social Psychology*, **10**: NY: Academic Press.

Geen, R.G. and Stonner, D. (1971), Effects of aggressiveness habit strength on behaviour in the presence of aggression-related stimuli, *Journal of Personality and Social Psychology*, **31**: 721–726.

Geen, R.G., Stonner, D., and Shope, G.L. (1975), The facilitation of aggression by aggression: Evidence against the catharsis hypothesis, *Journal of Personality and Social Psychology*, **31**: 721–726.

Geers, A.L., Handley, I.M., and McLarney, A.R. (2003), Discerning the role of optimism in persuasion: The valence-enhancement hypothesis, *Journal of Personality and Social Psychology*, **85**: 554–565.

Geertz, C. (1974), From the native's point of view: On the nature of anthropological understanding. In K. Basso and H. Selby (Eds.), *Meaning in Anthropology*, Albuquerque: University of New Mexico.

Geidt, F.H. (1955), Comparison of visual, content and auditory cues in interviewing, *Journal of Consulting Psychology*, **19**: 407–416.

Geis, M.L. (1995), *Speech Acts and Conversational Interaction*, NY: Cambridge University Press.

Gelles, R.J. and Cornell, C.P. (1990), *Intimate Violence in Families*, 2nd edn., Newbury Park, CA: Sage.

Gerard, H.B., Wilhelmy, R.A., and Conolley, E.S. (1968), Conformity and group size, *Journal of Personality and Social Psychology*, **8**: 79–82.

Gergen, K.J. (1978), Experimentation in social psychology: A reappraisal, *European Journal of Social Psychology*, **8**: 507–527.

Geschwind, N. (1972), Language and the brain, *Scientific American*, **220**: 76–83.

Getzels, J.W. (1969), A social psychology of education, In G. Lindzey and E. Arouson (Eds.), *The Handbook of Social Psychology*, 2nd edn., **5**: Reading, Mass: Addison-Wesley.

Ghosh, S.N. and Sharma, S. (1998), Trait anxiety and anger expression in patients with essential hypertension, *Journal of Indian Academy of Applied Psychology*, **24**: 9–14.

Gibb, C.A. Leadership, In G. Lindzey and E. Arous (Eds.), *Handbook of Social Psychology*, 2nd edn., Vol. 4, Reading Mass: Addison-Wesley.

Gibbons, F.X. (1990), Self-evaluation and self-perception: The role of attention in the experience of anxiety, *Anxiety Research*, **2**: 153–163.

Gibbons, F.X., Lane, D.J., Gerrad, M., Began–Reis, M., Lautrup, C.L., and Pexa, N.A. (2002), Comparison level preferences after performance: Is downward comparison theory still useful?, *Journal of Personality and Social Psychology*, **83**: 865–880.

Gibbons, F.X., Smith, T.W., Ingram, R.E., Pearce, K., Brehm, S.S., and Schroeder, D.J. (1985), Self-awareness and self-confrontation: Effects of self-focussed attention on members of a clinical population, *Journal of Personality and Social Psychology*, **48**: 662–675.

Gilbert, D.T. (1989), Thinking lightly about others: Automatic components of the social inference process, In J.S. Uleman and J.A. Bargh (Eds.), *Unintended Thought*. NY: Guilford Press.

Gilbert, D.T. and Malone, P.S. (1995), The correspondence bias, *Psychological Bulletin*, **117**: 21–38.

Gilbert, D.T., Tafarodi, R.W., and Malone, P.S. (1993), You cann't believe everything you read, *Journal of Personality and Social Psychology*, **65**: 221–233.

Gilbert, G.M. (1951), Stereotype persistence and change among college students, *Journal of Abnormal and Social Psychology*, **46**: 245–254.

Giles, H. and Coupland, N. (1991), *Language: Contexts and Consequences*, Pacific Grove, CA: Brooks/Cole.

Giles, H., Hervstone, M., and Clair, R. (1981), Speech as an independent variable of social situations: An introduction and new theoretical framework, In H. Giles and R. St. Clair (Eds.), *The Social Psychological Significance of Speech*, Hillsdale, NJ: Erlbaum.

Gill, J.S., Brar, R.S. Sandhu, K.S., and Mann, N.S. (1988), A comparative study of physical fitness and self-concept of college students, *NIS Scientific Journal*, **11**: 21–23.
Gillig, P.M. and Greenwald, A.G. (1974), Is it time to lay the sleeper effect to rest?, *Journal of Personality and Social Psychology*, **29**: 132–139.
Ginter, G. and Lindskold, S. (1975), Rate of participation and expertise as factors influencing leader choice, *Journal of Personality and Social Psychology*, **32**: 1085–1089.
Glanz, J., Geller, A.C., Shigaki, D., Maddock, J.E., and Isnec, M.R. (2002), A randomized trial of skin cancer prevention in aquatics settings: The pool cool program, *Health Psychology*, **21**(6): 579–587.
Glass, G.V. (1977), Integrating findings: The meta-analysis of research, In L. Shulman (Ed.), *Review of Research in Education*, IL: Peacock.
Gleitman, H. (1981), *Psychology*. NY: Norton and Company.
Glick, P. and Fiske, S.T. (1996), An ambivalent sexism inventory: Differentiating hostile and benevolent sexism, *Journal of Personality and Social Psychology*, **70**: 491–549.
Glick, P. and Fiske, S.T. (1999), Gender, power dynamics and social interaction, In M.M. Ferree, J. Corber and B.B. Hess (Eds.), *Revisioning Gender*, London: Sage Publications.
Glick, P. and Fiske, S.T. (2001), An ambivalent alliance: Hostile and benevolent sexism as complimentary justification for gender inequality, *American Psychologist*, **56**: 109–118.
Glick, P. and Fiske, S.T. et.al. (2000), Beyond prejudice as simple antipathy: Hostile and benevolent sexism across cultures, *Journal of Personality and Social Psychology*, **79**: 763–775.
Glick, P., Fiske, S.T., Mladinic, A., Saiz, J.L., Abrams, D., and Masser, B. (2000), Beyond prejudice as simple antipathy: Hostile and benevolent sexism across cultures, *Journal of Personality and Social Psychology*, **79**: 763–775.
Goeders, N.E (2004), Stress, motivation and drug addiction, *Current Directions in Psychological Science*, **13**: 35–35.
Goethals, G.R. and Darley, J. (1977), Social comparison theory: An attributional approach, In J.M. Suls and R.L. Miller (Eds.), *Social Comparison Processes: Theoretical and Empirical Perspectives*, 259–278, Washington, DC: Hemisphere.
Goffman, E. (1961), *Asylums*, Garden City, NY: Anchor Books.
Goldinger, S.D., Kelider, H.M., Tamiko, Azuma, and Beike, D.R. (2003), Blaming the victim under memory load, *Psychological Science*, **14**: 81–85.
Goodwin, S.A., Gubin, A., Fiske, S.T., and Yzerbyt, V.Y. (2000), Power can bias impression processes: Stereotyping subordinates by default and by design, *Group Processes and Intergroup Relations*, **3**: 227–256.
Goodwin, V.L., Wofford, J.C., and Whittington, J.L. (2001), A theoretical and empirical extension to the transformational leadership construct, *Journal of Occupational Behaviour*, **22**: 759–774.
Goranson, R.E. and Berkowitz, L. (1966), Reciprocity and responsibility reactions to prior help, *Journal of Personality and Social Psychology*, **3**: 227–232.
Gordon, R.A. (1993), The effect of strong versus weak evidence on the assessment of race stereotypical and non-stereotypical crimes, *Journal of Applied Social Psychology*, **23**: 734–749.
Gordon, R.A. (1996), Impact of ingratiation on judgements and evaluations: A meta-analysis investigation, *Journal of Personality and Social Psychology*, **71**: 54–70.
Gordon, T. (1970), *Parent Effectiveness Training*, NY: McGraw-Hill.
Gordon, T. (1974), *Teacher Effectiveness Training*, NY: David McKay.
Gracia, S.M., Weaver, K., Moskowitz, G.B., and Darley, J.M. (2002), Crowded minds: The implicit bystander effect, *Journal of Personality and Social Psychology*, **83**: 843–853.
Graen, G., Alvares, K., Orris, J.B., and Martella, J.A. (1970), Contingency model of leadership effectiveness: Antecedents and evidential results, *Psychological Bulletin*, **74**: 284–295.
Granberg, D. and Holmberg, S. (1990), The intention-behaviour relationship among US and Swedish voters, *Social Psychology Quarterly*, **53**: 44–54.

Gray, H.M., Ambady, N., Lowenthal, W.T., and Deldin, R. (2004), P 300 as an index of attention to self-relevant stimuli, *Journal of Experimental and Social Psychology,* **40**: 216–224.

Grayshon, M.C. (1980), Social grammar, social psychology and linguistic, In H. Giles, W.P. Robinson and P.M. Smith (Eds.), *Language Social Psychological Perspectives*, NY: Pergamon.

Graziano, W.G. and Eisenberg, N. (1997), Agreeableness: Dimensions of Personality, In R. Hogan, J. Johnson and S. Briggs (Eds.), *Handbook of Personality,* 795–825, San Diego, CA: Academic Press.

Graziano, W.G., Habashi, M., Sheese, B.E., and Tobin, R. (2004), Feeling compassion and helping the unfortunate: A social motivational analysis, In E.R. Smith and D.M. Mackie, *Social Psychology*, 3rd edn., Hove, NY: Psychology Press.

Green, L.R., Richardson, D.R., and Lago, T. (1996), How do friendship indirect and direct aggression relate? *Aggressive Behaviour,* **32**: 81–86.

Greenbaum P. and Rosenfield, H.W. (1978), Patterns of avoidance in responses to interpersonal staring and proximity: Effects of bystanders on drivers at a traffic intersection, *Journal of Personality and Social Psychology,* **36**: 575–587.

Greenberg, J., Solomon, S., and Pyszczynski, T. (1997), Terror management theory of self-esteem and cultural world views: Empirical assessments and conceptual refinements, *Advances in Experimental Social Psychology,* **29**: 61–142.

Greenberg, J., Solomon, S., Pyszczynski, T., Rosenblott, A., Burling, J., Lyon, D., Simon, L., and Pinel, E. (1992), Why do people need self-esteem? Converging evidence that self-esteem serves an anxiety-buffering function. *Journal of Personality and Social Psychology,* **63**: 913–922.

Greene, J. (1990), Topics in language and communication, In Rosh (Ed.), *Introduction to Psychology,* **2**: Hove: Lawrence Erlbaum.

Greenspoon, T. (1955), The reinforcing effect of two spoken sounds on the frequency of two responses, *American Journal of Psychology,* **62**: 409–416.

Greenwald, A.G. (2002), Constructs in student ratings of instructions, In H.I. Baraun and D.N. Douglas (Eds.), *The Role of Constructs in Psychological and Educational Measurement,* 277–297, Mahwah, NJ: Erlbaum.

Greenwald, A.G. and Farnham, S.D. (2000), Using the implicit association test to measure self-esteem and self-concept, *Journal of Personality and Social Psychology,* **79**: 1022–1038.

Greenwald, A.G., McGhee, D.E., and Schwartz, J.L.K. (1998), Measuring individual differences in implicit cognition: The implicit association test, *Journal of Personality and Social Psychology,* **74**: 1464–1480.

Greer, D.L. (1983), Spectator booing and the home advantage: A study of social influence in the basketball arena, *Social Psychology Quarterly,* **46**: 252–261.

Greetz, C. (1974), From the native's point of view: On the nature of anthropological understanding, In K. Basso and H. Selby (Eds.), *Meaning in Anthropology,* Albuquerque: University of New Mexico Press.

Grice, H.P. (1968), Utterer's meaning, sentence meaning and word meaning, *Foundations of Language,* **4**: 225–42.

Grice, P.H. (1975), Logic and conversation, In P. Gole and J.C. Morgan (Eds.), *Syntax and Semantics, Speech Acts,* Vol. 3, NY: Academic Press.

Griffitt, W. (1970), Environmental effects on interpersonal affective behaviour: Ambient effective temperature and attraction, *Journal of Personality and Social Psychology,* **15**: 240–244.

Griffitt, W. and Guay, P. (1969), Object evaluation and conditioned effect, *Journal of Experimental Research in Personality,* **4**: 1–8.

Griffitt, W. and Veitch, R. (1971), Hot and crowded: Influences of population density and temperature on interpersonal affective behaviour, *Journal of Personality and Social Psychology,* **17**: 92–98.

Grimshaw, A.D. (1990), *Talk and Social Control,* In M. Rosenberg and R.H. Turner (Eds.), *Social Psychology: Sociological Perspectives,* New Brunswick, NJ: Transaction.

Gross, A.E. and Latane, J.G. (1974), Receiving help, reciprocation and interpersonal attraction, *Journal of Applied Social Psychology,* **4**: 210–223.

Grusky, O. (1963), The effects of formal structure on managerial recruitment: A study of baseball organization, *Sociometry*, **26**: 345–353.

Guetzkow, N. and Simon, H.A. (1955), The impact of certain communication nets on organisation and performance in task-oriented groups, *Management Science*, **1**: 233–250.

Guinote, A., Judd, C.M. and Brauer, M. (2002), Effects of power on perceived and objective group variability: Evidence that more powerful groups are more variable, *Journal of Personality and Social Psychology*, **82**: 708–721.

Gump, B.B. and Kulik, J.A. (1997), Stress, affiliation and emotional contagion, *Journal of Personality and Social Psychology*, **72**: 305–319.

Gump, P.V. and Ross, R. (1977), The fit of milieu and programme in school environments, In H. McGurk (Ed.), *Ecological Factors in Human Development*, NY: North Holland.

Gunther, A. (1995), Overrating the X-rating: The third person perception and support for censorship of pornography, *Journal of Communication*, **45**: 27–38.

Gupta, S.P. (1976), A study of some selected inputs for improving education of secondary school teachers, In J. Pandey's (Ed.), *Psychology in India*, ND: Sage Publication.

Gurevitch, Z.D. (1990), The embrace: On the element of non-distance in human relations, *The Sociological Quarterly*, **31**: 187–201.

Gustafson, R. (1990), Wine and male physical aggression, *Journal of Drug Issues*, **20**: 75–86.

Guttman, L. (1950), The third component of scalable attitudes, *International Journal of Opinion and Attitude Research*, **7**: 247–80.

Hahn, J. and Blass, T. (1997), Dating partner preferences: A function of similarity of love styles, *Journal of Social Behaviour and Personality*, **12**: 595–610.

Haire, M. (1950), Projective techniques in marketing research, *Journal of Marketing*, **14**: 649–656.

Hall, E.T. (1959), *The Silent Language*, NY: Double-day.

Hall, G.S. (1954), *A Primer of Freudian Psychology*, NY: New American Library, Mentor Book.

Hall, J.A. (1998), How big are nonverbal sex difference? The case of smiling and sensitivity to nonverbal cues, In D.J. Canary and K. Dindia (Eds.), *Sex Differences and Similarities in Communication: Critical Essays and Empirical Investigation of Sex and Gender in Interaction*, Mahwah, NJ: Erlbaum.

Hall, J.A., Carter, J.D., and Horgan, T.G. (2000), Gender differences in nonverbal communication of emotion, In A.H. Fischer (Ed.), *Gender and Emotion: Social and Psychological Perspectives*. NY: Cambridge University Press.

Halliday, M.A. (1975), *Learning How to Mean: Exploration in the Development of Language*, London: Arnold.

Hallin, R. and Trope, Y. (2000), Facing faces: Studies on cognitive aspects of physiognomy, *Journal of Personality and Social Psychology*, **78**: 837–852.

Hallingworth, L.S. (1942), *Children above 180 IQ stanfod-Binet: Origin and Development*, Yonkerson Hudson, NY: World.

Halpin, A. (1954), The leadership behaviour and combat performances of airplane commanders, *Journal of Abnormal and Social Psychology*, **49**: 19–22.

Halpin, A.W. (1966), *Theory and Research in Administration*, NY: Macmillan.

Hamblin, R.L. (1958), Leadership and Crisis, *Sociometry*, **21**: 322–335.

Hamilton, D.L. (1981), Stereotyping and intergroup behaviour: Some thoughts on the cognitive approach, In D.L. Hamilton (Ed.), *Cognitive Processes in Stereotyping and Intergroup Behaviour*, Hillsdale, NJ: Erlbaum.

Hammond, K.R. (1948), Measuring attitudes by error-choice: An indirect method, *Journal of Abnormal and Social Psychology*, **43**: 38–48.

Hampson, S.E. (1998), When is an inconsistency not an inconsistency? Trait reconciliation in personality description and impression formation, *Journal of Personality and Social Psychology*, **74**: 102–117.

Handrick, C. and Hendrick, S.S. (1986), A theory and method of love, *Journal of Personality and Social Psychology*, **50**: 392–402.

Haney, C., Banks, W., and Zimbardo, P. (1973), Interpersonal dynamics in a simulated prison, *International Journal of Criminology*, **1**: 69–97.

Hardy, C. and Latane, B. (1986), Social loafing on a cheering task, *Social Science,* **71**: 165–172.

Hardy, C.L. and Van Vugt, M. (2006), Nice guys finish first: The competitive altruism hypothesis, *Personality and Social Psychology Bulletin*, **32**: 1402–1413.

Hardy, R.C. (1976), A test of the poor leader: Member relations calls of the contingency model in elementary school children, *Child Development*, **46**: 958–964.

Hare, A.P. (1976), *Handbook of Small Group Research*, NY: Free Press.

Hareli, S. and Weiner, B. (2000), Accounts for success as determinants of perceived arrogance and modesty, *Motivation and Emotion*, **24**: 215–236.

Harkins, S.G. and Petty, R.E. (1981), The multiple source effect in persuasion: The effects of distraction, *Personality and Social Psychology Bulletin,* **4**: 627–635.

Harkins, S.G. and Petty, R.E. (1982), Effects of task difficulty and task uniqueness on social loafing, *Journal of Personality and Social Psychology*, **43**: 1214–1229.

Harley, T.A. (1995), *The Psychology of Language: From Data to Theory*, Erlbaum: Taylor and Rancis.

Harrell, W.A. (1980), Aggression by high school basketball players: An observational study of the effects to opponents' aggression and frustration-inducing factors, *International Journal of Sport Psychology*, **11**: 290–298.

Harries, K.D. and Stadler, S.J. (1988), Heat and violence: New findings from Dallas field data, 1980–1981, *Journal of Applied Social Psychology*, **18**: 129–138.

Harris, M.B. (1974), Mediators between frustration and aggression in a field experiment, *Journal of Experimental Social Psychology*, **10**: 561–571.

Harris, M.B. (1992), Sex, race and experiences of aggression, *Aggressive Behaviour*, **18**: 201–217.

Harris, M.B. (1993), How provoking! What makes men and women angry?, *Journal of Applied Social Psychology*, **23**: 199–211.

Harris, M.B. (1994), Gender of subject and target as mediators of aggression, *Journal of Applied Social Psychology*, **12**: 503–516.

Harter, S. (1990), Self and identity development, In S.S. Feldman and G.R. Elliott (Eds.), *At the Threshold: The Developing Adolescent*, Cambridge, HA: Harvard University Press.

Hartland, J. (1991), *Language and Thought*, Leicester: BPS Books.

Hartup, W.W. (1983), Peer relations, In P.H. Mussen (Ed.), *Handbook of Child Psychology*, 4th edn, Vol. 4, NY: Wiley.

Harvey, O.J. and Consalvi, C. (1960), Status and conformity to pressures in informal groups, *Journal of Abnormal and Social Psychology*, **60**: 182–187.

Haslam, S.A. (2004), *Psychology in Organizations: The Social Identity Approach*, 2nd edn., London: Sage.

Haslam, S.A. and Platow, M.J. (2001), The link between leadership and fellowship: How affirming social identity translates vision into action, *Personality and Social Psychology Bulletin*, **27**: 1469–1479.

Hassan, M.K. (1981), *Prejudice in Indian Youth*, ND: Classical Publishing Company.

Hassan, M.K. (1983), Parental influence on children's prejudice, *Social Change*, **13**(2): 40–46.

Hassin, R. and Trope, Y. (2000), Facing faces: Studies on the cognitive aspects of physiognomy, *Journal of Personality and Social Psychology*, **78**: 837–852.

Hastie, R. and Kumar, P.A. (1979), Person memory: Personality traits as organizing principles in memory for behaviour, *Journal of Personality and Social Psychology*, **37**: 25–38.

Hatfield, E. and Sprecher, S. (1986a), *Mirror, Mirror...the Importance of Looks in Everyday Life*, Albany, NY: State University of New York Press.

Hatfield, E. and Sprecher, S. (1986b), Measuring passionate love in intimate relationship, *Journal of Adolescence*, **9**: 383–410.

Hatfield, E. and Walster, G.W. (1978), *A New Look at Love*, Reading, MA: Addison-Wesley.

Haugtvedt, C.P. and Wegener, D.J. (1994), Message order effects in persuasion: An attitude strength perspective, *Journal of Consumer Research*, **21**: 205–218.

Havighurst, R.J. (1972), *Developmental Tasks and Education*, NY: McKay.

Hayes, D.P., Melzer, L., and Bouma, G.D. (1968), Activity as a determinant of interpersonal perception, *American Psychological Association Proceedings,* **3**: 417–418.

Hearold, S. (1986), A synthesis of 1043 effects of television on social behaviour, In G. Comstock (Ed.), *Public Communication and Behaviour*, Vol. 1, Orlando, FL: Academic Press.

Heatherton, T.F. and Vohs, K.D. (2000), Personality processes and individual differences—interpersonal evaluations following threats to self: Role of self-esteem, *Journal of Personality and Social Psychology*, **78**: 725–736.

Hebl, H.R. and Mannix, L.M. (2003), The weight of obesity in evaluating others: A mere proximity effect, *Personality and Social Psychology*, **29**: 28–38.

Heider, F. (1944), Social perception and phenomenal causality, *Psychological Review*, **51**: 358–74.

Heider, F. (1946), Attitudes and cognitive organization, *Journal of Psychology*, **21**: 107–112.

Heider, F. (1958), *The Psychology of Interpersonal Relations*, NY: Wiley.

Heilman, M.E. and Stopeck, M.H. (1985), Attractiveness and corporate success: Different causal attributions for males and females, *Journal of Applied Psychology*, **70**: 379–388.

Heimpel, S.A., Wood, J.W., Marshall, M.A., and Brown, J.D. (2002), Do people with self-esteem really want to feel better?: Self-esteem differences in motivation to repair negative moods, *Journal of Personality and Social Psychology*, **82**: 128–147.

Heine, S.J., Lehman, D.R., Markus, H.R., and Kitayama, S. (1999), Is there a universal need for positive self-regard?, *Psychological Review*, **106**: 766–794.

Heiss, D. (1979), *Understanding Events, Affect and the Construction of Social Action*, NY: Cambridge University Press.

Heiss, J. (1990), Social roles, In M. Rosenberg and R. Turner (Eds.), *Social Psychology: Sociological Perspectives*, New Brunswick, NJ: Transaction.

Heiss, J. and Owens, S. (1972), Self-evaluations of blacks and whites, *American Journal of Sociology*, **78**: 360–370.

Helgeson, V.S. (1992), Moderators of relation between perceived control and adjustment to chronic illness, *Journal of Personality and Social Psychology*, **63**: 656–666.

Helgeson, V.S. (2005), *The Psychology of Gender*, Delhi: Pearson Education.

Helgeson, V.S. and Mickelson, K.D. (1995), Motives for social comparison, *Personality and Social Psychology Bulletin*, **21**: 1200–1209.

Hendrick, C., Hendrick, S.S., Foote, F.H., and Slapion-Foote, M.J. (1984), Do men and women love differently?, *Journal of Social and Personal Relationships*, **1**: 177–195.

Herbst, K.C., Gaertner, L., and Insko, C.A. (2003), My head says yes but my heart says no: Cognitive and affective attraction as a function of similarity to the ideal self, *Journal of Personality and Social Psychology*, **84**: 1206–1219.

Heritage, G.M. and Capitanio, J.P. (1996), Some of my best friends: Intergroup contact, concealable stigma and heterosexuals' attitudes towards gay men and lesbians, *Personality and Social Psychology Bulletin*, **22**: 412–424.

Heritage, J. and Greatbatch, D. (1986), Generating applause: A study of rhetoric and response at party political confuses, *American Journal of Sociology*, **92**: 110–157.

Herrera, N.C., Zajonc, R.B., Wieczovkowska, G., and Cichomski, B. (2003), Beliefs about birth rank and their reflection in reality, *Journal of Personality and Social Psychology*, **85**: 142–150.

Hersey, P. and Blanchard, K. (1969), Life-cycle theory of leadership, *Training and Development Journal*, **23**(5): 26–34.

Hersey, P. and Blanchard, K.H. (1977), *Management of Organisational Behaviour: Utilising human resources*, 3rd ed., New Jersey: Prentice Hall.

Heshka, J. and Nelson, Y. (1972), Interpersonal speaking distance as a function of age, sex and relationship, *Sociometry*, **35**: 491–498.

Hess, E.H. (1965), The pupil responds to changes in attitude as well as to changes in illumination, *Scientific American*, **212**: 46–54.

Hess, R.D. and Shipman, V.C. (1965), Early experience and the socialization of cognitive modes in children, *Child Development*, **36**: 869–886.

Hewitt, J.P. (1997), *Self and Society*, 7th edn., Boston: Allyn and Bacon.

Hewstone, M. and Jaspars, J. (1987), Covariation and causal attribution: A logical model of the intuitive analysis of variance, *Journal of Personality and Social Psychology*, **53**: 663–672.

Hewstone, M., Stoebe, W., and Stephenson, G. (Eds.), (1996), *Introduction to Social Psychology*, Oxford: Blackwell.

Higbee, K.L., Millard, R.J., and Folman, J.R. (1982), Social psychology research during the 1970s: Predominance of experimentation and college students, *Personality and Social Psychology Bulletin*, **8**: 180–183.

Higgins, E.J. (2000), Social cognition: Learning about what matters in the world, *European Journal of Social Psychology*, **30**: 3–39.

Higgins, E.T. (1989), Self-discrepancy theory: What patterns of self-beliefs cause people to suffer?, In L. Berkowitz (Ed.), *Advances in Experimental Psychology*, Vol. 22, NY: Academic Press.

Higgins, E.T. (1998), Promotion and prevention: Regulatory focus as a motivational principle, In M.P. Zanna (Ed.), *Advances in Experimental Social Psychology*, Vol. 30, NY: Academic Press.

Higgins, E.T. and Bargh, J.A. (1987), Social cognition and social perception, *Annual Review of Psychology*, **38**: 369–425.

Higgins, E.T. and Bryant, S.L. (1982), Consensus information and the fundamental attribution error: The role of development and in-group versus out-group knowledge, *Journal of Personality and Social Psychology*, **47**: 422–425.

Higgins, E.T., Klein, R., and Strauman, T. (1985), Self-concept discrepancy theory: A psychological model for distinguishing among different aspects of depression and anxiety, *Social Cognition*, **3**: 51–76.

Higgins, N.C. and Bhatt, G. (2001), Culture moderates the self-serving bias: Etic and emic features of causal attributions in India and in Canada, *Social Behaviour and Personality*, **29**(1): 46–61.

Higgins, N.C. and Shaw, J.K. (1999), Attributional style moderates the impact of causal controllability information on helping behaviour, *Social Behaviour and Personality*, **27**: 221–236.

Hightower, E. (1990), Adolescent interpersonal and familial precursors of positive mental health and midlife, *Journal of Youth and Adolescence*, **19**: 257–275.

Hill, C.J. and Stull, D.E. (1981), Sex differences in effects of social and value similarity in same sex relationship, *Journal of Personality and Social Psychology*, **41**: 488–502.

Hill, K.T. and Eaton, W.O. (1977), The interaction of test anxiety and success-failure experiences in determining children's arithmetic performance, *Developmental Psychology*, **13**: 205–211.

Hilton, N.Z., Harris, G.T., and Rice, M.E. (2000), The functions of aggression by male teenagers, *Journal of Personality and Social Psychology*, **79**: 988–994.

Hinsz, V.B. (1995), Goal setting by groups performing an additive task: A comparison with individual goal setting, *Journal of Applied Social Psychology*, **25**: 965–990.

Hockett, C.F. (1960), The origin of speech, *Scientific American*, **203**: 88–96.

Hodson, R. (1998), Organizational ethnographies: An underutilized resource in the sociology of work, *Social Forces*, **76**: 1173–208.

Hoelter, J.W. (1983), The effect of role evaluation and commitment on identity salience, *Social Psychology Quarterly*, **46**: 140–147.

Hoff–Ginsberg, E. and Tardif, T. (1995), Socio-economic status and parenting, In M.H. Bornstein (Ed.), *Children and Parenting*, Vol. 2, Hillsdale, NJ: Erlbaum.

Hoffman, L.R. and Maier, N.R.F. (1961), Quality and acceptance of problem solutions by members of homogeneous and heterogeneous groups, *Journal of Abnormal and Social Psychology*, **62**: 401–407.

Hogg, H., Turner, J.C., and Davidson, B. (1990), Polarised norms and social frames of reference: A test of self-categorization theory of group polarization, *Basic and Applied Social Psychology*, **11**: 77–100.

Hogg, M.A. (1992), *The Social Psychology of Group Cohesiveness: From Attraction to Social Identity*, London: Harvester Wheatsheaf.

Hogg, M.A. and Turner, J.C. (1985), Interpersonal attraction, social identification and psychological group formation, *European Journal of Social Psychology*, **15**: 51–66.

Hogg, M.A. and Vaughan, G.M. (1995), *Social Psychology: An Introduction*, London: Prentice-Hall/ Harvester.

Hogg, M.A., Terry, D.J., and White, K.M. (1995), A tale of two theories: A critical comparison of identity theory with social identity theory, *Social Psychology Quarterly*, **58**: 255–269.

Hollander, E.P. (1985), Leadership and Power, In G. Lindzey and E. Aronson (Ed.), *Handbook of Social Psychology*, 3rd edn., **2**: 485–537, NY: Random House.

Hollander, E.P. and Julian, J.W. (1970), Studies in leader legitimacy, influence and innovation, In L. Berkowitz (Ed.), *Advances in Experimental Social Psychology*, **5**: 33–69, NY: Academic Press.

Hollingworth, L.S. (1942), *Children above 180 IQ on Stanford–Binet; Origin and Development*, Yonkers-on-Hudson, NY: World.

Holmes, T.H. and Rahe, R.H. (1967), The social adjustment rating scale, *Journal of Psychosomatic Research*, **22**: 213–218.

Holtgraves, T. (1997), Styles of language use: Individual and cultural variability in conversational indirectness, *Journal of Personality and Social Psychology*, **73**: 624–637.

Holtgraves, T. and Srull, T.K. (1989), The effects of positive self-descriptions on impressions: General principles and individual differences, *Personality and Social Psychology Bulletin*, **15**: 452–462.

Homans, G.C. (1961 & 1974), *Social Behaviour: Its Elementary Forms*, NY: Harcourt, Brace and World.

Horney, K. (1950), *Neurosis and Human Growth: The Struggle Toward Self-realization*, NY: Norton.

Hornstein, G. (1985), Intimacy in conversational style as a function of the degree of closeness between members of a dyad, *Journal of Personality and Social Psychology*, **49**: 671–681.

Hornstein, H.A. (1970), The influence of social models on helping, In McCauley, J. and Berkowitz, L. (Eds.), *Altruism and Helping Behaviour*, NY: Academic Press.

Hornstein, H.A. (1978), Promotive tension and prosocial behaviour: A Lewinian analysis, In L. Wispe (Ed.), *Altruism, Sympathy and Helping*, NY: Academic Press.

House, J.S., Landis, K.R., and Umberson, D. (1988), *Social Relationship and Health Science*, **241**: 540–544.

House, R.J. (1971), A path-goal theory of leader effectiveness, *Administrative Science Quarterly*, **16**: 321–339.

House, R.J. and Baetz, M.L. (1979), Leadership: Some empirical generalizations and new search directions, *Research in Organization Behaviour*, **1**: 341–423.

House, R.J., Spangler, W.D., and Woycke, J. (1991), Personality and Charisma in the US presidency: A psychological theory of leader effectiveness, *Administrative Science Quarterly*, **36**: 364–396.

Hovland, C.I. and Janis, I.L. (1959), *Personality and Persuasibility*, New Haven, Conn: Yale University Press.

Hovland, C.I. and Mandell, W. (1952), An experimental comparison of conclusion-drawing by the communicator and the audience, *Journal of Abnormal and Social Psychology*, **47**: 581–588.

Hovland, C.I. and Pritzker, H.A. (1957), Extent of opinion change as a function of amount of change advocated, *Journal of Abnormal and Social Psychology*, **54**: 257–261.

Hovland, C.I. and Weiss, W. (1951), The influence of source credibility on communication effectiveness, *Public Opinion Quarterly*, **15**: 635–650.

Hovland, C.I., Janis, I.L., and Kelley, H.H. (1953), *Communication and Persuasion*, New Haven: Yale University Press.

Hovland, C.I., Lumsdaine, A.A., and Sheffield, F.D. (1949), Experiments on mass communication, *Studies in Social Psychology in World War II*, Vol. III, Princeton, NJ: Princeton University Press.

Hovland, C.J. and Sherif, M. (1952), Judgemental phenomena and scales of attitude measurement: Item displacement in thurston scales, *Journal of Abnormal and Social Psychology*, **47**: 822–832.

Hue, C. and Erickson, J.R. (1991), Normative studies of sequence strength of scene structures of 30 scripts, *American Journal of Psychology*, **104**: 229–240.

Huesman, L.R., Eron, L.D., and Yarmel, P.W. (1987), Intellectual functioning and aggression, *Journal of Personality and Social Psychology*, **52**: 232–240.

Huesmann, L.R. and Eron, L.D. (1986), *Television and the Aggressive Child: A Cross-national*, Hillsdale, NJ: Erlbaum.

Huesmann, L.R. and Moise, J. (1996), Media violence: A demonstrated public health threat to children, *Harvard Mental Health Letter*, **12**(12): 5–7.

Huesmann, L.R., Eron, L.D., Klein, R., Brice, P., and Fischer, P. (1983), Mitigating the imitation of aggressive behaviours by changing children's attitudes about media violence, *Journal of Personality and Social Psychology*, **44**: 899–910.

Hui, C.H. (1990), Work attitudes, leadership styles, and managerial behaviour in different cultures, In R.W. Brislin (Ed.), *Applied Cross-cultural Psychology*, 186–208, Newbury Park, CA: Sage.

Hundal, P.S. (1971), A study of entrepreneurial motivation: Comparison for fast and slow progressing small-scale industrial entrepreneurs in Punjab, *Journal of Applied Psychology*, **55**: 317–323.

Hundal, P.S. and Singh, S. (1975), Structure of personality characteristics and motive patterns of farmers, *Indian Journal of Psychology*, **50**: 33–43.

Husain, A. and Kureshi, A. (1979), Need-value similarity, interpersonal congruency and friendship, *Social Science Research Journal*, **3**: 63–69.

Husain, A. and Kureshi, A. (1982), evaluators' physique and self-evaluation as mode-rating variables in opposite sex physique attraction, *Perspectives in Psychology Researches*, **5**: 31–36.

Husain, A. and Kureshi, A. (1983a), Opposite sex attraction as a function of perceiver's self-evaluation and physical attractiveness of the perceiver and the perceived, *Personality Study and Group Behaviour*, **3**: 35–42.

Husain, A. and Kureshi, A. (1983b), Value similarity and friendship: A study of interpersonal attraction, *Psychologia*, **26**: 167–174.

Husain, M.G. (Ed.) (1983), *Psycho-ecological Dimensions of Poverty*, New Delhi: Manohar Publications.

Huston–Stein, A., Freidrich–cofer, L., and Susman, E.J. (1977), The relation of classroom structure to social behaviour, imaginative play, and self-regulation of economically disadvantaged children, *Child Development*, **48**: 908–916.

Hyman, H.H. and Sheatsley, P.B. (1954), The authoritarian personality: A methodological critique, In R. Christie and M. Hahoda (Eds.), *Studies in the Scope and Method of the Authoritarian Personality*, NY: Free Press of Glencoe.

Hymes, D. (1967), Models of the Interaction of Languages and Social Setting, *Journal of Social Issues*, **23**: 8–28.

Hymes, D. (1974), *Foundations in Sociolinguistics*, Lond: Tavistock.

Ilgen, D.R., Hellenbeck, J.R., Johnson, M., and Jundt, D. (2005), Terms in organizations: From input-process-output modes to IMOI models, *Annual Review of Psychology*, **56**: 517–543.

Insko, C.A., Dreenan, S., Soloman, M.R., Smith, R., and Wade, T.J. (1983), Conformity as a function of consistency of positive self-evaluation with being liked and being right, *Journal of Experimental Social Psychology*, **19**: 341–358.

Inzlicht, M. and Ben-Zeev, T. (2000), A threatening intellectual environment: Why females are susceptible to experiencing problem-solving deficits in the presence of males, *Psychological Science*, **11**: 365–371.

Isen, A.M. (1970), Success, failure, attention and reaction to others: The warm glow of success, *Journal of Personality and Social Psychology*, **15**: 294–301.

Isen, A.M. (1984), Toward understanding the role of affect in cognition, In S.C.R. Wyer and T.K. Srull (Eds.), *Handbook of Social Cognition*, **3**: 179–236, Hillsdale, NJ: Erlbaum.

Isen, A.M. and Levin, P.F. (1972), Effect of feeling good on helping: Cookies and kindness, *Journal of Personality and Social Psychology*, **21**: 384–388.

Isenberg, D.J. (1986), Group polarization: A critical review and meta-analysis, *Journal of Personality and Social Psychology*, **50**: 1141–1151.

Isozaki, M. (1984), The effect of discussion on polarization of judgements, *Japanese Psychological Research*, **26**: 187–193.
Itard, J. M.G. (1932), *The Wild Boy of Aveyron*, NY: Appleton, Century-Crofts.
Iyer, R.V. (2000), A study of development of reading and meta-phonological skills in Malayalam speaking children, In G. Misra's (Ed.), *Psychology in India*, Language and Communication, 5th ICSSR Survey, Delhi: Longman/Pearson.
Izard, C. (1991), *The Psychology of Emotions*, NY: Plenum.
Jackman, M.H. and Senter, M.S. (1981), Beliefs about race, gender and social class: Different therefore unequal, In D.J. Treiman and R.V. Robinson (Eds.), *Research in Stratification and Mobility*, Vol. 2, Greenwich: JAI Press.
Jackson, L.M., Esses, V.M., and Burris, C.T. (2001), Contemporary sexism and discrimination: The importance of respect for men and women, *Personality and Social Psychology Bulletin*, **27**: 48–61.
Jagdish, C. and Yadav, S. (1999), Relationship between home deprivation and mental health among school students, *Indian Journal of Psychometry and Education*, **30**: 35–38.
Jagdish, S.B. and Reddy, A.N.V. (2000), Study of level of stress among health professionals: A management perspective, *Journal of Community Guidance and Research*, **17**: 241–248.
Jai Prakash, I. and Suvarna, B.J. (1996), Sex role attitudes of college students, *Journal of Personality and Clinical Studies*, **12**(1.2): 61–65.
James, D. and Drakich, J. (1993), Understanding gender differences in amount of talk: A critical review of research, In D. Trannen (Ed.), *Gender and Conversational Interaction*, NY: Oxford University Press.
James, W. (1890), *Principles of Psychology*, NY: Holt, Rinehart and Winston.
Janis, I.L. (1982), *Groupthink: Psychological Studies of Policy Decision and Fiascos*, Boston: Houghton-Mifflin
Janis, I.L. and Feshbach, S. (1953), Effects of fear-arousing communications, *Journal of Abnormal and Social Psychology*, **48**: 78–92.
Janis, I.L. and King, B.T. (1954), The influence of role playing on opinion change, *Journal of Applied Social Psychology*, **48**: 211–218.
Jarvik, L.F., Klodin, V., and Matsuryama, S.S. (1973), Human aggression and the extra Y-chromosome: Fact or fantasy, *American Psychologist*, **28**: 674–682.
Jason, L.A., Reichler, A., Easton, J., Neal, A., and Wilson, M. (1984), Female harassment after ending a relationship: A preliminary study, *Alternative Lifestyles*, **6**: 259–269.
Jemmott, J.B., Pettigrew, T.F., and Johnson, J.T. (1983), The effect of in-group versus out-group membership in social perception, In R.S. Feldman, *Social Psychology*, International Student Edition, NY: McGraw-Hill.
Jenkins, W.O. (1947), A review of leadership studies with particular reference to military problems, *Psychological Bulletin*, **44**: 54–87.
Jensen–Campbell, L.A., West, S.G., and Graziano, W.G. (1995), Dominance, prosocial orientation and female preferences: Do nice guys really finish last?, *Journal of Personality and Social Psychology*, **68**: 427–440.
Jha, J.D. (1973), Student–teacher classroom interaction, *Indian Educational Review*, **8**: 63–76.
Jing, Q. (2000), International Psychology, In K. Pawlik and M.R. Rosenzweig (Eds.), *International Handbook of Psychology*, London: Sage.
Jobe, L.G. and Pope, C.A. (2002), The English methods class matters: Professor D. and the student teachers, *Reading Research and Instruction*, **42**: 1–29.
Johnson, B.T. (1994), Effects of outcome-relevant involvement and prior information on persuasion, *Journal of Experimental Social Psychology*, **30**: 566–579.
Johnson, C. (1994), Gender, legitimate authority and leader-subordinate conversations, *American Sociological Review*, **59**: 289–299.
Johnson, D.W., Marauyama, G., Johnson, R., Nelson, D., and Skon, L. (1981), Effects of cooperative, competitive and individualistic goal structurers on achievement: A meta-analysis. *Psychological Bulletin*, **89**: 47–62.
Johnson, J.D. and Lecci, L. (2003), Assessing anti-white attitudes and predicting perceived racism: The Johnson-Lecci Scale, *Personality and Social Psychology Bulletin*, **29**: 299–312.

Johnson, J.G., Cohen, P., Smeiles, E.M., Kasen, S.L., and Brooks, J.S. (2002), Television viewing and aggressive behaviour during adolescents and adulthood, *Science*, **295**: 2648–2471.

Johnson, K.J., Lund, D.A., and Diamond, M.F. (1986), Stress, self-esteem and coping during bereavement among the elderly, *Social Psychology Quarterly*, **49**: 273–279.

Johnson, M.K., Hashtroudi, S., and Lindsay, D.S. (1993), Source monitoring, *Psychological Bulletin*, **114**: 3–28.

Johnson, T.J., Feigenbaum, R. and Weibey, M. (1964), Some determinants and consequences of the teacher's perception of causality, *Journal of Educational Psychology*, **55**: 337–246.

Johnston, J. and Ettema, J. (1986), Using television to best advantage: Research for prosocial television, In J. Bryant and D. Zillman (Eds.), *Perspectives on Media Effects*, 143–164, Hillsdale, NJ: Lawrence-Erlbaum Associated.

Joireman, J., Anderson, J., and Strathman, A. (2003), The aggression paradox: Understanding links among aggression, sensation seeking and consideration of future consequences, *Journal of Personality and Social Psychology*, **84**: 1287–1302.

Jones, E.E. (1979), The rocky road from acts to dispositions, *American Psychologist*, **34**: 107–117.

Jones, E.E. (1990), *Interpersonal Perception*, NY: W.H. Freeman.

Jones, E.E. and Davis, K.E. (1965), From actions to dispositions: The attribution process in person perception, In Berkowitz, L. (Ed.), *Advances in Experimental Psychology*, Vol. 2, NY: Academic Press.

Jones, E.E. and McGillis, D. (1976), Correspondent inferences and the attribution cube: A comparative appraisal, In Jarvey, J.H., Ickes, W.J. and Kidd, R.F. (Eds.), *New Directions in Attribution Research*, Vol. 1, Hillsdale, NJ: Erlbaum.

Jones, E.E. and Nisbett, R. (1972), The actor and observer: Divergent perceptions of the causes of behaviour, In E.E. Jones, D.E. Kanouse, H.H. Kelley, R.E. Nisbett, S. Valins, and B.W. Weiner (Eds.), *Attribution: Perceiving the Causes of Behaviour*, Morristown, NJ: General Learning Press.

Jones, E.E. and Pittman, T. (1982), Toward a general theory of strategic self-presentation, In J. Suls (Ed.), *Psychological Perspectives on the Self*, **3**: 231–262, Hillsdale, NJ: Erlbaum.

Jones, E.E. and Sigall, H. (1971), The bogus pipeline: A new paradigm for measuring affect and attitude, *Psychological Bulletin*, **76**: 349–364.

Jones, E.E., Gregen, K.J., Gumpert, P., and Thibaut, J. (1965), Some conditions affecting the user of ingratiation to influence performance evaluation, *Journal of Personality and Social Psychology*, **1**: 613–626.

Jones, E.E., Rock, L., Shaver, K.G., Goeshals, G.R., and Ward, L.M. (1968), Pattern of performance and ability attribution: An unexpected primacy effect, *Journal of Personality and Social Psychology*, **10**: 317–340.

Jones, R.A. and Brehm, J.W. (1970), Persuasiveness of one and two-sided communications as a function of awareness: There are two sides, *Journal of Experimental Social Psychology*, **6**: 47–56.

Jordan, C.H., Spencer, S.J., Zanna, M.P., Hoshino–Browne, E., and Cowell, J. (2003), Secure and defensive self-esteem, *Journal of Personality and Social Psychology*, **62**: 26–37.

Joseph, N. and Alex, N. (1972), The Uniform: A sociological perspective, *American Journal of Sociology*, **77**: 719–730.

Josephs, R.A., Larrick, R.P., Steele, C.M., and Nisbett, R.E. (1992), Protecting the self from the negative consequences of risky decisions, *Journal of Personality and Social Psychology*, **62**: 26–37.

Joshi, M. and Aaron, P.G. (2000), The component model of reading: Simple view of reading made a little more complex, *Reading Psychology*, **21**: 85–97.

Judge, J.A. and Bono, J.E. (2000), Five-factor model of personality and transformational leadership, *Journal of Applied Psychology*, **85**: 751–765.

Judge, J.A. and Cable, T.A. (2004), The effect of physical height on workplace success and income, Preliminary test of theoretical model, *Journal of Applied Psychology*, **89**: 428–441.

Judge, T.A., Bono, T.E., Ilies, R., and Gerhgardt, M.W. (2002), Personality and leadership: A qualitative and qualitative review, *Journal of Applied Psychology*, **87**: 765–780.

Jussim, L. (2005), Accuracy in social perception: Criticisms, controversies, criteria, components and cognitive processes, *Advances in Experimental Social Sciences*, **37**: 1–93.

Jussim, L., Coleman, L. and Nassau, S. (1987), The influence of self-esteem on perception of performance and feedback, *Social Psychology Quarterly*, **50**: 95–99.

Kabasa, S. (1979), Stressful life events, personality and health: An inquiry into hardiness, *Journal of Personality and Social Psychology*, **37**(1): 1–11.

Kagan, S. (1977), Social motives and behaviours of Mexican-American and Anglo-American children, In J.L. Murtinez and R.H. Mendoza (Eds.), *Chicago Psychology*, 2nd edn., 289–333, NY: Academic Press.

Kahle, L.R. and Berman, J.J. (1979), Attitudes cause behaviours: A cross-lagged panel analysis, *Journal of Personality and Social Psychology*, **37**: 315–321.

Kahn, A., O'Leary, V.E., Krulewitz, J.E., and Lamm, H. (1980), Equity and equality: Male and female means to a just end, *Basic and Applied Social Psychology*, **1**: 173–197.

Kahneman, D. and Miller, D.T. (1986), Norm theory: Comparing reality to its alternatives, *Psychological Review*, **93**: 136–153.

Kahneman, D. and Tversky, A. (1982), The psychology of preferences, *Scientific American*, **246**: 160–173.

Kakkar, O.B. (1982), Teacher behaviour and student characteristics, *Indian Educational Review*, **17**: 71–79.

Kakar, S., (1971), The theme of authority in social relations in India, *Journal of Social Psychology*, **84**: 93–101.

Kakar, S. (1974), *Personality and Authority in Work*, Bombay: Somaiya Publication.

Kaliappan, R. and Kaliappan, K.V. (1993), Reduction of aggression in juvenile delinquents through behaviour therapy, *Journal of Psychological Researches*, **37**: 62–65.

Kammarath, L.K., Mendoza–Denton, R., and Mischel, W. (2005), Incorporating if…then…personality signatures in person perception: Beyond the person situation dichotomy, *Journal of Personality and Social Psychology*, **88**: 605–618.

Kanagawa, C., Cross, S.E., and Markus, H.R. (2001), "Who am I?" The cultural psychology of the conceptual self, *Personality and Social Psychology Bulletin*, **27**: 90–103.

Kanter, R. (1977), *Men and Women of the Corporation*, NY: Basic Books.

Kanungo, R.M. and Conger, J.A. (1992), Charisma: Exploring new dimensions of leadership behaviour, *Psychology and Developing Societies*, **4**(1): 21–38.

Kanungo, R.M. and Conger, J.A. (1994), Promoting altruism as a corporate goal, *Academy of Management Executive*, **7**: 37–48.

Kapoor, P. and Verma, P. (1997), Aggression in relation to television viewing, *Psycholingua*, **25**: 41–46.

Karanth, P. and Prakash, P. (1996), Developmental investigation on onset, progress and stages of literacy acquisition: Its implication for instruction processes, *Research Project Report submitted to NCERT*, Mysore: All India Institute of Speech and Hearing.

Karau, S.J. and Williams, K.D. (1993), Social loafing: A meta-analytic review and theoretical integration, *Journal of Personality and Social Psychology*, **65**: 681–706.

Kark, R., Shamir, B., and Cohen, G. (2003), The two faces of transformational leadership: Empowerment and dependency, *Journal of Applied Psychology*, **88**: 246–255.

Karlins, H., Coffman, T.L., and Walters, G. (1969), On the founding of social stereotypes: Studies in three generations of college students, *Journal of Personality and Social Psychology*, **13**: 1–16.

Karremans, J.C., Van Lange, P.A.H., Ouwerkerk, J.W., and Kluwer, E.S. (2003), When forgiving enhances psychological well-being: The role of interpersonal commitment, *Journal of Personality and Social Psychology*, **84**: 1011–1026.

Kassin, S.M. and Kiechel, K.L. (1996), The social psychology of false confessions, Compliance, internalization and confabulation, *Psychology Science*, **7**: 125–128.

Kassin, S.M. and McNall, K. (1991), Police interrogations and confessions: Communicating promises and threats by pragmatic implication, *Law and Human Behaviour*, **15**: 233–251.

Kassin, S.M. and Neumann, K. (1997), On the power of confession evidence: A experimental test for the fundamental difference hypothesis, *Law and Human Behaviour*, **21**: 469–484.

Kassin, S.M. and Wrightsman, L.S. (1985), Confession evidence, In S.M. Kassin and L.S. Wrightsman (Eds.), *The Psychology of Evidence and Trial Procedure*, Newbury Park, CA: Sage.

Katz, D. (1960), The functional approach to the study of attitude change, *Public Opinion Quarterly*, **24**: 163–204.
Katz, D. and Braly, K.W. (1933), Racial stereotypes of 100 college students, *Journal of Abnormal and Social Psychology*, **28**: 280–290.
Katz, D. and K.W. Braly (1933), Racial prejudice and racial stereotypes, *Journal of Abnormal and Social Psychology*, **30**: 175–193.
Katz, D. and Kahn, R.L. (1966), *The Social Psychology of Organizations*, NY: Wiley.
Katz, D. and Stotland, E. (1959), A preliminary statement to a theory of attitude structure and change, In S. Koch (Ed.), *Psychology: A Study of Science*, Vol. III, Formulations of the person and the social context, NY: McGraw-Hill.
Katz, D. Maccoby, N., Gurin, G., and Floor, L.G. (1951), *Productivity, supervision, and morale among rail-road workers*, Ann Arbor: Survey, Research Center, Institute for Social Research, University of Michigan.
Katz, E. (1957), The two-step flow of communication: An up-to-date report on a hypothesis, *Public Opinion Quarterly*, **21**: 61–78.
Katz, H., Cadoret, R., Hughes, K., and Abbey, D. (1965), Physiological correlates of acceptable and unacceptable attitude statements, *Psychological Reports*, **17**: 18.
Katz, J. and Beach, S.R.H. (2000), Looking for love?: Self-verification and self-enhancement effects on initial romantic attraction, *Personality and Social Psychology Bulletin*, **26**: 1526–1539.
Kawakami, K., Dovidio, J.F., Moll, J., Hermsen, S., and Russn, A. (2000), Just say 'No' (to stereotyping): Effects of training in the negation of stereotypic associations on stereotype activation, *Journal of Personality and Social Psychology*, **78**: 871–888.
Kazdin, A.E. (1982), Applying behaviour principles in schools, In C.R. Reynolds and J.B. Gutkin (Eds.), *The Handbook of School Psychology*, NY: Wiley.
Keating, J.P. and Brock, T.C. (1974), Acceptance of persuasion and the inhibition of counterargumentation under various distraction tasks, *Journal of Experimental Social Psychology*, **10**: 301–309.
Keller, L.N., Bouchard, T.J., Aarvey, R.D., Segal, N.L., and Davis, R.V. (1992), Work values: Genetics and environmental influences, *Journal of Applied Psychology*, **77**: 79–88.
Kellermann, A.L. (1993), Gun ownership as a risk factor for homicide in the home, *New England Journal of Medicine*, **329**: 1984–1991.
Kellermann, A.L. (1997), Comment: Gunsmoke-changing public attitudes towards smoking and firearms, *American Journal of Public Health*, **87**: 910–912.
Kelley, H.H. (1950), The warm-cold variable in first impressions, *Journal of Personality*, **18**: 431–439.
Kelley, H.H. (1967), Attribution theory in social psychology, *Nebraska Symposium on Motivation*, **41**: 192–241.
Kelley, H.H. (1972), Causal schemata and the attribution process, In E.E. Jones et al. (Eds.), *Attribution: Perceiving the Causes of Behaviour*, Morristown, NJ: General Learning Press.
Kelley, H.H. and Thibaut, J.W. (1978), *Interpersonal Relations, A Theory of Interdependence*, **31**: 457–501.
Kellogg, R.T. (1995), *Cognitive Psychology*, Thousand Oaks: Sage.
Kelly, A.E. and Nauta, M.M. (1997), Reactance and thought suppression, *Personality and Social Psychology Bulletin*, **23**: 1123–1132.
Kelman, H.C. (1961), Processes of opinion change, *Public Opinion Quarterly*, **25**: 57–78.
Kelman, H.C. (1974), Attitudes are alive and well and gainfully employed in the sphere of action, *American Psychologist*, **29**: 310–324.
Kelman, H.C. and Hovland, C.I. (1953), Reinstatement of the communicator in the delayed measurement of opinion change, *Journal of Abnormal and Social Psychology*, **48**: 327–335.
Kemper, T.D. (1973), The fundamental dimensions of social relationship: A theoretical statement, *Acta Psychologica*, **32**: 100–125.
Kendler, K.S. and Prescott, C.A. (1999), A population-based twin study of lifetime major depression in men and women, *Archives of General Psychiatry*, **56**(1): 39–44.
Kenny, D.A. (1975), Cross-lagged panel correlation: A test for spuriousness, *Psychological Bulletin*, **82**: 887–903.
Kenny, D.A. (1994), *Interpersonal Perception: A Social Relation Analysis*, NY: Guilford Press.

Kenrick, D.T. (1995), Evolutionary theory versus the confederacy of dunces, *Psychological Inquiry*, **6**: 56–62.
Kenrick, D.T., McCreath, H.E., Govern, J., King, R., and Brodin, J. (1990), Person-environment intersections: Everyday settings and common trait dimensions, *Journal of Personality and Social Psychology*, **58**: 685–698.
Keys, C. and Bartunek, J.M. (1979), Organization development in schools: God agreement, process skills and diffusion of change, *Journal of Applied Behavioural Science*, **15**: 61–78.
Khan, H. (1981), Parents of prejudiced and unprejudiced Muslim school students, *Unpublished Doctoral Dissertation*, Ranchi: Ranchi University.
Khan, H.R. (1978), Development of religious identity and prejudice in children, *Unpublished Doctoral Dissertation*, Bodh Gaya: Magadh University.
Khan, H.R. (1979), A study of development of religions prejudice in children, In S.N. Singh and H.R. Khan (Eds.), *Prejudice in Indian Society*, Varanasi: Rupa Psychological Center.
Khokle, V.S. (1994), Acquisition of segment (gh) in Marathi: A case study, In B. Lakshmi Bai and D. Vasanta (Eds.), *Language Development and Languages Disorders: Perspectives from Indian Languages*, 37–52, ND: Bahri Publications.
Kiesler, C.A. and Kiesler, S.B. (1969), *Conformity*, Reading, MA: Addison-Wesley.
Kiesler, S. and Sproull, L. (1992), Group decision-making and communication technology, *Organizational Behaviour and Human Decision Processes*, **52**: 96–123.
Kiessling, R.J. and Kalish, R.A. (1961), Correlates of success in leaderless group discussion, *Journal of Social Psychology*, **54**: 359–365.
Kilduff, M. and Day, D.V. (1994), Do chameleons gal ahead? The effects of self-monitoring on managerial careers, *Academy of Management Journal*, **37**: 1047–1060.
Kilham, W. and Mann, L. (1974), Level of destructive obedience as a function of transmitter and executants roles in the Milgram obedience paradigm, *Journal of Personality and Social Psychology*, **29**: 96–702.
Kim, H. and Markus, H.R. (1999), Deviance or uniqueness, harmony or conformity?: A cultural analysis, *Journal of Personality and Social Psychology*, **77**: 785–800.
Kipnis, D. (1976), *The Powerholders*, Chicago: University of Chicago Press.
Kipnis, D. (1984), The use of power in organizations and in interpersonal settings, In S. Oskamp (Ed.), *Applied Social Psychology Annual*, **5**: 179–210, Beverly Hills, CA: Sage.
Kirchler, E. and Davis, J.H. (1986), The influence of member status differences and task type on group consensus and member position change, *Journal of Personality and Social Psychology*, **51**: 83–91.
Kirkpatrick, S.A. and Locke, E.A. (1991), Leadership: D. traits matter?, *Academy of Management Executive*, **5**: 48–60.
Kitayama, S. and Burnstein, E. (1988), Automaticity in conversations: A reexamination of mindlessness hypothesis, *Journal of Personality and Social Psychology*, **54**: 219–224.
Kitayama, S. and Markus, H.R. (1995), Culture and self: Implications for internationalizing psychology, In N.R. Godlberger and J.B. Veroff (Eds.), *The Culture and Psychology Reader*, NY: New York University Press.
Kitayama, S. and Markus, H.R. (2000), The pursuit of happiness and the realization of sympathy: Cultural patterns of self, social relations and well-being. In E. Diener and E.M. Suh (Eds.), *Subjective Well-being Across Cultures*, Cambridge, MA: MIT Press.
Kitayama, S., Duffy, S., Kawamura, T., and Larsen, J.T. (2003), Perceiving an object and its context in different cultures: A cultural look at new look, *Psychological Science*, **22**, 201–205.
Klar, Y. (2002), Way beyond compare: The nonselective superiority and inferiority bias in judging randomly assigned group members relative to their pears, *Journal of Experimental Social Psychology*, **38**: 331–351.
Klein, A.L. (1976), Changes in leadership appraisal as a function of the stress of a simulated panic situation, *Journal of Personality and Social Psychology*, **34**(6): 1143–1154.
Klein, O., Synder, M., and Livingston, R.W. (2004), Prejudice on the state: Self-monitoring and public expression of group attitudes, *British Journal of Social Psychology*, **43**: 299–314.
Kleinke, C.L. (1986), Gaze and eye contact: A research review, *Psychological Bulletin*, **100**: 78–100.

Kleinmuntz, B. and Szucko, J.J. (1984), A field study of the fallibility of polygraph lie detection, *Nature*, **308**: 449–450.
Knowles, M.S. (1975), *Self-directed Learning: A Guide for Learners and Teachers*, NY: Association Press.
Kobasa, S. (1979), Stressful life events, personality and health: An inquiry into hardiness, *Journal of Personality and Social Psychology*, **37**: 1–11.
Kobasa, S.C., Maddi, S.R., and Kahu, S. (1982), Hardiness and health: A prospective study, *Journal of Personality and Social Psychology*, **42**: 168–177.
Koenig, F. (1971), Definition of self in France and Sweden, *American Psychological Association Proceedings*, **6**: 257–258.
Kohl, W.L., Steers, R., and Terborg, J. (1995), The effects of transformational leadership on teacher attitudes and students performance in Singapore, *Journal of Organizational Behaviour*, **73**: 695–703.
Kohlberg, L. (1969), Stage and sequence: The cognitive-developmental approach to socialization, In D. Goslin (Ed.), *Handbook of Socialization Theory and Research*, Chicago: Rand McNally.
Kohlberg, L. (1973), Stage and sequence: The cognitive-developmental approach, In D.A. Goslin (Ed.), *Handbook of Socialization Theory and Research*, 347–400, Chicago: Rand McNally.
Kohn, M. (1969), *Class and Conformity: A Study in Values*, Homewood, IL: Dorsey Press.
Kohn, M., Naoi, A., Schoenbach, C., Schooter, C., and Slomczynsksi, K.M. (1990), Position in the class structure and psychological functioning in the United States, Japan and Poland, *American Journal of Sociology*, **95**: 964–1008.
Korn, J.H. and Nicks, S.D. (1993), *The Rise and Decline of Deception in Social Psychology*, p. 31, American Psychological Society Convention.
Krantz, D.S. and Manuck, S.B. (1984), Acute psychophysiologic reactivity and risk of cardiovascular disease: A review and methodological critique, *Psychological Bulletin*, **96**: 435–464.
Krantz, D.S., Grunberg, N.E., and Baum, A. (1985), Health Psychology Annual Review of Psychology, **36**: 349–383.
Krantz, S.E. and Rude, S. (1984), Depressive attributions: Selection of different causes or assignment of different meanings?, *Journal of Personality and Social Psychology*, **47**: 103–203.
Kraus, S.J. (1995), Attitudes and the prediction of behaviour: A meta-analysis of the empirical literature, *Personality and Social Psychology Bulletin*, **21**: 58–75.
Krauss, R. and Chiu, C. (1998), Language and social behaviour, In D. Gilbert, S. Fiske and G. Lindzey (Eds.), *The Handbook of Social Psychology*, 4th edn., **2**: 41–88, Boston: McGraw-Hill.
Krauss, R.M. and Fussell, S.K. (1996), Social psychological models of interpersonal communication, In E.T. Higgins and A. Kruglanski (Eds.), *Social Psychology: Handbook of Basic Principles*, 655–701, NY: Guilford Press.
Krauss, R.M., Morrel–Samuels, P., and Colasante, C. (1991), Do conversational hand gestures communicate?, *Journal of Personality and Social Psychology*, **61**: 743–754.
Kraut, R., Kiesler, S., Boneva, B., Cummings, J., Helgeson, V. and Crawford, A. (2004), Internet paradox revisited, *Journal of Social Issues*, **58**: 49–74.
Kravitz, D.A. and Martin, B. (1986), Ringlemaun rediscovered: The original article, *Journal of Personality and Social Psychology*, **50**: 936–941.
Krebs, D. (1970), Altruism: An examination of the concept and a review of the literature, *Psychological Bulletin*, **73**: 258–302.
Krebs, D.L. and Miller, D.T. (1985), Altruism and aggression, In G. Lindzey and E. Arouson (Eds.), *The Handbook of Social Psychology*, 3rd edn., NY: Random House.
Krech, D., Crutchfield, R.S., and Ballachey, E.L. (1962), *Individual in Society*, NY: McGraw-Hill.
Kretschmer, E. (1925), *Physique and Character*, NY: Harcourt, Brace and Company.
Krishnan, L. (1981), Theory and research on reactions to aid, In J. Pandey (Ed.), *Perspectives on Experimental Social Psychology in India*, ND: Concept.

Krishnan, L. (2000), Resource, relationship and scarcity in reward allocation in India, *Psychologia,* **43**: 275–285.
Krosnick, J.A. (1989), Attitude importance and attitude accessibility, *Personality and Psychology Bulletin,* **15**: 297–308.
Krosnick, J.A., Betz, A.L., Jussim, L.J., and Lynn, A.R. (1992), Subliminal conditions of attitudes, *Personality and Social Psychology Bulletin,* **18**: 152–162.
Kugihara, N. (2001), Effects of aggressive behaviour and group size on collective escape in emergency: A test between a social identity model of deindividuation theory, *British Journal of Social Psychology,* **40**: 575–598.
Kulick, J.A. and Brown, R. (1979), Frustration, attribution of blame and aggression, *Journal of Experimental Social Psychology,* **15**: 183–194.
Kulka, R.A. and Kessler, J.B. (1978), Is justice really blind?: The influence of litigant's physical attractiveness on judicial judgement, *Journal of Applied Social Psychology,* **8**: 366–381.
Kumar, G. and Shankhdhar, R.R. (1998), Self-concept and modes of frustration in urban and rural schedule caste and female adolescents: A multi-dimensional comparative study, *Indian Educational Review,* **33**: 106–16.
Kumar, K. (1972), Social climate in school and characteristics of pupils, In J. Pandey's (Ed.), *Psychology in India,* Vol. 2, ND: Sage.
Kumar, K. (1975), Social climate in school and characteristics of pupils, *Indian Journal of Clinical Psychology,* **2**: 162–172.
Kumari, R. (1995), Relationship of sex role attitudes and self-esteem to fear of success among college women, *Psychological Studies,* **40**(2): 82–88.
Kunda, Z. (1999), *Social Cognition: Making Sense of People,* Cambridge, MA: MIT Press.
Kunda, Z. and Oleson, K.C. (1995), Maintaining stereotypes in the face of disconfirmation: Constructing grounds for subtyping deviants, *Journal of Personality and Social Psychology,* **68**: 565–579.
Kunda, Z. and Thagard, P. (1996), Forming impression from stereotypes, traits and behaviours: A parallel-constraint-satisfaction theory, *Psychological Review,* **103**: 284–308.
Kundu, R. and Biswas, C. (1980), Changing pattern of interpersonal communication patterns in Hindu joint family in India, *International Journal of Group Tensions,* **8**(1): 120–129.
Kundu, R. and Maiti, B. (1980), A study of ego-strength and its impact on interpersonal attractiveness, *Journal of Psychological Researches,* **24**(1): 29–33.
Kureshi, A. and Husain, A. (1982), Attraction, alienation and attitude similarity–dissimilarity, *Psychological Studies,* **27**(2): 41–43.
LaFrance, M., Hecht, M.A., and Paluck, E.L. (2003), The contingent smile: A meta-analysis of sex differences in smiling, *Psychological Bulletin,* **129**: 305–334.
Lakshmi Bai, B. (2000), *Sounds and Words in Early Language Acquisition: A Bilingual Account,* Shimla: Indian Institute of Advanced Study.
Lal, N.N. (1987), Social class differences in self-perception, *Perspectives in Psychological Researches,* **10**: 30–36.
Lambert, A.J. (1995), Stereotypes and social judgement: The consequences of group variability, *Journal of Personality and Social Psychology,* **68**: 388–403.
Lamm, I.T. and Myers, D.G. (1976), Machiavellianism, discussion time and group shift, *Social Behaviour and Personality,* **4**: 41–48.
Landy, D. and Sigall, H. (1974), Beauty is talent: Task evaluation as a function of performer's physical attractiveness, *Journal of Personality and Social Psychology,* **29**: 299–304.
Langer, E.J. and Imber, L. (1980), The role of mindlessness in the perception of deviance, *Journal of Personality and Social Psychology,* **39**: 360–367.
Langlois, J.H., Kalakanis, L., Rubenstein, A.J., Larson, A., Hallam, M., and Smoot, M. (2000), Maxims or myths of beauty?: A meta-analytic and theoretical review, *Psychological Bulletin,* **126**: 390–423.
Lang, P.J., Bradley, M.M. and Cuthbert, B.N. (1990), Emotion, attention, and the startle reflex, *Psychological Review,* **97**: 377–395.
LaPiere, R. (1934), Attitude versus Action, *Social Forces,* **13**: 230–237.

Laptane, B., and Rodin, J. (1969), A lady in distress: Inhibiting effects of friends and strangers on bystander intervention, *Journal of Experimental Social Psychology*, **5**: 189–202.

Larson, J.R., Chirtensen, C., Frantz, T.M and Abbott, A.S. (1998), Diagnosing groups: The pooling, management and impact of shared and unshared case information in team-based medical decision-making, *Journal of Personality and Social Psychology*, **75**: 93–108.

Larson, J.R., Foster–Fishman, P.G. and Keys, C.B. (1994), Discussion of shared and unshared information in decision-making groups, *Journal of Personality and Social Psychology*, **67**: 446–461.

Lassiter, G.D., Geers, A.L., and Apple, K.J. (2002), Communication set and the perception of ongoing behaviour, *Personality and Social Psychology Bulletin*, **28**: 158–171.

Latane, B. and Darley, J.M. (1968), Group intervention of bystander intervention in emergencies, *Journal of Personality and Social Psychology*, **10**: 215–221.

Latane, B. and Darley, J.M. (1970), *The Unresponsive Bystander: Why Does Not He Help?*, NY: Appleton-Century-Crofts.

Latane, B. and Nida, S. (1981), Ten years of research on group size and helping, *Psychology Bulletin*, **89**: 308–324.

Latane, B. and Rodin, J. (1969), A lady in distress: Inhibiting effects of friends and strangers on bystanders intervention, *Journal of Experimental Social Psychology*, **5**: 189–202.

Latane, B., Nida, S.A., and Witson, D.W. (1981), The effects of group size on helping behaviour, In Rushton, J.P. and Sorrentino, R.H. (Eds.), *Altruism and Helping Behaviour*, 287–313, Hillsdale, NJ: Erlbaum..

Latane, B., Williams, K., and Harkins, S. (1979), Many hands make work light: The causes and consequences of social loafing, *Journal of Personality and Social Psychology*, **37**: 822–832.

Latha, K.S. and Suresh, A. (2002), Knowledge, attitude and practice (KAP): A study in coronary artery disease, *Psychological Studies*, **47**: 100–105.

Lau, R.R. and Russel, D. (1980), Attributions in the sports pages, *Journal of Personality and Social Psychology*, **39**: 29–38.

Lavoie, F., Hebert, H., Tremplay, R., Vitaro, F., Vezina, L., and Mc. Duff, P. (2002), History of family dysfunction and perpetration of dating violence by adolescent boys: A longitudinal study, *Journal of Adolescent Health*, **30**: 375–383.

Laws, G., Davies, I., and Andrews, C. (1995), Linguistic structure and nonlinguistic cognition: English and Russian blues compared, *Language and Cognitive Processes*, **10**: 59–94.

Lay, C. and Nguyen, T.T.I. (1998), The role of acculturation-related and acculturation non-specific daily issues: Vietnamese-Canadian students and psychological distress, *Canadian Journal of Behavioural Sciences*, **30**(3): 172–181.

Lazarsfeld, P.F., Berelson, B., and Gaudet, H. (1948), *The People's Choice: How the Voter Makes up his Mind in a Presidential Campaign*, NY: Columbia University Press.

Lazarus, R.S. (1983), The costs and benefits of denial, In S. Bresnitz (Ed.), *Denial of Stress*, NY: International University Press.

Lazarus, R.S. (1993), From psychological stress to the emotions: A history of changing outlooks, *Annual Review of Psychology*, **44**: 140–143.

Lazarus, R.S. and Folkman, S. (1984), *Stress, Appraisal and Coping*, NY: Springer.

Leana, C.R. (1985), A partial test of Janis' groupthink model: Effects of group cohesiveness and leader behaviour on defective decision making, *Journal of Management*, **11**: 5–17.

Leaper, C., Anderson, K., and Sanders, P. (1998), Moderators of gender effects on parents' talk to their children: A Meta-analysis, *Developmental Psychology*, **34**: 3–27.

Leary, M., Tchividjian, L., and Kraxberger, B. (1994), Self-presentation can be hazardous to your health: Impression management and health risk, *Health Psychology*, **13**: 461–470.

Leary, M.R. (1999), Making sense of self-esteem, *Current Directions in Psychological Science*, **8**: 32–35.

Leary, M.R., Rogers, P.A., Canfield, R.W. and Coe, C. (1986), Boredom in interpersonal encounters: Antecedents and implications, *Journal of Personality and Social Psychology*, **51**: 1265–1168.

Leary, M.R., Wheeler, D.S., and Jenkins, T.B. (1986), Aspects of identity and behavioural preference: Studies of occupational and recreational choice, *Social Psychology Quarterly*, **49**: 11–18.

Leary, W.E. (1988), (November, 19), Novel methods unlock witnesses' memories, In R.A. Baron, D. Byrne and N.R. Branscombe's *Social Psychology*, 11th ed., New Delhi: Prentice-Hall of India.

Leavitt, H.J. (1951), Some effects of certain communication patterns on group performance, *Journal of Abnormal and Social Psychology*, **46**: 38–50.

LeDoux, J.E. (1996), The Emotional Brain: The mysterious understanding of emotional life, New York: Simon & Schuster.

Lee, A.Y. (2001), The mere exposure effect: An uncertainty reduction explanation revisited, *Personality and Social Psychology Bulletin*, **27**: 1255–1266.

Lee, A.Y., Aaker, J.L., and Gardner, W.L. (2000), The pleasures and pains of distinct self-construals: The role of interdependence in regulatory focus, *Journal of Personality and Social Psychology*, **78**: 1122–1134.

Leffler, A., Gillespie, D.L., and Conaty, J.C. (1982), The effects of status differentiation on nonverbal behaviour, *Social Psychology Quarterly*, **45**: 153–161.

Lefrancois, G.R. (1980), *Of Children: An Introduction to Child Development*, California: Wadsworth Publishing Company.

Lefrancois, G.R. (1983), *Psychology*, California: Wadsworth Publishing Company.

Leighton, A.H. (1945), *The Governing of men: General Principles and Recommendation Based on Experience at a Japanese Relocation Camp*, Princeton, NJ: Princeton University Press.

Leippe, M.R. and Eisenstadt, D. (1994), Generalization of dissonance reduction: Decreasing prejudice through induced compliance, *Journal of Personality and Social Psychology*, **67**: 395–413.

Lenneberg, E.H. (1967), *Biological Foundations of Language*, NY: Wiley.

Lenneberg, E.H. (1969), On explaining language, *Science*, **164**: 635–643.

Lenneberg, E.H., Reblesky, F.G., and Nichols, I.A. (1965), The vocalization of infants born to deaf and hearing patients, *Vita Humana*, **8**: 23–27.

Lennington, S. (1981), Child abuse: The limits of sociobiology, *Ethology and Sociology*, **2**: 17–29.

Lepowsky, M. (1994), Women, men and aggression in an egalitarian society, *Sex Roles*, **30**: 199–211.

Lepper, M., Greene, D., and Nisbett, R. (1973), Undermining children's intrinsic interest with extrinsic reward: A test of the overjustification hypothesis, *Journal of Personality and Social Psychology*, **28**: 129–137.

Leventhal, H. (1970), Findings and theory in the study of fear communications, In L. Berkowitz (Ed.), *Advances in Experimental Social Psychology*, Vol. 5, NY: Academic Press.

Leventhal, H. (1974), Attitudes, In C. Nemeth (Ed.), *Social Psychology: Classic and Contemporary Integration*, Chicago: Rand-McNally.

Leventhal, H. and Niles, P. (1965), Persistence of influence for varying duration of exposure to threat stimuli, *Psychological Report*, **16**: 223–233.

Leventhal, H., Singer, R., and Jones, S. (1965), The effects of fear and specificity of recommendation upon attitudes and behaviour, *Journal of Personality and Social Psychology*, **2**: 20–29.

Leventhal, H., Watts, J.C., and Pagano, F. (1967), Effects of fear and instructions on how to cope with danger, *Journal of Personality and Social Psychology*, **6**: 313–321.

Levine, J.M. and Moreland, R.L. (1998), *Small groups*, In D. Gilbert, S. Fiske, and G. Lindzey (Eds.), *The Handbook of Social Psychology*, 4th edn., Boston: McGraw-Hill.

Levine, P. (2000), *The Sexual Activity and Birth Control Use of American Teenagers*, Cambridge: National Bureau of Economic Research.

Levine, R.A. and Campbell, D.T. (1972), *Ethnocentrism: Theories of Conflict, Ethnic Attitudes, and Group Behaviour*, NY: Wiley.

Levine, R.V., Martinez, T.S., Brase, G., and Sorenson, K. (1994), Helping in 30 US cities, *Journal of Personality and Social Psychology*, **67**: 69–82.

Levy, B. and Langer, E. (1994), Aging free from negative stereotypes: Successful memory in China and among American deaf, *Journal of Personality and Social Psychology*, **66**: 989–997.

Levy, B.R., Slode, M.D., Kunkel, S.R., and Kasl, S.V. (2002), Longevity increased by positive perceptions of aging, *Journal of Personality and Social Psychology*, **83**: 261–270.
Levy, L. (1960), Studies in conformity behaviour: A methodological note, *Journal of Psychology*, **50**: 39–41.
Lewin, K. (1947), Group decision and social change, In T.M. Newcomb and E.L. Hartley (Eds.), *Readings in Social Psychology*, NY: Holt, Rinehart and Winston.
Lewin, K. (1948), *Resolving Social Conflicts*, NY: Harper.
Lewin, K. (1951), *Field Theory in Social Science*, NY Harper.
Lewin, K., Lippitt, R. and White, R. (1939), Patterns of aggressive behaviour in experimentally created social climates, *Journal of Psychology*, **10**: 271–299.
Lewis, M. and Brooks-Gum, J. (1979), Toward a theory of social cognition: The development of self, In I. Uzgiris (Ed.), *Social Interaction and Communication during Infancy: New Directions for Child Development*, Vol. 4, San Francisco: Jossey-Bass.
Lewis, R. (2001), Classroom discipline and student responsibility: The students' view, *Teaching and Teacher Education*, **17**: 307–319.
Lex, B.W. (1986), Measurement of alcohol consumption in fieldwork settings, *Medical Anthropological Quarterly*, **17**: 95–98.
Lickel, B., Rutchick, A.M., Hamilton, D.L., and Sherman, S.J. (2006), Intuitive theories of group types and relational principles, *Journal of Experimental Social Psychology*, **42**: 28–39.
Lieberman, S. (1965), The effect of changes of roles on the attitudes of role occupants, In H. Proshansky and B. Seidenberg (Eds.), *Basic Studies in Social Psychology*, NY: Holt, Rinehart and Winston.
Lightdale, J.R. and Prentice, D.A. (1994), Rethinking sex differences in aggression: Aggressive behaviour in the absence of social roles, *Personality and Social Psychology Bulletin*, **20**: 34–44.
Likert, R. (1932), A technique for measurement of attitude, *Archives of Psychology*, **22**: 40.
Likert, R.A. (1932), Technique for measurement of attitude, *Archives of Psychology*, No. 140.
Linden, R.C. and Mitchell, T.R. (1988), Ingratiatory behaviours in organizational settings, *Academy of Management Review*, **13**: 572–587.
Linder, D.E. and Worchel, S. (1970), Opinion change as a result of effortfully drawing a counter attitudinal conclusion, *Journal of Experimental Social Psychology*, **6**: 432–448.
Lindgren, H.C. (1973), Leadership and college grades. *Journal of Social Psychology*, **20**: 271–280.
Lindgren, H.C. (1978), Trends in social psychology research in reduction, In D. Bar-tal and L. Saxe (Eds.), *Social Psychology of Education: Theory and Research*, Washington, D.C.: Hemisphere.
Lindgren, H.C. (1985), *An Introduction to Social Psychology*, ND: Wiley Eastern Limited.
Linville, P.W., Fisher, G.W., and Salovey, P. (1989), Perceived distributions of the characteristics of in-group and out-group members: Empirical evidence and a computer simulation, *Journal of Personality and Social Psychology*, **57**: 165–188.
Linz, D., Donnerstein, E., and Penrod, S. (1988), Effects of long-term exposure to violent and sexually degrading depictions of women, *Journal of Personality and Social Psychology*, **55**: 758–768.
Lionberger, H.F. (1953), Some characteristics of farm operators sought as resources of farm information in a Missouri community, *Rural Sociology*, **18**: 327–338.
Lipe, M.G. (1991), Counterfactual reasoning as a framework for attribution theories, *Psychological Bulletin*, **109**: 456–471.
Lipkus, I.M., Green, J.D., Feaganes, J.R., and Sedikiles, C. (2001), The relationships between attitudinal ambivalence and desire to quit smoking among college smokers, *Journal of Applied Social Psychology*, **31**: 113–133.
Lipscomb, T.J., Larrien, J.A., McAllister, H.A., and Bregman, N.J. (1982), Modeling and children's generosity: A developmental perspective, *Merrill-Palmer Quarterly*, **28**: 275–282.
Lipscomb, T.J., McAllister, H.A., and Bregman, M.J. (1985), A developmental inquiry into the effects of multiple models' on children's generosity, *Merrill-Palmer Quarterly*, **31**: 335–344.

Littlepage, G.E., Schmidt, G.W., Whisler, E.W., and Frost, A.G. (1995), An input-process-output analysis of influence and performance in problem-solving groups, *Journal of Personality and Social Psychology*, **69**: 877–889.
Locke, K.D. and Horowitz, D. (1990), Satisfaction in interpersonal attractions as a function of similarity in level of dysphoria, *Journal of Personality and Social Psychology*, **58**: 823–831.
Lockwood, P. (2002), Could it happen to you? Predicting the impact of downward comparisons on the self, *Journal of Personality and Social Psychology*, **82**: 343–358.
Lockwood, P. and Kunda, Z. (1997), Superstars and me: Predicting the impact of role models on the self, *Journal of Personality and Social Psychology*, **73**: 91–103.
Loftus E.F. (1975), Leading questions and the eyewitness report, *Cognitive Psychology*, **7**: 560–572.
Loftus, E.F. (1979), *Eyewitness Testimony*, Cambridge MA: Harvard University Press.
Loftus, E.F. (1992), When a lie becomes memory's truth: Memory distortion after exposure to misinformation, *Current Directions in Psychological Science*, **1**: 121–123.
Loftus, E.F. (2003), Make-believe memories, *American Psychologist*, **58**: 867–873.
Loftus, E.F. and Palmer, J.C. (1974), Reconstruction of automobile destruction: An example of the interaction between language and memory, *Journal of Verbal Learning and Verbal Behaviour*, **13**: 585–589.
Lohr, J.M. and Staats, A. (1973), Attitude conditioning in Sino-Tibetan languages, *Journal of Personality and Social Psychology*, **26**: 196–200.
Lois, J. (1999), Socialization to heroism: Individualism and collectivism in a voluntary search and rescue group, *Social Psychology Quarterly*, **62**: 117–135.
Lord, C.G. and Saenz, D.S. (1985), Memory deficits and memory surfeits: Differential cognitive consequences of tokenism for tokens and observers, *Journal of Personality and Social Psychology*, **49**: 918–926.
Lord, T.R. (2001), 101 reasons for using cooperative learning in biology teaching, *The American Biology Teacher*, **63**(1): 30–38.
Lorenz, K.Z. (1935), Imprinting, In R.C. Birney and R.C. Teevan (Eds.), *Instinct*, London: Van Nostrand.
Losch, M.E. and Cacioppo, J.T. (1990), Cognitive dissonance may enhance sympathetic tonus but attitudes are changed to reduce negative effect rather than arousal, *Journal of Experimental Social Psychology*, **20**: 289–304.
Lott, A.J. and Lott, B.E. (1965), Group cohesiveness as interpersonal attraction: A review of relationships with antecedent and consequent variables, *Psychological Bulletin*, **64**: 259–309.
Lott, A.J. and Lott, B.E. (1974), The role of reward in the formation of positive interpersonal attitudes, In T.L. Huston (Ed.), *Foundations of Interpersonal Attraction*, 171–189, NY: Academic Press.
Lott, A.J. and Lott, B.E. and Mathews, F.M. (1969), Interpersonal attraction among children as a function of vicarious rewards, *Journal of Educational Psychology*, **60**(4): 274–283.
Lott, B.E. and Lott, A.J. (1960), The formation of positive attitudes towards group members, *Journal of Abnormal and Social Psychology*, **61**: 297–300.
Loy, J.W. and Sage, J.M. (1970), The effects of formal structure of organization leadership: An investigation of interscholastic baseball teams, In G.S. Kenyan (Ed.), *Contemporary Psychology of Sport*, Chicago: The Athletic Institute.
Luchins, A.S. (1957a), Experimental attempts to minimize the impact of first impressions, In C. Hovland et al. (Eds.), *The Order of Presentation in Persuasion*, 62–75, NH: Yale University Press.
Luchins, A.S. (1957b), Primacy-recency in impression formation, In C. Hovland et al. (Eds.), *The Order of Presentation in Persuasion*, 62–75, NH: Yale University Press.
Lucy, J.A. and Shweder, R.A. (1979), Whorf and his critics: Linguistic and nonlinguistic influences on colour memory, *American Anthropologist*, **81**: 581–615.
Luhman, R. (1990), Appalachian English Stereotypes: Language attitudes in Kentucky, *Language in Society*, **19**: 331–348.
Lumsdaine, A.A. and Janis, I.L. (1953), Resistance to counterpropaganda produced by one-sided and two-sided propaganda presentations, *Public Opinion Quarterly*, **17**: 311–318.

Lundgren, D.C. and Knight, D.J. (1978), Sequential stages of development in sensitivity training groups, *Journal of Applied Behavioural Science*, **14**: 204–222.
Lupfer, M., Kay, J., and Burnette, S.A. (1969), The influence of picketing on the purchase of toy guns, *Journal of Social Psychology*, **77**: 197–200.
Lydon, J.E., Jamieson, D.W. and Zanna, M.P. (1988), Interpersonal similarity and the social and intellectual dimensions of first impressions, *Social Cognition*, **6**(4), 260–286.
Lyubomirsky, S., Caldwell, N.D., and Nolen–Hoeksema, S. (1998), Effects of ruminative and distracting responses to the depressed mood on retrieval of autobiographical memories, *Journal of Personality and Social Psychology*, **75**: 166–177.
Maass, A. and Arcuri, L. (1992), The role of language in the persistence of stereotypes, In G.R. Semin and K. Fiedler (Eds.), *Language, Interaction and Social Cognition*, 129–143, Newburry Park CA: Sage.
Macaulay, J. (1970), *A still for charity*, In Macaulay and L. Berkowitz (Eds.), *Altruism and Helping Behaviour*, 43–49, NY: Academic Press.
MacCracken, M.J. and Stadulis, R.E. (1985), Social facilitation of young children's dynamic performance balance, *Journal of Sport Psychology*, **7**: 150–165.
Maccoby, E.E. and Martin, J.A. (1983), Socialisation in the context of the family: Parent-child interaction, In E.M. Hetherington (Ed.), *Handbook of Child Psychology: Socialisation, Personality and social development*, Vol. 4, New York: Wiley.
Mackie, D.M. and Hunter, S.B. (1979), Majority and minority influence: The interactions of social identity and social cognition mediators, In D. Abrams and M.A. Hogg (Eds.), *Social Identity and Social Cognition*, Oxford, England: Blackwell.
MacLeod, C. and Campbell, L. (1992), Memory accessibility and probability judgement: An experimental evaluation of the availability heuristic, *Journal of Personality and Social Psychology*, **63**: 890–902.
Macrae, C.N., Bodenhausen, G.V., Shcloerscheidt, A.M., and Milue, A.B. (1999), Tales of the unexpected: Executive function and person perception, *Journal of Personality and Social Psychology*, **76**: 200–213.
Macrae, C.N., Milne, A.B., and Bodenhausen, G.V. (1994), Stereotypes as energy saving devices: A peek inside the cognitive toolbox, *Journal of Personality and Social Psychology*, **66**: 37–47.
Madnawat, A.V.S. and Thakur, L. (1986), Self construct of contrast caste groups of children, *Perspectives in Psychological Researches*, **9**: 21–23.
Major, B. (1981), Gender patterns in teaching touching behaviour, In C. Meyo and N.M. Henley (Eds.), *Gender and Nonverbal Behaviour*. NY: Springer-Verlag.
Major, B., Barr, L., Zubek, J., and Babey, S.H. (1999), Gender and self-esteem: A meta-analysis, In W.B. Swann, J.H. Langlois and L.A. Gilbert (Eds.), *Sexism and Stereotypes in Modern Society*, 223–253, Washington, DC: American Psychological Association.
Malinowski, B. (1927), *Sex and Repression in Savage Society*, NY: Harcourt, Brace and World.
Maltz, D.N. and Broker, R.A. (1982), A cultural approach to male–female miscommunications, In J.J. Gumperz (Ed.), *Language and Social Identity*, Cambridge, MA: Cambridge University Press.
Mandel, D.R. and Lehman, D.R. (1996), Counterfactual thinking and ascriptions of cause and preventability, *Journal of Personality and Social Psychology*, **71**: 450–463.
Manian, N., Strauman, T.J., and Denney, N. (1998), Temperament, recall parenting styles, and self-regulation: Retrospective tests of developmental postulates of self-discrepancy theory, *Journal of Personality and Social Psychology*, **75**: 1321–1332.
Manis, M., Nelson, T.E., and Shedler, J. (1988), Stereotypes and social judgement: Extremity, assimilation and contrast, *Journal of Personality and Social Psychology*, **55**: 28–36.
Mann, R.D. (1959), A review of the relationship between personality and performance in small groups, *Psychological Bulletin*, **56**: 241–270.
Mann, S., Vrij, A., and Bull, R. (2004), Detecting true lies: Police officers ability to detect suspects' lies, *Journal of Applied Psychology*, **89**: 137–149.

Manstead, A.S.R., Proffitt, C., and Smart, J.L. (1983), Predicting and understanding mother's infant-feeding intentions and behaviour: Testing the theory of reasoned action, *Journal of Personality and Social Psychology*, **44**: 657–671.

Marcus, D.K. and Miller, R.S. (2003), Sex differences in judgements of physical attractiveness: A social relations analysis, *Personality and Social Psychology Bulletin*, **29**: 325–335.

Marcus–Newhall, A., Pedersen, W.C., Carlron, M., and Miller, N. (2000), Displaced aggression is alive and well: A meta–analytic review, *Journal of Personality and Social Psychology*, **78**: 670–698.

Marfatia, J.C. (1973), The psychology of teacher–pupil relationship, *Child Psychiatry Quarterly*, **6**: 9–14.

Marks, D.F., Murray, M., Evans, B., Willig, C., Woodall, C., and Sykes, C.M. (2008), *Health Psychology*, ND: Sage.

Marks, G. and Miller, N. (1982), Target attractiveness as a mediator of assumed attitude similarity, *Personality and Social Psychology Bulletin*, **8**: 728–735.

Marks, G. and Miller, N. (1987), Ten years of research on the false-consensus effect: An empirical and theoretical review, *Psychological Bulletin*, **102**: 72–90.

Marks, L. and Miller, G.A. (1964), The role of semantic and syntactic constraints in the memorization of English sentences, *Journal of Verbal Learning and Verbal Behaviour*, **3**: 1–5.

Markus, H. (1977), Self-schemas and processing information about the self, *Journal of Personality and Social Psychology*, **35**: 63–78.

Markus, H. and Wurf, E. (1987), The dynamic of self-Concept: A social psychological perspective, *Annual Review of Psychology*, **38**: 299–337.

Markus, H. and Zajonc, R.B. (1985), The cognitive perspective in social psychology, In G. Lindzey and E. Aronson (Eds.), *The Handbook of Social Psychology*, **1**: 137–230, NY: Random House.

Markus, H., Kitayama, S., and Heiman, R.J. (1996), Culture and basic psychological principles, In E.T. Higgins and A.W. Kruglanski (Eds.), *Social Psychology: Handbook of Basic Principles*, 857–914, NY: Guilford Press.

Markus, H.R. and Kitayama, S. (1991), A collective fear of the collective: Implications for selves and theories of selves, Cognitive Science and Psychotherapy, *Journal of Psychotherapy Integration*, **4**: 317–579.

Markus, H.R. and Kitayama, S. (1994), A collective fear of the collective: Implications for selves and theories of selves, The self and the collective, *Personality and Social Psychology Bulletin*, **20**: 568–579.

Marler, P.R. (1970), A comparative approach to vocal learning: Song development in white-crowned sparrows, *Journal of Comparative and Physiological Psychology Monographs*, **71**(2): 1–25.

Marsh, C.P. and Coleman, A.L. (1954), Farmers practice adoption rates in relation to adoption rates of leaders, *Rural Sociology*, **19**: 180–183.

Marsh, H.W. and Young, A.S. (1997), Causal effects of academic self-concept on academic achievement: Structural equation models of longitudinal data, *Journal of Educational Psychology*, **89**: 41–54.

Marshall, M.A. and Brown, J.D. (2006), Trait aggressiveness and situational provocation: A test of the traits as situational sensitivities (TASS) model, *Personality and Social Psychology Bulletin*, **32**: 1100–1113.

Martens, P. and Peterson, J.A. (1971), Group cohesiveness as a determinant of success and member satisfaction in team performance, *International Review of Sport Sociology*, **6**: 49–61.

Martin, R. (1997), Girls don't talk about garages!: Perception of conversation in same and cross-sex friendships, *Personal Relationships*, **4**: 115–130.

Maruta, T., Colligan, R.C., Malinchoc, M., and Offord, K.P. (2002), Optimism-pessimism assessed in the 1960s and self-reported health status 30 years later, *Mayo Clinic Proceedings*, **77**: 748–753.

Maruyama, G., Fraser, S.C., and Miller, N. (1982), Personal responsibility and altruism in children, *Journal of Personality and Social Psychology*, **82**: 781–791.

Mascovici, S. and Zavalloni, M. (1969), The group as a polarizer of attitudes, *Journal of Personality and Social Psychology*, **12**: 125–135.

Maslach, C., Stapp, J., and Santee, R.T. (1985), Individuation: Conceptual analysis and assessment, *Journal of Personality and Social Psychology*, **49**: 658–664.

Maslow, A.H. (1943), A theory of human motivation, *Psychological Review*, **50**: 370–396.

Maslow, A.H. (1970), *Motivation and Personality*, NY: Harper and Row.
Mathur, S.S. and Singh, G. (1975), Correlates of academic achievement as perceived by teachers of secondary schools of Chandigarh, *Educational and Psychological Research Journal*, **2**: 8–18.
May, J.L. and Hamilton, P.A. (1980), Effects of musically evoked affect on women's interpersonal attraction and perceptual judgements of physical attractiveness of men, *Motivation and Emotion*, **4**: 217–228.
Mayadas, N. and Glasser, P. (1985), Termination: A neglected aspect of social group work, In M. Sundel, P. Glasser, R. Sarri, and R. Vinter (Eds.), *Individual Change Through Small Groups*, 2nd edn., 251–261, NY: Free Press.
Maynard, D.W. (1983), Social order and plea bargaining in the court, *The Sociological Quarterly*, **24**: 215–233.
Mayo, C. and Henley, N.M. (Eds.), (1981), *Gender and Non-verbal Behaviour*, Seacaucus, NJ: Springer-Verlag.
Mazzoni, G. and Memon, A. (2003), Imagination can create false autobiographical memories, *Psychological Science*, **14**: 186–188.
McArthur, L.Z. (1972), The how and why of what: Some determinants and consequences of causal attributions, *Journal of Personality and Social Psychology*, **22**: 171–193.
McCall, G.J. and Simmons, J.L. (1978), *Identities and Interactions*, NY: Free Press.
McCauley, C. (1989), The nature of social influence in groupthink: Compliance and internalization, *Journal of Personality and Social Psychology*, **57**: 250–260.
McCauley, Stitt, C.L., and Segal, M. (1980), Stereotyping: From Prejudice to Prediction, *Psychological Bulletin*, **87**: 195–208.
McClelland, D.C. (1961), *The Achieving Society*, Princeton, NJ: Van Nostrand.
McClelland, D.C., Atkinson, J.W., Clark, R.A., and Lowell, E.L. (1953), (Eds.), *The Achievement Motive*, NY: Appleton-Century-Crofts.
McClintock, C.G. (1963), Group support and the behaviour of leaders and non-leaders, *Journal of Abnormal and Social Psychology*, **67**: 105–113.
McCloskey, M. and Zaragosa, M.S. (1985), Misleading post-event information and memory and events: Arguments and evidence against the memory impairment hypothesis, *Journal of Experimental Psychology: General*, **114**: 1–16.
McClure, E.B. (2000), A meta-analytic review of sex differences in facial processing and their development in infants, children and adolescents, *Psychological Bulletin*, **26**: 424–453.
McCullough, M.E., Fincham, F.D., and Tsang, J.A. (2003), Forgiveness, forbearance, and time: The temporal unfolding of transgression-related interpersonal motivations, *Journal of Personality and Social Psychology*, **84**: 540–557.
McDavid, J.W. and Harari, H. (1999), *Social Psychology*, ND: CBS Publishers and Distributors.
McDonald, H.E. and Hirt, E.R. (1997), When expectancy meets desire: Motivational effects in reconstructive memory, *Journal of Personality and Social Psychology*, **72**: 5–23.
McDonald, R.D. (1962), The effect of reward-punishment and affiliation need on interpersonal attraction, In R.A. Baron, Donn Byrne and M.R. Branscombe, *Social Psychology*, 11th edn., ND: Prentice-Hall of India.
McDougall, W. (1908), *Introduction to Social Psychology*, London: Methuen.
McGinley, H., LeFevre, R., and McGinley, P. (1975), The influence of a communicator's body position on opinion change in others, *Journal of Personality and Social Psychology*, **31**: 686–690.
McGrath, J.E. (1984), *Groups: Interaction and Performance*, NJ: Prentice-Hall.
McGrath, J.E. and Julian, J.W. (1963), Interaction process and task outcome in experimentally created negotiation groups, *Journal of Psychological Studies*, **14**: 117–138.
McGuire, W.J. (1961), Resistance to persuasion confirmed by active and passive prior refutation of the same and alternate counterarguments, *Journal of Abnormal and Social Psychology*, **63**: 326–332.
McGuire, W.J. (1969), The nature of attitudes and attitude change, In G. Lindzey and E. Aronson (Eds.), *Handbook of Social Psychology*, 3, Reading, MA: Addison-Wesley.
McGuire, W.J. (1985), Attitudes and attitude change, In G. Lindzey and E. Arouson (Eds.), *The Handbook of Social Psychology*, 3rd edn., **2**: 233–346, NY: Random House.

McGuire, W.J. (2003), The morphing of attitude change into social cognition research, In G.V. Bodenhansen and A.J. Lambert (Eds.), *Foundations of Social Cognition*, London: Lawrence Erlbaum Associates.
McGuire, W.J. and McGuire, C.V. (1996), Enhancing self-esteem by directed-thinking tasks: Cognitive and affective positivity asymmetries, *Journal of Personality and Social Psychology*, **70**: 1117–1125.
McGuire, W.J. and Papageorgis, D. (1961), The relative efficacy of various types of prior belief-defense in producing immunity against persuasion, *Journal of Abnormal and Social Psychology*, **62**: 327–337.
McGurie, W.J. (1968), Theory of the structure of human thought. In R. Abelson, E. Aronson, W. McGure, T. Newcomb, M. Rosenberg and P. Tannenbaum (Eds.), *Theories of Cognitive Consistency. A Sourcebook*. Chicago: Rand McGurie.
McHoskey, J.W. (1999), Machiavellianism, intrinsic versus extrinsic goals and social interest: A self-determination theory analysis, *Motivation and Emotion*, **23**: 267–283.
McKelvie, S.J. (1993), Stereotyping in perception of attractiveness, age, and gender in schematic faces, *Social Behaviour and Personality*, **21**: 121–128.
McLeod, J.D. and Eckberg, D.A. (1993), Concordance for depressive disorders and martial quality, *Journal of Marriage and Family*, **55**: 733–746.
McMullen, M.N. and Markman, K.D. (2000), Downward counterfactuals and motivation: The "wake-up call" and the "Pangloss" effect, *Personality and Social Psychology Bulletin*, **26**: 575–584.
McNeill, D. (1966a), The creation of language, *Discovery*, **27**: 34–38.
McNeill, D. (1966b), Developmental psycholinguistics, In F.L. Smith and G.A. Miller (Eds.), *The Genesis of Language: A Psycholinguistic Approach,* 15–84. Cambridge, Massachusetts: MIT Press.
McNeill, D. (1970), *The Acquisition of Language: The Study of Developmental Psycholinguistics*, NY: Harper and Row.
Mead, G.H. (1934 & 1937), *Mind, Self and Society*, Chicago: University of Chicago Press.
Mead, G.H. (1968), The genesis of the self and social control, *International Journal of Ethics*, **35**: 251–73.
Mealey, L., Bridgstock, R., and Townsend, G.C. (1999), Symmetry and perceived facial attractiveness: A monozygotic cotwin companion, *Journal of Personality and Social Psychology*, **76**: 151–158.
Mears, P. (1974), Structuring communication in working group, *Journal of Communication*, **24**: 71–79.
Medvec, V.H. and Savitsky, K. (1997), When doing better means feeling worse: The effects of categorical cut off points on counterfactual thinking and satisfaction, *Journal of Personality and Social Psychology*, **72**: 1284–1296.
Megargee, E.I. (1969), Influence of sex roles on the manifestation of leadership, *Journal of Applied Psychology*, **53**: 377–382.
Mehare, K.T. (1976), Education of administration of secondary teachers training colleges in Maharashtra with special reference to Principal's role, In J. Pandey's (Ed.), *Psychology in India*, Vol. 2, ND: Sage .
Mehrabian, A. (1968), Inference of attitudes from the positive orientation and distance of a communicator, *Journal of Consulting and Clinical Psychology*, **32**: 296–308.
Mehrabian, A. (1969), Significance of posture and position in the communication, attitude and status relationships, *Psychological Bulletin*, **71**: 359–72.
Mehrabian, A. (1972), *Nonverbal Communication,* Chicago, III: Aldine-Atherton.
Mehrabian, A. and Piercy, M. (1993), Affective and personality characteristics inferred from length of the first names, *Personality and Social Psychology Bulletin*, **19**: 755–758.
Mehrabian, A. and Williams, M. (1969), Non-verbal concomitants of perceived and intended persuasiveness, *Journal of Personality and Social Psychology*, **13**: 37–58.
Mehta, A. (1977), Institutional climate as a factor of staff morale and student control ideology in affiliated colleges of Gujarat University, In J. Pandey's (Ed.), *Psychology in India*, Vol. 2, ND: Sage.
Meier, B.P., Robinson, M.D., and Clore, G.L. (2004), Why good guys wear white: Automatic interferences about stimulus valence based on brightness, *Psychological Science*, **15**: 82–87.

Merei, F. (1949), Group leadership and institutionalization, *Human Relations*, **2**: 123–129.
Meyer, P. (2000), The sociobiology of human cooperation: The interplay of ultimate and proximate causes, In J.H.G. Van der Dennen, D. Smillie and D.R. Wilson (Eds.), *The Darwinian Heritage and Sociobiology*, Westport CT: Praeger.
Micheals, J.W., Blomwel, J.M., Brocato, R.M., Linkous, R.A., and Rowe, J.S. (1982), Social facilitation and inhibition in natural settings, *Replications in Social Psychology*, **2**: 21–24.
Michener, H.A. and Burt, M.R. (1974), Legitimacy as a base of social influence, In J. Tedeschi (Ed.), *Perspectives on Social Power*, Chicago: Aldine.
Michener, H.A. and Suchner, R. (1972), The tactical use of social power, In J. Tedeschi (Ed.), *The Social Influence Process*, Chicago: Aldine.
Michener, H.A. and Wasserman, M. (1995), *Group decision-making*, In K.S. Cook, G.A. Fine and J.S. House (Eds.), *Sociological Perspectives on Social Psychology*, 336–361, Boston: Allyn and Bacon.
Michener, H.A., Plazewski, J.G., and Vaske, J.J. (1979), Ingratiation tactics channelled by target values and threat capability, *Journal of Personality*, **47**: 36–56.
Milavsky, J.R., Kessler, R., Stipp, H., Rubens, W.S., Pearl, D., and Bouthilet, L. (Eds.), (1982), Television and behaviour: Ten years of scientific programs and implications for the eighties, Vol. 2, *Technical Reviews*, Washington, DC: US Government Printing Office.
Miles, D.R. and Carey, G. (1997), Genetic and environmental architecture on human aggression, *Journal of Personality and Social Psychology*, **72**: 207–217.
Milgram, S. (1963), Behaviour study of obedience, *Journal of Abnormal and Social Psychology*, **67**: 371–378.
Milgram, S. (1965), Some conditions of obedience and disobedience to authority, *Human Relations*, **18**: 57–76.
Milgram, S. (1974), *Obedience to Authority*, NY: Harper and Row.
Milgram, S. (1992), *The Individual in a Social World: Essays and Experiments*, 2nd edn., NY: McGraw-Hill.
Milgram, S., Mann, C. and Harter, S. (1965), The lost-letter technique: A tool of social research, *Public Opinion Quarterly*, **29**: 437–438.
Millar, M.G. and Tesser, A. (1986), Thought-induced attitude change: The effects of schema structure and commitment, *Journal of Personality and Social Psychology*, **51**: 259–269.
Millar, M.G. and Tesser, A. (1989), The effects of affective-cognitive consistency and thought on attitude behaviour relation, *Journal of Experimental Social Psychology*, **51**: 259–269.
Miller, A.G., Collins, B.E., and Brief, D.E. (1995), Perspective on obedience to authority: The legacy of the Milgram experiments, *Journal of Social Issues*, **51**(3): 1–19.
Miller, D.T. (1977), Altruism and threat to a belief in a just world, *Journal of Experimental Social Psychology*, **13**: 113–124.
Miller, D.T. and Ross, M. (1975), Self-serving biases in the attribution of causality: Fact or fiction?, *Psychological Bulletin*, **82**: 213–215.
Miller, G.A. and Isard, S. (1963), Some perceptual consequences of linguistic rules, *Journal of Verbal Learning and Verbal Behaviour*, **2**: 217–28.
Miller, J.G., Bersoff, D.M., and Harwood, R.L. (1990), Perceptions of social responsibility in India and the United States: Moral imperatives or personal decisions?, *Journal of Personality and Social Psychology*, **58**: 33–47.
Miller, L.H. and Smith, A.D. (1993), *The Stress Solution*, NY: Pocket Books.
Miller, L.K. and Hamblin, R.L. (1963), Interdependence, differential rewarding, and productivity, *American Sociological Review*, **28**: 768–778.
Miller, M. and Campbell, D.T. (1959), Recency and primacy in persuasion as a function of timing of speeches and measurements, *Journal of Abnormal and Social Psychology*, **59**: 1–9.
Miller, M. and Rahe, R.H. (1997), Life changes scaling for the 1990s, *Journal of Psychosomatic Research*, **43**(3): 279–292.
Miller, N., Maruyama, G., Beabe, R.J., and Valone, K. (1976), Speed at speech and persuasion, *Journal of Personality and Social Psychology*, **34**: 615–624.

Miller, N., Maruyama, G., Beaber, R.J., and Valone, K. (1976), Speed at speech and persuasion, *Journal of Pesonality and Social Psychology*, **62**: 327–337.
Miller, N.E. (1941), The frustration–aggression hypothesis, *Psychological Review*, **48**: 337–342.
Miller, N.E. and Dollard, J. (1941), *Learning and Imitation*, NH: Yale University Press.
Miller, T.W. (1982), Assertiveness training for coaches: The issue of healthy communication between coaches and players, *Journal of Sport Psychology*, **4**: 107–114.
Mills, J. and Aronson, E. (1965), Opinion change as a function of communicator's attractiveness and desire to influence, *Journal of Personality and Social Psychology*, **1**: 173–177.
Miner, J.B. (1992), *Industrial-organisational Psychology,* NewYork: McGraw-Hill.
Minhas, S. (2003), Coping strategies and Kashmiri migrant children, *Psychological Studies*, **48**: 22–27.
Minrad, R.D. (1952), Race relations in the Pocahontas coal field, *Journal of Social Issues*, **8**: 29–44.
Mintz, A. (1951), Non-adaptive behaviour, *Journal of Abnormal and Social Psychology*, **46**: 150–159.
Minuchin, P.P. and Shapiro, E.K. (1983), The school as a context for social development, In P.H. Mussen (Ed.), *Handbook of Child Psychology*, Vol. 4, NY: Wiley.
Mishra, A.K. (2001), Culture and self: Implications for psychological inquiry, *Journal of Indian Psychology*, **19**(1,2): 1–20.
Mishra, A.K., Akoijam, A.B., and Mishra, G. (2009), Social psychological perspectives on self and identity, In G. Mishra (Ed.), *Psychology in India*, Vol. 3, Delhi: Pearson.
Misra, B. (1994), Development of communicative interest in Hindi during mother–child interaction, In B. Lakshmi Bai and D. Vansta (Eds.), *Language Development and Language Disorders: Perspectives from Indian Languages*, 29–36, ND: Bahri Publications.
Misra, G. and Giri, R. (1995), Is Indian self-predominantly interdependent? *Journal of Indian Psychology,* **13**(1): 16–29.
Misra, M. and Agrawal, A. (2003), Coping and satisfaction with life in a working women, In A. Agarwal and A.K. Saxena (Eds.), *Psychological Perspectives in Environmental and Developmental Issues*, ND: Concept.
Misra, S., Kanungo, R.N., Rosentiel, L.V., and Stuthler, E.A. (1985), The motivational formulation of job and work involvement: A cross-national study, *Human Relations*, **38**(6): 501–518.
Misra, G. (Ed.) (2009), *Psychology in India,* Vol. 2, Delhi: Pearson.
Misra, G. (Ed.) (1990), *Applied Social Psychology in India*, New Delhi: Sage Publication.
Missal, V. (1995), Mental terms in mothers and children's speech: Its implication for developing a theory of mind, In G. Misra (Ed.), *Psychology in India,* 5th ICSSR Survey, **1**: 11–148.
Misumi, J. (1995), The development in Japan of the performance-maintenance (PM) theory of leadership, *Journal of Social Issues*, **51**: 213–228.
Mitchell, T.R., Biglan, A., Oncken, G.R., and Fielder, F. (1970), The contingency model: Criticism and suggestions, *Academy of Management Journal*, **13**: 253–267.
Mitchell, T.R., Smyser, C.M., and Weed, S.E. (1975), Locus of control: Supervision and work satisfaction, *Academy of Management Journal*, **18**: 623–631.
Mitra, S.K. (1972), Psychological research in India, In S.K. Mitra (Ed.), *A Survey of Research in Psychology*, Bombay: Popular Prakashan.
Mixon, D. (1972), Instead of deception, *Journal for the Theory of Social Behaviour*, **2**: 145–178.
Moberg, D.O. (1953), Church membership and personal adjustment in old age, *Journal of Gerontology*, **8**: 207–211.
Modigliani, A. (1971), Embarrassment, face-work, and eye-contact: Testing a theory of embarrassment, *Journal of Personality and Social Psychology*, **17**: 15–34.
Mohanty, A.K. (1994a), Bilingualism in multilingual society, Mysore: Central Institute of Indian Languages.
Mohanty, A.K. (1994b), Bilingualism in multilingual society: Implication for cultural integration and education, *23rd International Congress of Applied Psychology*, Madrid: Spain.
Mohanty, A.K. (1998), Mother-tongue education: The Gandhian view and a psycholinguistic analysis, In N. Hazary, S.C. Hazary, and A. Mishra (Eds.), *Eternal Gandhi*, 161–68, ND: APH publishing.

Mohanty, A.K. (2000), Language behaviour and processes, In J. Pandey (Ed.), *Psychology in India Revisited-development in the Discipline,* Vol. 1: Physiological foundation and human cognition, 208–55, ND: Sage.

Mohanty, A.K. (2001), Psycholinguistic issues in early development and education: A multilingual perspective, *National Seminar on Theoretical Approaches to Early Development: Implications for Intervention,* Vadodara, India: M.S. University.

Mohanty, A.K. (2003), Psychology of language acquisition in bilingualism in India, In J.W. Berry, R.C. Mishra and R.C. Tripathi (Eds.), *Psychology in Human and Social Development: Lessons from Diverse Cultures,* ND: Sage.

Mohanty, A.K. and Perregaux, C. (1996), Language acquisition and bilingualism. In J.W. Berry. P.R. Dasen and T.S. Saraswathi (Eds.), *Handbook of Cross-cultural Psychology,* Vol. 2, *Basic Processes and Human Development,* 2nd ed., Boston: Allyn and Bacon.

Mohanty, A.K., Panda, S., and Mishra, B. (1999), Language acquisition and bilingualism, In J.W. Berry, P.R. Dassen and T.S. Sarswathi (Eds.), *Handbook of Cross-cultural Psychology,* Vol. 2, Basic processes and human development, 217–53, Boston, MA.: Allyn and Bacon.

Mohanty, B. and Pani, B. (1979), Effect of student–teacher classroom interaction on academic performance of students, *Psychological Studies,* **24**: 35–39.

Monahan, J.L., Murphy, S.T., and Zajonc, R.B. (2000), Subliminal mere exposure: Specific, general and diffuse effects, *Psychological Science,* **11**: 462–466.

Moon, H., Hollenback, J.R., Humphrey, S.E., Ilgen, D.R., West, B.J., and Ellis, A.P.J. (2004), Asymmetric adaptability: Dynamic team structures as one-way street, *Academy of Management,* **47**: 681–695.

Moore, M.M. (1985), Nonverbal courtship patterns in Women: Context and consequences, *Ethology and Sociobilogy,* **6**: 237–247.

Moorhead, G. and Montanari, J.R. (1986), An empirical investigation of the groupthink phenomenon, *Human Relations,* **39**: 399–41.

Moran, G. and Cutler, B.L. (1991), The prejudicial impact of pretrial publicity, *Journal of Applied Social Psychology,* **21**: 345–367.

Moreland, R.I. and Beach, S.R. (1992), Exposure effects in the classroom: The development of affinity among students, *Journal of Experimental Social Psychology,* **28**: 255–276.

Moreland, R.L. (1987), The formation of small groups, In C. Hendrick (Ed.), *Group Processes,* 80–110, Beverley Hills, CA: Sage.

Moreno, J.L. (1953), *Who Shall Survive?,* Beacon, NY: Beacon House.

Morgan, W., Alwin, D., and Griffin, L. (1979), Social origins, parental values and the transmission of inequality, *American Journal of Sociology,* **85**: 156–166.

Moriarty, T. (1975), Crime, commitment and the responsive bystander: Two field experiments, *Journal of Personality and Social Psychology,* **31**: 370–376.

Morley, M.E. (1957), *The Development and Disorders of Speech in Childhood,* London: Livingstone.

Morris, C.G. and Hackman, J.R. (1969), Behavioural correlations of perceived leadership, *Journal of Personality and Social Psychology,* **13**: 350–361.

Morris, T. and Summers, J. (1995), *Sport Psychology: Theories, Applications and Issues,* Brisbane: John Wiley and Sons.

Morris, W.N. and Miller, R.S. (1975), The effects of consensus-breaking and consensus-preempting partners on reduction of conformity, *Journal of Experimental Social Psychology,* **11**: 215–223.

Morrison, E.W. and Bies, R.J. (1991), Impression management in the feedback-seeking process: A literature review and research agenda, *Academy of Management Review,* **16**: 322–341.

Moscovici, S. (1980), Toward a theory of conversion behaviour, In L. Berkowitz (Ed.), *Advances in Experimental Social Psychology,* **13**: 209–239, NY: Academic Press.

Moscovici, S., Lage, E., and Naffrechoux, M. (1969), Influence of a consistent minority on the responses of a majority on a colour perception task, *Sociometry,* **32**: 365–379.

Moss, M.K. and Page, R.A. (1972), Reinforcement and helping behaviour, *Journal of Applied Social Psychology*, **2**: 360–361.
Mowrer, O.H. (1960), *Learning Theory and Behaviour*, NY: Wiley.
Muczyk, J.P. and Reimann, B.C. (1987), The case of directive leadership, *Academy of Management Review*, **12**: 647–687.
Mukherjee, G. and Mukhopadhyay, A. (1998), Patterns of stress and motivation of upper and lower gastrointestinal disorder patients, *Psychological Studies*, **43**: 80–84.
Mukherjee, N.P. (1940), An investigation of ability in work in groups and in isolation, *British Journal of Psychology* **30**: 25–30.
Mulac, A. (1998), The gender-linked language effect: Do language differences really make a difference?, In D.J. Canary and K. Dindia (Eds.), *Sex Differences and Similarities in Communication*, Mahwah, NJ: Erlbaum.
Mulac, A., Bradac, J.J., and Gibbons, P. (2001), Empirical support for the gender-as-culture hypothesis: An intercultural analysis of male/female language differences, *Human Communication Research*, **27**: 121–152.
Mulder, M. and Stemerding, A. (1963), Threat, attraction to group and need for strong leadership: A laboratory experiment in natural setting, *Human Relations*, **16**(4): 317–334.
Mullen, B. and Cooper, C. (1994), The relation between group cohesion and performance: An integration, *Psychological Bulletin*, **115**: 210–227.
Mullen, B., Salas, E., and Driskell, J.E. (1989) Salience motivation and artifact as contributions to the relation between participation rate and leadership, *Journal of Experimental Social Psychology*, **25**: 545–549.
Mullen, R., Migdal, M.J., and Rozell, D. (2003), Self-awareness, deindividuation and social identity: Unraveling theoretical paradoxes by filling empirical lacunae, *Personality and Social Psychology Bulletin*, **29**: 1071–1081.
Munro, G.D. and Ditto, P.H. (1997), Biased assimilation, attitude polarization and affect in reactions to stereotype-relevant scientific information, *Personality and Social Psychology Bulletin*, **23**: 636–653.
Murphy, G. (1953), *In the Minds of Men*, NY: Basic Books.
Murphy, G., Murphy, L.B., and Newcomb, J.M. (1937), *Experimental Social Psychology*, NY: Harper and Row.
Murphy, L.R. (1995), Managing job stress: An employee assistance/human resource management partnership, *Personnel Review*, **24**(1): 41–50.
Murray, H.A. (1938), *Explorations in Personality*, NY: Oxford University Press.
Murray, J.P. and Kippax, S. (1979), From the early window to the late night show: International trends in the study of television's impact on children and adults, In L. Berkowitz (Ed.), *Advances in Experimental Social Psychology*, Vol. 12, NY: Academic Press.
Murray, S.L. and Holmes, J.G. (1999), The (mental) ties that bind: Cognitive structures that predict relationship resilience, *Journal of Personality and Social Psychology*, **77**: 1228–1244.
Murray, S.L., Holmes, J.G., Gellavita, G., Griffin, D.W., and Doldenman, D. (2002), Kindred spirits?: The benefits of egocentrism in closing relationship, *Journal of Personality and Social Psychology*, **82**: 563–581.
Muthayya, B.C., Naidu, K., and Aneesuddin, M. (1979), *Behavioural Dimensions of Rural Leaders*, Hyderabad: National Institute of Rural Development.
Myer, T. (1972), The effect of sexually arousing and violent films on aggression behaviour, *Journal of Sex Research*, **8**: 324–333.
Myers, D.G. (2005), *Social Psychology*, Boston: McGraw-Hill.
Myers, D.G. and Bishop, G.D. (1970), Discussion effect on racial attitudes, *Science,* **169**: 778–789.
Naidu, R.K. (2001), Personality, self and life events, In J. Pandey (Ed.), *Psychology in India Revisited: Developments in the Discipline*, **2**: 228–299, ND: Sage.
Naidu, R.K. and Pande, N. (1999), Anasakti: The Indian vision of potential, human transcendence beyond mechanistic motivations, In G. Misra (Ed.), *Psychological Perspectives on Stress and Health*, ND: Concept.
Nail, P.R., MacDonald, G., and Levy, D.A. (2000), Proposal of a four-dimensional model of social response, *Psychological Bulletin*, **126**: 454–470.

Nair, A.S. (1981), Some social familial variables causing underachievement in secondary school mathematics, *Journal of Educational Research and Extension*, **18**: 10–14.
Nandy, A. (1974), The non-paradigmatic crisis in Indian psychology: Reflection on recipient culture of science, *Indian Journal of Psychology*, **49**: 1–20.
Narasimhan, R. (1998), *Language Behaviour: Acquisition and Evolutionary History*, ND: Sage.
Neisser, U. (1967), *Cognitive Psychology*, NY: Appleton-Century-Crofts.
Nelson, K.E. (1977), Facilitating children's syntax acquisition, *Developmental Psychology*, **13**: 101–107.
Nesbitt, P. (1972), The effectiveness of student canvassers, *Journal of Applied Social Psychology*, **2**: 47–59.
Nevill, A.H. and Holder, R.L. (1999), Home advantage in sport: An overview of studies on the advantage of playing at home, *Sports Medicine*, **28**: 221–236.
Newby–Clark, I.R., and Ross, M. (2003), Conceiving the past and future, *Personality and Social Psychology Bulletin*, **29**: 807–818.
Newcomb, T. (1943), *Personality and Social Change*, NY: Dryden Press.
Newcomb, T. (1963), Stabilities underlying changes in interpersonal attraction, *Journal of Abnormal and Social Psychology*, **66**: 376–380.
Newcomb, T.M. (1950), *Social Psychology*, NY: Dryden.
Newcomb, T.M. (1953), An approach to the study of communicative acts, *Psychological Review*, **60**: 393–404.
Newcomb, T.M. (1956), The prediction of interpersonal attraction, *American Psychologist*, **11**: 575–586.
Newcomb, T.M. (1958), Attitude development as a function of reference group: The Bennington study, In E. Maccoby, T.M. Newcomb and E.L. Hartly (Eds.), *Readings in Social Psychology*, 265–273, NY: Holt, Rinehart and Winston.
Newcomb, T.M. (1961), *The Acquaintance Process*, NY: Holt, Rinehart and Winston.
Newcomb, T.M. (1968), Interpersonal Balance, In R.P. Abselson, W.J. McGuire, T.M. Newcomb, M.J. Rosenberg and P.H. Tannenbaum (Eds.), *Theories of Cognitive Consistency: A Sourcebook*, Chicago: Rand McNally.
Newman, H.M. and Langer, E.J. (1981), Post-divorce adaptation and the attribution of responsibility, *Sex Roles*, **7**: 223–231.
Newport, E.L. (1977), Aspects of language acquisition and form use from age 2 to age 20, *Journal of American Academy of Child Psychiatry*, **16**: 20–40.
Neyer, F.J. and Lang, E.R. (2003), Blood is thicker than water: Kinship orientation across adulthood, *Journal of Personality and Social Psychology*, **84**: 310–321.
Niaura, R., Todaro, J.F., Stroud, L., Spiro, A. III, Ward, K.D., and Weiss, S. (2002), Hostility, the metabolic syndrome, and incident coronary heart diseases, *Health Psychology*, **21**(6): 588–593.
Nienhuis, A.E., Manstead, A.S.R., and Spears, R. (2001), Multiple motives and persuasive communication: Creative elaboration as a result of impression motivation and accuracy motivation, *Personality and Social Psychology Bulletin*, **27**: 118–132.
Nisbett, R.E. (2003), *The Geography of Thought: How Asians and Westerners Think Differently and Why*, NY: Free Press.
Nisbett, R.E. and Cohen, D. (1996), *Culture of Honor: The Psychology of Violence in the South*, Boulder, CO: Westview Press.
Nisbett, R.E., Camputo, C., Legant, P., and Maracek, (1973), Behaviour as seen by the actor and as seen by the observer, *Journal of Personality and Social Psychology*, **27**: 154–164.
Norvell, N. and Worchel, S. (1981), A reexamination of the relation between equal status contact and intergroup attraction, *Journal of Personality and Social Psychology*, **41**: 902–908.
Novak, D.W. and Lerner, M.J. (1968), From private attitude to public opinion: A dynamic theory of social comparison, *Psychological Review*, **97**: 362–376.
Nussbaum, S., Trope, Y., and Liberman, N. (2003), Creeping dispositionism: The temporal dynamics of behaviour prediction, *Journal of Personality and Social Psychology*, **84**: 485–497.
O'Connor, S.C. and Rosenblood, L.K. (1996), Affiliation motivation in everyday experience: A theoretical comparison, *Journal of Personality and Social Psychology*, **70**: 513–522.

Oakes, P.J., Hoslam, S.A., Morrison, B., and Grace, D. (1995), Becoming an in-group: Reexamining the impact of familiarity on perceptions of group homogeneity, *Social Psychology Quarterly*, **28**: 52–60.

Oettingen, G. (1995), Explanatory style in the context of culture, In G.M. Buchanan and M.E.P. Seligman (Eds.), *Explanatory Style*, Hillsdale, NJ: Erlbaum.

Ofshe, R. and Watters, E. (1994), *Making Monsters: False Memories, Psychotherapy and Sexual Hysteria*, NY: Scibners.

Ohbuchi, K., Kameda, M., and Agarie, N. (1989), Apology as aggression control: Its role in mediating appraisal of and response to harm, *Journal of Personality and Social Psychology*, **56**: 219–227.

Ohman, A., Lundqvist, D., and Esteves, F. (2001), The face in the crowd revisited: Threat advantage with schematic stimuli, *Journal of Personality and Social Psychology*, **80**: 381–396.

Okamoto, D.G. and Smith–Lovin, L. (2001), Changing the subject: Gender, status and the dynamics of topic change, *American Sociological Review*, **66**: 852–873.

Olson, J.M. and Cal, A.V. (1984), Source credibility, attitudes and the recall of past behaviours, *European Journal of Social Psychology*, **14**: 203–210.

Olson, J.M. and Zanna, M.P. (1993), Attitudes and attitude change, *Annual Review of Psychology*, **44**: 117–654.

Olson, M.A. and Fazio, R.H. (2001), Implicit attitude formation through classical conditioning, *Psychological Science*, **12**: 413–417.

Olson, M.A. and Fazio, R.H. (2004), Implicit acquisition and manifestation of classically conditioned attitudes, *Social Cognition*, **20**: 89–104.

Omoto, A.M. and Synder, M. (2002), Considerations of community: The context and process of volunteerism, *American Behavioural Scientist*, **45**: 846–886.

Orbell, J.M., Van de Kragt, A.J.C., and Dawas, R.M. (1988), Explaining discussion-induced cooperation, *Journal of Personality and Social Psychology*, **54**: 811–819.

Orne, M.T. (1962), On the social psychology of the psychological experiment: With particular reference to demand characteristics and their implications, *American Psychologist*, **17**: 776–783.

Osborn, A.F. (1957), *Applied Imagination*, NY: Scribners.

Osgood, C.E. and Tannenbaum, P.H (1955), The principle of congruity in the prediction of attitude change, *Psychological Review*, **62**: 42–55.

Osgood, C.E., Suci, G.J., and Tannenbaum, P.H. (1957), *The Measurement of Meaning*, Urbana, IL: University of Illinois Press.

Ostrom, T. (1973), The bogus pipeline: A new ignis fatuus?, *Psychological Bulletin*, **79**: 252–259.

Owens, L., Shute, R., and Slee, P. (2000), Guess what I just heard: Indirect aggression among teenage girls in Australia, *Aggressive Behaviour*, **26**: 57–66.

Oyserman, D., Coon, H.M., and Kemmelmeir, M. (2002), Rethinking individualism and collectivism: Evaluation of theoretical assumptions and meta-analyses, *Psychological Bulletin*, **128**: 3–72.

Ozer, E.M. and Bandura, A. (1990), Mechanisms governing empowerment effects: A self-efficacy analysis, *Journal of Personality and Social Psychology*, **58**: 472–486.

Pace, A. and Carron, A.V. (1992), Travel and home advantage, *Canadian Journal of Sport Sciences*, **17**: 60–64.

Padakannaya, P. (2009), *Language and Communication*, In G. Misra (Ed.), *Psychology in India*, 5th ICSSR's Survey, **1**: 111–148.

Padakannaya, P. and Mohanty, A.K. (2004), Indian Orthography and teaching how to read : A psycholinguistic framework, *Psychological Studies*, **49**, 262–71.

Pal, D.K., Choudhary, G., Das, T., and Sen Gupta, S. (2002), Predictors of parental adjustment to children's epilepsy in rural India, *Children, Health and Development*, **28**: 295–300.

Pallak, S.R. (1983), Salience of a communicator's physical attractiveness and persuasion: A heuristic versus systematic processing interpretation, *Social Cognition*, 156–168.

Pallak, S.R., Murroni, E., and Koch, J. (1983), Communicator attractiveness and expertise, emotional versus rational appeals and perusal: A heuristic versus systematic processing interpretation, *Social Cognition*, **2**: 122–141.

Panda, B. (1991), *Children's understanding of lie and truth*, In G. Misra (Ed.), *Psychology in India*, 5th ICSSR's Survey, **1**: 111–148.

Panda, K.C. and Dash, P.C. (1980), Effect of simulated information on assessment of cognitive competence: A test of expectancy hypotheses, *Indian Educational Review*, **13**: 22–35.

Panda, M.D. (1983), The relationship of parental style to intellectual achievement, responsibility, adjustment and cognitive performance among underprivileged children. In J. Pandey (Ed.), *Psychology in India*, 2nd Vol., 3rd ICSSR survey, New Delhi: Sage Publications.

Pandey, A.P. (1993), Personality traits and self-esteem, *Perspective in Psychological Researches*, **16**(1–2), 17–19.

Pandey, J. (1981), Ingratiation as a social behaviour, In. J. Pandey (Ed.), *Perspective on Experimental Social Psychology in India*, ND: Concept.

Pandey, J. (2000), *Psychology in India revisited-developments in the discipline: Physiological foundation and human cognition* (4th ICSSR Survey), Vol. 1, New Delhi: Sage.

Pandey, J. (2001), *Psychology in India revisited-developments in the discipline: Personality and health psychology* (4th ICSSR Survey), Vol. 2, New Delhi: Sage.

Pandey, J. (Ed.) (1988), *Psychology in India*, The State-of-the-Art (3rd ICSSR survey), Vol. II, ND: Sage.

Pandey, J. (Ed.) (2004), *Psychology in India Revisited*, Vol. III (4th ICSSR survey), ND: Sage.

Pandey, J. and Rastogi, R. (1979), Machiavellianism and Ingratiation, *Journal of Social Psychology*, **108**: 221–225.

Pandey, J., Bisht, S. and Rani, S. (1987), Children's donation as a function of their age, sex and resource level, *Psychological Studies*, **38**: 26–30.

Pandey, J. and Griffitt, W. (1974), Attraction and helping, *Bulletin of Psychonomic Society*, 123–124.

Pandey, J. and Griffitt, W. (1977), Benefactor's sex and reference need, recipients' dependency and the effects of the number of potential helpers, on helping behaviours, *Journal of Personality*, **45**: 79–99

Pandey, N. and Naidu, A.K. (1992), Anasakti and health: A study of non-attachment, *Psychology and Developing Societies*, **4**: 89–104.

Pandey, J. and Singh, P. (1997), Allocation criteria as function of situational factors and caste, *Basic and Applied Social Psychology*, **19**: 121–132.

Pandey, S. (2003), An empirical study of the role of perceived control in coping with residential crowding, In A. Agrawal and A.K. Saxena (Eds.), *Psychological Perspectives in Environmental and Developmental Issues*, ND: Concept.

Panjiyar, I.D. and Rout, M. (1999), Adjustment as a function of social class and economic status: A sociopsychological study, *Indian Journal of Psychological Issues*, **7**: 55–58.

Paranjpe, A.C. (1998), *Self and Identity in Modern Psychology and Indian Thought*, NY: Plenum.

Parasher, R.P. (2000), Lifestyle for perfect health, *Psychological Studies*, **45**: 167–172.

Pareek, U. (1981), *A Survey of Research in Psychology*, 1971–76, Part 2: Bombay: Popular Publication.

Pareek, U. (1977), Dynamics of Cooperative and Competitive behavior, *ICSSR Research Abstracts Quarterly*, **4**(12): 1–27.

Pareek, U. (Ed.), (1980), *A Survey of Research in Psychology*, 1971–76, Part I, Bombay: Popular Prakashan.

Pareek, U. and Banerjee, D. (1974), Developmental trends in the dimensions of cooperative and competitive game behaviour in some subcultures, *Indian Educational Review*, **9**(1): 11–37.

Pareek, U. and Banerjee, D. (1976), Achievement motive and competitive behavior, *Manas*, **23**(1): 9–15.

Pareek, V. and Rao, T.V. (1970), The patterns of classroom influence behaviour of class V teachers of Delhi, *Indian Educational Review*, **5**: 55–70.

Park, J. and Banaji, M.R. (2000), Mood and heuristics: The influence of happy and sad states on sensitivity and bias in stereotyping, *Journal of Personality and Social Psychology*, **78**: 1005–1023.

Park, J., Turnbull, A.P., and Turnbull, A.R. (2002), Impacts of poverty on quality of life in families of children with disabilities, *Exceptional Children*, **68**: 151–170.

Parke, R. (1969), Effectiveness of punishment as an interaction of intensity, timing, agent nurturance and cognitive structure, *Child Development*, **40**: 213–235.

Parke, R. (1970), The role of punishment in the socialization process, In R. Hoppe, G. Milton, and E. Simmel (Eds.), *Early Experiences and Processes of Socialization*, NY: Academic Press.

Parke, R.D., Berkowitz, L., Leyens, J.P., West, S.G., and Sebastian, R.J. (1977), Some effects of violent and nonviolent movies on the behaviour of juvenile delinquents, In L. Berkowitz (Ed.), *Advances in Experimental Social Psychology*, **10**: 135–172, NY: Academic Press.

Patel, P.G. (2004), *Exploring Reading Acquisition and Dyslexia in India*, New Delhi: Sage.

Patrick, H., Neighbors, C., and Knee, C.R. (2004), Appearance related social comparisons: The role of contingent self-esteem and self-perceptions of attractiveness, *Personality and Social Psychology Bulletin*, **30**: 501–514.

Pattnaik, B. (1997), The relationship between children's acquisition of a theory of mind and their understanding of meta-representational languages, In G. Misra (Ed.), *Psychology in India*, 5th ICSSR's Survey, **I**: 111–148.

Pattnaik, B. and Babu, N. (2004), Recursive thinking and children's concept of friendship, *Annual Conference of MAOP*, Kharagpur.

Paulus, P.B. (1988), *Prison Crowding: A Psychological Perspective*, NY: Springer-Verlag.

Pavelchak, M.A. (1989), Piecemeal and category-based evaluation: An ideographic analysis, *Journal of Personality and Social Psychology*, **56**: 354–363.

Pavlov, I.P. (1928), *Conditioned Reflexes*, Translated by G.V. Anrep, London: Oxford University Press.

Paxton, P. and Moody, J. (2003), Structure and sentiment: Explaining emotional attachment to groups, *Social Psychology Quarterly*, **66**: 34–47.

Payne, B.K., Lambert, A.J., and Jacoby, L.L. (2002), Best laid plans: Effects of goals on accessibility bias and cognitive control in the race-based misperceptions of weapons, *Journal of Experimental Social Psychology*, **60**: 384–530.

Pennington, D.C., Gillen, K., and Hill, P. (1999), *Social Psychology*, London: Arnold.

Perls, T.T. and Silver, M.H. (1999), *Living to 100: Lessons in Living to Your Maximum Potential at Any Age*, NY: Basic Books.

Pessin, J. (1933), The comparative effects of social and mechanical stimulation on memorizing, *American Journal of Psychology*, **45**: 263–270.

Peterson, C., Schwartz, S.M., and Seligman, M.E.P. (1981), Self-blame and depression symptoms, *Journal of Personality and Social Psychology*, **41**: 253–259.

Peterson, R.S. (1997), A directive leadership style in group decision-making can be both a virtue and vice: Evidence from elite and experimental groups, *Journal of Personality and Social Psychology*, **72**: 1107–1121.

Pettigrew, T.E. (1958), Personality and sociocultural factors in intergroup studies: A cross-national comparison, *Journal of Conflict Resolution*, **2**: 29–42.

Pettigrew, T.E. (1980), Prejudice, In S. Thernstrom (Ed.), *Harvard Encyclopedia of American Ethnic Groups*, Cambridge, MA: Harvard University Press.

Pettigrew, T.F. (1979), The ultimate attribution error: Extending Allport's cognitive analysis of prejudice, *Personality and Social Psychology Bulletin*, **55**: 461–476.

Pettigrew, T.F. (1997), Generalized intergroup contact effects on prejudice, *Personality and Social Psychology Bulletin*, **23**: 173–185.

Pettigrew, T.F., Jackson, J.S., Brika, J.B., Lemaine, G., Meertens, R.W., Wagner, V., and Zick, A. (1998), Outgroup prejudice in Western Europe, *European Review of Social Psychology*, **8**: 241–273.

Petty, R.E. and Cacioppo, J.T. (1986 & 1986a), *Communication and Persuasion: Central and Peripheral Routes to Attitude Change*, NY: Springer-Verlag.

Petty, R.E. and Cacioppo, J.T. (1986b), The elaboration likelihood model of persuasion, In L. Berkowitz (Ed.), *Advances in Experimental Social Psychology*, **19**: 207–249, NY: Academic Press.

Petty, R.E., Cacioppo, J.T., and Goldman, R. (1981), Personal involvement as a determinant of argument-based persuasion, *Journal of Personality and Social Psychology*, **41**: 847–855.

Petty, R.E., Schumann, D.W., Richman, S.A., and Strathman, A.J. (1993), Positive mood and persuasion: Different roles for affect under high and low elaboration conditions, *Journal of Personality and Social Psychology*, **64**: 5–20.

Petty, R.E., Wheeler, C., and Tormala, Z.L. (2003), Persuasion and attitude change, In T. Million and M.J. Lerner (Eds.), *Handbook of Psychology: Personality and Social Psychology,* **5**: 353–382, NY: Wiley.

Phelps, E.A., O'connor, K.J., Cunningham, W.A., Punayama, E., Gatenby, J., Gove, J.C. (2000), Performance on indirect measures of race evaluation predicts amygdala activation, *Journal of Cognitive Neuroscience,* **12**: 729–738.

Phillips, D.P. (1986), Natural experiments on the effects of mass media violence on fatal aggression: Strengths and weaknesses of a new approach, In Berkowitz (Ed.), *Advances in Experimental Social Psychology,* **19**: 207–250, NY: Academic Press.

Piaget, J. (1965), *The Moral Judgement of the Child,* NY: Free Press.

Piaget, J. (1968), *Six Psychological Studies,* NY: Random House.

Pickel, K.L. (1999), The influence of the context on the weapon focus effect, *Law and Human Behaviour,* **23**: 299–312.

Piliavin, J.A. and LePore, P.C. (1995), Biology and social psychology: Beyond nature versus nurture, In K.S. Cook, G.A. Fine, and J.S. House (Eds.), *Sociological Perspectives in Social Psychology,* Boston: Allyn and Bacon.

Piliavin, J.A. and Unger, R.K. (1985), The helpful but helpless female: Myth or reality? In V.E. O'Leary, R.K. Unger, and B.S. Wallston (Eds.), *Women, Gender and Social Psychology,* Hillsdale, NJ: Erlbaum.

Piliavin, J.A., Callero, P.L., and Evans, D.E. (1982), Addiction to altruism? Opponent-process theory and habitual blood donation, *Journal of Personality and Social Psychology,* **43**: 1200–1213.

Piliavin, J.A., Dovidio, J.F., Gaertner, S.L., and Clark, R.D. (1981), *Emergency Intervention,* NY: Academic Press.

Pillai, K. (1973), Organizational climate, teacher morale and school quality, In J. Pandey's (Ed.), *Psychology in India,* Vol. 2, ND: Sage.

Pinker, S. (1998), *How the Mind Works.,* NY: Norton.

Plaks, J.E. and Higgins, E.T. (2000), Pragmatic use of stereotyping in teamwork: Social loafing and compensation a function of inferred partner-situation fit, *Journal of Personality and Social Psychology,* **79**: 962–974.

Plant, E.A., Hyde, J.S., Keltner, D., and Devine, P.G. (2000), The gender stereotyping of emotions, *Psychology Women Quarterly,* **24**: 81–92.

Pleban, R. and Tesser, A. (1981), The effects of relevance and quality of another's performance on interpersonal closeness, *Social Psychology Quarterly,* **44**: 278–285.

Pollard, R. (1986), Home advantage in soccer: A retrospective analysis, *Journal of Sport Sciences,* **4**: 237–248.

Postmes, T. and Spears, R. (1998), Deindividuation and anti-normative behaviour: A meta-analysis, *Psychological Bulletin,* **123**: 238–259.

Potter, R. and Brewer, M. (1999), Perceptions of Witness behaviour-accuracy relationships held by police, lawyers and jurors, *Psychiatry, Psychology and Law,* **6**: 97–103.

Powell, A.A., Branscombe, N.R., and Schmitt, M.T. (2005), Inequality as 'in-group privilege' or 'out-group disadvantage': The impact of group focus on collective guilt and interracial attitudes, *Personality and Social Psychology Bulletin,* **31**(4): 508–521.

Powell, K.E., Spain, K.G., Christenson, G.M., and Mollenkamp, M.P. (1986), The status of 1990 objectives for physical fitness and exercise, *Public Health Reports,* **101**: 15–21.

Poyatos, F. (1983), *New Perspectives in Nonverbal Communication: Studies in Cultural Anthropology, Social Psychology, Linguistics, Literature and Semantics,* Oxford, UK: Pergamon.

Prabhu, P.H. (1954), *Hindu Social Organization: A Study in Social-psychological and Ideological Foundations,* Bombay: Popular Book Depot.

Pradhan, G.P. and Shrivastava, S.K. (2003), Peptic ulcer and anxiety, *Indian Journal of Psychological Issues,* **11**: 114–119.

Pradhan, M. and Misra, M. (1995), Spouse support and quality of marital relationship as correlates of stress, *Journal of the Indian Academy of Applied Psychology,* **21**: 43–50.

Prasad, B.D. (2001), Child abuse: Violence against children, *The Indian Journal of Social Work,* **62**: 328–346.

Prasad, J. (1935), The psychology of rumour: A study relating to the great Indian earthquake of 1934, *British Journal of Psychology*, **26**: 1–15.

Prasad, J. (1950), A comparative study of rumors and reports in earthquakes, *British Journal of Psychology*, **41**: 129–144.

Prasad, M.B. (1976), Caste awareness in Bihari children, *Journal of Social and Economic Studies*, **4**(2): 293–300.

Prasad, M.B. (1973), Development of caste awareness in children: A theoretical model, *Journal of Social and Economic Studies*, **1**: 115–129.

Pratkanis, A.R. and Greenwald, A.G. (1989), A sociocognitive model of attitude structure and function, In Berkowitz (Ed.), *Advances in Experimental Social Psychology*, **22**: 245–285, NY: Academic Press.

Pranjpe, A.C. (1970), *Caste, prejudice and the individual,* Bombay: Lalwani Publishing House.

Price, J.M. and Doge, K.A. (1989), Reactive and proactive aggression in childhood: Relations to peer status and social context dimensions, *Journal of Abnormal Child Psychology*, **17**: 455–471.

Price, K.O., Harburg, E., and Newcomb, T.M. (1966), Psychological balance in situations of negative interpersonal attitudes, *Journal of Personality and Social Psychology*, **3**: 265–270.

Prins, K.S., Buunk, B.P., and Van Yperen, M.W. (1993), Equity, normative disapproval and extramarital relationships, *Journal of Social and Personal Relationship*, **10**: 39–53.

Priscilla, S. and Karunanidhi, S. (1996), Influence of self-disclosure on self-esteem, interpersonal communication, and apprehension among high school students, *Journal of Psychological Researches*, **40**(1,2): 81–86.

Pruitt, D.G. (1976), Power and bargaining, In B. Seidenberg and A. Snadowsky, *Social Psychology: An Introduction*, NY: Free Press.

Pruitt, D.G. and Insko, C.A. (1980), Extension of the Kelley attribution model: The role of comparison-model consensus, target-object consensus, distinctiveness and consistency, *Journal of Personality and Social Psychology*, **39**: 39–58.

Puente, S. and Cohen, D. (2003), Jealousy and the meaning non-(or meaning) of violence, *Personality and Social Psychology Bulletin*, **29**: 449–460.

Pullum, G.K. (1991), *The Great Eskimo Vocabulary Hoax: And other Irrelevant Essays on the Study of Language*, Chicago: The University of Chicago Press.

Punetar, V.B. (1989), Work values and industrial development: A comparison of the Indian and Japanese experience, *Indian Journal of Industrial Relations*, **24**: 243–257.

Pyszczynski, T. and Greenberg, J. (1987), Toward an integration of cognitive and motivational perspectives on social inference: A biased-hypothesis-testing model, *Advances in Experimental Social Psychology*, **20**: 297–302.

Quattrone, G.A. and Jones, E.E. (1980), The perception of variability within in-groups and act-groups: Implications for the law of small numbers, *Journal of Personality and Social Psychology*, **38**: 141–152.

Queller, S. and Smith, E.R. (2002), Subtyping versus bookkeeping in stereotype learning and change: Connectionist simulations and empirical findings, *Journal of Personality and Social Psychology*, **82**: 300–313.

Rabbie, J.M. and Bekkers, F. (1976), Threatened leadership and intergroup competition, In S. Worchal and J. Cooper, *Understanding Social Psychology*, Illinois: The Dorsey Press.

Rai, I. (1981), Parents of prejudiced Hindu female children: A study of their attitude and personality traits, *Unpublished Doctoral Dissertation*, Ranchi: Ranchi University.

Raj, S.S. and Krishnan, R. (1980), Intelligence, socioeconomic status and family size as correlates of achievement, *Journal of Institute of Educational Research*, **4**: 1–6.

Rajendra, R. and Cherian, R.R. (1992), Alcoholism and violent behaviour, *Journal of Personality and Clinical Studies*, **8**: 39–42.

Rajini, M.R. (1985), Measurement of self-concept, *Unpublished Ph.D. Thesis*, Bangalore: Banglore University.

Ram, V. (Ed.), (2000), Roots of anger and aggression: Wisdom from Bhagwad Gita, *The Korean Journal of Health*, **5**: 171–180.

Rankin, R.E. and Campbell, D. (1955), Galvanic skin response to Negro and white experimenters, *Journal of Applied Social Psychology*, **51**: 30–33.

Rao, I. (1976), Education of disadvantaged children, *Indian Educational Review*, **11**: 8–12.

Rao, T.V. and Pareek, U. (1976), Classroom interaction behaviour of teachers, and students' mental health, *Indian Educational Review*, **11**: 1–43.

Rao, Y.R. (1976), A study of the relationship of a few selected variables to the academic achievement indices of secondary schools, In J. Pandey's (Ed.), *Psychology in India*, Vol. 2, New Delhi: Sage.

Rashotte, L.S. (2002), What does that smile mean? The meaning of non-verbal behaviours in social interaction, *Social Psychology Quarterly*, **65**: 92–102.

Rastogi, R. and Kashyap, K. (2001), A study of occupational stress and mental health among married working women, *Journal of Community Guidance and Research*, **18**: 189–196.

Rath, R. (1972), Social psychology, In S.K. Mitra (Ed.), *A Survey of Research Psychology*, Bombay: Popular Prakashan.

Rath, R. and Sircar, N.C. (1960), Inter caste relationships as reflected in the study of attitudes and opening of six Hindu caste groups, *Journal of Social Psychology*, **51**: 3–25.

Raven, B. and French, J. (1958), Legitimate power, coercive power and observability in social influence, *Sociometry*, **21**: 83–97.

Raven, B.H. (1974), The comparative analysis of power and power reference, In J. Tedeschi (Ed.), *Perspectives on Social Power*, Chicago: Aldine-Atherton.

Raven, B.H. and Haley, R.W. (1980), Social influence in medical context, In I.L. Bickman (Ed.), *Applied Social Psychology Annual*, **1**: 255–278.

Reader, N. and English, H.B. (1947), Personality factors in adolescent female friendships, *Journal of Consulting Psychology*, **11**: 212–220.

Reber, A.S., Allen, R., and Reber, E.S. (2009), *The Penguin Dictionary of Psychology*, England: Penguin Books.

Redlich, A.D. and Goodman, G.S. (2003), Taking responsibility for an act not committed: The influence of age and suggestibility, *Law and Human Behaviour*, **27**: 141–156.

Regan, D.T. and Cheng, J.B. (1973), Distraction and attitude change: A resolution, *Journal of Experimental Social Psychology*, **9**: 138–147.

Regan, D.T. and Fazio, R. (1977), On the consistency between attitudes and behaviour: Look to the method of attitude formation, *Journal of Experimental Social Psychology*, **126**: 627–631.

Regan, D.T., Williams, M., and Sparling, S. (1972), Voluntary expiation of guilt: A field experiment, *Journal of Personality and Social Psychology*, **24**: 42–45.

Regan, P.C. (2000), The role of sexual desire and sexual activity in dating relationships, *Social Behaviour and Personality*, **28**: 51–60.

Reicher, S., Haslam, S.A., and Hopkins, N. (2005), Social identity and the dynamics of leadership: Leaders and followers as collaborative agents in the transformation of social reality, *Leadership Quarterly*, **16**: 547–568.

Reifenberg, R.J. (1986), The self-serving bias and the use of objective and subjective methods for measuring success and failure, *Journal of Experimental Social Psychology*, **126**: 627–631.

Renne, C.H. (1997), *Excellent Classroom Management*, Belmont, CA: Wadsworth.

Renner, M.J. and Mackin, R.S. (1998), A life stress instrument for classroom use, *Teaching of Psychology*, **25**: 47.

Reno, R., Cialdini, R., and Kallgren, C.A. (1993), The trans-situational influence of social norms, *Journal of Personality and Social Psychology*, **64**: 104–112.

Restak, R. (1968), *The Mind*, Toronto: Bantam.

Rhee, E., Uleman, J.S., Lee, H.K., and Roman, R.J. (1995), Spontaneous self-descriptions and ethnic identities in individualistic and collectivistic cultures, *Journal of Personality and Social Psychology*, **69**: 142–152.

Rhodes, N. and Wood, W. (1992), Self-esteem and intelligence affect influenceability: The Mediating role of message reception, *Psychological Bulletin*, **111**: 156–171.

Rhodewalt, F. and Davison, J. (1983), Reactance and the coronary-prone behaviour pattern: The role of self-attribution in response to reduced behaviour freedom, *Journal of Personality and Social Psychology*, **44**: 220–228.

Richeson, J.A. and Ambady, M. (2003), Effects of situational power on automatic racial prejudice, *Journal of Experimental Social Psychology*, **39**: 177–183.

Riecken, H.W. (1958), The effect of talkativeness on ability to influence group solutions of problems, *Sociometry*, **21**: 309–321.

Rigney, J. (1962), A developmental study of cognitive equivalence transformations and their use in the acquisition and processing of information, In J.D. Delamater and D.J. Myers, *Textbook of Social Psychology*, 2009, ND: Cengage Learning.

Robertson, J.F. and Simons, R.L. (1989), Family factors, self-esteem and adolescent depression, *Journal of Marriage and the Family*, **51**: 125–138.

Robins, R.W., Hendin, H.M., and Trzesniewski, K.H. (2001), *Personality and Social Psychology Bulletin*, **27**: 151–161.

Roccas, S. (2003), Identification and status revisited: the moderations role of self-enhancement and self-transcendence values, *Personality and Social Psychology Bulletin*, **29**: 726–736.

Rochat, F. and Modigliani, A. (1995), The ordinary quality of resistance: From Milgram's laboratory to the village of Le Chambon, *Journal of Social Issues*, **5**: 195–210.

Rodin, J. (1985), The application of social psychology, In G. Lindzey and E. Aronson (Eds.), *The Handbook of Social Psychology*, **II**: 805–882, NY: Random House.

Rodin, J. and Langer, E. (1980), Aging labels: The decline of control and fall of self-esteem, *Journal of Social Issues*, **36**: 12–29.

Rodrigues, A. (1967), Effects of balance, positivity and agreement in triadic social relations, *Journal of Personality and Social Psychology*, **5**: 472–476.

Roebers, C.M. and Schneider, W. (2000), The impact of misleading questions on eyewitness memory in children and adults, *Applied Cognitive Psychology*, **14**: 509–526.

Roese, N.J. (1997), Counterfactual thinking, *Psychological Bulletin*, **121**: 133–148.

Roese, N.J. and Olson, J.M. (1994), Attitude importance as a function of repeated attitude expression, *Journal of Experimental Social Psychology*, **30**: 39–51.

Roethlisberger, F.J. and Dickson, W.J. (1939), *Management and the Worker*, Cambridge, Mass: Harvard University Press.

Roff, M., Sells, S.B., and Golden, M.W. (1972), *Social Adjustment and Personality Development in Children*, Minneapolis: University of Minnesota press.

Rogers, R.W. (1984), Changing health-related attitudes and behaviour: The role of preventive health Psychology, In J.H. Harvey, J.E. Maddux, R.P. McGlynn, and C.D. Stoltenberg (Eds.), *Social Perception in Clinical and Counselling Psychology*, Vol. 2, Lubbock: Texas Tech University Press.

Rogers, R.W. and Ketcher, C.M. (1979), Effects of anonymity and arousal on aggression, *Journal of Psychology*, **102**: 13–19.

Rogers, R.W. and Mewborn, C.R. (1976), Fear appeals and attitude change: Effects of a threat's noxiousness, probability of occurrence and the efficacy of coping responses, *Journal of Personality and Social Psychology*, **34**: 54–61.

Rollins, B.C. and Thomas, D.L. (1979), Parental support, power and control techniques in the socialization of children, In W.R. Burr, R. Hill, I.L. Reiss and F.I. Nye (Eds.), *Contemporary Theories About Family*, **1**: 317–64, NY: Free Press.

Root, M. (1995), The Psychology of Asian-American Women, In H. Landrine (Ed.), *Bringing Cultural Diversity to Feminist Psychology: Theory, Research and Practice*, 241–263, Washington, DC: American Psychological Association.

Rosch, E. and Mervis, C. (1975), Family resemblances: Studies in the interval structure of categories, *Cognitive Psychology*, **7**: 573–605.

Rosch–Heider, E. (1972), Universals in colour naming and memory, *Journal of Experimental Psychology*, **93**: 10–20.
Rosch–Heider, E. and Oliver, D.C. (1972), The structure of colour space in naming and memory for two languages, *Cognitive Psychology*, **3**: 337–354.
Rosenbaum, M.E. (1986), The repulsion hypothesis: On the non-development of relationships, *Journal of Personality and Social Psychology*, **51**: 1156–1166.
Rosenberg, M., Schooler C., Schoenbach, C., and Rosenberg F. (1995), Global self-esteem and specific self-esteem: Different concepts and different outcomes, *American Sociological Review*, **60**: 141–156
Rosenberg, L.A. (1961), Group size, prior experience and conformity, *Journal of Abnormal and Social Psychology*, **63**: 436–437.
Rosenberg, M. (1965), *Society and the Adolescent Self-image*, Princeton, NJ: Princeton University Press.
Rosenberg, M., Schooler, C., and Schoenbach, C. (1989), Self-esteem and adolescent problems: Modeling reciprocal effects, *American Sociological Review*, **60**: 141–156.
Rosenberg, M.J. (1965), When dissonance fails: On eliminating evaluation apprehension from attitude measurement, *Journal of Personality and Social Psychology*, **1**: 28–42.
Rosenhan, D.L., Salovey, P., and Hargis, K. (1981), The joys of helping: Focus of attention mediates the impact of positive effect on altruism, *Journal of Personality and Social Psychology*, **40**: 899–905.
Rosenthal, R. (1969), Interpersonal expectations: effects of experimenter's hypothesis. In R. Rosenthal and L Rosenthal (Eds.), *Artifacts in Behavioural Research,* NY: Academic Press.
Rosenthal, R. (1991), Meta-analysis: A review, *Psychosomatic Medicine*, **53**: 247–271.
Rosenthal, R. and DePaulo, B.M. (1979), Sex differences in accommodation in non-verbal communication, In R. Rosenthal (Ed.), *Skill in Non-verbal Communication: Individual Differences*, 68–103, Cambridge, MA: Oelgeshchlager, Guun and Hain.
Rosenthal, R. and Fode, K.L. (1963), The effect of experiment bias on the performance of albino rat, *Behavioural Science*, **8**: 183–189.
Rosenthal, R. and Jacobson, L.F. (1968), *Pygmalion in the Classroom*, NY: Holt, Rinehart and Wilson.
Rosenthal, T.L., Zimmerman, B.J., and Durning, K. (1970), Observationally induced changes in children's interrogative classes, *Journal of Personality and Social Psychology*, **16**: 681–688.
Rosnow, R.H. (1981), *Paradigms in Transition: The Methodology of Social Enquiry,* Oxford: Open University Press.
Ross, A.S. (1971), Effect of increased responsibility on bystander intervention: The presence of children, *Journal of Personality and Social Psychology*, **19**: 306–310.
Ross, J. and Staw, B.M. (1993), Organizational escalation and exist: Lessons from the Shoreham to nuclear power plant, *Academy of Management Journal*, **36**: 701–732.
Ross, L. (1977), The intuitive psychologist and his shortcomings: Distortion in the attribution process, In L. Berkowitz (Ed.), *Advances in Experimental Psychology*, Vol. 10, NY: Academic Press.
Ross, L.D., Greene, D., and House, P. (1977), The false consensus effect: An egocentric bias in social perception and attribution processes, *Journal of Experimental Social Psychology*, **13**: 279–301.
Ross, M. and Fletcher, G. (1985), Attribution and social perception, In G. Lindzey and E. Aronson (Eds.), *The Handbook of Social Psychology*, 3rd edn., Reading, MA: Addison-Wesley.
Roth, D.L., Wiebe, D.J., Filligim, R.B., and Shay, K.A. (1989), Life events, fitness, hardiness and health: A simultaneous analysis of proposed stress-resistance effects, *Journal of Personality and Social Psychology*, **57**: 136–142.
Rothbart, M. (1981), Memory process and social beliefs, In D.L. Hamilton (Ed.), *Cognitive Processes in Stereotyping and Intergroup Behaviour*, 145–182, NJ: Lawrence Erlbaum Associates.
Rothbart, M. and John, O.P. (1985), Social categorization and behavioural episodes: A cognitive analysis of the effects of intergroup contact, *Journal of Social Issues*, **41**(3): 81–104.
Rothbart, M., Fulero, S., Jensen, C., Howard, J., and Birrell, P. (1978), From individual to group impressions: Availability heuristics in stereotype formation, *Journal of Experimental Social Psychology*, **14**: 237–255.

Rothman, A.J. and Schwarz, M. (1998), Constructing perceptions of vulnerability: Personal relevance and the use of experiential information in health judgements, *Personality and Social Psychology Bulletin*, **24**: 1053–1064.

Rotton, J. and Cohn, E.G. (2000), Violence is the curvilinear function of temperature in Dallas: A replication, *Journal of Personality and Social Psychology*, **78**: 1074–1081.

Rotton, J. and Frey, J. (1985), Air pollution Paulus, weather, and violent crimes: Concomitant time-series analysis of archival data, *Journal of Personality and Social Psychology*, **49**: 1207–1220.

Rozin, P. and Nemeroff, C. (1990), The laws of sympathetic magic: A psychological analysis of similarity and contagion, In W. Stigler, R.A. Shweder and G. Herdt (Eds.), *Cultural Psychology: Essays in Comparative Human Development*, 205–232, Cambridge, England: Cambridge University press.

Rozin, P., Lowery, L. and Ebert, R. (1994), Varieties of disgust faces and structure of disgust, *Journal of Personality and Social Psychology*, **66**: 870–881.

Rubin, J.Z. (1973), *Liking and Loving*, NY: Holt, Rinehart and Wilson.

Rubin, Z. (1970), Measurement of romantic love, *Journal of Personality and Social Psychology*, **16**: 265–273.

Ruble, D. (1983), The development of social comparison processes and their role in achievement-related self-socialization, In E.T. Higgins, D.N. Ruble and W.W. Hartup (Eds.), *Social Cognition and Development*, NY: Cambridge University Press.

Ruder, M. and Bless, H. (2003), Mood and the reliance on the ease of retrieval heuristic, *Journal of Personality and Social Psychology*, **85**: 20–32.

Ruiter, R.A.C., Kok, G., Verplanken, B., and Brug, J. (2001), Evolved fear and effects of appeals on attitudes to performing breast self-examination: An information-processing perspective, *Health Education Research*, **16**: 307–319.

Rule, B.G. and Nesdale, A.R. (1976), Emotional arousal and aggressive behaviour, *Psychological Bulletin*, **83**: 851–863.

Rule, B.G., Taylor, B.R., and Dobbs, A.R. (1987), Priming effects of heat on aggressive thoughts, *Social Cognition*, **5**: 131–143.

Rusbult, C.E. (1983), A longitudinal test of the investment model: The development (and deterioration) of satisfaction and commitment in heterosexual involvements, *Journal of Personality and Social Psychology*, **45**: 101–117.

Rusbult, C.E., Johnson, D.J., and Morrow, G.D. (1986), Predicting satisfaction and commitment in adult romantic involvements: An assessment of the generalizability of the investment model, *Social Psychology Quarterly*, **49**: 81–89.

Rushton, J.P. (1975), Generosity in children: Immediate and long-term effects of modeling, preaching and moral judgement, *Journal of Personality and Social Psychology*, **31**: 459–466.

Rushton, J.P. and Campbell, A.C. (1977), Modeling, vicarious reinforcement and extraversion on blood donating in adults: Immediate and long-term effects, *European Journal of Social Psychology*, **7**: 297–306.

Russell, J.J. (1994), Is there universal recognition of emotion from facial expressions, A review of the cross-cultural studies, *Psychological Bulletin*, **115**: 102–141.

Rutkowski, G.K., Gruder, C.L., and Romer, D. (1983), Group cohesiveness, social norms and bystander intervention, *Journal of Personality and Social Psychology*, **44**: 545–552.

Rutter, M. (1983), School effects on pupil progress: Research findings and policy implications, *Child Development*, **54**: 386–416.

Sachdeva, P. (1998), Sex on campus: A preliminary study of knowledge, attitudes and behaviour of university students in Delhi, *Journal of Biosocial Science*, **30**: 95–105.

Sadker, M. and Sadker, D. (1994), *Failing at fairness: How America's schools cheat girls*, NY: Charles Scribners Sons.

Sahasrabudhe, S.A. (1977), Institutional climate as a function of pupil control, ideology and student indiscipline, In J. Pandey's (Ed.), *Psychology in India*, Vol. II, ND: Sage.

Sahu, K. and Misra, M. (1995), Life stress and coping styles in teachers, *Psychological Studies*, **40**: 115–119.

Sahu, S. (2003), *Psychology of Reading: Role of Orthographic Features*, ND: Concept.
Sailaja, V. (1994), Role of word order in the acquisition of Telugu, In B. Lakshmi Bai and D. Vansta (Eds.), *Language Development and Language Disorders: Perspectives from Indian Languages*, 63–70, ND: Bahri Publications.
Salovey, P., Mayer, J.D., and Rosenhan, D.L. (1991), Mood and helping: Mood as a motivator of helping and helping as a regulator of mood, In M.S. Clark (Ed.), *Review of Personality and Social Psychology*, Vol. 12, *Prosocial Behaviour*, 215–237, Newbury Park, CA: Sage.
Sanders, G.S. and Baron, R.S. (1977), Is social comparison relevant for producing choice shift?, *Journal of Experimental Social Psychology*, **13**: 303–314.
Sanford, F. (1950), Authoritarianism and leadership, Philadelphia: Institute for Research in Human Relations.
Sani, F. and Todman, J. (2002), Should we stay or should we go? A social psychological model of schisms in groups, *Personality and Social Psychology Bulletin*, **28**: 1647–1655.
Sanitioso, R., Kunda, Z., and Fong, G.T. (1990), Motivated recruitment of autobiographical memories, *Journal of Personality and Social Psychology*, **59**: 229–241.
Sanitioso, R.B. and Wlodarski, R. (2004), In search of information that confirms a desired self-perception: Motivational processing of social feedback and choice of social interactions, *Personality and Social Psychology Bulletin*, **30**: 412–422.
Sanna, L.J. (1997), Self-efficacy and counterfactual thinking: Up a creek with and without paddle, *Personality and Social Psychology Bulletin*, **23**: 654–666.
Santrock, J.W. (2006), *Educational Psychology*, ND: Tata McGraw Hill.
Sarason, I.G., Johnson, J.H., and Siegel, J.M. (1978), Assessing the impact of life challenges: Development of the life experience survey, *Journal of Consulting and Clinical Psychology*, **46**: 932–946.
Sarbin, T.R. (1954), Role theory, In G. Lindzey (Ed.), *Handbook of Social Psychology*, **I**: 223–258, Cambridge, Mass: Addison-Wesley.
Sarbin, T.R. and Allen, V.L. (1968), Role theory, In G. Lindzey and E. Arouson (Eds.), *The Handbook of Social Psychology*, 2nd edn., Vol. 1, Reading, Mass: Addison-Wesley.
Saunders, G.G. (1983), An attentional process model of social facilitation, In A. Hare, H. Blumberg, V. Kent and M. Davies (Eds.), *Small Groups*, London: Wiley.
Saunders, G.S., Boran, R.S., and Moore, D.L. (1978), Distraction and social compassion as mediators of social facilitation effects, *Journal of Experimental Social Psychology*, **14**: 291–303.
Saxe, L., Dougherty, D., and Cross, T. (1985), The validity of polygraph testing: Scientific analysis and public controversy, *American Psychologist*, **40**: 355–366.
Schachter S. and Singer, J. (1962), Cognitive, social and physiological determinants of emotional state, *Psychological Review*, **69**, 379–399.
Schachter, D.L. and Kihlstrom, J.E. (1989), Functional amnesia, In F. Boller and J. Grafman (Eds.), *Handbook of Neuropsychology*, **3**: 209–230, NY: Elsevier.
Schachter, S. (1951), Deviation, rejection and communication, *Journal of Abnormal and Social Psychology*, **46**: 190–207.
Schachter, S. (1959), *The Psychology of Affiliation*, Stanford, CA: Stanford University Press.
Scheier, M.F., Weinteraub, J.K., and Carver, C.S. (1986), Coping with stress: Divergent strategies of optimists and pessimists, *Journal of Personality and Social Psychology*, **51**: 1257–1264.
Scheier, M.H. and Carver, C.S. (1985), Optimism, coping and health: Assessment and implications of generalized outcome expectancies, *Health Psychology*, **4**: 219–247.
Scherer, K.R. (1979), Non-linguistic indicators of emotion and psychopathology, In C.E. Izard (Ed.), *Emotions in Personality and Psychopathology*, NY: Plenum.
Schifter, D.E. and Ajzen, I. (1985), Intention, perceived control, and weight loss: An application of the theory of planned behaviour, *Journal of Personality and Social Psychology*, **45**: 843–851.
Schlenker, B.R. (1980), *Impression Management: The Self-concept, Social Identity and Interpersonal Relations*, Monterey, CA: Brooks/Cole.

Schlenker, B.R. and Miller, R.S. (1977), Group cohesiveness as a determinant of egocentric perceptions in cooperative groups, *Human Relations*, **30**: 1039–1055.

Schlenker, B.R., Weigold, M.E., and Hallam, J.K. (1990), Self-serving attributions in social context: Effects of self-esteem and social pressure, *Journal of Personality and Social Psychology*, **58**: 855–863.

Schlosberg, H. (1952), The description of facial expressions in terms of two dimensions. *Journal of Experimental Psychology*, **44**: 229–37.

Schlosberg, H. (1954), Three dimensions of emotion, *Psychological Review*, **61**: 81–88.

Schmitt, B.H., Gilovich, T., Goore, N. and Joseph, L. (1986), Mere presence and social facilitation: One more time, *Journal of Experimental Social Psychology*, **22**: 242–248.

Schmitt, D.P. (2004), Patterns and Universals of mate poaching across 53 nations: The effects of sex, culture and personality on romantically attracting another person's partner, *Journal of Personality and Social Psychology*, **86**: 560–584.

Schmitt, M.T. and Branscombe, N.R. (2002), The causal loci of attributions to prejudice, *Personality and Social Psychology Bulletin*, **28**: 484–492.

Schmitt, M.T., Silvia, P.J., and Branscombe, N.R. (2000), The intersection of self-evaluation maintenance and social identity theories: Intragroup judgement in interpersonal and intergroup contexts, *Personality and Social Psychology Bulletin*, **26**: 1598–1606.

Schmitz, C., Wagner, J., and Menke, E. (2001), The interconnection of childhood poverty and homelessness: Negative impact/points of access, *Families in Society*, **82**(1): 69–77.

Schmuck, R.A. and Miles, M.B. (1971), *Organization Development in Schools*, La Jolla, California: University Associates.

Schmuck, R.A. and Schmuck, P.A. (1975), *Group Processes in the Classroom*, 2nd edn., Dubuque, Iowa: William. C. Brown.

Schmuck, R.A., Runkel, P.J., Arends, J.H., and Arends, R.J. (1977), *Second Handbook of Organization Development in Schools*, Palo Alto, California: Mayfield.

Schmuck, R.A., Runkel, P.J., Saturin, S.L., Martel, R.T., and Derr, C.B. (1972), *Handbook of Organization Development in Schools*, NY: National Press.

Schopler, J. (1970), An attribution analysis of some determinants of reciprocating a benefit, In J. Macaulay and L. Berkowitz (Eds.), *Altruism and Helping Behaviour: Social Psychological Studies of Some Antecedents and Consequences*, NY: Academic Press.

Schopler, J., Insko, C.A., Wieselquist, J., Pemberton, M., Witcher, B., and Kolar, R. (2001), When groups are more competitive than individuals: The domain of the discontinuity effect, *Journal of Personality and Social Psychology*, **80**: 632–644.

Schroeder, D.A., Penner, L.A., Dovidio, J.F., and Piliavin, J.A. (1995), *The Psychology of Helping and Altruism: Problems and Puzzles*, NY: McGraw-Hill.

Schubert, T.W. (2004), The power in your hand: Gender differences in bodily feedback from making a first, *Personality and Social Psychology Bulletin*, **30**: 75–769.

Schultz, D.P. and Schultz, S.E. (1994), *Psychology and Work Today: An Introduction to Industrial and Organizational Psychology*, NY: Macmillan.

Schultz–Hardt, S., Frey, D., Luthgens, C., and Moscovici, S. (2000), Biased information search in group decision-making, *Journal of Personality and Social Psychology*, **78**: 655–669.

Schumacher, M., Corrigan, P.W., and Dejong, T. (2003), Examining cues that signal mental illness stigma, *Journal of Social and Clinical Psychology*, **22**: 467–476.

Schuster, E. and Elderton, E.M. (1907), *The Inheritance of Ability*, London: Dulav and Co.

Schutz, W.C. (1966), *The Interpersonal Underworld*, Palo Alto, CA: Science and Behaviour Books.

Schwartz, B. and Barsky, S.F. (1977), The home advantage, *Social Sciences*, **55**: 641–661.

Schwartz, S.H. (1975), The justice of need and the activation of humanitarian norms, *Journal of Social Issues*, **31**(3): 111–136.

Schwartz, S.H. and Gottlieb, A. (1980), Bystander anonymity and reactions to emergencies, *Journal of Personality and Social Psychology*, **39**: 418–430.
Scott, W.A. (1957), Attitude change through reward of verbal behaviour, *Journal of Abnormal and Social Psychology*, **55**: 72–75.
Searle, J.R. (1969), *Speech Acts: An Essay in the Philosophy of Language*, NY: Cambridge University Press.
Searle, J.R. (1979), *Expression and Meaning: Studies in the Theory of Speech Acts*, Cambridge, UK: Cambridge University Press.
Sears, D.O. (1983), The person-positivity bias, *Journal of Personality and Social Psychology*, **44**: 233–250.
Sears, D.O. (1986), College sophomores in the laboratory: Influences of a narrow data base on social psychology's view of human nature, *Journal of Personality and Social Psychology*, **51**: 515–530.
Sears, D.O. and Levy, S.R. (2003), Childhood and adult political development, In D.O. Sears, L. Huddy, and R. Jervis (Eds.), *The Oxford Handbook of Political Psychology*, NY: Oxford University Press.
Sears, R.R., Whiting, J.W.M., Nowlis, J., and Sears, P.S. (1953), Child rearing antecedents of aggression and dependency in young children, *Genetic Psychology Monographs*, **47**: 135–234.
Seblay, N., Dysart, J., Fulero, S., and Lindsley, R.C. (2001), Eyewitness accuracy rates in sequential and simultaneous line up presentations: A meta-analytic comparison, *Law and Human Behaviour*, **25**: 459–474.
Secord, P.F. (1959), Stereotyping and favourableness in the perception of Negro face, *Journal of Abnormal and Social Psychology*, **59**: 309–315.
Secord, P.F. and Backman, C.W. (1974), *Social Psychology*, 2nd ed., Tokyo: McGraw-Hill.
Secord, P.F. and Muthard, J.E. (1955), Personalities in faces: IV A descriptive analysis of the perception of woman's faces and the identification of some physiognomic determinants, *Journal of Psychology*, **39**: 269–278.
Secord, P.F., Dukes, W.F., and Bevan, W. (1954), An experiment in social perceiving, *Genetic Psychological Monography*, **49**: 231–279.
Segal, M.W. (1974), Alphabet and attraction: An unobtrusive measure of the effect of the propinquity in a field setting, *Journal of Personality and Social Psychology*, **30**: 654–637.
Segerstorm, S.C., Taylor, S.E., Kemeny, M.E., and Fahey, J.L. (1998), Optimism is associated with mood, coping and immune change in response to stress, *Journal of Personality and Social Psychology*, **74**(6): 1646–1655.
Seligman, M.E.P. (2002), *Authentic Happiness*, NY: Free Press.
Seligman, M.E.P., Abramson, L.Y., Semmel, A.R., and Von Baeyer, C. (1979), Depressive attributional style, *Journal of Abnormal Psychology*, **88**: 242–247.
Sengupta, N.N. and Singh, C.P.N. (1926), Mental work in isolation and in group, *Indian Journal of Psychology*, **1**: 106–110.
Serbin, L. and O'Leavy, K. (1975), How nursery schools teach girls to shut up, *Psychology Today*, **9**: 56–58.
Serpe, R.T. (1987), Stability and change in self: A structural symbolic interactionist explanation, *Social Psychology Quarterly*, **50**: 44–55.
Shah, J. (2003), Automatic for the people: How representations of significant others implicitly affect goal pursuit, *Journal of Personality and Social Psychology*, **84**: 661–681.
Shanab, M.E. and Yahga, K.A. (1978), A cross-cultural study of obedience, *Bulletin of the Psychonomic Society*, **11**: 267–269.
Shanab, M.E. and Yahya, K.A. (1977), A behavioural study of obedience in children, *Journal of Personality and Social Psychology*, **35**: 530–536.
Shane, S. (2003), *A General Theory of Entrepreneurship: The Individual-opportunity Nexus Approach to Entrepreneurship*, Aldershot, United Kingdom: Edward Elgar.
Shapiro, P.N. and Penrod, S. (1986), Meta-analysis of facial identification studies, *Psychological Bulletin*, **100**: 139–156.
Sharda, N. and Raju, M.V.R. (2001), Gender role stress in organizations, *Journal of Indian Psychology*, **19**: 50–55.
Sharma, M. (1971), Organizational climate and pupil achievement, *Rajasthan Board Journal of Education*, **7**: 34–40.
Sharma, M. (1973), An investigation into organizational climate of secondary schools of Rajasthan, In J. Pandey (Ed.), *Psychology of India*, Vol. II, ND: Sage.

Sharma, S. (1999), Social support, stress and psychological well-being, In G. Misra (Ed.), *Psychological Perspectives on Stress and Health*, ND: Concept.
Sharma, S. (2003), Life events stress, emotional vital signs and hypertension, *Psychological Studies*, **48**: 53–65.
Sharma, S. and Misra, G. (2010), Health psychology: Progress and challengers, In G. Misra (Ed.), *Psychology in India*, 5th ICSSR Survey, Vol. 3, Delhi: Sage.
Sharma, S., Ghosh, S.N. and Sharma, H. (2004), Life events stress, emotional vital signs and peptic ulcer, *Psychological Studies*, **49**: 167–176.
Sharp, M.J. and Getz, J.G. (1996), Substance use as impression management, *Personality and Social Psychology Bulletin*, **22**: 60–67.
Shatz, M. (1983), Communication, In P.H. Mussen (Ed.), *Handbook of Child Psychology*, Vol. 3, NY: Wiley.
Shaver, K.G. (1975), *An Introduction to Attraction Process*, Englewood Cliffs, NJ: Prentice-Hall.
Shavitt, S. (1990), The role of attitude objects in attitude functions, *Journal of Experimental Social Psychology*, **26**: 124–148.
Shaw, J.I. (1976), Response-contingent payoffs and cooperative behaviour in the prisoner's dilemma game, *Journal of Personality and Social Psychology*, **34**: 1024–1033.
Shaw, M.E. (1954 & 1954b), Some effects of unequal distribution of information upon group performance in various communication nets, *Journal of Abnormal and Social Psychology*, **49**: 547–553.
Shaw, M.E. (1954a), Communication networks, In L. Berkowitz (Ed.), *Advances in Experimental Social Psychology*, **48**: 211–17.
Shaw, M.E. (1955), A comparison of two types of leadership in various communication nets, *Journal of Abnormal and Social Psychology*, **50**: 127–134.
Shaw, M.E. (1958), Some motivational factors in cooperation and competition, *Journal of Personality*, **20**: 196–210.
Shaw, M.E. (1964), Communication networks. In L Berkowitz (Ed.), *Advances in Experimental Social Psychology*, Vol. 1, NY: Academic Press.
Shaw, M.E. (1971), *Group Dynamics: The Psychology of Small Group Behaviour*, NY: McGraw-Hill.
Shaw, M.E. (1981), *Group Dynamics: Social Psychology of Small Group Behaviour*, NY: McGraw-Hill.
Sheier, M.F. and Carver, C.S. (1992), Effects of optimism on psychological and physical well-being: Theoretical overview and empirical update, *Cognitive Therapy and Research*, **16**: 201–228.
Shelat, N. (1974), Concept of organizational climate, In D.B. Desai, D.C. Joshi, N. Shelat, and P. Buch (Eds.), *School Management and Change*, Baroda: Centre of Advanced Study in Education.
Shelat, N. (1979), Study of organizational climate, teacher made and pupil motivations awards institutions in secondary schools of Baroda district, *Doctoral Dissertation*, Baroda: MS University.
Sheldon, W.H. and Stevens, S.S. (1942), *The Varieties of Temperament: A Psychology of Constitutional Differences*, NY: Harper and Row Publishers.
Sheldon, W.H., Stavens, S.S., and Tucker, W.B. (1940), *The Varieties of Human Physique: An Introduction to Constitutional Psychology*, NY: Harper and Row Publishers.
Shepperd, J.A. and Wright, R.A. (1989), Individual contribution to a collective effort: An incentive analysis, *Personality and Social Psychology Bulletin*, **15**: 141–149.
Shepperd, J.A., Ouellette, J.A., and Fernandez, J.K. (1996), Abandoning unrealistic optimistic performance estimates and the temporal proximity of self-relevant feedback, *Journal of Personality and Social Psychology*, **70**: 844–855.
Sherif, M. (1936), *The Psychology of Norms*, NY: Harper.
Sherif, M. (1963), Social psychology: Problems and trends in interdisciplinary relationships, In S. Koch (Ed.), *Psychology: A Study of Science*, Vol. 6, NY: McGraw-Hill.
Sherif, M. (1966), *Group Conflict and Cooperation: Their Social Psychology*, London: Routledge and Kegan Paul.
Sherif, M. and Hovland, C.I. (1953), Judgemental phenomena and scales of attitude measurement: Placement of items with individual choice of number of categories, *Journal of Abnormal and Social Psychology*, **48**: 135–141.
Sherif, M. and Sherif, P. (1950), *Outlines of Social Psychology*, NY: Harper.

Sherif, M., Harvey, D.J., White, B.J., Hood, W.R., and Sherif, C.W. (1961), *The Robbers' cave Experiment*, Norman: Institute of Group Relations.
Sherif, M., Harvey, O.J., White, B.J., Hood, W.R., and Sherif, C.W. (1961), *Intergroup conflict and cooperation: Robber's cave experiment*, Norman OK: University of Oklahoma.
Sherman, J.W. and Klein, S.B. (1994), Development and representation of personality impressions, *Journal of Personality and Social Psychology*, **67**: 972–983.
Sherman, L.W. and Berk, R.A. (1984), The specific deterrent effects of arrest for domestic assault, *American Sociological Review*, **49**: 261–272.
Shibutani, T. (1961), *Society and Personality: An Interactionist's Approach to Social Psychology*, Englewood Cliffs, NJ: Prentice-Hall.
Shomer, R., Davis, A., and Kelley, H. (1966), Threats and the development of coordination: Further studies of the Deutsch and Krauss trucking game, *Journal of Personality and Social Psychology*, **4**: 119–126.
Shotland, R.L. and Huston, T.L. (1979), Emergencies: What are they and do they influence bystanders to intervene?, *Journal of Personality and Social Psychology*, **37**: 1822–1834.
Shotland, R.L. and Straw, M.K. (1976), Bystander response to an assault: When a man attacks a woman, *Journal of Personality and Social Psychology*, **34**: 990–999.
Shott, S. (1979), Emotion and social life: A symbolic interactionist analysis, *American Journal of Sociology*, **84**: 1317–1334.
Shraugher, J.S. (1975), Responses to evaluation as a function of initial self-perceptions, *Psychological Bulletin*, **82**: 581–596.
Shrivastava, S.K. (2004), Mental health and personality adjustment among optimistic and pessimistic students, *Indian Journal of Community Psychology*, **1**: 93–98.
Shukla, S. and Mohanty, A.K. (1995), Maternal influences on the development of speech style in Hindi children, In B. Lakshmi Bai and D. Vansta (Eds.), *Language Development and Language Disorders: Perspectives from Indian Languages*, 13–28, ND: Bahri Publications.
Sidana, U.R., Singh, R. and Shrivastava, P. (1976), Social agents in children's happiness, *Journal of Social Psychology*, **99**: 289–290.
Siegel, E. (1969), Education of women at Stanford University, *The Study of Education at Stanford*, **7**: 1–32.
Sigall, H. and Page, R. (1971), Current stereotypes: A little fading, a little faking, *Journal of Personality and Social Psychology*, **18**: 247–255.
Silverman, F.H. and Klees, J. (1989), Adolescents' attitudes press who wear visible hearing aids, *Journal of Communication Disorders*, **22**: 147–150.
Silverman, I. (1964), Self-esteem and differential responsiveness to success and failure, *Journal of Applied Social Psychology*, **69**: 1115–119.
Simmonds, D.B. (1985), The nature of the organizational grapevine, *Supervisory Management*, 39–42.
Simon, B. and Klandermans, B. (2001), Politicized collective identity: A social psychological analysis, *American Psychologist*, **56**: 319–331.
Simon, L., Greenberg, J., and Brehm, J. (1995), Trivialization: The forgotten mode of dissonance reduction, *Journal of Personality and Social Psychology*, **68**: 247–260.
Simon, M., Houghton, S.M. and Aquino, K. (2000), Cognitive biases, risk perceptions and venture formation: How individuals decide to start companies, *Journal of Business Venturing*, **15**: 113–134.
Sinclair, L. and Kunda, Z. (1999), Reactions to a black professional: Motivated inhibition and activation of conflicting stereotypes, *Journal of Personality and Social Psychology*, **77**: 885–904.
Sinclair, S., Dunn E., and Lowrey, B.S. (2005), The relationship between parental racial attitudes and children's implicit prejudice, *Journal of Experimental Social Psychology*, **41**: 283–289.
Singer, J.E. (1961), Verbal conditioning and generalization of prodemocratic responses, *Journal of Abnormal and Social Psychology*, **63**: 43–46.
Singer, J.L. and Singer, D.G. (1981), *Television, Imagination and Aggression: A Study of Preschoolers*, Hillsdale, NJ: Erlbaum.

Singh, A.K. (1980), *Prejudice and its Correlates in School Students*, ICSSR Project Report, Ranchi: Ranchi University.
Singh, A.K. (2011), *Tests, Measurements and Research Methods in Behavioural Sciences,* Patna: Bharti Bhavan.
Singh, A.K. (1988(a)), Intergroup relations and social tensions, In J. Pandey (Ed.), *Psychology in India: The state of the art,* Vol. 3., 159–224, New Delhi: Sage.
Singh, A.K. (1988(b)), Attitudes and social cognition, In J. Pandey (Ed.), *Psychology in India: The State of the Art,* Vol. 2, 19–54, New Delhi: Sage.
Singh, A.P. and Shrivastava, A.K. (1979), Performance in relation to different styles of supervision, *Decision,* **6**: 271–275.
Singh, J. and Mishra, G. (2004), Human response to population growth and environmental challenges: The Indian experience, *HHDP Update,* **4**: 8–9.
Singh, J.E. (1961), Verbal conditioning and generalization of prodemocratic responses, *Journal of Abnormal and Social Psychology,* **63**: 43–46.
Singh, P. and Bhandarkar, A. (1990), Corporate success and transformational leadership, ND: Wiley Eastern.
Singh, R. (1974), Teacher behaviour as determinant of pupil behaviour and achievement, *Journal of Educational Research and Extension,* **10**: 197–205.
Singh, R. (1981), Prediction of performance from motivation and ability: An appraisal of the cultural difference hypothesis, In J. Pandey (Ed.), *Perspectives on Experimental Social Psychology,* ND: Concept.
Singh, R. and Ho, S.Y. (2000), Attitudes and attraction: A new test of attraction repulsion and similarity-dissimilarity asymmetry hypotheses, *British Journal of Social Psychology,* **39**: 197–211.
Singh, R. and Misra, G. (1989), Variations in achievement cognitions: Role of ecology, age and gender, *International Journal of Intercultural Relations,* **13**: 93–107.
Singh, R. (1988(b), Attitudes and Social Cognition. In J. Pandey (Ed.) *Psychology in India: The state of the art,* Vol. 2, 19–54, New Delhi: Sage.
Singh, R., Gupta, M. and Dalal, A.K. (1979), Cultural difference in attribution of performance: An integrated theoretical analysis, *Journal of Personality and Social Psychology,* **37**: 1342–1351.
Singh, R. and Teoh, J.B.P. (2000), Impression formation and intellectual and social traits: Evidence for behaviour adaptation and cognitive processing, *British Journal of Social Psychology,* **39**: 529–54.
Singh, R., Choo, W.M., and Poh, L.L. (1998), In-group bias and fair-mindedness as strategies of self-presentation in intergroup perception, *Personality and Social Psychology Bulletin,* **24**: 147–162.
Singh, R., Tetlock, P.E., Bell, P.A., Crisp, R., May, J., Tay, A.Y.L., Kaur, S. Chong, D., and Junid, F.B. (2003), Intuitive prudent prosecution of person and group: East-west differences in holistic-analytic thoughts or schema usage?, *Unpublished manuscript,* Singapore: Department of Social Work and Psychology, National University of Singapore.
Singh, R.P. and Sharma, S.N. (1978), Effect of birth order on academic achievement, *Indian Journal of Psychology and Education,* **9**: 21–29.
Singh, S.D., Singh, K., and Singh, Y. (1960), Development of caste consciousness among children from 4 to 10, *Agra University Journal of Research,* **8**: 109–125.
Sinha, A.K. and Jain, A. (2004), Emotional intelligence imperatives for organizational outcomes, *Psychological Studies,* **49**, 87–96.
Sinha, A.K.P. and Upadhyaya, O.P. (1960), Change and persistence in stereotypes of university students towards different ethnic groups during Sino-Indian border dispute, *Journal of Social Psychology,* **52**: 31–39.
Sinha, D. and Kao, H.S.R. (1988), *Social Values and Development: Asian Perspectives,* New Delhi: Sage.
Sinha, D. (1952), Behaviour in catastrophic situation: A psychological study of reports and rumours, *British Journal of Psychology,* **43**: 20–09.
Sinha, D. (1986), *Psychology in a Third World Country: An Indian experience,* New Delhi: Sage.
Sinha, D. (1969), *Indian Villages in Transition: A Motivational Analysis,* ND: Associated Publishing.
Sinha, D. (1981), Social psychology in India: A historical perspective, In J. Pandey (Ed.), *Perspectives on Experimental Social Psychology in India,* 3–17, ND: Concept.

Sinha, D. (1990), Applied cross-cultural psychology and the developing world, *International Journal of Psychology*, **25**: 381–386.
Sinha, D. (1990), Concept of psychosocial well-being: Western and Indian perspectives, NIMHANS Journal, **8**: 1–11.
Sinha, J.B.P. (1968), The n-ach/n-cooperation under limited/unlimited resource conditions, *Journal of Experimental Social Psychology*, **4**: 233–246.
Sinha, J.B.P. (1980), *The Nurturant Task Leader: A Model of the Effective Executive*, ND: Learning Concept Press.
Sinha, J.B.P. (1984), A model of effective leadership styles in India, *International Studies of Management and Organization*, **14**(2–3): 86–98.
Sinha, J.B.P. (1984), *Towards Partnership for Relevant Research in the Third World*, ND: Concept.
Sinha, J.B.P. (1993), The bulk and the front of Psychology in India, *Psychology and Developing Societies*, **5**: 135–150.
Sinha, J.B.P. and Verma, J. (1987), Structure of collectivism, In C. Kagitcibasi (Ed.), *Growth and Progress in Cross-cultural Psychology*, 123–129, Lisse: Swets and Zeitlinger.
Sinha, J.B.P., Sinha, T.N., Verma, J., and Sinha, R.B.N. (2001), Collectivism coexisting with individualism: An Indian scenario, *Asian Journal of Social Psychology*, **4**(2): 133–145.
Sinha, J.B.P. and Sinha, M. (1974), Middle class values in organizational perspective, *Journal al Social and Economic Studies,* **2**: 95–104.
Sinha, J.B.P and Pandey, J. (1970), Strategies of high n-Ach persons, *Psychologia,* **13**: 210–216.
Sinha, J.B.P. (1988), Reorganising values for development. In D. Sinha and H.S.R. Kao (Eds.), *Social Values and Development: Asian Perspectives,* 275–284. New Delhi: Sage.
Sinha, J.B.P. (1994), *The Cultural Context of Leadership and Power,* New Delhi: Sage.
Sinha, J.B.P. (1977), The poverty syndrome, power motive and democratization of workplace, *Integrated Management,* **12**, 5–8.
Sinha, J.B.P. (1982), Power in Indian organisations, *Indian Journal of Industrial Relegations,* **17**(3), 339–352.
Simons, H.W., Berkowitz, N.N. and Moyer, R.J. (1970), Similarity, credibility and attitude change: A review and a theory, *Psychological Bulletin,* **73**(1), 1–16.
Sistrunk, F. and McDavid, J.W. (1971), Sex variable in conformity behaviour, *Journal of Personality and Social Psychology*, **17**: 200–207.
Sivacek, J. and Crano, W.D. (1982), Vested interest as a moderator of attitude-behaviour, *Journal of Personality and Social Psychology*, **43**: 210–221.
Skimer, B.F. (1957), *Verbal Behaviour*, NY: Appleton-Century-Crofts.
Skinner, B.F. (1953), *Science and Human Behaviour*, NY: Macmillan.
Slater, M.R. and Sewell, D.F. (1994), An examination of the cohesion-performance relationship in current hockey teams, *Journal of Sport Sciences*, **12**: 423–431.
Small, K.H. and Peterson, J. (1981), The divergent perceptions of actors and observers, *Journal of Social Psychology*, **113**: 123–132.
Smeaton, G., Byrne, D., and Murnen, S.K. (1989), The repulsion hypothesis revisited: Similarity irrelevance or dissimilarity bias?, *Journal of Personality and Social Psychology*, **56**: 54–59.
Smirles, K.E. (2004), Attributions of responsibility in cases of sexual harassment: The person and the situation, *Journal of Applied Social Psychology*, **34**: 342–365.
Smith, D. (2003), Angry thoughts, at-risk hearts, *Monitor on Psychology,* 46–47.
Smith, D.E., Gier, J.A., and Willis, F.N. (1982), Interpersonal touch and compliance with a marketing request, *Basic and Applied Social Psychology*, **3**: 35–38.
Smith, E.R. and Henry, S. (1996), An in-group becomes part of the self: Response time evidence, *Personality and Social Psychology Bulletin*, **22**: 635–642.
Smith, E.R. and Mackie, D.M. (1995), *Social Psychology*, NY: Worth Publishers.
Smith, E.R. and Mackie, D.M. (2007), *Social Psychology*, Hove: Psychology Press.
Smith, K.D., Keating, J.P., and Stotland, E. (1989), Altruism reconsidered: The effect of denying feedback on a victim's status to empathetic witnesses, *Journal of Personality and Social Psychology*, **57**: 641–650.

Smith, M.D. (1980), Hockey violence: Interring some myths. In F.W. Straub (Ed.), *Sport Psychology: An Analysis of Athlete Behaviour,* 2nd edn., Ithaca, NY: Mouvement Publications.

Smith, P.B. and Harris Bond, M. (1993), *Social Psychology Across Cultures: Analysis and Perspective*, London: Harvester Wheatsheaf.

Smith, R.E., Vanderbil, T.K., and Callen, M.B. (1973), Social comparison and bystander intervention in emergencies, *Journal of Applied Social Psychology*, **3**: 186–196.

Smith–Lovin, L. (1990), Emotions as confirmation and disconfirmation of identity: The affect control modal, In T.D. Kemper (Ed.), *Research Agendas in Sociology of Emotion*, Albany, NY: SUNY Press.

Smolowe, J. (1993), Intermarried... with children, *Time*, 54–59.

Snyder, M. and Swann, W.B. (1978), Hypothesis-tasking processes in social interaction, *Journal of Personality and Social Psychology*, **36**: 1202–1212.

Solso, R. (1991), *Cognitive Psychology,* 3rd edn., Boston: Allyn and Bacon.

Sommers–Flanagan, R., Sommers–Flanagan, J., and Davis, B. (1993), What's happening on music television? A gender role content analysis, *Sex Roles*, **28**: 745–753.

Sorrentino, D.M. and Boutillier, R.G. (1975), The effect of quantity and quality of verbal interaction on ratings of leadership ability, *Journal of Experimental Social Psychology*, **11**: 403–411.

Spence, J.T., Deaux, K., and Helmreich, R.L. (1985), Sex roles in contemporary American society, In G. Lindzey and E. Aronson (Eds.), *Handbook of Social Psychology*, 3rd edn., **2**: 149–178, NY: Random House.

Spencer, S.J., Steele, C.M., and Quinn, D.M. (1999), Stereotype threat and women's math performance, *Journal of Experimental Social Psychology*, **35**: 4–28.

Spink, K.S. (1992), Group cohesion and starting status in successful and less successful elite volleyball teams, *Journal of Sport Sciences*, **10**: 379–388.

Spink, K.S. (1995), Cohesion and intention to participate of female sport team athletes, *Journal of Sport and Exercise Psychology*, **17**: 416–427.

Sporer, S.L., Penrod, S.D., Read, J.D., and Cutler, B.L. (1995), Choosing, confidence and accuracy: A meta-analysis of the confidence-accuracy relation in eyewitness identification studies, *Psychological Bulletin*, **118**: 315–327.

Sprafkin, J.N., Liebert, R.M., and Poulous, R.W. (1975), Effects of a prosocial televised example on children's helping, *Journal of Personality and Social Psychology*, **48**: 35–46.

Sprecher, S. (1998), Insiders' perspectives on reasons for attraction to a close other, *Social Psychology Quarterly*, **61**(4): 287–300.

Sprecher, S. and Regan, P. (1998), Passionate and companionate love in courting and young married couples, *Sociological Inquiry*, **68**: 163–185.

Sprecher, S. and Regan, P.C. (2002), Likings something (in some people), more than others: Partner preference in romantic relationships and friendships, *Journal of Social and Personal Relationships*, **19**: 463–481.

Srivastava, R. and Bhatnagar, P. (2000), Quality of life of scheduled caste women in Uttar Pradesh village, *Journal of Community Guidance and Research*, **17**: 1–10.

Srivastava, R. and Misra, G. (1997), Self-construal and perceived control. In G. Misra (Ed.), *Psychology in India*, vol. II (5th ICSSR Survey), Delhi: Pearson.

Staats, A.W. (1961), Verbal habit—families, concepts and the operant conditioning of work classes, *Psychological Review,* **60**: 190–204.

Staats, A.W. (1968), *Learning, Language and Cognition*, NY: Holt, Rinehart and Winston.

Staats, A.W. (1975), *Social Behaviourism*, Homewood, Illinois: Dorsey.

Staats, A.W. and Staats, C.K. (1958), Attitude established by classical conditioning, *Journal of Abnormal and Social Psychology*, **57**: 37–40.

Staats, A.W., Staats, C.K., and Crawford, H.L. (1962), First order conditioning of meaning and the parallel conditioning of GSR, *Journal of General Psychology*, **67**: 159–167.

Stanford, G. (1977), *Developing Effective Classroom Groups: A Practical Guide for Teachers*, NY: Hart.

Stang, D.J. (1973), Effects of interaction rate on ratings of leadership and liking, *Journal of Personality and Social Psychology*, **27**: 405–408.

Stangor, C. and McMillian, D. (1992), Memory for expectancy-concurrent and expectancy-incongruent information: A review of social and social development literatures, *Psychological Bulletin*, **111**: 42–61.

Stangor, C. and Ruble, D.N. (1989), Strength of expectancies and memory for social information: What we remember depends on how much we know, *Journal of Experimental Social Psychology*, **25**: 18–35.

Stangor, C., Lynch, L., Duan, C., and Glass, B. (1992), Categorization of individuals on the basis of multiple social features, *Journal of Personality and Social Psychology*, **62**: 207–218.

Stangor, C., Sechrist, G.B., and Jost, J.T. (2001), Changing racial beliefs by providing consensus information, *Personality and Social Psychology Bulletin*, **27**: 486–496.

Starbuck, E.D. (1901), *The Psychology of Religion*, London: Scott.

Stasser, G., Taylor, L.A., and Hanna, G. (1989), Information sampling in structured and unstructured discussions of three and six-person groups, *Journal of Personality and Social Psychology*, **57**: 67–78.

Staub, E. (1970), A child in distress: The influence of age and number of witnesses on children's attempts to help, *Journal of Personality and Social Psychology*, **14**: 130–140.

Steblay, M.M. (1992), A meta-analytic review of the weapon focus effects, *Law and Human Behaviour*, **27**: 523–540.

Steblay, N., Dysart, J., Fulero, S., and Lindsay, R.C.L. (2003), Eyewitness accuracy rates in police showup and lineup presentations: A metaanalytic comparison, *Law and Human Behaviour*, **25**: 459–474.

Steblay, N.M. (1997), Social influence in eyewitness recall: A meta-analytic review of line up instructions effects, *Law and Human Behaviour*, **21**: 283–297.

Steele, C.M. (1997), A threat in the air: How stereotypes shape the intellectual identities and performance of women and Africans–American, *American Psychologist*, **52**: 613–629.

Steele, C.M. and Josephs, R.A. (1990), Alcohol myopia: Its prizes and dangerous effects, *American Psychologist*, **45**: 921–933.

Steele, C.M., Southwick, L.L., and Critchlow, B. (1981), Dissonance and alcohol: Drinking your troubles away, *Journal of Personality and Social Psychology*, **41**: 831–846.

Steenland, K., Henley, J., and Jhun, M. (2002), All-cause and cause-specific death rates by educational status for two million people in two American Cancer Society Cohorts, 1959–1996, *American Journal of Epidemiology*, **156**: 11–21.

Stein, A.K. and Friedrich, L.K. (1972), Television content and young children's behaviour, In J. Murray, E., Ruben–stein and C. Comstock (Eds.), *Television and Social Learning*, Washington, DC: US Government Printing Office.

Stein, R.I. and Nemeroff, C.J. (1995), Moral overtones of food: Judgements of others based on what they eat, *Personality and Social Psychology Bulletin*, **21**: 480–490.

Steiner, D.D. and Rain, J.S. (1989), Immediate and delayed primacy and recency effects in performance evaluation, *Journal of Applied Psychology*, **74**: 136–142.

Steiner, I.D. (1972), *Group Process and Productivity*, NY: Academic Press.

Steiner, I.D. and Spaulding, J. (1966), Preference for balanced situations, *Journal of Personality and Social Psychology*, **5**: 40–44.

Stephens, D.E. and Bredemeier, B.J.L. (1996), Moral atmosphere and judgements about aggression in girls' soccer: Relationships among moral and motivational variables, *Journal of Sport and Exercise Psychology*, **18**: 158–173.

Sternberg, R.J. (1986), A triangular theory of love, *Psychological Review*, **93**: 119–135.

Sternberg, R.J. (1987), Liking Versus Loving: A comparative evaluation of theories, *Psychological Bulletin*, **102**: 331–345.

Stewart, R.H. (1965), Effect of continuous responding on the order effect in personality impression formation, *Journal of Personality and Social Psychology*, **1**: 161–165.

Stewart, W. and Roth, P. (2001), Risk taking propensity differences between entrepreneurs and managers: A meta-analytic review, *Journal of Applied Psychology*, **86**: 145–53.

Stier, D.S. and Hall, J.A. (1984), Gender differences in touch: An empirical and theoretical review, *Journal of Personality and Social Psychology*, **47**: 440–459.

Stiles, W., Orth, J., Scherwitz, L., Hennrikus, D., and Vallbona, C. (1984), Role behaviours in routine medical interviews with hypertensive patients: A repertoire of verbal exchanges, *Social Psychology Quarterly*, **47**: 244–254.

Stogdill, R. (1948), Personal factors associated with leadership, *Journal of Psychology*, **25**: 36–71.

Stone, G.P. (1959), Clothing and social relations: A study of appearance in the context of community life. In P.F. Secord and C.W. Backman, 2nd ed., *Social Psychology,* Tokyo: McGraw-Hill.

Stone, G.P. (1962), Appearances and self. In A. Rose (Ed.), *Human Behaviour and Social Processes,* Boston: Houghton Mifflin.

Stoner, J.A.F. (1961), *A Comparison of Individual and Group Decision Involving Risk*, Cambridge, MA: Massachusetts Institute of Technology.

Storms, M.D. (1973), Videotape and attribution process: Reversing actors' and observers' points of view, *Journal of Personality and Social Psychology*, **27**: 165–175.

Stouffer, S.A., Suchman, E.A., De Vinney, L.C., Star, S.A., and Williams, R.M.J. (1949), *The American Soldier: Adjustment during Army Life,* Vol. 1, Princeton: Princeton University Press.

Straus, M. and Field, C. (2003), Psychological aggression by American parents: National data on prevalence, chronicity and severity, *Journal of Marriage and Family*, **65**: 761–767.

Straus, M. and Stewart, J. (1999), Corporal punishment by American parents: National data on prevalence, chronicity and severity and duration in relation to child and family characteristics, *Clinical Child and Family Psychology Review*, **2**: 55–70.

Straus, M., Sugarman, D., and Giles–Sims, J. (1997), Spanking by parents and subsequent antisocial behaviour of children, *Archives of Pediatric and Adolescent Medicine*, **151**: 761–767.

Strickland, B.R. (1965), The prediction of social action from a dimension of internal-external control, *Journal of Social Psychology*, **66**: 353–368.

Strickland, L.H. (1968), Changes in self-presentation in need for approval scores, *Perceptual and Motor Skills*, **27**: 335–337.

Strodtbeck, F.L. (1957), Social studies in jury deliberations, *American Sociological Review*, **22**: 713–719.

Stroh, L.K., Langlands, C.L., and Simpson, P.A. (2004), Shattering the glass ceiling in the new millennium, In M.S. Stockdale and F.J. Crosby (Eds.), *The Psychology and Management of Workplace Diversity*, 147–167, Molden, MA: Blackwell.

Stromwall, L.A. and Granhag, P.A. (2003), How to detect deception? Arresting the beliefs of police officers, prosecutors and judges, *Psychology Crime and Law*, **9**: 19–36.

Strube, M., Turner, C.W., Cerro, D., Stevens, J., and Hinchey, F. (1984), Interpersonal aggression and the Type A coronary-prone behaviour pattern: A theoretical distinction and practical implications, *Journal of Personality and Social Psychology*, **47**: 839–847.

Strube, M.J. and Garcia, J.E. (1981), A meta-analytic investigation of Fiedler's contingency model of leadership effectiveness, *Psychological Bulletin*, **90**: 307–321.

Struch, N. and Schwartz, S.H. (1989), Intergroup aggression: Its predictors and distinctness from in-group bias, *Journal of Personality and Social Psychology*, **56**: 364–373.

Stryker, S. (1980), *Symbolic Interactionism: A Social Structural Version*, Menlo Park, CA: Benjamin/ Cummings.

Stryker, S. and Serpe, R. (1981), Commitment, identity salience, and role behaviour: Theory and research example, In W. Ickes and E. Knowles (Eds.), *Personality, Roles and Social Behaviour*, NY: Springer-Verlag.

Suarez, E.D. (1998), Anger and cardiovascular health, *Psychosomatic Medicine*, **60**: 1–12.

Suls, J. and Mullen, B. (1981), Life change in psychological distress: The role of perceived control and desirability, *Journal or Applied Social Psychology*, **11**: 379–389.

Suls, J., Martin, R., and Wheeler, L. (2002), Social comparison: Why, with whom and with what effect?, *Current Directions in Psychological Science*, **11**: 159–163.

Suls, J.M. and Miller, R. (Eds.), (1977), *Social Comparison Processes: Theoretical and Empirical Perspectives*, NY: Wiley.

Summers, R.J. (1991), The influence of affirmative action on perceptions of beneficiaries' qualifications, *Journal of Applied Social Psychology*, **21**: 1265–1276.

Surin, K., Aikin, K., Hall, W.S., and Hunter, B.A. (1995), Sexism and racism: old-fashioned and modern prejudices, *Journal of Personality and Social Psychology*, **68**: 199–214.

Swain, J.B. and Sahu, S. (2002), Early reading in Oriya orthography, *Psycholingua*, **32**: 3–7.

Swann, W.B. and Predmore, S.C. (1985), Intimates as agents of social support: Sources of consolation or despair?, *Journal of Personality and Social Psychology*, **49**: 1609–1617.

Swann, W.B. and Schroeder, D.G. (1995), The search for beauty and truth: A framework for understanding reactions to evaluations, *Personality and Social Psychology Bulletin*, **21**: 1307–1318.

Swann, W.B., Jr., De La Ronde, C, and Hixon, J.G. (1994), Authenticity and positivity strivings in marriage and courtship, *Journal of Personality and Social Psychology*, **66**: 857–869.

Sweeney, P.D., Anderson, K. and Bailey, S. (1986), Attributional style in depression: A meta-analytic review, *Journal of Personality and Social Psychology*, **50**: 974–991.

Swim, J.K., Aikin, K.J., Hall, W.S., and Hunter, B.A. (1995), Sexism and racism: Old-fashioned and modern prejudices, *Journal of Personality and Social Psychology*, **68**: 199–214.

Symons, D. (1992), On the use and misuse of Darwinism in the study of human behaviour, In J. Barkow, L. Cosmides and J. Tooby (Eds.), *The Adapted Mind: Evolutionary Psychology and the Generation of Culture*, NY: Oxford University Press.

Synder, M., Tanke, E.D., and Berscheid, E. (1977), Social perception and interpersonal behaviour: On the self-fulfilling nature of social stereotypes, *Journal of Personality and Social Psychology*, **35**: 656–666.

Tafarodi, R.W. and Vu, C. (1997), Two-dimensional self-esteem and reactions to success and failure, *Personality and Social Psychology Bulletin*, **23**: 626–635.

Tafarodi, R.W., Marshall, T.C., and Miline, A.B. (2003), Self-esteem and memory, *Journal of Personality and Social Psychology*, **84**: 29–45.

Tagiuri, R. (1960), Movement as a cue in person perception, In H.P. David and J.C. Brengelmaun (Eds.), *Perspectives in Personality Research*, 175–195, NY: Springer.

Tajfel, H. (1972), La categorization Sociale, In E.R. Smith and D.M. Mackie, *Social Psychology*, NY: Psychology Press.

Tajfel, H. (1978), *Differentiation between Social Groups: Studies in the Social Psychology of Intergroup Relations*, London: Academic Press.

Tajfel, H. (1981), *Human Groups and Social Categories: Studies in Social Psychology*, Cambridge, UK: Cambridge University Press.

Tajfel, H. and Turner, J.C. (1986), The social identity theory of intergroup behaviour, In S. Worchel and W.G. Austin (Eds.), *The Social Psychology Intergroup Relations*, 2nd edn., Monterey, CA: Brooks-Cole.

Tajfel, H. and Turner, J.C. (1986), The social identity theory of intergroup behaviour, In S. Worchel and W.G. Austin (Eds.), *Psychology of Intergroup Relations*, 2nd edn., Chicago: Nelson-Hall.

Tajfel, H., Billig, M.G., Bundy, R.P., and Flament, C. (1971), Social categorization and intergroup behaviour, *European Journal of Social Psychology*, **1**: 149–178.

Talwar, P. (1995), Study of familial and non-familial influences in aggression among adolescents, *The Indian Journal of Social Work*, **56**: 467–476.

Tan, D.T.Y. and Singh, R. (1995), Attitudes and attraction: A developmental study of the similarity-attraction and dissimilarity-repulsion hypotheses, *Personality and Social Psychology Bulletin*, **21**: 975–986.

Taubes, G. (1992), Violence epidemiologists tests of hazards of gun ownership, *Science*, **258**: 213–215.

Taylor, D.M. and Jaggi, V. (1974), Ethnocentrism and casual attribution in South India concept, *Journal of Cross-cultural Psychology*, **5**: 162–171.

Taylor, K.M. and Sheppard, J.A. (1998), Bracing for the worst: Severity testing and feedback timing as moderators of optimistic bias, *Personality and Social Psychology Bulletin*, **24**: 915–926.

Taylor, S.E. (1981), A categorization approach to stereotyping, In D.L. Hamilton (Ed.), *Cognitive Processes in Stereotyping and Intergroup Behaviour*, 83–114, Hillsdale, NJ: Erlbaum.

Taylor, S.E. (1991), Asymmetrical effects of positive and negative events: The mobilization-minimization hypothesis, *Psychological Bulletin*, **110**: 67–85.

Taylor, S.E. (2002), *Health Psychology*, 5th edn., NY: McGraw-Hill.

Taylor, S.E. and Crocker, J. (1981), Schematic bases of social information processing, In E.T. Higgins, C.P. Herman and M.P. Zanna (Eds.), *Social Cognition: The Ontario Symposium*, Vol. 1, Hillsdale, NJ: Erlbaum.

Taylor, S.E. and Fiske, S.T. (1978), Salience, attention, and attribution: Top of the head phenomena, In L. Berkowitz (Ed.), *Advances in Experimental Social Psychology*, Vol. II, NY: Academic Press.

Taylor, S.E., Helgeson, V.S., Reed, G.M., and Skokan, L.A. (1991), Self-generated feelings of control and adjustment to physical illness, *Journal of Social Issues*, **47**: 91–109.

Taylor, S.E., Lerner, J.S., Sherman, D.K., Sage, R.M., and McDowell, N.K. (2003), Portrait of the self-enhancer: well-adjusted and well-liked or maladjusted and friendless?, *Journal of Personality and Social Psychology*, **64**: 165–176.

Taylor, S.E., Peplau, L.A., and Sears, D.O. (2006), *Social Psychology*, ND: Pearson Prentice Hall.

Taylor, S.P. and Gammon, C.B. (1975), Effects of type and dose of alcohol on human physical aggression, *Journal of Personality and Social Psychology*, **32**: 169–175.

Taylor, S.P., Gammon, C.B., and Capasso, D.R. (1976), Aggression as a function of the interaction of alcohol and frustration, *Journal of Personality and Social Psychology*, **34**: 938–941.

Taylor, S.P., Schmutte, G.T., Leanard, K.E., and Cranston, J.W. (1979), The effects of alcohol and extreme provocation on the use of a highly noxious electric shock, *Motivation and Emotion*, **3**: 73–81.

Tedeschi, J.J., Schlenker, B.R., and Bonoma, T.V. (1971), Cognitive dissonance: Private ratiocination or public spectacle?, *American Psychologist*, **26**: 685–695.

Tedeschi, J.T. (1974), *Perspectives on Social Power*, Chicago: Aldine.

Terry, D. (1993), Project tenants see island of safety washing away, *New York Times*, pp. A1, B4, April 11.

Terry, D.J., Hogg, M.A., and Duck, J.M. (1999), Group membership, social identity and attitudes, In D. Abrams and M.A. Hoggs (Eds.), *Social Identity and Social Cognition*, 280–314, Oxford: Blackwell.

Tesser, A. (1988), Toward a self-evaluation maintenance model of social behaviour, In L. Berkowitz (Ed.), *Advances in Experimental Social Psychology*, **21**: 181–227, San Diego: Academic Press.

Tesser, A. and Campbell, J. (1983), Self-definition self-evaluation maintenance, In J. Suls and A.G. Greenwald (Eds.), *Psychological Perspectives on Self*, Vol. 2, Hillsdale: Erlbaum.

Tesser, A. Martin, L.L., and Cornell, D.P. (1996), On the substitutability of the self-protecting mechanisms, In P. Gollovitzer and J. Bargh (Eds.), *The Psychology of Action*, 48–68, NY: Guilford.

Tetlock, P.E. and Manstead, A.S.R. (1985), Impression management versus intrapsychic explanations of social psychology: A useful dichotomy?, *Psychological Review*, **92**: 59–77.

Tetlock, P.E., Peterson, R.S., Mc Gurie, C., and Chang, S. (1992), Assessing political group dynamics: A test of the groupthink model, *Journal of Personality and Social Psychology*, **63**: 403–425.

Thakerar, J.N., Giles, H., and Cheshire, J. (1982), Psychological and linguistic parameters of speech accommodation theory, In C. Fraser and K.P. Scherer (Eds.), *Advances in the Social Psychology of Language*, Cambridge, UK: Cambridge University Press.

Thankachan, M.V. and Kodandaram, P. (1992), A study of life events and personality among alcohol dependent individuals, *Journal of Personality and Clinical Studies*, **8**: 27–34.

Thibaut, J.W. and Kelley, H.H. (1959), *The Social Psychology of Groups*, NY: Wiley.

Thompson, L.L. and Crocker, J. (1985), Prejudice following threat to the self-concept effect of performance expectations and attributions, In D.G. Myers, *Social Psychology*, 8th edn., Boston: McGraw-Hill.

Thompson, M.S., Judd, C.M., and Park B. (2000), The consequences of communicating social stereotypes, *Journal of Environmental Social Psychology*, **36**: 567–599.

Thompson, T.L. and Zerbinos, E. (1995), Gender roles in animated cartoons: Has the picture changed in 20 years?, *Sex Roles*, **32**: 651–673.

Thompson, W.C., Cowan, A.N., and Rosenhan, D.L. (1980), Focus of attention mediates the impact of negative effect on altruism, *Journal of Personality and Social Psychology*, **38**: 291–300.

Thorne, B. (1993), *Gender Play: Girls and Boys in School,* NJ: University Press.

Thornhill, R. and Grammar, K. (1999), The body and face of woman: One ornament that signals quality?, *Evolution and Human Behaviour*, **20**: 105–120.

Thurstone, L.L. (1929), Theory of attitude measurement, *Psychological Bulletin*, **5**: 221–41.

Thurstone, L.L. (1931), The measurement of social attitude, *Journal of Abnormal and Social Psychology*, **26**: 249–69.

Thurstone, L.L. and Chave, E.J. (1929), *The Measurement of Attitudes*, Chicago: University of Chicago Press.

Tice, D.M., Bratslavsky, E., and Baumeister, R.E. (2000), Emotion distress regulation takes precedence over impulse control: If you feel bad, do it!, *Journal of Personality and Social Psychology*, **80**: 53–67.

Tiedens, L.Z. and Fragale, A.R. (2003), Power moves: Complementarity in dominant and submissive non-verbal behaviour, *Journal of Personality and Social Psychology*, **84**: 558–568.

Toch, H. (1965), *The Social Psychology of Social Movements*, NY: Bobbs-Merrill.

Toch, H. (1969), *Violent Men,* Chicago: Aldine.

Toch, H. (1975), *Men in Crisis: Human Breakdowns in Prisons*, Chicago: Aldine.

Toi, M. and Batson, C.O. (1982), More evidence that empathy is a source of altruism, *Journal of Personality and Social Psychology*, **43**: 289–292.

Tomar, V. (1999), Aggression as a function of humour, economic status and gender, *Journal of Personality and Clinical Studies*, **15**: 52–55.

Tourangeau, R. (2004), Survey research and societal change, *Annual Review of Psychology*, **55**: 775–801.

Toweles-Schwen, T. and Fazoi, R.H. (2001), On the origin of racial attitudes: Correlates of childhood experiences, *Personality and Social Psychology Bulletin*, **27**: 162–175.

Travis, L.E. (1925), The effect of a small audience on eye-hand coordination, *Journal of Abnormal and Social Psychology*, **20**: 142–146.

Triandis, H.C. (1977), Cross-cultural social and personality psychology, *Personality and Social Psychology Bulletin*, **3**: 143–158.

Triandis, H.C. (1986), The measurement of etic aspect of individualism and collectivism across cultures, *Australian Journal of Psychology*, **38**: 257–267.

Triandis, H.C. (1995), *Individualism and Collectivism*, Boulder, CO: Westview Press.

Triandis, H.C. (2000), Culture and conflict, *International Journal of Psychology*, **55**: 145–152.

Triandis, H.C., Bontempo, R., Villareal, M.J., Asai, M., and Lucca, N. (1988), Individualism versus collectivism: Cross-cultural perspectives on self-in group relationships, *Journal of Personality and Social Psychology*, **54**: 323–338.

Tripathi, R.C. (1981), Machiavellianism and social manipulation, In J. Pandey (Ed.), *Perspectives on Experimental Social Psychology in India*, ND: Concept.

Tripathi, R.C., Caplan, R.D., and Naidu, R.K. (1986), Accepting advice: A modifier of social support's effect on well-being, *Journal of Social and Personal Relationships*, **3**: 213–218.

Tripathi, R.C. and Srivastava, R. (1981), Relative deprivation and intergroup attitudes, *European Journal of Psychology,* **11**: 313–318.

Tripathi, R.C. (1988), Applied Social Psychology, In J. Pandey (Ed.) *Psychology in India: The state of the art,* Vol. 2: 95–158, New Delhi: Sage.

Tripathi, L.B. and Misra, G. (1975), Cognitive activities as a function of prolonged deprivation, *Psychological Studies*, **21**: 54–61.

Trope, Y. and Cohen, O. (1989), Perceptual and inferential determinants of behaviour-correspondent attributions, *Journal of Experimental Social Psychology*, **25**: 165–177.

Trost, M.R., Maass, A., and Kenrick, D.T. (1992), Minority influence: Personal relevance biases, cognitive processes and reverses private acceptance, *Journal of Experimental Social Psychology*, **28**: 234–254.

Tuckman, B.W. (1965), Developmental sequences in small groups, *Psychological Bulletin*, **63**: 384–399.

Turner, C.W. and Berkowitz, L. (1972), Identification with film aggressor (overt role taking), *Journal of Personality and Social Psychology*, **21**: 256–264.

Turner, J.C. (1978), Social categorization and social discrimination in the minimal group paradigm, In Tajfel, H. (Ed.), *Differentiation between Different Groups*, NY: Academic Press.

Turner, J.C., Hogg, M.A., Oakes, P.J., Reicher, S.D., and Wetherell, M.S. (1987), *Rediscovering the Social Group: A Self-categorization Theory*, Oxford: Blackwell.

Turner, J.C., Wetherell, M.S., and Hogg, M.A. (1989), Referent informational influence and group polarization, *British Journal of Social Psychology*, **28**: 135–147.

Turner, R.J. (1983), Direct, indirect and moderating effects of social support on psychological distress and associated conditions, In H.B. Kaplan (Ed.), *Psychological Stress: Trends in Theory and Research*, NY: Academic Press.

Tushman, M.L. (1978), Technical communication in research and development laboratories: The impact of project work characteristics, *Academy of Management Journal*, **21**: 624–645.

Tversky, A. and Kahneman, D. (1974), Judgement under uncertainty: Heuristics and biases, *Science*, **185**: 1124–1131.

Tversky, A. and Kahneman, D. (1982), Judgement under uncertainty: Heuristics and biases, In D. Kahneman, P. Slovic and A. Tveisky (Eds.), *Judgement Under Uncertainty,* 3–20, NY: Cambridge University Press.

Twenge, J.M. (1999), Mapping gender: The multifactorial approach and the organization of gender related attributes, *Psychology of Women Quarterly*, **23**: 485–502.

Twenge, J.M. and Campbell, W.K. (2003), Is not it fun to get the respect that we are going to deserve?: Narcissism, social rejection and aggression, *Personality and Social Psychology Bulletin*, **29**(2): 261–272.

Tykocinski, O.E. (2001), I never had a chance: Using hindsight tactics to mitigate disappointments, *Personality and Social Psychology Bulletin*, **27**: 376–382.

Ungerer, J.A., Dolby, R., Waters, B., Barnett, B., Kelk, N., and Lewin, V. (1990), The early development of empathy: Self-regulation and individual differences in the first year, *Motivation and Emotion*, **14**: 93–106.

Unnikrishnan, N. and Bajpai, S. (1996), *The Impact of Television Advertising on Children*, ND: Sage.

Van Barren, R.B., Holland, R.W., Kawakami, K., and Van Knippenberg, A. (2004), Mimicry and prosocial behaviour, *Psychological Science*, **15**: 71–74.

Van Barren, R.B., Holland, R.W., Steenaert, B., and Van Knippenberg, A. (2003), A mimicry for money: Behavioural consequences of imitation, *Journal of Experimental Social Psychology*, **39**: 393–398.

Van Dick, R., Wagner, U., Pettigraw, T.F., Christ, O., Wolf, C., Petzel, T., Castro, V.S., and Jackson, J.S. (2004), Role of perceived importance in intergroup contact, *Journal of Personality and Social Psychology*, **87**: 211–227.

Van der Linden, S. (2011), Charitable intent: A moral or social construct? A revised theory of planned behaviour model, *Current Psychology*, **30**(4): 355–374.

Van Overwalle, F. (1997), Dispositional attributions require the joint application of the methods of difference and agreement, *Personality and Social Psychology Bulletin*, **23**: 974–980.

Van Vugt, M. and Hart, C.M. (2004), Social identity as a social glue: The origins of group loyalty, *Journal of Personality and Social Psychology*, **86**: 585–598.

Vandello, J.A. and Cohen, D. (2003), Male honor and female fidelity: Implicit cultural scripts that perpetuate domestic violence, *Journal of Personality and Social Psychology*, **84**: 997–1010.

Vanman, E.J., Paul, B.Y., Ito, T.A., and Miller, N. (1997), The modern face of prejudice and structural features that moderate the effect of cooperation on effect, *Journal of Personality and Social Psychology*, **73**: 941–959.

Vasanta, D. (1999), Beginning reading in a non-alphabetic system: Some observation based on second and fifth grade Telugu speaking children, In G. Misra's (Ed.), *Psychology in India,* 5th ICSSR Survey, Delhi: Loyan/Pearson.

Vaughan, D. (1992), Theory elaboration: The heuristics of case analysis, In C. Ragin and H. Becker (Eds.), *What is a Case? Exploring the Foundations of Social Inquiry*, 173–202, Cambridge: Cambridge University Press.
Vecchio, R.P. (1987), Situational leadership theory: An examination of a prescriptive theory, *Journal of Applied Psychology*, **72**(3): 444–451.
Veeraraghavan, V. and Singh, S. (1999), *HIV and AIDS: An Interdisciplinary Approach to Prevention and Management*, ND: Mosaic Books.
Veithch, R. and Griffitt, W. (1976), Good news, bad news: Affective and interpersonal effects, *Journal of Applied Social Psychology*, **6**: 69–75.
Venkataih, N. (1980), A study of achievement of students of different socio- economic status, *Journal of the Institute of Educational Research*, **4**(3): 42–45.
Verma, J. (1994), A note on an indigenous approach to understanding sorrow, *Psychology and Developing Societies*, **6**: 187–192.
Verma, J. (1998), The state of a healthy mind: The Indian worldview, *Journal of Indian Psychology*, **16**: 1–9.
Verma, J. (1992), *Collectivism as a Correlate of Endogenous Development,* New Delhi: ICSSR.
Vidyasagar, P. and Mishra, H. (1993), Effect of modeling on aggression, *Indian Journal of Clinical Psychology*, **20**: 50–52.
Viemero, V. and Paajanen, S. (1992), The role of fantasies and dreams in the TV viewing aggression relationship, *Aggressive Behaviour*, **18**: 109–116.
Vig, D. and Nanda, P. (1999), Aggressive behaviour of adolescent boys, *Prachi Journal of Psychocultural Dimensions*, **15**: 125–128.
Vindhya, U. (2011), Issues of gender in psychology: Traversing from sex differences to quality of women's lives, In Girishwar Mishra (Ed.), *Psychology in India*, **4**: 173–225, Delhi: Pearson.
Virani, P. (2001), Long wait for justice, *The Hindu*, March 4.
Virtz, A., Edward, K., and Bull, R. (2001), Police officers' ability to deceit: The benefit of indirect detection measures, *Legal and Criminological Psychology,* **81**: 365–376.
Vogel, D.A., Lake, M.A., Evans, S., and Karraker, K.H. (1991), Children's and adults' sex-stereotyped perceptions of infants, *Sex Roles*, **24**: 605–616.
Volpato, C., Maass, A., Mucchi–Faina, A., and Vitti, E. (1990), Minority influence and social categorization, *European Journal of Social Psychology*, **20**: 119–132.
Vonk, R. (1993), The negativity effect in trait ratings and in open-ended descriptions of persons, *Personal and Social Psychology Bulletin*, **19**: 269–278.
Vonk, R. (1998), The slime effect: Suspicion and dislike of likeable behaviour towards superiors, *Journal of Personality and Social Psychology*, **74**: 849–864.
Vonk, R. (2002), Self-serving interpretations of flattery: Why ingratiation works, *Journal of Personality and Social Psychology*, **82**: 515–526.
Vrij, A., Edward, K., and Bull, R. (2001), Stereotypical verbal and non-verbal responses while deceiving others, *Personality and Social Psychology Bulletin*, **27**: 899–909.
Vroom, V.H. (1976), *Leadership*, In M.D. Dunnette, *Handbook of Industrial and Organizational Psychology*, Chicago: Rand McNally.
Vroom, V.H. and Yetton, P.W. (1973), *Leadership and Decision-making,* Pittsburgh: University of Pittsburgh Press.
Vyas, S.K. (1973), The origin of prejudice in children, In T.E. Shanmugam (Ed.), *Researches in Personality and Social Problems*, Madras: University of Madras.
Vygotsky, L.S. (1962 & 1986), *Thought and Language,* Cambridge, MA: MIT Press.
Wade, M. (2002), Fight or Woo? Sex scents for male mouse, *NY Times*, February 26.
Waldman, D.A., Ramirez, G.G., House, R.J., and Puranam, P. (2001), Does leadership matter? CEO leadership attributes and profitability under conditions of perceived environmental uncertainty, *Academy of Management Journal*, **44**: 134–143.
Walker, S., Richardson, D.S., and Green, L.R. (2000), Aggression among older adults: The relationship of interaction networks and gender role to direct and indirect responses, *Aggressive Behaviour*, **26**: 145–154.

Waller, M.G., Kojetin, B.A., Bouchard, J.J., Lykken, D.T., and Tellegen, A. (1990), Genetic and environmental influences on religions interests, attitudes and values: A study of twins reared apart and together, *Psychological Science*, **1**: 138–142.
Walsh, E.J. and Taylor, M. (1982), Occupational correlates of multidimensional self-esteem: Comparisons among garbage collectors, bartenders, professors and other workers, *Sociology and Social Research*, **66**: 252–258.
Walster, E. and Festinger, L. (1962), The effectiveness of 'overhead' persuasive communications, *Journal of Abnormal and Social Psychology*, **65**: 395–402.
Walster, E., Aronson, E., and Abrahams, D. (1966), On increasing the persuasiveness of a low prestige communicator, *Journal of Experimental Social Psychology*, **2**: 325–342.
Walster, E., Walster, G.W., and Bercheid, E. (1978), Equity: Theory and research, *Journal of Personality and Social Psychology*, **36**: 82–92.
Walster, E., Walster, G.W., and Berscheid, E. (1977), *Equity: Theory and Research*, Boston: Allyn and Bacon.
Walters, J. and Walters, L. (1980), Parent-child relationship: A review (1970–1979), *Journal of Marriage and Family*, **42**: 807–822.
Walters, R. and Willows, D. (1968), Imitation behaviour of disturbed children following exposures to aggressive and non-aggressive models, *Child Development*, **39**: 79–91.
Walters, R.H. and Brown, M. (1963), Studies of reinforcement of aggression: III transfer of responses to an interpersonal situation, *Child Development*, **34**: 536–571.
Ward, C. and Rana–Deuba, A. (1999), Acculturation and adaptation revisited, *Journal of Cross-cultural Psychology*, **30**: 422–442.
Warren, B.L. (1966), A multiple variable approach to the assertive mating phenomenon, *Eugenics Quarterly*, **13**: 285–298.
Warren, P.E. and Walker, I. (1991), Empathy, effectiveness and donations to charity: Social psychology's contribution, *British Journal of Social Psychology*, **30**: 325–337.
Watkins, M.J. and Pegnircioglu, Z.P. (1984), Determining perceived meaning during impression formation: Another look at the meaning change hypothesis, *Journal of Personality and Social Psychology*, **46**: 1005–1016.
Watson, D. (1982), The actor and the observer: How are their perceptions of causality divergent?, *Psychological Bulletin*, **92**: 682–700.
Watson, D. and Clark, L.A. (1994), *The PANAS-X: Manual for the positive and negative affect schedule-expanded form*, Iowa City: University of Iowa.
Watson, D. and Johnson, D. (1972), *Social Psychology*, Philadelphia: JB Lippincott.
Watson, R.I. (1973), Investigation into deindividuation using a cross-cultural survey technique, *Journal of Personality and Social Psychology*, **25**: 342–345.
Wayne, S.J. and Ferris, G.R. (1990), Influence tactics and exchange quality in supervisor-subordinate interactions: A laboratory experiment and field study, *Journal of Applied Psychology*, **75**: 487–499.
Wayne, S.J. and Liden, R.C. (1995), Effects of impression management on performance ratings: A longitudinal study, *Academy of Management Journal*, **38**: 232–260.
Weatherley, D. (1961), Anti-semitism and the expression of fantasy aggression, *Journal of Abnormal Social Psychology*, **62**: 454–457.
Webb, E.J., Campbell, D.T., Schwartz, R.D. Secharest, L., and Grove, J.B. (1981), *Non-reactive Measures in the Social Sciences*, Boston: Houghton Mifflin.
Weber, R. and Crocker, J. (1983), Cognitive processes in the revision of stereotypic beliefs, *Journal of Personality and Social Psychology*, **45**: 961–977.
Wegner, D.M. (1992), You can't always think what you want: Problems in the suppression of unwanted thoughts, In M. Zanna (Ed.), *Advances in Experimental Social Psychology*, **25**: 193–225, San Diego, CA: Academic Press.
Wegner, D.M. and Schaefer, D. (1978), The concentration of responsibility: An objective self-awareness analysis of group size effects in helping situations, *Journal of Personality and Social Psychology*, **36**: 147–155.

Weiner, B. (1979), A theory of motivation for some classroom experiences, *Journal of Educational Psychology*, **71**: 3–25.
Weiner, B. (1980), A cognitive (attribution), emotion-action model of motivated behaviour: An analysis of judgements of help-giving, *Journal of Personality and Social Psychology*, **39**: 186–200.
Weiner, B. (1985), *An Attributional Theory of Achievement Motivation and Emotion*, NY: Springer-Verlag.
Weiner, B. (1986), *An Attribution Theory of Motivation and Emotion*, NY: Springer-Verlag.
Weiner, B. (1995), *Judgements of Responsibility*, NY: Guilford.
Weiner, B., Amir Khan, J., Folkes, V.S., and Verette, J.A. (1987), An attributional analysis of excuse giving: Studies of a naïve theory of emotion, *Journal of Personality and Social Psychology*, **52**: 316–324.
Weiner, B., Perry, R.P., and Magnusson, J. (1988), An attributional analysis of reactions to stigmas, *Journal of Personality and Social Psychology*, **55**: 738–748.
Weinstein, N.D. (1993), Testing four competing theories of health protective behaviour, *Health Psychology*, **12**: 324–333.
Weisenthal, D.L. and Endler, N.S. (1976), Reversibility of relative competence as a determinant of comformity across different perceptual tasks, *Representative Research in Social Psychology*, **7**: 35–43.
Weiss, M.R. and Friedrichs, W.D. (1986), The influence of leader behaviours, coach attributes and institutional variables on performance and satisfaction of collegiate basketball teams, *Journal of Sport Psychology*, **8**: 332–346.
Wells, G.L. (1984), The psychology of line up identifications, *Journal of Applied Social Psychology*, **66**: 688–696.
Wells, G.L. (1993), What do we know about eyewitness identification?, *American Psychologist*, **48**: 553–571.
Wells, G.L. (2002), Eyewitness identifications: Scientific status, In D.L. Faigman, D.H. Kaye, M.J. Saks and J. Sanders (Eds.), *Modern Scientific Evidence: The Law and Science of Expert Testimony*, 2nd edn., **2**: 230–262, St. Paul, MN: West Publishing.
Wells, G.L. and Luus, C.A.E. (1990), Police line ups as experiments: Social methodology as a framework for properly conducted line ups, *Personality and Social Psychology Bulletin*, **16**: 106–117.
Wells, G.L., Luus, C.A.E., and Windschitl, P.D. (1994), Maximizing the utility of eyewitness identification evidence, *Current Directions in Psychological Science*, **3**: 194–197.
Wells, W.D. (1973), Television and aggression: Replication of an experimental field study, In S. Worchel and J. Cooper, *Social Psychology's Understanding Social Psychology*, Homewood: The Dorsey Press.
Wentura, D., Rothermund, K., and Bak, P. (2000), Automatic vigilance: The attention-grabbing power of approach and avoidance-related social information, *Journal of Personality and Social Psychology*, **78**: 1024–1037.
Wentzel, K.R. (1996), Social goals and social relationships as motivators of school adjustment, In J. Juronen and R. Wentzel (Eds.), *Social Motivation*, NY: Cambridge University Press.
Wentzel, K.R. and Asher, S.R. (1995), The academic lives of neglected, rejected, popular and controversial children, *Child Development*, **66**: 754–763.
Wentzel, K.R. and Battle, A. (2001), Social relationship and school adjustment, In T. Urdan and F. Pejares (Eds.), *Adolescence and Education*, Greenwich, CJ: IAP.
Westre, K.R. and Weiss, M.R. (1991), The relationship between perceived coaching behaviours and group cohesion in a high school football team, *The Sport Psychologist*, **5**: 41–54.
Wetzel, C.G. and Insko, C.A. (1982), The similarity attraction relationship: Is there an ideal one?, *Journal of Experimental Social Psychology*, **18**: 253–276.
Weyant, J. (1978), The effect of mood states, costs and benefits on helping, *Journal of Personality and Social Psychology*, **36**: 1169–76.
Whalen, M.R. and Zimmerman, D.H. (1987), Sequential and institutional contexts in calls for help, *Social Psychology Quarterly*, **50**: 172–185.
Wheelan, S.A (1994), *Group Processes: A Developmental Perspective*, Boston: Allyn and Bacon.
Wheelan, S.A., Davidson, B., and Tilin, F. (2003), Group development across time: Reality or illusion?, *Small Group Research*, **34**: 323–245.

White, R.W. (1963), Ego and reality in psychoanalytic theory: A proposal for ego independent energies, *Psychological Issues*, Vol. 3.
Whitehurst, G. (1980), Imitation, observational learning and language acquisition, In E.M. Hetherington and R.D. Parke, *Child Psychology*, 3rd edn., NY: McGraw-Hill.
Whorf, B.L. (1956), *Language, Thought and Reality*, Cambridge: MIT Press.
Wichman, H. (1970), Effects of isolation and communication on cooperation in a two-person game, *Journal of Personality and Social Psychology*, **6**: 114–120.
Wicker. A.W. (1969), Attitudes versus actions: The relationship of verbal and behavioural responses to attitude objects, *Journal of Social Issues*, **25**(4): 41–78.
Wicklund, R.A. (1975), Objective self-awareness. In L. Berkowitz (Ed.), *Advances in Experimental Social Psychology*, Vol. 8, NY: Academic.
Widmeyer, W.N., Carron, A.W., and Brawley, L.R. (1993), Group cohesion in sport and exercise, In R.N. Singer, M. Murphey and L.K. Tennant (Eds.), *Handbook of Research on Sport Psychology*, NY: MacMillan.
Wigboldus, D., Semin, G., and Spears, R. (2000), How do we communicate stereotypes? Linguistic biases and inferential consequences, *Journal of Personality and Social Psychology*, **78**: 5–18.
Wigfiled, A. and Asher, S.R. (1984), Social and Motivational Influences on Reading, In P.D. Pearson, R. Barr, M.L. Kamil and P. Mosenthal (Eds.), *Handbook of Reading Research*, NY: Longman.
Wilder, D.A. (1990), Some determinants of persuasive power of in-groups and out-groups: Organization of information and attribution of independence, *Journal of Personality and Social Psychology*, **59**: 1202–1213.
Wilder D.A. and Shepiro, P.N. (1984), Role of outgroup cues in determining social identity, *Journal of Personality and Social Psychology,* **47**, 342–348.
Wilder, D.A. and Shapiro, P.N. (1984), Role of out-group cues in determining social identities, *Journal of Personality and Social Psychology*, **56**: 60–69.
Wilke, W.H. (1934), An experimental comparison of the speech, the radio, and the printed page as propaganda devices, *Archives of Psychology*, **25**: 169.
Williams, J.E. and Best, D.L. (1990), *Sex and Psyche: Gender and Selfview cross-culturally*, Newbury Park, CA: Sage.
Williams, J.E., Best, D.L., Haque, A., Pandey, J., and Verma, R.K. (1982), Sex-trait stereotypes in India and Pakistan, *The Journal of Psychology,* **111**: 167–181.
Williams, J.H. and Hacker, C.M. (1982), Causal relationships among cohesion, satisfaction and performance in women's intercollegiate field hockey teams, *Journal of Sport Psychology*, **4**: 334–337.
Williams, K.B., Radefeld, P.A., Binning, J.F., and Fuadk, J.R. (1993), When job candidates are 'hard' easy-to-get: Effects of candidate availability on employment decisions, *Journal of Applied Social Psychology*, **23**: 169–198.
Williams, K.D. and Karau, S.J. (1991), Social loafing and social compensation: The effects of expectations of co-worker performance, *Journal of Personality and Social Psychology*, **61**: 570–581.
Williams, K.D., Harkins, S., and Latane, B. (1981), Identifiability as a deterrent to social loafing: Two cheering experiments, *Journal of Personality and Social Psychology*, **74**: 849–864.
Williams, K.D., Harkins, S.G., and Karau, S.J. (2003), *Social Performance*, In M.A. Hogg and J. Cooper (Eds.), *The Sage Handbook of Social Psychology*, 327–346, Thousand Oaks, CA: Sage.
Wills, T.A. (1981), Downward comparison principles in social psychology, *Psychological Bulletin*, **90**: 245–271.
Wilson, E.O. (1975), *Sociobiology: The New Synthesis,* Cambridge: Harvard University Press.
Wilson, R.S. (1960), Personality patterns, source attractiveness and conformity, *Journal of Personality*, **28**: 186–199.
Wimmer, H. and Hummer, P. (1990), How German-speaking first graders read and spell: Doubts on importance of the logographic stage, *Applied Psycholinguistics*, **11**: 349–68.
Winerman, B. and Swanson, L. (1952), An ecological determinant of differential amounts of sociometric choice within college sororities, *Sociometry*, **15**: 326–929.

Winquist, J.R. and Larson, J.R. (1998), Information pooling: When it impacts group decision-making, *Journal of Personality and Social Psychology*, **74**: 317–377.
Witt, L.A. and Ferris, G.B. (2003), Social skill as moderator of the conscientiousness-performance relationship: Convergent results across four studies, *Journal of Applied Psychology*, **88**: 808–820.
Wittenbrink, B., Judd, C.M., and Park, B. (2001), Evaluative versus conceptual judgements in automatic stereotyping and prejudice, *Journal of Experimental Social Psychology*, **37**: 244–252.
Woike, B., Mcleod, S., and Goggin, M. (2003), Implicit and explicit motives influence accessibility to different autobiographical knowledge, *Personality and Social Psychology Bulletin*, **29**: 1046–1055.
Wood, J.U., Heimpel, S.A., and Michela, J.L. (2003), Savoring versus dampening: Self-esteem differences in regulating positive effect, *Journal of Personality and Social Psychology*, **85**: 566–580.
Wood, J.V. (1989), Theory and research concerning social comparisons of personal attributes, *Psychological Bulletin*, **106**: 231–248.
Wood, J.V., Heimpel, S.A., and Michela, J.L. (2003), Savoring versus dampening: Self-esteem differences in regulating positive affect, *Journal of Personality and Social Psychology*, **85**: 566–580.
Wood, W. and Quinn, J.M. (2003), Forewarned and forearmed? Two meta-analytic syntheses of forewarning of influence appeals, *Psychological Bulletin*, **129**: 119–138.
Wood, W., Lundgren, S., Ouellette, J.A., Busceme, S., and Blackstone, T. (1994), Minority influence: A meta-analytic review of social influence processes, *Psychological Bulletin*, **115**: 323–345.
Woodberry, R.D. and Smith, C.S. (1998), Fundamentalism et al., Conservative protestants in America, *Annual Review of Sociology*, **24**: 25–56.
Worchel, S. and Cooper, J. (1979), *Understanding Social Psychology*, Illinois: The Dorsey Press.
Worchel, S., Andreoli, V.A., and Folger, R. (1977), Intergroup cooperation and intergroup attraction: The effect of previous interaction and outcome of combined effort, *Journal of Experimental Social Psychology*, **13**: 131–140.
Wortman, C.B. and Linsenmeier, J.A. (1977), Interpersonal attraction and techniques of ingratiation in organizational settings. In B.M. Staw and G.R. Salancik (Eds.), *New Directions in Organizational Behaviour*, Chicago: St. Clair Press.
Wright, E.F., Voyer, D., Wright, R.D., and Roney, C. (1995), Supporting audiences and performance under pressure: The home-ice disadvantage in hockey championships, *Journal of Sport Behaviour*, **18**: 21–28.
Wright, S.C. (2001), Strategic collective action: Social psychology and social change, In R. Brown and S. Gaertner (Eds.), *Blackwell Handbook of Social Psychology: Intergroup Processes*, Oxford: Blackwell.
Wulfert, E. and Wan, C.K. (1995), Safer sex interactions and condom use viewed from a health belief, reasoned action and social cognitive perspective, *Journal of Sex Research*, **32**: 299–311.
Wyer, R.S. and Srull, T.K. (Eds.), (1984), *Handbook of Social Cognition*, 2nd edn., Vol. 1, Hillsdale, NJ: Erlbaum.
Yamada, J.E. (1990), *Laura: A Case for Modularity of Language*, Cambridge, MA: MIT Press.
Yammarino, F., Skinner, S., and Chiders, T. (1991), Understanding mail survey response behaviour: A meta-analysis, *Public Opinion Quarterly*, **55**: 613–640.
Ybarra, O. (1999), Misanthropic person memory when the need to self-enhance is absent, *Personality and Social Psychology Bulletin*, **25**: 261–269.
Yinger, J.M. (1971), Personality, character and the self, In E.P. Hollander and R.G. Hunt (Eds.), *Current Principles in Social Psychology*, 3rd edn., NY: Oxford University Press.
Yoder, J.D. and Berendsen, L.L. (2001), Outsider within the firehouse: African, American and white woman fighters, *Psychology of Women Quarterly*, **25**: 27–36.
Yzerbyt, V., Rocher, S., and Schradron, G. (1997), Stereotypes as explanations: A subjective essentialist view of group perception, In R. Spears, P.J. Oakes, N. Ellemers and S.A. Haslam (Eds.), *The Social Psychology of Stereotyping and Group Life*, 20–50, Oxford: Blackwell.
Yzerbyt, V.Y. and Leyens, J.P. (1991), Requesting information to form an impression: The influence of valence and confirmatory status, *Journal of Experimental Social Psychology*, **30**: 138–164.

Zaccaro, S.J., Forti, R.J., and Kenny, D.A. (1991), Self-monitoring and trait-based variance in leadership: An investigation of leader flexibility across multiple group situations, *Journal of Applied Psychology*, **76**: 308–315.

Zajonc, R.B. (1965), Social facilitation, *Science*, **149**: 269–274.

Zajonc, R.B. (1968), Attitudinal effects of mere exposure, *Journal of Personality and Social Psychology*, **9**: 1–27.

Zajonc, R.B. (2001), Mere exposure: A gateway to the subliminal, *Current Directions in Psychological Science*, **9**: 1–27.

Zajonc, R.B., Heingarter, A., and Herman, E.M. (1966), Social enhancement and impairment of performance of the cockroach, *Journal of Personality and Social Psychology*, **13**: 83–92.

Zajonc, R.B., Heingartner, A. and Herman, F.M. (1970), Social enhancement and impairment of performance in cockroach, *Journal of Social Psychology*, **13**: 83–92.

Zanna, M. and Fazio, R. (1982), The attitude behaviour relation: Moving toward a third generation of research, In M. Zanna, E. Higgins and C. Herman (Eds.), *Consistency in Social Behaviour: The Ontario Symposium*, Vol. 2, Hillsdale, NJ: Erlbaum.

Zanna, M.P. and Rempel, J.K. (1988), Attitudes: A new look at an old concept, In D. Bar-Tal and A. Kruglanski (Eds.), *The Social Psychology of Knowledge*, 315–334, NY: Cambridge University Press.

Zaragoza, M.S., Payment, K.E., Ackil, U.K., Drivdahl, S.B., and Beck, M. (2000), Interviewing witnesses: Forced confabulation and confirmative feedback increase false memories, *Psychological Science*, **12**: 473–478.

Zelazo, P.R., Kearsley, R.B., and Ungerer, J.A. (1984), *Learning to Speak: A Manual for Parents*, Hillsdale, NJ: Erlbaum.

Zelditch, M. (1955), Role differentiation in the nuclear family: A comparative study, In T. Parsons, R. Bales, et al., *Family, Socialization and Interaction Process*, Glencoe, Illinois: Free Press.

Zigler, E. and Child, I.L. (1973), *Socialization and Personality Development*, Reading Mass: Addison-Wesley.

Ziller, R.C., Behringr, R.D., and Goodchilds, J.D. (1962), Group creativity under conditions of success or failure and variation in group stability, *Journal of Applied Psychology*, **46**: 43–49.

Zillmann, D. (1979), *Hostility and Aggression*, Hillsdale, NJ: Erlbaum.

Zillmann, D. (1983), Transfer of excitation in emotional behaviour, In J.T. Cacioppo and R.E. Petty (Eds.), *Social Psychophysiology: A Source Book*, 115–240, NY: Guilford Press.

Zillmann, D. (1988), Cognition-excitation in interdependencies in aggressive behaviour, *Aggressive Behaviour*, **14**: 51–64.

Zimbardo, P.G. (1970), The human choice: Individuation, reason and order versus deindividuation, impulse and chaos, In N.J. Arnold and D. Levine (Eds.), *Nebraska Symposium on Motivation*, Lincoln: University of Nebraska Press.

Zimmerman, D.H. and West, C. (1975), Sex roles, interruptions and silences in conversations, In B. Thorne and N. Henley (Eds.), *Language and Sex: Difference and Dominance*, Rowley, MA: Newbury House.

Zuckerman, M., De Frank, R.S., Hall, J.A., Larrnce, D.T., and Rosenthal, R. (1979), Facial and vocal cues of deception and honesty, *Journal of Experimental Social Psychology*, **15**: 378–396.

Zuckerman, M., DePaulo, B.M., and Rosenthal, R. (1981), Verbal and nonverbal communication of deception, In L. Berkowitz (Ed.), *Advances in Experimental Social Psychology*, Vol. 14, NY: Academic Press.

Zukerman, M. (1979), Attribution of success and failure revisited or: The motivational bias is alive and well in attribution theory, *Journal of Personality*, **47**: 245–287.

Zukerman, M. (1994), *Behavioural expressions and biosocial bases of sensation seeking*, NY: Cambridge University Press.

Zuwerink, J.R. and Devine, P.G. (1996), Attitude importance and resistance to persuasion: It's not just the thought that counts, *Journal of Personality and Social Psychology*, **70**: 931–944.

INDEX

ABC components, 229
ABC model of attitude, 204
Above-average effect, 109
Acceptance, 348
Accessibility, 40
Acculturation, 550
Acculturative stress, 550
Accuracy, 2, 17
Achieved roles, 118
Achievement-oriented leadership, 384
Acquisition model (AM), 498
Action research, 60
Action zone, 191
Activation of stereotypes, 272
Activation of the attitude, 208
Actor-observer effect, 166
Actual self, 96
Additive model, 143
Adjustive or ulitarain function, 206
Adolescence, 180
Aerobic exercise, 557
Affect, 409
Affection, 581
Affective-cognitive aspects of attitude, 210
Affective component, 204, 479
Affective relationship, 230
Affiliative conflict theory, 523
Agents of socialisation, 187
Aggression, 437, 569
Aggression cues, 453
Agitation-related emotions, 97
Alderfer's model, 74
All-connect, 338

Alternatives, 398
Altruism, 467
Anaclitic identification, 178
Anasakti, 545
Anchoring and adjustment, 165
Anchoring and adjustment heuristic, 124
Antecedents or causes of groupthink, 325
Anticipatory socialisation, 199
Apology, 459
Applications of attribution theory, 169
Applications of dissonance theory, 238
Applied social psychology, 8
Apprehension-conflict model of social facilitation, 574
Archival research, 43
Arousal, 462
Arousal-cost-reward model, 471
Ascribed roles, 118
Assertive behaviour, 570
Assertiveness, 570, 581
Assimilation, 550
Assimilation-contrast theory, 246
Associational relationship, 28
Association or classical conditioning, 75
Associative assertion, 242
Assumed similarity effect, 289
Attachment, 421
Attention, 119
Attitude, 204
Attitude and behaviour, 207
Attitude change and persuasion, 216
Attitudes in spontaneous and automatic behaviour reactions, 213
Attitude-to-behaviour process model, 213

Attractiveness and likableness, 219
Attribution, 155, 291
Audience effect, 572
Audience inhibition, 472
Auditorium style, 537
Augmentation principle, 160
Authoritarian personality, 58, 287
Authoritarian style, 189
Authoritarian type of leader, 371
Authority, 432
Autocratic, 371
Autocratic-participative dimension, 370
Autokinetic effect, 347
Automatic priming, 124
Availability heuristic, 123
Average children, 191
Averaging model, 143

Balance, 231
Balance theory, 230
Barriers to verbal communication, 513
Base rate fallacy, 123
Basic components of love, 423
Basic dimensions of leader behaviour, 369
Basic purposes, 515
Behavioural component, 204, 421
Behavioural consequences, 111
Behavioural model, 471
Behavioural theory of leadership, 377
Belongingness and love needs, 73
Benevolent sexism, 278, 285
Bias and error in attribution, 164
Biased use of information in groups, 328
Big five dimensions of personality, 377
Big mouth theory of leadership, 366
Bilingualism, 508
Biosocial effect, 51
Bipolar depression, 169
Body language, 134
Bogardus scale, 259
Bogus pipeline technique, 255
Bolstering, 238
Bona fide pipe line, 255
Boomerang effect, 248
Bottom-up processing, 144
Bracketed morality, 570
Brainstorming, 317
Bredemeier's theory of aggression, 570
Bystander effect, 476

Caring, 421
Case study method, 45
Categorisation, 117, 289
Category group, 145
Catharsis, 458, 570
Causal relationship, 28
Causal schemata model, 160
Causes of aggressive behaviour, 438
Causes of stress, 548
Cautious shift, 323
Centralised network, 338
Centrality, 251
Central route processing, 217
Chain network, 520
Chain pattern, 338
Chance conditioning, 216
Change of meaning theory, 149
Characteristics of attitude, 208
Characteristics of language, 490
Characteristics of work environment, 385
Charismatic leader, 364
Charismatic leadership, 363
Circle network, 520
Circle pattern, 338
Circumstance attribution, 161
Classical conditioning, 75, 214
Classroom climate, 539
Closed classroom climate, 539
Code mixing, 509
Code switching, 509
Coerced-complaint false confession, 564
Coerced-internalised false confession, 564
Coercion method, 188
Coercive power, 394
Cognition, 40, 115
Cognitive
    approach, 286, 289
    competence, 194
    component, 204, 421, 423, 479
    conflict, 308
    consequences, 110
    consistency theories of attitude change, 229
    explanation, 168
    homeostasis, 232
    load, 120
    priming, 462
    processes, 3
    structure, 78
    theories, 78, 79, 80
    universalism, 505

Cohesiveness, 309
Collective effort model, 319
Collectivism, 93, 94
Combatting groupthink, 327
Combining verbal and non-verbal communication, 524
Comcon network, 520
Comcon pattern, 338
Common-bond group, 305
Common in-group identity model, 298
Common-knowledge effect, 328
Common types of action research, 61
Communication, 514
    and social structure, 527
    network, 338, 519
    patterns, 336
    style, 225
Comparison level, 77, 406
    for alternatives, 77, 406
Compassionate love, 422, 424
Competitive altruism approach, 483
Competitive reward structure, 335
Compliance, 245, 349, 428
Computer-assisted telephone interviewing (CATI), 41
Concept of adult socialisation, 198
Concept of prejudice and discrimination, 282
Conflict of interest, 308
Conformity, 216, 348
Confounding variables, 49
Congenial climate, 539
Congruent change, 216
Congruity theory, 242
Conscience, 178
Consensus information, 160
Consequences of groupthink, 327
Consideration behaviour (CB), 378
Consideration (social or people role), 369
Consistency, 252
    information, 161
Consonant, 234
Construction of theories, 55
Consummate love, 424
Contact, 296
Contact hypothesis, 275, 296
Content analysis, 44, 45
Contents of stereotypes, 268
Contextualised theory of self, 94
Contingencies, 104
Contingency theory or interactional theory of leadership, 388
Continuum model, 145

Contrast effect, 247, 276
Control, 581
Control question test, 566
Controllable-uncontrollable dimension, 163
Controversial children, 191
Conventional level, 184
Conversational rules, 491
Conversion, 275
Correlational methods, 34, 35
Correlational research, 58
Correspondence bias, 164
Counterfactual thinking, 127, 131, 568
Covariation model, 161
Creole, 500
Criminal defendants, 564
Critical period, 179, 494
    for language learning, 499
    hypothesis, 494
Criticisms of dissonance theory, 240
Cross-cultural research, 63, 64
Cross-lagged correlations, 36
Cross-lagged panel correlation, 36, 59
Cue theory of aggression, 453
Cultural basis of attribution, 171
Culture, 82
Culture of honour, 446
Cumulative scaling, 259

Dark side of self-esteem, 106
Deal technique, 565
Death instinct, 450
Debriefing, 54
Decentralised communication pattern, 338
Decision/commitment component, 423
Decision-making theories, 77
Decision tree, 467
Decoding speed, 510
Decontextualised theory of self, 93
Deep structure, 498
Defensive attribution, 171
Defining aggression, 437
Defining attitude and its components, 203
Defining leadership, 360
Defining prosocial behaviour and alturism, 467
Definition and nature of social psychology, 2
Degree of attitude, 251
Degree of integration, 89
Degree of stability, 89
Dehumanisation, 440

Deindividuation, 320, 321, 440
Dejection-related emotions, 97
Deliberate stage, 157
Demand characteristics, 31, 51
Democratic leader, 372
Dependency, 398
Descriptive norms, 353
Descriptive research, 58
Descriptive social norms, 344
Desensitisation, 462
Desire for individuation, 354
Determinants of
    cooperation and competition, 335
    interpersonal attraction, 409
    prosocial behaviour, 471
    social power, 397
Devil's advocate technique, 329
Diagnostic action research, 61
Differential respect, 278
Difficult escape condition, 481
Diffusion of
    responsibility, 469, 476
    hypothesis, 27
Dimensions of attitude, 251
Dimensions of self-esteem, 88
Direction, 251
Directive leadership, 384
Directive-permissive dimension, 370
Direct measures, 256
Direct personal experience, 209
Discounting principle, 160
Discrepant message, 221
Discrimination, 282, 283
Disinhibition, 440
Disposition, 549
Dispositional attribution, 155
Dissonance, 230, 234
Dissonant, 234
Distinctiveness, 291
    information, 161
Distraction conflict hypothesis, 317
Distraction conflict model, 317
Distraction-conflict theory, 573
Diversity in language acquisition, 506
Document analysis, 44
Dominant leaders, 371
Dominant response, 316, 572
Door-in-the face technique, 429
Downside of impression management, 153
Downward social comparison, 103

Drive theories of aggression, 452
Drive theory, 316
    of social facilitation, 573
Dual-process hypothesis, 356

Easy escape condition, 481
Echoic responses, 501
Ecological validity, 31, 49, 50
Ectomorphs, 138
Effect size, 47
Ego, 177
Egocentric speech, 506
Ego-defensive function, 207
Ego ideal, 178
Ego identity, 180
Egoism, 467
Elaboration likelihood model (ELM), 217
Embedded language, 510
Emblems, 136
Emergence of leadership, 361
Emic approach, 63
Emotional aggression, 438
Emotional component, 421
Emotional consequences, 110
Emotion-focused coping, 552
    strategies, 553
Empathetic joy hypothesis, 483
Empathy, 479, 480
    altruism model, 480, 482
Empirical action research, 61
Empty love, 423
Enacted role, 307
Encoder–decoder model, 515
Encoding, 119
Endomorphs, 138
Entitativity, 305
Entrepreneur, 566
Environmentalist perspective, 500
Equitable, 408
Equity theory, 407
Eriksonian perspective, 178
Eros, 450
Error-choice technique, 254
Escalation of commitment, 568
Esteem needs, 73
Estimator variables, 560
Etic approach, 63
Evaluation apprehension, 52, 477
    hypothesis, 317

Evaluation research, 62
Event schemas, 118
Evolutionary
  perspective, 84, 85
  social psychology, 83
  theories, 83
Exchange theory, 406
Excitation transfer theory, 443
Exclusive and inclusive groups, 313
Exclusive groups, 313
Exemplars, 150
Expected role, 307
Experience-based learning, 76
Experiential learning, 76
Experimental
  action research, 61
  mortality, 49
  realism, 31
  research, 59
  social psychology, 6
Experimenter effect, 31, 51
Expert power, 395
Explicit attitude, 205
Extent of conscious awareness, 89
External attribution, 156
External determinants of interpersonal attraction, 410
External factors, 577
External validity, 31, 49, 50
Extraneous variables, 30, 49
Eyewitness identification and testimony, 559

Face-to-face style, 537
Factors behind obedience, 433
Factors influencing conformity, 352
False confessions, 564
False consensus effect, 168
Family experience, 102
Fast-approaching-deadline technique, 432
Fatuous love, 424
Festinger's theory of cognitive dissonance, 233
Fidelity, 181
Fiedler's contingency theory, 580
  of leadership, 388
Field, 32
  experiment, 32, 33
  study, 36, 37, 38
First language learning, 494
First-shift rule, 322

First wave, 41
Five communication networks, 520
Five components, 492
Five different types of classroom arrangement styles, 537
Five steps of bystander intervention, 467
Fixed interval schedule, 185
Fixed ratio schedule, 185
Flattery, 152, 431
Focus of attention bias, 166
Foot-in-the-door technique, 430
Forewarning, 249
Forgetting hypothesis, 561
Forgiveness, 460
Formal group, 313
Formation and maintenance of attitudes, 214
Formation of social norms, 345
Formative evaluation research, 62
Free-rein leaders, 372
Frustration, 444
Frustration-aggression hypothesis, 444, 452
Frustration-aggression theory, 570
Frustration and aggression–scapegoat theory, 286
Functions of attitude, 206
Functions of language, 493
Functions of leaders, 362
Fundamental attribution error, 164, 291
Fundamental axioms of social psychology, 18
Fundamental interpersonal relations orientation behaviour questionnaire (FIRO-BQ), 581

Game-playing love, 422
Game stage, 91
Gaming, 32
Gender differences in
  communication, 527
  non-verbal communication, 526
  verbal communication, 512
Gender stereotype, 269, 277
General affective aggression model, 456
General aggression model (GAM), 456
Generalised other, 91
Generativity, 181
Genetic determinism model, 484
Genetic factors, 214
Glass ceiling effect, 277
Global attribution, 169
Grapevine, 339

Great man theory of leadership, 375, 376
Group, 305, 576
    cohesiveness, 309
    decision-making, 322
    environment questionnaire (GEQ), 578
    integration, 578
    interaction, 330
    memory, 318
    norms, 579
    orientation, 578
    polarisation, 323
    polarisation hypothesis, 323
    schemas, 118
    serving bias, 289
    stereotype, 150
    structure, 306
Groupthink, 325
Guidelines for effective decision-making, 330
Guttman scale, 259

Halo effect, 147
Hardiness, 556
Hassles, 548
Hawthorne effect, 50
Health, 545
Healthy lifestyle, 544
Heider's naive psychology attribution theory, 158
Heider's theory, 230
Heroism, 467
Heuristic function, 493
Heuristics, 122
Hierarchy of identities, 99
Hi-hi hypothesis, 369
Historical and socio-cultural approach, 286, 292
Historical organisational case study, 46
Home ground advantage, 574
Hostile aggression, 438, 569
Hostile attributional bias, 439, 440
Hostile expectation bias, 445
Hostile sexism, 285
Hypothesis, 56

Id, 177
Ideal self, 96
Identification, 245
    with aggressor, 178
Identities, 98
Identity control theory, 99

Imaginative function, 493
Imbalance, 231
Imitation, 75, 462
Impact of stereotypes on judgements and actions, 273
Implications of dissonance theory, 237
Implicit association test (IAT), 205
Implicit attitude, 205
Implicit bystander effect, 476
Implicit personality theory, 142
Implicit self-esteem, 89
Impression formation, 140
Impression management, 151
Impression motivation function, 207
Imprinting, 494
Improved interview, 563
Improving police line ups, 564
Incidental similarity, 431
Inclusion, 581
Inclusive groups, 313
Incongruent change, 216
Incongruous traits, 133
Inconsistency, 230
Independent self, 93
Indirect measures, 252
Individual attraction, 578
Individualism, 93
Inductive-control method, 188
Inequitable, 408
Infatuated love, 423
Inferential prison, 270
Informal group, 313
Informational power, 396
Informational social influence, 349
Information overload, 122
Informative function, 493
Informed consent, 53
Ingratiation, 152
In-group, 312
    differentiation, 271
    favouritism effect, 289
    homogeneity, 271
    and out-groups, 312
Inhibition, 76
Initiating structure, 580
Initiating structure behaviour (ISB), 378
Initiating structure (or task role), 369
Injunctive norms, 353
Inquisitorial approach, 558
Instinct theory, 570
    of aggression, 450

Institutional leader, 370
Instrumental aggression, 438, 569
Instrumental conditioning, 185
Instrumental function, 493
Instrumental or heuristic function, 206
Integration, 550
Intensity, 251
Intentional, 427
Intentionalist model, 517
Interactional approach, 388
Interactionist perspective, 504
Interaction process analysis, 37, 38
Interactive determinants, 414
Interactive voice response (IVR), 41
Interchannel discrepancies, 139
Interdependent self, 94
Interindividual communication, 493
Intermittent reinforcement schedule, 183
Internal anchor point, 247
Internal attribution, 156
Internal determinants of interpersonal attraction, 409
Internal-external dimension, 163
Internal factors, 577
Internalisation, 187, 348
Internal validity, 49
Internet research, 48
Interpersonal attraction, 402
Interpersonal function, 493
Interpersonal model of group, 309
Interpersonal perception, 132
Interrole conflict, 72
Intersubjectivity, 518
Intimacy, 181, 421, 529
Intimacy component, 423
Intrarole conflict, 72
Isolation, 181

Jigsaw, 296
Jones and davis' correspondent inference attribution theory, 158
Just world hypothesis, 474

Kelley's model of causal attribution, 160
Kelman's theory, 244
Kinesics, 134, 522
Kin selection theory, 484
Kinship selection theory, 477
Knowledge or schematic function, 206
Knowledge structures, 445

Laboratory experiment, 29, 30, 31
Laissez-faire, 372
Language, 489, 490, 492
    acquisition, 507
    acquisition device (LAD), 498
    mixing, 509
    properties and structure, 489
Latitude of acceptance, 247
Latitude of non-commitment, 247
Latitude of rejection, 247
Leader, 360
Leader behaviour description questionnaire (LBDQ), 378
Leader opinion questionnaire (LOQ), 378
Leadership, 360
Learning theories, 74
Learning theory or reinforcement model, 404
Least preferred co-worker or LPC, 390
Legitimate power, 396
Legitimation/justification, 462
Less-leads-to-move effect, 237, 239
Lie detection, 565
Life change unit (LCU), 548
Life instinct, 450
Likert scale, 258
Liking, 423
Line up biases, 562
Linguistic
    determinism, 504
    hierarchy, 496
    intergroup bias, 519
    relativity hypothesis, 504
Locus of control, 481
Logical love, 422
Logographic stage, 510
Looking-glass self, 91, 154
Love and loving, 420
Low-ball technique, 431

Magical thinking, 129
Mail questionnaire survey, 41
Maintenance specialist, 379
Majority wins, 322
Mand responses, 501
Marginalisation, 550
Maslow's theory of need hierarchy, 73
Mass media, 461
Material self, 89
Mate selection, 83
Matrix language, 510
Maturation, 49

Meaning and bases of social power, 393
Meaning and nature
   of compliance, 428
   of interpersonal attraction, 402
   of self, 88
   of social cognition, 115
   of social group, 305
Meaning of conformity behaviour, 348
Measurement of attitude, 252
Measurement of prejudice, 300
Measurement of self-esteem, 104
Mechanical and individualistic view, 93
Media violence, 445, 461
Membership groups, 313
Memory construction, 561
Mere exposure effect, 411
Mesomorphs, 138
Meta-analysis, 46, 47, 48
Metamotivation, 74
Microexpressions, 139
Middle-range theories, 18, 69
Minimisation, 564
Minority influence, 356
Miscellaneous factors, 215
Mixed-motive game, 32, 334
Mixed motive situation, 333
Model, 186
Modelling, 75, 186
Models of communication, 515
Models of information integration, 142
Mood congruence memory, 130
Mood-dependent memory, 130
Moral realism, 345
Morphemes, 492, 497
Morphological development, 500
Motivation, 40
Motivational
   approach, 286
   explanation, 168
   theories, 72, 73, 74
Multicase study, 46
Multilingualism, 508
Mundane realism, 31
Mutual evaluations, 419

Narcissism, 440
Nativist perspective, 498
Natural experiment, 33, 34
Naturalistic observation, 36

Nature and contents of stereotypes, 266
Nature of evaluation, 90
Need for achievement (nAch), 74
Need for affiliation (nAff), 74
Need for power (nPow), 74
Need to affiliate, 409
Negative attitude change, 249
Negative correlation, 35, 58
Negative identity, 181
Negative referent power, 395
Negative reinforcement, 75
Negative-state relief hypothesis, 479
Negative-state relief model, 482
Negativity bias, 125
Negativity effect, 147
Neglected children, 191
Neglectful parenting, 189
Newcomb's A-B-X model, 232, 403
Non-causal relationship, 28
Non-reactive research, 43
Non-standard speech, 528
Non-threatening location, 559
Non-verbal communication, 134, 515, 521
Non-zero-sum, 333
No reputation condition, 483
Normative focus theory, 353
Normative or social comparison perspective, 323
Normative social influence, 349
Norm of family privacy, 446
Norm of internality, 165
Norm of male aggression, 446
Norm of reciprocity, 396, 473
Norm of social responsibility, 474
Norms, 306
Norms of social responsibility, 396
Nurturant leader, 373
Nurturant task (NT) leader, 373

Obedience to authority, 432
Objectivity, 2, 17
Observational case study:, 46
Observational learning, 75, 186
Off-set style, 537
Open classroom climate, 539
Open-mindedness, 2, 18
Operant conditioning, 75
Operational definition, 27
Opinion, 205
Opposite orientation condition, 167

Optimising condition, 538
Optimism, 555
Optimistic bias, 126, 567
Organisation development, 543
Origin, development and maintenance of prejudice, 286
Orthographic stage, 510
Other-enhancement, 152
Ought self, 96
Outcomes of socialisation, 193
Out-group, 312
    homogeneity effect, 271, 290
Overbenefitted partner, 408
Overconfidence barrier, 126
Overwriting hypothesis, 561

Panel, 41
Panel survey, 41
Paralanguage, 138, 524
Parallel-constraint-satisfaction model, 146
Participant action research, 61
Participant effect, 51
Participant observation, 37
Participant (or subject) effect, 31, 52
Participative leadership, 384
Partner schema, 420
Passionate (or romantic) love, 421
Passion component, 423
Path-goal theory of leader effectiveness, 383
Perceived role, 307
Perfectionism, 555
Performance feedback, 104
Period of awareness of language, 509
Period of language differentiation, 509
Period of multilingual functioning, 509
Peripheral route processing, 217
Perseverance effect, 120
Personal causes of aggressive behaviour, 438
Personal characteristics of leaders, 366
Personal function, 493
Personal (internal) determinants of prosocial behaviour, 477
Personal interview, 40
Personality needs, 288
Personal role conflict, 72
Personal-social identity continuum, 89
Personal standards perfectionism, 555
Person perception, 132
Persons-centred leader behaviour, 378
Person schemas, 118

Perspective taking, 480
    model, 518
Persuasibility, 216
Persuasion, 216
Persuasive-information perspective, 324
Persuasive leaders, 371
Pessimism, 555
Phase of action or execution, 60
Phase of evaluation, 60
Phase of fact-finding, 60
Phase of feedback, 60
Phase of planning, 60
Phases of group development, 314
Phonemes, 492, 496
Phrases and sentences, 497
Physical reality, 347
Physiognomy, 135
Physiological needs, 73
Physiological techniques, 252
Piaget's view, 505
Pidgin language, 500
Piecemeal group, 145
Planning fallacy, 126, 567
Playing hard to get technique, 432
Play stage, 91
Pluralistic ignorance, 469
Pooled standard deviation, 47
Poor group coordination, 318
Popular children, 191
Positive correlation, 35, 58
Positive referent power, 395
Positive reinforcement, 75
Positivity bias, 147
Possessive love, 422
Postconventional level, 184
Post-decisional dissonance, 238
Post-event information, 562
Potential dangers of group decision-making, 322
Pragmatics, 493
Preattribution, 459
Preconventional level, 184
Pre-intellectual language, 506
Prejudice, 282
Prescriptive social norms, 344
Prevention and control of aggression, 457
Prevention focus, 569
Prevention goals, 97
Primacy effect, 148, 223
Primary group, 311
Priming, 124

Principle of cognitive consistency, 79
Principle of covariation, 160
Prisoner's dilemma game (PDG), 333
Private acceptance, 348
Private conformity, 348
Private conformity and public conformity, 348
Problem-focused coping, 552
    strategies, 553
Process in thought suppression, 128
Process of socialisation, 193
Production blocking, 318
Production orientation, 369
Projective techniques, 253
Promotion focus, 569
Promotion goals, 97
Prosocial behaviour, 466
Prototypes, 117, 150
Prototypicality, 117, 523
Proximity, 410
Psychoanalytic perspective, 177
Psychodynamic approach, 286
Psychological effect, 51
Psychological hardiness, 556
Psychologistics, 492
Psychology, 4
Public conformity, 348
Public opinion poll, 39
Punishment, 457

Questionnaire survey, 41

Racism, 284
Random assignment, 29, 59
Reactance, 249
Reading acquisition, 510
Realistic group conflict theory, 287, 438
Reason action, 212
Reasoned action model, 211, 546
Rebound effect, 129
Recategorisation, 298
Recency effect, 149, 223
Reciprocal determination theory, 484
Reciprocal liking or disliking, 419
Recognising deceptions in non-verbal cues, 139
Recovery from aphasia, 495
Red-tapism, 313
Reduction of prejudice and discrimination, 295
Reference groups, 313

Referent power, 395
Reflected appraisal, 92
Refutational defence condition, 251
Regulatory function, 493
Reinforcement, 75
Rejected children, 191
Relationship schema, 420
Relative deprivation, 287, 444
Reliability, 27
Rep defenders, 439
Representativeness heuristic, 122
Reputation condition, 483
Reservoir of psychological energy, 177
Resisting the effects of destructive obedience, 435
Resource, 397
Retrieval, 120
Reward power, 394
Ringlemann effect, 319
Risky shift effect, 323
Role, 90
    acquisition, 198
    confusion, 180, 181
    discontinuity, 199
    enactment, 70
    identities, 98
    negotiation, 72
    of non-verbal cues in person perception, 134
    schemas, 118
    socialisation, 72
    taking, 90
Role theory, 70, 71, 72
Romantic love, 424
Romantic relationship, 419
Rosenberg self-esteem scale, 104
Rosenthal effect, 51

Safety needs, 73
Salience, 252
    hierarchy, 101
Same orientation condition, 167
Samples, 28
Sanctioned aggression, 438
Sapir-Whorf hypothesis, 504
Scale discrimination technique, 260
Scalogram analysis, 259
Scapegoat theory, 286
Schema, 78, 79, 96, 117, 149
Schematic processing, 119
Schematic traits, 118

Schism, 311
School as a social system, 536
Secondary groups, 311, 312
Second language learning, 495
Second wave, 41
Seeking social support, 552, 553
Selection bias, 49
Selective avoidance, 250
Selective exposure, 250
Self, 88
Self-actualisation needs, 73
Self-administered questionnaires, 41
Self-awareness, 97
Self-categorisation theory, 324
Self-competence, 88
Self-concept, 88, 102
Self-critical perfectionism, 555
Self-discrepancy, 97
Self-efficacy, 482
Self-enhancement technique, 151
Self-esteem, 88, 102
Self-esteem function, 206
Self-fulfilling prophecy, 121
Self-image defenders, 439
Self-image promoters, 439
Selfless love, 422
Self-liking, 88
Self-perception, 154
Self-presentation, 151
Self-promotion, 151, 431
Self-reference effect, 104
Self-regulation, 97, 183
Self-schemas, 118, 420
Self-serving bias, 109, 168
Self-verification strategies, 101
Semantic differential scale, 261
Semantics, 492
Sensation seeking, 441
Sequential line ups, 563
Sexism, 285
Shaping, 185
Shaver's attribution model, 162
Show up, 562
Significant others, 81
Similarity, 414
Simple random sampling, 28, 42
Simulation, 32, 60, 125
    heuristic, 125
Simultaneous line ups, 563
Singalism, 281

Situational
    approach, 286, 295
    attribution, 155
    constraints, 210
    effect, 52
    (external) determinants of prosocial behaviour, 471
    factors of aggression, 447
    theory of leadership, 379
Situation-specific theories, 581
Skepticism, 2, 17
Sleeper effect, 218
Slime effect, 153
Social
    aggression, 438
    cognition, 116
    cohesion, 577, 578
    comparison, 92, 103, 107, 215
    comparison theory, 92
    compensation, 319
    consensus, 90
    contagion, 321
    decision schemes, 322
    dilemma, 337
    dominance orientation, 293
    emotional leader, 371
    exchange theory, 76
    facilitation, 6, 315, 572
    identity, 91, 98
    identity theory, 290
    impairment, 316
    inequalities, 293
    influence, 245, 427
    inhibition, 316
    interaction, 2
Socialisation, 3, 82, 175, 176, 293
Social learning perspective, 182
Social learning theory, 76, 454, 570
    of aggression, 454
    of attitude change, 243
Social loafing, 6, 318
Social norms, 308, 344, 347
Social perception, 132
Social power, 393
Social psychology, 1, 2, 4
    for education, 535
    of education, 8, 535
    of psychological experiment, 51
Social readjustment rating scale (SRRS), 548
Social reality, 347
Social roles, 306

Social self, 89
Social status, 307
Social system, 535
Socio-cultural factors of aggression, 443
Socio-cultural theories, 82
Socio-economic status, 556
Socio-emotional leader, 379
Sociology, 4
Sociometry, 7
Some barriers to stereotype change, 275
Source monitoring theory, 561
Special interest groups, 312
Spontaneous stage, 157
Sport aggression, 569
Sport psychology, 569
Stability of attitude, 209
Stable-unstable dimension, 163
Stage of
    adjourning, 315
    alphabetic, 510
    despair, 182
    forming, 314
    norming, 314
    performing, 314
    psychosocial development, 179
    reading acquisition, 510
    phases of group development, 314
    storming, 314
Stagnation, 181
Standard speech, 528
Staring, 136
Status, 529
Stereotype, 118, 266
    effect, 111
    negation condition, 299
Stratified random sample, 42
Strength of attitude, 209
Stress, 547
Structured situation, 346
Studies of obedience, 432
Styles of leader behaviour, 384
Subjective social norm, 212
Suggestibility, 217
Summative evaluation research, 62
Sunk cost, 568
Superego, 178
Superordinate goals, 299
Supportive defence condition, 251
Supportive leadership, 384
Surface structure, 498

Survey interview, 40
Survey method, 39, 42
Symbolic cognitive perspective, 183
Symbolic interaction theory, 80, 81, 82
Symbolic social influence, 427
Symptoms of groupthink, 326
Syntax, 492
Systematic development, 500
Systematic observation, 36
System variables, 562

Tactical impression management, 151
Tact responses, 501
Task-centred leader behaviour, 378
Task cohesion, 578
Task-oriented leaders, 371
Task-specialist, 379
Teacher variable, 538
Team, 576
    building, 580
    cohesion, 576
    homogeneity, 577
    perception, 578
Technique of other-enhancement, 152
Techniques of compliance, 429
Techniques of reducing social loafing, 320
Telephone survey, 41
Terror management theory, 109
Testing, 49
Thanatos, 450
That's-not-all technique, 429
Theoretical perspectives, 18, 69
    of socialisation, 177
Theories of
    aggressive behaviour, 450
    attitude organisation and change, 229
    attribution, 156
    interpersonal attraction, 402
    language development, 497
    leadership, 375
    social comparison and cognitive dissonance, 9
Theory of impression management, 241
Theory of mind, 507
Theory of planned behaviour, 213
They-group, 312
Third-party effect, 215
Thought suppression, 128
Threatening location, 559
Threats to self-esteem, 289

Thurstone scale, 256
Time or zeitgeist theory, 379
Time pressure condition, 538
Tit-for-tat effect, 473
Tokenism, 285
Top-down information processing, 144
Traits as situational sensitivities (TASS) model, 441
Trait theory, 580
Transactional leaders, 364, 365
Transformational and transactional leaders, 364
    grammar, 499
    leaders, 364
Triangular theory of love, 423
Trucking game, 332
Truth wins, 322
Two-stage model, 157
Two-step flow of communication, 225
Types of
    case studies, 46
    group, 311
    leaders, 370
    parenting style, 189
    research in social psychology, 57
    social influence, 427
    survey method, 40

Ultimate attribution error, 291
Unanimity, 322
Underbenefitted, 408
Underlying principles of compliance, 428
Unintentional, 427
Unit relationship, 230
Universal behaviour theories of leadership, 580

Unobtrusive measures, 37
Unrequited love, 422
Unstructured situation, 346
Upward social comparison, 103

Validity, 28
    experiment, 49
Variable interval schedule, 185
Variable ratio schedule, 185
Verbal communication, 515
Verbal reinforcement, 75
Voluntary false confession, 564
Vygotskian model, 509
Vygotsky's view, 506

Ways of improving group decisions, 329
Weapon effect, 449
Weapon focus effect, 560
We-group, 312
Weighted averaging model, 144
Weiner's attribution model, 163
Wheel network, 520
Wheel pattern, 338
White blood cells, 551
Whorf's view, 504
Wisdom, 182
Women are wonderful effect, 277

Y-pattern, 338
Y-shaped network, 520